The Oxford Guide to the
United States
Government

The Oxford Guide to the
United States Government

John J. Patrick
Richard M. Pious
Donald A. Ritchie

OXFORD
UNIVERSITY PRESS
2001

OXFORD
UNIVERSITY PRESS

Oxford New York
Athens   Auckland   Bangkok   Bogotá   Buenos Aires   Calcutta
Cape Town   Chennai   Dar es Salaam   Delhi   Florence   Hong Kong   Istanbul
Karachi   Kuala Lumpur   Madrid   Melbourne   Mexico City   Mumbai
Nairobi   Paris   São Paulo   Shanghai   Singapore   Taipei   Tokyo   Toronto   Warsaw

and associated companies in
Berlin   Ibadan

Copyright © 1993, 1994, 1998, 2001
by John J. Patrick, Richard M. Pious, Donald A. Ritchie

Published by Oxford University Press, Inc.
198 Madison Avenue, New York, NY 10016
http://www.oup-usa.org

Library of Congress Cataloging-in-Publication Data

Patrick, John J.
    The Oxford guide to the United States government / John J. Patrick, Richard M. Pious, Donald
A. Ritchie.
    p. cm.
    Includes bibliographical references and index.
    ISBN-13 978-0-19-514273-0
    ISBN 0-19-514273-X
    1. United States—Politics and government—Encyclopedias.   I. Pious, Richard M.
II. Ritchie, Donald A.   III. Title.
JK9 .P384 2001
320.473'03—dc21

                                                                00-051024

5 7 9 8 6 4

Printed in the United States of America
on acid-free paper

Contents

How To Use This Book

The articles in this book are arranged alphabetically, so you can look up words, concepts, or names as you come across them in other readings or in the media. You can then use the SEE ALSO listings at the end of an article to find entries about related subjects. Sometimes you may find that the book presents information under a different article name than what you looked up. In that case, the book will refer you to the proper article. For example, if you look up Apportionment, you will find the notation "SEE Gerrymandering; Reapportionment."

In addition, there are abundant cross-references at the ends of most articles. So, for example, the article on Terms of the Supreme Court will refer you to Decision days and Opening day of the Supreme Court for further information.

You can also use this book topically, by reading all the articles about a particular aspect of the Presidency, Congress, Supreme Court, federal government department, or issue. Below are several groupings of topics around common themes.

BIOGRAPHIES

Presidents and Vice Presidents   There are articles on all the Presidents and Vice Presidents of the United States and selected First Ladies. The biographical dates used throughout the book are generally accepted by scholars; readers may find that some dates vary in "standard sources." You can find a chronological list of Presidents and Vice Presidents in Appendix 2.

Members of Congress If you want to know about a particular senator or representative, look the person up by his or her surname. Many of the leaders of both houses and others who personified important eras in congressional history are included. Brief biographies of the nearly 12,000 people who have served over the past two hundred years can be found in the *Biographical Directory of the United States Congress, 1774–1989* (Washington D.C.: Government Printing Office, 1989).

Supreme Court justices The book contains articles on all the chief justices and associate justices of the Supreme Court, listed by surname. The biographical entries include personal data about each justice, and the articles emphasize participation in notable Court decisions and significant contributions to constitutional law. In Appendix 5 is a list of the Justices of the Supreme Court with their term dates.

Groups Some unofficial groups of people have played important roles in American government and history, and the book has separate articles on them. Some examples are Boll Weevils, Carpetbaggers, and Coxey's army.

BUILDINGS

Appendix 6 contains information about visiting the Capitol Building, the Supreme Court Building, and the White House. The article on the White House will tell you about the building's architecture and history. To learn more about the place where members of Congress work, you can look up Architect of the Capitol, Cloakrooms, or Subways. Further information on the Supreme Court building, as well as the Court's previous homes, can be found in Buildings, Supreme Court.

DEPARTMENTS OF THE FEDERAL GOVERNMENT

There are articles on the various executive departments and organizations, such as Department of Defense, as well as on the most important agencies, such as Central Intelligence Agency and Social Security Administration. There are also articles on various committees and administrative units of the Congress, such as the Congressional Research Service, as well as overview articles on Committees, Congressional; and House-Senate relations, among others.

EVENTS

The book contains articles on individual events of historic importance, such as Camp David peace talks; Credit Mobilier scandal; and Watergate, as well as categories of events, such as Assassinations, Presidential; and Scandals, congressional. There are also articles on periods or policies, such as Fair Deal, Great Society, and New Deal.

ISSUES AND CONCEPTS

If you are interested in an issue, you can find an article on that issue, such as Freedom of speech and press, which will in turn refer you via cross-references to relevant Supreme Court cases, such as *Abrams* v. *United States*. If you need information on campaign finance, you can find articles on Campaign committees, congressional; Campaign financing, congressional; Compaign finance, Presidential; as well as related articles on Election campaigns, Presidential; and Primaries, Presidential.

LAWS AND DECISIONS

Laws   For important events in congressional history and information about particular laws enacted by Congress, you might consult Impeachment of Andrew Johnson (1868), Treaty of Versailles, or Watergate investigation (1973).

Presidential decisions   To read about Presidential decision making, see such articles as Cuban Missile Crisis; Decision making, Presidential; Gulf of Tonkin Resolution; and Monroe Doctrine.

Supreme Court cases The book contains articles on one hundred of the most historically significant cases decided by the Supreme Court. Each article on a case opens with standard information. The name of the case is followed by the official citation from *United States Reports* (for cases since 1875). For example, for *Abington School District* v. *Schempp* the citation is 374 U.S. 203 (1963). This means that the opinion in the case is published in volume 374 of *United States Reports,* beginning on page 203. The year the case was decided follows in parenthesis.

Before 1875, official reports of Supreme Court cases were published under the names of the Court reporters. Thus, these names (full or abbreviated) appear in the citations of the Court's decisions before 1875. For example, the citation for *McCulloch* v. *Maryland* is 4 Wheat. 316 (1819). Wheat. is an abbreviation for Henry Wheaton, the Supreme Court Reporter from 1816 to 1827. Thus, this citation indicates that this case can be found in the fourth volume compiled by Wheaton, that it begins on page 316, and that it was decided in 1819.

Each case article also provides the vote of the justices on the case; who wrote the majority opinion for the Court; and who, if anyone, concurred or dissented. The articles include background information on the case; the issue or issues before the Court; the

Court's opinion and legal reasoning in deciding the case; the dissenting opinions, if any, and reasons for them; and the significance of the case in constitutional law and history.

POWERS
If you want to know about the constitutional powers of the President, you can read articles such as Appointment power, Commander in chief, Creation of the Presidency, and Veto power. Articles on checking and balancing Presidential power include the following: Censure, resolutions of; Checks and balances; Ethics, Presidential; Impeachment; and War Powers Resolution (WPR).

To learn about the constitutional powers of Congress, you can look up Advice and consent, Investigations, or Treaties. For information about Supreme Court powers, there are articles on Judicial activism and judicial restraint; Judical power, and Judicial review.

PROCEDURES AND PRACTICES
Presidential procedures and practices   Presidential nominations and elections are covered in a number of articles, including Congressional caucus; Debates, Presidential; and Ticket. Regarding succession, see such articles as Assassinations, Presidential; Disability, Presidential; Inauguration, Presidential; Transitions, Presidential; and 25th Amendment. Appendix 3 contains a table of results for all Presidential elections. For other Presidential matters, such as perks of office, for example, consult articles on Air Force One; Camp David; Salary, Presidential; Secret Service, U.S.; and White House.

Congressional procedures   You can read about the process by which Congress drafts, debates, and votes on legislation in entries on Acts, Committees, Hearings, and Resolutions, among others. A number of articles deal with congressional elections, including Campaign financing, Incumbents, and Term limits. The fascinating relationship between Congress and the executive branch is discussed under Bipartisan foreign policy, Executive privilege, and Separation of powers.

Supreme Court procedures   Some examples of entries explaining how the Supreme Court operates are: Administration of federal courts, Conference, Decision days, Discuss list, Opinions, Oral argument, Rules of the Court, and Seniority.

TERMS
There are useful short definitions of terms such as Cloture; Concurrent resolution, Ex rel, Obiter Dictum, and Pocket veto.

TRADITIONS
For each branch of the government, there are articles on its traditions, such as Bean soup; "Hail to the Chief"; and Robing room.

A

ABINGTON SCHOOL DISTRICT V. SCHEMPP

- 374 U.S. 203 (1963)
- Vote: 8–1
- For the Court: Clark
- Concurring: Brennan, Douglas, and Goldberg
- Dissenting: Stewart

A Pennsylvania law required that each public school day must be started with the reading of at least 10 verses from the Bible, without comment. A student could be excused from this requirement by presenting to school authorities a written request from a parent or guardian. The Schempp family challenged the state law. They refused to request an exception for their child, a student at Abington High School, from the Bible-reading exercise. And they refused to allow their child to attend this exercise. The Schempps brought suit against the Abington School District to block enforcement of the Bible-reading statute.

The Issue Did the Pennsylvania law on Bible reading in public schools violate the 1st Amendment provision against laws "respecting an establishment of religion"?

Opinion of the Court The Supreme Court decided in favor of the Schempp family and struck down the state law on Bible reading in public schools. Writing for the Court, Justice Tom Clark concluded that the government may not promote religion in public schools. For the first time, the Court specified a test for de-termining whether a law violates the establishment clause of the 1st Amendment. Justice Clark wrote:

> The test may be stated as follows: What are the purposes and primary effect of the enactment? If either is the advancement or inhibition of religion then the enactment exceeds the scope of legislative power as circumscribed by the Constitution. . . . [T]o withstand the strictures of the Establishment Clause there must be a secular legislative purpose and a primary effect that neither advances nor inhibits religion.

According to the Court, the Pennsylvania law on daily Bible reading in public schools failed to pass this establishment clause test. The state law failed because it advances religion. The Pennsylvania Bible-reading statute was therefore ruled unconstitutional.

Dissent Justice Potter Stewart claimed that the Court had incorrectly applied the 1st Amendment's establishment clause in this case. He emphasized that by striking down the state law, the Court was denying free exercise of religion to the majority of citizens. According to Justice Stewart, this Pennsylvania law was constitutional because it did not force students to participate in a religious exercise. Justice Stewart wrote:

> We err in the first place if we do not recognize, as a matter of history and as a matter of imperatives of our free society, that religion and government must necessarily interact in countless ways. . . .

[T]he central value embodied in the First Amendment . . . is the safeguarding of an individual's right to free exercise of his religion. . . . [T]here is involved in these cases a substantial free exercise claim on the part of those who affirmatively desire to have their children's school day open with the reading of passages from the Bible.

Significance This case clearly stated the Court's position that the government cannot foster or promote religious doctrine in public schools through state-legislated religious exercises. By reinforcing the *Engel* v. *Vitale* (1962) decision, the Court in this case seemed to settle the question of state-sponsored religious exercises in public schools. However, public opinion polls from the 1960s to the 1990s have shown that more than 60 percent of Americans disagree with the Court's decisions on the prohibition of prayer in public school–sanctioned programs. Vigorous debate about the separation of church and state continues.

SEE ALSO *Engel v. Vitale; Establishment clause; Religious issues under the Constitution*

ABORTION RIGHTS

Abortion is the termination of a pregnancy before the embryo or fetus is capable of survival outside the mother's womb. Should a woman have the right to decide whether or when to have an abortion?

In the United States, the state governments traditionally have regulated the performance of abortions. In 1960 every state government had a law making abortion a crime except when it was done to save the mother's life. By 1973, however, 14 states had passed laws permitting abortions under certain other conditions, such as when the pregnancy resulted from rape or incest, or when the baby, if born, would likely suffer from a severe defect. Alaska, Hawaii, and New York repealed most previous restrictions on the woman's right to an abortion.

In 1973 the U.S. Supreme Court made its landmark ruling on abortion rights in *Roe* v. *Wade*. The Court struck down a Texas law regulating abortion as an unconstitutional infringement of a woman's right to privacy, which had been established in *Griswold* v. *Connecticut* (1965). In *Griswold* the Court invalidated a Connecticut law prohibiting the use of birth control devices by ruling that it violated a person's constitutional right to a zone of privacy based on several provisions of the Bill of Rights and the due process clause of the 14th Amendment. In *Roe* the Court held that the "right of privacy [established in *Griswold*] is broad enough to encompass a woman's decision whether or not to terminate her pregnancy."

Writing for the Court, Justice Harry Blackmun stated that a woman's right to abortion could be limited, however, by "a compelling state interest" to protect her health and life. The Court decided that during the second trimester of a woman's pregnancy (months 4 to 6), the state might intervene to regulate abortion to protect the mother's health and that the state might regulate or prohibit abortion during the third trimester (months 7 to 9). During the first trimester (months 1 to 3) of a pregnancy, however, it seemed unlikely that there would be a reason to restrict abortion rights in order to protect the health and life of the mother.

Writing in dissent, Justice Byron White could not find in the Constitution the right to privacy upon which the *Roe* decision was based. Justice White helped to frame the controversy about abortion rights that has continued since the *Roe* decision. Many critics, like Justice White, have believed that questions about abortion rights should be resolved by state governments, not by the Court, as had been the long-standing practice in the American federal system of government.

Many critics of the *Roe* decision, however, have opposed it on religious or moral grounds. They reject abortion rights because, in their system of belief, abortion is a sin or morally wrong.

Activities to counter or overturn the *Roe* decision have persisted and have led to legal challenges in federal courts. But attempts to erect barriers to abortion rights have mostly failed, as have efforts to overturn *Roe*.

In *Harris* v. *McRae* (1980), however, the Court held that "although government may not place obstacles in the path of a woman's exercise of her freedom of choice [to have an abortion], it need not remove those not of its own creation. Indigency [being poor] falls in the latter category." As a result of this ruling, poor women who could not afford to pay for an abortion were no longer able to use federal Medicaid funds for one, except in cases of rape or incest or when the mother's life is threatened. Further, in *Ohio* v. *Akron Center for Reproductive Health* (1990), the Court upheld a state law that required minors (those below adult age) seeking an abortion either to notify one parent or get approval from a local court of law.

A major legal challenge to *Roe* emerged in *Webster* v. *Reproductive Health Services* (1989). This case concerned the constitutionality of a 1986 Missouri law that included several provisions for restricting a woman's right to an abortion. The Court upheld only two. One banned the use of public facilities or public employees to carry out an abortion. The other restriction pertained to the performance of an abortion on a woman carrying a fetus thought to be more than 20 weeks old. Before performing such an abortion, the physician must determine, through medical testing, whether the fetus is viable, or capable of living outside the mother's womb. If it is viable, the abortion may be prohibited.

The *Webster* decision thus modified the second-trimester rule in *Roe*, which held that all regulations on abortion rights must be related to protecting the health of the mother. The *Webster* decision, however, stopped short of overturning *Roe*, which antiabortion rights advocates had wanted. And the *Webster* decision held that while government regulation of abortion is permissible, such regulation could not impose "undue burdens" or unreasonable obstacles to a person seeking an abortion.

In 1992, in *Planned Parenthood* v. *Casey*, the Court used the "undue burden" standard to uphold most of the Pennsylvania Abortion Control Act. The sustained parts of this law required a woman to wait 24 hours to have an abortion after receiving specific information from a doctor about the procedure, the condition of the fetus, and the possible alternatives to abortion. The one part of the law that the Court found unconstitutional was the requirement that a married woman inform her husband about an intended abortion. As in the *Webster* case, however, the Court's majority refused to overturn the *Roe* decision.

In 2000 (*Stenberg* v. *Carhart*), the Supreme Court struck down a Nebraska law (and, in effect, 30 similar state laws) that banned a procedure called "partial-birth" abortion. Doctors have used this procedure, which they call D&X (dilation and extraction), to terminate late-term pregnancies. Writing for the Court's 5-to-4 majority, Justice Stephen Breyer declared the Nebraska law unconstitutional because it did not provide an exception for cases when the life or health of the mother is in danger. Further, he held the law was written so broadly that it could be used to prohibit abortion procedures other than D&X, which would violate the Court's *Roe* decision. Writing in dissent, Justice Anthony Kennedy deplored the Court's decision and said the 1997 Nebraska law was made "to forbid a procedure many decent and civilized people find so abhorrent as to be among the most serious of crimes against human life."

SEE ALSO *Griswold v. Connecticut; Privacy, right to; Roe v. Wade; Webster v. Reproductive Health Services*

SOURCES David J. Garrow, *Liberty and*

Sexuality: The Right to Privacy and the Making of Roe v. Wade, 1923–1973 (New York: Macmillan, 1993). Laurence H. Tribe, *Abortion: The Clash of Absolutes* (New York: Norton, 1990).

ABRAMS V. UNITED STATES

- 250 U.S. 616 (1919)
- Vote: 7–2
- For the Court: Clarke
- Dissenting: Holmes and Brandeis

Jacob Abrams was arrested in New York City on August 23, 1918. He and several friends had written, printed, and distributed copies of a leaflet that severely criticized President Woodrow Wilson and the U.S. government. The leaflet opposed President Wilson's decision to send a small U.S. military force to Russia during the civil war that followed the communist revolution of 1917. The communists, led by Vladimir Lenin, were fighting against anticommunist Russians and various foreign military forces to retain control of the government. Abrams's leaflet urged American workers to walk off their jobs in protest against President Wilson and the U.S. government and in support of the new communist government in Russia.

Abrams and his friends were arrested for violating the Espionage Act of 1917 and the Sedition Act of 1918. These laws made it a crime to write and publish disloyal or profane statements that were intended to interfere with production of goods necessary to the defense of the United States during wartime. The laws were passed to control antiwar activity after the United States entered World War I.

The Issue The specific question facing the Supreme Court pertained to the constitutionality of the Espionage Act and the Sedition Act. These federal laws were designed to limit freedom of expression in order to protect national security during wartime. However, the 1st Amendment says, "Congress shall make no law . . .

abridging the freedom of speech, or of the press, or the right of the people peaceably to assemble, and to petition the Government for a redress of grievances." Did enforcement of the Espionage Act and the Sedition Act violate the 1st Amendment free speech and press rights of Jacob Abrams?

Opinion of the Court Justice John H. Clarke, writing for the Court, decided against Abrams's claims that his 1st Amendment rights were violated. Clarke based his decision on the "clear and present danger" and "bad tendency" tests stated by Justice Oliver Wendell Holmes in *Schenck* v. *United States* (1919). According to these two tests, which Holmes used interchangeably in *Schenck,* free speech and press could be limited if they were intended to cause an illegal action or if they threatened national security.

Justice Clarke wrote that "men must be held to have intended, and to be accountable for, the effects which their acts were likely to produce." Clarke argued that "the obvious effect" of the leaflet "would be to persuade persons . . . not to work in ammunition factories, where their work would produce bullets, bayonets, cannons, and other munitions" needed by U.S. military forces in World War I.

Dissent Justice Oliver Wendell Holmes disagreed, for himself and Justice Louis Brandeis, with Justice Clarke's use of the "clear and present danger" test in this case. And he repudiated the "bad tendency" test. Justice Holmes maintained that the government had the right to protect itself against speech that immediately and directly threatens the security and safety of the country. He wrote that the 1st Amendment protected the expression of all opinions "unless they so imminently threaten immediate interference with the lawful and pressing purposes of the law that an immediate check is required to save the country." Justice Holmes denied that Abrams's actions and intentions represented a danger sufficient to justify limitation of his freedom of expression.

Justice Holmes concluded his dissent with a compelling theory of free speech in a constitutional democracy. Arguing for "free trade in ideas," Holmes said: "[T]he best test of truth is the power of the thought to get itself accepted in the competition of the market. . . . That at any rate is the theory of our Constitution. It is an experiment, as all life is an experiment."

Significance The Court's opinion in this case prevailed only in the short run. The dissent of Justice Holmes eventually had more influence on the Court and the American people. Holmes modified the "clear and present danger" test he had stated in *Schenck,* which had been used interchangeably with the "bad tendency" test. In *Abrams,* Holmes rejected the "bad tendency" test, which emphasized a person's intentions to encourage lawless behavior. Instead, Holmes stated in his *Abrams* dissent that a "clear and present danger" exists only when speech can be immediately and directly connected to specific actions that cause illegal behavior threatening the safety or security of the United States. If an imminent danger could not be demonstrated, then speech could not be lawfully limited. The *Abrams* dissent has been called the best defense of free speech ever written by an American.

SEE ALSO *Freedom of speech and press; Schenck v. United States; Seditious libel*
SOURCES Richard Polenberg, *Fighting Faiths: The Abrams Case, the Supreme Court, and Free Speech* (New York: Viking, 1987).

ACTS OF CONGRESS

An act of Congress is a bill that has passed both the House of Representatives and Senate and has been signed by the President or passed by a two-thirds vote of both houses over the President's veto. Each act of Congress is numbered as a public law or private law. PL 103-35 would be the 35th public law enacted by the 103rd Congress. Private laws are numbered separately, from Private Law 103-1 on up.

SEE ALSO *Bills; Private laws*

ADAMS, ABIGAIL
First Lady

- Born: Nov. 11, 1744, Weymouth, Mass.
- Wife of John Adams, 2nd President
- Died: Oct. 28, 1818, Braintree, Mass.

Wife of John Adams, second President of the United States, mother of John Quincy Adams, sixth President, and an early champion of women's rights, Abigail Adams spent much of her life in towns on the outskirts of Boston. She had no formal schooling and her spelling was poor, but she was widely read and learned to read and write French. In October 1764 she married John Adams, a young law student. She strongly supported his criticisms of British colonial policies. During the first 10 years of their marriage they had four children. Then revolutionary politics separated the couple for most of the next decade. During the Revolution, Abigail Adams ran the family farm and several business enterprises. In 1784 she rejoined her husband in France, then in 1785 traveled with him to London, where he was the American minister to Great Britain.

Abigail wrote numerous letters to her husband, relatives, and friends, among them leaders of the Revolution such as Thomas Jefferson. Her letter writing was not only a form of communication but also a form of expression through which she could develop her ideas and influence the leaders of the new American nation.

Among those things she wrote was an eloquent statement on women's equality. "I desire you would Remember the ladies," she wrote to her husband in 1776 while he was attending the Continental Congress in Philadelphia, "and be more generous and favourable to them than your ancestors." She added that "if perticuliar [sic] care and attention is not paid to the Laidies [sic] we are determined to foment a Rebellion, and will not hold ourselves bound by any Laws in which we have no voice, or Representation." But her plea was unavailing: at the end of the Revolution women had fewer rights in law and politics than they had been given by colonial governments. In November 1800, in the last year of her husband's Presidency, Abigail Adams became the first Presidential wife to occupy the White House in Washington, D.C. More than two decades after her death, in 1840, her grandson Charles Francis Adams began publishing her letters, which became an inspiration to many women seeking greater equality.

SOURCES L. H. Butterfield et al., eds., *The Book of Abigail and John: Selected Letters of the Adams Family 1762–1784* (Cambridge: Harvard University Press, 1975). Phyllis Lee Levin, *Abigail Adams: A Biography* (New York: St. Martin's, 1987). Paul C. Nagel, *The Adams Women: Abigail and Louisa Adams, Their Sisters and Daughters* (New York: Oxford University Press, 1989). Lynne Withey, *Dearest Friend: A Life of Abigail Adams* (New York: Free Press, 1981). Nancy Woloch, "Abigail Adams," in *The Reader's Companion to American History,* edited by Eric Foner and John Garraty (Boston: Houghton Mifflin, 1991).

ADAMS, JOHN
2nd President

- Born: Oct. 19, 1735, Braintree, Mass.
- Political party: Federalist
- Education: Harvard College, A.B., 1755
- Military service: none
- Previous government service: Continental Congress, 1774–1778; committee that drafted Declaration of Independence, 1776; wrote first draft of Massachusetts Constitution, 1779; minister to the Netherlands, 1780–84; minister to Great Britain, 1785–87; Vice President, 1789–97
- Elected President, 1796; served, 1797–1801
- Died: July 4, 1826, Quincy, Mass.

John Adams was the first President to occupy the White House and the first to be defeated for reelection and turn over his office to a member of an opposition party. Adams was one of the most experienced men ever to become President. As a young man, he taught school in Worcester, Massachusetts, and studied law, becoming a lawyer in Boston in 1758. He played a major role in the struggle for independence. On the principle that there should be "no taxation without representation," Adams led the opposition to the Stamp Act of 1765, which required the purchase of a stamp (effectively a tax) for all public documents. He showed his fierce independence, however, when he defended several British soldiers accused of killing four people in the Boston Massacre in 1770; most were acquitted.

As a member of the Second Continental Congress in 1775, Adams seconded the nomination of George Washington as commander of the Continental Army. The following year he seconded the motion for independence, introduced by Richard Henry Lee, that "these colonies are, and of a right ought to be, free and independent states." He then convinced Thomas Jefferson to draft the Declaration of Independence. He was, as Jefferson said, "the pillar of support" in the debate leading to its adoption.

Adams helped draft the Massachusetts Constitution of 1780. In 1781 and 1782 he helped negotiate the treaty with the British ending the war and then a commercial treaty with the Netherlands and a large loan to the United States.

In 1785 Adams was named minister to Great Britain. Two years later, while still in London, he published his book *A Defence of the Constitutions of Government of the United States of America,* which called for a balanced Constitution. The people would be represented in the lower house of the legislature, "the rich, well born and able" would serve in the upper house, and a chief executive would act as a monarch to balance the interests of the upper and lower classes.

Adams received the second highest total of electoral college votes (behind George Washington) in the Presidential election of 1789, and so he assumed the post of Vice President. "My country has in its wisdom contrived for me the most insignificant office that ever the invention of man contrived or his imagination conceived," Adams observed. But he was instrumental in devising procedures for the new Senate, and he cast several important tie votes to pass Washington's legislative measures. He was one of the organizers of the Federalist party during his second term and was the choice of President Washington and most party leaders to run for President in 1796. He defeated Thomas Jefferson, 71 electoral votes to 68. Under the rules then in effect, Jefferson, as the runner-up, became Vice President, although he was the leader of the opposition party, the Democratic-Republicans.

During his Presidency, Adams faced intrigues within his own party as Alexander Hamilton moved to influence his cabinet and his policies. The Jay Treaty, which he had helped negotiate with Great Britain in 1795, allowed British ships to seize American cargoes bound for France. The French, in retaliation, decreed that French warships would follow the same policy against American ships bound for Britain, and they then seized 317 American merchant vessels in 1796. A diplomatic mission sent by Adams was refused a hearing by the French unless bribes were paid to French agents (who were referred to as X, Y, and Z) and the United States agreed to lend France $10 million. Adams refused and made the affair public. "Millions for War but not one cent for Tribute" became the slogan of Federalists calling for war.

Adams ignored pressure from Alexander Hamilton and his followers in the Federalist party and instead sought a diplomatic solution, while Congress passed laws enlarging the navy and preparing war measures. Bowing to party pressure, Adams appointed George Washington commander in chief of the army, in effect ceding his constitutional powers.

Congress created the Navy Department, organized the Marine Corps, and canceled all treaties with France. Three new frigates, the *United States*, the *Constitution*, and the *Constellation*, were launched in 1797 and 1798 and soon put to service in a naval war with France. They were responsible for a number of American victories in the Caribbean. Although Congress had not declared this war, it did vote funds for it, and the Supreme Court held that the war was constitutional. With French emperor Napoleon's navy bottled up by the British fleet, and many French ships sunk by Admiral Horatio Nelson in the Battle of the Nile in 1798, France could not easily retaliate. Finally a diplomatic solution in 1799 averted further war. The decision to talk rather than continue fighting led to a final split between Adams and the Hamilton wing of the Federalist party. In 1800 Napoleon and Adams agreed to the Treaty of Montfortaine, which released the United States from its revolutionary war treaties with France.

During the conflict Adams assented to the passage of the Alien and Sedition Acts (1798), which made it a crime to publish anything "with the intent to defame" the President or the government. The sedition law was invoked in 25 cases and used by his party to arrest editors from the opposition ranks. Ten editors were convicted by Federalist judges and juries. But public opinion opposed the prosecutions. Madison and Jefferson worked to get the Virginia and Kentucky legislatures to pass resolutions that the laws were unconstitutional and would not be enforced.

Although Adams retained enough support from moderate Federalists to win his party's nomination for a second term, the split in his party led to his defeat by Thomas Jefferson in the election of 1800. Adams's final act in office, on the morning of March 4, 1801, was to send to the Senate his nomination of John Marshall to be chief justice of the United States.

SEE ALSO *Burr, Aaron; Jefferson, Thomas; Washington, George*

SOURCES James Truslow Adams, *The Ad-*

ams Family (Boston: Little, Brown, 1930). Ralph Adams Brown, *The Presidency of John Adams* (Lawrence: University Press of Kansas, 1975). Joseph J. Ellis, *Passionate Sage: The Character and Legacy of John Adams* (New York: Norton, 1993).

ADAMS, JOHN QUINCY
6th President

- Born: July 11, 1767, Braintree, Mass.
- Political party: Federalist, Democratic-Republican, Whig
- Education: Harvard College, A.B., 1787
- Military service: none
- Previous government service: minister to the Netherlands, 1794; minister to Prussia, 1797; Massachusetts Senate, 1802; U.S. Senate, 1803–8; minister to Russia, 1809–14; negotiator of Treaty of Ghent, 1814; minister to Great Britain, 1815–17; U.S. secretary of state, 1817–25
- Elected President, 1824; served, 1825–29
- Subsequent government service: U.S. House of Representatives, 1831–48
- Died: Feb. 23, 1848, Washington, D.C.

John Quincy Adams spent much of his youth accompanying his father, John Adams, on diplomatic missions. He was educated in Amsterdam, Leipzig, London, Leiden, and Paris. In 1781, at the age of 14, he served as private secretary to Francis Dana, the American envoy to Russia. The following year he served as secretary to the American emissaries negotiating peace with Great Britain. After graduating from Harvard in 1787 and becoming a lawyer, he served as the American envoy to the Netherlands in 1794, and Washington wrote to Vice President Adams that his son "is the most valuable public character we have abroad." In 1797 he served as minister to Prussia during his father's Presidency and negotiated a commercial treaty with Prussia.

Adams returned home shortly after his father left the White House in 1801 and served in the U.S. Senate. He supported

Jefferson's purchase of Louisiana and voted for Jefferson's Embargo Act of 1807. Both of these acts alienated the Federalists in Massachusetts and induced Adams to resign from the Senate a year early. He then joined the Democratic-Republicans and, after teaching at Harvard for two years, accepted the position of minister to Russia. He declined James Madison's offer of a Supreme Court appointment in 1810. He was one of three American commissioners who negotiated an end to the War of 1812 on terms favorable to America by negotiating the Treaty of Ghent (1814) with Great Britain.

Adams capped his career as a diplomat with eight years of service as James Monroe's secretary of state. He performed brilliantly, negotiating a treaty with Great Britain in 1818 to extend the U.S.–Canadian border along the 49th parallel; arranging future arbitration of the disputed Oregon boundary; and obtaining Florida from Spain in return for a renunciation of U.S. claims on Texas. His policy of benevolent neutrality, a "tilt" to the former colonies and away from Spanish efforts to reconquer them, assured the success of Latin American independence movements without leading to war with Spain. The Monroe Doctrine, which warned European states against interference in the Western Hemisphere, was largely Adams's work: President Monroe was willing to accept a joint declaration with the British to warn the French, Spanish, and Russians against attempts to dominate the Americas, but Adams insisted that the United States issue the doctrine unilaterally. Adams is considered by many to be the greatest secretary of state in American history.

Meanwhile, the Federalist party had disappeared, and in the misnamed Era of Good Feelings, as Monroe's Presidency was known, only the "National Republicans" under President Monroe remained. In the Presidential election of 1824, Adams was one of four regional candidates from this party. Andrew Jackson received a plurality of the popular vote (he got the most votes, but fewer than 50 percent), defeating Adams 153,000 to 114,000 in states where electors were chosen by popular vote. Jackson's 99 electoral college votes put him ahead of Adams's 84, Senator William Crawford's 41, and Representative Henry Clay's 37.

Since no one had received a majority of the electoral college votes, the election went to the House of Representatives, where each state would have one vote. Crawford had meanwhile suffered a stroke and was not in serious contention. Clay, who had come in fourth, was ineligible in the House election according to the 12th Amendment. But Clay was Speaker of the House and threw his influential support to Adams, who received a winning 13 votes to only 7 for Jackson and 4 for Crawford on the first ballot. Jackson's followers claimed there had been a "corrupt bargain." It is believable that a bargain had been involved—because Adams named Clay his secretary of state only three days after the election.

Adams's Presidency was tainted by the questions surrounding his election and the violent opposition of the Jacksonians. He had no personal following among the people or in Congress and accomplished little. He backed Clay's "American system," which called for protective tariffs that would raise the prices of foreign goods to encourage U.S. industry, land sales to encourage settlement of the West, and enlargement of foreign markets for American agricultural products. Adams also proposed the creation of a national university and naval academy, new scientific missions to explore American coastal waters and lands, and expeditions to the South Seas. His proposals were scornfully ignored in Congress. Adams, Clay, and Secretary of the Treasury Richard Rush did manage to get Congress to pass measures subsidizing canals, harbors, and roads. Adams was more successful in foreign affairs. Together with Secretary of State Clay, he negotiated commercial treaties that improved trade with a number of European nations and with Mexico.

The midterm elections of 1826 gave a large majority in Congress to anti-Adams factions. Meanwhile, Andrew Jackson organized his followers and in 1828, running under the label Democrat or Democratic-Republican, defeated Adams, who ran on the ticket of the National Republicans.

Adams was elected to the U.S. House of Representatives in 1830 and served there for 18 years. In the House he won the nickname Old Man Eloquent for speaking out vigorously against slavery and for defeating a "gag rule" that Southern representatives had imposed against antislavery petitions.

He was a tireless opponent of slavery and offered a plan for its gradual elimination. In 1841 he argued a case, *United States* v. *Amistad*, before the Supreme Court that resulted in overturning the convictions of the African crew members who had mutinied aboard the slave ship *Amistad*.

In 1848, John Quincy Adams suffered a stroke at his desk in the House chamber, shortly after making an impassioned speech against extending slavery to the Western territories won in the Mexican-American War. He died in a nearby room. A bronze marker on the floor indicates where Adams's desk once stood. Visitors to the Capitol know it as the "whispering spot" in Statuary Hall.

SEE ALSO *Jackson, Andrew; Monroe Doctrine; Monroe, James*

SOURCES James Truslow Adams, *The Adams Family* (Boston: Little, Brown, 1930). Mary Hargreaves, *The Presidency of John Quincy Adams* (Lawrence: University Press of Kansas, 1985). Leonard Richards, *The Life and Times of Congressman John Quincy Adams* (New York: Oxford University Press, 1988).

ADJOURNMENT, CONGRESSIONAL

Adjournment is the way in which Congress goes *out* of session. Whenever the House or Senate adjourns, it ,ormally ends a legislative day. The next time that chamber reconvenes, it must go through the general order of business, including the reading of the journals (the minutes of previous sessions, which provide information such as bills and resolutions introduced, committee referrals, and votes) and other morning business. The House usually adjourns each day, but because routine morning business can be prolonged as part of a Senate filibuster, a delaying tactic, the Senate may recess rather than adjourn. A recess keeps the chamber in the same legislative day. A single legislative day of the Senate once ran for 162 calendar days, from January 3 to June 12, 1980.

The Constitution forbids either house to adjourn for more than three days without the other's permission. During an annual session of Congress, the Senate and House from time to time will adjourn for a week to allow members to return to their districts and states, often in connection with a holiday. In nonelection years, Congress usually adjourns for the month of August. An adjournment resolution will set a specific date when the Senate and House plan to return. At the end of the session, the leadership will make a motion to adjourn *sine die*. This Latin phrase means "without a day," since the resolution sets no time for Congress to return before the beginning of the next session on January 3. If a national emergency or some other unexpected business develops after an adjournment, the President can call Congress back into special, or extraordinary, session. In recent years, adjournment resolutions have also authorized the House and Senate majority leaders jointly to call Congress back from a *sine die* adjournment.

SEE ALSO *Recess, congressional*

ADMINISTRATION OF FEDERAL COURTS

The Supreme Court is in charge of the administration of the federal judicial system. The chief justice and associate justices participate in the work of the Judicial Conference of the United States, the Administrative Office of the United States Courts, and the Federal Judicial Center.

Judicial Conference of the United States The chief justice presides over the Judicial Conference of the United States, a board of trustees for the federal courts. Created by an act of Congress in 1922, the Judicial Conference has 27 members who represent the district or trial courts, the intermediate appellate courts, and the Supreme Court. By law, the mission of the Judicial Conference of the United States is to oversee the practices and procedures of the federal courts and to recommend changes to improve the functioning of the federal judicial system. The conference meets twice a year at the Supreme Court Building in Washington, D.C.

Administrative Office of the United States Courts Budgeting services and staff support for the Judicial Conference of the United States are provided by the Administrative Office of the U.S. Courts. The Administrative Office, created in 1939 by an act of Congress, operates under direction of the Judicial Conference to oversee and provide administrative services for the lower federal courts. More than 600 people work for the Administrative Office. The director, appointed by the Supreme Court, reports to the Judicial Conference of the United States.

Federal Judicial Center In 1967 Congress enacted legislation to create the Federal Judicial Center, which carries out research and training programs to improve the operations of the federal courts. The chief justice presides over the seven-member board of the center, which meets four times each year and oversees the work of the center's staff of more than 100 people. Findings of the center's research projects are reported to the Judicial Conference of the United States.

ADMIRALTY AND MARITIME LAW

Article 3, Section 2, of the U.S. Constitution says, "The judicial Power shall extend

... to all Cases of admiralty and maritime Jurisdiction." Admiralty or maritime law pertains to ships on the sea, including civil and criminal actions. In 1815 Justice Joseph Story, writing for the Supreme Court in *De Lovio* v. *Boit*, defined the scope of the Court's admiralty jurisdiction by stating that it extended to all transactions "which relate to the navigation, business, or commerce of the sea."

ADVICE AND CONSENT

Presidents nominate people to federal office and negotiate treaties with other nations, but these actions become official only after the Senate gives its "advice and consent." Such sharing of power between the executive and legislative branches of the federal government is a critical part of the system of checks and balances. The Constitution (Article 2, Section 2) explains how the Senate can grant its consent: a majority vote confirms a nomination, and a two-thirds vote is necessary to ratify a treaty. Giving advice, however, is much less clear.

During the 1st Congress, senators wanted the President to appear in their chamber to present all nominations and treaties in person. President George Washington believed nominations would be too numerous to make appearing in person practical, and he preferred to submit them to the Senate in writing. But he agreed to consult with the Senate personally about treaties. On August 24, 1789, Washington came to the Senate chamber seeking advice on a series of proposed treaties with Indian nations. He presented a list of questions for debate and response. But because the senators felt uncomfortable discussing these matters in the imposing presence of George Washington, they decided instead to refer the questions to a committee for further study. "This defeats every purpose of my coming here!" Washington exclaimed. Unhappily, he agreed to return to the Senate at a later date to receive their answers. This marked the last time that

Washington, or any President, came to the chamber personally in search of advice as well as consent.

Over the years, however, both legislators and the President have devised various other means of involving the Senate in nominations and treaties prior to granting its consent. For instance, Presidents may invite senators to help negotiate treaties or to attend the negotiations as observers. The attorney general and other cabinet officers are careful to consult with key senators before the President nominates federal judges, U.S. attorneys, and other appointed officials. Modern Presidents regularly telephone or meet privately with senators to win their support for pending treaties and nominations.

SEE ALSO *Appointment power; Checks and balances; Nominations, confirmation of; Treaty powers*

ADVISORY OPINIONS

An advisory opinion is a legal opinion given before a case is tried. Federal judges do not provide advisory opinions because Article 3 of the U.S. Constitution says their jurisdiction extends only to real cases and controversies "in Law and Equity, arising under this Constitution," and they therefore cannot issue statements about hypothetical cases.

A precedent against advisory opinions was established in 1793, when President George Washington asked Chief Justice John Jay and the Supreme Court to advise him about the federal government's obligations stemming from a 1778 treaty made by the Continental Congress with France. John Jay replied in a letter (August 8, 1793) that it was wrong, under the Constitution, for the Court to provide an advisory opinion to the President or anyone else. Jay's letter explained that the justices should not provide opinions on any matter unless it was brought to the Court through formal legal procedures as a real case.

The letter set a precedent against advisory opinions. It reinforced the principle of separation of powers and judicial independence from the executive branch. Thus, the President turns to the attorney general of the United States or to his own counsel, both of whom are officials of the executive branch, for legal advice.

SEE ALSO *Separation of powers*

AFFIRMATIVE ACTION

During the 1950s and 1960s, the Supreme Court struck down laws that unfairly discriminated against individuals on the basis of race. Through its decisions in cases such as *Brown* v. *Board of Education* (1954) and *Heart of Atlanta Motel* v. *United States* (1964), the Court ruled that African Americans must have "equal protection of the laws," which the 14th Amendment says is a right available to all people in the United States. While lauding this major advance in civil rights for African Americans, many civil rights leaders said it was not sufficient to overcome the negative effects of more than two centuries of racial discrimination in the United States. So, during the 1970s and 1980s, leaders of civil rights organizations, such as the National Association for the Advancement of Colored People (NAACP) and the National Organization of Women (NOW), proposed programs designed to go beyond mere equality of opportunity to provide limited kinds of preferential treatment for victims of long-term racial or gender-based discrimination. These programs are called *affirmative action* because they involve plans designed, through specific actions, to bring about desired outcomes, such as increased job opportunities, job promotions, and admissions to colleges and universities.

Affirmative action plans, as conceived by civil rights leaders, have the following characteristics. First, they may be sponsored or instituted either by government agencies and public educational institutions or by private organizations, such as businesses, labor unions, vocational training schools, or private colleges.

Second, affirmative action plans take into account such personal factors as race, ethnicity, or gender when individuals are under consideration for employment in a job, promotion to a better job, or admission to a school or college. However, individuals must *not* receive education or employment benefits solely on the basis of such factors as race, ethnicity, or gender; rather, these personal factors will determine who receives or does not receive certain opportunities only when minority candidates are otherwise well qualified for the jobs, educational programs, and so forth that they seek to attain.

Third, affirmative action programs are based clearly on the educational or economic need of individuals resulting from unfair treatment in the past of racial, ethnic, or gender groups to which these people belong.

Fourth, affirmative action plans are supposed to be temporary remedies, not permanent programs.

Supporters of affirmative action plans have pointed out that most members of certain minority groups, such as African Americans, lag far behind most white Americans in income, educational attainment, job advancement, and general living standards. They claim that these differences are the result of long-term racial discrimination, rooted in the pre–Civil War institution of slavery. Further, they argue that affirmative action programs, whether required by the government or voluntarily undertaken by private employers and schools, are the best means to overcome the persistent negative consequences of past discrimination against minorities, especially African Americans.

Affirmative action programs have been widely established in education and economic institutions of the United States. These programs have raised a fundamental constitutional question. Does the 14th Amendment's guarantee of "equal protection of the laws" permit certain kinds of preferential treatment of certain categories of individuals, such as African Americans or women, in order to remedy the negative consequences of long-term discrimination against them?

The Supreme Court has upheld some affirmative action practices while striking down extreme versions of this concept. In *Regents of the University of California* v. *Bakke* (1978), for example, the Court ruled that a university could take into account race and ethnicity when making decisions about the admission of students. However, the Court ruled that an affirmative action plan based on rigid racial quotas to boost admission of minority students to a university was unconstitutional. In *United Steelworkers of America* v. *Weber* (1979), the Court permitted an employer's voluntarily imposed and temporary affirmative action program. That program would encourage unskilled black workers to obtain training that would lead to better, more skilled jobs, in which black Americans historically have been underrepresented. Once again, however, the Court rejected rigid, race-based quotas in hiring and job advancement.

In *United States* v. *Paradise* (1987) the Court upheld a temporary and "narrowly tailored" quota system to bring about job promotion for black state troopers in Alabama. The state's affirmative action plan imposed a "one black for one white" promotion quota. This was justified, the Court said, by the "long and shameful record of delay and resistance" to employment opportunities for black Americans in the Alabama state police.

In 1987, in *Johnson* v. *Transportation Agency of Santa Clara County,* the Court endorsed a carefully crafted, temporary, and voluntary affirmative action plan to boost job promotion opportunities for women. The Court held it was permissible to take into account a woman's gender as a positive factor in promotion to a higher-ranking position because women had been systematically denied access to such positions in the past.

In 1995, the Court ruled in *Adarand Constructors, Inc.* v. *Peña* that all public programs that give preferences to minorities should be subjected to the strictest judicial scrutiny. Race-based affirmative action programs would be upheld, the Court declared, only if they were narrowly designed to apply to individuals victimized by past acts of racial discrimination. Thus, the Court emphasized that equal protection of the laws is a right guaranteed by the Constitution to every individual.

In 1996, the Supreme Court let stand a decision of the 5th Circuit Court of Appeals against an affirmative action policy of the University of Texas Law School. The Court of Appeals struck down a policy that allowed admissions officers to consider racial identity as a a factor in making decisions about which students to admit to the law school. The policy's purpose was to increase significantly the number of law school students belonging to racial minority groups. In its decision to ban this policy, the Court of Appeals contradicted the Supreme Court's 1978 *Bakke* decision, in which the Court held that colleges or universities could consider race in their admissions policies as long as they did not establish rigid race-based quotas.

In a brief statement about its refusal to hear this University of Texas Law School case, the Court said that the case did not offer a favorable opportunity to decide the issue. Because the University of Texas had abolished the policy at issue in the case, Justice Ruth Bader Ginsburg explained that "we must await a final judgment on a program genuinely in controversy before addressing the important questions raised in this petition."

Due to a last-minute settlement, the Court did not hear an affirmative action case during the 1997–98 term. In 1997 the Court had declined to hear a challenge to a California law banning race- or sex-based preferences in school admissions, public employment, and government contracts. The Court let stand a decision by the Ninth Circuit that the statute at issue, passed by voters in a referendum on Proposition 209, was not unconstitutional. Affirmative action, however, remains a controversial political and legal issue.

SEE ALSO *Brown v. Board of Education; Civil rights; Equality under the Constitution; Heart of Atlanta Motel v. United States; Johnson v. Transportation Agency of Santa Clara County; National Association for the Advancement of Colored People (NAACP); Regents of the University of California v. Bakke; United Steelworkers of America v. Weber*

SOURCES Michel Rosenfeld, *Affirmative Action and Justice* (New Haven: Yale University Press, 1991). Bernard Schwartz, *Behind Bakke: Affirmative Action and the Supreme Court* (New York: New York University Press, 1988). Girardeau A. Spann, *The Law of Affirmative Action : Twenty-Five Years of Supreme Court Decisions on Race and Remedies* (New York: New York University Press, 2000).

AFRICAN AMERICANS IN GOVERNMENT

African Americans in Congress After the Civil War and the abolition of slavery, the 14th Amendment (1868) granted African Americans citizenship, and the 15th Amendment (1870) gave black men (but not women) the right to vote. In February 1870, Hiram Revels (Republican–Mississippi) became the first black senator, taking the seat once occupied by Jefferson Davis, President of the Confederacy. In December 1870, Joseph Rainey (Republican–South Carolina) became the first black representative.

Several Southern states sent African Americans to Congress during Reconstruction. But later efforts by white Southerners to restrict black voting, often through violence and intimidation, resulted in the defeat of most black incumbents. After 1901 no blacks served in Congress until the election of Oscar DePriest (Republican–Illinois) in 1928. By then, Washington had become a segregated city, and DePriest had to struggle

even for his staff members to eat in the Capitol restaurants. In 1934, Arthur Mitchell (Democrat–Illinois), also an African American, defeated DePriest, signifying a dramatic shift in African-American voters from the party of Lincoln to the party of Franklin D. Roosevelt. William Dawson (Democrat–Illinois) succeeded Mitchell and later became the first black member of Congress to chair a major committee. During the 1940s, Dawson and Adam Clayton Powell, Jr. (Democrat–New York) were the only black members of Congress. But beginning in the 1950s, the number of blacks winning election to the House slowly grew, first from Northern cities and then from Southern rural districts. In 1968, Shirley Chisholm (Democrat–New York) became the first black woman elected to Congress. By contrast to the growing number of black representatives, Edward Brooke (Republican–Massachusetts) and Carol Moseley-Braun (Democrat–Illinois) have been the only black senators to serve during the 20th century.

As their ranks increased, African-American representatives formed the Congressional Black Caucus. Begun in 1971, the Black Caucus has sought a leadership role among African Americans, speaking for their concerns and promoting their legislative interests. The Black Caucus has worked for civil rights and for equal opportunity in education, employment, and housing but also has taken stands on Presidential nominations and matters of foreign policy.

African Americans in the Executive Branch Despite the abolition of slavery in 1865 and the extension of the vote in 1870, African Americans remained largely outsiders in American democracy. Post–Civil War Reconstructionist politics was full of fierce dispute over the role blacks should have in the political system: many Republicans worked to empower African Americans politically while reactionary Democrats sought to rebuild the antebellum South. Presidents began appointing

African Americans to positions within the executive branch during the late 19th century. Former U.S. senator Blanche K. Bruce served as registrar of the Treasury, and the abolitionist Frederick Douglass was appointed U.S. minister to Haiti. Republican Presidents also appointed southern blacks as postmasters and to other federal patronage positions.

John Mercer Langston was elected clerk of a town in rural Ohio in 1855, making him the first black elected to public office. In organizing black political clubs around the country and helping to shape the post–Civil War Republican party's progressive relationship toward blacks, Langston had an important role in mobilizing African Americans. He was twice suggested as a candidate for Republican Vice President.

African Americans shifted political allegiance to the Democratic party during the Great Depression and New Deal in the 1930s. Under President Franklin D. Roosevelt, high-level African-American appointees in several agencies met regularly in what was popularly known as the Black Cabinet to discuss racial policy. Mary McLeod Bethune was the founder of the National Council of Negro Women in 1935, and Roosevelt appointed her director of the Division of Negro Affairs of the National Youth Administration in 1936, a position she held until 1944. Along with the rest of the Black Cabinet, Bethune forced politicians to see African Americans as a significant population of voters who deserved representation.

Another member of the Black Cabinet, Robert Weaver, became the first African American appointed to the Presidential cabinet, when Lyndon Johnson named him as secretary of housing and urban affairs in 1966.

The first African American to run for President was Jesse Jackson. Although he lost the Democratic party nomination in 1984 and 1988, his campaigns proved that a black candidate could command a large audience and reflect a broad range of political interests. In 1984 Jackson garnered 21 percent of the popular vote in the primaries, and in 1988 his campaign registered more than 2 million new voters.

Jackson also opened the door for future black Presidential hopefuls. In 1996 Colin Powell, the first African American to serve as chairman of the Joint Chiefs of Staff (1989–93), made a Presidential bid but ultimately decided not to run. Alan Keyes, a former member of Ronald Reagan's administration and a U.S. ambassador to the United Nations Social and Economic Council, also made two bids for the Republican nomination, in 1996 and 2000.

African Americans in the Federal Judiciary In 2000, 10.3 percent of the country's federal judges were African American, while more than 12 percent of the total U.S. population was African American. The Supreme Court included one black justice, Clarence Thomas. Only one other African American had ever sat on the Court: Thurgood Marshall, who served from 1967 to 1991.

Half of the 13 U.S. appellate courts included no one of African-American ancestry in 2000. The Fourth Circuit, which serves Maryland, Virginia, West Virginia, North Carolina, and South Carolina, has never had a black judge, even though 23 percent of the region's population is black. Civil rights organizations, such as the National Association for the Advancement of Colored People (NAACP) have persistently called for the appointment of more African Americans and other minorities to the federal judiciary.

SEE ALSO *Chisholm, Shirley; Civil rights; Powell, Adam Clayton, Jr.; Reconstruction, congressional; Revels, Hiram R.*

SOURCES William L. Clay, *Just Permanent Interests: Black Americans in Congress, 1870–1991* (New York: Penguin, 1992). Dewey M. Clayton, *African Americans and the Politics of Congressional Redistricting* (New York: Garland, 1999). Bruce A. Ragsdale and Joel D. Treese, eds., *Black Americans in Congress, 1870–1989* (Washington, D.C.: Government Printing Office,

1990). Carol M. Swain, *Black Faces, Black Interests: The Representation of African Americans in Congress* (Cambridge: Harvard University Press, 1993).

AGNEW, SPIRO T.
Vice President

- Born: Nov. 9, 1918, Baltimore, Md.
- Political party: Republican
- Education: Johns Hopkins University, 1937–40; Baltimore Law School, LL.B., 1947
- Military service: U.S. Army, 1943–45; Bronze Star
- Previous government service: county executive, Baltimore County, 1962–66; governor of Maryland, 1966–68
- Vice President under Richard Nixon, 1969–73
- Died: Sep. 17, 1996, Berlin, Md.

Spiro Agnew played no substantive role in the policies of the Nixon administration, but he was its spokesman, launching strident attacks against Nixon's political enemies. A speech he gave in Des Moines, Iowa, in 1969 attacked the "instant analysis" that news commentators offered after Presidential addresses. In a 1970 speech in San Diego he characterized opponents of the administration as "nattering nabobs of negativism." Agnew's favorite target was what he referred to as the "Eastern establishment." He called this group "effete snobs" and "limousine liberals," claiming they had lost touch with the interests of working Americans, whom he and Nixon referred to as the "New American Majority." Agnew campaigned in 1972 against the "permissiveness" of American society, a social issue that drove millions of Democrats to desert their liberal nominee, George McGovern, and give the Republican ticket one of the largest landslides in American history.

In 1973 Agnew was prosecuted for taking bribes from Baltimore land developer Lester Matz between 1962 and 1971 and failing to report the income on his federal tax returns. On October 9, 1973, he pleaded no contest; he was declared guilty and fined $10,000. Agnew was spared a jail sentence as part of a plea bargain with the prosecutors in which he resigned his office. He later became a public relations representative and lobbyist and then retired to California. In 1981 a civil suit brought by taxpayers in Maryland led to a judgment against Agnew that required him to pay the state of Maryland $248,735 in compensation for the bribes he had taken when he was governor and Vice President.

SEE ALSO *Ford, Gerald R.; Nixon, Richard M.; Vice President*

SOURCES Spiro T. Agnew, *Go Quietly . . . Or Else* (New York: Morrow, 1980). Richard M. Cohen and Jules Witcover, *A Heartbeat Away: The Investigation and Resignation of Spiro T. Agnew* (New York: Viking, 1974). Jules Witcover, *White Knight: The Rise of Spiro Agnew* (New York: Random House, 1972).

AGOSTINI V. FELTON

- 521 U.S. 203 (1997)
- Vote: 5–4
- For the Court: O'Connor
- Dissenting: Souter

Issues involving the relationship of church and state have challenged the Supreme Court throughout the second half of the 20th century. The justices have struggled to determine the extent to which the 1st Amendment's establishment clause requires separation of government and religion.

In *Aguilar* v. *Felton* (1985), the Supreme Court decided for strict separation. It held that New York City could not use government funds to send public school teachers into private religious schools to provide remedial education for disadvantaged children. This program had been authorized by a federal law, Title 1 of the Elementary and Secondary Education Act of 1965. The Court, however, concluded that this New York program led to excessive entanglement of church and state in violation of the U.S. Constitution.

In 1995, the New York City School Board filed a motion in the federal district court to seek reconsideration of the *Aguilar* decision. The petitioners argued that Supreme Court decisions subsequent to *Aguilar* had undermined the Court's ruling in this 1985 case. In *Zobrest* v. *Catalina School District* (1993), for example, the Supreme Court decided that a deaf student in a private religious school could be helped by a sign-language interpreter supported by government funds. The Court explained that this kind of public aid directly helps the student—and not the private religious school or the church that sponsors it—and therefore does not violate the 1st Amendment's establishment clause.

The Issue   The 1985 *Aguilar* decision seemed to be contradicted by the 1993 *Zobrest* decision. So the issue in *Aguilar* was raised again: can remedial instruction be provided constitutionally to disadvantaged students in private religious schools through a federal government program?

Opinion of the Court   The Supreme Court overturned the decision in *Aguilar* v. *Felton* (1985). By a narrow 5-to-4 majority, the justices repudiated the argument that all government aid to religious schools is unconstitutional. Public funds could be provided to support programs that directly aid students of private religious schools and clearly promote secular purposes that contribute to the public good. The establishment clause is not violated as long as the religious mission of the private school is neither advanced nor obstructed by a government program.

Dissent   Led by Justice David Souter, the four dissenters argued against overturning the *Aguilar* decision. They predicted that the Court's decision in the *Agostini* case would open the way to direct government aid of religious institutions and thereby to public support of particular religious missions. Thus, the establishment clause of the 1st Amendment would be grossly violated.

Significance   The *Agostini* decision buoyed advocates of accommodation between government and religious institutions. It dismayed those in favor of strict separation between church and state.

AIR FORCE ONE

Air Force One is the designation of the plane on which the President flies. Since 1989 the President has usually flown on one of two Boeing 747s, each able to carry 80 passengers and 23 crew members to any point on the globe. Each plane is outfitted as a mobile command center and is linked to all U.S. military and national security communications networks.

The planes are coated in silver and have blue trim, and they carry the Presidential seal on their sides. They are operated by the Special Missions Fleet of the 89th Military Airlift Wing at Andrews Air Force Base. Expenses for *Air Force One* come out of the Defense Department budget, unless the President is on a campaign trip, in which case the political party's national committee or campaign committee foots the bill.

Marine One is the designation of the VH-3 helicopter that transports the President from the helipad on the South Lawn of the White House to local destinations or to the hangar at Andrews Air Force Base in Maryland where he boards *Air Force One*. Marine Helicopter Squadron One usually consists of eight craft, located at a base just down the Potomac River from the White House. *Marine One* is often used to take the President and his guests to his rural retreat at Camp David in nearby Maryland.

The cost of operating *Air Force One* is $40,243 per hour of flight. Each year the Pentagon spends approximately $185 million on travel expenses for the President and his top aides, according to the House Post Office Committee's Subcommittee on Human Resources.

SOURCES Bradley Patterson, *The Ring of Power* (New York: Basic Books, 1988). Jerold F. TerHorst, *The Flying White House: The Story of Air Force One* (New

York: Coward, McCann & Geoghegan, 1979).

ALDRICH, NELSON W.

- Born: Nov. 6, 1841, Foster, R.I.
- Political party: Republican
- Senator from Rhode Island: 1881–1911
- Died: Apr. 16, 1915, New York, N.Y.

At the beginning of the 20th century, a powerful group of conservative Republicans known as the Senate Four held enormous influence over federal policy. "The four bosses of the Senate can and do control that body," one journalist wrote of senators Nelson Aldrich, William Allison, Orville Platt, and John C. Spooner. "This means that these four men can block and defeat anything that the president or the House may desire."

Of the four, Nelson Aldrich wielded the greatest power because he was chairman of the Finance Committee, which determined all tariff legislation (tariffs are taxes placed on imported goods and materials). American industry sought protection from foreign competition through high tariffs, and business leaders looked to Aldrich to protect their interests. Aldrich strongly opposed President Theodore Roosevelt's proposals to regulate big business and fought the attempts of progressive reformers to lower tariff rates. The press called Aldrich a "dictator," "tyrant," and "boss of the Senate," making him a symbol of the need for reform through direct election of senators.

SOURCES Horace Samuel Merrill and Marion Galbraith Merrill, *The Republican Command, 1897–1913* (Lexington: University Press of Kentucky, 1971).

ALIEN AND SEDITION ACTS (1798)

Congress has not always been able to tolerate criticism from the press. In 1798, there was a distinct threat of war between the United States and France because of the French navy's interference with American shipping. The majority Federalist party in Congress reacted angrily to attacks from the minority Democratic-Republican party press by enacting the Alien and Sedition Acts.

The Alien Act allowed the President to deport any noncitizen he considered "dangerous to the peace and safety of the United States." This provision was aimed at the many Democratic-Republican editors who were born abroad. The Sedition Act made it a crime to publish anything false or malicious about either house of Congress or about the executive branch. Benjamin Franklin Bache, editor of the *Philadelphia Aurora,* predicted that "to laugh at the cut of a coat of a member of Congress will soon be treason." In fact, many editors went to prison for writing critically about Congress and the President. Even Representative Matthew Lyon (Democratic-Republican–Vermont) spent time in jail for condemning the government in his newspaper. Democratic-Republicans considered these laws unconstitutional. "Men who engage in public life, or are members of legislative bodies, must expect to be exposed to . . . attacks on their principles and opinions," said Senator Charles Pinckney (Democratic-Republican–South Carolina). When they gained the majority in the election of 1800, Democratic-Republicans allowed the Alien and Sedition Acts to expire.

SEE ALSO *Media coverage of Congress*
SOURCES James Morton Smith, *Freedom's Fetters: The Alien and Sedition Laws and American Civil Liberties* (Ithaca, N.Y.: Cornell University Press, 1956).

AMENDMENTS, CONSTITUTIONAL

The authors of the U.S. Constitution realized that this document would have to be revised to meet new needs that would arise as times changed. George Washington expressed the inevitable need for, and value of, constitutional change in a letter to his nephew, Bushrod Washington (Nov. 10, 1787):

> The warmest friends and best supporters the Constitution has do not contend that it is free from imperfections. . . . I think the People (for it is with them to Judge) can . . . decide with as much propriety on the alterations and amendments which are necessary [as] ourselves. I do not think we are more inspired, have more wisdom, or possess more virtue than those who will come after us.

The amendment process George Washington, who presided at the Constitutional Convention of 1787, recognized the importance of Article 5 of the Constitution, which specifies how formal changes, or amendments, may be made. Article 5 says:

> The Congress, whenever two thirds of both Houses shall deem it necessary, shall propose Amendments to this Constitution, or, on the Application of the Legislatures of two thirds of the several States, shall call a Convention for proposing Amendments, which, in either Case, shall be valid to all Intents and Purposes, as Part of this Constitution, when ratified by the Legislatures of three fourths of the several States, or by Conventions in three fourths thereof, as the one or the other Mode of Ratification may be proposed by the Congress; Provided that no Amendment which may be made prior to the Year One thousand eight hundred and eight shall in any Manner affect the first and fourth Clauses in the Ninth Section of the first Article; and that no State, without its Consent, shall be deprived of its equal Suffrage in the Senate.

The usual procedure for making amendments is for two-thirds of the members of Congress to vote for the proposed amendments. Then the amendment is sent to the legislatures of the 50 states for approval. If three-fourths of the state legislatures ratify, or vote for, the proposal, it becomes an amendment to the U.S. Constitution. Of the 27 constitutional amendments, 26 of them have been made in this way. The 21st Amendment was approved by special conventions in three-fourths of the states, rather than by votes in state legislatures.

There is another method of proposing amendments to the Constitution—a method that has never been used. Congress, upon request of the states, can call for a special constitutional convention to write a proposed amendment. Article 5 states that Congress "shall call a convention for proposing amendments" whenever two-thirds of the states petition for one. This method of proposing amendments is known as an "Article 5 Convention."

The Bill of Rights The Constitution was first amended in 1791. Amendments 1 through 10, known as the Bill of Rights, were ratified together by the end of 1791. This Bill of Rights limits the power of the federal government in order to protect the civil liberties and rights of individuals. These rights include the freedom of speech, press, and religion; protection against unwarranted searches and seizures; and provision of due process and other rights for people accused of criminal behavior.

Amendments 11 and 12 The 11th Amendment became part of the Constitution in 1795. It was proposed and ratified in response to an unpopular Supreme Court decision, *Chisholm* v. *Georgia* (1793). The Court decided that the citizens of one state can sue another state in a federal court without the consent of the state being sued. The 11th Amendment reversed the Court's decision by barring citizens of another state or a foreign country from suing a state in a federal court without the state's consent.

Amendment 12 was ratified in 1804 to correct a defect in the procedures for electing the President and Vice President. Article 2, Section 1, of the Constitution said that Presidential electors would vote for two people for President. The person who received the most votes would be the President, provided that he also received a majority of the votes cast. The person who came in second would be the Vice President. If no one received a majority of the electoral votes, then the House of Representatives had to elect the President from among the five candidates with the most votes.

This system broke down in the election of 1800, when Thomas Jefferson and Aaron Burr received an equal number of votes. It was generally understood that Jefferson was the candidate for President and Burr the candidate for Vice President. The Constitution, however, provided only that each elector vote for two people, without specifying which vote was for the Vice Presidential candidate. When Jefferson and Burr received the same number of votes, Burr tried to take advantage of the confusion to win the Presidency. Instead of stepping aside for his partner, Jefferson, he insisted that the contest be decided by the House of Representatives, as provided by the Constitution. Jefferson was the winner in the House election, but it was clear that the Constitution had to be amended to prevent confusion of this kind from happening again. The 12th Amendment provided that electors would cast separate ballots for President and Vice President. If no one receives a majority of votes for President, the House of Representatives selects the President from the three candidates with the largest number of votes. Each state then has one vote, no matter how many representatives it has in the House. If no one receives a majority of the electoral votes for Vice President, then the Senate selects the Vice President from the two candidates with the most votes.

Civil War amendments Amendments 13, 14, and 15 are known as the Civil War amendments. They were passed in the wake of the Union victory over the slave-holding states of the Confederacy. These three amendments were passed to protect the rights of former slaves.

The 13th Amendment, approved in 1865, prohibits slavery or involuntary servitude. The 14th Amendment, added to the Constitution in 1868, defined citizenship in such a way that state governments could not deny former slaves their rights and privileges as citizens. This amendment says that all people born in the United States are citizens, as are all individuals who are naturalized (foreign-born persons who become citizens through a legal process defined by Congress). According to Amendment 14, all citizens (natural-born and naturalized) have the same legal rights and privileges. This amendment forbids state governments from making and enforcing laws that would deprive any person of life, liberty, or property "without due process of law"; it also says that a state government may not deny to any person under its authority "the equal protection of the laws."

Amendment 15, adopted in 1870, barred the federal and state governments from denying any citizen the right to vote on the basis of race, color, or previous enslavement.

20th-century amendments The 16th Amendment, passed in 1913, allows the federal government to collect taxes on income earned by citizens. In 1895, the Supreme Court had ruled that a federal income tax law passed in 1894 was unconstitutional. Representatives of the people in Congress and state legislatures overruled the Supreme Court through passage and ratification of this 16th Amendment.

The 17th Amendment was also passed in 1913. It provides for the election of two senators from each state by direct vote of the eligible voters of the state. Before passage of this amendment, two senators were selected by the legislature of each state.

The 18th Amendment, approved in 1919, prohibited the production, sale, or transportation of intoxicating liquors in the United States. The 21st Amendment was passed in 1933 to repeal the 18th Amendment.

Amendments 19, 23, 24, and 26 extended and protected the voting rights of certain groups of people. The 19th Amendment, ratified in 1920, guaranteed the voting rights of women. The 23rd Amendment, adopted in 1961, gave citizens residing in the District of Columbia the right to vote in Presidential elections. The 24th Amendment, ratified in 1964, prohibited state governments from requiring people to pay a tax to qualify to vote, thereby extending the right to vote to people who could not afford to pay a poll tax. The 26th Amendment, added to the Constitution in 1971, required that neither the federal nor state governments could deny to someone 18 years of age or older the right to vote on account of age.

The 20th Amendment, passed in 1933, provided that the term of office of the President and Vice President shall end at noon, January 20, of the year following the last Presidential election. The term of office of senators and representatives shall end at noon, January 3.

The 22nd Amendment was passed in 1951 to prevent a President from serving more than two four-year terms of office. It was passed in response to the four-time election of President Franklin D. Roosevelt. Previously, Presidents had followed a custom begun by George Washington and had retired from office after serving two terms. Many people feared that a President might gain too much power if permitted to hold office for too long. The Constitution was amended to avoid this risk.

The 25th Amendment, passed in 1967, specifies how vacancies are to be filled in the office of Vice President. The President nominates a Vice President to fill a vacancy, but this choice must be approved by a majority of the members of the Senate and House of Representatives. The 25th Amendment also specifies how the Vice President can assume the duties of the President if he is incapacitated. When the President recovers, he can take charge

again, but if recovery is not likely to occur, the Vice President can be approved as the new President by a two-thirds vote of both houses of Congress. The 25th Amendment allows a President to resign from office and be replaced by the Vice President. The new President has the power to appoint a new Vice President, subject to approval by a majority of the members of both houses of Congress.

The 27th Amendment, passed in 1992, holds that if members of Congress vote a pay raise for themselves, their constituents must have the opportunity, before the pay raise takes effect, to vote out of office the members who voted for it. This amendment was originally proposed in 1789, along with the amendments that became parts of the Bill of Rights, but it was rejected. In the 18th century, six states ratified the amendment, and one more state ratified it in the 19th century. Thirty-three states approved it between 1978 and May 7, 1992, when Michigan became the final state needed to ratify it.

SEE ALSO *Bill of Rights; Constitution, U.S.; Lame-duck sessions of Congress*

SOURCES Richard B. Bernstein with Jerome Agel, *Amending America : If We Love the Constitution So Much, Why Do We Keep Trying to Change It?* (1993; reprint, Lawrence: University Press of Kansas, 1995). David E. Kyvig, *Explicit and Authentic Acts: Amending the U.S. Constitution, 1776–1995* (1996; reprint, Lawrence: University Press of Kansas, 1998). Maggie McComas, "Amending the Constitution," *Constitution* 4, no. 2 (Spring-Summer 1992): 26–31. Donald A. Ritchie, *The Constitution* (New York: Chelsea House, 1989).

AMENDMENTS, LEGISLATIVE

Amendments modify legislation in a variety of ways. Amendments can add new language, strike out certain provisions, or otherwise revise and improve a bill to gain enough votes to win its passage. After the sponsors have introduced a bill, other members will offer amendments to make it more acceptable to them. Lobbyists for private groups and the executive branch will also encourage amendments to make a bill more to their liking. Most amendments are added in committee, but others are added on the floor or later in the conference committee. All amendments must be voted on by the full Senate and House before becoming part of the bill.

Opponents use amendments to weaken a bill's initial purpose. They may offer amendments that would offend enough legislators to defeat the entire bill. Those seeking to filibuster against a bill, to delay it in debate, will pile on numerous technical amendments, changing a word or just the punctuation, in order to extend the debate and delay or defeat the bill's final passage. Even after a bill becomes law, future legislation may amend it. Many bills that Congress enacts are really amendments to previous legislation.

SEE ALSO *Committees, congressional; Germaneness*

AMERICAN BAR ASSOCIATION COMMITTEE ON FEDERAL JUDICIARY

The American Bar Association (ABA) is the oldest and largest private organization of lawyers in the United States. In 1946 the ABA established a Standing Committee on Federal Judiciary to advise the government on the selection of Supreme Court justices and judges for federal district and appellate courts.

The committee has 15 members, appointed by the ABA president. Members represent different regions of the country. There is at least one member from each of the geographical areas of the United States in which a circuit court of appeals is located.

The ABA committee's advisory ratings are an important part of the selection of Supreme Court justices. After the President of the United States nominates a person to be a Supreme Court justice, the ABA committee investigates the nominee's background and record of achievement. Then the Committee rates the nominee according to this scale: well qualified, not opposed, or not qualified. These ratings, although advisory, tend to have great influence on the Senate Judiciary Committee and on the Senate as a whole, which has the power to confirm or reject the President's nominations to the Court.

The ABA committee is also involved in the nomination of federal district and appellate court judges. It rates such nominees according to a slightly different scale: well qualified, qualified, qualified/not qualified (indicating a split vote), or not qualified. Its rating is sent to the Senate Judiciary Committee, which has the responsibility of recommending that the Senate approve or reject the nominee. The ABA committee also tries to publicize its ratings through the mass media.

SEE ALSO *Appointment power; Nominations, confirmation of*

AMERICAN CIVIL LIBERTIES UNION (ACLU)

Founded in 1920, the American Civil Liberties Union (ACLU) is a private organization, supported by dues-paying members, with the mission of defending the rights and liberties of individuals guaranteed by the U.S. Constitution. ACLU staff lawyers offer free legal services to individuals who claim that the government has violated their civil liberties. The ACLU defines civil liberties as those freedoms or rights that the government may not abridge or deny.

The ACLU claims nonpartisan support of the principle of civil liberties, and it has therefore defended the right to free speech of various individuals with conflicting political viewpoints because of its dedication to the idea of free speech for everyone. Moreover, ACLU lawyers have defended the free speech rights of people with whom they personally disagree, such as communists or Nazis, because they are dedicated to protecting the *principle* of free speech, not the *content* of any particular speech.

The ACLU has participated in numerous landmark cases before the U.S. Supreme Court that have greatly expanded the range and reach of the Bill of Rights during the 20th century. For example, in *Gitlow* v. *New York* (1925), a case involving 1st Amendment free speech issues, ACLU lawyers served as counsel for Benjamin Gitlow. The ACLU helped to influence the Court to recognize that the due process clause of the 14th Amendment could absorb or incorporate 1st Amendment freedoms. This case laid the foundations for the incorporation doctrine, which has led to the case-by-case application of most of the Bill of Rights to state laws. Lawyers for the ACLU were involved in most of these cases. For example, *Stromberg* v. *California* (1931) involved the 1st Amendment right to freedom of speech; *Engel* v. *Vitale* (1962) dealt with the 1st Amendment prohibition against the establishment of a state religion; and *Miranda* v. *Arizona* (1966) upheld the 5th Amendment right to avoid self-incrimination. The ACLU also cooperated with the National Association for the Advancement of Colored People (NAACP) in landmark civil rights cases, such as *Brown* v. *Board of Education* (1954), which have used the "equal protection of the laws" clause of the 14th Amendment to end racial segregation and discrimination in public facilities and services.

During the 1990s, the ACLU was involved prominently in cases about freedom of expression on the Internet, separation of religion and government in public schools, and the rights of women and minorities.

The ACLU has more than 275,000 members. The national office in Washington, D.C., includes a legal staff, a public education department, and people working on several special projects on legal research and education. The ACLU also has a network of affiliates in all 50 states.

SEE ALSO *Civil rights; Gitlow v. New York; Incorporation doctrine; Miranda v. Arizona; Stromberg v. California*

SOURCES Peggy Lamson, *Roger Baldwin: Founder of the American Civil Liberties Union* (Boston: Houghton Mifflin, 1976). Samuel Walker, *In Defense of American Liberties: A History of the ACLU* (New York: Oxford University Press, 1990).

"AMERICAN HOUSE OF LORDS"

The press has sometimes compared the U.S. Senate to the House of Lords, the upper chamber of the British Parliament. But senators actually have far greater power than the Lords and are much more involved in legislation. The term "House of Lords" has also been used to suggest the special privileges and "lordly" behavior of the Senate.

SEE ALSO *"Millionaires' club"*

AMICUS CURIAE

Amicus curiae is a Latin term meaning "friend of the court." An amicus curiae brief is a document regarding a case presented by someone who is not a direct party to the legal controversy. A friend of the court brief may be filed voluntarily, or it may be invited by the court. An amicus curiae brief is usually filed by individuals or groups with a special interest in the outcome of a case. However, no one who would benefit or be penalized directly, in a personal way, by the outcome of a case may file an amicus curiae brief.

In *Mapp* v. *Ohio* (1961), for example, the American Civil Liberties Union

(ACLU) filed an amicus brief that argued for the exclusion from a criminal trial of evidence seized without a search warrant. Although this issue was not even mentioned by Mapp's own attorneys, the ACLU brief influenced the Supreme Court to apply the exclusionary rule against a state government for the first time.

SEE ALSO *Mapp v. Ohio*

AMNESTY, PRESIDENTIAL

The Constitution (Article 2, Section 2) gives the President the power "to grant reprieves and pardons for offences against the United States except in cases of impeachment." This power is exercised by Presidential proclamation.

In 1795 President George Washington issued an amnesty to all participants in the Whiskey Rebellion, which involved a protest by farmers in Pennsylvania against paying federal taxes. President Abraham Lincoln's proclamation of December 8, 1863, offered a full pardon to Confederates (rebels), on condition that they take an oath to support the Constitution, laws, decisions of the Supreme Court, and proclamations of the President of the United States. On May 29, 1865, President Andrew Johnson issued a proclamation excluding certain groups of rebel leaders from amnesty but pardoning most other participants in secessionist activities. Decrees of July 4, 1868, and December 25, 1868, provided for full pardons for all who had participated in "the rebellion." This action led to the return from exile in England of several members of Confederate President Jefferson Davis's wartime cabinet. All told, more than 200,000 people were covered by these Civil War amnesties.

In 1946 President Harry S. Truman issued an amnesty covering 1,500 draft resisters in World War II. Six years later he granted amnesty to 9,000 individuals who had deserted from the military during the Korean War. The power of amnesty was also used by Presidents Gerald Ford and Jimmy Carter for more than 10,000 individuals who had resisted the draft during the Vietnam War.

SEE ALSO *Carter, Jimmy; Ford, Gerald R.; Johnson, Andrew; Lincoln, Abraham; Pardon power; Washington, George*

SOURCES David Gray Adler, "The President's Pardon Powers," in *Inventing the American Presidency,* edited by Thomas E. Cronin (Lawrence: University Press of Kansas, 1989).

APPEAL

An appeal is the procedure by which a case is taken to a higher court for its review and possible reversal of the lower court's decision. The bases for an appeal are claims by the losing party that the lower court made an error or committed an injustice in reaching its decision. In most cases, the U.S. Supreme Court has discretion in deciding whether or not to accept the case for review. However, in some types of cases there is an automatic right of appeal to the U.S. Supreme Court. For example, decisions by the highest court of a state in cases involving federal constitutional issues are always open to appeal by the losing party to the U.S. Supreme Court. However, the Court may decide to let the decision of the lower court stand, without conducting a hearing into the case.

Cases reach the U.S. Supreme Court on appeal after either a lower federal court or a state court has made a decision on them. Decisions by the highest state court can be appealed directly to the U.S. Supreme Court if a constitutional question is involved. The losing party in a case generally has the right to appeal the case to a court of appellate jurisdiction. In the federal judicial system, the U.S. Supreme Court is the appellate court of last resort. It has the final decision, within the judicial system, on cases that come before it.

Courts of appellate jurisdiction give the losing party a new chance to win a case.

This extra chance will be granted if there were errors of legal procedures, interpretation, or evidence in the lower court. Further, cases of great constitutional or national significance are likely to be accepted for determination by the highest appellate court, the U.S. Supreme Court. SEE ALSO *Circuit Courts of Appeals; Courts of Appeals*

APPELLANT

A party who appeals a lower court decision to a higher court, such as the U.S. Supreme Court, is an appellant.

APPELLATE JURISDICTION

SEE *Jurisdiction*

APPELLEE

The party to an appeal whose position in the case has been upheld by a lower court decision is the appellee. The appellant requires the appellee to respond in the higher court that accepts the case on appeal.

APPOINTMENT POWER

The Constitution (Article 2, Section 2) gives the President the power to nominate and, with the advice and consent of the Senate, appoint officers of the United States. The Constitution also provides that Congress by law may vest the appointment of "inferior Officers" in the President alone, in the courts of law, or in the heads of departments. Presidents also appoint and promote all military officers subject to Senate consent.

The President appoints 1,000 top officials, who bear titles such as secretary, under secretary, deputy secretary, and assistant secretary of the departments.

These officials collectively are the President's "administration." The other million or so federal civilian employees are considered "inferior officers," and almost all of them are appointed by heads of departments under civil service regulations.

To preserve the principle of separation of powers—the balance among the executive, legislative, and judicial branches—no member of Congress can be an officer of the United States while he or she serves in the Congress. Legislators are often appointed to a President's administration after leaving Congress, however.

Presidents since John Adams have chosen mostly members of their own political party for executive office, though Congress by law can require that appointments to regulatory commissions be evenly divided between Democrats and Republicans. Some Presidents, such as John F. Kennedy, chose several members of the opposition party for key positions in order to gain public and congressional support. Customarily, the Senate allows the President to pick whomever he wants for his administration, even if the Senate is controlled by the opposition party. The Senate usually does not consider the politics of nominees but restricts itself to their character. The Senate cannot attach formal conditions to its consent. It does not tell nominees what they must do once in office.

Prior to the 1950s only seven cabinet nominations were turned down. More recently, Dwight Eisenhower's nomination of Lewis Strauss for secretary of commerce in 1959 and George Bush's nomination of John Tower for secretary of defense in 1989 were defeated. Some nominees will withdraw before a Senate vote if the President senses they will be defeated; President Jimmy Carter withdrew the nomination of Theodore Sorensen for the position of Director of Central Intelligence in 1977, and President Bill Clinton withdrew his first two nominees for attorney general, Zo Baird and Kimba Wood, because of Senate opposition in 1993. In 1962 Congress refused to create the Department of Urban Affairs because President Kennedy made it known that he intended to appoint Robert Weaver to head it—and he would have been the first African American in the cabinet. By 1967 President Lyndon B. Johnson won congressional approval for the department and then for Weaver's appointment.

Supreme Court nominations   Presidents also nominate justices of the U.S. Supreme Court and judges of the lower federal courts. In each term a President appoints, on average, two Supreme Court justices. On at least 60 occasions sitting justices have offered suggestions for filling vacancies, and senators often provide advice. Presidents also tend to rely upon advice from the attorney general and the Department of Justice and the White House staff. In addition, the American Bar Association Standing Committee on Federal Judiciary, established in 1946, is generally influential in the selection of justices. This committee rates Supreme Court nominees as well qualified, not opposed, or not qualified.

Many interest groups also express views about the selection of justices. For example, the National Association for the Advancement of Colored People (NAACP) tries to influence selection of justices who will protect and support civil rights for African Americans and other minority groups. Likewise, the National Organization of Women (NOW) pushes for selection of justices who are sympathetic to women's rights.

The Senate Judiciary Committee conducts hearings to investigate the qualifications and merits of a proposed Supreme Court justice. Witnesses are called before the committee to provide information and opinions about the nominee. And the nominee also appears before the committee to answer questions about his or her qualifications to be a justice. Today, these hearings are often broadcast live to large audiences and reported daily in the mass media.

The Senate Judiciary Committee concludes its hearings with a vote to recommend confirmation or rejection of the nomination by the full Senate. A nominee becomes a justice only after a favorable vote by a majority of the U.S. Senate. Of the 148 nominations through 2000, 119 were approved, 13 rejected, and 16 withdrawn. When a President's party controls the Senate, more than 90 percent of his Supreme Court nominations are typically approved; when the opposition controls the Senate, the approval rate for justices drops to 50 percent.

There are no legal requirements for appointment to the U.S. Supreme Court. However, only lawyers have been selected for the Court. And it is unlikely that a nonlawyer could win approval to become a justice. Most justices have been judges on lower courts before becoming members of the Supreme Court. Since 1937, for example, 20 of the 34 justices had prior experience as either a state court judge or as a federal judge. Some of the greatest justices, however, did not serve previously as judges. For example, John Marshall, Joseph Story, Louis Brandeis, Harlan Fiske Stone, and Earl Warren have been rated as great achievers on the Court, but none of them had prior experience as a judge.

Presidents make a strong effort to select justices who will reflect favorably upon them and their administration. Legal scholars have noted the following personal characteristics that are expected of a nominee to the Supreme Court: substantial legal training and knowledge of law, personal integrity and high ethical standards, a strong sense of fair play, high intelligence, capacity for clear and cogent written and oral expression, and sound physical and mental health.

Presidents tend to nominate justices whose political and legal views appear to be compatible with their own. They usually do not seek agreement on specific cases or examples. Rather, they tend to want a nominee who shares their general views about constitutional interpretation and the process of making legal judgments.

Advice from Congress   Presidents often place their appointment powers at the disposal of important members of Congress. Senators often provide names of people from their state to the President for nomination as federal district judges as well as for positions in federal government regional offices located within their state; the President then makes the formal nomination. Moreover, the practice of "senatorial courtesy" enables the senator of a state affected by a Presidential nomination to declare that the nominee is "personally obnoxious"—in which case the Senate will take no action on a Presidential nomination. The Senator must be of the President's party and the Presidential nomination must be to a position in which power is exercised within the senator's home state.

The Constitution authorizes the President to make recess appointments when the Senate is not in session. Such appointments last only until the end of the next session of the Senate and do not require Senate consent. If the head of a department vacates the office, Congress by law has provided that Presidents may make an interim, or temporary, appointment without the consent of the Senate if the Senate had previously consented to the new appointee for another position. The interim appointee may serve for 30 days in the new position without Senate consent.

SEE ALSO *American Bar Association Committee on Federal Judiciary; Cabinet; Nominations, confirmation of; Senate Judiciary Committee*

SOURCES Henry J. Abraham, *Justices and Presidents: A Political History of Appointments to the Supreme Court* (New York: Oxford University Press, 1992). Henry J. Abraham, *Justices, Presidents, and Senators: A History of the U.S. Supreme Court Appointments from Washington to Clinton* (Lanham, Md.: Rowman & Littlefield, 1999). Louis Fisher, *Constitutional Conflicts between Congress and the President* (Princeton, N.J.: Princeton University Press, 1985). Joseph Harris, *The Advice and Consent of the Senate* (Berkeley: University of California Press, 1953). G. Calvin

MacKenzie, *The Politics of Presidential Appointments* (New York: Free Press, 1981).

APPORTIONMENT

SEE *Gerrymandering; Reapportionment*

APPROPRIATIONS

Congress holds the "power of the purse," the power to control how the government spends money. Neither the military nor any civilian agency of the federal government can spend any federal money unless it receives an appropriation from Congress. Americans inherited this powerful check on the executive branch from the early struggles between the British Parliament and the king. The Constitution provided for the popularly elected House to originate all revenue and appropriations bills and for the Senate to vote on these bills and to amend them.

Control of federal spending carries great power and influence, so there is always much competition for assignment to the House and Senate Appropriations Committees. Every bill that authorizes federal spending to carry out its programs must go to the Appropriations Committees, which decide whether to fund the programs fully, partially, or not at all. During each session, the Appropriations Committees will also hear extensive testimony about the operations and costs of executive branch agencies. Appropriations bills are regularly the last major bills enacted each session. It is not unusual for Congress to debate an appropriations bill late at night or early in the morning, with the clock ticking toward adjournment.

Not until after the Civil War did Congress create separate Appropriations Committees, to relieve the burden of appropriations from committees charged with raising revenue and to give Congress better control over federal spending. In the House, the Ways and Means Committee handled appropriations until 1865. In the

Senate, the Finance Committee oversaw appropriations until 1867. The Appropriations Committees are the largest in both bodies, with 61 members in the House and 28 in the Senate.

SEE ALSO *Recision bills*

SOURCES Richard F. Fenno, Jr., *The Power of the Purse: Appropriations Politics in Congress* (Boston: Little, Brown, 1966).

APPROVAL RATING, PRESIDENTIAL

SEE *Public opinion*

ARCHITECT OF THE CAPITOL

Appointed by the President, the Architect of the Capitol is in charge of any construction and maintenance of the Capitol building, House and Senate office buildings, Library of Congress, Supreme Court, and other sites and landscaping on Capitol Hill.

The original designer of the Capitol, William Thornton, was a physician rather than an architect. Thornton frequently argued with the professionally trained architects and engineers during the initial construction of the Capitol. A British architect, Benjamin Henry Latrobe, took over the project in 1803 and added his own influence to the designs, especially to the Capitol's interior. An American-born architect, Charles Bulfinch, oversaw completion of the original Capitol. From 1830 to 1851 there was no position of official architect. To supervise the building of the massive wings to house the new Senate and House chambers, Thomas U. Walter was appointed Architect of the Capitol in 1851. Walter was also in charge of building the massive cast-iron dome over the rotunda.

In the 20th century, Architects of the Capitol planned the extension of the East Front, the renovation of the West Front, and the construction of the office buildings. The architect is a member of the U.S. Capitol police board and supervises a large staff that handles all the necessary engineering, electrical work, air-conditioning, and landscaping around the Capitol.

SOURCES Lonnelle M. Aikman, *We, the People: The Story of the United States Capitol, Its Past and Its Promise* (Washington, D.C.: U.S. Capitol Historical Society, 1991).

ARMED SERVICES COMMITTEES

After the immense expansion of American military forces during World War II, Congress reorganized its many separate committees on military affairs, naval affairs, and militia into the House and Senate Armed Services Committees. These committees hold hearings and report legislation on all aspects of national defense, including military spending, weapons systems, strategies, bases, military academies, and the promotion of military officers. The influence of the Armed Services Committees grew in direct proportion to the billion-dollar increases in the defense budget during the cold war. Three Georgians, Representative Carl Vinson and Senators Richard Russell and Sam Nunn, established strong national reputations and earned respect within Congress as chairmen of the Armed Services Committees.

SEE ALSO *Committees, congressional*

ARMY-McCARTHY HEARINGS (1954)

The televised hearings that investigated alleged communist infiltration of the U.S. Army diminished public support for Senator Joseph R. McCarthy (Republican–Wisconsin) and led to his censure (rebuke) by the Senate. McCarthy was at the height of his influence when, as chairman of the

Permanent Subcommittee on Investigations, he launched an investigation of espionage and subversion in the army. During the inquiry, McCarthy verbally assaulted an army general, calling him "not fit to wear that uniform." The army responded that McCarthy was browbeating and humiliating its officers. It accused the senator of seeking preferential treatment for one of his staff members who had recently been drafted into the army. McCarthy stepped down temporarily as chairman to let the subcommittee investigate these charges.

Television covered the 35 days of hearings, from April to June 1954, and gave many Americans the opportunity to observe McCarthy's bullying tactics and irresponsible charges. "Have you no sense of decency, sir?" demanded the army's counsel, Joseph Welch. The public and the Senate had seen enough. In December, the Senate censured McCarthy for conduct unbecoming a senator.

SEE ALSO *Censure; Investigations, congressional; McCarthy, Joseph R.*

SOURCES Arthur Herman, *Joseph McCarthy: Reexamining the Life and Legacy of America's Most Hated Senator* (New York: Free Press, 1999). H. Lew. Wallace, "The McCarthy Era, 1954," in *Congress Investigates: A Documented History, 1792–1974,* edited by Arthur M. Schlesinger, Jr., and Roger Bruns (New York: Bowker, 1975).

ARTHUR, CHESTER ALAN
21st President

- Born: Oct. 5, 1829, Fairfield, Vt. (or Waterville, N. Y.)
- Political party: Republican
- Education: Union College, B.A., 1848; read law in New York City, 1853
- Military service: quartermaster general and brigadier general of New York, 1861–62
- Previous government service: collector of the Port of New York, 1871–78; Vice President, 1881

- Succeeded to Presidency, 1881; served, 1881–85
- Died: Nov. 18, 1886, New York, N.Y.

Chester Alan Arthur was a loyal follower of the corrupt Conkling political machine, or organization, in New York State who owed his political positions to connections and party loyalty. Ironically, it was this machine politician who, as President, presided over the creation of the first merit system for the civil service, or government employees.

Arthur was the son of a clergyman. After graduating from Union College he taught school briefly, then studied law. His law practice involved several cases in which he defended fugitive slaves and other African Americans. He obtained a large financial settlement for a black woman named Lizzie Jennings who had been put off a horsecar (a bus pulled by horses) in New York City because of her race. He served in the Civil War as a general of the New York volunteer troops.

Arthur became active in New York State Republican politics in an era of spoils—the awarding of jobs according to political connections—and corruption. He was named collector of the Port of New York by President Ulysses S. Grant, a position in which he dominated patronage in New York on behalf of Senator Roscoe Conkling. He controlled 1,000 jobs, which he gave to party regulars. President Rutherford B. Hayes forced him out as a reform measure.

At the Republican convention of 1880 Arthur was one of the leading Stalwarts supporting Ulysses Grant's third-term bid. After James G. Blaine's Half-Breed wing of the party (so-called because their opponents did not consider them "real" Republicans but quasi-Democrats) helped James Garfield win the nomination, Arthur was put on the ticket to regain the support of the Stalwart faction.

As Vice President, Arthur could cast the deciding vote in the Senate, which was sometimes deadlocked on straight-party votes because there were 37 Democrats opposed by an equal number of Republicans. When President Garfield appointed someone to the post of collector of New York without consulting Arthur, the two men had a parting of the ways. Although Arthur had always been a political hack, upon succeeding to the Presidency after Garfield's assassination in 1881, he promised that he would avoid the excesses of patronage appointments that had marked his career. He overhauled the cabinet entirely, replacing all but one of Garfield's secretaries with his own. He took action against fraud in the post office. His first message to Congress called for the creation of a civil service system, and over the opposition of his Stalwart colleagues he strongly supported the Pendleton Act of 1883, which created a civil service commission and began the principle of hiring on merit rather than party affiliation. He classified 14,000 federal positions, 10 percent of the total, as subject to the merit system. He vetoed a large rivers and harbors bill that Republicans had passed. He also vetoed the Chinese Exclusion Act of 1882, which would have kept workers from China out of the country for 20 years but then signed the measure when the exclusion was limited to 10 years.

Arthur is considered the father of the "steel navy," replacing the "floating washtubs" of the Civil War with modern, state-of-the-art steam warships. This program would give the United States the fifth largest navy in the world by the turn of the century. His major mistake was in foreign affairs, when he signed a treaty with Nicaragua to build a canal, in violation of an existing U.S. treaty with the British. The Senate refused to act on it, and President Grover Cleveland later withdrew it.

"It would be hard to better President Arthur's administration" was Mark Twain's verdict. But Roscoe Conkling had broken with him over civil service reform and other issues, and Grant devoted his energies to blocking Arthur's bid for an elected term of his own. With the knowledge that he was dying of Bright's disease, Arthur did not put up much resistance to

James G. Blaine's attempt to win the Republican nomination in 1884. Arthur returned to New York City to practice law but died soon after leaving office.

SEE ALSO *Garfield, James A.*

SOURCES Justin D. Doenecke, *The Presidencies of James A. Garfield and Chester A. Arthur* (Lawrence: University Press of Kansas, 1981). George F. Howe, *Chester A. Arthur* (New York: Frederick Ungar, 1935).

ARTICLES OF CONFEDERATION

The Articles of Confederation was the document that organized a "perpetual Union" among the 13 states that had declared independence from Great Britain. The Articles were in effect between March 1, 1781, and March 4, 1789, when they were superseded by the Constitution of the United States of America.

The Articles set up a national legislature that could raise an army and navy, declare war and negotiate treaties, borrow and coin money, run a postal system, and handle relations with Native Americans. Each state could send two delegates to Congress but had only one vote. Delegates from 7 of the 13 states had to be present to establish a quorum and conduct business. Delegates were elected for one-year terms and could not serve for more than three years in any six-year period.

The single-body Congress under the Articles of Confederation comprised the entire national government. There was neither an executive nor a judicial branch. In fact, in November 1777 the draft of the Articles that the Continental Congress submitted to the states for ratification specifically rejected a plan for an executive proposed by James Dickinson and the Committee of Thirteen the year before. The Dickinson draft would have provided for a "Council of State" appointed by Congress and for other officers "for managing the general affairs of the United States." The council would have exercised broad powers: command of the military, administration of finances and diplomacy, and "the Execution of such Measures as may be resolved on by the United States."

The Articles of Confederation provided instead for a "Committee of States" to "execute in the recess of Congress, such of the powers of Congress as the United States, in Congress assembled, shall by the consent of nine states, from time to time, think expedient to vest them with." The committee could not exercise military, diplomatic, or fiscal powers or make any decisions to which the Articles required the assent of nine states.

Under the Articles, the president of the Continental Congress was simply the presiding officer of the legislature and had no executive functions. The importance of the office can best be understood by the fact that in the absence of the president, a clerk was designated to perform his duties. Presidents served one-year terms, and they were usually men whose talents matched their limited powers.

Beginning in 1776, ad hoc or permanent congressional committees, supplemented by boards of officials operating under their direction, performed administrative duties. The Marine Committee dealt with the navy, the Board of War and Ordnance with the army, and the Committee of Secret Correspondence handled diplomacy. By 1781 several departments were created, among them Foreign Affairs, War, Marine, and Treasury, each with a single head. Neither the president of the Congress nor the Committee of States supervised these officials.

SEE ALSO *Continental Congress; Creation of the Presidency; Executive branch*

SOURCES Edmund C. Burnett, *The Continental Congress* (New York: Norton, 1941). Merrill Jensen, *The Articles of Confederation* (Madison: University of Wisconsin Press, 1940). Richard B. Morris, *The Forging of the Union, 1781–1789* (New York: Harper & Row, 1987). Jack Rakove, *The Beginnings of National Politics: An Interpretive History of the Continental Congress* (New York: Knopf, 1979). Jennings San-

ders, *Evolution of the Executive Departments of the Continental Congress* (Chapel Hill: University of North Carolina Press, 1935). Jennings Sanders, *The Presidency of the Continental Congress* (Gloucester, Mass.: Peter Smith, 1961).

ASIAN AMERICANS IN CONGRESS

Before 1965, American immigration laws restricted Asians from coming to the United States. Asian-American communities existed in the larger cities, but their populations generally were not large enough to elect members to Congress. The territory of Hawaii contained a high proportion of Chinese-, Japanese-, and Polynesian-American citizens. Much of the opposition to making Hawaii a state came from racially biased members who feared that Hawaii would send to Congress Asian Americans sympathetic to civil rights legislation. Indeed, when Hawaii became a state in 1959, it elected the first Chinese-American member of the Senate, Hiram Fong (Republican) and the first Japanese-American member of the House, Daniel Inouye (Democrat). In 1964, Patsy Mink (Democrat–Hawaii) was the first Japanese-American woman elected to the House. Daniel Akaka (Democrat–Hawaii) became the first Polynesian-American member of the House in 1977 and the first in the Senate in 1990.

California has also sent several Asian Americans to the House and Senate, including the first Asian American ever elected to Congress, Dalip Singh Saund (Democrat). Born in India, Saund came to the United States to study at the University of California. He won a House seat in 1956 and served three terms. California sent Japanese American Norman Mineta (Democrat) to the House in 1974, and S. I. Hayakawa (Republican) to the Senate in 1976. In 1992 California voters elected Jay Kim (Republican) as the first Korean American to serve in the House.

SOURCES Daniel K. Inouye, *Journey to Washington* (Englewood Cliffs, N.J.:

Prentice-Hall, 1967). Dalip Singh Saund, *Congressman from India* (New York: Dutton, 1960).

ASSASSINATIONS, PRESIDENTIAL

Presidents Abraham Lincoln, James A. Garfield, William McKinley, and John F. Kennedy were assassinated in office, and unsuccessful attempts were made against Presidents Andrew Jackson, Harry S. Truman, Gerald Ford, and Ronald Reagan. Attempts were made against Lincoln and Franklin D. Roosevelt when they were Presidents-elect.

Abraham Lincoln was shot by actor John Wilkes Booth on the night of April 14, 1865, while sitting in the Presidential box at Ford's Theatre. Booth and other conspirators were caught, tried, convicted, and sentenced to death. President Andrew Johnson refused to commute the sentences, and the conspirators were hanged.

James A. Garfield was shot to death at a railroad station in Washington, D.C., by a disappointed office seeker and religious fanatic, Charles Julius Guiteau, on July 2, 1881. William McKinley was shot to death on September 6, 1901, by Leon Czolgosz, an anarchist, at the Pan-American Exposition in Buffalo, New York. John F. Kennedy was shot to death on November 22, 1963, while on a political trip to Dallas, Texas, by Lee Harvey Oswald. The Warren Commission, which investigated the Kennedy assassination, concluded that the President had been shot by Oswald acting alone, though some people have argued that at least one other gunman was involved.

In response to the Kennedy assassination, Congress enacted a law on August 28, 1965, making it a federal (no longer merely a state) crime to kill, kidnap, or assault the President, Vice President, or President-elect or to threaten these officials with death or bodily harm. The penalty for killing the President is life imprisonment or death. The punishment for an attempt on the President's life is imprisonment for a term up to life. Since passage of the law, attempts on the President's life have fallen under the primary jurisdiction of the Federal Bureau of Investigation and other federal law enforcement officials, not under the jurisdiction of the local police departments in the place where an attempt was made on the President's life.

SEE ALSO *Ford, Gerald R.; Garfield, James A.; Jackson, Andrew; Kennedy, John F.; Lincoln, Abraham; McKinley, William; Reagan, Ronald; Roosevelt, Franklin D.; Secret Service, U.S.; Truman, Harry S.*

SOURCES James McKinley, *Assassination in America* (New York: Harper & Row, 1977).

ASSEMBLY, ASSOCIATION, AND PETITION, RIGHTS TO

The 1st Amendment to the U.S. Constitution guarantees "the right of the people peaceably to assemble, and to petition the Government for a redress of grievances." The constitutional right of peaceful assembly means that people can gather in public to discuss their opinions about government or other concerns. This right to assemble also guarantees the right of association in groups, such as political parties, labor unions, and business organizations.

The right of petition means that individuals, acting alone or as part of a group, can freely send written criticisms or complaints to government officials. The right of petition also provides freedom to circulate documents for people to sign in order to demonstrate mass support for complaints against the government.

These fundamental freedoms of assembly and petition predate the U.S. Constitution, having their origins in the English legal heritage and the colonial governments of British North America. The English Bill of Rights of 1689 affirmed that "it is the right of the subjects to petition the King and all commitments and prosecutions for such petitioning are illegal." Forty-eight years earlier, in 1641, Section 12 of the Massachusetts Body of Liberties guaranteed freedom of speech and petition at public meetings, so that "Every man . . . shall have liberty to . . . present any necessary motion, complaint, petition, Bill or information."

From 1776 to 1783, the freedoms of assembly and petition were included in several of the original state constitutions, including the acclaimed Massachusetts Constitution of 1780, which greatly influenced the U.S. Constitution of 1787. By the 1780s, the twin freedoms of assembly and petition were recognized by Americans as rights of individuals that should be protected. Therefore, it would have been unusual if James Madison had not included them in his proposal to the first federal Congress, dated June 8, 1789, to add "the Great Rights of Mankind" to the Constitution.

In that address, Madison presciently said that "independent tribunals of justice will consider themselves in a peculiar manner the guardians of those rights; they will be an impenetrable bulwark against every assumption of power in the legislative or executive; they will be naturally led to resist every encroachment upon rights expressly stipulated for in the Constitution." Madison's prediction has proved correct, especially in this century, as the freedoms of assembly and petition, along with other fundamental constitutional rights of the people, have been protected by an independent federal judiciary using its power of judicial review.

First Amendment freedoms have been expanded through judicial interpretation throughout 200 years of American constitutional history, and today the rights of assembly and petition and, by extension, the right of association are protected against infringement by the states by the due process clause of the 14th Amendment. The Supreme Court affirmed these rights for the first time in *DeJonge* v. *Oregon* (1937) and *Hague* v. *Congress of Industrial Organ-*

izations (1939). In *DeJonge,* the Court ruled that the Oregon state government could not make it a crime for a member of a radical group, such as the Communist party, merely to conduct and participate in a public meeting. Writing for the Court, Chief Justice Charles Evans Hughes declared, "The right of peaceable assembly is a right cognate to those of free speech and free press and is equally fundamental," and "peaceable assembly for lawful discussion cannot be made a crime."

In *Hague,* the Court struck down a Jersey City, New Jersey, ordinance requiring permits from a "director of public safety" in order to hold meetings in public places within the city or to distribute printed material in streets, parks, or other locations.

The freedoms of assembly, association, and petition, like other constitutional rights, have limits. Justice Louis Brandeis wrote in 1927 (*Whitney* v. *California*), "Although the rights of free speech and assembly are fundamental, they are not in their nature absolute. Their exercise is subject to restriction, if the particular restriction proposed is required in order to protect the State from destruction or from serious injury, political, economic or moral." These limits must be justified, as Brandeis emphasized, by a compelling public interest. "Only an emergency can justify repression," said Brandeis. "Such must be the rule if authority is to be reconciled with freedom. Such, in my opinion, is the command of the Constitution. It is therefore always open to Americans to challenge a law abridging free speech [petition] and assembly by showing that there was no emergency justifying it."

Citizens of a constitutional democracy will forever be challenged to decide what constitutes an "emergency justifying" a particular limitation upon freedom of expression. They must respond, case by case, to this broad question: At what point, and under what circumstances, should majority rule be limited by the higher law of the Constitution in order to protect the fundamental freedoms and rights of individuals in the minority, such as their rights of peaceable assembly, association, petition, and speech? Justice Oliver Wendell Holmes reminded us about the occasional difficulty of answering this question, when he wrote, in *United States* v. *Schwimmer* (1929), "If there is any principle of the Constitution that more imperatively calls for attachment than any other, it is the principle of free thought—not free thought for those who agree with us but freedom for the thought that we hate."

An especially poignant example of Justice Holmes's "principle of free thought" was provided in *Collin* v. *Smith* (1978), a case decided by the U.S. Court of Appeals for the Seventh Circuit. In this decision, the federal appellate court decided to permit "followers of Nazism" flaunting the swastika to publicly and peaceably assemble to express their views in the village of Skokie, Illinois. In this decision, the court of appeals appeared to disregard the wishes of the majority in a community, as expressed by their representatives in government, who had passed ordinances prohibiting these American Nazis from publicly assembling to express their "hateful" political and social opinions. Judge Bernard Decker wrote:

> In this case, a small group of zealots, openly professing to be followers of Nazism, have succeeded in exacerbating the emotions of a large segment of the citizens of the Village of Skokie who are bitterly opposed to their views and revolted by the prospect of this public appearance.
>
> When feeling and tensions are at their highest peak, it is a temptation to reach for the exception to the rule announced by Mr. Justice Holmes, ... freedom for the thought we hate.
>
> Freedom of thought carries with it the freedom to speak and to publicly assemble to express one's thoughts. . . . [I]t is better to allow those who preach racial hate to expend their venom in rhetoric rather than to be panicked into embarking

on a dangerous course of permitting the government to decide what its citizens must say and hear.

The U.S. Supreme Court refused to review the lower court decision in *Collin* v. *Smith*. Thus, Judge Decker's decision to overturn the Skokie ordinances was upheld.

This case presaged a heated controversy in the 1980s and 1990s about the limits of 1st Amendment freedoms of speech, press, assembly, association, and petition when these rights are used to assault the beliefs and sensitivities of vulnerable minorities, whether racial, ethnic, sexual, or religious. Exclusion from private organizations on the basis of race, ethnicity, religion, gender, or another category of personal characteristics has also raised questions about the latitude or limits of an individual's rights to association. Do people, for example, have an absolute right of association that permits them to exclude unwanted individuals from their organization? Or can one's right to freedom of association be limited by a state law forbidding discrimination? The Supreme Court ruled in *Boy Scouts of America* v. *Dale* (2000) that the 1st Amendment's protection of the right to freedom of association trumped New Jersey's state law against discrimination in public accommodations. The Boy Scouts, it was decided, have a constitutional right to exclude gay members because to include them would contradict the organization's "expressive message"—that is, its widely known public identity, image, goals, and mission. The Court recognized that private organizations do not have an unlimited right to association and complete freedom from regulation based on compelling public interests, but in this case, the majority concluded that the law did not justify the state's restrictions of the "rights to freedom of expressive association" of the Boy Scouts.

Four members of the Court strongly disagreed with the majority's decision in the Boy Scouts case, and the dissent revealed the intensity of current debate about conflicts between private freedoms and public interests. We are challenged today to decide critical questions about how to balance the 1st Amendment rights of various types of individuals, including some who are hateful, with our sense of the public good.

SEE ALSO *Whitney v. California*
SOURCES Fred W. Friendly and Martha J. N. Elliott, "Protecting the Thought That We Hate: Freedom of Speech and the Right of Peaceable Assembly," in *The Constitution: That Delicate Balance* (New York: Random House, 1984).

ASSISTANTS, CONGRESSIONAL

Administrative assistants (AAs) serve as office managers and often as chief advisers for their senator or representative. Although responsibilities vary in different offices, AAs generally supervise the rest of the office staff, schedule appointments, and oversee correspondence and case files, such as military academy appointments. They also handle constituents' problems with Social Security payments, veterans' benefits, and dealings with federal government agencies.

SEE ALSO *Legislative assistants; Staff, congressional*

ASSISTANTS, PRESIDENTIAL

SEE *White House Office*

ATTAINDER, BILL OF

A bill of attainder is a law that punishes a person without permitting him a trial or fair hearing in a court of law. It is punishment by legislation. Article 1, Section 9, of the U.S. Constitution forbids Congress to pass a bill of attainder, and Article 1, Sec-

tion 10, prohibits any state government from enacting one. If the Constitution permitted bills of attainder, government officials could, by law, force the person *attained* or punished by legislative act to forfeit his liberty, property, or income. Using a bill of attainder, government officials could punish an individual who criticizes them or who belongs to an unpopular group. The U.S. Constitution protects the rights of individuals by denying to the government the power to pass a bill of attainder.

ATTORNEY GENERAL OF THE UNITED STATES

The attorney general is the chief legal adviser to the President and head of the Department of Justice. The attorney general is a member of the President's "inner cabinet" of close advisers, along with the secretaries of defense, state, and Treasury, and is appointed by the President with the advice and consent of the Senate. The attorney general also serves as chief legal adviser to heads of executive branch departments, interpreting at their request the laws of the United States. The attorney general publishes interpretations of the Constitution in volumes known as the *Opinions of the Attorney General.*

The office of attorney general was created by Congress in the Judiciary Act of 1789, and at the request of President George Washington the first attorney general, Edmund Randolph of Virginia, served in the President's cabinet. In 1870 Congress created the Department of Justice and placed the attorney general at its head. Legal officers for the various executive departments were put under the supervision of the Department of Justice, as were U.S. attorneys, clerks, and marshals assigned to federal courts. At that time the solicitor general, the third-ranking official in the Department of Justice, was given the duty of arguing government cases before the Supreme

Court, a duty that until then had been exercised by the attorney general.

Attorneys general administer the Justice Department to suit Presidential priorities. President John F. Kennedy even appointed his brother Robert, joking that he wanted his brother to get some legal experience as a government lawyer before entering private practice. President Richard Nixon appointed his campaign manager, John Mitchell, and President Ronald Reagan appointed one of his senior White House aides, Edmund Meese. Many attorneys general are appointed after having served in other cabinet or White House positions, or they move to other positions in the inner cabinet after their tour of duty at the Justice Department. Several have been subsequently named to the Supreme Court; the two most influential in modern times were Chief Justice Harlan Fiske Stone and Justice Robert Jackson. Janet Reno, the county prosecutor in Dade County, Florida, appointed by President Bill Clinton in 1993, was the first woman attorney general.

SEE ALSO *Cabinet; Counsel, Office of; Office of Management and Budget*

SOURCES Nancy V. Baker, *Conflicting Loyalties: Law and Politics in the Attorney General's Office, 1789–1990* (Lawrence: University Press of Kansas, 1992).

AUSTRALIAN BALLOT

The Australian ballot, invented in that country in 1858, is a ballot printed by the government with all candidates for each office listed, to be marked by voters in voting booths. This process permits a secret ballot. By 1892 the Australian ballot had been adopted by all the states. Prior to the 1880s most states did not have secret balloting for President. Voters would tell election officials whom they favored or put ballots printed by political parties into a ballot box. Both systems made it difficult to preserve confidentiality. Using party ballots also made split-ticket voting (voting for a President of one party and members of the House or Senate from another) impossible. The Australian ballot reduced fraud and increased split-ticket voting, but it also reduced turnout because voters had to be able to read the ballot, which had not been the case with party ballots.

SEE ALSO *Election campaigns, Presidential*

SOURCES Richard Hofstadter, *The Age of Reform: From Bryan to F.D.R.* (New York: Vintage, 1955). Richard P. McCormick, *The Presidential Game: The Origins of American Presidential Politics* (New York: Oxford University Press, 1982).

B

SEE *Abrams v. United States; Freedom of speech and press*

"BAD TENDENCY" TEST

SEE *Abrams v. United States; Freedom of speech and press*

BAIL

Bail is a pledge of money given by an accused person as security that he will appear in court for trial when requested. Bail enables the accused person to be out of jail during the period of time between the person's arrest and receipt of charges and the person's trial. Failure of the accused person to appear for trial may result in loss of the bail.

The 8th Amendment to the U.S. Constitution says, "Excessive bail shall not be required," thus assuring an accused person a fair opportunity to be free on bail. Permitting a person to be free on bail allows him to retain employment and income while awaiting trial. It also gives the defendant ample opportunity to prepare a defense to the charges. However, bail is usually denied to those accused of first-degree murder or other heinous crimes.

SOURCES Vincent Buranelli, *The Eighth Amendment* (Englewood Cliffs, N.J.: Silver Burdett, 1991).

BAKER V. CARR

- 369 U.S. 186 (1962)
- Vote: 6–2
- For the Court: Brennan
- Concurring: Stewart and Clark
- Dissenting: Frankfurter and Harlan
- Not participating: Whittaker

In 1959, Charles Baker was mayor of Millington, Tennessee, a rapidly growing suburb of Memphis. He requested help from the state government in coping with the problems of urban growth. But he got no satisfaction because the urban areas of Tennessee were underrepresented in the state legislature. By contrast, the rural areas of the state were overrepresented. Approximately 11 percent of the population lived in rural areas of Tennessee, but more than 50 percent of the representatives in the state legislature were elected by the rural areas of the state. The outcome was neglect of the problems and the needs of urban people. The floor leader of the Tennessee House of Representatives said: "I believe in collecting the taxes where the money is—in the cities—and spending it where it's needed—in the country."

Charles Baker decided that the only way to solve the financial problems of Tennessee's cities was to force the government to reapportion the legislature—to draw the legislative districts equally according to population. In this way every citizen of the state, whether living in a rural or urban area, would be represented equally in the legislature—the principle of "one person, one vote." People's votes are equal when each member of the legislature represents about the same number of people. Charles Baker brought suit against Joseph Cordell Carr, the Tennessee secretary of state, to force reapportionment of the legislature. But the federal district court dismissed the suit because the issue was political rather than legal. Thus, according to the trial court, the question should be resolved by the political (legislative and executive) branches of government, not the judicial branch (the courts).

The Issue   Baker argued that urban voters in Tennessee were denied the equal protection of the laws guaranteed by the 14th Amendment. He requested that the state be ordered to equalize its legislative districts so that each person's vote was of equal weight. The Supreme Court, however, restricted its decision to questions of jurisdiction, standing, and justiciability. Did the court have the jurisdiction (authority) to make decisions about state legislative apportionment? Did Baker have standing (the right) to bring suit in a case of this kind? And was this issue appropriate for judicial decision or should it be left to the political branches of the government to decide?

Opinion of the Court   Justice William Brennan, writing for the Supreme Court, ruled that the Court had jurisdiction in this case, Baker had standing to bring suit, and the issue was justiciable. He wrote that "the right [to equal districts in the Tennessee legislature] is within the reach of judicial protection under the Fourteenth Amendment."

Although the Court limited its decision to the questions of jurisdiction, standing, and justiciability, Justice Brennan clearly stated that failure to apportion legislative districts of a state equally was a violation of the equal protection clause of the 14th Amendment. He concluded that Baker was entitled to a trial, so the case was sent back to the federal district court.

Dissent   Justice Felix Frankfurter and Justice John Marshall Harlan II strongly dissented. Frankfurter argued that the issue was essentially political, not judicial, and should be left to the legislative and executive branches to decide. Harlan argued that there was nothing in the U.S. Constitution that required state legislatures to be apportioned so as to equally represent each voter.

Significance   This case was the first in a series that led to legislative reapportionment throughout the country. The culminating case was *Reynolds* v. *Sims* (1964), in which the Court decided that states were required to establish equally populated electoral districts for both houses of the state legislature. Within one year of the decision in *Baker* v. *Carr,* 36 states were involved in lawsuits about legislative reapportionment. Eventually, every state of the United States was required to redraw its legislative districts to provide equal representation for all voters of the state.

U.S. Attorney General Robert F. Kennedy called the *Baker* decision "a landmark in the development of representative government." And Chief Justice Earl Warren, near the end of his life, called this case the most important one decided during his 16 years as chief justice.

SEE ALSO *Reynolds v. Sims*
SOURCES Richard C. Cortner, *The Apportionment Cases* (Knoxville: University of Tennessee Press, 1970).

BALDWIN, HENRY
Associate Justice, 1830–44

- Born: Jan. 14, 1780, New Haven, Conn.
- Education: Yale College, LL.D., 1797; studied law under Alexander J. Dallas, Washington, D.C.
- Previous government service: U.S. representative from Pennsylvania, 1817–22
- Appointed by President Andrew Jackson Jan. 4, 1830; replaced Bushrod Washington, who died
- Supreme Court term: confirmed by the Senate Jan. 6, 1830, by a 41–2 vote; served until Apr. 21, 1844
- Died: Apr. 21, 1844, Philadelphia, Pa.

Henry Baldwin was a strong supporter of Andrew Jackson's 1828 Presidential campaign. In 1830, President Jackson rewarded Baldwin with an appointment to the Supreme Court. Justice Baldwin tended to support states' rights in cases involving conflict between federal power and state sovereignty. However, he argued against extreme positions in support of either state sovereignty or federal supremacy. He claimed to be searching for a middle-of-the-road position between the two extremes.

Justice Baldwin clashed with Chief Justice John Marshall and helped to destroy the unity of the Court. In 1831, for example, he dissented seven times from the majority opinions of the Court. This was a dramatic departure from the tradition of unanimity that Marshall had established.

Justice Baldwin became irritable and erratic as he aged, a striking change from the good humor of the early years of his career. Toward the end of his life, he was often angry and occasionally violent. He was deeply in debt by 1844, when he died of paralysis.

BARBOUR, PHILIP PENDLETON
Associate Justice, 1836–41

- Born: May 25, 1783, Orange County, Va.
- Education: read law on his own; attended one term, College of William and Mary, 1801
- Previous government service: Virginia House of Delegates, 1812–14; U.S. representative from Virginia, 1814–25, 1827–30; Speaker of the House of Representatives, 1821–23; state judge, Virginia, 1825–27; president, Virginia Constitutional Convention, 1829–30; U.S. district judge, Court of Eastern Virginia, 1830–36
- Appointed by President Andrew Jackson Feb. 28, 1836; replaced Gabriel Duvall, who resigned
- Supreme Court term: confirmed by the Senate Mar. 15, 1836, by a 30–11 vote; served until Feb. 25, 1841
- Died: Feb. 25, 1841, Washington, D.C.

Philip Pendleton Barbour belonged to a prominent family of Virginia landowners. He followed the family tradition to become a wealthy plantation owner and a leader in the state and federal governments. Barbour became an active supporter of Andrew Jackson's Democratic party and backed Jackson's successful campaign for the Presidency in 1828. Two years later, Jackson rewarded him with an appointment to the U.S. District Court for Eastern Virginia. In 1835, Jackson appointed Barbour to the U.S. Supreme Court.

During his brief period on the Court, Justice Barbour strongly supported states' rights and powers and strict limitations on the constitutional powers of the federal government. As a result, proponents of a strong federal government and those who believed in a loose interpretation of the Constitution opposed Justice Barbour. Daniel Webster, for example, wrote in 1837, "His fear, or hatred, of the powers of this [federal] government is so great, his devotion to states' rights so absolute, that perhaps [a case] could hardly arise, in which he would be willing to exercise the power of declaring a state law void."

BARKLEY, ALBEN W.
Vice President

- Born: Nov. 24, 1877, Lowes, Ky.
- Political party: Democrat
- Education: Marvin College, B.A., 1897; studied law, Emory College, 1897–98; University of Virginia Law School, 1902
- Military service: none
- Other government service: Paducah County, Ky., prosecuting attorney, 1905–8; state judge, Paducah County Court, 1909–11; U.S. House of Representatives, 1913–27; U.S. Senate, 1927–49, 1955–56; Senate majority leader, 1937–46; Senate minority leader, 1947–49
- Vice President under Harry S. Truman, 1949–53
- Died: Apr. 30, 1956, Lexington, Va.

Alben Barkley defined the role of majority leader as the President's man in the Senate. He devoted himself steadfastly to enacting the legislative programs of Presidents Franklin D. Roosevelt and Harry S. Truman. A liberal Democrat, Barkley had been assistant majority leader under Joseph Robinson. When Robinson died, President Roosevelt intervened in the leadership race to help Barkley win. As a result, many senators felt that Barkley spoke for the President to them, rather than for them to the President. This impression continued until 1944, when Barkley became angry about the President's veto of a tax bill against his advice. He urged Congress to override the veto—which it did—and then resigned as majority leader. Barkley's independent stand elevated his stature among Senate Democrats, and they immediately and unanimously reelected Barkley as leader.

Barkley had been the keynote speaker at Democratic nominating conventions in 1932, 1936, and 1940, and when Harry Truman allowed the convention delegates to select their choice for Vice President in 1948, Barkley was nominated, though he provided no regional balance on the ticket. Barkley was the last of the Vice Presidents who did nothing in office. His only duties during his Vice Presidential years involved helping Truman as a liaison with Congress on pending legislation. He spent most of his time courting his second wife. In 1952 Barkley gave some thought to running for President himself. But labor leaders declined to support him on the grounds of age (he was 75), and he decided not to run. Barkley was reelected to the U.S. Senate in 1954 and served until his death.

SEE ALSO *Majority leader; Robinson, Joseph T.; Roosevelt, Franklin D.; Truman, Harry S.*

SOURCES Alben Barkley, *That Reminds Me* (Garden City, N.Y.: Doubleday, 1954). Polly Davis, *Alben Barkley: Senate Majority Leader and Vice President* (New York: Garland, 1979). James K. Libbey, *Dear Alben: Mr. Barkley of Kentucky* (Lexington: University of Kentucky Press, 1979). Donald A. Ritchie, "Alben W. Barkley: The President's Man," in *First among Equals: Outstanding Senate Leaders of the Twentieth Century,* edited by Richard A. Baker and Roger H. Davidson (Washington, D.C.: Congressional Quarterly, 1991).

BAR OF THE SUPREME COURT

The bar of the Supreme Court consists of lawyers authorized by the Court to argue cases there. During the Supreme Court's first term in 1790, it established two main qualifications for these lawyers. First, the person must have a satisfactory professional and moral character and reputation. Second, the person must have met the standards to practice law before the highest court of one of the states or territories of the United States. The clerk of the Court's office examines all applications and notifies the lawyers whose applications are accepted.

Between 4,000 and 5,000 applicants are admitted each year to practice before the bar of the Court. After receiving notification of acceptance, the applicant is required to pay an admission fee of $100. Each applicant may then be officially admitted to the bar of the Supreme Court by taking an oath of admission either before a notary public or in the open Court. The oath asks the person to "solemnly swear that as an attorney and counselor of this Court, you will conduct yourself uprightly and according to law, and that you will support the Constitution of the United States. So help you God." The applicant replies, "I do."

BARRON V. BALTIMORE

- 7 Pet. 243 (1833)
- Vote: 7–0
- For the Court: Marshall

John Barron owned docks and warehouses at the east side of the harbor of Baltimore, Maryland. Barron's wharf was a popular place for ships to tie up for off-loading cargoes into nearby warehouses. Barron and his partners made big profits by renting their wharf to ship owners.

Barron's prosperity was being ruined,

however, by construction crews working for the city government of Baltimore. They were digging up land, building streets, and diverting streams. Rainfall caused dirt-laden runoff to flow into the Patapsco River, which deposited the debris under Barron's docks. As a result, the water level at Barron's wharf was lowered to the point of interfering with the safe entry of ships. Barron claimed his profitable business had been severely damaged, and he sued the city of Baltimore to compensate him for the financial losses it had caused.

The Issue   Barron claimed that the city of Baltimore had violated his consti-tutional rights under the 5th Amendment, which says that "private property" shall not "be taken for public use without just compensation." Barron's claim raised this question: Could the 5th Amendment, or any other part of the federal Bill of Rights, be used to limit the powers of a state gov-ernment? Or does the Bill of Rights re-strain only the federal government?

Opinion of the Court   Chief Justice John Marshall concluded that the first 10 amendments to the U.S. Constitution ap-plied only to the federal government. This, he said, was the original intention of the framers of the first 10 amendments. Thus, the 5th Amendment could not be used by Barron to require Baltimore to pay him "just compensation" for taking his prop-erty. According to Marshall, the Supreme Court had no jurisdiction in the case, and so it was dismissed.

Significance   This decision legally es-tablished the widely held view that the fed-eral Bill of Rights was intended by its framers in 1789 to bind only the federal government. The constitutional issue of this case was settled until passage of the 14th Amendment in 1868, which was de-signed to limit the powers of state govern-ments in order to protect the rights of individuals. However, the Supreme Court did not begin to use the 14th Amendment to incorporate, or apply, parts of the fed-eral Bill of Rights to state governments un-til the second quarter of the 20th century, beginning with *Gitlow* v. *New York* (1925).

SEE ALSO *Incorporation doctrine*
SOURCES Fred W. Friendly and Martha J. H. Elliott. "Barron's Wharf: The First Test of the Bill of Rights," in *The Constitution: That Delicate Balance* (New York: Random House, 1984). Burnham Holmes, *The Fifth Amendment* (Englewood Cliffs, N.J.: Silver Burdett, 1991).

BEAN SOUP

By tradition, bean soup is served daily in the House and Senate restaurants. One leg-end attributes this custom to the beginning of the twentieth century, when Senator Fred Thomas Dubois of Idaho chaired the committee that supervised the Senate res-taurant. Others credit Senator Knute Nel-son of Minnesota, who expressed fondness for the dish in 1903.

The House restaurant dates its practice back to 1904, when Speaker Joseph G. Cannon found the soup missing from the menu. "Thunderation," roared the Speaker, "I had my mouth set for bean soup! From now on, hot or cold, rain, snow, or shine, I want it on the menu every day." The House and Senate recipes are similar, except that the House version omits the onions:

Take two pounds of small navy beans, wash, and run hot water through them until slightly whitened. Place beans in pot with four quarts of hot water. Add 1½ pounds of smoked ham hocks and simmer approxi-mately three hours in a covered pot, stirring occasionally. Remove ham hocks and set aside to cool. Dice meat and return to soup. Lightly brown one chopped onion in two ta-blespoons of butter and add to the soup. Be-fore serving, bring to a boil and then season with salt and pepper. Serves eight.

BELLS, CONGRESSIONAL

When bells ring and the halls fill with hur-rying people, the U.S. Capitol resembles a school between classes. Bells keep senators and representatives informed of the activities on the floor and summon them for votes and quorum calls.

Originally, pages and messengers rushed to alert absent members of votes in the chambers, but a more efficient system was needed as the Capitol complex grew larger. In 1893, after the Capitol was wired for electricity, one journalist noted, "The wires are connected with bells, and these notify the petted legislators of every urgent demand for their official service." Today members' offices, committee rooms, restaurants, and other locations around the Capitol and Senate and House office buildings are fitted with sets of lights. Whenever a bell rings, a corresponding light comes on. One long bell and a single light indicate a vote. Members then have fifteen minutes to get to the chamber to cast their vote. When half the time has elapsed, five bells and five lights warn members to hurry. Other bells indicate quorum calls, the end of morning business, or adjournment.

Once, a new page escorted an elderly woman up to the galleries. "Why do these bells ring so constantly and stridently?" the woman asked. "I'm not quite sure," replied the page, "but I think maybe one of them has escaped."

BENTON, THOMAS HART

- Born: Mar. 14, 1782, Harts Mill, N.C.
- Political party: Democrat
- Senator from Missouri: 1821–51
- Representative from Missouri: 1853–55
- Died: Apr. 10, 1858, Washington, D.C.

Two great compromises framed Thomas Hart Benton's 30 years in the U.S. Senate. In 1820, the Missouri Compromise drew a line across the country, above which slavery was not to spread. This compromise also made Missouri a state, and Thomas Hart Benton became one of its first senators. As a border state senator, he sided with neither the North nor the South on the issue of slavery. Benton saw Northern

abolitionists and Southern sectionalists as two halves of the same pair of scissors, threatening to cut the nation in half. He thought that slavery would eventually become unprofitable and fade away. Benton fought his last Senate battles over the Compromise of 1850, to settle the issue of slavery in the new territories taken from Mexico. Emotions grew so heated that Senator Henry Foote (Whig–Mississippi) pulled a pistol on Benton during the debate. "Stand out of the way and let the assassin fire!" Benton shouted as other senators pulled them apart. Although he escaped without harm, Benton ultimately fell victim to sectional tensions and lost his race for reelection in 1850.

SEE ALSO *Compromise of 1850; Missouri Compromise (1821)*

SOURCES Thomas Hart Benton, *Thirty Years' View; or, A History of the American Government for Thirty Years, from 1820–1850,* 2 vols (1854–56; reprint, Westport, Conn.: Greenwood, 1968). E. B. Smith, *Magnificent Missourian: Thomas Hart Benton* (Philadelphia: Lippincott, 1957).

BENTON V. MARYLAND

- 395 U.S. 784 (1969)
- Vote: 7–2
- For the Court: Marshall
- Dissenting: Harlan and Stewart

Benton was charged by the state of Maryland with committing two crimes: larceny and burglary. The jury found Benton innocent of larceny and guilty of burglary. Benton appealed his conviction for burglary. This led to the reopening of the larceny charges. In the new trial, Benton was found guilty of both charges—larceny and burglary—and sent to prison.

The Issue   The 5th Amendment to the Constitution provides protection against what is known as double jeopardy. It says that no person shall "be subject for the same offense to be twice put in jeopardy of life or limb." However, Benton had been tried twice by the state of Maryland for the same offense. Benton said that the state had violated his 5th Amendment right to protection against double jeopardy.

The state's attorneys pointed to the Supreme Court decision in *Palko* v. *Connecticut* (1937), which held that the 5th Amendment right to protection against double jeopardy was not applicable to the states because the due process clause of the 14th Amendment did not apply this right to the state courts. Therefore, this 5th Amendment right, they said, limited only federal government actions, not those of state governments. Was the 5th Amendment ban on double jeopardy applicable to state governments?

Opinion of the Court The Supreme Court ruled that the 5th Amendment protection against double jeopardy applied to the states. Justice Thurgood Marshall wrote that this 5th Amendment guarantee "represents a fundamental ideal." This right, wrote Marshall, is certainly among those rights that are central to the American concept of justice.

Significance The *Benton* decision overruled *Palko* by holding that the double jeopardy prohibition of the 5th Amendment is applicable to the states through the 14th Amendment. This case became part of the gradual process by which the Court, during the 20th century, has applied most parts of the federal Bill of Rights to the states, on a case-by-case basis.

SEE ALSO *Double jeopardy; Palko v. Connecticut*

BETHEL SCHOOL DISTRICT NO. 403 V. FRASER

- 478 U.S. 675 (1986)
- Vote: 7–2
- For the Court: Burger
- Concurring: Blackmun and Brennan
- Dissenting: Marshall and Stevens

Matthew Fraser, a 12th-grade student at Bethel High School in Pierce County, Washington, made a brief speech at a school assembly, in support of a friend's candidacy for the student government. The audience included approximately 600 students in grades 9 through 12.

Fraser's speech included no profane or "dirty" words. But it was filled with sexually suggestive comments and gestures. Fraser's performance caused an uproar among many students in the audience, who hooted, cheered, laughed uproariously, and mimicked the sexual activities implied by the suggestive language of the speech. Many other members of the audience, however, appeared to be shocked and upset.

School officials punished Fraser by suspending him from school for three days. Fraser's name was removed from a list of students eligible to speak at graduation exercises. He was charged with violating the school's disruptive conduct rule. According to this rule, "Conduct which materially and substantially interferes with the educational process is prohibited, including the use of obscene, profane language or gestures."

Fraser protested that his 1st Amendment right to freedom of speech had been violated. He sued school district officials.

The Issue Did the public school officials in this case violate a student's constitutional right to free speech by punishing him for violating the school's disruptive conduct rule? Do school officials have authority to impose limits on student speech of the kind specified in the disruptive conduct rule?

Opinion of the Court Writing for the Supreme Court, Chief Justice Warren E. Burger decided against Fraser's suit against the Bethel School District. He said, "The First Amendment does not prevent the school officials from determining that to permit a vulgar and lewd speech such as [Fraser's] would undermine the school's mission." Burger noted, "The undoubted freedom to advocate unpopular and controversial views in schools and classrooms must be balanced against the society's countervailing interest in teaching students the boundaries of socially appropriate behavior." The chief justice stressed that "the constitutional rights of students in public schools are not automatically coextensive with the rights of adults in other settings. . . . Nothing in the Constitution prohibits the states from insisting that certain modes of expression are inappropriate [in schools of the state] and subject to sanctions."

Dissent In a brief dissent, Justice Thurgood Marshall disagreed with the Court majority's conclusion that the student's remarks were disruptive of the school's educational mission. In a separate dissent, Justice John Paul Stevens said that the school district's disruptive conduct rule was too vague to be enforced fairly under the 1st Amendment's guarantee of free speech. He said, "I believe a strong presumption of free speech should apply whenever an issue of this kind is arguable."

Significance The Court's decision contributed to the concept that students in a public school do not necessarily have the same constitutional rights as adults outside of school. This point was also made in *New Jersey* v. *T.L.O.* (1985), which dealt with 4th Amendment protections against unlawful searches, and *Hazelwood School District* v. *Kuhlmeier* (1988), concerning free press rights. However, in *Tinker* v. *Des Moines Independent Community School District* (1969), Justice Abe Fortas, writing for the Court, said, "It can hardly be argued that either students or teachers shed their constitutional rights to freedom of speech or expression at the schoolhouse gate."

SEE ALSO *Freedom of speech and press; Hazelwood School District v. Kuhlmeier; New Jersey v. T.L.O.; Tinker v. Des Moines Independent Community School District*

BETTS V. BRADY

- 316 U.S. 455 (1942)
- Vote: 6–3
- For the Court: Roberts

- Dissenting: Black, Douglas, and Murphy

Smith Betts, a 43-year-old unemployed man, was indicted for robbing a store in Carroll County, Maryland. He pleaded not guilty, and because he could not afford to pay for a lawyer, he asked the trial court to appoint an attorney to defend him. The trial judge refused Betts's request because the courts in Maryland commonly appointed counsel only in special circumstances, such as cases involving mentally incompetent defendants or cases that involved the possibility of the death penalty. Smith Betts represented himself in court and was judged guilty. The judge sentenced him to eight years in the Maryland penitentiary.

While in jail, Betts filed habeas corpus petitions, which required the state either to justify holding him in jail or release him. He demanded to be released on the grounds that he was wrongfully convicted because his constitutional right to a lawyer had been denied. The courts refused his petitions. So Betts appealed his case to the U.S. Supreme Court.

The Issue Smith Betts argued that he had been deprived of the right to a lawyer guaranteed by the 6th Amendment, which says: "In all criminal prosecutions, the accused shall enjoy the right . . . to have the assistance of counsel for his defense." Furthermore, the 14th Amendment says that no state government "shall deprive any person of life, liberty, or property without due process of law."

Did the U.S. Constitution require the state of Maryland to provide a lawyer for a defendant too poor to pay for legal help? Could the right to "assistance of counsel" specified in the 6th Amendment be applied to a state government through the due process clause of the 14th Amendment?

Opinion of the Court The Court decided that "the Sixth Amendment of the Constitution applied only to trials in federal courts." The Court concluded that the Maryland legal system had given Smith Betts ample means to defend himself during his trial. In cases that did not involve capital punishment, a state did not have to provide a lawyer for a defendant too poor to pay for one.

Dissent Justice Hugo Black was joined in dissent by Justices William O. Douglas and Frank Murphy. Black argued that the due process clause of the 14th Amendment "incorporates" those rights spelled out in the federal Bill of Rights, which includes the 6th Amendment guarantee of the right "to have the assistance of counsel." Justice Black therefore concluded that the state of Maryland had denied Smith Betts one of his constitutional rights.

Justice Black wrote that no person should "be deprived of counsel merely because of his poverty. To do so, seems to me to defeat the promise of our democratic society to provide equal justice under the law."

Significance The Court's decision in *Betts* v. *Brady* prevailed until the 1960s. Justice Black's ringing dissent was not forgotten, however. The Court eventually overruled the *Betts* v. *Brady* decision in *Gideon* v. *Wainwright* (1963). And Justice Black, a dissenter in the *Betts* case, wrote the opinion for the Court in the *Gideon* case.

SEE ALSO *Gideon* v. *Wainwright; Incorporation doctrine; Rights of the accused*
SOURCES Eden Force, *The Sixth Amendment* (Englewood Cliffs, N.J.: Silver Burdett, 1991).

BEVERIDGE, ALBERT J.

- Born: Oct. 6, 1862, Sugar Tree Ridge, Ind.
- Political party: Republican
- Senator from Indiana: 1899–1911
- Died: Apr. 27, 1927, Indianapolis, Ind.

As fruits of the Spanish-American War, the United States acquired control of the Philippines, Puerto Rico, and other overseas territories. Some members of Congress, including Speaker Thomas B. Reed, strongly opposed such an imperialist policy. But the cause of annexation—the acquisition of new territory—gained a dynamic champion in the young freshman senator Albert J. Beveridge. Making his first speech in the Senate, Beveridge declared that God "has made us the master organizers of the world to establish system where chaos reigns." He described the riches in raw materials that these colonies would provide for American industry and won thunderous applause from the galleries. Although Senator George F. Hoar (Republican–Massachusetts) objected that "the words Right, Justice, Duty, Freedom were absent" from the speech, Senator Beveridge successfully captured the spirit of American nationalism at the start of the 20th century.

SOURCES John Braeman, *Albert J. Beveridge: American Nationalist* (Chicago: University of Chicago Press, 1971).

BICAMERAL

Unlike the single-body Congress under the Articles of Confederation, the U.S. Congress is bicameral (from the Latin *bi,* meaning "two," and *camera,* meaning "chamber"). Congress consists of two separate bodies that share legislative powers. Members of the House and Senate have different qualifications for holding office, and they serve terms of different lengths. A House member represents a district within a state, and a senator represents an entire state. The two houses have different presiding officers, make their own rules, and have different ways of conducting business. Yet both houses of Congress must pass bills in exactly the same form in order for them to become law.

James Madison, a major author of the Constitution, reasoned that a single, popularly elected legislature might respond too quickly to changes in public opinion and would enact "defective laws which do mischief before they can be mended." Madison believed that a second legislative body "consisting of fewer and riper members, deliberating separately & independently of the other, may be expected to correct many errors and inaccuracies" of the other.

In theory, the House would represent the common people, while the Senate would represent wealthier property owners and serve as a check against the pressures of public opinion. But those who wanted a more democratic government objected to creating an aristocratic "upper" house. Thomas Jefferson supposedly asked George Washington why a Senate was necessary. "Why did you pour that coffee into your saucer?" Washington responded. "To cool it," Jefferson replied. "Even so," said Washington, "we pour legislation into the senatorial saucer to cool it."

Two centuries later, senators, like representatives, are elected directly by the people (originally, they were elected by state legislatures), but the two bodies continue to balance each other. House rules favor majority rule, and the Senate rules give greater voice to minority objections. The House responds more quickly to public opinion, whereas the Senate prefers to take time to deliberate. As journalist William S. White observed, "The House marches; the Senate thinks, and sometimes overlong."

SEE ALSO *Articles of Confederation; Checks and balances; Constitution, U.S.; House-Senate relations; Separation of powers*
SOURCES Ross K. Baker, *House and Senate* (New York: Norton, 1989). Catherine Drinker Bowen, *Miracle at Philadelphia: The Story of the Constitutional Convention, May to September 1787* (Boston: Little, Brown, 1966). Donald A. Ritchie, *The U.S. Constitution* (New York: Chelsea House, 1989).

BILL CLERKS

Bill clerks assign numbers to all bills and resolutions, and they record in the journals any actions that the Senate and House take on that legislation. They also supervise the printing of all bills, resolutions, reports, and amendments through the Govern-

ment Printing Office. Each day, the bill clerks enter all legislative activities into a computer system known as LEGIS so that members, staff, and others can have instant information on how far the bill has progressed through the legislative process and what amendments might have been added.

SEE ALSO *Bills; Journals, congressional; Legislative clerks; Resolutions, congressional*

BILL OF RIGHTS

A major accomplishment of the 1st Congress was the drafting of the first 10 amendments to the Constitution, known as the Bill of Rights, which sets limits on the power of government in order to protect the liberties and rights of individuals from the government's abuse of its power.

Creation of the Bill of Rights   "[A] Bill of Rights is what the people are entitled to against every government on earth, general or particular [that is, federal or state], and what no just government should refuse, or rest on inference," wrote Thomas Jefferson to James Madison on December 20, 1787.

Jefferson was in Paris, serving as U.S. minister to France, when he received a copy of the Constitution drafted at the federal convention in Philadelphia during the summer of 1787 and found that it lacked a bill of rights. Jefferson generally approved of the new Constitution and reported in detail to Madison the many features of the proposed federal government that satisfied him. Then Jefferson declared in his December 20 letter to Madison that he did not like "the omission of a bill of rights providing clearly and without the aid of sophisms for freedom of religion, freedom of the press, protection against standing armies . . . and trial by jury in all matters of fact triable by the laws of the land."

A bill of rights consists of statements of civil liberties and rights that a government may not take away from the people who live under the government's authority. A bill of rights sets legal limits on the power of government to prevent public officials from denying liberties and rights to individuals, which they possess on the basis of their humanity.

Thomas Jefferson was concerned that the strong powers of government provided for by the U.S. Constitution could be used to destroy inherent civil liberties and rights of the people. He noted with pleasure that the Constitution of 1787 included means to limit the power of government, such as the separation of powers among three branches of government—legislative, executive, and judicial—to prevent any person or group from exercising power tyrannically. However, Jefferson strongly believed that additional guarantees of individual freedoms and rights were needed. He therefore demanded a bill of rights to protect certain liberties of the people, such as freedom to express ideas in public, from infringement by the government. Many Americans agreed with Jefferson, and they supported ratification of the Constitution only on the condition that a bill of rights would be added to it.

James Madison took up this cause at the first federal Congress in 1789. As a member of the Virginia delegation to the House of Representatives, Madison proposed several amendments to the Constitution to place certain liberties and rights of individuals beyond the reach of the government. The Congress approved 12 of these constitutional changes and sent them to the state governments for ratification. In 1791, 10 of these amendments were approved by the states and added to the Constitution. These 10 amendments are known as the Bill of Rights.

Contents of the Bill of Rights
Amendment 1 protects freedom of thought, belief, and expression. It says, for example, that the Congress of the United States is forbidden to pass any law "respecting an establishment of religion" or depriving individuals of certain fundamental civil liberties: religious freedom, the freedom of speech and the press, and the right of the people to gather together peacefully and petition the government to satisfy complaints they have against public policies and officials. The history of the 1st Amendment has involved the expansion of individual freedoms and the separation of church and state. For example, the 1st Amendment has been interpreted to mean that government may not establish an official religion, favor any or all religions, or stop individuals from practicing religion in their own way. Further, the right to assembly has been extended to include the right of association in organizations. Finally, the rights of free speech and press are generally understood to be very broad, if not absolute. There are, however, legal limits concerning the time, place, and manner of speech.

Amendment 2 protects the right of the state governments and the people to maintain militia or armed companies to guard against threats to their social order, safety, and security; and in connection with that state right the federal government may not take away the right of the people to have and use weapons.

Amendment 3 forbids the government, during times of peace, to house soldiers in a private dwelling without the consent of the owner. In a time of war the government may use private dwellings to quarter troops, if this is done lawfully.

Amendment 4 protects individuals against unreasonable and unwarranted searches and seizures of their property. It establishes conditions for the lawful issuing and use of search warrants by government officials to protect the right of individuals to security "in their persons, houses, papers, and effects." There must be "probable cause" for issuing a warrant to authorize a search or arrest; and the place to be searched, the objects sought, and the person to be arrested must be precisely described.

Amendment 5 states certain legal and procedural rights of individuals. For example, the government may not act against an individual in the following ways:

- Hold an individual to answer for a serious crime unless the prosecution presents appropriate evidence to a grand jury that indicates the likely guilt of the individual.

- Try an individual more than once for the same offense.
- Force an individual to act as a witness against himself in a criminal case.
- Deprive an individual of life, liberty, or property without due process of law (fair and proper legal proceedings).
- Deprive an individual of his or her private property for public use without compensating the person fairly.

Amendment 6 guarantees individuals suspected or accused of a crime certain protections against the power of government. This amendment provides to individuals:

- The right to a speedy public trial before an unbiased jury picked from the community in which the crime was committed.
- The right to receive information about what the individual has been accused of and why the accusation has been made.
- The right to face, in court, witnesses offering testimony against the individual.
- The right to obtain favorable witnesses to testify for the defendant in court (that is, the right to subpoena witnesses).
- The right to help from a lawyer.

Amendment 7 provides for the right to a trial by jury in civil cases (common lawsuits or cases that do not involve a criminal action) where the value of the item(s) or the demanded settlement involved in the controversy exceeds $20.

Amendment 8 protects individuals from punishments that are too harsh, fines that are too high, and bail that is too high.

Amendment 9 says that the rights guaranteed in the Constitution are not the only rights that individuals may have. Individuals retain other rights, not mentioned in the Constitution, that the government may not take away.

Amendment 10 says that the state governments and the people of the United States retain any powers the Constitution does not specifically grant to the federal government or prohibit to the state governments, such as the power of the states to establish and manage public school systems.

Expanding the scope of the Bill of Rights The framers of the first 10 amendments to the U.S. Constitution intended to limit only the powers of the national government, not those of the state governments. This understanding was supported by the Supreme Court's decision in *Barron* v. *Baltimore* (1833). Writing for a unanimous Court, Chief Justice John Marshall concluded that the Bill of Rights could be used to limit the power only of the federal government, not of the states.

However, the passage of the 14th Amendment in 1868 opened new possibilities. This amendment states that "no state . . . shall deprive any person of life, liberty, or property, without due process of law."

During the 20th century the Supreme Court has interpreted the due process clause of the 14th Amendment to require state and local governments to comply with most of the provisions of the Bill of Rights. Therefore, state and local governments are now prohibited from encroaching on most of the civil liberties and rights found in the U.S. Constitution. Under provisions of Amendment 14, the federal government has been empowered to act on behalf of individuals against state and local governments or people who would try to abridge other individuals' constitutional rights or liberties.

SEE ALSO *Amendments, constitutional; Assembly, association, and petition, rights to; Civil rights; Constitution, U.S.; Counsel, right to; Freedom of speech and press; Incorporation doctrine; Gun control and the right to bear arms; Liberty under the Constitution; Madison, James; Privacy, right to; Property rights; Religious issues under the Constitution; Rights of the accused; Searches and seizures; Self-incrimination, privilege against; Student rights under the Constitution*
SOURCES David J. Bodenhamer and James W. Ely, Jr., *The Bill of Rights in Modern America after Two-Hundred Years* (Bloomington: Indiana University Press, 1993).

Kermit L. Hall, ed., *By and For the People: Constitutional Rights in American History* (Arlington Heights, Ill.: Harlan Davidson, 1991). Leonard Levy, "Why We Have a Bill of Rights," *Constitution* 3, no. 1 (Winter 1991): 6–13. Milton Meltzer, *The Bill of Rights: How We Got It and What It Means* (New York: Crowell, 1990). Jack Rakove, "Inspired Expedient: How James Madison Balanced Principle and Politics in Securing the Adoption of the Bill of Rights," *Constitution* 3, no. 1 (Winter 1991): 19–25. Donald A. Ritchie, *The Constitution* (New York: Chelsea House, 1989). Robert Allen Rutland, *The Birth of the Bill of Rights, 1776–1791* (New York: Collier, 1962).

BILLS

Any member of Congress with an idea for a law can introduce it as a bill. But many hurdles must be overcome before that bill becomes law. In a two-year Congress, some 20,000 bills may be introduced, only 5 percent of which will become law. Representatives introduce bills by dropping them in a box called a hopper. Senators rise at their desk in the chamber and request permission to introduce a bill. Bill clerks assign the bill a number. H.R. 1 would be the first bill introduced in the House during that Congress; S. 256 would be the 256th bill introduced in the Senate. Members often reserve special numbers, such as 1776, to draw attention to their legislation. The names of the bill's sponsors are printed at the top of the bill, and bills are often known by their sponsors, such as the Wagner Bill or the Taft-Hartley Bill.

The parliamentarian refers the bill to the committee (or committees) with jurisdiction over its subject matter. A bill to reform the federal courts would go to the Judiciary Committee; a bill dealing with auto pollution might be divided between the energy and environmental committees. Most bills die in committee because the committee fails to act on them. The successful few are usually considered first in a

subcommittee, which may hold hearings to gather information and may amend, substitute, or combine the bill with other related bills. The full committee will "mark up" a bill, making final changes before reporting it back to the House or Senate.

The bill then goes on the calendar until it is called up for consideration. With the committee chairman or the bill's chief sponsor acting as floor manager, members will debate and amend the bill before passing or defeating it. Once one house passes a bill, messengers carry the bill to the other body, and the entire process begins again. Invariably, the Senate and House pass bills in different forms. They will then appoint a conference committee to try to negotiate a common version. The House and Senate must vote "up or down" (yes or no, without amendment) on the conference report.

If Congress passes the bill, it goes to the President, who can sign the bill, allow it to become law without his signature after 10 days, or veto (reject) it. A two-thirds vote of both houses of Congress is necessary to override a veto.

SEE ALSO *Acts of Congress; Bill clerks; Resolutions, congressional; Veto power*

SOURCES T. R. Reid, *Congressional Odyssey: The Saga of a Senate Bill* (New York: Freeman, 1980). Edward Willett, Jr., ed., *How Our Laws Are Made* (Washington, D.C.: Government Printing Office, 1986).

BIPARTISAN FOREIGN POLICY

Bipartisanship occurs when the two major parties put aside their political differences and work together. In 1947, when the United States entered the cold war of international tensions and competition with the Soviet Union and its allied communist bloc nations, both parties in Congress rallied behind a common, bipartisan foreign policy.

Bipartisanship developed during the 80th Congress (1947–48), with Republicans in the majority on Capitol Hill and Democratic President Harry S. Truman in the White House. Although opposed to Truman's domestic programs, Republicans such as Senator Arthur H. Vandenberg argued that "politics should stop at the water's edge." Most congressional Republicans supported Truman's foreign policies to rebuild Europe and to contain the spread of communism.

Republican Dwight D. Eisenhower was elected President in 1952, and congressional Democrats continued the bipartisan foreign policy, believing that it allowed the United States to respond effectively to the communist nations. But bipartisanship also stifled debate and eroded the legislative role in foreign policy. Asserting "national security," the executive branch determined foreign policy on its own, with minimum consultation with Congress.

Decline of bipartisanship   Bipartisan policy contributed to the Vietnam War and came apart because of it. President Lyndon B. Johnson, a former Senate majority leader, expected Congress to support his Vietnam initiatives. In 1964, with little debate, Congress almost unanimously passed the Gulf of Tonkin Resolution, which supported the use of American military force in Vietnam. But as the war escalated, many members—especially in Johnson's own Democratic party—grew disillusioned and dismayed. When Republican Richard Nixon continued the war after 1969, Democrats increasingly opposed his policies. Congress asserted a much stronger voice and began to challenge Presidential foreign policies. Enactment of the War Powers Resolution in 1973, over President Nixon's veto, set specific limits on the President's power to deploy military forces and marked the end of bipartisanship. Congress placed a renewed emphasis on the separation of powers and checks and balances in foreign policy.

SEE ALSO   *Gulf of Tonkin Resolution (1964); Johnson, Lyndon B.; Vandenberg, Arthur H.; War powers*
SOURCES   Arthur M. Schlesinger, Jr., *The Imperial Presidency* (Boston: Houghton Mifflin, 1973).

BLACK CAUCUS

SEE *African Americans in government*

BLACK, HUGO LAFAYETTE
Associate Justice, 1937–71

- Born: Feb. 27, 1886, Harlan, Ala.
- Education: Birmingham Medical College, 1903–4; University of Alabama, LL.B., 1906
- Previous government service: police court judge, Birmingham, 1910–11; solicitor, Jefferson County, Ala., 1915–17; U.S. senator from Alabama, 1927–37
- Appointed by President Franklin D. Roosevelt Aug. 12, 1937; replaced Willis Van Devanter, who retired
- Supreme Court term: confirmed by the Senate Aug. 17, 1937, by a 63–16 vote; retired Sept. 17, 1971
- Died: Sept. 25, 1971, Bethesda, MD

Hugo Lafayette Black rose from humble origins to become one of the most highly regarded justices in the Supreme Court's history. He was the eighth child of a farmer and storekeeper in rural Clay County, Alabama. Through hard work and determination, Hugo Black overcame the hardships of his youth to earn a law degree from the University of Alabama and to begin a career as a lawyer and public official in his home state.

In 1926, Black won election to the U.S. Senate, and he was reelected in 1932. During his second term, Senator Black became a strong supporter of President Franklin D. Roosevelt's New Deal policies. Roosevelt responded in 1937 by making Black his first appointment to the U.S. Supreme Court.

Black's membership on the Court became controversial when newspaper reporters revealed that he had been a member of the Ku Klux Klan from 1923 until 1926. The Ku Klux Klan had been organized after the Civil War by white supremacists who wanted to limit the opportunities and rights of black people. Justice Black repudiated his brief association with the racist Ku Klux Klan in a nationwide radio broadcast. "I did join the Klan," said Black. "I later resigned. I have never rejoined. . . . Before becoming a Senator I dropped the Klan. I have had nothing to do with it since that time." From this controversial beginning on the Court, Justice Black developed into one of its leading members, often taking a strong stand on behalf of the constitutional rights of individuals.

Justice Black favored a strict, literal reading of the Constitution regarding the government's power to infringe individual rights. For example, he wrote that "the First Amendment does not speak equivocally. It prohibits any law 'abridging the freedom of speech, or of the press.' It must be taken as a command of the broadest scope that explicit language . . . will allow" (*Bridges* v. *California,* 1941). In line with this viewpoint, Justice Black joined numerous decisions and wrote several dissents, to advocate virtually unlimited freedom of speech and press. Near the end of his career, however, he dissented from the majority opinions in cases protecting picketing and other nonverbal expression as examples of free speech (*Cox* v. *Louisiana,* 1965, and *Tinker* v. *Des Moines Independent Community School District,* 1969). In the *Tinker* case, for example, Black dissented from the Court's decision to protect the right of students in a secondary school to wear black arm bands to protest U.S. government policy in the Vietnam War. The Court decided that by displaying the arm bands the students were expressing "symbolic speech."

Justice Black was a persistent leader of the Court's use of the federal Bill of Rights to limit the powers of state governments. He interpreted the due process clause of the 14th Amendment, which states, "No state shall . . . deprive any person of life, liberty, or property, without due process of law," to require state governments to comply with all provisions of the Bill of Rights. He stated this "total incorporation" position in his dissent in *Adamson* v. *California* (1947): "My study of the historical events that culminated in the Fourteenth Amendment . . . persuades me that one of the chief objects that the provisions of the Amendment's first section, separately, and as a whole, were intended to accomplish was to make the Bill of Rights applicable to the states."

The Court has not yet agreed with his "total incorporation" doctrine—the application of all provisions of the Bill of Rights to the states. Rather, the Court has continued to "incorporate" particular provisions of the Bill of Rights on a case-by-case basis. Through this process, most parts of the Bill of Rights have been incorporated under the due process clause of the 14th Amendment and applied to the states.

Although Justice Black's total incorporation doctrine has not prevailed, he greatly influenced the gradual application of more and more provisions of the Bill of Rights to the states. Thus, he greatly expanded the constitutional protection of individual rights available to the people of the United States.

Justice Black always carried a well-used copy of the Constitution in his pocket as a sign of his devotion to limited government and the rule of law. This faith in the Constitution lasted for the rest of his life. After 34 years of service on the Court, he retired on September 17, 1971, because of ill health; he died eight days later.

SEE ALSO *Due process of law; Tinker v. Des Moines Independent Community School District*

SOURCES Howard Ball and Phillip J. Cooper. *Of Power and Right: Hugo Black, William O. Douglas, and America's Constitutional Revolution* (New York: Oxford University Press, 1992). Gerald T. Dunne, *Hugo Black and the Judicial Revolution* (New York: Simon & Schuster, 1977). Roger K. Newman, *Hugo Black: A Biography,* 2nd ed. (New York: Fordham University Press, 1997). James F. Simon, "The

Antagonists: Hugo Black and Felix Frankfurter," *Constitution* 3, no. 1 (Winter 1991): 26–34.

BLACKMUN, HARRY A.
Associate Justice, 1970–94

- Born: Nov. 12, 1908, Nashville, Ill.
- Education: Harvard College, A.B., 1929; Harvard Law School, LL.B., 1932
- Previous government service: clerk, Eighth Circuit Court of Appeals, 1932–33; judge, Eighth Circuit Court of Appeals, 1959–70
- Appointed by President Richard M. Nixon Apr. 14, 1970, to replace Abe Fortas, who resigned
- Supreme Court term: confirmed by the Senate May 12, 1970, by a 94–0 vote; retired Aug. 3, 1994
- Died: Mar. 4, 1999, Arlington, Va.

Harry A. Blackmun spent most of his childhood in the Minneapolis–St. Paul area, where he began a lasting friendship with Warren E. Burger, a future chief justice of the United States. After graduation from Harvard Law School in 1932, Blackmun practiced law in Minnesota. In 1959 President Dwight Eisenhower appointed him to the Eighth Circuit Court of Appeals. In 1970 President Richard Nixon appointed him to the U.S. Supreme Court after the Senate had refused to confirm two preceding appointments (Clement F. Haynsworth of South Carolina and G. Harrold Carswell of Florida). The Senate confirmed Blackmun unanimously.

During his early years on the Court, Justice Blackmun tended to vote with his friend, Chief Justice Burger. Their opinions were so similar that news reporters named them "the Minnesota Twins." Later on, however, their views diverged and Blackmun often voted with Justices William Brennan and Thurgood Marshall, who were more liberal in decisions about civil liberties.

Justice Blackmun's most significant opinion was written for the majority in *Roe*

v. *Wade* (1973). In this case, the Court defended the right of a pregnant woman to decide whether or not to have an abortion. Criminal penalties against doctors for performing abortions were declared unconstitutional. Justice Blackmun, writing for the Court, based his decision on the division of a pregnancy into three periods, called trimesters. He held that a state government could have no authority to prevent an abortion during the first trimester (the first three months of a pregnancy). During the second trimester, the state could regulate abortion only to protect the mother's well-being. During the third trimester, however, the state could legally prevent a woman from undergoing an abortion.

The *Roe* v. *Wade* decision was controversial. Since 1973, public response has been intense, whether for or against the Court's decision in this case. In the years following *Roe* v. *Wade*, Justice Blackmun has continued to defend the right of a pregnant woman to choose an abortion, in consultation with her doctor, during the first two trimesters of a pregnancy.

SEE ALSO Privacy, right to; Roe v. Wade
SOURCES Bernard Schwartz, ed., *The Burger Court: Counter-Revolution or Confirmation?* (New York: Oxford University Press, 1998). Stephen L. Wasby, "Justice Harry A. Blackmun," in *The Burger Court: Political and Judicial Profiles*, edited by Charles M. Lamb and Stephen C. Halpern (Urbana: University of Illinois Press, 1991).

BLAINE, JAMES G.

- Born: Jan. 31, 1830, West Brownsville, Pa.
- Political party: Republican
- Representative from Maine: 1863–76
- Speaker of the House: 1869–76
- Senator from Maine: 1876–81
- Died: Jan. 27, 1893, Washington, D.C.

Aggressive in debate, bold in behavior, and greedy for wealth and power, James G. Blaine dominated American politics during the decades after the Civil War. "Other leaders were admired, loved, honored, revered, respected," one senator observed, "but the sentiment for Blaine was delirium." As presiding officer, Blaine used his power to recognize speakers in order to bring more order to the House by controlling floor scheduling. Blaine's forceful leadership made him a frontrunner for the Republican Presidential nomination in 1876, until he was accused of having taken railroad stocks as a bribe. A brokerage firm bookkeeper, James Mulligan, produced some incriminating letters that Blaine had written. Blaine went to Mulligan's room, seized the letters, and selectively read them to the House to vindicate himself. Although he lost the Presidential nomination, Blaine went on to serve as senator and secretary of state. At last, in 1884, he became the Republican candidate for President, but suspicions about his financial dealings still haunted him, and Blaine lost what was then considered the "dirtiest campaign in history" to the Democratic candidate, Grover Cleveland.

SOURCES David S. Muzzey, *James G. Blaine: A Political Idol of Other Days* (1934; reprint, Port Washington, N.Y.: Kennikat Press, 1963).

BLAIR, JOHN, JR.
Associate Justice, 1789–95

- Born: 1732, Williamsburg, Va.
- Education: College of William and Mary, B.A., 1754; studied law at Middle Temple, London, 1755–56
- Previous government service: Virginia House of Burgesses, 1766–70; clerk, Virginia Governor's Council, 1770–75; Virginia Constitutional Convention, 1776; Virginia Governor's Council, 1776; judge, Virginia General Court, 1777–78; chief justice, Virginia General Court, 1779; judge, first Virginia Court of Appeals, 1780–89; Constitutional Convention, 1787; judge, Virginia Supreme Court of Appeals, 1789

- Appointed by President George Washington Sept. 24, 1789, as one of the original members of the U.S. Supreme Court
- Supreme Court term: confirmed by the Senate Sept. 26, 1789, by a voice vote; resigned Oct. 25, 1795
- Died: Aug. 31, 1800, Williamsburg, Va.

John Blair, Jr., was a member of a prominent Virginia family. He was an outstanding political leader of colonial Virginia and after 1776 continued his career of public service in the new state of Virginia. He participated in the Virginia Constitutional Convention of 1776 and the U.S. Constitutional Convention of 1787. He was one of three Virginians who signed the U.S. Constitution.

In recognition of his outstanding career as a political leader and Virginia state judge, George Washington appointed Blair to be one of the original six members of the U.S. Supreme Court. Blair's most important opinion was written in support of the Court's ruling in *Chisholm* v. *Georgia* (1793). In this decision, the Court ruled that Article 3, Section 2, of the U.S. Constitution gave a citizen of one state the right to sue another state in a federal court. This decision was overturned in 1795 by the 11th Amendment to the Constitution.

Justice Blair resigned from the Court on January 27, 1796. He retired to his home in Williamsburg, Virginia, where he died in 1800.

SEE ALSO *Chisholm v. Georgia*

BLATCHFORD, SAMUEL
Associate Justice, 1882–93

- Born: Mar. 9, 1820, New York, N.Y.
- Education: Columbia College, B.A., 1837

Previous government service: judge, Southern District of New York, 1867–72; judge, Second Circuit Court of New York, 1872–82

- Appointed by President Chester Alan Arthur Mar. 13, 1882; replaced Ward Hunt, who retired

- Supreme Court term: confirmed by the Senate Mar. 27, 1882, by a voice vote; served until July 7, 1893
- Died: July 7, 1893, Newport, R.I.

Samuel Blatchford entered Columbia College at the age of 13 and graduated four years later at the top of his class. He spent the next four years preparing to become a lawyer by studying with and working for his father's friend New York governor William H. Seward. Samuel Blatchford became a lawyer in 1842 and practiced law first with his father and then with Seward's law firm. Later he established his own law firm.

After serving 15 years as a federal judge in New York (1867–82), Blatchford was appointed to the Supreme Court by President Chester Alan Arthur. Justice Blatchford served on the Supreme Court for 11 years, performing ably but without distinction. During the Court's memorial service for him in 1893, Attorney General Richard Olney said, "If he [Blatchford] was not brilliant, he was safe."

BOLLING, RICHARD W.

- Born: May 17, 1916, New York, N.Y.
- Political party: Democrat
- Representative from Missouri: 1949–83
- Died: Apr. 21, 1991, Washington, D.C.

Arguing that foreign and domestic problems had mushroomed after World War II, Representative Richard Bolling called for institutional reform to make the House of Representatives function "effectively and responsibly." Bolling wanted greater party discipline, stronger leadership from the Speaker, reduced powers of seniority, and general reform of the committee structure. As Speaker Sam Rayburn's "lieutenant and leg man" on the Rules Committee, Bolling led the opposition to the conservative faction under chairman Howard Smith, which was blocking debate on civil rights and other liberal legislation. In 1961, Bolling helped Rayburn win expansion of the membership of the Rules Committee to

break the conservatives' majority. Later, when he became chairman of the Rules Committee himself, Bolling helped carry out many of the reforms he had proposed.

SEE ALSO *Rayburn, Sam; Rules committees; Rules of the House and Senate; Smith, Howard W.*

SOURCES Richard Bolling, *House Out of Order* (New York: Dutton, 1965). Richard Bolling, *Power in the House: A History of the Leadership of the House of Representatives* (New York: Capricorn Press, 1974).

BOLL WEEVILS

When Ronald Reagan won the Presidency in 1980, he carried with him the first Republican majority in the Senate in 26 years. Democrats retained their majority in the House, but the margin between the parties was narrowed. The balance of power in the House was held by a group of conservative Democratic representatives from the South and West. They organized themselves as the Conservative Democratic Forum but were more popularly known as the Boll Weevils, after the beetle that infests Southern cotton.

Led by Representative Phil Gramm (Democrat–Texas), the Boll Weevils voted with Republicans to enact Reagan's economic program, which involved cuts in federal spending and a plan to stimulate the economy by cutting taxes. Democrats responded by removing Gramm from his seat on the Budget Committee. Gramm resigned and won reelection as a Republican and soon after was elected to the Senate. Several other Boll Weevils also changed their party affiliation, but with less electoral success.

BONUS MARCHERS

Twelve thousand American veterans of World War I stood on the Capitol lawn on June 17, 1932, while the Senate debated the "Bonus Bill." Already passed by the House, the bill would have authorized immediate payment of a bonus that the veterans were due to receive in 1945. The veterans demanded their bonus right away, to help them and their families survive the economic hardships of the Great Depression. Bonus Marchers came from all over the country, set up tents on vacant land around Washington, and then gathered at the Capitol to await the final vote. Some senators feared mob violence, but when the Senate defeated the Bonus Bill, the marchers vowed to continue their fight, sang "America," and returned to their camps. Yet the Bonus March ended tragically. U.S. Army troops under the command of General Douglas MacArthur drove the marchers from the city and burned their camps. There were 100 casualties, and two children died in tear-gas attacks. Still, the Bonus Marchers had demonstrated the seriousness of their plight and the need for federal action to end the depression.

SOURCES William Manchester, *The Glory and the Dream: A Narrative History of America, 1932–1972* (Boston: Little, Brown, 1974).

BORAH, WILLIAM E.

- Born: June 29, 1865, Fairfield, Ill.
- Political party: Republican
- Senator from Idaho: 1907–40
- Died: Jan. 19, 1940, Washington, D.C.

The cry "Borah's got the floor!" sent newspaper reporters rushing to the press gallery, and senators to their seats, to hear him speak. William E. Borah was an independent maverick whose position was often unpredictable but whose speeches were always well reasoned and magnificently delivered. Thoughtful and deliberate, he was never swayed by the prevailing passions but sought to influence and change public opinion. Borah came to the Senate during the Progressive Era, and his efforts led to the direct election of senators, lower tariffs, the graduated income tax, and other progressive reforms.

After World War I, Borah's attention shifted to foreign policy, and he spoke out strongly against the Treaty of Versailles, which ended the war. During the 1920s, as chairman of the Foreign Relations Committee, he promoted isolationist policies designed to keep the United States out of foreign wars. One observer found Borah "so thoroughly independent that there was hardly a person with whom he did not differ at one time or another." But even if they disagreed with him, liberals and conservatives alike found that Borah's independence helped give them sharper perspectives on the issues.

SEE ALSO *Treaty of Versailles*

SOURCES LeRoy Ashby, *The Spearless Leader, Senator Borah and the Progressive Movement in the 1920s* (Urbana: University of Illinois Press, 1972).

BRADLEY, JOSEPH P.
Associate Justice, 1870–92

- Born: Mar. 14, 1813, Berne, N.Y.
- Education: Rutgers University, B.A., 1836
- Previous government service: none
- Appointed by President Ulysses S. Grant Feb. 7, 1870; replaced James Wayne, who died in 1867 and whose seat was unoccupied by act of Congress until 1870
- Supreme Court term: confirmed by the Senate Mar. 21, 1870, by a 46–9 vote; served until Jan. 22, 1892
- Died: Jan. 22, 1892, Washington, D.C.

Joseph P. Bradley was a poor farm boy who became a very successful and wealthy man. He studied hard in school and attracted the attention of a local minister, who recommended him to Rutgers University. After graduating from Rutgers in 1836, Bradley studied law in the office of Arthur Gifford and became a lawyer in 1839. He worked hard and built a rewarding career as a lawyer.

In 1870, President Ulysses Grant appointed Joseph P. Bradley to the Supreme Court. During his 22 years of service on the Court, he was known for his careful research and detailed analysis of constitutional issues. He remained on the Court until the day of his death in 1892.

BRAINS TRUST

Brains Trust is the informal name for senior government officials who advise the president. A Brains Trust is different from a "kitchen cabinet" of Presidential friends, none of whom hold public office. The original Brains Trust was a group of advisers to New York governor and later President Franklin D. Roosevelt who helped him develop his New Deal program. Members included prominent Columbia University professors such as Adolph A. Berle, Jr., of the law school, Rexford G. Tugwell of the economics department, and Raymond Moley of the department of public law and government. It also included political adviser and speech writer Samuel Rosenman (who first told Roosevelt to recruit the professors) and Frances Perkins, industrial commissioner of New York State when FDR was governor of New York. Roosevelt appointed Perkins to the position of secretary of labor, and she was the first woman to serve in a president's cabinet.

SEE ALSO *Kitchen cabinet; New Deal; New Frontier; Roosevelt, Franklin D.*

SOURCES Elliot A. Rosen, *Hoover, Roosevelt and the Brains Trust* (New York: Columbia University Press, 1977). Rexford G. Tugwell, *The Brains Trust* (New York: Viking, 1967).

BRANDEIS BRIEF

In 1908 Louis D. Brandeis, as counsel for the state of Oregon in *Muller* v. *Oregon,* prepared a new kind of brief in support of an Oregon law that limited the number of hours that a woman could work each day in laundries and other industries. The brief included only two pages of discussion of the legal issues of the *Muller* case. The other 95 pages of this brief presented evidence about the harmful impact of long hours of strenuous labor on the "health, safety, and morals of women." The sociological evidence presented by Brandeis convinced the Court to support the Oregon law in order to protect public health and safety.

The success of the new kind of brief submitted by Brandeis in the *Muller* case influenced other lawyers to use sociological evidence, when appropriate, to make their arguments. This new kind of brief was named the Brandeis brief in honor of its creator, who later became a highly regarded justice of the U.S. Supreme Court. SEE ALSO *Brief*

BRANDEIS, LOUIS DEMBITZ
Associate Justice, 1916–39

- Born: Nov. 13, 1856, Louisville, Ky.
- Education: Harvard Law School, LL.B., 1877
- Previous government service: attorney, Massachusetts State Board of Trade, 1897–1911; counsel, Ballinger-Pinchot Investigation, 1910; chairman, arbitration board, New York garment workers' labor disputes, 1910–16
- Appointed by President Woodrow Wilson Jan. 28, 1916; replaced Joseph R. Lamar, who died
- Supreme Court term: confirmed by the Senate June 1, 1916, by a 47–22 vote; retired Feb. 13, 1939
- Died: Oct. 5, 1941, Washington, D.C.

Louis Dembitz Brandeis was the first Jew to serve on the Supreme Court of the United States. His parents, Adolph and Fredericka Dembitz Brandeis, were immigrants from Bohemia who came to the United States in 1848.

The Brandeis family settled in Louisville, Kentucky, where Adolph Brandeis became a successful grain merchant who provided Louis with extraordinary opportunities for education and personal development. Louis completed two years of study at the highly regarded Annen-Realschule in Dresden, Germany. Brandeis returned to the United States to enter Harvard Law School, from which he graduated first in his class in 1877.

Soon after graduation, Brandeis began a law practice in Boston with his close friend and classmate Samuel Warren. By the turn of the century, Brandeis had become a nationally famous lawyer. News reporters called him the "people's attorney" because Brandeis often charged no fee for defending the rights of poor and disadvantaged people. He was also an active supporter of public reforms to bring about equal opportunities and fairness in the operations of businesses and government.

As the defense attorney in *Muller* v. *Oregon* (1908), Brandeis invented a new kind of legal argument, one based on sociological and economic evidence rather than legal precedent. Brandeis argued successfully for an Oregon law that limited the number of hours that women could work in laundries and other businesses. Brandeis's use of social science evidence to support legal reform of workplace conditions became a model for other lawyers, a type of document that they called "the Brandeis brief."

President Woodrow Wilson greatly respected Brandeis and often relied upon his advice. In 1916 Wilson appointed him to the U.S. Supreme Court to fill a vacancy created by the death of Justice Joseph R. Lamar. A vicious public controversy erupted over the nomination.

Many opponents disliked Brandeis because of his record as a political and social reformer. Others were against him because he was a Jew. One of his strongest supporters, Arthur Hill of Harvard Law School, explained the opposition to Brandeis's Supreme Court nomination: "Mr. Brandeis is an outsider, successful and a Jew."

The storm over President Wilson's appointment of Brandeis lasted for more than four months. This was the longest and most bitter battle over confirmation of an associate justice in the history of the Court. The closest example in recent times was the furor over the 1986 nomination of

Robert Bork by President Ronald Reagan. Unlike the Bork nomination, however, the Brandeis appointment was eventually supported by the Senate Judiciary Committee, 10 votes to 8. Finally, the full Senate confirmed Brandeis by a vote of 47 to 22.

The new justice's troubles were not over, however. One of his new colleagues, Justice James Clark McReynolds, refused to speak to Brandeis for more than three years. He would leave the conference table whenever Brandeis spoke, revealing his prejudice against the first Jew to serve on the Court.

Brandeis overcame this kind of hostility to become one of the greatest justices of all time. His most important opinions dealt with the constitutional rights of individuals. He sought to protect helpless individuals against oppression by uncaring government officials or an intolerant majority of the people. In *Olmstead* v. *United States* (1928), for example, Brandeis argued in a dissenting opinion for a general constitutional right to privacy. The Court had decided that wiretapping by federal government officials was not a violation of the 4th Amendment. Brandeis disagreed: "The makers of our Constitution . . . sought to protect Americans in their beliefs, their thoughts, their emotions and their sensations. They conferred, as against the Government, the right to be let alone—the most comprehensive of rights and the right most valued by civilized men."

Brandeis's dissent was vindicated in *Katz* v. *United States* (1967), when the Court overturned the *Olmstead* decision. In *Griswold* v. *Connecticut* (1965), the Court recognized a constitutional right to privacy for which Brandeis had argued many years before.

Brandeis was a leader in the movement to apply the federal Bill of Rights to the states through the due process clause of the 14th Amendment, a concept known as the incorporation doctrine. He first stated this idea in *Gilbert* v. *Minnesota* (1920). A few years later, the Court recognized this idea in *Gitlow* v. *New York* (1925). Since then, more and more parts of the Bill of Rights have been used to protect the liberties of individuals against state government violations.

Justice Brandeis was an especially vigorous defender of 1st Amendment freedoms. Through his Supreme Court opinions, he contributed mightily to the gradual expansion of these individual rights. He memorably expressed his commitment to 1st Amendment liberties in *Whitney* v. *California* (1927): "Those who won our independence believed that the final end of the State was to make men free to develop their faculties. . . . They believed liberty to be the secret of happiness."

Louis Brandeis served on the Court for 23 years, retiring in 1939 at the age of 82. A *New York Times* reporter noted: "The storm against him [when he was appointed to the Court] seems almost incredible now." Today, legal experts rate Louis Dembitz Brandeis one of the greatest justices in the history of the Supreme Court.
SEE ALSO *Incorporation doctrine; Muller v. Oregon; Olmstead v. United States; Privacy, right to*
SOURCES Leonard Baker, *Brandeis and Frankfurter: A Dual Biography* (New York: New York University Press, 1984). Lewis J. Paper, *Brandeis* (Englewood Cliffs, N.J.: Prentice-Hall, 1983). Phillipa Strum, *Louis D. Brandeis: Justice for the People* (Cambridge: Harvard University Press, 1984).

BRANDENBURG V. OHIO

- 395 U.S. 444 (1969)
- Vote: Unanimous
- For the Court: Per curiam decision

Clarence Brandenburg, a leader of the Ku Klux Klan, a white supremacist organization, was convicted of violating Ohio's Criminal Syndicalism Act. This state law outlawed speech that advocated violence as a means of achieving social or political reform. Brandenburg had urged violence against black people during a televised Ku Klux Klan rally.

The Issue The Ohio statute used to

convict Brandenburg was identical to a California law upheld in *Whitney* v. *California* (1927). Brandenburg, however, claimed that his conviction violated his 1st Amendment free speech rights. What are the limits, if any, to an individual's right to free speech?

Opinion of the Court The Supreme Court decided in favor of Brandenburg and struck down as unconstitutional the Ohio Criminal Syndicalism Act. This decision overturned *Whitney* v. *California*. The Court held that the constitutional guarantees of free speech do not permit a state to forbid people from speaking in favor of the use of force or other illegal actions unless it was likely to result in immediate violations of the law. The right to free speech can be limited only when the speech can be directly and immediately connected to specific actions that could result in lawless behavior.

Significance This decision greatly expanded the scope of political speech. The "clear and present danger" test set forth in *Schenck* v. *United States* (1919) and used in subsequent cases allowed restrictions on speech if it had a "bad tendency"—that is, if it appeared to encourage or cause illegal actions. However, the Brandenburg test allows virtually all political speech, unless it is demonstrably linked to immediate lawless behavior.
SEE ALSO *Freedom of speech and press; Schenck v. United States; Whitney v. California*

BRECKINRIDGE, JOHN C.
Vice President

- Born: Jan. 21, 1821, outside Lexington, Ky.
- Political party: Democrat
- Education: Centre College, B.A., 1839; College of New Jersey (Princeton), 1839; studied law, Transylvania University, 1840
- Military service: U.S. Army, 1847–48; Confederate Army, 1862–64

- Previous government service: Kentucky House of Representatives, 1850–51; U.S. House of Representatives, 1851–55
- Vice President under James Buchanan, 1857–61
- Subsequent government service: U.S. Senate, 1861; Confederate secretary of war, 1865
- Died: May 17, 1875, Lexington, Ky.

John Breckinridge was a border-state Democrat who tried to preserve the Union. As James Buchanan's Vice President, he presided over the Senate with impartiality. Nominated for President by a group of pro-slavery Democrats in 1860, he carried all the cotton states and the border states of Delaware and Maryland, running third in the popular vote behind Abraham Lincoln and Stephen A. Douglas. He supported the peace convention organized by former President John Tyler in the spring of 1861, hoping it would avert secession. Appointed U.S. senator from Kentucky in 1861, he hoped to forge a compromise that would keep the South in the Union. When Kentucky came under military occupation in the fall of 1861, Breckinridge left the capital and accepted a commission as a major general in the Confederate Army, for which he was expelled from the Senate. Breckinridge distinguished himself in the Virginia campaigns of 1864 and became Confederate secretary of state in February 1865. At the end of the Civil War he fled to Cuba and then went to England. He returned to the United States after President Andrew Johnson proclaimed amnesty, or forgiveness, for important rebel leaders. He practiced law in Lexington, Kentucky, until his death.

SEE ALSO *Amnesty, Presidential; Buchanan, James; Lincoln, Abraham; Tyler, John*
SOURCES William C. Davis, *Breckinridge: Statesman, Soldier, Symbol* (Baton Rouge: Louisiana State University Press, 1974).

BRENNAN, WILLIAM J., JR.
Associate Justice, 1956–90

- Born: Apr. 25, 1906, Newark, N.J.
- Education: University of Pennsylvania, B.S., 1928; Harvard Law School, LL.B., 1931
- Previous government service: judge, New Jersey Superior Court, 1949–50; judge, New Jersey Appellate Division, 1950–52; associate judge, New Jersey Supreme Court, 1952–56
- Appointed by President Dwight D. Eisenhower as a recess appointment Oct. 16, 1956; replaced Sherman Minton, who resigned; nominated by Eisenhower Jan. 14, 1957
- Supreme Court term: confirmed by the Senate Mar. 19, 1957, by a voice vote; retired July 20, 1990
- Died: July 24, 1997, Arlington, Va.

William J. Brennan was a leader on the Supreme Court during most of his 34 years of service. Chief Justice Earl Warren viewed Brennan as his closest associate and relied upon him for wise advice and strong partnership. After Warren's retirement in 1969, Brennan continued to influence his colleagues, although not as strongly or decisively as before.

William Brennan rose to national prominence through hard work, persistence, and continuous development of his sharp intellect. He was the second of eight children of Roman Catholic immigrants from Ireland. His working-class parents encouraged him to pursue higher education and to achieve excellence in his life. In response to his parents' encouragement, Brennan became a brilliant student at the University of Pennsylvania and Harvard Law School.

After leaving Harvard, Brennan practiced law in Newark, New Jersey, and served in the army during World War II. After the war, he returned to his law practice and became a judge in the state courts of New Jersey.

In 1956, Republican President Dwight Eisenhower appointed Brennan, a Democrat, to the Supreme Court. He immediately joined forces with Chief Justice Warren and wrote several of the Warren Court's landmark decisions between 1956 and 1969.

Brennan wrote the Court's opinion in *Baker* v. *Carr* (1962), which Warren called "the most important case that we decided in my time." In this case, the Court opened the way to a redrawing of voting districts that transferred political power from rural areas to urban ones throughout the United States. Before the *Baker* v. *Carr* decision, rural districts in many states had been unfairly favored over the urban districts to give them more representation in government than was deserved on the basis of population. *Baker* v. *Carr* led to a series of Court decisions (such as *Reynolds* v. *Sims* in 1964) that required state governments to eliminate or redraw voting districts that did not fairly represent various classes of voters.

Another of Brennan's landmark opinions came in *New York Times Co.* v. *Sullivan* (1964), which expanded freedom of the press by making it very difficult for a public official to recover damages for defamatory statements that are untrue. Justice Brennan argued that "debate on public issues should be uninhibited, robust, and wide open." He held that "wide open" freedom of expression is the purpose of the 1st Amendment, which would be undermined if critics of government officials had to conform to "any test of truth." He claimed that "erroneous statement is inevitable in free debate; and it must be protected if the freedoms of expression are to have the breathing space they need." Brennan concluded that all speech about public officials was protected by the Constitution unless it was expressed "with actual malice," that is, expressed "with knowledge that it was false or with reckless disregard of whether it was false or not." Thus, an "actual malice" standard was established as part of constitutional law.

Justice Brennan was a loose constructionist; that is, he gave the Constitution a broad interpretation to promote the rights and opportunities of individuals. He believed in a dynamic Constitution that should be adapted to changing circumstances by judicial interpretation. He wrote in the *South Texas Law Review* (1986) that "the genius of the Constitution rests not in any static meaning it might have had in a world that is dead and gone, but in the adaptability of its great principles to cope with current problems and current needs."

Critics charged that Brennan tried to overextend the powers of the judicial branch to involve federal judges in making policy decisions that belong only to the people's elected representatives in Congress. They accused him and his followers of wanting to make law through their judicial decisions instead of limiting themselves to making judgments in specific cases about the meaning of the Constitution and federal statutes. Critics also said that Brennan was wrong to disregard the intentions of those who wrote the Constitution and its amendments in his broad interpretations of this fundamental document.

Brennan retired in 1990 because of declining health. Both his supporters and his critics recognized Brennan's decisive influence on the development of the Constitution in the latter half of the 20th century. SEE ALSO *Baker v. Carr; Judicial activism and judicial restraint; New York Times Co. v. Sullivan*

SOURCES Stanley H. Friedelbaum, "Justice William J. Brennan," in *The Burger Court: Political and Judicial Profiles,* edited by Charles M. Lamb and Stephen C. Halpern (Urbana: University of Illinois Press, 1991).

BREWER, DAVID
Associate Justice, 1890–1910

- Born: June 20, 1837, Smyrna, Turkey
- Education: Wesleyan University, 1852–

53; Yale College, B.A., 1856; Albany Law School, LL.B., 1858
- Previous government service: commissioner, U.S. Circuit Court, Leavenworth, Kans., 1861–62; judge of probate and criminal courts, Leavenworth County, 1863–64; judge, First Judicial District of Kansas, 1865–69; Leavenworth city attorney, 1869–70; justice, Kansas Supreme Court, 1870–84; judge, Eighth Federal Circuit Court, 1884–89
- Other government service: president, Venezuela–British Guiana Border Commission, 1895
- Appointed by President Benjamin Harrison Dec. 4, 1889; replaced Stanley Matthews, who died
- Supreme Court term: confirmed by the Senate Dec. 18, 1889, by a 53–11 vote; served until Mar. 28, 1910
- Died: Mar. 28, 1910, Washington, D.C.

David Brewer was the son of a Congregational missionary who lived in the Anatolian part of the Turkish Empire. The family returned to the United States while Brewer was an infant, and he was raised in Wethersfield, Connecticut.

After graduating from Albany Law School, Brewer went to Kansas, where he served on several state courts, including the Supreme Court of Kansas. During his nearly 21 years as an associate justice of the U.S. Supreme Court, Brewer tended to support decisions to limit government regulation of private businesses. He strongly believed in free enterprise, free markets, and private property rights as foundations of a free government. Brewer also spoke and wrote against acquisition of colonies by the United States after the victorious war against Spain in 1898.

BREYER, STEPHEN G.
Associate Justice, 1994–

- Born: Aug. 15, 1938, San Francisco, Calif.
- Education: Stanford University, A.B., 1959; Oxford University, B.A., 1961; Harvard Law School, LL.B., 1964

- Previous government service: law clerk to Justice Arthur Goldberg, 1964–65; assistant to the attorney general, U.S. Department of Justice, 1965–67; assistant special prosecutor of the Watergate Special Prosecution Force, 1973; special counsel of the Senate Judiciary Committee, 1974–75; chief counsel of the Senate Judiciary Committee, 1979–80; judge, U.S. Court of Appeals for the First Circuit, 1980–94
- Appointed by President Bill Clinton May 17, 1994; replaced Harry A. Blackmun, who resigned
- Supreme Court term: confirmed by the Senate July 29, 1994, by a 87–9 vote

Stephen G. Breyer showed great promise as a thinker and writer from the beginning of his legal career. As clerk to Associate Justice Arthur Goldberg, he wrote the first draft of Goldberg's landmark opinion on the right to privacy in *Griswold* v. *Connecticut* (1965).

From 1967 to 1981, Breyer moved back and forth between the academic life of Harvard and the civic life of the federal government. He served on the Watergate Special Prosecution Force, which conducted investigations that led to President Richard Nixon's resignation in 1974. During this period, Breyer also served on the faculty of Harvard Law School, where he developed a widely respected theory on government regulation of economic activity. He brought this theory to his subsequent service as a federal judge, from 1980 to 1994.

When President Bill Clinton appointed him to the Supreme Court in 1994, Breyer had earned a reputation as a practical and innovative thinker about fundamental problems of when and how government agencies should regulate various industries. In 1994 he expressed his views on this topic in a series of lectures at Harvard, which were published as *Breaking the Vicious Cycle: Towards Effective Risk and Regulation.*

During his 14-year term as a federal judge, Breyer achieved respect as a consensus builder and as a mediator of conflicting views. His reputation influenced the Senate to confirm his nomination to the Supreme Court in 1994.

During his first term on the Court, Breyer acted forcefully and decisively. He broke Court tradition by participating in the questioning during the first oral argument he heard and by dissenting from the Court's decision in his first written opinion. Further, he wrote a sharp dissent against the Court's decision in *United States* v. *Lopez* (1995). In this case, the Court overturned as unconstitutional a federal law regulating the possession of guns in school zones. The Court's majority decided that under the federal system of the United States, this type of regulation is a power of each state government. Justice Breyer, in his dissent, defended the authority of Congress to regulate this type of gun possession.

Justice Breyer has tended to support concerns of local communities for public order and safety in regard to criminal law issues. For example, he joined the Court's opinion permitting random drug testing of public school athletes in the 1995 case of *Vernonia School District* v. *Acton.*

BRICKER AMENDMENT (1954)

Congress came close to passing a constitutional amendment to limit the President's ability to enter into executive agreements with other nations. During World War II, President Franklin D. Roosevelt conducted extensive personal diplomacy with Allied leaders, involving many executive agreements. Unlike treaties, executive agreements do not require the Senate's advice and consent. Republicans in Congress objected to these secret agreements and sought to reverse the trend. In the 1950s, Senator John Bricker (Republican–Ohio) proposed a constitutional amendment to give Congress "power to regulate all executive and other agreements with any foreign power or international organization." Republican President

Dwight Eisenhower opposed the Bricker Amendment, believing it would diminish a President's ability to conduct foreign policy. "If it's true that when you die the things that bothered you most are engraved on your skull," Eisenhower once remarked, "I am sure I'll have there . . . the name of Senator Bricker." In 1954, Eisenhower convinced enough senators to reject both the Bricker Amendment and a Democratic substitute amendment, which came within one vote of passing.

SEE ALSO *Advice and consent; Treaty powers*

SOURCES Duane Tanenbaum, *The Bricker Amendment Controversy: A Test of Eisenhower's Political Leadership* (Ithaca, N.Y.: Cornell University Press, 1988).

BRIEF

A written document known as a brief is prepared by the lawyers on each side of a case and submitted to a court. A brief presents the facts of a case and the counsel's legal argument. The term was first used in 1631.

In cases before the U.S. Supreme Court, the attorneys rely upon their written briefs to persuade the Court. Supreme Court rules require that a "brief must be compact, . . . concise, and free from burdensome, irrelevant, immaterial, and scandalous matter." Since 1980 there has been a 50-page limit on all briefs submitted to the Supreme Court.

SEE ALSO *Brandeis brief*

BROWN, HENRY B.
Associate Justice, 1891–1906

- Born: Mar. 2, 1836, South Lee, Mass.
- Education: Yale College, B.A., 1856; studied briefly at Yale Law School and Harvard Law School
- Previous government service: U.S. deputy marshal, 1861; assistant U.S. attorney, Detroit, Mich., 1863–68; circuit judge, Wayne County, Mich., 1868;

federal judge, Eastern District of Michigan, 1875–90
- Appointed by President Benjamin Harrison Dec. 23, 1890; replaced Samuel Miller, who died
- Supreme Court term: confirmed by the Senate Dec. 29, 1890, by a voice vote; retired May 28, 1906
- Died: Sept. 4, 1913, New York, N.Y.

Henry B. Brown became a lawyer in 1860 in Detroit, Michigan, after finishing his formal education at Yale. After a 15-year career as a federal district judge in Michigan, Brown joined the U.S. Supreme Court.

Justice Brown's strong support of property rights and free enterprise, and his tendency to resist strong government regulation of business, reflected the dominant opinions of his time. So did Brown's views about civil rights for black Americans, which were expressed in his opinion for the Court in *Plessy* v. *Ferguson* (1896). The *Plessy* decision supported a Louisiana state law that required black and white railroad passengers to sit in separate railway cars. Justice Brown, writing for the Court, argued that this Louisiana law did not violate the "equal protection of the laws" clause of the 14th Amendment. Brown used a "separate but equal" doctrine to support the Court's decision. He stated that separate facilities could be required by law for blacks and whites as long as the facilities provided for one group were equal to the facilities provided for the other group. He wrote, "We consider the underlying fallacy of the plaintiff's argument to consist in the assumption that the enforced separation of the two races stamps the colored race with a badge of inferiority."

The Court's decision in the *Plessy* case led to widespread enactment of state laws to segregate blacks from whites, to keep them apart, in the use of public facilities, such as schools, rest rooms, parks, cemeteries, and so forth.

Justice Brown left the Court in 1906 because of failing eyesight. He was popular then, but is not well regarded today because of his opinion for the Court in the *Plessy* case. Most Americans today strongly reject the legal segregation of blacks and whites, which Justice Brown defended in the 1890s. However, Brown and his Supreme Court colleagues expressed the prevailing view of that era about black-white relationships.

SEE ALSO *Plessy v. Ferguson*

BROWN V. BOARD OF EDUCATION

- 347 U.S. 483 (1954)
- Vote: 9–0
- For the Court: Warren

The 14th Amendment declares, "No state shall . . . deny to any person within its jurisdiction the equal protection of the laws." In 1896 the Supreme Court handed down a landmark decision on the meaning of this equal protection clause. In *Plessy* v. *Ferguson,* the Court ruled that the 14th Amendment allowed a state to segregate whites and blacks by providing "separate but equal" facilities for blacks.

For nearly 60 years this doctrine of "separate but equal" served as a constitutional justification for racial segregation in the United States. This doctrine sanctioned separating blacks and whites in schools, housing, transportation, and recreation.

Not all Americans accepted the view that the Constitution allowed racial discrimination. Those opposed to segregation agreed with Justice John Harlan, who dissented in *Plessy,* declaring, "Our Constitution is color-blind." In 1909 a group of black and white Americans formed the National Association for the Advancement of Colored People (NAACP) to fight segregation and racial injustice. In the 1930s and 1940s, NAACP legal counsel successfully argued a number of Supreme Court cases in which the Court prohibited segregation in public universities, political primaries, and railroads. By 1950 many blacks and whites were ready to challenge the constitutionality of segregated elementary and high schools. In the early 1950s five separate cases—from South Carolina,

Virginia, Delaware, Kansas, and Washington, D.C.—made their way through the court system. In each case the parents of black schoolchildren asked lower courts to strike down laws requiring segregated schools. The NAACP provided these parents with legal help. Eventually, the Supreme Court heard these cases together as *Brown v. Board of Education.* The case received its name when Mr. and Mrs. Oliver Brown sued the Topeka, Kansas, school board for denying their eight-year-old daughter, Linda, admission to a school only five blocks from their house. She had to leave her home at 7:40 every morning and travel 21 blocks in order to reach her assigned school by 9:00. The school board refused to let Linda attend the school in her own neighborhood solely because she was black and the school nearest to her home was for whites only.

The Issue   Thurgood Marshall, later a Supreme Court justice, was director of the NAACP Legal Defense Fund. He provided legal counsel for the Browns and the other plaintiffs. Marshall presented evidence showing that separating black and white students discriminated against blacks, placing them at a severe disadvantage. He argued that segregated schools were not and could never be equal. Such schools, he said, violated the equal protection guarantee of the 14th Amendment.

John W. Davis, a distinguished attorney and a 1924 Presidential candidate, represented the defense. He argued that the authors of the 14th Amendment never intended that article to prevent segregation in the nation's schools. Further, he claimed, the courts did not possess the authority to order the states to desegregate their schools.

Those states with segregated schools claimed that the dual system provided "separate but equal" facilities for whites and blacks. In fact, virtually no black schools were equal to white schools. The South Carolina case, for example, began when the local school board, run by whites, refused to provide school buses for black children. The board also refused to pay for heating the black schools or to provide them with indoor plumbing—services and facilities provided to white students. In spite of these glaring inequities, the black plaintiffs did not argue that the school systems were separate but *unequal.* Rather, they focused on challenging the "separate but equal" doctrine itself. Did state-supported segregation in public schools, even when black and white schools had equal facilities, violate the equal protection clause of the 14th Amendment?

Opinion of the Court   The Supreme Court unanimously struck down the "separate but equal" doctrine as an unconstitutional violation of the 14th Amendment. Chief Justice Earl Warren said that segregation clearly gave black children "a feeling of inferiority as to their status in the community that may affect their hearts and minds in a way unlikely to ever be undone." Even if segregated schools gave blacks access to equal physical facilities, Warren argued, they deprived students of equal educational opportunities.

Warren declared, "We conclude that in the field of public education the doctrine of 'separate but equal' has no place. Separate educational facilities are inherently unequal."

Significance   The *Brown* decision overturned *Plessy* v. *Ferguson* (1896). The ruling in this case destroyed the constitutional foundations of all forms of state-supported segregation in the United States. It also prompted massive resistance to school integration in many states. That resistance, in turn, helped spur the growth of the civil rights movement. This movement encouraged the passage of the federal civil rights acts of 1957, 1960, 1964, 1965, and 1968, which increased black political and civil rights.

Resistance also slowed implementation of the *Brown* decision in schools and led to many additional court cases. For example, Prince Edward County, Virginia, closed all of its public schools—for whites as well as blacks—rather than integrate. The first additional case, *Brown* v. *Board of*

Education (349 U.S. 294), known as *Brown II*, came in 1955.

Brown II came before the Court because, as Chief Justice Warren wrote, "[W]e requested further argument on the question of relief." The Court wanted to consider the issue of how to implement the ruling of *Brown I* to end segregation in public schools. In *Brown II* the Court set forth guidelines that placed the primary responsibility for doing so on local school officials. Federal district courts were to continue their jurisdiction and oversight of school desegregation cases. They could allow school districts to proceed carefully and gradually to complete school desegregation.

Although the Supreme Court ordered school districts to begin desegregation "with all deliberate speed," in reality just the opposite occurred. Fourteen years after *Brown*, less than 20 percent of black students in the South attended integrated schools. Faced with continued resistance, the Supreme Court ruled in 1968, in *Green v. County School Board of New Kent County, Virginia,* that segregation must end "at once." Eventually, lower federal court rulings and the work of the federal executive branch agencies began to change this pattern. By the 1980s most Americans fully accepted the Court's ruling in the *Brown* case as the correct decision. Today, it is hailed as one of the greatest and most important decisions in the history of the Supreme Court.

SEE ALSO *Civil rights; Equality under the Constitution; Marshall, Thurgood; Plessy v. Ferguson*

SOURCES Daniel M. Berman, *It Is So Ordered: The Supreme Court Rules on School Segregation* (New York: Norton, 1966). Richard Kluger, *Simple Justice* (New York: Knopf, 1976).

BUCHANAN, JAMES
15th President

- Born: Apr. 23, 1791, Cove Gap (near Mercersburg), Pa.

- Political party: Democrat
- Education: Dickinson College, B.A., 1809
- Military service: volunteer of dragoons, 1812
- Previous government service: Pennsylvania House of Representatives, 1814–16; U.S. House of Representatives, 1821–31; minister to Russia, 1832–33; U.S. Senate, 1834–45; U.S. secretary of state, 1845–49; minister to Great Britain, 1853–56
- Elected President, 1856; served, 1857–61
- Died: June 1, 1868, near Lancaster, Pa.

James Buchanan was a loyal Democrat; as President he did all he could to hold his party together by adopting a conciliatory position on slavery. As a Northerner, he opposed slavery in principle, but he was willing to protect the rights of slaveholders under the Constitution. His inability to see that his first responsibility was to the Union rather than to sectional compromise cost him his office and created the conditions for the Civil War.

James Buchanan was the oldest son of a Scotch-Irish merchant in Mercersburg, Pennsylvania. After graduating first in his class from Dickinson College, he became a successful lawyer. An engagement to Anne Caroline Coleman was broken off by her family, and she committed suicide; Buchanan never married, becoming the country's only bachelor President. After serving during the War of 1812 in the defense of Baltimore, he went into politics, moving from his affiliation as a Federalist in the Pennsylvania legislature in 1814 to the National Republicans in the 1820s as a member of the U.S. House of Representatives. He then switched to the Democrats in 1828. He became a loyal follower of President Andrew Jackson, who rewarded him by making him U.S. minister to Russia, where he negotiated the first commercial treaty between the two nations. Buchanan then served for 11 years in the Senate. He declined President Martin Van Buren's offer to serve as attorney general.

After a long career in Congress, Buchanan was a "favorite son" candidate at the Democratic convention in 1844 but lost the nomination to James K. Polk. He then served as Polk's secretary of state, successfully negotiating the end of a dispute with Great Britain over the Oregon boundary and bringing Texas into the Union. His offer to purchase Cuba was rejected by Spain, however. Buchanan did not get along with Polk, who thought his secretary of state was too ambitious and wished to replace him.

Buchanan was defeated by Lewis Cass for the Democratic nomination for President in 1848. He retired to private life but almost won the nomination in 1852. During Franklin Pierce's Presidency (1853–57) he served as minister to Great Britain. His participation in drafting the Ostend Manifesto, threatening war with Spain if it did not sell Cuba to the United States, made him popular with Southern Democrats.

Buchanan was nominated for President by the Democrats in 1856 as a noncontroversial choice: he had been out of the country during the bruising battles over the Kansas-Nebraska Act. Though his predecessor had been a weak and ineffectual President, the prosperity of the nation made it seem likely to party leaders that they could retain the White House with a candidate who appealed to both sections. Buchanan defeated Republican candidate John C. Frmont and American party (also known as the Whig and Know-Nothing party) candidate Millard Fillmore, though he did not receive a majority of the popular vote. Buchanan's base of support was the slave states: he won all except Maryland, which voted for Fillmore.

Buchanan became a "doughface" President—a term for a Northerner with Southern leanings. Buchanan's cabinet, like Pierce's, was balanced between North and South but seemed to many people to have a Southern tilt. Bolstered by the Supreme Court decision in *Dred Scott* v. *Sandford* (1857) that African Americans— whether slave or free—were not citizens and had no legal rights that could be protected by federal courts, Buchanan enforced the Fugitive Slave Act and incensed the Northern wing of his party.

In his first year as President, Buchanan dealt with a challenge to federal authority in Utah. The governor, Mormon spiritual leader Brigham Young, refused to obey federal laws and defied federal officials in the state. Buchanan sent in troops, removed Young, and appointed a new governor. Buchanan reported to Congress that "the authority of the Constitution and the laws has been fully restored and peace prevails throughout the territory."

Buchanan's greatest failure involved the sectional split over slavery. His party split over his support for a Southern attempt to bring Kansas into the Union as a slave state, with abolitionists such as Stephen Douglas opposing him. In a referendum, Kansas voters overwhelmingly adopted an antislavery constitution and compelled Buchanan and Congress to admit Kansas into the Union as a free state early in 1861. Minnesota and Oregon also came into the Union as free states. Northern sentiment swung sharply against Buchanan, and many anti-Buchanan Democrats won in the midterm elections of 1858, among them Stephen Douglas in the Senate contest in Illinois. Buchanan was now fatally weakened, with no following in Congress.

After the election of Abraham Lincoln in November 1860, South Carolina seceded from the Union. Buchanan denounced the secession but did nothing to enforce the laws of the United States, hoping for a peaceful solution. In his message to Congress in December, Buchanan observed that a state had no constitutional right to secede from the Union, but he argued that no state could be compelled to remain. He warned the Northern states that if they did not repeal their laws obstructing the execution of the Fugitive Slave Act, "it is impossible for any human power to save the Union." He defended his inaction against secession by arguing, "The Union rests upon public opinion, and can never be cemented by the blood of its citizens shed in civil war."

Although seven states in the lower South seceded and formed the Confederacy on February 20, 1861, eight other border and Southern slave states remained in the Union, awaiting the results of efforts to compromise. Buchanan's goal was to keep these states from seceding. When he sent a ship, *Star of the West,* to reinforce Fort Sumter, South Carolina, with 200 troops, shore batteries fired on the vessel and forced it to withdraw. Yet Buchanan did nothing to provoke the remainder of the slave states, lest they leave the Union. To advance Buchanan's notion of a compromise, a peace convention was held in Richmond, Virginia, under the chairmanship of former President John Tyler, but even before his inauguration Abraham Lincoln rebuffed the compromise proposals introduced there.

After leaving office Buchanan supported the Union cause during the Civil War. He died on June 1, 1868, at Wheatland, his Pennsylvania estate.

SEE ALSO *Lincoln, Abraham*

SOURCES Philip Shriver Klein, *President James Buchanan: A Biography* (University Park: Pennsylvania State University Press, 1962). Elbert B. Smith, *The Presidency of James Buchanan* (Lawrence: University Press of Kansas, 1975).

BUDGET AND IMPOUNDMENT CONTROL ACT, CONGRESSIONAL (1974)

Each year the President submits a budget for the federal government, only to have Congress alter that budget to meet its own goals. "I've been around here a long time," said Senate Appropriations Committee chairman Robert C. Byrd in 1992, "and I can't remember when the President's budget passed the Congress." President Richard Nixon considered such congressional tinkering with his budget "undisciplined" and "fiscally irresponsible." Nixon took it upon himself to impound (not spend)

funds that Congress appropriated for programs that he thought unnecessary. Members of Congress angrily accused Nixon of encroaching on the separation of powers and dangerously expanding the "imperial Presidency."

Not until Nixon stumbled in the Watergate scandal was Congress able to pass the Congressional Budget and Impoundment Control Act of 1974, over Nixon's veto. In addition to prohibiting Presidential impoundment of funds, the act established the House and Senate Budget Committees. These committees hold hearings and submit a concurrent resolution to the House and the Senate with their estimates of the next year's expected revenues and expenditures. The Appropriations Committees must limit appropriations to the amount that the concurrent resolution sets, or else the House and Senate must "reconcile" the difference by amendment. In the 1980s, reconciliation combined the numerous budget decisions into an omnibus measure that could be enacted by a single vote. This consolidation helped President Ronald Reagan regain greater influence over the budget in Congress.

Although impounding funds is now prohibited, under the Budget Act the President can ask Congress for a recision—or cutback—of appropriated funds for projects no longer considered necessary.

SEE ALSO *Appropriations; Concurrent resolution; Nixon, Richard M.; Recision bills; Watergate investigation (1973–74)*

SOURCES Nelson W. Polsby, *Congress and the Presidency* (Englewood Cliffs, N.J.: Prentice-Hall, 1986).

BUDGET, PRESIDENTIAL

The Presidential budget is the request that the President submits to Congress for legal authority to spend federal funds. Fourteen days after the Monday on which Congress convenes each January, the President is required by the Budget and Accounting Act of 1921 to submit to Congress the budget of the U.S. government, along with a message outlining his budget priorities. The budget covers the fiscal, or business, year (from October 1 to September 30) and is named for the calendar year in which it ends. The FY 2000 budget, for example, covers the period from October 1, 1999, through September 30, 2000. (Prior to passage of this law, departments submitted requests for funds directly to Congress, bypassing the President entirely.)

Presidential budget requests are prepared by the Office of Management and Budget (OMB), based in part on spending justifications submitted to it by each executive branch department and independent agency of government. The OMB evaluates all agency spending requests according to White House priorities.

The Budget of the United States provides data on past expenditures and current spending authority for each agency, but it is only a set of recommendations to Congress for future spending. The Constitution (Article 1, Section 9) provides that "no Money shall be drawn from the Treasury but in Consequence of Appropriations made by law." This provision gives Congress the final word on spending money. Presidents have at times asserted a power to impound funds, or to refuse to spend money appropriated by Congress.

According to provisions of the Budget and Impoundment Control Act of 1974, the House and Senate Budget Committees set overall spending targets and guidelines in 13 categories (such as defense, natural resources, and the environment) by passing a concurrent budget resolution. (A concurrent resolution is a motion passed simultaneously by both houses of the Congress.) Congressional appropriations committees (and some other standing committees that are permitted by congressional rules to authorize spending) modify each Presidential spending request according to their own priorities. They then convert them into budget authority— permission to withdraw funds from the Treasury—in the form of an appropriation or other law, which they report to each chamber of Congress. These appropriations and other spending bills must be passed in identical form by both chambers of Congress. The Treasury uses these appropriations laws to set limits on the "checking accounts" maintained by each agency. The OMB monitors the spending by each agency to see that it does not exceed the allowable limits.

Since the 1930s the Presidential budget has usually projected a deficit, or an excess of expenditures over revenue. In 1986 Congress passed the Gramm-Rudman-Hollings Act, which required the President to pare the projected deficits in his budget from $180 billion to zero by fiscal year 1991 or face mandatory "sequesters" (or holdbacks by the OMB) of funds to meet the targets. In 1988, the zero-deficit deadline was pushed back to fiscal year 1993.

In 1990, with a projected deficit of $318 billion, there was no way to make the sequesters required by the law without making deep cuts in the defense budget and in social welfare programs. Instead, President George Bush and congressional leaders agreed at a "budget summit" meeting held at Andrews Air Force Base in October 1990 to scrap the Gramm-Rudman-Hollings deficit targets. They decided instead to try to limit overall spending, with the assumption that within a few years increases in revenues would produce a balanced budget.

To implement their agreement, Congress passed the Budget Enforcement Act of 1990, which provided for caps on government spending. The law provided that any tax cuts in the President's budget would have to be accompanied by an equal amount of spending reductions. Similarly, any spending increases would have to be offset by equivalent tax increases. In 1995, a Republican-dominated Congress failed to pass a balanced-budget amendment to the Constitution or a measure allowing the President to veto individual items in appropriations bills.

SEE ALSO *Impoundment of funds; Office of Management and Budget*

SOURCES Richard J. Carroll, *An Economic*

Record of Presidential Performance: From Truman to Bush (Westport, Conn.: Praeger, 1995). James D. Savage, *Balanced Budgets & American Politics* (Ithaca, N.Y.: Cornell University Press, 1988). Aaron Wildavsky, *The Politics of the Budgetary Process,* 5th ed. (Boston: Little, Brown, 1992).

BUILDINGS

SEE *Capitol building; Office Buildings, Supreme Court; White House*

BUNK

Speeches delivered by members of Congress, designed for home consumption and to promote a member's chances of reelection, got the name "bunk" from Representative Felix Walker of Buncombe County, North Carolina. In 1820, Walker interrupted debate over the Missouri Compromise to make a speech directed chiefly to his constituents. Other representatives need not bother to stay to listen, he advised them, because "this is for Buncombe."

BUREAU OF THE BUDGET

SEE *Office of Management and Budget*

BURGER, WARREN E.
Chief Justice, 1969–86

- Born: Sept. 17, 1907, St. Paul, Minn.
- Education: University of Minnesota, 1925–27; St. Paul College of Law, LL.B., 1931
- Previous government service: assistant U.S. attorney general, Civil Division, 1953–56; judge, U.S. Court of Appeals for the District of Columbia, 1956–69
- Appointed by President Richard Nixon May 29, 1969; replaced Chief Justice Earl Warren, who retired

- Supreme Court term: confirmed by the Senate June 9, 1969, by a 74–3 vote; retired Sept. 26, 1986
- Died: June 25, 1995, Washington, D.C.

Warren E. Burger worked hard to achieve an education. After high school, he worked at part-time jobs while going to college and law school in his home city of St. Paul, Minnesota. From 1931 to 1953, Burger practiced law and participated in Republican party politics in Minnesota. He attracted the attention of national Republican party leaders, and in 1953 President Dwight Eisenhower appointed Burger assistant attorney general of the United States.

In 1956, President Eisenhower named Burger to the U.S. Court of Appeals for the District of Columbia circuit. This position was a stepping-stone to the Supreme Court. In 1969, President Richard Nixon appointed Burger to be the 15th chief justice of the United States. He replaced Earl Warren, the strong leader of the Court during two decades of ground-breaking decisions that greatly expanded the legal opportunities and rights of minorities and individuals accused of crimes.

Chief Justice Burger tended to support the civil rights decisions of the Warren Court. However, in cases regarding the rights of criminal defendants, Burger tended to support the police and prosecutors. He believed that the Court under Earl Warren had moved too far in favor of supporting the rights of accused persons and criminals.

Burger's most important decision was in the case of *United States* v. *Nixon* (1974), when the Court turned down President Nixon's claim of executive privilege as a reason for withholding tape recordings of private White House conversations from criminal investigators. The Court ordered the President to turn over the tapes, a ruling that established an important limitation on the powers of the President. This decision also affirmed the primacy of the Supreme Court in the interpretation of the Constitution.

Chief Justice Burger retired in 1986 to

become chairman of the Commission on the Bicentennial of the United States Constitution. His greatest achievements as chief justice were his improvements in the ways in which the federal judicial system carries out its work. He reorganized many procedures for keeping records and for carrying out more efficiently the business of the federal courts. But Chief Justice Burger, unlike his predecessor, Earl Warren, did not exercise a decisive influence on the opinions of his associate justices.

SEE ALSO *Chief justice; United States v. Nixon*

SOURCES Charles M. Lamb, "Chief Justice Warren E. Burger," in *The Burger Court: Political and Judicial Profiles,* edited by Charles M. Lamb and Stephen C. Halpern (Urbana: University of Illinois Press, 1991).

BURR, AARON
Vice President

- Born: Feb. 6, 1756, Newark, N.J.
- Political party: Democratic-Republican
- Education: College of New Jersey (Princeton), B.A., 1772; read law with Tapping Reeve, Litchfield, Conn., 1783
- Military service: Continental Army, 1776–79
- Previous government service: attorney general of New York State, 1789–91; U.S. Senate, 1791–97; New York State Assembly, 1797–98
- Vice President under Thomas Jefferson, 1801–5
- Died: Sept. 14, 1836, Port Richmond, Staten Island, N.Y.

Clever and ambitious, Aaron Burr practiced law in New York City before entering government service. Elected to the U.S. Senate in 1790, he led the opposition to Treasury Secretary Alexander Hamilton's financial programs. "As a public man he is one of the worst sort," Hamilton complained, "a friend of nothing but as it suits his interest and ambition."

Burr was defeated for reelection in 1796, then served two terms in the New York State Assembly from 1797 to 1798. He was a founder of the Society of St. Tammany, a political club that won control of the state legislature in 1800. The Republican majority in the legislature delivered New York State's electoral college vote to Thomas Jefferson in 1800 (in those days Presidential electors in New York and some other states were chosen not by the voters, but by the state legislators), and Burr was himself elected Vice President.

Aaron Burr was at the center of two of the most unusual episodes in American political life. One involved the Presidential election of 1800. At that time, electors in the electoral college cast two ballots for President. Jefferson and Burr ran on the same ticket, and so each received the same number of votes in the electoral college. Even though it had been clearly understood by members of their party that Jefferson was running for President and Burr was running for Vice President, the tie vote meant that the election would have to be settled by the House of Representatives, with each state having one vote. Burr then conspired with the opposition Federalists, who controlled a number of state delegations, in an effort to block Jefferson and win the Presidency for himself.

Fortunately for Jefferson, one of his political enemies, Alexander Hamilton, hated Aaron Burr even more—perhaps because Burr had defeated Hamilton's father-in-law in the Senate election of 1790. Hamilton broke the deadlock in the House, and on the 36th ballot Jefferson won the election. Soon afterward, the 12th Amendment to the Constitution was adopted, giving each elector a separate ballot to cast for President and Vice President.

Because of Burr's conspiracy against him in the election, Jefferson gave him nothing to do during his term of office, and he dropped him from the ticket in 1804. The same year, Burr lost the New York gubernatorial election. He fled west after killing Alexander Hamilton in a duel at Weehawken, New Jersey, on July 11,

1804, over Hamilton's remarks during the election campaign that Burr was "dangerous" and "despicable."

Burr then became involved in a second bizarre situation. With several hundred armed followers, Burr traveled down the Mississippi River toward New Orleans. No one knew what he intended to do: get Western territories to secede from Union control; attack Mexico or a Central American country and carve out an empire for himself; or charter ships in New Orleans and sail back to the nation's capital and try to seize power. President Jefferson took no chances. He had Burr arrested in the West and transported back to Virginia to face trial for attempting to take some of the Louisiana Territory away from the Union. Although Burr was eventually acquitted of the charges, his political career was finished, and he spent the next several years in Europe before returning to New York City, where he practiced law from 1812 until his death in 1836.

SEE ALSO *Electoral college; Jefferson, Thomas; Ticket; 12th Amendment*

SOURCES Thomas J. Fleming, *Duel: Alexander Hamilton, Aaron Burr, and the Future of America* (New York: Basic Books, 1999). Roger G. Kennedy, *Burr, Hamilton, and Jefferson: A Study in Character* (New York: Oxford University Press, 2000). Milton Lomask, *Aaron Burr*, 2 vols. (1979; reprint, New York: Farrar, Straus & Giroux, 1982). Herbert S. Parmet and Marie Hecht, *Aaron Burr: Portrait of an Ambitious Man* (New York: Macmillan, 1967).

BURTON, HAROLD H.
Associate Justice, 1945–58

- Born: June 22, 1888, Jamaica Plain, Mass.
- Education: Bowdoin College, B.A., 1909; Harvard Law School, LL.B., 1912
- Previous government service: Ohio House of Representatives, 1929; director of law, Cleveland, Ohio, 1929–32;

mayor, Cleveland, 1935–40; U.S. senator from Ohio, 1941–45
- Appointed by President Harry S. Truman Sept. 19, 1945; replaced Owen J. Roberts, who resigned
- Supreme Court term: confirmed by the Senate Sept. 19, 1945, by a voice vote; retired Oct. 13, 1958
- Died: Oct. 28, 1964, Washington, D.C.

Harold Burton, a Republican, was Democratic President Harry Truman's first appointment to the U.S. Supreme Court. He was the only Republican appointed to the Court between 1933 and 1953. Burton achieved an outstanding career in public life before joining the Court. He practiced law in Cleveland, where he had also been the mayor, and served one term in the U.S. Senate.

Justice Burton became a leading advocate of expanding the constitutional rights of African Americans. He spoke strongly against racial segregation and the "separate but equal" doctrine. He participated enthusiastically in the Court's decision in *Brown* v. *Board of Education* (1954) to end racial segregation in public schools. Burton resigned from the Court in 1958 because of illness; he died in 1964.

BUSH, GEORGE
41st President

- Born: June 12, 1924, Milton, Mass.
- Education: Yale College, B.A., 1948
- Political party: Republican
- Military service: U.S. Navy, 1942–45; Distinguished Flying Cross, three Air Medals
- Previous government service: U.S. House of Representatives, 1967–71; U.S. ambassador to the United Nations, 1971–73; chief, U.S. Liaison Office, People's Republic of China, 1974–75; Director of Central Intelligence, 1976–77; Vice President, 1981–89
- Elected President, 1988; served, 1989–93

George Bush was the first Vice President

to move directly to the White House by election since Martin Van Buren did so in 1836. His term was marked by few domestic initiatives, but he took bold action in foreign affairs, using the military to depose Panamanian dictator Manuel Noriega in 1989 and to repel Iraq's invasion of Kuwait in 1991.

Bush came from a politically and socially connected family: his father was Prescott Bush, an investment banker and U.S. senator from Connecticut (1953–63). His mother was Dorothy Walker Bush, a member of the family that donated the Walker Cup, one of amateur golf's most prestigious tournaments. Bush grew up in the affluent town of Greenwich, Connecticut, and attended Phillips Academy in Andover, Massachusetts, one of the finest prep schools in the nation.

During World War II, Bush enlisted in the navy and became its youngest pilot at age 19, flying Grumman Torpedo bombers in the Pacific from the aircraft carrier *San Jacinto.*

After his war service Bush married Barbara Pierce and attended Yale University, where he was captain of the championship baseball team and a member of the secret society Skull and Bones. He founded his own oil company in Houston, which soon merged with another to form the Zapata Petroleum Corporation.

After making a small fortune in oil exploration, George Bush turned to Republican politics in Texas. In 1962 he became Harris County Republican party chairman. Two years later he won the Republican Senate nomination but was defeated by the Democratic incumbent. He was elected to the U.S. House of Representatives from Houston in 1966 and was reelected in 1968. Bush served on the Ways and Means Committee, which deals with tax matters. In 1970 he was defeated for the Senate again.

After serving as U.S. ambassador to the United Nations, Bush was appointed by President Richard Nixon to be chair of the Republican National Committee in 1973. President Gerald Ford appointed Bush to

serve as chief of the U.S. Liaison Office to the People's Republic of China and then to be Director of Central Intelligence.

Bush ran for President in 1980, but he was defeated by Ronald Reagan in the Republican primaries. Bush ended his campaign before the convention and was rewarded for his efforts to achieve party unity by receiving the Vice Presidential nomination.

As Vice President, Bush chaired the Task Force on Regulatory Relief, which took a pro-industry position on most issues: it watered down proposals from the Occupational Safety and Health Administration (OSHA) on toxic substances in the workplace, delayed Transportation Department requirements that air bags be installed in cars, and delayed Environmental Protection Agency proposals to reduce lead in gasoline and remove asbestos from the workplace. Bush presided over the crisis management team at the White House and the drug interdiction task force. When President Reagan underwent cancer surgery in 1985, the powers of the Presidency were transferred to Bush for several hours under the provisions of the 25th Amendment.

Bush defeated Senator Robert Dole and the Reverend Pat Robertson for the Republican Presidential nomination in 1988. He chose Dan Quayle, junior Republican senator from Indiana, as his running mate. In the general election, running against Massachusetts Democratic governor Michael Dukakis, Bush repeatedly promised voters, "Read my lips, no new taxes." He told them he opposed abortion and gun control, embracing a conservative social agenda. Bush won the election with 54 percent of the popular vote and 426 electoral votes to Dukakis's 111. Bush entered office facing large Democratic majorities in the House and Senate.

In his inaugural address, President Bush promised to "make kinder the face of the nation and gentler the face of the world" and called for more cooperation between Democrats in Congress and Republicans in the White House. In his first

Bush, George 73

year in office he followed a conciliatory line. He moved quickly past a dispute over the nomination of former senator John Tower to be secretary of defense (Tower was rejected by the Senate) and settled on the appointment of the less controversial Richard Cheney. He made a relatively non-controversial Supreme Court appointment of the low-keyed David Souter. Bush concluded bipartisan negotiations over the budget by agreeing to the possibility of an increase in taxes, even though that meant repudiating his campaign promises and alienating the conservatives in his own party.

In foreign affairs President Bush initially tried to avoid any major new international crisis, preferring not to confront either Libya or Syria over support for terrorists. Similarly, he took a soft line on China after its leaders ordered a massacre of leaders of the democracy movement at Tiananmen Square in Beijing in 1989. He invaded Panama in 1989 to seize its dictator, Manuel Noriega, and then put him on trial for drug trafficking, securing a conviction in 1992. In Central America, Bush all but abandoned military pressure on the Sandinista government of Nicaragua, a revolutionary government with strong ties to the Soviet Union and Cuba. He opted instead to support an agreement for free elections that produced a non-Sandinista government. The results of his conciliatory approach to Congress and international adversaries were high standings in the polls and a reputation for skill in managing foreign affairs.

In the second year of Bush's term the collapse of Soviet control over the nations of Eastern Europe made it seem as if no international crisis would occur for the remainder of his term. The President signed an agreement with Soviet president Mikhail Gorbachev that greatly reduced the number of North Atlantic Treaty Organization (NATO) and Warsaw Pact (the Soviet-bloc nations of Eastern Europe) troops and tanks in Europe. In August, however, Iraq invaded and annexed Kuwait. Bush sent more than 500,000 troops into the Persian

Gulf, escalated his rhetoric against Iraqi dictator Saddam Hussein, and obtained a U.N. resolution approving the use of force against Iraq. Public approval for his handling of the crisis diminished, however, and many other nations urged more time for sanctions and diplomacy to work. Eventually, he received authorization from Congress to use force against Iraq, and the combined forces of the United States and several European and Arab nations waged a quick and successful military campaign. The effort forced Iraq to withdraw from Kuwait, but Saddam Hussein remained in power.

Bush began his third year with the highest ratings since public opinion pollsters began gauging Presidential popularity. Bush's popularity went into the 90 percent range, yet he offered almost no new domestic programs to Congress, refusing to capitalize on his standing with the public. He pressured the Soviet Union to accelerate its pace of economic and political reform, a strategy that culminated in a strategic arms reduction agreement signed in Moscow in August 1991. He pressured Israel and its Arab neighbors to come to an international peace conference, which began meeting early in 1992. He dropped sanctions (trade restrictions) on South Africa and refused to call for sanctions on China to protest human rights violations. Both moves were unpopular with Democrats in Congress.

Bush supported Mikhail Gorbachev's program of Perestroika, or economic and political restructuring, in the Soviet Union and led a coalition of Western nations that opposed a coup attempt against Gorbachev in August 1991. But Bush opposed the efforts of some republics within the Soviet Union to secede. Gorbachev was succeeded in power by Boris Yeltsin, and the Soviet Union was transformed into the Commonwealth of Independent States at the beginning of 1992. Bush then began to work with Yeltsin and his team of free-market reformers on programs of aid, trade, and nuclear disarmament.

In domestic affairs Bush continued his

conservative stance. He scuttled a compromise civil rights measure sponsored by Republican moderates in the Senate, setting up a major dispute with Democrats and civil rights organizations, but eventually he signed a version of the bill into law. He pushed hard for a defense budget that contained funding of major new strategic weapons programs, but his budget had little money for domestic initiatives—even for his much-trumpeted educational initiatives. The White House lobbied hard in the Senate for approval of Bush's Supreme Court nomination of Clarence Thomas, a black conservative. Although Bush won most of his highly publicized confrontations with Congress, his legislative success record remained one of the lowest of any modern President, even as his popularity with the public continued to hover in the 70 percent range.

In his fourth year Bush continued his emphasis on foreign affairs. He put more pressure on Israel to end its construction of new settlements in the West Bank by linking continued American foreign aid to Israeli policies regarding that disputed territory. He insisted that Iraq dismantle its strategic weapons and won United Nations sanctions against Libya until that nation agreed to turn over terrorists for trial in the 1988 bombing of a Pan Am passenger jet. He vetoed a Democratic bill to end "most favored nation" treatment of China (a policy giving it the lowest tariffs on goods exported to the United States), and his veto was sustained. At the end of 1992 he sent marines and other military personnel into Somalia to provide protection for relief workers alleviating the famine in that country. In early 1993 the United States and Russia signed a nuclear arms reduction agreement.

In domestic affairs Bush was more confrontational with Congress, using or threatening to use his veto power on a wide range of legislation. He fired the director of the National Endowment for the Arts as a result of a dispute over federal funding of so-called "pornographic" art. He reiterated his position calling for an end to abortion. He refused to pledge American adherence to proposed new pollution controls that had gained worldwide backing. He insisted that the budget limitations on domestic spending (agreed to in 1990) remain in place, in spite of pressure to spend the "peace dividend" (money not spent on defense) on social programs. He blocked a range of Democratic economic measures with vetoes, all of which were sustained. Meanwhile, the President's popularity slid from better than 70 percent into the low 40s. By early spring President Bush had the lowest rating in the polls of any first-term President in his fourth year in office since Herbert Hoover.

In the November election, Bush was defeated by Arkansas governor Bill Clinton, who won 43 percent of the popular vote to Bush's 38 percent. Independent candidate Ross Perot received 19 percent. After leaving the White House, Bush made his home in Houston, Texas.

SEE ALSO *Director of Central Intelligence; Ford, Gerald R.; Nixon, Richard M.; Quayle, J. Danforth; Reagan, Ronald*
SOURCES Colin Campbell and Bert Rockman, eds., *The Bush Presidency: First Appraisals* (Chatham, N.J.: Chatham House, 1991). Michael Duffy and Dan Goodgame, *Marching in Place: The Status Quo Presidency of George Bush* (New York: Simon & Schuster, 1992). Herbert S. Parmet, *George Bush: The Life of a Lone Star Yankee* (New York: Scribner, 1997). Kenneth W. Thompson, ed., *The Bush Presidency: Ten Intimate Perspectives of George Bush* (Lanham, Md.: University Press of America, 1997).

BUSH, GEORGE W.
43rd President

- Born: July 6, 1946, New Haven, Conn.
- Education: Yale University, B.A., 1968
- Harvard University, M.B.A., 1975
- Political Party: Republican
- Military Service: Texas Air National Guard, 1968–73

- Previous government service: Governor of Texas, 1994–2001
- Elected President, 2000; served, 2001-

George W. Bush was elected to the presidency eight years after his father's defeat by Bill Clinton in 1992. He grew up in the booming oil town of Midland, Texas, and as a young man worked in the oil industry. He lost a race for Congress in 1978. In 1989 he was part of a group that purchased the Texas Rangers baseball team, and served as managing director until he became governor of Texas. Bush was the first Texas governor to win a second consecutive four-year term.

Governor Bush persuaded the legislature to pass tort reform and limit frivolous lawsuits, and pass welfare reform to require recipients to go for job training. He opposed the elimination of aid to illegal immigrants and focused on improving the quality of Texas education.

Bush became the frontrunner for the Republican nomination and defeated John McCain in the primaries. Running against Al Gore Jr., Bush proclaimed himself a "compassionate conservative." His program called for large tax cuts focused on the wealthy, new drug benefits in Medicare to appeal to the elderly, and an overhaul of Social Security to provide young contributors with the opportunity to invest some of their contributions in the stock market. In foreign affairs Bush strongly supported constructing an anti-missile system and was skeptical about America's role in peacekeeping and nation-building abroad. His addition of Dick Cheney on the ticket and his promise that he would appoint an experienced team to assist him assuaged voters worried about his lack of national experience. His call to restore "honor and dignity" to the White House was heeded by the voters, and Bush was elected narrowly with 48 percent of the vote, slightly less than Gore received, and 271 electoral college votes, after a contest marred by inaccurate vote counts in Florida and a lengthy set of legal challenges by Gore.

SEE ALSO *Cheney, Richard; Electoral College*
SOURCES Bill Minutaglio, *First Son: George W. Bush and the Bush Family Dynasty* (New York: Times Books, 1999).

BUTLER, PIERCE
Associate Justice, 1923–39

- Born: Mar. 17, 1866, Pine Bend, Minn.
- Education: Carleton College, B.A., B.S., 1887
- Previous government service: assistant county attorney, Ramsey County, Minn., 1891–93; state's attorney, Ramsey County, 1893–97
- Appointed by President Warren G. Harding Nov. 23, 1922; replaced William R. Day, who retired
- Supreme Court term: confirmed by the Senate Dec. 21, 1922, by a 61–8 vote; served until Nov. 16, 1939
- Died: Nov. 16, 1939, Washington, D.C.

Pierce Butler was only the fourth Roman Catholic to be appointed to the Court. He was also a Democrat who was appointed by a Republican President, Warren G. Harding. Before joining the Court, he had practiced law and served as a prosecuting attorney in Minnesota.

Justice Butler tended to oppose government regulation of businesses. He was a strong opponent of government welfare programs and became a bitter foe of President Franklin D. Roosevelt's New Deal program of the 1930s. He voted against every New Deal policy that came before the Court. He also tended to oppose changes in racial segregation and the "separate but equal" doctrine.

SOURCES Francis Joseph Brown, *The Social and Economic Philosophy of Pierce Butler* (Washington, D.C.: Catholic University Press, 1945).

BYRD, ROBERT C.

- Born: Nov. 20, 1917, North Wilkesboro, N.C.

- Political party: Democrat
- Representative from West Virginia: 1953–59
- Senator from West Virginia: 1959–
- Senate majority whip: 1971–77
- Senate majority leader: 1977–81, 1987–89
- Senate minority leader: 1981–87
- President pro tempore: 1989–95

A coal miner's son who worked as a meat cutter and ship welder before entering politics, Robert C. Byrd advanced as a legislator through diligent study. Not until after his election to the House in 1952 did he begin law school at night, and not until after his election to the Senate did he receive his law degree in 1963. Byrd showed the same persistence in mastering the Senate's rules of procedure, which led to his election as Democratic whip and, in 1977, as majority leader. Byrd explained his ability to move the Senate and enact his party's programs by noting that "to be an effective leader, one ought to know the rules and precedents and understand how to use them." In 1989, Byrd stepped aside as majority leader in order to chair the powerful Senate Appropriations Committee. He pledged to use his chairmanship to channel a billion dollars' worth of federal funds into his relatively poor home state of West Virginia.

SEE ALSO *Leadership in Congress; Majority leader*

SOURCES Robert C. Byrd, "Reflections of a Party Leader," in *The Senate, 1789–1989: Addresses on the History of the United States Senate,* vol. 2 (Washington, D.C.: Government Printing Office, 1991).

BYRNES, JAMES F.
Associate Justice, 1941–42

- Born: May 2, 1879, Charleston, S.C.
- Education: studied law privately
- Previous government service: court reporter, Second Circuit of South Carolina, 1900–1908; solicitor, Second Circuit of South Carolina, 1908–10; U.S. representative from South Carolina, 1911–25; U.S. senator from South Carolina, 1931–41
- Appointed by President Franklin D. Roosevelt June 12, 1941; replaced James McReynolds, who retired
- Supreme Court term: confirmed by the Senate June 12, 1941, by a voice vote; resigned Oct. 3, 1942
- Subsequent government service: director of the Office of Economic Stabilization, 1942–43; director of the Office of War Mobilization and Reconversion, 1943–45; U.S. secretary of state, 1945–47; governor of South Carolina, 1951–55
- Died: Apr. 9, 1972, Columbia, S.C.

James F. Byrnes was the son of Irish immigrants who settled in Charleston, South Carolina. His father died before the younger Byrnes was born. His mother raised the family alone, and James left school to help support himself and his family. He worked as a law clerk and then as a court reporter. These jobs led to an interest in the law, which he studied on his own. He passed the state bar exam in 1903 and began a career as solicitor, or district attorney, for South Carolina's Second Circuit.

In 1910, Byrnes became a Democratic party candidate for a seat in the House of Representatives. His victory launched a spectacular career in the federal government. He became a close friend of President Franklin D. Roosevelt and served in the U.S. Senate during Roosevelt's first two terms. The President rewarded Byrnes for his loyal support by appointing him to the Supreme Court in 1941.

Byrnes's service on the Court lasted less than 14 months. During this time he wrote only 16 opinions. He left the Court to serve President Roosevelt as director of the Office of Economic Stabilization (1942–43) and then as director of the Office of War Mobilization and Reconversion (1943–45). He was secretary of state from 1945 to 1947 under President Harry S. Truman. Byrnes was governor of South Carolina for one term, from 1951 to 1955.

C

CABINET

The cabinet is a Presidential advisory group composed of the secretaries of the executive branch departments and other invited officials. At the Constitutional Convention delegates assumed that the President might convene the heads of departments for advice, but the cabinet was never mentioned in the original Constitution. The 25th Amendment, however, gives the cabinet certain duties regarding succession to the Presidency in cases of Presidential disability.

George Washington created the cabinet in 1789 when he invited the secretaries of state, Treasury, and war and the attorney general to meet informally with him. At first these officials met the President with other advisers, such as the chief justice of the United States, and it was not until 1791 that the cabinet met separately with the President. The secretary of the navy was added in 1798 by President John Adams, and the postmaster general in 1829 by Andrew Jackson. Other secretaries were added when their departments were created; the postmaster general was dropped in 1970 when the post office department became the U.S. Postal Service, an independent agency. Richard Nixon was the first Vice President to sit regularly with the cabinet (Coolidge had done so occasionally).

From 1791 onward Washington frequently convened his secretaries to debate the most important issues of his administration, and the term *cabinet* gained currency in 1793 during a crisis with the French government, when it met in a small room almost every day for nearly a year. Secretary of the Treasury Alexander Hamilton and Secretary of State Thomas Jefferson were the major figures in the first cabinet. Their disagreements over foreign policy led them to create the Federalist and Republican parties. By 1795 Washington understood that his cabinet and administration should be united on the major principles of foreign and domestic policy. By 1801, when Thomas Jefferson became President, it was understood that the cabinet would consist of appointees who supported his principles. Since the Democratic-Republican party retained power until 1828, it became the practice for a new President to retain some of his predecessor's secretaries and to consult with them before taking any action. Presidents often counted the opinion of the cabinet as equal to their own, creating a system of cabinet government. Cabinet government ended with the election of Andrew Jackson in 1828. Jackson established new rules: the President convenes cabinet meetings at his pleasure; the cabinet has no right to be consulted or convened; Presidential appointees serve as his subordinates and take direction from him; and the President may fire secretaries who disagree with his instructions. Because of a dispute with the cabinet over its ostracism of the wife of Secretary of War John Eaton in 1829, Jackson did not convene a meeting for two years and instead relied on a group of informal advisers known as the "kitchen cabinet." But in 1831 he finally bowed to pressure from members of his own party to meet with his secretaries.

Jackson dropped the prior practice of polling the secretaries for their positions on issues and then following the majority. President Lincoln was reported to have taken a vote in which he was the only person to favor a certain course of action. He then announced, "The ayes have it." After the Civil War the cabinet met regularly twice a week and was used primarily to give the President advice on patronage—the awarding of government jobs on the basis of political ties—and party politics and to coordinate legislative and budget proposals to Congress from the executive departments.

Until the 1930s there was only a handful of examples of a President making major decisions without first consulting the cabinet. These include the Emancipation Proclamation issued by President Lincoln, who gathered his cabinet and said, "I do not wish your advice about the main matter. That, I have determined for myself." Nor did Woodrow Wilson consult his cabinet on most issues, including the decision that the United States should enter World War I. Recent Presidents have convened their cabinets irregularly, one or two times a month at best. John F. Kennedy thought that cabinet meetings were a waste of time, asking, "Why should the Postmaster General sit there and listen to a discussion of the problems of Laos?" Kennedy held only six meetings in three years.

Today cabinets provide the President with political advice, serve as sounding boards for his ideas, and enable secretaries to coordinate their public statements on administration policy. Presidents also use cabinet meetings for symbolic purposes: Jimmy Carter used his first meeting to order that high officials use fewer limousines.

The "inner cabinet" consists of the secretaries of state, defense, and Treasury and the attorney general. These positions are usually the most prestigious, and the opinions of these secretaries carry the most weight with the President. The President sees these officials often, together or individually. The "outer cabinet" consists of the secretaries of the clientele agencies such as the Departments of Agriculture, Commerce, Interior, and Labor. These secretaries deal with issues that concern constituencies such as union workers, farmers, and business executives. Presidents spend little time with these secretaries and often use the White House staff and agencies of the Executive Office of the President to supervise their work.

SEE ALSO *Attorney general of the United States; Brains Trust; Departments, executive; Executive branch; Executive Office of the President; Kitchen cabinet; Modern Presidency; Office of Management and Budget; Patronage; Removal power; Secretary of defense; Secretary of state; Succession to the Presidency; 25th Amendment*
SOURCES Richard Fenno, *The President's Cabinet* (Cambridge: Harvard University Press, 1959).

CALENDARS, CONGRESSIONAL

Published daily whenever Congress is in session, calendars list all pending bills, resolutions, motions, and House-Senate conference committee actions. Only after a committee reports out a bill and the bill is placed on the calendar can it be called up for the full House or Senate to debate and vote on it. The House Rules Committee and the Senate majority leader decide the order in which bills will be called from the calendar for action. The Senate publishes two calendars, one for legislative and one for executive business (treaties and nominations). The House publishes five calendars for different types of legislation: revenue and appropriations bills, nonrevenue bills, noncontroversial bills that need not be debated, private claims and individual immigration bills, and—in very rare cases—motions to discharge (remove) bills from committees that were slow to act.

CALHOUN, JOHN C.
Vice President

- Born: Mar. 18, 1782, Mount Carmel, S.C.
- Political party: Democratic-Republican, Democrat
- Education: Yale College, B.A., 1804; Tapping Reeve Law School, 1805
- Military service: none
- Previous government service: South Carolina House of Representatives, 1809–10; U.S. House of Representatives, 1811–17; U.S. secretary of war, 1817–24
- Vice President under John Quincy Adams, 1825–29, and Andrew Jackson, 1829–33
- Subsequent government service: U.S. Senate, 1833–44, 1845–50; U.S. secretary of state, 1844–45
- Died: Mar. 31, 1850, Washington, D.C.

He seemed a man with rock-solid, immovable beliefs, but John C. Calhoun changed his position completely during his many years in Congress. Calhoun entered the House of Representatives as a nationalist, supporting a national bank, protective tariffs, and internal improvements to build the nation as a whole. Forty years later, Calhoun died as a defender of states' rights, a man who had sacrificed his Presidential ambitions in his devotion to the slave-owning South.

Calhoun was the choice of various factions of his party for the Vice Presidency in 1824. His Southern background provided a balance to the newly elected President from Massachusetts, John Quincy Adams. Calhoun played virtually no role in the Adams administration, however. In 1828, even though the Presidency went to Adams's bitter rival Andrew Jackson, Calhoun was elected Vice President a second time.

Calhoun and Jackson soon differed on a variety of issues, but the most important rift between them involved the marriage of the secretary of war, John Eaton, to Peggy O'Neale. Because the new Mrs. Eaton was considered too scandalous for Washington society, Calhoun's wife led a campaign among cabinet wives to freeze her out. Jackson was furious. He began to favor Martin Van Buren as his successor instead of Calhoun. The Vice President retaliated by opposing Jackson's plan to destroy the Bank of the United States—an organization that Calhoun had played a key role in chartering while a member of the House in 1816. Another rift between the two men occurred when it was revealed that Calhoun, as secretary of war, had sought the censure of Jackson for his controversial invasion of Florida in 1818.

In 1832, Calhoun resigned in protest over the "Tariff of Abominations" enacted by Congress in 1828. The law levied high duties on imported goods, and many Southerners believed it discriminated against their region (because higher tariffs would force them to pay more for imported goods and because Northern industries could also raise prices of goods to the South). Outraged people in South Carolina talked about withdrawing from the Union. In danger of losing his political base, Calhoun secretly drafted a "nullification" plan by which a state could nullify a federal law. When President Jackson denounced nullification as treason, Calhoun became the first Vice President to resign.

Calhoun returned home and South Carolina promptly elected him U.S. senator. With increasing passion he spoke for his state and his section. "If we do not defend ourselves none will defend," he declared; "if we yield we will be more and more pressed as we recede; and if we submit we will be trampled under foot." Calhoun induced the South Carolina legislature to pass an ordinance of nullification, which declared that the new tariff law would not be enforced in that state. President Jackson made it clear that he would use military force, if necessary, to collect the tariffs in Southern ports, and the state backed down.

In his 1850 book *Disquisition on Government,* Calhoun argued that states should be allowed to nullify, or ignore, laws passed by Congress and that no national laws should go into effect unless a majority of the members of Congress from each region of the country approved. If a majority from any region dissented, that would be enough to kill the measure. Calhoun's ideas for amending the Constitution went nowhere. By 1850 he predicted that there would be a civil war within 12 years.

Calhoun served as John Tyler's secretary of state in 1844, then returned to the Senate in 1845. He died fighting against the Compromise of 1850, which was intended to defuse the slavery issue in new western territories but which Calhoun feared would restrict the spread of slavery and weaken the South. On his deathbed Calhoun's only wish was for one more hour to speak in the Senate for his cause.

SEE ALSO *Adams, John Quincy; Compromise of 1850; Jackson, Andrew; Monroe, James; Tariff of Abominations (1828); Tyler, John*

SOURCES Teresa Celsi, *John C. Calhoun and the Roots of War* (Englewood Cliffs, N.J.: Silver Burdett, 1991). John Niven, *John C. Calhoun and the Price of Union* (Baton Rouge: Louisiana State University Press, 1988). Clyde N. Wilson, ed., *The Essential Calhoun* (New Brunswick, N.J.: Transaction Publishers, 1992).

CAMPAIGN COMMITTEES, CONGRESSIONAL

Democrats and Republicans in the House and Senate appoint their own campaign committees to raise funds for their party's congressional campaigns. Senators and representatives chair these committees and direct money to promising candidates, es-

pecially those in close races. Individual candidates also establish their own campaign committees and raise their own funds. The success of these individual efforts has increasingly helped elect to Congress members who are independent of their state and national party organizations. These members are less subject to party discipline in Congress.

CAMPAIGN FINANCING, CONGRESSIONAL

The escalating cost of campaigning for Congress, especially the cost of political advertisements on television, has turned many senators and representatives into part-time legislators and full-time fundraisers. The "money chase" continues even in nonelection years, as members build up large campaign chests. Although the quest for campaign financing places a wearisome burden on members of Congress, they still have great advantage over rival candidates who try to unseat them. Organized interest groups traditionally donated more money to those already holding office, in recognition of the power of their office and the likelihood of their reelection. Incumbents also have the advantage of greater visibility in the news media, a paid staff to assist them, and the franking privilege to keep their names before their constituents. The growing imbalance in fund-raising between incumbents and challengers has been a major reason for the high rate of reelection to Congress and has provoked demands for reform in campaign fundraising and even for limiting the number of terms that members of Congress may serve.

The Federal Election Commission requires all congressional candidates to file statements showing all the funds they raised and spent. Federal election laws also limit individual contributions to campaigns, but in the 1976 case of *Buckley* v. *Valeo* the Supreme Court ruled that it was an unconstitutional violation of free speech to set any restriction on the amount of money that wealthy people could spend on their own campaigns. Many members of Congress complain that this ruling gives unfair advantage to wealthy candidates.

The largest share of money for congressional campaigns comes from political action committees (PACs) representing various special interest groups. The predominance of PACs has raised concern that these contributors are attempting to "buy" special influence over legislation. In 1991, the Senate ethics committee investigated five senators who received campaign contributions from wealthy savings and loan banker Charles Keating. The Keating Five investigation questioned whether the senators had intervened with a government agency on behalf of Keating's bank because he was a constituent or because he had contributed financially to their campaigns. The ethics committee found that four of the senators had used poor judgment but had not violated Senate rules. A fifth senator, Alan Cranston (Democrat–California)—who had raised nearly a million dollars in campaign funds from Keating—was reprimanded by the full Senate for engaging in "an impermissible pattern of conduct."

SEE ALSO *Incumbents*

SOURCES David B. Magleby and Candice J. Nelson, *The Money Chase: Congressional Campaign Finance Reform* (Washington, D.C.: Brookings Institution, 1990).

CAMPAIGN FINANCING, PRESIDENTIAL

The Presidential Election Campaign Fund is an account administered by the U.S. Treasury that provides funds to Presidential candidates in the nominating contest and the general election. The fund is authorized by the Revenue Act of 1971, which allows each taxpayer to allocate a

dollar of his income taxes to the Treasury's Presidential election account. The allocation does not increase the amount of tax a person pays. The law went into effect with the 1976 election.

To be eligible for federal funds, candidates must agree to abide by the reporting requirements and spending limitations of the Federal Election Campaign Act of 1971 and the amendments of 1974. Candidates qualify for federal funds during the nominating contest if they raise $5,000 in each of 20 states through individual contributions of $250 or less. Once qualified, they receive matching funds from the Treasury for all contributions of $250 or less, up to the limits established by law.

In the general election, candidates who agree not to accept any private contributions are eligible for Treasury funding of their campaigns, up to the legal limits. In addition, the two major parties receive $11 million each for their national conventions. They may accept private donations for "party building" activities such as voter registration drives, which in reality go toward Presidential campaign activities.

Candidates who choose not to accept public funding for their primary or general election campaigns have no spending limits. Since the law was enacted, the only two serious contenders for the Presidency who did not accept federal funds were John Connally, who spent millions in 1980 and won just a single delegate to the Republican national convention, and independent Ross Perot, who spent $60 million of his own funds and received almost 20 percent of the popular vote in 1992.

SEE ALSO *Election campaigns, Presidential; Primaries, Presidential*

CAMPAIGNS, PRESIDENTIAL ELECTION

SEE *Election campaigns, Presidential*

CAMPBELL, JOHN A.
Associate Justice, 1853–61

- Born: June 24, 1811, Washington, Ga.
- Education: University of Georgia, B.A., 1825; U.S. Military Academy, 1825–28
- Previous government service: Alabama House of Representatives, 1837, 1843
- Appointed by President Franklin Pierce Mar. 21, 1853; replaced Justice John McKinley, who died
- Supreme Court term: confirmed by the Senate Mar. 25, 1853, by a voice vote; resigned Apr. 30, 1861
- Died: Mar. 12, 1889, Baltimore, Md.

John A. Campbell was a brilliant child who entered college at the age of 11 and graduated three years later. In 1828, he was admitted to the bar by a special act of the Georgia legislature and started his legal career in Alabama two years later. Campbell quickly became one of the best lawyers in Alabama.

Campbell joined the Supreme Court in 1853, during the political crisis that led to the Civil War. Important questions about human rights and property rights faced the Court. In response to these issues, Campbell supported states' rights and slavery. In *Scott* v. *Sandford* (1857), he joined Chief Justice Roger Taney to protect the property rights of slave owners, ruling that Congress could not prohibit slavery in U.S. territories.

When the Civil War started, Campbell left the Court and became assistant secretary of war for the Confederate States of America. After the war, he resumed his career as a lawyer and often represented clients in cases that went to the Supreme Court. For example, he represented the Butchers' Benevolent Association in oral argument in the *Slaughterhouse Cases* (1873).

CAMP DAVID

Camp David is a Presidential weekend retreat in Maryland's Catoctin Mountains. Originally a military base, it was turned over to the White House during the Great Depression and was named Shangri-La by President Franklin D. Roosevelt. President Dwight Eisenhower renamed it Camp David for his grandson David. It consists of 180 forested acres, protected by a ring of three fences and marine guard patrols. It is maintained by 150 naval personnel and, when the President is in residence, by 250 other support staff. It contains a number of residence cabins for the President and his guests, who often include foreign heads of state. Camp David also has a heated pool, skeet range, tennis courts, and horseshoe pit. It has a conference center where administration officials can meet with the President when he is on a "working vacation." Expenses for Camp David are part of the Navy Department budget.
SEE ALSO *Camp David peace talks*

CAMP DAVID PEACE TALKS

From September 4 to 17, 1978, President Jimmy Carter held meetings at Camp David with Anwar Sadat, president of Egypt, and Menachem Begin, prime minister of Israel. These negotiations led to a peace treaty between Israel and Egypt. The proceedings were kept secret and the delegations from both nations remained at Camp David throughout the sessions, ensuring no premature newspaper leaks about the substance of the talks.

President Carter negotiated separately with Sadat and Begin, shuttling between their cabins. Carter and his diplomatic team then produced drafts of agreements and modified them to take each side's objections into account. Carter oversaw every aspect of the negotiations.

Carter's own position adhered to United Nations Resolution 242, which instructed Israel to withdraw from occupied Arab territory and Arab nations to recognize and make peace with Israel. Carter's proposals included Israeli withdrawal from the Sinai Peninsula and Gaza Strip, an autonomous "homeland" for Palestinians in Gaza and the West Bank, an end to Israeli settlements in the West Bank, and a five-year transitional period in which the final status of the West Bank would be determined. In return, there would be an end to the Egyptian economic boycott of Israel and full recognition. Egypt would also give Israel navigation rights through the Suez Canal and Straits of Tiran. The borders existing before the 1967 Arab-Israeli war would be restored.

Sadat was willing to go along with most of these proposals, but he also wanted reparations from Israel for the occupation of Egyptian territory and for oil it had taken from the Sinai. Israel was willing to withdraw from the Sinai and insisted that most of it be demilitarized but wished to keep some military facilities in the area as well as some of its settlements. Israelis would give the Palestinians administrative self-rule but wanted to retain the right to buy land and settle on the West Bank. Israel also expressed interest in a mutual defense treaty with the United States, an idea rebuffed by Carter.

The main disagreements were between Carter and Begin. Carter argued that international borders could not be changed, while Begin insisted that the 1967 war gave Israel the right to change its frontiers. Carter claimed that West Jerusalem was part of the West Bank; Begin insisted it was an integral part of Israel. Carter wanted a freeze on Israeli settlements; Begin resisted. The Israeli leader insisted that Carter honor a pledge made by President Gerald Ford: that the United States would coordinate with Israel any American proposal for a peace settlement before submitting it to the Arabs. Carter rejected this approach to the negotiations.

Begin made a number of concessions to Carter. These included agreeing to the principle of Egyptian sovereignty in the Sinai and to complete Israeli withdrawal from all military facilities and all settlements in the Sinai.

Sadat and Carter were in substantial agreement on most issues, and the two men became close friends as the conference proceeded. Sadat made a number of concessions to Carter, which alienated some of his own delegation, including his foreign minister (who resigned at the end of the conference). They believed that Sadat had made too many concessions to the Americans and had been outmaneuvered by the Israelis.

On September 17, the Camp David Accords were signed. The accords included a *Framework for Peace in the Middle East* and a *Framework for Conclusion of a Peace Treaty between Egypt and Israel,* together with *Accompanying Letters* exchanged between President Carter and the two leaders. Israel withdrew from Arab territories and dismantled settlements in the Sinai Peninsula and Gaza. It recognized the principle that there were Palestinian rights to be negotiated in the future. Egypt made peace with the Jewish state and formally recognized it. It agreed to limit its military presence in the Sinai and recognized that Israel had legitimate security interests subject to negotiation.

Carter appointed Robert Strauss, former chairman of the Democratic National Committee, as a Presidential special envoy to the Middle East to implement the agreement. After intensive negotiations, Sadat and Begin traveled to Washington and signed a peace treaty on March 26, 1979. For their efforts, the two men shared the Nobel Peace Prize.

SEE ALSO *Carter, Jimmy*

SOURCES George Lenczowski, *American Presidents and the Middle East* (Durham: Duke University Press, 1990). William Quandt, *Camp David: Peacemaking and Politics* (Washington, D.C.: Brookings Institution, 1986).

CANNON, JOSEPH G.

- Born: May 7, 1836, Guilford, N.C.
- Political party: Republican
- Education: studied law at the Cincinnati Law School

- Representative from Illinois: 1873–91, 1893–1913, 1915–23
- Speaker of the House: 1903–13
- Died: Nov. 12, 1926, Danville, Ill.

The most powerful Speaker of the House of Representatives, Joseph G. Cannon represented the Republican conservative Old Guard during the Progressive Era. Uncle Joe looked like a crusty old farmer, but he ruled the House with an iron fist. The growth of big business did not worry Cannon, and he used his control of the House rules to suppress debate on government regulation of the railroads and other industries. "The country don't need any legislation," he insisted in typically earthy style.

On March 19, 1910, 149 Democrats and 42 progressive Republicans banded together to overthrow Cannon's power. Representative George Norris (Republican–Nebraska) made a motion for the House to elect members of the Rules Committee, rather than let the Speaker appoint them, and to bar the Speaker from being a member of the committee. Cannon offered to resign, but the House voted to keep him as Speaker, now that his powers had been trimmed. Despised by progressives (especially those outside of Congress), Cannon remained personally popular with members of the House. Despite the "revolt" against him, the House named its first office building in his memory.

SEE ALSO *Norris, George W.; Rules committees; Speaker of the House*
SOURCES Richard B. Cheney and Lynne V. Cheney, *Kings of the Hill: Power and Personality in the House of Representatives* (New York: Continuum, 1983).

CAPITAL PUNISHMENT

The penalty of death for a person convicted of a serious crime, such as intentional murder, is called capital punishment. *Capital* is derived from the Latin word *capitalis,* which means "of the head." Throughout human history, beheading a person has been the most frequent form of killing someone as punishment for a serious crime. Current methods of carrying out capital punishment in the United States are electrocution, firing squad, hanging, poison gas, and lethal injection. The use of lethal injection has become the most common way of carrying out the death penalty in the United States; it is the method used in 17 states.

Capital punishment has been practiced in the United States since the founding of the republic. During the founding period, several crimes were punishable by death in the 13 states: murder, treason, piracy, arson, rape, robbery, burglary, sodomy, counterfeiting, horse theft, and slave rebellion. Today, in the 36 states that permit capital punishment, premeditated murder is virtually the only crime for which the punishment is death. Fourteen states and the District of Columbia have banned the death penalty. The United States government may impose the death penalty for certain federal crimes, such as treason.

In 1972 the U.S. Supreme Court ruled in *Furman* v. *Georgia* that the death penalty could not be imposed without legal guidelines that define precisely the crime and conditions for a sentence of death. A jury in Georgia had convicted William Furman, a black man, of murdering a white man and had sentenced him to death. Under Georgia law, the jury had complete power to decide whether a convicted murderer should receive the death penalty. The Legal Defense Fund of the National Association for the Advancement of Colored People (NAACP) filed an appeal on Furman's behalf. It argued that state laws that gave a jury free rein to impose capital punishment could be unfair. The NAACP lawyers pointed to evidence that blacks convicted of murdering whites were much more likely to be punished by death than whites convicted of murder.

A divided Court (5 to 4) agreed with the NAACP position and, for the first time, nullified a death penalty on the basis of the 8th Amendment, which forbids "cruel and unusual punishments." Justices William

Brennan and Thurgood Marshall argued, in separate concurring opinions, that the death penalty is morally wrong and is always a violation of the "cruel and unusual punishments" clause of the 8th Amendment, as applied to the states through the due process clause of the 14th Amendment. Three other Justices—William O. Douglas, Potter Stewart, and Byron White—wrote separate concurring opinions in which they agreed only that the Georgia system for imposing capital punishment, at issue in this case, was unconstitutional because it led to random and unfair decisions about who should receive the death penalty.

After the *Furman* decision, there was a halt in the use of the death penalty by all 50 state governments. The Georgia government passed a new law regarding capital punishment to address the problems raised by the Court in *Furman*. It created a two-phase procedure for imposing the death penalty in murder cases: the trial phase and the sentencing phase. In the trial phase, a jury would determine a defendant's guilt or innocence. If the defendant was found guilty, the state could request the death penalty. During phase two, there would be a second jury trial with the sole purpose of deciding whether to impose death penalty. The Georgia law specified mandatory guidelines for determining whether to impose capital punishment. Thus, the law was designed to limit the jury's discretion and eliminate the kind of arbitrary application of the death penalty to which the Court objected in the *Furman* case.

The new Georgia law on capital punishment was tested in *Gregg* v. *Georgia* (1976), in which the Court decided that the death penalty for people convicted of first-degree murder is constitutional. The Court also upheld the Georgia law and praised it as a model for other states to follow. Many states have either adopted the Georgia law or created a similar one. The *Gregg* decision appears to have settled the capital punishment issue in favor of the death penalty, as long as it is imposed only

in convictions for murder in the first degree and only according to certain clearly spelled out procedures and conditions.

Justices William Brennan and Thurgood Marshall were the two dissenters in the *Gregg* case. They continued to argue that capital punishment is always a violation of the 8th Amendment's "cruel and unusual punishments" clause. By contrast, the defenders of limited uses of capital punishment argue that the U.S. Constitution sanctions the death penalty. They point to the 5th and 14th Amendments, which restrain the government from taking away a person's "life, liberty, or property, without due process of law." These constitutional provisions imply that a person may, under certain conditions, be deprived of life, as long as due process of law is observed. A large majority of Americans have agreed, in public opinion polls, that the death penalty is an acceptable punishment for first-degree murder.

SEE ALSO *Cruel and unusual punishment*
SOURCES Hugo Adam Bedau, ed., *The Death Penalty in America* (New York: Oxford University Press, 1982). Vincent Buranelli, *The Eighth Amendment* (Englewood Cliffs, N.J.: Silver Burdett, 1991). Welsh S. White, *The Death Penalty in the Nineties: An Examination of the Modern System of Capital Punishment* (Ann Arbor: University of Michigan Press, 1991).

CAPITOL BUILDING

The most widely recognized symbol of American democracy, the U.S. Capitol building houses the Congress. The Capitol contains more than 500 rooms in addition to the massive House and Senate chambers. Outside, in the shadow of its magnificent dome, Presidents of the United States take their inaugural oath, and they return to the Capitol to deliver their annual State of the Union message. State funerals and other ceremonies take place within the Rotunda, and foreign leaders frequently visit the Capitol to address joint sessions of Congress.

Expansion of the Capitol   The Capitol expanded along with the nation. President George Washington selected the original building design by Dr. William Thornton, and Washington laid the cornerstone in 1793. When Congress arrived in November 1800, only the Senate wing of the Capitol was completed. Within this small, boxlike structure operated the Senate, House, Supreme Court, and Library of Congress. When the House wing opened in 1810, a wooden walkway connected the two structures. This was how the building looked in August 1814, when British troops invaded Washington. Piling up furniture and books, the British set fire to the Capitol and destroyed its interior. A heavy rain saved the exterior walls. Congress reconvened in the restored Capitol in 1819, and the oldest desks in the current Senate chamber date back to that year. Congress also purchased Thomas Jefferson's private library to replace the Library of Congress volumes consumed in the flames.

In the 1820s, construction of the central Rotunda, topped by a low copper dome, completed the original plans for the building. But the constant addition of new states—which resulted in more members of Congress—caused the Senate and House to outgrow their chambers. Massive wings were added to the north and south ends of the Capitol. The House moved into its new chamber in 1857 and the Senate in 1859. The Architect of the Capitol proposed that a higher cast-iron dome would better fit the newly enlarged building. Outbreak of the Civil War in 1861 temporarily halted work on this dome, but President Lincoln urged its completion as a symbol of the Union. In December 1863 the dome was completed and capped with a bronze statue of Freedom. The top of the statue reaches 287 feet and 5 inches above the base of the Capitol's East Front.

Beginning in 1874, Frederick Law Olmsted (designer of New York's Central Park) oversaw the landscaping and constructed terraces along the West Front to give the Capitol grounds a more formal appearance and add new office space. The West Front is the only portion of the original sandstone exterior still visible from outside the Capitol. The East Front was extended out some 30 feet and rebuilt in marble during renovation in 1958.

A colorful interior   In contrast to its austere white exterior, the Capitol's interior is colorfully decorated. Much of this embellishment was the work of the Italian painter Constantino Brumidi, known as the "Michelangelo of the Capitol." Trained in the art of fresco (the technique of applying paint to wet plaster so that it retains its colors), Brumidi began his work in the 1850s. In 1865 he painted a huge fresco under the dome, 180 feet above the Rotunda floor, depicting the "Apotheosis [glorification] of George Washington." Brumidi devoted the rest of his life to painting halls and committee rooms on the Senate side of the Capitol. He died in 1880 after falling from the scaffold while painting the frieze that rings the inside of the Rotunda. The House had declined Brumidi's services, but a century later, during the 1970s, artist Allyn Cox enlivened the House corridors with similar historical scenes.

Enormous paintings of historical events decorate the public areas of the Capitol, and the corridors are lined with marble and bronze statues. In 1864 the House declared its old chamber to be National Statuary Hall and invited each state to send statues of two of its most illustrious citizens. Additional statues and busts honor many Presidents, Vice Presidents, foreign dignitaries, American Indian chiefs, and national heroes.

Congressional office buildings   Because of limited working space within the Capitol, the House and Senate have had additional office buildings constructed. In 1908, the House occupied its first permanent office building, now known as the Cannon building, and the Senate moved into the matching Richard Brevard Russell building the following year. Linked to the Capitol by underground tunnels and subways, these office buildings provide offices for committees, members, and their staffs.

As its staff grew, the House built two additional office buildings, the Longworth (1933) and Rayburn (1965) buildings, and the Senate added the Everett McKinley Dirksen (1958) and Philip A. Hart (1982) buildings.

The Library of Congress operated out of the Capitol until 1897, when it transported its growing collection to a separate building across the street. Similarly, the Supreme Court met within the Capitol until 1935, when its own building was constructed. Today, the complex of massive structures surrounding the Capitol represents functions that once all took place within the small sandstone building that greeted Congress in 1800.

The U.S. Capitol remains the most open of federal buildings. Visitors on guided tours, senators, representatives, journalists, lobbyists, staff, and constituents all mingle in its corridors. The galleries stay open to the public whenever the Senate and House convene, except for those rare closed sessions dealing with highly classified information. Flags flying above the chambers indicate which house is meeting, and at night a beacon high up in the Capitol dome signifies that a night session of the Senate or House is in progress.

SEE ALSO *Architect of the Capitol; Library of Congress*

SOURCES Lonnelle M. Aikman, *We, the People: The Story of the United States Capitol, Its Past and Its Promise* (Washington, D.C.: U.S. Capitol Historical Society, 1991). Glenn Brown, *History of the United States Capitol*, 2 vols. (1903; reprint, New York: Da Capo Press, 1970).

CAPITOL HILL

While drawing up plans for the city of Washington, the French architect Pierre L'Enfant called Capitol Hill a "pedestal waiting for a monument." He chose the hill as the site of the U.S. Capitol building. Formerly known as Jenkins Hill, the plateau rises 88 feet above the nearby Potomac River. This high ground overlooking the city was renamed Capitol Hill after the Capitoline Hill of the ancient Roman Republic.

Construction of the Capitol began in 1793. During the next two centuries, as Congress grew, its functions spread to many other buildings clustered around the Capitol. *Capitol Hill* became a collective term for the entire complex of buildings that house and serve Congress, as well as for the neighborhood of shops and homes within sight of the Capitol. Capitol Hill (or just the Hill) also came to mean Congress itself, just as the White House has become synonymous with the President who occupies it.

CAPITOL HISTORICAL SOCIETY

In 1962 Representative Fred Schwengel (Republican–Iowa) founded the U.S. Capitol Historical Society to promote greater public awareness of the history of Congress and the Capitol building. This not-for-profit membership organization raises funds largely through the sales of its guidebook, *We, the People,* and other Congress-related publications and memorabilia at a gift stand in the Capitol.

CAPITOL POLICE

Separate from the Washington metropolitan police, the Capitol Police protect Congress and its visitors. In 1800, Congress needed only a single guard to patrol the Capitol. By 1828, the official date of the founding of the Capitol Police, the staff had increased to three non-uniformed watchmen. By the Civil War, Capitol Police wore uniforms and badges and carried heavy canes as weapons.

As the Capitol grounds expanded, so did the Capitol police force. Officers guarded entrances, patrolled the grounds, directed traffic, and controlled crowds. At first, most police officers were appointed through patronage—they were war veterans or college students sponsored by members of Congress. In 1968, faced with a growing number of political demonstrations and civil disturbances in Washington, Congress moved to end the patronage system and create a professional police force. By the 1990s, more than 1,300 professionally trained men and women were serving as Capitol Police. Security devices, such as electronic metal detectors, were installed at the entrances to all buildings. Despite these precautions, tragedy occurred in 1998 when an armed man entered the Capitol and began firing. Two Capitol Police officers died before he could be subdued. The incident convinced members of Congress to approve construction of a Capitol Visitors' Center, where all visitors could be screened before entering the building.

CARDOZO, BENJAMIN N.
Associate Justice, 1932–38

- Born: May 24, 1870, New York, N.Y.
- Education: Columbia College, B.A., 1889; M.A., 1890; Columbia Law School, 1891
- Previous government service: justice, New York State Supreme Court, 1914; judge, New York State Court of Appeals, 1914–32, chief judge, New York State Court of Appeals, 1926–32
- Appointed by President Herbert Hoover Feb. 15, 1932; replaced Oliver Wendell Holmes, who retired
- Supreme Court term: confirmed by the Senate Feb. 24, 1932, by a voice vote; served until July 9, 1938
- Died: July 9, 1938, Port Chester, N.Y.

Benjamin N. Cardozo was only the second Jew to be appointed to the Supreme Court. He served on the Court with the first Jewish justice, Louis Brandeis.

Benjamin Cardozo was the youngest son of Albert and Rebecca Washington Cardozo, whose ancestors had settled in New York in the 1850s. He was a very bright child and entered Columbia University at age 15, graduating with honors four years later. In 1891, he began to practice law in New York City. Later, he served as a judge of the New York Supreme Court and the New York Court of Appeals.

As a New York State judge, Cardozo achieved a national reputation for his wise decisions and exemplary legal reasoning, which emphasized the effects of law on the lives of people. Cardozo opposed an overemphasis on precedent and tradition as constricting, too formal, and too likely to cause injustice by preventing constitutional changes to fit changing times.

Justice Cardozo served only six years on the U.S. Supreme Court. During this brief period, however, he established the doctrine of "selective incorporation" to guide the Court's use of the 14th Amendment to apply federal Bill of Rights provisions to the states. Cardozo stated this position in *Palko* v. *Connecticut* (1937). He wrote that to be "incorporated" under the due process clause of the 14th Amendment, a provision of the Bill of Rights must be "fundamental"; that is, it must be a right without which "neither liberty nor justice would exist," and the right "must be implicit in the concept of ordered liberty."

Cardozo recommended a case-by-case application of the 14th Amendment to use one or more parts of the Bill of Rights to limit the power of a state government and protect individual rights. This position was opposed by Justice Hugo Black, who wanted "total incorporation" of the Bill of Rights. Cardozo's position has prevailed, and the Court uses it today.

SEE ALSO *Incorporation doctrine; Palko v. Connecticut*

SOURCES Benjamin N. Cardozo, *The Nature of the Judicial Process* (New Haven: Yale University Press, 1921). Andrew L. Kaufman, *Cardozo* (Cambridge: Harvard University Press, 1998). Richard A. Posner, *Cardozo: A Study in Reputation* (Chicago: University of Chicago Press, 1990).

CARPETBAGGERS

During Reconstruction of the South after the Civil War, federal troops protected the right of freedmen to vote. Black voters helped elect Republican state governments and sent Republican candidates—both white and black—to the House of Representatives and Senate from the Southern states. Many of these Southern Republicans were Northerners who had moved to the South after the war. Southern Democrats denounced them as "carpetbaggers," after the carpet-fabric bags in which many of these newcomers brought their belongings to the South. Among the carpetbaggers were some corrupt opportunists, but others wanted to rebuild the South and to help the freedmen during the transition from slavery to freedom.

Eventually, in state after state, Democrats overthrew the Republican Reconstruction governments. The last of the federal troops withdrew from the Southern states after the election of 1876. Violence and restrictive election laws took the vote away from the freedmen. After Reconstruction the "solid South" sent almost no Republicans to Congress again until the 1960s.

SEE ALSO *Reconstruction, congressional;* *"Solid South"*

SOURCES Richard N. Current, *Those Terrible Carpetbaggers* (New York: Oxford University Press, 1988).

CARROLL V. UNITED STATES

- 267 U.S. 132 (1925)
- Vote: 6–2
- For the Court: Taft
- Dissenting: McReynolds and Sutherland

In 1923, George Carroll and John Kiro were transporting alcoholic beverages in an automobile. Federal officers suspected they might be carrying liquor, stopped

their car, and searched it. They found liquor and arrested Carroll and Kiro, who were charged with violating the Volstead Act (the federal law prohibiting the sale or transportation of alcoholic beverages). Carroll and Kiro were convicted, but they appealed because the federal officers had searched their automobile without a warrant.

The Issue   Carroll claimed that the federal officers who searched his automobile had violated the 4th Amendment of the Constitution, which states, "The right of the people to be secure in their persons, houses, papers, and effects, against unreasonable searches and seizures, shall not be violated, and no Warrants shall issue, but upon probable cause, supported by Oath or affirmation, and particularly describing the place to be searched, and the persons or things to be seized." Carroll argued that the federal officers had no legal grounds for searching his car, so the evidence they found should have been excluded from his trial.

Opinion of the Court   The Supreme Court decided against Carroll. The warrantless search of the car was constitutional, said Chief Justice William Howard Taft, because the vehicle could be driven away and the people in it could escape before a warrant could be obtained. Thus, an exception to the 4th Amendment warrant requirement could be made.

Dissent   Justice George Sutherland joined Justice James McReynolds in dissent. McReynolds argued that no exceptions should be made in cases involving searches of cars to the 4th Amendment requirement of a warrant as protection against unreasonable searches and seizures. He concluded that Carroll had been wrongfully arrested.

Significance   This case established a rule about searches of automobiles that has been upheld in subsequent cases such as *United States* v. *Ross* (1982). In *California* v. *Acevedo* (1991), the rule was strengthened by the Court's decision to eliminate a warrant requirement for searches and seizures of closed containers found in an automobile.

SEE ALSO *Searches and seizures; United States v. Ross*

CARTER, JIMMY
39th President

- Born: Oct. 1, 1924, Plains, Ga.
- Political party: Democrat
- Education: U.S. Naval Academy, B.S., 1946
- Military service: U.S. Navy, 1947–53
- Previous government service: chair, Sumter County, Ga., Board of Education, 1955–62; Georgia Senate 1963–66; governor of Georgia, 1971–75
- Elected President, 1976; served, 1977–81

Promising a "government as good as the people," Jimmy Carter was elected in 1976 as a Washington outsider by voters fed up with the Watergate scandal and the weak economy. Carter shed many of the trappings of the "imperial" Presidency and pursued a foreign policy emphasizing human rights and peaceful solution of international conflict. But his unpopular Panama Canal Treaty and rocketing inflation and interest rates made him a one-term President.

Born in the small town of Plains, Georgia, James Earl Carter, Jr., was the first American President to be born in a hospital. He graduated from Plains High School as valedictorian in 1941, and in 1946 he graduated from the U.S. Naval Academy in the top tenth of his class. He served as an ensign on an experimental nuclear submarine with Captain (later Admiral) Hyman Rickover, the father of the nuclear navy. In 1953, after the death of his father, Carter resigned his commission to take over his family's peanut farm, which he turned into a thriving business.

Carter became a deacon and Sunday school teacher in the Plains Baptist Church, then chairman of the Sumter County School Board, where he peacefully promoted racial desegregation of the schools. As a state senator, Carter fought local segregationist groups, and he defeated racist opponents to win reelection to the senate. He encouraged blacks to join the Plains Baptist Church.

In 1966 Carter ran for governor but lost to arch-segregationist Lester Maddox. Carter's loss led him to become a born-again Christian. In the 1970 Democratic gubernatorial primary Carter declared his opposition to busing as a means of overcoming racial segregation in schools, leading the *Atlanta Constitution* to call him an "ignorant, racist, backward, ultraconservative, rednecked South Georgia peanut farmer." With evangelical and fundamentalist Christian support, he won the election.

Although elected with segregationist support, Carter was a progressive, especially on race relations. Carter reorganized the state government and consolidated many independent agencies into a few efficient departments. He increased minority hiring in state government by 50 percent, and he promoted environmental and educational programs. But he worked poorly with traditional politicians in the state legislature, gaining a reputation as an arrogant and isolated governor.

Carter began a steady rise in national Democratic politics, however. He became chair of the Democratic Governors' Campaign Committee in 1972 and campaign chair for the Democratic National Committee in 1974—a year in which the party scored major successes in congressional elections. By 1975 Carter was spending most of his time making speeches and traveling from one state to another seeking financial support and media attention.

Carter portrayed himself as an outsider who could clean up the mess in Washington. He promised never to lie to the American people, implicitly contrasting himself to politicians like Richard Nixon in the Watergate scandal. He called for "a government that is as honest and decent and fair and competent and truthful and idealistic as are the American people." Carter won the Iowa Presidential caucuses on

January 19, 1976, and propelled himself to the forefront of the Democratic field. He won the New Hampshire primary a few weeks later, and funds poured into his campaign. He won a number of other primaries and gained sufficient votes for a first-ballot nomination at the national convention. He defeated the incumbent President, Gerald Ford, in the general election by a narrow margin, due in large measure to a split in the opposition ranks between moderate Republicans and conservatives who had favored Ronald Reagan. The high unemployment rate and Ford's pardon of Nixon also worked in Carter's favor.

Although Carter took office with large Democratic majorities in Congress, he was unable to get them to support much of his program. His opposition to some rivers and harbors projects early in his term was fiercely resisted by his own party's congressional leaders, as was his 1978 veto of a public works measure on the grounds that it would be inflationary. Although Congress passed his proposal to create a department of energy, his comprehensive energy program was revised. When it did pass, it proved unpopular with the public because it emphasized conservation and higher prices. He cut back on federal aid to urban areas, causing a backlash among liberal Democrats. His decision to cancel the B-1 bomber upset party conservatives. When Congress transformed his tax reform plan into new favors for special interests, Carter referred to them as "a pack of ravenous wolves." Carter did have some successes: he got Congress to divide the Department of Health, Education, and Welfare into two new departments, one for education and the other for health and human services; the minimum wage was raised; and Congress deregulated the airline, trucking, and railroad industries. It also established a "Superfund" to clean up toxic waste sites.

In foreign affairs, too, Carter took actions that were unpopular. In 1977, although more than three-fourths of the American people wanted to keep the Panama Canal Zone, Carter negotiated two treaties with Panama that called for the United States to give up sovereign rights in the Panama Canal Zone and to turn over operation of the canal to Panama by the turn of the century. The Senate consented to the treaties by only a bare margin. In 1978 Carter presided over the Camp David peace accords between Israel and Egypt, which resulted in a treaty between the two nations the following year. In 1979 Carter recognized communist China and canceled a defense treaty with the anticommunist government on Taiwan—actions that upset Southern conservatives. He began an emphasis in American foreign policy on human rights, cutting off foreign aid to certain Latin American nations with repressive regimes. The second Strategic Arms Limitation Treaty (SALT II) with the Soviet Union was signed on June 18, 1979, but the Soviet invasion of Afghanistan put Senate consent to the treaty in doubt and Carter withdrew it from the Senate. Nevertheless, both governments adhered to its terms.

Carter's popularity fell during much of his term, as inflation increased to more than 15 percent and the unemployment rate, after dropping early in his term, rose again to more than 6 percent. Interest rates rose to the 20 percent range, which made it difficult for people to purchase homes and consumer goods. The seizure of American diplomats in the embassy in Iran by "student" militants on November 4, 1979, and Carter's inability to obtain their release by diplomatic means also caused his popularity to sink. An April 1980 attempt to rescue the hostages ended in failure with the death of eight U.S. servicemen in a helicopter crash in the Iranian desert. The abortive mission seemed to many Americans to symbolize U.S. military weakness in the post-Vietnam era. In July 1980 Carter's popularity slid to 20 percent in the polls—lower even than Nixon's during the Watergate scandal.

In the 1980 Democratic nominating contest, Senator Edward M. Kennedy almost defeated Carter, and much of Kennedy's liberal platform was adopted by the convention in a repudiation of the Carter Presidency. With the Democrats split, Republican conservative Ronald Reagan defeated Carter in a three-way race that also involved independent candidate John Anderson. On the day Carter's successor was inaugurated, the Iranian government released the 52 hostages they had held for 444 days. President Reagan asked Carter to fly to Germany to greet the returning hostages.

After his election defeat, Carter returned to Georgia. He gave courses in public affairs at Emory University, participated in the creation and work of the Carter Presidential Center in Atlanta, an organization devoted to human rights and humanitarian causes around the world. Carter became involved in monitoring elections in a number of foreign nations, which aided in their transformation from dictatorship to democracy.

SEE ALSO *Camp David peace talks; Ford, Gerald R.; Mondale, Walter F.; Reagan, Ronald*

SOURCES Douglas Brinkley, *The Unfinished Presidency: Jimmy Carter's Journey Beyond the White House* (New York: Viking, 1998). Jimmy Carter, *Keeping Faith: Memoirs of a President* (New York: Bantam, 1982). Gary M. Fink and Hugh Davis Graham, *The Carter Presidency: Policy Choices in the Post–New Deal Era* (Lawrence: University Press of Kansas, 1998). Betty Glad, *Jimmy Carter, In Search of the Great White House* (New York: Norton, 1980). Erwin C. Hargrove, *Jimmy Carter as President: Leadership and the Politics of the Public Good* (Baton Rouge: Louisiana State University Press, 1988). Kenneth E. Morris, *Jimmy Carter: American Moralist* (Athens: University of Georgia Press, 1996). Kenneth W. Thompson, *The Carter Presidency: Fourteen Intimate Perspectives of Jimmy Carter* (Lanham, Md.: University Press of America, 1990).

CATRON, JOHN
Associate Justice, 1837–65

- Born: 1786, Pennsylvania
- Education: self-educated, studied law on his own
- Previous government service: judge, Tennessee Supreme Court of Errors and Appeals, 1824–31; chief justice of Tennessee, 1831–34
- Appointed by President Andrew Jackson Mar. 3, 1837, to fill a newly created seat on the Court
- Supreme Court term: confirmed by the Senate Mar. 8, 1837, by a 28–15 vote; served until May 30, 1865
- Died: May 30, 1865, Nashville, Tenn.

John Catron was the son of German immigrants to Pennsylvania. The exact place of his birth is unknown, but the hardships of his childhood in Virginia and Kentucky, and his struggles to overcome them, have been recorded. Although Catron did not have an opportunity to go to school, he educated himself by reading at home.

Catron served under General Andrew Jackson in the War of 1812. His friendship with Jackson worked to his benefit after Jackson became President in 1828. Catron became a loyal Jacksonian Democrat, and the President rewarded him with an appointment to the U.S. Supreme Court in 1837. During his 28 years on the Court, Catron supported states' rights and slavery. But when the Civil War started, he remained loyal to the Union and remained at his job on the Supreme Court.

CAUCUSES, CONGRESSIONAL

The congressional caucus was a method of nominating Presidential candidates used by the Federalist party in 1800 and the Democratic-Republican party between 1800 and 1824.

Borrowing the word from the Algonquian Indians, members of the same political party *caucus*—or meet together—in closed session. Each party's congressional caucus consisted of its U.S. senators and representatives. At the end of the congressional session in the Presidential election year, the party members met at the Capitol or a local tavern or boardinghouse. A vote was taken, and the candidate receiving a majority would be declared the party nominee for President. A "committee of correspondence and arrangements" would then send word to party newspapers, which would announce the caucus decision to the public.

No congressional caucus was held in 1789, when George Washington was "nominated" by the public by acclamation at huge outdoor rallies. For the second Presidential election, a number of Republicans met in Philadelphia on October 16, 1792, to choose a candidate for Vice President. They decided to back George Clinton rather than Aaron Burr. A similar meeting took place in June 1796, at which time Thomas Jefferson and Burr were chosen as Republican nominees for President and Vice President. In both cases the caucuses were "mixed" because many politicians who were not members of Congress attended the sessions.

The first full-fledged congressional caucus was held by the Federalists on May 3, 1800, when they nominated John Adams for reelection as President and Charles Cotesworth Pinckney to be Vice President. The Republicans held their first nominating caucus on March 11, 1800, and chose Jefferson for President and Aaron Burr as his running mate. The Republicans held their first pure congressional caucus (limited to members of Congress) on February 25, 1804. Jefferson was renominated for President. The dispirited Federalists did not even hold a caucus that year.

Federalist representatives from eight states held an informal meeting in New York City in July 1808, but no formal caucus was held. Some Federalist party leaders caucused in 1812 and secretly agreed to back Clinton against James Madison, exploiting a split in the Republican party rather than nominating their own candidate.

Through 1824 Republican congressional caucuses nominated candidates, but from 1808 on, many of the representatives backing candidates not expected to win the nomination absented themselves, so the caucuses were really gatherings of the front-runner's supporters rather than a deliberative body. Proxy votes (a form of absentee ballot) for missing legislators were permitted in 1816 and 1824. The caucus of 1820 involved only 50 members of Congress, and it was not considered "expedient" to take a vote because James Monroe was the President and had no opposition to his renomination from within his party.

The congressional caucus was discredited in the election of 1824 by Andrew Jackson, who referred to it as "King Caucus" because of its allegedly corrupt and undemocratic proceedings. Tennessee and Maryland instructed their congressional delegations to boycott any caucus proceeding. Several state legislatures favorable to Jackson or John Quincy Adams held their own caucuses to "nominate" their choices. When the congressional caucus was convened on February 14, 1824, only 66 members of Congress, representing only 14 of 22 states, attended. Almost all of those who attended were backers of William H. Crawford. Adams and Jackson simply ignored the congressional caucus and its endorsement.

The caucus system fell into disuse because the Republican party disintegrated under Jackson's onslaught in 1828. That year several state legislatures "nominated" Jackson by passing resolutions recommending him to the electorate. Party conventions eventually assumed the role of nominating Presidential candidates.

After the end of the single-party Era of Good Feelings, which lasted from the War of 1812 until 1828, caucuses took on new importance as the lines in Congress once again became drawn between political parties. Beginning in 1845, the Senate party caucuses began preparing lists of majority and minority party members of the Senate committees. By the late 19th century, the chairman of the Senate's majority caucus (who was elected by the majority party senators) had taken on the duties of opening and closing the session and scheduling legislation, duties that would later be the responsibility of the majority leader.

In the House, strong Speakers such as Thomas B. Reed and Joseph G. Cannon effectively used the caucuses to exert leadership in passing legislation and to discipline political renegades. Republicans adopted "binding caucus" rules—meaning that whatever a majority of members voted for in caucus, *all* members of the caucus would vote for in the full House—to marshal the maximum strength of their forces behind their legislative programs. When Democrats won the majority in Congress in 1912, they adopted a similar rule to unify behind President Woodrow Wilson's progressive agenda. They agreed to debate the issues within the caucus and then to vote together as much as possible on the floor.

During the 1920s, the caucus declined as a vehicle of party unity and discipline. As caucuses developed a negative public image, Republicans in both houses and Democrats in the Senate began calling the caucuses party conferences; only the House Democratic Caucus retained the name. Whether caucus or conference, the groups devoted themselves to electing floor leaders and performing organizational duties rather than to setting legislative agendas. Party leaders became reluctant to call many conference meetings because they did not want to expose the divisions within their party.

Numerous smaller caucuses also operate on Capitol Hill. The first such organization was the Democratic Study Group, begun in 1958. Others include the Congressional Black Caucus, the Congressional Caucus on Women's Issues, the Dairy Caucus, and other like-minded or single-issue groups that meet, elect officers, hold discussions, and issue publications to forge unity behind their legislative proposals.

SEE ALSO *Adams, John; Adams, John Quincy; Burr, Aaron; Clinton, George; Jackson, Andrew; Jefferson, Thomas; Madison, James; Monroe, James; Washington, George* SOURCES Edward Stanwood, "The Defeat of King Caucus," in A *History of the Presidency* (Boston: Houghton Mifflin, 1898). C. S. Thompson, *The Rise and Fall of the Congressional Caucus* (New Haven: Yale University Academical Department, 1902).

CAUCUSES, PRESIDENTIAL NOMINATING

Nominating caucuses are one method used to select delegates to Presidential nominating conventions. Republicans select almost one-quarter and Democrats almost one-third of their national convention delegates from states that use nominating caucuses. Until the 1970s caucuses were administered as follows: Members of local political party organizations met in precinct, or district, caucuses to choose delegates to county or congressional district conventions. They made their choices by majority vote. The conventions, in turn, chose delegates to a state convention, which would select delegates to the national nominating convention. The delegates were not pledged to a particular Presidential candidate. This system produced uncommitted state delegations who would vote for whomever the party bosses told them to at the national convention.

In 1972 the Democratic party's McGovern-Fraser Commission reformed caucus procedures by requiring that precinct meetings be open to all registered Democrats. The Republicans then adopted similar rules. Caucuses have since been transformed into contests between the Presidential candidates. The delegates selected to the national convention from caucus-convention states are now declared supporters of particular candidates. Delegates from these states to the national convention are allotted in the Democratic party to each Presidential contender according to the rule of proportional representation; if three-quarters of the precincts vote for candidate A and one-quarter for candidate B, then three-quarters of the convention delegates will cast their convention ballots for candidate A and one-quarter for candidate B. In the Republican party a winner-take-all system is often used, so that with a similar caucus result, all of the state's delegates would vote for candidate A.

The precinct caucus usually takes place in a meeting hall, such as a high school gymnasium or auditorium. The people attending nominate their choices for delegates to the district conventions; each slate of delegates consists of supporters of a different Presidential candidate. Some caucuses provide for an open vote, which is often taken by having those attending move to different corners of the room to demonstrate support for competing slates of delegates. This method is known as "grouping." In some states, however, party rules allow a secret ballot.

The precinct caucus is run as a meeting, in which the deliberations are supposed to influence the eventual outcome, though many attending have already made up their minds. Although the turnout of registered voters in caucuses is lower than the turnout in primaries, some states have turnouts of 10 to 15 percent.

Because the Iowa caucuses, which usually occur in the first week of February, are the first contest for convention delegates, they have assumed great importance in the Presidential contest. The winner in Iowa receives more media coverage than other contenders and a boost in campaign contributions. Candidates who fare badly in Iowa may be forced to drop out of the race.
SEE ALSO *Election campaigns, Presidential; Nominating conventions, Presidential; Primaries, Presidential*
SOURCES James Ceaser, *Presidential Selection* (Princeton, N.J.: Princeton University Press, 1979). Byron Shafer, *Quiet Revolu-* *tion* (New York: Russell Sage, 1984). Stephen Wayne, *Road to the White House* (New York: St. Martin's, 1992).

CAUCUS ROOMS

Two grandly ornate rooms in the Cannon House Office Building and Russell Senate Office Building are designated as caucus rooms. The title suggests that they were originally reserved for political party meetings, but the rooms gained more notoriety as the setting for major congressional investigations. In 1912 the Senate caucus room was the site of an investigation into the sinking of the *Titanic.* It was followed by the Teapot Dome investigation, the Wall Street investigation, the Truman Committee investigation of the national defense program, the Army-McCarthy hearings, the Watergate investigation, and the Iran-Contra scandal investigation. Beginning with Estes Kefauver's organized crime investigation in 1950, television covered the bigger Senate investigations, making the room and its unusual furnishings familiar to millions of viewers.

The House, similarly, used its caucus room for major investigations, such as the House Un-American Activities Committee's Hiss-Chambers hearings in 1948, when Whittaker Chambers testified that former State Department official Alger Hiss had secretly been a member of the Communist party and had engaged in espionage. But Speaker Sam Rayburn refused to allow television to cover House hearings. Not until 1970 did the House permit radio and television coverage of its committee hearings. In addition to committee hearings, members of Congress have used the caucus rooms to announce their Presidential candidacies, to host foreign visitors, and to sponsor assorted exhibits and receptions.

CENSURE

By censuring one of its members, Congress formally rebukes that person for wrongdoing. However, members who are censured do not lose their seat, their committee assignments, or their seniority. A simple majority vote can censure, but it requires a two-thirds vote to expel a member of Congress.

In 1842, the House nearly censured Representative John Quincy Adams (Whig–Massachusetts) for presenting an antislavery petition in violation of House rules. But Adams successfully fought back and the House took no vote. Other representatives suffered censure for insulting the Speaker, making treasonable utterances, assaulting fellow members of Congress, and corruption.

In 1811, the Senate censured Timothy Pickering (Federalist–Massachusetts) for reading a still-secret document in a public session. In 1902 two senators from South Carolina were censured for having a fistfight in the Senate chamber. Senators have also been censured for the misuse of campaign funds and other financial irregularities.

The most infamous censure case involved Joseph R. McCarthy (Republican–Wisconsin). McCarthy's reckless charges and bullying tactics had long troubled senators, but they hesitated to act because of the popularity of his anticommunist crusade. When McCarthy launched an irresponsible attack on the U.S. Army in 1954, public opinion turned against him. Following the Army-McCarthy hearings, the Senate by a vote of 67 to 22 found McCarthy guilty of conduct unbecoming a senator and of bringing the Senate into disrepute.

Since the resolution used the word *condemn*, McCarthy's supporters argued that he had not been censured. Other senators pointed out that the two words had identical meanings. In later cases involving financial misconduct, the Senate "denounced" offenders. Both the Senate and House have also "reprimanded" members for lesser offenses.

Congress may also pass resolutions of censure to condemn the President for improper, illegal, or unconstitutional conduct. Although the Constitution makes no mention of censure, three Presidents have been involved in incidents involving the censure power of Congress.

The Senate censured Andrew Jackson for failing to turn over executive branch records relating to the removal of government deposits from the Bank of the United States. Jackson had declined to comply because he believed the executive branch was independent from the legislature and that Congress had no right to demand any of his communications with cabinet officers.

In 1843 President John Tyler was censured by the House of Representatives after it failed to impeach him for vetoing bills passed by the Whig congressional majority. Former President John Quincy Adams chaired a select committee that reported that Tyler had misused his veto power. Tyler, like Jackson, responded with a letter to the House defending his conduct. The House refused to enter it into its journal and the matter was dropped.

President James Buchanan was investigated in 1860 by a congressional committee chaired by Representative John Covode for alleged improprieties involving appointments and contracts for government printing. The Covode committee's work might have led to censure, but President Buchanan sent a message of protest to the House. No resolution of censure was voted.

In 1998, after President Bill Clinton admitted that he lied about his affair with a White House intern, House Democrats drafted a resolution of censure. By a nearly party-line vote, the Republican majority defeated the censure resolution and instead impeached the President, who was later acquitted by the Senate.

SEE ALSO *Buchanan, James; Discipline, congressional; Expulsion from Congress; Impeachment; Jackson, Andrew; McCarthy, Joseph R.; Tyler, John*

SOURCES Robert Griffith, *The Politics of Fear: Joseph R. McCarthy and the Senate*

(Lexington: University Press of Kentucky, 1970).

CENTRAL INTELLIGENCE AGENCY

Not until World War II did the United States feel the need for an intelligence-gathering espionage agency outside of the military. During the war, the Office of Strategic Services (OSS) collected information and sent agents behind enemy lines to work with resistance groups. When the war ended, the OSS was disbanded. But the start of a cold war with the Soviet Union soon revived the need for a permanent intelligence agency. The Central Intelligence Agency (CIA) was created in 1947 with the passage of the National Security Act.

The CIA is an independent agency that supports the President, the National Security Council, and all other government officials who make and execute national security policy. The CIA fulfills this responsibility by providing accurate, comprehensive, and timely foreign intelligence on national security topics. The agency also conducts counterintelligence activities as directed by the President.

The head of the agency, the Director of Central Intelligence (DCI), is the primary adviser to the President and the National Security Council on intelligence matters. The director is appointed by the President, with the confirmation of the Senate. The DCI is not a cabinet-level position, but some Presidents have elevated it to cabinet-level status by executive order.

In the 1950s, President Dwight Eisenhower relied on the CIA as an extension of U.S. foreign policy. In 1953 and 1954, the CIA directed the overthrow of what were seen as pro-communist governments in Iran and Guatemala. The CIA also flew high-altitude U-2 surveillance missions over communist nations to monitor missile deployment. In 1960, the Eisenhower administration was embarrassed when the Soviet Union shot down one of the U-2 planes and captured the pilot, who admitted to working for the CIA. In 1961 the CIA also sponsored the ill-fated Bay of Pigs invasion of Cuba. Congressional investigations in the 1970s also revealed that the CIA had plotted assassinations of several communist leaders.

To gain more control over the intelligence community, President Bill Clinton issued an executive order in 1995 that established a committee of officials from the Departments of State and Defense, as well as the White House, to oversee CIA operations.

SEE ALSO *Director of Central Intelligence*

CEREMONIAL PRESIDENCY

As head of state, the President represents the American people on many ceremonial occasions. The Constitution, however, mentions none of the President's ceremonial functions, nor does it assign to the President the role of head of state. Some of the President's ceremonial functions are required by law, but most of them have come to be regarded as customary.

Presidents light the national Christmas tree, preside over the Easter egg roll on the White House lawn, and throw out the first ball to open the major league baseball season. They hold receptions to honor Americans who have won international prizes, such as the Nobel Prize. They greet returning astronauts after important missions.

Presidents issue proclamations to draw attention to national priorities, such as National Poison Prevention Week and National Safety Belt Use Day. They give out the Presidential Medal of Freedom, the nation's highest civilian award. Charities such as the American Cancer Society receive Presidential recognition each year. Presidents (or more often Vice Presidents, secretaries of state, or former Presidents) attend funerals of foreign heads of state. They issue memorial statements commemorating the death of prominent

Americans and lead the nation in honoring the war dead by laying wreaths at the Tomb of the Unknown Soldier on Memorial Day and Veterans Day. Lincoln's Gettysburg Address is the most famous eulogy in American history. With congressional approval, Presidents proclaim national holidays, as George Washington did in 1789 when he created Thanksgiving Day and Ronald Reagan did in 1983 when he declared the third Monday in January to be Martin Luther King, Jr., Day. They also issue proclamations each year celebrating national holidays such as Thanksgiving and the Fourth of July.

SEE ALSO *Gettysburg Address*
SOURCES Barbara Hinckley, *The Symbolic Presidency* (New York: Routledge, 1990).

CERTIORARI, WRIT OF

The U.S. Supreme Court has the authority, given by Congress (according to Article 3, Section 2, of the Constitution), to issue a writ of certiorari, which is an order to a lower court to prepare the record of a case and submit it to the Supreme Court for review. The Latin term *certiorari* means "to be informed." A party to a case seeking review by the Supreme Court submits a petition to the Court for a writ of certiorari. If at least four justices vote in favor of it, "cert." is granted, and the case comes to the Court for its review and decision.

Each year approximately 5,000 petitions are sent to the Court seeking a writ of certiorari. Less than 5 percent are granted "cert." If the writ of certiorari is denied, the decision of the lower court is sustained. However, a denial of "cert." cannot be used as evidence of the Supreme Court's opinion on the issue in the case.

The rules of the Court provide general guidelines for accepting or rejecting appeals from lower courts. For example, the Court will likely accept a case for review if there appears to be an error in lower court proceedings, if the issue in the case involves an unsettled question of federal law,

or if there are conflicting opinions on the case from the highest state court and a federal court of appeals.

According to Rule 10 of the *Rules of the Supreme Court of the United States*, "A review on writ of certiorari is not a matter of right, but of judicial discretion, and will be granted only when there are special and important reasons therefor." Making decisions about which cases to review, and which ones to reject, is among the most important judgments the Court makes. These decisions go a long way toward setting the agenda of the Court and determining who will and will not have access to it. Although there are other means by which a case comes before the U.S. Supreme Court, the writ of certiorari is the primary means for bringing a case to the Court for its review and disposition.

SEE ALSO *Jurisdiction*

CHAIRS OF COMMITTEES

Through seniority, or length of service in Congress, members of the majority party advance to become committee chairs. Since most legislative work is done in committee, chairmen are extremely influential on Capitol Hill. The chair controls a committee's operating funds, appoints much of its staff, refers legislation to subcommittees, and sets the schedule for committee business. It is difficult for legislation to leave a committee without the chair's approval. In the past, committee chairs acted like autocratic barons of legislative fiefdoms, but modern reforms have whittled down their power and made committee operations more democratic. Junior members now chair subcommittees, and all members have staff on the committees on which they serve. Committee chairs must work harder to accommodate other members—particularly the ranking minority member—to establish as much unity and agreement as possible within their committee before reporting bills to the floor.

Senator Bob Dole (Republican–Kansas), who chaired the powerful Finance Committee from 1981 to 1984, noted that "a chairman leads by consensus, not command."

A committee chairmanship has been described as "a blank check" to be filled out by the personality and skill of each individual who holds the job. As a result of their seniority, chairs are extremely familiar with the subject areas over which their committee has jurisdiction. Other members frequently defer to their judgment on the issues, and the heads of executive agencies consult with committee chairs in matters of common interest as well as to request increases in appropriations for their agencies. Some committee chairs gain respect and even inspire fear through their force of personality and parliamentary skill. All of these factors determine a chair's success in managing bills through to passage.

SEE ALSO *Ranking members in Congress; Seniority in Congress*
SOURCES Stephen S. Smith and Christopher J. Deering, *Committees in Congress* (Washington, D.C.: Congressional Quarterly, 1984).

CHAMBERS, HOUSE AND SENATE

The Senate and House of Representatives occupy impressive chambers on the north and south ends of the Capitol building, respectively. The galleries of these chambers are open to visitors, and the proceedings that take place there are televised, making them increasingly familiar to the public.

The Senate moved into the smaller of the two chambers in 1859. Today, it has 100 desks arranged in semicircular rows, with the parties divided by the central aisle. At the front of the chamber, the presiding officer sits at a raised desk. The various clerks and parliamentarians sit at a lower desk. Senators speak from their desks and vote by voice.

Since 1857, the House has occupied the larger chamber and therefore hosts all joint sessions, such as State of the Union addresses. House members sat at desks until 1911, when the membership reached 435 and the chamber became too crowded. The desks were replaced by semicircles of padded benches, with the parties divided by the center aisle. Representatives address the house from podiums in the "well" in front of the Speaker's rostrum or from two tables on either side of the aisle. They vote electronically, using voting cards, and the tallies are illuminated on the wall above the Speaker. The Speaker sits at an elevated rostrum above two rows of desks for the various clerks and a podium for the President and other heads of state who occasionally address the Congress.

Over the years, both chambers have undergone extensive remodeling. Electric lighting made the original glass ceilings unnecessary, and recessed panels were removed to improve acoustics. But the chambers also retain many symbols of their past. Long after senators ceased to use snuff, the Senate has kept two small snuffboxes filled with ground tobacco. Ringing the Senate chamber are marble busts of the first 20 Vice Presidents, who served as the Senate's presiding officers.

The House chamber features 23 marble medallions of the great lawgivers of history, ranging from the Babylonian king Hammurabi to Thomas Jefferson, author of the Declaration of Independence. On either side of the Speaker's podium are full-length portraits of George Washington, the first U.S. President, and the Marquis de Lafayette, the first foreign dignitary to address the House.

SEE ALSO *Capitol building*

CHAMBERS, SUPREME COURT

The offices of Supreme Court justices are called chambers. Each justice has three connecting rooms on the main floor. One serves as the private office of the justice, and the other two are used by clerks and secretaries.

CHAPLAINS, CONGRESSIONAL

Chaplains, the official clergymen of Congress, open the daily sessions of the House and Senate with prayer. Begun by the Continental Congress in 1774, this practice was continued by the 1st Congress. On April 25, 1789, the Senate elected Samuel Provoost, an Episcopalian bishop, as its first chaplain. On May 1, the Reverend William Lynn was elected chaplain of the House.

When Congress first moved to Washington, there were few churches in the new city, so the House and Senate chaplains alternated conducting Sunday services in the House chamber. Chaplains have also performed marriages and funerals for members of Congress. Reflecting the religious affiliation of a majority of members, most of the chaplains were Protestants. A Roman Catholic priest served as Senate chaplain from 1832 to 1833, but not until 1999 did the House appoint a Catholic as chaplain. Although all chaplains have been Christians, Congress has invited religious leaders from many other faiths to deliver opening prayers. In 1860, Rabbi Morris Jacob Raphall became the first Jewish clergyman to pray at the opening of a House session. In 1971, a Native American holy man brought his peace pipe to open a Senate session. And in 1992, the imam Wallace D. Mohammed became the first Muslim to offer an invocation.

Occasional lawsuits have charged that the congressional chaplains violate the separation of church and state. However, the courts have ruled that the Constitution grants each house of Congress the power to elect its own officers and manage its own internal affairs as the majority sees fit. SOURCES Robert C. Byrd, "Senate Chaplain," in *The Senate, 1789–1989: Addresses on the History of the United States Senate*,

vol. 2 (Washington, D.C.: Government Printing Office, 1991).

CHARLES RIVER BRIDGE V. WARREN BRIDGE

- 11 Pet. 420 (1837)
- Vote: 4–3
- For the Court: Taney
- Dissenting: McLean, Story, and Thompson

In 1828, the state government of Massachusetts granted a charter, or permit, for construction of a bridge across the Charles River to connect Boston with Cambridge. This new bridge, the Warren Bridge, was to span the river near an older bridge, the Charles River Bridge. The owners of the Charles River Bridge Company claimed that their charter, which they had obtained in 1785, gave them the right to prevent the construction of a new bridge. They claimed the new bridge would cause them to lose profits by attracting the patronage and the payments of those who had formerly used their bridge. The Charles River Bridge Company earned profits by charging a toll, or fee, to users of their bridge. The owners did not want competition from a new company that would also collect tolls from bridge users. Worse, the new Warren Bridge would become toll-free after six years.

The owners of the Charles River Bridge Company argued that in violating their charter, the new Warren Bridge Company charter violated the contract clause of the U.S. Constitution. They pointed to the Supreme Court's decision in *Dartmouth College* v. *Woodward* (1819), which seemed to support their argument that the state should not violate the terms of a contract. They stated that the Court should not allow the Warren Bridge Company to compete with them.

The Issue Should a contract granted by a state government be interpreted so as to stop the state from granting another charter to build new public facilities that would meet important public needs? Would the granting of such a charter violate the contract clause of Article 1, Section 10, of the Constitution, which provides that no state shall pass a law "impairing the Obligation of Contracts"?

Opinion of the Court   The Supreme Court ruled against the Charles River Bridge Company. Chief Justice Roger Taney wrote the majority opinion, which emphasized that a state must interpret public charters so as to benefit public and community needs. Thus, the state of Massachusetts had the right, under the Constitution, to charter the building of a bridge that would compete with another bridge it had contracted for earlier.

Chief Justice Taney was not ignoring the contract clause of the Constitution. He believed in private property rights and the sanctity of contracts. However, he opposed any interpretation of a contract that infringed upon the rights or needs of the public. The contract granted to the Charles River Bridge Company did not say exactly that no other company could build a bridge nearby. Rather, the company interpreted the contract to give them exclusive rights. Taney and the majority of the Court, however, would not interpret the contract as giving exclusive rights to the older and established Charles River Bridge Company.

Dissent   Justice Joseph Story argued for upholding the exclusive contract of the Charles River Bridge Company. He feared that the Court's decision in this case would undermine the faith of property owners in contracts as the means to protect their property rights.

Significance   This decision opposed business monopolies (companies having exclusive control of the provision of goods or services) that hurt the public. It encouraged private businesses to compete freely with one another. The Court supported the right of state governments to decide, under the 10th Amendment,

whether to grant charters to build new facilities such as highways, railroads, and bridges to serve the public.

SEE ALSO *Contract clause; Dartmouth College v. Woodward*
SOURCES Henry F. Graff, "The Charles River Bridge Case," in *Quarrels That Have Shaped the Constitution,* edited by John A. Garraty (New York: Harper & Row, 1987).

CHASE, SALMON P.
Chief Justice, 1864–73

- Born: Jan. 13, 1808, Cornish, N.H.
- Education: Dartmouth College, A.B., 1826
- Previous government service: U.S. senator from Ohio, 1849–55, 1861; governor of Ohio, 1856–60; U.S. secretary of the Treasury, 1861–64
- Appointed by President Abraham Lincoln Dec. 6, 1864; replaced Chief Justice Roger B. Taney, who died
- Supreme Court term: confirmed by the Senate Dec. 6, 1864, by a voice vote; served until May 7, 1873
- Died: May 7, 1873, New York, N.Y.

Salmon P. Chase had a lifelong ambition to become President of the United States. He failed to realize his highest goal, but he did become the sixth chief justice of the United States.

After graduating from Dartmouth College in 1826, Chase studied law under U.S. Attorney General William Wirt and became a lawyer in Cincinnati. He achieved a national reputation as an opponent of slavery and a defender of escaped slaves who sought refuge in the free Northern states. His friends and foes called him the "attorney general for runaway Negroes."

In the 1850s, Chase became a leader in the new Republican party and its antislavery mission. After an unsuccessful bid to become the Republican party's Presidential candidate in 1860, he backed his party's choice, Abraham Lincoln. The new President appointed Chase to his cabinet as secretary of the Treasury. In 1864, Lincoln chose Chase to be chief justice of the United States, even though Chase had tried to take Lincoln's place as the Republican party Presidential candidate in the 1864 election.

As chief justice, Chase continued his concern for the rights of African Americans newly freed from slavery in 1865 by the 13th Amendment. Chief Justice Chase, however, also supported the constitutional rights of a Confederate sympathizer from Indiana in the landmark decision of *Ex parte Milligan* (1866). He joined in the unanimous decision that Lambdin Milligan, who lived in a non–war zone during the Civil War, had been unfairly and illegally tried in a military court, instead of a civilian court, for supposedly committing crimes against the federal government.

Chief Justice Chase presided with dignity and fairness over the 1868 impeachment trial of President Andrew Johnson. And he wrote an enduring opinion for the Court in *Texas* v. *White* (1869) that endorsed the Republican party position that a state did not have a right to secede from the federal Union. Chase argued that Texas's Confederate government had been unlawful and that its acts, therefore, were null and void. Chase argued conclusively that the Constitution created "an indestructible union, composed of indestructible states" and that secession was illegal. SEE ALSO *Chief Justice; Ex parte Milligan; Texas v. White*

SOURCES Frederick J. Blue, *Salmon P. Chase: A Life in Politics* (Kent, Ohio: Kent State University Press, 1987).

CHASE, SAMUEL
Associate Justice, 1796–1811

- Born: Apr. 17, 1741, Somerset County, Md.
- Education: tutored by father; studied law in an Annapolis, Md., law office
- Previous government service: Maryland General Assembly, 1764–84; Continental Congress, 1774–78, 1784–85;

Maryland Convention and Council of Safety, 1775; judge, Baltimore Criminal Court, 1788–96; chief judge, General Court of Maryland, 1791–96
- Appointed by President George Washington Jan. 26, 1796; replaced John Blair, who resigned
- Supreme Court term: confirmed by the Senate Jan. 27, 1796, by a voice vote; served until June 19, 1811
- Died: June 19, 1811, Baltimore, Md.

Samuel Chase was a patriot in the American revolutionary war. He belonged to the Sons of Liberty and signed the Declaration of Independence.

Justice Chase wrote several important opinions in early key decisions of the Supreme Court. In *Ware* v. *Hylton* (1796), for example, he helped to establish the supremacy of federal treaties over state laws that contradicted them. In *Hylton* v. *United States* (1796), Chase and the Supreme Court made a judgment about whether or not an act of Congress, the carriage tax of 1794, agreed with the Constitution. The Court supported the federal statute, which was its first judgment about the constitutionality of an act of the legislative branch of government. The Court, however, neither asserted or discussed the power of judicial review, which was established by Chief Justice John Marshall in *Marbury* v. *Madison* (1803).

Justice Chase was a harsh public critic of the Jeffersonian Republicans because he disagreed with their interpretations of the Constitution. When Thomas Jefferson became President in 1801, Chase sharpened his criticism of Jefferson and the Republican majority in Congress. In return, President Jefferson urged that Chase be removed from the Supreme Court. A majority of the House of Representatives voted to impeach Chase. As provided in the Constitution, the case went to the Senate for trial, where two-thirds of the Senators had to vote against Chase to remove him from office. Chase argued that he had done nothing wrong and that a federal judge should not be impeached and re-

moved from office for criticizing the President. Chase was acquitted and remained on the Court until his death in 1811.
SEE ALSO *Hylton v. United States; Impeachment; Ware v. Hylton*
SOURCES James Haw et al. *Stormy Patriot: The Life of Samuel Chase* (Baltimore: Maryland Historical Society, 1980).

CHECKS AND BALANCES

"Ambition must be made to counteract ambition," explained James Madison when defining how the framers intended the U.S. Constitution to work. According to that reasoning, the Constitution divided the powers and responsibilities of the federal government among the legislative, executive, and judicial branches and also between the two houses of Congress. Each part of the government provides a check and balance on the ambition of the others, preventing any one part from becoming too powerful or autocratic.

For example, the President serves as commander in chief of the armed forces, but Congress appropriates the funds for the military and votes to declare war, and the Senate must ratify any peace treaties. The President nominates federal officials, but the Senate must confirm those nominations. The President may veto legislation, but Congress can override that veto by a two-thirds vote. The Supreme Court may declare acts of Congress unconstitutional, but new legislation can reverse Court decisions.

The use of judicial review is also the principal judicial check against the President. The Supreme Court and other federal courts may exercise this power to declare a Presidential action unconstitutional, as the Supreme Court did when President Harry Truman seized steel mills to ensure the production of steel for defense industries during the Korean War. The principal Presidential check on the judiciary is the appointment power, which can change the direction of the federal courts, as it did under Ronald Reagan and George Bush. To safeguard the justices against Presidential retribution, federal judges and Supreme Court justices of the United States serve on "good behavior" for life—unless they resign or commit a major offense—and cannot be removed except by the congressional impeachment process. A secondary Presidential check on the judiciary is the power to pardon people convicted of offenses against the United States.

Within Congress, both houses must pass a bill in the same form for it to become law, and both must cast a two-thirds vote to override a Presidential veto. The House alone initiates revenue bills; the Senate alone confirms nominations and treaties. The House votes to impeach federal officials, and then the Senate sits as a court to convict or acquit them.

Article 1, Section 8, of the Constitution gives Congress the power to pass laws dealing with the powers of the Presidency. The War Powers Act of 1973, for example, specifies conditions under which the President may use force in hostilities. The Budget and Impoundment Control Act of 1974 permits the President to delay spending funds, subject to congressional approval.

"If men were angels" The system of checks and balances requires Congress and the President to work together if they wish to accomplish anything. The system also creates friction among the branches, and it has sometimes appeared dangerously inefficient in times of national crisis. Yet the system has worked through war and peace, depression and prosperity, for more than two centuries. Checks and balances remain a reflection of the political realism of the framers of the Constitution.

"If men were angels, no government would be necessary," Madison wrote in the *Federalist Papers*. "If angels were to govern men, neither external nor internal controls on government would be necessary. In framing a government which is to be administered by men over men, the great difficulty is this: You must first enable the government to control the governed; and in the next place, oblige it to control itself."

SEE ALSO *Appointment power; Bicameral; Constitution, U.S.; Creation of the Presidency; Impeachment; Pardon power; Pocket veto; Removal power; Separation of powers; Steel seizure (1952); Treaty powers; Veto power*

SOURCES Donald A. Ritchie, *The U.S. Constitution* (New York: Chelsea House, 1989).

CHENEY, RICHARD
Vice President

- Born: January 30, 1941, Lincoln, Neb.
- Education: University of Wyoming, B.A., 1965; M.A. 1996
- Political party: Republican
- Military service: None
- Previous government service: Office of Economic Opportunity, 1969–71; assistant director, Cost of Living Council, 1971–73; deputy assistant, White House Staff, 1974–5; White House chief of staff, 1975–76; U.S.
- representative from Wyoming, 1979–89; secretary of defense, 1989–93

Dick Cheney was captain of his football team and married his high school sweetheart, one of the team cheerleaders. Cheney worked in the oil business, then entered the Nixon administration as a staff assistant. Rising through the ranks, he became White House chief of staff. After serving in Congress as one of its most conservative members, he became secretary of defense. He presided over two successful military campaigns, Operation Just Cause in Panama and Operation Desert Storm in the Persian Gulf.

Cheney's nomination as vice presidential candidate in 2000 added experience and maturity to the ticket headed by George W. Bush. Cheney was expected to be a forceful proponent of conservative

views on social policy and hawkish views on national defense.

SEE ALSO *Bush, George W.*

CHIEF JUSTICE

The chief justice of the United States is the presiding officer of the Supreme Court and the head of the judicial branch of the federal government. The title chief justice is mentioned only once, however, in the U.S. Constitution: Article 1, Section 3, mandates that the chief justice serve as presiding officer of the Senate during an impeachment trial of a President. The office of chief justice is *not* mentioned in Article 3 of the Constitution, which deals with the judicial branch of the federal government.

The office of chief justice was established by the Judiciary Act of 1789. The position has truly been shaped by its occupants, who have established the roles and duties as they performed them. In addition, Congress contributed to development of this office through legislation.

Since 1789, the office of chief justice has developed into a complex and prestigious position. The person occupying this position must serve as Supreme Court leader, judge, administrator, and national symbol of justice under the law.

The chief justice, like the eight associate justices of the Supreme Court, is appointed by the President of the United States "with the Advice and Consent of the Senate," as provided by Article 2, Section 2, of the Constitution. The chief justice, the eight associate justices, and the federal judges of the lower courts "shall hold their Offices during good Behaviour," according to Article 3, Section 1, of the Constitution, which provides lifetime job security for judges who want it. Further, Article 3, Section 1, says the pay of federal judges "shall not be diminished during their Continuance in Office." Thus, the Constitution provides for the independence of the chief justice, the eight associate justices, and other federal judges.

The chief justice has been called "first among equals" in his relationships with the eight associate justices. He has only one vote, as they do, in deciding cases. The chief justice and the eight associate justices are equal in their virtual lifetime tenure, in their protection against decreases in income, and in their independence as judicial decision makers on cases before the Court. The chief justice also must perform the work of a judge, along with his eight associates. Together, the chief and his associates review and make decisions on all petitions for certiorari (appeals from lower courts for a hearing before the Supreme Court); he must also examine, discuss, and decide, like his associates, all the cases that come to the Court. The chief shares with his associates the work of writing opinions for the Court.

Unlike his associates, however, the chief justice is the sole presiding officer of the Supreme Court. He presides at the conference during which the Court decides which cases to accept from the large number of appeals over which it has discretionary power. He also presides over the public sessions, or hearings of cases, that come before the Court, and he chairs the private conference at which cases are discussed among the nine members of the Court and eventually decided by a vote of the justices. Finally, when the chief justice is in the majority, he has the authority to assign the task of writing the Court's opinion on the case either to himself or to one of the associate justices. Thus, the chief justice is able to influence directly or indirectly the style and substance of the Court's written opinion. When the chief justice is not part of the majority decision on a case, the most senior member of the majority assigns the writing of the Court's opinion.

In addition to his duties as presiding officer of the Supreme Court, the chief justice also serves as administrative head of the judicial branch of the federal government. He is chairman of the Judicial Conference of the United States. The conference includes 27 federal judges, who represent all the levels and regions of the federal judiciary. The conference meets twice a year to discuss common problems, to coordinate administrative policies, and to recommend to Congress measures for improving the operation of the federal courts. Administrative and budgetary functions for the conference are carried out by the Administrative Office of the United States Courts. The Administrative Office's director and deputy director are appointed by the Supreme Court and report to the chief justice. The chief justice is also the permanent chairman of the governing board of the Federal Judicial Center, which provides research and training services for the federal judiciary.

The chief justice has several extra-judicial responsibilities. He is manager of the Supreme Court Building. He serves as chancellor of the Smithsonian Institution, a complex of museums and research institutions operated by the federal government. And he is considered the head of the legal profession in the United States.

The chief justice is also the living symbol of the federal judiciary. In this role, the chief administers the oath of office to the President at every inauguration.

Since 1789, there have been 16 chief justices of the United States. The first chief justice was John Jay, appointed by President George Washington. President John Adams appointed the chief justice generally acclaimed as the greatest, John Marshall, who served from 1801 until his death in 1835. His tenure as chief justice was the longest. Other chief justices whom scholars and legal experts consider truly great are Roger B. Taney, Charles Evans Hughes, Harlan Fiske Stone, and Earl Warren. Five chief justices, nearly one-third of the total from 1789 to 1993, have performed well enough to receive such excellent ratings.

SEE ALSO *Administration of federal courts; Justices of the Supreme Court*

SOURCES Jeffrey B. Morris, *First Among*

Equals: The Office of the Chief Justice of the United States (Berkeley: University of California Press, 1993). Jeffrey B. Morris, "Hail to the Chief Justice," *Constitution* 4, no. 2 (Spring–Summer 1992): 40–50. Robert J. Steamer, *Chief Justice: Leadership and the Supreme Court* (Columbia: University of South Carolina Press, 1986).

CHIEF OF STAFF, WHITE HOUSE

SEE *White House Office*

CHILDREN OF PRESIDENTS

Thirty-five Presidents of the United States and their wives, through Bill and Hillary Clinton, had 89 boys and 61 girls. Six had no children: George Washington, James Madison, Andrew Jackson, James Polk, James Buchanan, and Warren Harding. Presidents with large families living in the White House included John Tyler, Benjamin Harrison, and Theodore Roosevelt. All the Presidential children were born in the United States except for George Washington Adams (son of John), who was born in Berlin; Herbert Clark Hoover, Jr., and Allen Henry Hoover, both born in London; and Franklin D. Roosevelt, Jr., born at the Roosevelt vacation home on Campobello Island, New Brunswick, Canada.

Theodore Roosevelt's children kept a small zoo and a pony on the White House grounds. His daughter Alice once interrupted a White House meeting, and Roosevelt said, "I can be President of the United States, or I can control Alice. I cannot possibly do both." John F. Kennedy's daughter, Caroline, was also known for her antics in the Oval Office, and his son John-John made the Presidential desk his secret hiding place. The Kennedy children also had a small zoo as well as a tree house and a playground with a slide and tunnel. The

Kennedys established a nursery school in the White House, which Caroline and nine other children attended. Jimmy Carter's daughter, Amy, went to a public school in the District of Columbia. She took advantage of the White House movie theater and used a telescope on the White House roof. When Chelsea Clinton, who had lived in government housing since she was two years old, exchanged her room in the White House for a dormitory cube at Stanford University in 1997, the country watched the transition with fascination and curiosity. Her parents had gone to great lengths to shield her from media intrusion into her private life, though once in college she began to travel to various foreign countries with them.

Some children of Presidents have grown up to have distinguished government careers of their own. John Quincy Adams was a secretary of state and the sixth President of the United States. Robert Todd Lincoln served as secretary of war for President James Garfield. Franklin D. Roosevelt, Jr., served as under secretary of commerce for President Lyndon Johnson after several terms in the U.S. House of Representatives. Other Presidential sons who served in the House include Charles Francis Adams (son of John Quincy), John Scott Harrison (son of William Henry), David Tyler (son of John), and James Roosevelt (son of Franklin). Robert Taft, Sr. (son of William Howard), was a U.S. senator and a candidate for the Republican Presidential nomination. Other sons who were involved in Presidential politics include John Van Buren, who declined the Free-Soil nomination in favor of his father, Martin; John Scott Harrison, who declined the Whig nomination in 1856; and Robert Todd Lincoln, who was defeated at Republican conventions in 1884 and 1888.

A number of Presidential children have served in the armed forces. Frederick D. Grant graduated from West Point. During the Spanish-American War, James Webb Cook Hayes, son of former President Rutherford B. Hayes, won a Medal of

Honor in the Philippines. Aviator Quentin Roosevelt, son of Theodore, was shot down and killed in a dogfight in France in World War I. Roosevelt's two other sons, Archibald Roosevelt and Theodore Roosevelt, Jr., also served in that war, and Theodore, Jr., was killed in the Normandy campaign during World War II. The four sons of Franklin D. Roosevelt—James, Elliott, Franklin, and John—also served in World War II. John Eisenhower graduated from West Point and served in the Korean War, turning down an opportunity to leave the combat zone offered by President Harry Truman, who finally ordered him to a different command.

In recent years the children of Presidents have gravitated to the media and entertainment fields. Margaret Truman became a mystery writer. Ron Reagan, Jr., was a ballet dancer and then host of a talk show; his sisters, Maureen Reagan and Patti Davis, wrote books about the First Family. Caroline Kennedy became a lawyer and wrote a best-selling book about the Bill of Rights. Several of George Bush's children have been involved in business and politics. His sons George W. and Jeb have served as governors and George W. became the 43rd President.

Several Presidential children have been married at the White House. These include Maria Hester Monroe, John Adams (son of John Quincy), Elizabeth Tyler, Nellie Grant, Alice Roosevelt (daughter of Theodore), Jessie Woodrow Wilson and Eleanor Wilson (who married her father's secretary of the treasury), Lynda Bird Johnson, and Tricia Nixon.
SEE ALSO *First Lady*

CHISHOLM, SHIRLEY

- Born: Nov. 30, 1924, New York, N.Y.
- Political party: Democrat
- Education: Brooklyn College, B.A., 1946; Columbia University, M.A., 1952
- Representative from New York: 1969–83

The first African-American woman elected to the House of Representatives, Shirley Chisholm represented a poor, inner-city district in Brooklyn, New York. So she was shocked when her party assigned her to the House Agriculture Committee. Because that committee had little to do with the desperate needs of her constituents, she refused to serve on it. Party leaders reassigned her to the Veterans' Affairs Committee and eventually to her first choice, the Education and Labor Committee.

Unafraid of a good fight, Chisholm went to Congress determined to right the wrongs that she had personally witnessed and experienced. In the House she championed equal rights for women and minorities, an Equal Rights Amendment to the Constitution, extension of the minimum wage to domestic workers, and federal day-care facilities.
SEE ALSO *African Americans in government*
SOURCES Shirley Chisholm, *The Good Fight* (New York: Harper & Row, 1973). Shirley Chisholm, *Unbought and Unbossed* (Boston: Houghton Mifflin, 1970).

CHISHOLM V. GEORGIA

- 2 Dall. 419 (1793)
- Vote: 4–1
- For the Court: seriatim opinions by Jay, Cushing, Wilson, and Blair
- Dissenting: Iredell

During the American War of Independence, agents of the state government of Georgia purchased clothing, blankets, and other goods from Robert Farquhar, a merchant in Charleston, South Carolina. Farquhar died in 1784, and the executor of his estate was Alexander Chisholm. Acting for a minor (non-adult) heir of Farquhar, Chisholm sought payment from the Georgia state government for money that he claimed it owed Farquhar. Georgia officials refused to pay, however, because the state had already paid its agents for the goods. Chisholm was unable to collect the money owed his client from these agents. So he took his case to the newly established federal courts and sued the state of Georgia for the monetary value of the goods supplied by Farquhar.

The Issue The state of Georgia refused to send a representative to the Supreme Court. Georgia argued that the Court did not have jurisdiction in this case because a state government could not be sued by a citizen from another state.

Opinion of the Court The Supreme Court ruled in favor of Chisholm. This decision was based on Article 3, Section 2, of the U.S. Constitution, which says, "The judicial Power shall extend to all Cases ... between a State and Citizens of another State." Chief Justice John Jay wrote, "Any one state in the Union may sue another state in this court, that is, all the people of one state may sue all the people of another state. It is plain, then, that a state may be sued, and hence it plainly follows that suability and state sovereignty are not incompatible." In other words, a suit brought by citizens of one state against the government of another state does not diminish or threaten the authority or independent power of that state government.

Dissent Justice James Iredell argued that under common law no state could be sued unless it consented to the action. This state right was necessary in order for the state to retain its sovereignty (supreme power within its borders, free of external influences), said Iredell.

Significance This decision caused an uproar in Congress. A large majority in the House of Representatives (81–9) and the Senate (23–2) voted in favor of a proposed constitutional amendment that would effectively overturn the Supreme Court's decision in *Chisholm* v. *Georgia*. The state governments ratified this proposal, which became the 11th Amendment to the Constitution: "The Judicial power of the United States shall not be construed to extend to any suit in law or equity, commenced or prosecuted against one of the United States by citizens of another State, or by Citizens or Subjects of any Foreign

State." This was the first time a Supreme Court decision was overturned by constitutional amendment.

What happened to Chisholm's financial claim against Georgia? It succeeded. Robert Farquhar's heir accepted securities (bonds) of the Georgia state government in full payment of his claim against the state. These bonds paid interest to the holder and could be exchanged for cash.

SOURCES John V. Orth, *The Judicial Power of the United States: The Eleventh Amendment in American History* (New York: Oxford University Press, 1987).

"CHRISTMAS TREE" BILLS

SEE *Pork barrel politics*

CIRCUIT COURTS OF APPEALS

The Judiciary Act of 1789 set up a system of lower federal courts, under the Supreme Court of the United States. At the bottom were federal district courts, one per state except for Massachusetts and Virginia, which had two apiece because of their greater population. Between the Supreme Court and the district courts were three circuit courts of appeal, one for each of three circuits, or districts, each of which included several states. In 1789 the Southern Circuit included South Carolina and Georgia (North Carolina was added in 1790 after it entered the Union). In 1789 the Eastern Circuit contained New York, Connecticut, Massachusetts, and New Hampshire (Rhode Island and Vermont were added when they joined the Union in 1790 and 1791, respectively). The Middle Circuit included Virginia, Maryland, Pennsylvania, Delaware, and New Jersey.

Until 1869 the circuit courts served both as trial courts and appellate courts; both federal district court judges and Supreme Court justices presided in these circuit courts. The judges and justices had to "ride circuit" in order to carry out their circuit court duties; that is, they had to travel from place to place, within the large area of the circuit, to hear cases and make decisions. In the early years of the United States, the judges and justices rode on horseback or in horse-drawn carriages.

Circuit riding was a great hardship, involving long hours of travel. The Supreme Court justices constantly complained to Congress, asking to be relieved of this heavy burden. In the Judiciary Act of 1869, Congress finally responded to their complaints. This law provided for the appointment of nine new circuit court judges, which relieved the Supreme Court justices of their ongoing circuit-riding duties. However, the law did require the justices to participate in circuit court duties once every two years.

The Judiciary Act of 1891 created, for the first time, the U.S. Circuit Courts of Appeals, one for each of nine regions, or circuits, to hear cases on appeal from the lower courts. The old circuit courts were retained, but their duties were merged with the federal district courts. So the federal judiciary consisted of two trial courts (circuit and district courts) and two appellate courts (the Supreme Court and the new Circuit Courts of Appeals). The act eliminated the circuit-riding duties of Supreme Court justices and assigned three judges to each of the nine new Circuit Courts of Appeals. This relieved the burden on the Supreme Court, which until then had carried out most of the federal appellate court work. In 1911 Congress acted to eliminate the old circuit courts because they merely duplicated the work of the district courts, which were retained as the trial courts of the federal judiciary. In 1948 the Circuit Courts of Appeals were given a new name, which they retain today, the Courts of Appeals.

SEE ALSO *Courts of Appeals*

CITATION

The way in which opinions of the U.S. Supreme Court are identified, or cited, in legal literature is referred to as a citation. A Supreme Court case citation includes the following information, in this order: the names of the parties to the case, separated by "v.," for *versus* (Latin for "against"); the volume of *United States Reports* in which the case appears (for cases since 1875), or the volume of private reports, for pre-1875 cases; the beginning page number on which the report of the case appears; and the year the decision was made. For example, *Abrams* v. *United States,* 250 U.S. 616 (1919) means that the Supreme Court decision and opinion in this case will be found in Volume 250 of *United States Reports,* beginning on page 616. The case was decided in 1919.

United States Reports, published by the U.S. Government Printing Office, is one of several sources of Supreme Court opinions. Other sources are *Supreme Court Reporter,* published by West Publishing Company, and *United States Supreme Court Reports, Lawyers' Edition,* published by the Lawyers Cooperative Publishing Company.

Before 1875, official reports of Supreme Court cases were cited with the names of the Court reporters. These names (full or abbreviated) appear in the citations for those years. For example, in *Marbury* v. *Madison,* 1 Cr. 137 (1803), "Cr." is an abbreviation for William Cranch, the Supreme Court reporter from 1801 to 1815. The reporters of decisions from 1790 to 1875 were Alexander J. Dallas (1790–1800), William Cranch (1801–15), Henry Wheaton (1816–27), Richard Peters, Jr. (1828–42), Benjamin C. Howard (1843–60), Jeremiah S. Black (1861–62), and John W. Wallace (1863–75).

SEE ALSO *Reporter of decisions*

CITIZENSHIP

The 14th Amendment to the Constitution defines citizenship in the United States as follows: "All persons born or naturalized in the United States, and subject to the jurisdiction thereof, are citizens of the United States and of the state wherein they reside." Citizenship can be acquired by birth; anyone born in any of the 50 states, the District of Columbia, the Commonwealth of Puerto Rico, or the territories of Guam and the Virgin Islands, for example, is a natural-born citizen of the United States. Children born outside the country to at least one American parent are also U.S. citizens by birth. However, before they are 21 years old, they must become residents of the United States or declare their intention to become a U.S. citizen.

A second way to become a U.S. citizen, according to the 14th Amendment, is by naturalization. Article 1, Section 8, of the Constitution provides Congress the power "to establish a uniform law of naturalization." A person becomes a naturalized citizen by taking certain steps required by federal law. After five years of residence in the United States (three years if the person is married to an American citizen), a person may file a petition to become a citizen. Two U.S. citizens must testify that the person has fulfilled the residence requirement, exhibits good moral behavior, and believes in the principles of the Constitution. Next, the person completes an examination to prove literacy in English and knowledge of U.S. history and government. Finally, the person pledges an oath of allegiance to the Constitution of the United States and signs a certificate of naturalization.

In *United States* v. *Wong Kim Ark* (1898), the Supreme Court ruled for the first time on a case arising under the 14th Amendment clause that defines citizenship. The Court decided that the race, ethnic identity, or place of birth of a person's parents could not be used to deny citizenship to a person born in the United States. The Court affirmed the fundamental importance of citizenship in *Trop* v. *Dulles* (1958) by refusing to take away a person's citizenship because he had deserted the army during wartime. Writing for the Court, Chief Justice Earl Warren held that such a loss of citizenship would be "cruel and unusual punishment," which is banned by the 8th Amendment.

Naturalized citizens have the same rights and duties as natural-born citizens, with one exception: they are not eligible to become President or Vice President of the United States (Article 2, Section 1, of the Constitution). According to the 14th Amendment, "No state shall make or enforce any law which shall abridge the privileges or immunities of citizens of the United States." Citizenship entitles a person to certain rights, such as the right to vote or to be a federal government official. (The Bill of Rights, however, applies to all individuals living in the United States, both citizens and noncitizens.) In return, all citizens have certain legal responsibilities, such as paying taxes, serving on a jury if called, serving in the country's armed forces if called, serving as a witness in court if summoned, and obeying the laws of the United States. (Noncitizens residing in the United States are also required to pay taxes and obey the law.) In exchange for the privileges and rights of citizenship, all citizens of the United States have the obligation of loyalty and allegiance to their Constitution and their country.

SEE ALSO *United States v. Wong Kim Ark*
SOURCES Peter Riesenberg, *Citizenship in the Western Tradition* (Chapel Hill: University of North Carolina Press, 1992).

CITY OF BOERNE, TEXAS V. FLORES

- 117 S.Ct. 2157 (1997)
- Vote: 6-3
- For the Court: Kennedy
- Dissenting: O'Connor, Souter, and Breyer

A Roman Catholic priest in a small West Texas city, Boerne, wanted to enlarge the

St. Peter's Church. But the city government refused to grant a construction permit for an addition to the small 70-year-old church because it was located in a neighborhood designated by the local government as a historic preservation zone. The purpose of this zoning law was to maintain historic sites by preventing or limiting new construction that would significantly change the appearance of the city's historic district.

Archbishop P. F. Flores of the Roman Catholic Diocese of San Antonio, in which the city of Boerne was located, filed suit to force the city government to permit enlargement of St. Peter's Church. He based his suit on the city's presumed violation of a federal law, the Religious Freedom Restoration Act (RFRA) of 1993.

The RFRA limited the power of federal, state, and local governments to enforce laws that "substantially burden" the free exercise of religion. Such a "burdensome" law could be carried out only if the government could demonstrate a "compelling" public justification for doing so, and if it was "the least restrictive means of furthering that compelling governmental interest." Those whose constitutional rights to free exercise of religion had been "substantially burdened," as Archbishop Flores claimed, could "in a judicial proceeding . . . obtain appropriate relief against a government."

Using the RFRA to support his case, Archbishop Flores argued that the city of Boerne, through its zoning laws, was illegally interfering with the practices of a religious institution and thereby substantially burdening its constitutionally protected free exercise of religion. The federal district court ruled in favor of the city of Boerne and concluded that the RFRA was unconstitutional. The 5th Circuit Court of Appeals, however, disagreed. It upheld the RFRA as constitutional and reversed the lower court's decision. So the case went to the U.S. Supreme Court for resolution.

The Issue   When Congress passed the Religious Freedom Restoration Act, it relied upon the U.S. Constitution's 14th Amendment. Section 1 of the amendment guarantees that a state cannot deprive a person of life, liberty, or property without due process of law, and it cannot deny to any person the equal protection of the laws. Section 5 of the 14th Amendment empowers Congress to enforce these guarantees through enactment of appropriate laws.

In its enactment of the RFRA, Congress claimed that this law was needed to effectively protect a person's 1st Amendment right to free exercise of religion at state and local levels of government. The majority in Congress was concerned about possible state government infringement of rights to religious liberty due to the Supreme Court's decision in *Employment Division Department of Human Resources of Oregon* v. *Smith* (1990). This ruling had overturned a constitutional standard set in *Sherbert* v. *Verner* (1963), which declared that to survive judicial scrutiny, a law restricting the free exercise of religion must advance a compelling public interest of government in the least restrictive manner possible. The RFRA was intended by Congress to restore the "compelling interest" and "least restrictive means" standards of the *Sherbert* v. *Verner* decision.

Counsel for the city of Boerne, Marcia Hamilton, argued that the RFRA, on which Archbishop Flores based his lawsuit against the city, was unconstitutional because it represented an expansion of Congress's authority beyond the scope allowed by the Constitution. Thus, the RFRA violated the constitutional principles of separation of powers and federalism.

Does Congress have power under the 14th Amendment to define rights to religious freedoms more broadly than the U.S. Supreme Court, as it did in the RFRA? And does the RFRA thereby violate the constitutional principles of separation of powers among the three branches of the federal government and the principles of federalism, the division of powers between the federal and state governments?

Opinion of the Court   Writing for the Court, Justice Anthony Kennedy held that Congress went beyond its constitutionally sanctioned power by attempting to substantially interpret the Constitution through legislation. Thus, Congress usurped a power belonging exclusively to the federal courts under the Constitution. This amounts to violation of the constitutional principle of separation of powers. Further, Justice Kennedy concluded that through the RFRA, Congress had unconstitutionally infringed upon the authority of state governments to regulate the health, safety, or general welfare of their citizens. So the RFRA was a violation of the constitutional principle of federalism.

Justice Kennedy wrote, "Congress's discretion is not unlimited . . . and the courts retain the power, as they have since *Marbury* v. *Madison*, to determine if Congress has exceeded its authority under the Constitution. Broad as the power of Congress is under the Enforcement Clause of the Fourteenth Amendment, RFRA contradicts vital principles necessary to maintain separation of powers and the federal balance."

Dissent   The dissenters, led by Justice Sandra Day O'Connor, agreed with the Court's majority that Congress cannot redefine or expand the scope of constitutional rights by legislation. However, she disagreed with the Court's majority in its use of the *Smith* decision (1990) as the ruling predent because she believed the holding in *Smith* had been decided wrongly. She argued for reconsidering the *Smith* decision as bad constitutional law instead of declaring the RFRA unconstitutional.

Significance   Although the city of Boerne won its case, city officials offered a compromise agreement to the local Roman Catholic Church officials. They agreed to allow an enlargement of St. Peter's Church by 850 seats. But 80 percent of the building was to be left intact.

Some public reactions to the Court's decision were not as generous or accommodating as the response of the city of Boerne's government. Senator Orrin Hatch of Utah, for example, said that the Court "once again acted to push religion to the fringes of society." The winning lawyer in this case, Marcia Hamilton, said, "Congress does not have the power to amend the Constitution unilaterally."

Although the *City of Boerne* decision had important consequences for church and state relationships, its primary significance pertained to limitations on Congress's authority to expand its constitutional powers in relationship to the other branches of the federal government and the state governments. The Supreme Court clearly and emphatically served notice to the other branches of government that it has the conclusive power to say what the Constitution means and what it does not mean.

CIVIL LAW

Within the legal system of the United States, civil law is a body of law pertaining to noncriminal private disputes among individuals, corporations, and governments. Thus, civil law is distinguished from criminal law, which deals with the enforcement of the laws against those accused of violating them. In a civil action, one private party takes legal action against another private party to seek relief in a court of law for an alleged wrong.

SEE ALSO *Criminal law*

CIVIL RIGHTS

Civil rights and civil liberties often mean the same thing. The words are frequently used interchangeably to signify the protection of rights to liberty and equality under the Constitution, such as freedom of speech, protection against "unreasonable searches and seizures," and the right to due process of law. The term *civil rights,* however, is also used to refer to positive actions by the government to protect or extend the rights of people—to provide for individuals or groups opportunities that were previously denied to them. These kinds of civil rights guarantees usually are provided through statutes, such as the Civil Rights Act of 1964, which gives the federal government the power to prevent an employer from denying a job to someone because of the person's race, gender, religion, or ethnic origin.

Civil rights movements are organized efforts to obtain long-denied constitutional rights for individuals and groups such as African Americans, Hispanics, Native Americans, and women. These segments of the American population have not always enjoyed their full rights of citizenship under the U.S. Constitution.

Civil rights legislation   For a century after the Civil War, Congress debated, filibustered against, and finally enacted significant civil rights legislation to guarantee the equal rights of African Americans and other minorities. In 1866, Congress passed the first Civil Rights Act over President Andrew Johnson's veto. This act granted African Americans full citizenship, thereby reversing the Supreme Court's *Dred Scott* decision of 1857, which had stated that blacks, whether slave or free, were not citizens.

When Southern states passed laws requiring segregation by race, Senator Charles Sumner (Republican–Massachusetts) sponsored the Civil Rights Act of 1875, which provided for equal accommodations in hotels, restaurants, trains, and other public facilities. In 1896, the Supreme Court, ruling in *Plessy* v. *Ferguson*, declared this act unconstitutional and upheld racial segregation. The Court ruled that "laws permitting, and even requiring their separation in places where they are liable to be brought into contact do not necessarily imply the inferiority of either race to the other." Although segregationists never had the votes in Congress to write segregation into national law, they were able to protect it by filibustering.

During most of the 20th century, the civil rights movement of African Americans has had a strong impact on the advancement of constitutional rights for all Americans, especially those who had been long-suffering victims of unjust discrimination and unfair treatment under the law. The early leader of this civil rights movement was the National Association for the Advancement of Colored People (NAACP), founded in 1909. After the formation in 1939 of its Legal Defense Fund (LDF), directed by Thurgood Marshall, the NAACP began to have a steady and significant effect on federal court rulings to obtain and expand the civil rights of African Americans with regard to voting and education. In *Smith* v. *Allwright* (1944) the Court ruled that a political party (the Democrats in this case) could not exclude blacks from voting in a primary election to nominate party candidates for a subsequent general election. In *Sweatt* v. *Painter* (1950) the Court decided that a state may not deny admission of qualified blacks to a state law school on the grounds that a separate law school for blacks is available. The biggest breakthrough came with the legal victory, led by Thurgood Marshall and other NAACP attorneys, in *Brown* v. *Board of Education* (1954), which established that racial segregation in public schools is unconstitutional.

After the *Brown* decision, various African-American civil rights organizations, including the NAACP, launched political protest movements to influence enforcement of the *Brown* decision and to demand that the federal government pass laws to protect and promote civil rights for African Americans. Martin Luther King, Jr., and the Southern Christian Leadership Conference (SCLC), which he led, moved to the forefront.

In 1957, Senate majority leader Lyndon B. Johnson (Democrat–Texas) took credit for passing the first civil rights bill since Reconstruction, but Southern opponents had severely weakened this measure by adding an amendment that required jury trials for offenders. Since Southern juries were still likely to be all white, few convictions could be expected.

As President in 1964, Johnson led the effort to achieve cloture and stop the filibuster against a much stronger civil rights bill that outlawed discrimination in any form of interstate commerce. The next year Johnson proposed, and Congress enacted, the Voting Rights Act to provide federal protection for African Americans' right to vote. The Civil Rights Act of 1964 and Voting Rights Act of 1965 had a profound impact on American politics, especially in the South, where Southern Democratic officeholders became more attuned to minority constituents, where African Americans were elected to Congress, and where the Republican party once again became a real challenge to the once solid Democratic South.

The Civil Rights Act forbids discrimination on the basis of race, color, religion, national origin, and, in employment, sex. The law provides protection from unfair discrimination in employment and in the use of public facilities. It also requires desegregation of public schools and facilities.

The Supreme Court has upheld as constitutional the major provisions of the Civil Rights Act of 1964. And the Court has interpreted this law broadly to expand the opportunities available to racial minorities often victimized by past discriminatory practices. In *Heart of Atlanta Motel* v. *United States* (1964), for example, the Court established beyond challenge that no person can be excluded, because of race or color, from any facility that is open to the general public. Further, the Court has upheld programs of employers to emphasize recruitment of racial minorities that have suffered from the employer's racial discrimination in hiring in the past.

The 1965 Voting Rights Act outlawed discrimination by state governments against African Americans and other minority groups in voter registration and voting in state and federal elections. The Supreme Court upheld the law in *South Carolina* v. *Katzenbach* (1966), ruling that the law is a constitutional use of Congress's power to enforce the 15th Amendment ban on denying a citizen the right to vote because of the person's race or color. Congress renewed and reinforced this voting

rights legislation in 1970, 1975, and 1982. The result has been a dramatic increase in the participation of African Americans in public elections as voters and candidates for government offices.

The African-American civil rights movement has become a model for other groups seeking to end legal discrimination against them, such as women, Hispanics, gays, the elderly, and the physically disabled. These groups, too, have tried to bring about favorable legislative acts and judicial decisions.

During the 1980s and 1990s, civil rights advocates have promoted affirmative action programs—the use of preferential treatment of racial, ethnic, or gender groups to provide access to education, employment, and other social benefits. The groups seeking and receiving these benefits are seen as having been victims of persistent and unfair discrimination. They look to affirmative action as a temporary means to overcome the harmful consequences of systematic discrimination in the past, which has unfairly denied opportunities to some people.

Congress passed the Civil Rights Act of 1991 to amend the Civil Rights Act of 1964. The purpose was to strengthen the scope of federal civil rights protections, which had been weakened by the Supreme Court's decision in *Ward's Cove Packing Company* v. *Atonio* (1989). In the *Ward's Cove* decision, the Court determined that those claiming discrimination by employers had to prove that a specific employment practice had been discriminatory. Even if the plaintiff were to provide the proof required, the employer could still claim that the discriminating practice was necessary to maintain his or her business.

The Civil Rights Act of 1991 overturned the *Ward's Cove* decision by eliminating, as illegal, an employer's claim of "business necessity" as a justification for intentional discrimination against an individual based on race, color, ethnic origin, and gender. Further, the Civil Rights Act of 1991 protects an employee against racial harassment after being hired. Finally, the 1991 law limits the opportunities to legally challenge employers' affirmative action programs.

SEE ALSO *Affirmative action; Brown v. Board of Education; Civil Rights Cases; Equality under the Constitution; Heart of Atlanta Motel v. United States; Johnson, Lyndon B.; Johnson v. Transportation Agency of Santa Clara County; Liberty under the Constitution; National Association for the Advancement of Colored People (NAACP); Smith v. Allwright; Sumner, Charles; Sweatt v. Painter*

SOURCES Taylor Branch, *Parting the Waters: America in the King Years, 1954–63* (New York: Simon & Schuster, 1988). John Hope Franklin and Alfred A. Moss, Jr., *From Slavery to Freedom* (New York: Knopf, 1988). Martin Luther King, Jr., *Stride Toward Freedom* (New York: Harper & Row, 1958). Martin Luther King, Jr., *Why We Can't Wait* (New York: Signet, 1964). Milton R. Konvitz, *Century of Civil Rights* (New York: Columbia University Press, 1961). Charles Whalen and Barbara Whalen, *The Longest Debate: A Legislative History of the 1964 Civil Rights Act* (Washington, D.C.: Seven Locks Press, 1985).

CIVIL RIGHTS CASES

- 109 U.S. 3 (1883)
- Vote: 8–1
- For the Court: Bradley
- Dissenting: Harlan

The *Civil Rights Cases* were five cases that the Supreme Court decided together. In all five situations, the federal Civil Rights Act of 1875 had been enforced by the federal government against private facilities—a railroad company, theater owners, and innkeepers. In each case, a black American had been denied the same accommodations or services enjoyed by white Americans. The Civil Rights Act of 1875 forbade denial of access on the basis of race to theaters, hotels, railroad cars, and other privately owned facilities that served the public. The Civil Rights Act also forbade segregation of blacks and whites in their

use of such privately owned facilities as hotels, theaters, and railroad cars. The defendants in these cases argued that the Civil Rights Act of 1875 was an unconstitutional regulation of their management of private property.

The Issue   Congress passed the Civil Rights Act of 1875 to implement the "equal protection of the laws" clause of the 14th Amendment. This amendment restricted the power of a state *government* to violate the civil rights of people within its boundaries. But the primary intention of the framers of the 14th Amendment was to secure the rights of black people, which had been at risk. At issue was whether the 14th Amendment enabled Congress to forbid discrimination based on race by owners of *private* facilities used by the public.

Opinion of the Court   The Supreme Court ruled that the 14th Amendment banned the violation of individual rights only by state governments. According to Justice Joseph Bradley, the Civil Rights Act of 1875 was unconstitutional because it attempted to regulate the private conduct of individuals with regard to racial discrimination—an action that was beyond the scope of the 14th Amendment. According to Bradley, individuals faced with racial discrimination in their use of privately owned hotels, theaters, railroad cars, and so forth had to seek help from their state government. The federal government, according to the Court, had no constitutional authority to act in these cases.

Dissent   Justice John Harlan stood against the Court in this case because its opinion rested "upon grounds entirely narrow and artificial." Harlan argued for a broad interpretation of the 13th and 14th Amendments as a suitable legal basis for the Civil Rights Act of 1875.

Harlan claimed that the federal government had the authority and the responsibility to protect individuals from racial discrimination in their access to privately owned facilities serving the public. He pointed out, for example, that roads and railroads were "established by the authority of these States" and theaters operated under state government licenses. Therefore, Harlan argued, the state's association with these facilities justified federal action to provide all individuals, black and white, equal opportunity to use the facilities. Justice Harlan concluded:

[T]here cannot be, in this republic, any class of human beings in practical subjection to another class, with power in the latter to dole out to the former just such privileges as they may choose to grant. The supreme law of the land has decreed that no authority shall be exercised in this country upon the basis of discrimination, in respect of civil rights, against freemen and citizens because of their race, color, or previous condition of servitude.

Significance Public opinion in the 1870s was solidly in support of the Court's ruling in the *Civil Rights Cases.* However, Harlan's dissent prevailed in the long run in federal legislation such as the Civil Rights Act of 1964 and in Supreme Court decisions such as *Heart of Atlanta Motel* v. *United States* (1964). It is Justice Harlan's dissent that is honored today, not Justice Bradley's opinion for the Court.

SEE ALSO *Heart of Atlanta Motel v. United States*

SOURCES Andrew Kull, "The 14th Amendment That Wasn't," *Constitution* 5, no. 1 (Winter 1993): 68–75. Alvin F. Westin, "The Case of the Prejudiced Doorkeeper: The Civil Rights Cases," in *Quarrels That Have Shaped the Constitution,* edited by John A. Garraty (New York: Harper & Row, 1987).

CLARKE, JOHN H.
Associate Justice, 1916–22

- Born: Sept. 18, 1857, New Lisbon, Ohio
- Education: Western Reserve University, B.A., 1877; M.A., 1880
- Previous government service: federal judge, U.S. District Court for the Northern District of Ohio, 1914–16

- Appointed by President Woodrow Wilson July 14, 1916; replaced Charles Evans Hughes, who resigned
- Supreme Court term: confirmed by the Senate July 24, 1916, by a voice vote; resigned Sept. 18, 1922
- Died: Mar. 22, 1945, San Diego, Calif.

John H. Clarke served only six years on the Supreme Court. During this brief period, he often sided with Justice Louis Brandeis. His cooperation with Brandeis brought the hostility of Justice James McReynolds, who was persistently nasty to his two colleagues because he strongly disagreed with their legal ideas. McReynolds also seems to have disliked Brandeis because of a personal prejudice against Jews. McReynolds's ugly behavior was one of the reasons Clarke left the Court. McReynolds refused to sign the official letter expressing regret at Clarke's resignation.

Justice Clarke wrote the Court's opinion in *Abrams* v. *United States* (1919), in which he upheld limitations on free speech under the Espionage Act of 1918. In this opinion Clarke departed from his usual agreement with Brandeis, who joined Oliver Wendell Holmes in a strong dissent against the *Abrams* decision.

After leaving the Supreme Court, Clarke devoted the rest of his life to promoting the cause of world peace. He supported the work of the League of Nations and the creation of the United Nations in 1945.

SEE ALSO *Abrams v. United States*

CLARK, JAMES BEAUCHAMP ("CHAMP")

- Born: Mar. 7, 1850, Lawrenceburg, Ky.
- Political party: Democrat
- Education: Kentucky University at Lexington; Bethany College, graduated, 1873; Cincinnati Law School, graduated, 1875
- Representative from Missouri: 1893–95, 1897–1921

- Speaker of the House: 1913–19
- House minority leader: 1909–13, 1919–21
- Died: Mar. 2, 1921, Washington, D.C.

By leading the fight to limit Speaker Joseph G. Cannon's power over the House in 1909, Democratic minority leader Champ Clark limited himself as well. "Although I am going to be Speaker next time," said Clark, "I am going to sacrifice the Speaker's power to change the rules." Clark forged an alliance with progressive Republicans to win a majority of votes for his resolution to enlarge the House Rules Committee and prohibit the Speaker from serving on that powerful committee. The next year, when Democrats won the majority in the House, Clark replaced Cannon as Speaker. Clark served chiefly as the House's presiding officer and left it to Majority Leader Oscar W. Underwood (Democrat–Alabama) to lead his party's floor fights. Clark accepted a further reduction in power when the Democratic Caucus took away the Speaker's power to make committee appointments. Although Champ Clark reduced the powers of his own office, he made sure that the House would not return to "one-man rule."

SEE ALSO Cannon, Joseph G.

SOURCES Champ Clark, My Quarter Century of American Politics, 2 vols. (New York: Harper, 1920).

CLARK, TOM
Associate Justice, 1949–67

- Born: Sept. 23, 1899, Dallas, Tex.
- Education: University of Texas, B.A., 1921; LL.B., 1922
- Previous government service: civil district attorney, Dallas County, Tex., 1927–32; special assistant, U.S. Department of Justice, 1937–43; assistant U.S. attorney general, 1943–45; U.S. attorney general, 1945–49
- Appointed by President Harry S. Truman Aug. 2, 1949; replaced Frank Murphy, who died
- Supreme Court term: confirmed by the Senate Aug. 18, 1949, by a 73–8 vote; retired June 12, 1967
- Died: June 13, 1977, New York, N.Y.

Tom Clark worked in the U.S. Department of Justice and became friendly with Harry Truman, a senator from Missouri. In 1944, Clark supported Truman's bid to become the Democratic candidate for Vice President. When President Franklin D. Roosevelt died in 1945, Truman became President and he appointed Clark to be his attorney general. Four years later, Truman named Clark to the Supreme Court.

Both as attorney general and associate justice, Tom Clark supported government efforts to protect national security against Communist party activity in the United States. He also wrote opinions for the Court on landmark cases that protected individual rights. In Mapp v. Ohio (1961), for example, Clark declared that evidence seized illegally must be "excluded from" a state government's prosecution of a person accused of a crime. This "exclusionary rule" set forth by Clark in 1961 has endured as a guide to Court decisions.

Clark retired from the Supreme Court in 1967 when his son, Ramsay Clark, was appointed by President Lyndon Johnson to the job of U.S. attorney general, a position that Tom Clark had once filled. Tom Clark left the Court to avoid any possibility of conflict of interest in cases brought to the Court by his son.

He continued to serve the federal government, however, until his death in 1977. He was a founder and the first director of the Federal Judicial Center, which conducts research and training programs to improve operations of the federal courts. He also occasionally served as a judge on various circuits of the U.S. Court of Appeals.

SEE ALSO Mapp v. Ohio

CLASS ACTION

A lawsuit brought to court by one or more individuals on behalf of a category, or class, of people is called a *class action.* This type of lawsuit is used when there is a very large number of parties to a dispute who have common interests and stakes in the outcome. In a class action, the case is tried by one or a few parties who represent many others, and the judgment in the case is binding on all members of the class involved in the dispute. Many cases dealing with the civil rights of African Americans were class actions.

CLAY, HENRY

• Born: Apr. 12, 1777, Hanover County, Va.
• Political party: Democratic-Republican, Whig
• Education: studied law in Richmond, Virginia
• Senator from Kentucky: 1810–11, 1831–42, 1849–52
• Representative from Kentucky: 1811–14, 1815–21, 1823–25
• Speaker of the House: 1811–14, 1815–20, 1823–25
• Died: June 29, 1852, Washington, D.C.

Known as the "Great Compromiser," Henry Clay dominated the House and Senate for more than four decades yet lost the election every time he ran for President. After a brief term in the Senate, he went to the House, where he was elected Speaker on his first day. Clay put forward an ambitious program of federally funded roads, canals, and other internal improvements, a national bank, and a protective tariff. His American System program took him into battle with President Andrew Jackson and the Democrats and led to the formation of the Whig party.

Clay also worked for years in Congress to achieve compromises between the North and South to reduce sectional tensions over slavery. From the Missouri Compromise to the Compromise of 1850, Clay played a major role. Although a pragmatic politician, he could also show passion and let his temper get the best of him. Members of Congress either adored or hated him. "I don't like Clay," said John C. Calhoun. "He is a bad man, an imposter, a creature of wicked schemes. I won't speak to him, but, by God, I love him!" Voters showed similarly mixed feelings.

SEE ALSO *Compromise; Compromise of 1850; Missouri Compromise (1821)*
SOURCES Robert Remini, *Henry Clay: Statesman for the Union* (New York: Norton,1991).

CLEAR AND PRESENT DANGER TEST

SEE *Abrams v. United States; Freedom of speech and press; Schenck v. United States*

CLERK OF THE COURT

During the U.S. Supreme Court's first term, in 1790, it established the office of the clerk to be responsible for managing the Court's administrative work. The clerk manages the dockets (calendars, agendas, and schedules of events) of the Court, receives and records all documents filed on the various dockets and distributes these pages to the justices, notifies lower courts of all formal acts and decisions of the Supreme Court, and provides advice to lawyers who need information about the Court's rules and procedures. The clerk has a clerical and administrative staff of 25 people.

SEE ALSO *Staff of the Supreme Court, nonjudicial*

CLERK OF THE HOUSE OF REPRESENTATIVES

Beginning in 1789, the clerk of the House served as administrative officer of the House of Representatives. Elected by the members, although not a representative himself, the clerk purchased stationery and office supplies, disbursed salaries, and supervised the staff necessary for the functioning of House sessions.

House rules stated that whenever it passed a bill, "it shall be certified by the clerk, noting the day of its passing" at the bottom of the page. The clerk was also assigned to read to the members any bills referred to the House as a committee of the whole. The clerk was put in charge of all the records of the House, especially the keeping and printing of the House journals. Two centuries after John Beckley was elected the first clerk, his successors continue to be responsible for many of these duties and more, including compiling the activity reports that all congressional lobbyists must file each year according to federal law.

In 1992, following scandals involving the House bank and post office (neither of which were under the clerk of the House), the House created a new post of director of non-legislative services. The director was assigned to handle all payrolls, office supplies, inside mail, restaurants, barber and beauty shops, and other administrative business that had once been supervised by the clerk of the House and sergeant at arms. Reforms in 1995 further shifted the clerk's responsibilities from administrative to legislative business, supervising the variety of clerks at the desk in the chamber and the reporters of debate.

SEE ALSO *Committee of the whole; Director of non-legislative services; Journals, congressional; Officers of the House and Senate; Secretary of the Senate*

CLERKS OF THE JUSTICES

Each Supreme Court justice may have a staff of four law clerks. Chief Justice William Rehnquist and Justice John Paul Stevens, however, chose to employ only three each. The justices have complete control over the hiring of these legal assistants. Most law clerks work at the job for only one year and use the prestigious position as a stepping stone to important jobs in law firms, on law school faculties, and in government service. Thirty-two former law

clerks have become federal judges, and three have become Supreme Court justices: William H. Rehnquist, who clerked for Robert H. Jackson; John Paul Stevens, who clerked for Wiley B. Rutledge; and Byron White, who clerked for Fred M. Vinson.

The law clerks provide valuable research assistance for the justices. They also read, analyze, and write summaries of certiorari petitions, the requests to the Court for review of cases. The justices often depend upon their clerks' summaries and recommendations in deciding which cases to select for review.

Justice Horace Gray was the first member of the Court to employ a law clerk. In 1885 Gray hired a recent graduate of Harvard Law School, whom he paid with his own money. In 1922 Congress provided funds for the employment of one law clerk by each justice. In 1924 Congress established permanent law clerk positions at the Supreme Court.

CLEVELAND, GROVER
22nd and 24th President

- Born: Mar. 18, 1837, Caldwell, N.J.
- Political party: Democrat
- Education: common school; read law, 1855–59
- Military service: none
- Previous government service: ward supervisor, Erie County, N.Y., 1863; assistant district attorney, Erie County, 1863–65; Erie County sheriff, 1871–73; mayor of Buffalo, 1882; governor of New York, 1883–84
- Elected President, 1884; served, 1885–89; elected, 1892; served, 1893–97
- Died: June 24, 1908, Princeton, N.J.

Grover Cleveland began his political career as Erie County sheriff in New York, and after a meteoric rise became the first Democratic President elected after the Civil War and the only President to be married in the White House. In dealing with Congress and state governors, he was the strongest President since Abraham Lincoln.

The son of a Presbyterian minister, Cleveland helped support his family by working in a local grocery store beginning at age 14. He worked on his uncle's farm in Buffalo, then studied law. He became assistant district attorney of Erie County during the Civil War, hiring a substitute to fight for him for $300 when he was drafted, a frequent and legal procedure at the time. In 1865 he was defeated in his first election bid when he ran for district attorney of Erie County.

Nine years later he was elected mayor of Buffalo. As mayor, and then as governor of New York, he ran honest administrations and vetoed patronage (political appointments) and pork barrel measures (special projects for the benefit of particular constituents) of the city council and state legislature. He also vetoed progressive legislation that would have held down transit fares and regulated transit workers' hours.

Cleveland won the Democratic nomination in 1884 because of his record as a reformer.

As President, Cleveland was a conservative in budget matters and a reformer when it came to patronage and the civil service. He expanded the classified "merit appointment" list of the civil service by 85,000 positions. His cabinet and other high-level appointments owed less to patronage and politics and more to merit; his new secretary of the navy, William Whitney, built a modern steel navy that proved its worth to future Presidents. He vetoed 200 of the 1,700 private pension bills Congress passed for veterans of the Civil War, arguing that many of these claims were fraudulent. He also vetoed measures to relieve farmers in the West from drought because he did not believe that the national government had the responsibility under the Constitution to solve the problems of people in need.

Although Cleveland's administration was free of scandal and corruption, he was not all that popular. In 1888, running against a high-tariff candidate, Republican Benjamin Harrison, he won a majority of the popular vote but lost in the electoral college, in part because he failed to carry New York.

After leaving the White House, Cleveland practiced law in New York City for four years, a period he termed the happiest in his life. In 1892, Cleveland was nominated by the Democrats a third time, and he won the rematch with Harrison. Cleveland ran on a platform of good government, lower tariffs, and a return to using only gold (rather than silver) to back the paper currency issued by the U.S. Treasury. His victory made him the only American President to serve two nonconsecutive terms.

Cleveland's eventful second term was a contrast to his first. The Panic of 1893 led to calls from populists and progressives for national government programs to regulate the banks, but Cleveland turned a deaf ear. He refused to inflate the currency and forced repeal of the Silver Purchase Act, which had guaranteed that the government would purchase a set amount of silver from mine owners each year. This led to a contraction in the supply of money that worsened already hard times in the West.

Labor unrest added to Cleveland's troubles. When Jacob S. Coxey led "Coxey's army," a group of unemployed men, to the capital to demand public service jobs, Cleveland had them dispersed by the police. When Pullman railway car workers went on strike in 1894, Cleveland won a court injunction and then sent 2,000 federal troops into Illinois to break the strike. At the behest of Attorney General Richard Olney, a former railroad lawyer himself, the socialist leader Eugene V. Debs, head of the American Railway Union, was jailed for his role in organizing a boycott of Pullman cars in support of the strikers.

In foreign affairs Cleveland refused to accept a petition from a white settlers' government that Hawaii be annexed by the United States, accurately describing the local "Committee of Safety" as unrepresentative of the native population and not elected by it. In 1895 he insisted that the British government accept an American determination of the boundary between Venezuela and British Guyana. Ultimately, the British and Venezuelans negotiated an end to their boundary dispute, and arbitration upheld most of the British claim. Cleveland refused to intervene in the Cuban revolt against Spanish rule, leaving the problem for his successor. When there was talk in Congress of declaring war against Spain, Cleveland let it be known that as commander in chief he would refuse to use the military to fight such a war. He also rejected the idea that the United States buy Cuba from Spain. Instead, he proposed that the Spanish offer "genuine autonomy" to the Cubans.

By 1896 Cleveland's leadership was repudiated by his own party. A coalition of populists and silver Democrats, who were interested in aid to farmers, regulation of business, and increased use of silver coins as currency, dominated the party convention. It turned away from conservative policies and nominated the fiery populist William Jennings Bryan.

Cleveland moved to Princeton, New Jersey, and became a trustee of Princeton University. When he died in 1908 he was buried in Princeton Cemetery, close to the grave of former Vice President Aaron Burr.

SEE ALSO Harrison, Benjamin

SOURCES Allan Nevins, *Grover Cleveland: A Study in Courage* (New York: Dodd, Mead, 1932). Richard E. Welch, *The Presidencies of Grover Cleveland* (Lawrence: University Press of Kansas, 1988).

CLIFFORD, NATHAN
Associate Justice, 1858–81

- Born: Aug. 18, 1803, Rumney, N.H.
- Education: studied law in the office of Josiah Quincy in Rumney
- Previous government service: Maine House of Representatives, 1830–34; attorney general of Maine, 1834–38; U.S. representative from Maine, 1839–43;

U.S. attorney general, 1846–48; U.S. minister to Mexico, 1848–49
- Appointed by President James Buchanan Dec. 9, 1857; replaced Benjamin R. Curtis, who resigned
- Supreme Court term: confirmed by the Senate Jan. 12, 1858, by a 26–23 vote; served until July 25, 1881
- Died: July 25, 1881, Cornish, Maine

Nathan Clifford was a self-educated man who built a successful political career in Maine and in the federal government. He served as attorney general under President James Polk and was appointed by President James Buchanan to the U.S. Supreme Court. He was confirmed in a close vote because Republican senators believed he sympathized with the slave states that were threatening to secede from the Union.

Justice Clifford wrote no major opinions for the Court. He chaired the commission set up to settle the dispute over the Presidential election of 1876. There had been controversy about the correct vote totals and charges of voter fraud in three southern states. Clifford supported the case of Democrat Samuel Tilden but the commission decided in favor of Rutherford B. Hayes, the Republican.

CLINTON, BILL
42nd President

- Born: Aug. 19, 1946, Hope, Ark.
- Political party: Democrat
- Education: Georgetown University, B.S., 1968; Rhodes scholar, Oxford University, 1968–70; Yale University, J.D., 1973
- Military service: none
- Previous government service: attorney general of Arkansas, 1977–79; governor of Arkansas, 1979–81, 1983–92
- Elected President, 1992; served 1993–

Bill (William Jefferson) Clinton was only the second Democrat to win the Presidency since 1968. Like Jimmy Carter, he had been a Southern governor identified with the moderate rather than the liberal wing of his party. He was also the first

President from the "baby boom" generation (born between 1946 and 1960).

Clinton's father was killed in an automobile accident three months before he was born, and he was adopted by his mother's second husband. Throughout his school years he was considered a leader. Selected for the Boys Nation Leadership Camp in 1963, he shook hands with John F. Kennedy at the White House. He worked for Arkansas senator J. William Fulbright as an intern during his college years at Georgetown University and won a Rhodes scholarship to study at Oxford University. In 1969 he organized two anti–Vietnam War rallies in London.

In 1972 Clinton worked for George McGovern as codirector of his Presidential campaign in Texas. That fall Clinton entered Yale Law School. He taught at the University of Arkansas law school from 1974 to 1976, becoming only the second future President to teach constitutional law (the first was Woodrow Wilson).

Clinton became active in Arkansas Democratic politics. After losing a race for the U.S. House of Representatives in 1974, he was elected attorney general of Arkansas in 1976 and then governor in 1978 with more than 60 percent of the vote. He raised taxes and was defeated for a second term, becoming the youngest ex-governor in U.S. history. He was again elected governor in 1982 and served until 1992. He was elected president of the National Governors Association and was instrumental in founding the Democratic Leadership Conference, an organization devoted to moving the Democratic party away from its liberal orientation toward a centrist position, designed to win back voters in the Southern and border states in Presidential elections.

In the spring of 1991, when President Bush's popularity stood at 91 percent in the aftermath of the Persian Gulf War, Clinton began his run for the 1992 Presidential nomination. He defeated a weak field of contenders in the primaries despite allegations that he had engaged in extramarital affairs, had smoked marijuana, and had avoided military service during the Vietnam War.

In a three-candidate race (involving the independent candidacy of Texas billionaire Ross Perot) Clinton positioned himself as the one best equipped to manage the economy. His selection of Tennessee Democratic senator Al Gore as his running mate added strength to the ticket and took away the Republican advantage in the Southern and border states.

Clinton broke new ground in campaign strategy. He appeared on a late-night television show wearing sunglasses and played the saxophone in a successful attempt to appeal to younger voters. He followed up with many appearances on daytime television and radio talk shows.

Clinton won his first election with 42 percent of the popular vote, against 37 percent for Bush and 19 percent for Perot. He won 370 electoral college votes, compared with 160 for Bush.

In his first term, Clinton cut the annual deficits in half, laying the groundwork for growth, as well as lower unemployment and inflation. His bill to provide health insurance to all Americans was defeated after health insurers lobbied against it in Congress. Questions about his character continued to dog Clinton, especially his role in a scandal involving a failed savings and loan institution in Arkansas. In the 1994 midterm elections, Republicans won control of Congress for the first time in 40 years, putting an end to Clinton's legislative agenda. Thereafter his threat to veto Republican measures enabled him to negotiate with House Speaker Newt Gingrich and Senate majority leader Robert Dole on welfare reform and environmental policy.

Clinton won reelection over former senator Bob Dole with almost half the vote of the electorate, but the Congress, which in the 1994 midterm elections had become controlled by Republicans, remained in the hands of the opposition party. Two years into his second term, Clinton had failed to win enactment of his major health care initiatives but otherwise had compiled a respectable legislative record by cooperating with the Republicans or outmaneuvering them. He reoriented the Democratic party toward the center by balancing the budget, winning crime control measures (crime rates plunged during his terms), and cooperating with the Republicans to end "welfare as we know it" by providing incentives for states to reform their programs to get recipients into jobs.

Clinton's administration also downsized the federal departments as part of a "reinventing government" initiative. Clinton worked hard to improve race relations by appointing minorities to high positions in his administartion and beginning a national dialogue on race. He appointed women to the highest positions in government, including for the first time secretary of state and attorney general. He presided over one of the longest periods of economic expansion in the 20th century, with low rates of interest, inflation, and unemployment and high rates of economic growth. In consequence, the stock market reached new highs, and so did his job approval rating in the polls.

Throughout his Presidency, Clinton remained a centrist, attacked by conservatives for his defense of affirmative action programs and abortion rights and attacked by liberals for his willingness to cut domestic programs.

In foreign affairs, Clinton acted cautiously. He pulled U.S. troops out of Somalia after they came under attack; negotiated with North Korea to halt its development of nuclear weapons; and allowed former President Jimmy Carter to negotiate an agreement with Haiti's military rulers that allowed for a peaceful occupation of Haiti. In other diplomatic efforts, Clinton worked to secure peace agreements between Protestants and Catholics in Northern Ireland and between Israelis and Palestinians in the Middle East.

Clinton and other Western leaders made the decision to launch air attacks in Bosnia against the Serbs, which led to the Dayton Accords. Then in 1999 NATO leaders acted militarily against Serbia for its repression of the Kosovars, a decision that required Clinton to use all his negotiating skills to lessen the confrontation between NATO and the Russians and between his administration and the Chinese.

Clinton also backed a "Partnership for Peace" that would eventually permit Eastern European nations to join NATO without antagonizing Russia. Twenty years after the end of the Vietnam War, he established diplomatic relations with the communist government of Vietnam. Despite its human rights violations, Clinton refused to sever U.S. commercial relations with China.

Clinton showed leadership in international trade issues. He led the United States into the North American Free Trade Agreement (NAFTA) with Canada and Mexico against the opposition of a majority of his party and made $20 billion available to Mexico during the transition to a free-trade zone. He won congressional approval for the 1994 General Agreement on Tariffs and Trade (GATT), which lowered tariffs and provided for a World Trade Organization (WTO). Both NAFTA and the WTO led to an increase in world trade.

In January 1998 the news media reported that Clinton had had an affair with White House intern Monica Lewinsky. At first the President denied the allegation, but by late August he had admitted to having an "improper relationship" with her. Independent Counsel Kenneth Starr submitted a referral to the House of Representatives outlining possible "high crimes and misdemeanors," and the House subsequently voted to impeach Clinton for perjury and obstruction of justice committed during the investigation of his sexual relationships with Paula Jones and Monica Lewinsky. The vote was highly partisan, with most Democrats defending the President and most Republicans voting for impeachment.

In February 1999 the crisis ended when the Senate failed to muster the two-thirds vote needed to convict—or, for that matter, failed to secure even a majority. Clinton remained in office, but he was unable to pursue much of his legislative agenda because of the impeachment crisis and the conflict in the Balkans.

SEE ALSO *Bush, George; Gore, Albert, Jr.; Truman, Harry S.*

SOURCES Colin Campbell and Bert A. Rockman, eds., *The Clinton Presidency: First Appraisals* (Chatham, N.J.: Chatham House, 1995). Elizabeth Drew, *On the Edge: The Clinton Presidency* (New York: Simon & Schuster, 1994). David Maraniss, *First in His Class* (New York: Simon & Schuster, 1995). Richard A. Posner, *An Affair of State: The Investigation, Impeachment, and Trial of President Clinton* (Cambridge: Harvard University Press, 1999). Stanley A. Renshon, *High Hopes: The Clinton Presidency and the Politics of Ambition* (New York: Routledge, 1998).

CLINTON, GEORGE
Vice President

- Born: July 26, 1739, Little Britain, N.Y.
- Political party: Democratic-Republican
- Education: no formal education
- Military service: New York Militia, 1775–77; Continental Army, 1777
- Previous government service: governor of New York, 1777–95, 1801–4; New York State Assembly, 1800–1801
- Vice President under Thomas Jefferson, 1805–9, and James Madison, 1809–12

Died: Apr. 20, 1812, Washington, D.C.

George Clinton was the first governor of New York, serving during and after the revolutionary war. He also served as a brigadier general during the war. He was a strong governor whose conduct in office served as a model for the delegates at the Constitutional Convention who wanted a strong executive. Clinton himself presided over the New York State Convention called to consider ratification. He opposed ratification of the Constitution in 1788 because he believed in strong state government and a weak national government. Like most of the early Anti-Federalists, he followed Thomas Jefferson and James

Madison into the Republican party, opposing President George Washington and Alexander Hamilton. He served again as governor of New York between 1801 and 1804. Clinton received some electoral college votes in 1789, 1792, and 1796, but not enough to win the Presidency or Vice Presidency.

In 1804 President Thomas Jefferson barred Vice President Aaron Burr from gaining the Republican party's renomination, and the Republicans nominated Clinton to take Burr's place on the ticket. Jefferson and Clinton defeated the Federalist candidates, Charles Cotesworth Pinckney and Rufus King. In 1808 Clinton was again nominated to serve as Vice President, and he was reelected on the Republican ticket led by James Madison.

Like most 19th-century Vice Presidents, Clinton did little in office. His most important act occurred in 1812, while he was presiding over the Senate: he cast the tiebreaking vote against the bill to recharter the Bank of the United States. He retained his hold on the Vice Presidency in 1812 but died in office before his third term began.

SEE ALSO *Burr, Aaron; Jefferson, Thomas; Madison, James*

SOURCES John P. Kaminski, *George Clinton: Yeoman Politician of the New Republic* (Madison, Wis.: Madison House, 1990).

CLINTON V. CITY OF NEW YORK

- 118 S.Ct. 2091 (1998)
- Vote: 6-3
- For the Court: Stevens
- Dissenting: Scalia, O'Connor, and Breyer

Article 1, Section 7, of the U.S. Constitution says that bills passed by Congress must be presented to the President, who can either accept or reject any proposal in full. For more than a century, however, Presidents have wanted the power to reject selectively one or more points of a multifaceted bill that they generally approved.

President Ulysses S. Grant, for example, asked Congress in 1873 to approve an amendment to the Constitution that would give the chief executive the power to veto particular items of a comprehensive bill enacted by Congress while generally approving the legislation. Congress refused to support the President in his quest for what later came to be called a "line-item veto." In the 20th century, Presidents Franklin Roosevelt and Ronald Reagan unsuccessfully sought the power of the line-item veto. Then in 1996, Congress passed the Line Item Veto Act, and President Bill Clinton signed it.

This new federal statute gave the President the power to "cancel" a particular item on expenditure of funds in an omnibus, or comprehensive, bill that the chief executive otherwise approved. This "cancellation" had to be done within five days after the President signed the bill into law. This law also gave Congress the power to restore the item or items "canceled" by the President by passing a new bill within the next 30 days. However, the President could comprehensively sign or veto that bill, and the Congress could overrule the veto by a two-thirds vote.

Six members of Congress, led by Senator Robert C. Byrd of West Virginia, quickly challenged the Line Item Veto Act. They claimed the law violated the "presentment clause" in Article 1, Section 7, of the Constitution. They argued that this constitutional clause requires the President comprehensively, not selectively, to sign or veto a bill enacted by Congress and presented intact to the chief executive.

Senator Byrd and his five colleagues filed a suit in a federal district court on January 2, 1997, that asked that the Line Item Veto Act be nullified as unconstitutional. The federal judge agreed with the congressional plaintiffs. The Supreme Court, however, decided in June 1997 (*Raines* v. *Byrd*) that the members of Congress had no legal standing to file the suit because none of them had suffered a personal injury.

In August 1997, President Clinton used his power under the Line Item Veto Act to "cancel" two items from the budget enacted by Congress. And he removed one item from the Taxpayer Relief Act. He had previously signed both bills, which, with the exception of the "canceled" items, became federal law.

Members of Congress from New York opposed President Clinton's cancellation of a budget item that benefited hospitals and health-care workers in New York City. And residents of Idaho objected to the President's veto of a line item giving tax breaks to potato farmers in their state. Representatives of the offended groups in New York City and Idaho filed suits challenging the constitutionality of Clinton's actions under the Line Item Veto Act.

The Issue Did the Line Item Veto Act violate the presentment clause of Article 1, Section 7, of the Constitution? Supporters of the law claimed it was crafted carefully to overcome arguments against its constitutionality. They pointed out, for example, that the President could cancel particular items from an omnibus bill only after he signed it. And, they argued, Congress was empowered by the act to restore canceled items. Opponents of the act argued that it clearly and directly contradicted a specific provision of the Constitution. Thus, it should be nullified.

Opinion of the Court The Court ruled for the plaintiffs and declared the Line Item Veto Act to be unconstitutional. Writing for the Court, Justice John Paul Stevens said that the law at issue violated the presentment clause of the Constitution. He wrote, "This Act gives the President the unilateral power to change the text of duly enacted statutes. . . . Congress cannot alter the procedures set out in Article 1, Section 7, without amending the Constitution."

Dissent The dissenting opinions defended the constitutionality of the statute at issue. In particular, Justice Antonin Scalia argued that there was no significant difference between a President's cancellation of a line item in an omnibus budget bill and a chief executive's refusal to spend funds that Congress had appropriated because of disapproval of the programs to be supported by the money.

Significance The Federal Office of Budget and Management released all the funds for items the President had vetoed. So the immediate consequence of the decision was the distribution of federal benefits to the plaintiffs and those they represented in New York and Idaho.

The constitutional principle of separation of powers was reinforced. "The Constitution is intact," exclaimed New York Senator Daniel Patrick Moynihan. It appears that the only way to give the President the power of the line-item veto is to amend the Constitution.

CLOAKROOMS, CONGRESSIONAL

L-shaped rooms at the rear of the House and Senate chambers, on either side of the central door, provide cloakrooms for Democratic and Republican members. Once rooms where senators and representatives could hang their hats and cloaks before they entered the chambers, the cloakrooms have become informal meeting rooms. Members meet there to work out legislative compromises, use the phones, or simply rest on the leather couches behind the swinging doors to the chambers. The cloakrooms have become synonymous with backstage political dealing, away from public view. As majority leader, Lyndon B. Johnson (Democrat–Texas) shifted much of the Senate's real deliberations from the floor to the cloakrooms. Johnson once advised Senator Hubert Humphrey (Democrat–Minnesota):

> Now you don't just come right out on the floor and lay important bills right out in front of God and all those voters. That's not the way it's done, and you could lose before you get started, which doesn't look good to the folks back home. You have to take it slow and easy, working your

colleagues over like gentlemen— not on the floor but in the cloakrooms—explaining and trading, but always letting them see what's in it for them. Then when you're sure—Ivory soap sure, and you know you have the votes buttoned up in your back pocket—you come out statesmanlike on the Senate floor and, in the spirit of democracy, have a little debate for the people.

CLOSED RULE

When a bill comes before the House of Representatives, the Rules Committee may set a "closed rule" for its debate and final vote. Under a closed rule, no additional amendments or substitutes to the bill may be offered from the floor.

CLOSED SESSIONS OF CONGRESS

SEE *Executive sessions of Congress*

CLOTURE

In the Senate, when opponents of a bill try to delay and defeat its passage, supporters of the bill will seek to vote cloture, to cut off debate and bring the bill to a vote. The House of Representatives, because of its larger number of members, made majority rule easier to achieve. In 1842, the House adopted a standing rule that no member could speak for more than one hour on any issue under debate. Subsequent five-minute rules and one-minute rules reduced even further the time that members could speak on amendments. The House Rules Committee controls how long the House will debate a bill, prohibits nongermane (irrelevant) amendments, and sets the time for a vote.

The Senate has remained more tolerant of the right to unlimited debate. Until 1917, the Senate had no effective way of shutting off a filibuster, or delaying tactics. During the closing days of the session that year, a group of isolationist senators, who were opposed to the United States entering World War I, filibustered against a bill to arm U.S. merchant ships. President Woodrow Wilson denounced them as a "little group of willful men" and called on the Senate to change its rules. The Senate responded by adopting Rule 22, which provided that a two-thirds vote of all senators could cut off debate.

Cloture difficult to achieve even with Rule 22 The Senate tried eleven times between 1927 and 1962 to invoke cloture but failed each time. Southern senators especially relied on the filibuster to block civil rights legislation. They gained allies in senators from smaller states who refused to vote for cloture because they themselves might need to filibuster to protect their states' interests. In 1957, Senate majority leader Lyndon B. Johnson (Democrat–Texas) won passage of the first civil rights legislation since Reconstruction but at the price of a severely watered-down bill. As President in 1964, Johnson called for stronger civil rights legislation. With the support of Republican minority leader Everett Dirksen, Northern Democrats and Republicans at last were able to invoke cloture and break the Southern filibuster.

In 1975, the Senate reduced the number of votes necessary for cloture from two-thirds (67) to three-fifths (60) of the 100-member Senate. Some senators wanted to change the rule to require only a simple majority (51), but Majority Leader Mike Mansfield (Democrat–Montana) objected. Mansfield believed it was important to retain some way for the minority to check the majority. By then, even moderate and liberal senators had resorted to filibusters to block legislation they found offensive.

Post-cloture tactics Invoking cloture does not automatically stop all delaying tactics. In the 1970s, after rule changes made cloture easier to achieve, Senator James Allen (Democrat–Alabama) invented the post-cloture filibuster. Opponents load a bill up with amendments before cloture because under the terms of cloture they will have 100 hours to debate any amendment. But in 1977 Senate majority leader Robert C. Byrd (Democrat–West Virginia) arranged for the Vice President, as presiding officer, to declare a long list of such amendments out of order. But a minority of senators can still find enough loopholes in the Senate cloture rule to stall a bill long enough to amend or kill it.

SEE ALSO *Filibuster*

SOURCES Walter J. Oleszek, *Congressional Procedures and the Policy Process* (Washington, D.C.: Congressional Quarterly, 1989).

COATTAILS, PRESIDENTIAL

Presidential coattails is a term that refers to the ability of a Presidential candidate to bring out supporters who then vote for his party's candidates for other offices. In effect, the other candidates are said to ride on his coattails. In the 19th century voters cast their ballots by taking a ticket provided by a party worker and putting it in the ballot box. The party-column ballot listed all candidates of the party in a single column and allowed the voter to mark off the party box at the top, which encouraged straight-party voting and the coattails effect. Straight-party voting was the norm, and winners in Presidential elections often had long coattails. They almost always began their term with majorities in the House and Senate.

In modern times voting machines have replaced the party-column ballot with the office-column ballot: candidates are grouped by office rather than party. Often there is no way to cast a party-line vote, and each office must be voted on separately. The proportion of voters choosing House and Presidential candidates of different parties increased from 13 percent in 1952 to more than 40 percent in the elections of 1972, 1980, and 1988. Consequently, Presidential coattails have been virtually eliminated in most elections, and a number of Presidents—including Richard Nixon, Ronald Reagan, and George Bush—have begun their terms with one or both chambers of Congress controlled by the opposition party.

Presidents may suffer from a "reverse coattail" effect, in which more votes are cast for their party's candidates for the House or Senate than are cast for them. In 1976, for example, Jimmy Carter won the White House and obtained a total of 40,828,587 votes, but Democratic candidates for the House that year received 41,749,411 votes. In 1992 almost all Democrats elected to Congress won more votes than the party's Presidential candidate, Bill Clinton.

There is also the "negative coattail" effect, in which an unpopular Presidential candidate may hurt candidates on the party's ticket running for lower offices. Barry Goldwater's poor showing in the Presidential election of 1964 led to the defeat of dozens of Republicans in the House of Representatives, leaving President Lyndon Johnson a large Democratic majority to pass his programs.

SEE ALSO *Election campaigns, Presidential; Johnson, Lyndon Baines*
SOURCES Randall Calvert and John Ferejohn, "Coattail Voting in Recent Presidential Elections," *American Political Science Review* 7 (June 1983): 407–419. James Campbell and Joe Sumners, "Presidential Coattails in Senate Elections," *American Political Science Review* 84 (June 1990): 513–524.

COHENS V. VIRGINIA

- 6 Wheat. 264 (1821)
- Vote: 6–0
- For the Court: Marshall

Two brothers, Philip and Mendes Cohen, were charged with violating a Virginia law by selling lottery tickets within the state. They were tried, convicted, and fined by a local court in Norfolk, Virginia. The Coh-

ens appealed the Virginia court decision to the U.S. Supreme Court under Section 25 of the Judiciary Act of 1789, which provides for review by the U.S. Supreme Court of decisions by state courts that involve issues of constitutional or federal law.

The Cohen brothers said that their lottery had been incorporated in Washington, D.C., according to terms of an act of Congress. Therefore they concluded that their lottery was conducted properly under federal law and could not be restricted by a state law.

The Issue Attorneys for the state of Virginia argued that according to the 11th Amendment to the Constitution, the U.S. Supreme Court could not have jurisdiction in this case. Furthermore, they held that there were no words in the U.S. Constitution that "set up the federal judiciary above the state judiciary." Therefore, they said, Section 25 of the Judiciary Act of 1789 could not be used to justify jurisdiction of the Supreme Court in this case. The issue was: Does the U.S. Supreme Court have jurisdiction in cases originating in state courts when these cases involve questions about federal law and the U.S. Constitution? Is the U.S. Supreme Court the final authority in such cases? Did the state of Virginia wrongfully convict the Cohens for violating a state law against lotteries?

Opinion of the Court Chief Justice John Marshall delivered the unanimous decision of the Supreme Court, which upheld the jurisdiction and authority of the U.S. Supreme Court to review decisions of state courts when they involve issues about federal law or the U.S. Constitution. He wrote eloquently in support of Section 25 of the Judiciary Act of 1789 and reaffirmed the Court's decision (written by Justice Joseph Story) in *Martin* v. *Hunter's Lessee* (1816).

Marshall also effectively dismissed Virginia's claim that the 11th Amendment precluded the Supreme Court from having jurisdiction in this case. Finally, after establishing the Court's authority and jurisdiction in this case, Marshall ruled against the Cohen brothers and upheld their conviction under Virginia state law.

Significance Chief Justice Marshall asserted the supremacy of the U.S. Constitution and federal law over state laws that conflicted with them. And he argued compellingly for the ultimate authority of the U.S. Supreme Court over state courts on *all* questions involving the U.S. Constitution and federal law. These views are no longer controversial, but in Marshall's time they were burning constitutional issues. The chief justice, however, framed and responded to these issues in a timeless fashion, and his decision undergirds our contemporary conceptions of federal-state relations.

SEE ALSO *Federalism; Judicial review; Jurisdiction; Martin v. Hunter's Lessee*

COLFAX, SCHUYLER
Vice President

- Born: Mar. 23, 1823, New York, N.Y.
- Political party: Republican
- Education: grammar school
- Military service: none
- Previous government service: U.S. House of Representatives, 1855–69; Speaker of the House, 1863–69
- Vice President under Ulysses S. Grant, 1869–73
- Died: Jan. 13, 1885, Mankato, Minn.

Schuyler Colfax worked as a journalist in Indiana before winning election to the U.S. House of Representatives in 1854. Colfax's nickname in the House was Smiler because of his genial manner. He was chosen Speaker of the House during the Civil War and by 1868 was frequently mentioned as a Republican candidate for President. Colfax supported Ulysses S. Grant and was rewarded with the Vice Presidential nomination.

Colfax served one undistinguished term as Grant's Vice President, and the Republicans declined to renominate him. After the Republican convention of 1872, the Credit Mobilier financial scandal erupted: directors of the Union Pacific railroad had given stock in their Credit Mobilier company to several members of Congress, including Colfax when he had been Speaker. There were some calls for his impeachment, but his term of office was ending and no action was taken. He spent the last years of his life as a public speaker.

SOURCES Willard Smith II. *Schuyler Colfax: The Changing Fortunes of a Political Idol* (Indianapolis: Indiana Historical Bureau, 1952).

COMMANDER IN CHIEF

Article 2, Section 2, of the Constitution refers to the President as "Commander in Chief of the Army and Navy of the United States, and of the Militia of the several states, when called into the actual service of the United States." This clause is the only mention the Constitution makes of Presidential war powers. By it the President becomes, in Alexander Hamilton's phrase, "first general and admiral," and no one may be placed over him by Congress. Nor can he be outvoted by his cabinet, his senior military commanders, or the National Security Council. Final military decisions rest solely with the President, as with Harry Truman when he alone ordered atomic bombs dropped on Japan in 1945.

The President issues orders through the chain of command that runs (by act of Congress) through the secretary of defense and the Joint Chiefs of Staff to the military theater (on-site, or field) commanders. The President's power to command troops, to assign them duties, and to move them anywhere he deems fit is generally not restricted by the courts.

It is not expected that the President will personally take command of troops, though like George Washington during the Whiskey Rebellion, he may review them to determine their combat readiness. And like Abraham Lincoln during the Civil War, he may visit senior commanders near the theater of operations. He may also, as Woodrow Wilson did in World War I, temporarily place American forces under a foreign commander.

The President is not himself a member of the armed forces even in his capacity as commander in chief. To preserve the principle of civilian control of the military, it is a custom, adhered to by all candidates beginning with Washington, that a member of the armed forces will resign before running for President or taking the oath of office. Ulysses S. Grant, for example, did so in 1868, and Dwight Eisenhower did so in 1952.

The President's most important role as commander in chief is to defend the United States, its territories and possessions, and its armed forces against attack, and he need not wait for Congress to declare war to do so. The President also supervises the establishment of military rule in theaters of war, proclaims and enforces martial law (military rule) and establishes military courts in conquered territories, establishes military governments to rule these territories, and can proclaim armistices and cease-fires and conduct peace negotiations with the enemy. The President does not have the power to permanently acquire territory, but he may govern by Presidential decree until Congress acts. The Panama Canal Zone was governed in this manner from 1905 to 1912. The President may seize enemy property according to the rules of international law, but he may not seize or take control of property in the United States to pursue his war aims, except under provision of laws passed by Congress.

The President does not have absolute power to choose his military subordinates. Congress by law determines the ranks and qualifications for commissioned officers, and the Senate must consent to the appointment of all officers. The President's power to dismiss officers from the service is confined in peacetime to dismissal after a court-martial, or trial, but he can dismiss any officer from a particular command by naming someone else in his or her place. In wartime the President has an absolute power of dismissal.

Thirteen presidents had no military experience: John Adams, Thomas Jefferson, John Quincy Adams, Martin Van Buren, Millard Fillmore, Grover Cleveland, William Taft, Woodrow Wilson, Warren Harding, Calvin Coolidge, Herbert Hoover, Franklin D. Roosevelt, and Bill Clinton. Another, Abraham Lincoln, served briefly in an Illinois volunteer regiment and was reprimanded twice for breaches of discipline. Of these Presidents, John Adams, Lincoln, Wilson, and Roosevelt presided over serious conflicts (the naval war with France, the Civil War, and World Wars I and II), and historians do not regard their lack of military experience as a handicap in functioning as commander in chief.

SEE ALSO *War powers; War Powers Resolution (1973)*

COMMEMORATIVES

For years Congress designated practically every week to commemorate something. A large number of bills enacted each session named a day, a week, or a month in honor of some worthy cause. Congress declared commemoratives for country music, diseases, ethnic groups, flowers, and sports. Although commemoratives often appeared to pander to special interests, members of Congress considered these resolutions a way to recognize groups that did good work or issues that deserved national attention. In 1995, the pressure of legislative business caused Congress to suspend the passing of resolutions declaring commemoratives, although individual members could still draw attention to causes in their own remarks in the *Congressional Record*.

COMMERCE POWER

Article 1, Section 8, of the U.S. Constitution gives Congress the power "to regulate Commerce with foreign Nations and

Development of the Commerce Power

- *Kidd* v. *Pearson* (1888) Manufacturing of goods, such as liquor, is not commerce. Congress cannot regulate such manufacturing as interstate commerce.
- *Champion* v. *Ames* (1903) Congress may use its power to regulate commerce to outlaw the interstate sale and shipment of lottery tickets.
- *McCray* v. *United States* (1904) Congress may regulate the sale of oleomargarine (a butter substitute) by placing a high tax on it. This decision, along with *Champion*, strengthened Congress's ability to use the commerce power as a regulatory power for the public good.
- *Swift and Co.* v. *United States* (1905) The Court announces the "stream of commerce" doctrine. The meatpacking industry is part of a "stream of commerce" from the time an animal is purchased until it is processed and sold as meat. Congress could regulate at any point along that "stream." The "stream of commerce" doctrine became a basic legal concept in the expansion of the federal commerce power.
- *Adair* v. *United States* (1908) Labor relations do not directly affect interstate commerce. Thus, Congress cannot use the commerce power to prohibit certain kinds of labor contracts.
- *Shreveport Rate Cases* (1914) Court announces the "Shreveport doctrine." The federal government has power to regulate rail rates within states (intrastate) as well as between states (interstate). This sets the key precedent that whenever intrastate and interstate transactions (such as rail rates) become so related that reg-

ulation of one involves control of the other, Congress—not the states—has final authority.
- *Hammer* v. *Dagenhart* (1918) Congress may not use the commerce power as a police power to regulate working conditions for child laborers or to prohibit the use of children in factories.
- *Bailey* v. *Drexel Furniture Co.* (1922) Congress may not use its police power to place a high tax on the profits of companies employing child laborers. This decision, along with *Hammer* in 1918, greatly narrowed the federal police power. With these two decisions, the Court frustrated attempts by Congress to end child labor.
- *Railroad Retirement Board* v. *Alton Railroad* (1935) The commerce clause does not give Congress the power to set up a pension system for railroad workers.
- *Carter* v. *Carter Coal Co.* (1936) Mining is not commerce and does not affect commerce directly. Thus, Congress may not regulate labor relations in the coal mining industry.
- *National Labor Relations Board* v. *Jones & Laughlin Steel Corp.* (1937) Congress may regulate labor relations in manufacturing to prevent possible interference with interstate commerce. With this decision, which overturned the *Adair* and *Carter* decisions, the Court gave up the narrow view of Congress's power to regulate commerce it had followed for many years. The Court based its decision on precedents set in the *Swift* and *Shreveport* cases.
- *Mulford* v. *Smith* (1939) The commerce power gives Congress the authority to regulate market quotas for agricultural production. That is, Congress has the power to limit the amount of a product transported via interstate commerce.

- *United States* v. *Darby Lumber Co.* (1941) Congress may use its commerce power to prohibit from interstate commerce goods made under substandard labor conditions. This decision overturns the *Hammer* decision.
- *Wickard* v. *Filburn* (1942) Congress may regulate agricultural production affecting interstate commerce even if the produce is not meant for sale.
- *Heart of Atlanta Motel* v. *United States* (1964) Congress may use its commerce power to prohibit public hotels and motels from discriminating against customers on the basis of race.
- *National League of Cities* v. *Usery* (1976) Congress cannot use its commerce power to establish wage and hour standards for state and local government employees.
- *Garcia* v. *San Antonio Metropolitan Transit Authority* (1985) Neither the 10th Amendment nor any other provision of the Constitution can be interpreted to limit the commerce power of Congress over the state governments. Thus, federal laws on minimum wages and overtime pay can be applied to workers of a transit system owned and operated by the city of San Antonio, Texas. This decision overruled *National League of Cities* v. *Usery.*
- *United States* v. *Lopez* (1995) The Court overturned a Federal law banning individuals from carrying a gun near a school. According to a 5-4 majority of the Court, the statute extended beyond the constitutional power of the federal government to regulate interstate commerce.
- *Reno* v. *Condon* (2000) The Supreme Court upheld the Driver's Privacy Protection Act against a challenge from South Carolina as a constitutional use of Congress's commerce power. This federal law bars states from releasing personal information about licensed motor vehicle drivers

without their consent. Thus, federal statutory protection of an individual's privacy rights outweighed states' rights in this case.

among the several States, and with the Indian Tribes." Commerce refers to the production, selling, and transportation of goods. If these commercial activities affect more than one state, the federal government may use its "commerce power" to regulate them. Since practically all business crosses state lines, Congress has increasingly used the commerce clause to regulate railroads and other interstate transportation; to pass antitrust laws to prevent monopoly (the control of entire industries by a few large corporations); to set up independent regulatory commissions such as the Federal Trade Commission, the Securities and Exchange Commission, and the Environmental Protection Agency; and to prohibit racial discrimination in hotels, restaurants, buses, or any other form of public accommodation or transportation. The commerce clause also permits Congress to set tariffs, or taxes, on imported goods to protect U.S. industries and farm products and to impose economic sanctions, or penalties, on other nations to support U.S. foreign policy. Commerce issues are handled primarily by the House Energy and Commerce Committee and the Senate Commerce, Science, and Transportation Committee.

Ever since the 1820s, the Supreme Court has tended to interpret broadly the meaning of Congress's power to regulate commerce. The Court's first major decision to define the meaning of the commerce power involved a controversy over steamboats. In the early 1800s Robert Fulton developed the steamboat as a practical means of travel. Fulton's smoke-belching vessel started a chain of events that led to the case of *Gibbons* v. *Ogden* (1824).

The *Gibbons* case involved two key questions. First, did "commerce" include navigation, and did the commerce clause of the Constitution therefore give Congress the power to regulate navigation? Second, did Congress possess exclusive power to regulate interstate commerce or did it share that power with the states?

The *Gibbons* case interpreted the meaning of the term *commerce* to encompass not only "navigation" but also other forms of trade, movement, and business. However, the Court did not spell out exactly what these other forms were. For instance, did commerce include coal mining?

As a result, *Gibbons* v. *Ogden* did not immediately lead to extensive federal regulation of interstate commerce. Yet the decision did open the door for the vast expansion of national control over commerce that we have today. The Court's broad interpretation of the meaning of "commerce" ultimately enabled Congress to regulate manufacturing, child labor, farm production, wages and hours, labor unions, civil rights, and criminal conduct as well as buying and selling. Any activity affecting interstate commerce is now subject to national control. Moreover, the Court's broad interpretation of the commerce power has led to a steady growth of the federal government's power in its relationships with state governments.

Though the *Gibbons* ruling established a precedent, it was left to later courts to determine the scope of the commerce power on a case-by-case basis. The accompanying table lists some of the Court's major decisions on the commerce power made in the years since *Gibbons* v. *Ogden*. Through these decisions the Court has further defined Congress's power to regulate commerce in accordance with the commerce clause.

SEE ALSO *Federalism; Gibbons v. Ogden; Hammer v. Dagenhart; Heart of Atlanta Motel v. United States; National Labor Relations Board v. Jones & Laughlin Steel Corp.; United States v. Darby Lumber Co.*
SOURCES Edward S. Corwin, *The Commerce Power Versus States' Rights* (Princeton, N.J.: Princeton University Press, 1959).

COMMISSION ON CIVIL RIGHTS

For almost a century after the Civil War, a system of racial segregation became entrenched in the South and racial discrimination prevailed throughout the nation. During and after World War II, a new movement for equal rights developed. President Harry Truman desegregated the armed forces in 1949, and the Supreme Court ruled in 1954 that the racial segregation of schools was unconstitutional. Civil rights organizations demonstrated across the South. The Montgomery, Alabama, bus boycott of 1954 was one of the most dramatic civil rights confrontations.

In 1957, Congress passed the first Civil Rights Act since Reconstruction. Although generally a weak bill, the Civil Rights Act created the Commission on Civil Rights. The commission serves as a fact-finding agency to examine legislation and the government's policy initiatives to assess the nature and extent of denials of equal protection of the laws, a guarantee under the 14th Amendment to the U.S. Constitution. The commission has eight commissioners, four of whom are appointed by the President and four by Congress. The President appoints one of the commissioners as chairperson, but that person must receive the approval of a majority of the commission's members.

The Commission on Civil Rights studies alleged violations of the equal protection standard based on race, color, religion, sex, national origin, age, or disability. Its studies focus on the areas of employment, voting rights, education, and housing. The commission reports to both the President and to Congress. It conducts hearings but has no enforcement powers. Instead, it refers complaints to the appropriate government agency for possible action.

COMMITTEE ASSIGNMENTS, CONGRESSIONAL

Appointment to a particular committee determines the areas of legislation over which a senator or representative will have the greatest say. Members try hard to persuade their party's steering committees to put them on committees that match their own interests and their constituents' needs. Until the 1950s, freshmen members routinely were assigned to such minor committees as the District of Columbia Committee and had to wait their turn for assignment to such major committees as Armed Services or Appropriations. Today, each new member joins at least one major committee. All members are limited to the number of major committees on which they can serve. Since individuals move up in seniority within a committee toward the chairmanship, they tend to retain the same committee assignments from year to year. On the average, a senator serves on three committees, one select or special committee, and seven subcommittees. A representative usually has two standing committee assignments, one special or select committee, and four subcommittees. Since House members serve on fewer committees, they tend to become specialists in those areas, whereas senators, who serve on more committees, are more likely to be generalists.
SEE ALSO *Committees, congressional*

COMMITTEE OF THE WHOLE

To suspend its rules and move ahead speedily on major bills, to which a committee may have added many amendments, the House of Representatives frequently becomes a committee of the whole (the official title is the Committee of the Whole House on the State of the Union). All House members serve on the committee of the whole, and it meets in the House chamber. A member of the majority other than the Speaker presides over the committee of the whole, and the House mace is moved to a lower pedestal than usual to indicate that the House is no longer in regular session. Although in a regular session 218 members are needed to provide a quorum—the number of members required to be present to conduct business—only 100 members are needed for a quorum in the committee of the whole. Debate is limited to five minutes on each side for each amendment. The committee of the whole may vote on these amendments but not on the final version of the bill. At the end of the debate, the bill's floor manager makes a motion to report the legislation. The House then returns to regular session and votes on the bill. The Senate does not conduct business as a committee of the whole.

COMMITTEES, CONGRESSIONAL

When a bill is introduced, the House or Senate parliamentarian determines its jurisdiction and refers it to the appropriate committee. Within the committee, the bill is usually considered by a subcommittee, which may hold hearings to collect testimony and other evidence. The subcommittee then reports the bill to the full committee for further debate and amendment. If the committee approves, it will report the bill to the House or Senate. The committee chairman or another designated floor manager from the committee will attempt to defend the bill against crippling amendments and win its passage. Once a bill becomes law, the same committee exercises oversight over the executive department agency that carries out the law.

Legislation is shaped more in committee than on the floor of the House and Senate. Bills tend to pass in a form so close to that in which they are reported (voted on and sent to the floor) by committees that the committees have been called "little legislatures." Members therefore have the most influence over bills considered in their own committees.

Select committees The first House and Senate were small bodies that often debated legislative proposals as a committee of the whole and then appointed a select (temporary) committee to perfect the bill's language. Select committees went out of existence as soon as they reported their specific legislation. The first standing (permanent) committees dealt with such house-keeping items as enrolled bills (enrolled bills are the final versions of enacted bills that have been checked for typographical errors and inconsistencies) and contested congressional elections. During the early Congresses, the House and Senate created hundreds of select committees. Committee members were elected by the entire chamber, and whoever received the most votes chaired the committee. Under this system, some members served on many committees, while others served on few or none.

Standing committees In 1792, the House created the Ways and Means Committee to consider and enact Treasury Secretary Alexander Hamilton's proposals for an ambitious national financial program. A Committee on Public Lands was established following the Louisiana Purchase of 1803. After the disastrous War of 1812, for which both the executive and legislative branches seemed unprepared, both houses of Congress saw the need for more legislative expertise and for conducting their business more efficiently. In December 1816, the Senate created a dozen standing committees, including Foreign Relations, Judiciary, and Finance, which continue to operate today. By 1816, the House had created 16 standing committees. Over time, the number of committees increased steadily, and then various legislative reorganizations reduced their number and settled their jurisdiction—which bills would be referred to them.

By the late 19th century, congressional committees had become powerful instruments of government. Committees conducted most of their work in secret, and committee rooms became the domain of chairmen so autocratic that they were sometimes described as barons. The most influential committees were the four "money" committees—Finance and Appropriations in the Senate—Ways and Means and Appropriations in the House—which determined how all federal money would be raised and spent. Other committees held authority over such areas as the military, foreign policy, the federal judiciary, commerce, and the interior. A few committees existed only to give their chairmen a room and a clerk and never received any legislation to consider. For example, the Senate established a Committee on Woman Suffrage decades before the all-male Senate took that issue seriously and maintained a Committee on Revolutionary Claims into the early 20th century, long after any revolutionary war veterans and widows were still living to file claims for pensions. Party caucuses selected committee members, who then advanced by seniority.

Committee reforms Reforms in the 20th century reduced the power of committee chairmen, provided for discharge of bills from committees that failed to report them, assigned staff to all committee members, and threatened uncooperative chairmen with removal by a majority vote of the majority caucus. "Sunshine" rules required all committee hearings, including markup sessions, to be open to the public.

SEE ALSO *Chairs of committees; Committee assignments, congressional; Conference committees; Investigations, congressional; Joint committees; Oversight; Ranking members in Congress; Referrals to congressional committees; Seniority in Congress; Subcommittees, congressional*

SOURCES Robert C. Byrd, "The Committee System," in *The Senate, 1789–1989: Addresses on the History of the United States Senate,* vol. 2 (Washington, D.C.: Government Printing Office, 1991). Stephen S. Smith and Christopher J. Deering, *Committees in Congress* (Washington, D.C.: Congressional Quarterly, 1984).

Congressional Committees

106th Congress,

1999–2001

Standing Committees of the Senate
Agriculture, Nutrition, and Forestry
Appropriations
Armed Services
Banking, Housing, and Urban Affairs
Budget
Commerce, Science, and Technology
Energy and Natural Resources
Environment and Public Works
Finance
Foreign Relations
Governmental Affairs
Judiciary
Health, Education, Labor and Pensions
Rules and Administration
Small Business
Veterans' Affairs

**Select and Special Committees
of the Senate**
Select Committee on Ethics
Select Committee on Intelligence
Special Committee on Aging
Indian Affairs

Standing Committees of the House
Agriculture
Appropriations
Armed Services
Budget
Economic and Educational
Opportunities
Energy and Commerce
Financial Services
Government Reform
House Oversight
International Relations
Judiciary
Resources
Rules
Science
Small Business
Standards of Official Conduct
Transportation and Infrastructure
Veterans' Affairs
Ways and Means

**Select and Special Committees
of the House**
Permanent Select Committee on
Intelligence

Joint Committees
Joint Committee of Congress on the
Library
Joint Committee on Printing
Joint Committee on Taxation
Joint Economic Committee

COMMON LAW

Law made by judges through decisions in specific cases is known as the common law. These case-by-case decisions were used again and again in similar cases and thereby become customary, or common to all people living under the authority of the court of law. The common law used in the United States originated in England and was compiled in the 18th century by Sir William Blackstone in his *Commentaries on the Law of England.*

The English common law was taken by emigrants from the Old Country to the American colonies. After the American Revolution, English common law became the foundation of legal procedures in the United States of America. Today, the legal system in every American state, except Louisiana, is based on the Anglo-American common law. In Louisiana, once a French colony, certain French legal customs have been maintained. For instance, the word *parish,* derived from the French, is used instead of *county* to label administrative areas within the state.

Statutory law, the written law passed by

a legislature, overrides the common law. Many statutes, however, are rooted in the common law tradition and are interpreted by judges according to this tradition.

There is no federal common law because the federal government functions on the basis of a written constitution, through which the people delegate power to the government. Federal judges, however, apply the common law to cases involving people from different states when there is no federal law that fits a particular case.

The U.S. Supreme Court's use of precedents in deciding cases is an example of the common law heritage. In its exercise of judicial review in particular cases, the Court sets precedents that apply to future cases. If a statute in a particular state is held unconstitutional, for example, this decision is applicable to similar statutes in all other states. The Supreme Court made this point strongly in *Cooper* v. *Aaron* (1958), in which the Court upheld the application of its decision in *Brown* v. *Board of Education* (1954), which concerned Kansas, to enforce an end to segregation of public schools in Arkansas.

SEE ALSO *Cooper v. Aaron; Precedents, judicial*

SOURCES Arthur R. Hogue, *Origins of the Common Law* (Indianapolis: Liberty Press, 1986). Lawrence H. Tribe, *American Constitutional Law* (Mineola, N.Y.: Foundation Press, 1978).

COMPROMISE

"Compromise is the name of the game in the legislative process," argued Representative Richard Bolling (Democrat–Missouri). Henry Clay (Whig–Kentucky) gained fame as the "Great Compromiser," but "Battling Bob" La Follette (Republican–Wisconsin) preferred to lose rather than to compromise. Most members of Congress want to win without sacrificing their principles, but they recognize that because Congress represents such a diverse nation, conflicts over legislation are inevitable. To accomplish anything, they have to accommodate many conflicting positions and forge a consensus. Senate majority leader Alben Barkley (Democrat–Kentucky) insisted that "all legislation is a matter of compromise" and that no member should expect a bill to be enacted exactly as he introduced it. Other senators and representatives, in committee or on the floor, would see things differently and offer amendments to correct whatever problems or deficiencies they found. Very few bills become law with more than 50 to 75 percent of what their authors originally proposed. However, a bill's sponsors must decide when too much compromise might defeat their purposes and make their bill ineffective.

SOURCES Richard Bolling, *Power in the House: A History of the Leadership of the House of Representatives* (New York: Dutton, 1968).

COMPROMISE OF 1850

After the United States won vast southwestern territories from Mexico in 1848, Congress was faced with the question of whether to permit slavery in this region. Antislavery Northerners endorsed the Wilmot Proviso, an amendment to ban the spread of slavery, while Southerners insisted that any restriction on slavery would split the Union. The House of Representatives was so divided that it could not even elect a new Speaker, so solving the territorial problem fell to the Senate. Henry Clay (Whig–Kentucky) returned from retirement to craft one more compromise to save the Union. Clay put together an omnibus bill that would admit California to the Union as a free state, allow New Mexicans to decide whether they wanted slavery, preserve slavery in the District of Columbia, and enact a tough fugitive slave law to allow slave owners to hunt down runaway slaves in the North. Daniel Webster (Whig–Massachusetts) delivered an eloquent appeal for the compromise, warning Southerners who threatened to secede from the Union that there could be "no such thing as peaceable secession." By contrast, John C. Calhoun (Democrat–South Carolina) spent the last days of his life fighting against the compromise. Clay's strategy was to have the Senate vote upon his compromise as a whole, so that senators would have to accept even the portions of the package they disliked. When this tactic failed, an exhausted Clay left Washington to rest. In his absence, the young Stephen A. Douglas (Democrat–Illinois) took apart the omnibus bill, put together different majorities for each of its parts, and won their passage separately. Although not popular in any section of the country, the Compromise of 1850 delayed civil war in the United States for another decade.

SEE ALSO *Benton, Thomas Hart; Calhoun, John C.; Clay, Henry; Webster, Daniel; Wilmot Proviso*

SOURCES Holman Hamilton, *Prologue to Conflict: The Crisis and the Compromise of 1850* (New York: Norton, 1964).

CONCURRENT RESOLUTION

A concurrent resolution is a formal statement passed by both houses of the Congress, stating the opinion of Congress or permitting some action that does not require the President's approval. A concurrent resolution must pass both the House and Senate in the same language, but because it does not have the President's signature, it does not have the force of law. Instead, Congress uses concurrent resolutions (designated as H. Con. Res. or S. Con. Res.) for such housekeeping functions as creating joint committees, authorizing the printing of congressional documents, and setting the date for Congress to adjourn. Concurrent resolutions also express the sense, or opinion, of Congress on many matters of foreign and domestic policy.

SEE ALSO *Bills; Joint resolutions; Resolutions, congressional*

CONCURRING OPINION

Justices of the U.S. Supreme Court write concurring opinions on cases when they agree with the outcome of the majority opinion but disagree with the Court's reasons or explanations for the decision. In such a case a justice writes a separate concurring opinion, offering his or her own reasons about a decision with which he or she concurs, or agrees. On a few occasions, there have been so many concurring opinions in a case that there was no majority opinion of the Court. For example, in *Regents of the University of California* v. *Bakke* (1978), the Court decided the case by a vote of 5 to 4. However, eight of the justices wrote separate opinions, concurring in part and dissenting in part from the decision. As a result, there was no distinct opinion of the Court in this case. Rather, Justice Lewis Powell wrote an opinion announcing "the judgment of the Court," rather than an opinion for the majority of the Court. Cases decided without a clear-cut majority opinion written for the Court do not establish clear precedents.

SEE ALSO *Majority opinion; Opinions of the Supreme Court; Plurality opinion*

CONFERENCE COMMITTEES

For a bill to become law, both houses of Congress must pass it in exactly the same form, word for word. But the Senate and House usually pass different versions of the same bill. One house may authorize more money to be spent or make the bill tougher or add some entirely new provision. After each house has voted on its version of a bill, the party leaders appoint a conference committee of House and Senate members to reconcile the differences. Members of the conference committee are usually members of the committees that first handled the legislation. Once the conference agrees on a single bill, it issues a conference report, which the Senate and House then vote to adopt—or to reject.

If the chief disagreement is about how much money to spend, conference committees tend to split the difference. Issues are more subject to bargaining, and the conference may simply drop the most controversial portions of the bill. Sometimes the bill's floor managers have accepted controversial amendments simply as "trading material," knowing that the conference committee will eventually reject them.

House members often succeed in conference because they serve on just one major committee and have specialized in the issue at hand. "Before the conference committee, the House members usually meet to plan their strategies, their tactics," observed Howard Shuman, a veteran Senate staff member. "They stay together. They're tough in conference." But senators can also present a united front because the Senate usually works to achieve a bipartisan consensus on legislation rather than voting by party line. Conference reports tend to resemble the last version of the bill enacted, whether by the House or the Senate. Lobbyists from both inside and outside the government will concentrate on the later bill to correct whatever problems they find with the earlier one.

SEE ALSO *Bicameral; Lobbying*
SOURCES Ross K. Baker, *House and Senate* (New York: Norton, 1989).

CONFERENCE, JUDICIAL

The justices of the Supreme Court meet regularly in the Conference Room of the Supreme Court Building to discuss cases on which they have heard oral arguments. They also use the conference to screen and select petitions for review of new cases and to conduct other Court business. At least six justices must be present for a quorum,

the minimum number required for the group to make a decision about a case.

In Wednesday afternoon conferences, the justices discuss cases argued orally before the Court on the previous Monday. The all-day conference on Friday is used to discuss cases argued orally the previous Tuesday and Wednesday.

Unlike the presentation of oral arguments in the Supreme Court chamber (courtroom), which is open to the public, the conference is always private and conducted in complete secrecy. Not even the justices' clerks or secretaries attend. No official records of the conferences are made, and no formal reports of the proceedings are issued. However, justices often make personal notes to help them recall main points or important details of a particular discussion.

Discussion of a case usually begins with the chief justice, who sets the context and reviews key facts and issues. The other justices present their views on the case in order of their seniority, beginning with the most senior. If a formal vote is taken on the case, the justices vote in the opposite order, beginning with the least senior. The chief justice is the last to vote. After everyone has voted, the chief justice announces the vote tally and goes on to the next case. Such a formal vote is often not taken, however, because the justices frequently reveal their votes in the preceding round of discussion.

A justice's views on a case sometimes change in the weeks following the conference, during which opinions are written and exchanged and informal discussions of the case continue. Before the final decision and the Court's opinion are announced, justices may modify the positions they expressed during the conference.

CONFERENCES, CONGRESSIONAL

SEE *Caucuses, congressional*

CONFIRMATION PROCESS

SEE *Appointment power; Nominations, confirmation of; Senate Judiciary Committee*

CONGRESS

Congress is the collective identity of the Senate and House of Representatives. The word is derived from the Latin for "coming together." Just as representatives of the American colonies came together in the 1st Continental Congress, the elected representatives of the American people continue to meet together in the U.S. Congress. Sometimes *Congress* is applied incorrectly to the House of Representatives alone because representatives use the alternate title of congressman and congresswoman (whereas senators are always addressed as senators).

The term *Congress* also refers to the two sessions between each congressional election. For instance, the 1st Congress met from 1789 to 1791, and the 101st Congress met from 1989 to 1991. Although the House and Senate do most of their work independently of each other, they must eventually come together to pass all legislation. Bills that were debated as S. Res. 45 or H. Res. 230 become an act of Congress when passed.

The fact that Congress represents the nation coming together can be heard in the many regional accents spoken in its chambers. Every state sends two senators and at least one representative. These legislators bring local concerns to national debates, and they work to make sure that the particular needs and concerns of their constituents are addressed in national legislation. These varying needs sometimes pit different sections of the country against each other, whether industrial versus agricultural, energy-producing versus energy-consuming, or the Sun Belt of the Southeast and Southwest versus the Rust Belt of the Northeast and Midwest. Congress provides the forum where the people's elected representatives can debate these conflicting positions and forge some legislative solutions.

Popularity of Congress As a collective entity, Congress has never been popular. Many members of Congress even run for reelection by running *against* Congress—by emphasizing their differences with the congressional majorities. This accounts for the contradiction that Congress as a whole rates low in public opinion polls while the individual members of Congress are reelected at a high rate. People like their own senators and representatives, who reflect their views and fight for their interests. They have less admiration for senators and representatives who represent other constituencies and promote other interests.

In 1925 House Speaker Nicholas Longworth (Republican–Ohio) noted that he had been a member of Congress for 20 years:

> During the whole of that time we have been attacked, denounced, despised, hunted, harried, blamed, looked down upon, excoriated, and flayed. I refuse to take it personally. I have looked into history. . . . We were unpopular when Lincoln was a Congressman. We were unpopular when John Quincy Adams was a Congressman. We were unpopular even when Henry Clay was a Congressman. We have always been unpopular. From the beginning of the Republic, it has been the duty of every free-born voter to look down upon us, and the duty of every free-born humorist to make jokes at us.

SEE ALSO *Articles of Confederation; Bicameral; Continental Congress; House of Representatives; Senate*

SOURCES Alvin M. Josephy, Jr., *On the Hill: A History of the American Congress* (New York: Simon & Schuster, 1979).

CONGRESSIONAL BUDGET OFFICE

Congress's growing distrust of the executive branch during the administration of Richard Nixon led to the creation of the Congressional Budget Office (CBO) in 1974. Economist Alice Rivlin served as the CBO's first director. She and her successors were chosen by the leadership of both houses of Congress. Rather than rely on the President's economic assessments, Congress now had its own independent, nonpartisan budget office. Members of the CBO staff spend much of their time preparing cost estimates of all bills reported out of committee—that is, they calculate how much the bill would cost over time. The CBO works closely with the House and Senate Budget Committees, as well as with other committees, and prepares many special reports on the costs of issues that the committees are studying. Congress also looks to the CBO to scrutinize the President's annual budget and other requests for funds from executive branch agencies. Although often critical of the administration's figures and statistics, the CBO tries diligently not to take sides with either political party.

SEE ALSO *Budget and Impoundment Control Act, Congressional (1974); Legislative agencies*

SOURCES Rudolph G. Penner, ed., *The Congressional Budget Office after Five Years* (Washington, D.C.: American Enterprise Institute, 1981).

CONGRESSIONAL CEMETERY

Although the Capitol Hill cemetery belongs to an Episcopalian church, Congress gave it the name Congressional—inscribed across its arched iron gate—in honor of the many early members of Congress who are buried there. Fourteen senators and 42 representatives are interred in Congressional Cemetery, together with Vice Pres-

ident Elbridge Gerry; the designer of the Capitol, William Thornton; and various congressional staff members, diplomats, journalists, and American Indian chiefs who died while in Washington. From 1820 to 1870, Congress erected stubby-looking sandstone cenotaphs (empty tombs) in Congressional Cemetery in memory of deceased members who were not buried there. The practice ended after Senator George F. Hoar (Republican–Massachusetts) complained that the cenotaphs were so ugly that they added a new terror to death. Establishment of Arlington National Cemetery during the Civil War made Congressional Cemetery less fashionable, and over time it became one of the least known and least visited historical sites in Washington. Congressional Cemetery is located at Potomac Avenue and E Street in Southeast Washington.

CONGRESSIONAL DIRECTORY

The indispensable guide to each session of Congress is the *Congressional Directory,* which contains biographical sketches of members of Congress, their committee assignments, seniority rankings, and seating charts in the chambers, as well as statistical data and other information about sessions, committees, staff, the Capitol, the press galleries, the diplomatic corps, and the executive and judicial branches of the federal government.

Begun as a private publication in the 1820s, the first directories listed the Washington residences of senators and representatives at a time when members lived in hotels or rented rooms in boardinghouses. Since the boarders ate their meals together, as at a military mess hall, these residences were known as "messes." The directories listed members' addresses as the Washington Mess at Mrs. Wilson's boardinghouse or Dowson's Crowd at Mrs. Dowson's of Capitol Hill.

In 1860, journalist Benjamin Perley Poore published an expanded *Congres-*

sional Directory that established many of the volume's current features. Poore later became clerk of the Senate Committee on Printing, which in 1865 made the *Congressional Directory* a government publication. The Joint Committee on Printing continues to edit the annual *Congressional Directory*, which the Government Printing Office publishes and sells.

SOURCES James Sterling Young, *The Washington Community, 1800–1828* (New York: Columbia University Press, 1966).

CONGRESSIONAL MEDAL OF HONOR

In the name of Congress, the President of the United States awards medals of honor to members of the armed services who have distinguished themselves through bravery in combat, risking their lives above and beyond the call of duty. Congress created the medals by legislation during the Civil War, and the first medals were awarded in March 1863. Each branch of the armed services nominates those soldiers, sailors, marines, and aviators most deserving of the honor. Veterans who have received the medal are also entitled to a special pension.

SOURCES *The Congressional Medal of Honor: The Names, the Deeds* (Forest Ranch, Calif.: Sharp & Dunnigan, 1984).

CONGRESSIONAL QUARTERLY INC.

Since 1945, Congressional Quarterly, a private editorial research service, has studied Congress from an objective, nonpartisan perspective and published a variety of journals and books—everything except a quarterly. CQ issues a *Weekly Report* that profiles members, legislation, media coverage, and institutional issues relating to Congress. This weekly information is combined into an annual *Congressional Quarterly Almanac,* a handy compilation of data

on legislation, including voting statistics, for each session of Congress. Information from the almanacs is further synthesized into a multivolume series called *Congress and the Nation,* which traces the development of legislation over time. CQ's *Guide to Congress* is a one-volume reference book on the history, powers, and procedures of Congress.

CONGRESSIONAL RECORD

Reporters of debate record everything said and done in the House and Senate chambers and publish an edited version of the proceedings the next day in the *Congressional Record.* Members may edit and revise their remarks and may include full texts in place of the condensed speeches they delivered on the floor. The *Record* reflects Congress's attitudes and legislative intent, making it the first place to begin any research on Congress and the legislative process.

The Constitution does not require the House and Senate to keep a verbatim, or word-for-word, record, only that they publish journals from time to time. These legislative and executive journals are short minutes of the proceedings. So the *Congressional Record* is not a legal requirement but something that evolved from the notes that journalists made of the speeches and published in their newspapers. Joseph Gales and William Seaton recorded the debates for their Washington newspaper, the *National Intelligencer.* In 1824, Gales and Seaton began publishing these as the *Register of Debates.* They also compiled the speeches of the earliest Congresses in a series called the *Annals of Congress.* In 1833, Francis Blair and John C. Rives launched a rival publication, the *Congressional Globe.* Because Gales and Seaton were Whigs and Blair and Rives were Democrats, members of Congress sometimes viewed reporters from their publications as partisans who deliberately distorted congressional speeches. But it was not partisanship so much as primitive stenography and poor acoustics that hobbled the reporters.

Beginning in 1848, Congress put the reporters of debate on its payroll to ensure impartiality. That same year, the new Pitman system of stenography greatly improved the reporters' accuracy. The *Congressional Globe* remained a private publication until 1873, when the Government Printing Office took over the project and began publishing the *Congressional Record* as a government document.

Over time the *Congressional Record* has undergone many stylistic changes. In addition to their speeches, members are permitted to reprint newspaper and magazine articles and other items that they want their colleagues to read. It is against the rules, however, to reprint editorial cartoons. That rule was made in 1913 after Senator Benjamin Tillman (Democrat–South Carolina) put in the *Record* a cartoon of a cow being fed by western farmers and milked by eastern financiers.

Remarks that representatives do not actually read on the floor are printed in the "Extensions of Remarks" section at the back of the *Record*. Senators rarely use this section and instead ask for unanimous consent that their remarks be included in the *Record* as if they had been delivered on the floor. Such provisions speed up proceedings on the floor while still allowing members to compile a comprehensive record on the issues.

Since 1947, a Daily Digest has appeared at the back of the *Congressional Record* as a summary and index of floor proceedings and committee business of the day. Once a Congress has ended, the Government Printing Office combines the daily *Congressional Record*s into a fully indexed, permanent edition.

SEE ALSO *Daily Digest; Reporters of debate*
SOURCES Donald A. Ritchie, *Press Gallery: Congress and the Washington Correspondents* (Cambridge: Harvard University Press, 1991).

CONGRESSIONAL RESEARCH SERVICE

With Congress ever hungry for information, the Congressional Research Service (CRS) provides a ready source of nonpartisan, thorough, and reliable data. During the Progressive Era, reformers advocated that state and national governments hire experts to assist in the drafting of legislation. In 1914, the Legislative Reference Service was established as part of the Library of Congress. The service remained relatively small until the Legislative Reorganization Act of 1946 doubled its appropriation and provided for the appointment of senior specialists for each of the fields covered by the standing committees. Renamed the Congressional Research Service in 1970, the agency grew to include several hundred experts in government, law, agriculture, energy, economics, environment, housing, defense, foreign policy, and taxation.

CRS staff members prepare "issue briefs" stating the pros and cons of major issues before Congress and giving legislative histories of bills under consideration. They also compile specific information for individual members of Congress who plan to introduce legislation. Senior specialists regularly brief members and congressional staff on current issues, and the CRS occasionally loans members of its staff to congressional committees to assist with hearings and other legislative matters.

SEE ALSO *Library of Congress*
SOURCES Andrew L. Simpson, *The Library of Congress* (New York: Chelsea House, 1989).

CONKLING, ROSCOE

- Born: Oct. 30, 1829, Albany, N.Y.
- Political party: Republican
- Education: studied law
- Representative from New York: 1859–63, 1865–67
- Senator from New York: 1867–81

• Died: Apr. 18, 1888, New York, N.Y.

Handsome, intelligent, and eloquent but also vain, pompous, and overbearing, Senator Roscoe Conkling built one of the most powerful political machines (a tightly run political organization based on patronage) of the Gilded Age. Representative James Garfield (Republican–Ohio) once observed that Conkling was "inspired more by his hates than his loves." When Garfield won the Presidency, he took on the New York senator. Conkling's machine depended upon patronage—awarding government jobs in return for political support—and the richest source of patronage was the collector of the port of New York, the person who collected tariff revenues at the nation's busiest port. Conkling wanted his own man in the post, but Garfield instead nominated Conkling's rival, Judge William Robertson. When a Senate clerk read out Robertson's nomination, Conkling "raged and roared like a bull," according to a fellow Republican senator. Estimating that Garfield had the votes to confirm the nomination, Conkling and fellow New York Republican Senator Thomas C. Platt resigned from the Senate. They expected the New York legislature to reelect them as a show of support. But in a tragic twist of fate, an assassin sympathetic to Conkling shot and fatally wounded President Garfield. The New York legislature declined to reelect either Conkling or Platt, and Conkling's machine collapsed, ending his political career. Garfield's death spurred Congress to enact the first civil service laws aimed at ending the abuses of federal patronage.

SEE ALSO *Patronage*

SOURCES David M. Jordan, *Roscoe Conkling of New York: Voice in the Senate* (Ithaca, N.Y.: Cornell University Press, 1971).

CONSTITUENT SERVICES

First and foremost, members of Congress represent their constituents, the residents of their district or state who vote them into office. Senators and representatives assist constituents who have problems with Social Security payments, Medicare, veterans' pensions, or with other federal programs and agencies. Constituent needs vary widely, depending on whether a member represents a farming district or a densely populated city and depending on the social, cultural, and political leanings of the people in that district or state. Members cast their votes on national issues with an eye to how the legislation will affect their own constituents.

Constituent services offer members much visibility in their district or state. "I sent all graduating high-school seniors in the Sixth District a certificate to mark their commencement," Bob Dole (Republican–Kansas) recalled of his service in the House. "No bride walked down the aisle without a copy of *The Congressional Cookbook*. I once mistakenly extended congratulations on the birth of a baby to a couple observing their golden wedding anniversary."

Members of Congress now maintain offices in their home state as well as in Washington. Recesses of Congress are called "district work periods." Members return home as often as possible to gauge their constituents' opinions on national issues and to determine their needs. They employ caseworkers to handle mail and telephone requests from constituents. "Some members devote nearly all of their personal energies to such matters and little or none of their time to legislation beyond answering roll calls," Representative Richard Bolling (Democrat–Missouri) observed. But members of Congress can also use their staff to attend to their constituents, freeing them to devote more of their time to legislation.

SOURCES Richard Bolling, *Power in the House: A History of the Leadership of the House of Representatives* (New York: Dutton, 1968). Richard F. Fenno, *Home Style: House Members in Their Districts* (Boston: Little, Brown, 1978).

CONSTITUTIONAL
CONSTRUCTION

One's method of interpreting the U.S. Constitution is called constitutional construction. Some interpreters of the Constitution favor a strict or narrow construction of the document. Strict constructionists interpret the Constitution according to their views of the framers' original intentions about the various parts of the document. Strict constructionists also tend to emphasize the literal meaning of the words of the Constitution.

Loose constructionists favor a broad interpretation of the ideas and words of the Constitution. They attempt to apply the purposes and the principles of the Constitution to meet changing circumstances and conditions. Loose constructionists point to the general welfare clause and the necessary and proper clause of Article 1, Section 8, of the Constitution, which grant Congress power "To ... provide for the ... general welfare of the United States" and "To make all Laws which shall be necessary and proper for carrying into Execution the foregoing Powers, and all other Powers vested by this Constitution in the Government of the United States or in any Department or Officer thereof."

Loose constructionists claim that the general welfare clause and the necessary and proper clause are the bases for broad or flexible interpretation of the Constitution to adjust its ideas to changing times. Loose constructionists also emphasize that they abide by the principles of the Constitution and respect precedents and historical developments.

A significant Supreme Court decision on the issue of strict versus broad construction was made in the landmark case of *McCulloch v. Maryland* (1819). The Court, under the leadership of Chief Justice John Marshall, argued strongly for loose construction and implied powers (powers not explicitly stated but considered logical extensions of Constitutional

language). Since then, the loose constructionist position has prevailed most of the time. Occasionally, however, strict constructionists have exerted influence on the Court's decisions.

SEE ALSO *Marshall, John; McCulloch v. Maryland*

CONSTITUTIONAL
DEMOCRACY

The government of the United States is called a constitutional democracy. It is a democracy because the government is based on the consent of the people. Further, the government operates according to the principle of majority rule. The people, for example, elect their representatives and senators in Congress by majority vote; and the members of Congress make laws according to majority rule.

The popular and democratic government of the United States, however, is limited by the higher law of the Constitution in order to secure, as the Declaration of Independence says, the "unalienable rights" of every person. These legal limitations on the people's government make the United States a constitutional democracy, not an unlimited democracy.

James Madison and other framers of the Constitution feared the new threat to liberty that could come from a tyrannical majority. In times past, the threat to liberty came from the unrestrained powers of a king or an aristocracy. Madison, however, saw a new danger, which he expressed in a letter to Thomas Jefferson (Oct. 17, 1788):

> Wherever the real power in a Government lies, there is the danger of oppression. In our Governments, the real power lies in the majority of the Community, and the invasion of private rights is *chiefly* to be apprehended, not from acts of Government contrary to the sense of its constituents, but from acts in which the Government is the mere instrument of the major number [major-

ity] of the constituents. This is a truth of great importance, but not yet sufficiently attended to.... Whenever there is an interest and power to do wrong, wrong will generally be done, and not less readily by [a majority of the people] than by a ... prince.

Madison wanted government by majority rule of duly elected representatives of the people, but the majority's power must be limited by the higher law of a written constitution. If not, people that the majority disliked could lose basic freedoms and opportunities.

In *The Federalist* Nos. 10 and 51, James Madison argued for constitutional limits on power in government in order to protect the liberty and security of individuals. He opposed equally the absolutism, or total power, of a monarch or military dictator (the tyranny of one), an aristocracy or oligarchy (tyranny of the few over the many), or a majority of the people (tyranny of the many over the few). In a republic or representative democracy (government by elected representatives of the people), the greatest threat to liberty would come from an unrestrained majority. This threat could be overcome by constructing constitutional limits on majority rule in order to protect minority rights.

A constitutional democracy, then, is government by majority rule with protection of minority rights. It is democratic because of its foundations of popular consent and majority rule. It is constitutional because the power of the majority to rule is limited by a supreme law.

In the constitutional democracy of the United States, the Supreme Court uses its power of judicial review to make decisions about issues in specific cases concerning limits on majority rule or on minority rights. In many landmark decisions, such as *West Virginia State Board of Education* v. *Barnette* (1943), the Court has limited the power of majority rule in order to protect the rights to liberty of individuals in the minority. Writing for the Court in the *Barnette* case, Justice Robert Jackson ar-

gued that a person's rights to liberty, such as the right to free exercise of religion, "are beyond the reach of majorities." They may not, he wrote, "be submitted to vote," and "they depend on the outcome of no elections."

In other landmark decisions, the Court has limited an individual's rights to liberty in order to maintain the democratic power of majority rule. For example, in *United States* v. *O'Brien* (1968), the Court upheld a federal law that made it a crime for anyone to destroy a draft card, the document that indicates that a person has registered with the government for possible induction into the armed forces. David O'Brien was denied the right to burn his draft card as a protest against the government. According to the Court, this violation of a federal law, enacted by majority rule of Congress, was not a permissible expression of freedom under the 1st Amendment.

SEE ALSO *Constitutionalism; Judicial review; Liberty under the Constitution; United States v. O'Brien; West Virginia State Board of Education v. Barnette*
SOURCES John Agresto, *The Supreme Court and Constitutional Democracy* (Ithaca, N.Y.: Cornell University Press, 1984). Walter Berns, *Taking the Constitution Seriously* (Lanham, Md.: Madison Books, 1992). Jon Elster and Rune Slagstad, eds., *Constitutionalism and Democracy* (New York: Cambridge, 1988).

CONSTITUTIONALISM

Limited government and the rule of law, as embodied in legal documents, institutions, and procedures, are the two essential elements of constitutionalism.

Limited government means that officials cannot act arbitrarily when they make and enforce public decisions. Public officials cannot simply do as they please. Rather, they are guided and limited by laws as they carry out the duties of their government offices. In the United States, the

Constitution is the supreme law that guides and limits the exercise of power by government officials. Laws made in conformity with the Constitution also guide and limit the actions of government officials.

The rule of law means that neither government officials nor common citizens are allowed to break the law. Furthermore, people accused of crimes should be treated equally under the law and accorded due process, or fair and proper legal proceedings, in all official actions against them. Law governs the actions of everyone in the system—public officials and the citizenry, from highest to lowest ranks in both government and society. All laws and the actions based on those laws must conform to the highest law of the land, the Constitution.

In the United States, constitutionalism means there is a supreme law by which the people establish and limit the powers of their government. In 1787 representatives of the people of the United States drafted and ratified a Constitution, which stands above all laws made by any legislative body in the United States. Article 6 of the Constitution states this principle: "The Constitution, and the Laws of the United States which shall be made in Pursuance thereof . . . shall be the supreme Law of the Land." All laws, passed either by Congress or by state legislatures, must conform to the supreme law—the Constitution. As Alexander Hamilton explained in *The Federalist* No. 78: "No legislative act contrary to the Constitution, therefore, can be valid." On the contrary, a legislative or executive action that violates the Constitution can be declared unconstitutional, or unlawful, by the Supreme Court.

In the United States, the ultimate purpose of constitutionalism is stated in the Declaration of Independence: to secure the "unalienable rights" of all people through a government established by "consent of the governed." According to the Declaration, a good constitution limits the power of a government in order to secure the rights of every person, which belong equally to all human beings. If a government fails to secure these rights of individuals, then it is a bad government and the people have the right to alter and replace it.

A continuing problem of constitutionalism, and of constitution makers, is how to establish a government with sufficient power to rule and maintain order yet with sufficient limitations on its power to prevent tyranny. The rights and liberties of individuals are supposed to be protected by law against abuses of power by government officials. However, if constitutional limits on government are too strict, the government will be too weak to carry out its duties effectively. A government that is too limited by law may not even be able to enforce the laws and maintain public order and security. By contrast, if the government is too strong, or unlimited in its use of power, then the liberties of individuals may be lost and tyranny might prevail. An effective constitutional government is neither too powerful nor too weak.

It is difficult to achieve a workable balance between power sufficient to govern effectively and limits on power sufficient to protect the people's liberties and rights. On the eve of the Civil War, Abraham Lincoln asked, "Must a government, of necessity, be too strong for the liberties of its own people, or too weak to maintain its own existence?" During the 1780s, James Madison and Alexander Hamilton argued in *The Federalist* that limited government under the Articles of Confederation (the document that formed the first government of the newly independent states) was too weak to maintain its own existence. The authors of *The Federalist* argued that limited government and the rule of law—principles of government reflected in the 1787 Constitution—would protect the people from abuses of power by would-be tyrants. They feared equally any unrestrained source of power. The power of an unlimited majority of the people, in their view, was just as dangerous to the rights of individuals as the unlimited power of a king. They argued that the best government is both "energetic" (strong enough to act decisively and effectively in the public interest) and "limited by law" to protect individual rights.

The problem of constitutionalism—how to combine the contrary factors of power and restraint, order and liberty, in one constitution—was stated memorably by James Madison in *The Federalist* No. 51:

> But what is government itself but the greatest of all reflections of human nature? If men were angels, no government would be necessary. If angels were to govern men, neither external nor internal controls on government would be necessary. In framing a government which is to be administered by men over men, the great difficulty lies in this: you must first enable the government to control the governed; and in the next place oblige it to control itself. A dependence on the people is, no doubt, the primary control on the government; but experience has taught mankind the necessity of auxiliary precautions [limited government based on the supreme law of a written constitution].

Constitutionalism—limited government and the rule of law—is a means to the elusive end of securing the human rights of all people. This is the ultimate purpose of government under the U.S. Constitution.

SEE ALSO *Constitutional democracy; Constitutional law; Constitution, U.S.; Federalist, The; Judicial review; Liberty under the Constitution*

SOURCES Ralph Ketchum, *Framed for Posterity: The Enduring Philosophy of the Constitution* (Lawrence: University Press of Kansas, 1993). Donald S. Lutz, *The Origins of American Constitutionalism* (Baton Rouge: Louisiana State University Press, 1988). David A. J. Richards, *Foundations of American Constitutionalism* (New York: Oxford University Press, 1989).

CONSTITUTIONAL LAW

Decisions by judges, who interpret and apply the Constitution to specific cases, create constitutional law. For example, judicial interpretation of the meaning of general phrases in the Constitution, such as "due process of law" or "unreasonable searches and seizures" or "interstate commerce," establishes constitutional law. In the United States, the Supreme Court plays a central role in developing constitutional law. In 1982, for instance, the Court decided in *United States* v. *Ross* that the 4th Amendment ban against "unreasonable searches and seizures" did not prevent police, under certain circumstances, from searching the contents of a car without a search warrant.

Constitutional law in the United States is the product of judicial interpretation of the U.S. Constitution in response to the constitutional issues in cases that come before the courts. Thus, the courts develop a body of case law. The decisions of the courts in these legal cases establish precedents, decisions that serve as models for future decisions. Thus, over time these precedents accumulate to become a body of constitutional law.

The development of American constitutional law is based on the power of the Supreme Court to consider whether particular federal and state laws and executive actions are consistent with the Constitution. If so, the laws or actions at issue are confirmed. If not, they are declared unconstitutional. Thus, the power of judicial review and the principle of constitutionalism are fundamental factors in the development of constitutional law by the judicial branch of government.

SEE ALSO *Constitutionalism; Judicial review; Precedents, judicial*

SOURCES Jethro K. Lieberman, *The Evolving Constitution: How the Supreme Court Has Ruled on Issues from Abortion to Zoning* (New York: Random House, 1993).

CONSTITUTION, U.S.

The basic and supreme law of the land is the Constitution of the United States of America. It consists of 7 articles, which were drafted by the Constitutional Convention of 1787 in Philadelphia, and 27 amendments. More than 200 years old, this document is the oldest written constitution of a national state in use anywhere in the world today. (The oldest written constitution of any sort in use today is the Massachusetts state constitution of 1780.) Most of the national constitutions around the world have existed only since about 1970.

Under the Constitution, ratified in 1788, Congress was divided into two houses and power was distributed among the legislative, executive, and judicial branches of the federal government and the states.

The two compromises critical to the success of the Constitutional Convention both involved Congress. In the Great Compromise, the states were assured equal representation in the Senate and proportional representation (representation in proportion to their population) in the House of Representatives. The Three-fifths Compromise, which allowed a slave to be counted as three-fifths of a person, satisfied the Southern states because it meant their slaves (called "other persons") would be counted for purposes of taxation and representation in Congress.

Article 1, the longest part of the Constitution, deals exclusively with Congress. It grants the House and Senate together the power to collect taxes, borrow and coin money, raise and support an army and navy, declare war, set up a federal court system, establish rules for the naturalization of foreigners seeking citizenship, fix standard weights and measurements, establish post offices and post roads, make copyright and patent laws to protect authors and inventors, and pass legislation to govern the District of Columbia. The Constitution also authorizes Congress "to make all laws which shall be necessary and proper for carrying into execution the foregoing powers." Because this provision is so broad and sweeping, it is known as the "elastic clause."

The Constitution placed some restrictions on congressional power. Congress could not stop the slave trade until 1808 nor could it restrict habeas corpus (the right of a person accused of a crime to know the charges against him), pass ex post facto laws (make something a crime after the fact), give preference to any port of commerce, or grant or allow any federal officeholder to accept a title of nobility. Nor could members of Congress serve simultaneously in any other civil office.

Like other national constitutions, the U.S. Constitution establishes a general framework for organizing and operating a government. It is not a detailed blueprint for governing on a day-to-day basis. The Constitution consists of only about 7,500 words. It does not attempt to consider the details of how to run the national government. Officials who run the government supply the details that fit the general framework.

As the government's framework, the Constitution must be interpreted as specific problems arise. For example, the 4th Amendment to the Constitution protects people against "unreasonable searches and seizures" by police or other government officials. But what does "unreasonable searches and seizures" mean? The automobile did not exist in 1787, when the Constitution was written. Does the 4th Amendment allow the police to stop and search a car? In the case of *United States* v. *Ross* (1982), the Supreme Court decided that they could.

The Supreme Court is often called upon to answer such questions. Its decisions help to update the Constitution to reflect changing times and circumstances. Decisions by judges who interpret and apply the Constitution to specific cases help to add substance to the general framework of government established by the Constitution. These judicial decisions formulate *constitutional law.*

In addition to the sections pertaining to Congress, several other parts of the Constitution assign duties and powers to the President and judiciary. For example, the President can dispatch military forces to put down civil disorder or rebellion or to enforce federal laws if necessary. The Constitution also places limits on the powers of officials such as the President, Supreme Court justices, and members of Congress.

Such limitations on the expressed powers granted to the government protect the liberties of the people. For example, although the U.S. Treasury Department collects taxes, an act of Congress must authorize any expenditure of that tax money. More generally, the first 10 amendments to the Constitution, known collectively as the Bill of Rights, protect the liberties of the people.

All government officials must follow the Constitution when carrying out their duties. For example, the Constitution (Article 6) says that "no religious test shall ever be required as a qualification to any office of public trust in the United States." Thus the President may not require any employees of the executive branch of government to attend church services in order to keep their jobs.

The Constitution grants powers in the name of the people, and the government draws its power from the consent of the governed. The document assumes that government officials will use their powers in the interests of the people. The preamble to the Constitution says, "We the People of the United States . . . do ordain and establish this Constitution for the United States of America."

Representatives of the people wrote and approved the Constitution of the United States. Granting certain powers to government in the name of the people gives legitimacy to the government because most of the people, viewing it as legal and proper, are likely to find it acceptable. SEE ALSO *Amendments, constitutional; Bill*

of Rights; Constitutional democracy; Constitutionalism; Constitutional law

SOURCES George Anastaplo, *The Constitution of 1787: A Commentary* (Baltimore: Johns Hopkins University Press, 1989). Catherine Drinker Bowen, *Miracle at Philadelphia: The Story of the Constitutional Convention, May to September 1787* (Boston: Little, Brown, 1966). David P. Currie, *The Constitution of the United States: A Primer for the People* (Chicago: University of Chicago Press, 1988). Donald A. Ritchie, *The U.S. Constitution* (New York: Chelsea House, 1989).

CONTEMPT OF CONGRESS

Contempt of Congress is any improper attempt to obstruct the legislative process, usually by a refusal to provide information that Congress has requested. The contempt power is critical to Congress's ability to investigate the activities of the executive branch or any issue about which it is considering enacting legislation. Congress can use contempt citations against witnesses who refuse to testify or to produce required evidence. Those found guilty of contempt of Congress may go to prison.

There are three methods of prosecuting for contempt of Congress. First, Congress can try contempt cases itself. In 1848 and 1871 the Senate did just that, imprisoning newspaper reporters in the Capitol for not revealing the source of the Senate secrets they had published. Congress can also turn contempt cases over to the Department of Justice for criminal prosecution. However, juries have often acquitted individuals charged with contempt, especially if it appears that the congressional committee abused its power. For example, between 1950 and 1966 the House Un-American Activities Committee issued 133 contempt citations, but only nine people were convicted. Finally, the Senate or House can also file civil charges of contempt. Using this procedure, a federal judge determines whether a question asked by Congress was legitimate. If the judge orders a witness to answer and the witness refuses, then the witness would be in contempt of court and could be fined or imprisoned. For example, during the Watergate investigation the House cited G. Gordon Liddy for contempt for refusing to testify before a House committee. A federal judge gave Liddy a suspended six-month sentence.

The Supreme Court has upheld Congress's power to punish for contempt but has specified some limitations against its unreasonable use. In the case of *McGrain* v. *Daugherty* in 1927, the Court ruled that "a legislative body cannot legislate wisely or effectively in the absence of information. . . . Experience has taught that mere requests for such information often are unavailing, and also that information which is volunteered is not always accurate or complete; so some means of compulsion are essential to obtain that which is needed."

Although Congress has issued hundreds of contempt citations against witnesses, it has found only one executive agency head in contempt. In 1982, the House voted Environmental Protection Agency administrator Anne Gorsuch Burford in contempt for refusing to provide documents that the House Committee on Public Works and Transportation had requested. She later agreed to give the documents to the committee. Other actions against cabinet members and high-ranking officials have been resolved before either the House or Senate voted.

SEE ALSO *Investigations, congressional*
SOURCES James Hamilton, *The Power to Probe: A Study of Congressional Investigations* (New York: Vintage, 1976).

CONTEMPT POWER OF THE COURTS

The Judiciary Act of 1789 gives federal courts the power to punish an individual for contempt. A person is deemed in contempt of court when he disobeys a court's order or shows disrespect for its authority.

CONTINENTAL CONGRESS

The first national American government was the Continental Congress. Colonial leaders came together in this Congress to oppose British policies that restricted their rights and taxed them without representation in Parliament. Called by the Virginia House of Burgesses, delegates from all of the thirteen colonies except Georgia gathered in Philadelphia in September 1774.

The 1st Continental Congress urged Americans not to import British goods and to form armed militia. But rather than advocate revolution, Congress called for "peace, liberty and security" within the British empire. The British Parliament saw the Congress as treasonous and ordered colonial governors to prevent another election. Yet the 2nd Continental Congress met in May 1775.

The 2nd Congress established the Continental army and chose George Washington as its commander in chief. A committee that included Thomas Jefferson, John Adams, and Benjamin Franklin drafted the Declaration of Independence.

The Congress negotiated with foreign nations, established a postal system, borrowed money to support the army, and printed currency known as "continentals." However, the government's poor finances led to the expression "not worth a continental." Since the Continental Congress lacked any formal constitution, in 1777 a committee drafted a charter for a more permanent form of government. The Articles of Confederation were ratified in 1781, at which time the Continental Congress became "The United States in Congress Assembled."

SEE ALSO *Articles of Confederation*
SOURCES Edmund S. Morgan, *The Birth of the Republic, 1763–89* (Chicago: University of Chicago Press, 1977).

CONTRACT CLAUSE

Article 1, Section 10, of the U.S. Constitution says, "No State shall . . . pass any . . . Law impairing the Obligation of Contracts." This contract clause prohibits any state government from passing a law that would interfere with contracts made by citizens, either by weakening the obligations assumed by parties to a contract or by making a contract difficult to enforce. The Supreme Court's decisions in *Fletcher v. Peck* (1810) and *Dartmouth College v. Woodward* (1819) were landmark decisions that used the contract clause to uphold the sanctity of contracts.

The contract clause applies to contracts between private individuals or contracts made by a state government. However, if a contract endangers the health, safety, or welfare of the public, the state may regulate or void it. The state's authority to protect the public in this way is known as its police power. During the 20th century, the Court has often ruled in favor of state regulation or modification of contracts in the public interest.

SEE ALSO *Dartmouth College v. Woodward; Fletcher v. Peck*

CONTRACT WITH AMERICA

During the 1994 elections, Republican candidates for the House of Representatives took the unusual step of signing a "contract with America." They pledged to enact this legislative agenda if their party won the majority. Rarely has a congressional election been waged on such a specific program. The Contract promised a balanced-budget amendment and a line-item veto to control federal spending; tougher anticrime legislation; welfare reform; a tax credit for families with children; reduced federal regulation; enhanced national security; reforms in product liability laws; and term limits for members. The Contract helped Republicans win con-

trol of the House for the first time in 40 years and elevated its primary author, Georgia Representative Newt Gingrich, to Speaker of the House.

During their first hundred days in the majority in 1995, House members passed most key elements of the Contract. But the Senate moved more slowly. Since Senate Republicans had not campaigned on the Contract, they felt freer to amend and even reject some of its provisions.

SEE ALSO *"First hundred days"; Gingrich, Newt*

CONVENTIONS

SEE *Nominating conventions, Presidential*

COOLIDGE, CALVIN
30th President

- Born: July 4, 1872, Plymouth, Vt.
- Political party: Republican
- Education: Amherst College, B.A., 1895
- Military service: none
- Previous government service: Northampton, Mass., City Council, 1898–1900; Northampton city solicitor, 1901; clerk of the Northampton courts, 1905–6; Massachusetts State Assembly, 1907–9; mayor of Northampton, 1910–11; Massachusetts Senate, 1911–15; president, Massachusetts Senate, 1913–15; lieutenant governor of Massachusetts, 1916–19; governor of Massachusetts, 1919–21; Vice President, 1921–23
- Succeeded to Presidency, 1923; served, 1923–29
- Died: Jan. 5, 1933, Northampton, Mass.

Calvin Coolidge succeeded to the Presidency in the midst of the Teapot Dome scandal, which involved corruption in the sale of leases on naval oil reserves to private investors. His firm resolve to investigate corruption, and his firing of Attorney General Harry Daugherty for refusing to respond to investigations of corruption, did much to restore public confidence in the Republican party. Coolidge did little, but he was immensely popular.

Coolidge was born in a small town in Vermont, where he worked in his father's general store and on his own farm. He graduated from Amherst College and two years later became a lawyer. He then became active in Republican politics, moving from local office to become president of the Massachusetts Senate, then lieutenant governor, and finally governor.

Calvin Coolidge gained national attention while governor for his handling of the Boston police strike of September 1919. The police force demanded union recognition, and when it went out on strike, looting and rioting occurred in the downtown stores. Coolidge ordered the state militia into the city to restore order, and on September 11 he took control of the police department. He backed the Boston mayor's refusal to reinstate the striking police officers. In a message to Samuel Gompers, president of the American Federation of Labor, he argued, "There is no right to strike against the public safety by anybody, anywhere, any time." That sentence brought him immediate acclaim and a large reelection margin.

Coolidge went on to campaign for the Republican Presidential nomination in 1920, but he lacked the support of Massachusetts senator Henry Cabot Lodge. The convention denied him the nomination, but the rank-and-file delegates selected him as Warren Harding's running mate. Coolidge had no part in the scandals that occurred during Harding's administration. He presided over the Senate and was the first Vice President to attend cabinet sessions.

After learning of President Harding's death on August 3, 1923, Coolidge was sworn in as President by his father, the justice of the peace in Plymouth, Vermont. He was the first President from New England since Franklin Pierce. Coolidge became a very popular President because of his unusual public diffidence—it was hard for anybody, anywhere, at any time, to get

a word out of Silent Cal. In the spring of 1924, when the Teapot Dome scandal broke, he appointed a special prosecutor and new attorney general to investigate the scandals, using the slogan "Let the guilty be punished."

That summer Coolidge won the Republican nomination on the first ballot, at the first convention to be broadcast on the radio. With his smashing election victory over Democrat John W. Davis and Progressive Robert La Follette, he became the second President, after Theodore Roosevelt, to win a term in his own right after completing the term of his deceased predecessor.

"The business of America is business," Coolidge had observed as Vice President, and once in the White House his priorities were to reduce government expenditures, lessen government regulation of corporations, promote subsidies for industries and protect them with high tariffs (taxes on imported products), and cut taxes. He vetoed 50 liberal spending bills passed by a coalition of progressive Republicans and Democrats. He used surpluses to reduce the national debt. He refused to take action in the coal strike of 1927. He got Congress to cut the income tax and inheritance tax. These policies fueled a boom in the stock market.

In foreign policy Coolidge continued the Republican opposition to American participation in the League of Nations. He won Senate approval of a treaty that provided for American adherence to the World Court, but the reservations attached by the Senate proved unacceptable to other nations and Coolidge dropped the issue. He moderated American disputes over the oil and mineral policy of the revolutionary government of Mexico. He sent marines into Nicaragua to preserve order at the request of its government, repulsing rebels led by Augusto Sandino. He negotiated the Kellogg-Briand Pact of 1927, which renounced war as an instrument of national policy, though it did little good in the next decade.

In 1927 Coolidge issued an announcement: "I do not choose to run for President in 1928." After leaving office he wrote an autobiography and with the proceeds lived in comfortable retirement.

SEE ALSO *Harding, Warren G.*

SOURCES Donald R. McCoy, *Calvin Coolidge: The Quiet President* (New York: Macmillan, 1967). William A. White, *A Puritan in Babylon* (New York: Macmillan, 1938).

COOPER V. AARON

- 358 U.S. 1 (1958)
- Vote: 9–0
- For the Court: Warren
- Concurring: Frankfurter

In *Brown* v. *Board of Education* (1954), the Supreme Court ruled against racial segregation in public schools. However, school districts in most southern states were slow to carry out the *Brown* decision.

In the fall of 1957, the people of Little Rock, Arkansas, faced the first phase of the school board's very deliberate school desegregation plan. The day before desegregation was to begin, Governor Orval Faubus placed soldiers of the Arkansas National Guard at Central High School. The governor said they were there to keep order. But the federal district court ordered the National Guard removed because of a well-founded suspicion that Governor Faubus would use them to stop black students from entering the school.

The National Guard was withdrawn, and white protesters around the school rioted to prevent the black children from entering the high school. President Dwight Eisenhower sent in the 101st Airborne paratroopers to keep order and protect the nine black students at Central High School.

In February 1958 the federal district court gave the Little Rock school board permission for a two-year delay in carrying out school desegregation. In addition, the Arkansas legislature passed a law authorizing the governor to close all public schools required by the federal courts to desegregate. In this way, Governor Faubus

and the state legislature directly challenged the supremacy of U.S. constitutional law—specifically, the *Brown* decision—with regard to the issue of school desegregation.

In response to the slow pace and threatened postponement of school desegregation in Little Rock, the National Association for the Advancement of Colored People (NAACP) filed suit in the federal district court. The suit was filed against William G. Cooper, president of the school board, on behalf of John Aaron and 32 other students.

The federal district and appellate courts had upheld the slow-paced desegregation plan. So the NAACP appealed to the U.S. Supreme Court. Chief Justice Earl Warren convened a special session of the Court in the summer of 1958 to hear this case.

The Issue The NAACP attorneys argued that the slow pace of school desegregation violated the Supreme Court's decision in *Brown* v. *Board of Education* (1954) and *Brown II* (1955) and the black students' rights to equal protection of the laws provided by the 14th Amendment. They pointed to the two-year postponement in implementation of desegregation permitted by the federal district court. Despite the importance of the NAACP's argument about the violation of constitutional rights, an even greater issue was enforcement of U.S. Supreme Court decisions. Could a state government enact and enforce legislation designed to prevent implementation of a Supreme Court decision?

Opinion of the Court The Supreme Court ruled against any delay by the Little Rock school board in carrying out its desegregation plan. And the Court strongly rejected the idea that a state government could ignore or actively oppose enforcement of U.S. Supreme Court decisions. Chief Justice Earl Warren wrote that the rights of black students could "neither be nullified openly and directly by state legislatures or state executive officials nor nullified indirectly by them by evasive schemes for segregation."

Significance The *Cooper* case was the Supreme Court's first opportunity to rule on the enforcement of its decision in *Brown* v. *Board of Education* (1954). Further, *Cooper* provided the Court a grand opportunity to assert the supremacy of constitutional law over the states. However, the immediate impact of the *Cooper* decision on school desegregation was slight. Not until the civil rights activities of the 1960s, and especially the passage of the Civil Rights Act of 1964, did school desegregation begin to occur extensively throughout the United States.

SEE ALSO *Brown v. Board of Education; Civil rights*

SOURCES Tony Freyer, *The Little Rock Crisis: A Constitutional Interpretation* (Westport, Conn.: Greenwood Press, 1984).

COUNCIL OF ECONOMIC ADVISERS

The Council of Economic Advisers (CEA) is a three-member unit of the Executive Office of the President that provides the President with economic advice. It was established by the Employment Act of 1946; its members are appointed by the President. The CEA provides the President with economic advice on policies to stimulate growth, maintain price stability, and provide for full employment and advises on issues of international economics. It conducts research on economic problems and prepares the annual *Economic Report of the President,* which, accompanied by the President's economic message, is transmitted to Congress each January.

The CEA helps make fiscal policy—decisions on the relationship between revenues and expenditures—through its forecasts of future economic performance and the revenues the government is likely to receive. These estimates are used to prepare the President's budget and tax requests to Congress. The CEA often projects lower revenues than the Treasury Department does as well as higher spending levels than the Office of Management

and Budget does. Such discrepancies sometimes lead to conflicts within the Presidential advisory system.

Some members of the CEA offer the President expert nonpolitical advice. The first chair of the CEA, Edwin Nourse, observed in a letter to President Harry Truman that "there is no occasion for the Council to become involved in any way in the advocacy of particular measures." Truman had no use for this approach and fired Nourse. He appointed as CEA chair a highly partisan Democrat, Leon Keyserling, who was not even a professional economist but who was willing to defend the administration's policy proposals. Gardner Ackley, who chaired the CEA under President Lyndon Johnson, concluded, "If his economic advisor refrains from advice on the gut questions of policy, the President should and will get another one."

The CEA may also play a major role in planning new domestic programs. Its members chaired or participated in task forces that created many of John Kennedy's New Frontier and Lyndon Johnson's Great Society programs, including the War on Poverty. In the administrations of Gerald Ford, Jimmy Carter, Ronald Reagan, and George Bush, CEA members served on task forces dealing with deregulation of industry, energy policy, and international economic negotiations.

In 1993 President Bill Clinton appointed the first woman to chair the CEA: Laura D'Andrea Tyson, an expert in revitalizing American industry and in trade negotiation.

SEE ALSO *Executive Office of the President; Office of Management and Budget*

SOURCES Edward S. Flash, *Economic Advice and Presidential Leadership* (New York: Columbia University Press, 1965). Erwin C. Hargrove and Samuel A. Morley, eds., *The President and the Council of Economic Advisers* (Boulder, Colo.: Westview, 1984). James Pfiffner, ed., *The President and Economic Policy* (Philadelphia: Institute for the Study of Human Issues, 1986).

COUNCIL ON ENVIRONMENTAL QUALITY

The Council on Environmental Quality (CEQ) is the unit of the Executive Office of the President that recommends to the President national policies to preserve and improve environmental quality. It also analyzes changes and trends in the environment, reviews government programs to determine their effects on environmental policy, conducts research relating to ecological systems and environmental quality, assists the President in the preparation of the annual environmental quality report to Congress, and oversees implementation of the National Environmental Policy Act of 1969 and the Environmental Quality Improvement Act of 1970.

The CEQ was established by the National Environmental Policy Act of 1969. It replaced the Environmental Quality Council, which had been created by President Richard Nixon's executive order in June 1969. The CEQ consists of three members appointed by the President with the advice and consent of the Senate. The chair of the CEQ also serves as chair of the President's Commission on Environmental Quality, an advisory group consisting of private citizens.

SEE ALSO *Executive Office of the President*

COUNSEL, OFFICE OF

The Office of Counsel is the unit within the White House Office that provides legal advice to the President and his aides on policy and personal matters, including conflict of interest and ethics laws. The Office of Counsel consists of approximately 20 lawyers and is headed by the White House counsel, who is appointed by the President.

Duties of the counsel include handling requests for Presidential pardons and commutation of sentences; advising the President on which gifts he may accept for the nation; ensuring compliance with campaign finance laws during election campaigns; and responding to subpoenas from Congress for information and, when necessary, invoking executive privilege (the right of the President to withhold information about his activities from Congress or the courts). The White House counsel advises the President whether to sign or veto legislation and supervises compliance with the War Powers Resolution, a law that requires the President to report to Congress when he introduces U.S. armed forces into hostilities or situations that might lead to hostilities. The counsel's office prepares a handbook on procedures to be followed in case of Presidential disability, according to the provisions of the 25th Amendment to the Constitution. The office reviews data on appointments with the White House Personnel Office and the Office of Government Ethics and may show copies of Federal Bureau of Investigation reports and tax-compliance summaries prepared by the Internal Revenue Service to Senate committees reviewing Presidential nominations.

The White House counsel interviews candidates for District of Columbia judgeships, reviews the nominations made by the attorney general for federal judgeships, and is a principal adviser to the President on Supreme Court nominations.

At the end of a President's term, the White House counsel handles legal matters in connection with the establishment of a Presidential library and the disposition of the Presidential papers.

SEE ALSO *Appointment power; Ethics; Office of Government Ethics; Pardon power; White House Office*

COUNSEL, RIGHT TO

The 6th Amendment to the U.S. Constitution provides that "in all criminal prosecutions, the accused shall . . . have the assistance of counsel for his defence." This right of an accused person was not applied consistently to state governments until 1963, when the Court ruled in *Gideon* v. *Wainwright* that counsel must be provided for defendants in all state felony cases. If a defendant could not afford to pay for the services of counsel, then the state would be required to provide counsel for him. The guarantee of the right to counsel was extended to all state-level misdemeanor cases in *Argersinger* v. *Hamlin* (1972).

The *Gideon* case applied the right to counsel to the states through the due process clause of the 14th Amendment. This is an example of the Court's use of the incorporation doctrine to extend rights in the federal Bill of Rights to the state level. SEE ALSO *Due process of law; Gideon v. Wainwright; Incorporation doctrine; Rights of the accused*

COURT-PACKING PLAN (1937)

On February 5, 1937, President Franklin D. Roosevelt sent to Congress his Judicial Reorganization Bill. It called for adding one justice to the Supreme Court for every member over 70 years of age, up to a total of six additional justices. The size of the court is not fixed by the Constitution but is set by Congress in Judiciary Acts and has varied from 6 to 10 members.

The President claimed that he wanted to add new justices to increase the Court's efficiency in dealing with a heavy work load. His real motive, however, was to pack the Court with justices favorable to his New Deal political and economic reforms. The Supreme Court had struck down, as unconstitutional, such New Deal programs as the National Industrial Recovery Act, the Railroad Retirement Act, and the Agricultural Adjustment Act.

Four justices, Willis Van Devanter, James McReynolds, George Sutherland, and Pierce Butler, were ardent opponents of the New Deal. Three justices had voted to uphold Roosevelt's program: Louis D. Brandeis, Harlan Fiske Stone, and Benjamin Cardozo. Chief Justice Charles Evans Hughes and Associate Justice Owen Roberts were swing voters; they sometimes upheld New Deal legislation, but they had voted to strike down several laws that they believed delegated too much power to New Deal agencies. None of these justices had been appointed by Roosevelt, who was the first President since James Monroe to serve a term without making any appointments.

President Roosevelt's court-packing plan was controversial. Opponents claimed he was trying to destroy the independence of the judiciary to gain political advantage. Roosevelt, however, pushed hard for Congress to pass his bill, and it seemed that he had the votes needed to do so.

In the midst of the struggle over the plan, Justices Hughes and Roberts voted to support several New Deal measures, including the Wagner Labor Relations Act and the Social Security Act. These votes were dubbed "the switch in time that saved nine." The momentum for the President's court-packing plan declined in the wake of the two decisions.

Realizing that his proposal was in trouble, Roosevelt accepted a compromise worked out by supporters in Congress. The President would make one additional appointment each year for every justice 75 or older. But it was too late to stem defections by congressional Democrats. On July 22, 1937, Roosevelt's court-packing plan was voted down by the Senate, 70 to 20. Although the retirement of several justices soon enabled Roosevelt to appoint a majority of the Court, defeat of his plan had shattered his congressional majority and halted the New Deal's legislative program. The coalition of conservative Democrats and Republicans forged during the Court plan fight remained the effective majority in Congress for the next two decades. SEE ALSO *Appointment power; New Deal; Roosevelt, Franklin D.*

SOURCES Leonard Baker, *Back to Back: The Duel between FDR and the Supreme*

Court (New York: Macmillan, 1967). William Leuchtenburg, "The Origins of Franklin D. Roosevelt's 'Court-Packing Plan,'" *Supreme Court Review* (1966): 347–400. William Leuchtenburg, *The Supreme Court Reborn: The Constitutional Revolution in the Age of Roosevelt* (New York: Oxford University Press, 1996). Michael Nelson, "The President and the Court: Reinterpreting the Court-packing Episode of 1937," *Political Science Quarterly* 103, no. 2 (1988): 267–93.

COURT REPORTERS

SEE *Reporter of decisions*

COURTS OF APPEALS

The U.S. Courts of Appeals are the middle level of the federal judicial system. They stand between the federal district courts at the bottom and the Supreme Court of the United States at the top.

The Courts of Appeals have no original jurisdiction; they do not hear the first trial of a case. They hear only cases on appeal from the lower courts. In turn, cases may be appealed from the Court of Appeal to the highest court, the Supreme Court.

At present, the United States and its territories are divided into 12 circuits, or geographical areas in which a court of appeals is located. There are appellate circuits numbered 1 through 11 plus the Court of Appeals for the District of Columbia. In addition, the Federal Courts Improvement Act of 1982 created the U.S. Court of Appeals for the Federal Circuit, which takes cases on appeal from such specialized lower courts as the Court of Claims, the Court of Customs and Patent Appeals, and the Court of Veterans Appeals. In 2000, 179 judges were authorized to serve on the Courts of Appeals. The U.S. Court of Appeals for the Ninth Circuit (West Coast) has 28 judges, the largest number. The U.S. Court of Appeals for the First Circuit (the New England states) has only 6 judges, the least number. All appellate court judges are appointed by the President with the advice and consent of the Senate, as provided by Article 2, Section 3, of the Constitution.

The U.S. Courts of Appeals have appellate jurisdiction—they review the decisions of lower courts—over two main types of cases. The first type involves civil and criminal case appeals from the federal district courts, including the U.S. territorial courts (in U.S. territories such as Guam and Puerto Rico) and special courts such as the U.S. Tax Court. The second type involves appeals by individuals of decisions made by federal administrative agencies and independent regulatory commissions, such as the National Labor Relations Board. Most cases that come to the Courts of Appeals are of the first type.

SEE ALSO *Circuit Courts of Appeals; Federal judicial system*

COXEY'S ARMY

The 1st Amendment amendment to the Constitution states that Congress shall not abridge the "right of the people peaceably to assemble, and to petition the Government for a redress of grievances." Whenever demonstrators have protested at the Capitol, Congress has had to balance the right of peaceful assembly against the need to maintain public safety. During the severe depression of 1893–94, Ohio businessman Jacob Coxey proposed that Congress enact a "good roads bill" to put people back to work building roads and other public works. When Congress failed to act, Coxey organized an "army" of unemployed men to march on Washington. "We'll send a petition to Washington with boots on," he declared. Coxey's army attracted much newspaper publicity, and eventually some 500 marchers reached Washington. Doubting the peaceable nature of the approaching mob, a fearful Congress called out the police and federal troops to stop the marchers before they reached the Capitol building. Jacob Coxey slipped through police lines and raced toward the Capitol steps, where he tried to speak. He was arrested, fined, and imprisoned for walking on the grass. Although unsuccessful, Coxey's army revealed the depth of unrest among the unemployed and their frustration with an unresponsive government.

SEE ALSO *Protest*

SOURCES Carlos Schwantes, *Coxey's Army: An American Odyssey* (Lincoln: University of Nebraska Press, 1985).

CREATION OF THE PRESIDENCY

The office of President of the United States was created at the Constitutional Convention of 1787. The framers had three options: to create a weak executive to administer the departments of government, whose powers would come solely from laws passed by Congress; to create a stronger executive that would be able to check and balance Congress; or to establish an executive with its own constitutional grants of power.

The Virginia Plan (designed by George Mason and James Madison of Virginia), with which delegates began their work, envisioned a weak plural executive that would be elected by Congress and subject to recall by a majority of state governors or state legislatures. In contrast, Alexander Hamilton proposed a supreme governor to be elected by the people or their delegates for life, with an absolute veto over laws passed by the legislature and armed with "Supreme Executive Power." The Constitutional Convention settled on a middle course, providing for an executive branch that could check the legislature. Eventually, it also accepted language that would allow the President to exercise vast constitutional powers on his own prerogative, without requiring Congress to pass laws giving him authority to act in many diplomatic or military matters.

Convention deliberations began with Robert Morris's motion, which carried unanimously, to make George Washington the presiding officer. It was obvious that delegates expected Washington to lead the new government. All deliberations about the powers of the executive were also debates about powers to be accorded to Washington. "The first man put at the helm will be a good one," Benjamin Franklin acknowledged; "nobody knows what sort may come afterwards."

The Virginia Plan created a "National Executive" consisting of several officials elected by Congress who would be vested with "general power to execute National laws," but it specified neither the length of the term nor the powers of the office. No person holding an executive office would be eligible to serve in Congress simultaneously, and Congress could not change the salary of the President during his term. Both of these provisions were designed to promote the separation of the executive and legislative branches that later appeared in the Constitution. The executive would have a check on laws passed by Congress, but that power would be shared by a Council of Revision consisting of members of the high court, called the "supreme tribunal." Congress could, however, pass a law over the veto. The members of the executive could be impeached, or tried for crimes, by the "supreme tribunal."

After two weeks of debate these provisions were replaced by an article that called for a single executive officer, chosen for a seven-year term by Congress, ineligible for reelection, with powers derived solely from laws passed by Congress and the ability to veto laws (though the veto could be overridden by a two-thirds vote of each house of Congress).

The Committee on Detail added several constitutional powers for the "President" (as the committee now referred to the executive). These powers sometimes were modified by floor debate and on other occasions by the Committee on Postponed Matters when the delegates could not come to an agreement. The President was to appoint officers not otherwise provided for by the Constitution, give Congress information on the state of the Union and recommend measures for its consideration, receive foreign ambassadors, grant reprieves and pardons to people convicted of crimes, convene Congress on extraordinary occasions, take care that the laws be faithfully executed, command the armed forces, and command the militia when it was called into federal service. The Constitution also provided for an oath of office. The Committee on Detail also provided that the House could impeach the President on the grounds of "treason, bribery or corruption" and the trial would be held by the Supreme Court.

The Committee on Postponed Matters turned the trial of a President over to the Senate. It also dropped the vague charge of "corruption," and the convention substituted for it the phrase "other High Crimes and Misdemeanors," which referred to serious abuses of Presidential power. The convention also raised the number of senators needed for conviction from a majority to two-thirds. After the Committee on Detail assigned the power to make treaties to the Senate rather than to the President, James Madison dissented, arguing that the President alone should have the power. The delegates referred the issue to the Committee on Postponed Matters, which split the difference: it decided that the President, with the advice and consent of two-thirds of the Senate, would make treaties. The committee also removed the power to appoint judges from the Senate and gave it to the President, subject to the advice and consent of the Senate.

Throughout the convention proponents of a strong Presidency argued for a short term of four years, no restrictions on eligibility for reelection, and a method that would remove selection from the legislature and make the President accountable to the people. At times an electoral college was proposed and once even briefly accepted, but on most occasions the convention rejected the idea and returned to legislative selection of the President. Eventually, the Committee on Postponed Matters incorporated the electoral college into the final draft of the Constitution. Its proposal to have the Senate elect a President in the event of an electoral college deadlock was changed after debate to a House contingency election; because the House was popularly elected, it was considered the more democratic chamber.

The Committee on Postponed Matters also provided that the President be 35 years old, a natural-born citizen (or a citizen at the time of the Constitution's adoption), and a resident of the United States for at least 14 years. The convention approved Charles Pinckney's motion that no religious test should be required or be part of the oath of office.

The Committee on Postponed Matters suggested the opening language of Article 2, that "the Executive Power of the United States shall be vested in a President of the United States." This wording made it clear that the powers of the office, especially the enumerated, or specified, powers that followed, were derived from the Constitution, not from legislation that might be passed by Congress. Thus Congress could not modify or rescind these powers, though Article 1, Section 8, would permit Congress to pass all laws "necessary and proper" for the President to carry out his constitutional powers. Moreover, the phrase "Executive Power" could itself be an open-ended grant of power that might be interpreted expansively by Presidents to include powers not specifically mentioned in the Constitution, such as the power to remove officials from office and the power to direct executive department secretaries.

At the Constitutional Convention the Committee on Style was chaired by Gouverneur Morris, an ally of Washington and a strong proponent of Presidential power. He left the "Executive Power" provision of Article 2 intact but provided in Article 1 that Congress could exercise only the legislative powers "herein granted." The difference in language between Article 1 and Article 2 is taken by proponents of a strong

Presidency to mean that the executive power may consist of more than the specific powers that follow in Article 2. The Committee on Style left the Constitution at key points ambiguous, incomplete, and undefined. Much of the subsequent history of the Presidency would involve the incumbent's claim that he had the power to act, refuted by critics' claims that his exercise of power was unconstitutional.

The unsettled issue of Presidential power was to trouble many of the delegates to state conventions to ratify the Constitution. "Your President may easily become a King," thundered Patrick Henry of Virginia, and he predicted "there will be no checks, no real balances in this government." James Monroe gloomily foresaw a President who might be reelected for life. In Paris, Thomas Jefferson noted tartly that "their President seems a bad edition of a Polish King" because he could be reelected indefinitely and commanded the armed forces. The Virginia and North Carolina conventions submitted proposed constitutional amendments to limit tenure in office to 8 years in any 16-year period.

Defenders of Article 2 tried to minimize the scope of Presidential powers that the Constitution had granted. They pointed out that the President could not become a king because there was no established church or aristocracy in the United States. The President did not appoint the Senate and was unlikely to combine with it in a conspiracy to usurp congressional power. He had no royal prerogatives, or privileges, and his limited diplomatic authority was subject to Senate approval. He would be nominated and elected by the electoral college to a short term in office and would remain accountable to the people.

SEE ALSO *Appointment power; Articles of Confederation; Checks and balances; Commander in chief; Electoral college; Eligibility for the Presidency; Executive power; Impeachment; Madison, James; Term of office, Presidential; Treaty powers; Veto power; War powers; Washington, George*

SOURCES Catherine Drinker Bowen, *Miracle at Philadelphia* (Boston: Little, Brown, 1966). Thomas Cronin, ed., *Inventing the American Presidency* (Lawrence: University Press of Kansas, 1989). Charles Thach, *The Creation of the Presidency* (Baltimore, Md.: Johns Hopkins University Press, 1922).

CREDIT MOBILIER SCANDAL (1872–73)

In the boom years after the Civil War, Congress made large land grants and appropriated funds to help the privately owned Union Pacific Railroad build a transcontinental railroad line. Union Pacific organized a construction company called Credit Mobilier to lay the track. Union Pacific's chief Washington agent, Representative Oakes Ames (Republican–Massachusetts), distributed stock in Credit Mobilier to key members of Congress, where, as he explained, "it will do the most good for us." The company expected that those members who got the stock would look favorably on the project and support the company's future needs. The story did not break in the newspapers until the Presidential election of 1872. "How the Credit Mobilier Bought Its Way Through Congress," read one headline in the *New York Sun*. The press revealed that stocks had gone to the Vice President, the Speaker of the House, and leading members of the House and Senate. House and Senate investigations led to the censure of Representatives Ames and James Brooks (Democrat–New York). The Credit Mobilier scandal damaged or destroyed many other political reputations and left a stigma of corruption on the Congress of the Gilded Age.

SEE ALSO *Scandals, congressional*
SOURCES W. Allan. Wilbur, "The Credit Mobilier Scandal, 1873," in *Congress Investigates: A Documented History, 1792–1974,* edited by Arthur M. Schlesinger, Jr.,

and Roger Bruns (New York: Bowker, 1975).

CRIMINAL LAW

The body of law that pertains to crimes against public authority—the federal or state governments, for example—is known as criminal law. These are the statutes that executive branch officials have the power to enforce. People who violate these laws may be apprehended by police and tried in a court of law. If convicted, they face the punishment prescribed by the trial court. If the convicted person feels that his constitutional rights have been violated, he may appeal the case to the Supreme Court.

SEE ALSO *Civil law; Rights of the accused*

CROCKETT, DAVID

* Born: Aug. 17, 1786, Greene County, Tenn.
* Political party: Whig
* Representative from Tennessee: 1827– 31, 1833–35
* Died: Mar. 6, 1836, San Antonio, Tex.

Perhaps the most colorful personality ever elected to Congress was the legendary bear hunter Davy Crockett, who represented Tennessee in the House of Representatives for three terms. Although he had commanded a battalion of riflemen under General Andrew Jackson in campaigns against the Creek Indians in 1813 and 1814, Crockett ran for office against Jackson's financial policies and became an outspoken Whig. The frontiersman Crockett often felt impatient with Congress's slow pace of business. "We generally lounge and squabble the greater part of the session, and crowd into a few days of the last term three or four times the business done during as many preceding months," he complained. When his constituents failed to reelect him, Crockett told them: "I am going to Texas and you can go to hell." He joined the Texans' struggle for independence from Mexico and died fighting at the Alamo.

SOURCES David Crockett, *A Narrative of the Life of David Crockett of the State of Tennessee* (Knoxville: University of Tennessee Press, 1973). James Atkins Shackford, *David Crockett: The Man and the Legend* (Chapel Hill: University of North Carolina Press, 1956).

CRUEL AND UNUSUAL PUNISHMENT

The 8th Amendment to the Constitution prohibits the government from inflicting "cruel and unusual punishments." Individuals are protected from inhumane punishments, such as torture, burning at the stake, or crucifixion. Further, any punishment considered too severe in relation to the crime committed has been judged by the Court as "cruel and unusual punishment." In *Weems* v. *United States* (1910), for example, the Court overturned a sentence of 12 to 20 years in chains for a person convicted of giving false testimony. The Court judged this sentence to be cruel and unusual punishment because the penalty was out of proportion to the crime.

In 1972, in *Furman* v. *Georgia,* the Court decided that the death penalty was cruel and unusual punishment. In 1976, however, the Court held in *Gregg* v. *Georgia* that the death penalty is not necessarily an example of cruel and unusual punishment as long as systematic procedures are followed to eliminate arbitrary or racially discriminatory use of capital punishment.

Chief Justice Earl Warren aptly described the intent of the ban against cruel and unusual punishment in *Trop* v. *Dulles* (1958): "The basic concept underlying the Eighth Amendment is nothing less than the dignity of man. While the State has the power to punish, the Amendment stands to assure that this power be exercised within the limits of civilized standards." Warren also discussed the relationship of the ban on cruel and unusual punishment to community standards: "The Court [has]

recognized ... that the words of the [Eighth] Amendment are not precise, and that their scope is not static. The Amendment draws its meaning from the evolving standards of decency that mark the progress of a maturing society."
SEE ALSO *Capital punishment; Furman v. Georgia*

C-SPAN

You can watch House and Senate debates on television over C-SPAN, the Cable Satellite Public Affairs Network. Beginning in 1979, the House of Representatives allowed television to cover its floor proceedings. The Senate opened its chamber to television in 1986. Since then, C-SPAN has broadcast the daily proceedings of the House and Senate "gavel to gavel"—that is, from the moment the presiding officer gavels the chamber into session to the moment it adjourns. C-SPAN was created and continues to be funded solely by the cable television industry. C-SPAN expanded the congressional galleries into millions of homes, allowing citizens to follow the floor debates as well as the more important committee hearings. Videotapes of the proceedings are deposited at the National Archives for future research use.
SOURCES Stephen Frantzich and John Sullivan. *The C-SPAN Revolution* (Norman: University of Oklahoma Press, 1996).

CUBAN MISSILE CRISIS

The Cuban Missile Crisis was a confrontation between the United States and the Soviet Union in October 1962 that threatened all-out nuclear war. The dispute involved the Soviet placement of intermediate-range ballistic missiles in Cuba.

On October 15, 1962, President John F. Kennedy received a briefing from intelligence advisers informing him that the Soviet Union was installing intermediate-range ballistic missiles, medium-range bombers, in Cuba and sending more

than 10,000 troops to that island nation. The Executive Committee of the National Security Council (known as Ex Comm) gave Kennedy four options. He could do nothing, use quiet diplomacy and not publicize the presence of the missiles, take the weapons out with an air strike, or impose a naval blockade against Cuba.

The "do nothing" option was not feasible because Congress had already passed a joint resolution backing military action if offensive weapons were found in Cuba, and Republicans were using the possibility of the existence of such weapons against Democrats in the upcoming midterm (1962) congressional elections. Six members of the Ex Comm favored an air strike. Kennedy decided against it because he thought American allies in Europe would not approve until other alternatives had been tried. Attorney General Robert Kennedy argued against bombing, calling the tactic "a Pearl Harbor in reverse." The State Department legal adviser argued that bombing would be a violation of international law. Moreover, there were logistical concerns. The bombing could not be done by a single "surgical" strike; 500 or more missions would be required, destroying hundreds of targets to prevent missiles or aircraft from attacking the United States. The magnitude of the operation would lead to high casualties (provoking international outrage) and losses among the Soviet military, which might bring on military action by its forces against the United States.

On October 17 Kennedy decided on a blockade, or "quarantine," as his advisers called it, because a blockade is prohibited under international law unless a nation is at war. It would begin only with further shipments of missiles but if necessary could expand to cover civilian goods. Implementing it in stages would permit time for diplomacy to work. The quarantine would take place near American waters, where the United States had overwhelming naval superiority.

On October 22 Kennedy gave a televised speech to the nation in which he called the presence of the missiles "a change in the status quo which cannot be accepted by this country if our courage and our commitments are ever to be trusted again, by friend or foe." He described the threat to the United States, saying that "the purpose of these bases can be none other than to provide a nuclear strike capability against the Western Hemisphere." He announced the quarantine and warned the Soviet Union that "it will be the policy of the United States Government to regard any missile launched from Cuba against any nation in the Western Hemisphere as an attack upon the United States by the Soviet Union, requiring a full retaliatory response." Soviet ships attempting to enter Cuban waters would be subject to search in international waters, and if Soviet ships tried to run the blockade, Kennedy would order American ships to fire on them. The following day the Council of the Organization of American States unanimously backed Kennedy's quarantine.

For several days Soviet ships headed toward the blockade line and work on missile sites in Cuba accelerated. Then the ships stopped dead in the water, leading the members of the Ex Comm to think that the crisis was over. But one ship started again toward Cuba, and a Soviet air-defense missile battery shot down an American U-2 reconnaissance plane flying over Cuba, heating the crisis up again.

The crisis was finally resolved by negotiations between President Kennedy and Soviet chairman Nikita Khrushchev. Khrushchev offered to remove the missiles if the President would pledge that the United States would not invade Cuba. Kennedy hinted, through Attorney General Robert Kennedy, that if the Soviets ended the crisis, the United States would remove intermediate-range missiles from bases in Turkey. On October 28, the Soviets agreed to withdraw their missiles (and accepted verification by United Nations observers). The United States ended the quarantine and pledged not to invade Cuba.

The Soviets withdrew 42 missiles and 42 long-range bombers as well as 5,000 troops. They also removed weapons that the United States did not know were on the island: 9 short-range missiles equipped with nuclear warheads, which would have been used in case of an American invasion, and 36 nuclear warheads for use on the medium-range Soviet missiles. The short-range missiles could have been fired by local commanders, without authorization from Moscow, a possibility of which the American side was completely unaware. After the crisis ended, the Soviets kept in Cuba 37,000 of the 42,000 troops already there—a number far higher than American estimates during the crisis—as well as fighter planes and antimissile weapons. (The size of the Soviet commitments was not revealed to the American side until Soviet and American officials who had been involved in the crisis held a series of meetings between 1987 and 1992.)

American intermediate-range Jupiter missiles were withdrawn from Turkey and Italy. Kennedy pledged not to invade Cuba, but on December 14, 1962, he wrote to Khrushchev that the United States would require "adequate assurances that all offensive weapons are removed from Cuba and are not reintroduced, and that Cuba itself commits no aggressive acts against any of the nations of the Western Hemisphere." He thus left open the possibility that the United States might invade Cuba if these assurances were not received.

SEE ALSO *Kennedy, John F.; National Security Council*

SOURCES Graham Allison, *Essence of Decision: The Cuban Missile Crisis* (Boston: Little, Brown, 1971). James Bright and David Welch, *On the Brink: America and Soviets Reexamine the Cuban Missile Crisis* (New York: Hill & Wang, 1991).

CURATOR, OFFICE OF THE

SEE *Staff of the Supreme Court, nonjudicial*

CURTIS, BENJAMIN R.
Associate Justice, 1851–57

- Born: Nov. 4, 1809, Watertown, Mass.
- Education: Harvard College, A.B., 1829; Harvard Law School, LL.B., 1832
- Previous government service: Massachusetts state representative, 1849–51
- Appointed by President Millard Fillmore as a recess appointment Sept. 22, 1851; replaced Levi Woodbury, who died; nominated by Fillmore Dec. 11, 1851
- Supreme Court term: confirmed by the Senate Dec. 20, 1851, by a voice vote; resigned Sept. 30, 1857
- Died: Sept. 15, 1874, Newport, R.I.

Benjamin R. Curtis served only six years as an associate justice of the U.S. Supreme Court. But his dissent in the Dred Scott case is a lasting monument of the struggle for equal rights by African Americans.

Dred Scott, a slave, brought suit against his master, claiming himself a free man because he had lived in areas that banned slavery. The Court decided against Scott and ruled that he had no right to bring a suit to the federal courts.

Justice Curtis disagreed with every major point of the majority opinion in Scott v. Sandford (1857). He argued that African Americans could be citizens of the United States, although the majority argued that slaves were merely property. If so, they had the right to bring suits to the federal courts. Curtis also held that the federal government had authority under the Constitution to regulate or prevent slavery in territories of the United States. By contrast, Chief Justice Roger Taney's argument for the Court was an attempt to protect slavery against federal government regulation and to deny all constitutional rights to African Americans.

Taney's ideas prevailed in the Dred Scott case, but Curtis won in the long run. The 14th Amendment, ratified in 1868, embodies Curtis's ideas about citizenship and constitutional rights. Today, Taney's

opinion in the Dred Scott case is generally viewed as one of the worst decisions in the history of the Court.

Curtis left the Court a few months after the Dred Scott decision. This case caused serious conflict and hostility between Curtis and his associates on the Court. He decided he could no longer work comfortably and cooperatively with Chief Justice Taney and some other justices, and so he resigned.

Curtis returned to the practice of law and continued to attract national attention for his achievements. In 1868, for example, he successfully defended President Andrew Johnson in his impeachment trial. He also argued more than 50 cases before the U.S. Supreme Court.

SEE ALSO Scott v. Sandford
SOURCES Don E. Fehrenbacher, The Dred Scott Case (New York: Oxford University Press, 1978).

CURTIS, CHARLES
Vice President

- Born: Jan. 25, 1860, North Topeka, Kans.
- Political party: Republican
- Education: read law, 1879–82
- Military service: none
- Previous government service: county attorney, Shawnee County, Kans., 1885–91; U.S. House of Representatives, 1893–1907; U.S. Senate, 1907–13, 1915–29
- Vice President under Herbert Hoover, 1929–33
- Died: Feb. 8, 1936, Washington, D.C.

Charles Curtis had an Indian grandparent and was born on an Indian reservation in Kansas. He dropped out of high school to study law privately and was admitted to the bar in 1879. After serving as county attorney for Shawnee County, he served seven terms in the House of Representatives. Elected to the U.S. Senate in 1906, he was defeated for reelection in 1912 but then elected again in 1914. His congressional career involved a steady rise in influence; though he authored few bills, his mastery of legislative politics made him a natural leader in efforts to pass Republican programs. He became Senate whip in 1915 and majority leader in 1924. President Calvin Coolidge was unimpressed with Curtis and rebuffed his efforts to win the Vice Presidential nomination in 1924.

Curtis ran for the Republican Presidential nomination in 1928 as a favorite son from Kansas. Herbert Hoover, the eventual nominee, chose Curtis as his running mate in a bid for party unity and to attract votes from Midwestern farmers. The ticket was the first in American history on which both candidates came from states west of the Mississippi.

Curtis played next to no role in the Hoover administration, because the President never asked him to join in cabinet meetings or gave him any assignments, and their relationship was always strained. Curtis was nominated for a second term in 1932, but after the ticket's defeat he retired from politics to practice law in Washington, D.C.

SOURCES Marvin Ewy, *Charles Curtis of Kansas: Vice President of the United States, 1929–1933* (Emporia: Kansas State Teachers College, 1961).

CUSHING, WILLIAM
Associate Justice, 1790–1810

- Born: Mar. 1, 1732, Scituate, Mass.
- Education: Harvard College, A.B.,

1751, M.A., 1754; Yale University, M.A., 1753 studied law under Jeremiah Gridley, Boston
- Previous government service: judge, probate court for Lincoln, Mass. (now Maine), 1760–61; judge, Superior Court of Massachusetts Bay Province, 1772–77; chief justice, Superior Court of the Commonwealth of Massachusetts, 1777–89; Massachusetts Constitutional Convention, 1779; vice president, Massachusetts Ratifying Convention, 1788; delegate to the electoral college, 1788
- Appointed by President George Washington Sept. 24, 1789, to fill one of the original six seats on the U.S. Supreme Court
- Supreme Court term: confirmed by the Senate Sept. 26, 1789, by a voice vote; served until Sept. 13, 1810
- Died: Sept. 13, 1810, Scituate, Mass.

William Cushing was an original member of the U.S. Supreme Court. He was the last judge in the United States to wear a full wig, a traditional adornment for British judges. Cushing did not stop wearing his wig until 1790.

Justice Cushing served 21 years on the Court, the longest term of President George Washington's original appointments, but wrote only 19 opinions. His most important opinion, *Ware v. Hylton* (1796), agreed with the Court's majority that a federal treaty cannot be violated by a state law.

SEE ALSO *Ware v. Hylton*

D

DAILY DIGEST

At the back of each daily issue of the *Congressional Record* is the Daily Digest. Since 1947 the Digest has served as a handy index to the *Record*, listing the bills and resolutions introduced and what measures were passed or rejected in each chamber and giving the page numbers where the reports can be found. The Daily Digest also lists all nominations received, confirmed, or rejected, together with page references to messages from the President, amendments, cosponsors, and related information. In addition to floor activities, the Daily Digest catalogs the previous day's committee meetings, including a brief description of topics of hearings, witnesses, and votes. The Digest concludes with announcements of the hearings that will be held the next day, listing the subject, time, and location of these meetings.

SEE ALSO *Congressional Record*

DALLAS, GEORGE
Vice President

- Born: July 10, 1792, Philadelphia, Pa.
- Education: College of New Jersey (Princeton), B.A., 1810
- Political party: Democrat
- Military service: none
- Previous government service: diplomatic mission to Russia, 1813; lawyer, Bank of the United States, 1815–17; U.S. Senate, 1831–32; attorney general of Pennsylvania, 1833–35; ambassador to Russia, 1837–39

- Vice President under James K. Polk, 1845–49
- Subsequent government service: ambassador to Great Britain, 1856–60
- Died: Dec. 31, 1864, Philadelphia, Pa.

In 1844 the Democratic national convention unanimously chose Silas Wright of New York to be its Vice Presidential nominee, but for the first and only time in American history, a candidate declined a major party nomination. George Dallas was nominated to take his place.

During his term Dallas broke several tie votes in the Senate in favor of tariff cuts. He also backed President James K. Polk's expansionist policies in Oregon and in the Southwest during the Mexican-American War. Polk broke with Dallas when he refused to accept Dallas's suggestions for judicial and other appointments, and he kept Dallas off the ticket in 1848. In gratitude for his support for the annexation of Texas, the city of Dallas was named for him in 1846. Dallas closed out his government career as ambassador to Great Britain from 1856 to 1860 under President James Buchanan.

SOURCES John M. Belohlavek, *George Mifflin Dallas: Jacksonian Patrician* (University Park: Pennsylvania State University Press, 1977).

DANIEL, PETER V.
Associate Justice, 1842–60

- Born: Apr. 24, 1784, Stafford County, Va.
- Education: College of New Jersey

(Princeton), 1802–3; studied law with Edmund Randolph in Richmond, Va.

- Previous government service: Virginia House of Delegates, 1809–12; Virginia Privy Council, 1812–35; lieutenant governor of Virginia, 1818–35; U.S. district judge, Eastern District of Virginia, 1836–41
- Appointed by President Martin Van Buren Feb. 26, 1841; replaced Philip Barbour, who died
- Supreme Court term: confirmed by the Senate Mar. 2, 1841, by a 22–5 vote; served until May 31, 1860
- Died: May 31, 1860, Richmond, Va.

Peter V. Daniel was a loyal supporter of Andrew Jackson and the Democratic party. After becoming President, Andrew Jackson rewarded Daniel with an appointment to the federal judiciary in Virginia.

Daniel continued his support of the Democrats and was appointed to the U.S. Supreme Court by President Martin Van Buren. Justice Daniel tended to support the rights and powers of state governments in cases regarding the exercise of power in the federal system.

SOURCES John P. Frank, *Justice Daniel Dissenting* (Cambridge: Harvard University Press, 1964).

DARK HORSE, PRESIDENTIAL

A dark horse is a candidate for the Presidential nomination who trails far behind the favorites going into a national convention. The dark horse may be the second or third choice of many delegates but the first choice of few. The strategy of the dark horse is to block the favorite and create a deadlock among the front-runners.

James K. Polk was the first dark horse, winning the Democratic nomination in 1844 on the 9th ballot. Franklin Pierce won the Democratic nomination on the 49th ballot in 1852. In 1876 Rutherford B. Hayes won the Republican nomination on the 7th ballot. Recent Republican dark

horses have included Warren G. Harding in 1920 and Wendell Willkie in 1940. All but Willkie won the Presidency.

Changes in party rules have diminished the role of the nominating conventions in choosing Presidential candidates. Today they tend to function as events that officially record the preferences of voters in state primaries and caucuses. It is highly unlikely that a national convention will choose a dark-horse candidate in the future.

SEE ALSO *Caucuses, Presidential nominating; Nominating conventions, Presidential; Primaries, Presidential*

DARTMOUTH COLLEGE V. WOODWARD

- 4 Wheat. 518 (1819)
- Vote: 5–1
- For the Court: Marshall
- Concurring: Story and Washington
- Dissenting: Duvall

Dartmouth College was established in 1769 by a charter from King George III of England. After the formation of the United States, the agreement with the king became an agreement with the state of New Hampshire. In 1816 that state's legislature passed several amendments to the college's charter. By placing the school under the authority of the state government, these amendments had the effect of changing the private college into a state university.

Officials and friends of Dartmouth College objected. They believed the state legislature should not possess the authority to destroy the private nature of their college.

The Issue Daniel Webster, arguing for the Dartmouth College trustees, maintained that the legislature had violated Article 1, Section 10, of the Constitution, which provides that "no State shall . . . pass any . . . Law impairing the Obligation of Contracts." In an 1810 case (*Fletcher v. Peck*), the Supreme Court had ruled that a land grant is a contract. Webster now argued that "a grant of corporate powers and privileges is as much a contract as a grant of land."

Is a charter a contract? Did the Constitution's contract clause protect private corporate charters, such as Dartmouth's?

Opinion of the Court The Supreme Court ruled in favor of Dartmouth College. Chief Justice John Marshall's opinion held that the charter of a private corporation was a contract. Thus, the Constitution forbade the state legislature from changing that agreement. For the first time, the Court extended the protection of the Constitution's contract clause to a corporate charter. Marshall intended this ruling to be an important limitation on the powers and rights of state governments within the federal Union.

Dissent Justice Gabriel Duvall dissented in this case. However, he did not file an opinion.

Significance The decision increased the power of the federal government over the states. It reaffirmed that the U.S. Supreme Court could invalidate state laws when it found those laws unconstitutional. Further, the case reinforced the practice begun by *Fletcher* v. *Peck* of imposing restrictions upon state legislatures with regard to the regulation of corporations. The national government would not allow state legislatures to void or change existing charters because to do so would violate the contract clause of Article 1, Section 9, of the Constitution.

The *Dartmouth College* decision did not attract the attention of the press at the time. Yet it deserves recognition as one of the early Court's important decisions. Business corporations were just forming in a young nation, and the Court's decision gave these businesses security against unexpected legislative interference.

Such security was vital to those who might invest money in new industries and corporations. Investors could be sure that any rights granted a corporation by one state legislature could not be taken away by some future legislature. Such assurances

encouraged investment in railroads and other new industries, which in turn stimulated the country's economic development. The *Dartmouth College* case did not, however, prevent states from regulating corporations. The decision merely held that a state government could not alter corporate charters it had already granted, unless the state reserved the right to do so when it initially granted the charter.

After the resolution of the *Dartmouth College* case, many state legislatures placed restrictions on companies they chartered. These new corporate charters often contained clauses allowing the state, under certain circumstances, to revoke the charters or to buy the companies. Nevertheless, the *Dartmouth College* decision encouraged investors by assuring them that the Supreme Court would regulate state grants and charters and that after the granting of a charter, the grantees could expect the courts to protect their rights.

SEE ALSO *Contract clause; Federalism; Fletcher v. Peck*

SOURCES Richard N. Current, "The Dartmouth College Case," in *Quarrels That Have Shaped the Constitution*, edited by John A. Garraty (New York: Harper & Row, 1987).

DASCHLE, TOM

- Born: Dec. 9, 1947, Aberdeen, S.D.
- Political party: Democrat
- Representative from South Dakota: 1979–87
- House majority whip-at-large: 1982–86
- Senator from South Dakota: 1987–
- Senate minority leader: 1994–

Tom Daschle was elected leader of the Senate Democrats just as they lost the majority in 1994. The rules of the Senate made it easier to be a minority leader than a majority leader. "It doesn't take much to stop stuff here," Daschle pointed out, "—it's getting things passed that's hard." But Senate Democrats were not content with blocking Republican initiatives. They wanted to assist President Bill Clinton in enacting his legislative agenda.

Tom Daschle knew his way around Capitol Hill, having come to the Senate in 1973 as a legislative assistant to his home state senator, James Abourezk. He returned to South Dakota to win a seat in the House and served in his party's leadership as majority whip-at-large. When he went to the Senate, Daschle became co-chairman of the Democratic Policy Committee. Both positions involved planning legislative strategy and maintaining party unity, training that well prepared him to become his party's floor leader.

Daschle was personally close to President Clinton, with whom he frequently jogged in the morning, and the President learned to trust his advice. As minority leader, Daschle proved successful in keeping his party's senators together to prevent the majority from invoking cloture to cut off a debate and to prevent the Senate from overriding the President's vetoes. But Daschle also helped Senate Democrats switch from the defense to the offense by crafting amendments they could attach to Republican legislation. This way, the minority was able to promote issues it considered essential, such as raising the minimum wage and protecting safe drinking water. The Democrats also introduced some bills they knew would not pass. "We're in the minority, we know that," Daschle explained. "But it's important to let the American people know what the Democrats might have done if we were in the majority."

DATA SYSTEMS OFFICE OF THE SUPREME COURT

The Data Systems Office maintains the technological facilities and equipment, such as computers, printers, and photocopy machines, for the Supreme Court. The office electronically transmits opinions of the Court to outside agencies.

Court documents are processed (typed, printed, and copied) for the justices through the Data Systems Office. In addition, the office works with the Public Information Office to electronically transmit the bench copies of the Court's opinions to organizations outside the Court.

DAVIS, DAVID
Associate Justice, 1862–77

- Born: Mar. 9, 1815, Sassafras Neck, Md.
- Education: Kenyon College, B.A., 1832; Yale Law School, 1835
- Previous government service: Illinois House of Representatives, 1845–47; Illinois Constitutional Convention, 1847; Illinois State circuit court judge, 1848–62
- Appointed by President Abraham Lincoln as a recess appointment Oct. 17, 1862; replaced John A. Campbell, who resigned; nominated by Lincoln Dec. 1, 1862
- Supreme Court term: confirmed by the Senate Dec. 8, 1862, by a voice vote; resigned Mar. 4, 1877
- Died: June 26, 1886, Bloomington, Ill.

David Davis practiced law in Illinois, where he met Abraham Lincoln. Their friendship had a strong influence on Davis's career. He supported Lincoln's losing 1854 campaign for the U.S. Senate. Davis was Lincoln's campaign manager in 1860, when Lincoln won the Republican nomination for the Presidency and became the 16th President of the United States. In 1862, Lincoln appointed Davis to the Supreme Court.

Davis's outstanding contribution as an associate justice was his opinion for the Court in *Ex parte Milligan* (1866), a landmark decision. In the *Milligan* case, the Court decided that a military court in Indiana, created by order of the President, had illegally tried and convicted a man for the crime of aiding the Confederacy during the Civil War. Justice Davis argued that Indiana had not been a war zone and the civilian courts had remained open. Therefore, it was a denial of Milligan's constitutional rights to try him in a military court. Davis concluded that the Constitution could not be suspended in a national crisis, not even during a civil war, and that the Constitution was "a law for rulers and people, equally in time of war and peace."

SEE ALSO *Ex parte Milligan*

DAVIS, JEFFERSON

- Born: June 3, 1808, Fairview, Ky.
- Political party: Democrat
- Education: St. Thomas College; Jefferson College; Wilkinson County Academy; Transylvania University; United States Military Academy, graduated, 1828
- Representative from Mississippi: 1845–46
- Senator from Mississippi: 1847–51, 1857–61
- President of the Confederate States of America: 1861–65
- Died: Dec. 6, 1889, New Orleans, La.

"I have an infirmity of which I am ashamed," Senator Jefferson Davis once admitted. "When I am aroused in a matter, I lose control of my feeling and become personal." A West Point graduate with military bearing and self-control, Davis could turn hot-tempered, ready to challenge an opponent to a duel. As the leading spokesman for the South in Congress just before the Civil War, Davis showed these contradictory tendencies. He denounced Northern "disunionists" but talked of secession to protect Southern interests. As the South moved toward secession, Davis joined the Committee of Thirteen to find a compromise to keep the nation united. But when Mississippi left the Union, Davis knew he must resign and return home. On January 21, 1861, he spoke in the Senate for the last time, forgiving his opponents for their offenses toward him and offering his apologies for any offenses he had given them. Applauded from both sides of the aisle, Davis left the Senate chamber looking "inexpressively sad." A month later he became President of the Confederacy.

SOURCES William C. Davis, *Jefferson Davis: The Man and His Hour* (New York: HarperCollins, 1991).

DAWES, CHARLES
Vice President

- Born: Aug. 27, 1865, Marietta, Ohio
- Education: Marietta College, B.A., 1884; Cincinnati Law School, LL.B., 1886
- Political party: Republican
- Military service: U.S. Army, 1918–19
- Previous government service: comptroller of the currency, 1898–1902; director, Bureau of the Budget, 1921–23
- Vice President under Calvin Coolidge, 1925–29
- Subsequent government service: Commission to Santo Domingo, 1929; ambassador to Great Britain, 1929–32; delegate to London Naval Conference, 1930; president, Reconstruction Finance Corporation, 1932
- Died: Apr. 23, 1951, Evanston, Ill.

Charles Dawes was a successful banker and one of the most distinguished public servants the United States has ever produced. He began his career as a lawyer for utility companies in the Midwest. He was appointed comptroller of the currency in 1898 and served until 1902. That year, he organized the Central Trust Company of Illinois, remaining president until 1921 and serving as honorary chair until 1931.

Dawes was a brigadier general in World War I, directing supply efforts for American troops. He then served as the first director of the federal Bureau of the Budget, bringing businesslike methods to budgeting for cabinet departments. "Cabinet secretaries are Vice-Presidents in charge of spending, and as such are the natural enemies of the President," he concluded about his work. He was appointed by the Allied Reparations Commission in 1923 to help devise a financial plan for Germany. The Dawes Plan, a revised schedule of war reparations for Germany—payments to the victorious Allied nations—was adopted in 1924 to much international acclaim, and Dawes shared the Nobel Peace Prize for 1925 with British foreign secretary Sir Austen Chamberlain.

Calvin Coolidge chose Dawes to be his running mate in 1924, and the ticket swept to a huge victory. Dawes expected to be an active Vice President but was given no assignments by Coolidge. Dawes himself told Coolidge that he did not wish to attend cabinet meetings. The two men never established any rapport. As presiding officer of the Senate, Dawes attempted to overhaul its rules but met with failure. He wrote a diary of each day's events in office, *Notes as Vice President, 1928–29,* which was published in 1935. Coolidge blocked Dawes's efforts to gain support of Republican politicians for the Presidential nomination in 1928.

President Herbert Hoover appointed Dawes ambassador to Great Britain in 1929 and made him president of the Reconstruction Finance Corporation in 1932, where he spearheaded attempts to combat the Great Depression. After leaving office Dawes served as chairman of City National Bank and Trust Company of Chicago.

SOURCES Charles Dawes, *Notes as Vice President, 1928–29* (Boston: Little, Brown, 1935).

DAY, WILLIAM R.
Associate Justice, 1903–22

- Born: Apr. 17, 1849, Ravenna, Ohio
- Education: University of Michigan, B.A., 1870; University of Michigan Law School, 1871–72
- Other government service: judge, Court of Common Pleas, Canton, Ohio, 1886–90; first assistant U.S. secretary of state, 1897–98; U.S. secretary of state, 1898; U.S. delegation, Paris Peace Conference, 1898–99; judge, U.S. Court of Appeals for the Sixth Circuit,

1899–1903; umpire, Mixed Claims Commission, 1922–23
- Appointed by President Theodore Roosevelt Feb. 19, 1903; replaced George Shiras, Jr., who resigned
- Supreme Court term: confirmed by the Senate Feb. 23, 1903, by a voice vote; resigned Nov. 13, 1922
- Died: July 9, 1923, Mackinac Island, Mich.

William R. Day became a prominent lawyer and Republican party leader in Ohio. He developed a close friendship with William McKinley, who relied upon Day for support and advice. After McKinley became President, he appointed Day assistant secretary of state and later secretary of state. In 1899, McKinley further rewarded Day with an appointment to the U.S. Court of Appeals for the Sixth Circuit. McKinley's successor as President, Theodore Roosevelt, named Day to the Supreme Court.

During his 19 years on the Court, Justice Day tended to be an advocate for state powers and rights in the federal system. However, Day did support the power of the federal government to regulate businesses under the Sherman Anti-Trust Act. SOURCES Joseph E. McLean, *William Rufus Day: Supreme Court Justice from Ohio* (Baltimore: Johns Hopkins University Press, 1946).

"DEAR COLLEAGUE" LETTERS

To alert fellow members of Congress to a particular issue or event, or encourage them to cosponsor legislation, senators and representatives send out "Dear Colleague" letters. These form letters are circulated through internal mail (rather than through the postal system) to all members' offices. "Dear Colleague" letters identify the sender with a certain issue and form an important unofficial link in the information chain around Capitol Hill.

SEE ALSO *Sponsoring and cosponsoring legislation*

DEATH IN OFFICE, PRESIDENTIAL

SEE *Garfield, James A.; Harding, Warren G.; Harrison, William Henry; Kennedy, John F.; Lincoln, Abraham; McKinley, William; Roosevelt, Franklin D.; Succession to the Presidency; Taylor, Zachary; 22nd Amendment*

DEATH PENALTY

SEE *Capital punishment*

DEBATES, CONGRESSIONAL

Debates in Congress are aimed at winning votes from other members, swaying public opinion, forcing the opposition into politically embarrassing positions, and establishing a record of legislative intentions. Under the "speech and debate" clause of the Constitution (Article 1, Section 6), any member can speak on any issue in Congress without fear of being prosecuted for libel or slander (that is, defaming someone else's character).

Beginning in the 1840s, the growing size of the House caused representatives to adopt rules that limited debate. Under House rules, no member can hold the floor for more than an hour. During some debates members are allowed only five minutes to speak. Often the House considers a bill under a "suspension of the rules," which limits the entire debate on a bill, by both sides, to 40 minutes. By contrast, the Senate, which is smaller, has retained unlimited debate, allowing members to speak as long as they feel necessary on any issue. However, when senators filibuster, or speak excessively in order to block passage of a bill, a vote of three-fifths of the Senate can enact cloture, which cuts off debate and forces a vote.

Many observers have questioned whether speeches really change any votes.

In 1806, Senator William Plumer (Federalist–New Hampshire) commented, "I have for some time been convinced that speeches in the Senate in most cases have very little influence upon the vote." And in 1820, former President Thomas Jefferson complained, "If the present Congress err in too much talking, how can it be otherwise, in a body to which the people send 150 lawyers, whose trade is to question everything, yield nothing, and talk by the hour?"

SEE ALSO *Decorum, congressional; Filibuster; Oratory, congressional*

DEBATES, PRESIDENTIAL

Televised debates were held between the major candidates for President in 1960 and in every election since 1976. A panel of reporters acceptable to the candidates questions them, and they are given time to rebut their opponents' statements. Debates are also held between Vice Presidential candidates. Originally sponsored by the League of Women Voters and the television networks, Presidential debates are now organized by the Commission on Presidential Debates, a bipartisan group created by Congress.

Presidential debates attract huge television audiences: 107 million adults in 1960, 122 million in 1976, and more than 100 million in 1980 and 1984. Only 70 million people watched in 1988, reflecting a decline in enthusiasm for the candidates. But in 1992, thanks to interest in independent candidate Ross Perot, the three Presidential debates attracted more viewers than ever before; more than 130 million Americans watched one or more. This was the first debate in which both major-party candidates appeared at the same time as an independent third candidate. The debates gave Perot's campaign a major boost, especially among independent voters. Debates raise voter interest and provide information about the candidates and their response under pressure. In close contests many voters wait for the debates before deciding for whom to vote. This is especially true of independents, voters not registered as members of a political party, and those without strong feelings for their party. Those who watch debates tend to vote on the basis of the issues, whereas those who do not watch are more likely to vote on the basis of personality. The media not only report on the debates but also announce the "winner." This verdict may also affect voter behavior as people jump on the "winner's" bandwagon.

Polls showed that in 1960 four million voters based their vote on the debates. Of these, John F. Kennedy won 72 percent, helping him into the White House. In 1980 Ronald Reagan gained ground with undecided voters and political independents, helping him defeat Jimmy Carter. In 1988 George Bush lost some of his lead after the first debate and neither gained nor lost any of his lead over Michael Dukakis after their second debate—a victory for Bush because Dukakis was trailing and needed to score a "knockout."

After the 1960 debates between Kennedy and Richard Nixon, none were held in 1964, 1968, and 1972 because in each instance one of the candidates was clearly ahead and felt he had nothing to gain. In 1976 debates resumed: President Gerald Ford wanted to debate because he was behind in the polls and had nothing to lose, and Jimmy Carter wanted debates because his lead had begun to slip. By 1984 debates had become an institution, and a candidate could not avoid them without making his refusal an issue in its own right.

Candidates can use debates to overcome negative perceptions about them, as Kennedy did when his performance changed people's opinions about his youth. Candidates can defuse issues in debates, as Ronald Reagan did when he joked, "I will not make an issue of my opponent's youth and inexperience." Debates can also torpedo a campaign, as when Walter Mondale announced in a 1984 debate against Reagan that if elected, he would raise taxes. In 1980 Ronald Reagan's performance against Jimmy Carter was aided by the fact that his campaign had obtained one of the "briefing books" that Carter used to prepare for the debates, so he knew what Carter would say and could prepare his rebuttals in advance.

SEE ALSO *Bush, George; Carter, Jimmy; Clinton, Bill; Ford, Gerald R.; Kennedy, John F.; Nixon, Richard M.; Reagan, Ronald* SOURCES Kathleen Jamieson and David Birdsell, *Presidential Debates: The Challenge of Creating an Informed Electorate* (New York: Oxford University Press, 1988). Austin Ranney, ed., *The Past, Present and Future of Presidential Debates* (Washington, D.C.: American Enterprise Institute, 1979).

DECISION DAYS

The Supreme Court's decisions on cases are announced orally to the public in the Supreme Court chamber (courtroom). The justice who wrote the Court's opinion on the case announces the decision. Justices who wrote concurring or dissenting opinions may also state their position. The writers of the opinions may either briefly summarize their positions or simply state the result.

From 1857 until 1965 the Court followed a tradition of announcing decisions only on Mondays. But on April 15, 1965, the Court announced that it was ending the "Decision Monday" tradition. Now, in weeks when the Court hears oral arguments, opinions are announced on Tuesdays and Wednesdays. During other weeks, decisions are announced on Mondays.

DECISION MAKING, PRESIDENTIAL

A successful Presidential decision is one that wins White House, public, and congressional support. Politically, a decision that unites the President's party and divides the opposition is much better than a decision that splits his own party and unites his opponents. When President Bill Clinton attempted to end the military ban on homosexuals in his first week in office, he failed to gain a consensus within his own party and quickly agreed to a compromise. When he pushed for a family leave law (allowing workers to take time off from their jobs for a new baby or for a family emergency), Clinton unified his party, put the opposition on the defensive, and won a major victory early in his term.

Each Presidential decision, therefore, can be considered part of the game of politics. Decisions Presidents make not only affect the immediate problems they are trying to solve but also affect their power to make decisions on future issues, in much the same way that a move in chess or checkers affects the rest of the game. For example, when John Kennedy was negotiating with Soviet premier Nikita Khrushchev in the Cuban Missile Crisis, his decisions had an impact on Soviet-American relations long after the crisis was resolved. Kennedy's willingness to make a deal with the Soviets paved the way for the Test-Ban Treaty of 1963.

Some Presidents make decisions based on the national interest and then work out the strategy and tactics to get Congress and the bureaucracy to implement them; others seem to make decisions by determining what is best for them. When Jimmy Carter told Congress he would veto bills containing unnecessary "pork barrel" public works projects, he was attempting to act in the national interest, yet he antagonized members of Congress (even members of his own party), who delayed working on much of his legislative program in retaliation until Carter gave in and approved their pet projects. Yet if a president does not lead the nation in the public interest, who else can or will? When President Clinton called for sacrifice from all Americans to reduce the deficit in his first address to Congress in 1993, he was not doing the popular thing, but most observers applauded him for acting in the national interest.

Some political scientists have argued that what is in the political interest of the President is in the interest of the entire nation. A President, in their view, should always do what is best for himself because that will result in the most viable public policy. This argument can be taken too far: few people would argue that Richard Nixon's actions in covering up the Watergate crimes of his aides was in the national interest. Moreover, the argument ignores the basic principles of the Constitution. Ours is a government of separate institutions sharing the power of decision in making public policy. If the President acts unilaterally and claims he has done so in the public interest, what role is there for Congress or the courts? In any event, Congress does not accept the idea that the President's decisions are the last word on the public interest. And the Supreme Court, at times, has checked Presidential assertions of power, as it did when it ordered Harry Truman to return to their owners the steel mills he had seized during the Korean War.

Presidents do not always act rationally when they make decisions, nor do they always make decisions in their own interest, let alone the national interest. A President might ignore, discount, deny, or misinterpret information that contradicted his own beliefs. John Kennedy, in the first stages of the Cuban Missile Crisis, simply could not believe the Soviets would go back on their promises to him and place missiles in Cuba. The Soviets had several additional weeks to construct their missile facilities until reconnaissance photos convinced the skeptical President. A President might procrastinate to reduce the stress of having to make hard decisions, as George Bush did in dealing with the economy in his fourth year in office—a delay that cost him a second term, as his inaction became an election issue. Alternatively, a President might push his administration to meet self-imposed deadlines to make a decision and be done with it. And once the decision is made, the President might not reconsider it, even if he obtained important new information casting doubt on his original decision. Lyndon

Johnson, for example, paid little attention to advisers, including top officials in the Central Intelligence Agency, who warned him that his escalation of the war in Vietnam could not lead to a military victory, once he had made his decision to use 500,000 troops. It was not until the chairman of the Joint Chiefs of Staff asked for an additional 200,000 troops that Johnson realized he could not win the war.

A President might miscalculate the costs and benefits of a decision, as Ronald Reagan did when he agreed to sell arms to Iran in return for the release of U.S. hostages held in Lebanon. His decision led to the release of three hostages—but three new hostages were taken so the Iranians could obtain even more arms from the United States.

A President might make decisions based on "lessons" of history when these lessons may not apply. Presidents Kennedy and Johnson compared the civil war in Vietnam to World War II. In their view, a communist victory in South Vietnam would result in other nations in Southeast Asia turning communist. Yet after 1975, when Vietnam was unified under communist rule, noncommunist nations in the area, such as Thailand, Burma, Malaysia, and Singapore, did not find their security threatened by the Vietnamese government.

A President must guard against "groupthink," a situation in which consensus, or agreement, is prized and dissenters are frozen out and their potential contributions minimized. Indeed, one tip-off that decision making is poor is early agreement among advisers on the nature of the problem and the preferred solution. If debate fails to cover the full range of options, and if there is no advocate for the unpopular options, the President is not well served. The President, in turn, must encourage debate and dissent, must seek advisers who will be candid with him, and must be suspicious of premature consensus. Lyndon Johnson was not happy with advisers who disagreed with him about the Vietnam War. He cut Vice President Hubert Humphrey out of his inner circle over the issue and replaced Defense Secretary Robert MacNamara when he became skeptical about the war. The role of Presidential staffers, when they perform their jobs correctly, is to explore all the options and let the President know the full range of choices, but no adviser can force a President to listen to unpleasant truths.

Successful Presidents, much like unsuccessful Presidents, make mistakes. The big difference is that successful Presidents know when to extricate themselves from failing policies, as Franklin Roosevelt did on many occasions with his New Deal domestic programs. Any army, it is said, can learn to advance; the best armies also know when and how to retreat. The same maxim applies to the White House: a decision to undo a bad decision may sometimes be the best decision of all.

SEE ALSO *Camp David peace talks; Cuban Missile Crisis; National security adviser; Steel seizure (1952); Treaty of Versailles; Watergate investigation (1973–74)*
SOURCES Alexander George, *Presidential Decisionmaking and Foreign Policy* (Boulder, Colo.: Westview, 1980). Richard Neustadt, *Presidential Power and the Modern Presidents* (New York: Free Press, 1991).

DECORUM, CONGRESSIONAL

Members of Congress use extremely polite, old-fashioned language and decorum (or etiquette) during their debates. Officially, members do not even address each other but speak always to the presiding officer: "Mr. President" in the Senate or "Mr. Speaker" in the House. They call other members by title rather than by name. References to "my esteemed colleague," "the very able senior senator from . . . ," and "the distinguished representative from . . ." litter the *Congressional Record*. House and Senate rules prohibit any speaker from questioning another member's motives or referring offensively to other states. If a senator breaks these rules, the presiding officer can require that senator to sit down and not speak again without the permission of the Senate. The Speaker may similarly call the name of any House member causing commotion and order that person to sit down.

When the French writer Alexis de Tocqueville visited Congress in 1831, he described the Senate as a body "of eloquent advocates . . . whose language would at times do honor to the most remarkable parliamentary debates in Europe," but he was dismayed by the "vulgar demeanor" of the House. Although often more boisterous in debate, the House, just as much as the Senate, expects its members to maintain proper decorum. Members of Congress call this comity (courtesy). In 1989, Representative Mickey Edwards (Republican–Oklahoma) described the rules of comity as "this kind of nineteenth-century Victorian etiquette which is very important to keep us working together and helps bridge some of the partisan and deeply felt divisions between us."
SEE ALSO *Debates, congressional*
SOURCES Ross K. Baker, *House and Senate* (New York: Norton, 1989). Donald R. Mathews, *U.S. Senators and Their World* (New York: Vintage, 1960).

DELEGATES TO THE HOUSE OF REPRESENTATIVES

Each U.S. territory can elect a delegate to the House of Representatives. In the 3rd Congress, from 1794 to 1795, the first nonvoting delegate, James White, represented the "territory south of the River Ohio," which later became Tennessee. During the 103rd Congress, from 1993 to 1995, five delegates represented American Samoa, the Commonwealth of Puerto Rico, the District of Columbia, Guam, and the Virgin Islands. Delegates receive office space and staff, serve on committees, and have traditionally worked to promote statehood for their territory. They can vote in committee, and in the 103rd Congress, rules

were changed so that delegates can also vote when the House meets as a committee of the whole, to debate and vote on amendments. Delegates can participate in all legislative business except the final vote on bills.

In the Senate, only states can be represented. Some territories and the District of Columbia have elected "shadow senators" to lobby for statehood, but they are not officially part of the Senate. They neither serve on committees nor participate in other proceedings.
SEE ALSO *Committee of the whole; Shadow senators*

DENNIS V. UNITED STATES

- 341 U.S. 494 (1951)
- Vote: 6–2
- For the Court: Vinson
- Concurring: Frankfurter and Jackson
- Dissenting: Black and Douglas
- Not participating: Clark

In 1940, Congress passed a law banning sedition. It was known as the Smith Act after its sponsor, Representative Howard Smith of Virginia. The Smith Act made it a crime "to knowingly and willfully advocate, abet, advise or teach the duty, necessity, desirability, or propriety of overthrowing or destroying any government in the United States by force or violence." Further, the Smith Act made it a crime for anyone to organize a group with the mission of violently overthrowing the U.S. government.

After World War II, the United States and the Soviet Union—allies during the war—became enemies locked in a cold war. Members of the Communist Party of the United States of America (CPUSA) were suspected of collaborating with the Communist party leaders of the Soviet Union. A central part of the communist ideology was the inevitability of violent revolution to advance the cause of communism throughout the world. Given this perceived threat, many American political leaders urged use of the Smith Act to crack down on American communists.

In 1949 the federal government arrested and convicted 11 members of the CPUSA, including Eugene Dennis, for violating the Smith Act. Dennis appealed on the grounds that the Smith Act was unconstitutional.

The Issue   The 1st Amendment of the Constitution says, "Congress shall make no law ... abridging the freedom of speech, or of the press." Eugene Dennis was convicted under the Smith Act, however, because of the political ideas he expressed. Did the Smith Act violate the 1st Amendment?

Opinion of the Court   The Supreme Court voted to uphold the conviction of Dennis and 10 other members of the CPUSA. Chief Justice Fred M. Vinson announced the decision in this case. He argued that protecting the national security of the United States justified use of the Smith Act to limit the free speech of individuals advocating forcible overthrow of the national government.

Vinson wrote, "Overthrow of the government by force and violence ... is certainly a substantial enough interest for the Government to limit speech. Indeed this is the ultimate value of any society, for if a society cannot protect its very structure from armed internal attack, it must follow that no subordinate value can be protected." According to Vinson's opinion, it was reasonable to limit free speech of communists to protect the security of the United States.

Dissent   Justices Hugo Black and William O. Douglas believed the Smith Act was unconstitutional. Justice Black wrote:

I cannot agree that the First Amendment permits us to sustain laws suppressing freedom of speech and press on the basis of Congress's or our own notions of mere "reasonableness." Such a doctrine waters down the First Amendment so that it amounts to little more than an admonition to Congress. The Amend-

ment as so construed is not likely to protect any but those "safe" or orthodox views which rarely need its protection. . . .

Public opinion being what it now is, few will protest the conviction of these Communist petitioners. There is hope, however, that in calmer times when present pressures, passions and fears subside, this or some later Court will restore the First Amendment liberties to the high preferred place where they belong in a free society.

Significance   In the short run, the *Dennis* judgment encouraged the U.S. Department of Justice to suppress free speech by Communist party members. In the long run, however, the Court did fulfill Justice Black's hope. In a similar case, *Yates* v. *United States* (1957), the Court refused to uphold the convictions of Communist party members for violating the Smith Act. From that point on, the Smith Act, though held to be constitutional, was no longer used to suppress political activities of communists or anyone else.

SEE ALSO *Freedom of speech and press; Yates v. United States*

DEPARTMENT OF AGRICULTURE

The U.S. Department of Agriculture (USDA) was created by Congress in 1862, but it did not attain the level of cabinet status until 1889. The department's stated mission is to enhance the quality of life for Americans by supporting agricultural production through a wide variety of programs. In 1996 the USDA employed more than 110,000 people.

Initially, the department's top priorities were agricultural research, food inspection, and the oversight of national forests. By the 1930s, during the Great Depression, the USDA began to administer programs designed to provide farmers with direct governmental support, including a system of price supports and productions controls. During this critical stage of the nation's history, the department also began to assist the needy in both rural and urban areas through the distribution of food surpluses. Since World War II, the USDA has been called upon to supervise even more extensive assistance programs while simultaneously attempting to help farmers meet the ever-increasing needs of overseas markets.

Currently, the USDA conducts and supports agricultural research through its Agricultural Research Service, and the department provides farmers with information needed to successfully market their products through the Agricultural Marketing Service. Other USDA agencies manage the national forests and supervise soil conservation and watershed protection projects. In addition, there are also agencies that regulate the manufacture and sale of products used to control pests and diseases associated with farming, that inspect meat- and poultry-processing plants, and that enforce safety and labeling standards.

The USDA's Commodity Credit Corporation administers price support and subsidy programs, and the Rural Housing Service and Rural Utilities Service are cornerstones of the department's rural development efforts. The USDA also administers the food-stamp and school-lunch programs. In a nation marked by urban growth, the department's immediate challenge is to help farmers increase production to meet increasing demands and to do so in ways that are environmentally sound.

DEPARTMENT OF COMMERCE

The Department of Commerce has declared that its mission is to promote the economic growth of the nation by working in partnership with businesses, universities, communities, and workers. More specifically, the department's goal is to promote the competitiveness of the United States in the global marketplace by strengthening the nation's economic infrastructure, dispensing information about the latest advances in science and technology, and providing effective management and stewardship of the nation's resources.

The Department of Commerce and Labor was established by Congress in 1903 following decades of rapid economic growth. Originally, the department was assigned the task of overseeing the various components of foreign and domestic commerce, including manufacturing, transportation, and labor. In 1913 a separate Department of Labor was established. In 1966 the Department of Transportation was founded, further evidence of the nation's continuing economic growth.

In 1996 the Department of Commerce had almost 36,000 employees working in its various agencies. One agency is the International Trade Administration, which reports on business conditions and investment opportunities abroad and enforces federal laws that protect U.S. businesses from unfair foreign competition. The Bureau of Export Administration helps safeguard national security by enforcing laws concerning the export of products, materials, and technology. The Bureau of Economic Analysis provides pertinent data on the vitality of the nation's economy, and the Technology Administration maintains uniform standards of weights and measures. The Commerce Department also includes the Minority Business Development Agency.

A few of the department's agencies are widely recognized by the general public: the Bureau of the Census conducts, every 10 years, the census that is necessary for the reapportionment of seats in the U.S. House of Representatives among the states; the Patent and Trademark Office issues patents and registers trademarks; and the National Oceanic and Atmospheric Administration studies the environment and operates the National Weather Service.

With more than 95 percent of the world's consumers currently living outside of the United States, the information and direction provided by the Department of Commerce in the arena of international trade is increasingly important to the nation's economic well-being. In 1999 Commerce Secretary William M. Daley identified the need to protect consumer privacy as a vital issue, given the increasing volume of computer-based business and financial transactions around the world.

DEPARTMENT OF DEFENSE

The mission of the Department of Defense (DOD) is to provide the military forces needed to deter war and to protect the security of the United States. To this end, in 1999, there were almost 1.4 million men and women on active duty, and more than 700,000 civilians employed by the department. With a budget of $270 billion for 1999, defense spending constituted approximately one-sixth of all the spending by the national government. The Department of Defense is the largest and most costly of the 14 executive departments.

There are three military branches within the DOD: the army, the navy (which includes the Marine Corps), and the air force. The army, navy, and Marine Corps were actually established in 1775, prior to the signing of the Declaration of Independence. The War Department, which encompassed all three of these military services, was formed in 1789. Nine years later, however, the navy formed its own department to manage naval and Marine Corps operations, while the army continued to be supervised by the War Department. Under this arrangement, which lasted through World War II, both the War and Navy Departments had a cabinet-level secretary.

After the war, in 1947, the National Security Act created the office of the secretary of defense to direct a single, unified department known as the National Military Establishment. This act of Congress also created a new branch of the military, the air force. In 1949 the De-

partment of Defense was formally established by Congress and, though the army, navy, and air force were to be administered separately, all three of the armed services came under the direct control of the secretary of defense. In addition to the three branches of the military, there are currently 14 defense agencies, including the Ballistic Missile Defense Organization, the Defense Intelligence Agency, the Defense Finance and Accounting Service, and the Defense Security Cooperation Agency.

The most pressing challenge that Presidents have faced in the post–cold war era has been how to reduce defense spending without placing the nation's security in jeopardy. Despite a reduction in funding (from $390 billion in 1989 to $270 billion in 1999), the Department of Defense reported a dramatic increase in the total number of military deployments between 1989 and 1999. The department also listed 285 responses to federal disasters and emergencies between 1994 and 1998, and from 1992 to 1996 there were almost 10,000 requests from civilian law enforcement agencies for military support.
SEE ALSO *Secretary of defense*

DEPARTMENT OF EDUCATION

A federal Department of Education was created in 1867. As an agency not represented in the President's cabinet, it quickly became a relatively minor bureau in the Department of the Interior. In 1939 the bureau was transferred to the Federal Security Agency, where it was renamed the Office of Education. In 1953 the Federal Security Agency was upgraded to cabinet-level status as the Department of Health, Education, and Welfare. A separate Department of Education was created by Congress in 1980 as an executive department represented in the cabinet.

The principal duty of the Department of Education, which in 1996 had less than 4,800 employees, is to provide federal assistance to the state and local agencies primarily responsible for education in the United States. Grants designed to improve education are administered by the department's Office of Elementary and Secondary Education, the Office of Postsecondary Education, the Office of Special Education and Rehabilitative Services, and the Office of Vocational and Adult Education. The department also maintains an Office of Educational Research and Improvement.

Following President Bill Clinton's State of the Union address in 1997, the Department of Education developed a list of priorities that included having every classroom connected to the Internet and all students technologically literate by the year 2000. Priorities also included the creation of clear standards of student achievement in all states. In addition, the department asserted the goal of having all students prepared for and able to afford a college education by the age of 18.

DEPARTMENT OF ENERGY

The origins of the Department of Energy can be traced to the Manhattan Project, whose team of scientists developed the atomic bomb during World War II. In 1946, after the war, Congress created the Atomic Energy Commission to ensure that the civilian government, rather than the military, would control atomic research and development. Exclusive government control, however, came to an end in 1954 when the Atomic Energy Act opened the door to private commercial ventures in the field of nuclear power, though the act did stipulate that this new industry would be regulated by the Atomic Energy Commission.

The Energy Reorganization Act of 1974 replaced the Atomic Energy Commission with two new agencies: the Nuclear Regulatory Agency to regulate the nuclear power industry, and the Energy Research and Development Administration to manage programs that involved nuclear weap-onry, naval reactors, and energy development. In the mid-1970s the Arab oil embargo heavily damaged an American economy, making it clear that the United States was ill equipped to deal with energy crises. It was argued that a single agency was needed to formulate and oversee a comprehensive energy program. In 1977 Congress responded to this challenge by creating the cabinet-level Department of Energy.

Initially the department's mission was to provide the framework for a comprehensive and balanced energy plan by coordinating and administering the various energy functions of the federal government. The department continues to be responsible for the research and development of energy technology, energy conservation, the nuclear weapons program, energy regulatory programs, and the collection and analysis of energy data. In 1996 the department employed approximately 18,000 people in its various programs.

In 1999 the Department of Energy identified national security as its primary focus. The department has accepted the responsibility for maintaining the safety and reliability of the nation's nuclear stockpile, cleaning up the environment from the legacy of the cold war, and developing innovations in science and technology.

DEPARTMENT OF HEALTH AND HUMAN SERVICES

The roots of the Department of Health and Human Services (HHS) extend back to the health services of the nation's earliest years. In 1798 the first Marine Hospital, a forerunner of today's Public Health Service, was established to care for ailing seafarers. The National Institutes of Health (NIH)—an enormous complex of medical research centers in Bethesda, Maryland—sprang from a one-room laboratory that the federal government funded on Staten

Island in 1887 to conduct research on disease. The NIH now constitutes the largest of HHS's 11 operating divisions.

Assuming cabinet-level status first as the Department of Health, Education, and Welfare (HEW) under President Dwight Eisenhower in 1953, HHS officially came into being on May 4, 1980, when the Department of Education Organization Act of 1979 split HEW into the Department of Education and the Department of Health and Human Services. HHS became the government's principal agency for protecting the health of all Americans and providing them with essential human services.

HHS's operating divisions address a broad scope of health and welfare needs. NIH is the world's premier research organization, supporting more than 35,000 research projects nationwide; the Food and Drug Administration, founded in 1906, inspects foods, cosmetics, and medicines to ensure safety; the Health Care Financing Administration administers the Medicare and Medicaid health insurance programs that provide health care to one out of four Americans. Encompassing more than 300 programs that range from providing early-education programs to children through Head Start to halting the spread of infectious diseases, HHS is the largest grant-making agency in the federal government, awarding more than 60,000 grants per year.

The other eight operating divisions of HHS are the Administration on Aging, Administration for Children and Families, Agency for Healthcare Research and Quality, Agency for Toxic Substances and Disease Registry, Centers for Disease Control and Prevention, Health Resources and Services Administration, Indian Health Service, and the Substance Abuse and Mental Health Services Administration.

DEPARTMENT OF HOUSING AND URBAN DEVELOPMENT

The Department of Housing and Urban Development (HUD) was created by Congress in 1965. By that time, more than 70 percent of the nation's population lived in urban and suburban areas. The department was initially charged with the responsibility of dealing with housing shortages and related problems. In 1968, following the assassination of civil rights leader Dr. Martin Luther King, Jr., which led to riots in many major cities, the Fair Housing Act outlawed housing discrimination and gave HUD the responsibility of enforcing the legislation. Congress also created the Government National Mortgage Association, known as Ginnie Mae, in 1968 to expand the availability of mortgage funds for moderate-income families eligible for loans that are guaranteed by the government.

In 1999 HUD stated that its mission was to ensure a decent, safe, and sanitary home and suitable living environment for every American. In an effort to meet this goal, the department, which has about 11,500 employees, administers several insurance, rent-subsidy, and grant programs. Some of the grant programs it supervises are intended to help state and local governments improve housing conditions in urban areas through, for example, rental assistance for low-income families and the rehabilitation of residential housing units.

The department guarantees loans to home buyers made by private lenders and administers loan programs that help borrowers, both public and private, finance housing projects for the elderly and the disabled. In addition, HUD assists Native Americans by providing housing for low-income families on and near reservations.

DEPARTMENT OF JUSTICE

Although the post of attorney general dates back to George Washington's first cabinet, Congress did not establish the Department of Justice until 1870. The department represents the United States in court, enforces federal laws, and supervises federal prisons. Its head, the attorney general, is the nation's top law-enforcement officer.

Within the Department of Justice, the Antitrust, Tax, and Civil Rights Divisions handle cases involving violations of federal laws in their specific areas. The Criminal Division handles court cases involving federal crimes not covered by the other divisions. The Environment and Natural Resources Division handles criminal and civil cases involving public lands and natural resources. The Civil Division handles other civil cases to which the United States is a party.

When cases involving the U.S. government reach the U.S. Supreme Court, the solicitor general represents the nation. A top official in the Department of Justice, the solicitor general decides which lower court decisions the federal government will appeal to the highest court as well as what positions the government will take in those appeals. The solicitor general often argues these cases personally before the Supreme Court.

The Federal Bureau of Investigation (FBI) also operates under the direction of the Department of Justice. Established in 1908, the FBI is the principal investigative arm of the department. When the FBI was created, there were relatively few federal criminal laws, but the jurisdiction of the FBI expanded in 1910 when the Mann Act allowed the federal government to investigate criminals who evaded state laws even without violating federal statutes. During the two World Wars, the FBI investigated acts of espionage, sabotage, and draft evasion. The bureau became even more visible during the 1920s and 1930s when its pursuit of bank robbers and those who violated the prohibition on the sale of alcoholic beverages captured national attention. In later years, the FBI investigated organized crime, civil rights violations, and acts of terrorism. J. Edgar Hoover, who directed the FBI for almost a half century, developed a national prestige that insulated the FBI from much supervision by the Department of Justice. After Hoover's death in 1972, at a time of accusations that the FBI had employed illegal practices in its surveillance of antiwar and radical political groups, the Department of Justice moved to exert more direct control over the agency. FBI directors are now appointed for a fixed 10-year term.

The U.S. Marshals Service, the Drug Enforcement Agency, and the Immigration and Naturalization Service carry out the other law-enforcement responsibilities of the Department of Justice. In addition, the department's Bureau of Prisons oversees the federal penal system.

SEE ALSO *Attorney general of the United States, Immigration and Naturalization Service*

DEPARTMENT OF LABOR

The federal government responded to the growth of the industrial labor force by creating a Bureau of Labor in 1884. At first it was administered by the Department of the Interior, then later merged into the Department of Commerce. In 1913, after Woodrow Wilson was elected President with the support of organized labor, he called on Congress to establish a separate Department of Labor with cabinet-level status, to "foster, promote and develop the welfare of the working people, to improve their working conditions, and to enhance their opportunities for profitable employment."

From its beginning, the department's

major concerns included wages, hours, working conditions, and employment opportunities. It was concerned with all issues involving the role of labor in the nation's productivity, better relations between labor and management, and cases of employment discrimination. Presidents also relied on the secretary of labor to help mediate strikes and other labor disputes that threatened the national economy.

In 1933, at the depth of the Great Depression, President Franklin D. Roosevelt appointed Frances Perkins as secretary of labor. The first woman to serve in the cabinet, Perkins had been a social worker in New York. During her unequaled 12-year tenure as labor secretary, Perkins lobbied Congress for passage of the Social Security Act, to provide workers with old-age pensions, and the Wagner Labor Act, to help unskilled workers organize labor unions. (The American Federation of Labor [AFL] already represented skilled trade unions.) The Wagner Act fostered creation of the Congress of Industrial Organizations (CIO), which vastly increased the number of union members. Labor exercised its new muscle with major strikes in key industries. When Republicans regained control of Congress in 1947, they passed the Taft-Hartley Act to restrain some of organized labor's power and to give the President authority to enforce a 90-day "cooling off" period for strikes that might damage the nation's welfare.

The Labor Department's Employment Training Administration directs job-training programs and helps the states administer unemployment compensation programs. The Employment Standards Administration enforces minimum-wage laws as well as laws that prohibit discrimination on construction projects supported by federal funds. The Office of the American Workplace provides technical assistance to employers and unions engaged in collective bargaining and regulates the internal procedures and finances of labor unions.

The department's Bureau of Labor Statistics collects, analyzes, and publishes data on labor economics. The Occupational Safety and Health Administration (OSHA) enforces federal laws that set safety and health standards in the workplace. The Department of Labor also includes the Pension and Welfare Benefits Administration and the Mine Safety and Health Administration.

DEPARTMENT OF STATE

Operating under the Articles of Confederation in 1781, Congress created a Department of Foreign Affairs. In 1789, shortly after the government had been reorganized under the Constitution, Congress established the Department of State, the first cabinet-level department, to handle the nation's foreign relations. In its current mission statement, the department defines diplomacy as an instrument of power that is essential for national security.

In 1996 the department had nearly 25,000 employees, about two-thirds of whom were serving abroad as foreign service personnel. The department has essentially divided the globe into six geographic regions, and a member of the foreign service could be assigned to the Bureau of African Affairs, Bureau of European and Canadian Affairs, Bureau of East Asian and Pacific Affairs, Bureau of Inter-American Affairs, Bureau of Near Eastern Affairs, or the Bureau of South Asian Affairs. The United States maintains diplomatic relations with more than 150 nations, and ambassadors represent both the department and the President in the countries to which they are assigned.

The department's Bureau of Economic and Business Affairs designs and administers the nation's policies concerning foreign economic matters. The Bureau of Political-Military Affairs makes decisions that affect the security of the nation. The Bureau of Intelligence and Research analyzes the department's intelligence reports as well as those produced by other government agencies. The Bureau of Internal Organization Affairs is responsible for the participation of the United States in international organizations and conferences. The Bureau of Public Affairs provides information to the public about U.S. foreign policy, and the Bureau of Consular Affairs issues millions of passports to U.S. citizens each year. The Department of State also maintains the Bureau of Human Rights and Humanitarian Affairs and the Bureau of Refugee Programs.

The role of the United States in international relations grew throughout the 20th century, especially in the years following World War II when the nation established itself as the most powerful one in the world. As the department that advises the President on the formulation and execution of foreign policy, negotiates foreign treaties, and oversees the nation's representation in the United Nations and other international organizations, the Department of State has grown in importance in direct proportion to the participation of the United States in international affairs.

SEE ALSO *Secretary of state; United States Agency for International Development*

DEPARTMENT OF THE INTERIOR

When the United States acquired its western territories, it operated on the principle that the land and resources belonged to all the people, not just those who settled there. As a result, vast tracts of land, mostly in the western states, still belong to the federal government. The Interior Department has jurisdiction over millions of acres of federal lands that serve as national parks, wildlife refuges, federal mining areas, timberlands, and wetlands. As the nation's principal conservation agency, the Interior Department aims to protect and provide public access to the nation's natural and cultural heritage.

Immediately after the United States acquired a large amount of territory in the southwest as a result of the Mexican War,

and after the settlement of the Oregon territory dispute with Great Britain in the northwest, Congress created the Interior Department in 1849. The department's primary mission included supervising Indian programs, the exploration of western lands, and research into the nation's natural and geological resources. Within the department, the Bureau of Land Management is responsible for more than 264 million acres of public lands and more than 560 acres of subsurface mineral resources. The Minerals Management Service supervises energy and mineral development on more than 3 billion acres of the Outer Continental Shelf, located offshore of the coastal states.

The Office of Surface Mining Reclamation and Enforcement works in cooperation with the states and Indian tribes to ensure that land is restored to beneficial use after being mined. The Bureau of Reclamation oversees projects that deliver water to more than 30 million people for agricultural, municipal, industrial, and domestic use.

The U.S. Geological Survey is the nation's primary provider of earth and biological sciences information concerning the environment. This bureau monitors volcanoes and earthquakes and the quality of surface water and also acts as the principal civilian mapping agency.

The U.S. Fish and Wildlife Service manages more than 90 million acres that constitute the National Wildlife Refuge System. The National Park Service manages more than 80 million acres of national parks, monuments and historic sites, from Yellowstone National Park in Wyoming to Independence Hall in Philadelphia. The Bureau of Indian Affairs provides services to more than 500 tribes, including an education system that serves more than 50,000 Native American students.

With such an immense domain to oversee, the Interior Department has regularly been the subject of much controversy. Many westerners object to the federal government's control over such large portions of their states. Timber and mining interests argue that lifting restrictions on government lands would add jobs and boost local economies. Environmentalists, by contrast, complain that the department has allowed far too much development of the lands under its control. The Interior Department must struggle to balance the interests and demands of those who wish to develop and those who wish to protect the natural resources on federal lands.

DEPARTMENT OF TRANSPORTATION

The Department of Transportation (DOT) was created by Congress in 1966. The department has declared that its mission is to ensure a fast, safe, efficient, accessible, and convenient transportation system for the nation. In 1996 the department had more than 63,000 employees, and the work of the department is now handled by 11 individual administrations.

The Bureau of Transportation Statistics compiles, analyzes, and publishes data relevant to the nation's transportation system. The Federal Aviation Administration oversees the safety of civil aviation by issuing and enforcing regulations related to the manufacture, operation, certification, and maintenance of aircraft. The Federal Railroad Administration sets standards and conducts inspections to promote the safety of railroad transportation. The Surface Transportation Board sets economic regulations for the surface transportation industry, primarily railroad companies. The Federal Highway Administration provides federal financial assistance to the states to construct and improve roadways and bridges. The National Highway Traffic Safety Administration sets and enforces performance standards for motor vehicles. The Federal Transit Administration helps plan, build, and operate mass-transit systems in communities throughout the nation. The Research and Special Programs Administration oversees the transportation of hazardous materials. The depart-

ment's Maritime Administration oversees the nation's merchant marine, while the Coast Guard, yet another branch of the DOT, strives to ensure safe transportation on America's waterways. The Saint Lawrence Seaway Development Corporation operates the vital waterway that links the Great Lakes with the Atlantic Ocean. Finally, the Transportation Administrative Service Center provides technical and administrative services for the DOT's various administrations and other government agencies.

Prior to the creation of the Department of Transportation, President John F. Kennedy called congressional efforts to coordinate the various modes of transportation in the United States "a chaotic patchwork of inconsistent and often obsolete legislation." The department has helped to end that chaos, but it now faces the challenge of directing a national transportation network able to meet the needs of a population and an economy that continue to grow.

DEPARTMENT OF THE TREASURY

Concerned with settling the new nation's war debts and strengthening its economy, Congress created the Department of the Treasury in 1789. The organizational skills of its first secretary, Alexander Hamilton, helped establish the department as the principal manager of the nation's finances. In order to pay off the national debt, Hamilton proposed tariffs to raise revenue (and also to protect the young nation's industries) and an excise tax on American whiskey. Hamilton also proposed that the federal government assume the states' war debts and that it charter a national bank to handle its tax receipts and to issue paper money backed by federal deposits. Over the years, the Treasury Department continued to handle all federal funds and taxes, and eventually it took over the issuing of currency itself.

Perhaps the best-known agency of the

Treasury Department is the Internal Revenue Service, which collects all federal taxes. The U.S. Customs Service collects duties on imports and enforces customs laws designed to prevent smuggling. Through its Financial Management Service, the department acts as the nation's bookkeeper. The Bureau of Public Debt supervises federal borrowing and manages the national debt. The Office of the Comptroller of the Currency supervises more than 3,000 national banks, and many federal and state-chartered savings institutions are regulated by the Office of Thrift Supervision. The Bureau of Engraving and Printing produces all U.S. currency and postage stamps, while the U.S. mint manufactures all coins.

Laws against counterfeiting are enforced by the U.S. Secret Service, an agency better known for protecting the President, Vice President, and members of their families. The Secret Service is also responsible for protecting former Presidents, Presidential candidates, and visiting foreign dignitaries. The Bureau of Alcohol, Tobacco, and Firearms enforces federal laws concerning firearms and explosives and also regulates the production, distribution, and use of alcohol and tobacco products.

Although the secretary of the Treasury has continued to serve as the President's primary economic adviser, Alexander Hamilton's successors have had to compete for authority with several independent economic agencies. In particular, the Office of Management and Budget and the Federal Reserve Board also exercise considerable control over federal financial policy.

SEE ALSO *Internal Revenue Service; Secret Service, U.S.*

DEPARTMENT OF VETERANS AFFAIRS

The Veterans Administration was created by an executive order issued by President Herbert Hoover in 1930. It was not until 1989, however, that the Department of Veterans Affairs was established as an entity with cabinet-level status. The department, which had more than 250,000 employees in 1996, is a reflection of the nation's concern for the health and welfare of the millions of men and women who have served in the armed forces.

The three main components of the department are the Veterans Health Administration, the Veterans Benefits Administration, and the National Cemetery System. The Veterans Health Administration operates more than 170 hospitals and 400 outpatient clinics across the nation. These facilities provide medical services for eligible veterans. The Veterans Benefits Administration manages the pension program and other forms of assistance for veterans. An independent Board of Veterans Appeals hears and decides appeals for benefits. Finally, the National Cemetery System oversees more than 100 cemeteries for veterans that are located throughout the United States.

DEPARTMENTS, EXECUTIVE

The executive departments are the units of government that are under the direct supervision of the President. These do not include independent regulatory commissions and other independent agencies, such as the Federal Reserve Board, which are insulated by law from Presidential control. Top Departmental officials are appointed by the President with the advice and consent of the Senate. They serve at the President's pleasure, and he may remove them at his discretion. The President uses his executive power to issue orders to the heads of the departments, usually called secretaries, and their subordinates. Their legislative and budget requests to Congress and the rules and regulations they intend to issue are cleared by a Presidential agency, the Office of Management and Budget. The heads of the executive departments constitute the President's cabinet.

SEE ALSO *Appointment power; Cabinet; department of Agriculture; Department of Commerce; Department of Defense; Department of Education; Department of Energy; Department of Housing and Urban Development; Department of Justice; Department of Labor; Department of State; Department of the Interior; Department of Transportation; Department of the Treasury; Department of Veterans Affairs; Executive branch; Executive orders; Executive power; Patronage; Removal power* SOURCES *United States Government Organization Manual* (Washington, D.C.: Government Printing Office, 1992).

DESKS IN CONGRESS

Both senators and representatives were originally assigned desks in their chambers. But after the 1910 census, when House membership grew to 435, the House no longer had room for a desk for every member. House desks were replaced by rows of leather-upholstered seats, where representatives sit at random (Republicans to the left of the center aisle, Democrats to the right of the aisle).

In the Senate, each of the 100 members has a desk in the chamber. Some of these mahogany desks date back to 1819, and the rest were built as new states joined the Union. Some senators carve their name inside the desk drawers to show the desk's lineage. Several desks are notable. Daniel Webster's desk is the only one with no writing table fixed to its top. Writing tables with hinged tops that open to provide additional storage space were added in the 1840s, but Webster refused to have his desk altered, and none of his successors has chosen to change it. By resolution, the Webster desk always goes to the senior senator from New Hampshire (Webster's original home state). Jefferson Davis's desk bears a small scar from the bayonet of a Union soldier who in 1861 took out his anger on the desk where the Confederate president once sat. A small block of mahogany has been inlaid in the desk to fill

the scar. Since 1965, Republican senators have maintained a "candy desk" in the back row near the entrance to the chamber. Each senator assigned to that desk has dutifully kept its drawer filled with assorted candies for the benefit of other legislators.

DIRECT ELECTION

SEE *Elections, congressional; Senate*

DIRECTOR OF CENTRAL INTELLIGENCE

The Director of Central Intelligence is the principal intelligence adviser to the President, the director of the Central Intelligence Agency (CIA), and a statutory adviser to the National Security Council (NSC). The position of DCI was established by the National Security Act of 1947 in order to provide a coordinating mechanism for providing foreign intelligence—information about the military and economic capabilities of other nations—to the President and to maintain civilian control over the compilation of intelligence estimates. National Security Decision Directive 276, issued by President Ronald Reagan in 1987, makes the DCI a member of the National Security Planning Group, a committee of the NSC that reviews and oversees the implementation of national security policies. The DCI also serves on the NSC crisis-monitoring committee and is generally a trusted inner-circle adviser to the President.

The DCI coordinates all the intelligence reports from the CIA, the intelligence agencies of the military services, the Defense Intelligence Agency, the National Security Agency (which deals with codes and electronic intelligence), and the State Department's Bureau of Intelligence. Based on the information supplied by these agencies, the DCI provides the President with a daily briefing that summarizes these intelligence reports. He also oversees preparation of the National Intelligence Estimates, which deal with the military and diplomatic capabilities and intentions of foreign nations. The DCI is required by law to assist the President in complying with legal provisions requiring consultation with Congress when covert activities are implemented. Covert activities are actions in which the government does not acknowledge its involvement, such as attempts to overthrow anti-American governments in Latin America.

The DCI may assist the President in evading compliance with congressional consultation or reporting requirements by exploiting loopholes in the laws. For example, during the Iran-Contra affair in 1986, President Reagan did not inform Congress that funds from sales of arms to Iran were being sent to the Contra forces who opposed the Nicaraguan government. The DCI may also set up one or more fall guys to take the blame for covert operations away from the President, a system of protection for the White House known as "plausible denial"; the President states that he was unaware of the intelligence operation. This system may have been used to shield Presidents when CIA assassination plots against Cuban leader Fidel Castro and other world leaders were uncovered in the 1970s by two congressional committees and a national commission chaired by Vice President Nelson Rockefeller.

SEE ALSO *National security adviser; National Security Council*
SOURCES Thomas Powers, *The Man Who Kept the Secrets* (New York: Knopf, 1979). Jeffrey Richelson, *The United States Intelligence Community* (Cambridge, Mass.: Ballinger, 1984). Stansfield Turner, *Secrecy and Democracy* (Boston: Houghton Mifflin, 1985).

DIRECTOR OF NON-LEGISLATIVE SERVICES

Rocked by a series of scandals involving management of the House of Representa-

tives bank and post office, House members voted to create the new post of director of non-legislative services. In 1992, with bipartisan support, retired army general Leonard P. Wishart III was appointed as the first director. His office was assigned a variety of functions once performed by the clerk of the House, the sergeant at arms, and the House postmaster. These responsibilities include handling the House payroll, all internal mail, office supplies, restaurants and cafeterias, and the barber and beauty shops that operate out of the House office buildings to serve the members and staff.

SEE ALSO *Clerk of the House of Representatives; Sergeant at arms*

DIRKSEN, EVERETT McKINLEY

- Born: Jan. 4, 1896, Pekin, Ill.
- Political party: Republican
- Education: University of Minnesota College of Law
- Representative from Illinois: 1933–49
- Senator from Illinois: 1951–69
- Senate minority leader: 1959–69
- Died: Sept. 7, 1969, Washington, D.C.

Called the "Wizard of Ooze," Everett Dirksen used his deep baritone to great effect as Senate Republican minority leader. "He was a natural-born orator—eloquent, persuasive, and forceful," said Senator Norris Cotton (Republican–New Hampshire), who cited Dirksen's careful use of words, enormous vocabulary, and seemingly endless supply of stories and anecdotes. More than just talk, Dirksen possessed skills at legislative maneuvering. He fostered mutual ties between Republicans and conservative Southern Democrats and maintained a close friendship with Democratic majority leader and later President Lyndon B. Johnson. Both sides bargained for his support, which gave Dirksen influence far beyond his minority party status. Dirksen made his influence most keenly felt in 1964, when Southerners filibustered to block Johnson's Civil Rights Bill. De-

claring the end of segregation "an idea whose time has come," Dirksen dramatically chose to support cloture to cut off the filibuster. Enough Republicans joined Dirksen and the liberal Democrats to cut off debate and pass the bill. For such reasons, other senators called Minority Leader Dirksen "the most powerful member of the Senate."
SEE ALSO *Civil rights; Cloture; Filibuster; Johnson, Lyndon B.; Leadership in Congress*
SOURCES Burdett Loomis, "Everett M. Dirksen: The Consummate Minority Leader," in *First among Equals: Outstanding Senate Leaders of the Twentieth Century,* edited by Richard A. Baker and Roger A. Davidson (Washington, D.C.: Congressional Quarterly, 1991). Neil MacNeil, *Portrait of a Public Man* (New York: World, 1970).

DISABILITY, PRESIDENTIAL

Presidential disability is any condition in which the President is unable to exercise the powers and duties of his office. Ten presidents have been disabled while in office. In six instances the disability resulted in the President's death. In 1841 William Henry Harrison was bedridden for a week before dying of pneumonia. Zachary Taylor was bedridden for five days before his death from an acute intestinal obstruction (or perhaps appendicitis) in 1850. Abraham Lincoln was unconscious for nine hours before dying of a gunshot wound in 1865. James Garfield was bedridden for 80 days and William McKinley for 8 days before they died from gunshot wounds. Warren Harding was incapacitated for four days before his death from food poisoning (or a heart attack).

Four Presidents recovered from major disabilities. Woodrow Wilson was incapacitated with a stroke for 280 days. During that time his wife communicated with government officials from his bedside, refusing to allow cabinet secretaries to see her husband while he was making his slow

and only partial recovery. Dwight Eisenhower was incapacitated for 143 days by his first heart attack in 1955 and later convalesced from a stroke. He was also incapacitated briefly during an operation for ileitis. Ronald Reagan was incapacitated for 20 hours while undergoing surgery after suffering a gunshot wound in 1981 and later while undergoing surgery for colon cancer.

The Constitution makes no mention of the procedures involved when a President is disabled and the Vice President must assume the duties of the office as acting President. After Eisenhower's heart attack, he wrote a letter to Vice President Richard Nixon stating that if he were again disabled, Nixon would serve as acting President until the President announced he was able to resume his duties. If Eisenhower could not communicate, then Nixon was to make the determination himself about taking over the duties. Presidents John F. Kennedy and Lyndon Johnson continued this arrangement, which was later superseded by the specific provisions of the 25th Amendment to the Constitution.
SEE ALSO *Succession to the Presidency; 25th Amendment*
SOURCES Robert E. Gilbert, *The Mortal Presidency* (New York: Basic Books, 1992). Richard Hansen, *The Year We Had No President* (Lincoln: University of Nebraska Press, 1962). John Moses and Wilbur Cross, *Presidential Courage,* (New York: Norton, 1980).

DISCHARGING A BILL

When legislators try to get a bill out of a committee that refuses to report it, or refer it to the full House or Senate, the procedure is called discharging the bill. Legislators generally prefer to let the committees do the bulk of the work on a bill, but sometimes a committee will not report out a bill that the majority of the full house favors but the majority of the committee does not. When this happens, members attempt to discharge bills, but only rarely do such attempts succeed. However, sometimes just the threat of a discharge petition persuades the committee to act.

As part of the progressive revolt against Speaker Joseph G. Cannon's dictatorial leadership in 1910, the House of Representatives adopted the discharge petition. Once a majority of the House has signed the petition, it goes on the Discharge Calendar. After seven days, any member who signed the petition can make a motion to discharge the bill from committee. If a majority votes for the motion, the bill becomes the immediate business of the House and can be debated, amended, and voted upon.

The Senate uses a different procedure, in which members can make discharge motions during morning business, at the beginning of a day's session. The motion must remain at the clerk's desk for one day before it can be debated and adopted by a majority vote. However, other members may filibuster or use other delaying tactics to block a vote on the discharge motion.

SEE ALSO *Cannon, Joseph G.; Committees, congressional; Morning business*
SOURCES Walter Oleszek, *Congressional Procedures and the Policy Process* (Washington, D.C.: Congressional Quarterly, 1989).

DISCIPLINE, CONGRESSIONAL

Congress finds it painful to discipline its own members. Seeking to maintain alliances on so many different issues and to remain on good terms with each other, legislators prefer not to question their colleagues' ethics. They prefer to leave such judgments to the voters in the next election. But pressure from the press and public outrage over alleged misconduct often force the House or the Senate to act.

The Constitution permits each house to punish its own members for disorderly behavior. The most serious offenses can result in expulsion: a member can be expelled by a two-thirds vote. Alternatively, the Senate or House can censure (rebuke) a member by a majority vote. For lesser offenses, members may simply be reprimanded. The House has a Committee of Standards of Official Conduct, and the Senate a Select Committee on Ethics, which monitor the activities of members and staff and advise them on compliance with the rules and laws affecting behavior, ethics, and finances.

SEE ALSO *Censure; Ethics; Expulsion from Congress; Impeachment; Scandals, congressional*

DISCUSS LIST

The Supreme Court justices make decisions at the Court's conference about which cases to hear. However, not all requests for hearings are discussed. The justices make decisions at the conference only on cases that appear on a discuss list, from which many requests have been eliminated. The chief justice is in charge of creating the discuss list. He includes cases that, in his judgment, merit discussion before a decision is made about whether the Court should review the cases.

The discuss list is circulated in advance of the conference to all the justices. Any justice who thinks a case has been wrongly omitted may add it to the list. Each appeal from lower courts for the Supreme Court to hear a case is reviewed by each justice. Only those cases on the discuss list, however, are discussed at the regular conference of the justices.

Only about 30 percent of all the cases sent to the Court for review make the discuss list. The other petitions for review are rejected without further consideration by the Court. The discuss list is a means for reducing the time-consuming work of the Court by greatly reducing the number of cases discussed at conferences.

DISSENTING OPINION

One or more justices often disagree with the majority of the Supreme Court on how to decide a case. Justices who disagree with the majority are dissenters. They interpret the law, as it applies to a case, in a way that differs from the majority's interpretation. A dissenting opinion is different from the concurring opinion, which agrees with the Court's decision but provides an explanation that differs from the majority opinion.

A justice who disagrees with the verdict in a case usually writes a dissenting opinion, though there is no requirement that a dissent be accompanied by an opinion. However, most dissenting justices do write one to explain why they disagree with the majority decision. For example, in *Plessy v. Ferguson* (1896), the Court let stand a state law requiring trains to provide "separate but equal" facilities for black and white passengers. Justice John Marshall Harlan wrote a dissenting opinion in which he said that "the Constitution is color-blind, and neither knows nor tolerates classes among citizens."

A dissenting opinion is not an attempt to change the minds of the Court's majority because the Court has already reached a final decision before the dissenting opinion is written. Rather, the dissenter hopes to arouse public opinion against the majority opinion.

Ultimately, the dissenting judge hopes that the Court will reconsider the majority opinion and overrule it and that his opinion will someday become the basis for a majority opinion in a similar case. Chief Justice Charles Evans Hughes wrote: "A dissent in a court of last resort is an appeal to the brooding spirit of the law, to the intelligence of a future day, when a later decision may possibly correct the error into which the dissenting judge believes the court to have been betrayed."

For example, Justice Harlan's 1896 dissent in *Plessy* was vindicated by the majority opinion in *Brown v. Board of Education* (1954), in which the Court unanimously rejected the "separate but equal" doctrine and ruled that racially segregated public schools were inherently unequal. Similarly, Justice Hugo Black's dissenting opinion in *Betts v. Brady* (1942), in which he wrote that criminal defendants in state courts have the right to counsel, became the majority opinion in *Gideon v. Wainwright* (1963).

Over the course of history, however, dissenting opinions have rarely been incorporated into later decisions. Justice Oliver Wendell Holmes, who was known as the Great Dissenter, wrote 173 dissenting opinions during 30 years on the Supreme Court. Yet few of Holmes's dissenting opinions sparked reversals of court decisions.

The Supreme Court does not readily admit errors and overrule past decisions. The principle of *stare decisis* ("Let the decision stand") has a powerful influence on the Court. Justices usually accept precedents established in earlier Court decisions as guides in deciding later cases.

SEE ALSO *Concurring opinion; Opinions of the Supreme Court; Precedents, judicial*

SOURCES Alan Barth, *Prophets With Honor: Great Dissents and Great Dissenters on the Supreme Court* (New York: Random House, 1974).

DISTRICT OF COLUMBIA

The Constitution (Article 1, Section 8) gives Congress authority to make laws for the District of Columbia, the seat of the federal government. This power has its origins in events that took place in 1783, when soldiers angry about not being paid surrounded the Congress under the Articles of Confederation in Philadelphia, where local officials offered no protection. To ensure that the new federal government would never be as helpless, the framers of the Constitution called for a district, not exceeding 10 square miles, to serve as the seat of government.

As a result of a deal in which Southern

members of Congress agreed to support the repayment of American revolutionary war debts, Northerners agreed to locate the new capital in the South. Congress approved a location for the district on the Potomac River, on a 10-square-mile site that included the existing cities of Georgetown, Maryland, and Alexandria, Virginia. Commissioners in charge of the project named the district in honor of Christopher Columbus, and the new capital city within the district in honor of President George Washington, whose home, Mount Vernon, lay just 20 miles south of the new district. In 1800, the federal government moved to the district.

In 1846, the citizens of the Virginia side of the district voted to return their area to Virginia, so that the current District of Columbia occupies only the land that Maryland ceded. Congress has established several different kinds of government in the district, both with elected mayors and appointed commissioners. For many years, House and Senate committees really ran the district. Dominated by Southerners, the committees did not address the needs of the city's African-American majority.

In 1968, following the assassination of the civil rights leader Dr. Martin Luther King, Jr., riots broke out in Washington. There was extensive looting and destruction of property. These events hastened plans to establish an elected city government with a mayor and city council. However, Congress retained a veto on all of the city finances. The House has a standing committee on the District of Columbia, and the Senate assigns these functions to a subcommittee of the Governmental Affairs Committee.

Although the 23rd Amendment to the Constitution, ratified in 1961, allowed district residents to vote for President, they still cannot elect senators or representatives. The District of Columbia sends only a delegate to the House of Representatives. In 1990, the district also elected two shadow senators, including the nationally prominent African-American leader Jesse Jackson, to work for its statehood.

SEE ALSO *Delegates to the House of Representatives; Shadow senators*
SOURCES Kenneth R. Bowling, *The Creation of Washington, D.C.: The Idea and Location of the American Capital* (Fairfax, Va.: George Mason University Press, 1991). David L. Lewis, *The District of Columbia: A Bicentennial History* (New York: Norton, 1976).

DIVIDED GOVERNMENT

Divided government occurs when different parties control the House and Senate or when the majority in Congress is not from the President's party. These divisions differentiate the American government from parliamentary systems such as Great Britain's, where the prime minister always heads the majority party. There, if the prime minister's party loses its majority, or loses a "vote of confidence," the country must hold new elections. Under the U.S. Constitution, the President remains in office for a set term, even if his party loses control of Congress.

During the 19th century, voters faithfully cast straight-party ballots, electing Presidents and congressional majorities from the same party. However, the President's party frequently lost seats in the midterm election two years later. In the 20th century, party loyalty declined, and it became more common for the President and congressional majority to represent different parties. Divided government existed for 26 out of the 40 years between 1952 and 1992. From 1955 to 1995, Democrats held the longest continuous majority in the House of any party in U.S. history. Yet during these same years, Republicans more often won the Presidency. Ironically, when Republicans won majorities in both the House and Senate in 1994, Democrat Bill Clinton occupied the White House.

Why do voters choose divided government? They often select Presidential candidates based on national issues and congressional candidates based on what a candidate can do for their state or district. The high cost of running for Congress and the advantages that incumbents enjoy have also tended to insulate Congress from the frequent switches of party majority that occurred in the past.

During long periods of divided government, Congress grew more suspicious of the executive branch, expanded its own staff, and developed its own independent sources of data and analysis. Divided government deprived Congress of Presidential leadership and pitted the executive and legislative branches against each other. Presidents could veto legislation but had difficulty enacting their own legislative initiatives. As a result, while not efficient or entirely effective, divided government has further strengthened the U.S. system of checks and balances.

SEE ALSO *Checks and balances; Separation of powers*

DOCTOR, WHITE HOUSE

SEE *Physician to the President*

DOLE, ROBERT J.

- Born: July 22, 1923, Russell, Kans.
- Political party: Republican
- Education: Washburn Municipal University, undergraduate and law degrees, 1952; Kansas University, 1941–43; University of Arizona, 1948–49
- Representative from Kansas: 1961–69
- Senator from Kansas: 1969–96
- Senate majority leader: 1985–87, 1995–96
- Senate minority leader: 1987–95

There is nothing wrong with partisanship, Bob Dole believes, as long as it remains constructive and focused on issues rather than personalities. Dole never shies away from partisan politics. He entered the Senate with the Republican party in the minority in both houses of Congress, but

with the Republican Richard Nixon in the White House. Having little influence in his committees as a freshman, Dole spent much time on the Senate floor defending the President's programs. Barry Goldwater (Republican–Arizona) called Dole "the first fellow we've had around here in a long time who can grab 'em by the hair and haul 'em down the aisle." Dole's outspoken partisanship, tough debating style, and sense of humor all gained him recognition. In 1971 President Nixon endorsed him for chairman of the Republican National Committee. Gerald Ford chose him to be the Vice Presidential running mate in 1976, and Senate Republicans elected Dole as their leader in 1985. Although he lost the Republican Presidential nomination to George Bush in 1988, Dole led Senate Republicans in support of the the administration's programs. Dole resigned as majority leader in 1996 to become his party's nominee for President, a race he lost to Bill Clinton.

SEE ALSO *Leadership in Congress*
SOURCES Richard Ben Cramer, *Bob Dole* (New York: Vintage, 1995).

DOORKEEPERS

Visitors waiting for seats in the House and Senate galleries are supervised by doorkeepers. These doorkeepers enforce the rules of the chamber, maintain decorum, and regulate the flow of traffic. They also make sure that only those with floor privileges enter the floor of the chamber, and they bar all visitors during closed executive sessions. The doorkeepers operate under the supervision of the Senate and House sergeants at arms. During the President's State of the Union message, it was traditionally the role of the House doorkeeper to announce loudly, "Mr. Speaker, the President of the United States." In 1995, the office of House doorkeeper was abolished and its duties divided among the clerk of the House and sergeant at arms.

The sergeant at arms now announces the President and other guests to the chamber.

SEE ALSO *Dress code, congressional; Executive sessions of Congress; Floor privileges; Galleries*

SOURCES William "Fishbait" Miller. *Fishbait: The Memoirs of a Congressional Doorkeeper* (New York: Warner, 1977).

DOUBLE JEOPARDY

The 5th Amendment to the U.S. Constitution provides that no person shall "be subject for the same offence to be twice put in jeopardy of life or limb." This provision is known as the double jeopardy clause. It protects individuals against repeated prosecution by the government for a single alleged crime. In *Benton* v. *Maryland* (1969), the Supreme Court decided that the 5th Amendment's double jeopardy clause is incorporated by the due process clause of the 14th Amendment and thereby applicable to the states.

The double jeopardy clause protects an individual in three ways. First, it protects a person from being prosecuted a second time for the same offense after being declared innocent of this offense. Second, it protects a person from a second prosecution for the same crime after conviction for this offense. Third, in addition to prohibiting more than one prosecution, the double jeopardy clause protects an individual from being *punished* more than once for the same crime.

The great importance of the double jeopardy clause of the Constitution was emphasized by Justice Hugo L. Black in *Green* v. *United States* (1957): "The underlying idea . . . is that the State with all its resources and power should not be allowed to make repeated attempts to convict an individual for an alleged offense, thereby subjecting him to embarrassment, expense and ordeal and compelling him to live in a continuing state of anxiety and insecurity; as well as enhancing the possi-

bility that even though innocent he may be found guilty."

SEE ALSO *Benton v. Maryland*

DOUBLE VACANCY

SEE *Succession to the Presidency*

DOUGLAS, STEPHEN A.

- Born: Apr. 23, 1813, Brandon, Vt.
- Political party: Democrat
- Education: studied law at Canandaigua Academy
- Senator from Illinois: 1847–61
- Died: June 3, 1861, Chicago, Ill.

The fragile compromises that glued the Union together began to dissolve in January 1854, when Senator Stephen A. Douglas introduced the Kansas-Nebraska Bill. His bill aimed to organize the territorial governments of Kansas and Nebraska for eventual statehood. The Kansas-Nebraska territory lay north of the Missouri Compromise line, where slavery was prohibited. Douglas promoted the bill because it would allow construction of a transcontinental railroad out of Chicago, in his state of Illinois. To win Southern support, his bill canceled the Missouri Compromise and allowed the residents of the territories to decide for themselves whether to permit or prohibit slavery—a plan he called "popular sovereignty" (rule by the people). Douglas expected these territories to remain free, assuming that slavery could never be economical there. A skillful politician, known popularly as the "Little Giant," Douglas knew that his bill would raise a storm of protest, but even he was surprised by the ferocity of Northern opposition. The Kansas-Nebraska Bill led to the formation of a Republican party dedicated to opposing the spread of slavery into the territories. Rather than uniting the nation, as he had hoped, Douglas's plan divided it even further.

In 1858, Douglas was challenged for re-election to the Senate by Republican Abraham Lincoln. The Lincoln-Douglas debates, held throughout Illinois and focusing largely on the slavery issue, drew national attention. Although Douglas defeated Lincoln in that Senate race, two years later in 1860 he lost to Lincoln in the campaign for President. Douglas fell political victim to the forces he had unleashed by repealing the Kansas-Nebraska Act.
SEE ALSO *Missouri Compromise (1821)*
SOURCES Robert W. Johannsen, *Stephen A. Douglas* (New York: Oxford University Press, 1973).

DOUGLAS, WILLIAM O.
Associate Justice, 1939–75

- Born: Oct. 16, 1898, Maine, Minn.
- Education: Whitman College, B.A., 1920; Columbia Law School, LL.B., 1925
- Previous government service: Securities and Exchange Commission, 1936–39; chairman, 1937–39
- Appointed by President Franklin D. Roosevelt Mar. 20, 1939; replaced Louis D. Brandeis, who retired
- Supreme Court term: confirmed by the Senate Apr. 4, 1939, by a 62–4 vote; retired Nov. 12, 1975
- Died: Jan. 19, 1980, Washington, D.C.

William O. Douglas served on the Supreme Court for 36 years, longer than any other justice. He wrote more opinions than any justice before or since. And he was honored, before his death, with a lasting monument: Congress designated a parkland in Washington as the William O. Douglas National Park to commemorate his concern for the environment.

Douglas overcame crushing poverty and a crippling illness in his childhood to earn the great achievements and honors of his adult life. His father died when Douglas was five years old, leaving his mother with three children and almost no money. Later, he struggled with polio, which seriously weakened his legs. He took long walks in the mountains near his home to build strength in his legs, and his contact with nature influenced him to become a lifelong advocate of environmental causes. His childhood experiences also led Douglas to have sympathy for the "underdog"—a person who copes with poverty, physical handicaps, or racial discrimination.

William Douglas was an outstanding student in school, which opened opportunities for him to become a teacher, lawyer, and government official. His achievements as a lawyer attracted the attention of President Franklin D. Roosevelt, who appointed him to the Securities and Exchange Commission. He became a strong supporter of Roosevelt's New Deal economic recovery programs, and the President appointed him to the Supreme Court in 1939, to fill the seat of Louis Brandeis, who had retired.

Justice Douglas sought to defend the constitutional rights of individuals and professed that the Bill of Rights was meant "to keep government off the backs of people." He joined Justice Hugo Black to extend the limits of free expression and to promote "incorporation" of the Bill of Rights into Section 1 of the 14th Amendment, so that these constitutional rights could be used to protect individuals against abuses by state and local governments. Further, Justice Douglas joined with the majority of the Court under Chief Justice Earl Warren to defend the rights of African Americans, as in *Brown* v. *Board of Education* (1954) and *Cooper* v. *Aaron* (1958).

Douglas's most notable opinion for the Court was *Griswold* v. *Connecticut* (1965), in which he argued for a constitutional right to privacy based on his interpretation of the 1st, 3rd, 4th, 5th, and 9th Amendments. Although this opinion has prevailed, it also has been controversial because a right to privacy is not written specifically into the Constitution.

Douglas was a frequent writer of dissenting opinions, usually in defense of the rights of unpopular persons. He dissented, for example, in *Dennis* v. *United States* (1951), to protest the Court's decision to uphold convictions of American Communist party members for stating and writing that the U.S. government should be overthrown and replaced by a communist form of government. Douglas believed that the 1st Amendment forbade all government limitations upon the content of speech, or what a person could say. According to Justice Douglas, the Constitution gives the government power only to regulate the conduct of the speaker, that is, actions that pose a serious threat to the safety or property of people.

Justice Douglas often spoke and wrote about his beliefs on many topics. Many of his public statements were controversial or in opposition to commonly held viewpoints. As a result, many people disliked Douglas. He faced three attempts to impeach him, the last and most serious occurring in 1970, five years before his retirement from the Court.

Justice Douglas suffered a stroke on Dec. 31, 1974, which partially paralyzed him. Nearly a year later, Douglas left the Court. He died some four years later, a hero to many for his unyielding advocacy of individual rights, especially the rights of persons disliked or neglected by a majority of the people.

SEE ALSO *Griswold v. Connecticut; Incorporation doctrine; Privacy, right to*
SOURCES Howard Ball and Phillip J. Cooper, *Of Power and Right: Hugo Black, William O. Douglas, and America's Constitutional Revolution* (New York: Oxford University Press, 1992). William O. Douglas, *The Court Years, 1939–1975: The Autobiography of William O. Douglas* (New York: Vintage, 1981). James F. Simon, *Independent Journey: The Life of William O. Douglas* (New York: Harper & Row, 1980). Melvin I. Urofsky, "William O. Douglas, Common-Law Judge," *Constitution* 4, no. 3 (Fall 1992): 48–58.

DRED SCOTT CASE

SEE *Scott v. Sandford*

DRESS CODE, CONGRESSIONAL

House Speaker Thomas P. ("Tip") O'Neill, Jr. (Democrat–Massachusetts) once advised a representative wearing a yellow suit to go home and change, which he did. Tradition, more than rules, determines appropriate dress for members of Congress. At first, members of the House wore their hats in the chamber, carrying on a tradition of the British House of Commons to show its independence from the king. But in 1837, the House adopted a rule prohibiting wearing a hat in the chamber, and that rule remains in effect for both men and women members.

By the late 19th century, members of Congress—then all men—wore formal attire: striped pants, vests, and cutaway coats. Today, formal wear is seen only at Presidential inaugurations. The last senator to dress daily in this manner was Clyde Hoey (Democrat–North Carolina), who died in office in 1954. Long after, however, editorial cartoonists continued to depict congressional characters dressed in formal attire.

DUE PROCESS OF LAW

The 5th and 14th Amendments to the U.S. Constitution guarantee individuals the right of due process of law, which is often referred to simply as "due process." The 5th Amendment states, "No person shall be . . . deprived of life, liberty, or property, without due process of law." The 14th Amendment states, "No state shall . . . deprive any person of life, liberty, or property, without due process of law."

These two due process clauses provide

that the government must act fairly, according to established legal procedures, with regard to a person's rights to life, liberty, and property. Due process means, for example, that an individual accused of a crime is guaranteed certain legal procedural rights, such as the right to know the charges against him, to confront his accusers in court, to have legal counsel, and to have a jury trial. These and other rights of the accused are specified in the 4th, 5th, 6th, and 8th Amendments to the Constitution.

Procedural due process   These rights of the accused are examples of *procedural due process,* and they are constitutional limits on the power of government designed to protect the rights and liberties of individuals.

Procedural due process—the idea that government must follow fair and generally accepted legal procedures in its actions against individuals—has been traced to the great English charter of liberty, the Magna Carta (1215). By signing this document, King John of England agreed to "obey the law of the land." This idea developed into the legal guarantee of procedural due process of law to protect people against arbitrary or lawless punishments or penalties imposed by the government.

Due process of law was included in an act of the English Parliament in 1354, which affirmed the Magna Carta and specified "that no man . . . shall be put out of Land or Tenement, nor taken, nor imprisoned, nor disinherited, nor put to death, without being brought to Answer by due Process of Law." This English concept of due process was brought to North America by English colonists and was included in their colonial charters and laws. The Massachusetts Body of Liberties (1641), for example, provided that an individual could not be deprived of life, liberty, and property except by "some express law of the country warranting the same, established by a General Court and sufficiently published." The first American statute to use the words "due process of law" was an act

of the colonial government of Massachusetts in 1682.

The original state constitutions, drafted during the founding era of the United States (1776–83), included rights of procedural due process. They typically limited these rights to the traditional "law of the land" idea that stems from the Magna Carta. The Northwest Ordinance, enacted by the U.S. Congress in 1787 to regulate new territories north and west of the Ohio River, also guaranteed procedural due process rights by declaring, "[N]o man shall be deprived of his liberty or property but by the judgment of his peers, or the law of the land."

By 1789, when the federal Bill of Rights was drafted by the first Congress, the concept of due process was an established part of American constitutions and criminal law. Consequently, it was expected that the right of due process would be included in the Bill of Rights.

Substantive due process   During the 20th century, the Supreme Court has reinforced and extended individual rights. This has been done through the development of *substantive due process* and the nationwide application of the federal Bill of Rights through the due process clause of the 14th Amendment.

Substantive due process concerns specific behaviors of individuals that, according to the Court, are generally beyond the reach of government power, such as the free exercise of religion or participation in private organizations that petition the government about public problems and issues. The government may not regulate these actions, not even by the use of the fairest legal procedures, because to do so would violate the most fundamental rights of individuals in a constitutional government, such as rights to liberty, property, and equality under the law. If government officials want to regulate these kinds of usually protected actions, they must demonstrate that they cannot achieve a legitimate public purpose by any other means.

From the 1890s through the 1920s, the Court tended to use substantive due process to protect the property rights of business owners against state government regulations of working conditions, wages paid to employees, and hours of work. Since the 1930s, and especially since the 1960s, the Court has used substantive due process to protect the civil rights of individuals, especially racial minorities and women, against state government actions that threatened these fundamental rights. Thus, the Court has used substantive due process to invalidate hundreds of state laws pertaining to a wide variety of social and economic concerns and civil rights, such as fair conditions of employment.

The Court has, however, permitted state governments to regulate minimum wages and the working hours of employees in private businesses. These state regulations have been upheld, as necessary for the public good, against claims by business owners that they violate private property rights of individuals. This was the Court's ruling in *West Coast Hotel Co. v. Parrish* (1937), an early example of the use of substantive due process to protect and extend the rights of employees.

In the 20th century, the Supreme Court has used the due process clause of the 14th Amendment, which limits the powers of state governments, to apply most of the rights guaranteed by the federal Bill of Rights to the states. This use of the due process clause to protect the individual rights specified in the Bill of Rights against infringement by state and local governments has been referred to as the incorporation doctrine. This process has occurred gradually, on a case-by-case basis.

The Court's use of the incorporation doctrine and substantive due process has been controversial. Critics charge that substantive due process is a distortion of the original meaning of due process, which involved only adherence to formal and fair procedures by government officials in actions against individuals. Further, critics say that substantive due process has been used by judges to interfere in matters that should be left to resolution by majority vote in Congress or state legislatures. Finally, critics claim that substantive due process and the incorporation doctrine have been used by the U.S. Supreme Court to wrongly suppress the authority and power of state governments.

Virtually no one challenges the general value of due process of law as a guarantee of procedural consistency and fairness. Justice Felix Frankfurter expressed a commonly held view about procedural due process in *Malinski* v. *New York* (1945): "The history of American freedom is, in no small measure, the history of procedure." And in *Shaughnessy* v. *United States* (1953), Justice Robert Jackson stressed that controversy about substantive due process does not change the most fundamental and general agreement about procedural fairness, which "is what it [due process] most uncompromisingly requires."

SEE ALSO *Bill of Rights; Incorporation doctrine; West Coast Hotel Co. v. Parrish*
SOURCES Fred Graham, *The Due Process Revolution: The Warren Court's Impact on Criminal Law* (New York: Hayden, 1970).

DUNCAN V. LOUISIANA

- 391 U.S. 145 (1968)
- Vote: 7–2
- For the Court: White
- Concurring: Black, Douglas, and Fortas
- Dissenting: Harlan and Stewart

Gary Duncan was convicted of a misdemeanor—battery—and sentenced to 60 days in jail and a fine of $150. The maximum penalty for this offense was two years in jail and a $300 fine. Duncan had requested a trial by jury. The request was denied because the Louisiana constitution did not require a jury trial in cases involving lesser felonies or misdemeanors. Duncan appealed on the grounds that his rights under the U.S. Constitution had been violated.

The Issue Duncan claimed a 6th Amendment right to a jury trial. However, the Supreme Court had not yet used the 14th Amendment to apply this part of the federal Bill of Rights to the states. Was it constitutional for the state of Louisiana to deny Duncan a trial by jury?

Opinion of the Court The Supreme Court decided to incorporate the 6th Amendment right to trial by jury under the due process clause of the 14th Amendment, which provides that no state may "deprive any person of life, liberty, or property, without due process of law." Thus, the state of Louisiana had to provide a jury trial in cases like this one. Duncan's conviction was reversed because his right to a jury trial had been unconstitutionally denied. The Court held, however, that prosecutions for certain very minor offenses may not require a jury trial. Since Duncan's case involved a possible maximum imprisonment of two years, the Court decided this case was too serious to be tried without a jury.

Significance This was the first time that the 6th Amendment right to trial by jury was applied to a state through the 14th Amendment. This case, therefore, was part of the gradual process by which the Court has applied most parts of the federal Bill of Rights to the states.

SEE ALSO *Incorporation doctrine; Trial by jury*

DUVALL, GABRIEL
Associate Justice, 1811–35

- Born: Dec. 6, 1752, Prince Georges County, Md.
- Education: studied law privately
- Previous government service: clerk, Maryland Convention, 1775–76; clerk, Maryland House of Delegates, 1777–87; Maryland State Council, 1782–85;

Maryland House of Delegates, 1787–94; U.S. representative from Maryland, 1794–96; chief justice, General Court of Maryland, 1796–1802; presidential elector, 1796, 1800; first comptroller of the U.S. Treasury, 1802–11
- Appointed by President James Madison Nov. 15, 1811; replaced Samuel Chase, who died
- Supreme Court term: confirmed by the Senate Nov. 18, 1811, by a voice vote; resigned Jan. 14, 1835
- Died: Mar. 6, 1844, Prince Georges County, Md.

Gabriel Duvall served on the Supreme Court for a little more than 23 years. Despite this long period of service, he had a very small impact on the work of the Court and neither wrote significant opinions nor developed ideas to guide the work of his successors.

Duvall's appointment to prominent positions in the federal government, including the Supreme Court, was his reward for many years of loyal service to the Republican party founded by Thomas Jefferson and James Madison. President Jefferson appointed Duvall to be comptroller of the U.S. Treasury in 1802. President Madison appointed Duvall to the Supreme Court in 1811.

During the final 10 years of his Supreme Court service, Duvall was chronically ill and gradually lost his hearing. The infirmities greatly interfered with his ability to do his job, and he was repeatedly asked by his colleagues to resign. Justice Duvall resisted this advice until satisfied that he would be replaced by someone of whom he approved. Duvall resigned in 1835 after President Andrew Jackson promised him that Roger B. Taney, a friend of Duvall's from Maryland, would be named to the Court. In 1835, President Jackson appointed Philip Barbour of Virginia to replace Duvall, and in 1836 he named Taney to replace John Marshall as chief justice.

E

EARMARKING

SEE *Pork barrel politics*

EISENHOWER, DWIGHT DAVID
34th President

- Born: Oct. 14, 1890, Denison, Tex.
- Political party: Republican
- Education: U.S. Military Academy, B.S., 1915; U.S. Army Command and General Staff School, 1925–26; Army War College, 1927–28; Industrial College of the Armed Forces, 1931–32
- Military service: U.S. Army: 2nd lieutenant, 1915; major (temporary), 1917; lieutenant colonel (temporary), 1918; major, 1918; Office of Assistant Secretary of War, 1929–33; Office of Army Chief of Staff, 1933–35; assistant military adviser, Commonwealth of the Philippines, 1935–39; colonel, 1939; chief of staff of 3rd Army, 1939–41; major general, 1941; War Plans Division, Army Staff, 1941–42; commander of U.S. forces in Europe, 1942; Allied commander for invasion of North Africa, 1942–43; Allied commander in chief, 1943–45; five-star general of the army and army chief of staff, 1945–47; Supreme Allied Commander, Europe, North Atlantic Treaty Organization, 1950–52
- Previous civilian government service: none

- Elected President, 1952; served, 1953–61
- Died: Mar. 28, 1969, Washington, D.C.

Dwight D. Eisenhower was the first Republican President elected after the Great Depression. A "middle of the road" leader, he retained most of the Democratic New Deal programs rather than attempt to repeal them. He continued Harry Truman's policy of containment against communism but sought unsuccessfully to engage the leaders of the Soviet Union in summit diplomacy to limit atomic weapons. Although he won two elections, he was unable to make the Republican party dominant in American politics.

Eisenhower was born in Texas and raised in Abilene, Kansas. He graduated from West Point in 1915, ranking 61st in a class of 168. During World War I he saw no action but spent the time in training camps. After the war he was posted for a time in the Canal Zone of Panama. He graduated at the top of his class from the Army Command and General Staff School, then went to the War College and the Industrial College of the Armed Forces. He then worked as an aide to General Douglas MacArthur, army chief of staff, in Washington and later in the Philippines, returning to the United States as a lieutenant colonel in 1939. In the spring of 1941, with the rank of colonel, he distinguished himself in training maneuvers commanding the Third Army, winning promotion to brigadier general.

During World War II, Eisenhower was named chief of operations of the army in

1942 with the rank of major general. He was then named commanding general of the European theater of operations, a promotion that jumped him over 350 more senior officers. He commanded the forces that invaded North Africa in November 1942 and defeated the Axis powers by May 1943; he commanded the Italian campaign in 1943 that led to an armistice with the Italians; and he was named Supreme Commander of Allied Forces in Europe on January 17, 1944. He made the decision to go ahead with the invasion of Normandy, France, on June 6, 1944 (D Day), in spite of bad weather that might have imperiled the operation. He later called it the most difficult decision he ever made. He achieved the highest rank in the American military, five-star general of the army, in December 1944. After the war he served as army chief of staff, helping President Truman organize the new Department of Defense.

In 1948 Eisenhower retired from the army, declined offers from both political parties to run for President, and served two years as president of Columbia University, the only civilian position (other than the U.S. Presidency) he ever held. His account of the war, *Crusade in Europe,* was a best-seller. In 1950 President Truman recalled him to active duty to serve as the first commander of supreme headquarters, Allied Powers in Europe (SHAPE), the military arm of NATO (the North Atlantic Treaty Organization, an alliance of the United States, Canada, and Western European nations), a position he held for two years.

Although both parties considered him for the 1952 Presidential nomination, Eisenhower chose to enter the Republican contest and gained the support of the liberal and moderate wings of the party. He won a bitter nomination fight over Republican conservatives, led by "Mr. Republican," Senator Robert Taft of Ohio. His victory was due in part to the efforts of Senator Richard Nixon, who helped organize the California convention delegation for Eisenhower. Nixon was rewarded with the Vice Presidential nomination. With the Republican campaign slogan "I like Ike" and a series of effective television commercials, Eisenhower won a landslide victory over Democratic nominee Adlai Stevenson. His coattails brought in a Republican Congress.

Eisenhower concentrated on foreign affairs. "I shall go to Korea," Eisenhower had promised the American people, and one of his first acts was to honor that pledge and end the Korean War. The final truce agreement was signed on July 27, 1953. The following year he refused a French request to use American military might against North Vietnamese forces and instead supported the Geneva Accords that ended French involvement in Indochina. Between 1954 and 1955 Eisenhower shored up the American position in Asia by concluding a mutual defense agreement with the Nationalist Chinese government on Taiwan, providing military assistance to the South Korean government, cementing a strategic alliance with Japan, and giving American support to an anticommunist regime organized with U.S. assistance in South Vietnam. The United States, along with Great Britain and France, also sponsored the Southeast Asian Treaty Organization (SEATO), an alliance of the United States, Great Britain, France, and several Asian nations including Pakistan and Thailand, to resist communist expansion.

There were foreign policy successes in other parts of the world as well. In 1953 the Central Intelligence Agency (CIA) organized a coup that brought down an anti-American government in Iran. Then the Eisenhower administration organized the Central Treaty Organization, a military alliance between several Middle Eastern nations and the United States. In 1954 the CIA organized a coup against Jacobo Arbenz, the leftist president of Guatemala, and installed a pro-American leader. In 1956 Eisenhower insisted that France and Great Britain withdraw their troops from Egypt and end their attempt to topple Egyptian leader Gamal Abdel Nasser. Eisenhower did not confront Soviet military power directly. When Soviet forces crushed East German workers in 1953 and a full-scale revolution in Hungary in 1956, the United States made no move to respond. In dealing with the Soviets, Eisenhower showed respect for their military might and preferred peaceful negotiation. In 1955 he held a summit meeting with Soviet leader Nikita Khrushchev in Geneva. There he made an "open skies" proposal to allow each nation's air force to fly over the other's territory in order to conduct peaceful surveillance and reduce the military threat on both sides. The Soviets turned him down.

In domestic affairs Eisenhower expected Congress to take the initiative. He proposed combining the New Deal social agencies into a Department of Health, Education, and Welfare, which Congress approved, as well as an increase in Social Security payments and the minimum wage. He proposed only one major new additional domestic program, the interstate highway system. Eisenhower concluded the St. Lawrence Seaway agreement with Canada, which benefited U.S. ports on the Great Lakes by improving their access to the Atlantic Ocean in winter months. He proposed a constitutional amendment to allow 18-year-olds to vote, but Congress took no action on it. In the 1954 midterm elections Congress went back to the Democrats, which forced Eisenhower to adopt a bipartisan stance in domestic and foreign policy. Rather than claiming credit as a Republican, he worked closely with Democratic leaders to gain their support.

The least successful aspect of Eisenhower's first term involved his failure to stand up forcefully to Senator Joseph McCarthy (Republican–Wisconsin). McCarthy had charged that some members of the State Department and the army were part of a communist conspiracy. Though almost all his allegations proved unfounded, his mean-spirited investigation severely hurt morale in many government agencies. Eisenhower was slow in responding to McCarthy, though some have argued that he played a "hidden hand," working with Vice President Nixon and Senate majority leader Lyndon Johnson in maneuvers designed to weaken the senator. Eventually the Senate censured McCarthy for his unfair tactics of smear and innuendo.

Although Eisenhower suffered a heart attack in 1955 and had an operation to relieve an intestinal blockage the following year, his health was good enough for a second term. He was reelected over Adlai Stevenson in a landslide victory in 1956. But Congress remained in the hands of the Democrats, the first time a President had been elected without winning either House since Zachary Taylor's victory in 1848. Eisenhower's second term was marked by health problems; he had a stroke in 1957. Alaska and Hawaii were admitted to the Union in 1959. Eisenhower used federal troops to enforce federal court orders desegregating the public schools in Little Rock, Arkansas, but gave tepid support to other civil rights initiatives, leading congressional Democrats to pass their own civil rights measures in 1957 and 1960.

In 1957 Eisenhower announced the Eisenhower Doctrine, approved by Congress, that assured stability to nations threatened by communist subversion or aggression. In July 1958, to back up this doctrine, U.S. Marines landed in Lebanon to bolster the government against threats of civil war. When communist China starting shelling the islands of Quemoy and Matsu and threatened to invade them, Eisenhower ordered the U.S. Navy to escort Nationalist Chinese ships to resupply the islands.

In 1957 the Soviets launched a Sputnik satellite into outer space, challenging the United States for technological dominance and leading many Americans to think that the nation needed new leadership. With unemployment rising and the nation entering a recession, the midterm elections of 1958 led to a stunning loss for the Republicans in Congress and in gubernatorial elections. The Democrats, now controlling both houses, assumed control of domestic policy-making. They held hearings on shortcomings in national preparedness, science, education, and the space program, and they passed the National Aeronautics and Space Act of 1958 as well as a law that provided federal funding for science and foreign language education. Eisenhower's foreign policy began to suffer setbacks as well. In 1959 Fidel Castro assumed power in Cuba, and it soon became apparent that he was establishing the first communist regime in the Western Hemisphere. Then in 1960 Eisenhower planned a summit meeting with the Soviets to advance his arms limitations proposals. On May 1, 1960, shortly before the summit, the Soviets shot down an American U-2 reconnaissance plane over their territory; Eisenhower denied that the plane had been over Soviet territory, then had to admit the truth when the Soviets displayed the captured American pilot, Gary Francis Powers. The Soviets insisted that Eisenhower apologize for these flights, and when he refused, they broke up the summit conference. Khrushchev withdrew an invitation for Eisenhower to visit the Soviet Union. Later, Eisenhower toured the Far East but was forced to cancel a visit to Japan because of anti-American sentiment.

Eisenhower was popular throughout his two terms and probably would have won the next election had he not been the first President forbidden by the 22nd Amendment to stand for a third term. Although he campaigned for Republican nominee Richard Nixon in 1960, Nixon was defeated by Democrat John F. Kennedy, who ran a campaign highly critical of the Eisenhower administration.

After the election, Eisenhower delivered a famous farewell address in which he warned the American people of the potential dangers involved in the "military industrial complex" that had been created to produce weapons for the armed forces.

After retiring to private life in 1961, Eisenhower published his Presidential memoirs and lived at his farm at Gettysburg, Pennsylvania. He died of heart failure in 1969.

SEE ALSO *Health, Presidential; Hidden-hand Presidency; Kennedy, John F.; Nixon, Richard M.; Succession to the Presidency; Truman, Harry S.; 22nd Amendment*
SOURCES Stephen Ambrose, *Eisenhower, The President* (New York: Simon & Schuster, 1984). Dwight D. Eisenhower, *Mandate for Change, 1953–56* (Garden City, N.Y.: Doubleday, 1963). Dwight D. Eisenhower, *Waging Peace, 1956–1961* (Garden City, N.Y.: Doubleday, 1965). Fred Greenstein, *The Hidden Hand Presidency* (New York: Basic Books, 1982).

ELECTION CAMPAIGNS, PRESIDENTIAL

Initially, candidates for President "stood" for election—they did not "run" for the office—so they would not be accused of being too ambitious for power. In 1789 and 1792 George Washington had no opponent and was selected unanimously by the electoral college without campaigning.

Since 1796 there have been contests between candidates belonging to different political parties, and for many years the party managers did the campaigning while the candidates remained at home. In 1840 William Henry Harrison took a short "tour" but did not discuss issues or seek votes. In 1844 James K. Polk began the custom of sending "letters" to his supporters on issues such as the tariff, though he did not make speeches on political subjects. In 1852 Winfield Scott became the first candidate to campaign. By 1860 it was expected that the candidate who trailed would campaign: Stephen Douglas campaigned throughout the South and Midwest while Abraham Lincoln stayed home in Springfield, Illinois.

In 1876 Rutherford B. Hayes began the practice of responding to his party's nomination with an "acceptance letter" that dealt with the candidate's position on the issues. He confined himself to a "front porch" campaign, in which supporters would visit him, and his discussions with them would then be reported by the wire services and appear in newspapers. Hayes later advised James Garfield to "sit cross-legged and look wise until after the election," something his successor managed to do quite well on his farm in Mentor, Ohio. That election, in 1880, started the custom in which the challenger campaigned while the incumbent seeking reelection remained at home. In 1892 Grover Cleveland held a "notification" ceremony before thousands of his supporters in New York's Madison Square Garden, but he did not take to the campaign trail.

In the 19th century there usually was no need for a popular Presidential candidate to campaign: in 1896 Democrat William Jennings Bryan went to 27 states, made 600 speeches to 5 million people, and got crushed by Republican William McKinley, who ran a front-porch campaign. In 1904 Theodore Roosevelt thought it improper for an incumbent President to go on the campaign trail. Instead, he wrote hundreds of letters to party leaders, making patronage appointments to secure their support. He won by the greatest landslide since 1832 yet hardly ever left his home in Oyster Bay, New York.

The first incumbent President to stump for votes was William Howard Taft in the election of 1912. He made an 18,000-mile, 400-speech tour. His Democratic opponent, Woodrow Wilson, also toured the nation, making this the first election in which both major-party candidates campaigned.

Just as candidates began to take to the campaign trail, their speeches were eclipsed by new ways of communicating with voters. In 1916 Wilson used newspapers, magazines, billboards, and motion pictures in his campaign for reelection. In 1924 Calvin Coolidge began the use of radio in campaigns when he spoke to more than a million listeners. In 1928 Alfred E. Smith used the radio to reach 8 million people, though his strident speeches could not keep him from being crushed by Herbert Hoover. In 1932 Hoover, in turn, was defeated by Franklin D. Roosevelt, who

broadcast a series of radio "chats" to the voters from his Hyde Park, New York, home.

Perhaps the greatest victory on the campaign trail was won by Harry Truman in 1948, who did it the old-fashioned way, speech by speech. In April, when surveys showed only 30 percent of the public approved of his Presidency, pollsters did not give him a chance. Fifty leading campaign analysts predicted that Republican Thomas E. Dewey would win by 376 electoral college votes. Truman boarded a train named the *Ferdinand Magellan* and traveled 31,000 miles, delivering 271 speeches. The press started referring favorably to Truman's "whistle stop" campaign. Truman struck hard at the "Do-Nothing 80th Congress." "Give 'em hell, Harry," a supporter yelled out in Seattle. "I'm going to give 'em hell," he responded. His opponent, Dewey, aboard the *Victory Special,* rode 16,000 miles, made 13 major speeches, and briefly spoke on 43 other occasions . Ahead in the polls, Dewey spoke in generalities, telling a crowd in Arizona, "Our future lies before us." Referring to the Grand Old Party, the nickname of the Republicans, Democrats said that "GOP with Dewey leading it means Grand Old Platitudes." On election night—despite the *Washington Post's* forecast that he would lose, Truman told his aides that he had won, then went to bed. He awoke the next morning and received Dewey's concession telegram. When he returned to the capital, a sign on the Washington Post building said, "Mr. President, we are ready to eat crow whenever you are ready to serve it."

In 1952 Dwight Eisenhower pioneered the use of television commercials. "Eisenhower answers Mr. and Mrs. America" was a series in which the candidate answered questions from a moderator. "To think that an old soldier should come to this," Eisenhower lamented between takes. He also made several 30-minute speeches on issues, which went over with the audience like lead balloons, but he defeated his Democratic opponent handily.

By the 1960s political TV commercials dominated Presidential campaigns. Candidates used private polls to find positions on issues that would demonstrate their leadership qualities to the electorate. John F. Kennedy, for example, used surveys conducted at the state level in his 1960 campaign to emphasize issues that would enhance his image as a leader ready to move the nation forward. "Issues are only a means to establish personal qualities with voters," Republican media adviser Robert Teeter later observed. By the 1970s, candidates were using focus groups of voters to pretest campaign commercials. Groups of voters, gathered in small settings, would preview speeches and commercials: themes that appealed to them would be retained; those that fell flat would be dropped.

Candidates experimented with new ways to reach the voters. The network campaign commercials of the 1960s gave way to commercials geared to specific states in the 1970s and to particular racial and ethnic audiences in the 1980s. In the 1980s, 30-second attack commercials and quick "sound bites" were combined with sentimental ads such as Ronald Reagan's "Morning in America."

In the 1992 election voters did not respond to carefully crafted commercials, which seemed too slick and contrived. Radio and television stations participated in the Adwatch and Truth Test public service programs, in which they scrutinized advertisements for "fairness," making attack advertisements more of a liability than an asset. Appearances on staid network news programs gave way to appearances on television talk shows and entertainment programs such as "Arsenio Hall" (on which Bill Clinton played the saxophone) and "Larry King Live" (on which Ross Perot made his campaign announcements). In these forums candidates seemed more spontaneous, and voters felt they could make a judgment about character.

Increasingly, voters have used the Presidential debates to obtain information about candidates. More than one-third of the electorate usually waits until the debates are concluded before deciding for whom to vote.

To reach voters concerned primarily about issues, candidates prepared short books, such as Clinton's *Putting People First—A National Economic Strategy for America* and George Bush's *Agenda for American Renewal*, which were distributed free to voters who called toll-free telephone numbers. Campaigns also established computer "bulletin boards" to reach voters who subscribed to on-line information services.

SEE ALSO *Campaign financing, Presidential; Caucuses, Presidential nominating; Caucuses, congressional; Dark horse, Presidential; Debates, Presidential; Federal Election Commission; Nominating conventions, Presidential; Primaries, Presidential; Ticket*

SOURCES Paul F. Boller, Jr., *Presidential Campaigns*, rev. ed. (New York: Oxford University Press, 1996). Clifford W. Brown, Jr., Lynda W. Powell, and Clyde Wilcox, *Serious Money: Fundraising and Contributing in Presidential Nomination Campaigns* (New York: Cambridge University Press, 1995). James E. Campbell, *American Campaign: U.S. Presidential Campaigns and the National Vote* (College Station: Texas A&M University Press, 2000). Kathleen Hall Jamieson, *Dirty Politics: Deception, Distraction, and Democracy* (New York: Oxford University Press, 1992). Kathleen Hall Jamieson, *Packaging the Presidency: A History and Criticism of Presidential Campaign Advertising*, 3rd ed. (New York: Oxford University Press, 1996). Elizabeth Kolbert, "Test-marketing a President," *New York Times Magazine*, August 30, 1992. Richard M. McCormick, *The Presidential Game: The Origins of American Presidential Politics* (New York: Oxford University Press, 1982). Keith Melder, *Hail to the Candidate: Presidential Campaigns from Banners to Broadcasts* (Washington, D.C.: Smithsonian Institution Press, 1992). Eileen Shields-West, *The World Almanac of Presidential Campaigns*

(New York: World Almanac, 1992). Gil Troy, *See How They Ran: The Changing Role of the Presidential Candidate* (New York: Free Press, 1991).

ELECTIONS, CONGRESSIONAL

In Congress an election is never more than two years away. Representative government requires that the citizens elect the people who will represent them. The Constitution specified that the House of Representatives be directly elected by the people. The entire House stands for election every two years. Senators are elected for six-year terms. The Senate is divided into three groups, so that one-third of the Senate stands for election every two years. Initially, senators were chosen by state legislatures, but in several instances state legislators were unable to agree on a candidate and Senate seats went vacant for an entire Congress. Other problems involving the election process led progressives to advocate direct election of senators. As a result, the 17th Amendment to the Constitution was ratified in 1913, and senators stood for popular election for the first time in 1914.

Before the direct election of senators, the House was more likely than the Senate to respond to shifts of public opinion. During the late 19th century, as many as 200 House seats might change party in a single election. The Senate was more insulated from popular passions and frenzy. But a century later, House incumbents enjoyed a high rate of reelection, and shifts in party became more pronounced in the Senate. House members sought to spend their careers in Congress, aided in their reelections by their visibility in the media, their franking (free mail) privileges, and their ability to raise more campaign contributions than their challengers could.

SEE ALSO *Campaign committees, congressional; Campaign financing, congressional; Incumbents*

ELECTORAL COLLEGE

The electoral college is the formal body, created by the Constitution (Article 2, Section 1), that elects the President of the United States. Each state has as many electors in the electoral college as it has senators and representatives in Congress. When citizens participate in a Presidential election, they are actually voting for electors pledged to vote for their candidate.

The method of choosing electors is determined by state election laws. At first many states left the decision to their legislatures; other states permitted the people to choose the electors. By 1832 all states except South Carolina had switched to popular election of Presidential electors, and that state joined the others in 1856.

There is no constitutional requirement that all the electors of a state vote for a single candidate, but all states except Michigan in the 1890s and Maine in modern times have provided for a winner-take-all system: the candidate who receives a majority of the popular vote in the state receives all the state's electoral votes, and the other candidates receive nothing. Maine has adopted a "congressional district" system that chooses electors based on the plurality (the most votes but not necessarily a majority) in each district. This means that a candidate might win 3 rather than all 4 electoral votes if he or she loses in one of the districts. (The winner of the statewide vote in Maine also receives the two "senatorial" electors.)

On a date fixed by Congress the people vote in each state (and the District of Columbia) for members of the electoral college. Although the names of the Presidential candidates appear on the ballot, the voters actually cast their ballots for a slate of electors pledged to vote for that candidate. After the popular voting, on a date fixed by Congress (currently, the first Monday after the second Wednesday in December), the winning electors meet in their respective state capitals to cast one ballot for President and one ballot for Vice

President. (The electoral college never meets in a single place to cast ballots because the framers of the Constitution feared that the electors could be coerced or bribed more easily in one location.) The ballots from each state are sent to Congress. The outgoing Vice President of the United States (who is the president of the Senate) counts the ballots in the presence of Congress and announces the name of the next President. In 1960 Richard Nixon, as president of the Senate, announced that he had lost the election to John F. Kennedy. In 1968, outgoing Vice President Hubert Humphrey announced that Nixon had defeated him for the Presidency.

The delegates to the Constitutional Convention thought that in most elections the electoral college would be dominated by electors from the large states, who would vote for candidates from their own states. In that situation, none of the five leading candidates would amass the necessary majority of votes to be elected. In the event of a deadlock, the election would go to the House of Representatives, where each state's delegation would cast a single vote for one of the top five contenders. In a sense, the electoral college was expected to function as a nominating body and the House as the final arbiter. (The 12th Amendment to the Constitution, adopted in 1804, restricts the House's choice to the top three candidates.) The Vice President would be chosen by the Senate from among the top two candidates in the event of an electoral college deadlock.

The cumbersome system of contingency elections provided by the Constitution would give the large states the chance to "nominate" candidates for President, while all states, large and small, would have an equal voice in the final selection. This compromise between large and small states is at the heart of the original electoral college scheme.

The framers thought that electors would operate as free agents, diligently searching to find the best candidates for President. But since 1796 electors have been the agents of political parties supporting candidates already seeking the office. The electoral college has become a registering device for the preferences of the voters. Only a few electors have ever violated their pledges and voted for someone else, and none of these "faithless electors" have ever influenced the outcome of an election by doing so.

There have been two elections in which the electoral college deadlocked and contingency elections were held. In 1800 Thomas Jefferson was the Presidential candidate and Aaron Burr the Vice Presidential candidate of the Republicans. At that time each elector cast two ballots for President; the top candidate was elected President and the runner-up assumed the Vice Presidency. Jefferson and Burr each received the same number of electoral college votes for President, and because neither received a majority, the election went to the House, which elected Jefferson. To forestall that possibility in future elections, the 12th Amendment, adopted for the election of 1804, provided that the electoral college cast separate ballots cast for President and Vice President.

In 1824, when no candidate received a majority of electors, the House chose John Quincy Adams for President, even though Andrew Jackson had received a higher popular vote. In 1836, Virginia electors refused to vote for Richard M. Johnson for Vice President, denying any candidate a majority. The Senate then voted to make Johnson Vice President.

In 1876, when Southern Democrats were contending with radical Republicans for control of their state governments, close contests in several Southern states led both parties to claim victory, and therefore Democratic and Republican electors sent their ballots to the Capitol. It took a special commission set up by Congress to decide which party had won the statewide vote and therefore which party's ballots should be counted. In what was effectively a deal to end military occupation of the South, the Southern Democrats accepted the commission's finding that the electoral votes of the Republicans would be counted, thus ensuring the election of Republican President Rutherford B. Hayes, who needed all the contested votes cast in his favor to defeat his Democratic opponent, Samuel Tilden, by a single electoral vote. In turn, federal troops were quickly withdrawn from Southern states and Reconstruction policies were ended.

In several elections the candidate with the most popular votes has been defeated: Andrew Jackson in 1824; Samuel Tilden in 1876; and Grover Cleveland in 1888.

In other situations, small shifts in the popular vote could have had major effects on the electoral vote. In 1976, if a total of 9,245 votes had shifted to Gerald Ford in Ohio and Hawaii, he would have been elected President, even though he would have received 1.7 million fewer votes than Jimmy Carter. In 1988, a shift of 547,000 votes in 11 states would have shifted the election from George Bush to Michael Dukakis, even though Bush would have retained a margin of 5 million votes.

In the election of 2000, Vice President Albert Gore won the popular vote but narrowly lost the electoral college to Texas Governor George W. Bush. Gore objected to the vote count in Florida, where Bush was certified as winning by 500 votes, but where 175,000 ballots were eliminated by voting machines that could not determine for whom the ballots had been cast. These "undercounted" ballots came disproportionately from districts that favored Gore. He demanded a hand recount of the disputed ballots to determine the intention of the voters, but Bush sued to stop the recount. By a vote of 5–4, in Bush v. Gore, the U.S. Supreme Court, prohibited a recount because not enough time remained to ensure the equal protection of all voters. Florida's electors, and with them the presidency, then went to Bush.

In the 1970s several constitutional amendments to abolish the electoral college were introduced in Congress, and on several occasions they have passed the House or Senate, but none has received the two-thirds vote necessary for adoption.
SEE ALSO Adams, John Quincy; Burr,

Aaron; Hayes, Rutherford B.; Humphrey, Hubert H.; Jackson, Andrew; Jefferson, Thomas; Johnson, Andrew; Kennedy, John F.; Nixon, Richard M.
SOURCES Lawrence D. Longley and Alan G. Braun, The Politics of Electoral College Reform (New Haven: Yale University Press, 1975). Neal R. Pierce and Lawrence D. Longley, The People's President, rev. ed. (New Haven: Yale University Press, 1981). Arthur M. Schlesinger, Jr., and Fred L. Israel, eds., Running for President (New York: Simon & Schuster, 1993).

ELIGIBILITY FOR THE PRESIDENCY

In Article 2, Section 1, the Constitution sets forth the eligibility requirements for the President. These requirements were modified by the 12th Amendment in 1804. To serve as President, one must be a natural-born citizen (an American citizen born abroad whose parents were citizens at the time meets this requirement), 35 years of age upon assuming office, and 14 years a resident of the United States (though not necessarily the 14 years immediately preceding the election). The Constitution bars any religious test for federal office and does not contain any racial or gender restrictions.

The 12th Amendment, which provides for separate electoral college ballots for President and Vice President, requires that the Vice President have the same qualifications for office as the President.
SEE ALSO 12th Amendment

ELLSWORTH, OLIVER
Chief Justice, 1796–1800

- Born: Apr. 29, 1745, Windsor, Conn.
- Education: College of New Jersey (Princeton), B.A., 1766
- Other government service: Connecticut General Assembly, 1773–76; state's attorney, Hartford County, Conn., 1777–85; Continental Congress, 1776–83;

Connecticut Council of Safety, 1779; Governor's Council, 1780–85, 1801–7; judge, Connecticut Supreme Court, 1785–89; Constitutional Convention, 1787; U.S. senator from Connecticut, 1789–96

• Appointed by President George Washington Mar. 3, 1796; replaced John Jay, who resigned

• Supreme Court term: confirmed by the Senate Mar. 4, 1796, by a 21–1 vote; resigned Dec. 15, 1800

• Died: Nov. 26, 1807, Windsor, Conn.

Oliver Ellsworth was one of the leading founders of the United States of America. He played a major role in writing and supporting ratification of the U.S. Constitution. Later, as a senator from Connecticut in the first U.S. Congress, Ellsworth drafted the Judiciary Act of 1789, which set up the federal judicial system in line with Article 3 of the Constitution.

In 1796 President George Washington named Ellsworth chief justice of the United States, a position he held for only three years. Ellsworth had very little influence on development of the Court during his brief term. In 1799, Ellsworth agreed to President John Adams's request that he travel to France to repair broken relationships between the United States and its former ally, with which the United States was fighting an undeclared naval war. Ellsworth helped to resolve the problems with France, but he became ill while overseas and resigned as chief justice before returning to the United States.

EMANCIPATION PROCLAMATIONS

During the Civil War, President Abraham Lincoln issued two Presidential proclamations that freed slaves from states in secession.

At the beginning of the Civil War Lincoln wanted the border states to remain in the Union, and so he resisted pressure from abolitionists to issue an order ending slavery everywhere in the nation. In Sep-

tember 1861 he ordered General John C. Frmont to revoke a military proclamation that had freed the slaves of Missourians who supported the Confederacy. In 1862 Congress passed several acts confiscating the slaves of rebels, measures that Lincoln did not support or enforce. He preferred to compensate slaveholders for the slaves who were freed. After the Union victory at Antietam, however, Lincoln decided on a bolder course. "The moment came," Lincoln said, "when I felt that slavery must die that the Union might live." On September 23, 1862, Lincoln issued a proclamation stating that as of the new year, all slaves within rebelling states "shall be, then, thenceforward and forever free."

On January 1, 1863, using his authority as commander in chief, Lincoln issued the Emancipation Proclamation, declaring that the slaves in areas "in rebellion against the United States" were free as of that date. It specifically exempted border states such as Tennessee, Kentucky, and Missouri, the western part of Virginia, and parts of Louisiana in order to retain the support of Unionists in those areas. (Tennessee, although exempted, ended slavery of its own volition.)

There was no mention of compensation in the Emancipation Proclamation. Lincoln described it as a war measure: it enabled Union armies to obtain the services of former slaves. The proclamation was a political triumph for Lincoln. It was opposed by the Democrats, who argued that it violated Lincoln's 1860 pledge never to interfere with slavery in states where it existed. It also seemed to violate the 5th Amendment: the Supreme Court had ruled in the 1857 *Dred Scott* case that slaves were property, and Lincoln had emancipated slave owners' property without due process of law or compensation. Emancipation was, of course, popular with abolitionists in the North. And because of Lincoln's policy, African Americans remained strong supporters of the Republican party into the 1930s.

The emancipation of all slaves was attained with the passage of the 13th

Amendment in 1865. Lincoln's refusal to compensate slave owners for their property was embodied as constitutional policy in the 14th Amendment, ratified in 1868.
SEE ALSO *Lincoln, Abraham*
SOURCES John Hope Franklin, *The Emancipation Proclamation* (1963; reprint, Wheeling, Ill.: Harlan Davidson, 1995).

EMINENT DOMAIN

The government's power to take land for public use is called eminent domain. According to the 5th Amendment, "No person shall . . . be deprived of life, liberty, or property, without due process of law; nor shall private property be taken for public use without just compensation."
SEE ALSO *Just compensation*

ENACTING CLAUSE

Each bill before Congress begins with the phrase "Be it enacted by the Senate and House of Representatives," which is the enacting clause. If a majority votes to strike, or remove, the enacting clause, then the entire bill is automatically killed, without requiring a vote on the bill as a whole.

ENGEL V. VITALE

• 370 U.S. 421 (1962)
• Vote: 7–1
• For the Court: Black
• Concurring: Douglas
• Dissenting: Stewart
• Not participating: White
The Board of Regents of the state of New York has the authority to supervise the state's educational system. In 1961, this state education board composed a short prayer: "Almighty God, we acknowledge our dependence upon Thee, and we beg Thy blessings upon us, our parents, our teachers, and our Country." The Board of Regents recommended daily recitation in schools of this nondenominational prayer, on a voluntary basis.

Although the Regents prayer was only a recommendation, the New Hyde Park Board of Education required that this prayer be said aloud at the beginning of each school day by each class of students in the district and in the presence of a teacher. The parents of 10 students objected to this requirement as a violation of the principle of separation of church and state in the 1st Amendment to the Constitution. They took legal action to compel the local board of education to discontinue the use in public schools of an official prayer that was contrary to their beliefs and practices.
The Issue Did the New York Board of Regents and the New Hyde Park Board of Education violate the 1st Amendment ban on laws "respecting an establishment of religion"?
Opinion of the Court The Supreme Court decided to strike down the Regents prayer. Justice Hugo Black, writing for the majority, said that the primary concern in this case was the creation of the prayer and the subsequent distribution of it throughout the state by an official agency of the state government. These actions violated the establishment clause of the 1st Amendment, which was applicable to the state of New York through the due process clause of the 14th Amendment. Justice Black concluded, "Neither the fact that the prayer may be denominationally neutral nor the fact that its observance on the part of the students is voluntary [in school districts other than New Hyde Park] can serve to free it from the limitations of the Establishment Clause [which] is violated by the enactment of laws which establish an official religion whether those laws operate directly to coerce nonobserving individuals or not."
Dissent Justice Potter Stewart dissented on the grounds that the Regents prayer was nondenominational and voluntary. Justice Stewart wrote: "With all due respect, I think the Court has misapplied a great constitutional principle. I cannot see how an 'official religion' is established by letting those who want to say

a prayer say it. On the contrary, I think that to deny the wish of these school children to join in reciting this prayer is to deny them the opportunity of sharing in the spiritual heritage of the Nation."

Significance This case, in combination with the decision in *Abington School District* v. *Schempp* (1963), established a strong position in favor of a strict separation of church and state. However, opponents have continued to challenge this view. In his dissent in *Wallace* v. *Jaffree* (1985), Justice William Rehnquist rejected the idea of strict separation of church and state. Rather, he argued, the establishment clause of the 1st Amendment was meant only to prevent the government from favoring one religion over another.

SEE ALSO *Abington School District v. Schempp; Establishment clause; Religious issues under the Constitution; Wallace v. Jaffree*

ENVIRONMENTAL PROTECTION AGENCY

For years the American people believed their country offered unlimited resources and were therefore careless in their treatment of the environment. Industrial smokestacks polluted the air. Town sewerage polluted the waters. Farmers used new pesticides and fertilizers without realizing what some of their harmful effects might be. In 1962 the biologist Rachel Carson published *Silent Spring*, an exposé of the dangers of toxic chemicals to the environment. Federal investigations supported her conclusions, and Congress enacted legislation mandating changes to ensure clean air and water.

In 1970 Congress established the Environmental Protection Agency (EPA) as an independent regulatory agency to set standards against pollution. In 1980 Congress also authorized a "superfund" to pay for the cleanup of hazardous and toxic wastes. This fund, supported primarily through the collection of taxes, was also to be used in response to

chemical accidents. The fund allocated billions of dollars to maintain a clean and safe environment.

The President appoints the head of the EPA, with the confirmation of Congress. During Ronald Reagan's administration, EPA administrator Anne Gorsuch came under criticism for not enforcing the laws as Congress had intended. A conservative, Gorsuch believed that federal environmental mandates were too expensive for businesses compliance and that the government had grown too intrusive in business and private land management. Her stand was unpopular, however, and she was forced to resign under fire. President Bill Clinton later elevated the position to cabinet status by executive order, extending a seat in the cabinet to EPA administrator Carol M. Browner.

EQUALITY UNDER THE CONSTITUTION

The United States was born with a Declaration of Independence that proclaimed, as a self-evident truth, that, "all Men are created equal, that they are endowed by their Creator with certain unalienable Rights, that among these are Life, Liberty, and the Pursuit of Happiness—That to secure these Rights, Governments are instituted among Men." According to the founders of the United States of America, all people are equal, by virtue of their humanity, in possession of certain rights (such as rights to liberty) that it is the responsibility of government to protect.

The founders were not claiming that all individuals are equal in their personal attributes, such as physical strength, intelligence, or artistic talent. They were not saying that a government is established to enforce equality or uniformity in the way people think, act, or live. Rather, the founders were committed to establishing a government that would guarantee equally to all individuals the rule of law and security for liberty under the law.

The word *equality*, however, did not appear in the Constitution of 1787 and the Bill of Rights of 1791. Further, the ideal of equal rights for all individuals under a government of laws was contradicted by the existence of slavery and the denial of rights to some people because of race or gender. Although the Constitution and Bill of Rights, as originally written, did not outlaw slavery and discrimination based on race or gender, one of the great early opponents of slavery and racial discrimination, Frederick Douglass, argued in a widely praised Fourth of July speech (1852) that "interpreted as it *ought* to be interpreted, the Constitution is a GLORIOUS LIBERTY DOCUMENT." According to Douglass—and many other opponents of slavery, racial discrimination, and gender discrimination—the Constitution of 1787 was neutral with regard to race and sex, thereby leaving the way open to equal protection under the law for women and racial minorities.

The American ideal of equal rights under law, however, was not explicitly included in the Constitution until after the Civil War, with passage of the three Reconstruction-era amendments. The 13th Amendment (1865) banned slavery. The 14th Amendment (1868) guaranteed equal rights of citizenship to all Americans, with the special intention of protecting the rights of former slaves. The 15th Amendment (1870) provided that voting rights of citizens "shall not be denied or abridged by the United States or by any State on account of race, color, or previous condition of servitude."

The 14th Amendment includes the word *equality* in Section 1, which prohibits a state government from denying "to any person within its jurisdiction the equal protection of the laws." This equal protection clause protects individuals from arbitrary discrimination by government officials. Federal courts have read the equal protection concept into their interpretation of the due process clause of the 5th Amendment, thereby applying the equal protection limitations to the federal government. Neither federal nor state governments may classify people in ways that violate their liberties or rights under the U.S. Constitution.

The equal protection clause does not require identical treatment in all circumstances. Discrimination is sometimes permitted. For example, laws denying people under 18 years old the right to vote or the right to marry without parental permission are considered reasonable classifications that do not violate the individual's constitutional rights and liberties because a relationship seems to exist between chronological age and the ability to perform in certain ways. However, a law prohibiting redheads from voting would be unreasonable and unconstitutional because no relationship exists between red hair and the ability to vote.

Racial equality and affirmative action   Despite the promise of the 14th Amendment, most black Americans did not enjoy equal protection of the laws until the second half of the 20th century. Indeed, the Supreme Court decision in *Plessy v. Ferguson* (1896) exemplified the denial of equality to black Americans in its sanction of "separate but equal" treatment of people based on race. Both before and after *Plessy*, racial segregation was a firmly established fact of American life, with the separate facilities for blacks hardly ever equal to those provided for white Americans.

If *Plessy* was a symbol of the unequal and unjust social conditions of racial segregation, it also contained a seed of social change toward legal equality. In the dissenting opinion, Justice John Marshall Harlan wrote, "Our Constitution is color-blind and neither knows nor tolerates classes among citizens. In respect of civil rights all citizens are equal before the law. . . . It is therefore to be regretted that this high tribunal . . . has reached the conclusion that it is competent for a state to regulate the enjoyment by citizens of their civil rights solely on the basis of race." Justice Harlan's argument for a color-blind Constitution became the rallying cry and goal of the National Association for the Advancement of Colored People (NAACP) and other participants in a civil rights movement committed to equal justice under the law.

The NAACP and its allies achieved several legal victories from the 1930s to the 1950s that advanced the cause of equal protection for the constitutional rights of black Americans. For example, *Smith v. Allwright* (1944) struck down barriers to participation by blacks in Democratic party primary elections. *Missouri ex rel. Gaines* v. *Canada* (1938) and *Sweatt* v. *Painter* (1950) provided access for black students to public law schools previously restricted to white students. The turning point, however, came in *Brown* v. *Board of Education* (1954), which overturned *Plessy* and outlawed state-sanctioned racial segregation in public schools. Several Court decisions after *Brown,* plus the federal Civil Rights Act of 1964, struck down racial segregation laws affecting all facets of American life and advanced the cause of equal security for the constitutional rights of all individuals, regardless of color or race. A key Court decision after *Brown* was *Cooper* v. *Aaron* (1958), which reaffirmed the court's decision in *Brown* against racial segregation in public schools. And *Heart of Atlanta Motel* v. *United States* (1964) buttressed the Civil Rights Act of 1964 in its prohibition of racial discrimination in privately owned accommodations open to the public, such as hotels and restaurants.

In 1967, in *Loving* v. *Virginia,* the Court struck down a state law prohibiting interracial marriages and held that all racial classifications are "inherently suspect classifications." Thus, any legal classification based on race would be subject to "strict scrutiny" by the Court. This means that the suspect classification would be judged unconstitutional unless the government could justify it with a compelling public interest, which is very difficult to do.

Since the 1970s the NAACP and other civil rights organizations have argued for both government-sponsored and private,

voluntary affirmative action programs. Such programs are designed to give preferential treatment to racial minorities in order to provide greater access to jobs, competitive college and university programs, promotions to high-level professional and management positions, and government contracts. Advocates of affirmative action have argued that African Americans, for example, lag far behind whites in income, educational achievement, job advancement, and living standards. They claim that these differences are the consequence of many generations of racial discrimination and that affirmative action is the best way to overcome quickly the continuing negative effects of past discrimination.

Opponents of affirmative action view it as "reverse discrimination" based on race and, therefore, a violation of the idea that the Constitution is "color-blind."

The Court has upheld aspects of affirmative action while striking down extreme versions of this concept. In *Regents of the University of California* v. *Bakke* (1978), for example, the Court ruled that a university could take into account race and ethnicity when making decisions about the admission of students. However, the Court ruled that an affirmative action plan based on rigid racial quotas to boost admission of minority students to a university was unconstitutional. In *United Steelworkers of America* v. *Weber* (1979), the Court permitted an employer's voluntarily imposed and temporary affirmative action program. That program would encourage unskilled black workers to obtain training that would lead to better, more skilled jobs, in which black Americans historically have been underrepresented. Once again, however, the Court rejected rigid, race-based quotas in hiring and job advancement.

In *United States* v. *Paradise* (1987), the Court upheld a temporary and "narrowly tailored" quota system to bring about job promotion for black state troopers in Alabama. The state's affirmative action plan imposed a "one black-for-one-white" promotion quota. This was justified, the Court said, by the "long and shameful record of delay and resistance" to employment opportunities for black Americans in the Alabama state police force.

Gender-based issues of equality Not until the 1970s did the Court extend to women the 14th Amendment's guarantee of "equal protection of the laws." One hundred years earlier, in *Bradwell* v. *Illinois* (1873), the Court had refused to use the equal protection clause to overturn a state government's ruling denying a woman a license to practice law. The denial was based strictly on the person's gender, but the Court ignored this flagrant violation of "equal protection of the laws." Writing for the Court, Justice Joseph P. Bradley justified the decision in *Bradwell* with a paternalistic explanation: "The natural and proper timidity and delicacy which belongs to the female sex evidently unfits it for many of the occupations of civil life [such as being a lawyer]. . . . [T]he domestic sphere [is] that which properly belongs to the domain and functions of womanhood."

The Court's paternalism toward women reflected the general view of the public in the latter half of the 19th century. The late 19th-century Court also ruled that the 14th Amendment did not require state governments to permit women to vote (*Minor* v. *Happersett,* 1875) or to serve on juries (*Strauder* v. *West Virginia,* 1880). It took the 19th Amendment to the Constitution (1920) to overturn the Court's decision against women's voting rights. Not until 1975, in *Taylor* v. *Louisiana,* did the Court overturn *Strauder* and rule against state exclusion of women from jury duty.

Since the 1970s women have successfully challenged restrictions that appear to violate the 14th Amendment's equal protection clause. In *Reed* v. *Reed* (1971), for example, the Court used the 14th Amendment to nullify a state law that discriminated against women in serving as the administrators of the estates of the deceased.

In 1987, in *Johnson* v. *Transportation Agency of Santa Clara County,* the Court endorsed a carefully crafted, temporary, and voluntary affirmative action plan to boost job promotion opportunities for women. The Court held it was permissible to take into account a woman's gender as a positive factor in promotion to a higher-ranking position because women had been systematically denied access to such positions in the past.

In 1996, in *Romer* v. *Evans,* the Supreme Court struck down an amendment to the constitution of Colorado that violated the 14th Amendment's equal protection clause by discriminating against a class of people including homosexuals, lesbians, and bisexuals. Gay people, as a class, had been singled out, said the Court, and denied the right to seek protection from the government against discrimination based on membership in that class.

Continuing controversy Since the 1970s Americans have tended to agree about the constitutionality and justice of guaranteeing equality of civil rights and liberties to all individuals in the United States, regardless of race, ethnicity, or gender. Also since the 1970s, however, Americans have argued about the issue of affirmative action to remedy the effects of past discrimination against racial minorities and women.

Is any kind of affirmative action plan a violation of the equal protection clause? Or is affirmative action the best short-term and temporary means of reversing many generations of unjust discrimination?

The U.S. Congress endorsed limited uses of affirmative action to redress past injustices in the Civil Rights Act of 1991. However, in *Adarand Construction, Inc.* v. *Pena* (1995), the Court held that all race-based classifications, including government affirmative action programs, should be subjected to the standard of strict scrutiny. According to Justice Sandra Day O'Connor, all government classifications by race "should be subjected to detailed judicial inquiry to ensure that the personal right to equal protection of the laws has not been infringed." Policies or programs based on racial classifications—including those designed to boost the opportunities of minorities in an attempt to overcome the negative effects of past discrimination—have to be narrowly defined and designed to advance a compelling government interest. Otherwise, they could be struck down as unconstitutional infringements of the 14th Amendment.

There has been continuous public controversy about the constitutionality and morality of affirmative action programs in education, government, and private enterprise. Citizens and the courts are likely to face tough decisions about modification or termination of policies that sanction unequal treatment of groups in the pursuit of rememdies for past injustices.

SEE ALSO *Affirmative action; Brown v. Board of Education; Civil rights; Cooper v. Aaron; Heart of Atlanta Motel v. United States; Johnson v. Transportation Agency of Santa Clara County; Plessy v. Ferguson; Reed v. Reed; Regents of the University of California v. Bakke; Smith v. Allwright; Sweatt v. Painter; United Steelworkers of America v. Weber*

SOURCES Judith A. Baer, *Equality under the Constitution* (Ithaca: Cornell University Press, 1983). Paul Finkelman, "Race and the Constitution," in *By and for the People: Constitutional Rights in American History,* edited by Kermit L. Hall (Arlington Heights, Ill.: Harlan Davidson, 1991). Donald W. Jackson, *Even the Children of Strangers: Equality under the U.S. Constitution* (Lawrence: University Press of Kansas, 1992). Andrew Kull, *The Color-Blind Constitution* (Cambridge: Harvard University Press, 1992). Paula Petrik, "Women and the Bill of Rights," in *By and for the People: Constitutional Rights in American History,* edited by Kermit L. Hall (Arlington Heights, Ill.: Harlan Davidson, 1991). J. R. Pole, *The Pursuit of Equality in American History,* 2nd ed. (Berkeley: University of California Press, 1993). Sandra F. Van Burkleo, "No Rights But Human Rights," *Constitution* 2, no. 2 (Spring–Summer 1990): 4–19.

EQUAL PROTECTION OF THE LAWS

The equal protection clause of the 14th Amendment states, "No state shall ... deny to any person within its jurisdiction the equal protection of the laws." The 14th Amendment, ratified in 1868, became part of the U.S. Constitution in the wake of the Civil War, with the direct purpose of protecting the legal rights of African Americans recently emancipated from slavery. The equal protection clause, however, has been applied by the courts to protect the rights of all individuals under the authority of the Constitution.

Until the 1940s, the equal protection clause was rarely used by the Supreme Court to overturn state laws as unconstitutional. Since the 1950s, however, the Court has used the equal protection clause to strike down, as unconstitutional, state laws supporting racial segregation in schools and other public facilities. For example, the Court's decision in *Brown* v. *Board of Education* (1954) was based on the equal protection clause. In *Reed* v. *Reed* (1971) the Court, for the first time, struck down a state law because it discriminated against women, in violation of the 14th Amendment's equal protection clause.

SEE ALSO *Equality under the Constitution*

ERVIN, SAMUEL J., JR.

- Born: Sept. 27, 1896, Morganton, N.C.
- Political party: Democrat
- Education: University of North Carolina at Chapel Hill, graduated, 1917; Harvard University Law School, graduated, 1922
- Representative from North Carolina: 1946–47
- Senator from North Carolina: 1954–74
- Died: Apr. 23, 1985, Winston-Salem, N.C.

When it became clear that the Watergate break-in had been more than just a "third-rate burglary" and that Congress needed to investigate the Nixon administration's tactics during the 1972 Presidential election, Senate majority leader Mike Mansfield (Democrat–Montana) wisely chose North Carolina senator Sam Ervin to chair the special investigating committee. The 76-year-old Ervin called himself "just a country lawyer." But despite his grandfatherly appearance, Ervin was a shrewd politician, constitutional scholar, and relentless investigator.

As a conservative Southern Democrat, Ervin had opposed civil rights legislation, but as the chairman of the Senate Subcommittee on Constitutional Rights, he had labored long in defense of civil liberties. From his reading of the Bill of Rights, Ervin opposed excessive government secrecy and defended individual privacy and freedom of the press. When he became chairman of the Select Committee on Presidential Campaign Activities, formed to investigate Watergate, Ervin captivated national attention with his folksy sayings and Southern drawl. At the same time, his probing of witnesses from the Nixon administration exposed the "dirty tricks" they had employed during the election. Ervin's persistence led to the indictment and conviction of many government officials and eventually to the resignation of President Richard M. Nixon.

SEE ALSO *Bill of Rights; Investigations, congressional; Watergate investigation (1973–74)*

SOURCES Dick Dabney, *A Good Man: The Life of Sam J. Ervin* (Boston: Houghton Mifflin, 1976). Sam Ervin, *Preserving the Constitution: An Autobiography of Senator Sam Ervin* (Charlottesville, Va.: Mitchie, 1984).

ESTABLISHMENT CLAUSE

The 1st Amendment to the U.S. Constitution states, "Congress shall make no law respecting an establishment of religion." This establishment clause has been used by the Supreme Court to overturn, or declare unconstitutional, state laws involving the government in religious activities, such as prayers or religious programs in public schools. For example, the Court used the establishment clause to strike down state government laws in *Engel v. Vitale* (1962) and *Wallace v. Jaffree* (1985).

There is general agreement that the establishment clause prohibits an official religion endorsed by the government or preferential support by the government of some religions over others. There have been continuous arguments, however, about whether the establishment clause strictly prohibits all involvement by the government in support of religious activity as long as the involvement is conducted nonpreferentially.

SEE ALSO *Engel v. Vitale; Religious issues under the Constitution; Wallace v. Jaffree*

ETHICS

The public expects its elected officials to have high ethical standards. But standards of ethical behavior have changed over time. When Daniel Webster served as a senator in the 1830s and 1840s, he carried on a private legal practice and argued cases before the Supreme Court. Since Congress met for only half the year, it was commonplace for members to continue their other business activities during the months of adjournment. Questions arose about members' conflict of interest, and Congress began to meet year-round. The Senate and House revised their rules to prohibit members from representing legal clients and engaging in other outside activities. The old practice of a member putting his wife and children on the congressional payroll was banned. Ethics laws also prohibited the use of campaign funds for personal expenses. But no set of ethics laws will ever be final because political and financial practices, and public opinion, are constantly changing.

Some private groups, including Common Cause and Ralph Nader's Citizens'

Watch on Congress Project, keep close watch on congressional behavior and publicize ethics lapses and abuses of position. The press also scrutinizes congressional ethics. The Senate Select Committee on Ethics and the House Standards of Official Conduct Committee advise members and staff and investigate charges of impropriety.

From time to time, scandals have stirred public opinion and caused Congress to reexamine its rules of behavior. In the 19th century, such lobbying scandals as the one involving Credit Mobilier in 1872—when high-ranking members of both houses accepted stock from a railroad company receiving subsidies from the federal government—began the movement to restrict members' outside business and financial activities. Similarly, the 1970s investigation of Abscam (in which an FBI agent posed as an Arab sheikh and offered bribes to members of Congress) and the savings and loan scandals of the 1990s—which caught some members offering their influence in return for campaign contributions—further tightened congressional rules of ethics. The public has also seen excessive perks of Congress, including travel junkets and check bouncing at the House bank, as indications of the need for continued reform.

Ethics in the executive branch Like members of Congress, Presidents and their appointees are supposed to have high ethical standards, avoiding conflicts of interest between their public duties and private affairs. Concerns about ethics fall into three general categories: personal gain, conflict of interest, and misuse of public funds.

Presidents place their financial assets in a "blind trust," a legal arrangement under which a trustee, chosen by the President, handles the President's personal financial affairs. During his term the President has no knowledge of the trustee's investment decisions, allowing him to make decisions without thinking of personal gain.

To avoid misusing public funds, modern Presidents pay for political activities out of their own pockets or through their political parties. Party national committees pay for such expenses as public opinion polls and the President's appearances at political events. Similarly, members of the administration are expected to reimburse the government for transportation and related expenses when they use government vehicles for personal or political trips. Sometimes officials misuse this privilege or blur the line between public and private or political business.

Restrictions on officials began in 1789, when the secretary of the Treasury was forbidden by law from investing in government securities. In 1853 Congress passed the first conflict-of-interest statute, but its criminal penalties were rarely enforced. Most Presidents in the 19th century, especially James Buchanan and Ulysses S. Grant, did not enforce ethical standards.

In modern times President Dwight Eisenhower was forced to dismiss his chief of staff, Sherman Adams, for accepting presents from a Boston financier. Jimmy Carter's director of the Office of Management and Budget, Bert Lance, resigned over charges involving his conduct as a banker in Georgia, though the charges were eventually dropped. In 1986 two officials of Ronald Reagan's administration, Michael Deaver and Lyn Nofziger, were prosecuted for violating a ban on lobbying the government for one year after leaving government service. Deaver was found guilty of perjury and Nofziger of violating the one-year ban, but his conviction was overturned on appeal. In 1987 Attorney General Edwin Meese was investigated by independent counsel for his efforts to help a friend build an oil pipeline between Iraq and Jordan. A 1988 report indicated that Meese had violated federal law, but not for personal gain. Meese was not prosecuted, but he resigned as attorney general.

In 1965 President Lyndon Johnson issued Executive Order 11222, which ordered officials to avoid actions that gave the appearance of using their offices for private gain, giving preferential treatment to any individual or organization, "affecting adversely the confidence of the public in the integrity of government," or making decisions outside official channels. President Jimmy Carter established strict standards for appointees, including disclosure of financial assets, divestiture or sale of assets that might create conflicts of interest, and restrictions on private employment after officials leave government, including a one-year prohibition on lobbying. These provisions were incorporated into the Ethics in Government Act of 1978, which established an Office of Ethics in the White House to monitor compliance with reporting provisions and to issue advisory opinions to government personnel.

The Presidential Transition Effectiveness Act of 1988 covers ethics issues during changes of administration. It provides that transition aides who make conduct investigations and make recommendations about policy in government departments and agencies must fill out disclosure forms, so that the public will know the names, recent employment history, and "sources of funding" (if not paid for by transition funds) of such transition officials. During the transition to Bill Clinton's administration, rules for transition staff included a six-month ban on subsequent lobbying of government agencies by staffers involved with these agencies.

President Clinton ordered the strictest code of ethics for political appointees ever instituted. By executive order, he prohibited officials from lobbying their former departments for five years after leaving government service (an increase from the one-year ban in the 1978 law), although they could lobby other government agencies after one year. In addition, high officials in many departments, including U.S. trade negotiators, would also be banned for life from representing the interests of foreign governments and political parties, though they would be free to represent foreign corporations and interest groups after five years (an increase from the three-year ban in existing law). These rules covered the top 1,100 government officials. An additional 3,500 top executive branch officials are prohibited from lobbying federal agencies for one year after they leave government service.

Ethics in the Judicial Branch Like members of the legislative and executive branches, federal judges are expected to have high standards of ethics. All federal judges follow the principles outlined in the *Code of Conduct for United States Judges,* which has been adopted by the Judicial Conference of the United States, the federal courts' national policy-making group. The *Code of Conduct* includes these guidelines:
• A judge should uphold the integrity and independence of the judiciary.
• A judge should avoid impropriety and the appearance of impropriety in all activities.
• A judge should perform the duties of the office impartially and diligently.
• A judge may engage in extrajudicial activities to improve the law, the legal system, and the administration of justice.
• A judge should regulate extrajudicial activities to minimize the risk of conflict with judicial duties.
• A judge should regularly file reports of compensation received for law-related and extrajudicial activities.
• A judge should refrain from political activity.

According to these ethical standards, judges should not hear cases in which they have a financial interest, a personal bias regarding a party to the case, or earlier involvement in the case as a lawyer. Further, judges are expected to participate in activities that contribute to the public good through improvement of the legal and judicial systems, and as a result, many judges are engaged in law-related education activities in schools.

SEE ALSO *Campaign financing, congressional; Carter, Jimmy; Cleveland, Grover; Clinton, Bill; Credit Mobilier scandal (1872–73); Discipline, congressional; Executive Office of the President; Grant, Ulysses S.; House bank scandal (1992); Independent counsel; Junkets; Perks, congressional; White House Office*

SOURCES Terry Eastland, *Energy in the Executive: The Case for the Strong Presidency* (New York: Free Press, 1992). Bruce Jennings and Daniel Callahan, eds., *Representation and Responsibility: Exploring Legislative Ethics* (New York: Plenum, 1985). Robert North Roberts, *White House Ethics: The History of the Politics of Conflict of Interest Regulation* (Westport, Conn.: Greenwood, 1988).

EVERSON V. BOARD OF EDUCATION OF EWING TOWNSHIP

- 330 U.S. 1 (1947)
- Vote: 5–4
- For the Court: Black
- Dissenting: Jackson, Frankfurter, Rutledge, and Burton

In 1941 the New Jersey legislature passed a law that said boards of education could pay the costs of bus transportation, to and from school, of students in public schools and Catholic parochial schools. Arch Everson, a resident of the school district governed by the Ewing Township Board of Education, claimed that this state law violated the 1st Amendment prohibition against the state establishment of religion. Everson claimed that it was unfair and illegal for the state government to use money from taxpayers, like himself, to pay for costs associated with private religious schools.

The Issue The 1st Amendment of the Constitution says, "Congress shall make no law respecting an establishment of religion." Furthermore, the 14th Amendment says, "No state shall . . . deprive any person of life, liberty, or property without due process of law." Everson argued that the 1st Amendment, which applies only to the U.S. Congress, could also be applied to state governments through the due process clause of the 14th Amendment.

The other constitutional issue was whether the New Jersey law challenged by Arch Everson actually involved the state government in religion in a way that violated the establishment clause of the 1st Amendment.

Opinion of the Court Justice Hugo Black, writing for the Supreme Court, argued that the 1st Amendment to the Constitution can be used to limit state governments through the due process clause of the 14th Amendment. On this issue, the Court agreed with Arch Everson. However, the Court disagreed with Everson with regard to the establishment clause and upheld the New Jersey law, which provided bus transportation for Catholic parochial school students at public expense. Justice Black claimed that this New Jersey law did not violate the establishment clause of the 1st Amendment.

Justice Black wrote the following rules to guide decisions about the establishment clause:

Neither a state nor the Federal Government can set up a church. Neither can pass laws which aid one religion, aid all religions, or prefer one religion over another. Neither can force nor influence a person to go to or remain away from church against his will or force him to profess a belief or disbelief in any religion. . . . In the words of Jefferson, the clause against establishment of religion by law was intended to erect "a wall of separation between Church and State."

Justice Black concluded that the New Jersey statute at issue in this case did not violate the 1st Amendment because public payment for bus transportation of parochial school students had nothing to do with government promoting religion. Rather, this was only a program for moving children safely and easily to and from school, regardless of the religion or school of the children.

Dissent Justice Robert Jackson wrote that he agreed totally with the Court's rules for deciding what is an "establishment of religion." But he disagreed with the Court's conclusion that the *Everson* case did not fit these rules.

Justice Wiley Rutledge wrote a second dissenting opinion that also agreed with Black's rules and held that the New Jersey law *was* an example of an "establishment of religion." He concluded, "The [1st] Amendment's purpose . . . was to create a complete and permanent separation of the spheres of religious activity and civil authority by comprehensively forbidding every form of public aid or support for religion."

Significance The *Everson* case was the first to apply the establishment clause of the 1st Amendment to the states through the 14th Amendment. And it set standards to guide interpretation of the establishment clause that have been used to resolve later controversies, such as *Engel* v. *Vitale* (1962) and *Abington School District* v. *Schempp* (1963).

SEE ALSO *Abington School District v. Schempp; Establishment clause; Engel v. Vitale; Religious issues under the Constitution*

SOURCES William Lee Miller, *The First Liberty: Religion and the American Republic* (New York: Paragon House, 1985).

EXCLUSIONARY RULE

Evidence obtained in violation of a person's constitutional rights cannot be used to prosecute the person. This restriction on the use of evidence obtained illegally is called the exclusionary rule, which was created in *Weeks* v. *United States* (1914). The Supreme Court applied the exclusionary rule to a state government for the first time in *Mapp* v. *Ohio* (1961).

The 4th Amendment to the Constitution protects individuals "against unreasonable searches and seizures" by government officials and provides that "no warrants [for searches and seizures] shall issue, but upon probable cause." If government officials seize evidence without a warrant, for example, it usually is excluded, or thrown out, from the legal proceedings against a person accused of a crime. However, in *United States* v.

Leon (1984), the Court established a "good faith" exception to the exclusionary rule. This means that evidence seized on the basis of a mistakenly issued search warrant can still be used in a trial, if the warrant was issued on good faith—the belief that there were valid reasons for issuing it.

SEE ALSO *Mapp v. Ohio; Searches and seizures; United States v. Leon; Weeks v. United States*

EXECUTIVE AGREEMENTS

A pact or understanding with a foreign government reached by the President or a Presidential agent is called an executive agreement. The agreement may be written or oral. Unlike a treaty, it does not require the advice and consent of the Senate.

Although executive agreements are not mentioned in the Constitution, Presidents claim the power to enter into such agreements based on their executive power, their duty to receive ambassadors from other nations, their power as commander in chief, and their duty to take care that the laws be faithfully executed.

The first known executive agreement involved a 1792 postal arrangement with Canada, negotiated by the American and Canadian postmasters general. The vast majority have involved agreements between departments of government and their foreign counterparts in agriculture, health, trade, communications, the environment, science, and defense.

Executive agreements have been crucial in foreign affairs. There are many examples: the Bagot-Rush agreement to limit American and British naval forces on the Great Lakes (1817); a coalition between the United States and several European powers to crush the Boxer rebellion in China (1900); the so-called Gentlemen's Agreement to regulate Japanese immigration to the United States (1905); and an armistice with Imperial Germany (1918). Agreements have been made to exchange

U.S. destroyers for British naval bases (1940); to end the fighting in Germany and establish the status of Berlin (1945); to end the Korean War (1953); to end U.S. involvement in the Vietnam War (1973); to implement a strategic arms limitation agreement with the Soviet Union (1979); to secure the release of U.S. diplomats from Iran (1981); and to forge a coalition to defeat Iraqi aggression against Kuwait (1990).

There are nearly 10 times as many executive agreements as there are treaties; on average, only 30 treaties but more than 250 agreements have been concluded each year since the 1960s. The majority of the executive agreements have been authorized by Congress in advance or ratified by Congress after being put into effect, and most require subsequent laws by Congress to be implemented.

Only about 5 percent of executive agreements are negotiated and implemented without any congressional role. Some of these are major American commitments to the defense of other nations or agreements to lease military bases in other countries, pacts that in effect create military alliances without any congressional participation.

In 1969 Congress passed the National Commitments Resolution, which stated that a national commitment of the United States could not be made by executive agreement but only by "affirmative action taken by the executive and legislative branches of the U.S. Government by means of a treaty, statute, or concurrent resolution of both Houses of Congress specifically providing for such commitment."

Presidents do not accept this interpretation of a national commitment, arguing that executive agreements are binding obligations of the United States. The courts have imposed some limits on executive agreements: they cannot be inconsistent with prior congressional legislation; agreements that affect prior laws passed by Congress must be implemented by new congressional legislation; and they cannot

impair the constitutional rights of American citizens.

Some executive agreements have been kept secret, especially those involving the Department of Defense and intelligence agencies. In 1972 Congress passed the Case Act, which provided that the secretary of state must transmit the text of any executive agreement to Congress within 60 days. Secret agreements must be submitted to the House Foreign Affairs and Senate Foreign Relations Committees, which keep them secret unless released from that obligation by the President. In 1977 the time limit under the Case Act was reduced by Congress to 20 days.

SEE ALSO *Treaty powers*
SOURCES Louis Fisher, *The Constitution between Friends* (New York: St. Martin's, 1978).

EXECUTIVE BRANCH

The departments and agencies that take political direction from the President, including the 14 cabinet-level departments, constitute the executive branch of the federal government. "The executive branch" is not a phrase found in the Constitution, but it is favored by Presidents because it assumes that these departments are under their sole direction. The Constitution, however, provides that officials of the departments are to take direction not only from the President but also from laws passed by Congress.

Top officials in the executive branch, generally referred to as "the administration," are appointed by the President with the advice and consent of the Senate, and they serve at the pleasure of the President. The President uses his Executive Office agencies to supervise their budgets, their legislative requests to Congress, and the regulations they make and enforce.

Independent regulatory agencies (such as the Federal Trade Commission), units of government that are insulated by Congress from political direction (such as the Federal Reserve Board), as well as several agencies that perform functions for Congress (such as the Congressional Budget Office) are not part of the executive branch. Presidential appointment and removal powers over officials in these agencies may be limited by Congress, and the President may not provide them with political direction.

SEE ALSO *Appointment power; Budget, Presidential; Cabinet; Executive Office of the President; Removal power*
SOURCES Christopher H. Pyle and Richard M. Pious, *The President, Congress, and the Constitution* (New York: Free Press, 1984).

EXECUTIVE OFFICE BUILDINGS

The two Executive Office Buildings near the White House provide offices for the Executive Office of the President and some units of the White House Office.

The Old Executive Office Building, located next to the White House on Pennsylvania Avenue, provides office space for much of the Vice Presidential staff, the White House Office, and the National Security Council staff, as well as for the Office of Management and Budget and the Council of Economic Advisers. It also contains the White House Library and Research Center.

Built in 1875, the building housed the State, War, and Navy Departments until 1947. It was designed in French Second Empire style, with ornate stonework, including dormer windows, tiers of columns, a green copper mansard roof, and two dozen chimneys. It has 553 rooms and 440,250 square feet of office space. It was completely renovated and redecorated during Ronald Reagan's administration.

The New Executive Office Building, completed in 1968, houses the remaining Presidential agencies, such as the Office of Personnel Management. It is a 10-story structure of red brick, with 307,000 square feet of office space. It is located one block from the Old Executive Office Building, off Pennsylvania Avenue on Jackson Place. Although modern in style, its rooflines were designed to harmonize with the mansard style.

EXECUTIVE OFFICE OF THE PRESIDENT

The Executive Office of the President (EOP) assists the President in supervising the executive branch. It was created by President Franklin D. Roosevelt in Reorganization Act No. 1, submitted to Congress in 1939. At various times the EOP has included agencies to improve the management and administration of the executive departments, such as the Council on Personnel Administration in the 1940s; economic advisory boards, such as the International Economic Policy Board of the 1970s; agencies for national security, such as the Board of Consultants on Foreign Intelligence Activities in the 1950s; and agencies for emergency preparedness, such as the Office of Civil and Defense Mobilization in the 1960s.

Sometimes the EOP has contained agencies that should have belonged in the departments but have been given "Presidential status" to signal their importance to the administration. Such agencies include the Disarmament Agency in the 1950s, the Office of Economic Opportunity (which administered antipoverty programs) in the 1960s, and the Office of Drug Abuse Policy in the 1970s.

In 1992 the offices within the EOP had a total of 2,000 employees and spent $200 million each year. These offices included the White House Office, which provides the President with assistance in communicating with Congress, special interest groups, and the general public; the Office of Management and Budget, which prepares the Budget of the United States, oversees departmental requests for legislation from Congress, assists the President with veto messages, and ensures that new government regulations are in accordance with Presidential priorities; the Council of Economic Advisers, which prepares the economic report of the President and gives advice on economic policy; the National Security Council, which provides advice to the President on foreign policy and military matters; the Office of the U.S. Trade Representative, which negotiates trade policies with other nations; the Council on Environmental Quality, which develops regulatory policies for clean air and water; the Office of Science and Technology Policy, which recommends new government programs in science; the Office of Policy Development, which provides long-range studies for new domestic legislation; the Office of the Vice President, which assists the incumbent with speeches and scheduling of activities; and the Office of Administration, which provides management support for the other agencies.

SEE ALSO *Council of Economic Advisers; Council on Environmental Quality; Executive Office Buildings; National Security Council; Office of Administration; Office of Management and Budget; Office of Science and Technology Policy; Office of U.S. Trade Representative; Vice President; White House Office*

SOURCES John P. Burke, *The Institutional Presidency* (Baltimore, Md.: Johns Hopkins University Press, 1992). Thomas Cronin, ed., *The Presidential Advisory System* (New York: Harper & Row, 1969). Richard Johnson, *Managing the White House* (New York: Harper & Row, 1974). Richard Nathan, *The Administrative Presidency* (New York: Wiley, 1986).

EXECUTIVE ORDERS

Executive orders are regulations issued by the President. Provided that they are based either on his constitutional powers or laws passed by Congress, they have the force of law. Federal courts will enforce them just as if they had been enacted by Congress, provided that they do not conflict with federal laws. An executive order that carries out a law may later be revoked by new legislation. An executive order can be nullified, or canceled, if the Supreme Court or lower federal courts find that it is unconstitutional. For instance, in 1952 the Supreme Court ruled that President Harry Truman's seizure of the steel mills during the Korean War violated the due process clause of the Constitution because the President had seized property without being given statutory authority by Congress.

Executive orders are filed in the Department of State after the President issues them. Between 1789 and 1907 Presidents issued approximately 2,400 such orders. Since 1907 the orders have been filed chronologically, and each is given a number, with more than 13,000 numbered between 1908 and 1991.

The first executive order, issued by George Washington on June 8, 1789, instructed the heads of departments to make a "clear account" of matters in their departments. Since then, the orders have been used to regulate the civil service, to determine holidays for federal workers, to recognize federal employee unions, to institute security programs, and to classify government documents as top secret or secret. They have been used to designate public lands as Indian reservations and for environmental protection. They are also used to organize federal disaster assistance efforts. Executive orders have been used by each President beginning with Dwight Eisenhower to organize the intelligence agencies at the beginning of his term in office and to set up other aspects of White House operations.

President Franklin D. Roosevelt used executive orders to create agencies without going through Congress. In 1944 Congress prohibited funding such agencies. In 1968 Congress prohibited the creation of Presidential commissions, councils, or study groups that were not authorized by Congress. President Richard Nixon tried to dismantle several agencies by executive order. This action was blocked by the federal courts because Congress had not abolished them by law.

Executive orders have been used to assert Presidential war powers in the Civil War and all subsequent wars. Franklin

Roosevelt seized defense plants to ensure production of aircraft in World War II. He also used a series of executive orders to establish a curfew for Japanese Americans on the West Coast, to exclude them from certain areas, and finally, to intern them in camps in the desert until 1944.

Executive orders have often been used for civil rights enforcement. Harry Truman issued an executive order in 1948 ending racial segregation in the armed forces. John Kennedy issued an executive order banning racial discrimination in newly constructed public housing and another banning pay discrimination against women by federal contractors. He issued orders prohibiting racial discrimination in federally funded libraries, hospitals, and other public facilities. Richard Nixon required government contractors to institute affirmative action hiring programs for women and members of minority groups.

SEE ALSO *Executive branch; Executive power; Imperial Presidency; Steel seizure (1952)*

SOURCES Louis Fisher, *President and Congress* (New York: Free Press, 1972).

EXECUTIVE POWER

Article 2 of the Constitution opens with the words, "The executive power shall be vested in a President of the United States." Presidents take the term *executive power* to mean a general responsibility to direct the bureaucracy.

The Presidential claim is controversial because the Constitution confers neither the title nor the powers of "chief executive" on the President, nor does it assign the President any powers to make a budget or remove other government officials. It does not explicitly say that the President can issue orders to heads of departments. Instead, it provides that he may "require the opinion in writing, of the principal officer in each of the departments, on any subject relating to the duties of their respective offices."

When Andrew Jackson asserted that he could give orders to the secretary of the Treasury, his claim led to a split within his own party and the rise of an opposition party known as the Whigs, who challenged the prerogatives of "King Andrew the First." The Whigs sought to minimize, if not entirely eliminate, Presidential control of the departments. Senator Daniel Webster countered that the Founding Fathers did not intend to make the President administrative chief. He argued that "the executive power" meant no more than the specific powers that appear after it in Article 2—most of which had nothing to do with administering the government. "I do not regard the declaration that the executive power shall be vested in a President as being any grant at all," Webster concluded. The Whigs believed that Presidents could not remove cabinet secretaries without the consent of Congress, nor could they control policy in the departments. Instead, the Whigs believed that Congress should make policy.

Modern Presidents, beginning with Theodore Roosevelt, have argued that the "executive power" constitutes an affirmative grant of power that allows them to supervise the executive departments' budget and legislative requests to Congress. Presidents Herbert Hoover and Franklin D. Roosevelt both argued that the principle of accountability to the people in a democracy requires that Presidents have absolute control over operations of the departments, that they be considered the "chief executive," and that they be able to issue orders to officials in the departments. Only with such powers, they concluded, could Presidents be fairly held accountable for the actions of officials in their administrations.

The conflict between Congress and the President over power to run the departments remains unsettled, in large part because of specific powers the Constitution grants to Congress in Article 1. The legislature creates all the departments, determines their powers, and creates all the offices (and the salaries that go with them)—all by passing laws. It also reorganizes the government bureaucracy to create new agencies or abolish existing ones.

Congress authorizes government programs, determines the powers and duties of all officials, and can prohibit activities of which it disapproves. Congress appropriates all funds for departments, and officials can spend only the money appropriated by its laws. Congress oversees the activities of the agencies to ensure that officials have obeyed the laws and spent money lawfully. Congress makes the rules that govern the civil and military personnel in the bureaucracies. The Supreme Court has stated the principle that officials are expected, in performing routine duties, to obey the laws of the United States rather than orders that the President might issue, if such orders conflict.

In modern times Presidents have vastly increased their executive powers. Since 1921 they have submitted an annual budget to Congress, rather than permitting departments to request funds directly. Since 1926 they have had the power to remove officials from departments. Since the late 1930s the Executive Office of the President has enabled the President to dominate personnel selection, program development, and legislative requests made to Congress by the departments. In the 1940s the President was given authority by Congress to formulate and then implement reorganization plans, subject only to prior congressional consent. By the 1970s Presidents were implementing new management techniques in the departments. In the 1980s they were approving or disapproving all departmental agency regulations prior to final adoption. They had indeed become "chief executives."

SEE ALSO *Appointment power; Budget, Presidential; Cabinet; Commander in chief; Departments, executive; Executive branch; Executive Office of the President; Executive orders; Executive privilege; Impoundment of funds; Modern presidency; Office of Management and Budget; Removal power; War powers*
SOURCES Christopher H. Pyle and Richard

M. Pious, *The President, Congress, and the Constitution* (New York: Free Press, 1984).

EXECUTIVE PRIVILEGE

From time to time, Presidents of the United States have claimed the executive privilege of withholding information from Congress, the federal courts, or the general public. The Constitution says nothing about secrecy in the executive branch and does not contain the phrase "executive privilege." Presidents claim the privilege by arguing that it is a functional necessity: the advice they receive and the deliberations in their administration will not be candid and truthful if they are subject to subsequent congressional and judicial scrutiny.

In the 19th century Presidents tried to withhold information about diplomatic and military ventures, but all eventually provided Congress with the information it sought. When President George Washington refused to give Congress information about the Jay Treaty with Great Britain, it was because he claimed such information should be submitted only to the Senate, which must consent to all treaties.

In 1834, Andrew Jackson refused a Senate request for certain cabinet records dealing with his feud with the Bank of the United States. In a message to the Senate, Jackson stated, "The Executive is a coordinate and independent branch of the Government equally with the Senate; and I have yet to learn under what constitutional authority that branch of the Legislature has to require of me an account of any communication, either verbally or in writing, made to the heads of department acting as a cabinet council."

The modern practice of withholding information was instituted by President William Howard Taft, whose Executive Order 1062 provided that the President could order heads of departments not to furnish information to Congress if it were "incompatible with the national interest." Prior to World War II, refusals to furnish Congress with information were rare. During the war, however, President Franklin D. Roosevelt refused to turn over some Federal Bureau of Investigation files to congressional committees, and President Harry Truman ordered that congressional requests for personnel files be submitted to him for a final decision about compliance.

The term *executive privilege* was invented by Dwight Eisenhower's administration. In 1954 the President refused to turn over military personnel records to the Permanent Investigations Subcommittee of the Senate Government Operations Committee, headed by Senator Joseph McCarthy. Most of Congress took Eisenhower's side because McCarthy—without any evidence to back up his allegations—was questioning the loyalty of career military and diplomatic officers, charging them with being communists or communist sympathizers. Then, in 1958, Attorney General William Rogers argued that Eisenhower need not disclose candid advice from his assistants nor provide Congress with any documents relating to Presidential activities.

Other Presidents have also used executive privilege against Congress. President John F. Kennedy ordered General Maxwell Taylor, the White House military adviser, to refuse to testify before a House committee investigating the failure of an American-backed invasion of Cuba in 1961. Richard Nixon refused to supply documents to the House Armed Services Committee when it investigated bombing raids on North Vietnam that occurred without prior Presidential authorization.

The most important use of executive privilege occurred during the Watergate crisis. President Nixon refused to turn over tapes made of conversations in the Oval Office to the Senate Select Committee on Presidential Campaign Activities, which was investigating the Watergate crimes. A federal appeals court upheld Nixon's refusal, agreeing that he did not need to supply evidence about Watergate crimes to a congressional committee whose mandate from Congress was to consider changes in campaign financing laws.

In *United States* v. *Nixon* (1974), however, the Supreme Court ruled that President Nixon was required, despite his claim of executive privilege, to give up to a federal court the tape recordings that were sought as evidence against Presidential assistants charged with criminal behavior. Grand juries and juries on federal cases, the Supreme Court held, are entitled to all the evidence in a criminal case. No one, not even a President, may withhold evidence from the courts. While agreeing with Nixon that there is "a valid need for protection of communications" between Presidents and those who advise them, the Supreme Court insisted that the President was required to turn over evidence to the federal judge trying the case. The judge would then decide whether or not Nixon's claim was valid and whether or not the evidence could be introduced at a trial. The Supreme Court concluded that it was up to the courts, not the President, to weigh the balance between legitimate national security interests that might require information to be kept secret and the right of juries to obtain information about crimes.

The *United States* v. *Nixon* case recognized for the first time the Presidential claim that there may be, under certain circumstances, a right of executive privilege. But it left the final decision about the validity of the claim to the federal courts.

During the impeachment of Bill Clinton, the White House claimed that the president and his aides were shielded by executive privilege, that his lawyers were shielded by attorney-client privilege, and that Secret Service agents were shielded by "protective privilege." The federal courts rejected all of these claims, relying on the settled law in the *United States* v. *Nixon* case that, absent a national security issue, the president and his aides are required to provide evidence of criminal wrongdoing to grand juries.

SEE ALSO *Checks and balances; Executive orders; Nixon, Richard M.; United States v. Nixon; Watergate investigation (1973–74)*
SOURCES Raoul Berger, *Executive Privilege: A Constitutional Myth* (Cambridge: Har-

vard University Press, 1974). Archibald Cox, "Executive Privilege," *University of Pennsylvania Law Review* (June 1974): 1383–1438. James Hamilton, *The Power to Probe: A Study of Congressional Investigations* (New York: Vintage, 1976). Mark J. Rozell, *Executive Privilege: The Dilemma of Secrecy and Democratic Accountability* (Baltimore, Md.: Johns Hopkins University Press, 1994). Arthur M. Schlesinger, Jr., *The Imperial Presidency* (Boston: Houghton Mifflin, 1973).

EXECUTIVE PROTECTIVE SERVICE

SEE *Secret Service, U.S.*

EXECUTIVE SESSIONS OF CONGRESS

An executive session of a committee or of the full House or Senate once meant a closed session, from which the public and the press were excluded. In committee, these closed sessions often dealt with the final marking up of bills, in which the substance and language of a bill were prepared to be reported to the floor. Committees also held closed sessions to hear information of a sensitive nature, notably reports containing classified information relating to national security. The term *executive* also refers to executive business, such as treaties and nominations, which the Senate handles exclusively. Until 1929, the Senate debated and voted on executive business in closed session. Since then, the Senate has conducted these executive sessions in public, closing the doors only on rare occasions when dealing with highly classified, or confidential, information.

EX PARTE

When the Latin phrase *ex parte* (meaning "from the part of") is used in the title of a court case, it means that the action was taken on behalf of the person named in the title of the case. It does not require the notification of or participation by an opposing party. For example, *Ex parte Milligan* (1866) was a legal action taken to the U.S. Supreme Court on behalf of Lambdin P. Milligan by his attorney. Milligan was in jail when the Supreme Court decided his case. He had been sentenced to death by a U.S. military court for treason against the United States during the Civil War. The Supreme Court ruled that the military court had no jurisdiction in this case, and Milligan was released.

EX PARTE MILLIGAN

- 4 Wall. 2 (1866)
- Vote: 9–0
- For the Court: Davis

In 1864, the general in command of the military district of Indiana arrested Lambdin P. Milligan. The Civil War still raged in other parts of the country. Federal agents alleged they had evidence of a conspiracy by Milligan and others to release and arm rebel prisoners so they could take part in a Confederate invasion of Indiana.

The army brought Milligan before a special military court instead of before the regular civil courts that were still operating in Indiana. The military court convicted Milligan of conspiracy and sentenced him to death.

Early in the Civil War, President Abraham Lincoln had placed some sections of the country under military rule and replaced civilian courts with military courts to try individuals accused of insurrection. Lincoln also suspended the writ of habeas corpus in such situations. A writ of habeas corpus orders an official who has a person in custody to bring the prisoner to court and explain why he is detaining the person. This basic civil liberty prevents arbitrary arrest and imprisonment.

Article 1, Section 9, of the Constitution says, "The privilege of the writ of habeas corpus shall not be suspended, unless when in cases of rebellion or invasion the public safety may require it." Lincoln believed that his order, later confirmed by Congress, was crucial to the preservation of the Union.

Milligan applied to a civilian court in Indiana for a writ of habeas corpus. He claimed his conviction was unconstitutional and asked for his right to a trial by jury in a civilian court.

The Issue The issue came before the Supreme Court in 1866, a year after the Civil War had ended with the defeat of the Confederacy. The appeal did not involve the question of Milligan's guilt or innocence. Rather, the Court dealt with the constitutional issue of whether the government in wartime could suspend citizens' constitutional rights under the 5th and 6th Amendments and set up military courts in areas that were free from invasion or rebellion and in which the civilian courts were still operating.

Opinion of the Court The Court ruled against the government on this question. It ruled that suspending the right of habeas corpus and trying civilians in military courts when civilian courts still operated violated the Constitution.

The Court declared that the civilian courts had been open in Indiana and that the state had been far removed from the battle zone. Thus, neither the President nor Congress could legally deny to an accused person a civilian trial by jury and due process of law as guaranteed by the 5th and 6th Amendments.

Significance The *Milligan* decision represented a great victory for American civil liberties in times of war or internal turmoil. The Court upheld the principle that civilian authorities should control the military even in times of great stress and emergency. Moreover, it reaffirmed that the right of citizens to due process of law remains absolute as long as civilian courts are operating.

SEE ALSO *Habeas corpus, writ of*
SOURCES Allan Nevins, "The Case of the Copperhead Conspirator," in *Quarrels That Have Shaped the Constitution,* edited

by John A. Garraty (New York: Harper & Row, 1987).

EX POST FACTO LAW

Ex post facto is a Latin term meaning "after the fact." Article 1, Section 9, of the Constitution prohibits the federal government from passing an ex post facto law, which is one that makes an action a crime even though it was not a crime when it was committed, or increases the penalty for a crime after it was committed, or changes the rules of evidence to make it easier to convict someone. Similarly, Article 1, Section 10, provides that no state shall pass an ex post facto law. The Constitution protects individuals by denying to the Congress or state legislatures the power to punish people by passing ex post facto laws.

EX-PRESIDENCY

In the 19th century former Presidents received no pensions or regular retirement income, but often Congress passed special acts providing funds for them or for their widows or for paying off their debts. The Office of the Ex-Presidency was created as a formal entity by Congress in 1958, when it passed the Former Presidents Act. This law provided former Presidents with an annual pension of $25,000, to be adjusted upward to equal the salary of cabinet secretaries ($143,800 in 1993).

The Presidential Transition Act of 1963 provides ex-Presidents with an additional $1 million to cover expenses for the first six months out of office. During that time the General Services Administration provides them with office space, funds to pay staff, and travel expenses. For the remainder of their lives they are given free mailing privileges, use of an official residence at 716 Jackson Place, near the White House, the privilege of addressing the Senate, and Secret Service protection for themselves and their immediate families. The pension for Presidential widows was set at $10,000 in 1958 and was increased to $20,000 in 1971. However, widows under age 60 who remarry forfeit this pension. All widows are granted free use of the mails, and since 1968 widows have received lifetime Secret Service protection. Presidential children are guarded by the Secret Service until the age of 16.

In 1957 the cost of providing for former Presidents was $74,836, which was paid toward the upkeep of Presidential libraries. By 1987 that cost had grown to $16,202,000 for Presidential libraries, $1,234,000 for office allowances, and $9,843,965 for Secret Service protection, for a total of $27,279,965. In constant dollars the amount spent to support ex-Presidents had increased more than seven times.

To reduce these costs, the Presidential Libraries Act of 1986 provided that Presidents leaving office after 1989 would have to use private funds to operate as well as build their Presidential libraries, and it imposed new size and space limits on the size of Presidential museums operated with federal funds.

SEE ALSO *Libraries, Presidential; Secret Service, U.S.; Transitions, Presidential*

SOURCES John Whiteclay Chambers II, "Presidents Emeritus," *American Heritage*, June/July 1979, 16–22.

EXPULSION FROM CONGRESS

The most severe form of punishment for a member of Congress is expulsion, which requires a two-thirds vote of the Senate or House. In 1797 the Senate expelled William Blount of Tennessee for treason, and during the Civil War it expelled another 14 senators for supporting the Confederacy. The House similarly expelled three of its members during the Civil War. In 1980 the House expelled Michael ("Ozzie") Myers (Democrat–Pennsylvania) for corruption. However, most members of Congress convicted in court of a crime have resigned rather than face expulsion.

SEE ALSO *Censure; Discipline, congressional*

EX REL

The term *ex rel* is an abbreviation of the Latin phrase *ex relative*, which means "on the relation of." When *ex rel* appears in the title of a Supreme Court case, it means that the legal proceeding was started by a government official in the name of the state or federal government but at the urging of a private individual with an interest in the issue of the case. For example, *Illinois ex rel. McCollum v. Board of Education* (1948) was a case brought by the state of Illinois against a local school board at the instigation of a private citizen, Ms. Vashti McCollum.

EXTRAORDINARY SESSIONS OF CONGRESS

SEE *Special sessions of Congress*

F

FAIRBANKS, CHARLES
Vice President

- Born: May 11, 1852, Unionville Center, Ohio
- Political party: Republican
- Education: Ohio Wesleyan University, B.A., 1872
- Military service: none
- Previous government service: U.S. Senate, 1898–1904
- Vice President under Theodore Roosevelt, 1905–9
- Died: June 4, 1918, Indianapolis, Ind.

Charles Fairbanks was a lawyer who became active in Republican state politics in Indiana. He was named the temporary chair and keynote speaker at the Republican national convention in 1896. The following year he was elected to the U.S. Senate, where he chaired several important committees and served on a diplomatic commission that settled the Canadian-Alaskan boundary.

Fairbanks was nominated to run for Vice President on Theodore Roosevelt's ticket in 1904 to provide geographic balance and secure the electoral votes of Indiana. A conservative, he exercised no influence in the progressive Roosevelt administration. He later supported William Howard Taft against Roosevelt in the 1912 Presidential election. The Republicans again nominated him for Vice President in 1916 on a ticket headed by Supreme Court Justice Charles Evans Hughes.

FAIR DEAL

The Fair Deal was the slogan that President Harry Truman applied to the 21-point program that he presented to Congress on September 5, 1945, to convert the economy from wartime to peacetime status. The message to Congress emphasized passage of the Full Employment Act to provide jobs for U.S. servicemen and servicewomen returning from World War II. When Congress passed the Employment Act of 1946 (dropping "Full" from the title), it converted the measure from a guarantee of employment into a bill creating an economic advisory system for the President.

In 1949, after winning reelection, Truman presented a State of the Union address that again referred to a Fair Deal program. He called for protecting the civil rights of black Americans by establishing a fair employment commission. He also proposed federal aid to education, more funding for public housing, national health insurance, an expansion of Social Security benefits, an increase in the minimum wage, new land reclamation and public power programs, and a program of technical assistance to underdeveloped nations.

SEE ALSO *Truman, Harry S.*

SOURCES Alonzo Hamby, *Beyond the New Deal* (New York: Columbia University Press, 1973).

FAMILIES IN CONGRESS

The political impulse often passes from one generation to the next within the same family, so that many senators and representatives can claim family members who served in Congress before them. Younger family members win election in part because of their name recognition, voters' emotional ties to their family, and their strong identification with a particular state or region.

The Breckinridge family of Kentucky, for instance, began its congressional tenure when John Breckinridge served as a senator from 1801 to 1805. A grandson, John C. Breckinridge, was a senator from 1851 to 1855 and again in 1861; another grandson, William C. Breckinridge, served in the House from 1885 to 1895. A great-great-grandson, John B. Breckinridge, was a House member from 1973 to 1979.

The Bayard family of Delaware, similarly, had four generations in the House and Senate. Henry Dodge (Democrat–Wisconsin) and Augustus Caesar Dodge (Democrat–Iowa) have been the only father and son to serve in the Senate at the same time. Frances Bolton and her son Oliver (Republicans–Ohio) served simultaneously in the House of Representatives— Frances's late husband, Chester Bolton, had also served in the House. When Senator Huey P. Long (Democrat–Louisiana) was assassinated in 1935, his widow, Rose Long, was appointed to fill the vacancy. Their son, Russell Long, was elected in 1948, making them the only father, mother, and son to sit in the Senate.

Carrying on the tradition Sometimes family members come to Congress to carry on the tradition of a famous predecessor, as did "Young Bob" La Follette (Republican/Progressive–Wisconsin), who followed his crusading father, "Battling Bob" La Follette, in the Senate. Or they may deliberately chart a different course. Henry Cabot Lodge, Jr. (Republican–Massachu-

setts) won fame as an internationalist, although his grandfather, Henry Cabot Lodge, Sr., had led the fight against the Treaty of Versailles and fostered isolationism.

Among the most notable congressional families was the dynasty founded by John Fitzgerald (Democrat–Massachusetts), who served in the House from 1895 to 1901. His grandson John Fitzgerald Kennedy (Democrat–Massachusetts) served in the House from 1947 to 1953 and in the Senate from 1953 to 1960 before becoming President. John Kennedy's brothers Robert Kennedy (Democrat–New York) and Edward Kennedy (Democrat–Massachusetts) were also elected senators, and his nephews Joseph Kennedy (Democrat–Massachusetts) and Patrick Kennedy (Democrat–Rhode Island) have continued the family tradition as members of the House.

SEE ALSO *Kennedy, Edward M.; Lodge, Henry Cabot, Sr.; Long, Huey P.*

SOURCES Doris Kearns Goodwin, *The Fitzgeralds and the Kennedys* (New York: Simon & Schuster, 1987). James C. Klotter, *The Breckinridges of Kentucky: Two Centuries of Leadership* (Lexington: University Press of Kentucky, 1986).

FEDERAL COMMUNICATIONS COMMISSION

Believing that the airways belong to the people and should not be monopolized by private interests, Congress created the Federal Communications Commission (FCC) in 1934 as a successor to the original Federal Radio Commission. As an independent regulatory agency, the FCC regulates communications by radio, television, wire, satellite, and cable across the United States.

The FCC is directed by five commissioners appointed by the president and confirmed by the Senate. Each commissioner serves a five-year term, and no more than three may be members of the same political party. The president designates one of the commissioners to serve as chairperson.

Because there are a limited number of radio frequencies, the FCC assigned radio stations their place on the dial and prohibited other stations from interfering with their signals. The FCC similarly protected the three major television networks. For years, the FCC ruled against proposals for "pay TV" that would add more channels through cable or satellite transmission, in part because of its commitment to the ideology of free television and also because the technology had not yet been perfected. In the 1970s the FCC relented and permitted greater cable access. In the 1980s Ronald Reagan's administration and Congress pressed for greater deregulation of communications, reducing many of the restrictions on radio and television station ownership and transmission.

For decades, the FCC had also enforced a Fairness Doctrine that required all candidates for political office to have equal time to respond to their challengers. With the proliferation of stations, the FCC suspended the equal-time provision, on the assumption that all candidates would have access to some form of media, depending upon their ability to pay for it.

FEDERAL DISTRICT COURTS

The U.S. district courts have original jurisdiction in federal criminal cases and civil cases; that is, they are the first to hear these cases. They are the trial courts of the federal judicial system.

There are 94 federal district courts: 90 in the 50 states and the District of Columbia and 4 in the U.S. territories. Each state has at least one federal district court. Three large states—California, New York, and Texas—have four federal district courts each. Nine other states have three federal district courts apiece. In addition, there is a federal district court for each of the four U.S. territories: Guam, Puerto Rico, the Northern Mariana Islands, and the Virgin Islands.

Approximately 650 federal judges staff the district courts. They are appointed by the President and approved by the Senate, as specified in Article 2, Section 2, of the Constitution.

SEE ALSO *Federal judicial system*

FEDERAL ELECTION COMMISSION

The Federal Election Commission (FEC) is a bipartisan independent regulatory agency that administers federal campaign finance laws. It was established by the Federal Election Campaign Act Amendments of 1975 in the aftermath of the Watergate scandals, when illegal corporate contributions to Presidential campaigns were uncovered by a Senate investigation. The FEC consists of six commissioners appointed by the President with the advice and consent of the Senate. No more than three commissioners may be members of the same political party.

The FEC provides information about campaign finance laws to the candidates and the public. It issues regulations about, and monitors compliance with, campaign funding limitations established by law. The FEC monitors the operation of the Treasury Department's Presidential Election Campaign Fund, which provides matching public funding to Presidential candidates who qualify in the nominating period by raising $5,000 in each of 20 states. The fund also provides money for national nominating conventions of the major parties and gives public funds to the Presidential nominees of the two major parties and qualifying minor parties.

SEE ALSO *Campaign financing, Presidential; Election campaigns, Presidential*

SOURCES Robert E. Mutch, *Campaigns, Congress, and the Courts: The Making of Federal Campaign Finance Law* (New York:

Praeger, 1988). Frank J. Sorauf, *Money in American Elections* (Glenview, Ill.: Scott Foresman, 1988).

FEDERALISM

Federalism refers to the division of governmental powers between the national and state governments. The Founding Fathers created a federal system to overcome a tough political obstacle. They needed to convince independent states to join together to create a strong central government. Writing to George Washington before the Constitutional Convention, James Madison considered the dilemma. He said that establishing "one simple republic" that would do away with the states would be "unattainable." Instead, Madison wrote, "I have sought for a middle ground which may at once support a due supremacy of national authority, and not exclude [the states]." Federalism was the answer.

Under federalism, both state and national governments may directly govern through their own officials and laws. Both levels of government derive their legitimacy from the Constitution, which endows each with supreme power over certain areas of government. Both state and federal governments must agree to changes in the Constitution. Both exercise power separately and directly over the people living under their authority, subject to the limits specified in the U.S. Constitution, the supreme law of the country. The Constitution and acts of the national government that conform to it are superior to constitutions, laws, and actions of state and local governments.

In the American federal system, the national (federal) government has certain powers that are granted only to it by the Constitution. The 50 state governments also have powers that the national government is not supposed to exercise. For example, only the federal government may coin money or declare war. Only the state government may establish local governments and conduct elections within the

state. Some powers are shared by both federal and state governments, such as the power to tax and borrow money. Some powers are denied to the federal and state governments, such as granting titles of nobility and passing bills of attainder.

In the American federal system, the powers of the national government are limited. However, within its field or range of powers, the national government is supreme. The states can neither ignore nor contradict federal laws and the Constitution. The core idea of American federalism is that two levels of government (national and state) exercise power separately and directly on the people at the same time. Under federalism, the state of Indiana has authority over its residents, but so does the federal government based in Washington, D.C. Indiana residents must obey the laws of their state government and their federal government.

Federalism is a central principle of the Constitution, but the balance of power between the state and national governments was not defined exactly at the Constitutional Convention of 1787. Since then, debates about the rights and powers of states in relation to the federal government have continued.

In *The Federalist* No. 45, James Madison gave his vision of how federalism would work:

The powers delegated by the Constitution to the federal government are few and defined. Those which are to remain in state governments are numerous and indefinite. The former will be exercised principally on external objects, as war, peace, negotiation, and foreign commerce. ... The powers reserved to the several states will extend to all objects which, in the ordinary course of affairs, concern the lives, liberties, and properties of the people, and the internal order, improvement, and prosperity of the states.

However, the balance of power within the federal system—between the national government and state governments—has changed steadily since Madison's time. Through constitutional amendments, Supreme Court decisions, federal statutes, and executive actions, the powers of the national government have generally expanded to overshadow those of the states.

The development of national government power within the federal system was advanced initially by decisions of the U.S. Supreme Court under Chief Justice John Marshall. For example, the Court's decisions in *Fletcher* v. *Peck* (1810), *McCulloch* v. *Maryland* (1819), *Cohens* v. *Virginia* (1821), and *Gibbons* v. *Ogden* (1824) struck down state government actions that were judged in violation of federal law and the U.S. Constitution.

The Civil War (1861–65) established, once and for all, that in American federalism a state has no right to secede from the federal Union. In the wake of this war, the U.S. Supreme Court set forth the inviolable terms of federal Union in *Texas* v. *White* (1869): "The Constitution in all its provisions looks to an indestructible Union, composed of indestructible States."

During the 20th century, the Supreme Court has tended to make decisions that have diminished the power of state governments in their relationships with the national government. This trend was advanced strongly after 1937, in cases such as *West Coast Hotel Co.* v. *Parrish* (1937), when the Supreme Court began to uphold actions of the federal government to regulate economic activities in the states. During the 1950s and 1960s, the Supreme Court under Chief Justice Earl Warren upheld federal civil rights laws that restricted the actions of state governments to deprive racial minorities of individual rights. Further, in numerous landmark decisions the Court used the due process clause of the 14th Amendment to apply most of the federal Bill of Rights to state governments. These kinds of decisions have limited the powers of state governments in regard to the civil rights and liberties of individuals.

From 1995 to 2000, however, the Supreme Court made some decisions that favored the rights and powers of state governments over the federal government. For example, the Court ruled in *United States* v. *Lopez* (1995) that the federal government's commerce power did not extend to the regulation of gun possession by individuals near schools. Rather, this matter was left to the discretion of state and local governments. In *Printz* v. *United States* (1997) the Court struck down part of a federal gun control law that required local officials to do a background check on a customer before a gun sale could be completed. The Court held that the Constitution's 10th Amendment prohibits federal government from controlling or commandeering certain acts of state or local officials that are conducted according to powers reserved to state governments. In *Alden* v. *Maine* (1999) the Court decided that the 11th Amendment prohibits private individuals from suing a state for violation of a federal law, in this instance the Fair Labor Standards Act of 1938. The Court again used the 11th Amendment in *Kimel* v. *Florida Board of Regents* (2000) to rule that another federal law, the Age Discrimination in Employment Act, could not be the basis for a private lawsuit against a state. According to the Supreme Court, such issues are to be resolved in state courts according to state laws.

SEE ALSO *Incorporation doctrine; Texas v. White; West Coast Hotel Co. v. Parrish*
SOURCES Daniel J. Elazar, *American Federalism: A View from the States* (New York: Harper & Row, 1984). Robert A. Goldwin and William A. Schambra, eds., *How Federal Is the Constitution?* (Washington, D.C.: American Enterprise Institute, 1987). Judith S. Kaye, "Federalism's Other Tier," *Constitution* 3, no. 1 (Winter 1991): 48–55.

FEDERALIST, THE

The Federalist, a collection of 85 papers, or essays, was written to explain and support ratification of the Constitution of 1787. Seventy-seven essays were first printed in New York City newspapers between October 27, 1787, and April 2, 1788. The complete set of 85 essays was published in May 1788 by McLean and Company of New York City.

Alexander Hamilton, the major author of *The Federalist*, wrote 51 of the 85 papers (Nos. 1, 6–9, 11–13, 15–17, 21–36, 59–61, and 65–85). James Madison wrote 29 essays (Nos. 10, 14, 18–20, 37–58, and 62–63). Illness forced John Jay to withdraw from the project, and he wrote only five essays (Nos. 2–5 and 64). Each paper was signed with the pseudonym Publius, after Publius Valerius Publicola, a great defender of the Roman Republic of ancient times.

The first objective of *The Federalist* was to persuade the people of New York to ratify the Constitution; each paper was addressed "To the People of the State of New York" and published first in a New York newspaper. A second objective was to influence Americans in all 13 states to approve the Constitution.

The authors submerged their political differences in the overall pursuit of a common goal—ratification of the Constitution. Madison and Jay agreed with Hamilton that the Constitution was "a compromise of . . . many dissimilar interests and inclinations." It did not exactly reflect the ideas on government of any one of the coauthors, but they agreed that it was the best frame of government achievable under the circumstances and far superior to the Articles of Confederation under which the country had functioned since 1781.

After ratification of the Constitution and formation of the federal government, Madison joined Thomas Jefferson in political clashes with Hamilton that led to the establishment of rival political parties: Federalist (Hamilton) versus Democratic-Republican (Jefferson/Madison). These conflicts, however, lay ahead. In 1787–88, Madison and Hamilton were a formidable team in defense of the Constitution.

Hamilton, Madison, and Jay readily agreed on the name of their projected series of essays, *The Federalist*. With this name, they scored a public relations victory against their opponents, who accepted by default the name of Anti-Federalists. This negative label connoted only opposition, with no constructive ideas to improve the government.

The authors of *The Federalist* agreed on certain fundamental principles of constitutional government: republicanism, federalism, separation of powers, and free government.

A republican government is one "in which the scheme of representation takes place" (*The Federalist* No. 10). It is based on the consent of the governed because power is delegated to a small number of citizens who are elected by the rest of the citizens.

In a federal republic, power is divided between a general (federal) government and several state governments. Two levels of government, each supreme in its own sphere, can exercise powers separately and directly on the people. But state governments can neither ignore nor contradict federal statutes that conform to the supreme law, the Constitution. This conception of federalism departed from traditional forms of government, known today as confederations, in which states retained full sovereignty over their internal affairs.

Publius proclaims in *The Federalist* No. 47: "The accumulation of all powers, legislative, executive, and judiciary, in the same hands . . . may justly be pronounced the very definition of tyranny." So the Constitution provides for a separation of governmental powers among three branches, according to function. But this separation of powers is not complete. Each branch has various constitutional means to participate in the affairs of the other branches, to check and balance their powers, and to prevent one branch of the government from dominating the others.

Republicanism, federalism, and separation of powers are all characteristics of free government. According to *The Federalist*, free government is popular government, limited by the supreme law of the Constitution, established to protect the security, liberty, and property of individuals. A free government is powerful enough to provide protection against external and internal threats and limited enough to prevent tyranny in any form. In particular, free government is designed to guard against the most insidious danger of government by the people—the tyranny of the majority over minorities. This principle applies equally to constitutional protection of religious, ethnic, racial, or other minority groups.

Since its publication in 1788, *The Federalist* has been viewed as an extraordinary work about the principles and practice of constitutional government. *The Federalist* is "the best commentary on the principles of government which ever was written," wrote Thomas Jefferson to James Madison (Nov. 18, 1788). Chief Justice John Marshall agreed in this instance with Jefferson, his longtime political opponent. In *McCulloch v. Maryland* (1819), John Marshall wrote that *The Federalist* was "entitled to great respect [by courts] expounding the Constitution." Moreover, he wrote in *Cohens v. Virginia* (1821): "[*The Federalist*] is a complete commentary on our Constitution, and it is appealed to by all parties in the questions to which that instrument gave birth." Ever since the founding period, lawyers, judges, politicians, and scholars have used *The Federalist* to guide their decisions about issues of constitutional government.

SEE ALSO *Constitutional democracy; Constitutionalism; Federalism; Republicanism; Separation of powers*

SOURCES George Carey, *The Federalist: Design for a Constitutional Republic* (Urbana: University of Illinois Press, 1989). Alexander Hamilton, James Madison, and John Jay, *The Federalist,* edited by Jacob E. Cooke (Middletown, Conn.: Wesleyan University Press, 1961).

FEDERAL JUDICIAL CENTER

EE *Administration of federal courts*

FEDERAL JUDICIAL SYSTEM

The judicial system of the United States has three levels: the Supreme Court at the top, the 13 Courts of Appeals in the middle, and the 94 district courts and several specialized courts at the bottom.

The district courts are the courts of original jurisdiction, or trial courts. There are from one to four districts in each state, one in the District of Columbia, and one in each of the four U.S. territories.

The lowest level of the federal judicial system also includes specialized courts. For example, the Court of Claims hears cases involving monetary claims against the United States. The Court of Military Appeals hears appeals of courts-martial, or military trials, of people in the U.S. armed forces. The Tax Court hears cases regarding federal taxes. The Court of Customs and Patent Appeals hears cases involving international trade and claims about the legality of patents (legal assurances of ownership rights granted by the government to inventors).

The 13 Courts of Appeals have appellate jurisdiction; that is, they hear cases on appeal from the federal district courts and other lower courts. There is one U.S. Court of Appeals for each of 11 geographical regions (circuits) of the United States. They are numbered 1 through 11. In addition, there is a U.S. Court of Appeals for the District of Columbia and a U.S. Court of Appeals for the Federal Circuit, which hears cases on appeal from specialized lower courts.

The U.S. Supreme Court is primarily an appellate court of last resort. It hears appeals from the federal courts of appeals and the highest state courts in cases involving federal issues or questions, such as claims that a state government action conflicts with the U.S. Constitution or federal law.

SEE ALSO *Circuit Courts of Appeals; Courts of Appeals; Federal district courts*
SOURCES Robert A. Carp and Ronald Stid-

ham, *The Federal Courts* (Washington, D.C.: Congressional Quarterly Press, 1991).

FEDERAL RESERVE SYSTEM

For 80 years after President Andrew Jackson vetoed the rechartering of the Bank of the United States in 1832, the U. S. government lacked a central mechanism for regulating the money supply to control inflation and deflation and to boost the economy in times of recession and depression. Debate raged between creating a powerful private central bank or giving the job to a government agency. During the Progressive Era, President Woodrow Wilson proposed, and Congress enacted, the Federal Reserve Act of 1913, which combined private banks with government regulation.

The Federal Reserve Board is an independent regulatory agency that acts as the nation's central bank. Congress established it to provide a safe, flexible, and stable monetary and financial system. The agency conducts the nation's monetary policies, supervises and regulates banks, guards the credit rights of consumers, and provides financial services and information to the government, financial institutions, and the general public.

The Federal Reserve System is directed by a board of governors, consisting of seven members who each serve a 14-year term. The President appoints the governors, who are confirmed by the Senate. The President also designates one of the governors to serve as the chairperson of the board for a 4-year renewable term. Once in office, the governors operate independently of the Presidential administration, at times frustrating Presidents by raising interest rates to prevent inflation and cooling down the economy, moves that are often politically unpopular.

In its effort to stabilize the economy and prevent wide fluctuations, the board of governors can set the interest rates that the 12 Federal Reserve Banks charge their member banks for loans as well as determine the amount of reserves that banks must keep on hand. The board sets margin requirements for financial securities traded on the stock exchanges. It also establishes maximum interest rates on time deposits and savings deposits for its member banks.

The Federal Reserve Board has generally responded well to financial crises, although critics charged that the board's tight-money policies following the stock market crash of 1929 worsened the subsequent depression. The board's efforts to end double-digit inflation in the late 1970s triggered a severe recession. In the 1990s, the board under chairman Alan Greenspan was widely credited with keeping inflation down during the longest uninterrupted period of sustained prosperity in the nation's history.

FEDERAL TRADE COMMISSION

At the beginning of the twentieth century, when company mergers and industrial growth created many big businesses, the federal government's only weapon against monopolies was its antitrust laws. Some argued that bigness in business was inevitable and could be beneficial to consumers and the national economy, if adequately regulated. Acting on President Woodrow Wilson's recommendation, Congress created the Federal Trade Commission (FTC) in 1914. The FTC was assigned to regulate interstate commerce. Its five commissioners are nominated by the President and confirmed by the Senate. They serve seven-year terms, and no more than three of the commissioners may be members of the same political party.

From its beginning, the FTC has worked to ensure that businesses operated competitively. An FTC investigation can be instigated as a result of a letter from a consumer or a business, a congressional inquiry, or even a newspaper article. The FTC also enforces the federal consumer protection laws.

An FTC investigation can lead to a formal hearing before an administrative law judge. If judges find a business to be acting in restraint of trade, they can issue cease-and-desist orders. Corporations can appeal these orders to the full commission. In turn, a decision by the commission can be appealed to a U.S. Court of Appeals and, ultimately, to the U.S. Supreme Court.

FELTON, REBECCA LATIMER

- Born: June 10, 1835, Decatur, Ga.
- Political party: Democrat
- Education: Madison Female College, graduated, 1852
- Senator from Georgia: 1922
- Died: Jan. 24, 1930, Atlanta, Ga.

The first woman senator, 87-year-old Rebecca Felton was also the oldest person to become a senator, and her single-day term set the record as the shortest. Two years after the 19th Amendment granted women the right to vote in 1920, the governor of Georgia appointed her to fill out the remaining days of a deceased senator's term. The appointment was a symbolic gesture because the Senate was not expected to be in session before her successor would be chosen in a special election. But when the Senate met in special session, Rebecca Felton persuaded her elected successor, Walter George (Democrat), to withhold his credentials and allow her to serve just briefly. The Senate debated for a day whether to accept her credentials. At last she took the oath of office and delivered a short speech in which she promised senators that "when the women of the country come in and sit with you, though there may be but very few in the next few years, I pledge you that you will get ability, you will get integrity of purpose, you will get exalted patriotism, and you will get un-

stinted usefulness." The next day, her elected successor replaced her, and Rebecca Felton returned to Georgia.

SEE ALSO *Women in government*
SOURCES John E. Talmadge, *Rebecca Latimer Felton: Nine Stormy Decades* (Athens: University of Georgia Press, 1960).

FIELD, STEPHEN JOHNSON
Associate Justice, 1863–97

- Born: Nov. 4, 1816, Haddam, Conn.
- Education: Williams College, B.A., 1837; studied law privately
- Previous government service: California House of Representatives, 1850–51; justice, California Supreme Court, 1857–63
- Appointed by President Abraham Lincoln Mar. 6, 1863, to a newly created position on the Court
- Supreme Court term: confirmed by the Senate Mar. 10, 1863, by a voice vote; retired Dec. 1, 1897
- Died: Apr. 9, 1899, Washington, D.C.

Stephen Field served more than 34 years on the Supreme Court, longer than any other justice except William O. Douglas. During Field's long term, he was a strong supporter of the property rights of individuals.

Justice Field was the Court's leader in using the due process clause of the 14th Amendment to prohibit state governments from regulating or interfering with the property rights of corporations and other businesses or industries. Justice Field viewed a corporation as an individual that could not be deprived of its rights by state governments because of the protection of individual rights guaranteed by Section 1 of the 14th Amendment.

Justice Field and his followers on the Court did not, however, show an equal concern for the rights of people, especially black people, for whose protection the 14th Amendment was drafted and ratified in 1868. They consistently voted as a majority to deny these individual rights to African Americans. Field, for example, voted with the Court's majority in *Plessy* v. *Ferguson* to establish the "separate but equal" doctrine. That doctrine remained the legal basis for racial segregation in the United States until it was overturned in 1954 by the Court's decision in *Brown* v. *Board of Education.* Justice Field argued that the "equal protection of the laws" required by the 14th Amendment required only equal treatment of people, not their freedom of choice.

In the 1890s, Field's ability to work declined as he became disabled by illness and the infirmities of advanced age. His colleagues repeatedly asked him to retire, but Field refused because he wanted to surpass John Marshall's record for length of service on the Court. He finally retired in 1897, but only after barely exceeding Chief Justice Marshall's record of service of 34 years and five months.

SOURCES Carl B. Swisher, *Stephen J. Field: Craftsman of the Law* (Washington, D.C.: Brookings Institution, 1930).

FILIBUSTER

The use of delaying tactics to block legislation is called a filibuster. The expression, from a Dutch word meaning "pirate," became popular in the 1850s when American adventurers went filibustering around the Caribbean, trying to overthrow governments and seize power for themselves. The word was soon applied to Congress, where it was used to describe roguish efforts to seize the floor and prevent the majority from acting.

Even in the 1st Congress, minority members delivered long speeches and used the rules to obstruct legislation they opposed. At first, representatives as well as senators could filibuster, but as the House grew larger, it tightened its rules on how long individuals could speak. The Senate, which had fewer members, retained the right of unlimited debate. Senators felt it important that every member have the ability to speak for as long as necessary on any issue.

One of the Senate's first organized filibusters took place in 1841, when the Democratic minority sought to prevent action on a bank bill promoted by Henry Clay (Whig–Kentucky). After many days of speeches and delaying maneuvers, Clay threatened to change the Senate's rules to permit the majority to act. But Thomas Hart Benton (Democrat–Missouri) angrily accused Clay of trying to "stifle debate," and John C. Calhoun (Democrat–South Carolina) denounced any attempt "to infringe the right of speech." Clay retreated and conceded defeat.

Cloture   Until 1917 the Senate had no way to cut off debate. At the urging of President Woodrow Wilson, the Senate adopted a rule that permitted a two-thirds vote of the Senate to end debate. In 1919 the Senate invoked cloture for the first time to shut off a filibuster against the Treaty of Versailles. But cloture proved difficult to achieve and filibusters flourished, especially during lame-duck sessions, which take place between the November election and the beginning of the next Congress. During these sessions, many members would be leaving Congress shortly and were therefore easily influenced by special interests. With only days left in the session, any member could disrupt business by filibustering or even threatening to filibuster. For this reason, Senator George Norris (Republican–Nebraska) sponsored the 20th Amendment to the Constitution, ratified in 1933, which effectively ended lame-duck filibustering by moving the opening of Congress from December of the following year back to January of that year so that lame ducks would have much less time to serve after they had been replaced by election. Since then, Congress has rarely met during the months between a November election and the convening of a new Congress on January 3.

Famous   filibusters   During the 1930s, Senator Huey P. Long (Democrat–Louisiana) frequently filibustered against bills that he thought gave away too much to the wealthy. Long frustrated the Senate and entertained the nation by reciting Shakespeare, the Bible, and recipes for "pot-likker" (a Southern dish of boiled roots or greens whose liquid is used for dipping cornbread in) for hours on the Senate floor. He once held the floor for 15 hours. The longest individual speech was delivered by J. Strom Thurmond (Democrat/Republican–South Carolina), when he filibustered for 24 hours and 18 minutes against the Civil Rights Act of 1957.

More commonly, groups of senators conduct filibusters by working in teams to hold the floor for days and weeks. They will object to unanimous consent agreements, force the previous day's journal entry to be read aloud, suggest the absence of a quorum (the minimum attendance to conduct business), and otherwise insist that all the rules be observed as a means of slowing down business and wearing out the majority. For many years, Southern senators were especially skillful in filibustering against civil rights legislation. Not until 1964 was the Senate able to invoke cloture against an anti–civil rights filibuster. In 1975, the Senate reduced the number of senators needed to invoke cloture from two-thirds to three-fifths.

Absences and arrests Along with making long-winded speeches, another favorite device of filibustering senators is simply to absent themselves from the chamber. If the minority party does not answer quorum calls, then the majority has to stay near the chamber at all times, day or night, to establish a quorum and keep business moving. At such times, the Senate majority leader will order that the sergeant at arms arrest absent senators. Deputy sergeants at arms go to the absent senators' offices and homes to accompany them to the chamber, and on occasion they have even physically carried senators in the door.

The Senate tolerates filibusters as a necessary evil. The ability to filibuster makes every senator, even the most junior member of the minority party, an important

force in Senate proceedings. Even more important, contrary to the general belief that in a democracy the majority should rule, the filibuster offers a defense of the minority's rights and opinions.

SEE ALSO *Cloture; Debates, congressional; Lame-duck sessions of Congress*
SOURCES Sarah A. Binder and Steven S. Smith. *Politics or Principle? Filibustering in the United States Senate* (Washington, D.C.: Brookings Institution, 1996).

FILLMORE, MILLARD
13th President

- Born: Jan. 7, 1800, Cayuga County, N.Y.
- Political party: Whig
- Education: six months of grade school; read law, 1822
- Military service: none
- Previous government service: New York State Assembly, 1829–33; U.S. House of Representatives, 1833–35, 1837–43; New York State comptroller, 1847–48; Vice President, 1849–50
- Succeeded to Presidency, 1850; served, 1850–53
- Died: Mar. 8, 1874, Buffalo, N.Y.

Millard Fillmore was the third and last Whig President, succeeding Zachary Taylor, who died in office. He was the first and only successor to the Presidency to appoint an entirely new cabinet. His support of the Compromise of 1850 preserved the Union for another decade but destroyed his own political career.

Fillmore was born on a frontier farm in upstate New York. He was apprenticed to a cloth maker at age 14, then became a schoolteacher. He read law with a county judge and became a lawyer in East Aurora, New York. He served three terms in the New York legislature, sponsoring legislation to close the debtors prison.

Fillmore began his career in national politics as an opponent of Andrew Jackson, joining the Whig Party during his first term in the House of Representatives in 1833 and becoming party congressional leader in 1841. He opposed the spoils system, under which government posts were filled according to the recommendations of party bosses, and was in favor of national funding for internal improvements. Two of the tariff bills he wrote as chair of the Ways and Means Committee were vetoed by President John Tyler, but a third was approved in 1842.

Fillmore lost the Whig nomination for Vice President in 1844 and was defeated in an election for New York governor that same year. In 1847 he was elected New York State's first comptroller. Fillmore received the Vice Presidential nomination in 1848 to appease Northern Whigs opposed to the nomination of slaveholder Zachary Taylor. As Vice President, he presided fairly and firmly in the Senate over the intense debates between Northern abolitionists and Southern slaveholders. When Fillmore became President, he broke his political alliance with New York State Whig party boss Thurlow Weed and appointed a completely new cabinet, including Daniel Webster as secretary of state. He reversed Taylor's opposition to Henry Clay's Compromise of 1850, a measure designed to effect a compromise over extension of slavery into the newly acquired territories. It admitted California to the Union as a free state, permitted slavery in the New Mexico and Utah territories, abolished slavery in the District of Columbia, and strengthened the fugitive slave law to allow Southern slaveholders to use Northern state courts and police in efforts to retrieve runaway slaves. Fillmore approved the compromise to avoid sectional conflict. His major accomplishment in foreign policy was the decision to send a fleet commanded by Commodore Matthew C. Perry to Japan, which resulted in an 1854 treaty that opened up that nation to U.S. trade.

As a result of his sectional compromises, Fillmore was discredited among Northern Whigs, and after 53 ballots he lost the bid for his party's Presidential nomination in 1852 to General Winfield Scott, the third war hero the Whigs had nominated for the Presidency. But the party destroyed itself over the slavery issue, and Fillmore turned the White House over to Democrat Franklin Pierce; he then retired to Buffalo to practice law.

Fillmore's 1856 Presidential campaign on the Know-Nothing ticket was an embarrassment; the party was opposed to foreigners and was strongly anti-Catholic, though Fillmore refused to endorse these prejudices in the campaign. He ran as a nationalist, attempting to preserve the Union from sectional divisions. He received 21 percent of the vote, a record for a third-party candidate until 1912. But after the election the party disappeared and he retired from politics.

Fillmore became active in local affairs in upstate New York. A man who had received only six months of schooling in his life, he had begun his political career in New York by developing the public school system. In later life he founded the University of Buffalo (becoming its first chancellor) and the Buffalo Fine Arts Academy. SOURCES Elbert B. Smith, *The Presidencies of Zachary Taylor and Millard Fillmore* (Lawrence: University Press of Kansas, 1988).

FIRESIDE CHAT

A fireside chat is a Presidential address to the nation characterized by a warm, intimate, and informal tone. It is designed to build confidence in the President's policies. The tradition of the fireside chat was begun by President Franklin D. Roosevelt on March 12, 1933, speaking to the nation by radio shortly after his inauguration, in the midst of the Great Depression. He discussed the banking crisis, the bank holiday he had declared on March 6 and its results, and his plan to reopen banks the next day. Entitled "An Intimate Talk with the People of the United States on Banking," it was delivered in plain English to ordinary people. As the humorist Will Rogers put it Roosevelt took up the subject of banking and "made everyone understand it, even the bankers." The talk was successful in preventing a run on deposits and restored stability to the banking system.

The term *fireside chat* was first used by a CBS radio executive to promote an audience for Roosevelt's second address. Roosevelt gave 30 such addresses throughout his Presidency. Many of the chats described the bills that Roosevelt had gotten Congress to pass to deal with the depression. Other chats offered lessons in democracy.

President Jimmy Carter gave a televised fireside chat in 1977, complete with roaring fire in the Oval Office, and wore a cardigan sweater instead of the customary suit. That gesture earned him the nickname Jimmy Cardigan.

SEE ALSO *Carter, Jimmy; Public opinion; Roosevelt, Franklin D.*

SOURCES Russell D. Biuhite and David W. Levy, eds., *The Fireside Chats of Franklin D. Roosevelt* (Norman: University of Oklahoma Press, 1991).

FIRST BRANCH OF GOVERNMENT

As the subject of the first and longest article of the Constitution, Congress has been called the "first branch of government." This phrase also reflects the Jeffersonian concept that the legislative branch is superior to the executive and judiciary because it more accurately reflects the needs and opinions of the people.

"FIRST HUNDRED DAYS"

At the depth of the Great Depression, Franklin D. Roosevelt took office as President on March 4, 1933, and called Congress into special session. Lasting from March 9 to June 15, 1933, this session became known as the "first hundred days" of the New Deal. Responding to the economic crisis, Congress passed an extraor-

dinary amount of major legislation in a remarkably short period.

During the hundred days, Congress enacted emergency banking legislation to restore stable banking, emergency relief legislation, a public works bill, a Civilian Conservation Corps bill to provide relief and create jobs, the National Industrial Recovery Administration to establish federal economic planning, the Federal Securities Act to regulate the sale of stocks, the Agricultural Adjustment Act and Farm Credit Act to help farmers, and the Tennessee Valley Authority to provide electrical power and jobs. These laws were designed to bring recovery, relief, and reform.

Although some of these programs had originated in Congress, the first hundred days in general represented congressional yielding to strong Presidential leadership. In later years other Presidents' legislative successes have been measured against—but few have come close to matching—Roosevelt's first hundred days. Acutely aware of this pressure, John F. Kennedy said in his inaugural address, "It won't be done in the first hundred days. . . ." By comparison, Ronald Reagan consciously sought to establish his policies during the important first hundred days. Similarly, when House Republicans regained the majority in 1995, they pledged to enact their Contract with America in the first hundred days as a sign of their determination to change the direction of government policies.

SOURCES Fred L. Israel, *Franklin Delano Roosevelt* (New York: Chelsea House, 1985).

FIRST LADY

Initially, the President's wife was referred to as Lady (as in "Lady Washington") or Mrs. President. The term *First Lady* was coined by Mary Clemmer Ames in an 1877 magazine article describing the inauguration of President Rutherford B. Hayes. It was popularized by a play about Dolley Madison entitled *The First Lady in the Land,* produced in New York City in 1911.

All Presidents except for James Buchanan married. Five remarried after the death of their first wife, and one (Ronald Reagan) remarried after a divorce. Some wives died before their husband reached the White House, including Martha Jefferson, Rachel Jackson, Hannah Van Buren, and Ellen Arthur. Presidents who were unmarried while in office relied on hostesses to assist them at state dinners, receptions, and other social functions. These include Martha Jefferson Randolph, daughter of Thomas Jefferson; Emily Donelson, niece of Andrew Jackson; Angelica Van Buren, daughter-in-law of Martin Van Buren; Harriet Lane, niece of James Buchanan; Martha Patterson, daughter of Andrew Johnson; and Mary Arthur McElroy, sister of Chester Arthur.

In the 19th century few First Ladies had much formal education and none had careers, with the exception of Abigail Fillmore, a teacher. Most occupied themselves by managing the White House, hosting its social functions, and raising their family. The first to attend school was Anna Harrison, wife of William Henry Harrison; the first to attend college was Lucretia Garfield, who graduated from Hiram College. "Lemonade" Lucy Hayes did charity work and promoted the temperance (antialcohol) movement; Caroline Harrison, wife of Benjamin Harrison, raised money for Johns Hopkins University and pressed it to accept women into the medical school.

The wedding of Grover Cleveland and Frances Folsom, which took place in the White House on June 2, 1886, marked the first time a President was married in the executive mansion. Press coverage of that event made the First Lady a nationally known figure. Edith Roosevelt (wife of Theodore) was the first to hire a social secretary to assist her in her duties. Woodrow Wilson's first wife, Ellen, was the first to take a public position on a bill being considered by Congress; his second wife, Edith, served as a liaison between her husband and the rest of government after he suffered a stroke in 1919.

Eleanor Roosevelt was the first Presidential wife to have a significant career; she was a teacher, journalist, and Democratic party activist. Others with careers include Jacqueline Kennedy (journalism and publishing), Patricia Nixon (teaching and government service), Lady Bird Johnson (communications), Nancy Reagan (acting), and Hillary Clinton (law), though none pursued their careers in the White House as Mrs. Roosevelt had done.

Lady Bird Johnson was the first wife to campaign alone on behalf of her husband in a Presidential campaign. Rosalynn Carter was the first to play an active role within the White House Office, acting as a staff aide to the President. She testified before Congress on legislation, supported the Equal Rights Amendment, was active in promoting mental health initiatives in government, met foreign heads of state as her husband's representative, and attended cabinet meetings. Nancy Reagan sponsored a "Just Say No" campaign against drug use. Barbara Bush, who dropped out of Smith College in her sophomore year to marry George Bush and raise a family, was active in organizing a campaign against illiteracy.

Hillary Clinton, a graduate of Yale Law School, was a partner in a large corporate law firm in Little Rock while her husband, Bill Clinton, served as governor of Arkansas. She also chaired the board of the Children's Defense Fund. During the transition to the Clinton administration, she used her influence to bring large numbers of women into high levels of government. She was given an office in the West Wing and was put in charge of a task force on health care reform, but after a bill embodying her plan failed to pass Congress, she backed away from a visible role in policy-making. She preferred instead to assume a more traditional role in public while retaining her place as one of the President's most important advisers. She did, however, become the first First Lady in American history to hold an elective office, when she won the New York Democratic seat in the U.S. Senate.

Traditionally, First Ladies took responsibility for furnishing the family quarters, assisted by the White House Curator, who is responsible for the maintenance and restoration of its public rooms with authentic period furniture; for hosting White House social functions, including choosing the menu and entertainment; and for representing the President on ceremonial occasions. Today they also serve as confidential advisers and policy formulators.

The First Lady earns no salary and holds no formal office. She employs more than 20 aides and has an office in the East Wing of the White House to answer mail, deal with the media, and supervise social functions. She uses her West Wing office to work on policies of interest to her.

SEE ALSO *Adams, Abigail; Kennedy, Jacqueline; Madison, Dolley; Roosevelt, Eleanor; White House*

SOURCES Paul F. Boller, Jr., *Presidential Wives* (New York: Oxford University Press, 1988). Betty Boyd Caroli, *First Ladies,* expanded ed. (New York: Oxford University Press, 1995). Lewis J. Gould, ed., *American First Ladies: Their Lives and Their Legacy* (New York: Garland, 1996). Lewis L. Gould, "First Ladies," *American Scholar* (Autumn 1986): 528–35. Lewis L. Gould, "Modern First Ladies and the Presidency," *Presidential Studies Quarterly* 20 (Fall 1990): 677–82.

FIRST MONDAY IN OCTOBER

SEE *Opening Day of the Supreme Court*

FLAG, PRESIDENTIAL

The Presidential flag denotes the presence of the President of the United States. It is displayed on the Presidential yacht and limousines and on ceremonial occasions at the White House. It may also be displayed when the President gives an address and when he meets with foreign heads of state.

The first official Presidential flag was adopted by President Woodrow Wilson on May 29, 1916. Against a field of blue, the Presidential seal in bronze and a large white star in each corner were placed. On October 25, 1945, President Harry Truman increased the number of stars to 48, one for each state. The number was increased to 50 in 1959 by President Dwight Eisenhower to take into account the admission of Alaska and Hawaii to the Union.

SEE ALSO *Seal, Presidential*

FLETCHER V. PECK

- 6 Cranch 87 (1810)
- Vote: 4–1
- For the Court: Marshall
- Dissenting: Johnson in part

In 1795 the state of Georgia sold 35 million acres in the Yazoo area to four land companies. However, the authorization of the land sales was tainted by fraud and bribery involving important members of the state legislature who were voted out of office in 1796. New members of the Georgia legislature promptly acted to repeal the statute that had authorized the Yazoo land sales. The 1796 legislation invalidated all property rights gained from the Yazoo Land Act of 1795. People who had purchased Yazoo land under the 1795 statute, however, continued to sell this land to third parties. In 1803 John Peck sold 15,000 acres of Yazoo land to Robert Fletcher. Then Fletcher sued Peck for selling him land that was not his to sell.

The Issue   Chief Justice John Marshall avoided any discussion of the reasons for the Georgia legislature's action in repealing the 1795 land act. He said that charges of political corruption associated with land titles and sales were a matter for the state government to decide. According to Marshall, the only question before the U.S. Supreme Court was whether the state legislature could deprive investors of land they had acquired under the corrupt grant authorized by the 1795 law. Was depriving investors of this land, by repealing the land grant that had authorized their purchase of it, a violation of the contract clause of Article 1, Section 10, of the U.S. Constitution?

Opinion of the Court   Writing for the Court, Chief Justice John Marshall held that the Georgia legislature's act repealing the Yazoo land grant law was unconstitutional because it violated the contract clause of Article 1, Section 10, of the Constitution. That clause says, "No State shall . . . pass any . . . Law impairing the Obligation of Contracts." Thus, concluded Marshall, a state government could not make laws that impaired contracts or interfered with land titles acquired in good faith.

Significance   This decision was a legal blow against advocates of stronger state powers and rights within the federal system. Chief Justice Marshall emphatically asserted the right of the U.S. Supreme Court to review and strike down a state law as unconstitutional. Further, Marshall established that contracts and property rights would be protected by the federal courts against state government interference. This constitutional protection of an individual's property rights and contracts encouraged large-scale economic development of the nation.

SEE ALSO *Contract clause; Federalism*

FLOOR MANAGERS

After a congressional committee reports out legislation, floor managers guide the bill to a final vote of the House and Senate. Usually, the committee or subcommittee chairman serves as floor manager, while the ranking minority member leads the opposition. Floor managers make the opening statements and schedule other members who want to debate the bill. They try to prevent any crippling amendments but will negotiate to reach whatever compromises are necessary to get a majority vote.

In the House, floor managers sit at the large tables on either side of the center aisle and may address the chamber from that location. In the Senate, floor managers move forward to occupy the leaders' front-row desks. The floor managers normally serve on the conference committee that determines the bill's final form, and they are traditionally photographed standing behind the president as their work is signed into law. Some sponsors and floor managers become so identified with legislation that it takes their names, such as the Taft-Hartley or Humphrey-Hawkins bills.

FLOOR PRIVILEGES

The rules of the House of Representatives and Senate limit who can go onto the floor of the chambers when Congress is in session. Those regularly admitted include members and their staff, committee staff, the staff who work at the front desks, and the pages. Floor privileges are also extended to the President and Vice President, members of the cabinet, governors, Supreme Court justices, senior military officers, the Architect of the Capitol, and the mayor of the District of Columbia. House and Senate doorkeepers direct all other visitors to the galleries. Former members of Congress also have floor privileges, which for a while gave them considerable advantage as lobbyists. But since 1945 the House has followed the Rayburn Rule, named after former Speaker Sam Rayburn, which bars former members from the floor during any debate or vote in which they have any personal or business interest. The Senate, similarly, discourages former members from using their floor privileges to lobby.

SEE ALSO *Doorkeepers; Lobbying; Rayburn, Sam*

FOLEY, THOMAS S.

- Born: Mar. 6, 1929, Spokane, Wash.
- Political party: Democrat

- Education: University of Washington, A.B., 1951; University of Washington Law School, J.D., 1957
- Representative from Washington: 1965–95
- House majority leader: 1987–89
- Speaker of the House: 1989–95

Tom Foley assumed the Speaker's chair in the House of Representatives at a difficult time of divided government (a Republican President but Democratic majorities in Congress), which led to legislative stalemate and frustration.

After the election of 1992, the White House and Congress were once again controlled by the same party. But conservative Republicans put up stiff resistance to Democratic proposals, killing President Bill Clinton's ambitious plan for national health care. House Republicans portrayed Foley as a symbol of the Democratic majority and its resistance to term limitations and a balanced-budget amendment. Foley misjudged the depth of voter anger and demand for change. In 1994, as Democrats lost their majority for the first time in 40 years, he became the first Speaker defeated for reelection in more than a century.

SEE ALSO *Speaker of the House*

FORD, GERALD R.
38th President

- Born: July 14, 1913, Omaha, Nebr.
- Political party: Republican
- Education: University of Michigan, B.A., 1935; Yale University Law School, LL.B., 1940
- Military service: U.S. Navy, 1942–45
- Previous government service: U.S. House of Representatives, 1949–73; House minority leader, 1965–73; Vice President, 1973–74
- Succeeded to Presidency, 1974; served, 1974–77

Gerald Ford was the first Vice President ever to serve without having been popularly elected (he was appointed under the provisions of the 25th Amendment), and he was the first to succeed a President who resigned from office. His pardon of Richard Nixon for all Watergate crimes and his weak performance in dealing with the economy contributed to his election defeat in 1976.

Ford was originally named Leslie King, Jr. When he was two years old, his parents divorced; he took the name of his stepfather, Gerald Rudolph Ford, when his mother remarried. He was an Eagle Scout and in high school was a star football player and member of the student council. While an undergraduate at the University of Michigan, Ford played football, and after graduation he received offers from the Detroit Lions and Green Bay Packers. Instead he went to Yale Law School and while there coached boxing, was the assistant football coach, and occasionally modeled for magazines. After receiving his law degree, Ford served as a lieutenant commander in the navy during World War II. He received 10 battle stars for action in the Pacific theater and almost lost his life when a typhoon hit the Third Fleet on December 18, 1944.

After the war Ford briefly practiced law, and in 1948 defeated an incumbent Republican and won election to the U.S. House of Representatives from Grand Rapids, Michigan. During the campaign he married Betty Bloomer Warren. He served 12 terms in the House, never receiving less than 60 percent of the vote. In 1965, after the Republican party suffered a major defeat in the Presidential and congressional elections, House Republicans ousted Charles Halleck and elected the younger and more aggressive Gerald Ford as minority leader. Ford proved an aggressive and successful leader who helped his party regain much of its lost stature. Ford frequently sparred with President Lyndon Johnson, who once remarked that Ford had "played too much football with his helmet off." Ford opposed most of Johnson's Great Society programs, including aid to education and Medicare for the elderly.

In 1973, Vice President Spiro Agnew was convicted of accepting bribes and resigned from office. President Richard Nixon then appointed Ford as Vice President, both to rebuild the his administration's crumbling relations with Congress and because the Senate would be likely to confirm him. This was the first time that the 25th Amendment was used to fill a Vice Presidential vacancy. Ford was sworn in, after receiving congressional approval, on December 6, 1973.

When Nixon resigned on August 9, 1974, Ford succeeded to the Presidency. "Our long national nightmare is over," he told a nation numbed by the Watergate scandal. On September 8 he gave Nixon a "full, free and absolute" pardon for all Watergate crimes. "I do believe, with all my heart and mind and spirit, that I, not as President but as a humble servant of God, will receive justice without mercy if I fail to show mercy," he told the American people in a televised address. Ford's popularity plummeted because of the pardon, and it never recovered. Many Americans believed there had been a secret deal, or at least an "understanding," between Nixon and Ford, that Ford would issue a pardon if he were appointed Vice President and later succeeded Nixon in the White House.

Ford recommended to Congress that Nixon be paid $850,000 in transition expenses, which also upset public opinion. Congress allocated only $200,000 to Nixon. Ford appeared before a congressional committee to discuss the pardon, becoming the first President ever to appear before Congress for questioning. In September 1974 Ford offered Vietnam War deserters Presidential clemency if they participated in a work program. The contrast with the unconditional pardon given to Nixon seemed outrageous to many people.

Ford's domestic program was stalled by the Democratic Congress. As a result of the 1974 midterm elections, Democrats gained 43 House and 3 Senate seats to provide them with almost veto-proof margins. One-quarter of Ford's vetoes were overridden, a figure much higher than the 7 percent that other Presidents averaged. His anti-inflation effort, called Whip Inflation

Now (WIN), was ignored, although the inflation rate dropped from 12 to 5 percent. His energy conservation program was derailed. Democrats passed their own education, public works, and housing measures. Ford vetoed many Democratic spending measures on domestic programs in 1976, but the vetoes were unpopular with Democrats and independent voters.

In foreign affairs, Ford's most notable achievements included an arms agreement with the Soviet Union on strategic weapons. In addition, the Helsinki Conference of 35 nations signed a pact in 1975 that recognized the borders of all states in Europe. It conferred legitimacy on Soviet expansionism after World War II but also required all nations to adhere to universal standards of human rights—provisions that eventually would make Soviet rule in Eastern Europe more difficult to sustain. In October 1975 Secretary of State Henry Kissinger helped put in place an interim peace agreement between Egypt and Israel in the Sinai Peninsula.

In 1975 the North Vietnamese army overran South Vietnam and put an end to the Vietnam War. President Ford ordered U.S. armed forces to evacuate Americans and South Vietnamese allies. Seven laws prohibited the use of the armed forces in Vietnam, and Ford went before a joint session of Congress to urge their repeal. After Congress deadlocked and did nothing, Ford ordered the evacuations anyway. He asked Congress to allocate almost half a billion dollars to settle 140,000 refugees from Indochina in the United States—one of his few legislative successes. Later, he sent the military to rescue crewmen of the merchant ship *Mayaguez* from Cambodian custody, losing 43 servicemen in the incident.

On September 22, 1975, Ford was almost assassinated by Sarah Jane Moore as he emerged from the St. Francis Hotel in San Francisco. The pistol was deflected by a bystander and Ford was not hit by the bullet.

In 1976 Ford was challenged by Ronald Reagan in the Republican primaries and barely defeated him for the nomination. The Republican platform, however, was written by conservatives and repudiated much of the Ford-Kissinger foreign policy of dtente, or relaxation of tensions with the Soviet Union. During the general election campaign, Ford made a major slip in a debate when he asserted that "there is no Soviet domination of Eastern Europe." Although he seemed to have meant that the Soviets could not crush the Polish, Hungarian, and Czechoslovak peoples' longing for freedom, his poor choice of words gave the Democrats a chance to argue that Ford simply did not have the brains to be President. Ford was defeated by Jimmy Carter in a close election, receiving slightly less than 49 percent of the vote.

After retiring from the White House, Ford wrote his memoirs and saw to the construction of his Presidential library in Ann Arbor and museum in Grand Rapids, Michigan. In 1980 there was an effort to put Ford on the Reagan ticket as Vice President, but Ford insisted on a virtual "co-Presidency" in which he would share Presidential powers, and the effort was aborted by the Reagan camp.

SEE ALSO *Agnew, Spiro T.; Carter, Jimmy; Nixon, Richard M.; Pardon power; 25th Amendment; Watergate investigation (1973–74)*

SOURCES Betty Ford with Chris Chase, *The Times of My Life* (New York: Harper & Row, 1978). Gerald Ford, *A Time to Heal: The Autobiography of Gerald R. Ford* (New York: Harper & Row, 1979). Robert Hartmann, *Palace Politics: An Inside Account of the Ford Years* (New York: McGraw-Hill, 1980). Jules Witcover, *Crapshoot: Rolling the Dice on the Vice Presidency* (New York: Crown, 1992).

FORTAS, ABE
Associate Justice, 1965–69

- Born: June 19, 1910, Memphis, Tenn.
- Education: Southwestern College, B.A., 1930; Yale Law School, LL.B., 1933

- Previous government service: assistant director, corporate reorganization study, Securities and Exchange Commission, 1934–37; assistant director, public utilities commission, Securities and Exchange Commission, 1938–39; counsel to the bituminous coal division, Department of the Interior, 1939–41; director, Division of Power, Department of the Interior, 1941–42; undersecretary of the interior, 1942–46
- Appointed by President Lyndon B. Johnson July 28, 1965; replaced Arthur J. Goldberg, who resigned
- Supreme Court term: confirmed by the Senate Aug. 11, 1965, by a voice vote; resigned May 14, 1969
- Died: Apr. 5, 1982, Washington, D.C.

Abe Fortas was the son of Jewish immigrants from England who settled in Tennessee. Through his hard work and intelligence, Fortas won scholarships to Southwestern College and Yale Law School and eventually established a very successful legal practice.

In 1948, Fortas successfully defended Lyndon B. Johnson, a member of Congress from Texas. Johnson's election victory had been challenged in court by his opponent, who charged that Johnson won through illegal procedures. Lyndon Johnson never forgot Fortas's help during a critical moment in his political career. After becoming President, Johnson appointed Abe Fortas to the Supreme Court to replace Arthur Goldberg, whom he had encouraged to resign by offering Goldberg the position of U.S. ambassador to the United Nations.

Abe Fortas had won national recognition two years before his appointment to the Supreme Court because he was the winning attorney in the landmark Supreme Court case of *Gideon v. Wainwright* (1963). This case established the right of a poor person to be provided with a lawyer by a state government in all criminal cases involving alleged violations of state law. This case reversed the Court's decision in *Betts* v. *Brady* (1942) and was a significant step forward in the gradual "incorporation" of individual rights in the Bill of

Rights under the due process clause of the 14th Amendment.

Fortas showed a strong commitment to the rights of individuals during his brief term on the Court. His two most important opinions involved the rights of children: *In re Gault* (1967) and *Tinker v. Des Moines Independent Community School District* (1969).

The *Gault* decision extended to juvenile offenders due process rights of the 5th and 14th Amendments that were previously limited to adults. The *Tinker* decision expanded the 1st Amendment freedom of speech right to include "symbolic speech" expressed through the wearing of black arm bands by students in school to protest U.S. participation in the Vietnam War. Fortas argued that a public school's ban on this form of protest was a violation of a student's right to free speech, as long as this form of protest did not disrupt the functioning of the school or violate the rights of other individuals. Fortas wrote, "It can hardly be argued that either students or teachers shed their constitutional rights to freedom of speech or expression at the schoolhouse gate."

In 1968, Fortas's Supreme Court term came to an abrupt and unhappy end. President Johnson nominated Fortas to be chief justice, replacing Earl Warren, who was retiring. But many senators opposed this appointment, and Johnson was pressured to withdraw the nomination. During this controversy, critics of Fortas charged that he had acted improperly in accepting a large fee, raised by donations from friends and former clients, to teach a course at American University. Several months later, a *Life* magazine article claimed that Justice Fortas behaved wrongly in accepting a large fee from a former client in return for serving on a charitable foundation. The *Life* article also reported that Fortas had returned the money.

These charges influenced some members of Congress to discuss the possibility of starting impeachment proceedings against Fortas in order to remove him from the Court. Fortas strongly denied any improper or illegal activity, but he decided to resign from the Court and returned to private law practice. Thus, he was the first justice to leave the Court because of the threat of impeachment.

SEE ALSO *Gideon v. Wainwright; In re Gault; Tinker v. Des Moines Independent Community School District*

SOURCES Laura Kalman, *Abe Fortas: A Biography* (New Haven: Yale University Press, 1990). James F. Shogan, *A Question of Judgment: The Fortas Case and the Struggle for the Supreme Court* (Indianapolis: Bobbs-Merrill, 1972).

FRANKED MAIL

Members of Congress can send official correspondence by frank—or free of postage (from the Latin word *francus*, meaning "for free"). A member's printed signature on an envelope takes the place of stamps. This privilege dates back to both the British House of Commons and the American Continental Congress. In 1789, members of the 1st Congress granted the frank to themselves, the President, and members of the cabinet. Originally, members simply signed their name on envelopes; today their signatures are printed on all franked envelopes.

During the 19th century there were numerous charges that members of Congress were abusing the frank. Some mailed their laundry home, and others sent household goods. One senator supposedly signed his name to his horse's saddle and had the post office deliver the animal to his home. Incumbents were accused of bombarding their constituents with transcripts of speeches, government documents, packages of seeds (from the Department of Agriculture), and other items designed to win their reelection. So many objections were raised that in 1873 Congress suspended the use of the frank. However, others defended the frank as essential for "free and unrestrained communications between the people and their representatives." Acting in stages, Congress restored the frank by 1891. Since then, various revisions of the ethics code have limited the amount of franked mail that members can send each year and set restrictions on the newsletters and other types of mail that can be legitimately sent via the frank.

FRANKFURTER, FELIX
Associate Justice, 1939–62

- Born: Nov. 15, 1882, Vienna, Austria
- Education: City College of New York, B.A., 1902; Harvard Law School, LL.B., 1906
- Previous government service: assistant U.S. attorney, Southern District of New York, 1906–9; law officer, Bureau of Insular Affairs, War Department, 1910–14; assistant to the secretary of war, secretary and counsel, President's Mediation Commission, assistant to the U.S. secretary of labor, 1917–18; chairman, War Labor Policies Board, 1918
- Appointed by President Franklin D. Roosevelt Jan. 5, 1939; replaced Benjamin Cardozo, who died
- Supreme Court term: confirmed by the Senate Jan. 17, 1939, by a voice vote; retired Aug. 28, 1962
- Died: Feb. 21, 1965, Washington, D.C.

Felix Frankfurter was the only naturalized citizen of the United States to serve on the Supreme Court. He was born into a Jewish family in Vienna, Austria, and came to New York City in 1894, at the age of 12. He was unable to speak English upon his arrival, but he learned the language quickly and thoroughly. He graduated with honors from the City College of New York and Harvard Law School.

Frankfurter served as the U.S. attorney for the southern district of New York (1906–9), as a federal government official from 1910 to 1918, and then as a law professor at Harvard until 1939, when President Franklin D. Roosevelt appointed him to the Supreme Court. During his 23 years on the Court, Justice Frankfurter was an

advocate of judicial restraint, the belief that justices should carefully recognize constitutional limitations and defer to legislative decisions, whenever reasonable, as the legitimate expression of the majority of the people. In line with his views on judicial restraint, Justice Frankfurter strongly opposed "total incorporation" of the Bill of Rights under the due process clause of the 14th Amendment, which was promoted by his colleague Justice Hugo Black. He argued, for example, that the framers of the 14th Amendment had not intended state governments to follow exactly the requirements of the federal Bill of Rights in dealing with people accused of violating state laws. In *Adamson* v. *California* (1947), he held that the 14th Amendment was "not the basis of a uniform code of criminal procedure federally imposed.... In a federal system it would be a function debilitating to the responsibility of state and local agencies."

Frankfurter was concerned with maintaining the vigor of state and local governments within the federal system. He deplored the trend toward an overwhelming federal government that tended to diminish the functions of state and local governments. He viewed this as a violation of the fundamental constitutional principle of federalism, which originally involved a substantial role for state governments within the Union.

Frankfurter retired from the Court in 1962 after suffering a stroke that greatly weakened him. He died three years later.

SEE ALSO *Federalism; Incorporation doctrine; Judicial activism and judicial restraint*
SOURCES Liva Baker, *Felix Frankfurter* (New York: Coward-McCann, 1969). Max Freedman, *Roosevelt and Frankfurter: Their Correspondence* (Boston: Little, Brown, 1967). Harry N. Hirsch, *The Enigma of Felix Frankfurter* (New York: Basic Books, 1981). Philip B. Kurland, *Mr. Justice Frankfurter and the Constitution* (Chicago: University of Chicago Press, 1971). Michael E. Parrish, *Felix Frankfurter and His Times* (New York: Macmillan, 1982). James F. Simon, "The Antagonists: Hugo

Black and Felix Frankfurter," *Constitution* 3, no. 1 (Winter 1991): 26–34.

FREEDMEN'S BUREAU ACTS (1865 AND 1866)

As the Civil War ended in 1865, Congress created the Bureau of Refugees, Freedmen, and Abandoned Land, popularly known as the Freedmen's Bureau, to help former slaves make the transition to freedom. Throughout the South, the Freedmen's Bureau established schools and hospitals, helped negotiate labor contracts, leased or sold confiscated lands to the freedmen, and generally tried to protect them from former masters.

The unpopularity of the Freedmen's Bureau among white Southerners caused President Andrew Johnson to veto an 1866 bill to extend the life of the bureau. The veto outraged both moderate and radical Republicans in Congress and united them against the President. Congress passed the second Freedmen's Bureau Act over the President's veto and started down the collision course that would result in Johnson's impeachment in 1868.

SEE ALSO *Reconstruction, congressional*
SOURCES Michael Les Benedict, *A Compromise of Principle: Congressional Republicans and Reconstruction, 1863–1868* (New York: Norton, 1974).

FREEDOM OF SPEECH AND PRESS

The 1st Amendment to the Constitution protects free expression through speech or press against suppression by the government: "Congress shall make no law . . . abridging the freedom of speech, or of the press." All 50 state constitutions contain guarantees of free expression similar to those in the U.S. Constitution. An additional protection for the individual's right to free expression comes from Section 1 of the 14th Amendment: "No State shall make or enforce any law which shall abridge the privileges or immunities of citizens of the United States; nor shall any State deprive any person of life, liberty, or property, without due process of law." The Supreme Court has used this section of the 14th Amendment to apply the 1st Amendment guarantee of freedom of speech and press to cases involving state and local governments.

The right to free speech and press means that individuals may publicly express ideas and information—including expressions generally considered to be unwise, untrue, or unpopular—without fear of punishment by the government. In this way, government officials may be criticized and new ways of thinking and behaving may be advanced. Forms of free speech include the use of symbols, orderly public demonstrations, and radio and television broadcasts. Freedom of speech is an essential characteristic of a constitutional democracy because by exercising this right, individuals can communicate opinions both to other citizens and to their representatives in the government. Through this free exchange of ideas, government officials may become responsive to the people they are supposed to represent.

The right to free speech stems from the right to freedom of the press established in England during the 17th century. At that time, however, the right to free speech was specifically extended only to members of Parliament. All presses had to be licensed until 1694, when the law requiring licenses lapsed and was not renewed. But controls on the press continued through prosecution for seditious libel, which is speech and writing critical of the government or public officials. In the British colonies of North America, several colonial charters and constitutions explicitly protected freedom of the press, but the right to free speech, as in England, was guaranteed only to members of the legislative branch of government.

The constitutions of most of the original 13 American states protected freedom of the press, but the right of free speech was again extended only to members of the state legislature. An exception was the Pennsylvania Declaration of Rights (1776), which guaranteed freedom of the press and speech to the people.

Proposals for a bill of rights in the U.S. Constitution, advanced in the first session of Congress by James Madison (June 8, 1789), included freedom of speech and press. These rights to freedom of expression became part of the Constitution's 1st Amendment, ratified by the states in 1791.

From 1791 until the early 1900s, the U.S. Supreme Court heard no cases regarding free speech and free press issues. Then, after World War I, the Court decided several cases arising from enforcement of wartime laws to limit freedom of expression that threatened national security. In *Schenck* v. *United States* and *Abrams* v. *United States* (both 1919), the Court upheld such federal laws, basing its decisions on its "clear and present danger" and "bad tendency" tests.

Not until 1925, in *Gitlow* v. *New York,* did the U.S. Supreme Court assert its authority to deal with free speech and press issues originating at the state level of government. Prior to *Gitlow,* the 1st Amendment rights of free speech and press were held to apply only to the federal government (*Barron* v. *Baltimore,* 1833). In *Gitlow,* the Court acknowledged for the first time that the 1st Amendment freedoms of speech and press were tied fundamentally to the ideas of liberty and due process in the 14th Amendment. Thus, the rights of free speech and press were viewed as part of an individual's liberty that, according to the 14th Amendment, could not be taken from any person without due process of law.

Since *Gitlow,* the U.S. Supreme Court has made several landmark decisions that have expanded free speech and press rights through limitations on state government power to restrain or interfere with these rights. Examples of key Court cases on free speech and press issues, originating in the state courts, are listed below:

- *Stromberg* v. *California* (1931): The Court struck down a California statute outlawing the display of a red flag because it symbolized opposition to the government. This state law was held to be a violation of constitutional rights to freedom of expression.

- *Near* v. *Minnesota* (1931): The Court overturned a state law that barred continued publication of a newspaper because it printed articles that insulted racial and religious minorities and said nasty things about certain people. This law was held to be an example of "prior restraint" of the press in violation of the 1st Amendment.

- *New York Times Co.* v. *Sullivan* (1964): The Court ruled that the 1st Amendment protects the press from libel suits that result from the printing of articles that harm the reputation of a public official.

- *Brandenburg* v. *Ohio* (1969): The Court ruled that a state may not forbid or limit speech merely because it advocates the use of force against the government or the violation of the law. Rather, government may limit speech only when it is directly and immediately connected to lawless behavior. The Court departed from the "clear and present danger" doctrine used in *Schenck* v. *United States* and *Abrams* v. *United States,* which permitted government prohibition of speech that had a tendency to encourage or cause lawless behavior.

- *Texas* v. *Johnson* (1989): The Court decided that the state of Texas could not convict and punish a person for burning an American flag during a peaceful political protest demonstration. The state's action in this case, said the Court, violated the 1st Amendment's guarantee of freedom of expression.

Since the 1960s, the Supreme Court has also broadened free speech and press rights in cases originating at the federal level of government. Examples of key cases are *Yates* v. *United States* (1957) and *New York Times Co.* v. *United States* (1971). In *Yates* the court ruled that to prosecute people for violating the Smith Act, which prohibited the advocacy of violent overthrow of the government, there must be proof of overt lawless actions, not just expression of ideas about illegal behavior. In the *New York Times* case, the Court prevented the federal government from exercising "prior restraint" to stop a newspaper from printing information about the Vietnam War that it wanted to withhold from the public.

Supreme Court decisions in cases originating at the state and federal levels of government have protected speech and press from prior restraint by government, from charges of seditious libel by public officials, and from acts by government to ban or restrict unpopular ideas in speech and print—such as antiwar protests, antigovernment protests, and burning of the country's flag.

Americans have great freedom to say and write what they please without fear of government restrictions. But this freedom has limits pertaining to the time, place, and manner of speech. For example, individuals certainly have the right to speak out for or against candidates competing to win government offices. But they may not use amplifiers to broadcast campaign messages so loudly that residents of a community are disturbed late at night, when most people are in bed. This kind of speech is restricted by law because it unreasonably "disturbs the peace" of a community (*Kovacs* v. *Cooper,* 1949). But the government may not make a law restricting freedom of expression because of the content of the speech. In the *Kovacs* case Justice Felix Frankfurter wrote, "So long as a legislature does not prescribe what ideas may be . . . expressed and what may not be, nor discriminates among those who would make inroads upon the public peace, it is not for us to supervise the limits the legislature may impose."

Further, individuals do not have freedom under the Constitution to provoke a riot or other violent behavior. In times of national crisis, such as war or rebellion, the government could be justified in limiting freedom of expression that would critically threaten national security. The individual's

right to freedom of expression must always be weighed against the community's need for stability and security. At issue is the point at which freedom of expression is sufficiently dangerous to the public welfare to justify constitutionally its limitation in speech, the press, television, or radio.

Issues about constitutional limits on freedom of expression have challenged every generation of Americans and will continue to do so. When and how much should the government limit a person's right to freedom of expression?

The answer of some authorities to this question has been an emphatic affirmation of practically unlimited free speech. Justice Hugo Black was an advocate of unfettered free speech. For example, consider this excerpt from his dissent in *Dennis* v. *United States* (1951):

[A] governmental policy of unfettered communication of ideas does entail dangers. To the Founders of this Nation, however, the benefits derived from free expression were worth the risk. They embodied this philosophy in the First Amendment's command that "Congress shall make no law . . . abridging the freedom of speech, or of the press. . . ." I have always believed that the First Amendment is the keystone of our government, that the freedoms it guarantees provide the best insurance against destruction of all freedom. . . . [I] cannot agree that the First Amendment permits us to sustain laws suppressing freedom of speech and press on the basis of Congress' or our own notions of mere "reasonableness." Such a doctrine waters down the First Amendment so that it amounts to little more than an admonition to Congress. The Amendment as so construed is not likely to protect any but those "safe" or orthodox views which rarely need its protection.

In contrast to Justice Black's view, Chief Justice Fred M. Vinson, in his majority opinion in *Dennis,* stated a more narrow view of free speech and press, which provides more room for restrictions by government in behalf of the public security:

> Overthrow of the Government by force and violence is certainly a substantial enough interest for the Government to limit speech. Indeed, this is the ultimate value of any society, for if a society cannot protect its very structure from armed internal attack, it must follow that no subordinate value can be protected.

An alternative viewpoint, which strongly supports freedom of speech, while recognizing the need for limits, was written by Justice Louis Brandeis in *Whitney* v. *California* (1927):

> [A]lthough the rights of free speech and assembly are fundamental, they are not in their nature absolute. Their exercise is subject to restriction, if the particular restriction proposed is required to protect the State from destruction or from serious injury, political, economic or moral. . . .
>
> To justify suppression of free speech there must be reasonable ground to fear that serious evil will result if free speech is practiced. . . .
>
> [N]o danger flowing from speech can be deemed clear and present, unless the incidence of the evil apprehended is so imminent that it may befall before there is opportunity for full discussion. If there be time to expose through discussion the falsehoods and fallacies, to avert the evil by the processes of education, the remedy to be applied is more speech, not enforced silence. Only an emergency can justify repression.

Brandeis's position—great latitude for free speech, with particular limits associated with the time, manner, and place of that speech—has been the prevalent viewpoint in the United States during most of the 20th century. This viewpoint, however,

poses the continuing and complex challenge of making case-by-case judgments about the delicate balance of liberty and order, about the limits on authority and the limits on freedom that in concert sustain a constitutional democracy.

The latitude and limits of free speech are being challenged by new forms of communications, such as e-mail and the Internet. In *Reno* v. *American Civil Liberties Union* (1997), for example, the Supreme Court confronted the issue of federal government regulation of free speech via the Internet. The Court responded by striking down a 1996 federal law, the Communications Decency Act (CDA), which prohibited indecent messages through e-mail or on the Internet in order to shield children from offensive material. In this instance, the right to freedom of expression prevailed over an attempt to regulate it on behalf of the public good.

In *United States* v. *Playboy Entertainment Group* (2000) the Court ruled against a federal law that broadly limited the transmission of sexually explicit programs by cable television operators. The purpose of the regulation was to shield children from images deemed harmful to their healthy development, either by blocking transmission or limiting viewer access to hours when children were unlikely to be watching TV. The Court decided these regulations were too restrictive and thereby in violation of the 1st Amendment's free speech guarantee. For most of each day, no one in the cable service areas could receive the programs, whether or not a viewer wanted to see them. The Court decided that a system in which viewers could order signal blocking for themselves without restricting others was "an effective, less restrictive alternative" to the federal law at issue.

The question of when and how to limit freedom of expression via new mass communications technologies is likely to persist, and the Court will continue to face challenges about the latitude and limits of free speech and press.

SEE ALSO *Abrams v. United States; Barron*

v. Baltimore; Brandenburg v. Ohio; Dennis v. United States; Gitlow v. New York; Miami Herald Publishing Co. v. Tornillo; Near v. Minnesota; New York Times Co. v. Sullivan; New York Times Co. v. United States; Prior restraint; Schenck v. United States; Stromberg v. California; Texas v. Johnson; Tinker v. Des Moines Independent Community School District; Whitney v. California; Yates v. United States
SOURCES Margaret A. Blanchard, *Revolutionary Sparks: Freedom of Expression in Modern America* (New York: Oxford University Press, 1992). Nat Hentoff, *Free Speech For Me–But Not for Thee: How the American Left and Right Relentlessly Censor Each Other* (New York: HarperCollins, 1992). Bert Neuborne, "Cycles of Censorship," *Constitution* 4, no. 1 (Winter 1992): 22–29. Lucas A. Powe, Jr., *The Fourth Estate and the Constitution: Freedom of the Press in America* (Berkeley: University of California Press, 1991). Norman Rosenberg, "Freedom of Speech" and "Freedom of the Press," in *By and for the People: Constitutional Rights in American History,* edited by Kermit L. Hall (Arlington Heights, Ill.: Harlan Davidson, 1991). Rodney A. Smolla, *Free Speech in an Open Society* (New York: Knopf, 1992).

FREE EXERCISE CLAUSE

The 1st Amendment to the Constitution states, "Congress shall make no law respecting an establishment of religion, or prohibiting the free exercise thereof." Through its free exercise clause, the 1st Amendment protects the individual's right to freedom of conscience and free expression of religious beliefs.
SEE ALSO *Religious issues under the Constitution*

FULBRIGHT, J. WILLIAM

- Born: Apr. 9, 1905, Sumner, Mo.
- Political party: Democrat
- Education: University of Arkansas at Fayetteville, graduated, 1925; Rhodes Scholar, Oxford University, 1928; George Washington University Law School, graduated, 1934
- Representative from Arkansas: 1943–45
- Senator from Arkansas: 1945–74
- Died: Feb. 9, 1995, Washington, D.C.

In 1964, as chairman of the Senate Foreign Relations Committee, J. William Fulbright led the effort to pass the Gulf of Tonkin Resolution. The resolution gave congressional support to President Lyndon B. Johnson to retaliate against any hostile military acts by North Vietnam. Fulbright assured other senators that the resolution was not an act of war and that President Johnson would consult with Congress before escalating the conflict. The next year, however, when President Johnson sent U.S. Marines to intervene in a rebellion within the Dominican Republic, Senator Fulbright became concerned that the President was not telling Congress and the public the full truth. If Johnson had exaggerated the situation in the Dominican Republic in order to justify sending troops, Fulbright wondered, might he be doing the same in Vietnam? In 1966, the Foreign Relations Committee launched a series of "educational" hearings on the Vietnam War, inviting both defenders and critics of the war to testify. The hearings began a national debate on the war and made Senator Fulbright one of the leading dissenters against American foreign policy.
SEE ALSO *Gulf of Tonkin Resolution (1964); Johnson, Lyndon B.*
SOURCES Randall Bennett Woods, *Fulbright: A Biography* (New York: Cambridge University Press, 1995).

FULLER, MELVILLE W.
Chief Justice, 1888–1910

- Born: Feb. 11, 1833, Augusta, Maine
- Education: Bowdoin College, B.A., 1853; Harvard Law School, 1853–55
- Previous government service: Illinois

Constitutional Convention, 1861; Illinois House of Representatives, 1863–64
• Appointed by President Grover Cleveland Apr. 30, 1888; replaced Morrison R. Waite, who died
• Supreme Court term: confirmed by the Senate July 20, 1888, by a 41–20 vote; served until July 4, 1910
• Died: July 4, 1910, Sorrento, Maine

Melville W. Fuller was an active and loyal member of the Democratic party. He was also a successful lawyer who regularly represented clients in cases before the U.S. Supreme Court. When Chief Justice Morrison Waite died in 1888, President Grover Cleveland, a Democrat, chose to replace him with Fuller, who seemed to share the President's views about politics and constitutional issues.

During his 22 years as chief justice, Fuller guided Supreme Court decisions that supported racial segregation based on the "separate but equal" doctrine. He opposed government regulation of private businesses and of the uses of private property by individuals. In particular, Fuller believed that government had no right to regulate an employer's dealings with workers, such as setting rules about working conditions, payment of wages, or hours of work. These matters, according to Fuller, should be left to free bargaining between employers and workers. In *Adair v. United States* (1908), Fuller wrote, "The employer and the employee have equality of right, and any legislation that disturbs that equality is an arbitrary interference with liberty of contract, which no government can legally justify in a free land."

During his term on the Court, Fuller also served on the Venezuela–British Guiana Border Commission and the Permanent Court of Arbitration in The Hague, Netherlands. In these roles, Fuller worked for the peaceful resolution of international conflicts.

SOURCES Willard L. King, *Melville Westin Fuller: Chief Justice of the United States* (Chicago: University of Chicago Press, 1950).

G

"GAG RULE"

In 1836 the House of Representatives established a "gag rule" to try to stop citizens from submitting antislavery petitions. Previously, the House and Senate had simply referred such petitions to committee without ever acting on them. But when petitioners called for Congress to abolish slavery in the District of Columbia, which Congress supervised, Southern representatives sought to put an end to this "agitation." Together with sympathetic Northerners, they voted 117 to 68 to adopt a "gag rule" that required the House to lay antislavery petitions on the table (meaning to put them aside) immediately, without printing them, referring them to committee, or in any way debating them. Representative John Quincy Adams (Whig–Massachusetts) led the opposition to what he called an unconstitutional attempt to suppress the freedom to petition. Adams lost repeated battles and came close to being censured. By 1844, enough Northerners had changed their position, and the House voted 105 to 80 to repeal the "gag rule."

SEE ALSO *Adams, John Quincy; Petition, citizens' right to*

SOURCES Leonard L. Richards, *The Life and Times of Congressman John Quincy Adams* (New York: Oxford University Press, 1986).

GALLERIES

Visitors watch the proceedings of the House of Representatives and Senate from galleries, or balconies, surrounding the chambers. The House, elected directly by the people, opened a public gallery when it first met in 1789, but the Senate, whose members were elected by state legislatures, saw no need for a gallery at first. The Senate's debates were closed until 1794, when a gallery at last was constructed. Today the galleries of both the House and Senate are open whenever that chamber is in session, at any hour of the day or night.

Congress appoints doorkeepers to supervise the galleries. Rules prohibit visitors to the galleries from taking notes or photographs. Visitors may not lean over the railing, a prohibition dating back to 1916, when President Woodrow Wilson addressed a joint session of Congress and activists draped a large banner down from the gallery that read, "Mr. President, What Will You Do For Woman Suffrage?" The rules of the Senate and House also forbid members from addressing the galleries or from calling attention to special visitors.

Before entering the galleries, visitors must obtain tickets from their senators or representatives. The first tickets were issued in 1868 to control the crowds seeking to witness the impeachment trial of President Andrew Johnson. Today, television cameras mounted in the galleries broadcast the proceedings live via C-SPAN. Television has become a nationwide extension of the House and Senate galleries.

In addition to the public galleries, the House and Senate also make gallery space available to their staff, to the members' families, to the foreign diplomatic corps, and to the press. To encourage the widest media coverage of its proceedings, Congress provides separate press galleries for newspaper correspondents, radio and television reporters, magazine writers, and press photographers.

SEE ALSO *C-SPAN; Doorkeepers; Media coverage of Congress*

GARFIELD,
JAMES A.
20th President

- Born: Nov. 19, 1831, Orange, Ohio
- Political party: Republican
- Education: Williams College, B.A., 1856
- Military service: 42nd Ohio Infantry, 1862–63
- Previous government service: Ohio Senate, 1859–61; U.S. House of Representatives, 1863–80; member of electoral commission, 1876
- Elected President, 1880; served, 1881
- Died: Sept. 19, 1881, Elberon, N.J.

James A. Garfield served the second-shortest term of any President (the shortest was served by William Henry Harrison). In the four months before he was shot, he accomplished next to nothing, but his death by a disappointed office seeker spurred the Congress several years later to pass a civil service reform bill.

Garfield was born on the Ohio frontier. He was a canal sailor, a teacher, and a farmer. After graduating from Williams College he became a professor of ancient languages and literature at Hiram Eclectic Institute.

Garfield entered Republican politics and was elected to the Ohio legislature. During the Civil War he headed a volun-

teer company that consisted of many of his former students. He distinguished himself with his bravery at the Battle of Chickamauga, receiving a promotion to major general.

Garfield served as a member of the House of Representatives for 17 years. He was a radical Republican who voted for the impeachment of Andrew Johnson and later was one of the two House Republicans to serve on the electoral commission that decided the disputed election of 1876 in favor of Rutherford B. Hayes.

James Garfield was a true dark horse Presidential candidate, one whose name first emerged at the convention itself. He received not a single vote on the first ballot for the Republican nomination in 1880. At the national convention he headed the faction supporting Secretary of Treasury John Sherman and opposing ex-President Ulysses S. Grant and Senator James G. Blaine. The three-way race deadlocked, and on the 36th ballot Garfield was nominated as a compromise candidate. He defeated the Democratic candidate, Civil War hero General Winfield Scott Hancock, by a tiny popular majority, though his electoral college margin was more substantial.

Garfield and Secretary of State Blaine, leaders of the Half-Breed faction of the Republican party (so called because their opponents thought they were half-Democrat), struggled against Senator Roscoe Conkling and other "Stalwart" Republicans over appointments to positions in his administration. Eventually, Garfield appointed his own man as collector of the Port of New York, signaling his victory. He also started an investigation of corruption in the post office department, which involved the awarding of certain mail routes to political favorites who then submitted inflated claims for payment.

On July 2, 1881, while standing at a railway station in Washington, D.C., Garfield was shot by Charles Julius Guiteau, who wanted to become an ambassador and had been rebuffed by Blaine. Guiteau, evidently insane, shouted, "I am a Stalwart. Arthur is now President of the United

States," implying that Vice President Chester Arthur would get jobs for the Stalwarts. For 11 weeks Garfield hung between life and death while the cabinet debated questions about Presidential succession, including whether Arthur should assume office as acting President while Garfield lay ill. Garfield died on September 19 and was succeeded by Arthur; his assassin was found guilty of murder and hanged.

SEE ALSO *Arthur, Chester Alan; Assassinations, Presidential; Hayes, Rutherford B.; Succession to the Presidency*
SOURCES Justus D. Doenicke, *The Presidencies of James A. Garfield and Chester A. Arthur* (Lawrence: University Press of Kansas, 1981).

GARNER, JOHN NANCE
Vice President

- Born: Nov. 22, 1868, Red River County, Tex.
- Political party: Democrat
- Education: Vanderbilt University, 1888
- Military service: none
- Previous government service: Texas House of Representatives, 1899–1902; U.S. House of Representatives, 1903–33; House minority leader, 1929–31; Speaker of the House, 1931–33
- Vice President under Franklin D. Roosevelt, 1933–41
- Died: Nov. 7, 1967, Uvalde, Tex.

The election of 1930 made "Cactus Jack" Garner (known for his prickly humor) the first Democratic Speaker of the House in a dozen years. With the nation sliding into a terrible economic depression, Garner seemed uncertain about what course to follow. At first he encouraged Democratic support for Republican President Herbert Hoover's programs, but when these seemed too limited and unsatisfactory, Garner looked for Democratic alternatives. In 1932, Garner proposed that the federal government spend billions of dollars on public works programs to put the unemployed back to work. Hoover vetoed this plan, but the following year it became a major initiative of the new Democratic President, Franklin D. Roosevelt. Garner was by then Vice President, having received the nomination as a reward for delivering the Texas delegation to Roosevelt.

Garner helped Roosevelt deal with Congress in the early days of the New Deal. But Roosevelt gave him no other duties, and he spent much of his time at his ranch in Uvalde, Texas, taking target practice on a spittoon on his front porch. It was there that he described the Vice Presidency as "not worth a pitcher of warm spit."

In his second term, Garner opposed Roosevelt's attempt in 1937 to "pack" the Supreme Court—Roosevelt wanted to appoint additional justices sympathetic to his social and economic policies—and his attempt to "purge" Democrats in Congress who opposed the New Deal program in the 1938 elections. When Roosevelt decided to run for a third term, Garner objected to this violation of the unwritten two-term custom that had prevailed since George Washington. His own campaign for the 1940 Presidential nomination went nowhere, and he retired from politics permanently.

SEE ALSO *New Deal*
SOURCES Richard Bolling, *Power in the House: A History of the Leadership of the House of Representatives* (New York: Dutton, 1969). Bascom Timmons, *Garner of Texas* (New York: Harper, 1948).

GERMANENESS

To be germane, or relevant, an amendment to legislation must have something to do with the rest of the bill it seeks to amend. House rules require that all amendments be germane. The rules of the Senate are different, and senators can attach favored amendments onto completely unrelated bills. These are sometimes called "riders" because they ride along on the larger bill. The Senate requires germaneness only for amendments to general appropriations bills and after cloture, the end of debate, has been voted on a bill. The

Senate might also require germaneness as part of a unanimous consent agreement that sets the conditions under which a bill can be debated and voted upon.

SEE ALSO *Riders to bills*

GERRY, ELBRIDGE
Vice President

- Born: July 17, 1744, Marblehead, Mass.
- Political party: Democratic-Republican
- Education: Harvard College, A.B., 1762
- Military service: none
- Previous government service: judge, Massachusetts General Court, 1772–74; signer of Declaration of Independence, 1776; Continental Congress, 1776–81, 1783–85; U.S. House of Representatives, 1789–93; governor of Massachusetts, 1810–11
- Vice President under James Madison, 1813–14
- Died: Nov. 23, 1814, Washington, D.C.

As a delegate to the Constitutional Convention, Elbridge Gerry was a strong proponent of states' rights. He spoke against popular election of either the President or the Senate. He also wanted to restrict the size of the army to 3,000 in times of peace. He refused to sign the final draft of the Constitution because it did not provide a Bill of Rights.

Gerry was elected to Congress in 1789 and served two terms. In 1797 President John Adams sent Gerry, along with John Marshall and Charles Cotesworth Pinckney, on a diplomatic mission to France. Three French diplomats, known as X, Y, and Z, insisted on bribes and a $10 million loan as compensation for alleged American "insults." The mission ended in failure when the Americans refused these demands and published details of the so-called XYZ affair in American newspapers. A naval war with France ensued.

As governor of Massachusetts, Gerry invented the gerrymander, a system of redrawing state legislative and congressional districts to benefit members of his party. The term *gerrymander* was a combination of *Gerry* and *salamander*, a reference to the odd shapes of the districts that resulted.

In 1812 Gerry ran for Vice President as James Madison's running mate on the Republican ticket and won the election. He strongly supported the War of 1812, although opposition in his native Massachusetts was strong and the Federalist party, which controlled state governments in New England, refused to help the war effort. Gerry died in office in 1814.

GERRYMANDERING

When Elbridge Gerry was governor of Massachusetts in 1812, his party redrew the state's congressional districts deliberately to favor its own candidates. One district had such an odd shape that it resembled a salamander. Combining *Gerry* and sala*mander* created *Gerrymander,* which came to mean any unfair and extremely partisan form of reapportionment of election districts.

SEE ALSO *Reapportionment*

GETTYSBURG ADDRESS

On November 19, 1863, President Abraham Lincoln gave a short speech in Gettysburg, Pennsylvania, commemorating the Battle of Gettysburg and dedicating a national cemetery for fallen Union soldiers. Lincoln's speech is the most famous address ever given by an American President, and it is one of the most eloquent expressions of democratic ideals ever uttered. He wrote it in the White House, though he made a few changes on the train ride to Gettysburg.

He was preceded at the podium by the noted orator Edward Everett, who had spoken for nearly two hours. Lincoln's speech, by contrast, took only a few minutes. Lincoln observed, "The world will little note nor long remember what we say here, but it can never forget what they did here." Although the crowd gave Lincoln only perfunctory applause, Everett was more appreciative. He told Lincoln,

"My speech will soon be forgotten; yours never will be. How gladly would I exchange my hundred pages for your twenty lines."

"Now we are engaged in a great civil war," Lincoln said, testing whether "any nation, conceived in liberty, and dedicated to the proposition that all men are created equal, can long endure." He urged Americans to resolve "that these dead shall not have died in vain; that this nation, under God, shall have a new birth of freedom; and that government of the people, by the people, and for the people, shall not perish from the earth." By emphasizing the equality of Americans, a value not mentioned even in the Constitution, Lincoln had provided a vision of the United States that could justify the carnage of the Civil War and would reshape the meaning of American politics for generations to follow.

SEE ALSO *Emancipation Proclamations; Lincoln, Abraham*

SOURCES Garry Wills, *Lincoln at Gettysburg* (New York: Simon & Schuster, 1992).

GIBBONS V. OGDEN

• 9 Wheat. 1 (1824)
• Vote: 6–0
• For the Court: Marshall
• Concurring: Johnson

In 1807 Robert Fulton made the first successful steamboat run from New York City to Albany. The New York legislature soon granted Fulton and a partner the exclusive right to navigate the waters of New York State. In turn, Fulton and his partner sold Aaron Ogden the right to operate between New York City and the New Jersey shore of the Hudson River.

Meanwhile, Thomas Gibbons secured a license from the U.S. Congress to run two steamships between New York and New Jersey. Competition between Gibbons and Ogden became fierce. Finally, Ogden petitioned a New York state court to order Gibbons to discontinue his business. The state court decided in Ogden's favor, and

Gibbons appealed the New York court's decision to the Supreme Court.

The Issue Gibbons argued that under the Constitution, Congress had complete power to regulate interstate commerce. Therefore, his federal license to operate steamboats remained valid despite the ruling of the New York State court. Ogden countered that the congressional commerce power applied only to the transportation and sale of goods, not to navigation. Therefore, he argued, his New York license should prevail and invalidate Gibbons's license. The case raised two issues. First, what did "commerce" include? Did Congress have the power under the commerce clause (Article 1, Section 8) to regulate navigation? Second, did Congress hold an exclusive power or did the states also possess the power to regulate interstate commerce within their boundaries?

Opinion of the Court Chief Justice John Marshall wrote for the Court, which ruled in favor of Gibbons. In doing so, it defined the term *commerce* broadly. Commerce is more than traffic, the Court said. It includes all kinds of business and trade "between nations and parts of nations [the states]," including navigation.

The Court also ruled that should a state law regulating commerce interfere with a federal law, the federal law was always supreme. Consequently, the New York law giving Ogden his monopoly was invalid because it interfered with the federal law under which Gibbons had acquired his license.

The Court did not, however, resolve the second issue in the case—whether states could regulate areas of commerce Congress had not regulated. Nor did the Court decide whether the states could simultaneously regulate commerce that the Congress was regulating. These issues would have to wait several decades to be settled by additional Court rulings.

Significance The *Gibbons* case established a basic precedent because it paved the way for later federal regulation of transportation, communication, buying and selling, and manufacturing. In the 20th century, for example, the Court has ruled that the commerce clause permits Congress to fine a farmer for producing a small amount of wheat for his own use in violation of the quota set by the Department of Agriculture. Little economic activity remains outside the regulatory power of Congress today.

SEE ALSO *Commerce power*

SOURCES Maurice G. Baxter, *The Steamboat Monopoly, Gibbons v. Ogden, 1824* (Philadelphia: Philadelphia Book Co., 1972). George Dangerfield, "The Steamboat Case," in *Quarrels That Have Shaped the Constitution,* edited by John A. Garraty (New York: Harper & Row, 1987).

GIDEON V. WAINWRIGHT

- 372 U.S. 335 (1963)
- Vote: 9–0
- For the Court: Black
- Concurring: Clark, Douglas, and Harlan

Clarence Earl Gideon, a penniless Florida drifter, was arrested for the burglary of a Florida pool hall. At his trial Gideon asked for a court-appointed attorney because he could not afford a lawyer. The court denied Gideon's request, and he conducted his own defense.

The Florida court convicted Gideon and sentenced him to five years in prison. In his jail cell, using a pencil and pad of paper, Gideon composed a petition asking the Supreme Court to review his case. "The question is very simple," wrote Gideon. "I requested the [Florida] court to appoint me an attorney and the court refused." He maintained that the state court's refusal to appoint counsel for him denied him rights "guaranteed by the Constitution and the Bill of Rights" in the 6th and 14th Amendments. The Supreme Court decided to review Gideon's case. Unlike the Florida court, however, the Supreme Court did not expect Gideon to ar-

gue his own case. Instead, the Court appointed Abe Fortas, a prominent Washington lawyer and a future Supreme Court justice, to argue Gideon's case. Fortas defended Gideon *pro bono publico* (for the good of the public), donating his time and money for the cause of justice.

The Issue The 6th Amendment states that "in all criminal prosecutions the accused shall enjoy the right . . . to have the assistance of counsel for his defense."

Despite the unmistakably clear meaning of this wording, the Supreme Court had ruled in earlier cases that in state courts, needy defendants had a constitutional right to court-appointed lawyers in only two situations: in cases involving the death penalty (*Powell* v. *Alabama,* 1932) and in cases where special circumstances, such as youth or mental incompetence, required furnishing an attorney to assure a fair trial (*Betts* v. *Brady,* 1942).

Does the 6th Amendment right to counsel apply to all criminal cases? Does the due process clause of the 14th Amendment require states to provide lawyers for defendants too poor to hire their own attorneys? Or should the Court continue to follow the precedent set in *Betts* v. *Brady*? The Supreme Court asked the attorneys arguing the *Gideon* case specifically to consider whether it should overrule *Betts* v. *Brady*.

Opinion of the Court The Court ruled unanimously in Gideon's favor and did overrule *Betts* v. *Brady*. The Court held that the right to counsel was so fundamental that the 14th Amendment due process clause extended the 6th Amendment guarantee of counsel to *all* defendants in criminal cases.

Justice Hugo Black, who had written a dissenting opinion in *Betts* v. *Brady* 21 years before, now had the pleasure of writing the Court's opinion to overturn the *Betts* decision.

Significance As a result of the ruling, the state of Florida granted Clarence Earl Gideon a new state trial in August 1963. Represented by a court-appointed lawyer,

Gideon was found not guilty. The Supreme Court's decision also caused states throughout the nation to review numerous cases. Defendants too poor to afford attorneys' fees, who had been tried without the benefit of counsel, received retrials. The courts acquitted many and released them from prison.

The *Gideon* case reflected the emergence of a nationwide concern with equal justice for the poor. It recognized that, left without the aid of counsel, even intelligent and educated people have very little chance of successfully defending themselves in criminal trials. Most large cities and some states have public defender offices that provide free legal help to poor people in criminal cases. In other areas, trial court judges appoint private lawyers to represent poor defendants.

SEE ALSO *Betts v. Brady; Powell v. Alabama; Rights of the accused; Counsel, right to*

SOURCES Anthony Lewis, *Gideon's Trumpet* (New York: Random House, 1964).

GINGRICH, NEWT

- Born: June 17, 1943, Harrisburg, Pa.
- Political party: Republican
- Education: Emory University, B.A., 1965; Tulane University, M.A., 1968 and Ph.D, 1971
- Representative from Georgia: 1979–99
- House minority whip: 1989–95
- Speaker of the House: 1995–99

The man credited with gaining the majority for House Republicans in the 1994 elections—after 40 years in the minority—was Georgia Representative Newt Gingrich. He aimed to change business as usual in Congress and to "wipe the slate clean" of many liberal programs.

As a brash new member of the House, Gingrich rejected compromise and consensus and adopted a more combative, confrontational position. When House proceedings began to be televised in 1979, Gingrich inaugurated the practice of giving late-afternoon speeches to an almost

empty chamber and to a television audience across the country. In 1988, Gingrich brought the ethics charges that caused Speaker Jim Wright to resign.

Gingrich rose to leadership in the House by appealing to the dissatisfaction of Republicans so long in the minority and by offering them a strategy to win the majority. He proposed that Republican candidates for the House in 1994 sign a Contract with America, outlining the reforms they would enact if elected. When Republicans won the election, Gingrich became Speaker of the House.

An often controversial Speaker, Gingrich was widely blamed for shutting down the federal government during a budget impasse with President Bill Clinton in 1995. When the House moved to impeach Clinton in 1998, voters reacted negatively in the congressional elections and narrowed the Republican majority to five votes. Faced with mounting opposition within his own party, Gingrich chose to resign as Speaker and as a member of Congress.

SEE ALSO *Contract with America; Speaker of the House; Wright, Jim*

SOURCES Newt Gingrich, *To Renew America* (New York: HarperCollins, 1995).

GINSBURG, RUTH BADER
Associate Justice, 1993–

- Born: Mar. 15, 1933, Brooklyn, N.Y.
- Education: Cornell University, B.A., 1954; Harvard Law School, 1956–58; Columbia University Law School, LL.B., 1959
- Previous government service: law secretary, U.S. District Court, 1959–61; judge, U.S. Court of Appeals for the District of Columbia Circuit, 1980–93
- Appointed by President Bill Clinton June 14, 1993, to replace Byron White, who resigned
- Supreme Court term: confirmed by the Senate Aug. 3, 1993, by a 96–3 vote

On June 14, 1993, President Bill Clinton

nominated Ruth Bader Ginsburg to replace Justice Byron White on the U.S. Supreme Court. She was the second woman, after Justice Sandra Day O'Connor (appointed in 1981), to be named to the Court. She was the first Jew appointed to the Court since Abe Fortas was nominated by President Lyndon B. Johnson in 1965.

In 1960 Justice Felix Frankfurter rejected Ginsburg's application to serve as his law clerk. She had been an honor student at the law schools of two universities, Harvard and Columbia, and had strong recommendations from her professors. While recognizing her great talent, Justice Frankfurter explained that he did not want a woman as his law clerk. This rebuff inspired Ruth Bader Ginsburg to make her mark on constitutional law.

From 1960 to 1980 Ginsburg moved from a job as a federal district court law clerk to an appointment by President Jimmy Carter as a federal appellate court judge. Judge Ginsburg served for 13 years on the U.S. Court of Appeals for the District of Columbia Circuit.

Before serving as a federal appellate court judge, Ginsburg was a professor of law at Rutgers University (1963–72) and Columbia University (1972–73). From 1973 to 1980 she was an attorney for the American Civil Liberties Union (ACLU), where she started the Women's Rights Project. As an ACLU lawyer, Ginsburg argued six cases before the U.S. Supreme Court and won five of them, including *Reed* v. *Reed*, in which the Court struck down an Idaho law that discriminated against women in the appointment of estate executors. These legal victories greatly advanced the cause of constitutional rights for women.

In nominating Judge Ginsburg for the Supreme Court, President Clinton recognized her outstanding contributions to the development of constitutional law and the rights of women. "Over the course of a lifetime in her pioneering work in behalf of the women of this country," he said, "she has compiled a truly historic record of achievement in the finest traditions of American law and citizenship."

In her opinions for the Court, Ginsburg has taken strong positions in favor of women's rights, civil rights, and 1st Amendment rights to freedom of expression. For example, she wrote the Court's opinion in *United States* v. *Virginia* (1996), which brought an end to the Virginia Military Academy's all-male admissions policy.

GITLOW V. NEW YORK

- 268 U.S. 652 (1925)
- Vote: 7–2
- For the Court: Sanford
- Dissenting: Holmes and Brandeis

Benjamin Gitlow was a member of the Communist Labor Party of the United States, organized in 1919. He participated in the writing and distribution of a pamphlet published by his party called the *Left Wing Manifesto*. This pamphlet urged the people of the United States to rise up and overthrow their government and bring about a communist revolution. Gitlow was arrested and convicted for violating New York's Criminal Anarchy Law, which made it a crime to advocate violent revolution against the government.

The Issue   Gitlow claimed the Criminal Anarchy Law was unconstitutional because it violated his constitutional rights to free speech and press. The 14th Amendment says that a state government cannot deprive a person of liberty without due process of law. Furthermore, Gitlow's lawyers argued that the due process clause of the 14th Amendment could be used to extend 1st Amendment rights of free speech and press to the states. Did New York's Criminal Anarchy Law deprive Gitlow of his constitutional rights to freedom of expression? Could the 14th Amendment's due process clause be used to hold state governments to the free speech and press standards of the 1st Amendment?

Opinion of the Court   The Supreme Court upheld Gitlow's conviction and concluded that the Criminal Anarchy Law was constitutional. Justice Edward T. Sanford wrote, "[A] state may punish utterances endangering the foundations of organized government and threatening its overthrow by unlawful means." He concluded that Gitlow's pamphlet was not a mere discussion of ideas. Rather, it was "the language of direct incitement" to violent revolution.

The Court, agreed, however, that 1st Amendment free speech and press rights could be applied to the states through the 14th Amendment. Justice Sanford wrote that "for present purposes we may and do assume that freedom of speech and of the press—which are protected by the First Amendment from abridgement by Congress—are among the fundamental personal rights and liberties protected by the due process clause of the Fourteenth Amendment from impairment by the states."

Dissent   Justice Oliver Wendell Holmes, with Justice Louis Brandeis concurring, disagreed with the Court's decision to uphold the conviction of Gitlow. Holmes argued that the mere expression of ideas, separated from action, could not be punished under the "clear and present danger" doctrine that he had defined in *Schenck* v. *United States* and modified in his dissent in *Abrams* v. *United States* (both 1919). In his *Gitlow* dissent, Holmes followed his line of reasoning in *Abrams,* in which he stated that unless speech could be linked clearly with immediate violent and unlawful action, it should be permitted. Holmes said, "Every idea is an incitement. It offers itself for belief and, if believed it is acted on unless some other belief outweighs it." Further, Holmes said that there was no evidence that Gitlow's pamphlet was likely to incite violent revolution and that it posed only a remote threat to social order. Holmes and Brandeis agreed strongly with the Court's conclusion that the 1st Amendment should apply to the states.

Significance   This case was the foundation for the incorporation of the 1st

Amendment under the due process clause of the 14th Amendment in order to limit the states' power to restrict the free speech and press rights of individuals. The incorporation doctrine has been used gradually to apply most of the federal Bill of Rights to the states. Furthermore, beginning in the 1960s the Court rejected the narrow interpretation of free speech expressed by Justice Sanford in this case. The broader interpretation of free speech, expressed by Justice Holmes in dissent, has become the prevailing position of the Court. Thus the *Gitlow* case is important because it provided a foundation for the future expansion of free speech and press rights of individuals.

SEE ALSO   *Abrams v. United States; Freedom of speech and press; Incorporation doctrine; Schenck v. United States*

GOLDBERG, ARTHUR J.
Associate Justice, 1962–65

- Born: Aug. 8, 1908, Chicago, Ill.
- Education: Northwestern University, B.S.L., 1929; J.D., 1929
- Previous government service: U.S. secretary of labor, 1961–62
- Appointed by President John F. Kennedy Aug. 29, 1962; replaced Felix Frankfurter, who retired
- Supreme Court term: confirmed by the Senate Sept. 25, 1962, by a voice vote; resigned July 25, 1965
- Subsequent government service: U.S. ambassador to the United Nations, 1965–68
- Died: Jan. 19, 1990, Washington, D.C.

Arthur J. Goldberg was the youngest child of Russian Jewish parents who settled in Chicago. He served less than three years on the Supreme Court, resigning to become the U.S. ambassador to the United Nations.

After graduating from law school, Goldberg became an expert on the legal concerns of labor unions. He often represented unions in legal disputes with employers. In 1961 President John Kennedy appointed Goldberg to be secretary of labor. One year later, the President named Goldberg to the Supreme Court.

During his brief term on the Court, Justice Goldberg supported the expansion of 1st Amendment freedoms of expression and association. He also backed the rights of individuals accused of crimes. In *Escobedo* v. *Illinois* (1964), for example, Justice Goldberg wrote the Court's opinion that overturned the murder conviction of a man who had been denied the 6th Amendment right to counsel during questioning by the police. Justice Goldberg also argued that the police had not advised Escobedo of his right to remain silent and had therefore violated Escobedo's 5th Amendment protection against self-incrimination.

After leaving the Court, Goldberg served for three years as U.S. ambassador to the United Nations. He then returned to the private practice of law in Washington, D.C.

GOLDWATER, BARRY M.

- Born: Jan. 1, 1909, Phoenix, Ariz.
- Political party: Republican
- Education: University of Tuscon, 1928
- Senator from Arizona: 1953–65, 1969–87
- Died: May 29, 1998, Phoenix, Ariz.

As a senator during the 1950s, Barry Goldwater objected to what he called "me too" Republicanism. He meant that under President Dwight D. Eisenhower, Republicans had embraced many of the social and economic programs of Democratic Presidents Franklin D. Roosevelt and Harry S. Truman. Goldwater rejected the idea of big government, social welfare programs, and regulation of business. "My aim is not to pass laws, but to repeal them," he insisted. "It is not to inaugurate new programs, but to cancel old ones that do violence to the Constitution."

Goldwater used the Senate as a pulpit to preach his conservative creed and be-

came the nation's leading conservative spokesman. In 1964 he won the Republican nomination for President, but his views seemed extreme and he lost to Lyndon B. Johnson in a landslide. Goldwater's followers retained control of the Republican party and steered it in the direction that led eventually to the election of Ronald Reagan on a platform of cutting back social programs and deregulating business. Goldwater himself returned to the Senate in 1969, where he continued to speak his mind.

SOURCES Robert A. Goldberg, *Barry Goldwater* (New Haven: Yale University Press, 1995). Barry M. Goldwater, *With No Apologies* (New York: Morrow, 1979).

GOOD FAITH EXCEPTION

SEE *Exclusionary rule; United States v. Leon*

GORE, ALBERT, JR.
Vice President

- Born: Mar. 31, 1948, Washington, D.C.
- Political party: Democrat
- Education: Harvard College, A.B., 1969; Vanderbilt University Graduate School of Religion, 1971–72; Vanderbilt University Law School, LL.B, 1974
- Military service: U.S. Army, 1969–71
- Previous government service: U.S. House of Representatives, 1977–85; U.S. Senate, 1985–1993
- Vice President under Bill Clinton, 1993–

Al Gore, Jr's father was for 32 years a Democratic representative and senator from Tennessee. Al, Jr., was raised in a Washington hotel owned by his family and attended St. Alban's School for Boys, where he won varsity letters in football, basketball, and track. He graduated from Harvard and later Vanderbilt Law School. After serving as an army journalist in Vietnam, he worked as a reporter and editorial writer for the *Nashville Tennessean.*

As a senator from Tennessee, Gore compiled a consistently liberal voting record. He ran unsuccessfully for the Democratic Presidential nomination in 1988. In 1992 he added tremendous strength to Bill Clinton's ticket in the border and Southern states.

As Vice President, Gore led the National Performance Review that recommended more businesslike methods in the bureaucracy and downsizing the federal work force. He played a major role in telecommunications policy, and in decisions involving budgets, international trade, and U.S.-Russian relations. Clinton relied on Gore as his chief liaison with Democratic party leaders in Congress.

In 1996 Gore was renominated and reelected on Clinton's ticket. During the Clinton impeachment crisis, Gore emerged as one of the President's chief defenders. Gore himself had to weather allegations that his fund raising in the 1996 campaign had violated campaign finance laws. The charges could not be proved, though, and in spite of the resulting drop in his poll ratings, Gore defeated former senator Bill Bradley for the Democratic Presidential nomination in 2000. Distancing himself from Clinton, Gore proposed protection for Social Security and Medicare, targeted tax cuts to encourage saving and education, healthcare for all children under five, and improvements in public education. His selection of Joe Lieberman, the first Jewish candidate on a major ticket, was lauded by most Americans, since Lieberman had been a strong critic of Clinton's behavior. In a tight race Gore was defeated in the electoral college count by Bush (although Gore won a majority of the popular vote) in spite of the peace and prosperity of the Clinton years.

SEE ALSO *Clinton, Bill; Electoral College*
SOURCES Al Gore, *Earth in the Balance* (Boston: Houghton Mifflin, 1992). Bill Turque, *Inventing Al Gore: A Biography* (Boston: Houghton Mifflin, 2000).

GRAND JURY

The 5th Amendment to the U.S. Constitution provides that "no person shall be held to answer for a capital, or otherwise infamous crime, unless on a presentment or indictment of a Grand Jury, except in cases arising in the land or naval forces, or in the Militia, when in actual service in time of War or public danger." A grand jury is a group of 12 to 20 people convened to hear, in private, evidence presented by the prosecutor against a person accused of a crime. If a majority of the jurors agree that the accused person has committed a crime, an indictment, or formal charge, is issued. In this way, the government is empowered to proceed with its legal action against the accused person.

The grand jury is a means of protecting an accused person against hasty and oppressive action by a prosecutor for the government. In *Wood* v. *Georgia* (1962) the U.S. Supreme Court clearly described the value of the grand jury in protecting the rights of an accused person: "[I]t serves the invaluable function of standing between the accuser and the accused . . . to determine whether a charge is founded upon reason or was dictated by an intimidating power or by malice and personal ill will."
SEE ALSO *Due process of law; Rights of the accused*

GRANT, ULYSSES S.
18th President

- Born: Apr. 27, 1822, Point Pleasant, Ohio
- Political party: Republican
- Education: U.S. Military Academy, B.S., 1843
- Military service: U.S. Army: lieutenant, 1843; regimental quartermaster, 1846–48; 1st lieutenant, 1848; brevet captain, 1848; captain, 1853–54; 1st Illinois Volunteers: colonel, 1861; Galena Illinois Company: brigadier general, 1861; major general, 1862–63; lieutenant

general and commander of all Union armies, 1864–65; general of the armies of the United States, 1866
- Previous civilian government service: interim U.S. secretary of war, 1867–68
- Elected President, 1868; served, 1869–77
- Died: July 23, 1885, Mount McGregor, N.Y.

Ulysses S. Grant was an excellent general but a mediocre politician. He won the Civil War, but his Presidency was a failure because Grant surrounded himself with corrupt men who embroiled his administration in one scandal after another.

Grant was born on a farm and studied at local schools until obtaining an appointment to West Point, where he graduated 23rd in a class of 39. He fought under Zachary Taylor in the Mexican-American War, winning citations for bravery in several battles. In 1854 he resigned as captain of infantry and went back to farming, this time in Missouri. In 1860 he was a clerk at a leather goods store run by his father and brothers. When the Civil War broke out, he organized a local militia, then became colonel of an Illinois militia regiment, rising to the rank of major general.

Grant achieved great success in the Western campaigns, forcing Confederate forces to retreat from Forts Henry and Donelson on the Tennessee and Cumberland rivers. He then won the Battle of Shiloh, and by July 4, 1863, the garrison at Vicksburg, Mississippi, surrendered. Grant was promoted to major general after this victory and became lieutenant general when he won a victory at Chattanooga. Lincoln later made him commander of all the Union armies. In May 1864 he began the final campaign of attrition against General Robert E. Lee in Virginia, and a year later, on April 9, 1865, Lee surrendered to Grant at Appomattox Court House. In 1866 Grant was named general of the armies, a rank that had been achieved by no one other than George Washington. He demobilized his armies, then became embroiled in civilian politics.

In the words of Woodrow Wilson, President Ulysses Simpson Grant "combined great gifts with great mediocrity." At first it seemed as if Grant were an astute politician at the end of the Civil War: he supported a strong military presence in the South to protect the rights of newly freed blacks, endearing himself to the radical Republicans in Congress. When President Andrew Johnson tried to replace Secretary of War Edwin Stanton in order to wrest Reconstruction policy from Congress, Grant accepted an appointment as interim secretary of war. But when Congress restored Stanton to the position, Grant turned his office back over to Stanton. Grant's refusal to support Johnson's actions gained him the unanimous first-ballot Republican nomination for President in 1868, and he won a narrow popular vote victory over Democrat Horatio Seymour in the election.

But Grant was not politically astute. His first mistake was in naming several cronies from his home state to his cabinet. Several cabinet secretaries and other high-level officials became implicated in financial scandals. Resignations included those of his secretary of the Treasury (for irregularities in revenue collection), his secretary of war (for corruption in purchasing contracts), and his attorney general and secretary of the interior (for the Credit Mobilier railroad scandal).

Grant knew nothing of high finance, and he was taken advantage of by his brother-in-law, who worked with financiers Jay Gould and Jim Fisk in a scheme to corner the market in gold. They convinced Grant not to sell any government gold on financial markets, no matter how high the price went, so that their own gold would become more valuable. Grant eventually realized that his relative was using him and ordered the sale of $4 million in Treasury gold. This action caused a crash in the price of gold and financial ruin for many investors, though Gould and Fisk made a great deal of money.

Grant managed to defuse criticism of the corruption in his administration by establishing the Civil Service Commission in

1871. He was renominated in 1872, again by a unanimous first ballot at the convention, and he defeated Democrat Horace Greeley by a landslide.

Grant had a tougher time in his second term. A financial panic that began in 1873 helped Democrats gain control of the House of Representatives in 1874. However, Congress cut taxes and repealed an income tax law, which proved to be popular actions.

In foreign affairs, Grant's attempts to annex the Caribbean island of Santo Domingo were defeated by the Senate. The President's policy of remaining strictly neutral in the conflict between Cuban nationalists and the Spanish occupiers was upheld by Congress, when it voted down a resolution recognizing the revolutionary government proclaimed by the Cuban belligerents.

He tried for a third term in 1880 but lost the Republican nomination to James Garfield.

Grant spent his retirement writing popular articles about his military exploits. Mark Twain published Grant's best-selling memoirs just weeks after the ex-President's death on July 23, 1885.

SEE ALSO *Garfield, James A.; Johnson, Andrew*

SOURCES William McFeely, *Grant: A Biography* (New York: Norton, 1981).

GRAY, HORACE
Associate Justice, 1882–1902

- Born: Mar. 24, 1828, Boston, Mass.
- Education: Harvard College, A.B., 1845; Harvard Law School, LL.B., 1849
- Previous government service: reporter, Massachusetts Supreme Court, 1853–61; associate justice, 1864–73, Massachusetts Supreme Court; chief justice, Massachusetts Supreme Court, 1873–81
- Appointed by Chester A. Arthur Dec. 19, 1881; replaced Nathan Clifford, who died

- Supreme Court term: confirmed by the Senate Dec. 20, 1881, by a 51–5 vote; served until Sept. 15, 1902
- Died: Sept. 15, 1902, Nahant, Mass.

Horace Gray was a notable legal scholar with a reputation for basing decisions on careful research. He believed in the separation of legal decisions from politics.

Justice Gray's most important opinion for the Supreme Court was in the case of *United States* v. *Wong Kim Ark* (1898). He interpreted the 14th Amendment to mean that anyone born in the United States, regardless of race or national origin, had a right to U.S. citizenship. Therefore, Wong Kim Ark, who was born in the United States to immigrant parents from China, had a natural right to citizenship that could not be denied by the government.

SEE ALSO *United States v. Wong Kim Ark*

GREAT COMPROMISE (1787)

The basic structure of the Senate and House of Representatives resulted from the Great Compromise of 1787. A dangerous stalemate had developed at the Constitutional Convention between delegates from the larger states, who wanted representation in both houses of Congress according to the size of a state's population, and delegates from the smaller states, who demanded equal representation for each state.

When the convention recessed to celebrate the Fourth of July, a special committee met to break the deadlock. The committee proposed a compromise, strongly advocated by the delegates from Connecticut, under which the House membership would be apportioned by population and the Senate would have an equal number of representatives from each state. William Samuel Johnson of Connecticut explained that the two houses of Congress would be "halves of a unique whole." The Great Compromise (sometimes called the Connecticut Compromise) saved the Constitution. Equality was so essential for the smaller states that they added a clause to the Constitution to make sure they would never lose it. Article 5 states that "no state without its consent, shall be deprived of its equal suffrage in the Senate." Today, as a result of the Great Compromise, California's 30 million people send 52 representatives to the House, and Wyoming's one-half million people send only one. Yet both states elect two senators apiece.

SOURCES Donald A. Ritchie, *The U.S. Constitution* (New York: Chelsea House, 1989).

GREAT SOCIETY

The Great Society was the phrase that President Lyndon B. Johnson gave to his domestic programs. Johnson spelled out his vision of the Great Society in a commencement speech at the University of Michigan on May 22, 1964. He called on the nation to move not only toward "the rich society and the powerful society, but upward to the Great Society," one that would "end poverty and racial injustice." The term came from the English socialist Graham Wallas, who wrote a book of that name in 1914; the term was also used by the English socialist Harold Laski in his 1931 book *Introduction to Politics*.

Johnson believed that low-income communities could be aided by providing a variety of social services to their residents. These services would enable them to obtain the education and training necessary to obtain jobs that would lift them from poverty. Programs for the poor included the following: Head Start, which provided preschool educational and health programs; the Job Corps and Neighborhood Youth Corps, along with the Vocational Education Act, which gave job training to inner-city teenagers; the Higher Education Act, which provided loans and scholarships to college students from low-income families; the Teachers Corps, Volunteers in Service to America (VISTA), VISTA Lawyers and Legal Services Program, which sent teachers, community organizers, and lawyers into poor neighborhoods; the Model Cities Program of 1966, which coordinated slum renewal and economic development; the Fair Housing Act of 1968, which barred racial discrimination in housing, provided more low-income housing, and experimented with rent-supplement payments to the poor; Medicaid and Neighborhood Health Services, which provided funding to hospitals and doctors serving the poor; and the Elementary and Secondary Education Act of 1965, which provided federal funding to schools and targeted the aid to low-income school districts.

Johnson created the Office of Economic Opportunity in 1964 in order to coordinate social programs in poor neighborhoods. It did so through community action programs that provided for participation by residents in the communities served, usually through the creation of public corporations with elected boards of directors to administer services. These community action programs came under fire at the local level from conservatives opposed to government services for the poor as well as from mayors who wanted local governments to administer such programs. By 1968 most of these programs had been reorganized to place them under the control of city officials.

Richard Nixon's administration attempted to abolish the Office of Economic Opportunity and gave departments such as Health, Education, and Welfare (HEW) and Housing and Urban Development (HUD) the responsibility to administer its programs. Ronald Reagan was an unabashed foe of these programs, campaigning in 1980 with the slogan "In the 1960s we fought a war against poverty and poverty won." During Reagan's Presidency many of these programs were abolished and others, including job training, housing, and community development programs, suffered significant cutbacks.

Democrats pointed out that the Great Society programs had significantly reduced the poverty rates in the 1960s, down from 19 percent to 12 percent of the population between 1964 and 1969. In the 1980s, by contrast, poverty rates increased to about 15 percent when conservative Republican administrations phased out Great Society programs. In the 1960s the income of young black families had risen more than 60 percent. In 1992 families with children headed by people younger than 30 had one-third less income, and young black families had half the income of their predecessors in 1972.

Democrats also noted that many Great Society programs benefited middle-class families. These included the College Work Study and Higher Education Act, which provided loans and work-study employment for college students, and the Medicare program, which provided health insurance for the elderly.

SEE ALSO *Johnson, Lyndon B.*

SOURCES Peter Marris and Martin Rein, *Dilemmas of Social Reform* (London: Routledge, 1967). Charles Murray, *Losing Ground: American Social Policy, 1950–1980* (New York: Basic Books, 1984).

GRIER, ROBERT C.
Associate Justice, 1846–70

- Born: Mar. 5, 1794, Cumberland County, Pa.
- Education: Dickinson College, B.A., 1812; studied law privately
- Previous government service: judge, Allegheny County District Court, Pa., 1833–46
- Appointed by President James K. Polk Aug. 3, 1846; replaced Henry Baldwin, who died
- Supreme Court term: confirmed by the Senate Aug. 4, 1846, by a voice vote; retired Jan. 31, 1870
- Died: Sept. 25, 1870, Philadelphia, Pa.

Robert C. Grier was a schoolteacher and principal before becoming a lawyer. He was an active supporter of the Jacksonian Democratic party. President James K. Polk

appointed Grier to the Supreme Court because of his loyalty to Democratic party ideas on government and law.

Justice Grier's most important opinion for the Court was the *Prize Cases* (1863), which supported President Abraham Lincoln's coastal blockade of Southern ports during the Civil War. Owners of ships and cargoes taken by the federal government as prizes of the war argued that Lincoln's blockade was illegal. Writing for the Court, Justice Grier emphasized the President's duty to preserve the federal union in a time of crisis as justification for the blockade and for the seizure of ships that violated the blockade.

GRISWOLD V. CONNECTICUT

- 381 U.S. 479 (1965)
- Vote: 7–2
- For the Court: Douglas
- Concurring: Goldberg, Harlan, and White
- Dissenting: Black and Stewart

Estelle Griswold, executive director of the Planned Parenthood League of Connecticut, provided information to married people about how to use birth control devices to prevent pregnancy. This behavior violated an 1879 Connecticut law, which banned the use of drugs, materials, or instruments to prevent conception. Griswold was convicted of the crime of giving married couples advice on birth control and contraceptive devices.

The Issue The defendant argued that she had a constitutional right to privacy that was violated by enforcement of the 1879 state law. Is there a constitutional right to privacy that prevents the government from intruding into certain areas of a person's life, such as his or her choices and actions involving birth control? Could this constitutional right to privacy be applied to the states through the due process clause of the 14th Amendment?

Opinion of the Court The Supreme Court struck down the 1879 Connecticut law as an unconstitutional invasion of the individual's right to privacy in personal relationships between consenting adults. However, the Court offered differing interpretations of the constitutional right to privacy.

Writing for the majority, Justice William O. Douglas said that the 1st, 4th, 5th, and 9th Amendments imply "zones of privacy that are the foundation for a general right to privacy." And, he wrote, the 14th Amendment allows these implications from the federal Bill of Rights to be used to limit state governments. That amendment states, "No State shall make or enforce any law which shall abridge the privileges or immunities of citizens of the United States; nor shall any State deprive any person of life, liberty, or property without due process of law."

Justice Arthur Goldberg argued for a broader view of the right to privacy by using the 9th Amendment: "The enumeration in the Constitution of certain rights shall not be construed to deny or disparage others retained by the people." According to Goldberg, the idea of liberty stated in the 14th Amendment protects personal rights that are not listed in the federal Bill of Rights. These additional rights, protected by the 9th Amendment, are "so rooted in the traditions and conscience of our people as to be ranked fundamental."

Justices Harlan and White presented concurring opinions based solely on the due process clause of the 14th Amendment. Justice Harlan argued that privacy is a fundamental right at the core of due process. There are two conceptions of due process: Procedural due process refers to the necessity of following the rules of the legal process. Substantive due process refers to unspecified rights that are included in the more general definition of due process as legal fairness. Justice Harlan used the idea of substantive due process to justify the protection of an individual's right to privacy from intrusion by the state government.

Dissent   The dissenting opinions by Justices Hugo Black and Potter Stewart

judged the 1879 Connecticut law to be flawed; Justice Stewart called it "an uncommonly silly law." However, both Black and Stewart argued that the 1879 law did not violate any constitutional right. Stewart wrote, "I can find no such general right of privacy in the Bill of Rights, in any other part of the Constitution, or in any case ever before decided before this Court."

Both Black and Stewart criticized the Court's majority for going beyond the Constitution to use their judicial power willfully to achieve a desired social outcome. Justice Black concluded, "Use of any such broad, unbounded judicial authority would make of this Court's members a day-to-day constitutional convention." According to Stewart, this unrestrained use of judicial power would lead to a "great unconstitutional shift of power to the courts" and away from the legislative and executive branches, the branches directly accountable to the people through regular elections.

Significance   The constitutional right to privacy, affirmed in the *Griswold* case, has been used to support the right to an abortion against restrictive state laws, as in the Court's decision in *Roe v. Wade* (1973). This right-to-privacy position has, however, remained controversial.

SEE ALSO   *Privacy, right to; Roe v. Wade*

GULF OF TONKIN RESOLUTION (1964)

Even though Congress never officially declared war against North Vietnam during the 1960s, President Lyndon B. Johnson cited the Gulf of Tonkin Resolution as congressional authorization for American military intervention in Vietnam. Congress passed the resolution in 1964 to support Johnson in taking measures to protect U.S. armed forces in Indochina.

As requested by Johnson, Congress passed the resolution in response to incidents between U.S. naval destroyers and North Vietnamese gunboats in the Gulf of Tonkin, off the coast of North Vietnam.

According to the navy, on August 2, 1964, three North Vietnamese torpedo boats fired on the U.S.S. *Maddox.* Two of these gunboats were damaged by aircraft from the U.S.S. *Ticonderoga.* On August 4, the *Maddox* and the U.S.S. *Turner Joy* were on patrol in international waters when they came under attack, but they were not damaged. On August 5, in retaliation for these attacks, U.S. planes destroyed or damaged 25 patrol boats.

President Johnson asked Congress for a resolution allowing him to take "all necessary measures" to repel any further armed attacks. Congress had previously passed similar resolutions to show support for Presidents in confronting such trouble spots as Formosa (now Taiwan), the Middle East, Berlin, and Cuba. Although some senators worried that these resolutions were "blank checks" and "predated declarations of war," no President had actually put one of these resolutions to use. The Gulf of Tonkin Resolution was rushed through Congress with little debate. The House voted unanimously in its support. Only two senators, Wayne Morse (Democrat–Oregon) and Ernest Gruening (Democrat–Alaska), voted against it. J. William Fulbright (Democrat–Arkansas), chairman of the Senate Foreign Relations Committee, assured senators that the resolution was not a declaration of war and that the President would consult with Congress before expanding U.S. military efforts in Vietnam.

The resolution reads in part: "That the Congress approves and supports the determination of the President, as commander-in-chief, to take all measures necessary to repel any armed attack against the forces of the United States and to prevent further aggression. . . . The United States is, therefore, prepared, as the President determines, to take all necessary steps, including the use of armed forces."

Johnson later used this resolution as justification for sending 500,000 troops into South Vietnam to defend it against communist armies attempting to overthrow the government. His administration claimed the resolution was the "functional equivalent" of a declaration of war.

Congressional critics argued that Johnson had deceived Congress and the American people. Congressional investigations revealed that Johnson's staff had drafted the resolution well before the Gulf of Tonkin incident. These investigations also raised questions about whether an attack had even taken place. Evidence strongly suggested that the American naval vessels had reacted to radar signals caused by weather conditions rather than by the North Vietnamese.

In 1970, Congress repealed the resolution, but by then Johnson's successor, President Richard M. Nixon, argued that the Gulf of Tonkin Resolution was not necessary to continue the war. Displeasure with the Gulf of Tonkin Resolution led Congress to enact the War Powers Resolution of 1973, over Nixon's veto. It requires Presidents to withdraw troops from combat after 60 days unless Congress has approved the military action.

SEE ALSO *Fulbright, J. William; Johnson, Lyndon B.; War powers; War Powers Resolution (1973)*

SOURCES George C. Herring, *America's Longest War: The United States and Vietnam, 1950–1975* (New York: Knopf, 1986). U.S. Congress, Senate Committee on Foreign Relations, *The Gulf of Tonkin: The 1964 Incidents* (90th Cong., 2nd sess., 1968).

GUN CONTROL AND THE RIGHT TO BEAR ARMS

The 2nd Amendment to the U.S. Constitution says, "A well regulated Militia, being necessary to the security of a free State, the right of the people to keep and bear Arms, shall not be infringed." This provision of the federal Bill of Rights was derived from the contents of the original 13 state constitutions. For example, the Virginia Declaration of Rights (1776) stated that "a well-regulated Militia, composed of the body of the people, trained to arms, is the proper, natural, and safe defense of a free State." The Pennsylvania Constitution of 1776 said, "The people have a right to bear arms for the defense of themselves and the state."

The provisions of the 2nd Amendment have raised many issues and arguments about gun control laws and the constitutional limits on the right of individuals to bear arms. Does the 2nd Amendment primarily protect an individual's right to bear arms and prohibit the government from making and enforcing gun control laws? Or does it primarily guarantee to individuals only the right to bear arms in connection with service in a state's militia forces? Does the 2nd Amendment apply only to the federal government, or does it also limit state governments? What has been the Supreme Court's interpretation?

In *Presser* v. *Illinois* (1886) the Court held that the 2nd Amendment applied only to the federal government and did not prohibit state governments from regulating an individual's ownership or use of guns. In 1982 the Court reaffirmed the *Presser* ruling by refusing to hear a case about an ordinance in Morton Grove, Illinois, that banned handgun possession within the city. The Court let stand a decision by the Seventh Circuit Court of Appeals, *Quilici* v. *Village of Morton Grove* (1983), which exempts state and local laws from 2nd Amendment restrictions. Thus, the 2nd Amendment remains one of the few provisions of the Bill of Rights that is not "incorporated" under the due process clause of the 14th Amendment and thereby applied to state governments.

The Court has upheld a federal gun control law, the National Firearms Act of 1934. This law required taxation and registration of sawed-off shotguns and automatic weapons. In *United States* v. *Miller* (1939), the Court ruled that the weapons controlled by the National Firearms Act had no "reasonable relationship to the preservation or efficiency of a well-regulated militia."

Since *Miller,* lower-level courts have upheld various gun control laws. Further, the government may regulate the type of weapon individuals keep. For example, individuals do not have the right to own or keep artillery or rockets for their private use. In *United States* v. *Hale* (1992), the U.S. Court of Appeals for the Eighth Circuit held that "it is not sufficient to prove that the weapon in question was susceptible to military use. . . . Rather, the claimant of Second Amendment protection must prove that his or her possession of the weapon was reasonably related to a well-regulated militia."

At present, state governments are not prohibited by the 2nd Amendment from enacting gun control laws. Legal issues about these laws have been left to the state legislatures and state courts to decide. State courts have tended to uphold local ordinances and state laws to regulate or control ownership of guns. In 1968, for example, the New Jersey Supreme Court (*Burton* v. *Sills*) upheld a state law that required individuals to obtain permits and licenses for their guns. The New Jersey Supreme Court argued that the 2nd Amendment was "framed in contemplation not of individual rights but of the maintenance of the states' active, organized militia." Further, the federal Seventh Circuit Court of Appeals ruled in the *Quilici* case that the 2nd Amendment "had no other effect than to restrict the power of the National Government" in matters pertaining to "those arms which are necessary to maintain well-regulated militia."

SEE ALSO *Incorporation doctrine*

SOURCES Ellen Alderman and Caroline Kennedy, "The Right to Keep and Bear Arms," *Constitution* 3, no. 1 (Winter 1991): 66–73. Lawrence Delbert Cress, "The Right to Bear Arms," in *By and for the People: Constitutional Rights in American History,* edited by Kermit L. Hall (Arlington Heights, Ill.: Harlan Davidson, 1991). Stephen P. Halbrook, *That Every Man Be Armed: The Evolution of a Constitutional Right* (Albuquerque: University of New Mexico Press, 1985).

H

HABEAS CORPUS, WRIT OF

Article 1, Section 9, of the U.S. Constitution states: "The privilege of the Writ of Habeas Corpus shall not be suspended, unless when in Cases of Rebellion or Invasion the public Safety may require it." The Latin term *habeas corpus* means "You shall have the body." A writ is a written order from a court of law that requires the performance of a specific act. A writ of habeas corpus requires officials to bring a person whom they have arrested and held in custody before a judge in a court of law, where they must convince the judge that there are lawful reasons for holding the prisoner. If the judge finds their reasons unlawful, then the court frees the suspect. The writ of habeas corpus is a strong protection for individuals from government officials who might want to jail them merely because they belong to unpopular groups or express criticisms of the government.

The privilege of the writ of habeas corpus is rooted in English common law and was specified in Section 39 of the Magna Carta (1215), through which English aristocrats imposed limits on the power of the king. Parliament enacted a habeas corpus statute in 1641, but because it was not entirely effectual, an amendment act was passed in 1679. The Crown was thus prevented from unjustly holding individuals in prison for personal or political reasons. By the end of the 17th century this individual right was solidly established as the appropriate process for curbing illegal imprisonment.

The English habeas corpus acts were not extended to the Anglo-American colonies. However, the writ was one of the widely recognized common law rights of individuals in the American colonies and was frequently invoked before the Revolution. After the Declaration of Independence, the privilege of the writ of habeas corpus was included in several state constitutions enacted prior to the U.S. Constitution of 1787. The Second Article of Compact of the Northwest Ordinance of 1787 also protected this right. The federal Judiciary Act of 1789 provided power to all federal courts "to grant writs of habeas corpus for the purpose of an inquiry into the cause of commitment." Every state of the United States of America has a similar law providing for writs of habeas corpus.

The U.S. Supreme Court has consistently upheld the individual's habeas corpus right, even when this right has been suspended by the federal government to guard public safety and security. In 1861, after the outbreak of the Civil War, President Abraham Lincoln suspended habeas corpus in parts of Maryland. This action was challenged in *Ex parte Merryman* (1861). Chief Justice Roger Taney, sitting as a circuit judge, ruled that only Congress had the right to suspend the writ, but Lincoln ignored the ruling. In *Ex parte Milligan* (1866) the Supreme Court decided that the writ could not be suspended in states (Indiana, in this case) where public order and safety were not endangered by the Civil War. In 1869 Chief Justice Salmon Chase wrote in *Ex parte Yerger* that the privilege of the writ of habeas corpus is "the best and only sufficient defense of personal freedom." Ever since the founding of the United States, Americans have believed the writ of habeas corpus to be a primary protection of their personal liberties.

SEE ALSO *Ex parte Milligan*
SOURCES Larry W. Yackle, "Habeas Corpus," *Constitution* 5, no. 1 (Winter 1993): 61–66.

"HAIL TO THE CHIEF"

"Hail to the Chief" is the march music played to announce the arrival or recognize the presence of the President of the United States. The music was first published in the United States in 1812, to the words of "Lady of the Lake" by Sir Walter Scott. It may have been composed by James Sanderson, a noted English songwriter, but because it is unknown in England, "Mr. Sanderson" is most likely a pseudonym for an American composer. "Hail to the Chief" was first played at the inauguration of President Martin Van Buren on March 4, 1837.

SEE ALSO *Marine Band, U.S.; "Ruffles and Flourishes"*
SOURCES James J. Fuld, *The Book of World-Famous Music*, 3rd ed. (New York: Dover, 1985). Elise Kirk, *Music at the White House* (Urbana: University of Illinois Press, 1986).

HAMLIN, HANNIBAL
Vice President

- Born: Aug. 27, 1809, Paris Hill, Maine
- Political party: Democrat, then Republican
- Education: secondary school; read law, 1832
- Military service: none
- Previous government service: Maine House of Representatives, 1836–41; U.S. House of Representatives, 1843–

47; U.S. Senate, 1848–56, 1857–60; governor of Maine, 1856
- Vice President under Abraham Lincoln, 1861–65
- Subsequent government service: collector of Port of Boston, 1865–66; U.S. Senate, 1869–81; minister to Spain, 1881
- Died: July 4, 1891, Bangor, Maine

Originally a "Jackson Democrat," a follower of Andrew Jackson, Hannibal Hamlin joined the new Republican party in 1856. He was nominated by the Republicans for the Vice Presidency in 1860 to provide regional balance on the ticket (Presidential candidate Abraham Lincoln was from Illinois). As a strong antislavery voice, he also provided ideological balance to the more moderate Lincoln. As Vice President, Hamlin was closely associated with the radical wing of the Republican party in Congress, pressing its case with Lincoln and supporting congressional efforts to emancipate the slaves.

Although Hamlin had been loyal to Lincoln, in 1864 the President decided to drop him from the ticket and replace him with Tennessee loyalist Andrew Johnson in a move to widen the appeal of the Union cause in the border states. Lincoln named Hamlin collector of the Port of Boston in 1865. Hamlin later returned to the Senate and became a leading advocate of harsh Reconstruction measures in the South. He then served as U.S. minister to Spain.

SEE ALSO *Lincoln, Abraham*
SOURCES H. Draper Hunt, *Hannibal Hamlin of Maine: Lincoln's First Vice President* (Syracuse: Syracuse University Press, 1969).

HAMMER V. DAGENHART

- 247 U.S. 251 (1918)
- Vote: 5–4
- For the Court: Day
- Dissenting: Holmes, McKenna, Brandeis, and Clarke

In 1916 Congress passed the Keating-

Owen Child Labor Act, which banned the interstate shipment of products made by child labor. This federal law applied to businesses that employed children younger than 14 years of age or employed children of ages 14 through 16 for more than eight hours a day or more than six days per week.

Roland H. Dagenhart's two sons, Reuben (under 14 years old) and John (between 14 and 16 years old), worked at a cotton mill in Charlotte, North Carolina. He did not want his sons to lose their jobs because of the federal law regulating child labor. So Dagenhart brought suit to prevent the federal government from enforcing the Child Labor Act.

The Issue The Child Labor Act was based on Article 1, Section 8, of the Constitution, which gives Congress power to "regulate commerce among the several states." Dagenhart claimed that the Child Labor Act was not a constitutional regulation of commerce. Rather, it regulated conditions of production at the workplace, a power reserved to the states under the 10th Amendment of the Constitution. Dagenhart also argued that the federal law violated the due process clause of the 5th Amendment by taking away his sons' liberty to work. Did Congress, in passing the Child Labor Act, exceed its power to regulate interstate commerce? Did the Child Labor Act violate the 5th Amendment rights of children desiring employment?

Opinion of the Court Justice William Day agreed with the federal government that child laborers need protection but said the state governments, not the federal government, were the proper source of legal regulation. In his opinion, Justice Day wrote that powers "not expressly delegated to the national government are reserved to the people and the states." This is an incorrect statement of the 10th Amendment, which does not include the word *expressly* but says, "The powers not delegated to the United States by the Constitution, nor prohibited by it to the States, are reserved to the States respectively, or to the people." Inclusion of *expressly* in a restatement of the 10th Amendment implies a narrow interpretation of Congress's commerce power and a broad view of powers reserved to the states, which is the position of the Supreme Court in this case. Day concluded that it was North Carolina's right to decide the appropriate age of child laborers or their conditions of work. Congress has no power under the Constitution to force child labor laws on the states. To permit it to do so, wrote Justice Day, would be to destroy the system of federalism established by the Constitution.

Dissent Justice Oliver Wendell Holmes argued for a broad interpretation of the federal government's power to regulate interstate commerce, which, he said, is "given . . . in unqualified terms, [and] the power to regulate [includes] the power to prohibit." Holmes also argued that the Constitution was designed to be adapted to "the felt necessities" and problems of different eras. The Court should interpret the Constitution, said Holmes, to respond to changing times unless the Constitution specifically prevents it from doing so. Holmes concluded: "The public policy of the United States is shaped with a view to the benefit of the nation as a whole. . . . The national welfare understood by Congress may require a different attitude within its sphere from that of some self-seeking state."

Significance The dissent of Justice Holmes eventually prevailed. In *United States* v. *Darby Lumber Company* (1941), the Court overturned the decision in *Hammer* v. *Dagenhart*. Justice Holmes's dissent in this case became the basis for the Court's decision in the *Darby* case.

SEE ALSO *Commerce power; Federalism; United States v. Darby Lumber Co.*

HARDING, WARREN G.
29th President

- Born: Nov. 2, 1865, Blooming Grove, Ohio

- Political party: Republican
- Education: Ohio Central College, 1879–82
- Military service: none
- Previous government service: Ohio Senate, 1899–1903; lieutenant governor of Ohio, 1903–4; U.S. Senate, 1915–21
- Elected President, 1920; served, 1921–23
- Died: Aug. 2, 1923, San Francisco, Calif.

Warren Harding was a handsome, amiable man who looked like a President but hardly acted like one. He won election by a landslide but did nothing with his mandate. A conservative Republican, he favored a return to "normalcy" after Woodrow Wilson's New Freedom program of business regulation. Scandals rocked Harding's Presidency and contributed to his untimely death in office.

Harding grew up on a farm in Ohio. He worked on his father's newspaper, then became a reporter and publisher of the *Marion Star*. He lost a race for county auditor in 1892, but in 1899 won election to the state senate. After serving two terms he became lieutenant governor of Ohio in 1903. He lost the election for governor in 1909. Harding won Ohio's first direct primary nomination for U.S. senator and was elected in 1914. He voted for two constitutional amendments in the Senate, one prohibiting the sale and consumption of alcohol (though he was a heavy drinker) and the other establishing woman suffrage. He voted against the Treaty of Versailles at the end of World War I.

In 1920 Harding was a compromise choice when a deadlock developed at the convention between front-runners Leonard Wood and Frank Lowden. Harding won the nomination on the 10th ballot. He defeated Democratic candidate James Cox, the governor of Ohio, by a huge margin.

Harding's Presidential policies were pro-business: high tariffs (taxes on imports) to protect American industry, lower government expenditures, tax cuts for corporations, and an end to antitrust enforcement (the regulation or breakup of large financial empires that established business monopolies). Secretary of the Treasury Andrew Mellon, one of the wealthiest men in the United States, got Congress to reduce income taxes on millionaires by two-thirds. Harding was the first President to broadcast a radio address, when he dedicated the Francis Scott Key Memorial at Fort McHenry in Baltimore, Maryland, on June 14, 1922.

In foreign affairs Harding proposed an association of nations in place of the newly formed League of Nations, but his idea got no support at home or abroad. His secretary of commerce, Herbert Hoover, provided $20 million in emergency food relief for the Soviet Union in 1921 to avert a famine, saving as many as 10 million people. Harding concluded a treaty with Colombia that provided $25 million in reparations for the U.S. role in detaching Panama from that nation. Secretary of State Charles Evans Hughes organized the Naval Disarmament Conference of 1921–22, a successful effort to limit naval expenditures of major military powers. It resulted in treaties establishing ceilings on the total number of battleships owned by the United States, Great Britain, Japan, and several other nations.

Harding presided over one of the most corrupt administrations in U.S. history. If George Washington could not tell a lie, then Warren Harding could not tell a liar. The Ohio Gang from his state party took key positions; his main political adviser, the director of the Veterans Bureau, Charles Forbes, received tens of millions of dollars in bribes for the construction of veterans hospitals. Forbes was forced to resign and eventually spent two years in jail.

The biggest scandal of all involved naval oil reserves at Teapot Dome, Wyoming. The President and Secretary of the Navy Edwin Denby transferred control of naval petroleum reserves from the Navy Department to the Department of the Interior, headed by Albert Fall. Fall then leased the Teapot Dome reserve to oil producer Harry Sinclair after receiving at least

$300,000 from him in bribes. (In 1927 the government canceled the leases and Fall went to prison.) Though Harding himself was not involved in these scandals, he was embarrassed by the way in which his friends betrayed his trust for personal gain. Harding's death, from a heart attack during a vacation trip in the West, released him from the White House before the scandals became public and before the full political effects of his corrupt administration could be visited upon him.

SEE ALSO *Coolidge, Calvin*
SOURCES Robert K. Murray, *The Harding Era: Warren G. Harding and His Administration* (Minneapolis: University of Minnesota Press, 1969). Eugene P. Trani and David L. Wilson, *The Presidency of Warren G. Harding* (Lawrence: University Press of Kansas, 1977).

HARLAN, JOHN MARSHALL
Associate Justice, 1877–1911

- Born: June 1, 1833, Boyle County, Ky.
- Education: Centre College, B.A., 1850; studied law at Transylvania University, 1851–53
- Previous government service: adjutant general of Kentucky, 1851; county judge, Franklin County, Ky., 1858; attorney general of Kentucky, 1863–67
- Appointed by President Rutherford B. Hayes Oct. 17, 1877; replaced David Davis, who resigned
- Supreme Court term: confirmed by the Senate Nov. 29, 1877, by a voice vote; served until Oct. 14, 1911
- Died: Oct. 14, 1911, Washington, D.C.

John Marshall Harlan belonged to a wealthy and prominent Kentucky family. They were slaveholders and participants in public affairs.

Harlan joined the Republican party and backed the nomination of Rutherford B. Hayes for President in 1876. President Hayes rewarded Harlan with an appointment to the Supreme Court in 1877. Harlan served on the Court for almost 34 years, one of the longest terms in the Court's history. He was known as the Great Dissenter because of his opposition to several important decisions.

Justice Harlan's most famous dissent was in response to the Court's decision in *Plessy* v. *Ferguson* (1896). The Court upheld a Louisiana law requiring black railroad passengers to sit in separate cars, apart from white passengers. The Court argued that this state law was in line with the 14th Amendment requirement of "equal protection of the laws" because black passengers were treated equally, though separately. Justice Harlan disagreed: "Our Constitution is color-blind, and neither knows nor tolerates classes among citizens." Harlan's dissenting opinion was vindicated in *Brown* v. *Board of Education* (1954), which struck down state laws requiring racial segregation in public schools. But at the time of *Plessy*, Harlan was the only member of the Court who had the vision of justice that would prevail later on, in the decisions of the Warren Court in the 1950s and 1960s.

SEE ALSO *Plessy v. Ferguson*

HARLAN, JOHN MARSHALL, II
Associate Justice, 1955–71

- Born: May 20, 1899, Chicago, Ill.
- Education: Princeton University, B.A., 1920; Oxford University, Rhodes Scholar, B.A., 1923; New York Law School, LL.B., 1925
- Previous government service: assistant U.S. attorney, Southern District of New York, 1925–27; special assistant attorney general of New York State, 1928–30; chief counsel, New York State Crime Commission, 1951–53; judge, U.S. Court of Appeals for the Second Circuit, 1954–55
- Appointed by President Dwight D. Eisenhower Nov. 8, 1954; replaced Robert Jackson, who died

- Supreme Court term: confirmed by the Senate Mar. 16, 1855, by a 71–11 vote; retired Sept. 23, 1971
- Died: Dec. 29, 1971, Washington, D.C.

John Marshall Harlan II was the grandson of Justice John Marshall Harlan, who served on the Supreme Court from 1877 to 1911. His family was wealthy and prominent and provided Harlan with the best educational opportunities. He studied hard and made the most of his opportunities, winning a prestigious Rhodes Scholarship to study at Oxford University in England.

A lifelong member of the Republican party, Harlan was appointed to the Supreme Court by Republican President Dwight D. Eisenhower. Two of Justice Harlan's most important opinions were written for *National Association for the Advancement of Colored People* v. *Alabama ex rel. Patterson* (1958) and *Poe* v. *Ullman* (1961).

Justice Harlan's opinion in *NAACP* v. *Alabama* was the first Court decision to include freedom of association within the 1st and 14th Amendment provisions for protection of individual liberties. His dissent in *Poe* v. *Ullman* argued for a right to privacy in marital relationships. Four years later, in *Griswold* v. *Connecticut* (1965), a majority of the Court generally agreed with Justice Harlan's ground-breaking views in the *Poe* case, affirming a constitutional right to privacy.

SEE ALSO *Griswold v. Connecticut; Privacy, right to*

SOURCES Tinsley E. Yarbrough, *John Marshall Harlan: Great Dissenter of the Warren Court* (New York: Oxford University Press, 1992).

HARRISON, BENJAMIN
23rd President

- Born: Aug. 20, 1833, North Bend, Ohio
- Political party: Republican
- Education: Miami University (Ohio), B.A., 1852

- Military service: 70th Regiment of Indiana Volunteers, 1861–65
- Previous government service: crier of the federal court, 1854; Indiana Supreme Court reporter, 1860–62; member, Mississippi River Commission, 1879; U.S. Senate, 1881–87
- Elected President, 1888; served, 1889–93
- Subsequent government service: chief counsel for Venezuela in arbitration of boundary dispute with British Guyana, 1898–99
- Died: Mar. 13, 1901, Indianapolis, Ind.

Benjamin Harrison was one of the few Presidents to be elected despite winning fewer popular votes than his opponent. He was an effective leader in international affairs, and his administration concluded commercial treaties with many nations and improved relations with Latin America. But the economy deteriorated during his Presidency, inflation and joblessness increased, and labor unrest made him a one-term President.

Harrison was descended from a family of Ohio politicians that included his great-grandfather, Virginia governor Benjamin Harrison (a signer of the Declaration of Independence); his grandfather, President William Henry Harrison; and his father, Whig congressman John Scott Harrison. A lawyer by vocation, Benjamin Harrison became a member of the newly formed Republican party in the 1850s and held various state party positions. During the Civil War his regiment saw fierce fighting in Georgia, and Harrison led his men several times in successful charges against enemy positions. After the war he resumed the practice of law. He tried but failed to win the nomination for Indiana governor in 1872, then lost a close election for governor in 1876.

In 1880 Harrison chaired the Indiana delegation to the Republican national convention. His switch to Garfield decided the nomination. He declined a cabinet position in order to serve in the U.S. Senate for one term but was defeated for reelection. At the Republican convention of 1888, the delegates could not decide between Ohio's John Sherman and Indiana's Walter Gresham. Harrison was the compromise choice. Although he received 100,000 fewer popular votes than President Grover Cleveland, Harrison defeated Cleveland in the electoral college.

Harrison opened Oklahoma to settlement in 1889 under the Homestead Act, and in a single day 20,000 settlers claimed all the acreage available. During his term six states (Washington, Idaho, Montana, Wyoming, North Dakota, and South Dakota) entered the Union, completing the westward expansion of the nation.

Harrison almost secured the annexation of Hawaii as well. American settlers and plantation owners overthrew the government of Queen Liliuokalani, established a new regime, and were recognized by U.S. minister John L. Stevens, who sent 150 marines to protect the new government. Harrison denied any interference in the internal affairs of the islands, but the Senate delayed until 1898 action on a treaty of annexation offered by the revolutionary government.

The most powerful man in the Harrison administration was Secretary of State James G. ("Jingo") Blaine, and its most notable accomplishments were in foreign affairs. The first Pan American Conference, a meeting of the nations of the Western Hemisphere, was held in 1889, leading to the formation of the Pan American Union. A dispute over trading privileges in Samoa resulted in an international conference and creation of a three-power protectorate (British, German, and American) so each could receive the same trading rights in the islands.

An October 16, 1891, riot in Valparaso, Chile, involving sailors from the U.S.S. *Baltimore*, left 2 American sailors dead, 17 injured, and many others imprisoned. In a special message to Congress on January 25, 1892, Harrison warned of war. Blaine sent an ultimatum to Chile on January 21 requiring an apology. Chile did so and paid a $75,000 reparation, even as Harrison's message was sent off, ending the crisis.

During Harrison's administration Congress was dominated by "Czar" Thomas Reed, the Speaker of the House, and several Republican senators. They included John Sherman, who in 1890 got Congress to pass the Sherman Anti-Trust Act. It was supposed to allow the government to bring lawsuits against organizers of business enterprises that acted to restrain competition, but it was not vigorously enforced. The concentration of trusts proceeded with no interference from Harrison's Justice Department. The Sherman Silver Purchase Act (1890) was designed to help the silver industry and to secure votes in the West and among farmers favoring cheap money by having the government buy silver and then increase the amount of coins in circulation. Pensions for Civil War veterans increased by 50 percent under the Pension Act of 1890, but the McKinley Tariff increased the rates on most imports of industrial goods and was so unpopular with farmers and consumers in the 1890 election that Congress went over to Democratic control. Two years later, with the country reeling from labor unrest, Harrison was defeated for reelection by Grover Cleveland.

Harrison returned to his law practice in Indiana and wrote two books, *This Country of Ours* and *Views of an Ex-President*. He served as counsel to Venezuela from 1898 to 1899 in its negotiation of a boundary dispute with Great Britain. He was a strong critic of U.S. colonial policies after the Spanish-American War.

SEE ALSO *Cleveland, Grover*

SOURCES Homer E. Socolofsky and Allen B. Spetter, *The Presidency of Benjamin Harrison* (Lawrence: University Press of Kansas, 1987).

HARRISON, WILLIAM HENRY
9th President

- Born: Feb. 9, 1773, Charles City County, Va.
- Political party: Whig
- Education: Hampden-Sydney College,

1787–89; Philadelphia College of Physicians and Surgeons, 1790
- Military service: U.S. Army, 1791–98, 1812–14
- Previous government service: secretary of Northwest Territory, 1798–99; nonvoting member of U.S. House of Representatives from Northwest Territory, 1800; governor of Indiana Territory, 1800–12; U.S. House of Representatives, 1817–1819; Ohio Senate, 1819–21; U.S. Senate, 1825–28; U.S. minister to Colombia, 1828–29
- Elected President, 1840; served, 1841
- Died: Apr. 4, 1841, Washington, D.C.

William Henry Harrison was the first member of the Whig party to be elected President. He served the shortest time of any President, only 32 days. Harrison was born at Berkeley, his family's Virginia plantation, and intended to study medicine to please his father. When his father died, however, he abandoned medicine for a military career, serving in the Northwest Territory and seeing action in the Battle of Fallen Timbers, in which the Indian Confederacy of the Northwest was defeated. He became governor of the Indiana Territory in 1800.

Harrison became a military hero, defeating the Shawnee Indians at the Battle of Tippecanoe on November 7, 1811, and again at the Battle of the Thames in Canada in October 1813. The death of the Shawnee chief Tecumseh in that battle secured the Northwest frontier of the United States. Harrison then moved to Ohio and served in the U.S. House of Representatives, the state legislature, and the U.S. Senate and as a diplomat. He was active in organizing the Whig party.

Although Democratic candidate Martin Van Buren won the election of 1836, Harrison was the most popular of the four Whig candidates who ran for the Presidency in that election. In 1839 the Whigs united to nominate Harrison and then added Democratic defector John Tyler to the ticket. They campaigned in 1840 with the slogan "Tippecanoe and Tyler, too." The Whigs did not adopt a party platform:

they relied on songs, parades, and symbolism to appeal to the emotions rather than to the brains of the voters. They claimed that Harrison had grown up in a log cabin and hid his aristocratic plantation origins.

Harrison was nationally known as a war hero, but he had no record on political issues and his appeal was enormous. His election was more significant for the new style of politics it demonstrated than for his subsequent tenure in office because he served only one month before dying of pneumonia. He may have contracted the illness at his inaugural ceremony, which took place on the coldest inauguration day in American history. Harrison was the first President to die in office.

SEE ALSO *Tyler, John; Van Buren, Martin*
SOURCES Norma Louis Peterson, *The Presidencies of William Henry Harrison and John Tyler* (Lawrence: University Press of Kansas, 1989).

HART, PHILIP A.

- Born: Dec. 10, 1912, Bryn Mawr, Pa.
- Political party: Democrat
- Education: Georgetown University, graduated, 1934; University of Michigan Law School at Ann Arbor, graduated, 1937
- Senator from Michigan: 1959–76
- Died: Dec. 26, 1976, Washington, D.C.

Known as the "conscience of the Senate," Philip Hart was a quiet man who never ducked a fight. As chairman of the antitrust subcommittee, Hart took on big business and the trend toward corporate mergers that he believed would stifle competition. He fought his own state's largest industry, the automobile manufacturers. Hart promoted handgun control laws, although his state had many hunters opposed to any form of gun control. He fought for truth-in-packaging and other consumer rights. He urged the Senate to liberalize its own rules, to make it easier to achieve cloture and shut off filibusters—especially against civil rights bills. Hart's children helped change his opinion about the Vietnam War, and he became sympathetic toward student antiwar protests. As a sign of his support for antiestablishment protest, Hart grew the only beard in the Senate during his era. When he was dying of cancer in 1976, his Senate colleagues recognized his valiant career by naming the newest Senate office building after him.

HASTERT, J. DENNIS

- Born: Jan. 2, 1942, Aurora, Ill.
- Political Party: Republican
- Representative from Illinois: 1987–
- Chief deputy whip: 1995–98
- Speaker of the House: 1999–

Dennis Hastert believed that his 16 years as a high school wrestling coach had prepared him well for legislative leadership. "A good coach doesn't rely on only a few star players," he explained. "Everyone on the squad has something to offer." Moreover, "a good coach knows when to step back and let others shine in the spotlight."

Elected to Congress in 1986, Hastert became chief deputy whip when House Republicans returned to the majority after 40 years in the minority. A quiet, low-keyed man, he worked best in the back rooms where he lined up support for his party's programs. Following the Republicans' poor showing in the elections of 1998, the flamboyant Speaker Newt Gingrich unexpectedly resigned from Congress, as did his designated successor, Robert Livingston. House Republicans turned to Hastert as the new Speaker. He took over in a highly charged atmosphere, in which Republican efforts to impeach President Bill Clinton had made bipartisan cooperation seemingly impossible.

Hastert set about trying to calm tempers and restore harmony to the House. "I believe all of us—regardless of party—can respect one another, even as we fiercely disagree on particular issues" he insisted. Called a "subtle arm-twister" and the "stealth Speaker," Hastert adopted a lower public profile than the outspoken Gingrich. Like the coach who stepped back and let others shine, he usually let other Republican leaders speak for the party and contented himself with building consensus behind the scenes.

Despite Hastert's efforts, the two parties remained sharply divided in the House, and although Republicans were usually able to muster majorities to pass their programs, they lacked sufficient votes to override President Clinton's vetoes.

HAYES, RUTHERFORD B.
19th President

- Born: Oct. 4, 1822, Delaware, Ohio
- Political party: Whig, then Republican
- Education: Kenyon College, B.A., 1842; Harvard Law School, LL.B., 1845
- Military service: Ohio Volunteers, 1861–65
- Previous government service: solicitor of Cincinnati, 1858; U.S. House of Representatives, 1865–68; governor of Ohio, 1868–72, 1876–77
- Elected President, 1876; served, 1877–81
- Died: Jan. 17, 1893, Fremont, Ohio

Rutherford B. Hayes was the President who ended Reconstruction in the South. His honest administration restored the nation's faith in the Republican party after the corruption that occurred during the administration of Ulysses S. Grant.

Hayes never knew his father, who died before his birth. After graduating at the head of his class from Kenyon College and completing his legal studies at Harvard, Hayes practiced law in Cincinnati, Ohio, where he was active in the Whig party. He became a Republican in 1856. During the Civil War he commanded an Ohio regiment, fought in six major campaigns, and received a medal "for gallant and distinguished services." At the Battle of Winchester he captured an artillery position in hand-to-hand fighting. In the Battle of South Mountain he suffered a severe arm wound that ended his military career.

Hayes was then elected to the U.S. House of Representatives, where he supported the moderate wing of his party, which wished for conciliation with the South, rather than the radical Republicans, who intended to impose a harsh military occupation on the defeated region. He served three terms as governor of Ohio, providing honest and competent government. But Hayes failed in his efforts in 1868 to amend the state constitution to allow African Americans to vote. In 1876, as a dark horse candidate, Hayes defeated James G. Blaine for the Republican nomination for President. In his letter accepting the nomination, he pledged that he would not be a candidate for a second term.

Throughout his career Hayes managed to win one close election after another: it took 13 ballots for the Cincinnati city council to elect him solicitor; he won three Ohio gubernatorial contests by less than 1 percent margins; and his Presidential election followed a similar pattern. At first it appeared that Democrat Samuel J. Tilden was the winner. But Republicans challenged the results in Florida, Louisiana, Oregon, and South Carolina. These states had 20 electoral votes—enough for Hayes to win the White House.

Hayes believed that many African Americans had been intimidated from voting and that fraud had been committed. In South Carolina, for example, the number of votes counted was larger than the state's population. The Republican Senate and Democratic House created a 15-member electoral commission to examine the returns from these states and to certify which electoral votes—Democratic or Republican—it would accept as valid. The commission awarded all 20 of the contested electoral votes from these states to Hayes by a party-line vote of 8 to 7. On March 2, 1877, the commission declared Hayes elected by 185 to 184 electoral college votes.

In what historians have termed the "great betrayal" of African Americans, the Southern Democrats agreed to accept the election of Hayes in return for the withdrawal of all federal troops from Louisiana and South Carolina, thus ending Reconstruction. The troops were withdrawn within two months of Hayes's inauguration. Republicans abandoned black voters, and without federal protection, white supremacy in politics and the segregation of public accommodations soon occurred. Republicans also promised the South financing for a transcontinental railroad line to link Southern and Western markets.

Early in his Presidency Hayes lost any chance of popular support through his actions during the railroad strikes of 1877. Workers faced wage cuts on the Baltimore and Ohio Railroad, and they went on strike. At the request of the governor of West Virginia, Hayes sent federal troops to guard the mails and ensure the safety of trains. Rail strikes spread to Baltimore, Philadelphia, Pittsburgh, and other cities. Eventually, the workers gave in to management, but the resentment against Hayes's use of troops led to the first congressional investigation of labor-management relations.

Hayes had campaigned for President as a reformer, distancing himself from the corrupt Grant administration. "He serves his party best who serves his country best," he said in his inaugural address. Once in office, he alienated members of his party by making merit appointments and reforming government departments. His secretary of the interior, Carl Schurz, rooted out corrupt practices in the Indian Bureau. In June 1877 Hayes issued an order that civil servants could not be assessed, or forced by the parties to make political contributions, but this order was disregarded. Because of the opposition of New York party leader Senator Roscoe Conkling, it took Hayes two years to secure the dismissal for mismanagement of Chester A. Arthur as collector of the Port of New York. But Conkling (whom he had defeated for the nomination in 1876) was able to thwart Hayes's efforts to obtain civil service legislation.

After the 1878 midterm election Democrats controlled both houses of Congress, and Hayes had little influence in the legislature. He often vetoed legislation passed by Congress. His most notable vetoes included the Bland-Allison Act, which required the resumption of silver coinage (Congress passed the bill over his veto); "riders" to appropriations bills sponsored by Southern Democrats that would have nullified federal election laws protecting black voting rights in Southern states; and a bill to exclude Chinese immigrants, on the grounds that it violated the Burlingame Treaty of 1868, an agreement between the United States and China that precluded the United States from a total exclusion of Chinese immigrants. Hayes bowed to anti-Chinese sentiment and negotiated a new treaty with China that limited immigration.

Hayes opposed a French scheme to build the Panama Canal, claiming it was a violation of the Monroe Doctrine. He sent a special message to Congress on March 8, 1880, stating that "the policy of this country is a canal under American control." He further proclaimed that the United States would insist on exercising "supervision and authority" over any canal that was built. When the French diplomat Ferdinand de Lesseps formed an "advisory committee" in the United States and paid the secretary of the navy, Richard W. Thompson, $25,000 to serve, Hayes put an end to this effort to buy influence in the capital by firing Thompson. De Lesseps tried to build his canal anyway but eventually abandoned the project.

In other foreign matters, Hayes ordered U.S. troops into Mexico to end raids by Indians, eventually obtaining cooperation from Mexican authorities so that troops could be withdrawn. He negotiated a treaty with Samoa that gave the U.S. Navy the use of the port of Pago Pago.

In 1880 Hayes honored his pledge not to seek reelection. He returned to his home in Fremont, Ohio, where he promoted educational reforms, especially for African-American industrial education in the South. From 1883 on, he served as presi-

dent of the National Prison Association, an organization established to promote improvements in the correctional system.

SEE ALSO *Arthur, Chester Alan; Electoral college; Grant, Ulysses S.; Monroe Doctrine; Veto power*

SOURCES Kenneth E. Davison, *The Presidency of Rutherford B. Hayes* (Westport, Conn.: Greenwood, 1972). Ari Hoogenboom, *The Presidency of Rutherford B. Hayes* (Lawrence: University Press of Kansas, 1988). Rayford Logan, *The Betrayal of the Negro* (New York: Collier, 1965).

HAZELWOOD SCHOOL DISTRICT V. KUHLMEIER

- 484 U.S. 260 (1988)
- Vote: 6–3
- For the Court: White
- Dissenting: Brennan, Marshall, and Stevens

Students in a high school journalism class were involved in the publication of a school-sponsored newspaper. Because the newspaper was produced in the journalism class, it was part of the school curriculum. The journalism students became upset when the school principal deleted two pages from an issue of their newspaper.

The deleted pages contained sensitive information about a student pregnancy and the use of birth control devices and about the divorce of another student's parents. The principal decided that the deleted articles were inappropriate for the intended readers of the school newspaper. But the student journalists claimed that their constitutional rights to freedom of expression were violated by the principal.

The Issue Did the school principal violate the student journalists' 1st Amendment right to freedom of the press when he deleted their articles from the school newspaper?

Opinion of the Court The Supreme Court held that the students' constitutional rights were *not* violated in this case. Justice Byron White wrote the majority opinion. He argued that "the First Amendment rights of students in the public schools are not automatically coextensive with the rights of adults in other settings." The application of these rights to students in schools, therefore, must be tempered by concern for the special conditions and purposes of the school setting.

White held that a "school need not tolerate student speech that is inconsistent with its basic educational mission, even though the government could not censor similar speech outside the school." The school officials have the authority to regulate the contents of a school newspaper because the student journalists are producing this publication as part of the regular program of studies in the school. Thus, the school officials acted in their capacity as educators of these journalism students when they deleted material from the school newspaper.

Justice White concluded, "It is only when the decision to censor a school-sponsored publication . . . has no valid educational purpose that the First Amendment is so [involved] as to require judicial intervention to protect students' constitutional rights." In this case, the Court felt that there was a valid educational purpose for limiting the students' freedom of expression.

Dissent   Justice William Brennan dissented in this case:

In my view the principal . . . violated the First Amendment's prohibitions against censorship of any student expression that neither disrupts classwork nor invades the rights of others. . . .

[E]ducators must accommodate some student expression even if it offends them or offers views or values that contradict those the school wishes to inculcate. . . .

The mere fact of school sponsorship does not, as the court suggests, license such thought control in the high school, whether through

school suppression of disfavored viewpoints or through official assessment of topic sensitivity. The former would constitute unabashed and unconstitutional viewpoint discrimination, as well as an impermissible infringement of the students' "right to receive information and ideas."

Significance   This decision reinforced the opinion in *Bethel School District No. 403 v. Fraser* (1986), which held that the 1st Amendment rights of public school students are not exactly the same as the rights of adults in other places. This narrow view of student rights in public schools also prevailed in *New Jersey* v. *T.L.O.* (1985), a case about 4th Amendment rights of protection against unwarranted searches and seizures of an individual's possessions.

SEE ALSO *Bethel School District No. 403 v. Fraser; Student rights under the Constitution; New Jersey v. T.L.O.*

HEAD COUNTING

Congressional leaders rarely expect a straight party-line vote—one in which all Democrats vote on one side and all Republicans on the other side of a bill. Modern senators and representatives feel free to vote their conscience or to vote for the good of their constituents, regardless of their party's position on an issue. So "head counters" regularly poll the members of their party (and even members of the opposition) to find out how many are in favor, how many opposed, and how many might be leaning either way before a roll call vote. The party whips and party secretaries do most of the head counting, and some gain a special reputation for their accurate predictions.

Head counters expect many members to cast predictable votes because of their ideology, district, or other political reasons. But they also know that personal considerations may sway a member's vote. "You can't just say because Barry Goldwater is a conservative therefore he will vote for a conservative position," one Republican head counter explained. "There may be a personality problem. There may be something somebody did for him and he's going to pay back a favor." The information gathered from head counting enables the party leadership to decide when best to schedule a vote and when to try to delay a vote to avoid defeat.

HEADNOTES

SEE *Reporter of decisions*

HEALTH, PRESIDENTIAL

Many Presidents have suffered illnesses prior to and during their terms of office. Four died in office of illness: William Henry Harrison caught pneumonia after delivering his inaugural address; Zachary Taylor and Warren Harding both died of heart disease while their performance in office was being harshly criticized; and Franklin Roosevelt died of a cerebral hemorrhage. In fact, 25 of the 35 deceased Presidents did not live as long as other people of their generation. White House "burnout" really does take the ultimate toll. The more active and successful the President, however, the less the "mortality gap"—the difference between the life expectancy of someone the President's age and the actual age at which the President dies.

In the 19th century medical problems were often poorly diagnosed and treated. Even after modern medicine permitted accurate diagnoses by the President's doctors, the custom until the 1950s was to keep such information confidential. But since Dwight Eisenhower's heart attack in 1955, the public has come to expect full disclosure, though often the condition of the President is still minimized by White House aides.

George Washington suffered more serious illnesses than any other President, including tuberculosis, smallpox, and pneumonia. In his first year in office, a cancerous tumor was removed from his thigh.

Andrew Jackson was in the worst medical condition of any President. One dueling wound had shattered his left shoulder, while another, a bullet that lodged in his left lung, caused bleeding throughout his life. He had chronic infections in his bronchial tubes. He also was partially blind, and his poor digestion and diarrhea from chronic dysentery left him emaciated. He took calomel, a medicine that gave him mercury poisoning and headaches, possibly contributing to his colossal temper.

Two Whig Presidents died in office from their illnesses. William Henry Harrison caught a chest cold at his inauguration, then became chilled at a cabinet meeting. He contracted pneumonia and jaundice. Purging and vomiting left him debilitated. He died of pneumonia, pleurisy, and septicemia. Zachary Taylor spent too much time in the sun at Fourth of July ceremonies in 1850. He became dehydrated and suffered cramps, fever, and vomiting before he died. Doctors today speculate that he might have had a perforation of the diverticulum of the colon or a ruptured appendix.

Franklin Pierce was an alcoholic and suffered from cirrhosis of the liver. Abraham Lincoln suffered periods of depression that made it impossible for him to function. He had hyperphoria in his left eye, a condition in which the eye rolled slightly upward, inducing headaches, indigestion, and nausea. He also suffered from diplopia, or double vision. He contracted smallpox just before giving the Gettysburg Address and was diagnosed with exhaustion in March 1865. Some doctors today believe that he had Marfan's syndrome, which might have induced fatal congestive heart failure. Grover Cleveland was diagnosed with cancer of the mouth and upper jaw in 1893. He kept it secret, telling his doctors, "If a rumor gets around that I'm dying, then the country is dead too." He did not even tell his pregnant wife. He had surgery on the *Oneida,* a yacht floating in New York City's East River, on July 1, 1893, and a few days later was fitted with an artificial jaw. Cleveland's operation was finally revealed in 1917 in the *Saturday Evening Post.*

Woodrow Wilson suffered from the flu in April 1918, and bouts of coughing and shortness of breath remained with him. On September 26, 1919, he collapsed from exhaustion while on a nationwide speaking tour to promote the Treaty of Versailles. On October 2 he suffered a stroke in Washington, and he was incapacitated for much of his second term.

Warren Harding died in 1923 of a massive heart attack, though at the time doctors diagnosed his illness as pneumonia, gastritis, food poisoning, and copper poisoning. His successor, Calvin Coolidge, often suffered from debilitating bouts of depression.

Franklin D. Roosevelt was struck with polio in 1921 and never regained the use of his legs. He was never photographed in a wheelchair, and newspapers and radio commentators never mentioned that he could not walk and required 30-pound steel braces on his legs. Camera angles always focused on the upper part of his body. By 1944 Roosevelt was also suffering from hypertension, partial cardiac failure, and acute bronchitis. He died in 1945 of a massive cerebral hemorrhage.

Dwight Eisenhower suffered a heart attack in 1955. The following year he had an operation for ileitis, an intestinal problem, and in 1957 he had a minor stroke.

Of the recent Presidents, the one with the worst health was John F. Kennedy. As a child he had numerous illnesses, including scarlet fever, bronchitis, whooping cough, diphtheria, allergies, and asthma. He had a duodenal ulcer, was color-blind in one eye, and later lost his hearing in one ear. He suffered from a bad back throughout his life and almost died from back surgery in 1954. Kennedy wore a back brace, was fitted for an elevated heel on one shoe,

and often used crutches. He used a hydraulic lift to enter and exit *Air Force One.* He did not take painkillers but used cortisone to reduce inflammation. He would swim in the White House heated pool twice a day and take three hot baths daily to alleviate his pain. Kennedy also suffered from adrenal insufficiency (later diagnosed as Addison's disease, a progressive deterioration of the adrenal glands that made it difficult for him to fight infections) and had malaria and sciatica. What was thought to be a suntan epitomizing good health was actually the bronzed skin typical of people suffering from Addison's disease. To treat the disease, Kennedy took medication (cortisone, a steroid hormone) while in the White House. There is no evidence that his use of the medication affected his ability to make decisions. There is, however, an ethical issue involved because Kennedy and his doctors denied that he had Addison's disease or was being treated for it.

Lyndon Johnson had a heart attack that almost took his life in 1955 but suffered no serious illness while President. Richard Nixon took his path-breaking trip to China while suffering from phlebitis, a potentially life-threatening inflammation of a vein in his leg. Ronald Reagan underwent surgery after an assassination attempt in 1981, suffering from a collapsed lung and massive blood loss. Only the quick work of surgeons at the George Washington University Medical Center saved his life. In 1984 he had surgery to remove noncancerous polyps from his large intestine, and in 1985 surgeons removed a cancerous growth from his colon.

President George Bush suffered from atrial fibrillation, or rapid heartbeat, and a thyroid problem in 1991. A combination of intestinal flu and medication caused him to pass out during a state visit on a trip to Japan.

Some political scientists who have studied Presidential health issues have recommended that a panel of physicians be appointed to assist the cabinet secretaries and Vice President in making decisions about when to invoke the 25th Amendment in cases when the President appears to be disabled. Other recommendations include upgrading the capacity of the White House doctors to treat Presidents for mental health problems, including stress and depression.

SEE ALSO *Disability, Presidential; Physician to the President; 25th Amendment*

SOURCES Robert E. Gilbert, *The Mortal Presidency* (New York: Basic Books, 1992). John B. Moses and Wilbur Cross, *Presidential Courage* (New York: Norton, 1980).

HEARINGS, CONGRESSIONAL

Congressional committees and their subcommittees hold hearings to collect testimony and evidence in favor of or against proposed legislation, nominations, and treaties. Committees generally schedule hearings in the mornings, when the House and Senate are not in session. Since many hearings take place at the same time, they therefore compete with each other for attention from the press and even from their own members. Senators and representatives serve on a number of committees and subcommittees whose scheduling conflicts force them to decide which hearings to attend and which to skip.

Committee staffs prepare for hearings by inviting witnesses from the executive branch and various experts who favor or oppose the issue at hand. Citizens' groups and private individuals may also request time to give testimony. Committees often invite movie stars, former high-ranking officials, and other celebrities to testify to draw public attention—and to generate public support for a bill.

The committee chair calls the hearing to order, introduces and sometimes swears in the witnesses, and begins the questioning. Other members of the committee are allotted time, usually according to their seniority, to question the witness. Reporters take down whatever is said, which the committee will publish as a transcript of the hearings. The committee will also prepare a report on the information gathered in the hearings to issue to the full Senate or House.

For many years committees held many hearings and markup sessions—to prepare the final version of a bill—in executive, or closed, session. Since the adoption of "sunshine" rules in the 1970s, which required open committee meetings, the public can attend most congressional hearings and markup sessions. Washington, D.C., newspapers publish lists of those committees holding hearings each day, and visitors may attend without tickets. The more important hearings, however, draw large crowds of newspaper and broadcast reporters, lobbyists, and others, creating long lines of people waiting for available seating. C-SPAN televises many congressional hearings, and the major networks also record segments of the testimony for broadcast on news programs.

SEE ALSO *Committees, congressional; Executive sessions of Congress; Markup sessions; "Sunshine" rules*

HEART OF ATLANTA MOTEL V. UNITED STATES

- 379 U.S. 241 (1964)
- Vote: 9–0
- For the Court: Clark
- Concurring: Black, Douglas, Goldberg

The Civil Rights Act of 1964 was the most comprehensive civil rights legislation passed by Congress since 1875. Title II of this law prohibited discrimination on the grounds of race, color, religion, or national origin in public accommodations involved in any way in interstate commerce. Its goal was to end discrimination in facilities such as hotels, motels, restaurants, concert halls, theaters, and sports arenas.

Congress based its power to regulate such businesses on the commerce clause in Article 1, Section 8, of the Constitution which gives Congress the power to regulate commerce among the states. A case challenging the use of the commerce power by Congress to prevent racial discrimination reached the Supreme Court only a few months after the passage of the 1964 Civil Rights Act.

The Heart of Atlanta Motel in downtown Atlanta, Georgia, defied the new law by refusing to rent rooms to blacks. The motel owner claimed that Congress had exceeded its authority under the commerce clause by enacting Title II to regulate local businesses, such as hotels, that were open to the public.

The owner also argued that Title II violated his 5th Amendment rights. The 5th Amendment says that no person shall be "deprived of life, liberty, or property, without due process of law." The motel owner claimed the new Civil Rights Act regulated his private property "without due process of law."

The Issue The case represented a major test of a key part of the new Civil Rights Act. The Constitution gave Congress the clear right to regulate interstate commerce. But did this commerce power permit Congress to prohibit discrimination in privately owned accommodations open to the public within a single state?

Opinion of the Court The Supreme Court unanimously upheld Title II of the Civil Rights Act as a legitimate exercise of the commerce power. Justice Tom Clark, a former district attorney from Texas, wrote that the motel did engage in interstate commerce because it sought out-of-state customers by advertising in national publications and 75 percent of its guests were interstate travelers. Citing testimony from the congressional hearing on the act, Justice Clark pointed out that the difficulty blacks encountered in obtaining accommodations frequently discouraged them from traveling. The motel's discrimination therefore obstructed interstate commerce.

Next, Clark defined the meaning of the commerce power of Congress. He declared that Congress's power to regulate interstate commerce also gave it the authority

to regulate local business that "might have a substantial and harmful effect" on interstate commerce.

Clark added that the fact that Congress had used its powers under the commerce clause to achieve a moral goal—stopping discrimination—had no bearing on the decision. "Congress was not restricted by the fact that the particular obstruction to interstate commerce with which it was dealing was also deemed a moral and social wrong," he wrote.

Finally, the Court rejected the charge that Title II violated the motel owner's 5th Amendment rights to private property. "In a long line of cases this Court has rejected the claim that the prohibition of racial discrimination in public accommodations interferes with personal liberty," declared the opinion.

Significance The Supreme Court's decision affirmed that Congress has the constitutional power to promote equality of opportunity and to prevent discrimination. The case greatly aided the cause of the civil rights movement of the 1960s, putting a solid constitutional foundation under legislative and political efforts to promote equal rights for African Americans.

SEE ALSO *Civil rights; Commerce power; Equality under the Constitution*

HENDRICKS, THOMAS
Vice President

- Born: Sept. 7, 1819, Zanesville, Ohio
- Political party: Democrat
- Education: Hanover College, B.A., 1841
- Military service: none
- Previous government service: Indiana House of Representatives, 1848–49; U.S. House of Representatives, 1851–55; commissioner, General Land Office, 1855–59; U.S. Senate, 1863–69; governor of Indiana, 1873–77
- Vice President under Grover Cleveland, 1885
- Died: Nov. 25, 1885, Indianapolis, Ind.

As a senator, Thomas Hendricks opposed vigorous prosecution of the Civil War and the harsh Reconstruction measures that followed. He was one of Andrew Johnson's strongest defenders in the Senate during his impeachment trial. Hendricks also opposed congressional passage of the 13th, 14th, and 15th Amendments, which dealt with, among other things, the abolition of slavery, voting rights for former slaves, and the application of the principle of due process of law to state governments. Though Hendricks was an unsuccessful candidate for the Democratic Presidential nomination in 1868, he was elected governor of Indiana in 1872. He won the Democratic Vice Presidential nomination in 1876 but was defeated as part of the regional compromise that elected Rutherford B. Hayes President.

Finally elected Vice President in 1884 on a ticket with Grover Cleveland, Hendricks died in office less than nine months later, without having performed any duties of his office.

SOURCES Ralph D. Gray, ed., *Gentlemen from Indiana: National Party Candidates, 1836–1940* (Indianapolis: Indiana Historical Society, 1977).

HIDDEN-HAND PRESIDENCY

The "hidden-hand Presidency" was the term used by Princeton political scientist Fred Greenstein to describe the Presidency of Dwight David Eisenhower. During his term most historians and political scientists viewed Eisenhower as a political amateur who reigned but did not rule. "This man neither liked the game he was engaged in nor had gained much understanding of its rules," argued political scientist Richard Neustadt in 1960.

Once other researchers gained access to Eisenhower's Presidential papers (which had not been available to Neustadt and other earlier scholars), the image of Eisenhower as an amateur in office underwent substantial revision. Greenstein concluded that Eisenhower was actually a sophisticated politician who had honed his grasp of politics while in the army. During World War II he had to smooth over disputes among Allied officers of several nations, and he eventually worked closely with three world statesmen: U.S. President Franklin D. Roosevelt, French Resistance leader Charles de Gaulle, and British prime minister Winston Churchill.

Greenstein argued that Eisenhower played politics the way he played poker: with a "hidden hand" that was much better than his opponents realized. There were five facets to Eisenhower's approach to politics. First, he was a skillful politician who chose not to let others realize that fact. He camouflaged his participation in politics by relying on others to take a partisan role while he himself played the role of "President of all the people." His adversaries would underestimate him as a politician, but the American people would support him for being "above politics." Yet in reality Eisenhower was extensively involved in Republican party politics. Second, Eisenhower often used language that was deliberately ambiguous or spoke in an evasive, noncommittal, or seemingly confused way. This tactic enabled him to avoid taking unpopular positions on controversial issues, but it also led his adversaries to underestimate him. Third, Eisenhower avoided dealing in personalities. He never attacked anyone else's motives or made statements that would convert his political adversaries into bitter enemies. He often masked his own negative feelings about those with whom he had to work—including leading members of Congress of his own party—in order to stay on friendly terms with them. Maintaining his image as a genial leader also contributed to Eisenhower's popularity. Fourth, Eisenhower had a keen grasp of psychology: he could step into other people's shoes in order to understand how they viewed the world. He always tried to know what his adversaries were thinking before he engaged them in a controversy. And he tried to think of ways to bring them over to his side. Finally,

Eisenhower gave his subordinates important assignments but never lost control of policy. He would share credit for success with subordinates but would let them take most of the blame for the failures, disassociating himself from them when necessary to preserve his own position as a statesman in the eyes of the American people.

Critics of the hidden-hand theory observe that sometimes the "hidden hand" seemed so well hidden that no one could detect Eisenhower's leadership. He never transferred his own popularity to his political party, which suffered disastrous defeats in state and congressional elections in 1958 and lost the Presidency by 1960. He exerted no moral leadership on civil rights for African Americans, which was the key domestic issue of the time. His economic policies resulted in slow rates of growth and two severe recessions. He never groomed anyone to succeed him, and Richard Nixon, who was far from his first choice for President, was able to win the Republican nomination in 1960. Nevertheless, the hidden-hand theory of the Presidency is a useful way to analyze any President's behavior, because it prevents us from underestimating the political skills of incumbents who may be deliberately concealing their role in party politics in order to maintain the image of a statesman.

SEE ALSO *Eisenhower, Dwight David*
SOURCES Fred Greenstein, *The Hidden-Hand Presidency: Eisenhower as Leader* (New York: Basic Books, 1982). Richard Neustadt, *Presidential Power and the Modern Presidents* (New York: Free Press, 1991).

HIDEAWAY OFFICES

Senior members of Congress, particularly senators, occupy "hideaway" offices in the Capitol building. Regardless of their seniority, all members have offices in the office buildings. There, they and their staffs conduct legislative business and greet visitors. But when space becomes available, senior members receive an extra room closer to the House or Senate floor. No names are posted on the doors, and the locations of these hideaways are not announced. Some members rarely use their hideaway, or they assign them to overflow staff. Others retreat to their hideaway to get a few moments of peace and quiet, while remaining near the chambers. Hideaway offices range from windowless rooms in the Capitol's basement to spacious suites with panoramic views of the Mall.

SEE ALSO *Capitol building*

HIRABAYASHI V. UNITED STATES

- 320 U.S. 81 (1943)
- Vote: 9–0
- For the Court: Stone
- Concurring: Douglas, Murphy, and Rutledge

On December 7, 1941, Japanese aircraft attacked the U.S. naval base at Pearl Harbor, Hawaii, and won a smashing victory against the surprised American defenders. On December 8, the United States declared war on Japan. A few days later, Germany and Italy declared war on the United States. Thus, the United States was drawn into World War II.

The U.S. government feared that the 112,000 people of Japanese ancestry (most of them citizens of the United States) who lived on the West Coast might be a threat to national security in wartime. On February 19, 1942, President Franklin D. Roosevelt issued Executive Order 9066, giving authority to military commanders to establish special zones in U.S. territory threatened by enemy attack. The order invested the military commanders with power to decide who could come, go, or remain in the special military areas. The President issued this executive order on his own authority, under the Constitution, as commander in chief of the nation's armed forces. On March 21, Congress passed a law in support of the President's executive order. On March 24 General John L.

DeWitt proclaimed a curfew between the hours of 8:00 P.M. and 6:00 A.M. for all people of Japanese ancestry living on the Pacific Coast.

Gordon Hirabayashi was an American citizen of Japanese ancestry. Born in the United States, he had never seen Japan. He had done nothing to suggest disloyalty to the United States. Hirabayashi was arrested and convicted for violating General DeWitt's curfew order and for failing to register at a control station in preparation for transportation to a relocation camp, which had been established by federal law.

At the time, Hirabayashi was studying at the University of Washington. He was a model citizen and well-liked student, active in the local YMCA and church organizations. Hirabayashi refused to report to a control center or obey the curfew order because he believed both orders were discriminatory edicts contrary to the very spirit of the United States. He later said: "I must maintain the democratic standards for which this nation lives. . . . I am objecting to the principle of this order which denies the rights of human beings, including citizens."

The Issue Did the U.S. government deprive certain individuals—Americans of Japanese ancestry—of their constitutional rights under the 5th Amendment? The amendment says, "No person shall be . . . deprived of life, liberty, or property, without due process of law." Did the national emergency of World War II permit the U.S. government to suspend the constitutional rights of Japanese Americans?

Opinion of the Court The Supreme Court unanimously upheld the curfew law for Japanese Americans living in Military Area No. 1, the Pacific coastal region of the United States. The Court ruled that the President and Congress had used the war powers provided in the Constitution appropriately. The Court also held that the curfew order did not violate the 5th Amendment.

Writing for the Court, Chief Justice Harlan Fiske Stone said that discrimina-

tion based only upon race was "odious to a free people whose institutions are founded upon the doctrine of equality." However, in this case, Stone said, the need to protect national security in time of war necessitated consideration of race and ancestry as reasons for confinement of a group of people.

Significance Gordon Hirabayashi spent more than three years in county jails and federal prisons for his refusal to comply with a law that discriminated against people because of their ancestry. However, he never accepted the judgment against him, and he resolved someday to overturn it. His new day in court came in 1983, when he filed a petition in a federal district court to reopen his case. He eventually won his case, when the Ninth Circuit Court of Appeals ruled in his favor in September 1987. His conviction was overturned on the grounds of misconduct by the law enforcement officials who arrested and detained him.

Throughout his long ordeal, Hirabayashi, like most other Japanese Americans who suffered injustice during World War II, remained a loyal American. After his 1987 legal victory he said: "When my case was before the Supreme Court in 1943, I fully expected that as a citizen the Constitution would protect me. . . . I did not abandon my beliefs and values."

SEE ALSO *Korematsu v. United States*
SOURCES Peter Irons, *The Courage of Their Convictions* (New York: Free Press, 1988). Peter Irons, *Justice at War* (New York: Oxford University Press, 1983). Carl Mydans, "Internment Remembered," *Constitution* 4, no. 1 (Winter 1992): 43. Rudolph S. Rauch, "Internment," *Constitution* 4, no. 1 (Winter 1992): 30–42.

HISPANIC AMERICANS IN GOVERNMENT

Hispanic Americans in Congress Hispanics are one of the fastest-growing minority groups in the United States, but political participation has been proportionately slow in coming, and gains have been made only after great struggles against racism.

Hispanic Americans are a small but steadily increasing group in Congress, although their proportion there is less than it is in the general population. In 1877 Governor Romualdo Pacheco (Republican–California) became the first Hispanic American to serve in Congress when he was elected to the House of Representatives. He served two terms and chaired the Committee on Private Land Claims. The first Hispanic-American senator was Octaviano Larrazolo (Republican–New Mexico), who was elected to fill the remaining three months of a vacant Senate seat. In 1935 Representative Dennis Chavez (Democrat–New Mexico) was appointed to fill another Senate vacancy. Chavez was reelected four times and became chairman of the Committee on Public Works. After Chavez's death the state of New Mexico sent a statue of him to stand in the Capitol. Herman Badillo (Democrat–New York) became the first Puerto Rican–born representative, and Ilena Ros-Lehtinen (Republican–Florida) became the first Cuban-born representative.

In 1976 as the number of Hispanic members of Congress grew, they formed the Congressional Hispanic Caucus. Drawing its members largely from California, Florida, Texas, and New Mexico, the Hispanic Caucus has also included the nonvoting delegates from Samoa, Puerto Rico, Guam, and the Virgin Islands.

After the 1990 census, Congress enacted legislation requiring states to give racial and ethnic minorities greater voting strength in the newly drawn congressional districts. A number of largely Hispanic districts was created, and in 1992 seven new Hispanic candidates won election to the House.

Hispanic Americans in the Executive Branch   In the 1950s, when Hector P. García began to work for labor and education reform as a community leader,

activist, and physician in Texas, he campaigned to eliminate the "No Dogs or Mexicans Allowed" signs in Texan restaurants and the beating of Mexican schoolchildren for speaking Spanish. In 1968 García was appointed by President Lyndon Johnson to the U.S. Commission on Civil Rights, where he continued the struggle for Hispanic rights on a national level. (Until the 1960s, the imposition of poll taxes prevented many Hispanics from registering to vote.) When García received the Presidential Medal of Freedom in 1984 and the Aztec Eagle (posthumously in 1998), the highest honors bestowed by the U.S. and Mexican governments, it was to recognize the achievements of all Hispanic Americans made possible by the untiring work of García.

Such strides in civil and voting rights paved the way for many firsts for Hispanic Americans in the executive branch. Ramona Acosta Bañuelos was sworn in as the first Hispanic treasurer of the United States on December 17, 1971. The Mexico City native Edward Hidalgo was appointed secretary of the U.S. Navy by President Jimmy Carter in 1979. And in 1990 Antonia C. Novella was the first woman and first Hispanic surgeon general of the United States. The Puerto Rican–born doctor had served as deputy director of the National Institute of Child Health and Human Development before President George Bush appointed her as surgeon general.

Since 1988, when Ronald Reagan appointed Lauro F. Cavazos as secretary of education—the first Hispanic cabinet member—Hispanic Americans have had an increasing presence in the cabinet. The Republican congressman from New Mexico, Manuel Lujan, Jr., became the first Hispanic-American secretary of the interior in 1989. Henry G. Cisneros was sworn into office as President Bill Clinton's secretary of housing and urban development on January 22, 1993, and served until 1996. (Cisneros had been a four-term mayor of San Antonio, Texas, from 1981 to 1989, and president of the National League of Cities in 1985.)

Federico F. Peña served as secretary of transportation in Clinton's first term after serving as mayor of Denver, Colorado, from 1983 to 1991. As secretary, he increased travel safety, enacted new standards for airplanes, and signed aviation agreements with more than 40 nations, expanding U.S. markets overseas. He also served for a brief time as Clinton's secretary of energy.

Bill Richardson, ultimately the highest-ranking Hispanic in the Clinton administration, replaced Peña as secretary of energy on August 18, 1998. Richardson had served as U.S. ambassador to the United Nations from 1987 to 1998 after seven terms as a U.S. congressman from New Mexico. Richardson's negotiation of hostage releases in North Korea, Iraq, Cuba, and Sudan led to his three-time nomination for the Nobel Peace Prize.

The number of Hispanics in the United States is projected to reach 41.1 million by 2010, and 52.7 million by 2020. As of 1998, according to government statistics, the percentage representation of Hispanics in the permanent executive branch work force equaled or exceeded their percentage representation in directly comparable civilian work force occupations, in 5 of 22 executive branch independent agencies of more than 500 employees.

Hispanic Americans in the Federal Judiciary Hispanic Americans constituted a mere 5 percent of the total number of federal judges in 2000. By contrast, non-Hispanic whites constituted 83 percent. There has never been a Supreme Court justice of Hispanic origin. In 2000, however, there were 9 Hispanic-American judges among the 179 authorized judicial positions on the U.S. Courts of Appeals. Two were appointed in 2000: Richard A. Paez to the Ninth Circuit and Julio Fuente to the Third Circuit.

SOURCES Peter Thomas Conmy, *Romualdo Pacheco: Distinguished Californian of the Mexican and American Periods* (San

Francisco: Native Sons of the Golden West, 1957).

HOBART, GARRET
Vice President

- Born: June 3, 1844, Long Branch, N.J.
- Education: Rutgers College, B.A., 1863
- Military service: none
- Previous government service: New Jersey Assembly, 1873–75; New Jersey Senate, 1877–82
- Vice President under William McKinley, 1897–99
- Died: November 21, 1899, Paterson, N.J.

Garret Hobart was named to the Republican National Committee in 1884 after losing an election for U.S. Senator. He was nominated for the Vice Presidency by Republicans in 1896 to represent the East and balance the Republican ticket geographically. He was one of the most effective presiding officers of the U.S. Senate, in large measure because of his experience presiding over the New Jersey Assembly and Senate. As Vice President, Hobart cast the tiebreaking vote in the Senate against an amendment to the Treaty of Paris (which ended the war with Spain) that would have promised eventual independence to the Philippines. He was considered a close political adviser of President William McKinley, especially in Republican party affairs. Hobart's death in office in 1899 paved the way for Theodore Roosevelt's Vice Presidential nomination in 1900.

SEE ALSO *McKinley, William*

SOURCES Margaret Leech, *In the Days of McKinley* (New York: Harper & Row, 1959).

HOLD

Any senator who objects to a particular bill can have the party leader place a "hold" on that bill. A hold suspends action and may freeze a bill for weeks or months. At the end of a session, when time is running out, such holds can kill a bill. Managers of the bill will try to negotiate with senators who have placed holds to make whatever changes they can agree upon. If they reach a compromise, the senator will notify the party leadership to lift the hold. Because the hold is an informal arrangement, the leadership can decide at any time to ignore the hold and bring the legislation to the floor. However, the bill's managers know that the senator who placed the hold might object to any unanimous consent agreements and might even launch a filibuster or other delaying tactics. Senators sometimes place reciprocal holds on each other's bills so they can offer to lift one hold in return for lifting the other.

SEE ALSO *Filibuster; Unanimous consent agreements*

HOLMES, OLIVER WENDELL, JR.
Associate Justice, 1902–32

- Born: Mar. 8, 1841, Boston, Mass.
- Education: Harvard College, A.B., 1861; Harvard Law School, LL.B., 1866
- Previous government service: associate justice, Supreme Judicial Court of Massachusetts, 1882–99; chief justice, Massachusetts Supreme Court, 1899–1902
- Appointed by President Theodore Roosevelt as a recess appointment Aug. 11, 1902; nominated by Roosevelt Dec. 2, 1902; replaced Horace Gray, who died
- Supreme Court term: confirmed by the Senate Dec. 2, 1902, by a voice vote; retired Jan. 12, 1932
- Died: Mar. 6, 1932, Washington, D.C.

Oliver Wendell Holmes, Jr., was the son and namesake of a famous Boston physician and writer. He, too, won lasting fame. As a young man, Holmes was honored for uncommon courage as a Union soldier in the Civil War. He was seriously wounded in battle three times. As an older man,

Holmes became the most important legal thinker and writer of his time.

In 1881 Holmes published *The Common Law*, which has been recognized as one of the greatest works of American legal scholarship. In this book he developed a "realist" view of law and judging that emphasized "the felt necessities of the time." He argued that law is dynamic and adaptable to the changing conditions of people and their society. He wrote, "The life of law has not been logic; it has been experience."

In 1902 President Theodore Roosevelt named Holmes to the Supreme Court, where he served with distinction. During nearly 30 years on the Court, he wrote 873 opinions, more than any other justice. Holmes wrote so gracefully, forcefully, and cogently that many of his opinions continued to influence the Court long after his death, and several of his memorable phrases have often been quoted by judges, legal scholars, and historians from Holmes's time until today.

Justice Holmes's most notable opinions were written in cases about the limits and latitude of free speech. In *Schenck* v. *United States* (1919), Holmes, writing for the Court, said that Congress could restrict speech and writing that threatened the safety and security of the United States. He argued that freedom of speech was not unlimited: a person could be punished for "falsely shouting fire in a theater" and causing a panic. Thus, Congress could make laws to punish speech that posed a "clear and present danger" to the security and safety of people .

In *Abrams* v. *United States* (1919), Holmes wrote in dissent to support honest expression of ideas, including highly unpopular views, that posed "no clear and present danger." He expressed his famous "free market of ideas" viewpoint: "The best test of truth is the power of the thought to get itself accepted in the competition of the market." Thus, political protest and criticism are permissible and even valuable because these dissenting views challenge and test the worth of our most cherished beliefs and practices. Through free and open exchange of ideas, including unusual and unpopular opinions, we seek the truth and find ways to improve our lives.

Throughout his long life, which ended in 1932 at the age of 94, Holmes had faith in law as the best means to settle peacefully and fairly the unavoidable conflicts of human life. And he persistently argued, with considerable influence on judges, lawyers, and scholars, for a dynamic and realistic view of the law. Thus, law would always be molded to fit the changing needs of people and their communities.

SEE ALSO *Abrams v. United States; Schenck v. United States*

SOURCES David Burton, *Oliver Wendell Holmes, Jr.* (Boston: Twayne, 1980). Morton J. Horowitz, "The Place of Justice Holmes in American Legal Thought," in *The Transformation of American Law, 1870–1960* (New York: Oxford University Press, 1992). Sheldon M. Novick, *Honorable Justice: The Life of Oliver Wendell Holmes* (New York: Dell, 1990). H. L. Pohlman, *Justice Oliver Wendell Holmes: Free Speech and the Living Constitution* (New York: New York University Press, 1991). Richard A. Posner, ed., *The Essential Holmes: Selections from the Letters, Speeches, Judicial Opinions, and Other Writings of Oliver Wendell Holmes, Jr.* (Chicago: University of Chicago Press, 1992). G. Edward White, *Justice Oliver Wendell Holmes: Law and the Inner Self* (New York: Oxford University Press, 1993).

HONEYMOON, PRESIDENTIAL

The Presidential "honeymoon" is the short period after a President is inaugurated when the opposition party refrains from attack, Congress is inclined to support some of the President's initiatives, and the President receives high public approval ratings. Within a month or two partisan attacks generally resume and the honeymoon period ends.

President John F. Kennedy extended the concept by calling on the Soviet Union to extend him a honeymoon period as a goodwill gesture. One of the shortest honeymoons on record was that of Gerald Ford, whose pardon of his predecessor, Richard M. Nixon, for all Watergate crimes sparked public outrage and led to a 30-point drop in popularity in public opinion polls after his first month in office.

HOOVER, HERBERT C.
31st President

- Born: Aug. 10, 1874, West Branch, Iowa
- Political party: Republican
- Education: Stanford University, B.A., 1895
- Military service: none
- Previous government service: U.S. food administrator, 1917–19; U.S. secretary of commerce, 1921–29
- Elected President, 1928; served, 1929–33
- Subsequent government service: administrator, civilian relief in Europe, 1945–47; chair of two Commissions on the Organization of the Executive Branch of Government, 1947–49, 1953–55
- Died: Oct. 20, 1964, New York, N.Y.

Herbert Clark Hoover became President just as the Great Depression put millions of Americans out of work. He had made his reputation as an engineer and business entrepreneur and then had been one of the most effective cabinet secretaries in the administrations of Warren G. Harding and Calvin Coolidge. Yet Hoover made minimal efforts to end the depression because he was convinced that the business cycle would take care of economic recovery with minimal intervention and that "prosperity was just around the corner." His failure to provide effective leadership doomed him to a one-term Presidency and gave the Democrats an opportunity to dominate national politics for a generation.

Hoover was the first President born west of the Mississippi River. His father was a blacksmith and his mother a schoolteacher; both died in his childhood, and he grew up in his uncle's house in Oregon. Hoover worked his way through school beginning at age 10. He studied geology and mining engineering at Stanford University, graduating in 1895, and he became a supervisor of mining operations in Australia and then in China. He and his wife, Lou, became fluent in Chinese and were active in the relief of foreigners trapped in the Boxer Rebellion. The Hoovers traveled all over the world on business. By 1908 Herbert Hoover was the head of his own engineering and oil exploration company. In 1909 his lectures at Columbia and Stanford Universities were published as *Principles of Mining*, which became a standard textbook.

In 1914 Hoover was asked by the U.S. consul general in London to supervise the evacuation of 120,000 Americans trapped in Europe at the outbreak of World War I. That same year he became chairman of the privately organized Committee for Relief in Belgium, with the mission of preventing famine in that nation. In three years he raised and spent $1 billion for food relief in Europe. When the United States entered the war in 1917, President Woodrow Wilson named him U.S. food administrator. In the next two years Hoover supervised the rationing and conservation of foodstuffs in the United States and the export of food to U.S. and Allied troops. At the end of the war he became the director general of European Relief and Rehabilitation, in charge of U.S. food relief efforts to more than 20 nations in Europe with a total population of more than 300 million. He supported Wilson's efforts to join the League of Nations. Hoover also found time to collect wartime manuscripts and documents from many nations, which formed the nucleus of the Hoover Library on War, Revolution, and Peace established at Stanford University.

In 1920 Hoover was an unsuccessful contender for the Republican Presidential nomination, due in part to the opposition of fellow Californian Senator Hiram Johnson, who did not forgive Hoover for his support of the League of Nations. Hoover was named secretary of commerce by President Harding in 1921 and was considered the most capable and honest official in the administration. President Coolidge kept him on and he served through 1928. His department tried to improve the productivity of American industry and to promote international trade and the conservation of resources. In 1924 he received 300 votes for Vice President at the Republican convention but did not get the nomination.

In 1928 Hoover was the favorite to win the Republican nomination for President, largely because of his capable handling of relief efforts during a disastrous flood in Mississippi in 1927. He won several primaries over the opposition of party leaders and was nominated on the second ballot at the national convention. He won a landslide victory over Alfred E. Smith, the first Catholic candidate for President. Hoover's campaign slogan was "a chicken in every pot and a car in every garage." His promise of continued prosperity ensured his election.

At first Hoover tried to modernize government by creating national commissions on conservation and law enforcement and study groups to improve management of Indian affairs, veterans hospitals, and federal prisons. He got Congress to create a new Federal Farm Board, which helped farmers market their products at stable prices. But Hoover's administration was soon preoccupied with the effects of the stock market crash of October 29, 1929, known as Black Tuesday. Following the crash, industrial production plummeted, the gross national product (the total amount of goods and services produced) fell by almost a third, and unemployment soared from 3 to 25 percent by the end of his term.

Hoover responded with a tax cut to stimulate demand for goods and $400 million in public works projects. He also got the Federal Reserve Board to increase the supply of money, which resulted in lower interest rates and enabled corporations to borrow money cheaply for new projects. In 1930 he signed the Smoot-Hawley Tariff, which raised tariff rates and depressed international trade. Though designed to protect U.S. industry, it further weakened the position of American companies by reducing their exports and led to even higher unemployment, especially in the farm sector, because of foreign retaliation against U.S. farm exports.

Democrats won control of the House in 1930 and came close to winning the Senate. By May 1931 the crash of European stock markets and the resultant depression in Europe made the situation in U.S. industries dependent on foreign trade and investment even worse. Hoover vetoed a bill passed by the Republican Senate to provide $1 billion in veterans' bonuses, an action Democrats seized upon as an indication of his callousness. In 1932 his administration convinced Congress to create and fund the Reconstruction Finance Corporation to lend money to new enterprises, banks, and city and state governments, but Hoover initially balked at the large amounts Congress was willing to appropriate. The nation viewed his efforts as too little, too late. When more than 100,000 unemployed veterans of World War I marched to Washington in 1932 to ask for early payment of their bonuses and other federal assistance, two of the Bonus Marchers were killed in clashes with local police. On July 28, Hoover ordered General Douglas MacArthur to use the army to disperse the marchers. MacArthur went beyond Hoover's orders and sent his troops in to destroy their tent city as well. Hoover had turned the military against the very soldiers who had fought for the flag in 1918.

Hoover's record in international affairs was dismal. The London Naval Treaty of 1930 acceded to the Japanese naval preeminence in the Pacific. In September 1931 the Japanese embarked on a course of aggression by attacking Manchuria, in northern China. Hoover refused to respond with economic sanctions. An attempt to gain U.S. entry to the World Court, the organization that applied international law to disputes between nations, was defeated by the Senate. The European depression made it difficult for Germany to pay World War I reparations to Allied nations or for those nations to pay back their war loans to the United States. Hoover refused to support proposals to cancel some debts, coordinate monetary policy with Europeans, or lower tariffs to stimulate trade. All the European nations except Finland reneged on their debts.

In 1932, although renominated by his party, Hoover was defeated by Democrat Franklin D. Roosevelt. His defeat was the worst suffered by an incumbent President since William Howard Taft's in 1912. In his last months in office, unemployment climbed to more than one-quarter of the work force. Banks failed in record numbers as people panicked and took their money out.

Hoover wrote 30 books after he retired from the White House, including three volumes of memoirs and *The Ordeal of Woodrow Wilson,* a study of Wilson's failure to obtain Senate consent to the Treaty of Versailles. It was the first time one former President had written a book about another former President. During World War II Hoover tried unsuccessfully to organize food relief efforts to nations occupied by Nazi Germany. After the war he served as coordinator of the European Food Program, advised the U.S. government on occupation policies in Germany and Austria, and chaired two Commissions on the Organization of the Executive Branch of Government that made recommendations for greater efficiency. He remained associated with the conservative wing of the Republican party, and he was asked for advice by leading politicians from his party, including Richard Nixon. Hoover died at the age of 90; John Adams was the only President who lived longer.

SEE ALSO *Coolidge, Calvin; Harding, Warren G.; Roosevelt, Franklin D.; Wilson, Woodrow*

SOURCES Martin Fausold, *The Presidency of Herbert C. Hoover* (Lawrence: University Press of Kansas, 1985). Herbert Hoover, *Memoirs,* 3 vols. (1951–52; reprint, New York: Garland, 1979). Joan Hoff Wilson, *Herbert Hoover: Forgotten Progressive* (Boston: Little, Brown, 1975).

HOUSE BANK SCANDAL (1992)

In 1992, angry about stalemated government, soaring deficits, and economic recession, the public focused its attention on check bouncing in the House of Representatives bank as a symbol of government perks, or special privileges. For 150 years the House sergeant at arms had operated a bank in the Capitol, where members could write checks based on their deposited salaries. A General Accounting Office (GAO) investigation revealed that many representatives had written checks with insufficient funds in their accounts to cover those checks, but the bank had taken no action to suspend or penalize those who bounced checks. Extensive media coverage caused the House to abolish the bank and reveal the names of more than 300 members who had bounced checks. An unusually large number of representatives chose not to run for reelection, and several other check bouncers were defeated. The bank scandal spurred the House to establish the position of director of non-legislative services, who would serve as a general manager of financial and other administrative activities.

SEE ALSO *Director of non-legislative services; Perks; Scandals, congressional*

HOUSE OF REPRESENTATIVES

The House of Representatives has been called the "people's body." No one ever became a member of the House by appointment or any means other than standing for election by the people. Because of the House's close connection to the voters, the Constitution gave the House authority to originate all bills to levy taxes and spend government money.

Representatives serve two-year terms. Each state has at least one representative. States with larger populations are divided into districts, whose lines are redrawn every ten years according to the latest federal census. The House has sole authority to determine any disputed elections and to expel members by a two-thirds vote.

Sheer numbers have shaped the House. The original House consisted of 65 members, one for every 30,000 citizens. After the first census the number rose to 105, and it grew steadily as the population increased and new states were added. In 1910 Congress fixed the membership at 435, and districts are reapportioned every ten years following a new census.

As its membership grew, the House changed its rules to limit time for debate and to strengthen majority rule. When Asher Hinds compiled the first volumes of House precedents in 1907, he observed that "the pages of these volumes show a constant subordination of the individual to the necessities of the whole House as the voice of the national will." Nearly a century later, in 1992, House majority leader Richard Gephardt (Democrat–Missouri) reconfirmed that "the Senate is a collection of individuals, while the House, by virtue of its size, forces you to function in a group."

Leadership in the House The House sets its own rules and elects its own officers, headed by the Speaker. Depending upon the personality and philosophy of the various Speakers, they have acted as impartial presiding officers or as strong partisan leaders. Speakers of the stature of Henry Clay, James G. Blaine, Thomas B. Reed, Joseph G. Cannon, Nicholas Longworth, Sam Rayburn, Thomas P. ("Tip") O'Neill, Jr., and Newt Gingrich have shaped the development of the House. So, too, have strong committee chairs, notably of the powerful Rules Committee and of the "money" committees: Appropriations and Ways and Means. Traditionally, a small number of committee chairs, ranking minority members, and other senior representatives have dominated the House, and junior members have had little influence. Committee reforms in 1975 opened the chairmanships, particularly of subcommittees, to more members and gave members of the majority party the opportunity to vote to remove committee chairs who acted arbitrarily.

Constituent services House members often receive less national press attention than do senators, and they tend to devote more time to constituent services. If effective, they assure that their district will have a voice in national—and international—affairs and that the federal government will be responsive to its needs, whether in road building, federal water projects, public housing, military bases, Social Security payments, or any number of other areas.

The atmosphere of the House chamber has traditionally differed from that of the more staid Senate. The larger body has often been the more boisterous one, with shouts of "Vote! Vote!" and other commotion on the floor, causing Woodrow Wilson to describe the House as a "mass of jarring elements." The Speaker, as presiding officer, holds the responsibility for keeping order. He is assisted by the sergeant at arms, who during particularly tumultuous moments has lifted the House mace, the symbol of the authority of the House, as a means of quieting the chamber.

After 200 years the House of Representatives remains the branch of government closest to the voters and the most conscious of operating with the "consent of the governed." Its members therefore constantly strive to make sure that their constituents' voices are heard and their interests are fairly considered within the federal system.

SEE ALSO *Committees, congressional; Congress; House-Senate relations; Mace of the House of Representatives; Speaker of the House*

SOURCES James T. Currie, *The United States House of Representatives* (Malabar, Fla.: Krieger, 1988). Bruce A. Ragsdale, *The House of Representatives* (New York: Chelsea House, 1989).

HOUSE-SENATE RELATIONS

Although they must work together to produce all legislation, the Senate and House of Representatives have very different rules, procedures, terms of election, and constituencies. These differences often cause tensions between the two bodies.

Some representatives, impatient with the many years that it will take them to achieve seniority and influence in the House, run for the Senate. In the 1940s and 1950s Speaker Sam Rayburn would try to persuade them to stay in the House, citing long lists of representatives who had gone to the Senate "and hadn't amounted to much." Those who choose to spend their entire legislative career in the House bristle at the notion that the Senate is an "upper body," or in any way superior. Donald Riegle (Republican/Democrat–Michigan), who served in both the House and Senate, observed that some of the older House members "detest the Senate and can always be counted upon to rise up indignantly any time someone suggests that the Senate is transgressing on House prerogatives, attempting to by-pass House rules or 'blackmailing' the House by attaching 'non-germane' [irrelevant] amendments to bills."

Checks and balances House members often focus more closely on the needs and opinions of their home district, whereas senators, with statewide constituencies, develop a more national outlook on issues. House members also serve on fewer committees and tend to become specialists in a few areas, whereas senators, with many committee assignments, become generalists. House rules favor the majority; Senate rules give greater leeway to individual members, whether in the majority or the minority party. These disparities often come to a head in conference committees, when senators and representatives seek to merge the Senate and House versions of a bill into a single piece of legislation.

In the spirit of checks and balances, the two houses insist upon their equality. During the 1st Congress, the House rejected a Senate plan that would have paid senators a higher salary than representatives. Members of the 1st Congress also devised the elaborate procedures by which clerks still deliver bills and messages from one chamber to the next. The clerks appear in the center door of the chamber to be announced to the presiding officer. They bow as they enter the chamber, deliver the bill to the front desk, and bow again when they leave, demonstrating through this 18th-century ritual the respect of one house of Congress for the other.

SEE ALSO *Bicameral; Conference committees; Congress; House of Representatives; Senate*

SOURCES Ross K. Baker, *House and Senate* (New York: Norton, 1989). Donald Riegle, *O Congress* (New York: Popular Library, 1976).

HUGHES, CHARLES EVANS
Associate Justice, 1910–16
Chief Justice, 1930–41

- Born: Apr. 11, 1862, Glens Falls, N.Y.
- Education: Colgate University, 1876–78; Brown University, B.A., 1881; M.A., 1884; Columbia Law School, LL.B., 1884
- Other government service: special counsel, New York State Investigating Commissions, 1905–6; governor of New York, 1907–11; U.S. secretary of state, 1921–25; U.S. delegate, Washington Armament Conference, 1921; U.S. member, Permanent Court of Arbitration, 1926–30; judge, Permanent Court of International Justice, 1928–30
- Appointed by President William Howard Taft to be associate justice Apr. 25,

1910; replaced David Brewer, who died; appointed by President Herbert Hoover to be chief justice Feb. 3, 1930; replaced Chief Justice William Howard Taft, who retired
- Supreme Court term: confirmed as associate justice by the Senate May 2, 1910, by a voice vote; resigned June 10, 1916, to become Republican party candidate for President; confirmed by the Senate as chief justice Feb. 13, 1930, by a 52–26 vote; retired July 1, 1941
- Died: Aug. 27, 1948, Cape Cod, Mass.

Charles Evans Hughes served two terms on the Supreme Court, first as an associate justice (1910–16) and then as the chief justice (1930–41). He resigned from his first Court term to become the Republican party candidate for President. He lost to his Democratic party opponent, President Woodrow Wilson, by only 23 electoral votes.

Hughes served two Republican Presidents, Harding and Coolidge, as secretary of state. In this role, he negotiated several important treaties to limit international weapons buildups and promote world peace. He was a judge on the Permanent Court of International Justice when President Herbert Hoover appointed him to succeed William Howard Taft as chief justice of the United States.

Under Hughes's leadership, the Supreme Court actively protected the constitutional rights of individuals. In *Stromberg* v. *California* (1931), *Near* v. *Minnesota* (1931), and *DeJonge* v. *Oregon* (1937), Hughes used the due process clause of the 14th Amendment to deny state governments the power to abridge 1st Amendment freedoms of speech, press, and assembly. He also weakened the "separate but equal" doctrine on racial segregation. In his opinion for the Court in *Missouri ex rel. Gaines* v. *Canada* (1938), Hughes wrote that a state university had violated the 14th Amendment's equal protection clause by its refusal to admit a qualified African-American student to its law school.

During President Franklin D. Roosevelt's first term (1933–37), Hughes influenced the Court to reject key parts of the President's New Deal program that, according to the Court's majority, gave the federal government too much power to regulate or direct private businesses in their relationships with workers and consumers. Hughes also successfully resisted Roosevelt's court-packing plan, by which the President had hoped to add justices to the Court who would support his New Deal.

After 1937, however, Hughes began to support important New Deal legislation, to the delight of President Roosevelt and his supporters. It seems that Hughes recognized that the vast majority of the American people supported Roosevelt's programs. They had voted overwhelmingly for his reelection in 1936. So Hughes bowed to the election returns and ceased to be a major obstacle to the President's program.

Upon his retirement in 1941, Hughes was hailed as a great chief justice. In 1942 the American Bar Association honored Hughes with its medal for distinguished contributions to the law.

SEE ALSO Court-packing plan (1937); Near v. Minnesota; Stromberg v. California
SOURCES Merlo Pusey, *Charles Evans Hughes*, 2 vols. (New York: Macmillan, 1951).

HUMOR, CONGRESSIONAL

Humor has always been a ready weapon for members of Congress but also one that has often been aimed against them. Debaters use humor to put down their opponents. "You speak for the present generation; I speak for posterity [future generations]," a long-winded representative asserted. "Yes," replied Henry Clay (Whig–Kentucky), "and you seem resolved to continue speaking until your audience arrives." When a Democratic member asked for unanimous consent to correct the printed version of a speech he had made attacking the Republicans, Speaker Thomas B. Reed (Republican–Maine) replied, "No correction needed. We didn't think it was so when you said it."

Senators and representatives have also used humor to grease the legislative process, to help defuse tensions, and to put their colleagues in a more cooperative mood. Members have been known to engage in pranks and horseplay to relieve the tension and sometimes the boredom. For instance, they initiate new pages, students who run errands and carry messages, by sending them in search of a mythical "bill stretcher."

Congress has also been the target of humorous abuse. "Suppose you were an idiot," said Mark Twain, "and suppose you were a member of Congress; but I repeat myself." Humorist Will Rogers claimed, "After I read that ancient Rome had a Senate, too, I knew then why it had declined." Editorial cartoons and comic strips have similarly poked fun at talkative senators, the enjoyment of perks or privileges of office, and other congressional foibles. House Speaker Carl Albert (Democrat–Oklahoma) speculated that Congress attracts such a large share of humorous abuse because it is less distant from the public than the other branches of government: "Congress is as near as the post office, as personal as an old neighbor. For that reason, it is Congress—not the courts, not the presidency—that usually bears the frustrations with government. And Americans are frustrated with government. They nearly always are."
SOURCES Paul F. Boller, Jr., *Congressional Anecdotes* (New York: Oxford University Press, 1991). Bill Hogan and Mike Hill, *Will the Gentleman Yield? The Congressional Record Humor Book* (Berkeley, Calif.: Ten Speed Press, 1987). Anthony Pitch, *Congressional Chronicles* (Potomac, Md.: Mino Publications, 1990).

HUMPHREY, HUBERT H.
Vice President

- Born: May 27, 1911, Wallace, S.D.
- Political party: Democrat
- Education: Denver College of Pharmacy, 1932–33; University of Minnesota, B.A., 1939; University of Louisiana, M.A., 1940
- Military service: none
- Previous government service: director, War Production Board, 1942; assistant director, War Manpower Commission for Minnesota, 1943; mayor of Minneapolis, 1945–48; U.S. Senate, 1949–65, 1971–78; Senate majority whip, 1961–65
- Vice President under Lyndon B. Johnson, 1965–69
- Died: Jan. 13, 1978, Waverly, Minn.

Hubert Humphrey, a New Deal Democrat, gained national attention at the Democratic Presidential nominating convention of 1948. He made a fiery speech in favor of a civil rights plank for the Democratic party platform, a proposal that led to the walkout of Southern Democratic delegates and to the formation of a Dixiecrat third party.

Humphrey was elected to the U.S. Senate in 1948. He started as an outsider but was brought into the inner circle of leadership by Senator Lyndon B. Johnson. In 1961 Humphrey became majority whip, the second-ranking position in the Senate. He favored arms control pacts with the Soviet Union, federal aid for education, and national health insurance, and he was instrumental in achieving passage of the Civil Rights Act of 1964. Lyndon Johnson chose Humphrey to be his running mate in 1964, not only for geographic and ideological balance but because he believed Humphrey best to succeed him.

As Vice President, Humphrey not only presided over the Senate but also played a role in the development of Johnson's Great Society social programs, often lobbying members of Congress to provide the margin of victory on close votes. He chaired the National Aeronautics and Space Council, the Council on Marine Resources and Engineering, the Council on Native American Opportunity, the Council on Youth Opportunity, and a cabinet-level task force to promote tourism.

Humphrey's influence on foreign policy was small, though he made important trips to Western Europe to discuss military affairs and to the Far East to discuss the Vietnam War. His influence sharply diminished when he began advocating a political settlement of the war. He never went public with his criticisms and remained the chief defender of Johnson's war policies with his public speeches, an activity that caused a break with many of his liberal supporters.

Though Gallup polls after 1965 showed little public support for his quest for the Presidency, Humphrey announced his intention to run after Johnson withdrew his own candidacy in March 1968. Humphrey entered no primaries, so he received less than 2 percent of the primary vote, mostly from write-in ballots. Humphrey still had the support of a majority of the national convention delegates, chosen by state party leaders.

Humphrey won the nomination, but antiwar protesters in the streets of Chicago were involved in violent confrontations with the police, which gave Republican Presidential candidate Richard Nixon an insurmountable lead in public opinion. Even Humphrey's call for a halt to the bombing of North Vietnam, a step opposed by Johnson, could not bring him a victory, though his momentum in the closing days made the race extremely close.

Because Humphrey had won the Democratic nomination despite trailing far behind Eugene McCarthy and Robert Kennedy in primary voting, the Democratic party appointed a commission headed by South Dakota senator George McGovern to reform party rules for the 1972 Presidential nomination.

Humphrey was reelected to the Senate

in 1970 but was defeated for the Democratic Presidential nomination in 1972 by George McGovern.

SEE ALSO *Great Society; Johnson, Lyndon B.; Nominating conventions, Presidential; Primaries, Presidential*

SOURCES Hubert Humphrey, *The Education of a Public Man* (Garden City, N.Y.: Doubleday, 1976). Carl Solberg, *Hubert Humphrey: A Biography* (New York: Norton, 1984).

HUNT, WARD
Associate Justice, 1873–82

- Born: June 14, 1810, Utica, N.Y.
- Education: Union College, B.A., 1828; Litchfield Law School, 1829
- Previous government service: New York Assembly, 1839; mayor, Utica, N.Y., 1844; judge, New York State Court of Appeals, 1866–69; New York State commissioner of appeals, 1869–73
- Appointed by President Ulysses S. Grant Dec. 3, 1872; replaced Samuel Nelson, who retired
- Supreme Court term: confirmed by the Senate Dec. 11, 1872, by a voice vote; retired Jan. 27, 1882
- Died: Mar. 24, 1886, Washington, D.C.

Ward Hunt served only seven years on the Supreme Court. He regularly sided with the Court's majority, led by Chief Justice Morrison R. Waite. Hunt tended to oppose claims by African Americans for equal protection of the laws under the 14th Amendment. He also opposed extension of voting rights for women.

Justice Hunt departed from his usual position to be the lone dissenter in *United States* v. *Reese* (1876), arguing that the federal government had the power to coerce state governments to recognize the voting rights of African Americans guaranteed by the 15th Amendment. However, he returned to his usual position in *United States* v. *Cruikshank* (1876) and went along with the Court's position of indifference to the voting rights of African Americans.

HYLTON V. UNITED STATES

- 3 Dall. 171 (1796)
- Vote: 3–0
- For the Court: Seriatim opinions by Iredell, Paterson, and Chase
- Not participating: Cushing, Wilson, and Ellsworth

In 1794 Congress passed a law to tax carriages used as passenger vehicles. Daniel Hylton of Virginia refused to pay the tax, and the U.S. government sued Hylton for nonpayment of taxes.

The Issue   Daniel Hylton said that the federal carriage tax was a direct tax of the kind prohibited by Article 1, Section 9, of the Constitution. Did Congress have the power to levy a carriage tax on passenger vehicles?

Opinion of the Court   The Supreme Court upheld Congress's power to tax carriages used as passenger vehicles. The carriage tax law was an *indirect* tax, said the Court, and was not prohibited by Article 1, Section 9, of the Constitution. Justice Paterson wrote, "All taxes on expenses or consumptions are indirect taxes."

Significance   This was the first time that the Supreme Court made a judgment about whether an act of Congress was constitutional. By upholding the federal carriage tax, the Court implied that it had the power to overturn it. The justices did not directly discuss the power of judicial review—the power of the Court to declare an act of Congress unconstitutional, or in violation of the Constitution, and therefore void. However, they seemed to believe that they had the power to nullify acts of Congress that conflicted with the higher law of the Constitution. Justice Samuel Chase wrote that he would use this power of judicial review only "in a very clear case."

In 1803 Chief Justice John Marshall used the case of *Marbury* v. *Madison* to explain and justify the Court's power of judicial review of acts of Congress.

SEE ALSO *Judicial power; Judicial review; Marbury v. Madison*

I

IMMIGRATION AND NATURALIZATION SERVICE

In the 18th and early 19th centuries, the United States swelled with immigrants who freely crossed its borders without having to face federal immigration and naturalization policies. They found their way to this country before immigration became a serious political and cultural concern and before the government passed the immigration laws that resulted in the forming of the Immigration and Naturalization Service (INS) in 1933.

Worsening economic conditions and a growing xenophobia prompted the immigration legislation that appeared in the late 1800s and early 1900s. The Immigration Act of 1882, the country's first firm stance in response to immigration, levied a one-time tax of 50 cents on each immigrant and excluded the entry of "idiots, lunatics, and persons likely to become a public charge." Similarly, to limit immigration more severely, the Immigration Acts of 1921 and 1924 assigned each nationality a quota of immigrants based on its representation in past U.S. censuses. The passage of laws such as these created the need for a federal enforcement agency, and the Immigration Act of 1891 established the Immigration Service to monitor the influx of immigrants and guard against illegal entry.

Because no uniform naturalization process existed among the nation's 5,000 naturalization courts, Congress passed the Naturalization Act of 1906 to systematize the rules for naturalization. The rules put forth in this act remain in effect today. The legislation also expanded the Bureau of Immigration into the Bureau of Immigration and Naturalization, which became the INS in 1933.

The duties of the INS have evolved over time, from its World War II–era policies (including the operation of internment camps and detention centers for enemy aliens) to its more recent crackdowns on illegal immigration through stronger border patrols. Today the INS is especially attentive to the nation's growing concern over illegal immigration. Laws such as the Immigration Reform and Control Act of 1986, conceived to discipline the employers of undocumented aliens, reflect this concern.

IMPEACHMENT

If a federal official commits a crime or otherwise acts improperly, Congress may impeach—formally charge—and remove that person from office. The House of Representatives votes to impeach, an action similar to an indictment in a court of law. Then the Senate sits as a court to determine guilt or innocence. It takes a two-thirds vote of the Senate to remove someone from office.

The Constitutional Convention decided that no one should be above the law and that even the President should be subject to impeachment. All civil officers of the government can be removed if im-

Impeachment Cases

1797: William Blount, U.S. senator, Tennessee. Expelled from Senate, charges dropped.

1803: John Pickering, federal judge. Guilty, removed from office.

1804: Samuel Chase, Supreme Court justice. Not guilty.

1830: James H. Peck, federal judge. Not guilty.

1862: West H. Humphreys, federal judge. Guilty, removed from office.

1868: Andrew Johnson, President. Not guilty.

1873: Mark H. Delahay, federal judge. Resigned, no action.

1876: William Belknap, secretary of war. Not guilty.

1904: Charles Swayne, federal judge. Not guilty.

1912: Robert Archbald, judge, U.S. Commerce Court. Guilty, removed from office.

1926: George W. English, federal judge. Resigned, charges dismissed.

1933: Harold Louderback, federal judge. Not guilty.

1936: Halsted Ritter, federal judge. Guilty, removed from office.

1986: Harry Claiborne, federal judge. Guilty, removed from office.

1988: Alcee Hastings, federal judge. Guilty, removed from office. (In 1992 Hastings was elected to the House as a Democrat from Florida.)

1989: Walter Nixon, federal judge. Guilty, removed from office.

1998: William Jefferson Clinton, President. Not guilty.

peached and convicted for "treason, bribery, or other high crimes and misdemeanors" (Article 3, Section 4). If a President is impeached, the Constitution specifies that the chief justice of the United States shall preside over the Senate trial.

Article 1, Section 3, of the Constitution states, "Judgment in Cases of Impeachment shall not extend further than to removal from Office, and disqualification to hold and enjoy any Office of honor, Trust or Profit under the United States; but the Party convicted shall nevertheless be liable and subject to Indictment, Trial, Judgment and Punishment, according to Law." So, if a person is impeached by the House of Representatives and convicted by the Senate, that person will be removed from federal office and prevented from holding another federal office at any time in the future.

When a resolution to impeach is introduced on the floor of the House, it is referred to the Judiciary Committee. That committee holds hearings, then takes a formal vote on the articles of impeachment. It reports its findings to the full House, which may drop, amend, approve, or reject the articles by a simple majority vote of those present. A quorum of members—half of the House plus one—is necessary to hold a vote.

If an official is impeached, the House then names a manager or a committee to serve as the prosecutor in the Senate trial. The articles of impeachment are signed by the Speaker of the House and conveyed to the Senate by the managers. They are then transmitted to the impeached official.

Impeached officials may appear on their own behalf or send legal counsel to represent them. Their counsel can question witnesses and present evidence on behalf of the official. At the end of the trial, the Senate votes separately on each article of impeachment. Two-thirds of the senators present are necessary to convict and remove a person from office.

The Senate in recent years has delegated the responsibility of hearing evidence in impeachment cases for judges and other officials (except for the President) to special committees, which then report their findings to the full Senate for a vote. Judge Walter Nixon protested that the entire Senate had not heard the full charges against him. However, in 1993, the Supreme Court ruled in *Nixon* v. *United States* that the Senate had the sole power to decide how to try such cases and allowed Judge Nixon's impeachment to stand.

When a president is impeached, the chief justice of the United States presides over the trial in the Senate. The Senate sits as a body to hear the evidence and arguments. Although the president may be represented by counsel of his choosing, the House managers argue the case for removal. Several articles of impeachment may be brought against the President, but a two-thirds vote in favor of conviction on any single article would be sufficient to remove him from office.

The first impeachment case, in 1797, targeted a U.S. senator, William Blount of Tennessee, who was accused of conspiring with the British to prevent Spanish control of Florida and Louisiana. Although the House voted to impeach Blount, the Senate refused to try him because it had already expelled him from office under its internal rules. This case set the precedent that individuals cannot be impeached after they have left office. In 1974 the House Judiciary Committee voted to recommend impeachment of President Richard M. Nixon for his role in the Watergate scandal, but Nixon's resignation stopped any further impeachment proceedings.

Only one Supreme Court justice has been impeached: Samuel Chase, in 1805, for behaving in a partisan manner. Justice Chase was an outspoken promoter of the Federalist party and an acid critic of the Jeffersonian Republican party. In 1801 Thomas Jefferson became President and the majority in Congress was made up of Jeffersonian Republicans. Justice Chase's flagrant anti-Republican behavior vexed many of the Jeffersonian Republicans, who were determined to strike back at him. The proper moment came in 1805, they be-

lieved, after the reelection of Jefferson and a Republican party majority in Congress. The House of Representatives voted to impeach Justice Chase. But the Senate voted not to convict him, and he remained a justice of the Supreme Court until his death in 1811.

The impeachment proceedings against Justice Chase set a precedent that a person should not be impeached and removed from office because of his political opinions. Article 3, Section 1, of the U.S. Constitution says, "The Judges, both of the supreme and inferior Courts, shall hold their Offices during good Behaviour." The key issue in Justice Chase's impeachment trial was whether expression of political opinions was a violation of the constitutional provision for holding office "during good Behaviour."

Impeachment of Presidents Congress has resorted to impeaching a President in only three cases: President Andrew Johnson was impeached by the House of Representatives but was acquitted by the Senate after a trial in 1868; the House Committee on the Judiciary reported three articles of impeachment against President Richard Nixon in 1974, but he resigned before the full House could vote on them; and President Bill Clinton was impeached by the House of Representatives but was acquitted by the Senate after a trial in 1999.

Although an impeachment proceeding bears a close similarity to a criminal trial, there are substantial differences. First, the President is not necessarily charged with a criminal offense but with improper conduct in performing the duties of his office. Impeachment is not meant to be a partisan proceeding, nor is it used simply to reflect a lack of confidence in the President's policies or leadership by other branches of government. The Constitutional Convention explicitly rejected attempts to make impeachment overtly political. The delegates rejected proposals to make the President removable on the application of a majority of state governors. They rejected impeachment by a mere majority vote of Congress. They also rejected grounds for impeachment that involved the President's political judgment or vague terms such as "maladministration." They specified instead that the only grounds for impeachment were "Treason, Bribery, or other High Crimes and Misdemeanors." These terms referred to the abuse of power, misapplication of public funds, corruption, criminal conduct, or violating the separation of powers mandated by the Constitution.

A President may also be held responsible for the conduct of his subordinates. He may be charged with a cover-up if he knowingly conceals information regarding a violation of the law or if he fails to remove such officials from office when evidence of their offenses comes to his attention. He may also be charged with failing to see that the laws are faithfully executed, with failing to institute procedures so that officials will act lawfully, or with a conspiracy to see that the laws are violated. A President who testifies falsely in a judicial proceeding may be charged with perjury or obstruction of justice.

The Senate managers of an impeachment may attempt to prove that the President committed a statutory crime, though criminal guilt is not necessary in a case involving abuse of power. If they cannot do so, they may present evidence that the President engaged in a course of action or a pattern of behavior that demonstrates "high crimes and misdemeanors." Those seeking a President's impeachment may argue that grounds need not be limited to federal statutes. The Association of the Bar of the City of New York, in assessing grounds for Nixon's impeachment, argued that a President could be removed "for conduct amounting to a gross breach of trust or serious abuse of power" and that these are "not limited to criminal offenses" but refer to acts that undermine the integrity of the government, whether technically criminal or not.

Presidents have several defenses against impeachment. They can argue that impeachment is a criminal trial, in which all the safeguards of the 5th Amendment, which guarantees the due process of law, must apply. And as Nixon put it, "A criminal offense on the part of the President is the requirement for impeachment." The Republicans defending Nixon in 1973 also took this position, although it repudiated their 1868 stand against Andrew Johnson. Presidents may also argue that they cannot be held responsible for the conduct of their subordinates.

Presidents can claim that they believed that their actions were constitutional. If they are charged with failure to execute the laws, they can claim that the laws conflicted with other laws or was itself unconstitutional. Or they can argue that the alleged offense was a mere technical violation for which impeachment is too severe a penalty. They can argue that the offense was a "low" crime involving personal matters rather than a "high" crime involving abuse of power or violation of the public trust. Or they may claim that the violation of the law was necessary for national security.

Ultimately, the Senate must assess the motives of the President. Did he act in good faith? Was he attempting to usurp or abuse power? Did the ends justify the means? The judgment the senators come to will be political rather than legalistic. The Senate in the Clinton impeachment trial was influenced by public opinion polls, which indicated that Clinton's job approval ratings remained high and that the public, by a 2-to-1 margin, opposed the conviction. Republicans argued that the constitutional law of impeachment was being supplanted by an illegitimate "popular law" nullifying the crimes the President had committed. Democrats argued that the Senate should take into account the judgment of the American people.

Conviction by the Senate does not result in criminal penalties. If the offense involved a crime, judicial proceedings may be instituted after the President is removed from office.

SEE ALSO *Chase, Samuel; Clinton, Bill; Independent judiciary; Nixon, Richard M.; Oath of office; Pardon power; Resignation,*

Presidential; Separation of powers; Watergate investigation (1973–74)
SOURCES Michael Les Benedict, *The Impeachment and Trial of Andrew Johnson* (New York: Norton, 1973). Raoul Berger, *Impeachment: The Constitutional Problems*, 2nd ed. (Cambridge: Harvard University Press, 1999). Charles Black, *Impeachment* (New Haven: Yale University Press, 1974). Irving Brant, *Impeachment* (New York: Knopf, 1972). Robert C. Byrd, "Impeachment," in *The Senate, 1789–1989: Addresses on the History of the United States Senate*, vol. 2 (Washington, D.C.: Government Printing Office, 1991). Michael J. Gerhardt, *The Federal Impeachment Process: A Constitutional and Historical Analysis*, 2nd ed. (Chicago: University of Chicago Press, 2000). William H. Rehnquist and Cynthia Adams Phillips, *Grand Inquests: The Historic Impeachments of Justice Samuel Chase and President Andrew Johnson* (New York: Quill, 1999). Hans L. Trefousse, *Impeachment of a President: Andrew Johnson, the Blacks, and Reconstruction* (New York: Fordham University Press, 1999).

IMPERIAL PRESIDENCY

"Imperial Presidency" is the phrase used by some historians and political scientists to refer to the Presidencies of Lyndon B. Johnson and Richard M. Nixon. The notion that the President is above the law and that what he orders is the law, despite conflicting provisions of the Constitution or laws passed by Congress, is the fundamental tenet of the imperial Presidency.

The characteristics of the imperial Presidency are disregard for certain provisions of the Constitution, particularly regarding the power of the Congress to declare war and appropriate funds; excessive reliance by the President on White House aides, rather than the cabinet secretaries; isolation of the President from members of Congress; secrecy in making decisions and the use of executive privilege to prevent congressional or judicial inquiries; and surveillance of political opponents and the

use of "dirty tricks" against them, in effect converting politics from a contest into a form of political warfare in which all means are used to defeat the opposition.

Critics of this theory argue that Presidents before and after Lyndon Johnson and Richard Nixon—including Abraham Lincoln, Franklin D. Roosevelt, and Harry Truman—also used their war and budget powers expansively. Johnson and Nixon, the critics maintain, were not the only Presidents to suspend execution of certain constitutional provisions or statutes. Secrecy and the claim of executive privilege have been relied on by several Presidents, including Dwight Eisenhower and John F. Kennedy. Some observers have argued that Presidents Gerald Ford, Jimmy Carter, and Ronald Reagan provide evidence for an "imperiled" rather than "imperial" Presidency. These men, they say, faced excessive congressional oversight, investigation, criticism, micro-management through legislation, and other congressional checks and balances carried to extremes.

SEE ALSO *Johnson, Lyndon B.; Nixon, Richard M.*

SOURCES Arthur M. Schlesinger, Jr., *The Imperial Presidency* (Boston: Houghton Mifflin, 1973).

IMPLIED POWERS

The Constitution of the United States delegates various powers to the three branches of government. For example, Article 1, Section 8, is an enumeration, of powers that Congress may exercise. The final item in this list gives Congress the power "To make all Laws which shall be necessary and proper for carrying into Execution the foregoing powers, and all other Powers vested by this Constitution in the Government of the United States, or in any Department or Officer thereof."

This necessary and proper clause permits Congress to exercise *implied powers;* that is, to identify and use powers that are logical extensions or implications of the other powers delegated in the Constitution. For example, the doctrine of implied powers gave Congress justification for making a law to charter a national bank in 1791, even though this power is not specifically listed in the Constitution as one delegated to Congress. This power was implied as "necessary and proper" for the federal government to carry out its enumerated powers, such as borrowing money, regulating currency, and providing for the general welfare of the country.

The issue of the scope of implied powers under the Constitution was first confronted by the Supreme Court in *McCulloch v. Maryland* (1819). This case raised the issue of whether Congress had the power to charter a bank under authority of the necessary and proper clause. Writing for a unanimous Court, Chief Justice John Marshall favored a broad construction of Congress's implied powers that clearly included the power to charter a national bank. Marshall wrote, "Let the end be legitimate, let it be within the scope of the Constitution, and all means which are appropriate, which are plainly adapted to that end, which are not prohibited, but consistent with the letter and spirit of the Constitution, are constitutional."

Chief Justice Marshall's viewpoint agreed with ideas expressed earlier by Alexander Hamilton in *The Federalist* No. 23. Hamilton wrote: "[I]t is both unwise and dangerous to deny the federal government an unconfirmed authority in respect to all those objects which are entrusted to its management [grants of power enumerated in the Constitution]." In *The Federalist* No. 44, James Madison wrote that the necessary and proper clause was essential to the effective operation of the federal government. He said, "Without the substance of this power, the whole Constitution would be a dead letter."

Ever since the founding of the United States, scholars, lawyers, judges, and political leaders have argued about the scope of implied powers under the Constitution. Since the decisive opinions of Chief Justice John Marshall, however, the doctrine of implied powers has been solidly established

as an important source of federal government power under the Constitution.

SEE ALSO *Constitutional construction; McCulloch v. Maryland*

IMPOUNDMENT OF FUNDS

Impoundment is the power of the President to withhold from federal departments or agencies some or all of the funds appropriated by Congress. The Constitution does not explicitly consider crucial questions about spending powers: Must the President spend the money appropriated by Congress? Or are such appropriations optional, rather than mandatory?

In some instances Congress passes laws permitting or directing the President to withhold funds for programs. The Antideficiency Act of 1950 allows the President to impound funds if a program can be administered more efficiently by spending less. Civil rights laws direct the President to withhold funds from states, counties, cities, and private organizations that discriminate on the basis of race or gender. Faced with budget deficits, Congress sometimes gives the President "across the board" authority to cut all programs by a specified percentage. In all other cases Congress assumes that its appropriations are mandatory.

Some Presidents have claimed that they have a constitutional power of impoundment, which does not require any congressional approval and which permits them to instruct the Treasury to withhold some or all of the funds for programs appropriated by Congress.

Presidents may claim military necessity: President Thomas Jefferson once declined to spend funds appropriated for gunboats on the grounds that the funds would be wasted on inferior ships. President Franklin D. Roosevelt asserted his power as commander in chief during World War II to justify wartime deferrals of nonessential domestic programs. Presidents Harry Truman and John F. Kennedy also cited their powers as commanders in chief to justify impounding money designated for weapons.

Richard Nixon was the first President to engage in impoundments on a massive scale. He used no national security rationale because he targeted domestic programs he opposed, such as antipoverty and environmental projects. More than 30 federal lawsuits challenged these impoundments, and all were decided against the President. None of the decisions directly challenged Nixon's assertion that he had a constitutional power of impoundment. Instead, the judges looked at the language of the law requiring that cabinet-level officials spend funds for programs and decided that these laws had not given officials discretion to withhold funding.

Congress also responded negatively to Nixon's impoundments. A 1970 hospital construction bill explicitly forbade impoundments, and that same year a federal highways act was accompanied by a "sense of Congress" resolution that said impoundments were unconstitutional. A foreign aid bill in 1971 contained a provision that no funds could be expended until funds impounded by several departments were released.

By late 1973 Nixon had cut so many pet projects of lawmakers that he had lost the support in Congress of his natural allies, conservative Republicans and Southern Democrats concerned with high levels of federal spending. The backlash against Nixon's actions enabled Congress to pass the Budget and Impoundment Control Act of 1974. Under Title X of that act, the President could defer spending funds to a later year only if the House and the Senate did not disapprove; he could rescind funds that had been appropriated by Congress only by getting it to pass a law to that effect. The law specifically stated that the President had no constitutional power to impound. Since then, most requests to rescind spending have been rejected by Congress, but requests to defer some spending to later years are often accepted.

SEE ALSO *Budget and Impoundment Control Act, Congressional (1974); Budget, Pres-* *idential; Checks and balances; Executive power; Nixon, Richard M.; Recision bills*

SOURCES Louis Fisher, *Presidential Spending Power* (Princeton, N.J.: Princeton University Press, 1975). James Pfiffner, *The President, the Budget, and Congress: Impoundment and the 1974 Budget Act* (Boulder, Colo.: Westview, 1979). Howard E. Shuman, *Politics and the Budget: The Struggle between the President and the Congress* (Englewood Cliffs, N.J.: Prentice-Hall, 1992).

INAUGURATION, PRESIDENTIAL

The inauguration is the ceremony marking the start of a new Presidential term. It consists of the oath of office, an inaugural address, a parade to the White House, and various inaugural balls. The Constitution specifies only the language of the oath that the President must take; it specifies no other inauguration ceremonies.

George Washington's first inauguration was held at Federal Hall in New York City. His second, as well as the inauguration of his successor, John Adams, was held in Philadelphia because the capital had moved there. Thomas Jefferson was the first President to be inaugurated in Washington, D.C. Presidents who assume office upon the death of their predecessor take the oath wherever they are and do not have inaugurations. When Chester Arthur succeeded to the Presidency, he took the oath in New York City; Theodore Roosevelt took the oath in Buffalo, New York; Calvin Coolidge in Plymouth, Vermont; and Lyndon Johnson in Dallas, Texas.

When the inaugural day, January 20, falls on a Sunday, the new President takes the oath in a private ceremony on that day. The public inauguration ceremonies take place on the following Monday, when the oath is repeated. Both Dwight Eisenhower and Ronald Reagan took two oaths.

The inaugural ceremony takes place at the Capitol, not the White House. It is customary for outgoing Presidents to attend the inaugural ceremony and to ride with the incoming President to the Capitol. But John Adams refused to attend Jefferson's inauguration because his son Charles had just died and he wanted to get home. Adams's son John Quincy Adams did not attend Andrew Jackson's inauguration in 1828; Martin Van Buren did not attend William Harrison's; and Andrew Johnson did not attend Ulysses S. Grant's.

Initially, Presidents took the oath and then went indoors to speak to Congress. The first fully outdoor inauguration was held in 1817 for James Monroe, who gave his inaugural address to the public. The first address to be telegraphed to another city was James K. Polk's in 1845. The first photograph of an inauguration was of James Buchanan's in 1857. Benjamin Harrison was the first President to watch the parade from a viewing stand rather than participate in it. Warren Harding was the first President to ride a car to his inauguration in 1921. Four years later, Calvin Coolidge's inaugural address was the first to be broadcast on radio. The first to be carried on television was Harry Truman's in 1949.

The Presidential inaugural address sets the tone for the administration. Presidents usually stress national unity and bipartisanship after what is sometimes a divisive and bitter Presidential campaign. Thomas Jefferson, for instance, reassured his political opponents: "We are all Republicans, we are all Federalists." Woodrow Wilson observed, "Here muster, not the forces of party, but the forces of humanity." A President may call for reconciliation, as Abraham Lincoln did in his second inaugural address when he stated his policy toward the defeated Confederacy: "With malice toward none, with charity for all, with firmness in the right as God gives us to see the right, let us strive on to . . . bind up the nation's wounds." The President may try to banish the doubts and fears that plague the public when his predecessor's policies have failed, as Franklin D. Roosevelt did with his observation that "the only thing we have to fear is fear itself." He may call

for change and sacrifice, as John F. Kennedy did when he challenged Americans to "ask not what your country can do for you. Ask what you can do for your country." The newly elected President takes the opportunity to discuss some of the measures he will take in office.

The inaugural day ends with the inaugural balls. The first ball was held by Dolley Madison for her husband, James, in 1809. Andrew Jackson, grief-stricken over the death of his wife, Rachel, did not organize a ball. Neither did Woodrow Wilson, Warren Harding, or Calvin Coolidge. Franklin D. Roosevelt held a ball at his first inaugural, but none thereafter. Jimmy Carter organized mere "parties" to signal a new mood of austerity in Washington and dropped the requirement for formal wear. The Reagan and Bush administrations restored the tradition of the formal inaugural ball, holding several at different locations for Republican supporters.

Several Presidents have thrown the White House open to the public. Andrew Jackson began the tradition, serving an enormous cake. Bill Clinton revived the open-house tradition in 1993.

SEE ALSO *Oath of office*

INCORPORATION DOCTRINE

The passage of the 14th Amendment in 1868 established new restrictions on the power of state governments to deprive individuals of civil rights and liberties. Over the course of the 20th century, the Supreme Court has decided that the 14th Amendment incorporates or absorbs most provisions of the federal Bill of Rights, thereby applying these rights to the states.

Prior to the passage of the 14th Amendment, the federal Bill of Rights (Amendments 1 through 10 to the Constitution) was understood to restrict only the actions of the federal government. This common understanding was confirmed by the Supreme Court's decision in *Barron* v. *Baltimore* (1833), which held that the 5th

Amendment could not be used to restrict a state or local government from taking private property for public use without providing "just compensation." Thus, following *Barron*, the 1st Amendment freedoms of religion, speech, press, assembly, and petition, for example, checked only the federal government, not the state governments, which retained power to deal with these matters according to their own constitutions and statutes.

In 1868 the 14th Amendment was passed, primarily to protect the civil rights and liberties of former slaves, who had been freed by the Civil War and the 13th Amendment, against state governments that might try to discriminate unfairly against them. Section 1 of the 14th Amendment says, "No State shall make or enforce any law which shall abridge the privileges or immunities of citizens of the United States; nor shall any State deprive any person of life, liberty, or property, without due process of law; nor deny to any person within its jurisdiction the equal protection of the laws." However, during the remainder of the 19th century and the first quarter of the 20th century, the Supreme Court tended to interpret the 14th Amendment narrowly and thus did not use it to enhance significantly the constitutional rights of former slaves or anyone else.

The first departure from this narrow view of the 14th Amendment came in 1897 with the decision in *Chicago, Burlington & Quincy Railroad Co. v. Chicago*. The Supreme Court decided that the due process clause of the 14th Amendment required the states, when taking private property for public use, to give the property owners fair compensation. This right is also provided by the just compensation clause of the 5th Amendment to the Constitution. Thus, for the first time, a provision of the Bill of Rights (Amendment 5 in this instance) had been used to limit the power of a state government via the due process clause of the 14th Amendment.

The next opening for the application of the Bill of Rights to the states came in 1908 with the decision in *Twining* v. *New Jersey*. The court decided against application of the self-incrimination clause of the 5th Amendment to the states via the due process clause of the 14th Amendment. The Court stipulated, however, that the due process clause could in principle *incorporate* some rights similar to those in the federal Bill of Rights because they were essential to the idea of due process of law. The Court provided this guideline for future decisions about which rights were due each individual: "Is it [the right in question] a fundamental principle of liberty and justice which inheres in the very idea of free government and is the inalienable right of a citizen of such a government?" With this guideline, *Twining* v. *New Jersey* opened the way to future applications to the states of rights in the federal Bill of Rights via the incorporation doctrine.

In 1925 the door to application of the federal Bill of Rights to the states was opened wider in the case of *Gitlow* v. *New York*. Benjamin Gitlow had been convicted for violating New York's Criminal Anarchy Law, which made it a crime to advocate violent revolution against the government. He claimed that the state of New York had unlawfully denied his 1st Amendment right to free expression under the due process clause of the 14th Amendment. The Court upheld Gitlow's conviction but acknowledged the doctrine of incorporation of 1st Amendment freedoms in the due process clause of the 14th Amendment and their application to the states. The Court asserted that for "present purposes we may and do assume that freedom of speech and of the press—which are protected by the First Amendment from abridgement by Congress—are among the fundamental personal rights and 'liberties' protected by the due process clause of the Fourteenth Amendment from impairment by the states." This idea was reinforced in *Fiske* v. *Kansas* (1927), in which the Court used the 14th Amendment to protect the free speech rights of individuals against a state law.

In 1931, the Court ruled again (in *Near* v. *Minnesota* and *Stromberg* v. *California*) that the 14th Amendment due process clause guaranteed the 1st Amendment rights of freedom of speech (*Stromberg*) and freedom of the press (*Near*) against the power of state governments. Chief Justice Charles Evans Hughes wrote (*Near*), "It is no longer open to doubt that the liberty of the press and of speech is within the liberty safeguarded by the due process clause of the Fourteenth Amendment. It was found impossible to conclude that this essential liberty of the citizen was left unprotected by the general guaranty of fundamental rights of person and property."

Thus the Supreme Court, through its power of judicial review, had extended to all the states beyond doubt the 1st Amendment freedoms of speech and press. What about the other rights in the Bill of Rights? Were they also applicable to the states through the due process clause of the 14th Amendment?

These questions were answered slowly, on a case-by-case basis, from the 1930s through the 1980s. At present, most provisions in the Bill of Rights have been extended nationwide through decisions of the Supreme Court and are generally accepted as legitimate limitations on the powers of state governments. The exceptions are Amendment 2 (the right to bear arms), Amendment 3 (restrictions on the quartering of soldiers), the grand jury indictment clause of Amendment 5, Amendment 7 (requirement of jury trials in civil cases), and the excessive fines and bail clause of Amendment 8.

James Madison, primary author of the Bill of Rights, had wanted to restrict the powers of state governments to interfere with the individual's rights to freedom of speech, press, and religion and to trial by jury in criminal cases. He had proposed to the first federal Congress, in the summer of 1789, that "No state shall infringe the equal rights of conscience, nor the freedom of speech, or of the press, nor of the right to trial by jury in criminal cases." However, this proposal was voted down in Congress, and the principle inherent in it was not revived until ratifi-

cation of the 14th Amendment in 1868. According to the records of the first Congress, "Mr. Madison conceived this to be the most valuable amendment on the whole list [of amendments that constituted the Bill of Rights]; if there was any reason to restrain the government of the United States from infringing upon these essential rights, it was equally necessary that they should be secured against the state governments."

The Supreme Court, in developing the incorporation doctrine to extend rights in the Bill of Rights to the states, has gradually and securely fulfilled Madison's great hope that the law would be used to limit the power of both federal and state governments in order to protect the inherent rights and liberties of individuals.

SEE ALSO *Barron v. Baltimore; Benton v. Maryland; Bill of Rights; Constitutional law; Due process of law; Duncan v. Louisiana; Everson v. Board of Education of Ewing Township; Gideon v. Wainwright; Gitlow v. New York; Mapp v. Ohio; Near v. Minnesota; Stromberg v. California; Wolf v. Colorado*

SOURCES Richard Cortner, *The Supreme Court and the Second Bill of Rights: The Fourteenth Amendment and the Nationalization of the Bill of Rights* (Madison: University of Wisconsin Press, 1981).

INCUMBENTS

A person currently holding an elected position is an incumbent. Although *incumbent* is derived from the French word meaning "to lie down on," those who lie down on the job will not hold their job for long. Voters want to know, "What have you done for me lately?" Incumbents in Congress must demonstrate their ability to legislate effectively and to provide services for their constituents. But incumbents generally enjoy a high rate of reelection over their challengers because of their greater ability to raise campaign funds and their use of the frank (free mailing) and other privileges of office that make them better known to the voters.

INDEPENDENT CANDIDATES FOR PRESIDENT

See *Third parties*

INDEPENDENT COUNSEL

Independent counsels were a post-Watergate attempt to establish a regular means of investigating alleged wrongdoing in the executive branch. Appointed by the Department of Justice or a special panel of judges, an independent counsel could prosecute cases in federal courts.

The independent counsel replaced the special prosecutor appointed by the attorney general, whose independence was guaranteed only by "guidelines" issued by the attorney general at the time of each appointment, by department regulations. Congress, responding to public lack of confidence in the aftermath of the Watergate crisis, wished to institute a system more independent of the Presidency and attorney general. Instead of leaving the initiative solely to the attorney general, it provided that a majority of either party's membership on the House or Senate Judiciary Committee could trigger a request for an independent counsel. Instead of leaving the appointment to the discretion of the attorney general, it provided that the appointment of independent counsel would be made by a special three-judge panel of the Court of Appeals for the District of Columbia. In this way Congress sought to restore public confidence in the integrity of prosecutors dealing in matters involving high administration officials.

Title VI of the Ethics in Government Act of 1978 provided for the appointment of an independent counsel to investigate and prosecute the President, Vice Presi-

dent, members of the cabinet, or other political executives appointed by the President if the attorney general received "specific information" about their possible violation of federal criminal law.

The attorney general conducted a preliminary investigation and then might request the appointment of an independent counsel. The Judiciary Committee of either the Senate or the House might also request the attorney general to conduct a "threshold inquiry," which is a preliminary investigation of allegations of wrongdoing. If the attorney general failed to apply for an independent counsel, he or she had to explain the decision to Congress within 30 days.

The independent counsel received funds from Congress to conduct the investigation and trials. Title VII of the law provided that he or she could not be dismissed by the President or by the attorney general except on grounds of "extraordinary impropriety," thus ensuring the integrity of the investigation.

In 1979 an independent counsel investigated President Jimmy Carter's chief of staff, Hamilton Jordan, on charges that he used cocaine but decided that prosecution was not warranted. President Ronald Reagan's attorney general, Edwin Meese, was subject to two investigations regarding his efforts to help a friend build an oil pipeline between Iraq and Jordan; he was not indicted. Two former Reagan White House aides, Lyn Nofziger and Michael Deaver, were investigated for lobbying activities within one year after leaving their government positions. An assistant to Samuel Pierce, Reagan's secretary of housing and urban development, was investigated for conflicts of interest involving the award of contracts. Secretary of Labor Ray Donovan was investigated for business activities that had occurred before he joined the Reagan administration. Reagan's secretary of defense, Caspar Weinberger, was indicted in 1992 for giving false statements to Congress about the Iran-Contra affair, in which U.S. arms were sold to Iran and the profits illegally diverted to the Nicaraguan

Contras, but he was pardoned by President George Bush in 1992.

The legality of the independent counsel law came under attack from Colonel Oliver North, who was also investigated by the special prosecutor in the Iran-Contra affair. North charged that the appointment of the counsel was a violation of the doctrine of separation of powers (because the prosecutor was appointed by judges and not by the attorney general, a member of the executive branch). The Reagan administration also argued that the statute was unconstitutional because it infringed upon the Presidential removal power. Nevertheless, the Supreme Court upheld the law.

The independent counsel law expired in 1992, and Bill Clinton supported its renewal. The three-judge panel appointed Kenneth Starr to investigate Clinton's Whitewater land dealings. Starr was unable to link Clinton to criminal acts. He referred to the House of Representatives charges that Clinton perjured himself and obstructed justice in court proceedings involving his personal affairs, and the House impeached Clinton. Because of criticism of how the investigation was handled, with Democrats charging that the prosecution had been overzealous and had denied witnesses their due process rights, Congress in 1999 allowed the independent counsel statute to expire.

SEE ALSO *Appointment power; Ethics; Removal power; Watergate investigation (1973–74)*

SOURCES Katy J. Harriger, *Independent Justice: The Federal Special Prosecutor in American Politics* (Lawrence: University Press of Kansas, 1991).

INDEPENDENT JUDICIARY

The independence of the federal judicial branch is based on the insulation of its members, once appointed and confirmed in their positions, from punitive actions by the legislative and executive branches. According to Article 3 of the Constitution, federal judges may hold their positions "during good Behaviour"; in effect, they have lifetime appointments as long as they satisfy the ethical and legal standards of their judicial offices. Furthermore, Article 3 provides that the legislative and executive branches may not combine to punish federal judges by decreasing payments for their services. The intention of these constitutional provisions is to guard the federal judges against undue influence from the legislative and executive branches in the exercise of their judicial power.

Alexander Hamilton argued for an independent judiciary in *The Federalist* No. 78. He wrote, "The complete independence of the courts of justice is peculiarly essential in a limited Constitution." Hamilton claimed that only an independent judicial branch of government would be able to impartially check excessive exercise of power by the other branches of government.

SEE ALSO *Separation of powers*

INDEPENDENTS, CONGRESSIONAL

Occasionally, senators and representatives who are independent of the major parties are elected to office. Independents, or third-party candidates, have become increasingly rare in modern times. In the 1950s, Oregon senator Wayne Morse quit the Republican party. Before he joined the Democrats, he demonstrated his independence by moving his chair into the aisle that divided the two parties. Generally, independent members choose to join one of the major party conferences, and they receive their committee assignments through that conference. For instance, James Buckley, elected to the Senate by the Conservative party in New York in 1970, joined the Republican conference. Bernard Saunders, elected as a Socialist in Vermont in 1990, joined the House Democratic Caucus. Independents have their greatest influence when the two major parties are closely balanced—then, third-party members can tip the scales one way or the other.

INDIVIDUAL RIGHTS

SEE *Bill of Rights; Civil rights; Liberty under the Constitution*

IN FORMA PAUPERIS

The Latin phrase *in forma pauperis* means "in the manner of a pauper." Appeals for a hearing before the U.S. Supreme Court that are brought by individuals unable to pay court costs are known as *in forma pauperis* petitions. Appellants in such cases are not required to pay the filing fee.

INJUNCTION

An injunction is a court order requiring a person to do, or not to do, something in order to protect another's personal or property rights. A person who violates an injunction is in contempt of court and the court may fine or imprison him. An injunction usually is issued to prohibit an action. When it is used to command a positive action, it is called a mandatory injunction.

During the 20th century, courts have used injunctions to protect and promote the civil rights of minorities, especially African Americans. For example, federal courts used injunctions to stop school district officials from continuing racial segregation in schools after the decision in *Brown* v. *Board of Education* (1954). Courts also used injunctions to take positive actions, such as redrawing school district boundaries and ordering the busing of students between districts to achieve racially mixed schools. Thus, federal injunctions have become an important way of protecting the constitutional rights of individuals against infringement by state governments.

SEE ALSO *Brown v. Board of Education*

"INNER CLUB"

Described as the most exclusive club in the world, the Senate for many years also contained an "inner club." Theoretically, all senators are equal, but members of the "inner club" were committee chairmen and other senior senators who held greater power and influence over legislation than the average senator did. Conservative Southern Democrats, because of their seniority, made up the largest share of this "inner club," which was also called the "Senate establishment." By contrast, Northern liberals were relegated to the "outer life of the Senate." By the 1970s committee reforms had given more senators subcommittee chairmanships and other access to power. Although some senators remained more powerful than others, the "inner club" faded away.

SOURCES William S. White, *Citadel: The Story of the U.S. Senate* (New York: Harper, 1956).

IN RE

In re is a Latin phrase meaning "in the matter of." When *in re* appears in the title of a court case, it means that the case does *not* have formal opposing parties. The use of *in re* refers to the object or person that is the primary subject of the case. For example, *In re Winship* (1970) was a case without adversaries. The state did not oppose the person to whom the title refers, Samuel Winship. Thus, Winship was not required in this case to defend himself in any way. Rather, this case dealt only with the standard of proof necessary to incarcerate a 12-year-old boy who had been sentenced and committed to a training school for juvenile offenders. The phrase *in re* is often used in cases involving preadult offenders, which are handled by the juvenile justice system.

SEE ALSO *In re Winship; Juvenile justice*

IN RE GAULT

- 387 U.S. 1 (1967)
- Vote: 8–1
- For the Court: Fortas
- Concurring: Black, White, and Harlan
- Dissenting: Stewart

Gerald Gault, a 15-year-old boy, made obscene telephone calls to a neighbor. At the time, he was on court-ordered probation for a different act of juvenile delinquency.

As a juvenile, Gault did not have the standard constitutional guarantees of due process, such as the right to counsel, the right to confront or cross-examine one's accuser, the privilege of protection from self-incrimination, and the right to notice of a legal hearing. The juvenile justice system was separated from the usual criminal processes applied to adults. The intention had been to protect juvenile offenders from the harshness of adult criminal law. But these good intentions could in some cases lead to injustice, which is what Gault's advocates claimed.

If Gault had been tried as an adult, his punishment would have been a $50 fine or two months in jail. As a juvenile offender, he was sentenced to the Arizona State Industrial School until the age of 21, a six-year sentence. Further, Arizona law provided juvenile offenders virtually no due process rights, such as those set out in the 5th and 6th Amendments to the U.S. Constitution.

A state juvenile court judge convicted and sentenced Gerald Gault after two hearings. Gault's father sought his son's release from state-imposed detention on the grounds that he had been denied due process rights guaranteed by the U.S. Constitution.

The Issue   Do the due process rights of individuals, specified in the 5th, 6th, and 14th Amendments, apply to juveniles, just as they do to adults accused of crimes?

Opinion of the Court   The Supreme Court decided that Gerald Gault had been denied his constitutional rights of due process. Justice Abe Fortas declared that "nei-

ther the Fourteenth Amendment nor the Bill of Rights is for adults alone. . . . Under our Constitution, the condition of being a boy does not justify a kangaroo court. . . . The essential difference between Gerald's case and a normal criminal case is that safeguards available to adults were discarded in Gerald's case."

Justice Fortas held that due process of law for juveniles required at least four procedural protections of individual rights: written notification of specific charges to the juvenile and his parents, assistance of a lawyer, confrontation and cross-examination of witnesses, and protection against self-incrimination.

Justice Fortas argued that the guarantee of these four due process rights for juveniles would not require the state to treat a juvenile accused of delinquency exactly like an adult accused of crime. Rather, these safeguards would protect a juvenile against injustices that otherwise might occur.

Significance   This is the Court's most important decision about the rights of juveniles accused of illegal actions. It established that juveniles have certain constitutional rights that cannot be taken away solely because of age. However, the *Gault* decision did not abolish distinctive qualities of a separate juvenile court system. In particular, the due process requirements of *Gault* apply only to the adjudication (hearing and deciding) phase of legal proceedings and not to the conviction phase. Thus, *Gault* does not interfere with the emphasis that juvenile courts have traditionally placed on personalized treatment for rehabilitation of the individual.

SEE ALSO *Due process of law; Juvenile justice*

SOURCES   Thomas J. Bernard, *The Cycle of Juvenile Justice* (New York: Oxford University Press, 1992).

IN RE WINSHIP

- 397 U.S. 358 (1970)
- Vote: 6–3

• For the Court: Brennan
• Concurring: Harlan
• Dissenting: Burger, Stewart, and Black

A 12-year-old boy, Samuel Winship, was charged with an act of juvenile delinquency that, if committed by an adult, would be considered larceny. The boy was convicted by a family court judge according to the prevailing New York statute, which required only a "preponderance of the evidence" to justify juvenile detention. Advocates for the convicted juvenile claimed that a higher standard of proof— guilt "beyond a reasonable doubt"— should have been used in this case. That higher standard of proof had historically been the one accepted by the Court in adult criminal proceedings.

The Issue   What standard of proof should be necessary to convict a juvenile for an act that would be considered a serious crime if committed by an adult? Should the due process clauses of the 5th and 14th Amendments be interpreted to require proof beyond a reasonable doubt as the standard for conviction of an accused juvenile?

Opinion of the Court   Justice William J. Brennan decided that defendants in juvenile proceedings have the constitutional right to the higher standard of proof—"beyond a reasonable doubt." Brennan wrote, "We explicitly hold that the Due Process Clause protects the accused against conviction except upon proof beyond a reasonable doubt of every fact necessary to constitute the crime with which he is charged." Brennan based his opinion on common law and precedent because the "beyond a reasonable doubt" standard is not specifically stated in the U.S. Constitution.

Dissent   Justice Hugo Black criticized the Supreme Court's majority in this case for stepping beyond the boundaries of its power in order to amend the Bill of Rights. He wrote, "Nowhere in that document is there any statement that conviction of crime requires proof of guilt beyond a reasonable doubt."

Significance   The *Winship* decision provided juveniles accused of unlawful behavior with new constitutional protection. As stated by the Court, this higher standard of proof was also legally established for adults accused of criminal behavior.

SEE ALSO *Juvenile justice*

SOURCES Thomas J. Bernard, *The Cycle of Juvenile Justice* (New York: Oxford University Press, 1992).

INSTRUCTION OF SENATORS

Because state legislatures originally elected senators, they believed they held the power to instruct those senators how to vote. During the 1790s and 1800s several state legislatures sent formal instructions to their senators. Senators generally ignored these instructions, and a few denounced them as unconstitutional.

SOURCES Roy Swanstom, *The United States Senate, 1789–1801: A Dissertation on the First Fourteen Years of the Upper House* (Washington, D.C.: Government Printing Office, 1989).

INSURGENTS

Those members of Congress who revolt against their party leadership are known as insurgents—from the Latin word meaning "to rise up." Insurgents have often risen up against what they perceive as dictatorial behavior by the leadership or against the suppression of legislative reforms that they favor. Insurgents run the risk of being punished by the leadership for their defections.

The most famous insurgency took place in 1909, when progressive Republicans joined with Democrats to reduce the powers of Speaker Joseph G. Cannon. On an individual level, William Proxmire (Democrat–Wisconsin), a freshman senator in 1958, publicly denounced the powerful Senate majority leader, Lyndon B. Johnson, for his domineering behavior. Proxmire spoke on George Washington's birthday, a day when the Senate traditionally hears a reading of Washington's Farewell Address. Reporters joked that there were two farewell addresses that day: Washington's and Proxmire's. But Proxmire's insurgent spirit did not hurt him with the voters in his state, who regularly reelected him to the Senate.

SEE ALSO *Cannon, Joseph G.; Johnson, Lyndon B.*

INTERNAL REVENUE SERVICE

In 1798 Congress assessed its first direct tax on the American people, a $2 million sum apportioned among the states on the basis of the most current census. The federal government used direct taxation during the early years of the country to support war efforts and other administrative expenditures, but it was not until the Tax Act of 1862 that the government first levied an income tax and founded the Bureau of Internal Revenue to collect it. President Abraham Lincoln passed this tax act with rates of 3 to 5 percent to finance the Civil War, and people responded favorably, eager to help the war effort.

In 1895 in the case of *Pollack* v. *Farmers Loan and Trust,* the Supreme Court found income taxation unconstitutional, putting the Bureau of Internal Revenue in jeopardy. However, with the passage of the 16th Amendment in 1913, legalizing the taxation of income, the bureau's existence was insured. In the 1920s, in addition to collecting taxes, the bureau was responsible for enforcing the Prohibition amendment. It continued enforcing similar alcohol and tobacco legislation until 1972, when it passed on these duties to the newly formed Bureau of Alcohol, Tobacco, and Firearms.

In 1953 the Bureau of Internal Revenue was reorganized as the Internal Revenue Service (IRS). Responsible for determining, assessing, and collecting internal revenue, the IRS remains the largest of the Treasury's branches. Revenue collected consists of personal and corporate income taxes; excise, estate, and gift taxes; as well as employment taxes for the nation's Social Security system.

INTERNS, CONGRESSIONAL

During the summer months, student interns swell the ranks of the congressional staff. These interns, working for pay or for college credit, gain experience in the legislative process. Most often, interns deliver messages, photocopy, and file. But some offices use interns to help with correspondence and to conduct preliminary legislative research. Most important, they observe the activities of Congress firsthand.

Though the majority of interns are undergraduates, others are graduate students and people at mid-career who receive fellowships from professional associations to spend a year working with Congress. Representative Steve Horn (Republican–California), for example, first came to Capitol Hill as a Congressional Fellow with the American Political Science Association. He then joined the Senate staff and eventually won a seat in Congress himself.

INTERPARLIAMENTARY RELATIONS

Although the U.S. Congress is structured very differently from most legislatures around the world, it has sought to build goodwill and working ties with other legislative bodies. Members of Congress regularly attend sessions of the Inter-Parliamentary Union, which consists of delegates from many different national legislatures who meet to discuss common issues and problems. Congress also appoints delegations to the Canada–U.S. and Mexico–U.S. interparliamentary groups. Members of foreign parliaments regularly visit Congress to observe its proceedings and up-to-date technology. Since the end of the cold war, Congress has worked especially with the new legislative bodies in eastern Europe and the former Soviet republics to demonstrate how the U.S. system of separation of powers and checks and balances works.

INVESTIGATIONS, CONGRESSIONAL

Aside from its legislative activities, Congress devotes much attention to investigations. Congressional investigations have uncovered wrongdoing within the executive branch, from obscure agencies up to the President's office. They have also focused on the military, private enterprise, and foreign agents. By uncovering this information and informing the public, investigations have often led to important reform legislation.

But critics have also dismissed congressional investigations as merely an opportunity for politicians to make headlines and appear on television. They have accused some investigations of trampling on the rights of witnesses and interfering with court proceedings. Critics have pointed out that many investigations produce no solid evidence and fail to lead to any legislation at all.

The first congressional investigation took place in 1792, when a special committee of the House looked into the disastrous expedition led by General Arthur St. Clair against the Shawnee and Miami Indians in Ohio, in which 657 American troops were killed. The House committee demanded that it see War Department records regarding this defeat. President George Washington complied with the committee's request, thereby acknowledging Congress's right to investigate.

Uncovering scandal During the 19th century Congress investigated the military conduct of the Civil War, Ku Klux Klan violence against freedmen after the war, the circumstances surrounding the purchase of Alaska, and such railroad scandals as that involving Credit Mobi-lier, which involved the payment of bribes to key members of Congress. In the 20th century congressional investigating increased steadily. In 1923 the Senate's investigation of the Teapot Dome scandal discredited President Warren G. Harding's administration and sent his secretary of the interior, Albert B. Fall, to prison. During the 1930s the Senate banking committee drew many headlines with its investigation of the stock market crash of 1929 and the causes of the depression. Senator Harry S. Truman first rose to public notice by chairing an investigation of the national defense program during World War II.

During the cold war of the 1940s and 1950s, congressional investigations stirred up a "Red scare" by looking for communists in the government. The House Un-American Activities Committee (HUAC) made news when Whittaker Chambers testified that former State Department official Alger Hiss had secretly been a communist and alleged that Hiss had engaged in espionage. Later, Senator Joseph R. McCarthy (Republican–Wisconsin) used his chairmanship of the Senate's Permanent Subcommittee on Investigations to pursue allegations that communists were operating in the military and other government agencies. Critics charged HUAC and Senator McCarthy with "witch hunting" and accused congressional investigators of bullying witnesses and ignoring their civil rights and liberties.

Court rulings on investigations
Periodically, the Supreme Court has helped to define the scope and limitations of Congress's power to investigate. In *McGrain v. Daugherty* (1927) the Court ruled that anyone, even private citizens, could be subpoenaed (compelled) to testify before a congressional committee. And in *Sinclair v. United States* (1929) the Court said that Congress had the power to investigate anything related to legislation or oversight, the monitoring of the activities of executive agencies. But in *Watkins v. United States* (1957)—which involved a witness who declined to give names of sus-

pected communists to HUAC—the Court ruled that Congress's investigative powers are limited by the Bill of Rights and that witnesses do not lose those rights when they testify.

Public approval of congressional investigations was restored in 1973 by the Watergate investigation. Chaired by Sam Ervin (Democrat–North Carolina), the special Senate committee painstakingly interrogated witnesses to link the White House to the burglary of Democratic National Committee headquarters at the Watergate building in 1972. The investigation led to the resignations of many administration officials, including President Richard M. Nixon. The Watergate investigators established that in order for congressional investigations to be successful, investigators must treat witnesses seriously and with some degree of humanity; do their homework, no matter how much drudgery it entails; and persist until they have kept the issue in the media long enough to educate the public, expose wrongdoing, and suggest corrective action.

SEE ALSO *Ervin, Samuel J., Jr.; McCarthy, Joseph R.; Wall Street investigation (1932–34); Watergate investigation (1973–74)*
SOURCES James Hamilton, *The Power to Probe: A Study of Congressional Investigation* (New York: Vintage, 1976). Arthur M. Schlesinger, Jr., and Roger Bruns, eds., *Congress Investigates, 1792–1974: A Documented History*, 5 vols. (New York: Bowker, 1975).

IRAN-CONTRA INVESTIGATION (1986)

In 1986 a joint committee of Congress investigated charges that President Ronald Reagan's administration had sold weapons to Iran and diverted the money received to the Contra forces seeking to overthrow the government of Nicaragua. In 1982, Congress had enacted Representative Edward Boland's amendment to the defense appropriations bill, forbidding any U.S. aid to the Contras. But high-level officials of the Reagan administration, including Central Intelligence Agency director William Casey and National Security Council aide Lieutenant Colonel Oliver North, bypassed the Boland Amendment by using money raised through secret arms sales to Iran. After the media and the joint committee revealed the details of the Iran-Contra scandal, a special prosecutor won indictments and convictions of North and other officials. However, the courts later overturned some of these convictions on the grounds that their televised testimony before the investigating committee, and grants of limited immunity to testify, had prejudiced their case.

SOURCES William S. Cohen and George J. Mitchell, *Men of Zeal: A Candid Inside Story of the Iran-Contra Hearings* (New York: Viking, 1988).

IREDELL, JAMES
Associate Justice, 1790–99

- Born: Oct. 5, 1751, Lewes, England
- Education: read law under Samuel Johnston of North Carolina
- Previous government service: comptroller of customs, Edenton, N.C., 1768–74; collector of customs, Port of North Carolina, 1774–76; judge, Superior Court of North Carolina, 1778; attorney general of North Carolina, 1779–81; North Carolina Council of State, 1787; North Carolina Ratifying Convention, 1788
- Appointed by President George Washington Feb. 8, 1790
- Supreme Court term: confirmed by the Senate Feb. 10, 1790, by a voice vote; served until Oct. 20, 1799
- Died: Oct. 20, 1799, Edenton, N.C.

James Iredell was an original member of the Supreme Court. President Washington decided to appoint Iredell because of his good reputation as a legal expert and his skill as a political leader in North Carolina, where he had argued decisively against opponents of the 1787 Constitution.

Iredell had attracted Washington's attention during the debates about ratification of the Constitution. Iredell published a pamphlet opposing the "Objections to the New Constitution" by George Mason, a delegate from Virginia. Iredell also stood firm against the majority of citizens in North Carolina who at first opposed the Constitution of 1787. He eventually helped to persuade North Carolinians to ratify the federal Constitution in 1789.

In dissent from the Court's decision in *Chisholm v. Georgia* (1793), Justice Iredell held that a state government could not be sued in a federal court by a person from another state. This position became part of the Constitution in 1795 with ratification of the 11th Amendment.

In *Calder v. Bull* (1798), Iredell argued that the Court had authority to declare laws null and void if they violated the Constitution of the United States, the supreme law. This position on the power of judicial review was also implied by the Court, including Iredell, in *Hylton v. United States* (1796). In the *Hylton* case, the Court upheld the constitutionality of a federal tax law, and the decision implied that the Court could have ruled this federal law unconstitutional. However, the Court did not discuss the power of judicial review in this case. A few years later, in *Marbury v. Madison* (1803), Chief Justice John Marshall argued compellingly for the Court's power of judicial review to strike down acts of Congress that were in violation of the U.S. Constitution.

SEE ALSO *Hylton v. United States; Judicial review*

J

JACKSON, ANDREW
7th President

- Born: Mar. 15, 1767, Waxhaw settlement, S.C.
- Political party: Democrat
- Education: read law in Salisbury, N.C., 1784–87
- Military service: Waxhaw settlement militia, 1780; Tennessee Militia, 1802–14; U.S. Army, 1814–18
- Previous government service: public prosecutor, Mero District, Tenn., 1787; Tennessee Constitutional Convention, 1796; U.S. House of Representatives, 1796–97; U.S. Senate, 1797–98; Superior Court justice and member of the Tennessee Supreme Court, 1799–1804; territorial governor of Florida, 1821; U.S. Senate, 1823–25
- Elected President, 1828; served, 1829–37
- Died: June 8, 1845, near Nashville, Tenn.

Andrew Jackson was born on the Carolina frontier, the only American President born of immigrant parents. He brought the ways of the West to American politics, revitalizing and democratizing it, and carrying with him a whole generation of men who owed their careers to him. He created the Democratic party, the longest-lasting political party in American history, and he was the dominant political figure between Jefferson and Lincoln.

Jackson's father died just before he was born, soon after arriving from Ireland, and his mother and two brothers died during the revolutionary war. Jackson entered the war as an orderly, was captured by the British in 1780, and suffered a scar from a saber injury delivered by one of his guards. Jackson read law in North Carolina and became a frontier gambler, lawyer, land speculator, and cotton and tobacco farmer at Hunter's Hill, his plantation near Nashville, Tennessee. He married Rachel Donelson Robards, the daughter of one of the founders of Nashville, worked as a lawyer in debt collection cases, and was closely allied politically with large landowners and local bankers. Jackson helped to draft the state constitution in 1795, served at the state constitutional convention in 1796, and was sent to the U.S. House the following year and then the Senate in 1797, serving one year. He served on the Tennessee Superior Court from 1799 to 1804 but resigned to devote himself to business. Several reverses forced him to sell Hunter's Hill and move to a smaller plantation, the Hermitage. He bred, raised, and raced horses successfully. In a duel on May 30, 1806, Jackson shot and killed Charles Dickinson for making unflattering remarks about Jackson's wife; one of Dickinson's bullets remained in his chest. In 1813 Jackson was shot in a hotel brawl with Thomas Hart Benton and Jesse Benton, two brothers who dominated politics in Missouri, and the bullet was not removed until 1832.

Jackson took command of the Tennessee state militia during the War of 1812. Fighting the Creek Indians, who were allied with the British, he won the Battle of Horseshoe Bend in Alabama in March

1814. This victory ended the Creek War, forcing the tribe to cede more than 23 million acres to the United States. In May he was commissioned a major general of the regular army. He then captured Pensacola, Florida, and defeated the British at the Battle of New Orleans in 1815. The British suffered more than 2,000 dead, including their commanding general; American losses totaled 8 killed and 13 wounded. These military victories made Jackson, known as Sharp Knife to the Indians and Old Hickory to the Americans, a national figure.

After the war Jackson fought other Indian tribes, defeating the Chickasaw, the Choctaw, and the Cherokee. In 1818 he commanded troops in the Seminole Wars in Georgia. He invaded Spanish Florida and executed two British subjects who had stirred up an Indian revolt, causing a diplomatic furor. Jackson defeated an attempt by the House of Representatives to censure him. After the United States acquired Florida from Spain, President James Monroe appointed him the first territorial governor.

Jackson was elected to the Senate in 1823, occupying a seat next to Thomas Hart Benton, the man who had nearly killed him in 1813. The two soon became political allies, and Jackson began campaigning for the Presidency. In the election of 1824 he received the most popular and electoral votes of any candidate in the four-person race but not enough to win election. In the contingency election—held because no candidate received a majority of electoral college votes—the House of Representatives chose John Quincy Adams over Jackson and William Crawford. As Speaker of the House, Henry Clay had controlled the key House votes that elected Adams. Adams then named Clay secretary of state, an appointment that led Jackson's followers to charge that a "corrupt bargain" had been made. Jackson resigned from the Senate in 1825 to organize his next run for the Presidency.

By 1828 the number of voters had almost quadrupled, and in every state except

South Carolina electors were chosen directly by the voters, not by the state legislatures. Jackson and Martin Van Buren organized state parties to mobilize and turn out this large electorate. The huge turnout in what was the first fully democratic election in the United States gave Jackson an overwhelming popular and electoral college vote over his opponent, John Quincy Adams, who ran on the National Republican ticket. But tragedy marred his victory: between his election and inauguration his wife, Rachel, died.

Jackson's accession to power in Washington was akin to a political, social, and economic revolution. By his clothing, his speech, and his manners, Jackson was a "man of the people" with little in common with the Virginia or Massachusetts aristocrats who had previously sat in the White House. He was a military man with little Washington experience, a man with almost no formal education, and the first "outsider" to win the White House. Jackson had swept away the party-less Era of Good Feelings and soon created a new political party, the Democrats, with a strong Southern and Western base among frontiersmen, small farmers, and workers.

Early in his term Jackson dismissed about one-tenth of the officeholders in Washington and replaced them with his followers. Jackson embraced the principle of rotation in office, in which government officials are appointed on the basis of political ties, rather than a permanent civil service with lifetime appointments.

Jackson soon became embroiled in traditional Washington society. Peggy O'Neale, the daughter of a saloon keeper, married Jackson's secretary of war, John Eaton, and was ostracized by other cabinet wives, who claimed she had been having an adulterous affair with Eaton prior to their marriage. Rumors about Mrs. Eaton were spread by the wife of Vice President John C. Calhoun. Jackson took Peggy Eaton's side against the leaders of Washington society. He began to rely on a "kitchen cabinet" of political advisers rather than his cabinet secretaries. Later, his disagreement with Calhoun over the Tariff of Abominations of 1828 led to an open split between them. In the spring of 1831 Jackson forced out the three members of the cabinet who would not accept Peggy Eaton. He established the principle, new in American government, that the cabinet secretaries serve at the pleasure of the President and are subordinate to his will.

Jackson took on the Second Bank of the United States, a private corporation created as the linchpin of national economic policy-making. The national government held one-fifth of the bank's stock and kept its deposits there, and the bank's notes were legal tender (currency). On July 10, 1832, Jackson vetoed a bill passed by Congress that would have rechartered the bank, which was due to expire in 1836, attacking it as a law "to make the rich richer and the potent more powerful." Congress was unable to override his veto.

Jackson made the veto a major issue in his 1832 reelection campaign. He identified the bank with "special privileges" that the government had given to local bankers affiliated with the national bank. He argued that government should remain neutral among financial institutions. The appeal made Jackson seem like a representative of the common man against the wealthy and privileged, though Jackson had not explicitly called for class conflict.

With Martin Van Buren on his ticket, Jackson won an overwhelming victory over Henry Clay. He claimed he had a mandate to destroy the bank. He ordered his secretary of the Treasury, William Duane, to remove Treasury deposits from that bank and place them in state banks that were affiliated with his new party. When Duane refused, Jackson fired him, appointed his attorney general, Roger Taney, to his place, and had the deposits removed. Jackson's opponents in Congress organized a new political party, the Whigs, to oppose his policies and his exercise of Presidential power. The bank went out of existence in 1836. By the end of Jackson's term, the national debt had been entirely

paid and the government was running a surplus that Jackson's successor, Van Buren, distributed to the states.

Jackson took personal charge of Indian policy. In 1830 he got Congress to pass a law authorizing him to create new Indian lands west of the Mississippi River and to transport Indians there. He then negotiated with Indian tribes, forcing the Chickasaw, the Choctaw, and the Creek to move west. In 1832 he encouraged Georgia to violate an 1831 Supreme Court ruling, *Cherokee Nation* v. *Georgia,* that was supposed to prevent Georgia from taking over Cherokee lands, and that tribe was removed forcibly after Jackson left office. Many Indians died along the "trail of tears" during these removals.

As the first President whose election rested on a truly popular base, Jackson translated electoral support directly into Presidential power. When Jackson vetoed a bill rechartering the Second Bank on the grounds that it was unconstitutional (even though the Supreme Court, in the case of *McCulloch* v. *Maryland,* had already ruled that the bank was constitutional), Jackson asserted his authority to make his own decisions about the constitutionality of laws. In firing Duane, he asserted the power of a President to remove cabinet-level officials whose appointments had been approved by the Senate, even though the Constitution makes no mention of a removal power for the President, and many senators thought that such removals would require the concurrence of the Senate as well. The Senate responded by rejecting Jackson's nominations for governors on the bank board and his nomination of Taney as associate justice of the Supreme Court. It also censured Jackson, adopting Henry Clay's resolution that "the President, in the late Executive proceedings in relation to the public revenue, has assumed upon himself authority and power not conferred by the Constitution and laws, but in derogation of both." Jackson protested this resolution, and in 1836 it was expunged by the Senate.

Jackson also used Presidential power in a nullification controversy. In November 1832, with Vice President Calhoun's support, South Carolina passed a resolution nullifying, or preventing enforcement of, the high tariffs of 1828 and 1832 within the state. In December, Jackson responded with a proclamation to the people of South Carolina warning them against nullification or secession and reminding them of the supremacy of the national government and its law. He warned the citizens who were preparing to defend South Carolina militarily that "disunion by armed force is treason." Calhoun resigned his office in protest over these tariffs and Jackson's strong stance. In March 1833 Jackson gained from Congress a "Force Bill" giving him the power to use federal force to ensure compliance with the tariff as well as a reduction in the high rates designed to defuse the crisis. After Jackson sent warships to Charleston Harbor, South Carolina backed down, withdrawing its nullification of the tariff on Jackson's birthday. The state tried to save face by passing a new bill nullifying Jackson's Force Bill, however.

The struggle between Jackson and Calhoun epitomized the strains that would eventually tear the Union apart. At a dinner in Washington in 1830 Jackson had given a famous toast: "Our federal Union— it must be preserved." But Vice President Calhoun had responded, "The Union— next to our liberty, most dear." The question of national supremacy would remain an open issue until the end of the Civil War.

After leaving the White House, Jackson retired to the Hermitage, where he lived in poor health until his death on June 8, 1845.
SEE ALSO *Adams, John Quincy; Calhoun, John C.; Removal power; Van Buren, Martin*
SOURCES Richard Ellis, *The Union at Risk: Jacksonian Democracy, States' Rights, and the Nullification Crisis* (New York: Oxford University Press, 1989). Robert V. Remini, *Andrew Jackson*, 3 vols. (New York: Harper & Row, 1970–84). Arthur M. Schlesinger,

Jr., *The Age of Jackson* (Boston: Little, Brown, 1945).

JACKSON, HOWELL E.
Associate Justice, 1893–95

- Born: Apr. 8, 1832, Paris, Tenn.
- Education: West Tennessee College, B.A., 1849; University of Virginia, 1851–52; Cumberland University, 1856
- Previous government service: judge, Court of Arbitration for Western Tennessee, 1875–79; Tennessee House of Representatives, 1880; U.S. senator from Tennessee, 1881–86; judge, Sixth Federal Circuit Court, 1886–91; judge, Circuit Court of Appeals, 1891–93
- Appointed by President Benjamin Harrison Feb. 2, 1893; replaced Lucius Q. C. Lamar, who died
- Supreme Court term: confirmed by the Senate Feb. 18, 1893, by a voice vote; served until Aug. 8, 1895
- Died: Aug. 8, 1895, Nashville, Tenn.

Howell E. Jackson achieved an outstanding record of public service in his home state, Tennessee. He was rewarded in 1881 by election to the U.S. Senate, where he developed a close friendship with a senator from Indiana, Benjamin Harrison, and with President Grover Cleveland. In 1886, Jackson left the Senate to accept President Cleveland's appointment to the U.S. Court of Appeals for the Sixth Circuit. In 1893, Jackson was appointed to the Supreme Court by his old friend from the Senate, President Benjamin Harrison.

Jackson served less than two years on the Court because of poor health. In fact, during this time his illness prevented him from participating in several important decisions of the Court.

Jackson's most notable opinion was his dissent in *Pollock* v. *Farmers' Loan and Trust Co.* (1895). The Court decided that the 1894 federal income tax law was unconstitutional. Jackson strongly disagreed, and his position was confirmed in 1913 with passage of the 16th Amendment to the Constitution, which grants power to the federal government to tax incomes "from whatever source derived"

JACKSON, ROBERT H.
Associate Justice, 1941–54

- Born: Feb. 13, 1842, Spring Creek, Pa.
- Education: Albany Law School, 1912
- Previous government service: general counsel, Internal Revenue Bureau, 1934–36; special counsel, Securities and Exchange Commission, 1935; assistant U.S. attorney general, 1936–38; U.S. solicitor general, 1938–39; U.S. attorney general, 1940–41
- Appointed by President Franklin D. Roosevelt June 12, 1941; replaced Harlan F. Stone, who became chief justice
- Supreme Court term: confirmed by the Senate July 7, 1941, by a voice vote; served until Oct. 9, 1954
- Died: Oct. 9, 1954, Washington, D.C.

Robert H. Jackson was a Democratic party activist before he became a lawyer. After completing law school, he continued his involvement in the Democratic party of New York and became an ally and close friend of Franklin D. Roosevelt. In 1934 Jackson went to Washington, D.C., to work in the federal government led by President Roosevelt. He eventually became solicitor general in 1938 and attorney general in 1940, and he was also an important adviser to the President. In 1941 President Roosevelt named Jackson to fill a vacancy on the Supreme Court.

Justice Jackson tended to defend the individual against threats of oppression by government officials or by an intolerant majority of the people. In *West Virginia State Board of Education* v. *Barnette* (1943), Jackson upheld the rights of a religious minority, Jehovah's Witnesses, to refrain from participating in a public exercise, saluting the flag and reciting the pledge of allegiance. He wrote: "If there is any fixed star in our constitutional constellation, it is that no official, high or petty, can prescribe what shall be orthodox in politics, nationalism, religion, or other matters of opinion or force citizens to confess by word or act their faith therein."

Jackson, however, also recognized the need for public safety and social order, which could be threatened by unlimited or extreme expressions of individual liberty. He therefore voted with the Court's majority in *Dennis* v. *United States* (1951) to uphold the convictions of American Communist party leaders who promoted the violent overthrow of the U.S. government.

In May 1945, at the end of World War II, President Harry Truman asked Jackson to serve as chief counsel for the United States in the prosecution of Nazi war criminals at the Nuremberg (Germany) war crimes trials. In this role, Jackson developed the legal principles and procedures by which leading Nazis were tried and convicted of war crimes against humanity.

SEE ALSO *West Virginia State Board of Education v. Barnette*

SOURCES Eugene C. Gerhart, *America's Advocate: Robert H. Jackson* (Indianapolis: Bobbs-Merrill, 1958).

JAY, JOHN
Chief Justice, 1789–95

- Born: Dec. 12, 1745, New York, N.Y.
- Education: King's College (Columbia University), B.A., 1764; read law with Benjamin Kissam in New York, N.Y.
- Previous government service: secretary, Royal Boundary Commission, 1773; Continental Congress, 1774, 1775, 1777, president, 1778–79; New York Provincial Congress, 1776–77; chief justice, New York State, 1777–78; U.S. minister to Spain, 1779; U.S. secretary of foreign affairs, 1784–89
- Appointed by President George Washington Sept. 24, 1789, to be the first chief justice of the United States

- Supreme Court term: confirmed by the Senate Sept. 26, 1789, by a voice vote; resigned June 29, 1795
- Subsequent government service: governor of New York, 1795–1801
- Died: May 17, 1829, Bedford, N.Y.

John Jay was one of the great founders of the United States. Jay was elected to the First Continental Congress in 1774 and at first resisted independence from Great Britain, but he became a fervent patriot in 1776, after the Declaration of Independence.

Jay was the main author of the New York state constitution of 1777. In 1778, he was elected president of the Continental Congress. During the 1780s he was involved in making and conducting foreign policy for the United States.

Although Jay did not attend the Constitutional Convention of 1787, he worked effectively for ratification of the federal Constitution. Toward this end, he wrote five of The Federalist Papers (Nos. 2, 3, 4, 5, and 64), which were originally printed in New York newspapers to support the ratification of the U.S. Constitution. Other authors were James Madison and Alexander Hamilton, who were leaders in the movement to write and ratify the Constitution. Later, Hamilton became U.S. secretary of the Treasury under President George Washington, and Madison served as a Virginia member of the House of Representatives in the first federal Congress. Madison became the fourth President of the United States in 1809.

President George Washington appointed Jay as the first chief justice of the United States. The most important decision over which Jay presided was Chisholm v. Georgia (1793), in which the Court ruled that citizens of one state could bring suit in a federal court against another state.

Overall, however, Jay was disappointed at the apparent weaknesses and insignificance of the Court in comparison to the executive and legislative branches of the federal government. Political leaders seemed to pay slight attention to the Court, and few cases were taken to it. For this reason, Jay resigned as chief justice in 1795 to become governor of New York, a position for which he was elected while serving as chief justice.

President John Adams wanted to reappoint Jay as chief justice in 1800, but Jay refused because he believed the Court lacked "the energy, weight and dignity which are essential to its affording due support to the national government." In 1801, he retired from public life.

SEE ALSO Chisholm v. Georgia

SOURCES Richard B. Morris, John Jay, the Nation and the Court (Boston: Boston University Press, 1967).

JAY TREATY (1795)

The Jay Treaty with Great Britain ignited political fireworks in Congress. President George Washington sent Chief Justice John Jay to London to negotiate a treaty that would settle American disputes with Great Britain and avoid another war between the two nations. Britain opened some of its ports in the British West Indies to U.S. trade and agreed to remove British troops from the American Northwest Territory. But the treaty did nothing to stop British searches of American ships or to settle other American grievances. Jay's controversial treaty brought into the open the growing political rift between Federalists and Jeffersonian Democratic-Republicans in Congress.

After an angry debate, the Senate ratified the treaty by a vote of 20 to 10 on June 24, 1795. Because the treaty required the United States to pay some pre–revolutionary war debts, the House of Representatives would also have to vote for the needed appropriation of funds. Senators argued that because they had ratified the treaty, the House must fund it. Members of the House felt free to act as they saw fit but eventually appropriated the money. The House has never yet failed to fund a treaty approved by the Senate.

SOURCES Alvin M. Josephy, Jr., *On the Hill: A History of the American Congress* (New York: Simon & Schuster, 1979).

JEFFERSON'S MANUAL

As Vice President from 1797 to 1801, Thomas Jefferson occupied his time by compiling a handbook on parliamentary procedure. He finished the project shortly before becoming President, and his *Manual of Parliamentary Practice* was published in 1801. Jefferson combined his reading of British parliamentary practice with his personal observations of the debates in the Senate. He concluded that specific rules were less important than the fairness and consistency with which they were enforced. It was essential, he wrote, "that order, decency, and regularity be preserved in a dignified public body."

The Senate never officially made Jefferson's manual part of its rules but regularly printed it in the *Senate Rules Manual* until 1977. By contrast, the House of Representatives formally adopted Jefferson's manual in 1837 as a supplement to its own rules and continues to include it in the *House Rules Manual*.

SOURCES Wilbur Samuel Howell, ed., *Jefferson's Parliamentary Writings* (Princeton, N.J.: Princeton University Press, 1988).

JEFFERSON, THOMAS
3rd President

- Born: Apr. 13, 1743, Goochland (now Albemarle) County, Va.
- Political party: Democratic-Republican
- Education: College of William and Mary, B.A., 1762
- Military service: none
- Previous government service: Virginia House of Burgesses, 1769–75; Second Continental Congress, 1775; committee that drafted Declaration of Independence, 1776; Virginia House of Delegates, 1776–78; governor of Virginia, 1779–81; Continental Congress,

1783–84; minister to France, 1785–89; U.S. secretary of state, 1790–93; Vice President, 1797–1801
- Elected President, 1800; served, 1801–9
- Subsequent public service: rector, University of Virginia, 1819–26
- Died: July 4, 1826, Monticello, Va.

Thomas Jefferson is considered by many to be the most intelligent man ever to occupy the White House. He was a scientist, architect, landscaper, lawyer, inventor, violinist, and philosopher (serving between 1797 and 1815 as president of the American Philosophical Society), as well as the founder and leader of the Democratic-Republican political party. At a White House reception for Nobel Prize winners, John F. Kennedy said he was hosting "probably the greatest concentration of talent and genius in this house except for perhaps those times when Thomas Jefferson ate alone."

Jefferson was born at Shadwell, his father's 10,000-acre plantation near Charlottesville, Virginia. After graduating from college, he read law for five years and was admitted to the bar in 1767. Five years later he had obtained 5,000 acres for a plantation to secure his financial independence. As a member of the Virginia Committee of Correspondence in 1774, he wrote a defense of American independence called "A Summary View of the Rights of British America," which argued that the British Parliament, elected by 150,000 British voters, had no right to control the legislatures or courts of millions of Americans, no right to prevent Americans from prohibiting the slave trade, no right to quarter British soldiers in American homes, and no right to use American taxes to support British troops in the colonies. Virginia's Williamsburg Convention could not accept all the principles and did not officially endorse the document, but it established Jefferson as one of the preeminent political theorists of the Revolution. In 1775, in response to prime minister Lord North's proposals to compromise with the colonies, Jefferson wrote "Causes for Taking

Up Arms," which inspired revolutionary sentiment and rejected the British offer. At the Continental Congress in 1776 he was chosen to write the Declaration of Independence, and with only a few changes his draft became the document signed on July 4, 1776.

Jefferson returned from Philadelphia in September 1776, was elected to the Virginia legislature, and set to work organizing a legal code for its new state government. He wrote the Statute of Virginia for Religious Freedom, which ended the status of the Episcopal church as the state's established religion and affirmed the principle of separation of church and state. He also wrote a new penal code and much of the state constitution. His bill to prohibit the importation of slaves into Virginia was passed in 1778.

In 1779 Jefferson was elected governor, but he proved an ineffective wartime leader. British troops under General Charles Cornwallis occupied the capital at Richmond, and Jefferson himself, shortly after leaving office in 1781, was almost captured by a British raiding party at his Monticello estate.

He then published *Notes on the State of Virginia,* which described the social and political life of his state. In 1783, after his wife's death, he returned to Congress, where he worked on a committee to consider the peace treaty with Great Britain and another to establish territorial government for the Northwest Territories ceded by the British; his proposals were later embodied in the Northwest Ordinance of 1787. Though Congress initially refused to include his ban on slavery in the territories when it considered his proposal in 1784, it did ban slavery in these territories in 1787. Between 1785 and 1789 Jefferson served as minister to France, so he did not participate in the Constitutional Convention of 1787. He supported adoption of the U.S. Constitution but urged the addition of a Bill of Rights.

Jefferson joined the administration of George Washington in 1790 as secretary of state. He soon became involved in a bitter rivalry with Secretary of the Treasury Alexander Hamilton over foreign policy. Hamilton favored a pro-British "neutrality" in the Franco-British wars, while Jefferson favored strict neutrality and took a pro-French position. Hamilton favored creation of a national bank; Jefferson argued that the bank exceeded the powers of the national government and favored Northern interests. At the end of 1793, after writing a report recommending closer ties to France, Jefferson resigned from the cabinet and, with James Madison, began to organize the Democratic Societies. These associations later became a political party in opposition to the Federalist faction then in power.

In 1796 Jefferson ran for President against Federalist John Adams. Jefferson received the second-highest total in the electoral college vote, and in accordance with the procedures then used, he assumed the Vice Presidency. When the Federalists passed the Alien and Sedition Acts of 1798, which made it a criminal offense to criticize the government, Jefferson opposed the tendency of the Federalists "to silence, by force and not by reason," the complaints and criticisms of the people. In response, he drafted the Kentucky Resolves, in which he argued that an unconstitutional act passed by the national government, in this case violating 1st Amendment freedoms of speech and press, may be nullified by state governments.

In the election of 1800 Jefferson and his running mate, Aaron Burr, each received the same number of votes in the electoral college (the electoral votes at that time did not distinguish between President and Vice President). Jefferson was chosen President in the contingency election held by the House of Representatives. This was the first election in the United States in which power was transferred from one party to another. It was also the first election in which the electoral college voting had been organized by parties: all but one elector voted for his party's nominees.

Jefferson was the first President to be inaugurated in the new capital, Washington, D.C. He rode to his inauguration on his own horse rather than in a carriage, and after taking the oath of office reassured his political opponents with the conciliatory words, "We are all Republicans, we are all Federalists." With the motto "That government is best which governs least," Jefferson began to overturn many of the Federalist policies. He abolished new federal judgeships that the Federalists had created in 1801; trimmed back the Treasury Department's attempts to direct the national economy; eliminated domestic taxes (especially on whiskey); turned domestic matters back to the states; and reduced the national debt. He modernized the navy but cut back on the army, though he did establish the military academy at West Point. He arranged for the purchase of the Louisiana Territory from Napoleon Bonaparte for $15 million, which doubled the area of the United States. Although the Constitution makes no mention of acquiring territory (referring only to admission of new states to the Union), Jefferson downplayed the constitutional issues to complete the transaction.

Jefferson authorized Meriwether Lewis and William Clark to organize an expedition to map and report on the vast expanse of land. Congress then established a military government for the territory, which was gradually organized into 13 states. Jefferson was also successful when he used the navy against the pasha of Tripoli and the Barbary pirates; within four years their threat to U.S. shipping was diminished after a series of American naval victories. Jefferson did have to pay $60,000 to secure the release of American prisoners of war, however.

With the nation peaceful and prosperous, in 1804 Jefferson crushed his Federalist opponent, Charles Cotesworth Pinckney, to win reelection to a second term. Jefferson then tried to remove Federalist Supreme Court justice Samuel Chase but could not secure the necessary two-thirds vote in the Senate, a result that confirmed the independence of the judiciary from political interference.

In foreign affairs Jefferson suffered setbacks. Napoleon refused to sell East or West Florida. Great Britain and France began to interfere with U.S. shipping. The Embargo Act of 1807, which forbade all foreign trade, meant hundreds of American ships sat and rotted in ports while sailors were idle and merchants lost their markets. The act was widely criticized and was repealed by Congress near the end of Jefferson's administration. Congress replaced it with the Non-Intercourse Act of 1809, a law that restored American trade to all nations except England and France, which would have to declare their respect for American shipping to restore trade. Jefferson's poor handling of maritime policy eroded his support within his own party. Though five state legislatures passed resolutions requesting that he run for a third term, Jefferson declined.

After retiring from office, Jefferson returned to Monticello and remained there for the rest of his life. The government purchased his magnificent library after the War of 1812 to form the nucleus of the second Library of Congress (the British having burned the first). Jefferson was responsible for the chartering of the University of Virginia in 1819. He designed the campus and its buildings and served as the first rector of the university. He also designed the state capitol building. Jefferson died on July 4, 1826, just a few hours before his great rival and friend John Adams, on the 50th anniversary of the signing of the Declaration of Independence.

SEE ALSO *Adams, John; Burr, Aaron; Electoral college; Madison, James; 12th Amendment; Washington, George*

SOURCES Noble E. Cunningham, Jr., *In Pursuit of Reason: The Life of Thomas Jefferson* (Baton Rouge: Louisiana State University Press, 1987). Noble E. Cunningham, Jr., *The Process of Government Under Jefferson* (Princeton, N.J.: Princeton University Press, 1978). Joseph J. Ellis, *American Sphinx: The Character of Thomas Jefferson* (New York: Knopf, 1997). Adrienne Koch, *Jefferson and Madison: The Great Collaboration* (New York:

Oxford University Press, 1969). Forrest McDonald, *The Presidency of Thomas Jefferson* (Lawrence: University Press of Kansas, 1997). Merrill D. Peterson, *Thomas Jefferson and the New Nation* (New York: Oxford University Press, 1970).

JOHNSON, ANDREW
17th President

- Born: Dec. 29, 1808, Raleigh, N.C.
- Political party: Democrat; elected Vice President as Unionist
- Education: no formal education
- Military service: military governor of Tennessee, 1862–64
- Previous government service: alderman, Greeneville, Tenn., 1829–30; mayor of Greeneville, 1831–35; Tennessee State Constitutional Convention, 1834; Tennessee House of Representatives, 1835–37, 1839–41; Tennessee Senate, 1841–43; U.S. House of Representatives, 1843–53; governor of Tennessee, 1853–57; U.S. Senate, 1857–62; Vice President, 1865
- Succeeded to Presidency, 1865; served, 1865–69
- Subsequent government service: U.S. Senate, 1875
- Died: July 31, 1875, Carter Station, Tenn.

Andrew Johnson was a Southern Democrat elected on the Unionist ticket with President Abraham Lincoln in 1864. His Southern sympathies and conciliatory Reconstruction policies caused him to flout the Reconstruction Acts passed by Congress, and he became the first and so far the only President to be impeached by the House of Representatives and tried by the Senate. This conflict with Congress weakened the Presidency for the remainder of the century.

Johnson's father was a laborer and his mother a barmaid. His father died when he was three, and his mother barely survived by sewing and taking in laundry. She could not afford to send him to school, and Johnson became a tailor's apprentice

at 14. He and his brother opened their own tailor shop in Carthage, North Carolina; then, at 18, he opened his own shop in Greeneville, Tennessee. He married the next year and his wife, Eliza, taught him how to read, write, and count. He learned how to speak in public by participating in a debating society at a nearby college.

Johnson became active in local politics, identifying with poor whites and denouncing the rich planters and financiers. As governor of Tennessee, he supported free public education. He also supported slavery (and actually owned several slaves himself) and attacked abolitionists. But he broke with his party while he was in the Senate to support homesteading on Western lands (providing 160 acres for each settler who worked the land for five years), eventually getting the Homestead Act passed by Congress in 1862.

Johnson ran for the Democratic nomination for President in 1860, but was never in real contention. He supported Democrat John C. Breckinridge over Lincoln in the election.

When the Civil War came, Johnson denounced the secessionists, and by June 1861 he was the only Southern senator to remain in his seat and refuse to join the Confederacy. He sponsored a resolution in the Senate declaring that the aim of the war was reunion and not the emancipation of slaves.

President Lincoln appointed Johnson military governor of Tennessee in 1862, and he managed to end rebellion in the state by 1864. Johnson was an obvious choice for the Vice Presidential nomination, running as a Democrat with the Republican Lincoln on a coalition Unionist ticket. Only 42 days into his second term Lincoln was shot, and Johnson succeeded to the Presidency on April 15, 1865.

Johnson began his Presidency by issuing a proclamation of amnesty on May 29, 1865, to all citizens in the states that had seceded except for certain civil and military officers and citizens with property worth more than $20,000; he appointed provisional civil governors in the Southern states; he reestablished state governments on lenient terms (requiring merely that they ratify the 13th Amendment, which abolished slavery and absolved the U.S. government from paying Confederate debts); and he issued pardons to 14,000 Southern officers who applied, including General Robert E. Lee. Johnson refused to confiscate the property of former rebels. He left questions of voting rights to the states and did nothing when the new state governments instituted "black codes" that deprived former slaves of the right to vote, serve on juries, testify in lawsuits, or possess firearms (and in many states banned them from occupations other than farming). In 1866 he vetoed a civil rights bill that would have extended citizenship and legal protection to the former slaves and denounced the proposed 14th Amendment, which would have accomplished the same thing. On August 20, 1866, Johnson announced that the "insurrection" was over and that "peace, order, tranquility and civil authority now exist in and throughout the whole of the United States."

Radical Republicans in Congress fought Johnson and pushed stiffer Reconstruction measures on the South. When Congress reconvened in December 1865, it refused to seat Southern congressional delegations, thus preventing the South from obtaining a majority in Congress. In April 1866 Congress developed its own plans for Reconstruction, which would guarantee blacks the right to vote but take it away from former Confederate soldiers. In June Congress passed the 14th Amendment, guaranteeing black voting rights and due process of law. All the Southern states except Tennessee refused to ratify it, and Congress refused to lift its ban on their representation in the national legislature. In July Congress extended the life of the Freedmen's Bureau, the agency to protect freed slaves, over Johnson's veto.

To defeat the radical Republicans, Johnson organized a National Union Movement of Democrats and conservative Republicans to try to elect supporters of his Reconstruction policies in the 1866 elections. He campaigned across the Midwest for his candidates and policies. The result was that voters chose radical Republicans over the Democrats favored by Johnson, and the new Congress had a veto-proof Republican majority determined to bend the President to its will.

On March 2, 1867, Congress passed the first Reconstruction act: it divided the South into five military districts, with Freedmen's Bureau officials and military tribunals protecting the rights of blacks. The military would create a new list of voters in each state, who would, in turn, organize state constitutional conventions. The military governors could purge civil officials and state legislators whom they viewed as "disloyal." An army of occupation, 20,000 strong, enforced military rule. Johnson vetoed this Reconstruction law, which was then passed over his veto, and thereafter did as little as possible to enforce it. He began removing Republican officeholders from the executive branch and replacing them with Democrats, and he encouraged Southern states to vote against ratification of the 14th Amendment.

To prevent Johnson from interfering with congressional policies, Congress passed the Tenure of Office Act on March 2, 1867. Johnson vetoed this law, but Congress passed it over his veto. It prevented Johnson from dismissing cabinet secretaries or other high-level officials until the Senate had consented to their successors, thus giving the final word on dismissals to the Senate. It also passed a law preventing Johnson from dismissing the commander of the army without Senate consent and requiring the President to issue his military orders through the general of the army, Ulysses S. Grant.

To test the law, Johnson asked for the resignation of Secretary of War Edwin M. Stanton and then suspended him when he refused to resign. On January 13, 1868, the Senate refused to concur in Stanton's suspension. Disregarding the Tenure of Office Act, Johnson fired Stanton on February 21. Three days later the House of Representatives impeached Johnson for "high crimes and misdemeanors." The articles of impeachment concentrated on this violation of the law but added that Johnson's conduct toward Congress had involved "disgrace, ridicule, hatred, contempt and reproach." It did not include the charge by one member, George S. Boutwell, that Johnson himself was part of the plot to murder Lincoln. The Senate acquitted Johnson on May 16, 1868. The vote was 35 for conviction and 19 for acquittal, one vote short of the two-thirds majority necessary for conviction. Seven Republicans voted to dismiss the charges. The acquittal was unpopular, and all five of these senators who sought reelection were defeated.

Why did the Senate acquit Johnson? A few Republicans who favored the nomination of Ulysses S. Grant in 1868 voted to acquit because if Johnson had been removed, the president pro tempore of the Senate, Benjamin Wade, would have become President. That would have made it likely that Wade would have secured the Republican party's next Presidential nomination over Grant. Johnson agreed, even before the vote, to end his defiance of the Senate and nominate General John M. Schofield—a military man who would follow the Reconstruction policy of the Congress—to become the new secretary of war. In effect, Johnson gave up the powers and influence of his office as the price of maintaining his place in office.

In spite of the domestic turmoil and impeachment crisis, in foreign affairs the Johnson administration was quite successful. Most of the credit rests with Secretary of State William Seward, who had a free hand to enforce the Monroe Doctrine, warning European powers not to interfere in the Western Hemisphere. In 1863 the French emperor Napoleon III had put Maximilian on the throne as emperor of Mexico. At the end of the Civil War, U.S. pressure forced the French to pull their troops out of Mexico and abandon Maximilian, who soon fell victim to a Mexican firing squad. The Johnson administration tamped down a crisis with Great Britain by enforcing neutrality

laws, which prohibited U.S. citizens from using military force against other nations, against the Irish-American Fenians who made several armed forays into Canada in an attempt to annex Canadian territory. Civil War claims against Great Britain for building Confederate naval vessels that sank Union ships were sent to arbitration. In another foreign policy triumph, Secretary Seward negotiated a treaty to purchase Alaska from Russia for $7.2 million. Though at the time it was ridiculed as "Johnson's Polar Bear Garden" and "Seward's Folly," the purchase of Alaska turned out to be a great bargain. But Seward was unable to get Senate consent to acquire the Virgin Islands, Hawaii, Cuba, Puerto Rico, Greenland, or Iceland.

Andrew Johnson left office embittered, riding out of the capital without even speaking to his successor on Inauguration Day. He was defeated in a House election in 1872. When he returned to the Senate in 1875, only 13 of the 35 senators who had voted for his impeachment remained. One of them, Oliver P. Morton of Indiana, shook his hand in a gesture of reconciliation. Three months later, on vacation at his daughter's home in Tennessee, Johnson collapsed from a stroke. He requested that he be buried with a copy of the Constitution as a pillow and the Stars and Stripes for his shroud.

SEE ALSO *Grant, Ulysses S.; Impeachment; Lincoln, Abraham; Removal power*

SOURCES Michael Les Benedict, *The Impeachment and Trial of Andrew Johnson* (New York: Norton, 1973). Eric L. McKitrick, *Andrew Johnson and Reconstruction* (New York: Oxford University Press, 1988). James Sefton, *Andrew Johnson and the Uses of Constitutional Power* (Boston: Little, Brown, 1980).

JOHNSON, LYNDON B.
36th President

- Born: Aug. 27, 1908, near Stonewall, Tex.
- Political party: Democrat

- Education: Southwest Texas State Teachers College, B.S., 1930; George-town Law School, 1934
- Military service: U.S. Navy, 1942
- Previous government service: aide to U.S. Representative Richard Kleberg, 1932–34; Texas director, National Youth Administration, 1935–37; U.S. House of Representatives, 1937–49; U.S. Senate, 1949–61; Senate majority whip: 1951–53; Senate minority leader, 1953–55; Senate majority leader, 1955–61; Vice President, 1961–63
- Succeeded to Presidency, 1963; served, 1963–69
- Died: Jan. 22, 1973, Johnson City, Tex.

Lyndon Baines Johnson assumed the Presidency after the assassination of John F. Kennedy. He won passage of his Great Society domestic programs and was elected President in one of the greatest landslides in American history. He escalated U.S. involvement in Vietnam, eventually sending more than 500,000 troops to fight. Mounting casualties in an unwinnable war led to his withdrawal from the race for a second elected term in 1968.

Johnson grew up in Johnson City, Texas, which was named for his grandfather. After high school he went to California for a year, then returned home and worked on a road gang. After graduating from Southwest Texas State Teachers College he taught at a high school in Houston and in 1932 worked for Richard Kleberg, a member of the House of Representatives. In 1935 he became Texas director of the National Youth Administration, a New Deal agency, and began building a campaign organization for his political career. Meanwhile, Johnson's wife bought an Austin radio station and gradually accumulated a large fortune that made the family financially secure.

Johnson was elected to Congress in a special election in 1937 as a New Deal Democrat, and remained in the House until 1949. In 1941 he was defeated in a special election for the U.S. Senate. He was the first member of Congress to go into active duty during World War II, winning a Silver Star for gallantry in action when his plane was fired upon in the South Pacific. In July 1942 President Franklin D. Roosevelt ordered all legislators in active service to report back to Congress, and Johnson returned to the House.

In 1948, after winning a runoff Democratic senatorial primary against Texas governor Coke Stevenson by only 87 votes out of a million cast, Johnson won the general election against his Republican opponent by a 2-to-1 margin. Because of the likelihood that some of his votes in the primary were obtained fraudulently, he became known to his enemies as "landslide Lyndon."

Johnson quickly moved up the ladder in the Senate. He became the Democratic party whip in 1951, chaired the Preparedness Committee, which investigated government contracts during the Korean War, was elected minority leader in 1953, and ran the Senate as majority leader after the 1954 election returned it to Democratic control. He instituted the Johnson Rule, giving every Democratic senator, no matter how junior, at least one good committee assignment.

As Senate majority leader, Lyndon Johnson insisted that he had no power except the "power to persuade." But Johnson could be masterful in persuasion. With his aide Bobby Baker, Johnson made careful "head counts" to anticipate when he had a majority vote. He did frequent personal favors for senators and gave important committee assignments to those who voted with him. When Johnson sought to persuade another senator, wrote newspaper columnists Rowland Evans and Robert Novak, he would move in close, "his face a scant millimeter from his target, his eyes widening and narrowing, his eyebrows rising and falling. From his pockets poured clippings, memos, statistics." Mixing logic, humor, and bullying tactics, Johnson would leave his target "stunned and helpless."

As majority leader, Johnson established a remarkable record of legislation, including passage of the Civil Rights Act of 1957, the first civil rights bill since Reconstruction, and the Civil Rights Acts of 1960. In doing so, Johnson became identified as a Westerner rather than a Southerner in order to advance his Presidential ambitions—no Southern officeholder had been elected President for more than a century.

In 1960 Johnson ran for the Democratic Presidential nomination but lost to Senator John F. Kennedy on the first ballot by a 2-to-1 margin. When Kennedy offered Johnson the Vice Presidency, he accepted, to the astonishment of many of Kennedy's aides. Johnson helped Kennedy win several Southern and Western states that were decisive in the Democratic victory. As Vice President, Johnson headed the space council, which decided to put the headquarters for manned space flight in Houston, Texas. He also chaired the President's Committee on Equal Employment Opportunity and the Peace Corps Advisory Council.

On November 22, 1963, John Kennedy was assassinated in Dallas, Texas. Johnson had been in the President's motorcade, and he took the oath of office on *Air Force One,* which flew the new President, along with Jacqueline Kennedy and her slain husband, back to Washington. "All that I have I would have given gladly not to be standing here today," Johnson told the grief-stricken nation when he addressed a joint session of Congress. "Let us continue," he told the nation, announcing that he would keep Kennedy's cabinet and top aides.

Johnson continued with Kennedy's domestic programs, expanding them and labeling them the Great Society. He won passage of the Civil Rights Act of 1964, which ended racial discrimination in public accommodations, and passage of a set of programs to reduce poverty, which led to the creation of the Office of Economic Opportunity in 1964.

In the summer of 1964, Johnson was nominated by the Democrats by acclamation. He crushed his Republican opponent, conservative Barry Goldwater, winning more than 61 percent of the popular vote.

Johnson swept a large number of liberal Democrats into Congress and used his party majority to win passage of his Great Society programs. In the next two years Congress passed a federal aid to education act, health care reimbursement programs for the aged and the poor, new urban programs (including the Department of Urban Affairs), a tax cut that sparked economic growth, and a foreign trade bill that spurred U.S. exports. In 1967 Congress approved a new Department of Transportation.

Perhaps the most significant law Johnson won from Congress was the Voting Rights Act of 1965, a measure to protect the voting rights of blacks in the South; it tripled the number of black registered voters within three years, and within a decade changed the Democratic party from a party of white conservative segregationists into a biracial coalition of moderates.

In foreign affairs Johnson concentrated on U.S. involvement in Vietnam. In August 1964, after reports of attacks on U.S. naval vessels in the Gulf of Tonkin, he asked Congress for a resolution authorizing him to take all necessary measures to protect the armed forces. Soon thereafter Johnson escalated U.S. involvement, first by ordering the bombing of North Vietnam in the winter of 1965, then by ordering U.S. troops into combat in the spring. U.S. troops in Vietnam increased to 100,000 by the fall, and more than half a million by the end of 1966.

Democrats suffered large losses in the midterm elections of 1966 because of antiwar sentiment, though they retained majorities in both the House and Senate. Antiwar sentiment in the United States led to demonstrations against the war on college campuses and in Washington. With no end to the war in sight and American casualties growing rapidly, Johnson's popularity slid. By late 1966 his ability to get Congress to pass his programs had diminished.

Johnson made progress in arms control talks with the Soviet Union, though in January 1967 he signed the Outer Space Treaty with Soviet premier Aleksei Kosygin, which banned placement of nuclear weapons in earth orbit, on the moon or other planets, or in deep space. In 1968 the United States became a party to the Nuclear Nonproliferation Treaty, which prohibited the transfer of nuclear weapons to other nations and prohibited assistance to nonnuclear nations in the making or acquisition of nuclear arms.

In January 1968 the North Vietnamese launched the Tet Offensive in Saigon and other cities. Americans watched television images of the American embassy under siege, and public opposition to the war increased. In March Johnson barely defeated an antiwar Democratic challenger, Eugene McCarthy, in the New Hampshire primary. Knowing that with the Democrats so divided his renomination would be worthless, Johnson withdrew from the race on March 31. He also announced a reduction in the bombings of North Vietnam in an attempt to seek peace. But the war continued with no letup on the ground, and American casualties passed the 40,000 mark. Johnson helped his Vice President, Hubert Humphrey, secure the Democratic nomination, but his war policies hurt Humphrey, who lost the election to Richard Nixon.

In giving up his office after one elected term, Johnson followed the pattern set by other Vice Presidents who took office after the death of an incumbent. Although Theodore Roosevelt, Calvin Coolidge, and Harry Truman were subsequently elected in their own right, none of them ran immediately for a second elected term. In January 1969, an exhausted and emotionally spent Johnson retired to his ranch near Johnson City, Texas. He worked on his memoirs and helped organize his Presidential library at the University of Texas in Austin. He died of a heart attack on his beloved ranch, just one day before the Paris Peace Accord, which ended U.S. involvement in the Vietnam War, was concluded.

SEE ALSO *Gulf of Tonkin Resolution (1964); Humphrey, Hubert H.; Kennedy, John F.; Nixon, Richard M.*

SOURCES Joseph Califano, *The Triumph and Tragedy of Lyndon Johnson: The White House Years* (New York: Simon & Schuster, 1991). Robert Dallek, *Flawed Giant: Lyndon B. Johnson, 1960–1973* (New York: Oxford University Press, 1998). Robert Dallek, *Lone Star Rising: Lyndon Johnson and His Times, 1908–1960* (New York: Oxford University Press, 1991). Rowland Evans and Robert Novak, *Lyndon B. Johnson: The Exercise of Power* (New York: New American Library, 1966). Doris Kearns Goodwin, *Lyndon Johnson and the American Dream* (New York: Harper & Row, 1976). Lyndon Johnson, *Vantage Point: Perspectives of the Presidency* (New York: Holt, Rinehart & Winston, 1971). Howard E. Shuman, "Lyndon B. Johnson: The Senate's Powerful Persuader," in *First among Equals: Outstanding Senate Leaders of the Twentieth Century,* edited by Richard A. Baker and Roger Davidson (Washington, D.C.: Congressional Quarterly, 1991).

JOHNSON, RICHARD M.
Vice President

- Born: Oct. 17, 1780, Beargrass (Louisville), Ky.
- Political party: Democrat
- Education: studied law at Transylvania University, 1800–1801
- Military service: Kentucky Rifle Regiment, 1812–13
- Previous government service: Kentucky House of Representatives, 1805–6; U.S. House of Representatives, 1807–12, 1814–19, 1830–36; U.S. Senate, 1820–29
- Vice President under Martin Van Buren, 1837–41
- Subsequent government service: Kentucky House of Representatives, 1841–42
- Died: Nov. 19, 1850, Frankfort, Ky.

Richard Johnson was the only Vice President ever chosen by the U.S. Senate in a contingency election. He served in the War of 1812 as colonel of a Kentucky rifle regiment and claimed to have killed the Indian chief Tecumseh at the Battle of the Thames in 1813, a feat for which he received a sash from Congress. While a member of Congress, Richard Johnson pressed President James Madison to declare war against Great Britain. He became Andrew Jackson's key political lieutenant in Congress and helped the President break the social isolation of Peggy Eaton, the wife of the secretary of war who was accused of adultery, in Washington society. He was rewarded in 1836 when Jackson advised Martin Van Buren, the Democratic Presidential nominee, to put Johnson on the ticket as his running mate.

The Democratic national convention had little enthusiasm for Johnson, fearing that his reputation for running a saloon in Louisville and his relationship with an African-American slave woman would hurt the ticket. Virginia announced that it would not support the Vice Presidential nominee in the election. The Whigs ran William Harrison, known as the Hero of Tippecanoe, for President, and the Democrats countered with a song that went, "Rumpsey Dumpsey, rumpsey dumpsey, Colonel Johnson killed Tecumseh!" With Virginia supporting William Smith and Maryland, South Carolina, Georgia, and Tennessee supporting John Tyler, the electoral college did not give Johnson a majority vote. He got 147 electoral votes, missing a majority by one vote, while his running mate, Van Buren, won the Presidency handily with 170. The Senate, in accordance with the 12th Amendment, chose the Vice President. It had to choose between the top two vote-getters, Johnson and Whig candidate Francis Granger. On the first vote the Senate elected Johnson, 33 to 16.

Johnson played no significant role in Van Buren's administration. The Democrats refused to renominate him in 1840 and, in fact, made no nomination for Vice President. Nevertheless, Johnson received 48 electoral college votes for Vice President—almost half of those coming from his old enemy Virginia—but the Whig ticket won the election.

In 1841 Johnson returned to Kentucky to serve in the legislature. In 1844 he made a tour of Northern states, hoping in vain to drum up support for a run for the Presidency, but he received few votes at the Democratic convention.

SEE ALSO *Electoral college; 12th Amendment*

SOURCES Leland W. Meyer, *The Life and Times of Colonel Richard M. Johnson of Kentucky* (New York: Columbia University Press, 1932).

JOHNSON, THOMAS
Associate Justice, 1791–93

- Born: Nov. 4, 1732, Calvert County, Md.
- Education: Studied law under Stephen Bordley, Annapolis, Md.
- Previous government service: Maryland Provincial Assembly, 1762; Annapolis Convention, 1774; Continental Congress, 1774–77; governor of Maryland, 1777–80; Maryland House of Delegates, 1780, 1786–88; Maryland Ratifying Convention, 1788; chief judge, General Court of Maryland, 1790–91
- Appointed by President George Washington as a recess appointment Aug. 5, 1791; replaced John Rutledge, who resigned; nominated by Washington Oct. 31, 1791
- Supreme Court term: confirmed by the Senate Nov. 7, 1791, by a voice vote; resigned Jan. 16, 1793
- Died: Oct. 26, 1819, Frederick, Md.

Thomas Johnson was an American patriot who fought for the United States in the War of Independence. He became a friend of George Washington, who appointed him to the Supreme Court in 1791.

Johnson served on the Court for only 14 months and wrote only one opinion for the Court. President Washington later appointed Johnson to the committee that planned the new federal city. In 1795, Johnson refused Washington's offer to become secretary of state, and he retired from public life.

JOHNSON V. TRANSPORTATION AGENCY OF SANTA CLARA COUNTY

- 480 U.S. 616 (1987)
- Vote: 6–3
- For the Court: Brennan
- Concurring: O'Connor and Stevens
- Dissenting: White, Scalia, and Rehnquist

In 1978 the Transportation Agency of Santa Clara County, California, created an affirmative action plan to bring about fair representation in its work force of women, minorities, and disabled people. Affirmative action refers to programs or policies to provide opportunities to individuals on the basis of membership in certain groups, such as racial, ethnic, or gender categories that have been discriminated against in the past. The Santa Clara plan did not set aside a certain number of jobs for minorities, women, or the disabled. Rather, it set annual goals as guidelines for decisions about hiring and promoting workers so that eventually there would be "a work force whose composition reflected the proportion of minorities and women in the labor force."

In 1979 the Santa Clara County Transportation Agency gave notice of a vacancy for the job of road dispatcher. This was a craftworker position, a high-level, skilled job category. None of the 238 jobs in the agency's craftworker category was held by a woman. Paul Johnson and Diana Joyce were the leading candidates, among 12 applicants, for the vacant position.

The interviewers rated both Johnson and Joyce as well qualified. Johnson, however, had a slightly higher job interview score than Joyce did, and the selection

panel recommended that he get the position. Nevertheless, Diana Joyce got the job. So Johnson filed a complaint under the federal Civil Rights Act of 1964. He claimed that he was denied the job because of his sex.

The Issue This was the first case to test the legality of sex-based affirmative action plans under Title VII of the Civil Rights Act of 1964. Did the Santa Clara affirmative action plan violate Title VII of the 1964 Civil Rights Act, which prohibits an employer from depriving "any individual of employment opportunities . . . because of such individual's race, color, religion, sex, or national origin"? Did Santa Clara's voluntary sex-based affirmative action plan deprive Johnson of his 14th Amendment right to "equal protection of the laws"?

Opinion of the Court The Supreme Court upheld the Santa Clara Transportation Agency's affirmative action plan. Justice William Brennan wrote that it could be legal under Title VII of the 1964 Civil Rights Act to remedy imbalances of female and male workers in a skilled job category. This affirmative action plan was legal, Brennan wrote, because it merely set goals but did not establish quotas for hiring female employees. Further, this plan recognized gender as only one of several factors in decisions about hiring and promotion. Finally, the plan was acceptable because it was only a temporary means to overcome past discrimination against workers based on sex.

Dissent Justice Antonin Scalia argued that this sex-based affirmative action plan was in conflict with the specific words of Title VII of the 1964 Civil Rights Act. He wrote, "The court today completes the process of converting this [Civil Rights Act of 1964] from a guarantee that race or sex will *not* be the basis for employment discrimination, to a guarantee that it often *will*. [W]e effectively replace the goal of a discrimination-free society with the quite incompatible goal of proportionate representation by race and by sex in the workplace."

Significance For the first time, the Court decided that a voluntary sex-based affirmative action plan can be used to overcome the effects of past job discrimination based on gender. Further, the *Johnson* decision clearly endorsed affirmative action as a remedy for past discrimination, as long as it is temporary.

SEE ALSO *Affirmative action; Equality under the Constitution*
SOURCES Melvin I. Urofsky, *A Conflict of Rights: The Supreme Court and Affirmative Action* (New York: Scribners, 1991).

JOHNSON, WILLIAM
Associate Justice, 1804–34

- Born: Dec. 27, 1771, Charleston, S.C.
- Education: College of New Jersey (Princeton), B.A., 1790; studied law with Charles Cotesworth Pinckney in Charleston
- Previous government service: South Carolina House of Representatives, 1794–98, Speaker, 1798; judge, South Carolina Constitutional Court, 1799–1804
- Appointed by President Thomas Jefferson Mar. 22, 1804; replaced Alfred Moore, who resigned
- Supreme Court term: confirmed by the Senate Mar. 24, 1804, by a voice vote; served until Aug. 4, 1834
- Died: Aug. 4, 1834, Brooklyn, N.Y.

William Johnson was President Thomas Jefferson's first appointee to the Supreme Court. Of all the justices of the Court under John Marshall, Johnson was the one most likely to disagree with the dominating chief justice. He has been remembered as the first great dissenter of the Supreme Court.

Justice Johnson was a hardworking member of the Court who wrote 112 majority opinions, 21 concurrences, and 34 dissents during 29 years on the Court. Only John Marshall and Joseph Story produced more opinions during Johnson's tenure on the Court.

SOURCES Donald G. Morgan, *Justice William Johnson: The First Dissenter* (Columbia: University of South Carolina Press, 1954).

JOINT COMMITTEES

Consisting of both senators and representatives, joint committees avoid the duplication of House and Senate committee hearings on the same subject. During the Civil War, Congress created a Joint Committee on the Conduct of the War. Later, it created a Joint Committee of Fifteen to oversee the reconstruction of the Southern states. The greatest effort to establish joint committees came from the Legislative Reorganization Act of 1946, which promoted joint committees as a means of streamlining and modernizing Congress. Several joint committees were established as a result of this act. At first, senators always chaired such joint committees, but the Joint Committee on Atomic Energy developed the practice of alternating the chairmanship and vice chairmanship of the committee between senators and representatives, a practice that other joint committees also adopted. By the time of the Legislative Reorganization Act of 1970, however, members of both houses had found no indication that joint committees speeded up their work and recommended against continuing them. With the exception of the Joint Economic Committee and the Joint Committees on Taxation and on the Library, the use of joint committees was abandoned. During the Iran-Contra investigation of 1987 a joint committee was appointed, but its large membership made it unwieldy and reduced its effectiveness.

SEE ALSO *Committees, congressional; Legislative Reorganization Acts (1946 and 1970)*

JOINT MEETINGS

SEE *Joint sessions*

JOINT RESOLUTIONS

Congress uses joint resolutions to propose amendments to the Constitution and to address certain specific and limited issues. Joint resolutions are identified as H. J. Res. (House Joint Resolution) or S. J. Res. (Senate Joint Resolution) followed by their number. Like bills, joint resolutions require the President's signature, and they can be vetoed. However, joint resolutions proposing constitutional amendments require state ratification rather than a Presidential signature.

Congress has frequently used joint resolutions to express its sentiments on different policies and to encourage the administration to take a stand. For instance, Congress by joint resolution called on the United States to recognize Texas's independence from Mexico in 1836. Another significant joint resolution was the Gulf of Tonkin Resolution of 1964, by which the Congress authorized President Lyndon B. Johnson to take any military action necessary to prevent communist aggression in South Vietnam.

SEE ALSO *Bills; Gulf of Tonkin Resolution (1964); Legislation; Resolutions, congressional*

JOINT SESSIONS

The Senate and House of Representatives meet in joint session to hear the President's State of the Union message and to witness the counting of the electoral ballots for President and Vice President. The first joint session took place on April 6, 1789, for the counting of the electoral ballots that chose George Washington for President.

The Senate and House are in session during joint sessions. By contrast, the two bodies recess to attend joint meetings to hear distinguished speakers such as foreign heads of state and military heroes. Joint sessions and joint meetings take place in the House chamber, which is larger than the Senate. Senators march in procession from their chamber through the Capitol to the House chamber, where seats at the front are reserved for them. Members of the cabinet and Supreme Court usually attend joint sessions. Since 1947, most joint sessions and joint meetings have been televised.

JOURNALS, CONGRESSIONAL

The Constitution (Article 1, Section 5) requires both houses of Congress to keep and publish journals of their legislative business. The Senate also keeps a journal of its executive business (treaties and nominations). Unlike the *Congressional Record*, with its lengthy speeches, the journals are short minutes that list such information as bills and resolutions introduced, committee referrals, amendments, and votes. The indexes to the journals provide a short history of all legislation, nominations, and treaties for easy reference. Journals are available for research in the government documents section of most large libraries throughout the country.

Each legislative day in the House and Senate must begin with the reading of the journal, although this formality is usually suspended by unanimous consent. Journal clerks take notes on the proceedings and prepare the histories of bills and resolutions for publication in the annual journals.

JUDICIAL ACTIVISM AND JUDICIAL RESTRAINT

Article 3, Section 1, of the U.S. Constitution says, "The judicial Power of the United States, shall be vested in one supreme Court, and in such inferior Courts as the Congress may from time to time ordain and establish." Article 3, Section 2, provides that the "judicial Power shall extend to all Cases in Law and Equity, arising under this Constitution, the Laws of the United States, and Treaties made, or which shall be made, under their Authority." Thus, the justices of the U.S. Supreme Court have the power to interpret the Constitution, and laws and treaties of the United States, in response to cases that come before the Court.

In 1796, in *Ware* v. *Hylton,* the Supreme Court held a Virginia statute void because it violated a 1783 peace treaty with Great Britain. In *Marbury* v. *Madison* (1803) the Supreme Court declared a federal law unconstitutional. These cases established the power of judicial review in the Supreme Court—the power to declare acts of the state governments and of the legislative and executive branches of the federal government null and void if they violate provisions of the Constitution. Since the early 19th century, debate has continued over how federal judges should use their powers. Should they practice restraint, or should they actively expand the scope of the Constitution in their interpretations of law, treaties, and constitutional provisions?

Judicial restraint Those who advocate judicial restraint believe the courts should uphold all acts of Congress and state legislatures unless they clearly violate a specific section of the Constitution. In practicing judicial restraint, the courts should defer to the constitutional interpretations of Congress, the President, and others whenever possible. The courts should hesitate to use judicial review to promote new ideas or policy preferences. In short, the courts should interpret the law and not intervene in policy-making.

Over the years eminent Supreme Court Justices such as Felix Frankfurter have called for judicial self-restraint. In *West Virginia State Board of Education* v. *Barnette* (1943), Frankfurter said, "As a member of this Court I am not justified in writing my opinions into the Constitution, no matter how deeply I may cherish them. . . . It can never be emphasized too much that one's own opinion about the wisdom or evil of a law should be excluded alto-

gether when one is doing one's duty on the bench."

Judicial activism Sometimes judges appear to exceed their power in deciding cases before the Court. They are supposed to exercise judgment in interpreting the law, according to the Constitution. Judicial activists, however, seem to exercise their will to *make* law in response to legal issues before the Court.

According to the idea of judicial activism, judges should use their powers to correct injustices, especially when the other branches of government do not act to do so. In short, the courts should play an active role in shaping social policy on such issues as civil rights, protection of individual rights, political unfairness, and public morality.

Chief Justice Earl Warren (who served from 1954 to 1969) and many members of the Warren Court, such as William O. Douglas, practiced judicial activism when they boldly used the Constitution to make sweeping social changes promoting such policies as school desegregation and to insure that all Americans had the opportunity to vote and to participate in U.S. society. In 1956 Justice Douglas wrote, "[T]he judiciary must do more than dispense justice in cases and controversies. It must also keep the charter of government current with the times and not allow it to become archaic or out of tune with the needs of the day."

Arguments against judicial activism Opponents of judicial activism argue that activist judges make laws, not just interpret them, which is an abuse of their constitutional power. The issue, they claim, is not whether social problems need to be solved but whether the courts should involve themselves in such problem solving. By making decisions about how to run prisons or schools, argue the critics of judicial activism, the courts assume responsibilities that belong exclusively to the legislative and executive branches of government.

Critics of judicial activism worry that court decisions that so freely "interpret" the meaning of the Constitution will undermine public confidence in and respect for the courts. Justice Byron R. White wrote in *Bowers* v. *Hardwick* (1986), "The Court is most vulnerable and comes nearest to illegitimacy when it deals with judge-made constitutional law having little or no cognizable [knowable] roots in the language or design of the Constitution."

In addition, critics point out that federal judges are not elected; they are appointed for life terms. As a result, when judges begin making policy decisions about social or political changes society should make, they become unelected legislators. Consequently, the people lose control of the right to govern themselves. Further, unlike legislatures, courts are not supposed to be open to influence from interest groups. As a result, the courts may not hear different points of view on complex social issues. In legislatures, by contrast, elected officials are responsive to such interests.

Finally, opponents of judicial activism argue that judges lack special expertise in handling such complex tasks as running prisons, administering schools, or determining hiring policies for businesses. Judges are experts in the law, not in managing social institutions.

Opponents of judicial activism point to the constitutional principle of separation of powers (the division of power among the executive, legislative, and judicial branches of the federal government) and federalism (the division of power between the states and the federal government) to justify judicial restraint. They claim that judicial activism leads to unconstitutional intrusions of federal judicial power into the duties and powers of the executive and legislative branches of government and into the state governments. In *Griswold* v. *Connecticut* (1965), Justice John M. Harlan wrote, "Judicial self-restraint . . . will be achieved . . . only by continual insistence upon . . . the great roles that the doctrines of federalism and separation of powers have played in establishing and preserving American freedoms."

Arguments for judicial activism

Supporters of judicial activism argue that it is necessary to correct injustices and promote needed social changes. They view the courts as institutions of last resort for those in society who lack the political power to influence the other branches of government.

Supporters of judicial activism point out that the courts often step in only after governors and state legislatures have refused to do anything about a problem. For example, neither state legislatures nor Congress acted to ban racially segregated schools, trains, city buses, parks, and other public facilities for decades. Segregation might still exist legally if the Supreme Court had not declared it unconstitutional in 1954.

Supporters of judicial activism also mention that local courts and judges are uniquely qualified to ensure that local officials uphold the guarantees of the Constitution. In fact, with a few exceptions, district court judges have written most of the decisions affecting local institutions. For example, an Alabama judge took over the administration of the prison system in that state because he decided that the conditions in the prisons violated the Constitution's prohibition of "cruel and unusual punishments." Similarly, a Texas judge, a man born and raised in the Lone Star State, ordered sweeping changes in the Texas prison system. And a Massachusetts judge, himself a Boston resident, ordered massive school desegregation in that northern city. In each case, the district judge adopted an activist solution to a problem. But each pursued an activist course because he felt that only such measures would enforce the dictates of the Constitution.

Judicial activists argue that the courts do not create policy as legislatures do. Judges inevitably shape policy, however, as they interpret the law. And, they argue, interpreting the law is the job of the courts. Chief Justice Earl Warren put it this way: "When two [people] come into Court, one may say: 'an act of Congress means this.' The other says it means the opposite. We [the Court] then say it means one of the two or something else in between. In that way we *are* making the law, aren't we?"

Finally, judicial activists argue that the framers of the Constitution expected the courts to interpret the Constitution actively in order to react to new conditions. As Justice Frank Murphy wrote in *Schneiderman* v. *United States* (1943), "The constitutional fathers, fresh from a revolution, did not forge a political strait-jacket for the generations to come."

SEE ALSO *Constitutional construction; Judicial power; Judicial review; Separation of powers*

SOURCES Harry H. Wellington, *Interpreting the Constitution: The Supreme Court and the Process of Adjudication* (New Haven: Yale University Press, 1991).

JUDICIAL CONFERENCE OF THE UNITED STATES

SEE *Administration of federal courts*

JUDICIAL POWER

Article 3, Section 1, of the U.S. Constitution says, "The judicial Power of the United States shall be vested in one supreme Court, and in such inferior Courts as the Congress may from time to time order and establish." Section 2 says, "The judicial Power shall extend to all Cases, in Law and Equity, arising under this Constitution, the laws of the United States, and Treaties made, or which shall be made, under their Authority."

The judicial power specified in the Constitution is the capacity and authority of the U.S. Supreme Court and lower federal courts to hear and decide cases brought before them on the basis of the supreme law—the Constitution—and federal statutes and treaties that conform to the Constitution. The judicial power of the Supreme Court therefore involves interpretation of the law to make decisions in actual controversies that adversaries bring to the Court. Hypothetical cases are not subjects for Supreme Court decisions.

Article 3, Section 2, of the Constitution says that the judicial power of the federal courts can be exercised in two categories of cases: cases defined by the parties to the controversy and cases defined by their substance. The first category includes legal disputes in which the United States is a party, in which the opposing parties are different states of the federal system, or in which the parties are citizens of different states. The second category includes cases about the meaning or application of provisions of the Constitution, federal statutes, or treaties. It also includes cases pertaining to admiralty and maritime law and to ambassadors and officials from other countries.

Judicial review, although not mentioned in the Constitution, has become an important power of the federal judiciary. Judicial review is the power of a court to declare an act of the federal or state government unconstitutional, or unlawful and void. According to this concept, judges in courts of law appraise acts of the legislative and executive branches of federal and state governments to decide whether they are in conflict with the Constitution. All courts, federal and state, may practice judicial review. The Supreme Court of the United States, however, has final say within the judicial system on whether laws or actions violate or are in accord with the U.S. Constitution.

Judicial review is based on three ideas: that the Constitution is the supreme law, that acts contrary to the Constitution are null and void, and that judges in courts of law are responsible for determining if acts violate or agree with the Constitution.

The judicial power, including the power of judicial review, is one of three coordinate and separate powers of government in the United States: legislative, executive, and judicial. Chief Justice John Marshall, in *Osborn* v. *Bank of the United States* (1824), summarized the relationships of the three branches of government:

"[T]he legislative, executive, and judicial powers, of every well constructed government, are co-extensive with each other. . . . The executive department may constitutionally execute every law which the Legislative may constitutionally make, and the judicial department [has] . . . the power of construing every such law." As Marshall wrote in *Marbury* v. *Madison* (1803), "It is emphatically, the province and duty of the judicial department, to say what the law is." The federal judicial power, then, has the authority and capacity to interpret the Constitution and laws and treaties made under it; to apply the law to decisions about cases brought before the courts; and to declare laws unconstitutional if they do not conform to the supreme law, the U.S. Constitution.

SEE ALSO *Judicial review; Jurisdiction; Marbury v. Madison; Separation of powers*

SOURCES Henry J. Abraham, *The Judicial Process* (New York: Oxford University Press, 1993).

JUDICIAL REVIEW

Judicial review is the power of the judiciary, or the courts, to determine whether the acts of other branches of government are in accordance with the Constitution. All courts, federal and state, may exercise the power of judicial review, but the Supreme Court of the United States has the final judicial decision on whether laws or actions of local, state, or federal governments violate or conform to the U.S. Constitution, the highest law of the land.

Judges use their power of judicial review only in cases brought before the courts. They consider only actual controversies, not hypothetical questions about the Constitution. Congress cannot, for example, ask the Supreme Court for its advice about whether a bill is constitutional. The Court would make this kind of decision only if the bill became a law and someone challenged it.

Judicial review is not mentioned in the Constitution. However, before 1787 this power was used by courts in several of the American states to overturn laws that conflicted with the state constitution.

Judicial review of state laws The federal judiciary's power to review state laws is implied in Articles 3 and 6 of the U.S. Constitution. Article 3 says that the federal courts have power to make judgments in all cases pertaining to the Constitution, statutes, and treaties of the United States.

Article 6 implies that the judicial power must be used to protect and defend the authority of the U.S. Constitution with respect to the laws and constitutions of the states: "This Constitution, and the Laws of the United States which shall be made in Pursuance thereof; and all Treaties made, or which shall be made under the authority of the United States, shall be the supreme Law of the Land; and the Judges in every State shall be bound thereby, any Thing in the Constitution or Laws of any State to the Contrary notwithstanding." Furthermore, Article 6 declares that all officials of the federal and state governments, including all "judicial Officers, both of the United States and of the several States, shall be bound by Oath or Affirmation, to support this Constitution."

To establish a judicial system for the United States, Congress enacted the Judiciary Act of 1789. Section 25 of this statute provided for review by the U.S. Supreme Court of decisions by state courts that involved issues of federal law.

On the basis of Articles 3 and 6 of the U.S. Constitution and Section 25 of the Judiciary Act of 1789, the Supreme Court in 1796 (*Ware* v. *Hylton*) exercised the power of judicial review to strike down a law of the state government of Virginia. According to the Supreme Court, the Virginia law, which protected Virginia citizens with debts to British creditors from having to pay, was unconstitutional because it violated the 1783 Treaty of Paris, which guaranteed that prewar debts owed to the British would be paid. This judicial decision was generally viewed as consistent with the words of the U.S. Constitution and the intentions of its framers.

Judicial review of federal laws and actions An open-ended and troublesome question of the founding period was whether the power of judicial review could be used to nullify acts of the legislative or executive branches of the federal government.

In 1788 Alexander Hamilton argued in *The Federalist* No. 78 for judicial review as a means to void all governmental actions contrary to the Constitution. He maintained that limitations on the power of the federal legislative and executive branches in order to protect the rights of individuals "can be preserved in practice no other way than through . . . courts of justice, whose duty it must be to declare all acts contrary to . . . the Constitution void. Without this [power of judicial review], all the reservations of particular rights or privileges would amount to nothing."

Hamilton concluded, "No legislative act, therefore, contrary to the Constitution, can be valid. . . . [T]he interpretation of the laws is the proper and peculiar province of the courts. A constitution is . . . a fundamental law. It therefore belongs to [judges] to ascertain its meaning as well as the meaning of any particular act proceeding from the legislative body."

Marbury v. Madison The ideas on judicial review in *The Federalist* No. 78 were applied by John Marshall, chief justice of the United States, in *Marbury* v. *Madison* (1803). The specific issue and decision in this case are of little interest or consequence today. However, Chief Justice Marshall's argument for judicial review, which firmly established this power in the federal government's system of checks and balances, has become a strong instrument of the federal courts in securing the constitutional rights of individuals.

In *Marbury* v. *Madison,* the Supreme Court was confronted with an act of Congress that conflicted with a provision of the United States Constitution. The question,

in Marshall's words, was "whether an act, repugnant to the constitution, can become the law of the land." He answered that the Constitution is "the fundamental and paramount law of the nation, and consequently, . . . an act of the legislature repugnant to the constitution is void." Marshall argued, from the supremacy clause of Article 6, that *no* act of Congress that violates any part of the Constitution can be valid. Rather, he wrote, it must be declared unconstitutional and repealed.

Marshall concluded with his justification for the Supreme Court's power of judicial review:

It is, emphatically, the province and duty of the judicial department, to say what the law is. . . . So, if a law be in opposition to the constitution; if both the law and the constitution apply to a particular case, so that the court must either decide that case, conformable to the law, disregarding the constitution; or conformable to the constitution, disregarding the law; the court must determine which of these conflicting rules governs the case; this is of the very essence of judicial duty. If then, the courts are to regard the constitution, and the constitution is superior to any ordinary act of the legislature, the constitution, and not such ordinary act, must govern the case to which both apply.

Marshall used three provisions of the Constitution to justify his arguments for judicial review. The first was Article 3, Section 2, which extends the judicial power to "all Cases, in Law and Equity, arising under this Constitution." Marshall argued, "Could it be the intention of those who gave this power, to say, that in using it, the constitution should not be looked into? That a case arising under the constitution should be decided, without examining the instrument under which it arises? This is too extravagant to be maintained."

Second, Article 6 requires judges to pledge "to support this Constitution."

Marshall wrote, "How immoral to impose [this oath] on them, if they were to be used as the instruments . . . for violating what they swear to support!"

Third, Marshall pointed out "that in declaring what shall be the supreme law of the land [Article 6], the constitution itself is first mentioned; and not the laws of the United States, generally, but those only which shall be made in pursuance of the constitution, have that rank."

Finally, Chief Justice Marshall stated "the principle, supposed to be essential to all written constitutions, that a law repugnant to the constitution is void; and that courts, as well as other departments [of the government], are bound by that instrument."

Checking and balancing At times, the Supreme Court's use of judicial review has frustrated and angered both Presidents and Congress. Sometimes the federal judiciary lags behind public opinion—for instance, when conservative Supreme Court justices declared popular New Deal programs unconstitutional during the 1930s. Yet in 1937, when President Franklin D. Roosevelt proposed to "pack" the Court with extra justices to protect New Deal programs, Congress blocked the plan and defended the independence of the judiciary.

Sometimes the judiciary takes the lead in promoting new policies before the public—or their elected representatives in Congress—have accepted them. Many members of Congress were outraged over such decisions as *Brown v. Board of Education* (1954), which ended racially segregated schools, *Engle v. Vitale* (1962), which prohibited prayer in public schools, and *Roe v. Wade* (1971), which permitted abortion.

Congress can pass legislation to try to meet the Court's objections to a law it has overturned. Or two-thirds of Congress can propose a new amendment to the Constitution to overturn the Court's ruling. For instance, when the Supreme Court ruled a federal income tax unconstitutional, Congress responded with the 16th Amendment (ratified in 1913) to permit such a tax.

At other times, the Court makes changes by itself. Some have said that the Supreme Court "follows the election returns." This means that the Court has reversed some of its opinions because of shifts in national politics and public attitudes. For instance, even though Franklin Roosevelt failed to "pack" the Court, some of the conservative justices began to shift their votes in favor of the New Deal's liberal programs, which the public had endorsed by overwhelmingly reelecting Roosevelt and his supporters in Congress. New Presidents appoint new judges who often think differently about legal issues than the previous majority on the Court. Congress has the power to impeach federal judges, but it can do so only in cases of criminal misbehavior, rather than because of the way a judge thinks and votes. Instead, the Senate scrutinizes federal judges before they go on the bench and does not hesitate to reject a judge it considers too extreme or out of step with public opinion.

Significance of judicial review James Madison spoke with foresight during the first federal Congress when, on June 8, 1789, he predicted that the "independent tribunals of justice [federal courts] will consider themselves in a peculiar manner the guardians of those [constitutional] rights . . . [and] resist every encroachment upon rights expressly stipulated . . . by the declaration [bill] of rights."

During the more than 200 years of its existence, the Supreme Court has used its power of judicial review to overturn more than 150 acts of Congress and more than 1,000 state laws. The great majority of these invalidations of federal and state acts have occurred during the 20th century. The Supreme Court declared only 3 federal acts and 53 state laws unconstitutional from 1789 until 1868. Most of the laws declared unconstitutional since 1925 have involved civil liberties guaranteed by the Bill of Rights and subsequent amendments concerned with the rights of individuals. Thus, the Supreme Court has become the guardian of the people's liberties that James Madison said it would be at the inception of the republic.

SEE ALSO *Constitutional democracy; Constitutionalism; Court-packing plan (1937); Judicial power; Marbury v. Madison; Nominations, confirmation of; Separation of powers; Ware v. Hylton*

SOURCES Robert Lowry Clinton, *Marbury v. Madison and Judicial Review* (Lawrence: University Press of Kansas, 1989). John H. Ely, *Democracy and Distrust: A Theory of Judicial Review* (Cambridge: Harvard University Press, 1980). Leon Friedman, *The Supreme Court* (New York: Chelsea House, 1987). Kermit L. Hall, *The Supreme Court and Judicial Review in American History* (Washington, D.C.: American Historical Association, 1985). Edward Keynes with Randall K. Miller, *The Court vs. Congress: Prayer, Busing, and Abortion* (Durham, N.C.: Duke University Press, 1989). Christopher Wolfe, *The Rise of Modern Judicial Review* (New York: Basic Books, 1986).

JUDICIARY ACT OF 1789

Article 3 of the U.S. Constitution provides for a Supreme Court to exercise the "judicial Power of the United States." It also empowers Congress to provide through legislation "such inferior Courts as [it] may from time to time ordain and establish." The first federal Congress passed the Judiciary Act of 1789 to establish the structure of the federal court system under the Supreme Court of the United States.

This 1789 law created two lower levels of federal courts. At the lowest level, it created 13 federal district courts, one for each of the 13 states. At the next level, it established three circuit courts to hear appeals from the district courts. At the top of the three-level federal judiciary was the Supreme Court, consisting of the chief justice of the United States and five associate jus-

tices. (In 1863 Congress increased the number to eight associate justices.)

The Judiciary Act of 1789 stipulated that the Supreme Court, as the court of last resort, would hear questions of law on appeal from lower federal courts. Section 25 of this law gave the Supreme Court the power to exercise judicial review over the highest state courts when they made decisions that involved issues of federal law or the U.S. Constitution.

Greatly expanded and with the addition of appellate courts, the basic structure of the federal judiciary remains today essentially the same as when it was first created.

SEE ALSO *Federal judicial system*

SOURCES Maeva Marcus, ed., *Origins of the Federal Judiciary: Essays on the Judiciary Act of 1789* (New York: Oxford University Press, 1992).

JUDICIARY ACT OF 1869

This federal law set the number of Supreme Court justices at nine, the number that sits on the Court today. It also reformed the circuit courts by establishing a separate circuit court judiciary of nine members, one for each of nine new circuits or regions of the United States. Justices of the Supreme Court still had circuit-riding duties, but they were greatly decreased by the law; now they had to attend circuit court proceedings only once every two years.

SEE ALSO *Circuit Courts of Appeals*

JUDICIARY ACT OF 1891

This federal law created a new intermediate level for the federal judiciary—nine U.S. Circuit Courts of Appeals (renamed Courts of Appeals in 1948). It eliminated the need for Supreme Court justices to participate in deciding circuit court cases.

However, it retained the old circuit courts, which were not eliminated until 1911, when their work was assigned to the federal district courts, the lowest level of the federal judicial system.

The nine Courts of Appeals were staffed with three judges each. Since 1891 the number of the Courts of Appeals has increased to 13, one for each of 11 circuits or regions of the United States. In addition, there is the Court of Appeals for the District of Columbia Circuit and the Court of Appeals for the Federal Circuit. The basic structure of the federal judiciary today, however, was put in place by the Judiciary Act of 1891.

SEE ALSO *Courts of Appeals; Federal judicial system*

JUDICIARY ACT OF 1925

This Judiciary Act gave the U.S. Supreme Court expanded power to decide which cases it would accept or reject from lower courts. By limiting the number of cases the Court was required to accept, the Judiciary Act left the Court free to concentrate on cases of great national and constitutional significance.

By sharply limiting the number of cases that would go to the Supreme Court, the 1925 act enhanced the authority and prestige of the Courts of Appeals. These appellate courts became the final review courts for the great majority of appellate cases.

JUNKETS

The press often criticizes members of Congress who travel abroad at government expense for taking "junkets." The term implies that the trip is as much or more for personal pleasure as for official business and is just another congressional perk, or privilege of office. Indeed, the origin of the word *junket* suggests a good time: it comes from an old English word, *jonket*,

for the woven reed baskets used to carry foods for picnics and other outings. Some members travel more frequently than others, but most congressional travel is related to the members' committee assignments, including military policy, foreign relations, international commerce, and interparliamentary activities (that is, meetings with legislative branches in other countries).

To explain the purpose and findings of their trips to the public, members usually prepare a formal report for publication after their return. Advocates of congressional travel argue that regardless of the official reason, international travel is useful because it allows members to escape from parochialism (cultural and geographic narrowness) and broaden their perspectives on the world issues upon which they must vote.

SEE ALSO *Interparliamentary relations; Perks, congressional*

JURISDICTION

The extent or scope of a court's authority to hear and decide a case properly brought to it is its jurisdiction. There are two types of jurisdiction: original and appellate.

Original jurisdiction is the authority of a court to hear and decide a case for the first time. In general, courts of original jurisdiction are minor courts or trial courts. Federal district courts, for example, are courts of original jurisdiction. Article 3, Section 2, of the U.S. Constitution states that the U.S. Supreme Court has original jurisdiction only in suits involving ambassadors from other countries and in suits to which a state of the United States is a party. For instance, the Court had original jurisdiction in *Georgia* v. *South Carolina* (1990), a case involving the correct location of a boundary between the two states. In all cases except the types listed above, the U.S. Supreme Court has appellate jurisdiction, which is the authority of a court to hear and decide cases brought on appeal from a lower court.

Indeed, the U.S. Supreme Court is primarily an appellate court. Throughout its history, the Court has exercised original jurisdiction in fewer than 160 cases. Article 3, Section 2, of the Constitution provides that "the Supreme Court shall have appellate Jurisdiction, both as to law and fact" with only a few exceptions. However, Article 3 also says that Congress has the power to regulate the nature and scope of the Supreme Court's power of appellate jurisdiction. Using this power, Congress passed the Judiciary Act of 1925 to give greater authority to the Court to decide which cases it would accept or reject on appeal from lower courts. The result was to greatly reduce the number of cases in the Court's caseload.

SEE ALSO *Judicial power*

JUST COMPENSATION

The 5th Amendment to the U.S. Constitution states, "No person shall be . . . deprived of life, liberty, or property, without due process of law; nor shall private property be taken for public use without just compensation." The 5th Amendment recognizes the property rights of individuals and guarantees that the government must provide fair payment to a person whose property is taken for public use. Just compensation is determined by the market value of the property—the amount of money a willing buyer would pay a willing seller for the property in an open and free marketplace. In *Chicago, Burlington & Quincy Railroad Co. v. Chicago* (1897) the Supreme Court ruled that state and local governments are required to pay "just compensation" when taking private property for public use. In this case a public street in Chicago was opened across a privately owned railroad track.

SEE ALSO *Eminent domain*

JUSTICES OF THE SUPREME COURT

There are nine seats on the U.S. Supreme Court: one chief justice and eight associate

justices. The number of justices is set by Congress. The Judiciary Act of 1789 created a Supreme Court of six members: five associate justices and a chief justice.

The size of the Court remained at six members until the Judiciary Act of 1801 reduced the number to five. A year later, however, the Judiciary Act of 1802 restored the six-member Court. Congress added a seventh justice in 1807, eighth and ninth justices in 1837, and a tenth justice in 1863.

In 1866, however, Congress reduced the Court to seven members. Through this measure, the Republican party majority in Congress deprived President Andrew Johnson, whom it opposed, of an opportunity to appoint new justices to the Court. After the election of the popular Ulysses S. Grant to the Presidency, Congress passed the Judiciary Act of 1869, which set the Court's membership at nine. This number has remained the same ever since. In 1937, President Franklin Roosevelt attempted unsuccessfully to expand the membership of the court to gain support on the Court for his New Deal programs. He proposed adding one justice to the Supreme Court for every member over 70 years of age, up to a total of six additional justices.

Duties and powers   The chief justice of the United States is the presiding officer of the Supreme Court and the head of the federal judiciary. The eight associate justices work with the chief justice to decide cases that come before the Court. They are expected to make and justify these decisions within the framework of the Constitution and the system of law based on it. The associate justices also collaborate with each other and the chief justice to review all petitions for certiorari (appeals from lower courts for a hearing before the Supreme Court) and decide which of these appeals will be accepted for Supreme Court review.

All associate justices are equal in their formal power. Each associate justice has one vote, and each vote has the same weight. Some justices, however, tend to have more influence than others on Court decisions because they have more skill in reasoning and arguing about legal issues. Some are better at managing human relationships and leading their peers. The justices with more ability to persuade through the force of intellect or personal style are likely to have a greater impact on the deliberations and decisions of the Court. For example, Justice William Brennan, who served on the Court from 1956 to 1990, had great ability to influence other justices. His colleague Thurgood Marshall said, "There's nobody here that can persuade the way Brennan can persuade."

The chief justice has more authority and power than the associate justices, even though he, too, has only one vote. The chief justice, in presiding over the Court in conference, is able to direct and structure the discussion of cases and thereby to influence the outcome. Further, the chief justice has authority to make up the first version of the discuss list, which is the list of petitions for Supreme Court review that will be considered. By carrying out this task, the chief justice has great power in determining which cases are to be denied a hearing by the Court. Another example of the special role of the chief justice is his power to assign the task of writing the Court's opinion on a case, whenever he is part of the majority in the initial vote in conference. When the chief justice is not part of the majority, the senior justice in the majority makes the assignment. The chief justice tends to make most of the assignments and is thereby able to influence the contents and style of the Court's opinion. For example, the chief may decide to write the opinion of the Court in very important cases, or he may choose an associate justice who tends to agree with him.

Appointment and terms   Both the chief justice and associate justices are appointed by the President of the United States "with the Advice and Consent of the Senate," as provided by Article 2, Section 2, of the U.S. Constitution. They "hold their Offices during good Behaviour," as prescribed by Article 3, Section 1, of the Constitution. This clause practically guarantees appointment for life for those who

desire it. Fifty justices have died in office. The justice who served the longest on the Court was William O. Douglas, whose tenure was 36 years and 7 months (1939–75). Justice Oliver Wendell Holmes was the oldest person to serve on the Court. He retired in 1932 at age 90, after 30 years on the Court. By contrast, two associate justices served less than two years. Thomas Johnson had served less than 14 months when he died in 1793, the shortest tenure in the history of the Court. Justice James F. Byrnes served only 16 months before resigning in 1942 to take another job in the federal government.

Salaries of the justices   Article 3, Section 1, of the Constitution says, "The Judges, both of the supreme and inferior Courts, shall . . . at stated Times, receive for their Services, a Compensation, which shall not be diminished during their Continuance in Office." This provision was designed to keep the judiciary independent by protecting federal judges from threats of pay cuts that might influence their decisions.

The Judiciary Act of 1789 set the chief justice's annual salary at $4,000 and an associate justice's salary at $3,500. Since then, Congress has appropriated larger amounts for judicial salaries. The 1989 Ethics Reform Act provided an annual salary of $124,000 for the chief justice and $118,600 for the associate justices. In 2000 the associate justices received an annual salary of $173,600, and the chief justice was paid $181,400.

Membership of the Court   Since 1789, 96 people have served as associate justices of the U.S. Supreme Court. Five of the 16 chief justices served as associate justices before becoming chief justice: John Rutledge, Edward D. White, Charles Evans Hughes, Harlan F. Stone, and William H. Rehnquist. The overwhelming majority of the justices, including 14 of 16 chief justices, have been white men affiliated with Protestant religions.

The first woman associate justice is Sandra Day O'Connor, who was appointed in 1981 by President Ronald Reagan. Ruth

Bader Ginsburg, appointed by President Bill Clinton in 1993, is the second woman to become an associate justice. Two associate justices have been African Americans: Thurgood Marshall, who served from 1967 to 1991, and Clarence Thomas, who was appointed in 1991 to replace Justice Marshall.

Six associate justices have been Jewish: Louis D. Brandeis, Benjamin Cardozo, Felix Frankfurter, Arthur Goldberg, Abe Fortas, and Ruth Bader Ginsburg.

Eight associate justices have been Roman Catholics: Edward D. White, Joseph McKenna, Pierce Butler, Frank Murphy, William Brennan, Antonin Scalia, Anthony Kennedy, and Clarence Thomas. White also served as chief justice. Another Roman Catholic, Roger B. Taney, served only as chief justice.

SEE ALSO *Chief justice; Court-packing plan (1937); Judiciary Act of 1789; Judiciary Act of 1869; Opinions of the Supreme Court; Seniority on the Supreme Court*

JUSTICIABLE QUESTIONS

The U.S. Supreme Court has held that federal courts may deal only with cases or questions that are justiciable, that is, questions "appropriate for judicial determination" (*Aetna Life Insurance Co.* v. *Haworth,* 1937). In the *Aetna* case Chief Justice Charles Evans Hughes discussed the differences between justiciable questions or issues and those not justiciable. He emphasized that justiciable questions involve a "real and substantial controversy" that can be resolved by a conclusive decision of a court of law.

The U.S. Supreme Court does not provide advisory opinions because they do not pertain to justiciable questions: real cases that are appropriate for a judicial decision. The Court also does not accept cases that require decisions on political questions because they cannot, in the Court's opinion, be resolved on legal or constitutional grounds. Rather, political questions are those appropriate for resolution by the legislative and executive branches of government. For instance, the President, not the Court, decides whether the United States should recognize and maintain diplomatic relations with foreign governments. The Congress, not the Court, decides political questions such as how much federal money should be appropriated to maintain the U.S. armed forces.

SEE ALSO *Advisory opinions; Jurisdiction; Political questions*

JUVENILE JUSTICE

People who have not reached the legal age of adulthood (usually 18 years old) are considered juveniles under the law. There are special courts of law throughout the United States designed to meet the presumed needs of preadult lawbreakers. These juvenile courts are the core of a system of juvenile justice, with legal procedures that specify what can and cannot be done with, to, and for juveniles by various public officials, including police, prosecutors, judges, and probation officers. The juvenile justice system is separate from the adult criminal justice system.

Juveniles are required to obey the same federal, state, and local laws that adults must obey. Both juveniles and adults, for example, are required to obey laws forbidding such criminal offenses as burglary, arson, rape, and murder. Juveniles also are required to obey laws that adults do not have to obey, such as laws against running away from home, disobeying parents, refusing to attend school (truancy), drinking alcoholic beverages, or participating in consensual sexual activity. Such laws pertain to *status offenses,* so called because they apply only to those with the status of a juvenile.

In most states, people under 18 years old are sent to a juvenile court when they break the law. In a few states, such as New York, those older than 15 who commit criminal offenses are sent to an adult criminal court. In general, juveniles may be tried in an adult court when they commit serious or frequent crimes.

In a few states, such as Pennsylvania, all juveniles accused of homicide (no matter what their age) are sent directly to an adult criminal court. There, the juvenile's lawyer can try to persuade the judge that the accused youth should be transferred to a juvenile court. If the judge agrees, the case can be sent to a juvenile court.

The original purpose of juvenile courts was to provide special care and treatment for preadult offenders, with the intention of rehabilitating the offender in order to prevent repeated illegal behavior. A symbol of the special concern for preadult offenders in juvenile courts is the manner of naming the cases. The typical title of a juvenile court case is *In re Joe Dokes*, which means "in the matter of 20...." By contrast, the usual title of a criminal court case is *State* v. *Joe Dokes*, which implies that the defendant is involved in a legal contest with the state. There usually is no suggestion in the name of a juvenile court case that the preadult (Joe Dokes) must defend himself against the state. In return for the special care provided to offenders in the juvenile justice system, juveniles did not have the constitutional rights to due process of law guaranteed to adults in criminal courts, such as the right to counsel, the right to confront and cross-examine witnesses, and the protection against self-incrimination.

During the 1950s critics pointed out that juvenile courts often did not provide special concern for preadult offenders or act in their best interests. Rather, the juvenile justice system often appeared only to punish juveniles for their offenses and not to remedy their problems or address their particular needs. So the critics recommended that juveniles accused of criminal offenses should have the constitutional rights of due process, just like adults in criminal courts.

In the case of *In re Gault* (1967), the Supreme Court for the first time confronted the issue of due process rights for juvenile offenders. The Court rejected the traditional claim that a juvenile's rights are sufficiently protected by judges in juvenile courts, who act as substitute parents. Rather, the Court held that juvenile courts must provide the same basic due process rights that the U.S. Constitution guarantees to adults. Writing for the Court, Justice Abe Fortas specified four due process rights that must be provided: written notification of specific charges to the juvenile and his or her parents, assistance of a lawyer, confrontational cross-examination of witnesses, and protection against self-incrimination (the right to remain silent when questioned by prosecutors).

The constitutional rights of preadults in juvenile courts were expanded by the Court in the case of *In re Winship* (1970). The offender, Samuel Winship, was convicted of theft by a juvenile court judge. However, the evidence used to convict Winship was slight. It would not have met the standard of proof typically used in an adult criminal case, which is referred to as proof "beyond a reasonable doubt." This means that the evidence against the accused person is so great that there can be little or no doubt that the person committed the crime. The Court decided that preadults in a juvenile court should have the right to the higher standard of proof available in criminal court proceedings.

In *McKeiver* v. *Pennsylvania* (1971), a juvenile was charged with robbery, larceny, and receiving stolen goods. The defendant's lawyer requested a trial by jury because punishment for these serious offenses could be as much as five years of detention. The state refused the lawyer's request and the defendant was convicted and sentenced without a jury trial. He appealed on the grounds that the right to trial by jury, granted to adults accused of criminal offenses, was unconstitutionally denied to him.

The Supreme Court decided that due process of law for juveniles does not require a trial by jury. Writing for the Court, Justice Harry Blackmun argued that a jury trial would subject juveniles to unnecessary and disruptive adversarial proceedings without the compensating benefits of greater accuracy in fact-finding or determination of guilt or innocence. The *McKeiver* decision indicated that the Court was unwilling to extend all the rights of the criminally accused to juveniles charged with criminal offenses.

In *Schall* v. *Martin* (1984) the Court made another decision that limits the due process rights of juveniles. The Court upheld a New York law that permits a judge to order pretrial confinement for up to 17 days of a juvenile accused of a criminal offense, when there is a significant risk that the juvenile may commit a serious crime before the trial. Justice William Rehnquist emphasized that it is the state's duty to protect the community against criminal acts. The *Schall* decision has influenced other states to enact preventive detention laws similar to the New York law upheld by the Court. Justice Thurgood Marshall dissented from the Court's opinion in *Schall* v. *Martin*. He argued that preventive detention laws give power to judges to treat different juveniles unequally and unfairly.

The *McKeiver* and *Schall* decisions put certain limitations on due process rights in the juvenile justice system. The due process protections provided by the *Gault* and *Winship* decisions, however, have been firmly established. They have profoundly changed the juvenile justice system in the United States.

Before the *Gault* decision, juveniles had no due process rights. But in exchange for the lack of legal protection from the state, juveniles were supposed to receive benevolent treatment from officials. This pre-*Gault* juvenile justice system permitted competent, caring officials to readily help children. There were no complex due process procedures to get in the way of direct, discreet, and benign behavior on the part of good officials to assist troubled youths. The problem with the pre-*Gault* system was that bad or stupid officials could hurt juveniles, who had no recourse to due process procedures to protect them from abuses of the system.

The post-*Gault* juvenile justice system is concerned more with punishment and prevention of crime than with treatment and reform of troubled youth. Thus, it has become more like the adult criminal justice system, with its adversarial proceedings and guarantees of constitutional due process rights to protect the accused person against the power of the state. Older juveniles accused of serious criminal offenses are likely to be transferred to the criminal courts. Status offenses, such as truancy or disobedience, are still handled by juvenile courts in the traditional paternal and caring manner, with an emphasis on diagnosis and treatment of the psychological and social problems of the offenders.

SEE ALSO *Due process of law; In re Gault; In re Winship; McKeiver v. Pennsylvania*
SOURCES Thomas J. Bernard, *The Cycle of Juvenile Justice* (New York: Oxford University Press, 1992).

K

KANSAS-NEBRASKA ACT

SEE *Douglas, Stephen A.*

KATZ V. UNITED STATES

- 389 U.S. 347 (1967)
- Vote: 7–1
- For the Court: Stewart
- Concurring: Harlan and White
- Dissenting: Black
- Not Participating: Marshall

Charles Katz was known to be a gambler, and the Federal Bureau of Investigation (FBI) suspected him of engaging in illegal activities in making bets. In particular, the FBI believed he was using a public telephone booth to transmit information about wagers from Los Angeles to Miami and Boston. So FBI agents placed electronic devices outside a telephone booth regularly used by Katz to make his calls. The agents recorded Katz's telephone conversations in order to gather evidence of his illegal gambling activity.

At Katz's trial, the federal government used evidence of his telephone conversations to win a conviction. Katz appealed his conviction on grounds that the evidence introduced against him had been obtained illegally.

The Issue Charles Katz argued that the government had violated his 4th Amendment rights—"The right of the people to be secure in their persons, houses, papers, and effects, against unreasonable searches and seizures." Katz said that the illegally gathered evidence against him should have been excluded from his trial.

Lawyers for the federal government argued that placing a tap on the outside of a public telephone booth was not a violation of the 4th Amendment. They based their argument on the case of *Olmstead* v. *United States* (1928), which had permitted federal government use of electronic surveillance and wiretapping on the grounds that those actions outside a person's home fell outside the scope of the 4th Amendment.

Opinion of the Court In *Katz*, the Supreme Court overturned the decision in *Olmstead* v. *United States*. Justice Potter Stewart argued that the 4th Amendment protects people, not places. It protects an individual's right even in a place accessible to the public, such as a telephone booth on a street corner. Justice Stewart wrote, "[T]he Government's activities in electronically listening to and recording [Katz's] words violated the privacy upon which he justifiably relied while using the telephone booth and thus constituted a 'search and seizure' within the meaning of the Fourth Amendment."

Significance The *Katz* case expanded the scope of 4th Amendment rights to include protection against certain kinds of electronic invasions of an individual's privacy. Since the *Katz* decision, the 4th Amendment has been a means to protect individual privacy in places open to the public.

SEE ALSO *Olmstead v. United States; Searches and seizures*
SOURCES Alvin F. Westin, "Civil Liberties in the Technology Age," *Constitution* 3, no. 1 (Winter 1991): 56–64.

KENNEDY, ANTHONY M.
Associate Justice, 1988–

- Born: July 23, 1936, Sacramento, Calif.
- Education: Stanford University, B.A., 1958; London School of Economics, 1957–58; Harvard Law School, LL.B., 1961
- Previous government service: judge, Ninth Circuit Court of Appeals, 1975–88
- Appointed by President Ronald Reagan Nov. 30, 1987; replaced Louis F. Powell, Jr., who retired
- Supreme Court term: confirmed by the Senate Feb. 3, 1988, by a 97–0 vote

Anthony M. Kennedy was, for most of his career, a partner in a law firm and a teacher at the McGeorge School of Law of the University of the Pacific in Stockton, California. President Gerald Ford appointed Kennedy to be a federal appellate court judge, and between 1975 and 1988, Kennedy wrote more than 400 opinions as a federal judge on the Ninth Circuit Court of Appeals.

After his appointment to the Supreme Court in 1988, Justice Kennedy, as a moderate conservative, tended to vote in agreement with Chief Justice William Rehnquist during the 1988–89 term. In 90 percent of the cases, he voted in agreement with the chief justice. Since then, he has shown more independence.

In *Church of the Lukumi Babalu Aye v. City of Hialeah* (1993), Kennedy wrote the decision for the Court to strike down a city's ban on ritual animal sacrifice, practiced by the followers of the Santera religion. Kennedy held that the city government of Hialeah, Florida, had violated the 1st Amendment right to free exercise of religion.

In *Romer* v. *Evans* (1996), Justice Kennedy wrote the Court's opinion to strike down an amendment to the Colorado constitution that prohibited legislation created specifically to protect the rights of homosexuals.

KENNEDY, EDWARD M.

- Born: Feb. 22, 1932, Boston, Mass.
- Political party: Democrat
- Education: Harvard College, A.B., 1956; International Law School, The Hague, graduated, 1958; University of Virginia Law School, graduated, 1959
- Senator from Massachusetts: 1962–
- Senate majority whip: 1969–71

Edward M. Kennedy began his Senate career in the shadow of his famous brothers, John, who was President of the United States, and Robert, who was attorney general. All three Kennedy brothers served in the Senate, but in many ways Edward Kennedy became the most effective legislator among them. Despite personal tragedies that came close to derailing his political career, over time he surprised his critics by building one of the most effective staffs on Capitol Hill and taking strong leadership on a wide variety of legislation. When Kennedy speaks, whether against apartheid— the policy of racial segregation—in South Africa or in favor of a jobs program or medical insurance, he attracts the media and focuses national attention on that issue. Nowhere did he demonstrate his ability to galvanize public opinion and frame the debate better than by his successful effort to block the Supreme Court nomination of Judge Robert Bork in 1986.

SEE ALSO *Families in Congress*
SOURCES James MacGregor Burns, *Edward Kennedy and the Camelot Legacy* (New York: Norton, 1976).

KENNEDY, JACQUELINE
First Lady

- Born: July 28, 1929, Southampton, N.Y.
- Wife of John F. Kennedy, 35th President
- Died: May 19, 1994, New York, New York

Jackie Bouvier came from a wealthy, socially prominent family and was educated in private schools. She attended Vassar College and graduated from George Washington University in 1951. She became a photographer and columnist for the *Washington Times-Herald* until she married Senator John F. Kennedy in 1953. They had two children (another died in infancy), Caroline and John, Jr. As First Lady, Jackie Kennedy became an international celebrity. Her beauty and her sense of fashion set the style for the New Frontier, for the capital, and for much of the nation. Her husband once said admiringly, "I am the man who accompanied Jacqueline Kennedy to Paris." She busied herself in a project to renovate and restore several of the public rooms of the White House with authentic period antiques. In February 1962 she showed off the results of her work in a televised tour of the White House. The program, and her efforts at restoration, received widespread acclaim. She took several trips abroad with her husband and one trip by herself to India, which were widely covered by the news media. She accompanied her husband to Dallas, Texas, and was with him on November 22, 1963, when he was assassinated. The films of her reaching over her husband's body to pull a Secret Service officer into the limousine, then standing with Lyndon Johnson as he took the oath of office on *Air Force One*, and finally accompanying her husband's remains from the plane when it landed in Washington, with blood still on her dress, are images that remain indelibly part of the national consciousness.

Jackie Kennedy emerged from seclusion after the assassination to be romantically linked with several of the wealthiest men in the world. She married Greek shipping magnate Aristotle Onassis in 1968. In 1975, after his death, she became a book editor for a New York publishing house.

SEE ALSO *First Lady; Kennedy, John F.; White House*

SOURCES Stephen Birmingham, *Jacqueline Bouvier Kennedy Onassis* (New York: Grosset & Dunlap, 1978). Mary B. Gallagher, *My Life with Jacqueline Kennedy* (New York: David McKay, 1969). Kitty Kelley, *Jackie Oh!* (Secaucus, N.J.: Lyle Stuart, 1978).

KENNEDY, JOHN F.
35th President

- Born: May 29, 1917, Brookline, Mass.
- Political party: Democrat
- Education: Harvard College, A.B., 1940; Stanford University Business School, 1940
- Military service: U.S. Navy, 1941–45
- Previous government service: U.S. House of Representatives, 1949–53; U.S. Senate, 1953–60
- Elected President, 1960; served, 1961–63
- Died: Nov. 22, 1963, Dallas, Tex.

John Fitzgerald Kennedy was the youngest person ever elected President and the first Catholic to serve as the nation's chief executive. His Presidency continued the New Deal and Fair Deal domestic programs of Franklin D. Roosevelt and Harry Truman and attempted to maintain a position of world leadership for the United States. He died in office before the promise of his Presidency could be fulfilled.

Kennedy was the second son of Rose Fitzgerald Kennedy and Joseph P. Kennedy. His father was a financier and former chairman of the Securities and Exchange Commission who was active in the Democratic party. John Kennedy was voted "most likely to succeed" at the Choate School. After serving for a time as secretary to his father, who in 1937 had been appointed ambassador to Great Britain by President Franklin D. Roosevelt, Kennedy graduated from Harvard in 1940. His senior thesis, "Appeasement at Munich," a study of the British appeasement of Adolf Hitler, was awarded high honors. It was published that same year under the title *Why England Slept*, becoming a bestseller.

Kennedy enlisted in the navy in October 1941, and on August 2, 1943, his PT Boat 109 was sunk by a Japanese destroyer. Two of the crew died, but Kennedy helped to rescue his 10 surviving crew members and was awarded the U.S. Navy and Marine Corps medal and a Purple Heart for injury. He returned home a hero, though a naval inquiry into the sinking indicated poor seamanship and command on Kennedy's part.

In 1945 Kennedy was discharged from the navy, worked briefly as a reporter for the Hearst newspapers, and the following year won election to the House of Representatives from a district in Boston. He was reelected twice and in 1952 defeated incumbent Republican Henry Cabot Lodge, Jr., for a Senate seat. Kennedy's accomplishments in Congress were minimal. He had one of the worst attendance records, which may have been due to his having Addison's disease, which required daily implantation of a steroid compound in his thighs.

Kennedy had a spinal operation in 1954, and while recuperating he wrote *Profiles in Courage*, a series of biographies of American politicians who had gone against public opinion to do what they believed was right. It was published in 1955 and won a Pulitzer Prize for biography the following year. In 1956 Kennedy campaigned for the Vice Presidential slot on the Democratic ticket, but the convention nominated Estes Kefauver instead. Later, Kennedy would say that losing that contest was the best thing that could have happened to him, because the Democratic ticket went down to a crushing defeat. Kennedy was reelected to the Senate by a large margin and began organizing a campaign for the next Presidential nomination.

In 1960 Kennedy defeated Hubert Humphrey and several others in the Democratic field in seven primary contests: in West Virginia his victory demonstrated that an overwhelmingly Protestant state would vote for a Catholic candidate. He was nominated by the Democratic convention on the first ballot, defeating Senate majority leader Lyndon Johnson handily. He then offered Johnson the second spot on the ticket, and to the surprise of many of Kennedy's advisers, Johnson accepted. Kennedy's July 15 acceptance speech offered Americans a "New Frontier" and promised "to get America moving again."

In the November election Kennedy and Johnson won a majority of electoral college votes against Republican nominee Richard M. Nixon and his running mate, Henry Cabot Lodge, but they received less than half the popular vote. At age 43, Kennedy was the youngest man ever elected President (though Theodore Roosevelt had been a year younger when he succeeded to the office).

"Ask not what your country can do for you," Kennedy said in his inaugural address, "ask what you can do for your country." He challenged youthful idealists to join the Peace Corps, which he created by executive order a few weeks later, to help with the development of other nations. He got Congress to create an Alliance of Progress in Latin America to provide foreign aid in the Western Hemisphere. He created an arms control agency to pursue arms limitations talks with the Soviet Union. He challenged the nation to put a man on the moon by the end of the decade, a feat accomplished in 1969, right on schedule.

Kennedy's New Frontier legislative program was designed to get the U.S. economy moving again after the recession and slow growth of the years under Dwight Eisenhower. It emphasized an investment tax credit and other tax breaks for business. His proposed social programs were extensions of the New Deal: federal aid to education, medical care for the elderly, urban mass transit, a new Department of Urban Affairs, and regional development for Appalachia. Much of this legislation was stalled in Congress by a coalition of Republicans and conservative Southern Democrats, though Congress did pass an increase in the minimum wage, higher Social Security benefits, and a public housing bill. It also passed a trade expansion act that significantly increased U.S. exports and opened up foreign markets.

Kennedy's refusal to provide for aid to parochial (church-run) schools in his federal aid to education bill doomed its chances. In 1962 Kennedy sent federal troops to Mississippi to ensure that James Meredith, an African-American student, could enroll at the University of Mississippi and attend classes without harassment. In 1963 he used federal troops in Alabama to enforce federal court desegregation orders. But Kennedy delayed introducing civil rights legislation until late spring 1963. On August 28, 1963, a March on Washington for Peace and Justice, which attracted more than 200,000 people, convinced Kennedy to push Congress harder for comprehensive civil rights laws. In a televised speech Kennedy identified with the marchers, saying that the grandchildren of the slaves freed by Lincoln "are not yet freed from the bonds of injustice . . . and this nation, for all its hopes and all its boasts, will not be fully free until all its citizens are free."

Kennedy's foreign policy emphasized militant anticommunism. In his inaugural address he laid down a gauntlet to communists: "Let every nation know, whether it wishes us well or ill, that we shall pay any price, bear any burden, meet any hardship, support any friend, oppose any foe to assure the survival and the success of liberty."

On April 17, 1961, an operation sponsored by the Central Intelligence Agency (CIA) against Cuban communist leader Fidel Castro began: 1,500 Cuban exiles landed in Cuba at the Bay of Pigs, hoping to spark an uprising. They were surrounded and defeated by the Cuban army.

At the last minute Kennedy refused to provide them with air cover for their operation in order to avoid overt U.S. involvement. Kennedy accepted full responsibility for the fiasco, however, noting that "victory has a hundred fathers, but defeat is an orphan." The 1,100 prisoners held by Castro were ransomed by the United States for $53 million in food and medical supplies.

After East Germany constructed the Berlin Wall to seal off the communist side of the city from the West in August 1961, Kennedy traveled to Berlin to show solidarity with its citizens. He proclaimed in German, "Ich bin ein Berliner" (I am a Berliner). In October 1962 Kennedy found out that the Soviet Union had shipped offensive missiles and bombers to Cuba; after quarantining the island with U.S. naval forces, he insisted that the Soviets remove their offensive forces, and after a tense standoff they did so. In August 1963 Kennedy and Soviet leader Nikita Khrushchev signed the Limited Test Ban Treaty, which banned nuclear testing in the atmosphere, outer space, and the oceans. Only underground testing, which presented no risk of radioactive fallout, would be permitted.

Kennedy ordered U.S. military advisers and trainers to South Vietnam, 18,000 in all, to prop up a pro-American government against attempts by communist guerrillas to undermine it. But he also decided to allow South Vietnamese military units to overthrow President Ngo Dinh Diem and install a new military leader. Although Kennedy hoped the new regime would improve the situation, the November 1, 1963, coup began a prolonged period of instability in South Vietnam that all but ensured that U.S. troops would be needed for the war.

On November 22, 1963, while visiting Dallas, Texas, to help unify the feuding state Democrats, John Kennedy was shot and killed by two bullets fired from the Book Depository building while riding in a motorcade through the center of town. Texas governor John Connally was wounded. Lee Harvey Oswald, the suspected assassin, was taken into custody by Dallas police, but two days later he was killed by Dallas nightclub owner Jack Ruby while being transferred from his cell to an office for questioning. A national commission headed by Chief Justice Earl Warren concluded that Oswald, acting alone, had shot the President in the rear of the head with a rifle and that Oswald had been mentally ill.

The conclusions of the Warren Commission remain controversial. The House Select Committee on Assassinations argued in 1979 that there were at least three shots fired rather than two. Others believe that Kennedy was killed by a bullet, fired from a nearby grassy knoll, that entered the front of his head; that theory would point to a conspiracy rather than a lone assassin. But the House panel's final conclusion was that Oswald had fired all three shots, two of which hit Kennedy and one missed. Nevertheless, conspiracy theories continue to capture the public imagination, and the answer to the question "Who killed Kennedy?" remains unclear to many Americans.

The Kennedy era was brief. It began the transition from an era of confrontation to an era of negotiation in the cold war. Kennedy was the first President born in the 20th century: his youth, vigor, and style under pressure created a "Camelot on the Potomac" for a generation of Americans who came of age during World War II and the first years of the cold war.

SEE ALSO *Assassinations, Presidential; Cuban Missile Crisis; Debates, Presidential; Health, Presidential; Johnson, Lyndon B.; Kennedy, Jacqueline; Monroe Doctrine; New Frontier; Nixon, Richard M.; Primaries, Presidential*

SOURCES Benjamin Bradley, *Conversations with Kennedy* (New York: Norton, 1975). Herbert Parmet, *J.F.K.: The Presidency of John F. Kennedy* (New York: Dial, 1983). Arthur M. Schlesinger, Jr., *A Thousand Days: John F. Kennedy in the White House* (Boston: Houghton Mifflin, 1965).

KING, WILLIAM
Vice President

- Born: Apr. 7, 1786, Sampson County, N.C.
- Political party: Democrat
- Education: University of North Carolina, B.A., 1803
- Military service: none
- Previous government service: North Carolina House of Commons, 1808–10; U.S. House of Representatives, 1810–16; secretary of legation, U.S. mission to Russia, 1816–18; U.S. Senate, 1818–44, 1848–52; president pro tempore of the Senate, 1850–52; minister to France, 1844–46
- Vice President under Franklin Pierce, 1853
- Died: Apr. 18, 1853, Cahaba, Ala.

As a Democratic party leader in the Senate, William King represented Southern regional interests, and he received votes for Vice President at several Democratic conventions. At the 1852 convention he supported James Buchanan, but when Franklin Pierce was nominated, the second spot went to King to unify the party. King was elected but was dying of tuberculosis. He went to Cuba to seek a cure, and Congress passed a law that allowed him to take the oath of office there on March 4, 1853. He returned to his plantation in Alabama and died a few weeks later. He never set foot in Washington or performed any official duties during his brief term.

KITCHEN CABINET

The kitchen cabinet is the name given to Presidential advisers who do not hold high public office but who wield great influence in the White House. President Andrew Jackson, upset because his cabinet secretaries did not rein in their wives during the Peggy Eaton affair (in which the wife of the secretary of war was accused of a prior adulterous act), relied on two newspaper editors and three minor officials in the

Treasury Department instead of convening cabinet meetings. His political enemies accused him of using a "kitchen cabinet" instead of the real one.

Earlier, Thomas Jefferson had been accused of forming an "invisible cabinet" that dealt in "backstairs influence" at the White House. Later, Theodore Roosevelt had a "tennis cabinet" and Warren Harding a "poker cabinet" of advisers. Harry Truman was criticized for relying on his Missouri Gang, and he struck back at critics by claiming to have organized his own kitchen cabinet, which included a secretary for inflation, secretary of reaction, secretary for columnists, and secretary of semantics. President Ronald Reagan invited a group of California business entrepreneurs who had been active in funding his campaigns to serve as informal advisers, but after some bad publicity the White House staff got Reagan to distance himself from them.

SEE ALSO *Brains Trust; Cabinet; Jackson, Andrew*

SOURCES William Safire, *Safire's Political Dictionary* (New York: Ballantine, 1978).

KOREMATSU V. UNITED STATES

- 323 U.S. 214 (1944)
- Vote: 6–3
- For the Court: Black
- Concurring: Frankfurter
- Dissenting: Roberts, Murphy, and Jackson

After Japan's attack on Pearl Harbor, Hawaii, on December 7, 1941, more than 100,000 Americans of Japanese ancestry were removed from their homes on the Pacific Coast of the United States and sent to internment camps in the interior of the country. Most of them spent the duration of the war, until August 1945, confined in one of these camps, even though they were loyal U.S. citizens who had done nothing to harm their homeland, the United States. One such U.S. citizen was Fred Korematsu, born and raised in Alameda County, California. He had never visited Japan and knew little or nothing about the Japanese way of life.

In June 1941, before the official U.S. declaration of war, Fred Korematsu had tried to enlist in the navy. Although the navy was actively recruiting men in anticipation of the U.S. entry into the war, the service did not allow Korematsu to enlist because of poor health. He then went to work in a shipyard as a welder. When the war began, he lost his job because of his Japanese heritage.

On May 9, 1942, General John L. DeWitt ordered all people of Japanese background or ancestry excluded from Military Area No. 1, the Pacific coastal region of the United States. This military order was authorized by an executive order of President Franklin D. Roosevelt (issued on February 19) and an act of Congress (passed on March 21).

Hoping to move to Nevada with his fiance, who was not of Japanese ancestry, Korematsu ignored the evacuation orders when they came. As a U.S. citizen, he felt the orders should not apply to him in any event. The FBI arrested Korematsu, and he was convicted of violating the orders of the commander of Military Area No. 1.

The Issue The U.S. government justified the internment in two ways. The government claimed that American citizens of Japanese ancestry were more loyal to Japan than to their own country and would spy for Japan. Second, the government claimed that because Japan had attacked the U.S. territory of Hawaii, those Americans of Japanese ancestry might have helped Japan.

Korematsu claimed that military commanders, acting under authority granted by the President and Congress, had denied more than 75,000 U.S. citizens their constitutional rights of due process. The 5th Amendment says, "No person shall be ... deprived of life, liberty, or property, without due process of law." Had the government wrongly taken away the constitutional rights of Japanese Americans?

Opinion of the Court   The Supreme Court upheld the exclusion of Japanese Americans from the Pacific coastal region. The needs of national security in a time of crisis, it said, justified the exclusion orders. The war powers of the President and Congress, specified by the Constitution, provided the legal basis for the majority decision.

Justice Hugo Black admitted that the exclusion orders forced citizens of Japanese ancestry to endure severe hardships. "But hardships are a part of war," said Black, "and war is an aggregation of hardships."

Justice Black maintained that the orders had not excluded Korematsu primarily for reasons of race but for reasons of military security. The majority ruling really did not say whether the relocation of Japanese Americans was constitutional. Rather, the Court sidestepped that touchy issue, emphasizing instead the national crisis caused by the war.

Dissent   Three justices—Frank Murphy, Robert Jackson, and Owen Roberts—disagreed with the majority. Justice Roberts thought it a plain "case of convicting a citizen as punishment for not submitting to imprisonment in a concentration camp solely because of his ancestry," without evidence concerning his loyalty to the United States.

Justice Murphy said that the exclusion orders violated the right of citizens to due process of law. Furthermore, Murphy protested that the decision of the Court's majority amounted to the "legalization of racism. Racial discrimination in any form and in any degree has no justifiable part whatever in our democratic way of life."

Murphy admitted that the argument citing military necessity carried weight, but he insisted that such a claim must "subject itself to the judicial process" to determine "whether the deprivation is reasonably related to a public danger that is so 'immediate, imminent, and impending.'"

Finally, Murphy concluded that "individuals must not be left impoverished in their constitutional rights on a plea of military necessity that has neither substance nor support."

Justice Jackson expressed grave concern about the future uses of the precedent set in this case. He wrote:

A military order, however unconstitutional, is not apt to last longer than the military emergency.... But once a judicial opinion rationalizes such an order to show that it conforms to the Constitution ... the Court for all time has validated the principle of racial discrimination in criminal procedures and of transplanting American citizens. The principle then lies about like a loaded weapon ready for the hand of any authority that can bring forward a plausible claim of an urgent need.

Significance   The *Korematsu* ruling has never been revoked by law or Supreme Court ruling. In 1980, however, Congress reopened investigations into the treatment of Japanese Americans during World War II and created the Commission on Wartime Relocation and Internment of Civilians. After nearly three years of careful examination of the evidence, which included testimony from 750 witnesses, the commission issued a report on February 25, 1983. The report concluded: "A grave injustice was done to American citizens and resident aliens of Japanese ancestry who, without individual review or any probative evidence against them, were excluded, removed, and detained by the United States during World War II."

In 1988, on the basis of the 1983 report, Congress officially recognized the "grave injustice" of the relocation and internment experience and offered payments of $20,000 as compensation to each person still living who had been detained in a relocation center.

SEE ALSO *Hirabayashi v. United States*
SOURCES Peter Irons, *Justice at War* (New

York: Oxford University Press, 1983). Carl Mydans, "Internment Remembered," *Constitution* 4, no. 1 (Winter 1992): 43. Rudolph S. Rauch, "Internment," *Constitution* 4, no. 1 (Winter 1992): 30–42.

KUNZ V. NEW YORK

- 340 U.S. 290 (1951)
- Vote: 8–1
- For the Court: Vinson
- Concurring: Black and Frankfurter
- Dissenting: Jackson

A Baptist minister, Carl J. Kunz, was denied a permit to preach on the streets of New York City by the city police commissioner. A city ordinance prohibited religious services on public streets without a permit from the city government. The ordinance did not spell out the reasons for denying someone a permit. The Reverend Mr. Kunz was denied a permit because he had a reputation for using obscene words in his speeches to denounce Catholics and Jews. Kunz defied the city ordinance and preached on a street corner without a permit. He was arrested and convicted for violating the city ordinance.

The Issue Were Carl Kunz's rights to freedom of speech and free exercise of religion, guaranteed by the 1st and 14th Amendments, violated by the New York City ordinance that was used to deny him a permit to preach in public?

Opinion of the Court The Supreme Court struck down as unconstitutional the New York City ordinance that barred worship services on public streets without a permit. Chief Justice Fred Vinson said that enforcement of the ordinance was an unconstitutional "prior restraint" (advance censorship) on an individual's rights to free speech and free exercise of religion. Vinson ruled that New York could not legally give an administrative official control over the right to speak on religious subjects without "appropriate standards to guide his action."

Dissent Justice Robert Jackson defended the restrictions on Kunz's freedom of expression because the reverend had used "fighting words." Justice Jackson based his dissenting opinion on the "fighting words" doctrine used by the Court in *Chaplinski* v. *New Hampshire* (1942), which held that "the lewd and obscene, the profane, the libelous" and insulting or "fighting words" did not have any "social value" in the search for truth, public order, and safety. Therefore, the Court had ruled that "fighting words" are outside the protection of 1st Amendment guarantees of free speech.

Significance The *Kunz* case established that any broadly worded law restricting freedom of expression in public places is an unconstitutional exercise of prior restraint. The "fighting words" doctrine, employed in the dissenting opinion, has subsequently declined as an argument for restrictions on speech. The only prevailing justification for restricting speech is to prevent direct, immediate, and substantial harm to a vital social interest, such as national security, public order, and the safety of individuals.

SEE ALSO *Freedom of speech and press*

L

LAMAR, JOSEPH R.
Associate Justice, 1911–16

- Born: Oct. 14, 1857, Ruckersville, Ga.
- Education: University of Georgia, 1874–75; Bethany College, B.A., 1877; Washington and Lee University, 1877
- Previous government service: Georgia House of Representatives, 1886–89; commissioner to codify Georgia laws, 1893; associate justice, Georgia Supreme Court, 1903–5
- Appointed by President William Howard Taft Dec. 12, 1910; replaced William Henry Moody, who retired
- Supreme Court term: confirmed by the Senate Dec. 15, 1910, by a voice vote; served until Jan. 2, 1916
- Died: Jan. 2, 1916, Washington, D.C.

Joseph R. Lamar belonged to a socially prominent family in Georgia. His ardent studies of law and legal history led to his appointment to a state commission to codify the laws of Georgia. He alone wrote the resulting volume on civil law in Georgia. He later wrote several books on the history of law in Georgia.

During his brief term on the Court, Justice Lamar tended to vote with the majority. He wrote only eight dissents. His only notable opinion for the Court was in a 1911 case, *United States* v. *Grimaud*, which upheld a federal law, the Forest Reserve Act of 1911. This decision gave leeway to federal administrations to "fill in details" when carrying out laws.

LAMAR, LUCIUS Q. C.
Associate Justice, 1888–93

- Born: Sept. 17, 1825, Eatonton, Ga.
- Education: Emory College, B.A., 1845
- Previous government service: Georgia House of Representatives, 1853; U.S. representative from Mississippi, 1857–60, 1873–77; U.S. senator from Mississippi, 1877–85; U.S. secretary of the interior, 1885–88
- Appointed by President Grover Cleveland Dec. 6, 1887; replaced William Woods, who died
- Supreme Court term: confirmed by the Senate Jan. 16, 1888, by a 42–38 vote; served until Jan. 23, 1893
- Died: Jan. 23, 1893, Macon, Ga.

Lucius Lamar was a prominent leader of the Confederate States of America and wrote the state of Mississippi's ordinance of secession from the United States. In 1861 he resigned from the U.S. Congress to become a colonel in the Confederate army and fight against the Union in the Civil War. Years later, Lucius Lamar was called the "Great Pacificator" because of his efforts to reconcile the differences between Americans who had fought on opposing sides in the Civil War.

During the latter half of the 1800s, Lamar served in all three branches of the federal government: as a member of Congress, as the secretary of the interior, and as an associate justice of the Supreme

Court. His nomination to the Court by President Grover Cleveland was bitterly opposed by diehard foes of anyone associated with the Confederate cause. As a result, Lamar was narrowly confirmed by a Senate vote of 42 to 38. He was the first Southerner to take a seat on the Court since his own cousin, John A. Campbell, in 1853. During his brief term on the Court, Lamar tended to vote with the Court majority in opposition to strong state regulation of economic activity.
SOURCES James B. Murphy, *L. Q. C. Lamar, Pragmatic Patriot* (Baton Rouge: Louisiana State University Press, 1973).

LAME-DUCK SESSIONS OF CONGRESS

If the outgoing Congress comes back into session between the November election and the beginning of the new Congress in January, it is called a lame-duck session. The British first used the term *lame duck* to refer to bankrupt businessmen, and eventually it was extended to defeated politicians. Members of Congress who lose or do not stand for reelection can still attend a postelection session and vote on legislation. But because they have been defeated or are about to retire, they are as hobbled as lame ducks in terms of influence.

Throughout the 19th century, Congress regularly held lame-duck sessions. But reformers believed that lame-duck legislators were less responsive to the public and more susceptible to influence by special interests. Led by Senator George Norris (Republican–Nebraska), reformers proposed the 20th Amendment to the Constitution, which in 1933 changed the opening of a new Congress from the first Monday in December in odd-numbered years (13 months after the election) to January 3 (just two months after the election). Since then, Congress has held lame-duck sessions only on rare occasions, to address some important unfinished business.
SEE ALSO *Norris, George W.; Sessions of Congress*

LAWS

SEE *Acts of Congress; Bills; Legislation*

LAWYERS' EDITION

One of the unofficial publications of U.S. Supreme Court decisions is produced by the Lawyers Cooperative Publishing Company. This publication, *United States Supreme Court Reports,* Lawyers' Edition, began in 1882. It is commonly referred to as the *Lawyers' Edition.* Special features of this publication are summaries of briefs in selected cases and annotations of key ideas and arguments in some very significant cases.

The single official version of all U.S. Supreme Court decisions is *United States Reports,* which is published by the U.S. Government Printing Office.
SEE ALSO *Supreme Court Reporter; United States Reports*

LEADERSHIP IN CONGRESS

THE TWO houses of Congress depend on many different types of leadership. The Constitution provides for presiding officers for both chambers: the Speaker of the House; the president of the Senate (who is the Vice President of the United States); and the president pro tempore of the Senate, who presides in the Vice President's absence.

Once political parties were established, their members in Congress formed party caucuses, each of which elected a chairman. In the Senate the caucus chairman often acted as a party floor leader. Over time the party leadership positions of majority and minority leader and majority and minority whip evolved as formal leadership posts. Leadership is also provided by the chairmen and ranking minority members of the House and Senate committees. Additionally, members of both

Houses have formed blocs, or caucuses, united by region, race, or issues, whose leaders develop prominence and power within their chamber. Although leadership generally comes through seniority or election to a formal party post, strong, assertive, and charismatic personalities have also exerted influence and leadership over their colleagues even without holding a formal position.

SEE ALSO *Majority leader; Minority leader; President pro tempore of the Senate; Speaker of the House; Vice President; Whip*

LEAKS, CONGRESSIONAL

SEE *Secrecy in Congress*

LEGAL COUNSEL, OFFICE OF THE

SEE *Staff of the Supreme Court, nonjudicial*

LEGISLATION

In Latin, *legis lator* means "a proposer of laws." Legislation is therefore proposed laws, in the form of bills and resolutions. Making legislation is Congress's chief function. Ideas for legislation originate with members of Congress, their staff, lobbyists, constituents, the media, and the executive branch. Once members have introduced legislation, it is referred to the appropriate committees, made the subject of hearings, voted upon, and reported out to the full House or Senate. Both chambers must adopt the legislation in the same form for it to be sent to the President, who may sign or veto it. Once the President has signed the legislation, or Congress has overridden the veto, the legislation becomes law.

SEE ALSO *Acts of Congress; Bills; Resolutions, congressional*

LEGISLATIVE AGENCIES

In addition to the staff of members and committees, several large agencies are part of the legislative branch of the federal government. The General Accounting Office (GAO) assists Congress by investigating how executive branch agencies handle federal funds. The Congressional Budget Office helps Congress assess the President's annual budget requests and estimates the cost of all bills reported out of committee. The Library of Congress provides a vast amount of reference and research materials for the Congress, both through its general collections and through the work of the Congressional Research Service. The Office of Technology Assessment analyzes scientific and technological policy issues for Congress. The Government Printing Office publishes the *Congressional Record,* hearing transcripts, and reports of Congress. It also publishes government documents for the executive and judicial branches. These agencies have nonpartisan, professional staffs who are all included in the legislative branch payroll.

SEE ALSO *Congressional Budget Office; Congressional Research Service; Library of Congress*

LEGISLATIVE ASSISTANTS

Each member of the House of Representatives and Senate hires legislative assistants to work on different types of legislation in which that member is particularly interested. One legislative assistant might handle all agricultural and environmental issues, while another handles military and foreign policy issues. The larger a member's staff, the more a legislative assistant can specialize in certain types of legislation. Legislative assistants are responsible for following bills in their areas of specialization, briefing the senator or representative for whom they work, working with the staff of committees and with other members, and suggesting bills and amendments for their senator or representative to introduce. In general, legislative assistants make sure that their senator or representative is well informed when voting in committee or in the full chamber.

LEGISLATIVE CLERKS

Sitting at the front desk, below the presiding officer of the House or Senate, the legislative clerks serve as official readers of bills, resolutions, and amendments, as well as the journals. In the Senate, legislative clerks also call the roll for roll call votes and for quorum calls (to establish that enough members are present to conduct business), functions that have been automated in the larger House. Legislative clerks assign numbers to all bills and reports from the committees on those bills, and they publish the *Calendar of Business*. Because these clerks also maintain the official copies of all legislation under debate, they are responsible for preparing bills and resolutions for the *Congressional Record*.
SEE ALSO *Bills; Calendars, congressional; Journals, congressional; Resolutions, congressional; Voting in Congress*

LEGISLATIVE COUNSEL

The House of Representatives and Senate each employ a nonpartisan legislative counsel to assist in drafting bills. These trained lawyers, appointed to the staff with the approval of the leadership of both parties, do not take sides on a bill but make sure that the legislation is correctly and coherently written and that its language achieves what its sponsors want to accomplish. Legislative counsels also work with conference committees on perfecting the final language of the bills.

LEGISLATIVE DAY

Congressional days sometimes last longer than 24 hours. In an average day the House

and Senate convene in the morning and work through the late afternoon or early evening, when they adjourn. But sometimes, for tactical reasons, the House or Senate may recess rather than adjourn. When the members meet again on the next calendar day, the "legislative day" will not have changed. For instance, immediately following the date in the Senate section of the *Congressional Record* for Wednesday, July 2, 1980, was the notation "(Legislative day of Thursday, June 12, 1980)." That meant that while the calendar date for the rest of the world was July 2, the Senate was still operating on the legislative day of June 12. Especially in the Senate, this tactic of extending the legislative day reduces the amount of routine daily business, such as the reading of the journal, that opponents of a bill might use to slow down procedures and obstruct a vote.

LEGISLATIVE INTENT

The reports that congressional committees produce when they send a bill to the floor, as well as the speeches that the bill's supporters make, help to establish the bill's legislative intent—the reasons why Congress passed the legislation. Laws will often include specific language telling executive departments how they should be administered. When questions arise, the courts often consider legislative intent when they interpret those laws and how they have been administered.

LEGISLATIVE
REORGANIZATION
ACTS (1946 AND 1970)

In order to modernize and streamline the way it handles legislative business, Congress has twice conducted a major reexamination and reorganization of its internal operations. During World War II many senators and representatives became concerned about the slow and often cumbersome ways that Congress was doing business. The Legislative Reorganization Act of 1946 reduced the number of committees, recommended establishment of joint committees, increased the personal staffs of members, and established the first professional, nonpartisan committee staffs.

The Legislative Reorganization Act of 1970 increased the number of committee staff members, permitting the hiring of minority-party staff members. The act called for committees to open their doors and do more business in public (later specified in the "sunshine" rules of the Senate and House) and set the month of August as a regular recess period for Congress (except during times of war). It also upgraded the Legislative Reference Service into the Congressional Research Service to provide expanded research, reference, and information services to members and committees.

LEGISLATIVE VETO

Because the Constitution permits the President to veto, or reject, legislation passed by Congress, Congress has tried to create its own legislative veto. The legislative veto began as a way to give the President an opportunity to create policies that would stand unless either the House or the Senate (or both) voted against them. In 1932, Congress enacted legislation that permitted President Herbert Hoover to reorganize the executive branch. His reorganization plans would automatically go into effect after 60 days if neither house disapproved. After Hoover was defeated for reelection, he issued executive orders to consolidate government activities. The Democratic majority in the House rejected all of his plans.

During the 1970s Congress considerably expanded its use of the legislative veto over many executive agency regulations. In the case of *Immigration and Naturalization Service v. Chadha* (1983), the Supreme Court ruled that a one-house legislative veto was an unconstitutional violation of the separation of powers. In cases where people's legal rights are at stake, the Court declared, both houses of Congress must enact legislation or pass a joint resolution to be signed by the President. Although the Supreme Court's ruling undermined the legislative veto's legal standing, Congress has not been willing to abandon the practice completely in its attempt to restrain the executive branch. Future court challenges will likely follow.

SEE ALSO *Judicial review; Veto power*
SOURCES Louis Fisher, *Constitutional Conflicts between Congress and the President* (Princeton, N.J.: Princeton University Press, 1985).

LEMON TEST

In *Lemon v. Kurtzman* (1971), the Supreme Court stated three standards, or criteria, by which to decide cases involving disputes about the meaning of the 1st Amendment's establishment clause, which concerns government involvement with religion. These three standards are known as the Lemon Test. In order for a statute *not* to violate the establishment clause, it must meet these three conditions: First, it must have a secular or nonreligious purpose. Second, it must neither promote nor restrict religion in its primary effects. Third, it must not bring about an excessive entanglement with religion.

SEE ALSO *Establishment clause; Lemon v. Kurtzman; Religious issues under the Constitution*

LEMON V. KURTZMAN

- 403 U.S. 602 (1971)
- Vote: 8–0
- For the Court: Burger
- Concurring: Brennan and White
- Not participating: Marshall

According to Pennsylvania's Non-Public Elementary and Secondary Education Act of 1968, the state could directly support salaries of teachers of secular (nonreligious) subjects in parochial (church-run) and other private schools. The state could also reimburse the nonpublic schools for the purchase of textbooks and other instructional materials used to teach secular subjects. Alton Lemon, a taxpayer and resident of Pennsylvania, believed these state government payments of expenses for parochial schools, which had the primary mission of promoting particular religious beliefs, were unconstitutional. So Lemon brought suit against David Kurtzman, the state superintendent of schools, to stop state payments to parochial schools.

The Issue   Did the Pennsylvania law, which authorized state payments to Roman Catholic schools and other private schools with a religious mission, violate the 1st Amendment's religious freedom clause, which said, "Congress shall make no law respecting an establishment of religion, or prohibiting the free exercise thereof"?

Opinion of the Court   The Supreme Court struck down the Pennsylvania law at issue in this case because it provided for an "excessive entanglement" of the state with institutions (parochial schools) set up for the purpose of promoting religious doctrine. Chief Justice Warren Burger wrote, "The Constitution decrees that religion must be a private matter for the individual, the family, and the institutions of private choice, and that while some involvement and entanglements are inevitable, lines must be drawn."

The Court drew three lines, known ever since as the Lemon Test, to guide decisions in similar cases. For a statute to be constitutional under the establishment clause of the 1st Amendment, it had to meet these three standards of the Lemon Test: it must have a secular or nonreligious purpose; it must neither promote nor interfere with religion; and it cannot cause an excessive entanglement of government with religion.

Although the Court had maintained a barrier between church and state, Chief Justice Burger said it was "far from being a wall." He was referring to Thomas Jefferson's famous phrase—"a wall of separation between church and state"—which the Court had used previously to interpret the establishment clause of the 1st Amendment. Burger claimed that separation of church and state is "a blurred, indistinct, and a variable barrier depending on all the circumstances of a particular relationship."

Significance   The Court maintained a separation of church and state, as it had in several other cases since the 1940s, such as *Everson* v. *Board of Education of Ewing Township* (1947), *Engel* v. *Vitale* (1962), and *Abington School District* v. *Schempp* (1963). Further, the Court attempted to clarify the meaning of the separation of church and state through its three-part Lemon Test. However, the Court, through the opinion of Chief Justice Burger, exhibited uncertainty about when or how this "variable barrier" of separation between church and state might be lowered.

In 1993 the Court upheld student-led prayers at graduation ceremonies when it let stand the Fifth Circuit Court of Appeals decision in *Jones* v. *Clear Creek Independent School District.* But in *Lee* v. *Weisman* (1992), the Court struck down a Rhode Island policy that permitted school officials to include prayers in public high school graduation ceremonies. Further, in *Zobrest* v. *Catalina School District (1993)*, the court ruled that government funds can be used to pay for a sign-language interpreter to assist a deaf student in a Catholic school.

SEE ALSO *Abington School District v. Schempp; Engel v. Vitale; Everson v. Board of Education of Ewing Township; Lemon Test; Religious issues under the Constitution*

LEXIS

LEXIS is a computerized legal research service operated by a private corporation, Mead Data Central, Inc. It contains the full text of all Supreme Court decisions from 1790 to the present. The Court electronically transmits its decisions to the LEXIS database on the same day they are made. LEXIS users can access either the citations or the full text of particular Supreme Court decisions and print them out.

United States Law Week, a weekly publication providing current news about Supreme Court personnel and proceedings, is part of the LEXIS database.

SEE ALSO *WESTLAW*

LIBERTY UNDER THE CONSTITUTION

Liberty means that a person is free to make choices about, for example, what to say or to do. A primary purpose of constitutional government in the United States is to make the liberty of individuals secure. The preamble to the Constitution proclaims that a principal reason for establishing the federal government is to "secure the Blessings of Liberty to ourselves and our Posterity."

The Bill of Rights, Amendments 1 to 10 of the Constitution, protects the individual's rights to liberty from the power of government. The 1st Amendment, for example, says that Congress shall not take away a person's freedoms of religion, speech, press, assembly, and petition. The 4th Amendment protects personal liberty; it guarantees the right of the people to be secure against unwarranted intrusions into their private lives by forbidding "unreasonable searches and seizures" by government officials. The 5th Amendment prohibits the federal government from taking away a person's "life, liberty, or property, without due process of law." And the 14th Amendment applies the same prohibition against abuses of a person's liberty by state governments.

The freedoms spelled out in the U.S. Constitution are called civil liberties. However, these civil liberties are not granted by government to individuals. Rather, the Constitution assumes that all people automatically have these civil liberties and therefore restrains the government from using its power to abuse individuals. Thus, there is a private realm of life, which government officials cannot invade without violating the Constitution. Within this domain of privacy, individuals have certain liberties of thought, belief, and action.

The Constitution also guarantees liberty for the people to participate publicly in the political life of their society. The 1st Amendment freedoms, for example, protect a person's right to participate freely in activities to elect representatives in government and to influence public decisions of elected and appointed government officials.

Liberty under the Constitution, then, is secured by limiting the power of government in order to protect the people's rights to freedom. But if the government has too little power, so that law and order break down, then the people's liberties may be lost. Neither freedom of thought nor action is secure in a lawless and disorderly society, where there are no law enforcement officers to protect people against criminals who would abuse them.

So an overriding purpose of constitutional government in the United States has been to provide for the use of sufficient power to maintain order, stability, and security for the liberties of the people. The American Declaration of Independence (1776), for example, clearly and emphatically states, "That to secure these Rights [to Life, Liberty, and the Pursuit of Happiness] Governments are instituted among Men."

Ordered liberty is the desirable condition whereby both public order and personal liberty are secured for the individuals in a society. How can liberty and authority, freedom and power, be combined and balanced? This was the basic political problem of the founding period in the United States, and it continues to challenge Americans today. During the debate on ratification of the Constitution, for example, James Madison wrote to Thomas Jefferson in 1788, "It is a melancholy reflection that liberty should be equally exposed to danger whether the Government have too much or too little power; and that the line which divides these extremes should be so inaccurately defined by experience."

Madison noted the standing threat to liberty posed by insufficient constitutional limits on government. He also recognized that liberty carried to the extreme of license, as in a riot, is equally dangerous to the freedom and rights of individuals. A good constitution is a source of liberty and order, but the right mix of these two factors is sometimes difficult to find and maintain. The challenging questions, of course, are these two: At what point, and under what conditions, should the power of government be limited to protect the rights to liberty of individuals? At what point, and under what conditions, should limits be placed on the freedoms and rights of individuals to protect public order, upon which the security for liberty depends?

In the United States, the Supreme Court has the power and the constitutional responsibility to address authoritatively these broad questions and to resolve disputes about them on a case-by-case basis. Through its power of judicial review, the Court can uphold or overturn, as violations of the Constitution, acts of federal and state governments pertaining to questions of liberty and order. But the questions are never answered for all time. They remain as challenges of a constitutional democracy.

In many of its landmark decisions, the Supreme Court has decided to protect the individual's rights to liberty under the Constitution from an unconstitutional exercise of power by government officials. In *Katz* v. *United States* (1967), for example, the Court prohibited federal law enforcement officials from using evidence against a defendant gained by electronic surveillance (listening in) of his telephone conversations. According to the Court, the federal agents had violated the 4th Amendment guarantee of security "against unreasonable searches and seizures." And in *Texas* v. *Johnson* (1989) the Court struck down, as an unconstitutional violation of 1st Amendment rights to freedom of expression, a state law that banned public protest involving the burning of the American flag.

In other significant decisions, the Court

has upheld the constitutional exercise of government power and thereby restricted the rights to liberty of individuals. In *United States* v. *Ross* (1982) the Court upheld the authority of police officers to search an entire automobile they have stopped, without obtaining a warrant (required by the 4th Amendment), if they have "probable cause" to suspect that drugs or other illegally possessed objects are in the vehicle. And in *Kovacs* v. *Cooper* (1949) the Court upheld as constitutional a local law that banned the use of sound-amplifying equipment on city streets to transmit information. In this case, the Court favored the community's desire to avoid noisy disturbances over the individual's presumed constitutional right to freedom of expression.

SEE ALSO *Bill of Rights; Civil rights; Constitutional democracy; Constitutionalism; Judicial review; Katz v. United States; Texas v. Johnson; United States v. Ross*

SOURCES Learned Hand, *The Spirit of Liberty* (New York: Knopf, 1960). Michael Kammen, *Spheres of Liberty: Changing Perceptions of Liberty in American Culture* (Ithaca, N.Y.: Cornell University Press, 1986). Herbert J. Muller, *Freedom in the Western World* (New York: Harper & Row, 1963). Orlando Patterson, *Freedom in the Making of Western Culture* (New York: Basic Books, 1991). Ellis Sandoz, ed., *The Roots of Liberty* (Columbia: University of Missouri Press, 1993).

LIBRARIAN, SUPREME COURT

SEE *Staff of the Supreme Court, nonjudicial*

LIBRARIES, PRESIDENTIAL

Presidential libraries preserve Presidential papers and documents; acquire books, films, and videotapes about Presidents; conduct oral history interviews with members of Presidential administrations; sponsor research conferences; and provide scholars with access to Presidential documents.

The White House papers and documents of all Presidents from George Washington through Warren Harding are located in the manuscript division of the Library of Congress in Washington, D.C. All Presidents beginning with Herbert Hoover have donated their White House papers to separate Presidential libraries. The libraries are built with private funds. The Presidential Libraries Act of 1955 provided that the National Archives and the National Park Service would maintain the libraries and grounds and would fund professional archivists to take care of and catalog all Presidential papers. These libraries are supervised by their own governing boards and library staffs. The Presidential Libraries Act of 1986 provided that George Bush and his successors would have to use private funds to operate as well as build their Presidential libraries.

The Richard M. Nixon Library is an entirely private operation that receives no public funding and does not contain any original Presidential documents. According to the terms of the Presidential Recordings and Materials Preservation Act of 1974 and subsequent laws, Nixon's original papers and tapes are stored in a warehouse controlled by the National Archives.

Presidential libraries opened prior to 1978 are subject to restrictions imposed by each individual President on the use of his White House papers. The Presidential Records Act of 1978 divides materials for all Presidents elected after 1980 into two categories: Presidential papers and personal papers. The personal papers are those that "do not relate to or have an effect upon the carrying out of the constitutional, statutory, or other official or ceremonial duties of the President," such as a personal diary or personal correspondence. Presidents may put whatever restrictions they wish on their personal papers.

In the category of Presidential papers,

former Presidents can restrict national security information and personnel files for up to 12 years; all other types of Presidential papers must be open within 5 years. Individuals such as cabinet secretaries or White House aides who donate materials (including oral histories) to Presidential libraries may place their own restrictions on use.

SEE ALSO *Ex-Presidency*
SOURCES Larry Berman, "Presidential Libraries: How Not to Be a Stranger in a Strange Land," in *Studying the Presidency,* edited by George C. Edwards and Stephen J. Wayne (Knoxville: University of Tennessee Press, 1983). Martha Joynt Kumar, "Presidential Libraries: Gold Mine, Booby Trap, or Both?," in *Studying the Presidency,* edited by George C. Edwards and Stephen J. Wayne (Knoxville: University of Tennessee Press, 1983). Frank S. Schick, *Records of the Presidency: Presidential Papers and Libraries from Washington to Reagan* (Phoenix, Ariz.: Oryx, 1989).

LIBRARY OF CONGRESS

Always in need of information, Congress established its own library, which eventually became a national library. In April 1800, while preparing to move from Philadelphia to the then-wilderness of the District of Columbia, Congress realized that it would no longer be able to depend upon Philadelphia's libraries. So members appropriated $5,000 to purchase books for "the use of Congress." This was the beginning of the Library of Congress.

In 1802, Clerk of the House John Beckley became the first librarian of Congress, at a time when its catalog consisted of 740 volumes. These books were destroyed when British troops burned down the Capitol in 1814. Former President Thomas Jefferson then offered as a replacement his personal library, which Congress purchased. The old collection had consisted largely of law books and other reference materials. But Jefferson's library ranged more broadly over history, philosophy, and the arts and sciences. As new volumes were added in these fields, the Library of Congress grew into one of the world's most diverse research centers.

From 1824 until 1897 the Library of Congress occupied three stories along the West Front of the Capitol, an equal distance between the House and Senate wings. When its collection outgrew this space, Congress authorized the construction of a separate library building across the plaza from the Capitol. This magnificently decorated building with its high-domed central reading room has been named the Thomas Jefferson Building. Two additional buildings, named for John Adams and James Madison, were later constructed nearby.

Funded mostly by Congress but also through some private donations, the library has become an unparalleled research collection. In 1990 the library held an estimated 12 million books, newspapers, and magazines; 4 million maps; 16 million photographs, prints, and motion pictures; and 39 million manuscript documents (including the papers of many prominent senators and representatives of the past). The Library of Congress also operates the Congressional Research Service, which provides nonpartisan research assistance to committees and members of Congress. Its services to the general public include a national library of braille, large-print, and recorded materials for the blind and physically handicapped.

SEE ALSO *Congressional Research Service; Legislative agencies*
SOURCES Charles A. Goodrum, *Treasures of the Library of Congress* (New York: Abrams, 1991). Andrew L. Simpson, *The Library of Congress* (New York: Chelsea House, 1989).

LIMITED GOVERNMENT

SEE *Constitutional democracy; Constitutionalism; Separation of powers*

LINCOLN, ABRAHAM
16th President

- Born: Feb. 12, 1809, near Hodgenville, Ky.
- Political party: Whig (in Congress); Republican
- Education: sporadic schooling in lower grades
- Military service: Illinois volunteer regiment, 1832
- Previous government service: postmaster, New Salem, Ill., 1833–36; Illinois General Assembly, 1834–41; U.S. House of Representatives, 1847–49
- Elected President, 1860; served, 1861–65
- Died: Apr. 15, 1865, Washington, D.C.

Using military force to defeat the Southern secessionists and win the Civil War, Abraham Lincoln acted in accordance with his oath of office to preserve the Union. In doing so, he used emergency powers that no previous President had exercised. His twin policies, emancipation of slaves and reconciliation of North and South, were his greatest legacies to a war-torn nation.

Lincoln was born in a log cabin in Kentucky. He was the first President born outside the original 13 states that formed the Union. When he was seven, his family moved to another log cabin in Indiana, where his father cleared and farmed 160 acres. His mother died when he was nine and his father married Sarah Bush Johnston, whose three children moved into the log cabin with Lincoln and his sister, Sarah. After his farm chores young Abe educated himself by lantern light, borrowing books from neighbors and nearby towns. He grew to his full size of six feet, four inches and gained a reputation not only as a scholar but also as a wrestler and axeman.

At age 22 Lincoln struck out on his own and settled in New Salem, Illinois. He worked as a storekeeper and was a captain in a campaign against the Black Hawk Indians, but he saw no action and his store failed. He then worked as a surveyor and postmaster. He lost a contest for the state legislature in 1832 ("The only time I have ever been beaten by the people," he later said), but he was elected two years later on the Whig ticket. He also studied law and was admitted to the bar in 1836. Lincoln became a successful lawyer in Springfield, and his clients included the Illinois Central Railroad and other corporations. In 1839 he met Mary Todd, and they married in 1842.

Lincoln entered national politics in 1846, when he was elected as a Whig to the U.S. House of Representatives. He introduced a bill to end slavery in the nation's capital, but it was never brought to a vote. His support for the Wilmot Proviso (a bill to outlaw slavery in territories acquired from Mexico), his opposition to the Mexican-American War (he voted for a resolution in Congress that described it as "a war unconstitutionally and unjustly begun by the President"), and his campaigning for Zachary Taylor in the election of 1848 were unpopular positions in Illinois, and he declined to seek reelection.

In various speeches in 1854, Lincoln opposed the Kansas-Nebraska Bill sponsored by Senator Stephen A. Douglas. The bill provided for a popular vote on the question of slavery in each of the territories. In two debates with Douglas, Lincoln argued that the Missouri Compromise of 1820, which forbade slavery north of Missouri's southern boundary, should be retained. He argued that only in free states could poor white workers improve their circumstances, because there they would not be competing against slave labor.

Lincoln failed in a bid to obtain a Senate seat in 1855, but the following year he helped organize the Republican party and nearly won its Vice Presidential nomination. In 1858 Lincoln challenged Douglas for his Senate seat. "A house divided against itself cannot stand," he told the Illinois Republican party convention in his acceptance speech, adding "I believe this Government cannot endure permanently half slave and half free." In a second series of Lincoln-Douglas debates held around the state, Lincoln hammered at Douglas for ignoring the moral dimension of the slavery question, calling slavery a "moral, social and political evil." Lincoln lost the election but gained a national reputation.

In February 1860 Lincoln delivered an antislavery speech in New York City and was applauded by his audience and by New York newspapers, which made him a contender for the Republican Presidential nomination. In May, he won the nomination by defeating the favorite, William H. Seward, on the third ballot, after his campaign managers promised cabinet positions to politicians from Ohio, Indiana, and Pennsylvania.

The Whigs nominated John Bell, the Northern Democrats nominated Stephen A. Douglas, and the Southern Democrats bolted from their party to nominate John C. Breckinridge. Lincoln, along with Vice Presidential nominee Hannibal Hamlin, was elected with a 39.8 percent plurality of the popular vote but a large majority in the electoral college. He said farewell to his friends in Springfield and took a train east. Because of a plot against his life, he left his train in Philadelphia and arrived without notice in Washington, D.C., on February 23, 1861. By that time seven states of the lower South had already left the Union, and a peace convention in Richmond, Virginia, was trying to forge a compromise under the auspices of former President John Tyler. Lincoln gave the delegates to the convention no encouragement, however.

Lincoln took the oath of office on March 4, 1861. "We must not be enemies," he pleaded with Southern leaders in his inaugural address. He reminded them that no state had a right to leave the Union "upon its own mere motion" and warned that he had taken an oath of office to enforce federal laws. "In your hands, my dissatisfied fellow-countrymen, and not in mine, is the momentous issue of civil war." He rejected the Crittenden Compromise, which would have permitted slavery in the Western states below the Mason-Dixon line. Lincoln would allow slavery to continue where it already was but would hear nothing of extending it across the lower states to the West.

After his inauguration Lincoln informed the governor of South Carolina that he would resupply the federal garrison at Fort Sumter in Charleston Harbor with ammunition, food, and medicine, but would send no reinforcements or weapons. On April 12, 1861, the South Carolina government responded by opening fire on Fort Sumter, and two days later its commander surrendered. Congress was not in session, and Lincoln did not call it into emergency session. Instead, relying on his own Presidential powers, on April 15 he proclaimed a blockade of Southern ports, called on the states for 75,000 volunteers to join the army and enforce federal laws, suspended the privilege of the writ of habeas corpus (so that he could arrest and hold people without taking them to court), rounded up thousands of Confederate sympathizers in the border states, and spent funds from the U.S. Treasury without obtaining congressional appropriations. Then, on July 4, Lincoln called Congress into session and informed the legislators of what he had done. Within the month Congress retroactively ratified his actions.

For several years the war went badly for the North. In July the First Battle at Bull Run in Virginia was a defeat for Union forces, with more than 3,500 dead and wounded. A campaign to capture Richmond bogged down. The South won victories at Fredericksburg and at the Second Battle of Bull Run. The Union instituted a draft to replace troops fallen in battle. In New York City draft riots showed strong antiwar sentiment among many Northerners. But eventually the war effort succeeded. In 1862 Union forces led by Generals Ulysses S. Grant and Don C. Buell began to win victories along the Mississippi River, and Admiral David Farragut captured New Orleans. On January 1,

1863, Lincoln issued a Proclamation of Emancipation that freed slaves in states in secession. As Union forces advanced into enemy territory, former slaves became a decisive source of manpower for the Union forces.

In 1863 the fortunes of war turned toward the North. On July 3, Union forces defeated more than 90,000 troops led by Robert E. Lee at Gettysburg, Pennsylvania. The following day Grant divided the Confederacy with the capture of Vicksburg, Mississippi. President Lincoln named him commander of the Union armies early in 1864, and he faced off against Lee in Virginia, taking huge losses but steadily moving forward. Meanwhile, General William Tecumseh Sherman began a successful march from Tennessee into Georgia, eventually seizing and burning Atlanta.

The election of 1864 would decide whether or not the war would continue. Lincoln received the Republican nomination and chose the military governor of Tennessee, Andrew Johnson, a Democrat, to run with him on a coalition Unionist ticket. Democrats challenged Lincoln's exertion of Presidential power, called for a halt to hostilities and the return of slaveholding states to the Union, and nominated General George B. McClellan, whom Lincoln had relieved of command. Successes in the field, especially the capture of the last port on the Gulf of Mexico at Mobile Bay by Admiral Farragut, led many voters to believe the war would soon be over. Lincoln won 55 percent of the popular vote and almost all the electoral votes in the election.

Lincoln's second inaugural address stressed a policy of reconciliation toward the South: "With malice toward none, with charity for all, with firmness in the right as God gives us to see the right, let us strive on to finish the work we are in, to bind up the nation's wounds, to care for him who shall have borne the battle and for his widow and his orphan—to do all which may achieve and cherish a just and lasting piece among ourselves and with all nations." In 1864 he had vetoed the Wade-

Davis Reconstruction bill passed by Congress because he opposed its harsh terms. Louisiana, Arkansas, Tennessee, and Virginia reestablished state governments and petitioned Congress for recognition but were denied. On April 11, two days after Robert E. Lee surrendered his army to Grant, Lincoln again called for the former Confederate states to be readmitted to the Union on lenient terms.

On the evening of April 14, while attending a performance of *Our American Cousin* at Ford's Theatre in Washington, Lincoln was shot by John Wilkes Booth, an actor and Southern sympathizer, and died the next morning. As his body was taken back to Springfield, mourners lined the 1,700-mile route to pay their respects to the Great Emancipator.

SEE ALSO *Amnesty, Presidential; Assassinations, Presidential; Buchanan, James; Emancipation Proclamations; Gettysburg Address; Grant, Ulysses S.; Hamlin, Hannibal; Johnson, Andrew; War powers*
SOURCES Richard N. Current, *The Lincoln Nobody Knows* (Westport, Conn.: Greenwood, 1980). David Herbert Donald, *Lincoln Reconsidered* (New York: Vintage, 1961). Philip B. Kunhardt, Jr., et al. *Lincoln: An Illustrated Biography* (New York: Knopf, 1992). James M. McPherson, *Abraham Lincoln and the Second American Revolution* (New York: Oxford University Press, 1991). Mark E. Neely, *The Abraham Lincoln Encyclopedia* (New York: McGraw-Hill, 1982).

LINE-ITEM VETO

Unlike most state governors, the President does not have the line-item veto. This means that the President must approve or veto an entire appropriations bill and may not veto any single part of the bill. Presidents Ronald Reagan, George Bush, and Bill Clinton all called for a constitutional amendment to give them such a partial veto as a means of controlling federal spending and reducing the deficit. With this power they could disapprove of what

they considered wasteful "pork barrel" spending without having to reject the many more worthy projects in the rest of an appropriations bill. Lacking the two-thirds vote needed for a constitutional amendment, Congress in 1996 passed a law giving the President the line-item veto. The line-item veto constituted a major part of the "Contract with America" that had helped the Republicans recapture the majority in Congress.

President Clinton exercised this power sparingly, but many in Congress—including some who had supported the line-item veto—protested when he used it to veto their projects. In 1998 the Supreme Court ruled the line-item veto unconstitutional on the grounds that it violated the constitutional requirement that legislation be passed by both houses of Congress and presented in its entirety to the President for his signature or veto. On hearing this news, Senator Robert Byrd of West Virginia exclaimed, "God save this honorable Court!"

SEE ALSO *Pork barrel politics; Veto power*

LIVINGSTON, HENRY BROCKHOLST
Associate Justice, 1807–23

- Born: Nov. 25, 1757, New York, N.Y.
- Education: College of New Jersey (Princeton), B.A., 1774; studied law with Peter Yates in New York, N.Y.
- Previous government service: New York Assembly, 1786, 1798–99; judge, New York State Supreme Court, 1802–7
- Appointed by President Thomas Jefferson as a recess appointment Nov. 10, 1806; replaced William Paterson, who died; nominated by Jefferson Dec. 13, 1806
- Supreme Court term: confirmed by the Senate Dec. 17, 1806, by a voice vote; served until Mar. 18, 1823
- Died: Mar. 18, 1823, Washington, D.C.

Henry Brockholst Livingston was a patriot who served in the Continental Army during the American War of Independence. After the war, he practiced law in New York and became a leading judge of the New York State Supreme Court.

Justice Livingston was a minor figure on the U.S. Supreme Court, which was dominated at that time by Chief Justice John Marshall. However, he was considered an expert on commercial law.

LOBBYING

Lobbyists are people hired by groups or organizations with particular interests to convince members of Congress to pass or defeat legislation. They may work for business corporations, labor unions, executive branch agencies, foreign governments, or private or public interest groups. Although lobbyists were present during the 1st Congress—and in the British Parliament before that—the term did not come into use until the 1820s. As the name suggests, lobbyists often work the lobbies and corridors surrounding the House and Senate chamber, intercepting members and arguing their client's case. Maurice Rosenblatt, a lobbyist for many causes, described the job as "one man, one buttonhole. It is that personal eye-to-eye contact that has the maximum effect."

Because of scandals in which lobbyists employed questionable tactics to win legislation for special interests, they acquired a sinister image. Senator Norris Cotton (Republican–New Hampshire) considered this image unjust because most lobbyists perform a legitimate and necessary function by "presenting diverse social and economic viewpoints to Congress" and by providing legal knowledge and technical skills to help frame legislation. Since 1876 Congress has enacted increasingly tighter requirements for lobbyists to register and to identify their clients and fees. Many loopholes remain in these regulations, but Congress has been concerned that further limitations on lobbying might also restrict the constitutional rights of free speech and freedom to petition.

Rather than return to their home state, some former members of Congress stay in Washington as lobbyists, making use of their experience on Capitol Hill—and their floor privileges in the House and Senate chambers and access to the cloakrooms and dining rooms. George Smathers (Democrat–Florida) explained that as a former senator he could "get in to see senators a lot more quickly than you can if you're just a normal lobbyist." Over time, however, former members often find that their advantages as lobbyists diminish as fewer of their old colleagues remain in office.

SEE ALSO *Floor privileges*
SOURCES Robert C. Byrd, "Lobbyists," in *The Senate, 1789–1989: Addresses on the History of the United States Senate*, vol. 2 (Washington, D.C.: Government Printing Office, 1991). Margaret Susan Thompson, *The "Spider's Web": Congress and Lobbying in the Age of Grant* (Ithaca, N.Y.: Cornell University Press, 1985).

LOCHNER V. NEW YORK

- 198 U.S. 45 (1905)
- Vote: 5–4
- For the Court: Peckham
- Dissenting: Harlan, White, Day, and Holmes

Joseph Lochner owned a small bakery shop in Utica, New York. In 1901 the state charged him with violating the Bakeshop Act, a New York law that banned bakers from working more than 10 hours a day or 60 hours a week. Lochner had required an employee, Aman Schmitter, to work more than the 60 hours per week permitted by the state law. The Oneida County Court convicted Lochner, and he appealed his case. After losing in the New York State appellate courts, Lochner appealed to the U.S. Supreme Court.

The Issue Lochner said that the Bakeshop Act violated the 14th Amendment because it deprived him of "life, liberty, or property, without due process of law." Lochner claimed that the Bakeshop Act unconstitutionally interfered with his freedom to make a contract with his workers about pay and hours of work. State officials countered that the Bakeshop Act was intended to protect the health and well-being of workers against employers who might otherwise exploit them.

Opinion of the Court Justice Rufus Peckham, writing for the Court, said the Bakeshop Act was unconstitutional because it took away "the right of the individual to liberty of person and freedom of contract." Under the 14th Amendment, Peckham argued, individuals were free to purchase and sell labor. Therefore, any state law interfering with this "liberty of contract" would be unconstitutional "unless there are circumstances which exclude that right."

This right was not stated in the Constitution. Rather, the Court "found" this right through its interpretation of the due process clause of the 14th Amendment, which says that no state government shall "deprive any person of life, liberty, or property without due process of law." Thus, the Court developed the doctrine of substantive due process, by which it claimed the power to examine the content of laws to determine their fairness. In this way, the Court decides whether laws violate any fundamental rights of individuals, such as rights the Court believes to be associated with "life, liberty, or property." This doctrine of substantive due process was a departure from the traditional understanding of due process solely as government procedures that follow rules of fairness.

Dissent Justice Oliver Wendell Holmes sharply disagreed with the *Lochner* decision and the doctrine of substantive due process upon which it was based. He argued that the Bakeshop Act was a "reasonable" regulation of private business in behalf of a compelling public interest, as determined by a majority of the people's representatives in the state government.

According to Holmes, the Court had no authority to strike down laws made by legislative majorities on the basis of the personal opinions of the justices, which they read into the Constitution through the specious doctrine of substantive due process. Holmes believed that "liberty in the Fourteenth Amendment" was "perverted" when "held to prevent the natural outcome of a dominant opinion" (the legislative majority) unless a "rational and fair man" would conclude that the law violated "fundamental principles" of law and tradition. Holmes charged that the Court overstepped the boundaries of its judicial powers by using substantive due process to substitute its opinion of wise social policy for that of the popularly elected state legislature.

Significance The *Lochner* decision did not stop the movement for legal regulation of the workplace to protect employees. In *Muller v. Oregon* (1908), for example, the Court upheld a state law limiting the number of hours per day that women could work. And in *Bunting v. Oregon* (1917), the Court sustained a 10-hour workday limit for male workers. However, the Court continued to use the *Lochner* decision as the basis for overseeing legislative regulations of businesses. In 1937, however, the Court overruled *Lochner v. New York* with its decision in *West Coast Hotel Co. v. Parrish* (1937). In this case, the Court upheld a state law regulating minimum wages for children and women workers.

SEE ALSO *Due process of law; Muller v. Oregon; West Coast Hotel Co. v. Parrish*

LODGE, HENRY CABOT, SR.

- Born: May 12, 1850, Boston, Mass.
- Political party: Republican
- Education: Harvard University, graduated, 1871; Harvard Law School, graduated, 1874; Harvard University, Ph.D, 1876
- Representative from Massachusetts: 1887–93

- Senator from Massachusetts: 1893–1924
- President pro tempore: 1911–13
- Senate majority leader: 1919–24
- Died: Nov. 9, 1924, Cambridge, Mass.

A scholar in politics, Henry Cabot Lodge taught history at Harvard before he was elected to Congress. Known to be strong in his dislikes, Lodge displayed a deep antagonism toward another scholar in politics, Woodrow Wilson, who became President in 1913. Recognizing that a split in the Republican party in the 1912 election had put a Democrat in the White House, Lodge worked to reunite his party and defeat Wilson. When the Republicans regained the majority in the Senate in the 1918 elections, Lodge, as majority leader and chairman of the Foreign Relations Committee, was determined to deny Wilson and the Democratic party the triumph of writing the treaty that ended World War I. Lodge added a series of Republican reservations to Wilson's Treaty of Versailles. Such reservations could alter the interpretation of the treaty and could affect whether the other parties to the treaty would still accept it. Wilson, an equally stubborn man, refused to compromise and took his case directly to the people.

Without the compromise offered by the Republican reservations, the Senate twice defeated the Treaty of Versailles. Republicans triumphed in the elections of 1920, but victory also brought disappointment. Despite Lodge's objections to the treaty, he wanted the United States to play a strong role in international affairs. Instead, his policies resulted in the United States's embrace of isolationism during the decades between the world wars.

SEE ALSO *Treaty of Versailles*

SOURCES John A. Garraty, *Henry Cabot Lodge: A Biography* (New York: Knopf, 1968). William C. Widenor, "Henry Cabot Lodge: The Astute Parliamentarian," in *First among Equals: Outstanding Senate Leaders of the Twentieth Century,* edited by Richard A. Baker and Roger H. Davidson (Washington, D.C.: Congressional Quarterly, 1991).

LONG, HUEY P.

- Born: Aug. 30, 1893, Winnfield, La.
- Political party: Democrat
- Education: University of Oklahoma School of Law; studied law at Tulane University
- Senator from Louisiana: 1931–35
- Died: Sept. 10, 1935, Baton Rouge, La.

Huey Long served less than a single term in the Senate and never chaired a committee—in fact, he resigned from the committees to which he was appointed. Within Congress he was more of a gadfly than an effective legislator. Yet he held great influence because of his strong political base in Louisiana, his unpredictability, and his ability to sway the public. Long preferred to do his work out in public on the Senate floor, or on the radio and in the newspapers, rather than away from view in the committee rooms. He mocked and taunted his party's leaders, and he used the filibuster and other legislative tactics to force the majority to pay attention to his populist views, which were more radical, antiestablishment, and aimed toward the common people than those of the political mainstream. During the Great Depression of the 1930s Long proposed to tax the rich more heavily in order to "share the wealth" more evenly among all citizens. His motto was "Every Man a King." Although other senators considered Long a "wild man," they recognized the popular appeal of his message. Senator Long set his sights on the Presidency, even writing a book called *My First Days in the White House,* which mixed his outrageous humor and his platform for the future. But the flamboyant politician's career ended with his assassination in 1935.

SOURCES T. Harry Williams, *Huey Long* (New York: Knopf, 1969).

LONGWORTH, NICHOLAS

- Born: Nov. 5, 1869, Cincinnati, Ohio
- Political party: Republican

- Education: Harvard University, graduated, 1891; Harvard Law School; Cincinnati Law School, graduated, 1894
- Representative from Ohio: 1903–13, 1915–31
- House majority leader: 1923–25
- Speaker of the House: 1925–31
- Died: Apr. 9, 1931, Aiken, S.C.

The aristocratic Nicholas Longworth seemed too much a dandy to be an effective politician. He played the violin, dressed impeccably, and loved fine food, card playing, and dancing. But Nick Longworth could also be a tough politician who knew how to bargain and compromise and when to hold the line and fight. As Speaker of the House, he ruled his party and the House firmly. He ordered that progressive Republicans who had bolted their party during the election of 1924 be barred from the Republican conference, removed from their committee assignments, and denied their seniority. He won changes in the House rules to strengthen majority control by making it more difficult to discharge a bill from committee against the wishes of the leadership. Although he demanded discipline within his party, Longworth worked closely with the minority leader, John Nance Garner, to make the House work as efficiently as possible. Republicans sometimes protested that the Speaker was *too* fair to the Democrats. As a testament to Longworth's popularity among members of both parties, the House later named one of its office buildings in his honor.

SOURCES Richard B. Cheney and Lynne V. Cheney, *Kings of the Hill: Power and Personality in the House of Representatives* (New York: Continuum, 1983).

LOTT, TRENT

- Born: Oct. 9, 1941, Grenada, Miss.
- Political Party: Republican
- Representative from Mississippi: 1973–89
- Senator from Mississippi: 1989–
- House minority whip: 1981–89
- Senate majority whip: 1995–96
- Senate majority leader:1996–

As a Republican from Mississippi, Trent Lott represented the political upheaval of the once "Solid South." From the 1870s until the 1970s, practically all southern senators and representatives had been Democrats. Lott himself first went to Washington as the administrative assistant to a Democrat, Representative William Colmer. When Colmer retired, Lott was elected to succeed him—as a Republican. It was the beginning of a trend that saw many southerners change party allegiance and the political base of the Republican party shift from the North to the South.

As a congressman, Lott aligned himself with a group of conservative House members known as the "Conservative Opportunity Society," led by Georgia Representative Newt Gingrich. Seeking to return the Republicans to the majority after decades in the minority, the young conservatives pursued more aggressive legislative tactics than their party's moderate leadership did. They provoked frequent confrontations with the majority party over policy and procedure. Among this group of mavericks, Lott was the first to move into his party's leadership by becoming the minority whip.

In 1988 Lott ran for the Senate and within a few years moved into its leadership as well. He served first as whip and then as majority leader. Since the rules of the Senate give more voice to the minority than the rules of the House, Lott needed to pursue different tactics as a Senate leader. "A Senate majority leader has to be a legislator, moderator, partisan activist, consensus builder, and traffic cop," he commented, "—often all at the same time." Although still strongly conservative in outlook, he worked with his Democratic counterparts to accommodate senators of all views.

A skilled legislative tactician, Lott steered the Senate through the emotional impeachment trial of President Bill Clinton in 1999. Rather than run the trial as a partisan affair, Lott convened an extraordinary joint conference of all 100 Republican and

Democratic senators. They met in the Old Senate Chamber to discuss behind closed doors the fairest way to conduct the trial. By the time they had emerged, the senators had voted unanimously for a set of procedures, a testament to Majority Leader Lott's grasp of how the often cumbersome Senate could best operate.

LOUISIANA PURCHASE
(1803)

France's offer to sell the vast Louisiana Territory to the United States in 1803 sparked a constitutional dilemma. President Thomas Jefferson wanted to purchase the territory, which would double the size of the United States. But Jefferson also favored a narrow interpretation of the Constitution—and nowhere did it provide for acquiring additional territory. Because of the need to act quickly on the deal, there was no time to amend the Constitution. Instead, the Jeffersonian Democratic-Republicans in Congress passed legislation that gave the President permission to sign a treaty to receive the territory, and Congress appropriated the money to pay for it. Congress acted under the provision of the Constitution (Article 5, Section 3) that gave Congress the power to regulate the territories, arguing that that power included the right to purchase new territories. Congress and the President therefore stretched the Constitution to fit new circumstances and solve their dilemma.

SOURCES Marshall Smelser, *The Democratic Republic, 1801–1815* (New York: Harper & Row, 1968).

LURTON, HORACE H.
Associate Justice, 1910–14

- Born: Feb. 26, 1844, Newport, Ky.
- Education: Douglas University, 1860; Cumberland Law School, LL.B., 1867
- Previous government service: judge, Tennessee Supreme Court, 1886–93; judge, U.S. Court of Appeals for the Sixth Circuit, 1893–1909
- Appointed by President William Howard Taft Dec. 13, 1909; replaced Rufus W. Peckham, who died
- Supreme Court term: confirmed by the Senate Dec. 20, 1909, by a voice vote; served until July 12, 1914
- Died: July 12, 1914, Atlantic City, N.J.

Horace H. Lurton served in the Confederate Army during the Civil War. He was captured by Union forces and kept in a camp for prisoners of war. After the war, Lurton studied law and set up a private law practice in Clarksville, Tennessee.

During his brief term on the Court, Justice Lurton wrote few opinions. Instead, he usually went along with the Court's majority in deciding cases. He tended to support a strict construction of the Constitution and judicial restraint. Justice Lurton strongly opposed the use of judicial power to overcome social problems. In 1911 he wrote in *North American Review*, "The contention that . . . the Constitution is to be disregarded if it stands in the way of that which is deemed of public advantage . . . is destructive of the whole theory upon which our American Commonwealths have been founded."

M

MACE OF THE HOUSE OF REPRESENTATIVES

The symbol of authority of the House sergeant at arms is a 46-inch silver mace decorated with lashed rods and axes that are topped by a flying eagle. The House first adopted a mace, modeled after the mace of ancient Roman officials, in 1789. At the beginning of each day's session of the House, an assistant sergeant at arms brings the mace from its cabinet and sets it to the right of the Speaker's chair. There the mace stands upright on a marble pedestal for as long as the House remains in session. During moments of extreme turmoil in the House, the sergeant at arms will hold up the mace to restore order in the chamber. The Senate does not use a mace, but the symbol of the mace appears frequently in the decoration around the Senate and House chambers and office buildings.

SEE ALSO *Sergeant at arms*

MACLAY, WILLIAM

- Born: July 20, 1737, New Garden, Pa.
- Political party: Anti-Federalist
- Senator from Pennsylvania: 1789–91
- Died: Apr. 16, 1804, Harrisburg, Pa.

The diary of Senator William Maclay gives a rare glimpse of the Senate during the 1st Congress, when the Senate met entirely behind closed doors. The official records of its earliest debates and activities are thin and unrevealing. But Maclay kept a lively and highly opinionated diary of his personal observations. An Anti-Federalist who believed in simplicity of manners, Maclay was sharply critical and suspicious of the Senate's first president, John Adams, and other Federalists. His diary described in detail President Washington's first inauguration in the Senate chamber and the President's personal visit to receive the Senate's advice and consent on a treaty with the Indian nations. The diary also gives modern readers a glimpse into the first Senate committees, the earliest lobbyists, and the hectic last-minute business before the Senate adjourned. The first senators drew lots to see whether they would serve a full six-year term, a four-year term, or a two-year term, so that one-third of the Senate would stand for election every two years thereafter. Since Maclay drew a two-year term, his Senate service ended with the 1st Congress, and so did his diary.

SOURCES Kenneth R. Bowling and Helen E. Veit, eds., *The Diary of William Maclay and Other Notes on Senate Debates* (Baltimore, Md.: Johns Hopkins University Press, 1988).

MADISON, DOLLEY
First Lady

- Born: May 20, 1768, Guilford County, N.C.
- Wife of James Madison, 4th President
- Died: July 12, 1849, Washington, D.C.

Born Dorothea Payne, Dolley (also spelled Dolly) Madison grew up on a plantation in Virginia. In 1783 her father freed his slaves, sold his plantation, and started a factory in Philadelphia. Dolley Payne was married to John Todd, a Philadelphia lawyer, in 1789. Four years later Todd and their newborn son died of yellow fever. Dolley and her oldest son survived.

Dolley remained in Philadelphia. After a four-month courtship, she married James Madison in 1794. He was 17 years older than his bride, but they maintained a close and loving relationship for 42 years. While James Madison was shy and industrious, Dolley was outgoing and loved to entertain. She was noted for her beautiful gowns and elaborate makeup and hairstyling.

When Thomas Jefferson appointed Madison his secretary of state in 1801, the couple moved from Madison's Virginia plantation to Washington, D.C., where Dolley soon became the center of the Jefferson administration's social life. Both Jefferson and Aaron Burr were widowers, and Dolley was asked, as the wife of the senior department secretary, to preside over Presidential dinners and receptions. Her friendship with President Jefferson made her an unofficial First Lady in his administration. In 1809, when her husband became President, Dolley Madison simply continued with her duties as Washington's hostess.

Dolley Madison insisted on formal etiquette at all state functions. Beginning in May 1809 she held an informal Wednesday evening "salon" that was open not only to Washington officials but also to the general public. In August 1814, during the War of 1812, British troops captured the capital and burned many of its buildings. Dolley Madison managed to safeguard historical paintings, the White House silver, velvet curtains, a clock, and important state papers from the White House before fleeing to Virginia. After the British withdrew, the Madisons returned to Washington, where they lived in the Octagon House, which was loaned to them by the French government, until the White House could be rebuilt.

After Madison's retirement from the Presidency, the couple lived for 20 years at their plantation, Montpelier. After her husband's death in 1836, Dolley returned to Washington, where she lived for 13 years until her death.

SEE ALSO *First Lady; Madison, James*
SOURCES Elizabeth L. Dean, *Dolly Madison: The Nation's Hostess* (Boston: Lothrop, Lee & Shepard, 1928).

MADISON, JAMES
4th President

- Born: Mar. 16, 1751, Port Conway, Va.
- Political party: Democratic-Republican
- Education: College of New Jersey (Princeton), B.A., 1771
- Military service: none
- Previous government service: Committee of Safety, 1774; Virginia Constitutional Convention, 1776; Virginia House of Delegates, 1777, 1784–86; Virginia Governor's Council, 1778–80; Continental Congress, 1780–83; Annapolis Convention, 1786; federal Constitutional Convention, 1787; Virginia constitutional ratifying convention, 1788; U.S. House of Representatives, 1789–97; U.S. secretary of state, 1801–9
- Elected President, 1808; served, 1809–17
- Subsequent public service: Virginia Constitutional Convention, 1829; rector, University of Virginia, 1826–36
- Died: June 28, 1836, Montpelier, Va.

James Madison is known as the "father of the Constitution" because he played a major role at the Constitutional Convention of 1787. He drafted the Virginia Plan, with which the convention began its work, and he was instrumental in adding to the powers of Congress and the Presidency and in providing for a system of checks and balances among the branches of government. His own Presidency, however, was beset with difficulties, largely because of the workings of the checks and balances he had helped to create.

Madison grew up on his affluent family's plantation, Montpelier. Educated at the College of New Jersey, he then studied law and became a member of Orange County's Committee of Safety in 1774, at the start of the Revolution. At Virginia's constitutional convention of 1776 he fought for a clause protecting freedom of religion. He served in the Governor's Council for most of the remainder of the war. In the 1780s, as a member of the Continental Congress under the Articles of Confederation, he advocated strengthening its powers (particularly the power of taxation) to provide more effective government. In 1785, in the Virginia House of Delegates, he fought successfully for separation of church and state. With Alexander Hamilton he helped to organize the Annapolis Convention of 1786, a meeting of five states that proposed stronger powers for the national government in interstate commerce, and the Constitutional Convention in Philadelphia in 1787.

At that convention Madison helped put together the key compromises that kept the convention going, though the delegates rejected a number of his proposals, including a council of state to share executive power, a congressional veto on state laws, a Senate share in the Presidential power to pardon, a Supreme Court power to impeach the President, and a Supreme Court share in the Presidential veto power. Madison also unsuccessfully opposed any extension of the slave trade, which the convention decided to protect until 1808. Madison later published his notes on the convention debates, which are today the primary source for historians studying the convention.

Madison teamed up with Hamilton and John Jay to write *The Federalist Papers,* a set of essays defending the Constitution against attack by its critics and calling for its ratification. Madison wrote under the pen name Publius. He led the pro-Constitution faction at the Virginia ratifying convention, opposing the Anti-Federalists led by Patrick Henry and James Monroe.

Madison was passed over by the Virginia legislature for election to the U.S. Senate because the state legislators doubted that he would "obey instructions" on how to vote in the Senate. In 1788, however, he defeated James Monroe in the first elections held for the House of Representatives. As a member of the first Congress, Madison fulfilled a campaign pledge by proposing a Bill of Rights to protect civil liberties from actions of the national government. He also drafted legislation that organized the Departments of Foreign Affairs, War, and the Treasury. Although he held no official title, Madison served as floor leader of the House for President George Washington's administration during the 1st Congress. However, he soon came to oppose the financial program of the first Treasury secretary, Alexander Hamilton, particularly the protective tariff (a tax on imported goods), as well as Washington's Proclamation of Neutrality, which kept the United States out of the war between Great Britain and France. Together with Thomas Jefferson, Madison organized an opposition faction that later became the Democratic-Republican party, and they attracted to it most of the Anti-Federalists of the 1780s.

During the undeclared naval war with France in 1798 the Federalist Congress passed the Alien and Sedition Acts, which made it a crime to publish criticism of government war policies. In response, in 1798 Madison and Jefferson wrote the Kentucky and Virginia Resolutions, which stated that the Alien and Sedition Acts were unconstitutional and which implied that the states need not enforce them. This was a reversal of Madison's strong "nationalist" position of the 1780s, when he wanted national law to be supreme over state laws.

After Jefferson was elected President in 1800, Madison became his secretary of state. He defended the Louisiana Purchase and supported Jefferson's decision to ask Congress to pass an Embargo Act, which would ban trade with European nations while they were at war. His negotiations with Spain to acquire Florida were unsuccessful.

In 1808 the Republican congressional

caucus nominated Madison for the Presidency. He defeated his Federalist opponent, Charles Cotesworth Pinckney, 122 electoral votes to 47.

Foreign policy preoccupied the Madison Presidency; the President acted as his own secretary of state until the appointment of James Monroe in 1811 to replace the incompetent Robert Smith. In 1809 Congress repealed Jefferson's Embargo Act, which forbade carrying foreign goods on American ships, and replaced it with the Non-Intercourse Act, which banned all trade with England and France until those countries ceased interfering with U.S. shipping. Madison declared that trade with Great Britain would be permitted but soon found that assurances that U.S. ships would be left alone were not honored by the British government. Madison issued a nonintercourse proclamation against Great Britain in November 1810. Congress then passed a bill that ended all restrictions on U.S. trade with Europe. It promised, however, that if the British would cease harassing American ships, the United States would bar trade with its enemy France, and if the French would cease harassment, the United States would bar trade with Great Britain. French emperor Napoleon promised freedom of the seas to U.S. ships, and Madison issued a nonintercourse proclamation against the British. Then Napoleon betrayed Madison by issuing new decrees against U.S. shipping, forcing the President to admit to Congress that his policy had failed.

The "war hawks" in Congress urged Madison to declare war against Great Britain, and they pressed for an invasion of Canada. Although the nation was unprepared for war and large parts of New England opposed it, on June 1, 1812, Madison bowed to the war hawks in his party and sent a secret message to Congress asking for a declaration of war. Not everyone approved of war, and the declaration carried in the House by 79 to 49 and in the Senate by only 19 to 13. Madison signed the declaration on June 18, 1812. He had already been unanimously renominated by the Republican caucus, and in the general election he defeated DeWitt Clinton.

The War of 1812 was a disaster. A U.S. invasion of Canada failed, and much of the Northwest Territory, including the key outpost at Detroit, was retaken by the British. By 1813 the British navy had bottled up U.S. naval vessels and blockaded the American coast. After defeating Napoleon in Europe, the British were able to transfer 14 new regiments to the war effort in the United States. They marched into Washington, D.C., on August 24, 1814, and burned the Capitol, the President's House, and other public buildings in retaliation for a U.S. raid on Toronto the year before. When Madison returned to the capital, he took up residence in the Octagon House, near the ruined President's House. Congress reassembled in the old patents and post office building next to the ruined Capitol Building. Disgruntled Federalists met in Hartford, Connecticut, in December 1814 to demand that Madison end the war. Republicans claimed that Federalists at the meeting, known as the Hartford Convention, were plotting to secede from the Union.

But the news was not all bad. Heroic resistance by the defenders of Fort McHenry prevented the British from capturing Baltimore and inspired Francis Scott Key, who was imprisoned on a British ship attacking the fort, to write "The Star-Spangled Banner." The British suffered major defeats in northern New York State and Mobile, Alabama. Then Andrew Jackson won the Battle of New Orleans. Even before that battle, the British and U.S. peace negotiators had signed the Treaty of Ghent (though news had not yet reached the United States), and Madison urged the Senate to consent to it. The United States failed to gain any of its war aims and was lucky to keep all its territory intact. But Americans had not conceded any rights to a greater power and had demonstrated their willingness to fight for freedom of the seas.

At the end of the war Madison turned

to domestic matters. He called for a larger military, a protective tariff, a system of roads and canals, and a national university. Congress authorized a stronger military establishment and passed the first protective tariff in U.S. history but did not act on the bill for a university—something Madison had tried to put in the Constitution in 1787. He also won congressional approval to charter the Second Bank of the United States.

Madison retired to his plantation at Montpelier in 1817. He participated in the Virginia Constitutional Convention of 1829, organized his notes of the federal convention of 1787 for publication, and was rector of the University of Virginia from 1826 until his death in 1836.

SEE ALSO *Creation of the Presidency; Jefferson, Thomas; Madison, Dolley; Monroe, James; Washington, George*

SOURCES Irving Brant, *James Madison* (Indianapolis: Bobbs-Merrill, 1961). Ralph Ketcham, *James Madison: A Biography* (Charlottesville: University of Virginia Press, 1990). Jack N. Rakove, *James Madison and the Creation of the American Republic* (Glenview, Ill.: Scott, Foresman, 1990). Robert A. Rutland, *James Madison: The Founding Father* (New York: Macmillan, 1987).

MAJORITY LEADER

Members of the majority party in both the House of Representatives and the Senate elect a leader to represent them in floor proceedings and to serve as a spokesperson for their party's position on the issues. The majority leader schedules business on the floor, plans party strategy, and attempts to keep the majority party as united as possible when casting roll call votes. Majority leaders receive a higher salary than other members, a car and driver, and a separate leadership office and staff within the Capitol.

The Constitution provides for presiding officers for the House and Senate but says nothing about party floor leadership.

This was because the framers of the Constitution hoped that the United States might avoid parties—or factions, as they called them. But within a few years after the federal government had started, such controversial issues as the Jay Treaty divided Americans, and their congressional representatives, into opposing political parties. Early Presidents turned to certain members of the House and Senate to act as their spokesmen, to promote their programs, and to make sure other members of their party voted with them. Formal party leadership positions, such as majority and minority leaders and whips, evolved over time.

House majority leaders Because of the House's larger size, its parties were first to require active floor leadership to keep their members informed and in line. The Speaker would designate one member to act as his spokesman on the floor, often choosing the chairman of the powerful Ways and Means Committee or the Appropriations Committee. By the Civil War the press was using the terms *majority* and *minority leader* to describe the top party officials in the House.

After progressive House members revolted against the dictatorial leadership of Speaker Joseph G. Cannon in 1910, Speakers lost the power to name the floor leader. Instead, the party conferences elected the leader. These leaders devoted their attention to floor business and no longer chaired committees. Majority leaders also became the prime candidates to move up to the Speakership.

Senate majority leaders During the 19th century, leadership in the Senate was divided among the majority party caucus (or conference) leader and the most powerful committee chairmen. "No one is *the* Senator, no one may speak for his party as well as himself," Woodrow Wilson wrote in his study of Congress in 1885. By the time Wilson became President in 1913, Senate party leaders began to emerge. Democratic conference chairman John Worth Kern and later Republican conference chairman Henry Cabot Lodge per-

Majority Leaders of the House

Serano E. Payne (Republican-New York), 1899-1911

Oscar W. Underwood (Democrat-Alabama), 1911-15

Claude Kitchin (Democrat-North Carolina), 1915-19

Franklin W. Mondell (Republican-Wyoming), 1919-23

Nicholas Longworth (Republican-Ohio), 1923-25

John Q. Tilson (Republican-Connecticut), 1925-31

Henry T. Rainey (Democrat-Illinois), 1931-33

Joseph W. Byrns (Democrat-Tennessee), 1933-35

William Bankhead (Democrat-Alabama), 1935-36

Sam Rayburn (Democrat-Texas), 1937-40

John W. McCormack (Democrat-Massachusetts) 1940-47, 1949-53, 1955-61

Charles A. Halleck (Republican-Indiana), 1947-49, 1953-55

Carl Albert (Democrat-Oklahoma), 1961-69

Hale Boggs (Democrat-Louisiana), 1969-72

Thomas P. ("Tip") O'Neill, Jr. (Democrat-Massachusetts), 1973-77

Jim Wright (Democrat-Texas), 1977-87

Thomas S. Foley (Democrat-Washington), 1987-89

Richard A. Gephardt (Democrat-Missouri), 1989-95

Richard Armey (Republican-Texas), 1995

Identification of majority leaders in the 19th century was unofficial, and a comprehensive list is unavailable.

Majority Leaders of the Senate

John Worth Kern (Democrat-Indiana), 1913-17*

Thomas S. Martin (Democrat-Virginia), 1917-19*

Henry Cabot Lodge, Sr. (Republican-Massachusetts), 1919-24*

Charles Curtis (Republican-Kansas), 1925-29

James S. Watson (Republican-Indiana), 1929-33

Joseph T. Robinson (Democrat-Arkansas), 1933-37

Alben W. Barkley (Democrat-Kentucky), 1937-47

Wallace H. White, Jr. (Republican-Maine), 1947-49

Scott Lucas (Democrat-Illinois), 1949-51

Ernest McFarland (Democrat-Arizona), 1951-53

Robert A. Taft, Sr. (Republican-Ohio), 1953

William F. Knowland (Republican-California), 1953-55

Lyndon B. Johnson (Democrat-Texas), 1955-61

Mike Mansfield (Democrat-Montana), 1961-77

Robert C. Byrd (Democrat-West Virginia), 1977-81, 1987-89

Howard Baker (Republican-Tennessee), 1981-85

Robert Dole (Republican-Kansas), 1985-87, 1995-96

George S. Mitchell (Democrat-Maine), 1989-95

Trent Lott (Republican-Mississippi), 1996-

*conference chairman; not officially designated majority leader formed all the functions of modern majority leaders, although neither formally held the title. The Democrats first designated a floor leader in 1921. They elected Oscar W. Underwood (Democrat–Alabama), who had previously served as House majority leader from 1911 to 1915. In 1925 the Republicans designated Charles Curtis (Republican–Kansas) as their first official majority leader.

House rules favor the majority party and limit the role of the minority—as long as the majority stays united. Senate rules give more authority to individual members of both the majority and minority parties and provide few specific powers for the leaders. Senate rules require that the presiding officer must recognize the majority and minority leaders before other senators seeking recognition to speak. This procedure gives the leadership increased control over the proceedings. The floor leaders also chair their party steering committees, which determine committee assignments. But otherwise the job carries few specific powers. The power of the majority leader depends instead on the skill, intelligence, and personality of the person who holds the post.

SEE ALSO *Leadership in Congress; Minority leader*

MAJORITY OPINION

The opinion of the U.S. Supreme Court in cases that it decides is usually a majority opinion. A majority is one more than half of the justices participating in a decision. When five of the nine justices agree with the opinion of the Court, there is a majority opinion of the Court. When four of seven justices agree (with two justices not participating), there is a majority opinion. All decisions of the Court are by majority vote. In some cases, however, there is not a majority opinion because too many justices write their own concurring opinions. These justices vote with the majority to reach a decision on a case, but they write separate concurring opinions. For exam-

ple, in 1989 the Court decided *Webster* v. *Reproductive Health Services* by a 5 to 4 vote. However, two justices voting with the majority wrote separate concurring opinions. Only three justices joined the opinion announced by the Court. As a result, there was a plurality opinion in the case, not a majority opinion.

SEE ALSO *Concurring opinion; Dissenting opinion; Opinions of the Supreme Court; Plurality opinion*

SOURCES Fred W. Friendly and Martha J. H. Elliott. "A Knock at the Door: How the Supreme Court Created a Rule to Enforce the Fourth Amendment," in *The Constitution: That Delicate Balance* (New York: Random House, 1984).

MANSFIELD, MIKE

- Born: Mar. 19, 1903, New York, N.Y.
- Political party: Democrat
- Education: Montana State University at Missoula, graduated, 1933, and M.A., 1934; University of California at Los Angeles, 1936, 1937
- Representative from Montana: 1943–53
- Senator from Montana: 1953–77
- Senate majority whip: 1957–61
- Senate majority leader: 1961–77

It was not easy following Lyndon B. Johnson as Senate majority leader. Although many senators were glad to see the domineering Johnson leave, others wanted Johnson's strong style of leadership to continue. Mansfield believed that all senators should be equal and should act out of a sense of their own responsibility rather than be driven by a powerful leader. Explaining his leadership style, Mansfield said, "I am neither a circus ringmaster, the master of ceremonies of a Senate night club, a tamer of Senate lions, or a wheeler and dealer." Instead, he argued that senators needed to work out their own agreements and accommodations through mutual respect for each other. Although some people, including President Lyndon B. Johnson, grumbled over Mansfield's permissive style, it helped promote a burst of legislative activity in the 1960s and made Mansfield the longest-serving majority leader in Senate history.

SEE ALSO *Johnson, Lyndon B.; Leadership in Congress; Majority leader*

SOURCES Ross K. Baker, "Mike Mansfield and the Birth of the Modern Senate," in *First among Equals: Outstanding Senate Leaders of the Twentieth Century,* edited by Richard A. Baker and Roger Davidson (Washington, D.C.: Congressional Quarterly, 1991).

MAPP V. OHIO

- 367 U.S. 643 (1961)
- Vote: 6–3
- For the Court: Clark
- Concurring: Black, Douglas, and Stewart
- Dissenting: Harlan, Frankfurter, and Whittaker

On May 23, 1957, police officers forced their way into the home of Dollree Mapp, whom they suspected of criminal activities. The police claimed they had a search warrant, which is required under the 4th Amendment to the Constitution, but they never proved it. During their unwarranted search of Mapp's house, the police seized obscene pictures, which under an Ohio law were illegal objects for someone to have. Mapp was convicted of possessing obscene pictures and sentenced to prison. Her lawyer appealed to the U.S. Supreme Court.

The Issue The police obtained evidence of Dollree Mapp's illegal behavior through actions that violated the 4th Amendment guarantee against unreasonable searches and seizures. Can evidence obtained through an illegally conducted search be used to convict a person of violating a state law?

Opinion of the Court The Court overturned Dollree Mapp's conviction. Justice Tom Clark wrote that evidence obtained in violation of the 4th Amendment of the U.S. Constitution must be excluded from use in state as well as federal criminal

trials. The Court thus applied the exclusionary rule for the first time in ruling against a state government.

Dissent The dissenting opinions were based on opposition to the incorporation doctrine, by which the exclusionary rule associated with the 4th Amendment was applied to a state government through the due process clause of the 14th Amendment. The dissenting justices believed that the 4th Amendment guarantees of individual rights were applicable only to the federal government.

Significance The exclusionary rule was created by the Court in *Weeks* v. *United States* (1914). Before the *Mapp* case, however, this rule had never been used against a state government. During the 1980s the Court recognized certain exceptions to the exclusionary rule as used in the *Mapp* case. For example, in *United States* v. *Leon* (1984), the Court ruled that evidence seized on the basis of a mistakenly issued search warrant can be used in a trial, if the warrant was issued in good faith—that is, on presumption that there were valid reasons for issuing the warrant. As a result, the exclusionary rule has been narrowed by this "good faith" exception.

SEE ALSO *Exclusionary rule; Incorporation doctrine; Searches and seizures; United States v. Leon; Weeks v. United States*

MARBURY V. MADISON

- 1 Cranch 137 (1803)
- Vote: 5–0
- For the Court: Marshall

In the Presidential election of 1800, Thomas Jefferson, the candidate of the Democratic-Republican party, defeated the Federalist candidate, John Adams. Not only had Adams lost the Presidency but the Federalists had lost control of Congress. Adams and his party feared that Jefferson would ruin the country by undoing everything the Federalists had accomplished in the previous 12 years. Between the November election and the March inauguration, the Federalists tried to ensure that they would continue to play a role in the U.S. government.

On January 20, 1801, Adams appointed Secretary of State John Marshall to be chief justice of the United States. Although the Senate confirmed this nomination in less than two weeks, Marshall remained secretary of state until Jefferson took office.

Throughout February the Federalists, who controlled Congress, created offices for Adams to fill with loyal supporters. During his last month as President, Adams nominated more than 200 men to new offices. These nominations included 42 justices of the peace for the new national capital at Washington, D.C. Adams appointed William Marbury as one of these justices of the peace.

The Senate received the nominations of the new justices of the peace on March 2 and confirmed them on March 3, Adams's last day in office. In order for the confirmed appointees to assume office, the executive had to complete one more procedure: the President had to sign commissions empowering each man to hold office, and the secretary of state had to place the official seal of the U.S. government on those commissions and supervise their delivery. In those days, officials prepared the commissions by hand. Thus, Adams spent his last evening as President signing commissions. The secretary of state, John Marshall, worked well into the night, affixing the Great Seal of the United States to the commissions and sending them off for delivery. However, in the chaos of Adams's last day in office, a number of commissions, including William Marbury's, though signed and sealed, remained undelivered.

On March 4, 1801, Jefferson became President. Soon after, Marbury asked the new secretary of state, James Madison, for his commission. Madison, after consulting with Jefferson, refused to give Marbury the commission. Marbury then appealed to the Supreme Court for help.

Marbury asked the Court to issue a writ of mandamus directed to Secretary of State James Madison. A writ of mandamus orders a public official to carry out his duties. Marbury argued that he was legally entitled to his commission and that Madison should give it to him. Madison ignored these legal proceedings. Neither he nor Jefferson believed that the Supreme Court could give orders to the other two branches of government. Thus, the Court had to rule on Marbury's case with the knowledge that Madison might ignore the ruling. The man responsible for making the ruling was John Marshall, who as secretary of state had failed to send Marbury his commission in the first place.

The Issue   Marbury argued that Section 13 of the Judiciary Act of 1789 gave the Supreme Court authority to issue a writ of mandamus under its original jurisdiction, its power to hear and decide such a case for the first time. The writ would require Secretary of State Madison to deliver Marbury's commission. Marbury pointed out that an act of Congress had created the office and the Senate had confirmed his Presidential appointment. With the commission legally signed and sealed, delivery of the commission was not, in Marbury's view, a discretionary act on the part of the secretary of state. Madison did not, Marbury claimed, have the authority to choose whether to deliver the commission. Rather, his job required him to deliver it.

Did Marbury have a right to the commission, and did the law provide him a means to obtain it? These were the apparent issues of the case. Chief Justice Marshall, however, asserted another issue: Could the Supreme Court, under the U.S. Constitution, have original jurisdiction in this case? Or, to put it another way, did Section 13 of the Judiciary Act of 1789 contradict or violate the U.S. Constitution?

Opinion of the Court   The Court ruled that Marbury was due his commission. Chief Justice John Marshall said, "To withhold his commission is an act" that violates the law.

Marshall held that the writ of mandamus was the proper legal procedure to require a public official to do his duty.

Marshall also acknowledged that the Judiciary Act of 1789 authorized the Supreme Court to issue such a writ.

Marshall knew, however, that if he ruled in favor of Marbury, Madison would probably ignore the Court's order to deliver the commission and cause a constitutional crisis. Above all else, Marshall hoped to avoid such a controversy. So one more question remained for Marshall to answer. Could the Supreme Court actually issue the writ of mandamus? If it could, then Marshall had backed himself into a corner. Having admitted that Marbury deserved the writ, he would then have to issue one. But Marshall had an out.

Marbury had directed his request for a writ of mandamus to the Supreme Court. By asking the Supreme Court to issue the writ, Marbury had asked the Court to take original jurisdiction in the case, to be the first court to consider the request. In complying with such a request, the Supreme Court would act as a trial court. However, the founders of the Supreme Court had designed the Supreme Court as an appellate court—a court to hear appeals from other federal courts and from the state courts. The Constitution, in Article 3, Section 2, Clause 2, spelled out the few types of cases over which the Supreme Court would exercise original jurisdiction. Marshall examined that clause of the Constitution and concluded it did not authorize the Supreme Court to issue a writ of mandamus. Such a writ, he decided, could come only from a lower court.

Thus, Marshall concluded that Section 13 of the Judiciary Act of 1789, which authorized the Court to issue a writ of mandamus, violated the Constitution. Because the Supreme Court could not enforce an unconstitutional law, Marbury did not get his writ.

Marshall's opinion avoided generating a confrontation with Madison and Jefferson. He did not order Madison to give Marbury his commission. Marshall also succeeded in lecturing Madison and Jefferson on their respective responsibilities as secretary of state and President. In addition, by his opinion Marshall successfully asserted the Supreme Court's power to declare acts of Congress unconstitutional. This power is known as judicial review.

Marshall used three provisions of the Constitution to justify his arguments for judicial review. The first was Article 3, Section 2, which extends the judicial power to "all Cases, in Law and Equity, arising under this Constitution." Marshall argued: "Could it be the intention of those who gave this power, to say, that in using it, the constitution should not be looked into? That a case arising under the constitution should be decided, without examining the instrument under which it arises? This is too extravagant to be maintained."

Second, Article 6 requires judges to pledge "to support this Constitution." Marshall wrote, "How immoral to impose [this oath] on them, if they were to be used as the instruments . . . for violating what they swear to support!"

Third, Marshall pointed out that "in declaring what shall be the supreme law of the land [Article 6], the constitution itself is first mentioned; and not the laws of the United States, generally, but those only which shall be made in pursuance of the constitution, have that rank." Marshall argued from the supremacy clause of Article 6 that no act of Congress that violates any part of the Constitution, the highest law, can be valid. Rather, it must be declared unconstitutional and repealed.

Marshall memorably defined the Supreme Court's duty under the U.S. Constitution:

> It is, emphatically, the province and duty of the judicial department, to say what the law is. . . . So, if a law be in opposition to the constitution; if both the law and the constitution apply to a particular case, so that the court must either decide that case, conformable to the law, disregarding the constitution; or conformable to the constitution, disregarding the law; the court must determine which of these conflicting rules gov-

erns the case; this is of the very essence of judicial duty. If then, the courts are to regard the constitution, and the constitution is superior to any ordinary act of the legislature, the constitution, and not such ordinary act, must govern the case to which both apply.

Significance The *Marbury* decision provided the constitutional basis for the Supreme Court's power of judicial review of the actions and laws of the federal government. This decision asserted the Court's power to declare invalid those federal laws it finds in conflict with the Constitution. The Court's decision laid the foundation on which the Supreme Court eventually developed into an important branch of the federal government.

Full acceptance of judicial review would not happen until after the Civil War. Regardless, this case established the principle that the courts and government should not enforce unconstitutional federal laws.

SEE ALSO *Judicial power; Judicial review; Judiciary Act of 1789*

SOURCES Robert Lowry Clinton, *Marbury v. Madison and Judicial Review* (Lawrence: University Press of Kansas, 1989). John A. Garraty, "The Case of the Missing Commissions," *in Quarrels That Have Shaped the Constitution,* edited by John A. Garraty (New York: Harper & Row, 1987).

MARINE BAND, U.S.

The Marine Band, known as "the President's own," is a unit of the U.S. Marine Corps. It is assigned to play at the White House on ceremonial occasions, such as the arrival of a foreign head of state, state dinners, and cultural events. The director of the Marine Band serves as the musical adviser to the President in organizing the music for ceremonial occasions.

Established on July 11, 1798, by President John Adams, the band is the oldest musical organization in the U.S. armed forces and the oldest continuous unit of the Marine Corps. It has played at every Presidential inauguration since Thomas Jefferson's in 1801 and at every inaugural ball since James Madison's in 1809. The first dancing at the White House occurred in 1828, during the Presidency of John Quincy Adams, to the music of the Marine Band.

The band achieved its greatest prominence after 1880 when John Philip Sousa assumed the position of musical director and transformed it into the best band in the nation. Its concerts in Washington, D.C., became cultural events when it premiered Sousa's new marches, such as "Semper Fidelis" and "The Washington Post" march, which inspired a dance craze in the United States and Europe. In 1891 Sousa took the band on its first national tour, and since then the band has made such tours every fall except during wartime. The Marine Band's recordings of Sousa marches were some of the first ever made for Thomas Edison's phonograph.

Today the band or its individual performers play more than 600 times each year. In 1990 it made an 18-day concert tour of the Soviet Union as part of a historic Soviet-American Armed Forces Band Exchange designed to promote better understanding between the two nations.

SEE ALSO *"Hail to the Chief"; "Ruffles and Flourishes"*

SOURCES Elise Kirk, *Music at the White House* (Urbana: University of Illinois Press, 1986).

MARKUP SESSIONS

After congressional hearings have been held on a bill, the members of the subcommittee or full committee will meet to "mark up" the bill. This means that they will make final changes, adding and removing words and provisions, revising the amounts of money authorized, and otherwise polishing and perfecting the text before reporting it to the floor. The name dates back to the time when committee members and clerks literally "marked up" bills by writing the new amendments on the original text. Until the 1970s, markup sessions were held behind closed doors and were the occasion for much last-minute compromising and deal making. But "sunshine" rules adopted by the House in 1973 and the Senate in 1975 required that committees hold their markups in public session.

SEE ALSO *Committees, congressional; Hearings, congressional; "Sunshine" rules*

MARSHALL, JOHN
Chief Justice, 1801–35

- Born: Sept. 24, 1755, Germantown, Va.
- Education: taught at home by his father and two clergymen; self-educated in law; attended one course on law, College of William and Mary, 1780
- Previous government service: Virginia House of Delegates, 1782–85, 1787–90, 1795–96; Executive Council of State, Virginia, 1782–84; recorder, Richmond City Hustings Court, Virginia, 1785–88; U.S. minister to France, 1797–98; Virginia Ratifying Convention, 1788; U.S. representative from Virginia, 1799–1800; U.S. secretary of state, 1800–1801
- Appointed by President John Adams Jan. 20, 1801; replaced Oliver Ellsworth, who resigned
- Supreme Court term: confirmed by the Senate Jan. 27, 1801, by a voice vote; served until July 6, 1835
- Died: July 6, 1835, Philadelphia, Pa.

John Marshall was the fourth chief justice of the United States. From his time to ours, he has been called the Great Chief Justice.

Born and raised in the backcountry of Virginia, Marshall was educated mostly at home, with his father as the main teacher. His formal education in the law consisted of one course of lectures by George Wythe, a leading Virginia political leader and legal authority at the College of William and Mary. Marshall, however, had a keen mind that he filled with knowledge through a lifetime of reading, thinking, and interact-

ing with political leaders in the public affairs of Virginia and the United States.

Participation in the American Revolution shaped John Marshall's lifetime loyalty to the United States. He later expressed this loyalty decisively during his tenure on the Supreme Court through opinions that reinforced the power and authority of the federal government over the states. He served in the Continental Army for nearly six years, fought in the battles of Great Bridge, Brandywine, Germantown, and Monmouth and spent the grueling winter with George Washington's forces at Valley Forge. He left the Continental Army in 1781 with the rank of captain. Marshall exhibited intense patriotism and had great admiration for George Washington, which he expressed later in his five-volume biography *Life of George Washington,* published in 1804–7.

President John Adams appointed Marshall to be chief justice in 1801 as one of his final actions before leaving office. Adams's first choice for the job was John Jay, who had been the first chief justice. Jay, however, declined because in his view, widely shared at the time, the Supreme Court was too weak and unimportant; he said that he would not be head of "a system so defective." So John Marshall took the job that Jay refused and transformed it into the most powerful and prominent judicial position in the world.

Marshall brought unity and order to the Court by practically ending *seriatim* opinions (the writing of opinions by various justices). Before Chief Justice Marshall, the Court did not issue a single majority opinion. He, however, influenced the Court's majority to speak with one voice, through an opinion for the Court on each case before it. Of course, members of the Court occasionally wrote concurring or dissenting opinions, as they do today.

Often the Court's voice was John Marshall's. During his 34 years on the Court, the longest tenure of any chief justice, Marshall wrote 519 of the 1,100 opinions issued during that period, and he dissented only eight times.

Chief Justice Marshall's greatest opinions were masterworks of legal reasoning and graceful writing. They stand today as an authoritative commentary on the core principles of the U.S. Constitution. Marshall's first great decision came in *Marbury* v. *Madison* (1803), in which he ruled that Section 13 of the Judiciary Act of 1789 was void because it violated Article 3 of the Constitution. In this opinion, Marshall made a compelling argument for judicial review, the Court's power to decide whether an act of Congress violates the Constitution. If it does, Marshall wrote, then the legislative act contrary to the Constitution is unconstitutional, or illegal, and could not be enforced. Marshall wrote, "It is emphatically the province and duty of the judicial department to say what the law is. . . . So if a law be in opposition to the constitution . . . the constitution and not such ordinary Act, must govern the case to which they both apply."

In a series of great decisions, Marshall also established, beyond legal challenge, the Court's power of judicial review over acts of state government. In *Fletcher* v. *Peck* (1810), *Dartmouth College* v. *Woodward* (1819), *McCulloch* v. *Maryland* (1819), and *Cohens* v. *Virginia* (1821), Marshall wrote for the Court that acts of state government in violation of federal statutes or the federal Constitution were unconstitutional or void.

The Marshall Court's decisions also defended the sanctity of contracts and private property rights against would-be violators in the cases of *Fletcher* v. *Peck* and *Dartmouth College* v. *Woodward*. In *Gibbons* v. *Ogden* (1824), Marshall broadly interpreted Congress's power to regulate commerce (Article 1, Section 8, of the Constitution) and prohibited states from passing laws to interfere with the flow of goods and transportation across state lines.

Chief Justice Marshall's greatest opinions protected private property rights as a foundation of individual liberty. They also rejected claims of state sovereignty in favor of a federal Constitution based on the sovereignty of the people of the United States.

Finally, Marshall clearly and convincingly argued for the Constitution as a permanent supreme law that the Supreme Court was established to interpret and defend. "Ours is a Constitution," Marshall wrote in 1819 (*McCulloch* v. *Maryland*), "intended to endure for ages to come, and consequently, to be adapted to the various crises of human affairs."

Only through broad construction of the federal government's powers could the Constitution of 1787 be "adapted" to meet changing times. And only through strict limits on excessive use of the government's powers could the Constitution endure as a guardian of individual rights. The special duty of the Supreme Court, according to Marshall, was to make the difficult judgments, based on the Constitution, about when to impose limits or to permit broad exercise of the federal government's powers.

In 1833, near the end of John Marshall's career, his associate on the Supreme Court, Justice Joseph Story, wrote a "Dedication to John Marshall" that included these words of high praise: "Your expositions of constitutional law . . . constitute a monument of fame far beyond the ordinary memorials of political or military glory. They are destined to enlighten, instruct and convince future generations; and can scarcely perish but with the memory of the Constitution itself." And so it has been, from Marshall's time until our own, that his judgments and commentaries on the Constitution have instructed and inspired Americans.

SEE ALSO *Cohens v. Virginia; Dartmouth College v. Woodward; Fletcher v. Peck; Judicial review; Marbury v. Madison; McCulloch v. Maryland*

SOURCES Leonard Baker, *John Marshall: A Life in Law* (New York: Macmillan, 1974). Charles F. Hobson, *The Great Chief Justice: John Marshall and the Rule of Law* (Lawrence: University Press of Kansas, 2000). Herbert A. Johnson, *The Chief Justiceship of John Marshall, 1801–1835* (Columbia: University of South Carolina Press, 1998). Frances H. Rudko, *John Mar-*

shall, Statesman, and Chief Justice (Westport, Conn.: Greenwood Press, 1991). Francis N. Stites, *John Marshall: Defender of the Constitution* (Boston: Little, Brown, 1981). G. Edward White, *The Marshall Court and Cultural Change* (New York: Oxford University Press, 1991).

MARSHALL, THOMAS
Vice President

- Born: Mar. 14, 1854, North Manchester, Ind.
- Political party: Democrat
- Education: Wabash College, 1873; read law, 1874–75
- Previous government service: governor of Indiana, 1909–10
- Vice President under Woodrow Wilson, 1913–21
- Subsequent government service: U.S. Coal Commission, 1922–23
- Died: June 1, 1925, Washington, D.C.

Thomas Marshall was a lawyer active in Democratic party campaigns, and he served one term as governor of Indiana. He was a favorite-son candidate for President in 1912, and after switching his delegation to Woodrow Wilson he was rewarded with the Vice Presidential nomination. He served for two terms, the first Vice President to do so in nearly a century. He presided over the Senate with fairness and over the cabinet when Wilson was in Paris negotiating the Treaty of Versailles after World War I. Marshall told the secretaries that he was presiding "informally and personally" and not seeking "to exercise any official duty or function." At first opposed to U.S. entry into World War I, Marshall loyally supported Wilson's decision to intervene as well as the Treaty of Versailles. He opposed the woman suffrage amendment in the postwar period. He offered a definitive word on the Vice Presidency when he quipped: "There were two brothers. One ran away to sea, the other was elected Vice President, and nothing was ever heard from either of them again."

Marshall is also remembered as the man who said, "What this country needs is a good five cent cigar." Marshall had Presidential ambitions of his own, but Wilson successfully blocked him. After his Vice Presidency, Marshall served on the U.S. Coal Commission.

SEE ALSO *Wilson, Woodrow*
SOURCES Thomas Marshall, *Recollections of Thomas R. Marshall, Vice President and Hoosier Philosopher* (Indianapolis: Bobbs-Merrill, 1925). Charles M. Thomas, *Thomas Riley Marshall: Hoosier Statesman* (Oxford University Press, Ohio: Mississippi Valley Press, 1939).

MARSHALL, THURGOOD
Associate Justice, 1967–91

- Born: July 2, 1908, Baltimore, Md.
- Education: Lincoln University, B.A., 1930; Howard University Law School, LL.B., 1933
- Previous government service: judge, Second Circuit Court of Appeals, 1961–65; U.S. solicitor general, 1965–67
- Appointed by President Lyndon B. Johnson June 13, 1967; replaced Tom C. Clark, who retired
- Supreme Court term: confirmed by the Senate Aug. 30, 1967, by a 69–11 vote; retired Oct. 1, 1991
- Died: Jan. 24, 1993, Bethesda, Md.

Thurgood Marshall, the great-grandson of a slave, was the first African-American justice of the Supreme Court. He began his historic career in 1933, as a civil rights lawyer for the National Association for the Advancement of Colored People (NAACP). In 1940 Marshall became head of the NAACP Legal Defense Fund. In this position, he led the NAACP's legal fight against racial segregation and denial of individual rights of black people. Marshall successfully argued 29 out of 32 cases before the U.S. Supreme Court.

In 1954 Thurgood Marshall achieved his biggest victory for the NAACP in

Brown v. *Board of Education.* In this landmark case, Marshall convinced the Supreme Court to decide that racial segregation in public schools was unconstitutional. This was the beginning of the eventual ending of state government laws that denied equal rights to black people.

In 1961 President John F. Kennedy appointed Marshall to the U.S. Court of Appeals for the Second Circuit. In 1965 President Lyndon B. Johnson selected Marshall to be solicitor general of the United States, the top lawyer for the U.S. government in federal court cases. Marshall was the first African American to serve as the solicitor general and to argue cases for the government at the Supreme Court.

During his 24 years on the Court, Justice Marshall wrote many opinions on various issues pertaining to federal jurisdiction, antitrust laws, and civil rights. He wrote numerous dissenting opinions about equal protection of the laws, the rights of minorities, and capital punishment. He strongly opposed the death penalty, which in his opinion was a violation of the 8th Amendment prohibition of "cruel and unusual punishment." Throughout his long career in law, Thurgood Marshall was an outspoken advocate for the rights and opportunities of minorities, especially for African Americans and poor people.

During his final years on the Court, Justice Marshall often wrote strong dissents to call attention to his views about unmet needs for social justice. He opposed the conservative tendencies of the Court during the 1980s and was a staunch ally of Justice William Brennan in arguing for liberal positions. He remained on the Court only one term after Brennan retired, citing declining health as a major reason for his retirement. Marshall's death in 1993 brought an outpouring of praise for his remarkable career.

SEE ALSO *Brown v. Board of Education; Civil rights; National Association for the Advancement of Colored People (NAACP)*

SOURCES Lisa Aldred, *Thurgood Marshall*

(New York: Chelsea House, 1990). Carl T. Rowan, *Dream Makers, Dream Breakers: The World of Thurgood Marshall* (Boston: Little, Brown, 1993). Mark V. Tushnet, *Making Civil Rights Law: Thurgood Marshall and the Supreme Court, 1936–1961* (New York: Oxford University Press, 1993).

MARSHAL, SUPREME COURT

SEE *Staff of the Supreme Court, nonjudicial*

MARTIN V. HUNTER'S LESSEE

- 1 Wheat. 304 (1816)
- Vote: 6–0
- For the Court: Story
- Not participating: Marshall

Thomas, sixth Lord Fairfax, owned more than 5 million acres of valuable land in the northern area of western Virginia. In 1781 Lord Fairfax died and left his property to a nephew, Denny Martin, a British subject. However, during the War of Independence, Virginia had passed laws confiscating the property of Loyalists, such as Lord Fairfax, who supported Great Britain. The state sold the land to private owners, including David Hunter, who denied Denny Martin's claim to his uncle's property. Martin challenged Hunter's right to this property and filed a lawsuit against him.

The state courts of Virginia decided in favor of Hunter, so Martin took his case to the U.S. Supreme Court. In *Fairfax's Devisee* v. *Hunter's Lessee* (1813), the Court decided in favor of Martin. (Chief Justice John Marshall did not participate in this decision because of financial interests in the land at issue.)

Writing for the Court, Justice Joseph Story overturned the Virginia laws used to take the Fairfax lands, reasoning that Martin's inheritance was protected by the Treaty of Paris (1783) and Jay's Treaty (1794). Both of these treaties between the

United States and Great Britain pledged that the property of Loyalists in the United States would be protected by the federal government. Justice Story pointed to Article 6 of the Constitution, which included treaties of the United States as part of the "supreme Law of the Land." Further, Article 6 said that "the Judges in every State shall be bound thereby, any thing in the Constitution or Laws of any State to the Contrary notwithstanding." Finally, Justice Story referred to Section 25 of the Judiciary Act of 1789, which provided for review by the U.S. Supreme Court of decisions by state courts that involved the U.S. Constitution, federal laws, and treaties.

Justice Story ordered the Virginia Court of Appeals to carry out the decision of the U.S. Supreme Court. The Virginia judges refused to obey the order, however. They claimed that Section 25 of the Judiciary Act of 1789 was not valid because it violated the powers and rights of state governments in the federal Union.

The Issue Virginia's refusal to comply with Justice Story's ruling brought the case back to the U.S. Supreme Court. The issue cut to the heart of the federal Union. Did the Supreme Court have authority over all state laws and state judicial decisions that involved the U.S. Constitution, federal laws, and treaties? Or did each state have authority under the U.S. Constitution to defy certain kinds of federal treaties or decisions if it did not approve of them?

Opinion of the Court Once again, Joseph Story wrote for the Court. (Chief Justice Marshall again declined to participate because of a possible conflict of interest.) Justice Story decided that the U.S. Supreme Court had jurisdiction in this case, and he rebuked the Virginia judges who had refused to comply with the Court's orders. Contrary to the views of the Virginia judges, Story argued that the U.S. Supreme Court's appellate jurisdiction extended to all cases involving federal issues, not merely to cases coming to it from lower federal courts.

Story asserted that Article 25 of the Ju-

diciary Act of 1789 was constitutional and was necessary to the enforcement of federal laws and treaties as part of the supreme law of the land, as defined by Article 6 of the Constitution. He rejected Virginia's claim to equal sovereignty with the United States and argued that the American people, not the states, had created the federal Union.

Finally, Justice Story insisted that to enforce the supremacy clause of Article 6, the U.S. Supreme Court had the final power to interpret the U.S. Constitution. Without this power over state governments, Story insisted, there could be no enduring federal Union.

Significance The Court's judgment, expressed by Justice Story, has been called the greatest argument ever made for judicial review of state laws and court decisions by the U.S. Supreme Court. Story's opinion also gave great strength to the nationalists' side of the ongoing argument about state powers and rights in the federal system of the United States. The claims of extreme states' rights advocates, however, were not subdued until after the Civil War.
SEE ALSO *Federalism; Judicial power; Judicial review; Jurisdiction*

MATTHEWS, STANLEY
Associate Justice, 1881–89

- Born: July 21, 1824, Cincinnati, Ohio
- Education: Kenyon College, B.A., 1840
- Previous government service: assistant prosecuting attorney, Hamilton County, Ohio, 1845; clerk, Ohio House of Representatives, 1848–49; judge, Hamilton County Court of Common Pleas, 1851–53; Ohio Senate, 1855–58; U.S. attorney for the Southern District of Ohio, 1858–61; judge, Superior Court of Cincinnati, 1863–65; counsel, Hayes-Tilden electoral commission, 1877; U.S. senator from Ohio, 1877–79
- Appointed by President James A. Garfield Mar. 14, 1881; replaced Noah Swayne, who retired
- Supreme Court term: confirmed by the

Senate May 12, 1881, by a 24–23 vote; served until Mar. 22, 1889
• Died: Mar. 22, 1889, Washington, D.C.

Stanley Matthews's political connections led to his appointment to the Supreme Court. He campaigned for Presidential candidate Rutherford B. Hayes in 1876. Then he served as a lawyer for Hayes at the 1877 electoral commission that decided the contested Presidential election in favor of Hayes. Consequently, Hayes appointed Matthews to fill a vacancy on the Court, but the Senate blocked the nomination. They recalled his involvement in a controversial federal case in 1859, when Matthews served as the U.S. attorney for southern Ohio. Although Matthews had sided publicly with the cause of abolishing slavery, he vigorously prosecuted an abolitionist for helping two fugitive slaves to escape to freedom. Many senators objected to Matthews because of his role as prosecuting attorney in this case. Matthews was renominated by President Hayes's successor, James A. Garfield, but he was still opposed by many senators and was barely confirmed, by a vote of 24–23.

The controversy about Matthews's appointment to the Court eventually died down and he served satisfactorily as an associate justice. He wrote 232 opinions for the Court and 5 dissents in a Supreme Court career of less than eight years.

MAVERICKS

Although most members of Congress still follow the advice of Speaker Sam Rayburn (Democrat–Texas) that "to get along you have to go along," a few senators and representatives made their career not by "going along" but by becoming legislative mavericks. Mavericks tend to represent a minority viewpoint within their own party and tend to refuse to bend their principles to prevailing attitudes. Mavericks are often showmen who enjoy the spotlight of publicity. They will employ disruptive tactics to stop or slow down action on a bill, trying to make the majority agree with their

demands. They may show contempt for the rules, courtesies, and elaborate forms of politeness that other legislators adopt with each other.

Robert La Follette, Sr. (Republican–Wisconsin) would rather lose a legislative battle than to accept "half a loaf." George Norris (Republican–Nebraska) challenged powerful Speaker of the House Joseph G. Cannon and was successful in reducing the Speaker's powers. Huey P. Long (Democrat–Louisiana) resigned from his committee assignments and devoted his attention to flamboyant speeches on the Senate floor, often mimicking and mocking other senators. Joseph R. McCarthy (Republican–Wisconsin) flaunted the Senate's rules and decorum until he was censured. Mavericks generally work outside of their party's official leadership. By contrast, Representative Newt Gingrich (Republican–Georgia) gained enough notoriety from his maverick stands to be elected one of his party's leaders in the House.

SEE ALSO *Independents, congressional*

McCARTHY, JOSEPH R.

• Born: Nov. 14, 1908, Grand Chute, Wis.
• Political party: Republican
• Education: Marquette University, law degree, 1935
• Senator from Wisconsin: 1947–57
• Died: May 2, 1957, Bethesda, Md.

As a relatively obscure freshman senator, Joe McCarthy made himself a household name when he declared at a political rally in Wheeling, West Virginia, in 1950 that he held in his hand a list of 205 known communists within the State Department. McCarthy exploited the tense cold war atmosphere of the time to shock his audience—and the nation as well. In fact, he had no hard evidence of communists in government, but people willingly believed him just the same. McCarthy's influence increased in 1953 when he used his chairmanship of the Permanent Subcommittee on Investigations to hold a series of dramatic hearings, bullying witnesses and intimidating senators who opposed him. Justifying his actions as necessary to combat communist subversion, McCarthy disrupted the Senate's normal rules, customs, and decorum. Eventually, his charges and behavior became too outrageous. Following the Army-McCarthy hearings in 1954, when McCarthy recklessly accused the U.S. Army of harboring communists, public opinion shifted away from McCarthy, and the Senate censured him by a vote of 67 to 22 for conduct "contrary to senatorial traditions."

SEE ALSO *Army-McCarthy hearings (1954); Censure; Investigations, congressional*
SOURCES Robert Griffith, *The Politics of Fear: Joseph R. McCarthy and the Senate*, 2nd ed. (Amherst: University of Massachusetts Press, 1987). Arthur Herman, *Joseph McCarthy: Reexamining the Life and Legacy of America's Most Hated Senator* (New York: Free Press, 1999). David Oshinsky, *A Conspiracy So Immense: The World of Joseph McCarthy* (New York: Free Press, 1983). Thomas C. Reeves, *The Life and Times of Joe McCarthy: A Biography* (1982; reprint, Lanham, Md.: Madison Books, 1997). Ellen Schrecker, *The Age of McCarthyism* (New York: Bedford/St. Martin's, 1994). Ellen Schrecker, *Many Are the Crimes: McCarthyism in America* (Boston: Little, Brown, 1998).

McCULLOCH V. MARYLAND

- 4 Wheat. 316 (1819)
- Vote: 7–0
- For the Court: Marshall

Congress chartered the Second Bank of the United States in 1816 to provide a sound national currency. But the bank soon proved very unpopular in many states. Maryland passed a law that levied an extremely high tax on any bank in the state without a state charter. At the time, the Second Bank of the United States was the only bank operating in Maryland that was not chartered by the state. McCulloch, the cashier of the Baltimore branch of the Bank of the United States, refused to pay the tax. Maryland sued McCulloch and won in the Maryland courts.

Officials of the bank appealed to the U.S. Supreme Court. They claimed the state tax interfered unconstitutionally with the federally chartered bank. Maryland argued that Congress had no power to charter the bank and that the state had the power to tax the bank.

The Issue The Constitution did not expressly give Congress the power to charter a national bank. However, Article 1, Section 8, Clause 18, did grant Congress the power to "make all laws which shall be necessary and proper for carrying into Execution the foregoing Powers." Did this "necessary and proper" clause give Congress adequate power only to do those few things indispensable for carrying out its listed, or delegated, powers? Or did it ensure that Congress could do nearly anything it wanted, such as chartering a national bank, to exercise its delegated powers?

In addition, did states have the power to tax a national bank? Was national law or state law supreme in this case?

Opinion of the Court The Court upheld the power of Congress to create a national bank. Chief Justice John Marshall wrote that the Constitution did not need to expressly authorize Congress to establish a bank. Such expressly listed congressional powers as the power to tax, to spend money, to borrow money, and to support the army and navy implied that Congress had the power to establish a bank.

At the same time, the Court ruled that the states could not tax the bank. Marshall declared that allowing states to tax part of the national government would interfere with national supremacy. "The power to tax involves the power to destroy."

Thus, the Court established two important constitutional principles. The first, the implied powers doctrine, stated that the legal system should interpret broadly the necessary and proper clause of the Constitution to let Congress choose the means it wished to employ to carry out the powers the Constitution expressly gave it. Marshall wrote, "Let the end be legitimate, let it be within the scope of the Constitution, and all means which are appropriate, which are plainly adapted to that end, which are not prohibited, but consist with the letter and spirit of the Constitution, are constitutional."

The second principle, national supremacy, forbids the states to intrude into the constitutional operations of the federal government. It reinforced the supremacy of the Constitution and federal laws over state laws that conflict with them.

Significance The *McCulloch* decision has been used to support a broad construction of the Constitution that enables the federal government to apply the supreme law flexibly to meet the new problems of changing times. In the *McCulloch* case Chief Justice Marshall made a memorable statement, which is often quoted to support a broad interpretation of the federal government's constitutional powers: "This ... is ... a constitution we are expounding, intended to endure for ages to come, and consequently, to be adapted to the various crises of human affairs."

Today, many bills Congress passes to some extent draw their legitimacy from the necessary and proper clause and the broad construction of the Constitution exemplified in Marshall's *McCulloch* opinion. For example, federal laws pertaining to the regulation of airlines or broadcasting are based on the necessary and proper clause, not on express powers of Congress specified in the Constitution.

The *McCulloch* decision also strengthened the Court's powers of judicial review over acts of state governments. Thus, it pleased advocates of federal supremacy and infuriated supporters of state powers and rights. The vision of national supremacy under the Constitution, expressed in

Chief Justice Marshall's *McCulloch* opinion, has prevailed in the 20th century.

SEE ALSO *Constitutional construction; Federalism; Implied powers*

SOURCES Gerald Gunther, *John Marshall's Defense of McCulloch v. Maryland* (Stanford, Calif.: Stanford University Press, 1969). Bray Hammond, "The Bank Cases," in *Quarrels That Have Shaped the Constitution,* edited by John A. Garraty (New York: Harper & Row, 1987).

McKEIVER V. PENNSYLVANIA

- 403 U.S. 528 (1971)
- Vote: 6–3
- For the Court: Blackmun
- Concurring: White, Harlan, and Brennan
- Dissenting: Douglas, Black, and Marshall

Joseph McKeiver, 16 years old, was a juvenile defendant who had been accused of serious acts of delinquency—robbery and receiving stolen goods. He faced the possible punishment of detention for five years. McKeiver asked for a trial by jury, but the state of Pennsylvania denied his request. McKeiver was convicted and sentenced without a jury trial. He appealed his conviction on the grounds that his constitutional right to a trial by jury had been violated.

The Issue Adults accused of crimes have a constitutional right to trial by jury. This right is included in the 6th Amendment, and it is applicable to the states through the due process clause of the 14th Amendment. Is this right to trial by jury required in state proceedings against a juvenile accused of unlawful behavior?

Opinion of the Court The Supreme Court decided that due process of law for juveniles does not require a trial by jury. Justice Harry Blackmun stated a standard of "fundamental fairness" for due process in juvenile cases. Thus, a right to trial by jury in juvenile cases had to be balanced against the special requirements of juvenile justice. Justice Blackmun feared that a jury trial would subject juveniles to unnecessary and disruptive adversarial proceedings without providing compensating benefits of greater accuracy in fact-finding or determination of guilt.

Significance   The Court decided in another case about a juvenile offender, *In re Gault* (1967), to extend constitutional rights of due process to juvenile court proceedings. The *McKeiver* decision, however, indicated that the Court was unwilling to extend all the rights of the criminally accused to juveniles accused of serious crimes. According to this decision, states are not required to provide a jury trial for a juvenile, but they may choose to do so. To date, none has done so.

SEE ALSO   *In re Gault; Juvenile justice; Trial by jury*

SOURCES   Thomas J. Bernard, *The Cycle of Juvenile Justice* (New York: Oxford University Press, 1992).

McKENNA, JOSEPH
Associate Justice, 1898–1925

- Born: Aug. 10, 1843, Philadelphia, Pa.
- Education: Benicia Collegiate Institute, 1865
- Previous government service: district attorney, Solano County, Calif., 1866–70; California Assembly, 1875–76; U.S. representative from California, 1885–92; judge, U.S. Court of Appeals for the Ninth Circuit, 1892–97; U.S. attorney general, 1897
- Appointed by President William McKinley Dec. 16, 1897; replaced Stephen J. Field, who retired
- Supreme Court term: confirmed by the Senate Jan. 21, 1898, by a voice vote; retired Jan. 5, 1925
- Died: Nov. 21, 1926, Washington, D.C.

Joseph McKenna was the son of immigrants from Ireland. He was a successful politician who served seven years in the U.S. House of Representatives, where he became a friend of William McKinley.

When McKinley became President, he appointed his old friend to fill a vacancy on the Supreme Court.

Justice McKenna served on the Court for 27 years. He joined in the Court's opinions to regulate various kinds of economic activity under the "commerce clause" of Article 1, Section 8, of the Constitution. He also supported regulation of businesses under the Pure Food and Drug Act.

During his later years on the Court, McKenna's reasoning powers seemed to decline. His associates urged him to resign, which he did in 1925, at age 83.

SOURCES   Matthew McDevitt, *Joseph McKenna* (1946; reprint, New York: Da Capo, 1974).

McKINLEY, JOHN
Associate Justice, 1837–52

- Born: May 1, 1780, Culpeper County, Va.
- Education: self-educated in the law
- Previous government service: Alabama House of Representatives, 1820, 1831, 1836; U.S. senator from Alabama, 1826–31; U.S. representative from Alabama, 1833–35
- Appointed by President Martin Van Buren as a recess appointment Apr. 22, 1837, to a newly created position on the Supreme Court; nominated by Van Buren Sept. 18, 1837
- Supreme Court term: confirmed by the Senate Sept. 25, 1837, by a voice vote; served until July 19, 1852
- Died: July 19, 1852, Lexington, Ky.

John McKinley was a loyal supporter of the Jacksonian Democrats, who backed the Presidential candidacies of Andrew Jackson and Martin Van Buren. After Van Buren became President, he rewarded McKinley with an appointment to the Supreme Court.

Justice McKinley was a strong supporter of states' rights and slavery. However, he was an unproductive and mediocre associate justice who wrote only 20 opinions for the Court during his 15 years of service. He usually voted with the Court's majority and dissented only when joined by at least one other justice. He wrote no opinions that contributed significantly to the development of constitutional law.

McKINLEY, WILLIAM
25th President

- Born: Jan. 29, 1843, Niles, Ohio
- Political party: Republican
- Education: Allegheny College, 1860; Albany Law School, 1866
- Military service: 23rd Ohio Volunteer Infantry, 1861–65
- Previous government service: prosecuting attorney, Stark County, Ohio, 1870–71; U.S. House of Representatives, 1877–85, 1887–91; governor of Ohio, 1892–96
- Elected President, 1896; served, 1897–1901
- Died: Sept. 14, 1901, Buffalo, N.Y.

William McKinley protected the interests of big business while doing little to alleviate the social problems caused by industrialization. McKinley's victory in the Spanish-American War made the United States into a world power and transformed the Presidency into an office of world leadership.

McKinley grew up in a small town in Ohio. During the Civil War he enlisted in the 23rd Ohio Volunteer Infantry, serving as an aide to Colonel Rutherford B. Hayes. He was promoted to major for bravery in the Battle of Fisher's Hill.

After the war McKinley studied law. He was elected prosecuting attorney of Stark County in 1869 but was defeated for reelection two years later. In 1876 he was elected to the U.S. House of Representatives, where he gained a reputation for supporting high tariffs. His grandfather and father were iron manufacturers, which may explain why he championed business interests as chair of the Committee on Ways and Means. But the high rates of the McKinley Tariff Act of 1890 were so un-

popular with the voters that he was defeated in the next election. He then organized two successful campaigns for governor of Ohio with the help of Mark Hanna, a Cleveland businessman and political fund-raiser.

In 1896 the Republican convention nominated McKinley for President on the first ballot, and Hanna organized his successful campaign. McKinley sat on his front porch in Canton, Ohio, and greeted 750,000 visitors from 30 states while his Democratic opponent, William Jennings Bryan, frantically traveled 18,000 miles by rail. Hanna organized a pro-tariff, pro-business coalition for McKinley, who won by a healthy margin in the electoral college.

McKinley presided over a period of industrial expansion. He supported the record-high Dingley Tariff of 1897. Soon he had to turn his attention to foreign affairs. Spain was trying to put down a rebellion in its Cuban province that had begun in 1895. The Spanish commander, known as Butcher Weyler, put Cuban civilians into concentration camps and American opinion swung solidly behind the rebellion. The sinking of the U.S.S. *Maine* in Havana Harbor on February 15, 1898, with the loss of 260 lives, fanned the war fever in the United States. On March 1, the U.S. Naval Court of Inquiry sent its findings to Washington—results that implicated Spain (though the U.S. Navy much later, in 1976, agreed with the results of the Spanish investigation that claimed that the explosion was an accident). McKinley tried to prevent war by winning some concessions from Spain, including the closing of the concentration camps and an armistice with the Cuban rebels. But two days after the Spanish made those concessions, McKinley finally bowed to public opinion and asked Congress for a declaration of war. On April 19 Congress passed a joint resolution authorizing U.S. intervention to win Cuban independence from Spain.

With Admiral George Dewey's destruction of the Spanish Pacific fleet in Manila, the Philippines, on May 1, 1898, the United States became a world power with global influence. Three days later, Congress approved a long-standing resolution of annexation for the Hawaiian Islands. According to the terms of the Treaty of Paris with Spain in December 1898, the United States became a colonial power, occupying Cuba (temporarily), Puerto Rico, and Guam and gaining Wake Island and Samoa in 1899.

McKinley then won a series of victories in Congress for his foreign policy. He got Senate consent for the Treaty of Paris in spite of the opposition of House Speaker Thomas Reed and the Anti-Imperialist League, an American organization opposed to the acquisition of colonies. McKinley's tariff reciprocity policies, designed to encourage free trade in selected markets—trade under low or no tariffs—were accepted by Congress even though they contradicted traditional Republican support for protectionist tariffs. He won passage of the Spooner Amendment, which allowed him to institute military government in the Philippines, and the Platt Amendment, which permitted U.S. intervention in Cuban affairs.

In his annual message to Congress in 1899, McKinley denied the claim of the Philippine leader Emilio Aguinaldo that Admiral Dewey had promised independence to the islands in return for local help against the Spanish. The McKinley administration was determined to keep the islands. To do so, it put down a bloody rebellion of Philippine patriots that lasted three years and employed 120,000 U.S. soldiers.

In 1900 the McKinley administration intervened in China with 2,500 troops (along with Japan and several Western nations) to put down the Boxer Rebellion against Westerners in Beijing. The United States received a payment of $25 million from China for damages suffered but returned $18 million so that Chinese students could study in the United States. McKinley also intervened twice in Nicaragua to protect lives and property.

McKinley's Vice President, Garret Hobart, died in office in 1899, and McKinley accepted Theodore Roosevelt as the choice of the Republican convention to be his running mate in 1900. Mark Hanna opposed the nomination. "Don't you realize there's only one life between this madman and the Presidency?" he asked convention delegates. McKinley's margin over William Jennings Bryan improved in their 1900 rematch, and he became the first President since Ulysses S. Grant to win a second consecutive term.

McKinley was shot by Leon Czolgosz, an anarchist, at the Pan-American Exposition in Buffalo, New York, on September 6, 1901, and died of his wounds eight days later. Hanna and the Republican party would now have to deal with Teddy Roosevelt and his progressive policies.

SEE ALSO *Hobart, Garret; Roosevelt, Theodore; Treaty powers*
SOURCES Margaret Leech, *In the Days of McKinley* (New York: Harper, 1959). Lewis L. Gould, *The Presidency of William McKinley* (Lawrence: Regents Press of Kansas, 1980). H. Wayne Morgan, *William McKinley and His America* (Syracuse, N.Y.: Syracuse University Press, 1963).

McLEAN, JOHN
Associate Justice, 1830–61

- Born: Mar. 11, 1785, Morris County, N.J.
- Education: studied at home with private tutors; read law in the office of Arthur St. Clair, Jr., in Cincinnati
- Previous government service: examiner, U.S. Land Office, Cincinnati, Ohio, 1811–12; U.S. representative from Ohio, 1813–16; judge, Ohio Supreme Court, 1816–22; commissioner, General Land Office, 1822–23; U.S. postmaster general, 1823–29
- Appointed by President Andrew Jackson Mar. 6, 1829; replaced Robert Trimble, who died
- Supreme Court term: confirmed by the Senate Mar. 7, 1829, by a voice vote; served until Apr. 4, 1861
- Died: Apr. 4, 1861, Cincinnati, Ohio

John McLean was President Andrew Jackson's first appointment to the Supreme Court. During his 32 years on the Court, however, Justice McLean moved away from Jacksonian views, which favored states' rights, to support nationalism and the federal government's power to regulate foreign and interstate commerce.

Justice McLean's dislike of slavery and states' rights was expressed in his famous dissent in the Dred Scott case (*Scott* v. *Sandford,* 1857). In opposition to the Court's majority, he argued that Congress could ban slavery in the territories of the United States, that blacks could be citizens, and that Dred Scott was a free man because he had lived in a free state and a free territory. This dissent was vindicated by ratification of the 13th and 14th Amendments, which overturned the *Dred Scott* decision.

SEE ALSO *Scott v. Sandford*

SOURCES Francis P. Weisenburger, *The Life of John McLean* (1937; reprint, New York: Da Capo, 1971).

McNARY, CHARLES L.

- Born: June 12, 1874, Salem, Oreg.
- Political party: Republican
- Education: Leland Stanford Junior University; studied law
- Senator from Oregon: 1917–44
- Senate minority leader: 1933–44
- Died: Feb. 25, 1944, Fort Lauderdale, Fla.

No minority leader ever commanded so few members as effectively as Charles McNary did. After the 1936 election the number of Senate Republicans shrank to 16, against 76 Democrats and 4 independents. But McNary led his party by coaxing and accommodation, rather than by confrontation, and he was a shrewd judge of legislative behavior. In 1937 when President Franklin D. Roosevelt announced his plan to "pack" the Supreme Court with liberal justices (to prevent conservative justices from ruling New Deal programs

unconstitutional), Republican senators wanted to lead the fight against the plan. McNary cautioned restraint, urging them to let Democrats take the lead against the plan instead. He reasoned that if the Republicans remained quiet, the Democrats would fight among themselves and split their swollen majority. McNary's strategy worked, the Court plan was defeated, the Democrats became divided, and the small band of Republicans was able to form an effective coalition with the Democratic conservatives to dominate the Senate for many years.

SEE ALSO *Court-packing plan (1937); Minority leader*

SOURCES Steve Neal, *McNary of Oregon: A Political Biography* (Portland, Oreg.: Western Imprints, 1983).

McREYNOLDS, JAMES CLARK
Associate Justice, 1914–41

- Born: Feb. 3, 1862, Elkton, Ky.
- Education: Vanderbilt University, B.S., 1882; University of Virginia, LL.B., 1884
- Previous government service: assistant U.S. attorney, 1903–7; U.S. attorney general, 1913–14
- Appointed by President Woodrow Wilson Aug. 19, 1914; replaced Horace H. Lurton, who died
- Supreme Court term: confirmed by the Senate Aug. 29, 1914, by a 44–6 vote; retired Jan. 31, 1941
- Died: Aug. 24, 1946, Washington, D.C.

James McReynolds was an outspoken man with strong views and a disagreeable personality. He was intolerant of colleagues with opposing views and expressed his feelings through rude behavior. He disliked Associate Justices Louis Brandeis and Benjamin Cardozo so much that he would not speak to them. Brandeis and Cardozo were Jews and critics accused McReynolds of anti-Semitism. He also seemed to favor racial segregation and to be prejudiced against female attorneys.

Justice McReynolds was a harsh critic of President Franklin D. Roosevelt's New Deal programs and joined several majority opinions to strike down New Deal legislation between 1934 and 1936. During President Roosevelt's second term, however, the Court shifted to majority support of New Deal enactments. Justice McReynolds therefore became a bitter dissenter during his last years on the Court.

MEDIA COVERAGE OF CONGRESS

Of the three branches of the federal government, Congress traditionally has been the most open to newspaper and broadcast journalists. While the executive and judicial branches do much of their work in private, Congress holds hearings, debates, and votes in public. Representing both parties and a wide range of ideologies, members of Congress are usually willing to give interviews and information to the press.

In 1789 the popularly elected House opened its floor debates and voting to the public and the press. Senators, still elected by state legislatures, debated in closed session until 1794. The first reporters to cover Congress were really stenographers paid by private newspapers to record the debates. From their notes evolved the *Congressional Record*. By the 1820s "letter writers," or correspondents, sat in the congressional galleries gathering information for more interpretive reporting.

When the number of these correspondents increased, the Senate set aside the first press gallery in 1841, and the House did so soon afterward. These press galleries guaranteed accredited reporters regular seats in the Senate and House chambers and also provided them a room behind the galleries in which to write their stories. By the 1850s telegraph facilities were set up within the press galleries to decrease the time it took correspondents to wire the news to their papers. In the 20th century Congress established separate radio-television galleries as well as recording studios where members could prepare taped remarks for broadcast.

The press, President, and Congress Despite Congress's openness, press attention has shifted steadily toward the White House since the 1930s. A single President is easier to visualize and portray than 535 voting members of Congress. Presidents have gained easier access to the media than to individual members of Congress, and they can use television to appeal directly to public opinion.

Yet there are some 5,000 reporters who hold passes to the House and Senate press galleries. To become accredited and receive a congressional press pass, reporters must show that they work full-time as journalists, have no affiliation with any government agency, and are not involved in lobbying Congress for any private interests. Gallery space could never accommodate these thousands of reporters, but only a small number is present regularly at the Capitol to cover committee hearings and floor proceedings. A larger number of reporters appears only occasionally, in search of some specific information or to interview members and staff about the issues of the day.

Regional reporting Some journalists report for national news networks, magazines, and major metropolitan newspapers. But most on Capitol Hill are "regional reporters" who report for smaller papers or chains of papers located in a particular state or region. Regional reporters seek news that will be of special interest to local or regional readers and viewers. They generally form mutual working relationships with the members of Congress from their region, who are their best sources of news. In return, the members of Congress seek favorable publicity to keep their name and their activities before the voters back home.

Impact of the Internet By the mid-1990s, the global digital communications system known as the Internet had made an impact on Congress. Every member established a Web site to provide information directly to constituents and other "browsers." Newspapers, magazines, and radio and television stations also set up on-line departments to provide constantly updated news, 24 hours a day. Internet reporters began appearing on Capitol Hill, forcing the various press galleries to determine if they were legitimately part of the news media and whether to issue them press credentials.

SEE ALSO *Press secretary; News conferences, Presidential*

SOURCES Donald A. Ritchie, *Press Gallery: Congress and the Washington Correspondents* (Cambridge: Harvard University Press, 1991).

MESSAGES, PRESIDENTIAL

Article 2, Section 3, of the Constitution provides that the President shall "from time to time give to the Congress information of the State of the Union and recommend to their consideration such measures as he shall judge necessary and expedient."

Between 1801 and 1911 Presidents from Thomas Jefferson through William Howard Taft transmitted an annual message to Congress at the opening of each session. It included reports from all the departments of government. President James Monroe used his 1823 message to announce the Monroe Doctrine as a matter of U.S. foreign policy. Lincoln used his messages to discuss the military situation in the Civil War. Theodore Roosevelt used his messages to educate the American people about child labor and the protection of the environment. William Howard Taft called for reforms in the federal budget process.

Woodrow Wilson revived the practice of George Washington and John Adams of speaking to a joint session of Congress, rather than sending an annual written message. Since 1945 this speech has been known as the State of the Union address.

Presidents may also send messages to Congress while it is in session. These have included Andrew Jackson's messages to the

Senate during the controversies over the Bank of the United States, James Buchanan's 1860 messages to Congress about the impending secession of Southern states; Abraham Lincoln's Civil War messages; Franklin D. Roosevelt's messages on legislation proposed for recovery from the Great Depression; and Harry Truman's message proposing a Fair Deal for postwar economic conversion to civilian industries.

The Constitution also requires the President to send Congress a message outlining his reasons for vetoing legislation. Sometimes, Presidents send Congress messages that explain their understanding of the law when they sign bills.

Other Presidential messages required by law include the ones that accompany the Budget of the United States and the Economic Report of the President. Both are delivered each January as Congress begins its new session.

SEE ALSO *Budget, Presidential; Council of Economic Advisers; Fair Deal; Monroe Doctrine; New Deal; Veto power*

MIAMI HERALD PUBLISHING CO. V. TORNILLO

- 418 U.S. 241 (1974)
- Vote: 9–0
- For the Court: Burger
- Concurring: Brennan, Rehnquist, and White

In September 1972, the *Miami Herald* printed editorials that were highly critical of Pat Tornillo, a candidate for the Florida House of Representatives. The editorials faulted Tornillo's judgment and character and advised voters not to support him.

Tornillo demanded that the *Miami Herald* print his response to its critical editorials. When the newspaper's publisher refused, Tornillo pointed to a 1913 Florida law that provided that "if a candidate for nomination in election is assailed regarding his personal character or official record by any newspaper, the candidate has a right to demand that the newspaper print ... any reply the candidate may make to the newspaper's charges."

The *Miami Herald*'s publisher continued to ignore Tornillo's request, so Tornillo filed suit, asking that the Florida "right to reply" law be enforced in his behalf.

The Florida Supreme Court upheld the "right to reply" law as furthering the "broad societal interest in the free flow of information to the public." The *Miami Herald* appealed to the U.S. Supreme Court.

The Issue The 1st Amendment to the U.S. Constitution says, "Congress shall make no law ... abridging the freedom of speech, or of the press." The 1st Amendment freedoms of speech and press have been applied by the Court to the states through the due process clause of the 14th Amendment. Did the Florida "right to reply" law violate the *Miami Herald*'s constitutional right to freedom of the press?

Opinion of the Court The Court reversed the Florida Supreme Court judgment and declared the "right to reply" law unconstitutional. Chief Justice Warren Burger concluded that the 1913 Florida statute was a clear violation of the 1st Amendment guarantee of a free press. Burger wrote, "The choice of material to go into a newspaper, and the decisions made as to ... treatment of public issues and public officials—whether fair or unfair—constitute the exercise of editorial control and judgment."

Significance This case established that the government cannot force a newspaper publisher to print and distribute particular information. However, the Court has upheld government "right to reply" regulations with regard to news broadcasting, as in *Red Lion Broadcasting Co., Inc.* v. *Federal Communications Commission* (1969). That is because the broadcast media, unlike print media, have a limited number of frequencies or channels available, so the only way to provide for access to different points of view is a "right to reply" regulation that can be imposed by the Federal Communications Commission.

SEE ALSO *Freedom of speech and press; Incorporation doctrine*
SOURCES Lucas A. Powe, Jr., *American Broadcasting and the First Amendment* (Berkeley: University of California Press, 1987).

MICHEL, ROBERT H.

- Born: Mar. 2, 1923, Peoria, Ill.
- Political party: Republican
- Education: Bradley University, B.S., 1948
- Representative from Illinois: 1957–95
- House minority whip: 1975–81
- House minority leader: 1981–95

Bob Michel set the record for having spent the longest time in the minority of any member of Congress. He was first elected to the House in 1956, shortly after Democrats regained the majority. Michel gained a seat on the powerful House Appropriations Committee but noted that it took three terms before the "crusty old chairman named Clarence Cannon" (Democrat–Missouri) seemed to recognize that the freshman Republican was a member of his committee. After 38 years of service, Michel retired as a member of the minority, although by then he had become the Republican floor leader and one of the best-known members of the House. During his years in the minority, Michel often worked closely with the leaders of the majority. By understanding when to accommodate the majority and when to stand up against it, he offered effective support for Republican Presidents Ronald Reagan and George Bush despite the lack of a Republican majority in the House.

MILLER, SAMUEL FREEMAN
Associate Justice, 1862–90

- Born: Apr. 5, 1816, Richmond, Ky.
- Education: Transylvania University, M.D., 1838; studied law privately

- Previous government service: justice of the peace and member of the Knox County Court, Ky., 1840s
- Appointed by President Abraham Lincoln July 6, 1862; replaced Peter V. Daniel, who died
- Supreme Court term: confirmed by the Senate July 16, 1862, by voice vote; served until Oct. 13, 1890
- Died: Oct. 13, 1890, Washington, D.C.

Samuel Miller participated in more than 5,000 decisions of the Supreme Court during his 28 years of service. Before Justice Miller, no other member of the Court had written as many opinions.

During and after the Civil War, Miller voted to sustain President Abraham Lincoln's actions to suspend habeas corpus and to try civilians in military courts in cases involving charges of disloyalty to the Union. A writ of habeas corpus requires officials to bring a person whom they have arrested and held in custody before a judge in a court of law. If a judge finds their reasons for holding the person unlawful, then the court frees the suspect.

However, Justice Miller's greatest influence on constitutional law was in his decision to support state government rights and powers. Thus, he opposed a broad interpretation of the 14th Amendment that would involve the Court as "a perpetual censor upon all legislation of the states." He asserted this opinion for the Court in the *Slaughterhouse Cases* (1873). In this decision, Justice Miller advanced a narrow interpretation of the 14th Amendment that supported state government authority over the privileges and immunities of citizenship instead of emphasizing the federal government's power in these matters. Justice Miller concluded that it would be a violation of the Constitution to bring protection of all civil rights under the authority of the federal government. This would, he wrote, "fetter and degrade the state governments by subjecting them to the control of Congress."

Justice Miller and his supporters on the Court effectively blocked the use of the 14th Amendment to protect black Americans from state government acts that would restrict their civil rights, especially their right to "equal protection of the laws." This narrow interpretation of the 14th Amendment persisted until the middle of the 20th century.

SEE ALSO *Slaughterhouse Cases*

SOURCES Charles Fairman, *Mr. Justice Miller and the Supreme Court* (Cambridge: Harvard University Press, 1938).

"MILLIONAIRES' CLUB"

By the end of the 19th century, so many rich men had been elected to the Senate that critics dubbed it a "millionaires' club." Reformers charged that wealthy senators were neither representative of average citizens nor sensitive to their needs. The image of the "millionaires' club" was a contributing factor to the movement toward direct election of senators. Even after direct election, however, the great expense of running for national office continued to favor wealthy candidates.

MINERSVILLE SCHOOL DISTRICT V. GOBITIS

- 310 U.S. 586 (1940)
- Vote: 8–1
- For the Court: Frankfurter
- Dissenting: Stone

One day in 1936, Lillian Gobitis, age 12, and her brother William, age 10, came home from school with news that distressed their parents. They had been expelled from their Minersville, Pennsylvania, school for refusing to salute the American flag during the morning patriotic exercises.

The Gobitis family belonged to the Jehovah's Witnesses faith. This religion taught that saluting the flag was like worshiping a graven image (an idol), an offense against God's law.

Lillian and William's parents asked the Minersville school board to excuse their children from the flag salute requirement.

The board refused, and the Gobitises placed their children in a private school. Mr. Gobitis then sued the school board to stop it from requiring children attending the public schools to salute the flag. Federal district and appellate judges upheld Gobitis's suit. The Minersville school board then appealed to the Supreme Court.

The Issue   Could public school officials force Jehovah's Witnesses to salute the American flag even though doing so contradicted their religious beliefs? The Witnesses claimed the Minersville school board's regulation violated their 1st Amendment right to the "free exercise" of religion.

Opinion of the Court   The Court voted to sustain the lower courts' rulings and uphold the flag salute requirement. Justice Felix Frankfurter wrote the majority opinion. He argued that religious liberty had to give way to state authority as long as the state did not directly promote or restrict religion. Because it met this requirement, the school board's flag salute requirement was constitutional.

Frankfurter called the controversy a "tragic issue" that defied the Court to find a clear-cut solution. However, he argued that national unity is the basis for national security. If a local school board believed that a compulsory flag salute promoted national unity, then the Court should not prevent it from requiring students to salute the flag.

Dissent   Justice Harlan Fiske Stone was the lone dissenter in the *Gobitis* case. He considered religious freedom to be outside the jurisdiction of political authority. Stone argued that when the state attempts to force children to express a belief they do not really hold, it violates their 1st Amendment rights to freedom of speech and free exercise of religion. Furthermore, he suggested that there were other ways to instill patriotism in students.

Significance   Within three years, the majority of the Court would come to agree with Stone's opposition to the *Gobitis* de-

cision. *Gobitis* established a precedent, but that precedent did not last. Two factors influenced the Court's determination to overrule it: the reaction of the public and the legal community and changes in the Court's membership.

To Justice Frankfurter's surprise, a substantial public outburst greeted the *Gobitis* decision. More than 170 newspapers opposed the decision. The stance of the *St. Louis Post-Dispatch* typified the nationwide criticism. "We think this decision of the United States Supreme Court is dead wrong," declared its editorial. Members of the legal profession, exerting influence on the justices, strongly condemned the decision. Articles in legal journals opposed the decision nearly unanimously and agreed with the dissent of Justice Stone.

Over a three-year period the membership of the Court changed. This change proved a second factor leading to the overruling of *Gobitis*. The first new member was Robert H. Jackson, an advocate of civil liberties for minorities. Then Wiley B. Rutledge, known for strong views in favor of freedom of religion, joined the Court. In addition, Justice Stone, who had stood alone against the *Gobitis* decision, became chief justice. A new point of view prevailed on the Court after these changes in membership.

The Court reversed the *Gobitis* decision in 1943 in the case of *West Virginia State Board of Education* v. *Barnette,* which said that Jehovah's Witnesses in public schools had the right to refuse to participate in required flag salute ceremonies.

SEE ALSO *Religious issues under the Constitution; West Virginia State Board of Education v. Barnette*

SOURCES Peter Irons, *The Courage of Their Convictions* (New York: Free Press, 1988).

MINORITY LEADER

Elected by the members of the minority party in each house of Congress, minority leaders represent the interests of their party on the Senate and House floors—but with fewer votes to count on than majority leaders do. Minority leaders work to keep their party united and to attract enough votes from the majority party to affect legislation. Like majority leaders, minority leaders receive a higher salary than regular members, a car and driver, and a separate leadership office in the Capitol.

Minority leaders work with majority leaders on scheduling, but they lack the majority leaders' control over calling up legislation. House rules generally favor the majority, but in the Senate, where much of the business is done by unanimous consent, the minority leader's cooperation is more crucial. That is because the minority leader, or any other minority member, can stop an action by objecting, thereby requiring time-consuming legislative procedures and voting. Senator Robert C. Byrd (Democrat–West Virginia) noted the need for cooperation between the leaders: "An element of compromise and forbearance [tolerance] is crucial if the Senate is to function properly—or if, indeed, it is to function at all."

When the President's party holds the majority in Congress, the minority leaders become the chief voices of opposition to administration programs. They are featured prominently in the media and are often given television time to respond to the President's broadcast speeches. When the President's party is in the minority in Congress, the minority leaders serve as his spokesmen. Representative Robert Michel (Republican–Illinois) has described this as a "dual role" that requires a leader to look at issues from two perspectives, "your own district's and the President's."

SEE ALSO *Majority leader; Michel, Robert H.*

SOURCES Richard A. Baker and Roger H. Davidson, eds., *First among Equals: Outstanding Senate Leaders of the Twentieth Century* (Washington, D.C.: Congressional Quarterly, 1991). Robert C. Byrd, "Party Floor Leaders," in *The Senate, 1789–1989: Addresses on the History of the United States*

Senate, vol. 2 (Washington, D.C.: Government Printing Office, 1991).

MINORITY RIGHTS

SEE *Affirmative action; Constitutional democracy; Civil rights; Equality under the Constitution; Liberty under the Constitution*

MINTON, SHERMAN
Associate Justice, 1949–56

- Born: Oct. 20, 1890, Georgetown, Ind.
- Education: Indiana University, LL.B., 1925; Yale University, LL.M., 1927
- Previous government service: Indiana public counselor, 1933–34; U.S. senator from Indiana, 1935–41; administrative assistant to the President, 1941; federal judge, Seventh Circuit Court of Appeals, 1941–49
- Appointed by President Harry S. Truman Sept. 15, 1949; replaced Wiley B. Rutledge, who died
- Supreme Court term: confirmed by the Senate Oct. 4, 1949, by a 48–16 vote; retired Oct. 15, 1956
- Died: Apr. 9, 1965, New Albany, Ind.

Sherman Minton graduated from Indiana University, where he excelled as a scholar and a varsity athlete in football and basketball. After holding a minor position in the state government, he entered national politics in 1934, winning a seat in the U.S. Senate. A Democrat, he strongly supported the New Deal programs of President Franklin D. Roosevelt.

Justice Minton supported the authority of the executive and legislative branches to make policies without interference from the judiciary. So he tended to favor a broad interpretation of the constitutional powers of the federal government.

Minton's term on the Court was cut short by a severe case of anemia that caused physical weakness and exhaustion. This condition forced him to retire after only seven years of service. As a result, his impact on constitutional law was minimal. He tended to favor government regulations over the civil liberties and rights of individuals. Justice Minton was an avid supporter of national security objectives, which he expressed as the writer of the Court's opinion in *Adler* v. *Board of Education*. This ruling upheld a New York law that banned members of subversive organizations, such as the Communist party, from teaching in public schools.

SOURCES Linda C. Gugin and James E. St. Clair, *Sherman Minton: New Deal Senator, Cold War Justice* (Indianapolis: Indiana Historical Society, 1997).

MIRANDA V. ARIZONA

- 384 U.S. 436 (1966)
- Vote: 5–4
- For the Court: Warren
- Dissenting: Clark, Harlan, White, and Stewart

In 1963 Ernesto Miranda was arrested for kidnapping and attacking a young woman near Phoenix. The woman identified him at the police station and the police questioned him for two hours. No one told him that he had the right to refuse to answer questions or to see a lawyer. Miranda confessed. He was tried and convicted on the basis of his confession.

Miranda appealed his conviction to the U.S. Supreme Court. His lawyer claimed the police violated Miranda's 5th Amendment protection against self-incrimination. The 5th Amendment says, "No person . . . shall be compelled in any criminal case to be a witness against himself."

Arizona's lawyers argued that Miranda could have asked for a lawyer at any time during questioning. He had not done so. They also said no one had forced him to confess. Because he had given his confession voluntarily, the prosecution could use it in court.

The Issue Does the 5th Amendment require the police to inform suspects of their right to remain silent and that any-

thing they say can be held against them? Could the police use evidence obtained without such warnings in court?

Opinion of the Court The Court struck down Miranda's conviction, ruling that the 5th Amendment requires police to inform suspects in their custody that they have the right to remain silent, that anything they say can be held against them, and that they have a right to consult a lawyer. The police must give these warnings, the Court said, before any questioning of a suspect can take place. A defendant can then voluntarily waive these rights.

The Court added that if a suspect wants to remain silent or to contact a lawyer, police interrogation must stop until the suspect is ready to talk again or a lawyer is present. The prosecution cannot use any confessions obtained in violation of this rule in court.

Chief Justice Earl Warren argued that the U.S. system of justice is based on the idea that an individual is innocent until proved guilty. The government, he claimed, must produce evidence against an accused person. It cannot resort to forcing suspects to prove themselves guilty.

Dissent In a strong dissent, Justice John Harlan argued: "It's obviously going to mean the disappearance of confessions as a legitimate tool of law enforcement." He concluded, "[T]he thrust of the new rule is to negate all pressures, to reinforce the nervous or ignorant suspect, and ultimately to discourage any confession at all."

Significance The *Miranda* decision was controversial. Many law enforcement officials complained the decision "handcuffed the police." However, in 1986, in *Moran* v. *Burbine*, the Court referred to the *Miranda* case as a decision that "embodies a carefully crafted balance designed to fully protect both the defendant's and society's interests."

Ever since the *Miranda* decision, police have carried cards that they use to read suspects their rights. This message has become known as the Miranda warnings, which consist of four points: the right to remain silent, the reminder that anything said by the suspect can be used against him, the right to a lawyer, and the reminder that a lawyer will be provided free if the suspect cannot afford to hire one.

The Court reaffirmed, by a 7-to-2 vote, the Miranda rights of suspects in *Dickerson v. United States* (2000). At issue was a 1968 federal law that held it was not always necessary to read Miranda warnings to suspects before they confessed voluntarily to crimes. In striking down this statute, Chief Justice William Rehnquist, in his opinion for the Court, said, "Miranda has become embedded in routine police practice to the point where the warnings have become part of our national culture." The police must continue to give the Miranda warnings or risk having a suspect's confession excluded as evidence against him.

SEE ALSO *Counsel, right to; Rights of the accused*

SOURCES Liva Baker, *Miranda: Crime, Law and Politics* (New York: Atheneum, 1983).

MISSOURI
COMPROMISE
(1821)

The first great legislative compromise designed to quiet and settle the slavery issue was the Missouri Compromise, which drew a line on the map that slavery was not to spread across. Having acquired the vast territory of the Louisiana Purchase in 1803, the United States faced the question of whether slave owners could take slaves into the new territories. In 1818, when Missouri asked to join the Union, Northern members of Congress supported an amendment requiring emancipation of any slaves in Missouri. Slave owners, however, objected to any limit on their right to own slaves. At the time, the Senate was evenly divided between slaveholding and non-slaveholding states. Neither the North nor the South wanted to become the minority. After dramatic and heated debates,

Congress agreed to admit Missouri as a slaveholding state and Maine, at the same time, as a free state, preserving the balance of political power between the sections in the Senate. Congress also set the 36th parallel as the boundary above which slavery could not spread. The Missouri Compromise held until Congress repealed its dividing line with the Kansas-Nebraska Act of 1854.

MITCHELL,
GEORGE J.

- Born: Aug. 20, 1933, Waterville, Maine
- Political party: Democrat
- Education: Bowdoin College, graduated, 1954; Georgetown University Law Center, graduated, 1960
- Senator from Maine: 1980–95
- Majority leader: 1989–95

What qualities lift senators into their party's leadership? Candidates are judged by their fellow senators on how articulate they will be in presenting their party's programs in the Senate and to the national media. They are chosen for their skills as legislative strategists. And they are often measured by their success in raising campaign funds for their colleagues. All of these qualities helped George Mitchell become Democratic majority leader in 1989.

Mitchell first learned the legislative process when he served on the Senate staff from 1962 to 1965 as executive assistant to Edmund Muskie (Democrat–Maine). In 1980 he was appointed to succeed Muskie (who had resigned to become secretary of state). Mitchell chaired the Democratic Senatorial Campaign Committee in 1986, raising funds that helped the Democrats win back the majority in the Senate. He campaigned for the position of majority leader with a promise to improve the "quality of life" for the members by scheduling Senate business to avoid late-night sessions and to allow members to return home over long weekends. Mitchell's eloquence and persistence as a member of the committee investigating the Iran-Contra scandal also convinced Democratic senators of his ability to serve as their spokesman.

SEE ALSO *Iran-Contra investigation (1986); Majority leader*

MODERN PRESIDENCY

The modern Presidency is the term used by historians and political scientists to describe the Presidential office since the early 1930s. The characteristics of the modern Presidency, as developed by Franklin D. Roosevelt and consolidated by Harry Truman, Dwight Eisenhower, and John F. Kennedy, are as follows: increased constitutional powers in foreign affairs and national security; use of the White House Office and the Executive Office of the President to supervise the bureaucracy; greater willingness to use the powers of the office to deal with economic and social problems; greater attempts to win passage of the Presidential legislative agenda; and greater ability to dominate public opinion by using radio and television.

SEE ALSO *Eisenhower, Dwight David; Kennedy, John F.; Roosevelt, Franklin D.; Truman, Harry S.*
SOURCES Fred I. Greenstein, ed., *Leadership in the Modern Presidency* (Cambridge: Harvard University Press, 1988).

MONDALE, WALTER F.
Vice President

- Born: Jan. 5, 1928, Ceylon, Minn.
- Political party: Democrat
- Education: University of Minnesota, B.A., 1951; LL.B., 1956
- Military service: U.S. Army, 1951–53
- Previous government service: attorney general of Minnesota, 1960–64; U.S. Senate, 1964–77
- Vice President under Jimmy Carter, 1977–81

Walter ("FRITZ") Mondale rose through the ranks of the Minnesota Democratic Farmer Labor party (DFL), which is affiliated with the national Democratic party. The DFL supports small business owners, farmers, and union workers and is part of the liberal wing of the Democratic party.

Mondale was appointed attorney general of Minnesota in 1960, then appointed to the U.S. Senate in 1964 to fill the unexpired term of Hubert Humphrey. He was elected to the Senate in 1966 and reelected in 1972.

Throughout Mondale's career in state politics and the Senate, he was an effective advocate for liberal programs. In 1976 he was mentioned as a possible Presidential candidate but decided, in his words, that he did not have the "fire in the belly" to run for the Presidency. As a Northern liberal and Washington insider, he was a perfect balance on the 1976 ticket to Southern moderate and Washington outsider Jimmy Carter.

As Vice President, Mondale presided over the Senate, and during a debate on an energy bill made a number of important rulings that made it easier to shut off a filibuster. But his real influence was felt in the White House itself. He worked closely with Carter, who gave Mondale a White House office right next to his own, let him attend any high-level meetings he wished, and had a private lunch with him at least once a week.

Carter named Mondale a senior adviser, with concurrent authority over the entire White House staff. Key staffers such as Chief of Staff Hamilton Jordan and Press Secretary Jody Powell publicly termed themselves his subordinates.

Mondale headed several Vice Presidential task forces assigned to develop new programs for the administration, including a group dealing with long-range goals. He was a principal legislative tactician in dealings with Congress and an adviser on economic policy. He even helped Carter choose many of his cabinet secretaries.

Carter described his relationship with Mondale this way: "I see Fritz four to five hours a day. There is not a single aspect of my own responsibilities in which Fritz is not intimately associated. He is the only person that I have with both the substantive knowledge and political stature to whom I can turn over a major assignment."

Mondale did not always succeed in pushing Carter in a liberal direction. He strongly supported a proposed tax rebate, but Carter withdrew his proposal when it appeared it would be defeated. Mondale favored higher minimum wages and higher government payments to farmers for surplus crops—positions Carter did not adopt. Mondale was more successful in national security matters, as when he convinced Carter to cancel the B-1 bomber project.

Mondale was part of an informal group that Carter used to keep in contact with the "network"—the campaign workers who would be needed for the reelection effort of 1980—and he helped Carter defeat the strong challenge of Senator Edward Kennedy for the Democratic Presidential nomination in 1980.

"I have been closer to a President than maybe any Vice President in history," Mondale concluded at the end of his term. He might have added that he also played a major part in the transformation of the Vice Presidency from a ceremonial and constitutional position to one with important functions within the executive branch.

SEE ALSO *Vice President*

SOURCES Steven M. Gillon, *The Democrat's Dilemma: Walter F. Mondale and the Liberal Legacy* (New York: Columbia University Press, 1992). Finlay Lewis, *Mondale: Portrait of an American Politician*, rev. ed. (New York: Harper & Row, 1984). Walter Mondale, *The Accountability of Power* (New York: David McKay, 1975).

MONROE DOCTRINE

In his annual message to Congress on December 2, 1823, President James Monroe stated, "The American continents, by the free and independent condition which they have assumed, are henceforth not to be considered as subjects for future colonization by any European power."

Monroe was responding to Russian claims to the Oregon Territory and to an attempt by the Russian-American Trading Company to exclude U.S. ships from the waters near its trading post in Spanish California. In October 1823 Russian czar Alexander I sent a letter to his allies in the Holy Alliance—France, Spain, and Austria—in which he observed that newly independent Latin American nations had set up republics contrary to the European "political system." He called for allied European governments to join in overthrowing those republics and replacing them with monarchies. Monroe warned in his message, "We could not view any interposition for the purpose of oppressing them or controlling in any other manner their destiny, by any European power" as other than an unfriendly act. Monroe added, "It is impossible that the allied powers should extend their political system to any portion of either continent without endangering our peace and happiness."

Monroe based the right of the United States to protest against European intervention upon the practice of the United States to keep out of all entangling alliances in Europe. He disclaimed any intention of interfering in Latin American internal affairs, and he pledged not to interfere with existing colonies or dependencies of any European power.

Monroe decided to make his statements after strong pressure from Secretary of State John Quincy Adams. In 1822 the United States had recognized several Latin American states and exchanged ministers with them. In 1823 the restored Spanish monarch Ferdinand VII called for an international conference to consider the claims to independence made by these states. On August 20, 1823, the British foreign minister, George Canning, proposed to Richard Rush, the U.S. minister in London, that the United States and Great Britain join in a declaration that the two nations were opposed to intervention in American affairs by European powers. President Monroe at first agreed to Canning's proposal, with the strong endorsement of former Presidents Thomas Jefferson and James Madison, but Adams proposed that the United States issue its own declaration. He had a strong influence on Monroe's eventual decision and the language of his message to Congress.

The Monroe Doctrine, combined with the support of the British navy, put an end to all plans for intervention in Latin America by European powers. By 1824 the United States negotiated with Russia a treaty by which Russia withdrew any territorial claims on the Oregon Territory, and in 1867 the U.S. acquisition of Alaska ended Russian colonization in North America.

The French fared no better: although they successfully intervened in Argentina in 1840, their attempt to establish a sphere of influence in Mexico met with failure. During the U.S. Civil War, French troops established the Austrian Maximilian as emperor of Mexico. The United States protested, and after the Civil War ended 50,000 U.S. troops were posted near the Mexican border, and Mexican troops loyal to the Mexican rebel Benito Juarez pressured the French to withdraw. Maximilian was killed by a Mexican firing squad at Quertaro in 1867.

The Monroe Doctrine was extended in 1905 by Secretary of State Richard Olney, who asserted that existing European colonies in the Americas were "unnatural and inexpedient," that "the United States is practically the sovereign on this continent, and its fiat is law upon the subjects to which it confines its interposition." He further argued that to disregard the Monroe Doctrine would be a violation of international law, that it would require arbitration between European colonies and Latin American nations, and that refusal to adhere to the Monroe Doctrine would be grounds for war. The Roosevelt Corollary, named for President Theodore Roosevelt, stated that the United States would not permit other nations to collect debts in this hemisphere but would do what it could to collect them itself.

The Olney and Roosevelt corollaries were highly unpopular in Latin America. They were eventually revoked by the State Department in 1928 in a memorandum that stated that the United States would no longer take military action on behalf of other nations to collect debts owed by Latin American nations. President Franklin D. Roosevelt instituted a Good Neighbor Policy. By the Montevideo Treaty of 1933 and the Buenos Aires Protocol of 1936, the United States renounced the right of intervention in Latin American affairs.

During World War II the Monroe Doctrine was "pan-Americanized" so that all nations in the hemisphere would participate. The Latin nations and the United States met in Panama in 1939 to sign the "Resolution on the Transfer of Sovereignty of Geographic Regions of the Americas Held by Non-American States," a long title for a simple agreement to prevent European possessions from falling into the hands of the Axis nations—Germany, Italy, and Japan. During the cold war the United States intervened in Latin American affairs to reduce what it perceived to be communist influence in the hemisphere. In 1954 President Dwight Eisenhower ordered the Central Intelligence Agency (CIA) to back Colonel Castillo Armas in an invasion to eliminate the leftist government of Gautemala headed by Jacobo Arbenz. After Fidel Castro established a pro-Soviet regime in Cuba in 1959, Soviet military advisers, combat troops, airplanes, and offensive missiles were brought to the island. President John F. Kennedy used the Monroe Doctrine during the Cuban Missile Crisis of 1962 as one of the justifications for imposing a quarantine on that nation until the Soviet Union removed its offensive weapons from Cuba. On October 23, 1962, the Organization of American States gave the United States a mandate to use force if necessary in compelling their removal.

SEE ALSO *Adams, John Quincy; Cuban Missile Crisis; Kennedy, John F.; Monroe, James*
SOURCES Ernest R. May, *The Making of the Monroe Doctrine* (Cambridge: Harvard University Press, 1975). Dexter Perkins, *Hands Off: A History of the Monroe Doctrine*, rev. ed. (Boston: Little, Brown, 1963).

MONROE, JAMES
5th President

- Born: Apr. 28, 1758, Westmoreland County, Va.
- Political party: Democratic-Republican
- Education: College of William and Mary, 1774–76
- Military service: 3rd Virginia Infantry, 1776–80
- Previous government service: Virginia House of Delegates, 1782, 1787, 1810; Virginia Governor's Council, 1781–83; Continental Congress, 1783–86; Annapolis Convention, 1786; Virginia constitutional ratifying convention, 1788; U.S. Senate, 1790–94; minister to France, 1794–97; governor of Virginia, 1799–1802, 1811; minister to Great Britain, 1803–7; U.S. secretary of state, 1811–17; U.S. secretary of war, 1814–15
- Elected President, 1816; served, 1817–25
- Subsequent public service: Virginia Constitutional Convention, 1829; regent, University of Virginia, 1826–31
- Died: July 4, 1831, New York, N.Y.

James Monroe was a brilliant secretary of state whose Presidency restored peace and prosperity in the aftermath of the War of 1812. Monroe was born into a family without much money, but relatives helped him attend the College of William and Mary. He left after two years to fight with the 3rd Virginia Infantry under General George Washington during the revolutionary war. He fought in several battles and was wounded while leading a charge at the Battle of Trenton. In 1780 he left the military and studied law under Thomas Jefferson, who was at that time governor of Virginia. In 1782 he served in the Virginia Governor's Council, then in the Congress under the Articles of Confederation from 1783 to 1786. Although he opposed ratifying the new U.S. Constitution, Monroe soon took part in national politics. He was defeated by James Madison for a seat in the House of Representatives in 1788, but two years later was selected by the Virginia legislature for a seat in the U.S. Senate, where he opposed the Federalist economic programs of Alexander Hamilton.

President George Washington appointed Monroe to be U.S. minister to France. He refused to defend the Jay Treaty with Great Britain to the French government, believing the terms to favor British interests against the French, and Washington recalled him. He published a defense of his conduct and an attack on the Federalist foreign policy in a book, *A View of the Conduct of the Executive in the Foreign Affairs of the United States* (1797). He then served three terms as governor of Virginia.

In 1803 President Jefferson appointed Monroe to a mission to France to purchase New Orleans. Finding that Emperor Napoleon wished to sell even more land, Monroe exceeded his instructions and negotiated a treaty to purchase the entire Louisiana Territory. The following year, however, he failed in an attempt to negotiate the purchase of Florida from Spain. In 1806 he negotiated a commercial treaty with Great Britain that seemed so favorable to the British that President Jefferson refused to submit it to the Senate. In response, Monroe entered the Presidential contest in an attempt to defeat Jefferson's protégé, James Madison. But in a replay of their 1788 contest, Madison defeated Monroe once again, this time for the Democratic-Republican caucus nomination.

In spite of their political rivalry, Madison appointed Monroe secretary of state in 1811. Simultaneously appointed secretary of war just after the British sacking of the capital in 1814, Monroe prevented an outright British victory, and he oversaw a favorable peace treaty that ended the War of 1812. By a narrow margin the Democratic-Republican congressional caucus nominated him for the Presidency in 1816. He handily won the general election against Federalist candidate Rufus King.

Since the Capitol had been burned to the ground by the British, Monroe's inauguration took place at the Brick Capitol, a temporary meeting hall for Congress. The Monroes could not move into the President's House, soon to be known as the White House, for six months, and Congress could not use the Capitol again until 1819.

Monroe's two terms saw the disappearance of the Federalist party and the brief establishment of a "no party" period known as the Era of Good Feelings. Sectional conflicts among the North, South, and West took the place of party competition. Monroe was reelected in 1820 by a 231-to-1 vote in the electoral college. The one dissenting vote was cast by William Plumer, an elector from New Hampshire, because he wished to reserve the honor of a unanimous vote for Washington alone.

Monroe appointed an exceptional cabinet: John Quincy Adams as secretary of state, John C. Calhoun as secretary of war, William Crawford as secretary of the Treasury, and William Wirt as attorney general—all men of Presidential stature. The cabinet met 180 times during Monroe's two terms, and most decisions were made by consensus.

In domestic affairs Monroe reduced taxes and paid off much of the public debt. He signed the Missouri Compromise of 1820, which forbade slavery in the Louisiana Territory above the southern boundary of Missouri, in spite of his doubts that Congress had the constitutional power to exclude slavery from any part of the Union. The compromise preserved sectional peace. Monroe vetoed the Cumberland Road Bill in 1822 because he did not think it was constitutional for the national government to charge tolls for national roads. The following year, however, he submitted his own public works program

for construction of roads and canals, to be funded by the national government out of general revenues.

Monroe's major accomplishments were in foreign affairs. In 1818 the United States settled its fishing disputes with Canada, which involved the right of Americans to fish off the coast of Labrador. By the Adams-Onis Treaty (1819) the United States acquired Florida from Spain and all Spanish claims to the Oregon Territory were granted instead to the United States. The United States recognized the newly independent nations of Latin America, and the Monroe Doctrine established the principles that European states were neither to colonize in the New World nor interfere with the governments there. Monroe's only significant failure involved the Senate, which refused to consent to a treaty with Great Britain that would have allowed navies of both nations to put an end to the illegal trade in African slaves.

Monroe retired in 1825 to Oak Hill, his Virginia plantation. He was the last of the "Virginia dynasty" to occupy the White House. Monroe acted as a regent of the University of Virginia and presided over the Virginia state constitutional convention in 1829. He died on a visit to New York City on July 4, 1831.

SEE ALSO *Caucuses, congressional; Jefferson, Thomas; Madison, James; Monroe Doctrine; Washington, George*
SOURCES Harry Ammon, *James Monroe: The Quest for National Identity* (New York: McGraw-Hill, 1971). George Dangerfield, *The Era of Good Feelings* (New York: Harcourt, Brace, 1952).

MOODY, WILLIAM HENRY
Associate Justice, 1906–10

- Born: Dec. 23, 1853, Newbury, Mass.
- Education: Harvard College, A.B., 1876; Harvard Law School, 1876–77
- Previous government service: city solicitor, Haverhill, Mass., 1888–90; district

attorney, Eastern District of Massachusetts, 1890–95; U.S. representative from Massachusetts, 1895–1902; U.S. secretary of the navy, 1902–4; U.S. attorney general, 1904–6
• Appointed by President Theodore Roosevelt Dec. 3, 1906; replaced Henry B. Brown, who retired
• Supreme Court term: confirmed by the Senate Dec. 12, 1906, by a voice vote; retired Nov. 20, 1910
• Died: July 2, 1917, Haverhill, Mass.

William Moody became a friend of Theodore Roosevelt in 1895. The two men shared similar interests and ideas; when Roosevelt became President, he appointed Moody as secretary of the navy. In 1904, President Roosevelt chose Moody to be the U.S. attorney general. In 1906, he named Moody an associate justice of the Supreme Court.

Justice Moody's most important opinion for the Court came in *Twining* v. *New Jersey* (1908). Moody, writing for the Court, refused to apply to a state government the 5th Amendment right of an accused person to refuse to testify against himself, to avoid self-incrimination. He argued that this right of the individual, as granted in the federal Bill of Rights, could not be used to restrict state governments because the Bill of Rights applies only to the federal government. This decision was later overturned, but it had force and influence for many years.

Justice Moody's impact on constitutional law was limited by his very short term of service on the Court. He was forced to retire because of the crippling disease of rheumatism.

SEE ALSO *Twining v. New Jersey*

MOORE, ALFRED
Associate Justice, 1800–1804

• Born: May 21, 1755, New Hanover County, N.C.
• Education: studied law under his father
• Previous government service: North Carolina General Assembly, 1782, 1792; attorney general of North Carolina, 1782–91; judge, North Carolina Superior Court, 1799
• Appointed by President John Adams Dec. 6, 1799; replaced James Iredell, who died
• Supreme Court term: confirmed by the Senate Dec. 10, 1799, by a voice vote; resigned Jan. 26, 1804
• Died: Oct. 15, 1810, Bladen County, N.C.

Alfred Moore was a strong supporter of an independent United States of America during the 1770s conflict with the British. He served in the First North Carolina Regiment in the War of Independence and was recognized for his courage and ability as a military leader.

During the 1780s, Moore backed the movement for a strong federal government, which resulted in the framing of the Constitution of 1787. He helped to achieve ratification of the Constitution in North Carolina.

Moore served briefly on the Supreme Court because of ill health. In 1800, he wrote his only opinion for the Court in a case involving the capture of a French vessel by the U.S. navy during the undeclared naval war with France in 1798. The vessel had been owned by an American before its capture by the French. The court ruled that the former owner had to pay one-half the value of the ship in order to reclaim it from the U.S. government.

MORNING BUSINESS

The first thing that the House of Representatives and the Senate do each legislative day is to set aside a period called the Morning Hour for introducing bills, resolutions, memorials, committee reports, and messages from the President, department heads, or the other body. These activities are known as morning business. On each new legislative day, morning business follows the reading of the journal and comes at the beginning of the Morning Hour.

SEE ALSO *Legislative day; Morning Hour*

MORNING HOUR

At the beginning of a new legislative day, the House of Representatives and Senate have a period called the Morning Hour when morning business is conducted and during which members may make brief speeches on any subject. In the House Morning Hour speeches are limited to one minute per member. The Senate sets aside the first two hours of a new legislative day as Morning Hour, and members speak briefly, although without set time limitations. Morning Hour gives members the opportunity to speak on the current issues of the day, even if there is no pending legislation dealing with those issues.

SEE ALSO *Legislative day; Morning business*

MORRILL, JUSTIN S.

- Born: Apr. 14, 1810, Strafford, Vt.
- Political party: Whig, Republican
- Representative from Vermont: 1855–67
- Senator from Vermont: 1867–98
- Died: Dec. 28, 1898, Washington, D.C.

When the Southern Democrats left Congress as their states seceded in 1860 and 1861, they opened the way for the new Republican majority to enact its domestic legislation. Even as the Civil War was being fought, Congress still had to deal with nonmilitary measures. One of the most important of these was the Morrill Land Grant College Act, sponsored by Representative Justin Morrill of Vermont. The Morrill Act set aside public land that could be sold to establish and operate state agricultural and mechanical arts (A&M) colleges. Many state universities today owe their origins to this act, passed in 1862. Justin Morrill remained in the House and Senate for 43 years of continuous service

as a powerful committee chairman (of the House Ways and Means and Senate Finance Committees) and a productive legislator. He turned down repeated requests to join Presidential cabinets, noting that there was no appointed office that would cause him to resign from Congress, which he considered "the highest honor" and "the highest function that I could perform."

MORTON, LEVI
Vice President

- Born: May 16, 1824, Shoreham, Vt.
- Political party: Republican
- Education: no formal education
- Military service: none
- Previous government service: U.S. House of Representatives, 1879–81; minister to France, 1881–85
- Vice President under Benjamin Harrison, 1889–93
- Subsequent government service: governor of New York, 1895–96
- Died: May 16, 1920, Rhinebeck, N.Y.

Levi Morton was successful as a financier, establishing the large Wall Street banking firm of L. P. Morton and Company. In the 1870s the firm, by then known as Morton, Bliss and Co., helped refinance the national debt. Morton moved into politics and was elected to the U.S. House of Representatives in 1878. Three years later, President James Garfield appointed him U.S. minister to France.

Morton was nominated for Vice President on the Republican ticket in 1888 to provide geographic balance and access to the administration for Wall Street. As Benjamin Harrison's Vice President, Morton was an advocate of civil service reforms and good-government practices designed to reduce fraud and corruption. These measures were supported by much of the business community.

After the Democrats took back the White House in 1893 Morton served one term as governor of New York. He then returned to Wall Street and founded another financial company, retiring from business in 1909.

SEE ALSO *Harrison, Benjamin*

MOTIONS, PARLIAMENTARY

When legislators seek some action, whether in committee or on the floor, they make a motion. To make a motion, members first must be recognized, or called upon, by the chair or presiding officer. The member then announces, for example, "Mr. Chairman, I move that we report the bill as amended." Or "Madam President, I move that the yeas and nays be called." Or "Mr. Speaker, I move that the reading of the journal be dispensed with." The motion must be seconded (that is, at least one other member must indicate support) and be voted upon by voice or roll call vote. Motions trigger different types of parliamentary actions, and the rules of the Senate and House establish the priority of motions (that is, which ones must be taken up first and in what order).

MUHLENBERG, FREDERICK AUGUSTUS

- Born: Jan 1, 1750, Trappe, Pa.
- Political party: Federalist, Democratic-Republican
- Education: studied theology at the University of Halle, Germany
- Delegate to the Continental Congress: 1779–80
- Representative from Pennsylvania: 1789–97
- Speaker of the House: 1789–91, 1793–95
- Died: June 4, 1801, Lancaster, Pa.

The first Speaker of the House of Representatives, Frederick Muhlenberg, was a Lutheran minister who had previously served as a member of the Continental Congress, speaker of the Pennsylvania As-

sembly, and president of the Pennsylvania State Convention that ratified the Constitution. His experience in government and his representation of a middle state (whereas George Washington was a Southerner and Vice President John Adams came from New England) led to Muhlenberg's election as Speaker. A portly, distinguished-looking man, he brought honesty, integrity, and dignity to his office. However, because he attempted to rule with impartiality, following the model of the speakers of the British House of Commons, Muhlenberg displeased members of the Federalist party. They removed him as Speaker in favor of a more ardent champion of Federalist policies. Muhlenberg later switched to the Democratic-Republican party.

MULLER V. OREGON

- 208 U.S. 412 (1908)
- Vote: 9–0
- For the Court: Brewer

In the early 1900s state legislatures began passing laws aimed at reforming working conditions. Employers soon challenged the new laws. As a result, the Supreme Court began to face questions regarding the constitutionality of these reform laws.

A case arose in 1907 that dramatically changed how the Supreme Court made decisions about such social reform legislation. That year, Curt Muller, a Portland, Oregon, laundry owner, was charged with violating an Oregon law that set a maximum 10-hour workday for women working in laundries. Muller challenged the law as a violation of his "liberty to contract," which he claimed was guaranteed by the 14th Amendment.

Muller argued that the due process clause of the 14th Amendment prevented the state from interfering with his liberty to enter into any contracts, including those setting wages and hours for workers, necessary for running his business. (The amendment states, in part, "nor shall any

State deprive any person of life, liberty, or property, without due process of law.") The Supreme Court had supported this interpretation of the 14th Amendment in several earlier cases.

Louis D. Brandeis, a brilliant lawyer who later became a distinguished Supreme Court justice, argued the case for Oregon. Brandeis took a startling new approach. He presented sociological, medical, and statistical information to show that long hours of hard labor had a harmful effect upon women's health. He claimed the Court must consider whether the Oregon law was a reasonable attempt to protect public health and safety. A state law might be allowed to interfere with the 14th Amendment's presumed guarantee of liberty of contract if it could be justified as protecting public health against real dangers.

How could the Court decide when a state law met such a standard? Brandeis argued that the Court could not rely merely on legal precedents and the vague words of the Constitution in judging such cases. It also had to consider relevant facts about the social conditions that led to the law in the first place.

The Issue   Brandeis defined the question before the Court: Did the consideration of social conditions justify the Oregon law's interference with the 14th Amendment supposed guarantee of liberty of contract?

Would the Court accept Brandeis's novel thesis that it should consider relevant social facts in deciding the case? Or would the Court, as it had in the past, decide the case strictly through reference to legal arguments?

Opinion of the Court   The Court accepted Brandeis's argument, ruling unanimously to uphold Oregon's law. The factual evidence Brandeis supplied proved convincing. The Court ruled that longer working hours might harm women's ability to bear children. Thus, the state's limitation of those hours was a justified interference with liberty of contract and property and within the state's regulatory power.

Significance   The *Muller* case established that lawyers could use social facts and statistics as well as strictly legal arguments in the briefs they presented to the Supreme Court. A brief is a document summarizing the facts and legal arguments that a lawyer gives to a court when appealing a case. Today we call a brief that contains substantial nonlegal data a *Brandeis brief*. Ever since the *Muller* case, lawyers have used relevant social data in their arguments before the Court. When deciding subsequent cases—*Brown* v. *Board of Education* (1954), for example—the Supreme Court has recognized that information about social conditions could appropriately supplement legal principles.

SEE ALSO   *Brandeis brief*

SOURCES   Alpheus Thomas Mason, "The Case of the Overworked Laundress," in *Quarrels That Have Shaped the Constitution,* edited by John A. Garraty (New York: Harper & Row, 1987). Nancy Woloch, *Muller v. Oregon: A Brief History with Documents* (New York: Bedford/St. Martin's, 1996).

MUNN V. ILLINOIS

- 94 U.S. 113 (1877)
- Vote: 7–2
- For the Court: Waite
- Dissenting: Field and Strong

Munn v. *Illinois* was the first of a famous series of cases known as the *Granger Cases.* These cases dealt with issues resulting from the rapid growth of manufacturing and transportation companies that began after the Civil War ended in 1865.

Many of these companies, particularly those formed by railroad concerns and operators of huge grain warehouses, began to abuse the nearly complete control they had over hauling and storing farm products, especially grain. The railroads and grain warehouses charged farmers very high prices and often tried to cheat them. By the 1870s, the situation had deteriorated so much that even the *Chicago Tribune,* a newspaper known for its pro-business sympathies, called the grain warehouses "blood-sucking insects."

In response to such conditions, a large, politically powerful farm group, the Grange, developed. Farmers in the Granger movement influenced state legislatures in the Midwest to pass laws regulating the prices railroads, warehouses, and public utilities charged for hauling freight and storing grain.

The Issue The railroads and grain warehouses fought against state regulation of their businesses in the courts. They claimed the states' Granger laws violated the Constitution in three ways: they infringed on Congress's right to regulate interstate commerce, they violated the Constitution's prohibition against interfering with contracts, and they violated the 14th Amendment by depriving businesses of their liberty and property without due process of law.

The *Munn* case posed a clear and important question for a nation with rapidly developing industries. Did the Constitution permit a state to regulate privately owned businesses?

Opinion of the Court The Supreme Court ruled in favor of the states. It said the Illinois state legislature could fix maximum rates for grain storage in Chicago and other places in the state. Chief Justice Morrison R. Waite set forth a doctrine that both Congress and state legislatures still use to regulate many private business activities—the doctrine of "business affected with a public interest."

Waite said that when the activity of a company "has public consequences and affect(s) the community at large," it is a "business affected with a public interest." Under the Constitution the states can regulate such a business, and the owner of such a business "must submit to be controlled by the public for the common good."

Dissent Justice Stephen J. Field argued against the *Munn* opinion as an invasion of private property rights, which he said were protected against state power by the due process clause of the 14th Amendment. Justice Field wanted to limit the use of state "police power" to regulate businesses.

Significance The Court's decision established the power of state government to regulate businesses other than public utilities. Today, state legislatures exercise tremendous regulatory powers over such matters as working conditions, transportation of goods and people, and manufacturing of products for sale to the public. The constitutional basis for much of this activity rests directly on the Court's decision in *Munn* v. *Illinois*.

MURPHY, FRANK
Associate Justice, 1940–49

- Born: Apr. 13, 1890, Harbor Beach, Mich.
- Education: University of Michigan, B.A., 1912; LL.B., 1914
- Previous government service: chief assistant attorney general, Eastern District of Michigan, 1919–20; judge, Recorder's Court, Detroit, Mich., 1923–30; mayor of Detroit, 1930–33; governor general of the Philippines, 1933–35; U.S. high commissioner to the Philippines, 1935–36; governor of Michigan, 1937–39; U.S. attorney general, 1939–40
- Appointed by President Franklin D. Roosevelt Jan. 4, 1940; replaced Pierce Butler, who died
- Supreme Court term: confirmed by the Senate Jan. 15, 1940, by a voice vote; served until July 19, 1949
- Died: July 19, 1949, Detroit, Mich.

Frank Murphy was a strong supporter of Franklin D. Roosevelt's 1932 campaign for the Presidency. After serving as an administrator of the U.S. territory of the Philippines and as U.S. attorney general, Murphy was appointed by President Roosevelt to the Supreme Court.

As an associate justice, Murphy was a strong defender of minority rights. His most notable opinions were written in dissent of the Court's decisions to favor federal or state government interests above the rights of individuals.

Justice Murphy's dissent in *Korematsu v. United States* (1944) has been regarded as an example of the best opinions to be found in the Supreme Court literature. In this wartime case, the Court upheld the right of the government to relocate and confine all persons of Japanese ancestry living on the Pacific coast of the United States. The Court's majority argued that this action was necessary to protect national security during the war against Japan. Justice Murphy disagreed and said the relocation was "utterly revolting among a free people who have embraced the principles set forth in the Constitution of the United States."

Murphy's dissent in the *Korematsu* case is honored today as a courageous and correct view of the case. And the majority opinion in that case tends to be criticized, in Murphy's terms, as "legalization of racism."

SEE ALSO *Korematsu v. United States*

SOURCES Sidney Fine, *Frank Murphy: The Washington Years* (Ann Arbor: University of Michigan Press, 1984). J. Woodford Howard, *Mr. Justice Murphy: A Political Biography* (Princeton, N.J.: Princeton University Press, 1968).

N

NATIONAL AERONAUTICS AND SPACE ADMINISTRATION

Prior to the successful launch of the satellite known as *Sputnik* by the Soviet Union in 1957, interest in space exploration in the United States was primarily the domain of the National Advisory Committee for Aeronautics (NACA). In 1958, however, Congress responded to the Soviet space venture with the passage of the National Aeronautics and Space Act. This legislation, with the support of President Dwight Eisenhower, established the National Aeronautics and Space Administration (NASA) as an independent agency to direct the nation's space flight and research programs. NASA is directed by an administrator who is nominated by the President and confirmed by the Senate for an indefinite term.

NASA's human space flight efforts began in the 1960s, first with Project Mercury and, later, Project Gemini. In 1969 Project Apollo accomplished the goal of "landing a man on the moon and returning him safely to Earth," which had been announced by President John F. Kennedy in 1961. By 1981 NASA had ushered in a new stage in the evolution of space flight with the introduction of the space shuttle program. The program utilizes space shuttles, rocket-powered space crafts that look like bulky jet planes and are capable of landing on runways, to ferry people and equipment between the ground and Earth orbit. The first space shuttle, *Columbia*, was launched into orbit on April 12, 1981, but the most memorable space shuttle launch was on January 25, 1986, when the shuttle *Challenger* exploded soon after leaving the launch pad because of a fuel leak. The seven astronauts on board were killed.

Other than human space flights, NASA successes over the years have included the exploration of the solar system by scientific probes such as the *Pioneer* and *Voyager* spacecraft. The *Viking* and *Pathfinder* missions provided valuable information about Mars, and the Hubble space telescope has enabled scientists to make a number of important astronomical discoveries. NASA has also launched communications satellites, including the *Echo, Telstar,* and *Syncom* satellites.

NATIONAL ARCHIVES AND RECORDS ADMINISTRATION

Every year, the federal government produces vast quantities of records on paper and tape, in photographs and microfilm, and increasingly in electronic format. These records document every government action and are vital evidence in documenting the history of the nation, for reviewing past policies, for conducting investigations, for scholarly research, and for genealogical studies. For many years, no central repository for these records existed. Government agencies stored their records in basements, attics, and warehouses. As a result, many records were lost, destroyed, or allowed to deteriorate.

In 1934 Congress established the National Archives to identify, preserve, and provide access to significant government documents and records. In 1949 the archives was incorporated into the General Services Administration and renamed the National Archives and Records Service. As such, it worked with records administrators in every agency, advising them on what records they could dispose of and what they needed to maintain for permanent preservation. In 1984 Congress reestablished it as an independent agency, designated the National Archives and Records Administration (NARA). The archivist of the United States, appointed by the President and confirmed by the Senate for a 10-year term, oversees the agency.

In the National Archives building on the Mall in Washington are housed and displayed the nation's most famous documents: the Declaration of Independence, the original Constitution of the United States, and the Bill of Rights. Back in the stacks of that building, and in the sprawling Archives II, in nearby College Park, Maryland, are billions of other documents, along with millions of maps, photographs, motion pictures, and video and sound recordings. In addition, NARA includes the Office of Presidential Libraries, which preserve the records of recent Presidents in their home states.

The introduction of computers in the years following World War II created a whole new form of federal record keeping. At first used by the military and by the census, computers spread to every agency, and electronic mail (e-mail) steadily replaced postal mail. Although computer tapes were more compact than the equivalent paper copy, computer systems quickly became obsolete and conversion from one generation of computer technology to the next was often difficult and expensive, creating new dilemmas for archivists seeking to preserve as complete documentation as possible.

SEE ALSO *Libraries, Presidential*

NATIONAL ASSOCIATION FOR THE ADVANCEMENT OF COLORED PEOPLE (NAACP)

The National Association for the Advancement of Colored People (NAACP) is a private, not-for-profit organization founded in 1909 to protect and expand the civil rights of African Americans. The NAACP has used both political and legal strategies to carry out its mission. In 1939 the NAACP Legal Defense Fund (LDF) was created to support legal strategies on behalf of civil rights for African Americans. From 1940 to 1961 Thurgood Marshall was the director of the LDF. He was primarily responsible for winning 29 victories for the LDF in cases before the Supreme Court. Marshall and the LDF helped the NAACP to win its greatest legal victory, the Supreme Court decision in *Brown* v. *Board of Education* (1954), which outlawed racial segregation in public schools. Marshall went on to become an associate justice of the Supreme Court.

The NAACP carefully monitors the President's nominations of Supreme Court justices and other federal judges. The purpose is to encourage the appointment of people who are likely to agree with the organization's views on civil rights.

SEE ALSO *Brown v. Board of Education; Civil rights*

NATIONAL ENDOWMENT FOR THE ARTS

The National Endowment for the Arts (NEA) is an independent agency that was created by Congress in 1965. The NEA has proclaimed that its mission is to foster the excellence, diversity, and vitality of the arts and to broaden public access to the arts in the United States. The head of the NEA is a chairperson who serves a four-year term after being appointed by the President and confirmed by the Senate. The chairperson is advised by a council of 26 people who are also nominated by the President and subject to Senate confirmation.

Since 1965 the NEA has awarded more than 100,000 grants to support projects such as orchestra concerts; dance and opera performances; radio and television broadcasts; music, theater, and film festivals; and a wide variety of other arts programs. The NEA awards grants to nonprofit arts organizations and nonmatching fellowships to individual artists. Currently the agency devotes about 40 percent of its budget to partnerships with state and regional arts agencies. The NEA also maintains a number of partnerships with other federal agencies, including the Department of Education, the Department of Justice, the Center for Substance Abuse Prevention, and the National Science Foundation.

NATIONAL ENDOWMENT FOR THE HUMANITIES

The National Endowment for the Humanities (NEH) is an independent agency that was created by Congress in 1965. The NEH has stated that its mission is to enrich the cultural life of the nation by promoting knowledge of human history, thought, and culture. The agency is directed by a chairperson who is appointed by the President and confirmed by the Senate for a term of four years. The National Council on the Humanities, a board of 26 people who are also appointed by the President and confirmed by the Senate, advises the chairperson.

The NEH promotes the humanities by making grants in four areas: education, research, public programs, and providing access to cultural resources. Grants are typically awarded to cultural institutions such as museums, archives, libraries, universities, and public television and radio stations, though individual scholars can also qualify for NEH grants. The legislation that established the NEH stated that the term *humanities* includes, but is not limited to, the study of history, philosophy, languages, linguistics, literature, archaeology, jurisprudence, comparative religion, and ethics.

NATIONAL LABOR RELATIONS BOARD V. JONES & LAUGHLIN STEEL CORP.

- 301 U.S. 1 (1937)
- Vote: 5–4
- For the Court: Hughes
- Dissenting: Sutherland, Van Devanter, McReynolds, and Butler

In July 1935 the Jones & Laughlin Steel Corporation fired 10 workers at its Aliquippa, Pennsylvania, plant. They were leaders of a local unit of the American Federation of Labor (AFL), a national labor union. The managers of the steel company wanted to stop their workers from joining the labor union.

On July 5, 1935, four days before Jones & Laughlin dismissed the 10 labor union leaders, President Franklin D. Roosevelt signed into law the National Labor Relations Act, often called the Wagner Act after New York senator Robert Wagner, the law's major sponsor in Congress. This new federal law made it illegal for an employer to fire or otherwise harass a worker because he belonged to a labor union. The law also protected the right of workers at a company to designate, by majority vote, a labor union to represent them as their sole bargaining agent with their employer. The Wagner Act applied to all businesses either engaged directly in interstate commerce or whose operations affected interstate commerce. Thus, the law could be applied to a business such as Jones & Laughlin Steel Corporation, which shipped steel across state lines.

The government set up the National

Labor Relations Board (NLRB) to enforce the Wagner Act. On April 9, 1936, the NLRB charged Jones & Laughlin with violating the Wagner Act by discharging the 10 workers because they were labor union leaders. The company was ordered to reinstate the men and to give them back pay for the period they were not permitted to work. Jones & Laughlin's response was to challenge the NLRB and the Wagner Act as unconstitutional.

The Issue Lawyers for Jones & Laughlin argued that the Wagner Act was based on an excessively broad interpretation of the commerce powers of Congress specified in Article 1, Section 8, of the U.S. Constitution. According to Jones & Laughlin, Congress did not have power under the commerce clause to regulate the relationships of managers and workers of a private corporation. Furthermore, the company claimed, the Wagner Act violated the due process clause of the 5th Amendment, which had been held in previous decisions of the Supreme Court to protect the "liberty of contract" between employers and employees. The federal government had no power, said the Jones & Laughlin lawyers, to interfere with the rights of private property owners and workers to bargain about wages, hours of work, and working conditions.

Opinion of the Court The Court sustained the Wagner Act as a constitutional exercise of Congress's commerce power and ruled that it did not violate the 5th Amendment's due process clause. Chief Justice Charles Evans Hughes wrote that the Wagner Act's purpose was to reduce the possibility of strikes, which could disrupt the production and distribution of products and thereby increase the bargaining power to achieve satisfactory working conditions. Strikes could be prevented, Hughes said, by protecting the right of workers to organize labor unions. Hughes also rejected the "liberty of contract" argument based on the due process clause of the 5th Amendment. He emphasized that the Wagner Act in fact *enhanced* workers'

power to bargain through a democratically elected representative of a labor union.

Significance In this decision, the Court affirmed President Roosevelt's position that the federal government has the power under the Constitution to regulate the economic system. The *Jones & Laughlin* decision was a departure from several decisions between 1933 and 1937 in which the Court had firmly rejected President Roosevelt's New Deal programs.

The Court's opposition had so angered the President that, following his landslide victory in the 1936 election, he threatened to change the membership of the Court in his favor. On February 5, 1937, Roosevelt announced that he would ask Congress to enact legislation to enable the President to add up to six additional justices to the Court. With such a law, he could immediately add new justices to the Court who would be likely to vote for his economic regulation policies. This Court-packing plan was abandoned by President Roosevelt after the Court made decisions he agreed with in *Jones & Laughlin* and other 1937 cases.

The upholding of the Wagner Act by the Court greatly changed labor-management relations throughout the United States. It led to an enormous growth in the membership and power of labor unions, which were influential in improving wages, hours of work, and working conditions.

SEE ALSO *Commerce power; Court-packing plan (1937)*
SOURCES Richard C. Cortner, *The Jones & Laughlin Case* (New York: Knopf, 1970).

NATIONAL SECURITY ADVISER

The national security adviser (NSA) serves as the principal adviser to the President on national security matters, supervises the staff of the National Security Council (NSC), and organizes the meetings of the NSC. The NSA prepares initial drafts of

National Security Decision Directives (NSDD) for NSC consideration and monitors the implementation of national security decisions made by the President. Appointed by the President without Senate consent, the NSA is a White House aide with no statutory powers or duties and is not a member of the National Security Council.

The NSA may play several different roles in Presidential decision making. President Dwight Eisenhower used Robert Cutler, his special assistant for national security affairs, as a "custodian manager" to see that all options were being considered, especially for long-range planning. Cutler also had to ensure that the elaborate staffing method Eisenhower put in place (with 76 aides to the National Security Council) was operating smoothly.

President John F. Kennedy used McGeorge Bundy as one of his key advisers and policymakers. Bundy was less concerned with process and paperwork than with policy advocacy, especially in short-term crisis management. Similarly, Lyndon Johnson used Walt Rostow as a policy advocate for escalating the Vietnam War and as a defender of that policy before Congress.

President Richard Nixon relied on Henry Kissinger as his principal adviser in foreign policy and national security, sent him on a top secret diplomatic mission to the People's Republic of China, and entrusted him with negotiating arms control agreements with the Soviet Union. Kissinger used the NSC staff to dominate interdepartmental committees concerned with arms control negotiations with the Soviets and with defense budgeting.

President Jimmy Carter used Zbigniew Brzezinski to formulate his foreign policy goals and as a counterweight to his secretary of state, Cyrus Vance, making him the first national security adviser with cabinet rank. Brzezinski presided over NSC committees dealing with intelligence, arms control, and crisis management.

During Ronald Reagan's administration, two advisers with a military background, marine colonel Robert McFarlane and navy admiral John Poindexter, took operational control of policy when they oversaw the sale of arms to Iran and the transfer of some of the profits to the Contra resistance movement in Nicaragua. Instead of developing policy proposals for the President and the NSC, the NSA and the Political-Military Affairs Directorate of the NSC developed policies and implemented them on their own.

In the aftermath of the Iran-Contra affair, President Reagan appointed Frank Carlucci and then Colin Powell as NSA. They implemented the recommendations of the Tower Commission, the panel appointed by Reagan to investigate the affair. They dissolved the Political-Military Affairs Directorate, making the NSA accountable to all members of the NSC; allowed all departments to present policy options to the President; and served as impartial custodians of the national security advisory process.

SEE ALSO *Commander in chief; Cuban Missile Crisis; Decision making, Presidential; National Security Council; Secretary of state*
SOURCES Zbigniew Brzezinski, *Power and Principle* (New York: Farrar, Straus & Giroux, 1983). Henry Kissinger, *White House Years* (Boston: Little, Brown, 1979).

NATIONAL SECURITY COUNCIL

The National Security Council (NSC) is the unit of the Executive Office of the President that assists the President in making and executing national security decisions. It was established by the National Security Act of 1947, according to which it consisted of the President, who chaired its meetings, the secretary of state, the secretary of defense, and the service secretaries of the army, navy, and air force. The Director of Central Intelligence was not a member but would serve as an adviser.

In 1949 Congress amended the law to

change the composition of the council: the three service secretaries were dropped and the Vice President was added. The chair of the Joint Chiefs of Staff became an adviser to the council and attended its meetings. The President might "from time to time" designate other officials to sit on the council or attend its meetings, and 20 or more officials have often been invited. The NSC has a staff of 40 or more aides, supervised by the assistant to the President for national security.

The NSC has no powers of its own, takes no votes, and makes no decisions. Presidential decisions made after NSC deliberations are embodied in National Security Decision Directives and are implemented by the executive departments of the federal government.

The NSC staff monitors national security communications in the Situation Room, located in the White House basement, and in a Crisis Management Center located in the Executive Office Building (equipped with computers and projection facilities for the display of information). These communications include State Department instructions to U.S. embassies and missions, Defense Department messages to military commands, and Joint Chiefs of Staff orders to the regional military commanders in chief. Data from the Pentagon's National Military Command Center in Colorado Springs, Colorado, can be simultaneously displayed in the Situation Room.

Although Presidents Harry Truman and Dwight Eisenhower convened the NSC frequently, most Presidents rely on very small meetings with their key national security advisers much more than on meetings of the council itself. President Kennedy used the Ex Comm, a smaller "executive committee" of the national security officials, to deliberate in crisis situations such as the Berlin Crisis and the Cuban Missile Crisis. Lyndon Johnson relied on his Tuesday lunch with the secretaries of war and defense, the Director of Central Intelligence, chair of the Joint Chiefs, and his national security adviser, to

plan strategy for the war in Vietnam. Richard Nixon worked closely with Henry Kissinger, his national security adviser, on improving relations with the People's Republic of China and the Soviet Union, and sometimes they were referred to as the "two-man band." Jimmy Carter held Friday breakfasts with his Vice President, the secretaries of state and defense, and his national security adviser to deal with the Iran hostage crisis and relations with the Soviets. Ronald Reagan used the National Security Planning Group, consisting of the members of the NSC, the Director of Central Intelligence, the national security adviser, and three top White House political aides. Reagan was the first President to include political advisers in national security decision making.

SEE ALSO *Cuban Missile Crisis; Decision making, Presidential; Director of Central Intelligence; National security adviser; Secretary of defense; Secretary of state*

SOURCES *Report of the President's Special Review Board* [Tower Commission] (Washington, D.C.: Government Printing Office, 1987).

NATIVE AMERICANS IN CONGRESS

Although Congress has long had committees and subcommittees that deal with issues related to American Indians, few Native Americans have served in the House or Senate. Originally, the Constitution treated the Indian tribes as separate nations. Indians were not citizens and were not counted for purposes of taxes or for determining a state's representation in the House (Article 1, Section 2). Not until the Dawes Act of 1887 did Congress grant U.S. citizenship to the Indians.

The first member of Congress to claim Native American ancestry was Charles Curtis (Republican–Kansas), who was one-eighth Kaw-Osage. His mother died when he was three, and Curtis was for a while raised by his Indian grandmother. He often visited the Kaw reservation in

Oklahoma. Even after he was elected to the House in 1892 and to the Senate in 1906, Curtis was listed on the rolls of the Interior Department as an Indian ward of the government. A few other members, largely from Oklahoma, were also part Indian.

Benjamin Reifel (Republican–South Dakota), a Sioux born on the Rosebud Indian Reservation, served in the House from 1961 to 1971. Ben Nighthorse Campbell (Democrat/Republican–Colorado), a Cheyenne who designs Indian jewelry and dresses and wears his hair in Indian style, was elected to the House in 1986 and to the Senate in 1992. Senator Daniel Akaka (Democrat– Hawaii) notes that his Polynesian heritage also makes him a Native American.

SOURCES William E. Unrau, *Mixed-Bloods and Tribal Dissolution: Charles Curtis and the Quest for Indian Identity* (Lawrence: University Press of Kansas, 1989).

NATURAL LAW

The theory of natural law holds that there is a certain order in nature from which humans, by use of their reason, can derive standards for human conduct. For example, Saint Thomas Aquinas (a 13th-century European scholar and Roman Catholic priest), in his *Summa Theologica,* attempted to derive natural law from his understanding of the divine law revealed by God.

By contrast, philosophers of the European Age of Enlightenment (from the 1680s through the 1700s) such as John Locke in his *Two Treatises of Government* (1690) ignored the idea of divine law and based their concept of natural law on the fundamental human desire for self-preservation and fulfillment. Accordingly, Locke and other Enlightenment thinkers held that the laws of nature imply government based on consent of the governed as the way to secure natural rights of individuals to life, liberty, and property. The natural law standard for judging the worth of government was the effectiveness of the government in securing the natural rights of individuals. These rights were thought to exist prior to the people's establishment of their government, and all people were entitled to these rights by virtue of their humanity. All were bound to respect and abide by these natural rights because of their capacity to know and justify them through human reason.

The Enlightenment conception of natural law and natural rights influenced the founders of constitutional government in the United States. This influence is evident in the text of the Declaration of Independence and the preambles to the first state constitutions of the original 13 states. However, there were other important influences on the constitutional thought of the founders, such as the political and legal ideas brought to America from England and the experiences in establishing and developing their colonial governments.

The idea of natural law was used from time to time in debates about constitutional issues. For example, both sides in the slavery controversy, from the 1780s to the 1860s, appealed to natural law as justification for their views. Nineteenth-century opponents of strong government regulation of private business also appealed to natural law to support their constitutional arguments. However, during the 20th century, natural law theories have had little influence on the decisions of Supreme Court justices or the thoughts of most legal scholars. Legal protection of individual rights has not been based on natural law doctrines but on the principles and precedents stemming from interpretation of the U.S. Constitution and federal statutes.

SEE ALSO *Constitutional democracy; Constitutionalism; Constitutional law*
SOURCES Hadley Arkes, "Natural Law," *Constitution* 4, no. 1 (Winter 1992): 13–20.

NEAR V. MINNESOTA

- 283 U.S. 697 (1931)
- Vote: 5–4

• For the Court: Hughes
• Dissenting: Butler, Van Devanter, Sutherland, and McReynolds

In 1927 Jay Near and Howard Guilford established the *Saturday Press* in Minneapolis. Near, an experienced journalist, was known for his bigotry against Catholics, blacks, Jews, and organized labor. He specialized in reporting scandals in a sensational manner.

From its first issue, the *Saturday Press* hammered away at alleged ties between gangsters and police in a series of sensational stories. The paper proved especially tough on city and county government officials.

The *Saturday Press* attacked, among others, county prosecutor Floyd Olson, who later became a three-term Minnesota governor. The *Saturday Press* called him "Jew lover" Olson and accused him of dragging his feet in the investigation of organized crime. Olson was enraged. On November 21, 1927, he filed a complaint under Minnesota's Public Nuisance Abatement Law with the county district judge. Olson charged that the *Saturday Press* had defamed various politicians, the county grand jury, and the entire Jewish community.

The county judge issued a temporary restraining order against the *Saturday Press* prohibiting publication of the paper under the Public Nuisance Abatement Law. That law was known as a "gag law" because it authorized a form of censorship called prior restraint. Prior restraint allows government officials to restrict a newspaper or magazine *in advance* from publishing materials of which they disapprove.

Near and Guilford obeyed the restraining order issued against them. They claimed, however, that it was unconstitutional. As the Minnesota courts dealt with this case, Howard Guilford withdrew from the legal battle. More important, Near recruited a rich and powerful ally. Robert McCormick, the publisher of the *Chicago Tribune,* sympathized with Near for a number of reasons. Like Near, the bigoted McCormick disliked blacks, Jews, and other minorities. McCormick had also fought numerous legal battles over articles published in his paper. These struggles had taught McCormick the importance of defending the 1st Amendment. He did not want the Illinois legislature to copy the Minnesota gag law. And so the interests of the rich publisher in Chicago and those of the poor scandalmonger in Minnesota coincided. Near wanted his little paper back in business; McCormick wanted a free press. McCormick committed the *Tribune's* full resources to the case. His lawyers represented Near in future legal proceedings.

The Minnesota Supreme Court decided against Near and upheld the Public Nuisance Abatement Law. Near, with McCormick's support, appealed to the U.S. Supreme Court.

The Issue Near's attorney claimed that the Minnesota Public Nuisance Abatement Law allowed prior restraint and thus violated the 1st Amendment, which guarantees freedom of speech and press, and the 14th Amendment, which forbids the states to "deprive any person of life, liberty, or property, without due process of law." He argued that the Constitution guaranteed freedom of the press as a fundamental right. No state could take the right away through prior restraint.

Near's attorney admitted that the *Saturday Press* article was "defamatory" of government officials. But, he added, "So long as men do evil, so long will newspapers publish defamation." The attorney argued, "Every person does have a constitutional right to publish malicious, scandalous and defamatory matter, though untrue and with bad motives, and for unjustifiable ends." Such a person could be punished afterward. The remedy, then, was not censorship of an offending newspaper by prior restraint. Rather, the state should bring specific criminal charges against such a newspaper after it published the material.

Minnesota argued that the Public Nuisance Abatement Law was constitutional and that the injunction against the *Satur-*

day Press was not prior restraint. The injunction was issued only after the *Saturday Press* had attacked the reputations of public officials. Thus, the law punished an offense already committed. The Constitution was designed to protect individual freedoms, not serve the purposes of wrongdoers, such as Near and his scandalous *Saturday Press.*

Opinion of the Court The Court ruled in favor of Jay Near and held that the Minnesota Public Nuisance Abatement Law was a prior restraint on the press that violated both the 1st Amendment and the due process clause of the 14th Amendment.

Chief Justice Charles Evans Hughes, in the majority opinion, declared the Minnesota law "the essence of censorship." He stated that libel laws, not newspaper closures, should counter false charges and character assassinations. He emphasized that the right to criticize government officials was one of the foundations of the American nation.

Hughes stressed that "this statute [the Public Nuisance Abatement Law] raises questions of grave importance transcending the local interests involved in the particular action. It is no longer open to doubt that the liberty of the press . . . is within the liberty safeguarded by the due process clause of the Fourteenth Amendment from invasion by state action."

Dissent Justice Pierce Butler argued that the Minnesota law was not an example of prior restraint. Rather, it allowed public officials to control unacceptable publications after reading the published material. Butler also argued that the U.S. Supreme Court had imposed on a state government "a federal restriction that is without precedent." He was referring to the fact that this decision was the first time that the Court used the due process clause of the 14th Amendment to apply the 1st Amendment right to freedom of the press to a state. Butler and his colleagues in dissent said this should not be done.

Significance Jay Near was triumphant when he learned of the Court's verdict. In October 1932 Near again began to publish the *Saturday Press.* The paper did not survive, however, and in April 1936 Near died in obscurity.

The Court's ruling also pleased Colonel McCormick. He wrote Chief Justice Hughes: "I think your decision in the Gag Law case will forever remain one of the buttresses of free government."

As a result of *Near v. Minnesota,* the United States has built a tradition against prior restraints unlike any other in the world. This tradition has helped keep the free press from censorship by government officials merely because it is critical of them.

In 1971 the Supreme Court relied on the *Near* precedent in the Pentagon Papers case (*New York Times Co. v. United States*). In that case the federal government attempted to stop the *New York Times* from publishing secret documents describing the history of U.S. involvement in the Vietnam War. The Court ruled against the government and permitted publication of the documents.

SEE ALSO *Freedom of press and speech; Incorporation doctrine; New York Times Co. v. United States; Prior restraint*
SOURCES Fred W. Friendly, *Minnesota Rag: The Dramatic Story of the Landmark Court Case That Gave New Meaning to Freedom of the Press* (New York: Random House, 1981). Paul L. Murphy, "The Case of the Miscreant Purveyor of Scandal," in *Quarrels That Have Shaped the Constitution,* edited by John A. Garraty (New York: Harper & Row, 1987).

NECESSARY AND PROPER CLAUSE

SEE *Constitutional construction; Implied powers*

NELSON, SAMUEL
Associate Justice, 1845–72

- Born: Nov. 10, 1792, Hebron, N.Y.
- Education: Middlebury College, B.A., 1813

- Previous government service: postmaster, Cortland, N.Y., 1820–23; New York State Constitutional Convention, 1821; Presidential elector, 1820; judge, Sixth Circuit Court of New York, 1823–31; associate justice, New York Supreme Court, 1831–37; chief justice, New York Supreme Court, 1837–45
- Appointed by President John Tyler Feb. 4, 1845; replaced Smith Thompson, who died
- Supreme Court term: confirmed by the Senate Feb. 14, 1845, by a voice vote; retired Nov. 28, 1872
- Died: Dec. 13, 1873, Cooperstown, N.Y.

Samuel Nelson was the son of Scotch-Irish parents who came to North America in the 1760s. After admission to the New York bar in 1817, he began a career in law and politics. In 1823 he was appointed to the position of judge on the Sixth Circuit Court of New York. For nearly the rest of his life, Nelson occupied judicial positions in the state of New York and on the U.S. Supreme Court.

During his 27 years on the Supreme Court, Nelson performed satisfactorily but without distinction. His decisions tended to favor states' rights and judicial self-restraint. In his opinion for the Court in *Georgia* v. *Stanton* (1868), Justice Nelson showed his strong belief in judicial restraint to the point of deciding against states' rights. He decided against the attempts of two Southern states to obstruct Reconstruction policies of the federal government. He held that the case presented by the Southern states should be dismissed because it involved "political questions" that the Supreme Court could not decide.

NEW DEAL

The New Deal was the term used by Franklin D. Roosevelt to describe his domestic program. "I pledge to you," Roosevelt told the Democratic national convention in Chicago in his 1932 acceptance speech, "I pledge myself, to a new deal for the American people." According to speech writers Raymond Moley and Samuel Rosenman, both of whom used the term in drafts of the speech, neither they nor Roosevelt had any idea that the phrase, designed simply as campaign rhetoric, would become so significant. The term had been used earlier at the convention, when John McDuffie of Alabama nominated John Nance Garner for Vice President with the words, "There is a demand for a new deal in the management of the affairs of the American people."

The phrase may have been borrowed from the British campaign of David Lloyd George, who ran for prime minister in 1919 with the slogan "A New Deal for Everyone." American reformers had also used the phrase, including Senator Carl Schurz of Missouri in 1871, Woodrow Wilson in his campaign for New Jersey governor in 1910, and Senator Robert La Follette of Wisconsin in 1912.

The New Deal involved three activities: First, Roosevelt had to restore confidence in the banking system and end the panicked withdrawals of funds that threatened thousands of banks. Then he had to stabilize prices in order to encourage businesses and farmers to resume production. Finally, he had to provide new federal assistance to those he described in his second inaugural address as the third of the nation that was "ill-housed, ill-clad, ill-nourished."

Roosevelt's efforts began on March 6, 1933, when he proclaimed a bank holiday and called Congress into special session. In the hundred days of that session, from March 9 through June 15, Congress passed Roosevelt's program: the Emergency Banking Act, the Agricultural Adjustment Act, and the National Industrial Recovery Act, as well as the bills creating the Tennessee Valley Authority (which built dams and power stations to provide power in a six-state region), the Home Owners Loan Corporation (which made mortgage loans to encourage home owning), and the Federal Emergency Relief Administration (which provided funds to the jobless).

Roosevelt also took the United States off the gold standard to prevent a run on government gold reserves by people worried about the value of the currency.

Later New Deal laws created public housing for workers, unemployment insurance, and Social Security benefits (pensions) for workers when they retired. Other laws made federal grants to states to provide welfare for needy families with children and established a legal framework for organizing labor unions and for collective bargaining with management (to discourage companies from breaking strikes by employing nonunion labor or intimidating workers from joining unions). New Deal legislation also created public service jobs for the unemployed, including the Civilian Conservation Corps for youths and the Works Progress Administration, which sponsored environmental and cultural public works projects. Other new government agencies included the Federal Communications Commission (which regulated radio broadcasting and telephone companies), the Securities and Exchange Commission (which regulated stock markets to ensure fair trading practices), the National Labor Relations Board (which ensured the rights of workers to unionize and bargain collectively with management), the Federal Housing Administration (which constructed public housing), and the Rural Electrification Administration (which brought electric lines to rural areas that had never had power before).

SEE ALSO *Brains Trust; Roosevelt, Franklin D.*

SOURCES Melvyn Dubofsky and Stephen Burwood, eds., *The New Deal* (New York: Garland, 1990). Robert Eden, ed., *The New Deal and Its Legacy* (Westport, Conn.: Greenwood, 1989). Katie Louchheim, ed., *The Making of the New Deal* (Cambridge: Harvard University Press, 1983). Robert S. McElvaine, *The Depression and New Deal: A History in Documents* (New York: Oxford University Press, 1999).

NEW FREEDOM

The New Freedom was the term used by Woodrow Wilson in the 1912 Presidential campaign to describe his domestic program. Wilson believed that "private monopoly is indefensible and intolerable" and that national government should break up such large concentrations of corporate wealth. This view distinguished him clearly from his two opponents. Wilson claimed that President William Howard Taft stood for the interests of big business and that ex-President Theodore Roosevelt's New Nationalism program to regulate big business would prove unworkable.

Wilson also argued for lower tariffs (taxes on imported goods) to benefit consumers. He called for reform of the banking system to ensure stability in the money supply and end financial panics as well as to provide more credit (lending money), especially to small businesses.

Congress approved most of the New Freedom program in 1913 and 1914, including the Underwood Tariff Act, which cut tariffs by about 25 percent; the Federal Reserve Act, which established the Federal Reserve Board to regulate the banks and the money supply; the Clayton Anti-Trust Act, which made it more difficult to establish a monopoly in an industry; and the Federal Trade Commission Act, which prevented business practices that unfairly restrained trade. Later in his administration Wilson got Congress to pass laws to aid merchant seamen in dealing with ship owners, to provide an eight-hour day for railroad workers, and to help farmers repay their loans. Congress passed his proposal to ban child labor but the law was declared unconstitutional by the Supreme Court.

SEE ALSO *Wilson, Woodrow*
SOURCES Woodrow Wilson, *The New Freedom* (1913; reprint, Englewood Cliffs, N.J.: Prentice-Hall, 1961).

NEW FRONTIER

The New Frontier was the term used by John F. Kennedy to describe the challenges facing the United States. In his acceptance speech for the Democratic nomination for President in 1960, Kennedy said, "We stand today on the edge of a new frontier—the frontier of the 1960s, a frontier of unknown opportunities and paths." He added, "The new frontier of which I speak is not a set of promises—it is a set of challenges. It sums up not what I intend to offer the American people, but what I intend to ask of them."

Kennedy's speech was drafted by his speech writer Theodore Sorensen. The term *New Frontier* had previously been used in 1934 as the title of a book written by Secretary of Agriculture Henry A. Wallace, in 1936 speeches by Presidential candidate Alf Landon, and in a 1959 speech by historian Arthur Schlesinger, Jr.

The term *New Frontiersmen* refers to the kind of appointees Kennedy brought into government: relatives such as Robert F. Kennedy and Sargent Shriver; academics such as Schlesinger; and Democratic party liberals such as Adlai Stevenson and Chester Bowles. New Frontiersmen joined Kennedy in touch football and other active sports, and several were noted for their wit and style.

Many of the Kennedy administration programs are referred to as New Frontier measures. These include the Peace Corps, the Alliance for Progress in Latin America, a trade expansion act, an increase in the minimum wage, a federal housing act, and an Area Redevelopment Act to benefit depressed rural areas. Kennedy suffered defeats on many bills, however, including federal aid to education, creation of the Department of Urban Affairs, medical insurance for the elderly, and urban mass transit. Most of the unfinished New Frontier agenda was passed by Congress during the Presidency of Lyndon Johnson.

SEE ALSO *Kennedy, John F.*

SOURCES Theodore Sorensen, *Kennedy* (New York: Harper & Row, 1965).

NEW JERSEY V. T.L.O.

- 469 U.S. 325 (1985)
- Vote: 6–3
- For the Court: White
- Dissenting: Stevens, Brennan, and Marshall

A teacher at a New Jersey high school discovered a student smoking cigarettes in a school bathroom, which was a violation of school rules. The teacher took the student to the principal's office. The assistant principal questioned the student, who denied she had been smoking in the bathroom. The school official then demanded to see her purse. After opening it, he found cigarettes, cigarette rolling papers that are commonly associated with the use of marijuana, a pipe, plastic bags, money, a list of students who owed her money, and two letters that contained evidence that she had been involved in marijuana dealings.

As a result of this search of the student's purse and the seizure of items in it, the state brought delinquency charges against the student in New Jersey Juvenile Court. The student (identified in the case only by her initials, T.L.O.) countered with a motion to suppress evidence found in her purse as a violation of her constitutional rights against unreasonable and unwarranted searches and seizures.

The Issue Is the 4th Amendment prohibition of unreasonable and unwarranted searches and seizures applicable to officials in a public school with regard to its students?

Opinion of the Court The Supreme Court decided that the 4th Amendment prohibition of *unreasonable* searches and seizures is applicable to searches conducted by public school officials, but that in this case a warrantless search of the student's purse *was* reasonable and permissible.

Justice Byron White wrote the opinion of the Court. He said that school officials may search a student in school as long as "there are reasonable grounds for suspecting that the search will turn up evidence that the student has violated or is violating either the law or the rules of the school."

Dissent Justice John Paul Stevens wrote in dissent:

The search of a young woman's purse by a school administrator is a serious invasion of her legitimate expectations of privacy.... Because [the student's] conduct was neither unlawful nor significantly disruptive of school order or the educational process, the invasion of privacy associated with the forcible opening of T.L.O.'s purse was entirely unjustified at its inception.... The rule the Court adopts today is so open-ended that it may make the Fourth Amendment virtually meaningless in the school context. Although I agree that school administrators must have broad latitude to maintain order and discipline in our classrooms, that authority is not unlimited.

Significance This decision indicated that the Court did not view the rights of students in a public school as equivalent to the rights of adults in a nonschool setting. Police need to demonstrate "probable cause" that individuals they search have violated or are violating a law. School officials, by contrast, need to have only "reasonable suspicion" of unlawful conduct to justify a search of students in school. School authorities, in this view, may restrict the rights of students in behalf of the school's compelling educational purpose.

SEE ALSO *Searches and seizures; Student rights under the Constitution*

NEWS CONFERENCES, PRESIDENTIAL

News conferences are official meetings between the President and journalists that are reported in newspapers and on television and radio.

Theodore Roosevelt was the first President to invite reporters into the White House, providing the press with a room in the newly constructed executive office wing. He hired a press secretary to give news releases to reporters. Roosevelt also talked to reporters himself but only off the record. William Howard Taft discontinued the practice of meeting with reporters and had as little to do with them as possible.

Formal news conferences were begun by Woodrow Wilson, who met with reporters once or twice a week for more than two years. He canceled these meetings in 1915, citing "national security" reasons after the sinking of the *Lusitania* by Germany, but that was only an excuse. Wilson was fed up with reporters asking him personal questions about his family.

Warren Harding, a former newspaper publisher, played cards and golf with White House reporters. He held news conferences twice a week and opened them to all accredited reporters. He invented the title "White House spokesman" to allow the press to quote the President without direct attribution to him. Calvin Coolidge held conferences with reporters, but they could not quote the President or attribute anything to him; consequently there was no "news" in the conference. Herbert Hoover required that questions be submitted one day in advance, and during the depression he suggested that reporters submit their stories to the White House for "clearance." He held meetings with publishers to complain about their White House reporters and excluded reporters whose stories were critical of him from attending the conferences.

News conferences were used extensively by Franklin Roosevelt, who allowed 20 or so reporters to crowd into the Oval Office twice each week. He eliminated the practice of submitting questions in advance and enjoyed sparring and joking with the reporters. After his first session, they applauded Roosevelt's performance. Harry Truman was more formal, holding news conferences in the State Department's Indian Treaty Room (in what is now the Old Executive Office Building). He stood at a podium looking down at the reporters; he required them to identify themselves before asking questions; and he reduced the sessions to one a week. He also allowed radio stations to broadcast taped excerpts, making news conferences public events.

Dwight Eisenhower filmed conferences for television news and allowed reporters to quote him directly. For the first time, Eisenhower also permitted reporters to transcribe questions and answers, and the *New York Times* began to print them. Five days after his inauguration, John Kennedy decided to move his news conferences from the White House to an auditorium in the new State Department building that could seat more than 400 reporters. He also permitted live television coverage. The most recent innovation came from Gerald Ford, who allowed reporters to ask follow-up questions after the President responded to the first inquiry.

A news conference typically begins with a brief statement by the President. The reporters then raise their hands and the President recognizes them, often by name. The first questioners are usually the representatives of the wire services, followed by correspondents for the national television or radio networks, and then by other reporters. The conference ends when the senior wire service correspondent says, "Thank you, Mr. President."

Presidents need not hold news conferences. Coolidge held more than 100 every year; Franklin Roosevelt held them weekly, but Kennedy held them only every other month. Lyndon Johnson was so apprehensive about appearing on television without a prepared speech that he delayed holding a televised conference until February 29, 1964, nearly three months after he had succeeded to the office. He held few conferences during the Vietnam War after reporters accused him of a "credibility gap."

Richard Nixon also held few news conferences; in his first he told reporters that he would not discuss serious issues in "off-the-cuff responses." Sometimes he engaged in hostile exchanges with reporters, most notably CBS News correspondent Dan Rather. He refused to hold conferences during the last months of the Watergate crisis. Jimmy Carter held 59 conferences but very few during the Iran hostage crisis because he did not want to report on his lack of progress in freeing the hostages. Ronald Reagan, the "Great Communicator," held only 27 during his first term and held none through most of the Iran-Contra affair. During his second term, Bill Clinton held hardly any news conferences, particularly during the impeachment crisis.

SEE ALSO *Press secretary; Media coverage of Congress*

SOURCES Douglas Cater, *The Fourth Branch of Government* (New York: Vintage, 1959). Blaire A. French, *The Presidential Press Conference: Its History and Role in the American Political System* (Washington, D.C.: University Press of America, 1982). Carolyn Smith, *Presidential Press Conferences* (Westport, Conn.: Praeger, 1990).

NEW YORK TIMES CO. V. SULLIVAN

- 376 U.S. 254 (1964)
- Vote: 9–0
- For the Court: Brennan

On March 29, 1960, the *New York Times* printed a full-page advertisement paid for by two black civil rights organizations. L. B. Sullivan, an elected city commissioner of Montgomery, Alabama, read the advertisement and decided to bring a libel suit against the *New York Times* and the sponsors of the advertisement. Libel is the act of slandering, or hurting a person's reputation by saying negative things about him that are untrue or misleading.

Sullivan was upset about the advertisement because it described civil rights activities in southern states, including Alabama, and appealed for donations of money to support the programs of the ad's two sponsors. The ad also included an eight-line description of events in Montgomery, Alabama, that criticized the city police for abuses against black demonstrators. Sullivan's name was not mentioned, but he was offended because he was in charge of the Montgomery police department. So he claimed that false and exaggerated charges against the city police were slanders against him in his role as police commissioner.

State courts in Alabama decided in favor of Sullivan. Sullivan proved that there were several errors about details, but not main points, in the advertisement. The state courts concluded that he had been libeled and awarded him $500,000 in damages. The *New York Times* appealed this decision to the U.S. Supreme Court.

The Issue L. B. Sullivan argued that the advertisement in this case was libelous because it contained untrue statements. He claimed that the Constitution does not protect speech that is false or misleading about the actions of a person. The *New York Times* argued that the libel law of Alabama, which permitted restrictions on untrue speech, was an infringement on 1st Amendment freedoms to express criticisms of public officials. To what extent do constitutional protections of free speech limit a state government's power to award damages in a libel action brought by a government official against his critics?

Opinion of the Court The U.S. Supreme Court reversed the decision of the Alabama Supreme Court. Justice William Brennan argued that the Alabama libel law threatened 1st Amendment freedoms of speech and press by "raising . . . the possibility that a good-faith critic of government will be penalized for his criticism." Brennan said that "debate on public issues should be uninhibited, robust, and wide-open, and that it may well include vehement, caustic, and sometimes unpleasantly sharp attacks on government and public officials."

Brennan maintained that "erroneous statement is inevitable in free debate." Therefore, even false statements about public officials must be protected if citizens and the media are to act effectively as critics of their government. Therefore, the Court concluded, public officials may not be awarded damages for defamatory statements about their official conduct merely because the statements are false. Rather, the offended public official must prove actual malice. That is, he must demonstrate that "the statement was made with . . . knowledge that it was false or with reckless disregard of whether it was false or not."

Significance This decision has made it very difficult for public officials to bring libel actions against the media. As a result, freedom of expression about the actions of government has been greatly expanded. The media have been encouraged to play the role of watchdog and exposer of questionable or improper actions by public officials, such as corrupt or foolish behavior.

SEE ALSO *Freedom of speech and press*
SOURCES Anthony Lewis, *Make No Law: The Sullivan Case and the First Amendment* (New York: Random House, 1991). *The Pentagon Papers as Published by the New York Times* (New York: Bantam, 1971). S. J. Unger, *The Papers and the Papers: An Account of the Legal and Political Battles over the Pentagon Papers* (New York: Dutton, 1972).

NEW YORK TIMES CO. V. UNITED STATES

- 403 U.S. 713 (1971)
- Vote: 6–3
- For the Court: per curiam opinion; Douglas, Stewart, White, Marshall, Black, and Brennan writing separately
- Dissenting: Burger, Blackmun, and Harlan

In June 1971, the *New York Times* and the *Washington Post* started to publish a series of articles based on U.S. government documents that became known as the Pentagon Papers. The Pentagon is the headquarters of the U.S. Department of Defense, the compiler of these documents, which included information about U.S. military involvement in Vietnam and federal government policies on the Vietnam War that was classified as top secret. Federal officials did not want the Pentagon Papers released to the public and printed only 15 copies. Daniel Ellsberg, a researcher involved in compiling and editing the Pentagon Papers, made a photocopy of these documents and gave most of them to Neil Sheehan of the *New York Times.*

A team of *Times* reporters wrote a series of articles on U.S. involvement in the Vietnam War based on the top secret information in the Pentagon Papers. A short time later, Daniel Ellsberg also provided materials from the Pentagon Papers to the *Washington Post,* and articles based on these documents began to appear in that paper, too.

The federal government objected to the publication in daily newspapers of information it classified as top secret. Government officials claimed that wide distribution of information in the Pentagon Papers would be damaging to national security. So the government brought legal action against the *New York Times* and the *Washington Post* to stop them, and other newspapers, from publishing articles about the Pentagon Papers.

The Issue   Representatives of the *New York Times* said the federal government's attempt to stop publication of articles about the Pentagon Papers was an example of prior restraint—when the government restricts a publication in advance from publishing certain information—and a violation of freedom of the press guaranteed in the 1st Amendment. The federal government argued that publication of this top secret information would put the lives of soldiers in danger and give assistance during wartime to enemies of the United States. Do the needs of national security during wartime outweigh the value of free and open communication of information? Does the President's constitutional duty as commander in chief of the armed forces require that he have power to restrict publication of military secrets? What are the constitutional limits on a free press during wartime?

Opinion of the Court   The Supreme Court rejected the federal government's arguments for prior restraint on the publication of information from the Pentagon Papers. The Court concluded that the government failed to show that publication of this information about the Vietnam War would cause such serious harm as to outweigh the value of free expression of information.

Dissent   Chief Justice Warren Burger emphasized the complexity of this kind of case. He agreed in principle with constitutional limits on prior restraint. But he also argued that there are limits on 1st Amendment freedoms. He said, "[T]he imperative of a free and unfettered press comes into collision with another imperative, the effective functioning of a complex modern government and specifically the effective exercise of certain constitutional powers of the Executive." He referred to the constitutional powers of the President pertaining to conduct of foreign policy and command of military forces.

Significance   The Supreme Court decision in this case was a clear defeat for advocates of prior restraint under conditions of wartime or other national crises. The decision also encouraged the media in their efforts to check federal government officials or hold them accountable by obtaining and publishing information that the government wants to keep from public view.

SEE ALSO *Freedom of speech and press; Prior restraint*

NIXON, RICHARD M.
37th President

- Born: Jan. 9, 1913, Yorba Linda, Calif.
- Political party: Republican
- Education: Whittier College, B.A., 1934; Duke University Law School, LL.B., 1937
- Military service: U.S. Navy, 1942–46
- Previous government service: U.S. House of Representatives, 1947–51;

U.S. Senate, 1951–53; Vice President, 1953–61
- Elected President, 1968; served, 1969–74; resigned, 1974
- Died: Apr. 22, 1994, New York, N.Y.

Richard Nixon was the only President ever to resign his office and the second (after Andrew Johnson) to be involved in impeachment proceedings in the House of Representatives. Some historians called him an "imperial" President because he relied excessively on Presidential powers and failed to collaborate with Congress. Although he ended U.S. involvement in the Vietnam War and won diplomatic agreements with the Soviet Union and China, his misuses of power destroyed his Presidency.

Nixon's parents ran a lemon grove and a grocery store, and Richard worked for them before and after school. He graduated second in his class from Whittier College and third in his class from Duke University Law School, then practiced law in Whittier. He met Thelma ("Pat") Ryan at a dramatic society and married her in 1940. At the start of World War II Nixon worked for the Office of Price Administration, implementing rationing of automobile tires. He joined the navy and served as an operations officer for an air transport squadron flying in the South Pacific, then as a lawyer negotiating contracts, until his discharge in 1946 with the rank of lieutenant commander.

Just as Nixon was leaving the navy, a group of prominent Republicans in Whittier began looking for a prospective candidate, preferably a young veteran, to run for Congress against the liberal Democratic incumbent Jerry Voorhis. Nixon was offered the nomination, and he defeated Voorhis in a series of debates, charging his opponent with accepting the support of pro-communist labor unions. While in Congress, Nixon served on the House Un-American Activities Committee and was instrumental in the investigation of State Department official Alger Hiss, who had been charged by Whittaker Chambers, a senior editor of *Time* magazine, with being a member of a communist spy ring during World War II. Hiss vigorously denied the charges and many high-ranking officials who had worked with him doubted these charges, but Nixon's support of Chambers was considered vindicated when a jury found Hiss guilty of perjury (lying under oath). He was sentenced to five years in prison for denying to the committee that he had ever met Chambers.

Nixon's work on the committee gained him a national reputation as a hard-line anticommunist. He also served on the House Committee on Education and Labor, which wrote the pro-business Taft-Hartley Act. He strongly supported Harry Truman's proposal for the Marshall Plan for European reconstruction after World War II. Nixon ran for the Senate in 1950, defeating liberal Democrat Helen Gahagan Douglas by insinuating that her voting record was "pink" (pro-communist) and referring to her as the "pink lady." He became the youngest Republican in the U.S. Senate.

In 1952 Nixon convinced members of the California delegation to the Republican convention to support Dwight Eisenhower's candidacy rather than Robert Taft or favorite son Earl Warren. Eisenhower then chose Nixon to run with him. Newspapers charged that while Nixon was a senator, he had accepted $18,000 from supporters to defray his personal expenses. Eisenhower insisted that Nixon make a full and public explanation. Nixon made a nationwide television broadcast on September 23, 1952, in which he defended his actions and won over the public when he insisted that whatever else might happen, he would never return one gift—a dog that his children had named Checkers. The overwhelmingly positive response to his "Checkers speech" convinced Eisenhower to keep Nixon on the ticket, and they were elected by a large margin. Nixon was the youngest person ever to be elected Vice President.

Nixon worked tirelessly to elect Republican candidates to Congress and state offices. When Eisenhower was ill, he presided with great discretion over 19 meetings of the cabinet and 26 meetings of the National Security Council. He made numerous trips abroad and was the target of violent anti-U.S. demonstrations in several Latin American nations in 1958. He debated Soviet premier Nikita Khrushchev at the American National Exposition in Moscow in 1959, reinforcing his anticommunist image with the American television audience.

Nixon was the odds-on favorite to win the Republican Presidential nomination in 1960. He won the primaries without opposition but then faced a last-minute bid by New York governor Nelson Rockefeller. With Eisenhower's endorsement, Nixon fended off Rockefeller, then compromised with him on a Republican party platform that implicitly criticized the performance of the Eisenhower administration. This agreement alienated Eisenhower, who did little campaigning for the ticket.

Nixon engaged in four Presidential debates with Democratic candidate John F. Kennedy, and a majority of television viewers thought that he lost the first one badly. With the economy in a recession, Nixon lost several key states, and vote fraud may have played a part in his losses in Illinois and Texas. Nixon lost the election but refused to contest the results.

In 1962 Nixon ran for governor of California but was defeated by incumbent governor Edmund G. Brown, Jr. He held a press conference after the election in which he attacked the media for bias and insisted, "You won't have Nixon to kick around anymore." He moved to New York City and practiced law with the newly renamed firm of Nixon, Mudge, Rose, Guthrie, Alexander and Mitchell. But Nixon had not retired from politics: he campaigned effectively for Republican congressional candidates in the 1966 midterm elections.

In 1968 Nixon again won the Republican nomination, defeating George Romney, Nelson Rockefeller, and Ronald Reagan. With the Democratic party split between hawks who supported Hubert Humphrey and antiwar activists who favored Eugene McCarthy and Robert Kennedy (assassinated in June after winning the California primary), Nixon entered the general election well ahead of Humphrey. But the race tightened up after his opponent endorsed a halt to the bombing of Vietnam. In a three-person race (the other candidate was Southerner George Wallace, running on a segregationist platform of the American Independent party), Nixon won only 43.4 percent of the popular vote, defeating Humphrey by less than 1 percent.

Nixon was only the fifth Presidential candidate to win the office after a prior defeat (the others were Thomas Jefferson, Andrew Jackson, William Henry Harrison, and Grover Cleveland), and the only one to win against a new opponent rather than against the candidate who had previously defeated him. He was also the first former Vice President since Martin Van Buren in 1836 to be elected to the Presidency without first having succeeded to the position after the death of a President.

"I shall consecrate my office," Nixon pledged in his inaugural address, "to the cause of peace among nations." He announced a policy to "Vietnamize" the war in Vietnam and remove most of the 500,000 U.S. ground combat forces. Soon U.S. combat casualties were sharply reduced. In 1970 he invaded neighboring Cambodia in pursuit of Vietnamese communist forces, an action that led to widespread protests and demonstrations in the United States. By 1972 almost all U.S. forces had been removed from South Vietnam, and on January 27, 1973, after a Christmas bombing campaign against North Vietnam, the United States came to an agreement with the North Vietnamese: a cease-fire was proclaimed, U.S. prisoners of war were returned, and U.S. military involvement in the Vietnam War ended. Air force bombing continued against the communists in Cambodia, however, until Congress overrode a Nixon veto and ordered a halt to the bombing by August 15, 1973. Then Congress passed the War Powers Resolution of 1973, also over Nixon's veto, which provided that Congress must approve of any military action by a President within 60 days or the forces must be withdrawn.

Although Nixon had made his career as a staunch anticommunist, in 1971 he reversed his long-standing opposition to seating communist China in the United Nations. Then, in February 1972, he became the first President to visit the People's Republic of China. He established low-level diplomatic relations with that nation, naming George Bush to head a "mission" to Beijing, though without formal recognition of its government. In May 1972 Nixon made a trip to the Soviet Union and completed a significant arms control agreement involving limitations on intercontinental ballistic missiles. On May 28 he made a televised speech to the people of the Soviet Union, reassuring them that the United States did not have aggressive intentions against them. This summit conference ushered in a period of détente, or relaxation of tensions, between the two superpowers. Numerous other agreements in science, space, technology, and trade were also signed over the next two years.

In domestic affairs Nixon was checked by Congress and the courts. He opposed busing to overcome racial imbalance in public schools. Instead, he proposed $2 billion in funding to bring inner-city schools up to par with those in more affluent communities, but Congress refused to consider his proposal. He nominated two conservative Southerners to the Supreme Court, Clement Haynesworth and G. Harrold Carswell, neither of whom was accepted by the Democrat-dominated Senate. He tried to eliminate many of Lyndon Johnson's Great Society programs, including the Office of Economic Opportunity, which ran the War on Poverty, and he impounded funds for many programs. But he was blocked from implementing his plans by the Democratic Congress and federal court orders requiring him to spend impounded funds.

Although Nixon positioned himself as a conservative, spending for many social welfare programs, including Social Security, Medicare, and Medicaid, increased greatly during his tenure. A national system of food stamps costing billions of dollars was developed as part of the welfare system. Nixon proposed, and Congress accepted, a reallocation of government funds to state and local governments. This plan replaced many grants for specific programs with broader "bloc" grants, giving states more flexibility. He also won passage of a revenue-sharing measure that provided $5 billion annually from the national Treasury to state and local governments. However, Congress refused to pass his program for "family allowances" to replace welfare, an idea that would have significantly increased social welfare spending.

Although Nixon was a free-market Republican, opposed to much government regulation of the economy, for the first time in U.S. history he presided over the use of wage and price controls in peacetime (from 1971 to 1973) in order to check inflation. He also proposed large increases in spending for the environment and created the Council on Environmental Quality. An Arab oil embargo against the United States, imposed during the Yom Kippur War involving Israel and Syria and Egypt in 1973, led Nixon to impose new regulations on energy producers and users. Nixon proposed Project Independence, a plan to make the United States economy energy-independent of Arab oil producers within a decade. Nixon vetoed a Democratic bill that would have regulated energy prices, preferring to rely in part on higher oil prices as an incentive for U.S. oil producers to increase domestic production.

Nixon won a landslide reelection victory in 1972 over his Democratic opponent, Senator George McGovern of South Dakota. This election set the pattern for the next two decades in all elections except 1976: liberal Democrats were trounced by conservative Republicans who won Southern states on the basis of "backlash" politics. But Republicans continued to be a minority in both Congress and in state governments—part of the pattern of "split government."

Early in Nixon's second term, it was revealed that operatives working for the Committee to Re-Elect the President had burglarized the Democratic National Committee headquarters in the Watergate office complex in 1972. The scandal gradually enveloped many senior White House aides and three cabinet secretaries, and as it came closer to the President his popularity dropped.

On October 10, 1973, Vice President Spiro T. Agnew resigned as part of a plea bargain in a court case involving bribes paid to him by Maryland construction contractors before and during his tenure as Vice President. Congress approved Nixon's nomination of House minority leader Gerald Ford to fill the vacancy.

In 1974 the House Judiciary Committee began an inquiry into the Watergate scandal to determine if Nixon should be impeached. Late in July the Supreme Court issued a ruling requiring Nixon to turn over evidence in criminal trials of his aides, in spite of his claim that it was his executive privilege to keep information about Presidential decisions from the courts. The tape recordings Nixon made of conversations in the Oval Office indicated that he had participated in a cover-up of the Watergate burglary.

Nixon resigned his office on August 9, 1974, shortly after the House committee voted to recommend three articles of impeachment to the full House. He was succeeded by Vice President Gerald Ford, who on September 8, 1974, issued Nixon a "full, free and absolute pardon" for all crimes committed during his Presidency. Nixon accepted the pardon, admitting "mistakes" in the way he had handled Watergate, but made no admission that he was guilty of any crimes.

In retirement Nixon moved to an affluent community in New Jersey, completed his memoirs, RN, and wrote many books on foreign policy. He gradually assumed a role as a senior foreign policy adviser to Republican Presidents.

Richard Nixon died of a stroke at the age of 81.

SEE ALSO Agnew, Spiro T.; Amnesty, Presidential; Debates, Presidential; Eisenhower, Dwight David; Executive privilege; Ex-Presidency; Ford, Gerald R.; Humphrey, Hubert H.; Impeachment; Imperial Presidency; Kennedy, John F.; Pardon power; Succession to the Presidency; United States v. Nixon; War powers; War Powers Resolution (1973); Watergate investigation (1973–74)

SOURCES Stephen Ambrose, Nixon, 2 vols. (New York: Simon & Schuster, 1987). Roger Morris, Richard Milhous Nixon (New York: Henry Holt, 1990). Richard Nixon, RN: The Memoirs of Richard Nixon (New York: Grosset & Dunlap, 1978). Herbert Parmet, Richard Nixon and His America (Boston: Little, Brown, 1990). Richard M. Pious, Richard Nixon: A Political Life (Englewood Cliffs, N.J.: Silver Burdett, 1992).

NOMINATING CONVENTIONS, PRESIDENTIAL

Every four years, delegates from state political parties meet to nominate their party candidate for President of the United States. Conventions replaced the congressional caucus, in which the senators and representatives would nominate a candidate, which was discredited after the election of 1824.

The Anti-Masons held the first national convention in September 1830 to organize themselves as a political party. They aimed to stop what they believed was a plot by the Masonic order (a fraternal group) to seize political power. They decided to hold a Presidential nominating convention on September 26, 1831, and nominated William Wirt of Maryland, who then confessed that he had once been a member of the Masons. The convention stood by its nomination. The second convention was held by the National Republican party on

December 12, 1831; it nominated Henry Clay.

The Democratic party held its first convention at the saloon in the Baltimore Athenaeum in May 1832. It accepted President Andrew Jackson's request that it nominate Martin Van Buren for Vice President. Since Jackson was already President, the convention did not actually nominate him but passed a resolution that concurred in the "nominations" he had received "in various parts of the Union" by Democratic state parties. The Democrats also passed a rule requiring nominees to win the votes of two-thirds of the delegates—a rule that was not discarded in favor of a simple majority vote until 1936. The two-thirds rule gave the South a "veto" over Democratic nominees and led to nominations of several Northern Democrats with Southern sympathies, such as James Buchanan, just prior to the Civil War. It also contributed to convention deadlocks; the 1924 Democratic convention endured 103 rounds of balloting.

From the 1830s through the 1960s state delegations were chosen and controlled by state party leaders. "Less than one hundred men in any convention really dictate what occurs," explained Bronx, New York, Democratic party boss Ed Flynn in 1948. The unit rule required all delegates in a state to vote the way the majority of the delegates wished, ensuring boss control of a unified state delegation. "What the party wants," British commentator Lord Bryce observed, "is not a good President but a good candidate," one who would distribute the spoils of victory, appointments and government contracts, to the bosses and their party followers. Although major-party candidates did not appear at their party's convention until Franklin Roosevelt flew to Chicago to claim his nomination in 1932, their managers bargained with the bosses who controlled state delegations over future Presidential appointments and other political favors.

"I authorize no bargains and will be bound by none," Abraham Lincoln telegraphed his managers in 1860. "Damn Lincoln," his zealous managers responded. They won Indiana's support for Lincoln by offering Caleb Smith the post of secretary of the interior; took Pennsylvania by giving Simon Cameron the War Department; and made New York's Salmon Chase secretary of the Treasury to seal their victory. Lincoln fretted over the public reaction to these deals: "What will they think of their honest Abe when he appoints Simon Cameron?" Similarly, Woodrow Wilson publicly rejected deal making to win the 1912 Democratic nomination. Yet his campaign managers dealt away cabinet positions and the Vice Presidency to gain Wilson his victory on the 46th ballot, a strategy also used by Franklin Roosevelt in his 1932 nominating battle.

In 1968 the boss-dominated convention system lost its legitimacy. Although voters in Democratic party primaries overwhelmingly chose antiwar contenders Robert Kennedy and Eugene McCarthy, the bosses at the Chicago convention chose Vice President Hubert Humphrey to be the party's Presidential nominee—even though Humphrey had not entered the primaries. After the Democratic election defeat, a party reform commission recommended changes in party rules that would take control of the selection of convention delegates away from state parties and give it to the party voters. The Republicans soon followed suit.

Since the 1970s the 4,288 Democratic and 2,209 Republican delegates have been selected by the party voters in primaries or open caucuses. In the Democratic party, a candidate receives a share of convention delegates proportional to the percentage of votes he or she has won in the primary. The Republican party uses a winner-take-all procedure in which the candidate with the most votes wins an entire state delegation. In either event, the candidates, not the party bosses, control the state delegations once the voters have given them their specified share through the primary voting. The candidate for President who wins the majority of the delegates dominates the convention.

"The rise of the primaries has made it inevitable that the nomination is settled before the convention begins," noted New York senator Daniel Moynihan, adding, "The convention does not decide and it does not debate." Nevertheless, delegates decide on the content of the party platform and determine changes in party rules for the next nominating convention.

Delegates from both parties are generally better educated and more affluent than the rank-and-file members of the parties. Most Republican delegates call themselves conservatives, while Democratic delegates are almost evenly split between liberals and moderates. Democratic delegates usually take positions more liberal than the party rank-and-file members or all voters, whereas Republicans are more conservative, especially on issues such as abortion, prayer in the schools, gun control, and gay rights.

Democratic party rules require that half the delegates be women; the Republicans do not have such a rule, but more than two-fifths of their delegates in 1992 were women. Since the 1970s the Democrats have had more Catholic, Jewish, and African-American representation at their convention than the Republicans.

Convention delegates are experienced in elective politics: more than two-thirds at most conventions have held public or party office, and more than half have attended previous conventions. Democratic rules provide for a category of superdelegates: most Democratic members of the House and Senate are added automatically to their state delegation. They may vote for whomever they wish, though they invariably vote according to the preferences of the majority of the delegates at the convention, adding to the front-runner's advantage.

Modern conventions usually last four days, with most of the proceedings organized by the contender who has won the primaries. The first evening's proceedings are devoted to speeches and films introducing the candidate and party to televi-

sion viewers and to "housekeeping" business—accepting the credentials of the delegates, dealing with challenges to delegates, and adopting convention rules. The second day is devoted to discussion of the party platform, which is adopted that evening. Platforms do not bind candidates, but once in office most Presidents implement the large majority of platform pledges.

The third evening is devoted to nominating speeches for the Presidential candidate, followed by the vote for the candidate. The victorious candidate then addresses the convention and a nationwide television audience either that evening or the following evening. On the fourth evening the Vice President is nominated and makes an acceptance speech.

Prime-time convention coverage in 1968 by the three networks consisted of 90 hours; by 1992 it was down to less than 30. In 1984 the networks dropped gavel-to-gavel coverage in the evening and by 1992 their prime-time coverage averaged 1 to 2 hours per day. The networks reduced coverage because viewership had diminished.

If the country knows who will be nominated before the first ballot is even cast, what then is the point of holding a convention? "Our activists and leaders still need to meet with each other," Georgia Republican representative Newt Gingrich points out, to confer about "their beliefs and about the future." The public can watch television summaries of the proceedings on the networks or gavel-to-gavel coverage on C-SPAN. Conventions provide an opportunity for newspapers and magazines to comment on the direction being taken by the candidate and party.

Television coverage of the nominating and acceptance speeches is an important part of the campaign: the acceptance speech can win the confidence of the nation or destroy the campaign even before it starts. Barry Goldwater self-destructed at the Republican convention in 1964 when he told his conservative supporters that "extremism in the defense of liberty is no vice." Walter Mondale's candor at the Democratic convention held in 1984—"Taxes will go up, and anyone who says they won't is not telling the truth"—provided the Republicans with campaign ammunition.

Candidates who avoid these traps usually benefit from a "convention bounce," rising in the polls after favorable television coverage. According to *New York Times/CBS* polls, in 1992 Bill Clinton jumped an incredible 24 points, taking a 56-to-31 percent lead over George Bush. Just after the Republican convention, Bush bounced back, cutting Clinton's lead substantially.

A party convention sets the stage not only for the general election but also for the next nomination. It gives party leaders across the nation a chance to see potential candidates in action: holding receptions, giving interviews, making speeches, and participating in platform fights. The news media may even poll delegates about their choices for the next election, establishing the field of contenders, though this technique must be taken with a grain of salt.

SEE ALSO *Caucuses, congressional; Humphrey, Hubert H.; Jackson, Andrew; Lincoln, Abraham; Mondale, Walter F.; Roosevelt, Franklin D.; Van Buren, Martin; Wilson, Woodrow*

SOURCES James Ceasar, *Presidential Selection* (Princeton, N.J.: Princeton University Press, 1979). James S. Chase, *Emergence of the Presidential Nominating Convention, 1789–1832* (Urbana: University of Illinois Press, 1973). James Davis, *National Conventions in an Age of Party Reform* (Westport, Conn.: Greenwood, 1983).

NOMINATIONS, CONFIRMATION OF

According to the Constitution (Article 2, Section 2), the Senate alone has the authority to advise and consent on nominations made by the President. These nominations include those of members of the cabinet, executive agency heads, diplomats, judges, federal attorneys, and military officers. This power is critically important to the federal system of checks and balances. Along with the development of "senatorial courtesy"—by which senators usually will not vote to confirm nominees opposed by their home-state senators—the confirmation power has given the Senate great influence over certain types of appointments. For instance, Presidents generally nominate federal judges and U.S. marshals from lists provided by senators and key members of the House of Representatives.

Both the executive branch and the Senate committees handling the nominations carefully screen the nominees. Often, the Federal Bureau of Investigation (FBI) conducts an investigation of the nominee's life. The staff of the Senate committee to which the nomination is referred also compiles information, and witnesses testify at committee hearings about the nominee's qualifications. For instance, the Senate agriculture committee holds nomination hearings for the secretary of agriculture, and the Foreign Relations Committee handles the nomination of the secretary of state.

Cabinet versus Court nominations Out of the many hundreds of cabinet nominations made since 1789, the Senate has rejected only nine (another six were withdrawn because they would probably not have been confirmed). The low number of rejections suggests that the Senate believes that Presidents should have the right to name their own cabinets, as long as those nominees appear fully fit for office. By contrast, from 1789 to 2000 the Senate either rejected by formal vote, or informally turned away, 27 Presidential nominees to the Supreme Court. The Senate officially rejected 11 nominees by majority vote. Seventeen nominations were either withdrawn by the President before a formal vote, or no action was taken by the Senate on the nomination, thereby defeating it. This considerably larger percentage of rejections suggests that the Senate seeks a larger role in the choice of members of the independent judicial branch.

Rejection of Supreme Court nominees   The Senate first formally voted to reject a Supreme Court nominee in 1811, when the senators refused to confirm President James Madison's nomination of Alexander Wolcott, by a vote of 24 to 9. The main reason for rejection was doubt about his competence.

Four nominees have been voted down by the Senate during the period from 1900 to 1993: John Parker, nominated by President Herbert Hoover in 1930 (by a vote of 39 to 41); Clement Haynsworth, nominated by President Richard Nixon in 1969 (by a vote of 45 to 55); G. Harrold Carswell in 1970, nominated by Nixon (by a vote of 45 to 51); and Robert H. Bork, nominated by President Ronald Reagan in 1987 (by a vote of 42 to 58).

Both John Parker and Robert Bork were defeated because important interest groups opposed them. Parker was defeated because of pressure exerted by labor unions, whose leaders believed him to be opposed to more federal regulation of businesses to improve wages and working conditions. Bork's defeat was influenced by civil rights and feminist groups, who disliked his conservative ideas about a woman's right to an abortion and government programs to advance opportunities of minorities and women. Furthermore, some senators opposed Bork because they disagreed with his conservative legal philosophy, which emphasized judicial restraint and a strict construction of the Constitution. For example, Bork could find no justification in the Constitution for the Supreme Court's decision in *Roe* v. *Wade* (1973), which affirmed a woman's right to an abortion during a certain period of pregnancy. He believed that the issue of abortion rights should be decided by state legislatures, not by the federal judiciary. Despite disagreements with his legal and political ideas, most of Bork's opponents respected the high quality of his

intellect, legal work, and personal integrity.

By contrast, President Nixon's nomination of Clement Haynsworth in 1969 failed largely because most senators had doubts about his competence and character. The Senate also rejected Nixon's nomination of G. Harrold Carswell the following year because of doubts about Carswell's ability to do the job.

Some critics have argued that in dealing with judicial nominations, the Senate should confine itself to examining each nominee's personal integrity and legal qualifications. But the Senate has also rejected nominees because of political opposition to the President making the nomination; disagreement with the nominee's views on controversial public issues; and strong opposition to the nominee by large or influential special interest groups.

During the late twentieth century, Presidents more often than not faced opposition party majorities in the Senate. Political conflicts added to the length of time that it took for the Senate to confirm nominations, particularly for the judiciary. Liberal Democrats objected to the appointment of many conservatives during the Nixon, Ford, Reagan, and Bush administrations, while the Republican majority during much of Bill Clinton's Presidency similarly delayed or blocked altogether the confirmation of liberal judges. A favored tactic is putting "holds" on nominations. In placing "holds," individual senators notify the leaders that they have a problem with a particular nominee and would object if the Senate attempted to confirm the nomination by unanimous consent. Usually the Senate leadership will not call up for a vote any nominations with "holds." White House congressional liaisons then work with the individual senators in an attempt to satisfy their concerns. Trading often goes on, with the president agreeing to make a nomination that the senators want in return for their allowing other nominations to come to a vote.

SEE ALSO *Advice and consent; Appointment power; Checks and balances; Senate Judiciary Committee; Senatorial courtesy*
SOURCES Robert C. Byrd, "Nominations," in *The Senate, 1789–1989: Addresses on the History of the United States Senate*, vol. 2 (Washington, D.C.: Government Printing Office, 1991).

NONVOTING DELEGATES TO THE HOUSE OF REPRE- SENTATIVES

SEE *Delegates to the House of Representatives*

NORRIS, GEORGE W.

- Born: July 11, 1861, Clyde, Ohio
- Political party: Republican
- Education: Baldwin University; Northern Indiana Normal School at Valparaiso; Valparaiso University, graduated, 1883
- Representative from Nebraska: 1903–13
- Senator from Nebraska: 1913–43
- Died: Sept. 2, 1944, McCook, Nebr.

Hailed as a "Great Insurgent" in Congress, George Norris devoted his long career to reforming government and improving the nation's general welfare. In 1910 he led the revolt against House Speaker Joseph G. Cannon to reduce the power of the conservative Speaker and make it easier to enact reform legislation. Norris was a persistent man, willing to devote years to a good fight. From 1918 to 1933 he advocated that the federal government build dams in the Tennessee River Valley to provide low-cost electricity to an impoverished area and to create a model for public power programs elsewhere. Although Presidents Calvin Coolidge and Herbert Hoover vetoed his bills, Norris fought on.

Finally, as part of the first hundred days of the New Deal, Congress again enacted the bill, and President Franklin D. Roosevelt signed the Tennessee Valley Authority (TVA) into law. Under TVA, the government built dams and powerhouses, replanted forests, and brought electricity to remote areas. "Changed times change attitudes," Norris explained. He owed his success to standing firmly by his principles until national attitudes changed to support him.

SEE ALSO *Cannon, Joseph G.; "First hundred days"; Insurgents*
SOURCES Richard Lowitt, *George W. Norris: The Making of a Progressive, 1861–1912* (1963; reprint, Westport, Conn.: Greenwood, 1980). Richard Lowitt, *George W. Norris: The Persistence of a Progressive, 1913–1933* (Urbana: University of Illinois Press, 1971). Richard Lowitt, *George W. Norris: The Triumph of a Progressive: 1933–1944* (Urbana: University of Illinois Press, 1978).

NORTHERN SECURITIES CO. V. UNITED STATES

- 193 U.S. 197 (1904)
- Vote: 5–4
- For the Court: Harlan
- Concurring: Brewer
- Dissenting: White, Holmes, Fuller, and Peckham

J. P. Morgan, James J. Hill, and Edward H. Harriman were powerful stock market speculators and investors who were interested mainly in railroads. Each desperately desired to control the three leading railroads linking the Great Lakes and the Pacific Northwest. In 1901 they battled fiercely on the stock exchange to gain control of the railroads. None of the three succeeded, so they settled their differences and joined together to form the Northern Securities Company to control the three railroads. They chartered their company under New Jersey laws.

In 1890, however, Congress had passed

the Sherman Antitrust Act in an effort to prevent the growth of business monopolies. (A monopoly is the exclusive control of an industry by a single owner or company.) This law prohibited trusts, or business combinations "in restraint of trade or commerce among the several States." Congress had the power to pass that law under the commerce clause of the Constitution (Article 1, Section 8), which had been defined broadly in the Supreme Court case *Gibbons* v. *Ogden* (1824). But the Sherman Antitrust Act was vague. What did "restraint of trade and commerce" mean?

The government argued that the Northern Securities Company was guilty of the very thing the law forbade. The Sherman Act aimed to prevent monopolies from taking over an industry or an aspect of an industry. The Northern Securities Company controlled *all* of the major railroads throughout a huge section of the country. If the Court allowed the three competing railroads to merge into one giant company, competition in the area would disappear. Because people had no alternative method of transportation, the Northern Securities Company would have been able to charge them exorbitant fees. Serving only the narrow interests of Morgan, Hill, and Harriman, this monopoly would harm the public and nation.

The Northern Securities Company argued that the federal government could not interfere with its affairs because it was merely a holding company created by a stock transaction. (A holding company is created solely to hold the ownership rights to two or more companies. But the holding company, as an administrative convenience, does not by itself deal in commerce.) Legally, under New Jersey laws, the corporation therefore did not deal in commerce. Federal government interference would violate state powers as protected by the 10th Amendment.

The Issue   Did the combination of railroads under the Northern Securities Company represent a "restraint of trade or commerce" covered by the Sherman Antitrust Act? Or was the combination just a stock transaction, not commerce? If it was the latter, it merited legal recognition under New Jersey law and 10th Amendment protection.

As often happens in Supreme Court cases, however, this specific question reflected a larger, more general issue. Could the national government regulate the activities of the huge, powerful businesses that were developing in the nation? A decision in favor of the Northern Securities Company would greatly limit the effectiveness of the Sherman Antitrust Act and the ability of the government to gain some control over business.

Opinion of the Court   The Supreme Court ruled in favor of the government. It found that the Northern Securities Company intended to eliminate competition among the railroads involved. Hence, the company was "a combination in restraint of interstate commerce" and was illegal under the Sherman Antitrust Act.

The Court interpreted the act broadly. Justice John Harlan wrote that a combination of businesses, a trust, did not need to engage directly in commerce to violate the act. If it restrained commerce in any way, a trust was illegal.

Dismissing the argument that the Sherman Act violated state powers under the Constitution, Harlan said a state law could not confer immunity from federal law. In regulating interstate commerce, Congress superseded the states' power to create corporations. Acting within its legitimate sphere, such as regulating commerce, the national government was supreme.

Dissent   Chief Justice Edward D. White argued that Congress could not regulate the ownership of stock through laws such as the Sherman Antitrust Act because this was a violation of powers reserved to the states by the 10th Amendment. He also claimed that a broad interpretation of the Sherman Act would have a negative effect on business.

Significance   The Court's decision helped establish increased government control of trusts and monopolies. The *Northern Securities* case symbolized the federal government's right and duty to regulate the national economy for the public good. The Court's ruling gave the federal government the authority to begin to exercise stricter supervision of the growing number of large American corporations. For example, the Federal Trade Commission Act of 1914 provided for regulation of businesses to prevent activities that would reduce competition in the marketplace or cheat consumers.

SEE ALSO *Commerce power*
SOURCES R. W. Apple, Jr., "The Case of the Monopolistic Railroadmen," in *Quarrels That Have Shaped the Constitution,* edited by John A. Garraty (New York: Harper & Row, 1987).

NUCLEAR REGULATORY COMMISSION

The Nuclear Regulatory Commission (NRC) was created by Congress in 1974 with the passage of the Energy Reorganization Act. The NRC is an independent regulatory agency directed by five commissioners who are appointed by the President and confirmed by the Senate. Commissioners serve five-year terms; no more than three of the five appointees may be members of the same political party, and one of the five commissioners is designated by the President to serve as the agency's chairperson. When the NRC was established, it replaced the Atomic Energy Commission, which was simultaneously abolished.

In addition to contributing to the defense and security of the nation by regulating the nuclear weapons program, the NRC has proclaimed that its mission is also to regulate the use of nuclear materials so as to protect the environment and public health and safety. To this end, the NRC regulates commercial nuclear power reactors and oversees reactors that are used for research, testing, and training purposes. In addition, the NRC regulates medical, academic, and industrial uses of nuclear materials and the transportation, storage, and disposal of nuclear materials and nuclear waste.

NULLIFICATION

In the years preceding the Civil War, some supporters of state powers and rights developed the doctrine of nullification. Advocates of nullification claimed that state governments had the power, under the U.S. Constitution, to declare a federal law unconstitutional, or unlawful and void.

John C. Calhoun of South Carolina, then Vice President of the United States, was the leading proponent of nullification. In the essay *South Carolina Exposition and Protest* (1828), Calhoun argued that the Constitution and federal Union were established by sovereign states, not by the people of the United States. Thus, the state governments have authority to decide whether acts of the federal government are constitutional or not. If a state government decided that the federal government had exceeded constitutional limits on its powers, then the state could call a special convention to nullify the law, thereby declaring that the law would *not* be enforced in the state. The nullification doctrine was linked to the claim that a state had a right to secede from, or leave, the federal Union.

In 1832, during a controversy about a federal tariff law, South Carolina attempted to use Calhoun's nullification doctrine to declare the federal statute unconstitutional. There was talk of secession. President Andrew Jackson responded with the threat of military force to suppress actions that he viewed as rebellious violations of the U.S. Constitution. The crisis ended with a compromise about the terms of the disputed federal tariff law.

Arguments about the nullification doctrine and the right of secession were settled, once and for all, by the Civil War (1861–65). After the Union victory over the Confederate states, there was no more serious advocacy of a state's right to nullify a federal law or to secede from the federal Union. The Supreme Court, in *Texas v. White* (1869), concluded that the Constitution created "an indestructible Union, composed of indestructible states."

SEE ALSO *Calhoun, John C.; Constitutionalism; Federalism; Implied powers; Texas v. White*

SOURCES Ross M. Lence, ed., *Union and Liberty: The Political Philosophy of John C. Calhoun* (Indianapolis: Liberty Fund, 1992).

O

OATH OF OFFICE

In Congress, all members take the same oath of office when they begin a new term. The Vice President usually administers the oath to senators, and the Speaker of the House administers the oath to representatives:

I, [member's name], do solemnly swear (or affirm) that I will support and defend the Constitution of the United States against all enemies, foreign and domestic; that I will bear true faith and allegiance to the same; that I take this obligation freely, without any mental reservation or purpose of evasion; and that I will well and faithfully discharge the duties of the office on which I am about to enter: So help me God.

The Constitution (Article 2, Section 1) provides that before assuming office the President must take the following oath or affirmation: "I do solemnly swear (or affirm) that I will faithfully execute the office of President of the United States, and will, to the best of my ability, preserve, protect and defend the Constitution of the United States."

George Washington added the words "so help me God" at the first inauguration, a practice followed by all his successors. He took the oath with his left hand on a Bible and his right hand raised toward heaven. Although the Constitution does not require that the oath be taken on a Bible, most other Presidents have done so. The Bible is always opened to a passage, and no

two Presidents have chosen the same one. Franklin Pierce was the only President to affirm rather than swear his oath.

Usually, the President takes the oath in the public inaugural ceremony. However, when the Presidential term begins on a Sunday, it is the custom to delay the inauguration until Monday. In that case the President takes the oath of office privately at noon on Sunday and repeats it at the inauguration the next day.

The Constitution does not specify who administers the oath. At George Washington's inauguration the oath was administered by the chief justice of New York State, Robert R. Livingston, because the Supreme Court had not yet been appointed. Since the inauguration of John Adams, it has been the custom for the oath to be administered by the chief justice of the United States at all regular inaugurations.

However, federal judges, magistrates, state judges, and even a notary public have administered oaths when Vice Presidents assumed the Presidency after the sudden death of the incumbent. Only three of nine men who succeeded to the Presidency because of death or resignation took their oath from the chief justice of the United States.

Some Presidents have argued that the oath confers a responsibility on the President not otherwise mentioned in the Constitution to cease the "faithful execution of the law" if he believes such a law to be unconstitutional. Andrew Jackson, in his message to Congress vetoing the Second Bank of the United States, argued that he had a right to refuse to enforce laws or judicial decisions if he did not believe them to be constitutional. He claimed that this duty was required by his oath of office. President Abraham Lincoln justified his use of emergency powers during the Civil War by referring to his oath to "preserve, protect, and defend the Constitution." President Andrew Johnson, during his impeachment trial, also argued that the President need not execute laws he deemed unconstitutional.

The Constitution says in Article 6 that "judicial officers, both of the United States and of the several states, shall be bound by oath or affirmation, to support this Constitution." In line with this clause, the federal Judiciary Act of 1789 specifies an oath of office to be taken by all federal judges before they assume their official duties: "I, [judge's name], do solemnly swear or affirm, that I will administer justice without respect to persons, and do equal right to the poor and to the rich, and that I will faithfully and impartially discharge and perform all the duties incumbent on me as [title or position], according to the best of my abilities and understanding, agreeably to the Constitution and laws of the United States. So help me God."

SEE ALSO *Inauguration, Presidential*

OBITER DICTUM

In writing an opinion, justices of the Supreme Court or judges of a lower court sometimes make statements that are not necessary to the legal reasoning of the decision in the case. Such a statement is called *obiter dictum*, which is Latin for "said in passing." Occasionally, obiter dicta (the plural of the term) have become important in the development of constitutional law. Justice Edward T. Sanford, for example, made a statement in passing (obiter dictum) in *Gitlow* v. *New York* (1925) that greatly influenced the incorporation of 1st Amendment free speech and press rights under the due process clause of the 14th Amendment. Justice

Sanford wrote, "[W]e may act to assume that freedom of speech and of the press . . . are among the fundamental personal rights and liberties protected by the due process clause of the Fourteenth Amendment from impairment by the States."

Justice Sanford's statement was not part of his reasoning in the decision of this case. Nevertheless, it soon influenced decisions of the Court in two important cases: *Near* v. *Minnesota* and *Stromberg* v. *California* (both 1931), which applied the 1st Amendment freedoms of speech (*Stromberg*) and the press (*Near*) to the states through the due process clause of the 14th Amendment.

SEE ALSO *Gitlow v. New York; Near v. Minnesota; Stromberg v. California*

O'CONNOR, SANDRA DAY
Associate Justice, 1981–

- Born: Mar. 26, 1930, El Paso, Tex.
- Education: Stanford College, B.A., 1950; Stanford University Law School, LL.B., 1952
- Previous government service: assistant attorney general, Arizona, 1965–69; Arizona Senate, 1969–75, majority leader of the Arizona Senate, 1973–74; judge, Maricopa County Superior Court, Arizona, 1975–79; judge, Arizona Court of Appeals, 1979–81
- Appointed by President Ronald Reagan Aug. 19, 1981; replaced Potter Stewart, who retired
- Supreme Court term: confirmed by the Senate Sept. 21, 1981, by a 99–0 vote

Sandra Day O'Connor was the first woman to be appointed and confirmed to the U.S. Supreme Court . She was a brilliant student, and her record at Stanford University Law School was outstanding. However, she had difficulty, at first, in pursuing a career in the law because of her gender. She was an outstanding woman in a profession traditionally dominated by men. Many male lawyers did not want to work with women, and O'Connor had a hard time getting a job she wanted. One prominent law firm offered her a job as a secretary.

Through persistence and competence, O'Connor earned recognition as a lawyer, as a state senator in Arizona, and as a judge in the Arizona state court system. She also found time to raise three sons with her husband, John O'Connor.

In 1981, President Ronald Reagan appointed Sandra Day O'Connor to the U.S. Supreme Court. Justice O'Connor has appeared to resist overturning *Roe* v. *Wade* (1973), which granted women the right to have an abortion, although she has tended to narrow the scope of that decision by upholding state-level regulations "not unduly burdensome" to the woman. She has also shaped Supreme Court rulings on affirmative action and separation of church and state with regard to state government actions. She appears to favor strict neutrality over strict separation in the state's treatment of religion. And in response to state-level affirmative action cases, she has tended to favor a strict scrutiny test that would permit programs to rectify prior discrimination by the state government.

Justice O'Connor wrote the Court's first opinion to restrict the use of race as a category in determining the boundaries of state legislative and congressional districts (*Shaw* v. *Reno,* 1998). She has, however, expressed opposition to the complete removal of the consideration of race in redistricting cases, as long as it is not the primary factor in drawing boundaries of election districts (*Bush* v. *Vera,* 1996).

SOURCES Beverly B. Cook, "Justice Sandra Day O'Connor: Transition to a Republican Court Agenda," in *The Burger Court: Political and Judicial Profiles,* edited by Charles M. Lamb and Stephen C. Halpern (Urbana: University of Illinois Press, 1991). Beverly Gherman, *Sandra Day O'Connor: Justice for All* (New York: Viking, 1991). Peter Huber, *Sandra Day O'Connor* (New York: Chelsea House, 1990). Nancy Maveety, *Justice Sandra Day O'Connor: Strategist on the Supreme Court* (Lanham, Md.: Rowman & Littlefield, 1996).

OFFICE BUILDINGS, CONGRESSIONAL

SEE *Capitol building*

OFFICE BUILDINGS, SUPREME COURT

The Supreme Court has had several homes since its first meeting, on February 1, 1790, in New York City.

The first federal government of the United States was located in New York from 1789 to 1790. The Supreme Court met, at first, on the second floor of the Royal Exchange Building at the intersection of Broad and Water streets.

In December 1790 the federal government moved to Philadelphia, where the Court occupied a room on the first floor of the State House, known today as Independence Hall. In August 1791, the Court moved to the newly built City Hall, located on the east side of State House Square, where it remained until 1801.

Early Years in Washington At this time, the Court followed the rest of the federal government to its permanent headquarters, the new city of Washington, in the District of Columbia. Buildings had been constructed especially for the President and the Congress in the new federal city, but there was no new building for the Supreme Court. So Congress permitted the justices to use a small room on the first floor of its still unfinished Capitol building. The Court stayed there until 1808, when it moved to another room in the Capitol that also housed the Library of Congress. But the Library was so crowded and inconvenient that the Court often met in a nearby tavern.

From February 1810 until August 1814, the Supreme Court met in a room specially created for it. This courtroom was located in the Capitol basement beneath the new chamber for the U.S. Senate. On the night of August 24, 1814, British troops invaded Washington, during the War of 1812, and burned the Capitol. The Supreme Court was therefore forced to meet in various temporary quarters until its former courtroom was repaired and ready for use in 1819. The Court remained in this location for 41 years. This room, known today as the Old Supreme Court Chamber, is open to visitors. It is furnished as it was when the Court met there long ago. This small courtroom has mahogany desks on a slightly raised platform, behind which the justices sat. There was also a very small room for the clerk of the Court. But there were neither offices nor a library for the justices. So, much of their work was done at home.

By 1860, two wings had been added to the Capitol to provide new, spacious chambers for the House of Representatives and the Senate. The Supreme Court moved from its cramped basement room to the old Senate chamber on the first floor of the Capitol. This large room, with anterooms for offices and storage, was by far the best home the Court had ever had. And the justices occupied the old Senate chamber for the next 75 years, until 1935.

The Supreme Court Building The modern Supreme Court Building, opened in 1935, fulfilled the dream of Chief Justice William Howard Taft. He worked for several years to convince Congress to appropriate money to build a suitable, permanent home for the Court. The site chosen for the new Supreme Court Building was a full square block on First Street, across from the Capitol.

In 1928, Chief Justice Taft became chairman of the Supreme Court Building Commission, created by Congress. He picked Cass Gilbert to be the architect for the new Supreme Court Building and worked closely with him in overseeing development of the plans. The cornerstone was laid on October 13, 1932, but Taft was not there to see it, having died on March 8, 1930. Gilbert died in 1934, but his son, Cass Gilbert, Jr., and John Rockart finished the project, under the supervision of David Lynn, Architect of the Capitol. The Court held its first session in its new home on October 7, 1935.

Gilbert, with Taft's approval, used the classical Greek style of architecture as his model. He selected marble to be the primary material for the building, which has four floors and a basement.

The basement contains a garage, laundry, carpentry shop, and police roll-call room. It also has offices and equipment storage rooms for the facilities manager and 32 maintenance workers.

The ground floor houses some of the administrative offices, including the Public Information Office, the clerk's office, the publications office, and police offices. It also has exhibit halls, a cafeteria, and a gift shop.

The first floor includes the courtroom, the chambers (offices) of the justices, the robing room, and conference rooms. The courtroom has seating for about 300 people. There is a raised bench along the east wall, where the justices sit to hear oral arguments on cases. The courtroom, at the center of the first floor, is surrounded by the justices' chambers. There is also a robing room, where justices go before sessions of the Court to put on their black judicial robes. Next to the robing room is the Justices' Conference Room, where cases are privately discussed and decided. Two other conference rooms (East and West Conference Rooms) are used for social events and meetings of Supreme Court staff members.

The second floor contains the dining room and library of the justices, the offices of the reporter of decisions and law clerks, and the legal office, which is occupied by the Court counsel and staff who do legal research for the justices.

The third floor is given to the large library. The fourth floor includes a gymnasium with a basketball court and exercise equipment, as well as storage space.

Both the exterior and interior of the Supreme Court Building are decorated with symbols of law and justice, liberty and order. On either side of the steps to the main (west) entrance to the building, for example, are two marble figures: the one at the left is a female symbolizing justice, the one at the right a male representing the authority of law. Also at the main entrance is a pediment with sculptures representing liberty, order, and authority, with an inscription below the panel of sculptures: "Equal Justice Under Law." Panels on the main door feature sculpted scenes in the history of law.

At the building's east side entrance, there is a pediment with a sculpted figure representing the benefits of law and the judicial resolution of conflicts. An inscription below this panel proclaims, "Justice, the Guardian of Liberty."

On the inside, along both sides of the Great Hall, are busts of former chief justices, profiles of great lawgivers in history, and other symbols of law and justice. The Great Hall leads to the Court chamber, or courtroom. Among the various sculpted symbols in this grand room, where the justices hear oral arguments, are figures and objects representing law, government, and the rights and liberty of the people.

OFFICE OF ADMINISTRATION

The Office of Administration is the unit of the Executive Office of the President that handles housekeeping functions for the White House Office, including payroll and accounting, central purchasing, and the law and general reference libraries. Its Reference Center, with access to government and commercial computer databases, provides the President and White House staff with background research under deadline pressures.

The office trains White House aides in the use of computers and has equipped more than 1,100 White House staffers and members of the Executive Office of the President with personal computers. Its OASIS system software provides electronic mail, calendar and time management software, and access to wire services and databases using modems, and it allows staffers to fax documents from their computers. It does not store documents centrally, nor does it handle classified and top secret information.

In the early 1990s the system was organized around three minicomputers in the data center named Chip, Dale, and Opus, with backup memory units named Bugs and Daffy. The OASIS network is connected to *Air Force One,* the President's airplane, via satellite. All White House computers with the exception of the one used personally by the President are networked so that information can move rapidly throughout the White House Office. Because much of the system was installed in 1988, the Clinton administration replaced most of it with an advanced network of workstations and laptop computers in the first months of 1993.

SEE ALSO *Executive Office of the President; White House Office*

SOURCES Nick Sullivan, "The Ultimate Home Office: The White House," *Home Office Computing,* February 1992, 44–45.

OFFICE OF CONGRESSIONAL RELATIONS

Also known as the Congressional Liaison Office or Legislative Affairs Office, the Office of Congressional Relations (OCR) is a unit of the White House Office that assists the President in communicating with members of Congress about legislation. It also handles congressional mail and requests for information addressed to the White House. Its offices are in the West Wing of the White House; on Capitol Hill staffers operate out of the Vice President's suite on the Senate side and the office of the leader of the President's party on the House side.

Prior to World War II, White House

liaison with Congress was handled by cabinet- and subcabinet-level officials, especially those who had served in Congress. Woodrow Wilson instituted the Common Council Club, a group of 30 subcabinet officials (including Assistant Secretary of the Navy Franklin D. Roosevelt) to round up support on Capitol Hill. Roosevelt used his postmaster general, James Farley, and he reserved the position of assistant secretary of commerce for an official in charge of congressional liaison.

During World War II the War Department performed liaison for the Roosevelt administration, with more than 200 officers assigned to its Legislation and Liaison Division. The Bureau of the Budget's Legislative Reference Division also lobbied in Congress. After the war the newly created Department of Defense established an assistant secretary for congressional liaison, the Department of State named an assistant secretary for congressional relations, and between 1949 and 1963 the other departments followed suit, assigning more than 500 officials to these units.

Departmental liaison offices were supervised by White House aides. Dwight Eisenhower created the first such formal unit in the White House Office. John F. Kennedy retained the unit. Richard Nixon, who named the office the Office of Congressional Relations, organized it into Senate and House divisions. President Jimmy Carter also relied on Vice President Walter Mondale, a former senator. Presidents George Bush and Bill Clinton used Vice Presidents Dan Quayle and Albert Gore in the same capacity.

SEE ALSO *Executive Office of the President*
SOURCES Jon R. Bond and Richard Fleisher, eds., *Polarized Politics: Congress and the President in a Partisan Era* (Washington, D.C.: Congressional Quarterly Books, 2000). Louis Fisher, *Constitutional Conflicts Between Congress and the President*, 4th ed., rev. (Lawrence: University Press of Kansas, 1997). Rebecca K. C.

Hersman, *Friends and Foes: How Congress and the President Really Make Foreign Policy* (Washington, D.C.: Brookings Institution, 2000). Ralph K. Huitt, "White House Channels to the Hill," in *Congress against the President*, edited by Harvey C. Mansfield, Sr. (New York: Academy of Political Science, 1975). John Manley, "Presidential Power and White House Lobbying," *Political Science Quarterly* 93, no. 2 (Summer 1978): 255–75. Christopher H. Pyle and Richard M. Pious, eds., *The President, Congress, and the Constitution: Power and Legitimacy in American Politics* (New York: Free Press, 1984).

OFFICE OF GOVERNMENT ETHICS

The Office of Government Ethics oversees ethical standards for the White House Office, the Executive Office of the President, and for the executive branch departments. It was created by the Ethics in Government Act of 1978. The director is appointed by the President with the advice and consent of the Senate for a five-year term. Every two years the director submits to Congress a report about implementation of ethics laws.

The Office of Government Ethics develops rules and regulations regarding standards of conduct, identification of conflicts of interest, and financial disclosure in consultation with the attorney general and the Office of Personnel Management. They are officially promulgated by the President, and the Office of Government Ethics then supervises compliance by providing government officials with advisory letters and formal advisory opinions that deal with their particular situations.

SEE ALSO *Ethics; Executive Office of the President; White House Office*
SOURCES Terry Eastland, *Energy in the Executive: The Case for the Strong Presidency* (New York: Free Press, 1992).

OFFICE OF MANAGEMENT AND BUDGET

The Office of Management and Budget (OMB) prepares the Budget of the United States, which constitutes the President's annual budget request to Congress. It was created as the Bureau of the Budget (BOB) by the Budget and Accounting Act of 1921. Originally located in the Treasury Department, the BOB was moved to the Executive Office of the President in 1939 and renamed the Office of Management and Budget in 1970.

The OMB has 500 or so professional staff members. Its Budget Division prepares the Budget of the United States and drafts of the President's annual budget message. It also reviews and revises the congressional testimony of department secretaries when they request funds from the appropriations committees. Once Congress has appropriated funds, the OMB controls the rate of spending by departments through a system of quarterly allotments. It can also recommend to the President that he defer spending to future years or even rescind scheduled spending—both actions that require ultimate approval by Congress. It can order the reprogramming of funds (transferring money from one activity to another) within an agency or across agency lines.

The OMB's Management Division suggests to department secretaries ways for the departments to be run more efficiently. Its Division of Federal Procurement Policy recommends ways of cutting purchasing costs. Its Legislative Division performs a legislative clearance function: it reviews all requests by departments to Congress for new legislation and decides if such requests should become "part of the President's program" (bills that the President personally endorses), "in accordance with the program of the President" (merely acceptable to the White House), or should be blocked as "not in accord with the pro-

gram of the President." It reviews all legislation passed by Congress within five days and advises the President on whether these "enrolled bills" should be signed or vetoed. Finally, the OMB Division of Information and Regulatory Affairs reviews all regulations proposed by departments to see if they are consistent with the President's policies and should go into effect, a system known as regulatory clearance.

Until the 1970s the Bureau of the Budget was committed to the concept of "neutral competence." This meant that its career civil servants would provide expert advice to a succession of Presidents from both parties and would work dispassionately for the President's goals, whether liberal or conservative. The BOB's first director, Charles Dawes, established the rule that "the Budget Bureau must be impartial, impersonal, and nonpolitical."

President Richard Nixon preferred a partisan and political operation. He reorganized the BOB into the Office of Management and Budget. He installed the OMB director in the West Wing of the White House with other senior political advisers. Political appointees, called program associate directors, were placed over career civil servants to make the agency more responsive to Presidential politics. A majority of the division managers and their top-ranking aides soon left, reducing OMB's expertise. Presidents Gerald Ford, Jimmy Carter, Ronald Reagan, and George Bush all appointed key political advisers as OMB directors, reducing to some extent the competence of the agency in forecasting expenditures and consequently reducing its influence with Congress as well.

SEE ALSO *Budget, Presidential; Executive Office of the President; Impoundment of funds*

SOURCES Larry Berman, *The Office of Management and Budget, 1921–1979* (Princeton, N.J.: Princeton University Press, 1979). Frederic C. Mosher, *A Tale of Two Agencies: A Comparative Analysis of the General Accounting Office and the Office of Management and Budget* (Baton Rouge: Louisiana State University Press, 1984).

462 Office of Science and Technology Policy

Shelley Lynne Tomkin, *Inside OMB: Politics and Process in the President's Budget Office* (Armonk, N.Y.: M. E. Sharpe, 1998).

OFFICE OF SCIENCE AND TECHNOLOGY POLICY

The Office of Science and Technology Policy (OSTP) is a unit of the Executive Office of the President whose director serves as the principal scientific adviser to the President. The office was established by the National Science and Technology Policy, Organization, and Priorities Act of 1976 to advise the President on scientific and technological matters; evaluate the scale, quality, and effectiveness of national government policies in science and technology; and advise the President on proposed funding for scientific research and development. The agency also prepares reports on science and technology that are mandated by Congress. The agency coordinates its work with the Office of Management and Budget and helps prepare those parts of the federal budget that deal with science and technology, such as the space program.

The director of the Office of Science and Technology Policy chairs the cabinet-level Federal Coordinating Council for Science, Engineering, and Technology, which uses task forces of government officials to recommend policies to promote more effective planning for federal scientific, engineering, and technology programs that affect more than a single federal agency or department.

The President's Council of Advisers on Science and Technology is a group of nongovernment scientists who provide the President with independent advice so that he is not entirely reliant on the director of the OSTP in formulating policy.

SEE ALSO *Decision making, Presidential; Executive Office of the President; Office of Management and Budget*

SOURCES *Technology and Economic Performance: Organizing the Executive Branch for a Stronger National Technology Base* (New York: Carnegie Commission on Science, Technology, and Government, 1991).

OFFICE OF U.S. TRADE REPRESENTATIVE

The Office of U.S. Trade Representative is a unit of the Executive Office of the President that develops the United States's policies on international trade. Created by an executive order of President John F. Kennedy in 1963, the office is headed by the U.S. trade representative, a cabinet-level officer with the rank of ambassador, who reports directly to the President.

The U.S. trade representative is the chief representative of the United States for all activities concerning the General Agreement on Tariffs and Trade (GATT), an international agreement subscribed to by most nations, including negotiations on future GATT tariff adjustments. The trade representative negotiates with the Organization for Economic Cooperation and Development (OECD), a 24-nation organization of advanced industrial nations, when the OECD takes up trade and agricultural commodity issues. The trade representative also serves as a member of the boards of directors of the Export-Import Bank (which makes low-cost loans to foreign purchasers) and the Overseas Private Investment Corporation (which insures overseas private investments) and serves on the National Advisory Council for International Monetary and Financial Policy.

The Omnibus Trade and Competitiveness Act of 1988 gave the trade representative authority to implement sanctions against foreign nations that have not abided by the principles of free trade stated in international trade agreements with the United States. The threat of sanctions provides the trade representative with a negotiating tool that is used for "managed trade" agreements with nations that export more to the United States than they import from this country.

SEE ALSO *Executive Office of the President*
SOURCES Ann Scott Tyson, "U.S. Ambassador Hides Steel Behind Silk Scarves" (*Christian Science Monitor*, Apr. 30, 1999, p. 1).

OFFICERS OF THE HOUSE AND SENATE

The Vice President of the United States, various elected members of Congress, and elected staff members are the officers of the House and Senate. The Constitution assigns the Vice President to serve as presiding officer of the Senate (or president of the Senate), with the power to cast tiebreaking votes. Article 1, Section 3, of the Constitution instructs the Senate to elect a president pro tempore (temporary president) to preside in the absence of the Vice President. In recent years, the president pro tempore has been the longest-serving member of the majority party. Article 1, Section 2, of the Constitution instructs the House to elect a Speaker as its presiding officer. The Vice President, the Speaker of the House, and the president pro tempore are therefore the three constitutional officers of Congress, and they stand in that order in the line of Presidential succession (that is, the order in which they would move up to the Presidency in the case of a vacancy).

Each house also elects its own administrative officers. The Senate elects the secretary of the Senate, sergeant at arms, chaplain, and secretaries for the majority and minority parties. None of these officers are senators. The House elects the clerk of the House, sergeant at arms, doorkeeper, and chaplain, none of whom are representatives.

The political parties represented in Congress also elect officers, including majority and minority leaders, conference (caucus) chairs, and party secretaries.

SEE ALSO *Chaplains, congressional; Clerk of the House of Representatives; Constitution,* *U.S.; President pro tempore of the Senate; Sergeant at arms; Speaker of the House; Vice President*

OLMSTEAD V. UNITED STATES

• 277 U.S. 438 (1928)
• Vote: 5–4
• For the Court: Taft
• Dissenting: Holmes, Brandeis, Butler, and Stone

In 1919, the 18th Amendment to the U.S. Constitution was ratified. It banned the sale, transportation, and importation of alcoholic beverages. Congress passed the National Prohibition Act to implement the 18th Amendment. Roy Olmstead, however, defied the National Prohibition Act by conducting a large-scale business to transport liquor throughout the state of Washington and British Columbia in Canada.

Federal agents gained evidence of Olmstead's illegal business by tapping the telephone line in one of his company's offices and the telephone lines into the homes of four of his workers. The agents listened to his telephone conversations and took notes about illegal activities.

Roy Olmstead and several others were convicted of conspiracy to violate the National Prohibition Act. Olmstead appealed his conviction to the Supreme Court. He claimed that the wiretap violated his rights under the 4th Amendment, which says, "The right of the people to be secure in their persons, houses, papers, and effects, against unreasonable searches and seizures, shall not be violated." Further, he argued that searches and seizures are unreasonable unless officials conducting them have obtained warrants only for "probable cause" that the person to be searched has violated or is violating the law. He also pointed to the 5th Amendment right that "no person . . . shall be compelled in any criminal case to be a witness against himself."

The Issue   Was the use of evidence obtained through a telephone wiretap a violation of an individual's 4th and 5th Amendment rights? Should evidence obtained through a telephone wiretap be excluded from the trial of a person accused of a crime?

Opinion of the Court   The Supreme Court upheld Olmstead's conviction. Chief Justice William Howard Taft wrote that conversations were not protected by the 4th Amendment and that the wiretaps on the telephone lines were not an invasion of the defendant's house or office. Taft agreed with the decision in *Weeks* v. *United States* (1914) that evidence obtained illegally must be excluded from a defendant's trial. However, he concluded that the evidence against Roy Olmstead was gathered legally.

Dissent   Justice Louis D. Brandeis wrote an eloquent dissent that took account of the new technologies involved in this case; the electronic devices involved in the case did not exist when the 4th Amendment was written and ratified.

The wiretaps by federal agents, said Brandeis, were an invasion of privacy, which violated the intention of those who wrote and ratified the Constitution. According to Brandeis, they "sought to protect Americans in their beliefs, their thoughts, their emotions and their sensations. They conferred, as against the government, the right to be let alone—the most comprehensive of rights and the right most valued by civilized men." He asserted that to protect the person's right to privacy, every "unjustifiable intrusion by the government . . . whatever the means employed" must be viewed as a violation of the 4th Amendment. In addition, he said, use of evidence gathered illegally, such as through telephone wiretaps, violates the 5th Amendment.

Significance   The *Olmstead* case was the first one in which the Court considered the impact of new electronic technology on the constitutional rights of individuals accused of criminal activity. It was also the first case in which a general right to privacy was asserted as a fundamental right—the basis of the dissenting opinion by Justice Brandeis.

The Court's decision in *Olmstead* was overturned in *Katz* v. *United States* (1967), which concluded that wiretaps and other forms of electronic surveillance are violations of the 4th Amendment. In Title III of the Crime Control and Safe Streets Act of 1968, Congress banned wiretapping to gain evidence against individuals in the United States except when it was approved in advance by a federal judge according to guidelines in the 1968 act. In the long run the dissenting views of Justice Brandeis prevailed concerning the use of wiretapping to gather evidence of criminal behavior. Brandeis's views about privacy as a general constitutional right are still controversial, although this idea has influenced opinions in several key cases. These include *Griswold* v. *Connecticut* (1965) and *Roe* v. *Wade* (1973), which dealt with the issues of birth control and abortion.

SEE ALSO   *Griswold v. Connecticut; Katz v. United States; Privacy, right to; Roe v. Wade; Searches and seizures*

SOURCES   Walter F. Murphy, *Wiretapping on Trial: A Case Study in the Judicial Process* (New York: Random House, 1965).

O'NEILL, THOMAS P. ("TIP"), JR.

- Born: Dec. 9, 1912, Cambridge, Mass.
- Political party: Democrat
- Education: Boston College, graduated, 1936
- Representative from Massachusetts: 1953–87
- House majority whip: 1971–73
- House majority leader: 1973–77
- Speaker of the House: 1977–87
- Died: Jan.5, 1994, Boston, Mass.

When he first ran for public office, Tip O'Neill received some shrewd advice from his father, who said: "All politics is local." During his long career in the House of

Representatives, O'Neill would repeat that advice to new members. What he meant was that regardless of the issue, representatives must consider the interests, needs, and opinions of their own local district. "You can be the most important congressman in the country, but you had better not forget the people back home," he would tell them. When members become so involved in national issues that they lose connection with their own constituents, then the next election might send them packing. Keeping his father's advice in mind, O'Neill won reelection repeatedly. He served for 34 years in the House, becoming Democratic whip, majority leader, and Speaker of the House. From 1981 through 1986, when the Republicans held the majority in the Senate and Ronald Reagan was President, Speaker O'Neill found himself the highest-ranking Democrat in the federal government. Although O'Neill had little success in opposing Reagan's conservative economic program, he was able to marshal House Democrats to prevent the dismantling of federal health, education, and social welfare programs.

SOURCES Thomas P. O'Neill, Jr., and William Novak, *Man of the House: The Life and Political Memoirs of Speaker Tip O'Neill* (New York: Random House, 1987).

ONE PERSON, ONE VOTE

SEE *Baker v. Carr; Reynolds v. Sims*

OPENING DAY OF THE SUPREME COURT

Since 1917 the first Monday in October has been the official opening day of the annual term of the Supreme Court. The chief justice ceremoniously opens the session at 10:00 A.M. New justices, if any, take their oath of office, and attorneys are admitted to the bar of the Supreme Court. The Court shows its respect to retired and deceased colleagues and Supreme Court officers through brief statements of tribute. Since 1975 the opening day has also included oral arguments.

OPINIONS OF THE SUPREME COURT

The Supreme Court presents its decisions on cases to the public through written opinions. The opinions announce the outcomes of cases decided by the Court and provide the legal reasoning in support of the decisions.

When the chief justice is part of the majority opinion on a case, he may either write the Court's opinion himself or assign it to another justice in the majority group. When the chief justice is not part of the Court's majority, the most senior associate justice in the majority group assigns the task of writing the opinion. The writing of minority or dissenting opinions is not assigned. The justices who wish to write them merely assume this responsibility voluntarily.

When the justice assigned to write the Court's opinion completes a first draft, the opinion is distributed to the other eight justices, who may join the opinion. Sometimes, the opinion is modified to satisfy one or more justices, who otherwise will not sign it. These differences and compromises are discussed among the justices in meetings and in written messages in response to drafts of opinions that have been circulated.

If a justice agrees with the Court's decision but disagrees somewhat with the written opinion of the Court, he or she may write a concurring opinion, one that reaches the same conclusion but using different legal reasoning. Justices who disagree with the Court's decision on a case may write a dissenting opinion.

SEE ALSO *Concurring opinion; Dissenting opinion; Majority opinion; Per curiam; Plurality opinion; Seriatim opinions*

ORAL ARGUMENT

After the Supreme Court decides to hear a case, the clerk of the Court schedules the oral argument on the case. At this time, attorneys for both sides of the case speak before the justices in the Supreme Court chamber, or courtroom. Each side is limited to a 30-minute oral presentation. The attorneys may not read a set speech. They usually interact with the justices, who ask them questions. The justices may interrupt an advocate with questions or comments whenever they wish. About one-third of the counsel's 30-minute presentation is taken up with questions or remarks by justices. The effective advocate makes skillful responses to the questions of the justices. Those who stumble in responding or try to evade the question are likely to make a bad impression on the Court. During oral arguments, passionate exchanges at times occur between advocate and justices or between different justices who take exception to the reasoning or style of the commentary.

The justices read briefs, which are the lawyers' summaries of their arguments, and other documents regarding each case, such as memoranda about the case prepared by their law clerks and records from the trial court, before the day of the oral argument. As a result, they are likely to bring questions and concerns about the issues to the oral argument. This hearing gives the justices an opportunity to test the worth of the arguments on both sides of the case. Moreover, through this open hearing the justices demonstrate to the public that arguments on both sides of the case will be considered and challenged before a decision is made.

ORATORY, CONGRESSIONAL

The era before the Civil War was known as the golden age of debate, when oratory, the art of public speaking, flourished in Congress. But the quality of oratory in Congress declined substantially in later years. Modern visitors to the galleries who expect to hear great speech making or dramatic debates are often disappointed to find someone reading a dry and technical speech to a largely empty chamber. Regardless of the empty chairs, members speak to establish a record of support for or disapproval of some legislation, as their words are recorded in the *Congressional Record* and broadcast on television.

By contrast, the speeches of many 19th-century senators and representatives could pack the chambers and the galleries. Daniel Webster (Whig–Massachusetts), for instance, used oratory to sway public opinion and influence his colleagues' votes. Such speeches carried great moral and intellectual authority and were reprinted widely in newspapers and pamphlets. Students memorized the most stirring passages. Eloquence and the skillful use of rhetoric helped establish a member's reputation as a wise statesman. By the 20th century, members known for oratory, such as Everett M. Dirksen (Republican–Illinois), seemed amusingly eccentric.

Many factors eroded the use of oratory as a legislative tool. To speed business, in 1847 the House, with its many members, established a five-minute rule limiting how long its members could speak on amendments. When the new House and Senate chambers were opened in the late 1850s, poor acoustics made it more difficult for speakers to be heard; one representative called the House chamber "the worst place in America for a man to speak." Not for another century would microphones be installed for amplification.

Styles of political campaigning also changed. Stump speaking (addressing a crowd usually from an elevated area or impromptu stage) required strong lungs, a loud voice, and colorful language to reach and hold audiences. But the introduction of television required members of Congress to tone down their voices and their rhetoric for the new "cool" medium. Long, thoughtful speeches might establish a record, but only a few seconds would ever be carried on an evening news broadcast. So politicians learned to use catchy phrases, and sound bites replaced oratory.

Effective legislators also suspect that most floor speeches are aimed more at attracting attention from the media and constituents at home than at persuading colleagues. Senator Warren Magnuson (Democrat–Washington) summed up this attitude: "If you've got the votes, you don't need a speech. If you need the speech, you don't have the votes."

SEE ALSO *Debates, congressional; Webster, Daniel*

SOURCES Kenneth Cmiel, *Democratic Eloquence: The Fight over Popular Speech in Nineteenth-Century America* (New York: Morrow, 1990).

ORDERS LIST

The clerk of the Supreme Court prepares orders lists that appear near the end of volumes of the *United States Reports,* the official record of the Court's opinions. Each orders list is made up of brief summaries of the Court's actions on a particular day regarding certain cases under review but does not include opinions. For example, the Court may decide to refuse or accept a writ of appeal; it may deny or accept petitions for a writ of certiorari (an order for a lower court to send the official record of a case to the Supreme Court). Orders may treat such matters as stays of execution for a person scheduled for capital punishment, permissions to file amicus curiae briefs (which are filed by individuals or organizations not involved in a particular case but who have a special interest in the issue under review), or actions on disbarment of attorneys (expulsion from the legal profession).

SEE ALSO *United States Reports*

ORGANIZED CRIME INVESTIGATION (1950)

The first nationally televised congressional investigation looked into the underworld of organized crime in the United States. The hearings drew a large audience and made the special investigating committee's chairman, Estes Kefauver (Democrat–Tennessee), a major contender for his party's Presidential nomination. A notable moment occurred when mobster Frank Costello refused to allow the television cameras to film his face while he testified. Instead, the cameras followed Costello's hands, whose nervous gestures betrayed his otherwise cool appearance. Although the Kefauver hearings had little impact on legislation, they provided the first indication of the power that the new medium of television would have in future investigations.

SEE ALSO *Investigations, congressional; Media coverage of Congress*

SOURCES Joseph Bruce Gorman, *Kefauver: A Political Biography* (New York: Oxford University Press, 1971).

ORIGINAL INTENT

The method of interpreting the U.S. Constitution according to the literal intentions of its authors is known as original intent. Advocates of this method of constitutional interpretation claim that judges are obligated to find out what the framers intended by the words they used in writing the Constitution. Robert H. Bork, a legal scholar who favors original intent, stated in 1984, "It is necessary to establish the proposition that the framers' intentions . . . are the sole premise from which constitutional analysis may proceed."

Critics of the original intent method say that most of the framers did not expect those who came after them to be bound strictly by their work. Rather, they claim, the framers expected that the basic principles of the Constitution would be retained but details would be adapted to meet the changing and unforeseen circumstances of the future.

Justice William J. Brennan, for example, opposed the doctrine of original intent. He said in a 1985 speech, "We current Justices read the Constitution in the only way we can: as Twentieth Century Americans. We look to the history of the time of framing and to the intervening history of interpretation. But the ultimate question must be, what do the words of the text mean in our time. For the genius of the Constitution rests not in any static meaning it might have had in a world that is dead and gone, but in the adaptability of its great principles to cope with current problems and current needs."

Defenders of original intent, however, argue that the rule of law cannot be maintained unless judges apply the Constitution to current controversies as the framers intended it to be applied. If original intent is ignored, they claim, then judges become lawmakers, not law interpreters, as they are supposed to be. Robert H. Bork, for example, told the Senate Judiciary Committee in 1987, "How should a judge go about finding the law? The only legitimate way, in my opinion, is by attempting to discern what those who made the law intended. . . . If a judge abandons intention as his guide, there is no law available to him and he begins to legislate a social agenda for the American people. That goes way beyond his legitimate power."

Is it the duty of the judges to keep the Constitution in tune with the times? No, say the advocates of original intent. Rather, they argue, it is the duty of judges to maintain an unbroken continuity of constitutional meaning from the founding era to their own times.

SEE ALSO *Constitutional construction; Judicial activism and judicial restraint*

ORIGINAL JURISDICTION

SEE *Jurisdiction*

"OTHER BODY"

When Vice President Thomas Jefferson wrote his manual of parliamentary procedure, he observed that it was poor form for members of one house of Congress to refer to the debates or actions of the other house. "The opinion of each house should be left to its own independency," Jefferson wrote, "not to be influenced by the proceedings of the other." In this spirit of independence, and in an effort to avoid misunderstanding and ill will between the two bodies, members of the House generally do not mention the Senate by name and simply call it the "other body." Senators, who no longer use Jefferson's manual as part of their rules, are more likely to refer to the House by name, although by tradition they do not speak critically of the House or question the motives of its members. House members find "other body" preferable to "upper body" when referring to the Senate and consider the phrase more in keeping with the equality of the two chambers.

SEE ALSO *Jefferson's manual;* "*Upper house*"

OVAL OFFICE

The Oval Office is the informal name for the President's office in the West Wing of the White House. The original Oval Office was located in the center of the West Wing when it was constructed in 1909. The office was moved to the southeast corner of the West Wing in 1934, during the Presidency of Franklin D. Roosevelt, when the wing was renovated. It opens onto the Rose Garden and faces the rear lawn.

The Presidential office is oval in shape. Its exterior wall holds a large bay window with steel sash frames and bulletproof glass panes. The bay window allows the office to be flooded with southern sun through much of the day. The ceiling is decorated with a medallion of the Presidential seal. The United States and Presidential flags are located behind the President's desk. Near the fireplace is a seating area for casual conversation.

The name Oval Office came into general use during Richard Nixon's administration. It is also used by reporters as a substitute for the name of the President, as in "The Oval Office has decided . . ." The White House Historical Association began referring to the Oval Office rather than the President's Office in 1973.

SEE ALSO *White House*

OVERSIGHT

In general usage, *oversight* usually means something that has been forgotten or overlooked. But in Congress it means just the opposite. When Congress performs its oversight functions, it is supervising, or looking over, the business of executive branch departments. The Legislative Reorganization Act of 1946 assigned to each committee or subcommittee with jurisdiction over legislation relating to a particular agency, or with the power to appropriate its funds, the power to exercise "continuous watchfulness" over that agency. Through their oversight functions, congressional committees monitor how well agencies are administering the laws and if they are spending federal money properly. The General Accounting Office conducts regular audits of agency finances. Committees also call agency heads to testify during oversight hearings. By contrast to investigations, which are usually special hearings concerned with a single issue or event, oversight is a regular, year-to-year, ongoing procedure. Consequently, Congress's oversight functions get less attention from the media than do splashier investigations.

SEE ALSO *Investigations, congressional; Legislative Reorganization Acts (1946 and 1970)*

SOURCES Walter J. Oleszek, "Legislative Oversight," in *Congressional Procedures and Policy Process* (Washington, D.C.: Congressional Quarterly, 1989). Randall B. Ripley, *Congress: Process and Policy* (New York: Norton, 1988).

P

PAGES, CONGRESSIONAL

During each session of Congress, high school juniors from every state work as pages for the House and Senate. Dressed in blue uniforms, they sit on either side of the presiding officers in the chambers, ready to run errands, set up podiums for speakers, and generally help out in the chambers and cloakrooms. From 6:15 A.M. to 10:30 A.M. they attend high school classes at a special page school before beginning their daily duties for Congress.

The term *page* dates back to the medieval European practice of having youths serve as attendants to knights and other nobles. In 1827 the House appointed its first pages, Charles B. Chalmers, Edward Dunn, and John C. Burch. Shortly afterward, Senator Daniel Webster employed 9-year-old Grafton Dulany Hanson and 12-year-old Isaac Bassett as the Senate's first two pages. Bassett devoted the next 64 years of his life to Senate service, working as a messenger and doorkeeper. John Burch similarly spent a long career on Capitol Hill and was eventually elected secretary of the Senate. Other pages grew up to win election as senators and representatives, including Senator David Pryor (Democrat–Arkansas) and Representative John Dingell, Jr. (Democrat–Michigan).

Before the Capitol was wired for electricity and signal bells were installed, pages raced from room to room summoning members to vote. Before telephones, pages rode horseback to the White House and executive departments, delivering bills and correspondence. Pages also worked as the first telephone operators in the Capitol. Although technology replaced these functions, pages can still be seen darting through the Capitol carrying messages for the members.

Initially, only boys served as pages. The first female page, Gene Cox, the 13-year-old daughter of Representative Eugene Cox (Democrat–Georgia), served for a single day in 1939. Not until the 1970s were girls as well as boys regularly appointed congressional pages. One page described her experiences as "a chance to watch [Congress] day by day. . . . When you look at one piece—one day—it means nothing, but after a while you discover how it all fits and locks together."

SOURCES Bill Severn, *Democracy's Messengers: The Capitol Pages* (New York: Hawthorn, 1975).

PAIR VOTING

A senator or representative who expects to be absent during a recorded vote (in which a member's name will be listed as voting yea or nay) can arrange to be paired with another member who plans to vote the opposite way and is also going to be absent. With this voluntary agreement the two absent members show how they would have voted and that their votes would not have changed the final result. If one of the pair is present for the vote, it is called a "live pair." In a live pair the member votes "present" and announces how the pair of them would have voted on that issue. Paired votes appear in the *Congressional Record* at the end of the recorded vote tally.

PALKO V. CONNECTICUT

- 302 U.S. 319 (1937)
- Vote: 8–1
- For the Court: Cardozo
- Dissenting: Butler

Frank Palko robbed a store in Connecticut and shot and killed two police officers. He was tried for first-degree murder. The jury, however, found Palko guilty of the lesser crime of second-degree murder. He was sentenced to life in prison. The state prosecutors appealed this conviction and won a second trial, at which new evidence against Palko was introduced.

The judge at the first trial had refused to allow Palko's confession to be used as evidence against him. The absence of this evidence led to a lesser sentence for the defendant. At the second trial, however, all available evidence was used. As a result, Palko was convicted of the more serious charge of first-degree murder and sentenced to death.

Frank Palko appealed to the U.S. Supreme Court. His appeal was based on the 5th Amendment, which guarantees that no one should endure double jeopardy—that is, be put on trial twice for the same crime. The 5th Amendment, however, applies only to actions of the federal government. So Palko also pointed to the 14th Amendment provision that no state can "deprive any person of life, liberty, or property, without due process of law." Palko claimed that the 5th Amendment protection against double jeopardy could be applied to a state government through the due process clause of the 14th Amendment.

The Issue   There was no question about Palko's guilt or innocence. The issue was whether he had been unconstitutionally subjected to double jeopardy. Does the 14th Amendment's due process clause en-

compass the 5th Amendment's prohibition of double jeopardy? Or does the 5th Amendment apply only to actions of the federal government?

Opinion of the Court   Palko's appeal was denied. His basic argument— "[W]hatever is forbidden by the Fifth Amendment is forbidden by the Fourteenth also"—was rejected. In reaching this conclusion, the Court proposed a new test to determine which rights of an accused person, as stated in the federal Bill of Rights, are so fundamental that they apply equally to the state and federal governments. Justice Benjamin Cardozo wrote that fundamental rights are "the very essence of a scheme of ordered liberty," without which justice is not possible. To deprive an individual of these rights is "a hardship so acute and shocking that our polity will not endure it."

According to Cardozo, the 5th Amendment rights claimed by Palko in this case were important but were not "principles of justice so rooted in the traditions and conscience of our people as to be ranked fundamental." Thus, the Court would not apply to the states in this case the 5th Amendment right of protection against double jeopardy.

Significance   The *Palko* case was an important contribution in creating an acceptable test to guide the Court's use of the 14th Amendment's due process clause in limiting the actions of state governments. Justice Cardozo created the "fundamental rights" test in the *Palko* opinion. According to this test, the 14th Amendment's due process clause does not necessarily incorporate the federal Bill of Rights. However, it does open the way for a case-by-case consideration of what and how to select parts of the federal Bill of Rights to apply them to the states. In 1969 the Court overruled *Palko* in *Benton* v. *Maryland*. Double jeopardy became one of the provisions of the federal Bill of Rights to be selectively incorporated into the 14th Amendment and applied to the states.

SEE ALSO *Benton v. Maryland; Double jeopardy; Incorporation doctrine*

PARDON POWER

The Constitution (Article 2, Section 2) grants the President the power to reprieve and pardon individuals who have committed crimes or other offenses against the United States. A reprieve is a temporary postponement of a court's sentence, designed to give the President time to consider a request for a pardon or a reduction of the sentence. A pardon stops any further criminal judicial process from proceeding and, in effect, makes a "new person" of the offender. Amnesty is a pardon granted to a class of offenders. In the case *Ex parte Garland* (1867) the Supreme Court said of a pardon that "in the eye of the law the offender is as innocent as if he had never committed the offense." A pardon restores to the offender all civil and political rights.

The framers of the Constitution gave the President the pardon power to prevent miscarriages of justice and also to provide the President with a way to end treasonous activities such as rebellion.

The President may not use the pardon power to overrule the impeachment process. Indeed, if the President used a pardon to prevent the execution of the laws, that would constitute an impeachable offense, according to Chief Justice William Howard Taft in *Ex parte Grossman* (1925). Any conditions that a President attaches to a pardon issued to an individual are subject to review by the Supreme Court. In two cases, *Ex parte Garland* and *Klein v. United States* (1872), the Supreme Court ruled that the pardon power could not be regulated by congressional legislation, leaving the judiciary itself as the only check on the pardon power.

Pardons are administered by the Department of Justice. The attorney general provides the President with recommendations about pardons. The attorney general, in turn, relies on the department's Office of Pardon Attorney.

After Thomas Jefferson assumed the Presidency in 1801, he pardoned members of the Democratic Societies, most of them

his political supporters, who had been convicted of violating the Alien and Sedition Acts of 1798. At the end of the Civil War, President Andrew Johnson proclaimed amnesty for most Confederate soldiers and pardoned Jefferson Davis, President of the Confederate States of America. He also pardoned Dr. Samuel Mudd, the doctor who set John Wilkes Booth's broken leg after Booth assassinated Abraham Lincoln. In 1921 President Warren G. Harding issued a pardon to labor organizer and Socialist party leader Eugene V. Debs for antiwar organizing with only one condition: Debs had to travel to Washington and meet Harding in person to receive his pardon. In 1971 President Richard Nixon commuted the prison term of a former president of the Teamsters Union, Jimmy Hoffa, on condition that Hoffa take no further part in union activities.

The most unpopular pardon was issued by Gerald Ford to his predecessor, Richard Nixon, in 1974 for all offenses against the United States that he had committed "or may have committed or taken part in." These offenses involved the obstruction of justice in the Watergate scandal of 1972, because of which Nixon resigned his office. Ford's public approval rating nose-dived from 71 to 49 percent within a week after he issued the pardon. His press secretary resigned in protest, and the pardon probably cost Ford the Presidential election of 1976. He appeared before the House Judiciary Committee to answer questions about the pardon, claiming "there never was at any time any agreement whatsoever concerning a pardon to Mr. Nixon if he were to resign and I were to become President." Ford insisted that he had issued the pardon to Nixon to end "the long national nightmare" of Watergate. By a 55-to-24 vote, the Senate passed a resolution opposing pardons for other Watergate conspirators.

President Ronald Reagan did not offer pardons to any of those accused of violating federal laws in the Iran-Contra affair, but near the end of his term President

George Bush pardoned six participants, including Caspar Weinberger, former defense secretary. Some critics charged that President Bush had pardoned Weinberger in order to prevent testimony or the introduction of evidence at the trial that might have implicated Bush directly in the cover-up. The independent counsel for Iran-Contra prosecutions, Lawrence Walsh, condemned the Presidential pardon, charging that "The Iran-Contra cover-up, which has continued for more than six years, has now been completed."

SEE ALSO *Amnesty, Presidential; Bush, George; Ford, Gerald R.; Nixon, Richard M.; Reagan, Ronald; Watergate investigation (1973–74)*

SOURCES David Gray Adler, "The President's Pardon Power," in *Inventing the American Presidency,* edited by Thomas Cronin (Lawrence: University Press of Kansas, 1989).

PARLIAMENTARIAN

The rules of the Senate and House are few in number, but the precedents—the previous actions of the two bodies and the rulings of their presiding officers—are voluminous. The accumulated precedents serve as guides for future actions. In order to operate properly within the boundaries of these precedents, and to plan strategies for passing or defeating legislation, the Senate and House each appoint staff members to serve as parliamentarians.

Before the 1920s various clerks kept track of the rules and precedents and offered advice to the presiding officers. In 1928 Speaker Nicholas Longworth appointed Lewis Deschler as the first House parliamentarian. It was a tribute to Deschler's nonpartisanship that he continued in the job until 1974, through both Republican and Democratic majorities. In 1937 Charles Watkins became the Senate's first official parliamentarian, and he, too, remained in his post under both parties until his retirement in 1964.

"Ventriloquists" The parliamentarian sits at the front desk, immediately below the presiding officer. When a question about some matter of parliamentary procedure arises from the floor, the presiding officer leans over and consults the parliamentarian. Because the presiding officers invariably announce aloud exactly what the parliamentarians have just whispered, the parliamentarians have been called the "ventriloquists" of the House and Senate. But presiding officers have learned the wisdom of following the parliamentarian's advice. Those who ignore the parliamentarian and rule differently face being overridden by a majority vote of the House or Senate. Some members of Congress rely entirely on the parliamentarian for advice, while others study the rules and precedents independently and win recognition on Capitol Hill for their mastery of parliamentary procedure. These members are often members of the minority who can be especially effective in using their knowledge of the rules to block passage of legislation that the majority favors.

The parliamentarians are responsible for publishing the collected precedents of their chamber so that members and staff can become aware of them. Recently, the precedents have also been compiled in computers, and terminals have been installed at the front desks, giving the parliamentarians much faster access. Parliamentarians try to avoid taking sides in parliamentary disputes, and they offer advice to the leaders and members of both parties.

SEE ALSO *Parliamentary procedure; Precedents, congressional; Rules of the House and Senate*

SOURCES Floyd M. Riddick and Alan S. Frumin, *Riddick's Senate Procedure: Precedents and Practices* (Washington, D.C.: Government Printing Office, 1992).

PARLIAMENTARY GOVERNMENT

Most national legislatures around the world operate under parliamentary systems that are very different from the U.S. government under which Congress operates. Parliamentary governments separate the ceremonial head of state (the king, queen, or president) from the political head of government (the prime minister or premier). Though most parliaments have two chambers, the upper body, such as the British House of Lords, may be hereditary (members inherit their seat from family members) rather than elected and is usually very limited in its powers. The popularly elected lower house, such as the British House of Commons, holds the real legislative power.

The majority party in the lower house elects the prime minister, who appoints cabinet secretaries from among other members of the parliamentary majority. The leader of the opposition party appoints a "shadow" cabinet as a counterpart to promote the minority party's interests. If the prime minister's party loses its majority through the death, resignation, or defection of some of its members, or if it loses on a major issue, then new parliamentary elections are held. The British Parliament also developed the "vote of confidence" procedure by which members of the majority party are called to stand in a new election with their prime minister. A prime minister who loses a vote of confidence will call for a new election. Party loyalty and regularity are therefore essential in parliamentary governments. In parliamentary systems where the major parties are unable to win a clear majority, they must enter into coalitions with one or more minor parties or hold new elections.

The legislative chambers of parliamentary governments even look unlike the Congress. U.S. senators and representatives sit in semicircular rows facing the presiding officer, with the center aisle separating the parties. By contrast, in the British House of Commons and many other similar legislatures, members of Parliament (MPs) sit with opposing parties facing each other. On key issues, MPs line up to vote (a procedure called a division). Those who choose not to vote with their party must walk to the other side, a physical act that requires considerable political courage. Party defections are therefore much more rare in a parliamentary government than in Congress, where members feel free to vote according to their conscience and are not bound to follow their party's leaders.

Parliamentary governments usually feature a question period when members may address questions directly to the prime minister and cabinet secretaries, who appear personally in the chamber to respond. The U.S. Congress cannot call the President to answer such questions, but congressional committees regularly call upon cabinet secretaries to testify.

Parliamentary systems offer efficient and effective leadership under majority rule, but they also diminish minority rights. In nations where one party holds the overwhelming majority, this situation can foster a "tyranny of the majority" and "constitutional dictatorship." The U.S. system of separation of powers and of checks and balances is less efficient, but it is deliberately so, to prevent the development of arbitrary power.

SOURCES Richard M. Pious, "A Prime Minister for America?" *Constitution* 4 (Fall 1992): 4–12.

PARLIAMENTARY PROCEDURE

"So much of what we do around here [in Congress]," House Republican leader Robert Michel observed, "is determined by how we do it." Parliamentary procedure is the "how" by which Congress operates. It is the collected rules and precedents—the previous actions of the Senate and House and rulings of their presiding officers. It is also the customs, courtesies, and accepted behavior of Congress. Parliamentary procedure establishes the daily routines of the House and Senate. It sets the ways in which members seek recognition on the floor, address the chair and each other, introduce bills and resolutions, and seek to win the passage of legislation or to block it through objections, amendments, filibusters, and other tactics within the rules of order.

The United States inherited its basic parliamentary procedures from the British Parliament during the colonial era. New England town meetings and colonial legislatures followed these traditional methods of operating, as did the Continental Congress, the Congress under the Articles of Confederation, the Constitutional Convention, and the U.S. Congress. In 1801 President Thomas Jefferson published the first volume of parliamentary procedure in the United States, known as Jefferson's manual, which is still part of the House rules.

The House and Senate adopt their own rules and set precedents by their actions. Parliamentarians on the staff of both houses compile and study these rules and precedents in order to advise the presiding officers on how to keep the floor proceedings moving fairly and properly.

To casual visitors in the galleries, the procedures on the House and Senate floor may seem excessively formal. But the parliamentary procedure that they are witnessing evolved over 200 years of legislative activity to enable the Senate and House to function in ways that are reasonably fair and efficient. The procedures prevent presiding officers from ruling arbitrarily, and they ensure that both sides have an opportunity to be heard and to offer their own bills and amendments. Although their emotions often rise over the immediate issues before them, members of Congress have adopted parliamentary procedures that enable them to operate in a rational and orderly manner.

SEE ALSO *Jefferson's manual; Precedents, congressional; Rules of the House and Senate*

PARTY ORGANIZATIONS IN CONGRESS

Democratic and Republican party organizations in the Senate and House help the members of the two parties formulate and defend their programs and get enough members elected to enact them. The basic party organization is the conference or caucus, made up of all the members of one party in that house, such as all the Democrats in the House of Representatives or all the Republicans in the Senate. The conference elects its own chairman (the Democratic floor leader also chairs the Senate Democratic Conference, and the other conferences or caucuses elect separate floor leaders and chairs) and secretary. The conferences also elect the Speaker of the House, the president pro tempore of the Senate, and the majority and minority floor leaders and whips for each chamber. The party conferences also appoint steering committees to assign members of that party to congressional committees.

Although the parties are essentially private organizations, the Legislative Reorganization Act of 1946 acknowledged their legitimate role in the operations of the Congress by enabling each major party to establish a Policy Committee and by funding their staffs. Congress also funds the operations of the majority and minority party secretaries, elected staff members who assist the floor leaders.

Republican and Democratic Senatorial Campaign Committees and Congressional Campaign Committees are appointed by the party conferences to raise funds and otherwise assist party candidates for election to Congress.

SEE ALSO *Caucuses, congressional; Majority leader; Minority leader*

PATERSON, WILLIAM
Associate Justice, 1793–1806

- Born: Dec. 24, 1745, County Antrim, Ireland
- Education: College of New Jersey (Princeton), B.A., 1763, M.A., 1766; studied law under Richard Stockton
- Previous government service: New Jersey Provincial Congress, 1775–76; New Jersey State Constitutional Convention,

1776; attorney general of New Jersey, 1776–83; Constitutional Convention, 1787; U.S. senator from New Jersey, 1789–90; governor of New Jersey, 1790–93

- Appointed by President George Washington Mar. 4, 1793; replaced Thomas Johnson, who resigned
- Supreme Court term: confirmed by the Senate Mar. 4, 1793, by a voice vote; served until Sept. 9, 1806
- Died: Sept. 9, 1806, Albany, N.Y.

William Paterson, born in Ireland, was one of the founders of the United States of America. He helped to draft the first constitution of New Jersey in 1776 and the U.S. Constitution in 1787. At the Constitutional Convention, Paterson was the main author of the New Jersey Plan, an outline of how the government should be set up that he introduced as an alternative to the Virginia Plan of James Madison and Edmund Randolph. Several parts of the New Jersey Plan were combined with the Virginia Plan to create the foundation of the U.S. Constitution.

Paterson participated in the 1st Congress of the United States as a senator from New Jersey. He worked with Oliver Ellsworth of Connecticut to draft the Judiciary Act of 1789, which created the federal judicial system.

President George Washington appointed Paterson to the Supreme Court in 1793. Justice Paterson consistently argued for the supremacy of the federal government in cases about state powers and rights. For example, in *Ware* v. *Hylton* (1796), he decided that an act of the Virginia state government was unconstitutional because it violated the U.S. government's treaty of peace with Great Britain. According to Article 6 of the U.S. Constitution, valid treaties of the United States are part of the supreme law of the land, which all state governments are bound to obey.

William Paterson was injured critically in 1804 while riding circuit for the Court. In those days, justices of the Supreme Court were responsible also for duties on the federal Circuit Courts of Appeals. Each circuit court encompassed a certain region of the United States. Riding circuit involved traveling from place to place to hear cases on appeal from lower courts. During one of those trips in 1804, the horses pulling Justice Paterson's carriage bolted, overturning the vehicle and severely injuring Paterson. He never recovered and died in 1806. The city of Paterson, New Jersey, which he helped to plan, is named after him.

SEE ALSO *Ware* v. *Hylton*

SOURCES John E. O'Connor, *William Paterson: Lawyer and Statesman* (New Brunswick, N.J.: Rutgers University Press, 1979).

PATRONAGE

The awarding of government jobs, appointments, and other considerations on the basis of political ties or favors is known as patronage—that is, a patron or official sponsor arranged it. During the first century of the federal government, almost all nonelected posts went by patronage to elected officials' supporters and fellow party members. After each election, the patronage jobholders from the losing party found themselves out of work.

Initially, there were few Presidential appointments, and President George Washington named his revolutionary war colleagues to these posts. Thomas Jefferson used appointments to build up the new state parties. "No duty the President had to perform was so trying as to put the right man in the right place," he observed.

Andrew Jackson established the principle of "rotation in office," by which he meant that when a new party took over the White House, the President would appoint new officeholders in the bureaucracy, not just the cabinet. These appointments were designed to build up the Democratic party that Jackson had created. Senator William Marcy of New York, in a speech delivered to the Senate in January 1832, observed that the Jacksonians "see nothing wrong in the rule that to the victors belong the spoils of the enemy." (Patronage was also called the "spoils system.") Postal routes and postmasterships were awarded to local politicians in Jackson's party. The collectors of the ports, collectors of fees, Indian agents, and other federal officials were usually well connected to state parties or Jackson's congressional supporters.

Many patronage appointees, however, were poorly qualified for their jobs. Election turnovers disrupted agency operations and removed experienced staff. Office seekers besieged members of Congress and new Presidents, demanding high government jobs in return for their party service. After a disappointed job seeker shot and killed President James Garfield in 1881, Congress enacted the first civil service law in 1883. It required the executive branch to assign most jobs according to merit rather than political influence. To obtain a civil service position, an applicant must take a qualifying examination or demonstrate sufficient professional training and experience. Once appointed, civil servants cannot be fired for political reasons. The Office of Personnel Management now enforces all rules relating to civil service hiring.

Presidents still used patronage, however, to increase their influence with members of Congress and political party leaders. Benjamin Harrison and William McKinley used patronage to pass tariffs, and McKinley used it to assure Senate approval of the Treaty of Paris. William Howard Taft denied patronage to members of his party who refused to support his legislative program, which infuriated them and led to a split within the Republican party.

No President can afford to ignore the demands of his party. Postmaster General Albert Burleson advised President Woodrow Wilson that "these little offices mean a great deal to the Senators and Representatives in Congress. . . . If they are turned down, they will hate you and will not vote for anything you want." Franklin Roosevelt used patronage to win support for crucial military preparedness legislation prior to the attack at Pearl Harbor.

President Dwight Eisenhower acted as if he were above the pettiness of party politics, but actually he was very much involved. He came out of a cabinet meeting one day and wrote in his diary, "Everything seems to have been patronage this morning." Lyndon Johnson used patronage to cement a relationship with the opposition party. By taking care of the patronage requests made by Senate minority leader Everett Dirksen, Johnson won crucial Republican votes for his Civil Rights Act of 1964 and his Voting Rights Act of 1965.

Assigning jobs on Capitol Hill   Even after establishing a civil service system for the executive branch, Congress continued to assign most of its own jobs according to patronage. At first this was because Congress met for only half the year and hired a small staff for only those months. Only a few committees, such as Finance, Ways and Means, Printing, and Claims, which received correspondence and other documents even after Congress had adjourned, were authorized to employ a year-round staff. Members of the House and Senate appointed their own office staffs. Sometimes members appointed their wives, children, and other relatives as their secretaries, messengers, or committee clerks. New ethics laws eventually outlawed nepotism, but members continued to appoint their campaign supporters to posts in their own offices and committees and to other jobs around the Capitol. Both parties had patronage committees to assign clerks, elevator operators, and Capitol police to their members for patronage appointments.

Patronage began to decline after World War II, as Congress began to meet on a year-round basis and as the growth in members' personal staffs relieved the pressure of making patronage appointments elsewhere. But outside of members' own offices (where staffs generally reflect the member's political leaning), the trend in the general operations of Congress has continued toward a permanent, professional, and nonpartisan staff.

SEE ALSO *Appointment power*

SOURCES Woodrow Wilson, *Congressional Government* (New York: Meridian, 1956).

PEACE CORPS

The Peace Corps is an independent agency that was created on March 1, 1961, by an executive order issued by President John F. Kennedy. On September 22, 1961, Congress approved legislation that formally authorized the Peace Corps to promote world peace through friendship. Congress also set three goals for the agency that have remained the mission of the Peace Corps to this day: to help the people of interested countries in fulfilling their needs for professionally trained men and women, to help promote a better understanding of Americans on the part of the peoples served, and to help promote a better understanding of other peoples on the part of Americans. The head of the Peace Corps is a director who is appointed by the President and confirmed by the Senate for an indefinite term.

During the first four decades of its existence, the agency has stationed approximately 155,000 volunteers in more than 130 countries. In 1999 there were about 7,000 Peace Corps volunteers serving in 78 foreign nations. Currently, 40 percent of the volunteers are engaged in educational work, 18 percent are working in health-related fields, 17 percent are assigned to environmental projects, 13 percent are involved in business ventures, and 9 percent do agricultural work.

SEE ALSO *Kennedy, John F.*

PECKHAM, RUFUS W.
Associate Justice, 1896–1909

- Born: Nov. 8, 1838, Albany, N.Y.
- Education: studied law in his father's law firm
- Previous government service: district attorney, Albany County, N.Y., 1869–72; judge, New York Supreme Court, 1883–86; judge, New York Court of Appeals, 1886–95
- Appointed by President Grover Cleveland Dec. 3, 1895; replaced Howell Jackson, who died
- Supreme Court term: confirmed by the Senate Dec. 9, 1895, by a voice vote; served until Oct. 24, 1909
- Died: Oct. 24, 1909, Altamont, N.Y.

Rufus W. Peckham was named to the Supreme Court in 1895. In the previous year, his brother, Wheeler H. Peckham, had been nominated by President Grover Cleveland and rejected by the Senate. The Senate, however, readily confirmed Rufus Peckham's nomination.

During his 13 years on the Court, Justice Peckham favored property rights and contract rights of individuals. He usually opposed state government regulation of businesses and working conditions in favor of economic liberty. His most notable opinion for the Court was in *Lochner* v. *New York* (1905). He ruled that a New York law limiting the length of the workday for bakers was unconstitutional because it violated the rights of workers and employers to freely make contracts.

SEE ALSO *Lochner v. New York*

PER CURIAM

Per curiam is Latin for "by the court." An opinion designated by the Supreme Court as a body, instead of by one member, is called a per curiam decision. In *Brandenburg* v. *Ohio* (1969), for example, the opinion of the Court was not attributed to a particular justice. Instead, it was announced as a per curiam decision. This kind of opinion is used to summarily deal with an issue in a concise and unsigned opinion that signifies the general authority of the Court.

PERKS

Elected officials enjoy many benefits of office, known as perquisites, or "perks." Members of Congress send mail free of charge, park in special lots at Washington airports, and are reimbursed for trips they make to their home state and abroad. At the Capitol they have special subways, elevators, restaurants, low-cost gymnasiums, shops that offer discount-price supplies, and free plants from the Botanical Gardens to decorate their offices. Some congressional leaders are also assigned cars and drivers.

Critics of perks argue that the people's representatives should not receive special privileges at the taxpayers' expense. But questions arise about what privileges are necessary for the performance of congressional duties. Members need to keep in close contact with their constituents, which requires extensive communication and travel. They maintain homes in Washington and in their home state and have to decide where to raise their family. They must get to the floor quickly to vote, and their crowded daily schedules give them little time to shop, dine, or even get their hair trimmed away from the Capitol. They exercise in the Capitol gyms to keep fit and to relieve the stress of their job.

Over the years, members have viewed perks in different ways. In the 1st Congress James Madison declined to accept the free stationery supplies provided to each representative but noted that he was "the sole exception." In the 1920s a reporter tried to question Senator William E. Borah (Republican–Idaho) about the then-free haircuts for members. Borah grumbled, "You tell that reporter to go to the devil. I want the same service that was received here by Henry Clay and John C. Calhoun." But periodic criticism by the press and by constituents has caused Congress to abandon such perks as free haircuts and shaving mugs so that they are more in line with costs elsewhere. In 1992 the House abolished its 150-year-old bank after published reports revealed that members had been able to bounce checks—that is, write checks for more money than they had deposited—without penalty. Although no public funds were involved, voters saw the House bank scandal as just another example of a perk that allowed members of Congress to operate under different rules than did average citizens.

Presidential perks   Presidents receive perks that entitle them to special extensions of power. Certain luxuries, such as the fully staffed White House residence, Camp David retreat, *Air Force One,* and presidential helicopters and limousines, are provided as much to symbolize presidential power as to facilitate the conduct of official business. In addition to their salaries, Presidents receive generous expense accounts to pay for official entertaining and travel, and they retire with a pension and a government-funded office and staff. Former Presidents and their spouses are also entitled to Secret Service protection. Recent Presidents have all established Presidential libraries to house their papers and to commemorate the accomplishments of their administrations. Although constructed with private money, the libraries are maintained by the federal government under the jurisdiction of the National Archives and Records Administration.

SEE ALSO *House bank scandal (1992)*

PERSIAN GULF DEBATE (1991)

After Iraq invaded Kuwait in August 1990, threatening the world's oil supplies, President George Bush sent U.S. troops to the Persian Gulf. Claiming this was a defensive action—and calling it Operation Desert Shield—to protect neighboring Saudi Arabia, the President did not initially ask for congressional approval. But in January 1991 the President sought congressional approval to use military force—Operation Desert Storm—in support of United Nations resolutions that set a deadline for Iraq to withdraw from Kuwait.

Recalling that in 1964 the Gulf of Tonkin Resolution had led to the Vietnam War, senators and representatives recognized that their approval would be the equivalent of a declaration of war. With a large national audience watching on television, Congress held a dramatic debate over the Persian Gulf Resolution. Most Republicans supported the President, while most Democrats favored continuing the use of economic sanctions against Iraq. But enough Democrats joined Republicans to pass the Persian Gulf Resolution by a vote of 52 to 47 in the Senate and 250 to 183 in the House. Combat began four days later, and U.S.-led forces drove Iraq out of Kuwait.

Notable in this incident was Congress's failure to invoke the War Powers Act, which raised serious doubts about that act's effectiveness. Under the War Powers Act, military troops must be withdrawn from combat after 60 days unless Congress has declared war or otherwise authorized the use of military force. The President's supporters in Congress believed that applying the War Powers Act would limit his ability to act. Opponents of the war feared that triggering the War Powers Act would actually sanction the use of the military in combat for 60 days. Therefore, neither side called for enforcement of the War Powers Act.

SEE ALSO *Gulf of Tonkin Resolution (1964); War powers*

PETITION, CITIZENS' RIGHT TO

The 1st Amendment to the Constitution guarantees citizens the right "to petition the Government for a redress of grievances." People have readily exercised this right, sending Congress petitions on any number of issues. A petitioner can be a single individual or a long list of signatures. In the early 19th century, reformers petitioned Congress to ban alcohol, abolish slavery, and give the vote to women. After the Civil War, many individuals (known as claimants) petitioned the government for military pensions or for compensation for property destroyed during the war. During the depression of the late 1920s

and 1930s, Congress received petitions to improve roads, censor the movies, and provide economic relief.

When citizens write to their senators and representatives for help with their Social Security payments, veterans' pensions, and other problems with the bureaucracy, they are utilizing their right to petition.

PHYSICIAN TO THE PRESIDENT

From George Washington's administration through Andrew Jackson's, Presidents used their own doctors, who brought in specialists when necessary. Jackson and many of his successors, especially after the Civil War, relied on military physicians, who provided care to the First Family without charge.

In modern times Presidents have used a combination of private and military doctors. The President's personal doctor and several military assistants and nurses form the White House Medical Unit. Their facilities include a medical suite in the White House itself and facilities in the Executive Office Building, where there is also a dental suite.

The President has medical checkups and is treated for illness at Walter Reed Army Hospital or Bethesda Naval Medical Center. When the President travels, a doctor is part of his entourage and an emergency medical unit is available at all times. A blood supply for the President is always available at a local hospital, and an ambulance is often stationed near the most convenient exit from the place where the President is staying.

SEE ALSO *Disability, Presidential; Health, Presidential; Succession to the Presidency*
SOURCES Robert E. Gilbert, *The Mortal Presidency* (New York: Basic Books, 1992). Thomas C. Wiegele, "Presidential Physicians and Presidential Health Care," *Presidential Studies Quarterly* 20 (Winter 1990): 71–89.

PIERCE, FRANKLIN
14th President

- Born: Nov. 23, 1804, Hillsborough, N.H.
- Political party: Democrat
- Education: Bowdoin College, B.A., 1824
- Military service: New Hampshire Volunteers, 1846–48
- Previous government service: New Hampshire House of Representatives, 1829–33; U.S. House of Representatives, 1834–36; U.S. Senate, 1837–42; U.S. attorney for New Hampshire, 1842–46
- Elected President, 1852; served, 1853–57
- Died: Oct. 8, 1869, Concord, N.H.

Franklin Pierce's Presidency was marked by family tragedy. Two months before Pierce assumed office, his son Benjamin was killed in a railroad accident. Mrs. Pierce did not attend her husband's inauguration, and she secluded herself in the White House for two years. She wore black mourning clothes each day and refused to take part in Washington life. Distracted by his wife's grief, Pierce was an ineffectual leader in domestic and foreign affairs.

Franklin Pierce was the son of Benjamin Pierce, a revolutionary war hero who was twice elected governor of New Hampshire. Franklin attended Bowdoin College, where he became friendly with Nathaniel Hawthorne, who later wrote his biography. At age 23 he became a lawyer and began his own spectacular rise in state Democratic politics, becoming speaker of the state legislature at age 26. He then served several terms in Congress, where he strongly supported the policies of President Andrew Jackson, especially the veto of the national bank. He became a U.S. senator at age 36. Pierce served in the Mexican-American War as a brigadier general of volunteers from his state under the overall command of General Winfield Scott and was injured at the Battle of Contreras when he fell off his horse. He re-

turned to his New Hampshire law practice at the end of the war.

Pierce was a dark-horse contender for the Democratic nomination in 1852. The convention deadlocked between leading candidates James Buchanan and Lewis Cass, and Pierce was the convention's compromise choice on the 49th ballot. He defeated General Scott, who had won the Whig nomination, by a large margin, in a campaign that emphasized sectional unity. His sweep of states (he lost just four) was the greatest landslide since the election of James Monroe. It began the disintegration of the Whig party. At age 48, Pierce had capped his political career by becoming the youngest President up to that time.

Pierce tried to give the South a major role in his administration by appointing Jefferson Davis from Mississippi as his secretary of war and a coalition of Southern planters and Northern financiers to his cabinet, none of whom wished to push the abolitionist cause. Pierce and the cabinet agreed on most issues: he made not a single change of personnel during his entire term.

Pierce used federal law enforcement to implement the Fugitive Slave Act, which required federal and state officials to assist slave owners in recovering slaves who had fled to free states in the North. He encouraged the construction of transcontinental railroads to bind the nation together, and the Gadsden Purchase from Mexico (for $10 million) was made with a new southern rail link in mind. In 1854 Pierce signed the Kansas-Nebraska Act, establishing new territorial governments and ending the Missouri Compromise. It provided that when the Kansas and Nebraska territories applied for statehood, their citizens would determine whether or not the state would be free or slave. Soon Kansas was in flames as pro-slavery "border ruffians" and fiery abolitionists such as John Brown fought over its future.

Pierce blundered in foreign affairs. He believed that territorial expansion might be a way to unite North and South. In his inaugural address he hinted at his goal of annexing Cuba, and he even had his Vice President take his inaugural oath on that island. Pierce instructed the U.S. ministers to Spain, Great Britain, and France to meet in Ostend, Belgium, to prepare recommendations about the possible purchase of Cuba from Spain. Their memorandum to Pierce, known as the Ostend Manifesto, proposed to offer the Spanish up to $110 million, but it advocated an invasion to seize the island if the Spanish refused to sell. The secret dispatch was leaked to Whig newspapers, causing great embarrassment to the administration and aborting diplomatic efforts for the sale.

Pierce was more successful in opening Japan to foreign trade through the expedition of Commodore Matthew Perry in 1853. In 1856 Pierce recognized a dictatorship in Nicaragua established by William Walker, an American who had taken over that nation by force and had begun to introduce slavery as a prelude to having Nicaragua apply for admission to the Union as a slave state. Although an expansionist, Pierce rejected Hawaii's application to join the Union, though he agreed to a request by King Kamehameha to place the islands under U.S. protection from European powers seeking conquest or trade concessions.

Because of his domestic and foreign policy blunders, Pierce was ignored at the Democratic convention of 1856, and he returned to Concord, New Hampshire. During the Civil War he gained local notoriety by opposing the policies of the Republican party and claiming that the Emancipation Proclamation was unconstitutional.

SEE ALSO Buchanan, James
SOURCES Larry Gara, *The Presidency of Franklin Pierce* (Lawrence: University Press of Kansas, 1991). Roy Franklin Nichols, *Franklin Pierce: Young Hickory of the Granite Hills* (Philadelphia: University of Pennsylvania Press, 1958).

PITNEY, MAHLON
Associate Justice, 1912–22

- Born: Feb. 5, 1858, Morristown, N.J.
- Education: College of New Jersey (Princeton), B.A., 1879, M.A., 1882
- Previous government service: U.S. representative from New Jersey, 1895–99; New Jersey Senate, 1899–1901; president, New Jersey Senate, 1901; associate justice, New Jersey Supreme Court, 1901–8; chancellor of New Jersey, 1908–12
- Appointed by President William Howard Taft Feb. 19, 1912; replaced John Marshall Harlan, who died
- Supreme Court term: confirmed by the Senate Mar. 13, 1912, by a 50–26 vote; retired Dec. 31, 1922
- Died: Dec. 9, 1924, Washington, D.C.

Mahlon Pitney was a strong supporter of individual rights, especially economic liberty and property rights. He tended to oppose strong government regulation of economic activities. He, however, tended to support limits on freedom of expression when it appeared to threaten national security. In *Pierce* v. *United States* (1920), for example, Justice Pitney upheld the prosecution of individuals under the Espionage Act of 1917 because their freedom of expression, he argued, threatened the security of the U.S. government.

Justice Pitney believed that the individual's right to contract was the most important constitutional right. He, therefore, tended to oppose the interests of labor unions as a threat to the economic liberty of individuals. However, he showed great concern for compensation of workers injured at the workplace. In *New York Railroad Company* v. *White* (1917) and several subsequent cases, Justice Pitney upheld state government laws that required employers to compensate workers for injuries suffered during their employment.

PLEA BARGAINING

Plea bargaining is the process by which a person accused of a crime may bargain with the prosecutor to receive a lesser punishment. Typically, the accused person will plead guilty, sometimes to a lesser charge than the original one (to manslaughter rather than murder, for example). This process saves the government the time and cost of a jury trial in exchange for a reduced sentence.

Defendants who plead guilty as part of a plea bargain give up three constitutional rights: the right of trial by jury, the right to confront and question one's accusers, and the right to refuse to incriminate oneself. In *Boykin* v. *Alabama* (1969) the Court ruled that plea bargaining is constitutional as long as the defendant gives up his constitutional rights voluntarily and with full comprehension of the trade-offs of the deal.

PLESSY V. FERGUSON

- 163 U.S. 537 (1896)
- Vote: 7–1
- For the Court: Brown
- Dissenting: Harlan
- Not participating: Brewer

The ratification of the 13th Amendment in 1865, shortly after the end of the Civil War, abolished slavery in the United States. However, prejudices against blacks remained strong. Southern states began to pass laws to keep blacks separated from whites. A group of black leaders in Louisiana formed a Citizens' Committee to deliberately test the constitutionality of one such law, the Separate Car Law.

Acting for the Citizens' Committee, Homer Plessy, a Louisiana resident who was one-eighth black, bought a first-class ticket for a train in Louisiana. Plessy took a seat in the railroad car reserved for whites only, ignoring the coach marked "colored only." When Plessy refused to move to the coach reserved for "colored," he was arrested. He had violated the Louisiana law requiring separate railroad accommodations for blacks and whites.

The Citizens' Committee and Plessy claimed the Louisiana law denied him the "equal protection of the laws" guaranteed by the 14th Amendment. Plessy's lawyers also claimed the law violated the 13th Amendment ban on slavery by destroying the legal equality of the races and, in effect, reintroducing slavery.

The Issue Did a state law requiring segregation of the races violate the 13th Amendment ban on slavery or the 14th Amendment guarantee of equal protection of the laws for all citizens?

Opinion of the Court The Supreme Court ruled against Plessy. The Court held that the "equal protection of the laws" clause of the 14th Amendment allowed a state to provide "separate but equal" facilities for blacks. Justice Henry Brown wrote that the 14th Amendment aimed "to enforce the absolute equality of the two races before the law, but in the nature of things it could not have been intended to abolish distinctions based upon color, or to enforce social . . . equality."

The Court also ruled that the Louisiana law did not violate the 13th Amendment ban on slavery. Brown said a law "which implies merely a legal distinction between the white and colored races . . . has no tendency to . . . reestablish a state of involuntary servitude [slavery]."

Dissent Justice John M. Harlan dissented in the *Plessy* decision. Harlan, a native of Kentucky and a former slaveholder, argued strongly against dividing people by race. He declared, "[I]n the eye of the law there is in this country no superior, dominant, ruling class of citizens. There is no caste here. Our Constitution is color-blind and neither knows nor tolerates classes among citizens." Justice Harlan's view finally prevailed in 1954, when the Supreme Court overruled the *Plessy* decision in the case of *Brown* v. *Board of Education*.

Significance The "separate but equal" doctrine established by the Court served to justify segregation in many states for the next half century. The *Plessy* decision reinforced state-ordered segregation, which had become a fact of life in the southern states. State laws required blacks to use separate toilets, water fountains, streetcars, and waiting rooms. Blacks had to attend different schools and remained separated from whites in prisons, hospitals, parks, theaters, and other public facilities. By 1920 segregation regulated every facet of life in the South. Blacks and whites could not eat at the same restaurants, stay in the same hotels, use the same elevators, or visit the same beaches, swimming pools, or amusement parks. Blacks and whites attended separate public schools, and in some states at the end of each school year the school board had to store the books from black schools separately from the books from white schools. One state required the segregation of public telephones, while another prohibited blacks and whites from playing checkers together.

Born in segregated hospitals, educated in segregated schools, employed at workplaces that kept blacks and whites separated, and buried in the segregated cemeteries of segregated churches, the people of the South endured the all-pervasive influence of segregation. The separation of the races was one of the most important aspects of southern life. *Plessy* v. *Ferguson* gave this entire system legitimacy. Although that decision established the well-known doctrine of "separate but equal," in actual practice separate but *unequal* was the rule throughout the South.

The "separate but equal" doctrine was upheld by Supreme Court rulings for the next 50 years. For decades, however, the Court refused to examine the actual conditions in the South to determine if equality existed along with separateness. Not until the 1930s and 1940s did the Supreme Court begin to enforce the "equal" part of the doctrine. And not until 1954 did the Court directly face the more basic question of whether separating whites and blacks

was an inherently discriminating act that by nature ensured unequal treatment. In *Brown* v. *Board of Education* (1954), the Court overturned the *Plessy* decision, declaring, in a now-famous phrase, "Separate educational facilities are inherently unequal."

SEE ALSO *Brown v. Board of Education; Civil rights; Equality under the Constitution; Segregation, de facto and de jure*

SOURCES Andrew Kull, "The 14th Amendment That Wasn't," *Constitution* 5, no. 1 (Winter 1993): 68–75. Brook Thomas, ed., *Plessy v. Ferguson: A Brief History with Documents* (New York: St. Martin's, 1996). C. Vann Woodward, "The Case of the Louisiana Traveler," in *Quarrels That Have Shaped the Constitution,* edited by John A. Garraty (New York: Harper & Row, 1987).

PLURALITY OPINION

The U.S. Supreme Court decides cases by majority vote; more than half of the justices participating must vote in favor of the decision. If the justices in the majority agree to sign a single opinion, they produce a majority opinion for the Court. Now and then, however, there are so many individual concurring opinions that the opinion that garners the most votes is called not a majority opinion but a plurality opinion.

For example, in *Dennis* v. *United States* (1951), the Court decided the case by a vote of 6 to 2 (one justice did not participate). Two justices wrote separate concurring opinions and thereby made it impossible for there to be a single majority opinion for the Court. Instead, there was a plurality opinion (signed by four justices), supported in many respects by two justices' concurring opinions, and opposed by the other two justices' dissenting opinions. Thus, Chief Justice Vinson announced the decision of the Court based on a plurality opinion.

SEE ALSO *Concurring opinion; Dissenting*

opinion; Majority opinion; Opinions of the Supreme Court

POCKET VETO

The pocket veto is the power of the President to veto a bill sent to him within the 10-day period prior to congressional adjournment, without any possibility of a congressional override. The Constitution (Article 1, Section 7) provides that if Congress passes a bill and sends it to the President, he has 10 days in which to veto the bill and return it with his objections. But if Congress adjourns within that 10-day period, the President cannot return the bill with a veto message and any bill that has already been sent to the President is automatically vetoed unless he decides to sign it into law. The end-of-session pocket veto (named for the practice of putting the bill in the President's pocket until Congress adjourns) cannot be overridden by a two-thirds vote of each chamber; it is irreversible. The President sends no message to Congress indicating his objections to the measure, nor does he return the bill to either chamber for further action. A new bill must be introduced and go through the entire legislative process.

In the *Pocket Veto Case* (1929), the Supreme Court decided that "adjournment" meant not only end-of-session adjournments but could also mean recesses, or district work periods, within a congressional session. The key issue was not whether Congress intended to return but whether its absence prevented return of the bill within the designated 10-day period.

Presidents have sometimes abused the pocket veto. They have killed measures when Congress adjourned or recessed for short periods, even when Congress intended to return within 10 days and could easily have received the President's regular veto message. Both Presidents Richard Nixon and Gerald Ford used the pocket veto during interim adjournments of a few days during a session of Congress—Nixon

to kill a health care bill and Ford to veto vocational rehabilitation, farm labor, and wildlife refuge measures. Congress responded to this misuse of the pocket veto by designating officers in each chamber to receive veto messages from the President, thereby attempting to retain the ordinary veto system. In the 1970s Senate leaders began the practice of waiting until Congress returned from short recesses before sending bills it had passed to the White House in order to avoid the entire issue.

In 1974 the U.S. Court of Appeals for Washington, D.C., ruling in *Kennedy* v. *Sampson,* barred the President's use of the pocket veto during short congressional recesses, provided an officer was appointed by Congress to receive an ordinary Presidential veto message.

SEE ALSO *Checks and balances; Veto power*
SOURCES U.S. Congress, Senate Committee on the Judiciary, Subcommittee on Separation of Powers, *Constitutionality of the President's Pocket Veto Power* (92nd Cong., 1st sess., 1971). Clement Vose, "The Memorandum Pocket Veto," *Journal of Politics* 26, no. 2 (May 1964): 397–405.

POINT OF ORDER

SEE *Precedents, congressional*

POLITICAL ACTION COMMITTEES (PACS)

SEE *Campaign financing, congressional*

POLITICAL PARTIES IN CONGRESS

The authors of the U.S. Constitution hoped that the federal government could avoid political parties. They wanted a government run by independent-minded people who served out of a sense of civic virtue. They envisioned parties ("factions") as the tool of the politically ambitious and as a source of corruption. However, not long after the new government began, many of those who opposed parties became the founders and leaders of political parties. They discovered that a two-party system could contribute to the constitutional system of checks and balances. The competing parties would help keep any one group from becoming powerful enough to threaten citizens' rights.

First parties in Congress Although they were not as organized as modern political parties, identifiable parties first emerged in the 1790s. The Federalist party consolidated those who supported the policies of the Washington administration, particularly the financial program of Treasury Secretary Alexander Hamilton. In 1792 James Madison and Thomas Jefferson launched an opposition Democratic-Republican party, which gained the majority in the House of Representatives that year. Opposing a strong, activist central government, Democratic-Republicans rallied against Hamilton's programs. Their strength in Congress came largely from Southern and Western districts, while the Federalists were strongest in New England. By 1800 political caucuses in Congress were selecting their party's Presidential candidates. The Federalist party shrank steadily until it expired in the essentially one-party Era of Good Feelings after the War of 1812.

The second party system During the 1820s the political system split apart again. Denouncing "King Caucus"—the congressionally dominated system of nominating Presidential candidates—Andrew Jackson won the Presidency in 1828. Behind the scenes, New York Senator Martin Van Buren built a new political instrument, the Democratic party, to support Jackson's policies. Jackson's veto of a bill renewing the charter of the Bank of the United States in 1832 led to the rise of the opposition Whig party. Kentucky Senator Henry Clay served as the Whigs' leader in Congress. By the 1840s the two parties had become such

permanent fixtures on Capitol Hill that they took over the assignment of senators and representatives to committees and shaped much of the daily operations of Congress. Party leaders began to emerge in the House, while senators continued to insist that because they were all equal, they needed no formal leadership. The Democrats and Whigs were both national parties—that is, they elected members from every region of the country. Then, in the 1850s, agitation over the slavery issue disrupted these national coalitions. New parties such as the Free Soil and American (Know-Nothing) parties emerged but did not attract a majority of the voters. By 1856 the new Republican party had absorbed these smaller parties and supplanted the Whigs as the chief opposition to the Democrats.

Republicans versus Democrats The election of 1860, followed by the secession of the Southern states, gave the Republicans control of the White House and the majority in both houses of Congress. The Republicans remained the majority party for the rest of the 19th century, although after the last of the Southern states had been readmitted to the Union in 1870, Democrats often controlled one of the houses of Congress. The "solid South," consisting of the 11 former Confederate states, remained overwhelmingly Democratic. The North, with the exception of such major cities as New York and Boston, remained overwhelmingly Republican. Border states and some Midwestern and Western states swung back and forth, changing the majorities in Congress. When the Republican party's conservative and progressive wings split apart in 1912 (with Theodore Roosevelt leading the progressives in a campaign for greater social, economic, and political reform), Woodrow Wilson won the Presidency and Democrats captured the House and Senate. Six years later the Republicans regained their congressional majorities, which they held until the stock market crash of 1929 and the Great Depression that followed. It was during the 1920s that the two parties formally elected majority and minority leaders in the Senate.

The long Democratic majority In the 1930s New Deal programs to combat the depression won widespread popular approval, and Democratic majorities in Congress grew to enormous proportions. At their peak, after the 1936 election, there were 76 Democrats in the Senate (opposed to 16 Republicans and 4 independents) and 334 Democrats in the House (opposed to 88 Republicans and 13 independents). For the next six decades, with only rare exceptions, the Democrats retained their majorities in Congress, even when they lost the White House to the Republicans.

Third parties Although a two-party system has prevailed through most of American history, many third parties have appeared and have elected members to Congress. Third parties generally have had more success in winning election in smaller House districts than in statewide Senate races. In the 19th century, the Anti-Masonic, Nullifiers, American (Know-Nothing), Free Soil, States' Rightists, Unionists, Constitutional Union, Liberal Republican, National (Greenback), People's (Populist), and Silver Republican parties all sent members to Congress. Third parties in the 20th century have included the Socialist, Progressive (Bull Moose), Prohibition, and Conservative parties.

If a third party is large enough, its members can form their own caucus, as the Progressives did after the 1912 election. But usually they are too few in number and choose to join either the Republican or Democratic caucus, which will give them their committee assignments. The major parties are not always tolerant of third parties, however. Victor Berger of Wisconsin became the first Socialist elected to Congress, serving in the House from 1911 to 1913. Although he was elected again in 1918 and 1920, the House refused to let him take his seat because of his opposition to U.S. participation in World War I.

SEE ALSO *Caucuses, congressional*
SOURCES Kenneth C. Martis, *The Historical Atlas of Political Parties in the United States Congress, 1789–1989* (New York: Macmillan, 1989).

POLITICAL QUESTIONS

The Supreme Court may decide not to accept a case because it involves what it considers to be political questions, which are outside the scope of the Court's authority. Political questions may include problems clearly in the domain of Congress or the President. These are questions that, in the Court's opinion, defy resolution on legal or constitutional grounds. For example, the Court has ruled that the President, not the Court, should determine whether the United States should recognize a certain foreign government.

The political questions doctrine is a limitation that the Court has imposed upon its own powers of judicial review. Only the Supreme Court itself decides which cases involve political questions, thereby disqualifying them for review and judgment by the Court. Such political questions are referred to as non-justiciable. Justiciable questions, by contrast, are those the Supreme Court accepts as appropriate for its review and judgment.

In *Pacific States Telephone & Telegraph v. Oregon* (1912), the Court faced an issue that it decided was outside the scope of judicial review. The issue pertained to Article 4, Section 4, of the Constitution, which says, "The United States shall guarantee to every State in the Union a Republican Form of Government. . . ." The Pacific States Telephone & Telegraph Company argued that the state of Oregon was enacting laws in a non-republican manner, which violated Article 4, Section 4. The state had passed a tax of 2 percent on the income of all telephone and telegraph companies in the state. This tax law was passed through a popular initiative and referendum, not strictly and exclusively by the state legislature. The people of the state used an initiative to petition the government to pass the tax law; in response to this initiative, the voters of Oregon were permitted to decide in a public election (a referendum, which was also called for by the voters) whether to pass the law.

SEE ALSO *Judicial power; Judicial review; Justiciable questions*

POLK, JAMES K.
11th President

- Born: Nov. 2, 1795, Mecklenburg County, N.C.
- Political party: Democrat
- Education: University of North Carolina, B.A., 1818
- Military service: none
- Previous government service: Tennessee House of Representatives, 1823–25; U.S. House of Representatives, 1825–39; Speaker of the House, 1835–39; governor of Tennessee, 1839–40
- Elected President, 1844; served, 1845–49
- Died: June 15, 1849, Nashville, Tenn.

James K. Polk was a Jacksonian Democrat whose expansionist policies led to the Mexican-American War and the acquisition of vast territories in the Southwest. He was the first President to decline to seek a second term.

Polk was born on a small farm on the North Carolina frontier. His father became a large landowner in Tennessee and Polk was able to attend college. Two years after graduating he began to practice law in Columbia, Tennessee. Polk began his political career by serving with Andrew Jackson in the Tennessee legislature, and later he was the leading spokesman in Congress for the Jackson administration, serving as majority leader of the Democrats and chair of the powerful Ways and Means Committee. He was elected Speaker in 1835. He helped to secure the repeal of the Second Bank of the United States, earning the name Young

Hickory because of his support for the President, Old Hickory. In 1839 he won election as governor of Tennessee but was defeated in the 1841 and 1843 elections.

Polk made a political comeback in Presidential politics in 1844. He favored the annexation of the independent nation of Texas and negotiations with Great Britain to acquire territory in the Northwest, which later became known as the Oregon Territory. He received Jackson's support over John Tyler, who opposed annexing Texas. Polk was the Democratic party's first dark horse, or unknown nominee, winning in a sectional compromise on the ninth ballot. The word was sent from Baltimore to the capital by telegraph—the first use by a political party of Samuel F. B. Morse's new invention—and the recipients thought the machine was not working because it seemed so improbable that Polk was the nominee.

In the Presidential election Polk's rival, Whig candidate Henry Clay, exclaimed, "Who is James K. Polk?" The Democrats took up the question as a defiant campaign slogan, and in a fierce campaign Polk defeated Clay, receiving 49.6 percent of the popular vote to Clay's 48.1. At age 49 he was the youngest person yet to serve as President.

Polk's Presidency was distinguished for its expansionist policies. Polk claimed it was the "manifest destiny" of the nation to expand from the Atlantic to the Pacific. He added more territory to the Union than any President except Thomas Jefferson. His quiet diplomacy secured an 1846 boundary agreement with Great Britain that settled the northern borders of the United States along the 49th parallel; the United States and Britain each gave up about half their claims. His policy was more warlike in the Southwest. Even before Polk's inauguration, his predecessor, John Tyler, claimed that the election was a mandate to annex Texas, and he supported a joint resolution of Congress to start the procedure. Texas entered the Union in December 1845, which caused Mexico to sever diplomatic relations with the United States. Polk's attempts to buy California and disputed Texas territory from Mexico for $25 million were rebuffed: the Mexicans would not permit U.S. envoys to present their proposal. In late 1845 Polk ordered 3,000 U.S. troops under the command of Zachary Taylor into a disputed border area between the Rio Grande and Rio Nueces in the state of Texas.

On May 9, 1846, Polk laid before his cabinet a proposal for a declaration of war, on the grounds that Mexico had refused to receive his envoy and had refused to pay damage claims for losses of U.S. lives and property. Just that evening, word reached the capital that there had been a skirmish between Mexican and U.S. forces that had resulted in death or injury to 16 U.S. soldiers. Polk had Congress declare war on May 13, 1846, saying that Mexican forces had "invaded our territory and shed American blood upon the American soil." In fact, the events occurred in disputed territory after U.S. forces trained their cannons on the town square of Matamoros.

The war was a military success: General Winfield Scott captured Mexico City on September 14, 1847, while Colonel Stephen Kearny took control of New Mexico and California. The Treaty of Guadalupe Hidalgo, signed February 2, 1848, ended the war. The United States took possession of the Mexican provinces of Upper California and New Mexico, and the two countries established a border at the Rio Grande in Texas. Polk agreed to pay Mexico $15 million for the territories and also to pay $3,250,000 in claims made by U.S. citizens against Mexico. Nevertheless, the treaty was unpopular with abolitionists in the North, who saw it as a way to extend slavery. Ulysses S. Grant, who served in the war, called it "one of the most unjust ever waged by a stronger against a weaker nation." Abraham Lincoln, a Whig member of Congress at the time, devoted his first speech in the House of Representatives to criticizing Polk's decision, saying that Mexico "was in no way molesting or menacing the United States." Needless to say, the Mexicans have never forgotten Polk for taking away half their nation. In 1848 Polk's effort to buy Cuba for $100 million was rejected by Spain.

In domestic policy, Polk secured passage of the Walker Tariff Act of 1846, which reduced tariffs, or taxes on imported products, and thus fulfilled a campaign promise popular in the South and among farmers. He later blocked the Whig programs of high tariffs, federally funded internal improvements, and a national bank, which the Whigs proposed when they took control of Congress in the midterm elections of 1846. Polk also vetoed measures to use federal funds to improve rivers and harbors.

Polk alienated the antislavery faction of his party with his Mexican policy. He opposed the Wilmot Proviso, a congressional measure intended to bar slavery from the territories newly conquered from Mexico but that failed to pass. His own idea to extend the Missouri Compromise line west and bar slavery below the 36th parallel was ignored. Congress was unable to pass laws governing the new territories because of the slavery issue. Polk was exhausted from his efforts to hold his party together and fend off the Whig majority in Congress, and decided not to seek a second term. His last message to Congress spoke of an "abundance of gold" in California, setting off the gold rush of 1849. Polk died during a cholera epidemic shortly after leaving office.

SEE ALSO *Jackson, Andrew; Tyler, John; Van Buren, Martin*

SOURCES Paul H. Bergeron, *The Presidency of James K. Polk* (Lawrence: University Press of Kansas, 1987). Charles Greer Sellers, *James K. Polk, Continentalist, 1843–1846* (Princeton, N.J.: Princeton University Press, 1966).

POLLS, PRESIDENTIAL

SEE *Public opinion*

POPULAR SOVEREIGNTY

Popular sovereignty is government based on the consent of the people. Government, established by free choice of the people, is expected to serve the people, who have sovereignty, or supreme power.

Popular sovereignty is the basis of constitutional government in the United States. The U.S. Constitution clearly establishes government in the name of the people. The preamble says: "We the people of the United States . . . do ordain and establish this Constitution for the United States of America."

Popular sovereignty was exercised according to Article 7 of the Constitution, which required that nine states approve the proposed frame of government before it could become the supreme law of the United States. The people chose representatives to ratification conventions who freely decided to approve the Constitution in the name of those who elected them. Popular sovereignty was also recognized in Article 5 of the Constitution, which provides for amendments to the Constitution through decisions by elected representatives of the people. Finally, popular sovereignty is reflected in Article 1, which requires that representatives to Congress be elected by the people.

Popular sovereignty, or government by the people, implies majority rule. People elect representatives in government by majority vote, and these representatives of the people make laws by majority vote.

SEE ALSO *Constitutional democracy; Constitutionalism; Republicanism*

SOURCES Edmund S. Morgan, *Inventing the People: The Rise of Popular Sovereignty in England and America* (New York: Norton, 1988).

PORK BARREL POLITICS

When members of Congress try to gain federal funds for projects in their district or state, they are often accused of playing "pork barrel politics." This curious expression dates back to the days of plantation slavery before the Civil War, when field hands dipped into large barrels of salt pork for their food. Similarly, those senators and representatives who win special projects for their constituents are "bringing home the bacon."

Legislation authorizing improvements in rivers and harbors, flood control and dams, construction of federal buildings, and highway construction traditionally caused members to scramble to get something in for their state or district. More recently, energy and defense appropriations bills have attracted pork barrel amendments. Members of Congress defend their pork barrel efforts as a way of more evenly distributing federal money throughout the nation. But critics charge that Congress often diverts funds to projects and places not out of national need but to enhance members' chances of reelection. Senator Norris Cotton (Republican–New Hampshire), who served on the Appropriations Committee, spoke for many when he called pork barrel politics "one of the worst features of the whole system of federal grants and subsidies."

Pork barrel politics has become associated with a variety of colorful legislative terms. When members seize upon a bill that the President is likely to sign into law and then add pork barrel amendments, it is called a "Christmas tree" bill. Special projects are hung upon the bill the way ornaments adorn a Christmas tree. When Congress specifies exactly where and how federal money should be spent—for example, specifying the awarding of a grant to a certain university to conduct weapons research—it is "earmarking" the funds, just as some farm animals are marked on the ear to identify who owns them. And when members trade their votes for each other's pork barrel projects, the practice is called "logrolling." This expression dates back to the frontier practice of neighbors working together to clear their farmland and gather logs for building their homes, barns, and fences. Whoever helped his neighbors in logrolling would receive their help in return.

SOURCES Norris Cotton, *In the Senate: Amidst the Conflict and the Turmoil* (New York: Dodd, Mead, 1978).

POSTMODERN PRESIDENCY

The postmodern Presidency is a term used by some political scientists to describe the Presidential office since Jimmy Carter's administration of the late 1970s. They argue that the White House does not have the fiscal or political resources necessary to meet the President's international responsibilities. In large measure this is because of the increased relative economic strength of other industrial nations, which prevents the United States from dominating international trade and finance, and the lack of American public support for foreign aid and other international commitments.

To succeed in the White House, the President must operate in a world of increasing international interdependency rather than U.S. superiority. The President must cooperate with other nations rather than act unilaterally; he must understand the limits of U.S. economic, diplomatic, and military power and keep U.S. commitments in balance; he must obtain support in the international community for U.S. goals from other world leaders and international organizations such as the United Nations, the North Atlantic Treaty Organization, and the Group of Seven Industrialized Nations.

According to Richard Rose, a political scientist at the University of Strathclyde, Scotland, postmodern Presidents can be classified as follows: world leaders who have a strong influence on policy and have the support of the international community; vulnerable Presidents who have great policy influence but are opposed by much of the international community; isolated Presidents who have support from around the world but face opposition within the United States; and failing Presidents who have neither foreign nor domestic support.

Presidents may, during the course of their terms, fit into more than one of these categories. George Bush was a *world leader* during the Persian Gulf War because he forged an international coalition at the United Nations that voted to use force if necessary to repel Iraqi aggression. Members of the coalition then contributed money and armed forces to the effort. He was also a world leader in his efforts to ensure the safety of relief workers delivering food to the starving people of Somalia.

In contrast, Jimmy Carter was an *isolated President* when he tried to promote a policy of energy independence. He was unable to win public or congressional support for his initiatives and was also opposed by many foreign nations. His failure to impose serious conservation measures contributed to continued U.S. dependence on foreign oil.

Ronald Reagan was a *vulnerable President* in much of his foreign policy. He had considerable support within the United States for increased defense expenditures and development of the Star Wars antimissile system, but he lacked support from many allies for these policies. Reagan was a *global failure* in his policy of trying to overthrow the Sandinista regime in Nicaragua. His funding of the Contra opposition violated the law and was not supported by a majority of the American people.

SEE ALSO *Bush, George; Carter, Jimmy; Reagan, Ronald*

SOURCES Richard Rose, *The Postmodern President*, 2nd ed. (Chatham, N.J.: Chatham House, 1991).

POWELL, ADAM CLAYTON, JR.

- Born: Nov. 29, 1908, New Haven, Conn.
- Political party: Democrat
- Education: Colgate University, graduated, 1930; Columbia University, graduated, 1932; Shaw University (theological department), graduated, 1934
- Representative from New York: 1945–67, 1969–71
- Died: Apr. 4, 1972, Miami, Fla.

Adam Clayton Powell excelled in the politics of confrontation. An African American, he won election to Congress in 1944, when racial segregation existed in much of the country and when Southerners who advocated white supremacy chaired most of the congressional committees. Instead of acting deferentially and seeking compromise, Powell ridiculed segregation, attacked discrimination, and promoted equality and civil rights at every opportunity. He set out to be an "irritant," believing that "whenever a person keeps prodding, keeps them squirming ... it serves a purpose." Between 1950 and 1960, he repeatedly attached a "Powell Amendment" to other bills, seeking to ban federal funds for segregated facilities.

Seniority eventually made him chairman of the House Committee on Education and Labor, where he managed many important bills. But Powell's antagonistic style worked better when he was an "outsider" rather than an "insider." Friends and enemies alike found him increasingly unreliable, and he was frequently absent from the House. In 1967, after much criticism of his behavior, the House removed Powell as committee chairman and voted not to seat him as a member. The Supreme Court ruled 7 to 1 that Powell's exclusion had been unconstitutional. He won his seat back in a special election. But by 1970 Powell's constituents had lost patience, and they defeated him in the Democratic primary when he ran for renomination.

SEE ALSO *African Americans in government; Insurgents*

SOURCES Charles Hamilton, *Adam Clayton Powell, Jr.: The Political Biography of an American Dilemma* (New York: Macmillan, 1991). Adam Clayton Powell, *Adam by Adam* (New York: Dial, 1971).

POWELL, LEWIS F., JR.
Associate Justice, 1972–87

- Born: Sept. 19, 1907, Suffolk, Va.
- Education: Washington and Lee University, B.S., 1929; Washington and Lee University Law School, LL.B., 1931; Harvard Law School, LL.M., 1932
- Previous government service: chairman, Richmond School Board, Va., 1952–61; Virginia State Board of Education, 1961–69; president, Virginia State Board of Education, 1968–69
- Appointed by President Richard Nixon Oct. 21, 1971; replaced Hugo L. Black, who retired
- Supreme Court term: confirmed by the Senate Dec. 6, 1971, by an 89–1 vote; retired June 26, 1987
- Died: Aug. 25, 1998, Richmond, Va.

Lewis F. Powell, Jr., belonged to a respected family with deep roots in Virginia. The first American Powell was one of the original settlers of Jamestown in 1607.

Though a member of the Virginia establishment, Powell opposed the long-established practice of racial segregation in the public schools. As chairman of the Richmond School Board, he presided over the peaceful integration of the city's schools in the wake of the *Brown* v. *Board of Education* (1954) decision. He also stood up to leading Virginians who resisted statewide integration of schools. As a member of the Virginia State Board of Education, he led the successful racial integration of the state's public schools.

As a justice of the Supreme Court, Powell tried to balance the needs of society against the rights of individuals. His most famous opinion for the Court was *Regents of the University of California* v. *Bakke* (1978), a case about the legality of a plan that provided special opportunities for minority group applicants (such as African Americans) to gain admission to the university. Powell characteristically sought the middle ground between competing claims for preferences based on race and equality of individual rights in decisions about whom to admit to the state university. Powell decided against the establishment of rigid racial quotas for minorities seeking admission to the university. However, he also upheld the principle of "affirmative action" as one factor, among others, that could be considered in making decisions about admitting students to the university. Affirmative action means making a special effort to provide opportunities for members of groups that had been discriminated against in the past. Considering the racial identity of an applicant as a positive factor in making a decision about student admissions could be done to compensate for the negative effects of past discrimination.

SEE ALSO *Regents of the University of California v. Bakke*

SOURCES Donna. Haupt, "A Justice Reflects," *Constitution* 2, no. 3 (Fall 1990): 16–25. Jacob W. Landynski, "Justice Lewis F. Powell, Jr.: Balance Wheel of the Court," in *The Burger Court: Political and Judicial Profiles,* edited by Charles M. Lamb and Stephen C. Halpern (Urbana: University of Illinois Press, 1991).

POWELL V. ALABAMA

- 287 U.S. 45 (1932)
- Vote: 7–2
- For the Court: Sutherland
- Dissenting: Butler and McReynolds

On March 25, 1931, nine African-American youths, ranging in age from 12 to 20, were arrested near Scottsboro, Alabama. They were accused of having raped two white women. A hostile crowd gathered outside the jail in Scottsboro and shouted insults at the young men.

The nine youths were quickly indicted and a trial date was set for six days later. The nine defendants were too poor to hire an attorney to represent them. According to Alabama law, the judge was required to appoint counsel to assist them because they were accused of a capital offense (a crime punishable by death). The judge responded to this legal requirement by declaring that every licensed lawyer in Scottsboro was assigned to represent the nine men. No one attorney, however, took personal responsibility for their defense.

On the day of the trial, two attorneys did show up to defend the accused youths. They asked the judge to postpone the trial so they could have time to prepare their defense. But the judge refused, and the lawyers had only 30 minutes before the trial started to consult with the defendants.

The trial was conducted quickly. Eight of the nine defendants were found guilty and sentenced to death. The jury was unable to reach a decision about one of the defendants.

The decision was appealed to the Alabama Supreme Court, which upheld the conviction of seven of the defendants. The conviction of one defendant was reversed because he was a juvenile (only 12 years old). The Alabama Supreme Court ruling with regard to the other seven was appealed to the U.S. Supreme Court.

The Issue The defendants, too poor to hire a lawyer, were tried, convicted, and sentenced to death without effective assistance of an attorney. However, the 14th Amendment to the U.S. Constitution says, "No state shall . . . deprive any person of life, liberty, or property, without due process of law."

Were due process rights denied to the

defendants in this case? Do people without means to obtain a lawyer have the right to counsel at the government's expense?

Opinion of the Court Writing for the Court, Justice George Sutherland overturned the convictions of the defendants. This decision was based on the due process clause of the 14th Amendment. Justice Sutherland argued that the right to counsel is an essential element of due process. Further, he rejected claims by the prosecutors that the defendants were given effective legal assistance. He pointed to the last-minute assignment of counsel for the defense as inadequate.

Justice Sutherland wrote about the critical importance of effective legal counsel, without which a fair trial is impossible. A defendant, he said, "lacks both the skill and knowledge adequately to prepare his defense, even though he has a perfect one. He requires the guiding hand of counsel at every step in the proceedings against him. Without it, though he be not guilty, he faces the danger of conviction because he does not know how to establish his innocence."

Dissent Justice Pierce Butler, joined in dissent by Justice James McReynolds, argued that the defendants had received adequate legal assistance. Further, they said that the Court's reversal of the convictions was unjustified interference with the operations of a state court system.

Significance In the *Powell* case the Court decided for the first time that the 14th Amendment required states to provide legal help for poor defendants in order to guarantee a fair trial. After *Powell*, state governments were required to provide counsel for poor defendants in all capital cases.

By contrast, the assistance of counsel clause of the 6th Amendment to the Constitution required the federal government to provide counsel for indigent defendants in both capital and noncapital cases. Federal and state government requirements regarding the assistance of counsel were not brought into conformity until 1963 with the decision in *Gideon* v. *Wainwright*.

In this landmark case, the Court ruled for the first time that the 6th Amendment assistance of counsel clause applied to state governments. The Court incorporated the 6th Amendment right to an attorney under the due process clause of the 14th Amendment. The states have to provide legal assistance to indigent defendants, in both capital and noncapital cases, in order to guarantee that the defendant receives the constitutional right to due process in criminal justice proceedings.

Following the Court's decision in *Powell*, the case was returned to Alabama for retrial of the seven youths on rape charges. This time, the defendants were represented by counsel, as required by the Supreme Court decision. However, they were again convicted and sentenced to death. Once again, they appealed their conviction and the case returned to the U.S. Supreme Court as *Norris* v. *Alabama* (1935). This appeal was based on the exclusion of blacks from the jury pool for the trial. The Court again overturned the convictions on the grounds that the 14th Amendment due process rights of the defendants were violated by systematic exclusion of jurors because of race.

The case was returned once more to Alabama for a jury trial. In subsequent state trials, the defendants were convicted again. However, none of them was sentenced to the death penalty. After several years of very complicated proceedings, all of the defendants were released from prison on parole, the last one in 1950.

SEE ALSO *Counsel, right to; Due process of law; Gideon v. Wainwright; Incorporation doctrine*

SOURCES Dan T. Carter, *Scottsboro: A Tragedy of the American South*, rev. ed. (Baton Rouge: Louisiana State University Press, 1979).

PRECEDENTS, CONGRESSIONAL

The rules of the House and Senate are relatively few in number, but each time that either body interprets those rules, it establishes a precedent, or guide to future behavior. Senate and House precedents number in the thousands. A member who objects to some procedural action on the floor will rise to make a point of order. The presiding officer will then rule on the point of order, based on the parliamentarian's reading of the rules and precedents. If no one appeals the ruling, then it becomes a new precedent. If members object to the chair's ruling, they can vote by a simple majority to overturn the ruling—and in their own way set a precedent. Precedents established by a vote carry the greatest weight in future actions. However, a different majority voting at a different time can reverse an earlier precedent.

For instance, the rules of the Senate prohibit a senator from making more than two speeches on the same subject in a single day. In 1935 the presiding officer ruled that if a senator made a motion to suggest the absence of a quorum (that not enough members were present to conduct business), the motion counted as a "speech." Over the next 50 years that precedent was rarely applied, but in 1986 one senator objected that another senator had spoken twice against a bill—including suggesting the absence of a quorum—and should not speak again. Citing the 1935 precedent, the presiding officer agreed. A heated debate followed, and by a vote of 92 to 5 the senators overturned the chair's ruling, voided the 1935 precedent, and thereby set a new precedent for the future.

Those involved in planning legislative strategy must know the precedents as well as the rules. Because there are so many precedents, the House and Senate parliamentarians from time to time publish volumes of the precedents, arranged by subject. Computer programs have also compiled precedents for the parliamentarians' ready access during debate.

SEE ALSO *Parliamentarian; Parliamentary procedure; Rules of the House and Senate*

PRECEDENTS, JUDICIAL

Appeals courts in the United States, including the Supreme Court, follow precedent, or past decisions, in making new ones. Once a case has been decided, similar cases are supposed to be decided in the same way. This practice is based on the doctrine of *stare decisis,* a Latin phrase meaning "Let the decision stand." The principle of *stare decisis* gives stability and predictability to the law. Decisions of the Supreme Court are binding on all lower courts in the United States, and they also serve as guidelines for subsequent Supreme Court decisions.

Occasionally, however, the Court departs from precedent to decide a case in a new way. Its decision in *Brown* v. *Board of Education* (1954), for example, rejected the precedent of "separate but equal" that had been established in *Plessy* v. *Ferguson* (1896) to support racial segregation.

SEE ALSO *Constitutional law; Dissenting opinion; Judicial review*

PRESIDENTIAL RELATIONS WITH CONGRESS

The President and Congress both share and compete for power. The Constitution suggests Presidential involvement in legislation in two ways: First, in the annual State of the Union message the President may recommend for Congress's consideration "such measures as he shall judge necessary" (Article 2, Section 3). Second, the President can veto measures he disapproves of (though the veto is subject to being overridden by a two-thirds vote of both the House and Senate) (Article 1, Section 7). Though 19th-century Presidents often adopted a passive role, limiting themselves to administering the laws that Congress enacted, modern Presidents have defined their role as "chief legislator" as well as "chief executive" and have attempted to exert strong influence over Congress.

As the leader of his political party, the President tends to work through his party in Congress. When a President's party holds the majority in Congress, the likelihood of passing the President's legislative program is great. When a President's party is in the minority, stalemate can occur, a situation that has been called the "deadlock of democracy." When such a "divided government" occurs, Presidents can seek to build bipartisan policies, as Democratic President Harry S. Truman did in promoting a bipartisan foreign policy during the Republican 80th Congress (1947–49). Alternatively, they can lambast Congress for opposing their policies and being a "do nothing" Congress, as Truman did effectively during the election of 1948.

Mandates to lead Popular Presidents who have won election by a large margin assert that they have a mandate to lead. Under these circumstances, Congress will often follow the President's lead on the assumption that his program represents the popular will. But members of Congress also feel they have a mandate from their constituents, and they will often remain fiercely independent from Presidential leadership. Franklin D. Roosevelt won reelection by one of the largest margins in history in 1936, but the next year Congress blocked his plan to "pack" the Supreme Court, feeling he had overstepped himself. House Speaker Sam Rayburn, whose service in Congress extended from the Presidency of Woodrow Wilson to John F. Kennedy, insisted that he served *under* no President, "but I have served *with* eight of them."

Since a President's success is often judged by his ability to win passage of legislation, he spends much time trying to convince Congress to support him. In addition to personal addresses to Congress, Presidents assign certain staff members to act as liaisons with the Senate and House, lobbying for the administration's proposals and finding out what members of Congress want from the administration in return. Presidents will telephone members to solicit their votes, invite them to the White House, and otherwise twist arms, appeal to patriotism, and offer favors in return for congressional support. When all else fails, Presidents can use the threat of vetoing legislation as a means to force at least a compromise.

Disputes over foreign policy In dealing with military and foreign policies, Presidents have often acted independently of Congress. Although Congress has the constitutional power to declare war, and the Senate ratifies treaties and confirms diplomatic nominations, Presidents often take action without consulting first with Congress. Congressional leaders complain that they are called in for briefings only after the major decisions have been made and that Presidents seek their consent rather than their advice. Members of Congress expressed a desire to be consulted during the takeoff as well as during the crash landing. They enacted the War Powers Act in 1973 to require the President to notify them whenever he sent troops into a combat situation.

SOURCES John R. Bond and Richard Fleisher, *The President in the Legislative Arena* (Chicago: University of Chicago Press, 1990). James McGregor Burns, *The Deadlock of Democracy: Four-Party Politics in America* (Englewood Cliffs, N.J.: Prentice-Hall, 1963).

PRESIDENT PRO TEMPORE OF THE SENATE

The Constitution (Article 1, Section 3) requires the Senate to elect a president pro tempore (*pro tempore* is a Latin phrase meaning "for the time being") to serve as presiding officer when the Vice President is absent. The president pro tempore can preside over the Senate, swear in senators, and sign legislation. Originally, when Vice Presidents presided daily over the Senate, presidents pro tempore were elected to serve only during a particular absence of the Vice President or for the duration of the term of a Vice President who died in office or succeeded to the Presidency. In the 5th Congress (1797–99), for instance, the Senate elected five different presidents pro tem. To give the office more continuity, in 1890 the Senate changed the term of president pro tempore to last until another was elected, so the term might last for several Congresses. During the 20th century the Senate began electing the senior member of the majority party as president pro tem, to hold the office until he retired or his party lost the majority.

Since modern Vice Presidents generally appear in the Senate only for ceremonial occasions or to break tie votes, the president pro tem opens each session and then assigns junior senators in the majority party to take rotating turns presiding during the day's session. The president pro tempore also stands third in line, behind the Vice President and Speaker of the House, in the order of Presidential succession.

SEE ALSO *Officers of the House and Senate; Vice President*
SOURCES Robert C. Byrd, "The President Pro Tempore," in *The Senate, 1789–1989: Addresses on the History of the United States Senate,* vol. 2 (Washington, D.C.: Government Printing Office, 1991).

PRESIDENT'S COUNCIL ON PHYSICAL FITNESS AND SPORTS

The President's Council on Physical Fitness and Sports (PCPFS) is an advisory council, part of the Executive Office of the President, that promotes and encourages the development of physical fitness and sports programs in American life. The PCPFS was created by executive order by President Dwight Eisenhower in 1956 and was first chaired by Vice President Richard Nixon.

The PCPFS encourages schools, business and industry, government, recreation agencies, and sports organizations to increase support for activities that promote physical fitness. It has established local Councils on Physical Fitness and Sports; a Presidential Sports Award Program to encourage fitness through regular participation in sports; the Healthy American Fitness Leader Awards, in cooperation with private industry; and the President's Challenge, a physical fitness awards program for children in the fourth through sixth grades. Each year the PCPFS recognizes outstanding school physical fitness programs in each state with special awards. Selected schools serve as demonstration sites for teacher education programs and foreign visitors. By Presidential proclamation, each May is National Physical Fitness and Sports Month, and the council prepares radio and television announcements and public service information on physical fitness during that month. It also sponsors an annual "running and fitness week" in cooperation with the American Running and Fitness Association. The PCPFS has also sponsored programs for the estimated one in six children who are "physically underdeveloped." It encourages schools to identify these children and establish programs designed specifically to improve their physical fitness and sports performance.

Twenty private citizens serve on the council. Members have included such sports celebrities as bodybuilder Arnold Schwarzenegger, basketball star Earvin ("Magic") Johnson, Olympic gold medal runner Jackie Joyner-Kersee, and tennis stars Chris Evert and Pam Shriver. They are appointed by the President and report to the President and the secretary of the Department of Health and Human Services. A full-time staff of eight carries out the programs of the council.

PRESS

SEE *Media coverage of Congress; Public opinion*

PRESS CONFERENCES

SEE *News conferences, Presidential*

PRESS SECRETARY

The press secretary, who is also director of the White House Press Office, is the Presidential assistant in charge of relations with the media. The title was first used in the Hoover administration.

The press secretary is the only official who "speaks for the President" to the press. The press secretary holds one or two daily briefings for correspondents in the West Terrace briefing room of the White House, during which correspondents are briefed about appointments, the President's daily schedule, upcoming travel plans, and Presidential messages and speeches. (This information is also summarized in daily news releases distributed to White House reporters.) Then the press secretary takes questions.

The Press Office issues credentials, or permission to attend White House news conferences, to about 1,500 journalists and provides office space in the West Terrace for 30 White House correspondents. Its Office of Public Liaison also provides services to newspapers and television stations across the country, including interviews with officials using the White House television studios. It prepares a "press plan" for all Presidential domestic and overseas trips to encourage favorable media coverage. It makes travel arrangements for as many as 300 reporters on major Presidential trips.

The press secretary organizes the President's news conferences and prepares briefing books for the President to study before the conference. The secretary helps the President prepare. After the conference the secretary issues corrections of any Presidential misstatements.

Pierre Salinger was one of the most successful press secretaries. A member of John Kennedy's inner circle of political advisers, he also had good rapport with the Washington press corps. Unlike many of the tall and athletic New Frontiersmen, Salinger was short, overweight, and decidedly unathletic. He joked about himself and about everyone else, but he was a consummate professional when it came to helping reporters meet their deadlines with reliable and interesting stories. He quickly became one of the most popular figures in Washington and one of the most adept at getting good press for his boss.

Press secretaries, usually former reporters, frequently have conflicts with other senior Presidential aides, often because they are not given advance notice of important Presidential decisions and then are accused by their former colleagues of deception. Press Secretary Jerry Horst resigned from Gerald Ford's administration because he was not told in advance about Richard Nixon's pardon.

Press secretaries are often accused of trying to manipulate the media by "managing" the news. In 1985, at a summit with Soviet president Mikhail Gorbachev, Larry Speakes was concerned that President Ronald Reagan receive favorable press coverage. He made up some Presidential statements. Many months later, he admitted what he had done and apologized. But the damage had been done: in the future no one could be sure that a Presidential quote passed on by the press secretary had actually been said by the President. In recent years the person in charge of relations with the media has taken the title "director of communications," and the director's assistant is known as the press secretary.

SEE ALSO *Public opinion; White House Office*

SOURCES W. Dale Nelson, *Who Speaks for the President?: The White House Press Secretary from Cleveland to Clinton* (Syracuse,

N.Y.: Syracuse University Press, 1998). Ron Nessen, *It Sure Looks Different on the Inside* (Chicago: Playboy Press, 1978). Jody Powell, *The Other Side of the Story* (New York: Morrow, 1984). Larry Speakes, *Speaking Out: Inside the Reagan White House* (New York: Scribners, 1988). George Stephanopoulos, *All Too Human: A Political Education* (Boston: Back Bay, 2000).

PREVIOUS QUESTION

The previous question is a procedural device used in the House of Representatives to limit debate and avoid potentially damaging amendments by a bill's opponents. Managers of a bill can make a motion calling for the previous question—"question" in this case meaning the bill being debated. If the motion passes, no further amendments can be introduced and the House must vote on the original bill. Although the House permits this parliamentary tactic, the Senate has resisted it. Senate rules have traditionally been more tolerant of the minority and make it more difficult to cut off debate. Rather than needing a majority vote (51 percent) for the previous question, the Senate must achieve a three-fifths vote (60 percent) to invoke cloture and cut off debate.

SEE ALSO *Cloture; Motions, parliamentary; Parliamentary procedure*

PRIMARIES, PRESIDENTIAL

Presidential primaries are contests held by state political parties to determine the composition of state delegations to the national nominating conventions. State election laws establish the rules for primaries: in *closed primaries* only voters registered in the state party may vote; in *open primaries* independents may also vote; in *crossover primaries* voters from any party as well as independents may participate. Turnouts in

primaries are low. Through the 1970s, approximately 11 percent of the eligible voters participated; since then, the percentage has almost doubled, to 21 percent.

The first Presidential primary was held in Florida, which in 1904 created a "preference" primary that did not bind its state's convention delegates. In 1905 Governor Robert M. La Follette of Wisconsin won passage of the first state law creating a delegate-selection primary in time for the 1908 conventions. That same year Oregon adopted a "first ballot" primary that bound the state delegation to vote for the winner of the primary on the first convention ballot. North Dakota, Nebraska, Wisconsin, and New Jersey followed suit.

By 1912 a dozen states had established primaries, including California, Illinois, Maryland, Massachusetts, Michigan, and South Dakota, but many were "preference" primaries, in which voters could not only choose delegates but also express a preference for their party's nomination. Sometimes this could lead to confusing results. In Massachusetts, for instance, the state's voters selected a slate of Theodore Roosevelt supporters to go to the convention but expressed their "preference" for William Howard Taft. Ex-President Roosevelt, after losing the Republican nomination and deciding to run on the Progressive party ticket, called for a national primary that would end such anomalies and allow voters in each party to choose the Presidential nominee without the need for a convention.

As of 1916, 20 states held primaries, and President Woodrow Wilson also endorsed the idea of a national primary. But the pendulum swung in the other direction: in the 1920s, because of high costs and low voter participation, eight states dropped primaries and returned to the caucus system. Until the 1970s, between 12 and 17 states used the primary system, while the remainder used the caucus system.

Candidates could lose a majority of primaries—or not enter them—and still win their party's Presidential nomination. The list includes Woodrow Wilson and William Howard Taft in 1912; Warren Harding in 1920; Herbert Hoover in 1932; Thomas Dewey in 1948; Dwight Eisenhower in 1952; and Hubert Humphrey in 1968. Conversely, winning primaries did not ensure a contender of winning the Presidential nomination. In 1912 Theodore Roosevelt won every primary but was defeated for the Republican nomination by incumbent President William Howard Taft, primarily because Taft controlled patronage vital to state parties. In 1948 Harold Stassen won three early Republican primaries but could not derail the candidacy of Thomas Dewey.

Entering primaries enabled candidates to dispel doubts about their electability and gain the support of political bosses who controlled a majority of the convention delegates. In 1960 John F. Kennedy won primaries in Wisconsin and West Virginia, demonstrating that a Catholic could do well with Protestant voters. In 1968 Richard Nixon won enough primaries to dispel his "loser" reputation.

By 1968 primaries were held in 17 states, accounting for 37.5 percent of the Democratic and 34.3 percent of the Republican convention delegates. That year, Hubert Humphrey won the Democratic nomination without having entered a single Democratic primary. To rank-and-file Democrats, many of whom had voted for Humphrey's rivals Eugene McCarthy and Robert Kennedy, the system seemed undemocratic.

Democrats, stung by their defeat in the 1968 Presidential election, organized the Commission on Party Structure and Delegate Selection, known as the McGovern-Fraser Commission. As a result of its recommendations, six more states adopted the primary system by 1972, and another eight by 1976. There were 35 Democratic Presidential primaries by 1980 and 39 by 2000. Republican state parties followed suit.

Today, in any given election between two-thirds and three-quarters of each party's convention delegates are chosen in primaries. Even more significant, party rules require that the preferences of the voters be translated directly into election of delegates. Gone are the "preference" primaries that had no effect on the composition of the state delegation.

A string of primary victories now translates into large numbers of convention delegates committed to a candidate. Primary winners also get momentum; they receive more campaign contributions and favorable media exposure, and they rise in the public opinion polls. In 1976 Jimmy Carter went from less than 1 percent support in the polls to more than 30 percent on the basis of his victory in the New Hampshire primary.

Contenders who do poorly in early primaries find that their contributions dry up and Treasury funding for their campaign is cut off. The early primaries winnow the field down to two or three serious contenders. Then a regional grouping (such as Super Tuesday in the South, on which day six or more states hold primaries) or primaries in large states such as New York may propel one of the contenders far to the front. Since 1972, any front-runner who has emerged from the primary season with more than 41 percent of the delegates has been nominated.

SEE ALSO *Carter, Jimmy; Caucuses, Presidential nominating; Election campaigns, Presidential; Kennedy, John F.; Nixon, Richard M.; Nominating conventions, Presidential; Wilson, Woodrow*

SOURCES Rhodes Cook, *United States Presidential Primary Elections 1968–1996: A Handbook of Election Statistics* (Washington, D.C.: Congressional Quarterly Books, 2000). James W. Davis, *Presidential Primaries: Road to the White House* (Westport, Conn.: Greenwood, 1980). Austin Ranney, *Curing the Mischiefs of Faction: Party Reform in America* (Berkeley: University of California Press, 1975). Byron E. Shafer, *Quiet Revolution: The Struggle for the Democratic Party and the Shaping of Post-Reform Politics* (New York: Russell Sage Foundation, 1983).

PRIOR RESTRAINT

Prior restraint is a form of censorship in which government officials restrict a newspaper or magazine in advance from publishing materials of which they disapprove. The 1st Amendment guarantee of a free press precludes the government's use of prior restraint to control the content of a publication. This 1st Amendment ban on prior restraint was applied to state governments through the due process clause of the 14th Amendment in *Near* v. *Minnesota* (1931). In this landmark decision, the Supreme Court ruled that an injunction to stop publication of a newspaper with objectionable content was an example of prior restraint and therefore unconstitutional. The Court did not rule, however, that a publisher was protected from legal action *after* publishing questionable material.

SEE ALSO *Freedom of speech and press; Near v. Minnesota; New York Times Co. v. United States*

PRIVACY, RIGHT TO

The word *privacy* cannot be found in the Constitution of the United States. Yet Americans have tended to believe in a constitutional right to privacy—the right to be secure against unlawful intrusions by government into certain protected areas of life. Ever since the founding era, most Americans have recognized public and private domains of society. The public domain is open to regulation by government. For example, the people expect their police officers to keep order on the streets of a community, a function that involves certain limits on the free movement of people. The private domain, by contrast, is generally closed to invasion and control by government and can be entered and reg-

ulated by police officers only for a compelling public purpose and according to due process of law.

There are continuing legal issues about the boundaries between the public and private domains of society because these two realms of life are inextricably bound together. Thus, for example, the government can constitutionally justify certain regulations of private property owners to protect the public against abuses, such as pollution of the environment. Further, the government may constitutionally enter a person's home to prevent individuals from conducting activities that violate the public interest, such as molesting children. When, and under what circumstances, does a person's right to privacy end and the public's authority to regulate behavior in the public interest begin? This is an ongoing problem in the courts.

Justice Louis D. Brandeis argued for a general constitutional right to privacy in a famous dissent in the Supreme Court case of *Olmstead* v. *United States* (1928): "The makers of our Constitution undertook to secure conditions favorable to the pursuit of happiness.... They conferred, as against the Government, the right to be let alone—the most comprehensive of rights and the right most valued by civilized men." Justice Brandeis pointed to the 4th Amendment protections against "unreasonable searches and seizures" and the 5th Amendment guarantees against self-incrimination as examples of constitutional protection against "unjustifiable intrusion by the Government upon the privacy of the individual."

For more than 30 years after the *Olmstead* case, the Court avoided serious discussions of a constitutional right to privacy. Then, in *Poe* v. *Ullman* (1961), Justices John Marshall Harlan and William O. Douglas argued in dissent for the individual's right to privacy against a Connecticut law banning the use of birth control devices, even by married couples. Harlan pointed to the 14th Amendment's provision that "no State shall make or enforce any law which shall . . . deprive any person of life, liberty, or property, without due process of law." According to Harlan, the state law at issue unconstitutionally deprived individuals of their liberty, without due process of law, to use birth control devices, which was "an intolerable and unjustifiable invasion of privacy." Thus, Harlan linked the 14th Amendment's guarantee of liberty to the right to privacy.

In *Griswold* v. *Connecticut* (1965), the Court overturned the decision in *Poe* v. *Ullman* (1961). The Court decided that the Connecticut law against contraception was unconstitutional and based its decision on a constitutional right to privacy. However, the justices disagreed about where in the Constitution this right to privacy could be found.

Justice William O. Douglas found a general right to privacy which, he believed, can be interpreted from the words of parts of the Bill of Rights (the 1st, 3rd, 4th, and 5th Amendments). He argued that the state of Connecticut had specifically violated the right to marital privacy, which fits within the "zone of privacy" one can infer from the text of the Bill of Rights.

Justice Arthur Goldberg's concurring opinion in *Griswold* emphasized the 9th Amendment: "The enumeration in the Constitution of certain rights shall not be construed to deny or disparage others retained by the people." Justice Goldberg held that the right to privacy in marital relationships was one of those rights not written in the Constitution that was nonetheless "retained by the people." Justice Goldberg wrote, "To hold that a right so basic and fundamental and so deep-rooted in our society as the right to privacy in marriage may be infringed because the right is not guaranteed in so many words by the first eight amendments to the Constitution is to ignore the Ninth Amendment and to give it no effect whatsoever."

Justice John Marshall Harlan also concurred with the Court's opinion in the *Griswold* case. However, Harlan based his decision on the due process clause of the 14th Amendment, as he had done in

his dissent in the *Poe* case four years earlier.

Justices Hugo L. Black and Potter Stewart dissented from the Court's opinion in *Griswold*. They argued that a general right to privacy cannot be inferred from any part of the Constitution. Further, they criticized the Court's majority for deciding this case according to personal opinion instead of following the text of the Constitution. Justice Black wrote, "I like my privacy as well as the next one, but I am nevertheless compelled to admit that government has a right to invade it unless prohibited by some specific constitutional provision." In *Griswold*, Black found no "specific constitutional provision" that prohibited the state government's regulation of the private behavior at issue in this case.

Support for a right to privacy has continued since the *Griswold* decision. In *Katz* v. *United States* (1967), the Court overturned the decision in *Olmstead* v. *United States* (1928). The Court held that the 4th and 5th Amendments protect an individual's right to privacy against electronic surveillance and wiretapping by government agents, even in a place open to the public, such as a telephone booth on a city street. In *Roe* v. *Wade* (1973), the Court ruled that the right to privacy included a woman's choice to have an abortion during the first three months of pregnancy.

While continuing to recognize a constitutional right to privacy, the Court has acted recently to set limits on it. In *Skinner* v. *Railway Labor Executives Association* (1989) and *National Treasury Employees Union* v. *Von Raab* (1989), the Court has upheld federal regulations that provide for drug testing of railroad and customs workers, even without warrants or reasonable suspicion of drug use. In these cases, the Court decided that the need for public safety was a compelling reason for limiting the individual's right to privacy against government regulation.

Since the 1960s the often-contested right to privacy has been established in a line of Supreme Court decisions. As Justice

Harry A. Blackmun wrote in *Thornburgh v. American College of Obstetricians and Gynecologists* (1986), "Our cases long have recognized that the Constitution embodies a promise that a certain private sphere of individual liberty will be kept largely beyond the reach of government."

An individual's right to privacy was reinforced in *Reno* v. *Condon* (2000), in which South Carolina challenged a federal law, the Driver's Privacy Protection Act (DPPA). This statute prevents states from releasing personal information in motor vehicle records without consent. The South Carolina attorney general claimed that the DPPA violated the constitutional powers and rights of a state within the federal system of the United States. The Court rejected the claim and upheld the DPPA as a constitutional means of protecting the privacy of licensed drivers. In this case, an individual's privacy rights were upheld over states' rights.

The exact meaning and limits of this widely recognized right to privacy, however, will continue to be controversial. Every extension of the right to privacy limits the power of government to regulate behavior for the public good, which citizens of a constitutional democracy expect. By contrast, every expansion of government's power to regulate the behavior of individuals diminishes the "private sphere of individual liberty" cherished by citizens of a constitutional democracy. How to justly balance and blend these contending factors, so that both are addressed but neither one is sacrificed to the other, is an ongoing issue of the Supreme Court and the citizenry of the United States.

SEE ALSO *Griswold v. Connecticut; Katz v. United States; Olmstead v. United States; Roe v. Wade*

SOURCES Ellen Alderman and Caroline Kennedy, *The Right to Privacy* (1995; reprint, New York: Vintage, 1997). Randy Barnett, ed., *The Rights Retained by the People: The History and Meaning of the Ninth Amendment* (Fairfax, Va.: George Mason University Press, 1989). Sandra F. Van Burkleo, "The Right to Privacy," in *By and for the People: Constitutional Rights in American History*, edited by Kermit L. Hall (Arlington Heights, Ill.: Harlan Davidson, 1991). Alan F. Westin, *Privacy and Freedom* (New York: Atheneum, 1968).

PRIVATE LAWS

When Congress acts to aid a specific individual, family, or other small group, it passes a private law. Public laws, by comparison, deal with society as a whole. The first private bill, which was passed in September 1789, awarded 17 months' back pay to a military officer. Many other private bills that followed dealt with military pensions or claims of citizens whose property was damaged during wartime. Other private bills permitted specifically named foreigners to immigrate and become naturalized citizens of the United States. By 1900 private bills far outnumbered the public bills that Congress considered. Later, Congress turned settlement of most private claims over to the executive departments and enacted more comprehensive veterans' pensions and immigration laws that reduced the need to address them case by case. Legislation has also more narrowly defined the circumstances in which Congress will consider private claims. However, Congress continues to enact private laws to aid citizens who have been injured by government programs or who have appealed an executive agency ruling, such as one requiring the deportation of a noncitizen. Private laws are numbered separately from public laws. During the 102nd Congress, for example, they were numbered Private Law 102-1 and up.

SEE ALSO *Acts of Congress*

PROBABLE CAUSE

The 4th Amendment to the U.S. Constitution requires that "no [search or arrest] warrants shall issue, but upon probable cause." Thus, government officials may not obtain a warrant to search or arrest someone unless they have probable cause, or good reasons, to believe that the person may be involved in criminal behavior of some kind. Judges, not law enforcement officers, have the authority to decide if there is probable cause for issuing a warrant to search or arrest someone. In *Terry v. Ohio* (1968), however, the Supreme Court adjusted this standard to allow police officers to stop and frisk suspects if they consider it necessary to protect themselves, even without probable cause for arrest.

SEE ALSO *Searches and seizures; Terry v. Ohio*

PRO FORMA SESSIONS OF CONGRESS

Visitors to the galleries sometimes are puzzled to see the Senate or House come into session and then adjourn within a few seconds. Why does Congress bother with these short pro forma (a Latin phrase meaning "as a matter of form") sessions? The Constitution says that neither the Senate nor the House may adjourn for more than three days without the other's consent (Article 1, Section 5). This requirement prevents either house from trying to delay legislation by refusing to meet. Rather than always having to ask the other body's permission not to meet, the Senate or House simply holds a pro forma session in which one member gavels the chamber to order and then immediately declares it adjourned. Regardless of how briefly this session lasts, it counts as a day's session. Pro forma sessions allow senators or representatives more time to spend in committee hearings or other business off the floor.

PROPERTY RIGHTS

The founders of the United States believed that the right to acquire, own, and use private property was an essential element of a free society. John Adams expressed a prevailing opinion of his times when he wrote in 1790, "Property must be secured or liberty cannot exist."

Land ownership was one kind of property right the founders wanted to protect. They were also concerned about rights to other kinds of property, such as personal goods (clothing, tools, houses, and animals, for instance), ideas, inventions, and money. Property takes many forms that represent both wealth and the means of creating or producing wealth.

A main purpose of the U.S. Constitution of 1787 was to limit the power of government in order to protect individual rights, including property rights. The framers used separation of powers, with checks and balances, to constitutionally limit the government for the purpose of guarding individual property rights and other fundamental rights. The framers of the Constitution and of the Bill of Rights also provided protections for property rights in specific clauses.

For example, Article 1, Section 10, states, "No State shall . . . pass any Bill of Attainder . . . or Law impairing the Obligation of Contracts." By prohibiting bills of attainder, or the punishment of a person by a legislative act (rather than by a court of law), the Constitution protects individuals from legislative actions to arbitrarily deprive them of property or punish them in some other way. By prohibiting legislative actions interfering with the terms of a contract, the Constitution protects property rights involved in the contract. Further, in Article 1, Section 8, Congress is granted the power to protect the property rights of inventors and writers to their ideas and creations "by securing for limited Times to Authors and Inventors the exclusive Right to their respective Writings and Discoveries." Finally, Article 1, Section 9, prohibits Congress from levying direct taxes on individuals unless they are apportioned according to population. This constitutional provision limited the Congress's power to impose land taxes, thereby protecting a person's private property from acquisition by the federal government. (The 16th Amendment, passed in 1913, permits the federal government to levy taxes on the income of individuals, whatever the source.)

The 5th Amendment to the U.S. Constitution (ratified in 1791 as part of the Bill of Rights) says, "No person shall be . . . deprived of life, liberty, or property, without due process of law; nor shall private property be taken for public use without just compensation." The 14th Amendment (ratified in 1868) provides protection for private property rights by prohibiting any state government from taking a person's property "without due process of law." The 5th and 14th Amendments limit the power of the federal and state governments to abuse the property rights of individuals.

Chief Justice John Marshall strongly supported private property rights of individuals as a bulwark of personal liberty and as a stimulus to productive use of resources. Marshall believed, as did most other leaders of his time, that security in the ownership of property helped a person to resist domination by others, especially government officials. Chief Justice Marshall's opinions in *Fletcher* v. *Peck* (1810) and *Dartmouth College* v. *Woodward* (1819) bolstered the "Obligation of Contracts" cited in Article 1, Section 10, of the Constitution as a guarantee of private property rights.

If the Constitution set limits on the power of government to violate property rights, it also implied that there are limits on the rights of individuals in behalf of the public good. For example, Chief Justice Roger Taney was a strong supporter of private property rights. In *Charles River Bridge* v. *Warren Bridge* (1837), however, Taney held that property rights in a contract could sometimes be overridden to permit development of innovations or improvements to benefit the public. In *West River Bridge Co.* v. *Dix* (1848), the Taney Court held that the contract clause of the Constitution did not protect a corporation from the state's right of eminent domain— its power to take private property, with fair compensation, to use for the public good.

There has been persistent tension between the private property rights of individuals and the public's need for limitations or regulations on private property rights. Justice John M. Harlan stressed in *Chicago, Burlington & Quincy Railroad Company* v. *Chicago* (1897), "Due protection of the rights of property has been regarded as a vital principle of republican institutions." Justice Harlan also wrote (*Mugler* v. *Kansas*, 1887), "All property in this country is held under the implied obligation that the owner's use of it shall not be injurious to the community." However, he qualified this recognition of the government's authority to regulate property rights by insisting that there were "limits beyond which legislation cannot rightfully go."

At times the Supreme Court has tilted to the government-regulation side of the debate on property rights. In *Munn* v. *Illinois* (1877), for instance, the Court upheld an Illinois law regulating the price for storing grain in privately owned storage elevators. Chief Justice Morrison R. Waite wrote, "When private property is devoted to a public use, it is subject to public regulation."

More often, however, from the 1870s until the 1930s the Court seemed to oppose any government laws that interfered with the free market, such as state laws regulating wages or working conditions of employees. In *Lochner* v. *New York* (1905), for example, the Court overturned a New York law that restricted hours of work in bakeries. Writing for the Court, Justice Rufus W. Peckham argued that the New York law violated the "liberty of contract" protected by the 14th Amendment.

The *Lochner* decision set the trend for Court rulings on state regulation of private property rights for the next 30 years. Not until 1937, when the Court upheld federal laws regulating the economy for the public good (in *National Labor Relations Board* v. *Jones & Laughlin Steel Corp.* and *West Coast Hotel Co.* v. *Parrish*), did the trend shift away from the resistance to many kinds of public regulations of private

property rights. In the *Parrish* case, Chief
Justice Charles Evans Hughes rejected the
"liberty of contract" idea that had prevailed in the *Lochner* decision and other
subsequent decisions. He wrote for the
Court, "Liberty under the Constitution is
... necessarily subject to the restraints of
due process, and regulation [of a private
business by a state government to protect
the health, welfare, and personal rights of
workers] which is adopted in the interests
of the community is due process."

During the middle years of the 20th
century, from 1937 until the 1960s, the
Court tilted strongly toward public regulation of private property for the public
good and away from 19th-century views
on the connection of private property
rights to personal liberty. For example,
Justice Hugo Black wrote in *Marsh* v. *Alabama* (1946), "Ownership does not always mean absolute domination. The
more an owner, for his advantage, opens
up his property for use by the public in
general, the more do his rights become cir-
cumscribed by the statutory and constitutional rights of those who use it....
Thus, the owners of privately held bridges,
ferries, turnpikes, and railroads may not
operate them as freely as a farmer does his
farm. Since these facilities are built and operated primarily to benefit the public and
since their operation is essentially a public
function, it is subject to state regulation."

Since the 1970s, however, the Court has
tended to reemphasize private property
rights in a continuing quest for a just balance between private property rights and
the public good. Justice Potter Stewart expressed in *Lynch* v. *Household Finance Corporation* (1972) the Court's renewed
emphasis on property rights as a key to
liberty and a free society: "In fact, a fundamental interdependence exists between
the personal right to liberty and the personal right to property. Neither could have
meaning without the other."

SEE ALSO *Charles River Bridge* v. *Warren
Bridge; Contract clause; Dartmouth College
v. Woodward; Fletcher v. Peck; Lochner v.
New York; Munn v. Illinois; National Labor*

Relations Board v. *Jones & Laughlin Steel
Corp.; West Coast Hotel Co.* v. *Parrish*
SOURCES Gordon Morris Bakken, "Prop-
erty Rights," in *By and for the People: Con-
stitutional Rights in American History*,
edited by Kermit L. Hall (Arlington
Heights, Ill.: Harlan Davidson, 1991).
James W. Ely, Jr., *The Guardian of Every
Other Right: A Constitutional History of
Property Rights* (New York: Oxford Uni-
versity Press, 1992). Richard Epstein, *Tak-
ings: Private Property and the Power of
Eminent Domain* (Cambridge: Harvard
University Press, 1985).

PROTEST

On any day, you might observe a rally or
demonstration on the Capitol grounds.
Concerned citizens, labor unions,
women's rights organizations, civil rights
activists, environmentalists, and advocates
of special interests of every kind assemble
at the Capitol, unfurl their banners, listen
to their speakers, and then seek out their
senators and representatives to lobby for
their cause.

The 1st Amendment to the Constitution protects the "right of the people
peaceably to assemble," and the Capitol
has often provided the backdrop for citizens' peaceful assembly. In 1894, during a
severe economic depression, Ohio business executive Jacob Coxey led an army of
unemployed men and women to Washington to demand federal job programs.
"General" Coxey's army reached the Capitol but was prohibited from walking on
the grass or displaying any banners or
signs. When Coxey stepped forward to
speak, he was arrested for walking on the
grass. During another great depression, in
1932, an army of Bonus Marchers appeared on the Capitol grounds. World
War I army veterans assembled outside the
Capitol while the Senate debated making
an early bonus payment to help them
through the hard times. Although many
people expected trouble when the Senate
voted down the Bonus Bill, the marchers

sang "America" and dispersed. Later, regular army troops forced the veterans out of Washington.

During the Vietnam War in the 1960s, antiwar protestors regularly picketed and protested at the Capitol. Every January on the anniversary of the Supreme Court's 1972 ruling in *Roe v. Wade,* which legalized abortion, antiabortion protestors have marched on the Capitol. Smaller groups often gather on the Capitol steps to protest political oppression and human rights violations in their native land. Regardless of the issues, these groups can receive a permit to assemble peacefully at the Capitol to exercise their constitutional rights.

SEE ALSO *Bonus Marchers; Coxey's army*

PROXY VOTING

When members of Congress expect to be absent from a committee meeting, they will arrange for a colleague to cast their vote by proxy (from a Latin word meaning "to take care of"), or written permission. The chair usually holds proxies for absent members of the majority, and at times a sole member will cast proxies for all the members of the minority. Critics call this procedure "ghost voting" and accuse absent members of not performing their job. However, those who vote by proxy may be at another committee hearing, participating in a floor debate, or conducting some other legislative business. Because of the competing demands on members' time, committees would find it difficult to carry on business without proxy voting. No proxies are allowed in roll call votes on the floor of either the House or Senate, but absent members may "pair" their vote—that is, couple it with that of another member who would have voted the opposite way to show that these two votes would not have changed the outcome.

SEE ALSO *Pair voting*

PUBLIC INFORMATION OFFICE OF THE SUPREME COURT

SEE *Staff of the Supreme Court, nonjudicial*

PUBLIC OPINION

James Madison observed that "public opinion sets bounds to every government, and is the real sovereign in every free one." Edmund Burke, a member of the British Parliament in the 18th century, expressed a different attitude when he told his constituents, "Your representative owes you, not his industry only, but his judgment; and he betrays, instead of serving you, if he sacrifices it to your opinion."

Members of Congress generally win election because they reflect the views of the majority in their home state or districts. Once in office, senators and representatives keep in constant contact with their constituents. They travel home regularly, hold public meetings, circulate questionnaires in their newsletters, and read public opinion polls. Members of Congress remain keenly interested in the mail and telephone responses of their constituents to current issues, and they take these into consideration when casting their votes. "Without public opinion on its side," commented Representative Dante Fascell (Democrat–Florida), "Congress can't move very much one way or the other." Yet polls constantly change, reflecting the public's shifting moods and attitudes and indicating that effective leadership can alter public opinion.

Presidents and the people In modern times, Presidents have frequently found it in their interest to appeal directly to the public for support on issues. The framers of the Constitution, however, did not expect Presidents to make such appeals or to be popular figures. They were concerned that Presidents might become "hard" demagogues, by dividing the people along class or territorial lines, or "soft" demagogues, flattering the voters in order to mislead them. The system of indirect election by the electoral college was, in part, a safeguard against a President's appealing to the people or holding himself directly accountable to the electorate.

In the 19th century, one of the articles of impeachment against President Andrew Johnson involved the charge that he had made speeches in an attempt to gain public support for his Reconstruction policies. During his battles with Congress over these policies, Johnson became the first President to give an interview for publication to a reporter. "I want to give these fellows hell," Johnson said, gesturing toward the Capitol, "and I think I can do it better through your paper than through a message [to Congress], because the people read the papers more than they do messages." Presidents were not expected to show up at their party's national convention to accept the nomination, nor were they expected to campaign for office. They did not give a State of the Union address to Congress but sent a detailed written message instead. They did not make political or policy speeches but stuck to vague platitudes of "civic republicanism" when addressing audiences. They had no direct dealings with the press.

The first President to depart from these practices (after Johnson) was Theodore Roosevelt, who used the Presidency as a bully pulpit in furthering his Square Deal program and who met regularly with reporters. Woodrow Wilson revived Thomas Jefferson's practice of delivering an annual address to Congress, and he held press conferences. Wilson sent messages to Congress outlining his New Freedom legislative program, and he made three speeches and held conferences to get his ideas before the public and gain support for his program. Wilson believed that Presidential

rhetoric was appropriate and did not have to be demagogic, or inflammatory, provided that it attempted to educate the public rather than simply manipulate it and provided it was for the public interest rather than partisan political advantage.

Franklin Roosevelt was the first President to use public opinion polls, taking advantage of polls already being conducted by the Department of Agriculture about support for the New Deal. He also used private pollsters under contract to the Democratic National Committee. To influence public opinion in favor of the New Deal, he used radio "fireside chats," provided movie theaters with newsreel footage of New Deal programs, and had government agencies send press releases about his programs to newspapers. He created public information offices in New Deal agencies and coordinated them through the White House Press Office.

Modern Presidents use their State of the Union addresses and special messages to Congress as media events to present their position to television audiences. Their communications directors and press secretaries provide the media with briefings and with the White House "spin" on, or interpretation of, events.

Presidents make televised addresses during crises, obtaining free time from the major networks. Occasionally, a request for free time will be rejected if it seems too partisan. Presidents are reluctant to bump popular prime-time programs, and the White House limits speeches so as not to jade its audience.

Presidents also rely on pseudo-events, events staged simply for media coverage. President Ronald Reagan visited schools, where he read from Shakespeare's plays to dramatize his theme that "back to basics" was more important than more federal financial aid. Presidents Jimmy Carter and Bill Clinton held "town meetings" to discuss issues with concerned citizens.

The White House relies on pollsters to conduct public opinion surveys whose results help shape their programs. President

Reagan received nightly "tracking" polls that indicated shifts in opinion on issues and support for the President.

Most Presidents have been poor media performers, ill at ease in front of cameras and the press, including Presidents Lyndon Johnson, Richard Nixon, Gerald Ford, Jimmy Carter, and George Bush. Many Presidential speeches that try to sway public opinion are unsuccessful. President Ford's speech unveiling his economic program, complete with a WIN button (standing for "Whip Inflation Now"), became a national joke. The more President Carter appealed for support for his energy program, the lower his approval ratings fell. One study by political scientists of 56 public issues showed that on only a few did Presidents sway public opinion, and then only when they were popular; otherwise, their efforts often made things worse.

At best, Presidents draw attention to problems and get the media and the public to focus on them. Sometimes they do so by their speeches and messages and sometimes by making decisions that set events in motion. But rarely do they persuade the American public; more likely, they activate opinions that already were present.

Presidents who have high public approval ratings are much more likely to hold press conferences, give speeches on issues, and pressure Congress to pass ambitious legislative programs. Popular Presidents have some persuasive ability in dealing with the public and with Congress. A popular President usually gets more support from members of his party than an unpopular President, especially on veto override votes. The proportion of Presidential requests in Congress that pass often varies directly with Presidential popularity. According to some political scientists, with every percentage point increase in public support, there is an increase in the probability that his bills will pass Congress. Unpopular Presidents are less likely to propose major new initiatives and are more likely to face restrictions on their powers by Congress. The unpopular Presidents are more likely to veto bills but are also more likely to have them overridden by Congress.

Unpopular Presidents may face renomination challenges in an election year. Such challenges caused Presidents Harry Truman and Lyndon Johnson to withdraw from the race. Presidents who win such challenges are likely to lose in the general election, the fate that befell Presidents Ford, Carter, and Bush. An unpopular President may bequeath problems to his party: every 10-point decline in the President's approval rating results, on average, in a 4-point drop in the percentage of the popular vote his party will obtain in the next Presidential election. An unpopular President drives voters away from identifying with his party; a succession of popular Presidents brings voters into the party.

SEE ALSO *Fireside chat; Media coverage of Congress; Messages, Presidential; News conferences, Presidential; Press secretary; Reagan, Ronald; Roosevelt, Franklin D.; Roosevelt, Theodore; Speech writers, Presidential; State of the Union address*

SOURCES Richard A. Brody, *Assessing the President: The Media, Elite Opinion, and Public Support* (Stanford, Calif.: Stanford University Press, 1992). George Edwards III, *The Public Presidency: The Pursuit of Popular Support* (New York: St. Martin's, 1983). Fred L. Israel, "The Public Looks at Congress," in *Understanding Congress: Research Perspectives,* edited by Roger H. Davidson and Richard C. Sachs (Washington, D.C.: Government Printing Office, 1991). Samuel Kernell, *Going Public: New Strategies of Presidential Leadership,* 3rd ed. (Washington, D.C.: Congressional Quarterly Books, 1997). Benjamin Page and Robert Shapiro, *The Rational Public* (Chicago: University of Chicago Press, 1991). Stephen Ponder, *Managing the Press: Origins of the Media Presidency, 1897–1933* (New York: St. Martin's, 1999). Richard Rubin, *Press, Party, and Presidency* (New York: Norton, 1978).

Q

QUALIFICATIONS FOR CONGRESS

The Constitution specifically lists the qualifications necessary to become a member of the House or Senate. A representative must be at least 25 years old, have been a U.S. citizen for seven years, and be a resident of the state (although not necessarily the district) from which he or she is chosen (Article 1, Section 2). A senator must be at least 30 years old, have been a citizen for nine years, and be a resident of his or her state (Article 1, Section 3).

When the House refused to seat Adam Clayton Powell, Jr., in 1967, citing his prolonged absences and other objectionable behavior, the Supreme Court ruled the action unconstitutional. The Court said that no requirements besides age, citizenship, and residence could be considered in seating a member. In the earlier years, a few members served while younger than the minimum age specified by the Constitution, but no action was taken against them. Henry Clay, for instance, was only 29 when he first took his seat as a senator. When another senator questioned this, Clay responded, "I hope my colleague will propound that question to my constituents." By this Clay meant that the voters should decide who is eligible. In later years, however, Congress insisted that those elected while still too young to serve must wait until they have reached the required age before they can take the oath of office and become a member of Congress.

SEE ALSO *Clay, Henry; Powell, Adam Clayton, Jr.*

QUALIFICATIONS FOR THE PRESIDENCY

SEE *Eligibility for the Presidency*

QUALIFICATIONS FOR THE SUPREME COURT

SEE *Appointment power*

QUAYLE, J. DANFORTH
Vice President

- Born: Feb. 4, 1947, Indianapolis, Ind.
- Political party: Republican
- Education: DePauw University, B.S., 1969; Indiana University Law School, J.D., 1974
- Military service: Indiana National Guard, 1969–75
- Previous government service: chief investigator, Consumer Protection Division, Office of Indiana Attorney General, 1970–71; administrative assistant to governor of Indiana, 1971–73; director, Inheritance Tax Division, Indiana Department of Treasury, 1973–74; U.S. House of Representatives, 1977–81; U.S. Senate, 1981–89
- Vice President under George Bush, **1989–93**

Dan Quayle left public life to work in his

family's newspaper business as associate publisher of the *Huntington Herald-Press* from 1974 to 1976. He returned to politics when he was elected to the U.S. House of Representatives in 1976, serving two terms. He was twice elected to the U.S. Senate from Indiana by large margins.

George Bush astonished his party and the nation by choosing Dan Quayle to be his running mate in 1988. Quayle had not been considered one of the leaders of the Senate, but his strongly conservative voting record helped Bush to solidify his base with the dominant wing of the Republican party. Press coverage was overwhelmingly negative throughout his tenure in office. Though Quayle had some accomplishments in the Senate (such as passage of an important job training bill), media coverage made it seem as if he were an intellectual lightweight.

As Vice President Quayle gathered a staff of experienced conservative intellectuals who helped him stake out his own policy positions and he lobbied with his former colleagues in the Senate for Bush's domestic program. As chair of the National Aeronautics and Space Council, he oversaw a major study on the effectiveness of the space program and was an advocate of a manned landing on Mars. As chair of the White House Council on Competitiveness, he promoted deregulation of business. He also implemented a "privatization" policy whereby cities and counties might sell airports and other facilities built with federal funds to the private sector. He was considered a strong supporter of Israel and was a strong proponent of military action against Iraq after it invaded Kuwait in 1990.

Quayle played a highly visible role in the 1992 Presidential campaign, attempting to shore up the Republican party's conservative base by campaigning against "the cultural elites" of the United States. He claimed that journalists, professors, abortion rights activists, and Hollywood television and music producers did not share the values of mainstream Americans.

He attacked the television character Murphy Brown for having a child out of wedlock and thereby weakening "family values."

A majority of the American public disapproved of Quayle's divisive campaign style; in the summer of 1992 national public opinion polls put his popularity at around 20 percent, and 60 percent of the public wanted Bush to choose another running mate. His failure to spell *potato* correctly at a spelling bee (he spelled it *potatoe*) prompted the comedian Jay Leno to quip, "Maybe he should stop watching 'Murphy Brown' and start watching 'Sesame Street.'"

SEE ALSO *Bush, George*

SOURCES David S. Broder and Bob Woodward, *The Man Who Would Be President: Dan Quayle* (New York: Simon & Schuster, 1992). Richard Fenno, *The Making of a Senator: Dan Quayle* (Washington, D.C.: Congressional Quarterly, 1989). Andrew Rosenthal, "Quayle's Moment," *New York Times Magazine,* July 5, 1992.

QUORUM

A quorum is the minimum attendance—half the members plus one—necessary for either the Senate or House to conduct business. If a quorum is not present, no business can be transacted. Normally, far fewer than half the senators and representatives are present on the floor. However, a quorum is assumed to be present until any member suggests its absence. When that happens, bells ring to summon absent members to the floor.

In the House, members respond to quorum calls by going to the chamber and answering when their name is called. During the 19th century, members of the minority could stall House business simply by not answering quorum calls. But in 1890 House Speaker Thomas B. Reed stopped this practice by counting anyone he saw, even if they had not responded when their name was called.

Senators use quorum calls as a delaying tactic to suspend floor activity between speeches or while working out some legislative compromise off the floor. The clerk slowly calls the roll, but senators do not need to respond. As soon as they are ready to proceed, a senator will ask unanimous consent to suspend the quorum call, and business will pick up where it left off. Only for "live" quorums (three bells rather than two) must senators respond to a quorum call. Those trying to filibuster will often use quorum calls to delay or stop business altogether. The leadership will also use "live" quorum calls to bring as many members as possible to the floor to be present for some important business.

SEE ALSO *Bells, congressional; Filibuster; Reed, Thomas B.; Unanimous consent agreements*

R

RANKING MEMBERS IN CONGRESS

At the beginning of each Congress, minority party members of each committee elect their ranking member, usually the person with the most seniority on that committee. However, party rules limit the number of committees and subcommittees on which someone may be the ranking member. In cases where the most senior member is already the ranking member of another committee, the next most senior member generally moves up to the ranking position.

The ranking member appoints and supervises the minority staff of a committee or subcommittee and looks out for the minority party's interests in all committee business. A committee chairman will try to work closely with the ranking member in order to maintain goodwill and to keep their committee as united as possible when reporting legislation out to the full House or Senate.

SEE ALSO *Chairs of committees; Seniority in Congress*

RANKIN, JEANNETTE

- Born: June 11, 1880, Missoula, Mont.
- Political party: Republican
- Education: University of Montana at Missoula, graduated, 1902; School of Philanthropy, New York City, 1908, 1909
- Representative from Montana: 1917–19, 1941–43

- Died: May 18, 1973, Carmel, Calif.

A leader in the campaign to give women the right to vote in Montana, Jeannette Rankin in 1916 became the first woman elected to Congress. In the House of Representatives, she initially devoted herself to winning national suffrage (voting rights) for women, but her attentions were soon diverted to the war in Europe. A pacifist, Rankin joined 49 other antiwar members of the House to vote against U.S. entry into World War I in 1917. The following year she lost a bid to be elected to the Senate. Ironically, in 1940 Rankin again won a seat in the House, and she was there when the Japanese bombed Pearl Harbor on December 7, 1941. Standing firm for her beliefs against enormous pressure, she became the only member of Congress to vote against war with Japan.

Rankin never again ran for Congress but resumed her private activities on behalf of peace and women's rights. At 90, she was protesting the Vietnam War. After her death, the state of Montana sent a statue of Jeannette Rankin to the U.S. Capitol, bearing the motto "I cannot vote for war."

SEE ALSO *Women in government*
SOURCES Hannah Josephson, *Jeannette Rankin, First Lady in Congress* (Indianapolis: Bobbs-Merrill, 1974).

RAYBURN, SAM

- Born: Jan. 6, 1882, Kingston, Tenn.
- Political party: Democrat
- Education: East Texas Normal College,

graduated, 1903; studied law at the University of Texas at Austin
- Representative from Texas: 1913–61
- House majority leader: 1937–40
- Speaker of the House: 1940–47, 1949–53, 1955–61
- Died: Nov. 16, 1961, Bonham, Tex.

"To get along, go along," Sam Rayburn would advise new members of the House of Representatives. An extremely effective legislator himself, "Mr. Sam" was famous for hard work, fair play, and keeping his word to other members. "He's so damned sincere and dedicated to a cause and he knows his country and his job inside out so well," said another representative, "that I would feel pretty dirty to turn him down and not trust him." Except for two Republican Congresses, Rayburn served as Speaker of the House from 1940 to 1961. Democratic Presidents depended upon him to get the votes in the House for their programs. But despite the Democratic majorities, Rayburn had to contend with a coalition between conservative Democrats and Republicans. They especially dominated the House Rules Committee, chaired by former judge Howard Smith of Virginia. As one of his last acts as Speaker, Rayburn threw his prestige behind a plan to enlarge the Rules Committee and break the conservatives' control. "Boys, are you with me or with Judge Smith?" he asked House members. Rayburn won the vote by 217 to 212, clearing the way for the liberal legislation of the administrations of John F. Kennedy and Lyndon B. Johnson in the 1960s. In 1965 the Rayburn House Office Building opened, named in honor of the House's longest-serving Speaker.

SEE ALSO *Speaker of the House*
SOURCES Richard B. Cheney and Lynne V. Cheney, *Kings of the Hill: Power and Personality in the House of Representatives* (New York: Continuum, 1983). D. B. Hardeman and Donald C. Bacon, *Rayburn: A Biography* (Austin: Texas Monthly Press, 1987).

REAGAN, RONALD
40th President

- Born: Feb. 6, 1911, Tampico, Ill.
- Political party: Republican
- Education: Eureka College, B.A., 1932
- Military service: U.S. Army Air Force, 1942–45
- Previous government service: governor of California, 1967–74
- Elected President, 1980; served, 1981–89

Ronald Wilson Reagan was the first actor to be elected President. He was also the oldest man ever elected and the first to have been divorced. Reagan brought conservatives to power in the Republican party and in the nation. His economic program of tax and spending cuts led to a boom between 1982 and 1987 that stimulated economic growth, but it also led to high federal budget deficits and the conversion of the United States from the largest creditor to the largest debtor in the world. His popularity declined during the Iran-Contra crisis but returned to high levels as he left office. The most popular President since Dwight Eisenhower, he was the first since Franklin Roosevelt to serve two or more full terms and hand over the office to a member of his own party.

Reagan's father worked in a shoe store and for the Works Progress Administration during the New Deal, and his mother was a store clerk. Reagan was a popular football player in high school and won election as student government president. At Eureka College he also played football, participated in student government, and joined the drama society.

After graduating from college in 1932 with a major in economics, he began his career as a radio sports announcer in Iowa. In 1937 he became a contract motion picture actor for Warner Brothers, starring in such movies as *Knute Rockne—All Ameri-*

can, *King's Row,* and *Bedtime for Bonzo.* He married actress Jane Wyman in 1940; they had two children (one adopted), then divorced in 1948.

During World War II, Reagan served as a captain in the army, making films for the military. He was elected president of the Screen Actors Guild in 1947 and served through 1952, devoting much of his time to combating the influence of communists in the union. He was active in Democratic politics, supporting Harry Truman for President in 1948 and Helen Gahagan Douglas against Richard Nixon in the California senatorial contest of 1950. In 1952 he married Nancy Davis, a contract actress at MGM, and they had two children. Between 1954 and 1962 he was the host of the television show *General Electric Theater.* In 1959 Reagan again led the Screen Actors Guild, this time in a strike that gave actors a share in television profits from their movies.

Reagan became more conservative in the 1950s and supported the Presidential candidacies of Eisenhower in 1952 and 1956 and Nixon in 1960. He switched his voter registration to the Republican party in 1962. In October 1964 Reagan gave a televised speech for Barry Goldwater, the Republican candidate for President. After Goldwater's defeat, Reagan became one of the leading conservative spokesmen.

Reagan was twice elected governor of California, in 1966 and 1970, but for six of his eight years in office he had to work with a Democratic legislature. He cut the welfare rolls, instituted the Medi-Cal program to pay medical bills for the poor, increased income taxes in order to eliminate a projected budget deficit (but later gave rebates when the government ran a surplus), and managed to lower property taxes. He took a strong stance against student demonstrators against the Vietnam War who closed down many campuses of the state university system, and he more than doubled funding for California's public colleges and universities.

Reagan was a dark-horse candidate for the Republican Presidential nomination in

1968, but Nixon won the nomination on the first ballot. Reagan declined to run for a third gubernatorial term and challenged President Gerald Ford for the Republican nomination in 1976. Reagan lost the nomination by a slim margin. His followers did influence the Republican party platform, which repudiated much of Ford's foreign policy of détente, or accommodation, with the Soviet Union.

In 1980 Reagan ran again for the Republican nomination, defeating George Bush handily. Reagan attempted to get ex-President Ford to join the ticket, but Ford insisted on a "co-Presidency" arrangement in which he would share responsibility for policy-making. Reagan then chose Bush to complete the ticket.

With interest rates close to 20 percent, inflation around 12 percent, and unemployment near 10 percent, the voters responded by giving Reagan a landslide victory over President Jimmy Carter and independent candidate John Anderson. Reagan's coattails brought in a Republican-controlled Senate, though the House remained strongly Democratic.

Reagan's inaugural address emphasized economic recovery and putting all Americans back to work. He called for fewer government regulations and lower taxes. Reagan's first State of the Union address offered a four-point program of reduced expenditures, tax cuts, lessened government regulation, and policies to reduce inflation.

Reagan had a "hands off" management style that involved setting overall priorities but then delegating to others the work of translating these into specific policies. He often seemed lackadaisical in his duties: "It's true that hard work never killed anybody, but why take the chance?" he would joke.

Reagan was known as the Great Communicator. No President in the 20th century, with the possible exception of Teddy and Franklin Roosevelt, could match his ability as a speech maker. He presented his arguments to the American people in the form of stories. He used concrete examples involving real people rather than abstract principles to make his points. And often the public responded to his down-to-earth analogies. The Democrats had no one who could match him, and often the President would bypass Congress and appeal directly to the people to support his conservative policies.

Eventually, Reagan's inattention to details and disinterest in economic theory would catch up with him. His budget and tax numbers never did add up. A few of his subordinates were involved in conflicts of interest that led to embarrassing investigations. In his second term, his national security advisers took advantage of his management style to launch illegal operations, then covered up their involvement by lying to Congress.

On March 30, 1981, Reagan was shot outside a hotel in Washington, D.C., by John W. Hinckley, Jr., in an attempted assassination. The President lost a great deal of blood and at one point was near death, but the bullet had not hit any vital organs and he soon recovered. His popularity soared, which helped him deal with Congress in promoting his plan, popularly known as Reaganomics. Much of what Reagan asked for was passed by Congress in June. But instead of promoting prosperity, Reaganomics took the nation into a steep recession, a time of decline in the gross national product and an increase in unemployment. As joblessness increased, Reagan's popularity plummeted, down to the levels of Nixon during the Watergate scandal.

In foreign affairs Reagan took a confrontational line with the Soviets, referring to the U.S.S.R. as the "evil empire." He announced plans to equip NATO forces in Europe with new medium-range Pershing nuclear-tipped missiles. He asked for funds to deploy a new generation of intercontinental MX missiles. He reversed President Jimmy Carter's decision to cancel the B-1 bomber and ordered development of the radar-evading Stealth bombers and fighters. He increased the size of the navy

to 600 surface ships and ordered new submarines and aircraft carriers. He announced a Strategic Defense Initiative program of antimissile weapons to defend against Soviet attack, which his critics promptly dubbed Star Wars. Over five years he increased the annual level of defense spending from $200 billion to $300 billion.

Reagan equipped the government of El Salvador in its fight against leftist guerrillas and also supported the Contra rebels in their struggle against the Sandinista government of Nicaragua. He provided covert funding for anticommunist rebels in Afghanistan. He ordered the invasion of Grenada in October 1983, ostensibly to protect American medical students during disorders between two factions of the Marxist government; this action led to the replacement of the leftist government with leaders backed by the United States. Reagan also used U.S. Marines as part of an international peacekeeping force in Lebanon but withdrew the forces several months after guerrillas blew up the marine barracks, killing 241 marines in October 1983.

The economy started to revive in 1983 and with it Reagan's standing in the polls. Reagan was almost unanimously renominated in 1984 for the Presidency. He handily defeated the Democratic nominee, former Vice President Walter Mondale.

In Reagan's second term the economy continued to expand, resulting in millions of new jobs, record corporate profits, and lower inflation. Reagan adhered to the supply-side theory of economics, concentrating on stimulating the supply of goods and services. He felt that lower tax rates on producers would stimulate the economy and produce greater tax revenues, which could shrink the deficit. But the result of tax cuts turned out to be massive budget deficits: in the Reagan years the total national debt rose from $1 trillion (accumulated through 190 years of U.S. history) to $3 trillion. Moreover, the nation had entered the Reagan years with a surplus in its accounts with foreign nations but began to run large trade deficits and became a debtor nation for the first time since before World War I. The stock market rose dramatically, then dropped sharply on October 19, 1987; the Dow-Jones average (of stock prices) lost a third of its value in a few days. Deregulation of financial institutions led to a savings and loan scandal, in which bank officials used poor judgment in making loans and some then engaged in criminal behavior to cover up their losses. The eventual bailout by the national government to keep the financial system stable would cost taxpayers at least $150 billion. The Tax Reform Act of 1986 reduced personal income tax rates, contributing to a great accumulation of wealth for those in the top 10 percent of the population. But the bottom fifth of the population was paying a higher percentage of their income in taxes at the end of the decade than at the beginning because of increases in Social Security taxes.

The Reagan years were marked by an increase in economic inequality, as the rich got richer much faster than others benefited. Young adults with children actually found their incomes decreasing through the decade. The percentage of Americans in poverty increased during the decade from 12 to 15 percent. Meanwhile, Reagan had won cuts in various social welfare programs for the poor: job training, Medicaid, food stamps, and welfare. Although the total amount spent on these programs increased, individuals often found their allotments cut.

During the Reagan years Republican appointments to the Supreme Court and lower federal courts gave conservatives much more influence than they had enjoyed before. Reagan appointed Supreme Court justices Sandra Day O'Connor, the first woman on the high court, and conservative law professor Antonin Scalia. The Senate rejected two of Reagan's other Supreme Court nominees, Court of Appeals judges Robert Bork and Douglas Ginsburg, but Reagan managed to gain confirmation

of another federal judge, Anthony Kennedy. Reagan also promoted Associate Justice William Rehnquist to chief justice upon the retirement of Warren Burger.

In foreign affairs the defense buildup brought the Soviets to the negotiating table in a position of weakness. In 1987 the United States and the Soviet Union signed the Intermediate-Range Nuclear Forces Treaty, which provided for gradual dismantling of all Soviet and U.S. medium- and short-range missiles in Europe. Another Reagan success occurred in the Middle East: the President deterred Libya from organizing international terrorist forces when he ordered a bombing raid on Libya in 1986 in retaliation for a bombing on a disco in West Germany frequented by U.S. troops. That bombing killed 37 people, including the daughter of Libyan leader Mu'ammar Qaddafi. In 1987 Reagan used the navy to convoy Kuwaiti ships in the Persian Gulf and prevent the Iranian navy from imposing a blockade on oil tankers.

Reagan committed a major foreign policy blunder, however, that nearly destroyed his Presidency. He agreed to sell arms to Iran in a secret attempt to bolster moderates in that nation's government who were willing to free Western hostages. Some of the profits from the sales were then transferred to the Contra rebels to help fund their battle against the Nicaraguan government. The funding violated the Boland Amendment, a law passed by Congress that had cut off U.S. government funds to the Contras.

The arms sales and fund transfers were disclosed in the fall of 1986, just after the Democrats regained control of the Senate in the congressional elections. The Democrats then organized a full-scale investigation of the Iran-Contra affair. For months Reagan seemed preoccupied with the crisis and his government was paralyzed. His national security adviser, members of the NSC staff, several top White House aides, and his chief of staff resigned. There was no evidence linking Reagan directly to the transfer of funds to the Contras, but the Tower Commission, appointed by the President to study the incident, determined that national security affairs in the White House had been mismanaged. The President implemented most of the reforms in procedures suggested by the commission.

In retirement Reagan worked at his ranch near Santa Barbara, California, gave occasional speeches, and wrote his memoirs until he was incapable of doing so because of Alzheimer's disease.

SEE ALSO *Budget, Presidential; Bush, George; Carter, Jimmy; Ford, Gerald R.; War Powers Resolution (1973)*

SOURCES Paul Boyer, ed., *Reagan As President: Contemporary Views of the Man, His Politics, and His Policies* (Chicago: Ivan R. Dee, 1990). Lou Cannon, *President Reagan: The Role of a Lifetime* (New York: Simon & Schuster, 1991). Dinesh D'Souza, *Ronald Reagan: How an Ordinary Man Became an Extraordinary Leader* (New York: Free Press, 1997). Haynes Johnson, *Sleepwalking through History: America in the Reagan Years* (New York: Norton, 1991). William Ker Muir, Jr., and Robert B. Hawkins, *The Bully Pulpit: The Presidential Leadership of Ronald Reagan* (San Francisco: Institute for Contemporary Studies Press, 1992). Kenneth W. Thompson, ed., *Leadership in the Reagan Presidency: Seven Intimate Perspectives.* (Lanham, Md.: Madison Books, 1992).

REAPPORTIONMENT

Every ten years the United States conducts a census of its population, after which the House of Representatives is reapportioned—that is, the seats are reallocated in proportion to the states' populations. Some states gain congressional districts, some lose districts, and some keep the same number.

By statute, Congress sets the total number of representatives in the House. At first, the House simply enlarged its membership to accommodate new states and a growing population. After the 1790 census the House expanded from 65 to 105 members. The numbers increased steadily until 1911, when House membership reached 435. Since then, that number has remained the ceiling. After each census the states redraw the lines of their congressional districts to conform to any changes in the population. (In addition to the 435 voting members, the House of Representatives also has various delegates who represent U.S. territories.)

In the 1790s each member of the House represented about 33,000 people. By the 1990s each member represented nearly 600,000 people. However, at times the population size of congressional districts has varied widely. For many years the state legislatures that drew the boundaries for their state's congressional districts favored less-populated rural areas over cities by giving the rural areas greater proportional representation. In the 1964 case of *Wesberry* v. *Sanders,* the Supreme Court ruled such inequalities unconstitutional. The Court ordered that congressional districts be drawn to provide "one person, one vote."

The majority party in the state legislature invariably tries to draw the reapportionment lines to favor its own candidates in elections. Sometimes they resort to gerrymandering—drawing oddly shaped districts to combine areas where their party registration is the strongest. The Voting Rights Act of 1982 encouraged states not to divide up districts in such a way that minority groups cannot elect their own candidates.

In the redistricting that followed the 1990 census, this led to the creation of many more districts where African-American and Hispanic-American candidates stood a better chance of election. But the Supreme Court restrained this trend by ruling in *Miller* v. *Johnson* (1995) that states could not use race as the predominant reason for drawing a district's boundaries.

SEE ALSO *Gerrymandering*

RECESS, CONGRESSIONAL

Between the opening of a session and its final adjournment, or closing, Congress calls the time it takes off "recesses." During the 19th century, Congress took few long recesses because it generally met for only half the year and then adjourned so that members could spend the other half back home. But in recent years, the first session of a two-year Congress begins on January 3 and runs to the middle of December, averaging more than 300 days. The second session begins the following January 3 and adjourns in October, a month before the November election, averaging more than 250 days. Congress does not meet every day during these sessions. The Senate and House often do not meet on either Friday or Monday, recessing to give members long weekends to return to their home state.

Congress will also recess for a week corresponding with major federal holidays. And some members of the House call these recesses "district work periods" because instead of taking vacations, many members spend the time working directly with their constituents in their home district. Other members use recesses for international travel or simply to spend time with their families. The Legislative Reorganization Act of 1970 also provided that Congress take a 30-day recess each August, except in time of war.

Whenever Congress is in recess, Presidents gain some additional leeway. During longer congressional recesses, the President can kill a bill with a pocket veto—in a sense, putting the bill unsigned in his pocket—which Congress cannot override. Presidents also make recess appointments, giving the individual named some time in the post before the Senate returns to begin the confirmation process. This gives the nominee the chance to perform the duties of the office. But the Senate can still reject a recess appointee if the President resubmits the nomination for a full term.

SEE ALSO *Adjournment, congressional; Legislative Reorganization Acts (1946 and 1970); Nominations, confirmation of; Veto power*

RECISION BILLS

The Congressional Budget and Impoundment Control Act of 1974 forbade Presidents from impounding, or withholding, money that Congress had appropriated for federal projects. But it permitted the President to ask Congress for a recision, a cancellation or cutback, of any appropriation that was no longer needed. Because of the soaring federal deficits, proposals before Congress have suggested giving the President an "enhanced recision" power. The President could then cut back appropriated funds unless a majority in both houses voted to restore those funds.

SEE ALSO *Appropriations; Budget and Impoundment Control Act, Congressional (1974)*

RECONSTRUCTION, CONGRESSIONAL

Congress and President Andrew Johnson fought bitterly over the Reconstruction of the South after the Civil War. Johnson believed he was following the wishes of the assassinated Abraham Lincoln by pursuing a quick and lenient return of the South into the Union. Radical Republicans, led by Representative Thaddeus Stevens, argued that these former Confederate states had committed "state suicide" and reverted to the status of territories. Radicals wanted to readmit the Southern states only if they ensured the civil rights and liberties of the freedmen (the term used for former slaves). Moderates in Congress hoped to work with Johnson but were dismayed when he vetoed the Freedmen's Bureau Bill, which provided funds to build and run schools for the freedmen. The bill's sponsor, Senator William Fessenden (Republican–Maine) declared that Johnson had "broken the faith, betrayed his trust, and must sink from detestation to contempt." Johnson's veto drove moderate and radical Republicans together in support of tough Reconstruction measures, and it eventually led to the failed effort to impeach and remove the President.

Congress took control of Reconstruction policies away from the President, drafting the 14th and 15th Amendments to the Constitution to protect the civil liberties and voting rights of African Americans. In 1866 and 1875 Congress also enacted civil rights bills to guarantee all citizens equal rights in hotels, restaurants, trains, and other public accommodations and transportation facilities. Federal troops occupied many Southern states during Reconstruction, enabling the freedmen to vote and to elect Republican candidates—both black and white—to Congress. When these federal troops left, following the election of 1876, Congressional Reconstruction collapsed. The Supreme Court later ruled the civil rights acts unconstitutional. In the following decades African Americans lost the right to vote, and racial segregation became the law throughout the South.

SEE ALSO *African Americans in government; Civil rights; Stevens, Thaddeus*
SOURCES Eric Foner, *Reconstruction: America's Unfinished Revolution, 1863–1877* (New York: Harper & Row, 1988).

RECORDS OF CONGRESS

After the hearings and debates end and Congress has adopted or rejected a piece of legislation, a nomination, or a treaty, the official records go to the National Archives and Records Administration in Washington, D.C. There, archivists catalog, box, and open the records for research, subject to the rules of the Senate and House. Although congressional records are not included under the Freedom of Information Act (which sets the terms for access to executive branch records), most Senate records open automatically after 20 years, and House records after 30 years. Records involving national security and personal privacy are closed for as much as 50 years. Official records are those of the committees and support staff. Senators' and representatives' papers are considered their personal property. Although in the past many members of Congress destroyed their papers, today most members send their papers to home-state libraries and historical societies.

Before the National Archives opened in 1936, the records of Congress were stored haphazardly throughout the Capitol building. Conditions were often so bad that the documents deteriorated or were destroyed. Congressional documents include copies of bills and resolutions, transcripts of hearings, nominations, treaties, correspondence, and petitions that range from individual postcards to great rolls containing thousands of signatures.

Nineteenth-century clerks of Congress folded documents in thirds to fit within the pigeonholes of their desks and tied bundles of documents with red tape. "Cutting through the red tape" referred to removing the tape to find needed documents—and the expression is still used for getting something done in the bureaucracy. In recent years many records have been microfilmed, or they exist only in computers. Such technological advances both facilitate and complicate the jobs of those archivists who preserve, catalog, and make available for research the records of Congress.

SOURCES Herman J. Viola, *The National Archives of the United States* (New York: Abrams, 1984).

RECRUITMENT INTO CONGRESS

Who runs for Congress? The kind of candidate has changed significantly over time. When political parties were strong institutions, they chose candidates based on party loyalty. Local party bosses and political "machines" in the larger cities determined all local and congressional candidates. For instance, in 1934 the Democratic machine in Kansas City, Missouri, picked Harry S. Truman for the Senate. A political machine is a tightly run political organization based on patronage. Many machine politicians who became candidates were far less talented and honest than Truman. Party endorsements were particularly important to senatorial candidates when senators were chosen by state legislatures rather than by popular vote. Since Senate candidates had to have strong support within the state legislature, most 19th-century senators served first in a state legislature or as governor of their state. Because they identified strongly with their party, they tended to vote with other members of their party in Congress.

After the 17th Amendment established direct election of senators in 1913, and after many states provided for primaries where voters could choose party candidates, the influence of party organizations declined and reform candidates often successfully challenged the machines.

Self-selected candidates Congressional candidates became increasingly self-selected rather than party-selected. Fewer candidates for federal office had any experience in local or state government. Many congressional candidates had never run for public office before but had gained their experience in law, business, or universities. Some gained public attention as astronauts, athletes, or actors: Senator John Glenn (Democrat–Ohio) won fame as the first American astronaut to orbit the earth. Senator Bill Bradley (Democrat–New Jersey) played professional basketball for the New York Knicks. And Representative Fred Grandy (Republican–Iowa) had a featured role in a television series called "The Love Boat."

Instead of state legislators and governors running for the Senate, many members of the House became Senate candidates. Congressional staff members also began to run for office themselves. In the 102nd Congress, both Speaker of the House Thomas Foley and Senate majority leader George Mitchell were former members of the congressional staff.

The chances of self-selected candidates winning election improved with the growth of broadcast news. In the 19th century, newspapers identified strongly with one political party or the other and strongly endorsed that party's candidates. Candidates could address only limited audiences during a campaign, and they had to rely on party organizations to organize rallies, put up posters, and get party members out to vote. But the development of radio, and more important, of television, allowed candidates to talk directly to the voters. With enough money, and with effective advertisements, an individual unknown to 99 percent of the voters at the beginning of a race can become known well enough to upset the incumbent, the person currently serving in the office.

The value of a family name Having a prominent family name has always been an asset in winning party nomination and election to Congress. At age 30, Russell Long (Democrat–Louisiana) followed his famous father, Huey P. Long, to the Senate. Also at age 30, Edward M. Kennedy (Democrat–Massachusetts) won the Senate seat once held by his brother John F. Kennedy. His Republican opponent, George Cabot Lodge, was the son of another former Massachusetts senator, Henry Cabot Lodge, Jr. Similarly, in 1990 Representative Susan Molinari (Republican–New York) took the House seat that her father, Guy Molinari, had held for a decade.

Republican and Democratic campaign committees in both the House and Senate try to recruit strong candidates to run against incumbents from the opposition party. Campaign committees promise to raise funds for these candidates and to help them gain name recognition. Other candidates draw their support and financial base from their past connections with chambers of commerce, labor unions, consumer and environmental organizations, the civil rights and women's rights movements, antiabortion activists, and other single- and multi-issue groups.

SEE ALSO *Campaign committees, congressional; Families in Congress*

SOURCES David T. Cannon, *Actors, Athletes, and Astronauts: Political Amateurs in the United States Congress* (Chicago: University of Chicago Press, 1990).

RECUSAL

A judge may recuse himself or herself, or refuse to participate in deciding a case, because of a special interest in the outcome that could influence his or her decision. The term *recuse* is derived from the Latin word *recusare*, which means "to refuse." Chief Justice John Marshall, for example, recused himself in the case of *Martin* v. *Hunter's Lessee* (1816) because he had served as attorney to one of the parties (Martin) in an earlier phase of the case. In addition, he had a financial stake in the outcome of the case.

REED, STANLEY F.
Associate Justice, 1938–57

- Born: Dec. 31, 1884, Minerva, Ky.
- Education: Kentucky Wesleyan College, B.A., 1902; Yale College, B.A., 1906; legal studies at University of Virginia and Columbia University
- Previous government service: Kentucky General Assembly, 1912–16; general counsel, Federal Farm Board, 1929–32; general counsel, Reconstruction Finance Corporation, 1932–35; special assistant to the U.S. attorney general, 1935; U.S. solicitor general, 1935–38
- Appointed by President Franklin D. Roosevelt Jan. 15, 1938; replaced George Sutherland, who retired
- Supreme Court term: confirmed by the Senate Jan. 25, 1938, by a voice vote; retired Feb. 25, 1957
- Died: Apr. 2, 1980, Huntington, N.Y.

Stanley Reed was a prominent defender of the New Deal policies of President Franklin D. Roosevelt. As a lawyer for the federal government, he defended New Deal programs in several important Supreme Court cases. His reward was appointment in 1938 by President Roosevelt to a vacancy on the Supreme Court.

Justice Reed continued to support the economic programs of President Roosevelt's New Deal. He tended to favor broad exercise of the federal government's power to regulate commerce or trade among the states (Article 1, Section 8, of the Constitution). However, Justice Reed tended to have a narrow view of freedom of expression when he thought it threatened national security or public order.

Reed retired from the Court in 1957, but he continued to assist the Court of Claims and the Court of Appeals for the District of Columbia. In 1980, he died at the age of 95, having lived longer than any other justice of the Supreme Court.

REED, THOMAS B.

- Born: Oct. 18, 1839, Portland, Maine
- Political party: Republican
- Education: Bowdoin College, graduated, 1860; studied law
- Representative from Maine: 1877–99
- Speaker of the House: 1889–91, 1895–99
- Died: Dec. 7, 1902, Washington, D.C.

Six feet, three inches tall and weighing nearly 300 pounds, Speaker Thomas B. Reed ruled the House of Representatives so firmly that people called him "Czar" Reed. After years of weak leadership, Reed was unwilling to sit helplessly in the Speaker's chair and watch the majority become powerless to pass legislation. The minority Democrats had been disrupting House business by making motions to adjourn and then demanding roll call votes.

Reed declared these motions "dilatory," or deliberately delaying, and ruled them out of order. The minority also tried to stall House business by not answering quorum calls—a practice known as the "disappearing quorum." Reed simply took it upon himself to count anyone he saw, even if they had not answered "present." One furious Kentucky Democrat shouted, "I deny your right, Mr. Speaker, to count me present." Reed calmly responded, "The Chair is making a statement of fact that the gentleman from Kentucky is present. Does he wish to deny it?"

Reed got his way, and the rules of the House were changed to recognize the Speaker's right to count a quorum and to declare delaying motions out of order. The rules of the House, he insisted, were designed not to protect the minority but "to promote the orderly conduct of business." Reed used his power as Speaker to promote the Republican party's conservative financial programs. But even Reed could not stop the House stampede to vote for war with Spain in 1898. After the war he strongly opposed the taking of Puerto Rico and the Philippines as U.S. territories. He retired as Speaker when he failed to persuade his party to abandon its expansionist foreign policies.

SEE ALSO *Quorum; Rules of the House and Senate; Speaker of the House*
SOURCES Richard B. Cheney and Lynne V. Cheney *Kings of the Hill: Power and Personality in the House of Representatives* (New York: Continuum, 1983).

REED V. REED

- 404 U.S. 71 (1971)
- Vote: 7–0
- For the Court: Burger

Sally and Cecil Reed were the separated parents of a deceased son, Richard Reed. Both parents petitioned an Idaho court for appointment as the administrator of their son's estate. The court denied Sally Reed's petition in favor of Cecil Reed. This deci-

sion was based on an Idaho statute that preferred males to females in choosing administrators of estates.

Sally Reed sued Cecil for the right to administer Richard's estate, which was valued at less than $1,000. She claimed that the Idaho law giving preference to a male over a female violated the 14th Amendment guarantee of "equal protection of the laws." Ruth Bader Ginsburg, as a lawyer for the American Civil Liberties Union, argued Sally Reed's case before the Supreme Court.

The Issue The 14th Amendment says, "No State shall . . . deny to any person within its jurisdiction the equal protection of the laws." However, in past cases the Court had not used the "equal protection" clause of the 14th Amendment to overturn laws that discriminated against individuals on the basis of gender. The Court had used what it called a rational basis test to uphold sex-based laws. According to this test, such laws were constitutional unless one could prove they were not reasonably connected to a compelling public interest. Did the Idaho law in this case violate the equal protection clause of the 14th Amendment? Was there any compelling public reason for sustaining this law?

Opinion of the Court The Court decided this case in favor of Sally Reed, ruling that the Idaho statute did not meet the rational basis test. Chief Justice Warren E. Burger wrote, "To give a mandatory preference to members of either sex . . . merely to accomplish the elimination of hearings on the merits, is to make the very kind of arbitrary legislative choice forbidden by the Equal Protection Clause of the Fourteenth Amendment."

Significance This case was the first to rule that laws mandating gender discrimination are violations of the 14th Amendment. The Court has used the precedent established in the *Reed* case to strike down many laws that unfairly discriminated against women. For instance, in *Kahn* v. *Shevin* (1974) it ruled that a Florida law that gave a property tax exemption to widowers (males), but not to widows (females) was unconstitutional.

SEE ALSO *Equality under the Constitution*

REFERRALS TO CONGRESSIONAL COMMITTEES

Once a bill or resolution is introduced, the parliamentarian, acting for the presiding officer, refers it to the appropriate committee. The rules of the Senate and House spell out which committees should handle what types of legislation. For instance, bills dealing with the federal courts would be referred to the Judiciary Committees, whereas bills dealing with education would go to the education and labor committees. Sometimes, however, one bill covers issues over which more than one committee has jurisdiction. In these cases the parliamentarian makes multiple referrals. In the Senate, a bill setting clean air standards for automobile exhaust systems might be referred to both the Committee on Energy and Natural Resources and the Committee on Environment and Public Works. An entire bill could be referred to two or more committees, or the individual sections of the bill might be separated and distributed to the committees that deal with such issues. Authors therefore try to draft bills in such a way as to increase the likelihood that they will be referred to the most sympathetic committees.

SEE ALSO *Committees, congressional; Parliamentarian*

REGENTS OF THE UNIVERSITY OF CALIFORNIA V. BAKKE

- 438 U.S. 265 (1978)
- Vote: 5–4
- For the Court: Powell
- Concurring: Burger, Rehnquist, Stevens, and Stewart

- Dissenting: Blackmun, Brennan, Marshall, and White

In 1972 there were 2,664 applicants for admission to the medical school of the University of California at Davis. From this large pool of applicants, the medical school intended to select 100 students. Eighty-four of the 100 openings were to be filled according to usual procedures of the standard admissions program. Sixteen of the 100 places were to be filled through a special affirmative action program designed to increase the number of disadvantaged students from certain minority groups, such as African Americans, Latinos, and Native Americans.

Students applying for admission through the affirmative action program did not have to meet the same standards as students applying through the regular admissions program. For example, requirements for grade point averages and scores on standardized tests of scholastic aptitude and achievement were lower for those seeking admission through the special program.

Allan Bakke, a white male, wanted to become a doctor. In 1972 he applied through the regular program for admission to the Davis medical school. He was rejected even though his grade point average and standardized test scores were higher than those of several students admitted to the medical school through the affirmative action program.

In 1973 Bakke again tried to gain admission to the Davis medical school. This time he was one of 3,737 applicants for 100 vacancies. Once again, 16 places were set aside for applicants through the special affirmative action program. Bakke was rejected a second time, even though he appeared to be more qualified, based on certain statistical indicators, than several applicants admitted through both the affirmative action program and the regular process.

Bakke claimed he was a victim of unequal and unfair treatment. He sued for admission to the state medical school.

The Issue Bakke argued that the

medical school's admissions program violated the "equal protection of the laws" guarantee of the 14th Amendment. Bakke also claimed that the university's affirmative action admissions program conflicted with Title VI of the Civil Rights Act of 1964, which forbids discrimination based on race or ethnicity in programs supported by federal funds.

The University of California defended its special admissions program as necessary to compensate for past injustices suffered by members of certain disadvantaged groups. The special admissions program, university officials said, was one way to open new opportunities for individual members of groups that in the past had not enjoyed these opportunities to the same degree as other members of society.

Allan Bakke, however, questioned whether the affirmative action admissions program went too far in trying to provide new opportunities for members of certain disadvantaged groups. To Bakke, the medical school's affirmative action admissions program seemed to be "reverse discrimination" based on race or ethnicity. Therefore, he asserted, it violated federal statutes and the U.S. Constitution.

Opinion of the Court The Supreme Court was so sharply divided in its response to this case that the majority could not agree on a common opinion for the Court. Lewis F. Powell was designated to announce the decision, but the four concurring justices wrote separate opinions, which were mixed in their reasons for supporting or opposing different aspects of the Court's decision.

A majority decided that Allan Bakke must be admitted to the University of California Medical School at Davis. Justice Powell noted that Bakke had been excluded from competition for one of the 16 positions reserved for individuals seeking admission through the special affirmative action program. Therefore, Powell concluded, Bakke had been denied "equal protection of the laws" as required by the 14th Amendment.

Justice Powell wrote, "The guarantees

of the Fourteenth Amendment extend to all persons.... The guarantee of equal protection cannot mean one thing when applied to one individual and something else when applied to a person of another color. If both are not accorded the same protection, then it is not equal."

The Court held that a university may use admissions standards involving race or ethnicity as one part of a complex admissions process. But "fixed quotas"— guaranteeing a certain number of positions for students of a particular race or ethnicity—cannot be used. Race and ethnic background may be viewed favorably in making decisions about when to admit a person to a university program. But they cannot be the sole factor in determining whether to admit or reject someone.

Dissent Justices William Brennan, Byron White, Thurgood Marshall, and Harry Blackmun voted against admission of Bakke to the medical school. And they would have upheld the quota-based admissions system of the medical school. However, they joined with Justice Powell to permit "race conscious programs in the future," as long as they are only one factor considered in a multifactor admissions process. Thus, the four dissenters from the decision to admit Bakke to the medical school blocked the other four justices (Warren Burger, William Rehnquist, John Paul Stevens, and Potter Stewart), who would have prohibited any use of a person's race as a factor in deciding whom to admit to a university program.

The four dissenters defended the affirmative action admissions program of the medical school:

The Davis program does not simply advance less qualified applicants; rather it compensates applicants, who it is uncontested are fully qualified to study medicine, for educational disadvantages that it was reasonable to conclude were a product of state-fostered discrimination. Once admitted, these students must satisfy the same degree requirements as regularly admitted students.

Significance This case was the Court's first major statement on whether affirmative action programs are constitutional. And the results were mixed. The rejection of Allan Bakke as a result of the medical school's special admissions program was declared in violation of the U.S. Constitution. However, race could be an important factor in admissions programs, as long as it was not the sole or dominating factor in making an admissions decision.

Allan Bakke certainly benefited from the Court's decision. He graduated in 1982 from the University of California Medical School at Davis and later served as a resident at the prestigious Mayo Clinic in Rochester, Minnesota. However, the *Bakke* decision has had only slight impact on university admissions programs, which shun explicitly stated quotas but tend to consider race and ethnicity as important factors in admissions decisions. This matter remains complex and controversial.

SEE ALSO *Affirmative action*

SOURCES Fred W. Friendly and Martha J. H. Elliott, "Bakke and the Equal Protection Clause," in *The Constitution: That Delicate Balance* (New York: Random House, 1984). J. Harvie Wilkinson, *From Brown to Bakke: The Supreme Court and School Integration, 1954–1978* (New York: Oxford University Press, 1979).

REGULATION OF COMMERCE

SEE *Commerce power*

REHNQUIST, WILLIAM H.
Associate Justice, 1972–86
Chief Justice, 1986–

- Born: Oct. 1, 1924, Milwaukee, Wis.
- Education: Stanford University, B.A., 1948, M.A., 1949; Harvard University,

M.A., 1950; Stanford University Law School, LL.B., 1951

- Previous government service: law clerk to Justice Robert H. Jackson of the Supreme Court, 1952–53; assistant U.S. attorney general, 1969–71
- Appointed by President Richard Nixon to the position of associate justice Oct. 21, 1971; replaced John Marshall Harlan II, who retired; appointed chief justice by President Ronald Reagan June 20, 1986; replaced Chief Justice Warren E. Burger, who retired
- Supreme Court term: confirmed by the Senate as associate justice Dec. 10, 1971, by a 68–26 vote; confirmed by the Senate as chief justice Sept. 17, 1986, by a 65–33 vote

William H. Rehnquist ranked first in his class at Stanford Law School, which also included Justice Sandra Day O'Connor. And he was a distinctive member of the Supreme Court under Chief Justice Warren Burger. Justice Rehnquist dissented more than any other member of that Court. In 1986, President Ronald Reagan named Rehnquist the Chief Justice of the United States.

Rehnquist has tended to support the rights and powers of state governments within the federal system. He strongly believes that the Constitution limits the federal government so that the state governments have substantial powers in many areas. He has favored state law enforcement powers over the rights of accused persons, as in *New York* v. *Quarles* (1984) and *United States* v. *Leon* (1984). He also has upheld state rules that restrict abortion rights but has stopped short of total opposition to *Roe* v. *Wade* (1973), the landmark case restricting states from taking away the abortion rights of women.

Rehnquist emphasizes limitations of judicial power and tries to avoid judicial infringement of the legitimate powers of the legislative and executive branches of government. The judicial branch, according to Rehnquist, should scrupulously avoid political questions and restrict itself to exercising judgment according to the words of the Constitution and the intentions of the framers.

In 1999 Chief Justice Rehnquist presided at the Senate's impeachment trial of President Bill Clinton, as required by the Constitution. The Senate voted against conviction of the President.

SOURCES Sue Davis, *Justice Rehnquist and the Constitution* (Princeton, N.J.: Princeton University Press, 1989). Sue Davis, "Justice William H. Rehnquist: Right-Wing Ideologue or Majoritarian Democrat?" in *The Burger Court: Political and Judicial Profiles,* edited by Charles M. Lamb and Stephen C. Halpern (Urbana: University of Illinois Press, 1991). William H. Rehnquist, *The Supreme Court: How It Was, How It Is* (New York: Morrow, 1987). David G. Savage, *Turning Right: The Making of the Rehnquist Supreme Court* (New York: Wiley, 1992). Tinsley E. Yarbrough, *The Rehnquist Court and the Constitution* (New York: Oxford University Press, 2000).

RELIGIOUS ISSUES UNDER THE CONSTITUTION

The 1st Amendment to the U.S. Constitution requires that "Congress shall make no law respecting an establishment of religion, or prohibiting the free exercise thereof." There are two parts to this constitutional provision about religion: the establishment clause and the free exercise clause.

Establishment clause Americans have always agreed that the establishment clause bans government actions establishing or promoting an official religion. Americans have argued vehemently, however, about whether the establishment clause strictly prohibits all government involvement in support of religion.

Thomas Jefferson wrote in 1802 that the intent of the 1st Amendment was to build "a wall of separation between church and state." Justice Hugo Black agreed with

Jefferson in writing for the Supreme Court in *Everson* v. *Board of Education of Ewing Township* (1947), the case that began the ongoing contemporary debate about the meaning of the establishment clause. Justice Black wrote that neither federal nor state governments can act to "aid one religion, aid all religions, or prefer one religion over another." The *Everson* decision was the first time the Court applied the 1st Amendment's establishment clause to the states through the due process clause of the 14th Amendment.

Justice Black, like Thomas Jefferson, held an *absolutist* position on the meaning of the establishment clause. Absolutists argue for complete separation of government from religious activity. According to the absolutists, religious activity should be carried out solely in the private sphere of society, free of both government interference and government support.

Since the earliest years of the republic, many Americans have disagreed with the absolutist position on church-state relations. For example, Justice William O. Douglas, writing for the Court in *Zorach* v. *Clauson* (1952), argued that the 1st Amendment "does not say that in every and all respect there shall be a separation of church and state." In *Zorach,* the Court approved a program whereby public school students could be released during school hours to receive religious instruction, but not within the public school facilities. The *Zorach* decision was the first in which the Court accommodated a relationship between church and state in a nonpreferential and voluntary program of religious education. However, *Zorach* was a very small breach in the "wall of separation" supported by the *Everson* case and later Court rulings.

Since the *Everson* decision in 1947, the Court has for the most part rejected the nonpreferentialist interpretation of the establishment clause, in which minimal government support of religion is permitted as long as it does not give preference to a particular religious denomination. Other key cases supporting strict separation of church and state are *Engel* v. *Vitale* (1962), *Abington School District* v. *Schempp* (1963), and *Wallace* v. *Jaffree* (1985). With these decisions, the Court has overturned state laws that require or sanction prayer and Bible-reading activities in public schools. These prohibitions apply even when the prayers or religious activities at issue are nondenominational, nonpreferential, and voluntary.

In *Lee* v. *Weisman* (1992) the Court prohibited prayers as part of a public school's formal graduation ceremony. A major factor in the case was the direction of the ceremony by school officials. The Court stressed that under the establishment clause, public authorities are forbidden to sanction even nondenominational or supposedly voluntary prayers. Finally, in this case, as in others of its type, the Court emphasized the importance of protecting the rights of individuals in the minority against the control or coercion of majority rule and peer pressure. However, students remain free to organize, on their own and without school support, voluntary religious programs associated with graduation from school. In 1993 the Supreme Court let stand, without comment, a decision of the U.S. Court of Appeals for the Fifth Circuit that upheld a Texas public school district's policy of permitting students to lead voluntary prayers at graduation ceremonies.

In *Santa Fe Independent School District* v. *Doe* (2000) the Court maintained a long-standing prohibition against prayer at public school events and ruled that student-led prayer at public high school football games was unconstitutional. Chief Justice William Rehnquist dissented, as did Antonin Scalia and Clarence Thomas, and continued in his opposition to the strict separation of government and religion.

In 1985 Rehnquist had expressed strong opposition to the absolutist position developed by the Court since the *Everson* decision. In his dissent in *Wallace* v. *Jaffree*, Rehnquist wrote, "The establishment clause did not require government neutrality between religion and irreligion

nor did it prohibit the federal government from providing nondiscriminatory aid to religions."

Justice Rehnquist and others support a position referred to as *nonpreferentialist.* The position rejects Jefferson's "wall of separation" viewpoint. Nonpreferentialists assert that government should be able to aid religious activity, as long as the support would be provided equally to all religions. That is, no religious denomination would be favored or preferred over others.

The Lemon Test, developed by the Court in *Lemon* v. *Kurtzman* (1971), was an attempt to accommodate some modest relationships between church and state. The test involves three standards for deciding whether federal or state aid to religious schools or programs is constitutional. The Lemon Test says that a statute does not violate the establishment clause if its purpose is secular or nonreligious, if it neither promotes nor restricts religion in its primary effects, and if it does not bring about excessive government entanglement with religion.

During the 1980s the Supreme Court moved slightly in the direction of accommodation between church and state. In *Marsh* v. *Chambers* (1983), the Court held that the Nebraska legislature could begin its sessions with prayers led by a paid chaplain. In *Lynch* v. *Donnelly* (1984) the Court upheld the placing of a crèche, a Christian nativity scene, at public expense on public property in front of a city hall at Christmastime. The display, the Court held, was permissible because it was within the context of a larger exhibit that emphasized secular or nonreligious objects, such as a Santa Claus, reindeers, and talking wishing wells. However, in *Allegheny County* v. *American Civil Liberties Union, Greater Pittsburgh Chapter* (1989), the Court ruled that an exclusively religious exhibit, a Jewish menorah and a crèche, could not be displayed in a government building because this kind of religious exhibit violated the establishment clause.

Another move toward accommodation of church and state was made by the Court in *Zobrest* v. *Catalina School District* (1993). The Court ruled that a deaf student at a private parochial school (run by the Catholic church) could be assisted by a publicly funded sign-language interpreter. This kind of aid helps the student, not the Church, said the Court. It therefore does not violate the 1st Amendment's establishment clause.

Free exercise clause   The free exercise clause of the 1st Amendment has not provoked as much controversy as the establishment clause. This clause clearly indicates that government must neither interfere with religious practices of individuals nor prescribe their religious beliefs. From the founding era of the United States until today, most Americans have heartily agreed that individuals have the right to freely express their religious beliefs in the private sphere of society.

The Supreme Court has protected the free-exercise rights of religious minorities since the 1940s. In *Cantwell* v. *Connecticut* (1940) the free exercise clause was for the first time "incorporated" by the Court under the due process clause of the 14th Amendment and applied to state governments. The outcome was the protection of the right of Jehovah's Witnesses, a minority religion, to peacefully distribute religious information to people in their neighborhoods with the aim of winning converts.

In *West Virginia State Board of Education* v. *Barnette* (1943) the Court struck down a state flag-salute law because it forced some students, who were Jehovah's Witnesses, to violate their religious beliefs. Writing for the Court, Justice Robert Jackson emphasized that the individual's right to free exercise of religion was placed by the 1st Amendment "beyond the reach of majorities and officials." He emphasized that it was the Court's responsibility to protect this constitutional right of individuals against the power of majority rule, whenever the majority, acting through representatives in government, might try to deny that right to unpopular minority groups.

Like freedom of speech, the individual's free exercise of religion is not absolute. The Court has ruled that in some instances religious expression may be limited on behalf of the public good.

In *Reynolds* v. *United States* (1879), for example, the Supreme Court upheld a federal law against the practice of polygamy—having multiple spouses—in federal territories. The Court ruled that the anti-polygamy law did not violate the right to free exercise of religion of a member of the Church of Jesus Christ of Latter-Day Saints (Mormons), who claimed it was his religious obligation to have more than one wife. Writing for the Court, Chief Justice Morrison Waite argued that the federal law prohibiting polygamy, even when practiced for religious reasons, was necessary for the good of the community. He wrote, "Suppose one believed that human sacrifices were a necessary part of religious worship, would it be seriously contended that the civil government [could] not interfere to prevent a sacrifice?"

In order to restrict an individual's free exercise of religion, the government must demonstrate a compelling public interest. In *Sherbert* v. *Verner* (1963), the Court ruled that a state could not refuse unemployment benefits to a worker who would not make herself available for employment on Saturday because this was her special day of worship (she was a Seventh-Day Adventist). An entitlement such as state unemployment benefits cannot be denied to someone because of her religious practices.

By contrast, in *Employment Division, Department of Human Resources of Oregon* v. *Smith* (1990), the Court ruled against state employees who were denied unemployment benefits after being dismissed from their jobs for religion-related reasons. The employees, who were Native Americans, practiced a religion with rituals involving the smoking of peyote, an illegal substance under state law. Because they were dismissed for violating a state law, the Court upheld the denial of unemployment compensation. Writing for the Court, Justice Antonin Scalia argued that "the right of free exercise does not relieve an individual of the obligation to comply with a valid and neutral law of general applicability."

In 1993, however, the Court struck down a city ordinance that banned ritual animal sacrifice by a religious group. The Court held in *Church of the Lukumi Babalu Aye* v. *City of Hialeah* (1993) that the ordinance violated the 1st Amendment's free exercise clause because it suppressed, without a compelling argument on behalf of the public good, a religious ceremony fundamental to members of a church.

Deciding when the free exercise of religion needs protection, however, is not always a straightforward task. When the city of Boerne, Texas, refused a Roman Catholic church's request to build a larger sanctuary, the Supreme Court ruled for the city. In *City of Boerne, Texas* v. *Flores* (1997), speaking for the majority, Justice Anthony Kennedy struck down the Religious Freedom Restoration Act, a federal law passed in 1993 that limited the power of federal, state, and local governments to enforce laws that "substantially burden" the free exercise of religion. Kennedy emphasized that the power to determine violations of the Constitution is reserved for government's judicial branch.

Continuing controversies   The fiercest arguments today about religion-related constitutional rights pertain to the establishment clause, not the free exercise clause. The absolutists and the nonpreferentialists strongly disagree about such issues as state-sponsored prayer in schools and neutral or nonpreferential support for religious practices in public places or with public funds. Public opinion polls have revealed more than 70 percent of Americans to be against the absolutist, or strict separation, position.

Recent Court decisions indicate a movement toward more accommodation and less separation of religion from the state. In *Capitol Square Review and Advisory Board* v. *Pinette* (1995), the Court ruled that a private group may put religious symbols on government property if

there is no appearance of government support for the religious message. And the Court decided in 1995 that a state university cannot discriminate against a student religious publication by denying it financial support on equal terms with other student publications (*Rosenberg* v. *Rector and Visitors of University of Virginia*).

The Supreme Court's movement toward accommodation between government and religion continued in *Agostini* v. *Felton* (1997). This decision, which overturned *Aguilar* v. *Felton* (1985), held that government funds can be used to provide remedial education for disadvantaged students in private religious schools. As long as the public funds aid students directly and do not promote religion or excessively entangle government with a religious institution, then the government-funded program is constitutional.

In *Mitchell* v. *Helms* (2000) the Court upheld a federal program that provided computer equipment and software and other media materials to religiously affiliated schools. In a plurality opinion, Justice Clarence Thomas, joined by Rehnquist, Scalia, and Kennedy, held that federal programs in agreement with "the principles of neutrality and private choice" are not in violation of the 1st Amendment's establishment clause. Justices Sandra Day O'Connor and Stephen Breyer concurred that the federal program at issue was constitutional, but they did not agree with Thomas's "neutrality principle." The Supreme Court clearly has moved strikingly toward an accommodationist position in church-state relationships. How far this accommodation may go, however, is the subject of a lively debate.

SEE ALSO *Abington School District v. Schempp; City of Boerne, Texas v. Flores; Engel v. Vitale; Establishment clause; Everson v. Board of Education of Ewing Township; Free exercise clause; Lemon Test; Lemon v. Kurtzman; Wallace v. Jaffree; West Virginia State Board of Education v. Barnette; Zorach v. Clauson*

SOURCES Robert S. Alley, ed., *The Constitution & Religion: Leading Supreme Court*

Cases on Church and State (Amherst, N.Y.: Prometheus, 1999). Robert S. Alley, ed., James Madison on Religious Liberty (Buffalo, N.Y.: Prometheus Books, 1985). Robert S. Alley, ed., The Supreme Court on Church and State (New York: Oxford University Press, 1988). Thomas J. Curry, The First Freedoms: Church and State in America to the Passage of the First Amendment (New York: Oxford University Press, 1986). Edwin S. Gaustad, Church and State in America (New York: Oxford University Press, 1999). Leonard W. Levy, The Establishment Clause: Religion and the First Amendment (New York: Macmillan, 1986). William Lee Miller, The First Liberty: Religion and the American Republic (New York: Paragon House, 1985). Melvin I. Urofsky, "The Religion Clauses," in By and for the People: Constitutional Rights in American History, edited by Kermit L. Hall (Arlington Heights, Ill.: Harlan Davidson, 1991).

REMOVAL OF THE PRESIDENT

SEE Impeachment

REMOVAL POWER

Article 2 of the Constitution, which gives the President the power to appoint government officials, does not explicitly provide the President with the power to remove officials. In Federalist Paper No. 77, one of a series of newspaper articles written in 1788 in support of the Constitution, Alexander Hamilton argued that the Senate's power of "advice and consent" to Presidential nominations also extended to removals unless Congress legislated otherwise. But James Madison, in the 1789 congressional debates over a removal clause in the law creating the Department of Foreign Affairs, argued for an unrestricted Presidential removal power. When Congress created the War and Treasury Departments, it followed Madison's argu-

ment and acknowledged the removal power of the President.

George Washington secured the resignation of Edmund Randolph as secretary of state in 1795. An intercepted letter implied that Randolph would pursue a pro-French policy in exchange for a bribe; when Washington showed the letter to Randolph, he promptly submitted his resignation. All told, Washington removed 17 officials whose appointments had been approved by the Senate.

John Adams was the first President to remove a cabinet secretary without the formality of a resignation. Incensed at Secretary of State Timothy Pickering's interference with his French policy and his failure to support Adams's nomination of his son-in-law for adjutant general, Adams wrote to Pickering asking for his resignation. When Pickering did not respond, Adams fired him with an abrupt written notice. Adams also removed 20 other civil officers.

President Thomas Jefferson fired John Adams's son-in-law, Colonel William Smith, surveyor of the Port of New York. Smith had taken part in a plot against Spanish possessions in South America, a violation of U.S. law. Jefferson removed a total of 109 officers. James Madison fired his secretary of state, Robert Smith, for incompetence, claiming that whatever talents Smith had, he did not "possess those adapted to his station." Madison also obtained the resignation under pressure of General John Armstrong as secretary of war after Armstrong failed to prepare the capital against the arrival of British troops during the War of 1812 and the city was sacked.

For the most part the removals by Presidents through the 1820s involved wrongdoing in office, not partisan politics. In 1820 Congress had little problem with Presidential removals: it passed a Tenure of Office Act specifying fixed four-year terms for officers handling funds but made them removable at the pleasure of the President.

Controversy erupted in the administration of Andrew Jackson, who established the principle of rotation in office on partisan grounds. Jackson's removal of his political enemies was abrupt, arbitrary, and unrestrained by law. But in all nonpolitical cases involving employees, it was Jackson's common practice to provide them with notice and the elements of due process, similar to a fair trial, and to discharge them only after a complete investigation of allegations.

Jackson was the first President to claim the power to remove cabinet officials simply for disagreeing with Presidential policy, if they did not follow his orders. By law, the Treasury secretary had the responsibility of depositing the funds of the United States in such banks as he saw fit. Jackson asked Secretary of the Treasury William J. Duane to remove the funds from the Bank of the United States and deposit them in state banks. Duane declined to do so, arguing, "Congress confers discretionary power." Jackson responded, "A secretary, sir, is merely an executive agent, a subordinate." When Duane defied Jackson's orders, he was fired.

The opposition Whigs argued against an unrestricted Presidential right of removal. Henry Clay offered a Senate resolution in 1834 stating, "The Constitution of the United States does not vest in the President the power to remove, at his pleasure, officers under the Government of the United States, whose officers have been established by law." Instead, Congress would legislate the length of their service. Clay further proposed a law requiring that the power of removal be exercised only "in concurrence with the Senate," but Jackson used his influence to defeat this and other similar proposals.

The Whig-dominated Senate did manage to pass a Resolution of Censure against Jackson, who sent a "Response" claiming that he possessed the right of "removing those officers who are to aid [him] in the execution of the laws." The Whigs put in their 1836 platform the notion that Congress possessed sole removal power. One of their Presidential nominees, William

Henry Harrison, pledged never to remove a Treasury secretary without approval of Congress.

During the Civil War, Congress established the office of comptroller of the currency, specifying a five-year term and authorizing his removal only with the consent of the Senate. In 1864 Congress passed a statute requiring the President to submit to Congress the reasons for removal of consular clerks in the Department of State. An 1865 law gave military officers dismissed by the President the right to apply for a trial.

In the aftermath of the Civil War, Congress passed two measures to protect its Reconstruction policies from President Andrew Johnson, who wished to pursue policies favorable to the Southern states. The Command of the Army Act, passed on March 2, 1867, provided that "the General of the Army shall not be removed, suspended, or relieved from command, or assigned to duty elsewhere than at said headquarters, except at his own request, without the previous approval of the Senate." The Tenure of Office Act, passed the same day, provided that "every person holding any civil office to which he has been appointed by and with the advice and consent of the Senate . . . shall be entitled to hold such office until a successor shall have been in like manner appointed and duly qualified." During a Senate recess the President could suspend an official for reason of misconduct in office, criminal activity, incapacity, or legal disqualification, but he would be restored to his office if the Senate refused to endorse the President's action. Both acts were passed over Johnson's veto.

After Congress adjourned, Johnson asked Secretary of War Edwin Stanton to resign. When Stanton refused, in August 1867, the President, seemingly acting in accordance with the laws, suspended him and authorized General Ulysses S. Grant to act as secretary of war. Johnson had outmaneuvered Congress, using a provision in the law that permitted him to suspend a department secretary until the Senate reconvened. But when the Senate did so, it reinstated Stanton. Now Johnson acted for the first time in apparent violation of the Tenure of Office Act. He removed Stanton while the Senate was in session and appointed General Lorenzo Thomas secretary of war. The House then voted articles of impeachment against Johnson.

At his Senate trial Johnson argued that the Tenure of Office Act was unconstitutional. He also argued that even if the act were constitutional, his removal of Stanton did not violate it. Stanton had been appointed by Lincoln; Johnson argued that the law could not prevent a President from removing an official nominated by his predecessor but covered only those nominations he himself had made. Johnson was tried in the Senate and escaped removal by just one vote, and Stanton surrendered his office. Congress did not repeal the last provisions of the law until 1887.

In the landmark 1926 Supreme Court case *Myers* v. *United States,* Chief Justice William Howard Taft recognized the removal power as a Presidential power and struck down all congressional efforts to pass legislation about the Presidential removal power.

In *Humphrey's Executor* v. *United States* (1935), the Court retreated somewhat from the *Myers* case. It distinguished between officials doing executive tasks and those engaged in "quasi-legislative" and "quasi-judicial" ones. Quasi-judicial officials, such as commissioners of regulatory agencies like the Federal Trade Commission, could be insulated from the Presidential removal power by legislation. Moreover, in *Wiener* v. *United States* (1958) the Supreme Court held that Presidential removal power did not extend to such officials even when Congress has not protected them by law.

The courts and Congress have also protected special prosecutors and independent counsels who investigate high-level scandals involving the Presidency, such as the special prosecutor in the Watergate investigation. President Richard Nixon ordered Attorney General Elliott Richardson

to dismiss Archibald Cox for pursuing the inquiry further than Nixon wished. Richardson, who had given the Senate his word that he would not do so except for "extraordinary improprieties on his [Cox's] part" and who had issued regulations protecting Cox, promptly resigned. The deputy attorney general, William Ruckelshaus, was ordered to fire Cox, and when he refused, Nixon fired him, too. Finally, Solicitor General Robert Bork, who had become acting attorney general, fired Cox.

In *Nader* v. *Bork* (1973) a district court agreed that Cox had been illegally removed from office because the removal violated the department's regulations regarding the special prosecutor. Subsequently, the Ethics in Government Act of 1978 prohibited the removal of an independent counsel (or special prosecutor) except for extraordinary impropriety, physical disability, mental incapacity, or "any other condition that substantially impairs the performance of such special prosecutor's duties."

SEE ALSO *Appointment power; Censure; Executive branch; Executive power; Impeachment; Independent counsel; Jackson, Andrew; Johnson, Andrew*
SOURCES Edward S. Corwin, *The President's Removal Power under the Constitution* (New York: National Municipal League, 1927). Louis Fisher, *Constitutional Conflicts between President and Congress* (Princeton, N.J.: Princeton University Press, 1985).

RENO V. AMERICAN CIVIL LIBERTIES UNION

- 117 S.Ct. 2329 (1997)
- Vote: 9–0
- For the Court: Stevens
- Concurring: O'Connor and Rehnquist

In 1996 Congress, with the strong support of President Bill Clinton, passed the Communications Decency Act (CDA) to prohibit the transmission of indecent or pornographic messages via e-mail or the Internet. The law made it a crime for a person to send indecent messages by way of an interactive computer network to anyone younger than 18. It also banned Internet displays of pornography that would be accessible to someone under 18. The law did not clearly or precisely define the material to be banned. Rather the act referred to "patently offensive" and "indecent" portrayals of sexual or excretory activities. Convicted violators of the CDA could be fined $25,000, sentenced to two years in prison, or both.

Supporters of the CDA argued that the law served a compelling public interest—the common good of protecting the moral development of preadults. Opponents, however, denounced the CDA as an unconstitutional limitation on 1st Amendment rights to freedom of expression.

The American Civil Liberties Union (ACLU), in concert with other groups including the American Library Association (ALA), filed suit against enforcement of the CDA by the attorney general of the United States, Janet Reno. A three-judge panel of a federal district court agreed with the plaintiffs and ruled that the CDA was unconstitutional. Then the case was appealed to the U.S. Supreme Court.

The Issue This case raised questions about the extent to which the federal government may regulate the transmission of messages via the new electronically driven mass media, such as the Internet. Should the Court view the Internet as similar to newspapers and books and provide the highest level of constitutional protection to freedom of expression? Or should it treat the Internet the way it has responded to broadcast and cable television and permit greater regulation by government on behalf of the public good? Can all communication on the Internet be limited by federal law for the purpose of protecting children against exposure to indecent messages? Or is the Constitution's 1st Amendment violated by a federal law that would limit all speech on the Internet to the level of a child?

Opinion of the Court Justice John Paul Stevens wrote, "Not withstanding the legitimacy and importance of the congressional goal of protecting children from harmful materials, we agree . . . that the statute abridges the freedom of speech protected by the First Amendment. . . . The interest in encouraging freedom of expression in a democratic society outweighs any theoretical but unproven benefit of censorship." So the Communications Decency Act's prohibition of indecent material on the Internet was declared unconstitutional.

Justice Sandra Day O'Connor was joined by Chief Justice William Rehnquist in a concurring opinion. She argued that a federal law, such as the CDA, could be upheld only in cases where it is clear that the transmitter of the material intended the messages exclusively for preadults. She also agreed with Justice Stevens that the CDA was flawed because it did not clearly define or specify the material to be excluded.

Significance The Court's decision left the Internet to expand freely without strict regulation by government of its content. The executive director of the Center for Democracy and Technology applauded the ruling and claimed, "The Supreme Court has written the Bill of Rights for the 21st century." Many others, however, sided with Indiana Senator Dan Coats, who regretted that "the Court was telling families to fend for themselves on an Internet of raw indecency." So parents and other private guardians of the moral development of youth were left with the responsibility of regulating the Internet access of children and teenagers.

REPORTER OF DECISIONS

In 1816 Congress officially created the office of reporter of decisions of the Supreme Court. The reporter, with a staff of nine, records and edits all the Court's case decisions. Since 1955 audio tapes have been made of oral arguments before the Court. These recordings are stored at the National Archives. The reporter oversees the process of printing and publishing the record of the Court's decisions in *United States Reports*, the official publication of the Court's decisions.

The reporter also supervises the printing of a headnote for each decision of the Court. The headnote is a summary of the case that includes background facts, the legal reasoning used in the decision, and the voting record of the justices on the case. The headnote also tells whether the lower court's ruling has been affirmed or overturned by the Supreme Court's decision. Each headnote contains this statement: "The syllabus [headnote] constitutes no part of the opinion of the Court but has been prepared by the Reporter of Decisions for the convenience of the reader."

The first reporter of decisions was Alexander Dallas, who served unofficially on the job from 1790 to 1800. He was self-appointed, but the Court gave its approval to his work. He was not paid by the federal government, but he tried to make a profit through sales of his published reports. William Cranch, the second reporter, also worked unofficially at this job from 1801 to 1815. Henry Wheaton, who served from 1816 to 1827, was the first official reporter of the Supreme Court. The early reporters of decisions did their work laboriously by hand. Today, the reporter and his staff use audiotape and recorders, photocopy machines, and high-speed computers and printers to process information and produce the formal record of the Court's work.

SEE ALSO *Staff of the Supreme Court, nonjudicial; United States Reports*

REPORTERS OF DEBATE

During debates in the Senate and House chamber, a reporter of debate takes down whatever the members say or do. The next morning, the entire debate, floor statements, and votes will be published in the daily *Congressional Record*. There are many steps in this amazingly fast process.

Since the 1840s the Senate and House have each employed teams of reporters of debate. (Prior to 1840 these reporters—or stenographers—were employees of the newspapers that published the debates.) When the chamber is in session, reporters go on the floor in 10-minute rotations, taking down what they hear before returning to transcribe their notes. Since speakers are not always clear, and reporters make mistakes, members of Congress (or their staffs) are permitted to review the reporters' notes and make corrections before the *Record* is published. Some members also correct grammatical errors and otherwise polish their remarks. Occasionally, when tempers flare, members will say things that they regret, perhaps insulting a colleague. They may delete such offending remarks entirely from the transcript.

More often, the *Record* tells more than what happened, rather than less. Instead of reading an entire speech, a speaker might read just the opening paragraphs and ask for unanimous consent to "revise and extend" these remarks for the *Record*. The speaker then hands the reporter a copy of the unread text. Congress grants these unanimous consent requests to speed up the proceedings and to avoid having to listen to endless speeches.

Modern reporters of debate take shorthand notes on a device similar to a court reporting machine. The machine enters their notes immediately into a computer system that converts the text into standard English. The computer system facilitates editing, speeds typesetting, and reduces costs and printing errors. Even with such assistance, however, reporters still provide a human touch to editing the daily proceedings of Congress—and members appreciate their help in making their remarks presentable. As Senator Everett Dirksen (Republican–Illinois) once observed, "Congress is really the home of the split infinitive . . . ; this is the place where the dangling participle is certainly nourished; this is the home of the broken sentence;

and if there were no dashes I do not know what the distinguished reporters of debate would do ... and yet, somehow, out of this great funnel it all comes out all right, and it is always readable."

SEE ALSO *Congressional Record*

REPRESENTATION IN CONGRESS

As a result of the Great Compromise of 1787, the Constitution provided for fundamentally different types of representation in the House and Senate. Membership in the House is proportional to the population of the state. The number of representatives to which each state is entitled is determined every 10 years after a national census, or head count, has been taken. In the 1st Congress each member of the House represented about 30,000 constituents. By the 103rd Congress the average House member represented nearly 600,000 constituents. At first the number of representatives grew with each census, from 105 after the 1790 census to 435 after the 1910 census. Then Congress froze the number at 435 to keep the House at a manageable size.

The membership of the Senate grows by two each time a new state joins the Union. Every state is entitled to two senators, regardless of the size of its population. Before the ratification of the 17th Amendment in 1913, when senators were still elected by state legislatures, senators were compared to ambassadors, representing their state's political establishment in the national legislature. With direct election of senators, however, senators see themselves as representing the people of their state, who voted them into office.

SEE ALSO *Bicameral; Great Compromise (1787); Reapportionment*

REPUBLICANISM

Republicanism is the belief in the worth of a republic, a type of government that is based on the consent of the governed and is conducted by elected representatives of the people. In a republican government, the people are sovereign, or supreme, because their representatives serve at their pleasure for the common good. Today, people tend to use the terms *republic* and *representative democracy* interchangeably. In contrast to a republic, a *pure* or *direct democracy* is a form of government in which the people govern directly—in a town meeting, for example—instead of through representatives whom they elect.

In *The Federalist* No. 39, James Madison presented the idea of republicanism that is embodied in the U.S. Constitution:

> What, then, are the distinctive characters of the republican form? ...
> If we resort for a criterion ... we may define a republic to be ... a government which derives all its powers directly or indirectly from the great body of the people, and is administered by persons holding their offices during pleasure for a limited period, or during good behavior. It is essential to such a government that it be derived from the great body of the society, not from an inconsiderable proportion or a favored class of it.... It is *sufficient* for such a government that the persons administering it be appointed, either directly or indirectly, by the people; and that they hold their appointments by either of the tenures just specified.

In the world of the 1780s, the republican form of government was rare; monarchies and aristocracies prevailed. These non-republican forms of government function without representation of or participation by the common people. In an absolute monarchy, the monarch (the king or queen or both) rules; and in an aristocracy, a small elite group of aristocrats or nobles exercises power in government. Power usually is based on heredity in a monarchy or aristocracy; titles are passed from father to children (usually sons).

Americans in the 1780s were committed to republicanism, rather than a monarchy, aristocracy, or other non-republican form of government. They agreed that the rights and liberty of individuals could best be secured through a republican form of government. As a result, they built republicanism into the U.S. Constitution. Article 4, Section 4, says, "The United States [federal government] shall guarantee to every State in this Union a Republican Form of Government."

SEE ALSO *Constitutional democracy; Constitutionalism; Liberty under the Constitution*

SOURCES Paul Rahe, *Republics Ancient and Modern* (Chapel Hill: University of North Carolina Press, 1992).

RESIGNATION, PRESIDENTIAL

The Constitution (Article 2, Section 1) specifies that if the President resigns, the office of President devolves on the Vice President. The 25th Amendment states that in case of resignation, the Vice President "shall become President."

The mechanisms for a Presidential resignation are as follows: The President signs a letter, addressed to the secretary of state, specifying the time at which resignation from the office becomes effective. The Vice President is notified by the secretary of state and takes the oath of office at the designated time.

Only one President has ever resigned. Richard Nixon resigned at noon on August 9, 1974, to avoid impeachment by the House of Representatives for high crimes and misdemeanors for his involvement in the Watergate scandal. He was succeeded by Gerald Ford, who took the oath in a ceremony at the Capitol.

SEE ALSO *Ford, Gerald R.; Nixon, Richard M.; Secretary of state; Succession to the Presidency; Watergate investigation (1973–74)*

RESOLUTIONS, CONGRESSIONAL

To state its decisions or declare its opinions, Congress uses three different types of resolutions. A single house can pass a simple resolution for such internal business as adopting rules, creating special committees, or printing documents. Simple resolutions also express the sense of one house on a matter, such as a Senate resolution congratulating the Washington Redskins on their victory in the Super Bowl. Because only one house enacts such a resolution, and the President does not sign it, the resolution does not become law. Resolutions are identified as H. Res. or S. Res., and they are numbered consecutively during a Congress.

Concurrent resolutions When both houses express the opinion of Congress on some issue, set the date of adjournment, or deal with some other internal matter affecting both houses, they adopt a concurrent resolution. For instance, in 1992 Congress by concurrent resolution declared that the 27th Amendment to the Constitution, proposed 202 years earlier to regulate increases in congressional salaries, had finally been ratified by three-quarters of the states and had become part of the Constitution. Presidents do not sign concurrent resolutions. Concurrent resolutions are numbered, with the prefix H. Con. Res. when introduced in the House and S. Con. Res. when introduced in the Senate.

Joint resolutions Unlike simple and concurrent resolutions, joint resolutions become law if the President signs them. Congress proposes amendments to the Constitution, creates joint committees, and expresses the joint opinion of Congress on specific issues using joint resolutions. Joint resolutions are numbered, with the prefix H. J. Res. when introduced in the House and S. J. Res. when introduced in the Senate.

SEE ALSO *Bills; Concurrent resolutions; Joint resolutions; Legislation*

REVELS, HIRAM R.

* Born: Sept. 27, 1827, Fayetteville, N.C.
* Political party: Republican
* Education: Knox College
* Senator from Mississippi: 1870–71
* Died: Jan. 16, 1901, Aberdeen, Miss.

The first African American elected to the Senate was Hiram Revels. Although born in North Carolina during slavery, Revels's parents had been free and he was never a slave. He attended Knox College in Illinois and became a minister in the African Methodist Episcopal Church in Baltimore, Maryland. During the Civil War, Revels raised two black regiments to fight for the Union and served as a chaplain in a black regiment at Vicksburg, Mississippi. He remained in Mississippi after the war and became active in Reconstruction politics. In 1870 the state legislature chose Revels to fill a seat in the Senate that had been vacant since the start of the Civil War. Although he served only a brief term, Revels established a significant precedent just by taking his seat, against the objection of white Southerners. As a senator, Revels won notice for speaking out against racial segregation.

SEE ALSO *African Americans in government; Reconstruction, congressional*
SOURCES Julius Thompson, *Hiram R. Revels, 1827–1901: A Biography* (New York: Arno Press, 1982).

REVENUE BILLS

In order for the federal government to function, it must be able to raise revenue, or money. A chief limitation of the Continental Congress and the Congress under the Articles of Confederation was their reliance on the states for all funds. Because the states were slow to act, Congress was always short of funds, even to pay troops during and after the revolutionary war. The Constitution (Article 1, Section 8) therefore gave Congress the power to "lay [set] and collect taxes, duties, imposts and excises, to pay the debts and provide for the common defense and general welfare of the United States." The framers of the Constitution regarded the "power of the purse" to be so important that they decided that the House of Representatives— at that time the only members of Congress directly elected by the people—should be able to originate any revenue bill. However, according to the Constitution (Article 1, Section 7), the Senate could amend these bills just as it could any other legislation.

At first Congress raised revenues chiefly through tariffs, which are duties or taxes set on imported goods. During the Civil War, and after enactment of the 16th Amendment to the Constitution in 1913, Congress also levied income taxes on individuals and corporations. Revenue bills are handled by the House Ways and Means Committee and the Senate Finance Committee, a responsibility that has traditionally made them two of the most powerful committees of Congress. Not until 1944 did a President—Franklin D. Roosevelt— veto a revenue bill. Congress, always jealous of its power of the purse, immediately voted to override his veto.

SEE ALSO *Appropriations*

REVERSALS OF SUPREME COURT DECISIONS

The Supreme Court has the last word, within the American judicial system, on questions of constitutional interpretation. However, a Supreme Court decision regarding interpretation of the Constitution can be overturned by a constitutional amendment. A Court decision on interpretation of federal laws can be overturned by Congressional enactment of a new law.

Reversals   by   Constitutional

Amendment The people, through their representatives in government, can use Article 5 of the Constitution to overturn the Court's decisions. Article 5 provides that constitutional amendments can be proposed by a two-thirds vote of the members of each house of Congress or by a special convention that Congress calls after two-thirds of the state legislatures have voted to request it. For a proposed amendment to be ratified, three-fourths of the states must approve it, either by their legislatures or by conventions especially convened for this purpose. To date, all amendments have been proposed by Congress, and all but one (the 21st) have been ratified by state legislatures. The 21st Amendment was ratified by state conventions.

Of the 27 amendments to the Constitution, 4 clearly were enacted to overturn unpopular Supreme Court decisions. The 11th Amendment overturned *Chisholm* v. *Georgia* (1793) by guaranteeing the immunity of states from lawsuits by citizens of another state or a foreign country. The 14th Amendment nullified *Scott* v. *Sandford* (1857) by guaranteeing the civil rights and citizenship of African Americans. The 16th Amendment overrode *Pollock* v. *Farmers' Loan and Trust Co.* (1895) by giving Congress the power to levy an income tax. The 26th Amendment negated *Oregon* v. *Mitchell* (1970) by permitting 18-year-olds to vote in state elections. Many other attempts to enact constitutional amendments to override Supreme Court decisions have failed.

Reversals of Court decisions by Congress Congress has a rather simple and direct way to negate unpopular decisions of the Court that have nullified federal statutes: It can pass a new law. For example, Congress passed the Civil Rights Act of 1991 to overturn the Court's decision in *Ward's Cove Packing Company* v. *Atonio* (1989). In *Ward's Cove,* the Court decided that an individual proving discrimination by an employer could still be dismissed or demoted from a desired job as long as the employer could prove that the discriminating practice was necessary

to maintain his business. The Civil Rights Act of 1991 makes it illegal for an employer to claim "business necessity" as a reason for intentional job discrimination against an individual based on race, color, ethnic origin, and gender.

Although most bills that have been introduced to overturn Supreme Court decisions have *not* been passed, the power of Congress to negate certain kinds of Court decisions is an important part of the American constitutional system of separation of powers and checks and balances. SEE ALSO *Amendments to the Constitution; Precedents, judicial; Separation of powers*

REYNOLDS V. SIMS

- 377 U.S. 533 (1964)
- Vote: 8–1
- For the Court: Warren
- Concurring: Stewart and Clark
- Dissenting: Harlan

By the early 1920s the distribution of the U.S. population had clearly changed since the 19th century. For the first time, more Americans were living in cities than in rural areas. This change created inequities between the populations of urban and rural state legislative districts.

By 1960 nearly every state had some urban legislative districts populated by at least twice as many people as rural districts in the state. In Alabama, for example, the smallest congressional district had a population of 6,700 and the largest had a population of 104,000. In a representative democracy people's votes possess equal value only when each member of a legislative body represents the same number of people. Clearly, the people in more populous urban districts and the people in less populous rural districts were not represented equally. As a result, city and suburban problems did not receive appropriate attention in state legislatures dominated by representatives from farming and rural districts.

The domination by rural interests also meant that state legislatures refused to redistrict to ensure that each member of the legislature would represent roughly the same number of people. Some simply ignored sections in their state constitutions requiring redistricting every 10 years. Others merely redistricted in ways that continued to favor rural interests. There was little voters could do to change things through the ballot box.

During the 1960s the Supreme Court heard a series of cases challenging the apportionment (distribution) of state legislative districts. In *Reynolds* v. *Sims,* voters in Jefferson County, Alabama, claimed that the unequal representation of citizens in Alabama districts violated the equal protection clause of the 14th Amendment.

The Issue   The 14th Amendment declares: "No state . . . shall deny to any person within its jurisdiction the equal protection of the laws." Did Alabama and other states violate the equal protection rights of voters by setting up legislative districts that contained unequal numbers of people?

Opinion of the Court   The Supreme Court ruled that the 14th Amendment required states to establish equally populated electoral districts for both houses of state legislatures. Chief Justice Earl Warren declared that plans for setting up legislative districts could not discriminate against people on the basis of where they live (city versus country, in this case) any more than they could on the basis of race or economic status.

The Court rejected the idea that state legislatures, like Congress, could create senate districts on the basis of area rather than population. The Constitution, which allotted equal representation to states in the U.S. Senate no matter what their size, recognized the states as "sovereign entities." Political subdivisions within a state (such as counties or regions), however, did not possess the status of sovereign entities. Thus, Warren argued, the people of a state must benefit from equal representation in *both* houses of a state legislature. "Legislators represent people, not trees or acres," Warren declared.

The Court ruled that state legislatures did not have to draw legislative districts with "mathematical exactness or precision." However, such districts did have to be based "substantially" on equal population. The Court thus established the key principle of "one person, one vote."

Dissent   Justice John Marshall Harlan argued that this case did not pertain to violation of constitutional rights. Rather, he said, it involved a political question that should be decided by elected representatives of the people, not by the Court.

Significance   The *Reynolds* decision had a major impact on state legislatures. After the decision, 49 state legislatures reapportioned their legislative districts on the basis of equal population. Oregon had already done so in 1961. The decision caused a fundamental shift in American politics by declaring unconstitutional the practices that enabled rural minorities to control state legislatures. The decision also affected national politics because state legislatures draw the lines for U.S. congressional districts.

SOURCES   Richard C. Cortner, *The Apportionment Cases* (Knoxville: University of Tennessee Press, 1970).

RIDERS TO BILLS

Like a hitchhiker thumbing a ride, a "rider" is an amendment looking for a vehicle to take it where it wants to go. Members of Congress with a bill that cannot attract enough votes on its own will add it as an amendment to a popular bill that is likely to pass. Riders usually are not germane to the bill—that is, they have little or nothing in common with the bill on which they are riding. House rules prohibit non-germane amendments, so riders are used in the Senate, with the hope that the House will accept them in the conference committee that hammers out the differences between the House and Senate versions of the bill. Appropriations bills, which provide for payment of federal money for many different projects, are favorite vehicles for these legislative riders.

SEE ALSO *Appropriations; Conference committees; Germaneness*

RIGHTS OF THE ACCUSED

A primary purpose of government is to enforce law and order. The federal and state constitutions of the United States, for example, grant certain powers to government officials so they can maintain an orderly society and protect the lives, property, and rights of the people. Federal and state government officials have the duty of preventing some individuals from harming others through criminal acts such as theft, assault, rape, and murder. Nevertheless, criminal behavior has become a serious threat to many American communities where violence, theft, and illegal drug use are rampant. Most Americans, therefore, want law enforcement officials to be tough on criminals, to apprehend and punish them.

There are, however, constitutional limits on the power of government officials in order to prevent them from abusing the rights of individuals, including those accused of criminal behavior. From colonial times until the present, Americans have believed in an old English saying: "It is better for 99 guilty persons to go free than for one innocent person to be punished." In the United States, a person accused of a crime is presumed innocent until proved guilty. The burden of proving the suspect guilty is upon the government prosecutors.

Americans want their federal and state governments to be both powerful and limited, so that freedom and order are balanced. On the one side, government officials should have enough power to keep order so that people are safe and secure. On the other side, the power of government officials to enforce law and order should be sufficiently limited so that they cannot oppress anyone.

Constitutional rights of the accused   The U.S. Constitution, especially the Bill of Rights (Amendments 1 to 10), protects individuals from wrong or unjust accusations and punishments by law enforcement officials.

Amendment 4 protects individuals against unreasonable and unwarranted searches and seizures of their property. It establishes conditions for the lawful issuing and use of search warrants by government officials in order to protect the right of individuals to security "in their persons, houses, papers and effects." There must be a "probable cause" for issuing a warrant to authorize a search or arrest, and the place to be searched, the objects sought, and the person to be arrested must be precisely described.

Amendment 5 states certain legal and procedural rights of individuals. For example, the government may not act against an individual in the following ways:

- Hold an individual to answer for a serious crime unless the prosecution presents appropriate evidence to a grand jury that indicates the likely guilt of the individual.
- Try an individual more than once for the same offense.
- Force an individual to act as a witness against himself in a criminal case.
- Deprive an individual of life, liberty, or property without due process of law (fair and proper legal proceedings).

Amendment 6 guarantees people suspected or accused of a crime certain protections against the power of government. It provides these rights to individuals:

- A speedy public trial before an unbiased jury picked from the state and community in which the crime was committed.
- Information about what the individual has been accused of and why the accusation has been made.
- A meeting with witnesses offering testimony against the individual.
- Means of obtaining favorable witnesses, including the right to subpoena, or le-

gally compel, witnesses to testify in court.

• Help from a lawyer.

Amendment 8 protects individuals from overly harsh punishments and excessive fines and bail (the amount of money required to secure a person's release from custody while awaiting trial).

Amendment 14 provides general protection for the rights of the accused against the powers of state governments. This amendment forbids state governments from making and enforcing laws that will deprive any individual of life, liberty, or property "without due process of law"; it also says that a state government may not deny to any person under its authority "the equal protection of the laws."

The U.S. Constitution includes other protections of individual rights that are not in the Bill of Rights or subsequent amendments. For example, Article 1, Section 9, prohibits government from suspending the privilege of the writ of habeas corpus. A writ of habeas corpus requires officials to bring a person whom they have arrested and held in custody before a judge in a court of law. The officials must convince the judge that there are lawful reasons for holding the person. If the judge finds their reasons unlawful, then the court frees the suspect. Thus, the writ of habeas corpus protects individuals from government officials who might want to jail them arbitrarily—because they belong to unpopular groups or express criticisms of the government, for instance.

Article 1, Section 9, also prohibits enactment by the federal government of bills of attainder and ex post facto laws. A bill of attainder is a law that punishes an individual solely by means of legislation, without a trial or fair hearing in a court of law. An ex post facto (literally, "after the fact") law makes an action a crime after it was committed.

Article 1, Section 10, prohibits state governments from enacting bills of attainder and ex post facto laws.

Article 3, Section 2, provides individuals accused of a crime the right to trial by jury.

Article 3, Section 3, protects individuals against arbitrary accusations of treason—an attempt to overthrow the government or to give aid and support to enemies of the United States, such as countries waging war against it. This article also establishes rigorous standards for convicting a person of treason.

Sources of rights of the accused- American ideas about the rights of the accused—criminal defendants—can be traced to the great English documents of liberty, such as the Magna Carta (1215), the Petition of Right (1628), and the English Bill of Rights (1689). These documents embodied the principles of limited government and the rule of law, which all were bound to obey, even the king. For example, Section 39 of the Magna Carta said that no "freeman" could be put in prison except "by the lawful judgment of peers or the law of the land." This was the beginning of due process of law and rights for individuals accused of crimes. These ideas were developed in England and brought to the North American colonies in the 1600s.

American colonists expanded their English legal heritage to provide new and higher levels of protection for the rights of the accused. The Massachusetts Body of Liberties (1641), for example, established many provisions that appeared later in the federal Bill of Rights, such as the rights to trial by jury, to challenge jurors, to have assistance of counsel, to know the charges of criminal behavior, to reasonable bail, and to protection against cruel or unusual punishment.

By the time of the American Revolution, legal protections for those accused of crimes were a generally accepted part of government. The Declaration of Independence (1776) accused the British king of, among other charges, violating the due process rights of Americans, such as "depriving us, in many cases, of the Benefits of Trial by Jury."

The new constitutions of the first 13 states of the United States, written between 1776 and 1783, included ample provisions for the rights of the accused. These state constitutions reflected an American consensus about the general importance of due process of law in criminal proceedings and about specific protections for the rights of accused persons. The rights of the accused expressed in the U.S. Constitution (1787) and Bill of Rights (1791) were drawn from the provisions in the original 13 state constitutions.

Rights of the accused under constitutional law   Throughout most of U.S. history, the federal Bill of Rights had little impact on individuals accused of crimes. Most criminal cases in the American federal system were (and will be) within the jurisdiction of state governments. And the U.S. Supreme Court ruled in *Barron* v. *Baltimore* (1833) that the federal Bill of Rights restrained only the federal government. As a result, the rights of the accused guaranteed by Amendments 4, 5, 6, and 8 of the U.S. Constitution were not applicable to law enforcement activities of state governments. Most defendants, therefore, could look only to their state constitutions and bills of rights for legal protection against police power.

The 14th Amendment, ratified in 1868, appeared to impose certain legal restrictions on the states in criminal proceedings. This amendment stated, "No state shall . . . deprive any person of life, liberty, or property, without due process of law, nor deny to any person within its jurisdiction the equal protection of the laws."

In *Hurtado* v. *California* (1884), the U.S. Supreme Court faced the question of whether the due process clause of the 14th Amendment required a state government to provide the 5th amendment guarantee of a grand jury indictment in criminal proceedings. The Court ruled that the 14th Amendment did not incorporate, or include, any part of the 5th Amendment and thereby make it binding on state governments. *Hurtado*, like *Barron* v. *Baltimore*,

implied that the federal Bill of Rights could be used only to limit the federal government.

Justice John Marshall Harlan dissented from the Court's opinion in *Hurtado* v. *California*. He argued that the intent of the 14th Amendment was "to impose upon the States the same restrictions, in respect of proceedings involving life, liberty, and property, which had been imposed upon the general government." Harlan concluded that the rights of the accused in the federal Bill of Rights could be applied to the states through the 14th Amendment's due process clause.

Justice Harlan's dissent in *Hurtado* prevailed in the long run. In *Powell* v. *Alabama* (1932) the U.S. Supreme Court ruled that the due process clause of the 14th Amendment required assistance of a lawyer for defendants charged in a state court with a crime punishable by death. In *Cole* v. *Arkansas* (1947) the Court used the 14th Amendment's due process clause to apply to a state the 6th Amendment's requirement of notice of accusation to a defendant. And in *In re Oliver* (1948), the 6th Amendment requirement of a public trial was imposed upon the states through the 14th Amendment. Further, in *Wolf* v. *Colorado* (1949), the Court incorporated the 4th Amendment's protections against unreasonable searches and seizures into the 14th Amendment.

The Supreme Court's case-by-case application of the rights of the accused listed in the federal Bill of Rights to the states moved ahead dramatically during the 1960s. This rapid change, often called a "due process revolution," took place under the leadership of Chief Justice Earl Warren. The following cases applied virtually all of the 4th, 5th, 6th, and 8th Amendment rights of the accused to the states through the due process clause of the 14th Amendment:

- *Mapp* v. *Ohio* (1961): Evidence obtained in violation of 4th Amendment rights must be excluded from the state's prosecution of criminal defendants.

- *Robinson* v. *California* (1962): State governments cannot use cruel and unusual punishments in violation of the 8th Amendment.
- *Gideon* v. *Wainwright* (1963): The 6th Amendment right to counsel must be provided to all defendants.
- *Malloy* v. *Hogan* (1964): Defendants in state courts have the 5th Amendment right of protection against self-incrimination.
- *Pointer* v. *Texas* (1965): States must observe the 6th Amendment right of defendants to confront witnesses against them.
- *Parker* v. *Gladden* (1966): Defendants in state courts have the 6th Amendment right to an impartial jury.
- *Miranda* v. *Arizona* (1966): Police are required to advise suspects of their 5th Amendment right of protection against self-incrimination and 6th Amendment right to an attorney.
- *Klopfer* v. *North Carolina* (1967): Defendants in state courts have the 6th Amendment right to a speedy trial.
- *Washington* v. *Texas* (1967): Defendants in state courts have the 6th Amendment right to subpoena witnesses to testify in their favor.
- *Duncan* v. *Louisiana* (1968): States must guarantee the defendant's 6th Amendment right to a jury trial in criminal cases.
- *Benton* v. *Maryland* (1969): State law enforcers cannot subject a person to double jeopardy; that is, they cannot deprive individuals of their 5th Amendment right not to be tried twice for the same crime.

Controversies about rights of the accused The Warren Court's due process revolution nationalized the rights of the accused in the federal Bill of Rights; that is, people accused of crimes anywhere in the United States could expect the same legal protections.

Many Americans hailed the due process revolution. Others, however, criticized it for caring too much for the rights of accused criminals and too little for the victims of crime and the law-abiding majority of the people. The critics claimed that such decisions as *Mapp*, *Malloy*, and *Miranda* restricted police too much and made it too easy for criminals to evade punishment.

During his 1968 Presidential campaign, Richard Nixon sided with the critics when he said, "Let us always respect, as I do, our courts and those who serve on them, but let us also recognize that some of our courts have gone too far in weakening the peace forces as against the criminal forces in this country." After winning the Presidency, Nixon appointed a new chief justice, Warren Burger, who agreed with him about issues of law, order, and the rights of the accused. From 1970 to 1971 President Nixon appointed three more justices: Harry Blackmun, Lewis Powell, and William Rehnquist. Later, Presidents Ronald Reagan and George Bush also expressed strong concern for the rights of crime victims and criticized the overemphasis on the rights of criminal suspects.

Despite high-level objections to some aspects of the due process revolution of the Warren Court, none of the Court's rulings on the rights of the accused has been overruled. Only minor modifications have been made in the *Mapp* and *Miranda* decisions about certain 4th and 5th Amendment rights. In *New York* v. *Quarles* (1984), the Court decided that police officers could, in order to protect themselves against harm, question a suspect about possession of weapons before advising the suspect of his Miranda rights to remain silent and obtain counsel. In *United States* v. *Leon* (1984) the Court adopted a "good faith exception" to the exclusionary rule established by the *Mapp* decision. This means that evidence obtained illegally may be used to prosecute a defendant if the police who obtained it thought they were acting legally at the time. In *Dickerson* v. *United States* (2000), however, the Court acted to reinforce the rights of a suspect by deciding that Congress cannot enact legislation to overrule the long-standing Miranda warnings requirement.

In a free society, there will always be arguments about the proper balance between liberty and order, between the rights of criminal suspects and the public's need for safety and security against crime. The exact meaning and practical applications of due process of law will continue to be debated in public forums and courts of law. Such constructive controversies are signs of a healthy constitutional democracy.

SEE ALSO *Benton v. Maryland; Bill of Rights; Counsel, right to; Double jeopardy; Due process of law; Duncan v. Louisiana; Exclusionary rule; Gideon v. Wainwright; Grand jury; Habeas corpus, writ of; Incorporation doctrine; Juvenile justice; Mapp v. Ohio; Miranda v. Arizona; Powell v. Alabama; Searches and seizures; Trial by jury; United States v. Leon; Wolf v. Colorado*

SOURCES David J. Bodenhamer, *Fair Trial: Rights of the Accused in American History* (New York: Oxford, 1992). David J. Bodenhamer, "Trial Rights of the Accused," in *By and for the People: Constitutional Rights in American History,* edited by Kermit L. Hall (Arlington Heights, Ill.: Harlan Davidson, 1991). David J. Bodenhamer and James W. Ely, Jr., *The Bill of Rights in Modern America after Two Hundred Years* (Bloomington: Indiana University Press, 1993). Fred Graham, *The Due Process Revolution: The Warren Court's Impact on Criminal Law* (New York: Hayden, 1970). Samuel Walker, *Popular Justice: A History of American Criminal Law* (New York: Oxford University Press, 1980). Samuel Walker, "Rights Before Trial," in *By and for the People: Constitutional Rights in American History,* edited by Kermit L. Hall (Arlington Heights, Ill.: Harlan Davidson, 1991).

ROBERTS, OWEN J.
Associate Justice, 1930–1945

- Born: May 2, 1875, Germantown, Pa.
- Education: University of Pennsylvania, A.B., 1895, LL.B., 1898
- Previous government service: special deputy attorney general, Eastern District of Pennsylvania, 1918; special U.S. attorney, 1924–30

- Appointed by President Herbert Hoover May 9, 1930; replaced Justice Edward Terry Sanford, who died
- Supreme Court term: confirmed by the Senate May 20, 1930, by a voice vote; resigned July 31, 1945
- Died: May 17, 1955, West Vincent Township, Pa.

Owen J. Roberts served on the Supreme Court during an era of crisis and controversy, which included the Great Depression and World War II. He initially participated with the Court's majority in opposing President Franklin Roosevelt's New Deal programs. Later, he switched his position to join the Court's majority in favor of New Deal programs and laws. His change in position seemed to reflect a great change in popular opinion signaled by President Roosevelt's landslide victory in the 1936 election.

Justice Roberts's most notable Supreme Court opinion came in dissent in *Korematsu v. United States* (1944). The Court upheld the compulsory movement of Japanese Americans during World War II to internment centers because they were viewed as a threat to national security following Japan's attack on Pearl Harbor in Hawaii. Roberts, however, disagreed and wrote: "[This] is the case of convicting a citizen as a punishment for not submitting to imprisonment in a concentration camp, based on his ancestry . . . without evidence or inquiry concerning his loyalty and good disposition towards the United States. . . . I need hardly labor the conclusion that constitutional rights have been violated." Justice Roberts's dissent in the *Korematsu* case is viewed by most Americans today as the correct opinion.

SEE ALSO *Korematsu v. United States*

ROBING ROOM

Before each session of the Supreme Court, the justices go to the robing room on the main floor of the Supreme Court Building, next to the Conference Room. The robing room contains nine closets, one for each justice, which hold the judicial robes. In this room, the justices put on their robes before appearing in public for a session of the Court.

ROBINSON, JOSEPH T.

- Born: Aug. 26, 1872, Lonoke, Ark.
- Political party: Democrat
- Education: University of Arkansas; law department of the University of Virginia
- Representative from Arkansas: 1903–13
- Senator from Arkansas: 1913–37
- Senate minority leader: 1923–33
- Senate majority leader: 1933–37
- Died: July 14, 1937, Washington, D.C.

As Democratic majority leader during the first years of the New Deal, Joe Robinson got the Senate's usually slow machinery to work with amazing speed. He personally served as floor manager of President Franklin D. Roosevelt's emergency banking bill and drove it through the Senate in one afternoon. Robinson similarly volunteered to manage other New Deal bills. Many committee chairmen were happy to give up this responsibility because they were conservative Southern Democrats who felt uncomfortable with liberal New Deal proposals but did not want to stand in the way of ending the depression. Most senators liked and trusted Robinson and willingly followed his lead. But if they crossed him, Robinson would bellow and bang his fist on his desk until he whipped the Senate into line. A big, bluff, tough man, he gave the impression of "brute animal strength," said one reporter, "and a willingness to use it."

When President Roosevelt proposed expanding the Supreme Court in 1937, in order to add more liberal justices, Robinson reluctantly went along. Against strong opposition from members of his own party, he put together a slim majority in favor of the bill. But during an intense fight Robinson died of a heart attack. Without his leadership, the court plan collapsed and the Democratic majority split badly for the remainder of the New Deal years.

SEE ALSO Court-packing plan (1937); "First hundred days"; Majority leader

SOURCES Donald C. Bacon, "Joseph Taylor Robinson: The Good Soldier," in First among Equals: Outstanding Senate Leaders of the Twentieth Century, edited by Richard A. Baker and Roger H. Davidson (Washington, D.C.: Congressional Quarterly, 1991).

ROCKEFELLER, NELSON
Vice President

- Born: July 8, 1908, Bar Harbor, Maine
- Political party: Republican
- Education: Dartmouth College, B.A., 1930
- Military service: none
- Previous government service: director, Office of Inter-American Affairs, U.S. Department of State, 1940–44; assistant secretary of state for Latin American Affairs, 1944–45; chair, Advisory Board on International Development, 1950–51; chair, Advisory Committee on Government Organization, 1953–58; under secretary of health, education, and welfare, 1953–54; special assistant to the President for foreign affairs, 1954–55; governor of New York, 1959–73
- Vice President under Gerald R. Ford, 1975–77
- Died: Jan. 26, 1979, New York, N.Y.

Nelson Rockefeller was the second Vice President to be nominated by a President and confirmed by Congress under the 25th Amendment. The son of one of the richest men in the United States, John D. Rockefeller, founder of Standard Oil, Nelson Rockefeller devoted most of his career to government service. He held executive appointments under Presidents Franklin Roosevelt, Harry Truman, and Dwight Eisenhower, and he served as one of Eisenhower's principal foreign policy advisers on arms control in the mid-1950s.

Rockefeller first won elective office in

1958, when he defeated Averell Harriman to become governor of New York. Reelected three times, he was responsible for building a huge state office complex in Albany, constructing the New York State thruway system, and establishing the State University of New York as one of the largest university systems in the nation.

Rockefeller tried for the Republican Presidential nomination in 1960 but withdrew before the Republican convention in a deal with front-runner Richard Nixon that led to the liberalization of the party's platform on civil rights and foreign policy. In 1964 he led the liberal wing of the Republican party and again tried for the nomination but was defeated by the conservative Barry Goldwater after a bruising primary season. In 1968 he lost a third nomination bid, again to Nixon.

On August 20, 1975, President Gerald Ford used the provisions of the 25th Amendment to fill the vacancy in the Vice Presidency (caused by Ford's succession to the Presidency after Nixon's resignation). Ford nominated Rockefeller for Vice President. To do so, he had to override the wishes of conservatives who preferred George Bush. Four months later, after lengthy hearings, the Senate and House both consented to Rockefeller.

As presiding officer of the Senate, Rockefeller played a major role in weakening the tradition of unlimited debate. He made several rulings that closed off debate by a three-fifths vote instead of the customary two-thirds. Rockefeller became one of Ford's key domestic advisers. He had a weekly lunch with the President and unlimited access to him. Ford accepted Rockefeller's proposal for a government corporation to develop energy self-sufficiency for the nation but opposed his suggestion that the national government help New York City through a fiscal crisis. Ford incorporated 6 of Rockefeller's 19 suggestions for domestic policy in his 1976 State of the Union address. Rockefeller developed these proposals by serving as chair of the Domestic Council. He also chaired a number of Presidential commissions,

such as the National Commission on Productivity and Work Quality and the National Commission on Water Quality, and he was a member of the Commission on the Organization of Government and the Conduct of Foreign Policy. He conducted a major review of the Central Intelligence Agency. But he admitted to the Senate, when presiding over it for the last time, that "these past two years, in all candor, cannot be said to have sorely tried either my talents or my stamina."

Rockefeller helped Ford secure renomination in 1976 against a determined challenge by Ronald Reagan. He delivered the New York delegation to Ford at the convention and later helped raise large sums of money for Ford's campaign. But Ford felt he could not afford to have Rockefeller run for Vice President because he would risk losing the nomination to the conservative Reagan. Rockefeller voluntarily withdrew from the ticket before the nominating season began and retired from public service at the end of his term.

SEE ALSO *Ford, Gerald R.; Nixon, Richard M.; 25th Amendment*

SOURCES Gerald Benjamin and T. Norman Hurd, eds., *Rockefeller in Retrospect* (Albany, N.Y.: Rockefeller Institute of Government, 1984). Michael Kramer and Sam Roberts, *I Never Wanted to Be Vice President of Anything* (New York: Basic Books, 1976). Cary Reich, *The Life of Nelson A. Rockefeller: Worlds to Conquer, 1908–1958* (New York: Doubleday, 1996). Michael Turner, *The Vice President as Policy Maker: Rockefeller in the Ford White House* (Westport, Conn.: Greenwood, 1982).

ROE V. WADE

- 410 U.S. 113 (1973)
- Vote: 7–2
- For the Court: Blackmun
- Concurring: Douglas, Stewart, and Burger
- Dissenting: White and Rehnquist

In August 1969 an unmarried pregnant

woman living in Texas wanted to terminate her pregnancy by having an abortion. Her doctor refused this request because Texas law made it a crime to have an abortion unless the operation was necessary to save the mother's life. So the woman sought legal help and filed suit against Henry Wade, district attorney for Dallas County, Texas. Throughout the legal proceedings, the woman was identified as Jane Roe to protect her anonymity. The plaintiff later was identified by the media as Norma McCorvey.

Jane Roe argued that the Texas abortion laws were unconstitutional. So she requested an injunction to restrain Henry Wade from enforcing them.

The Issue   Roe's lawyers claimed that the Texas abortion laws violated her rights under the due process clause of the 14th Amendment, which prohibited states from depriving their citizens of life, liberty, or property without due process of law. Does the 14th Amendment protect the right of a woman to have an abortion? Are state laws prohibiting abortion unconstitutional?

Opinion of the Court   The Supreme Court ruled that the Texas statutes on abortion were unconstitutional and that a woman did have the right to terminate her pregnancy. Justice Harry Blackmun wrote, "The right of privacy . . . whether it is to be found in the Fourteenth Amendment's concept of personal liberty . . . or . . . in the Ninth Amendment's reservation of rights to the people, is broad enough to encompass a woman's decision whether or not to terminate her pregnancy."

Justice Blackmun recognized that a woman's right to an abortion could be limited by "a compelling state interest" to protect her health and life. Based on medical evidence, Justice Blackmun concluded that during the "second trimester" of a woman's pregnancy (months 4 to 6), the state might intervene to regulate abortion to protect the mother's well-being. And the state could regulate or prohibit abortion during the third trimester (months 7 to 9). However, during the first trimester (months 1 to 3) of a pregnancy, it seemed unlikely that there would be "a compelling state interest" to restrict abortion rights to protect the health and life of the mother.

Dissent   Justice Byron White could not find in the Constitution the right to privacy upon which the *Roe* decision was based. He wrote, "I find nothing in the language or history of the Constitution to support the Court's judgment. . . . This issue, for the most part, should be left with the people and the political processes the people have devised to govern their affairs." Justices White and William Rehnquist both objected to the Court's involvement in a question they believed should be left to state governments to decide, without interference from the federal courts. They also believed that the *Roe* decision unjustly disregarded the protection due to the life of the fetus.

Significance   The *Roe* decision has generated continuing controversy. Women's rights advocates have hailed *Roe* as a landmark victory. Its critics can be roughly divided into two groups: those who oppose the decision because they believe abortion is murder and those who believe that the Court improperly substituted its policy preference for the will of the people as expressed through their elected representatives in state governments.

Justice Byron White accurately remarked in his dissent that the right to an abortion is an issue about which "reasonable men may easily and heatedly differ." And so it has been since 1973, when the *Roe* case was decided.

Efforts to modify or overturn the *Roe* decision have continued. In *Webster* v. *Reproductive Health Services* (1989), for example, the Court upheld provisions of a Missouri law that restricted the right to an abortion, a retreat from the *Roe* decision that stopped short of overturning it. *Rust* v. *Sullivan* (1991) limited the access of poor women to abortions by forbidding federally funded clinics, such as those run by Planned Parenthood, to advise patients about abortion. In *Steinberg v. Carhart* (2000), the Court ruled against state laws banning a type of late-term abortion known as "partial-birth" abortion.

SEE ALSO *Abortion rights; Privacy, right to; Webster v. Reproductive Health Services*
SOURCES Marian Faux, *Roe v. Wade* (New York: Macmillan, 1988). David J. Garrow, *Liberty and Sexuality: The Right to Privacy and the Making of Roe v. Wade, 1923–1973* (New York: Macmillan, 1993). Rosalind Rosenberg, "The Abortion Case," in *Quarrels That Have Shaped the Constitution,* edited by John A. Garraty (New York: Harper & Row, 1987). Laurence H. Tribe, *Abortion: The Clash of Absolutes* (New York: Norton, 1990). Sarah Weddington, *A Question of Choice* (New York: Putnam, 1992).

ROOSEVELT, ELEANOR
First Lady

- Born: Oct. 11, 1884, New York, N.Y.
- Wife of Franklin D. Roosevelt, 32nd President
- Died: Nov. 7, 1962, New York, N.Y.

Eleanor Roosevelt was a leader of the liberal wing of the Democratic party and the wife of Franklin D. Roosevelt, the 32nd President. Her parents died during her childhood, and she was raised by her grandmother and educated in England. In 1905 she married her fifth cousin (once removed) Franklin Delano Roosevelt. At her wedding she was given away by her uncle, President Theodore Roosevelt.

Eleanor Roosevelt helped her husband in the early stages of his political career, acting as his confidante and adviser. They had six children, one of whom died in infancy. She cared for her husband after he became ill with polio and while he was convalescing at Warm Springs, Georgia. Then she embarked on her own career as a teacher at the Todhunter School in New York City. She fought against racial segregation in the South and headed the

women's platform committee at the 1924 Democratic national convention, which proposed many liberal programs later adopted by her husband in the 1930s.

Eleanor Roosevelt became active in her own right in trade union causes. She worked with her husband in his successful campaign for the New York governorship in 1928. When she became First Lady in 1933, she strongly lobbied her husband to adopt liberal causes.

In 1933 Eleanor Roosevelt became the first First Lady to hold a press conference so that women reporters, then barred from the regular Presidential news conferences, could be accommodated. She broadcast a regular 15-minute radio program in which she commented on politics. She wrote a syndicated newspaper column, "My Day," which concentrated on women's issues until 1939 and then on public affairs in general, and in 1941 she began writing a column, "If you ask me," for the *Ladies Home Journal.* She resigned in 1939 from the Daughters of the American Revolution because the organization refused to allow the African-American opera singer Marian Anderson to give a concert in Washington's Constitution Hall. She took many trips across the country during the depression to see how New Deal recovery programs were working, serving as her husband's "eyes and ears." During World War II she traveled as her husband's emissary to raise troop morale on three fronts.

In 1945 President Harry Truman named Eleanor Roosevelt a U.S. delegate to the United Nations. She played a major role in securing UN adoption of the Universal Declaration of Human Rights in 1948, although the U.S. Senate refused its consent. She left her post in 1952. But she remained active in Democratic politics, working for liberal candidates and causes, especially those involving civil rights and liberties, and her endorsements were highly sought after and often crucial in New York State and national elections. In 1961 President John F. Kennedy reappointed her to the U.S. delegation to the UN, where she served until her death.

SEE ALSO *New Deal; Roosevelt, Franklin D.*
SOURCES Blanche Wiesen Cook, *Eleanor Roosevelt, 1884–1933* (New York: Viking, 1992). Blanche Wiesen Cook, *Eleanor Roosevelt: The Defining Years, 1933–1938* (New York: Viking, 1999). Joseph P. Lash, *Eleanor and Franklin* (New York: Norton, 1971). Eleanor Roosevelt, *The Autobiography of Eleanor Roosevelt* (New York: Harper, 1961). Eleanor Roosevelt, *On My Own* (New York: Harper, 1958). Eleanor Roosevelt, *This I Remember* (1949; reprint, Westport, Conn.: Greenwood Press, 1975).

ROOSEVELT, FRANKLIN D.
32nd President

- Born: Jan. 30, 1882, Hyde Park, N.Y.
- Political party: Democrat
- Education: Harvard College, A.B., 1903; Columbia University Law School, 1904–7
- Military service: none
- Previous government service: New York Senate, 1911–13; assistant secretary of the navy, 1913–20; governor of New York, 1929–33
- Elected President, 1932; served, 1933–45
- Died: Apr. 12, 1945, Warm Springs, Ga.

Franklin Delano Roosevelt was President during the Great Depression and World War II. He demonstrated the power of the modern Presidency to restore public confidence and win speedy passage of recovery legislation. In spite of considerable isolationist sentiment in Congress, he provided aid to Great Britain and the Soviet Union that prevented their defeat at the hands of Adolf Hitler, and after U.S. entry into World War II he led the Allied coalition to victory over Germany. Roosevelt created the New Deal coalition within the Democratic party, which dominated national politics through the 1960s.

Roosevelt was descended from a wealthy family of Dutch settlers and was a fifth cousin of President Theodore Roosevelt. He was educated by private tutors, then at the elite Groton School and at Harvard College, where he studied history and became editor of the student newspaper, the Harvard *Crimson*. He studied law at Columbia University but did not graduate. He married his fifth cousin Eleanor Roosevelt, passed the bar, and began to practice law in New York City in 1908.

In 1910 Roosevelt won election to the state senate from rural Duchess County (a seat that no Democrat had won since the Civil War). He was appointed assistant secretary of the navy in 1913 by Woodrow Wilson and served until 1920. That year he won the Democratic Vice Presidential nomination and campaigned strenuously for the League of Nations and Treaty of Versailles, but he was defeated. The following year, while vacationing at his family retreat on Campobello Island in Canada, he came down with polio. For the rest of his life he was paralyzed below the waist, though he went through arduous rehabilitation at a spa in Warm Springs, Georgia. In 1927 Roosevelt founded the Warm Springs Foundation to treat other victims of polio.

Although he used a wheelchair and was weighed down with heavy leg braces, Roosevelt remained an important figure in New York Democratic politics. He attended his party's national conventions in 1924 and 1928, both times giving nominating speeches for the "Happy Warrior," Al Smith. Although Smith was crushed in 1928, in part because he was a Roman Catholic, Roosevelt spoke out against religious intolerance and won the governorship of New York.

As governor, Roosevelt lowered taxes and electric rates and created a state power authority, state parks, and state highways. In 1930, in the midst of the depression, he created the first state public relief agency and the first system of unemployment insurance. He was reelected by the greatest landslide ever received by a New York gubernatorial candidate.

In 1932 Roosevelt won the Democratic

nomination for President, becoming the first person ever to win a Presidential nomination after being defeated in a Vice Presidential election. He flew to Chicago and became the first Presidential nominee in U.S. history to deliver his acceptance speech in person. "I pledge you, I pledge myself," he told the delegates, "to a New Deal for the American people." He defeated Herbert Hoover by a landslide. Riding his political coattails, the Democrats increased their majorities in the House and Senate.

Roosevelt's 1932 election and the three that followed brought into power the New Deal coalition: white Protestant Southerners, Northern Jews and Catholics, blacks, labor union members, and small farmers. That coalition would convert the Democrats into the majority party, dominate the Presidential elections (with only two exceptions) through the 1960s, and control most of the Congresses into the 1990s.

Roosevelt continued Woodrow Wilson's transformation of the Democratic party from its Jeffersonian and Jacksonian traditions of states' rights and limited governmental regulation to an emphasis on national economic regulation and social welfare programs for the poor, the unemployed, the sick, and the elderly.

As Roosevelt took his oath of office, there were millions unemployed, farmers and home owners had seen their land or homes foreclosed, industrial production was sinking, and thousands of banks had been closed by state governors to prevent a run on their deposits. "Let me assert my firm belief that the only thing we have to fear is fear itself," Roosevelt told the American people in his inaugural address, "nameless, unreasoning, unjustified terror which paralyzes needed efforts to convert retreat into advance." He took measures to end that fear. He declared a bank holiday to end the run on deposits, then got Congress to pass an emergency banking bill to regulate banks. Only those that were declared solvent were allowed to reopen. By executive order he took the nation off the gold standard to protect dwindling Trea-sury reserves from people who wanted to exchange dollars for gold, which they thought would be more valuable in hard times. The bank panic was over.

Roosevelt began his administration with the "hundred days" of emergency legislation. Banking deposits were guaranteed by the Federal Deposit Insurance Corporation, restoring depositor confidence. An Economy Act permitted the President to cut federal employees' salaries and veterans' pensions. The Federal Emergency Relief Administration gave states funds to provide public works jobs to the unemployed, and the Civilian Conservation Corps gave work to young people. The Home Owners Loan Corporation helped home owners avoid foreclosures. The Farm Credit Administration provided funds for farmers in the growing season; the Farm Mortgage Refinancing Act provided them with loans to make mortgage payments; and the Agricultural Adjustment Administration helped stabilize farm prices by limiting production and establishing marketing quotas. The National Industrial Recovery Act allowed industrial producers to stabilize prices and restore production. The Tennessee Valley Authority built 30 dams that provided cheap power for farms and industry and better agricultural techniques to parts of seven states in the poverty-stricken Tennessee Valley. The Works Progress Administration funded artists and writers and photographers to undertake public cultural projects such as painting murals in government buildings.

Roosevelt continued his recovery program by creating more New Deal agencies, such as the Securities and Exchange Commission to regulate financial markets, the Federal Communications Commission to regulate telephone and radio (and later television), and the National Industrial Relations Board to regulate labor-management relations. He got the national government involved in public housing, rural electrification, public service jobs, unemployment insurance, and old-age pensions.

Although Roosevelt did not lift the nation out of the depression, his active and energetic leadership and his ability to restore public confidence helped alleviate the worst suffering. In 1936 he won a landslide victory against Republican Alf Landon, winning a greater percentage of the popular vote than in 1932.

In Roosevelt's second inaugural address he pledged to relieve the poverty of "one third of a nation ill-housed, ill-clad, ill-nourished." To do so, he moved against the Supreme Court, which had declared several recovery laws unconstitutional. Roosevelt proposed to "pack" the court with an additional appointee for every justice over the age of 70—giving him six new appointments. Members of Congress, even those from his own party, were reluctant to see Roosevelt dominate the court.

Roosevelt's court-packing plan was defeated in Congress in 1937. He would later appoint enough justices to secure a firm liberal majority on the court. But after the court-packing fight, a conservative coalition of Southern Democrats and Republicans in Congress blocked most of Roosevelt's New Deal proposals.

Roosevelt maintained strict neutrality in European affairs until the summer of 1939. But after a trip to the United States by the British king and queen, he recommended that Congress amend the neutrality laws to allow nations that might go to war with the Axis powers (Germany, Italy, and Japan) the right to buy supplies from the United States. After Germany invaded Poland on September 1, 1939, Roosevelt initiated a "cash and carry" policy to arm the British. The British paid cash and carried the goods away in their own ships.

In the summer of 1940 Roosevelt began a national preparedness program, had Congress give him authority to draft troops, and raised the ceiling on the national debt. In September, using an executive order to bypass the Senate's advice and consent power over treaties, Roosevelt concluded a "destroyer deal" with Great Britain: in return for providing the British with 50 old destroyers useful for submarine warfare, the United States received the use of British military bases in the Caribbean.

Because of the ominous international situation, Roosevelt broke with tradition and accepted a unanimous third nomination for President. He promised the American people, "Your sons will not fight in a foreign war," and he defeated Republican Wendell Willkie. In his State of the Union address in 1941, he put forth his vision of a postwar world when he enunciated the Four Freedoms: freedom of speech and expression; freedom of every person to worship God in his own way; freedom from want; and freedom from fear.

In 1941 Congress passed the Lend-Lease Act, which provided military assistance to Great Britain and the Soviet Union. The United States, in the President's words, became the "arsenal of democracy" against the Axis dictatorships. Although Roosevelt gave "shoot on sight" orders to the navy against German submarines in the North Atlantic in 1941, landed U.S. troops in Iceland, closed Italian and German consulates, and froze Japanese assets in the United States, he did not ask Congress for a declaration of war because most Americans opposed it. In August 1941 Roosevelt met with British prime minister Winston Churchill to draft the Atlantic Charter, an eight-point plan on common principles of a democratic postwar world. The following month the U.S. Navy began to convoy British merchant ships carrying lend-lease supplies.

The Japanese attacks on Pearl Harbor (in the Hawaiian Islands), on the Philippines, and on Guam, which all took place on December 7, 1941, led Roosevelt to ask Congress to declare war not only on Japan but on Germany and Italy as well. Early in 1942 a coalition of 26 nations subscribed to the Atlantic Charter. Following Roosevelt's suggestions, these nations called themselves the United Nations. In 1943 Roosevelt and Churchill called for an unconditional Axis surrender.

In June 1944 Allied troops under the command of General Dwight D. Eisenhower launched the Normandy invasion in France. With the war going successfully, Roosevelt received a fourth Democratic nomination and defeated Republican challenger Thomas E. Dewey.

In February 1945 Roosevelt traveled to Yalta in the Soviet Union to discuss plans for peace with Churchill and Soviet dictator Joseph Stalin. Stalin and Churchill discussed spheres of influence for their nations, parts of Europe and the Middle East where they would have dominant political and economic influence. Roosevelt, in poor health, was not in a position to argue forcefully against them and in favor of the U.S. position of open markets and equal access for all the great powers. This led some critics to claim that Roosevelt had "sold out" the nations of eastern Europe to Stalin. While resting at Warm Springs, Georgia, in preparation for the San Francisco conference that was to create the United Nations, Roosevelt died of a cerebral hemorrhage on April 12, 1945.

SEE ALSO *Brains Trust; Court-packing plan (1937); Executive Office of the President; Garner, John Nance; Hoover, Herbert C.; Modern Presidency; New Deal; Roosevelt, Eleanor; Term of office, Presidential; Truman, Harry S.; Two-term tradition; Wallace, Henry; White House Office*
SOURCES James MacGregor Burns, *The Lion and the Fox* (New York: Harcourt Brace, 1956). Robert Dallek, *Franklin Roosevelt and American Foreign Policy, 1932–1945* (New York: Oxford University Press, 1979). Kenneth Sydney Davis, *FDR: Into the Storm, 1937–1940: A History* (New York: Random House, 1993). William E. Leuchtenburg, *Franklin D. Roosevelt and the New Deal* (New York: Harper & Row, 1963).

ROOSEVELT, THEODORE
26th President

- Born: Oct. 27, 1858, New York, N.Y.
- Political party: Republican
- Education: Harvard College, A.B.,

1880; Columbia University School of Law, 1881
- Military service: 1st U.S. Volunteer Cavalry, 1898
- Previous government service: New York State Assembly, 1881–84; U.S. Civil Service commissioner, 1889–95; president, New York City Board of Police Commissioners, 1895–96; assistant secretary of the navy, 1897–98; governor of New York, 1899–1901; Vice President, 1901
- Succeeded to Presidency, 1901; served, 1901–9
- Died: Jan. 6, 1919, Oyster Bay, N.Y.

Theodore ("Teddy") Roosevelt was the youngest person ever to serve as President of the United States and the first Vice President who succeeded to the Presidency to win election in his own right. He used the powers of the Presidency to the hilt, especially in foreign affairs, and he was the first President to act as the leader of a world power. His motto was "Speak softly and carry a big stick," yet in spite of his militaristic attitudes, the nation remained at peace. Not a single member of the armed forces died in combat during his term—almost a unique accomplishment among U.S. Presidents.

Roosevelt was afflicted with asthma as a boy but built himself up with exercise. He graduated from Harvard and attended law school briefly. In the New York Assembly he strayed frequently from the Republican party to take an independent position. He wrote several popular histories, beginning with *The Naval War of 1812*. When his wife Alice Lee died in childbirth in 1884 (on the same day he learned of the death of his mother), he went out West to a ranch in the Dakota Territory to recover from his grief.

Roosevelt returned to the East to run for mayor of New York City in 1886, but he finished third and went back to the ranch with his new wife, his childhood friend Edith Carow. There he wrote biographies of Senator Thomas Hart Benton and Gouverneur Morris (an influential delegate to the federal Constitutional Convention), and the two volumes of *The Winning of the West*. In 1889 he returned East again and was named to the U.S. Civil Service Commission by President Benjamin Harrison. He transferred thousands of patronage jobs to the merit system. In 1895 he became president of the New York City Board of Police Commissioners.

When President William McKinley took office in 1897, he named Roosevelt assistant secretary of the navy. Roosevelt promoted ship construction and deployed much of the fleet in the Far East, where Admiral George Dewey was able to secure Manila Bay and win control of the Philippines at the beginning of the Spanish-American War. Roosevelt himself organized the 1st U.S. Volunteer Cavalry, known as the Rough Riders. As their commander, he led them into battle at Kettle Hill near Santiago de Cuba, which newspaper accounts called the "charge up San Juan Hill."

Roosevelt's battlefield exploits, recounted in his book *The Rough Riders* (1899), won him the governorship of New York. His reform program so upset party leaders that they arranged for him to receive the Vice Presidential nomination in 1900. Roosevelt was so bored with the inactivity of the Vice Presidency that he seriously considered finishing law school. But six months after his inauguration, on September 14, 1901, President William McKinley died of an assassin's bullet and Roosevelt took the Presidential oath.

At 42, Roosevelt was the youngest person ever to assume the office. He pledged to continue McKinley's policies but soon demonstrated his reformist and independent streak, much to the chagrin of the Republican leaders who had put him on the ticket. He developed the "stewardship" theory of the Presidency: the chief executive could and should take all measures necessary for the welfare of the American people, even if they were not specifically mentioned in the Constitution.

Roosevelt instituted more than 30 court cases against corporations, charging them with violations of antitrust laws—conspiring to control markets or fix prices. He insisted that coal mine owners negotiate with their miners. This was the first time that a President had acted as a neutral umpire in a dispute between management and labor. In 1902 he secured passage of the Newlands Reclamation Act, which funded irrigation projects in the West. He increased the acreage of national parks and forests fivefold, much of it by executive orders creating five national parks. He also established the first federal bird reservation and 50 bird sanctuaries to protect endangered species. For the first time, a President focused public attention on conservation and the environment, and he got Congress to establish the U.S. Forest Service. In 1903 Congress created the Department of Commerce and Labor, and to head it, Roosevelt nominated the first Jewish cabinet secretary, Oscar Straus.

In foreign affairs Roosevelt presided over the expansion of American naval power, sending the Great White Fleet on a tour around the world from 1907 to 1909 to demonstrate the power of the United States to other nations. He insisted that the United States be the dominant naval power in the Pacific. When the government of Colombia refused to ratify an agreement that would allow the United States to begin construction of a canal across the isthmus of Panama (then a Colombian province), Roosevelt encouraged revolutionists to declare Panama independent and used the navy to prevent Colombian warships from quelling the revolt. Soon, he concluded an agreement with the new nation, granting the United States a zone in which to construct a canal. In 1904 the President announced the Roosevelt Corollary to the Monroe Doctrine, which, in effect, made the United States the "policeman" in the Western Hemisphere.

In 1904 Roosevelt was unanimously nominated for President by the Republican party, and he won election in his own right by defeating Democrat Alton B. Parker. He declared that he viewed his first three years in the White House as a full first term, and that, therefore, his second term would be his last.

Roosevelt continued his activist foreign policies. He took full control of the finances of the Dominican Republic in 1905 in order to pay its debts to U.S. and European creditors. When the Senate balked at consenting to a commercial treaty with the Dominican Republic because Southern senators considered it harmful to Southern sugar growers, Roosevelt implemented its terms by calling it an executive agreement, which did not require Senate consent. That same year Roosevelt mediated an end to the Russo-Japanese War at the Portsmouth Conference, receiving the 1906 Nobel Peace Prize for his efforts. He donated his $40,000 prize to a foundation for promoting better labor-management relations.

With solid Republican majorities in both chambers of Congress, in 1906 Roosevelt won passage of three important laws: the Pure Food and Drug Act and the Meat Inspection Act, which established new safety standards for consumers, and the Hepburn Railroad Act, which strengthened the enforcement power of the Interstate Commerce Commission over railroads.

In 1908 Roosevelt honored his two-term pledge and helped secure the Republican Presidential nomination for his protégé William Howard Taft. The two men eventually broke over Taft's conservative policies, and in 1910 Roosevelt went on a nationwide speaking tour, promoting a program of New Nationalism. To Roosevelt, the issue was simple: the Republican party should be the "party of the plain people," not "the party of privilege and of special interests." He called for government regulation of corporations and natural resources, a minimum wage, and limitations on the length of the workday.

In 1912 Taft defeated Roosevelt for the Republican nomination. Roosevelt's followers then organized a new party, the Progressive party, and nominated him. Roosevelt told them he felt "as strong as a bull moose," and the press then dubbed it the Bull Moose party. His platform emphasized democratization of U.S. politics; its proposals included the reversal of judicial decisions by popular vote, direct election of U.S. senators, woman suffrage, and referenda (direct popular votes) on legislation.

With Republican voters split between the regular Taft and the insurgent Roosevelt, Democrat Woodrow Wilson won the White House. Toward the end of his life, Roosevelt attempted unsuccessfully to get Wilson to offer him a commission so he could lead a new group of volunteers to fight in World War I. He died in 1919, shortly after the war's end.

SEE ALSO *Executive agreements; McKinley, William; Monroe Doctrine; Taft, William Howard; Two-term tradition; Wilson, Woodrow*

SOURCES John Milton Cooper, Jr., *The Warrior and the Priest: Woodrow Wilson and Theodore Roosevelt* (Cambridge: Harvard University Press, 1983). Lewis L. Gould, *The Presidency of Theodore Roosevelt* (Lawrence: University Press of Kansas, 1991). William H. Harbaugh, *Power and Responsibility: The Life and Times of Theodore Roosevelt* (New York: Oxford University Press, 1975). David McCullough, *Mornings on Horseback* (New York: Simon & Schuster, 1981). Edmund Morris, *The Rise of Theodore Roosevelt* (New York: Coward, McCann & Geoghegan, 1979).

"RUFFLES AND FLOURISHES"

"Ruffles and flourishes" is the trumpet fanfare that traditionally heralds the arrival of a head of state. When it announces the President, it is followed by the playing of "Hail to the Chief." The "ruffles" (short drumrolls) and the "flourishes" (a bugle call) are generally played four times.

SEE ALSO *"Hail to the Chief"; Marine Band, U.S.*

RULE OF FOUR

Petitioners seeking review of a case by the Supreme Court will petition the Court for a writ of certiorari, an order from the Supreme Court to a lower court requiring that a record of a case be sent to the Court for review. If at least four of the nine justices vote in favor of this action, the Court will grant a petition for certiorari. This procedure is known as the Rule of Four.

SEE ALSO *Certiorari, writ of*

RULE OF LAW

SEE *Constitutionalism*

RULES COMMITTEES

Like the rules of the two bodies, the House of Representatives and Senate rules committees operate very differently. The House Rules Committee plays a powerful role in all House proceedings. When bills are reported out of committee, but before they are debated by the full House, the House Rules Committee determines the rules under which the bill will be debated, setting time limits and other conditions for the debate.

The House Rules Committee can adopt an open rule, a closed rule, or a modified rule. If it adopts no rule at all, the bill will not get to the House floor. Under an open rule, members can debate and amend a bill as much as they want. Under a closed rule, members may not introduce amendments from the floor, and they can debate the bill only for a limited time, with the time divided equally between the opposing sides. A modified rule is not as restrictive as a closed rule but spells out how many and what types of amendments may be introduced from the floor.

By the type of rule it adopts, the Rules Committee can therefore make it much easier for the House majority to get its way, or it can block the passage of a bill or at least make it more difficult. Before 1910, when progressives led a revolt against the conservative Speaker Joseph G. Cannon for blocking their reform legislation, Speakers of the House appointed the chairman of the Rules Committee and served on the committee themselves, which increased the Speaker's control over legislation. After 1910 the chairmanship went to the committee member from the majority party who had the most seniority. In the 1950s a conservative coalition of Republicans and Democrats controlled the Rules Committee under chairman Howard Smith (Democrat–Virginia). Because this conservative coalition frustrated many liberal initiatives, Speaker Sam Rayburn led the movement to enlarge the Rules Committee and make it more representative of the majority party as a whole rather than just its conservative wing. Legislative reforms in the 1970s also increased the influence of the Speaker and the majority party leadership over the Rules Committee.

Although the House has separate committees for rules and administration, the Senate has combined these functions into a single Rules and Administration Committee. Time limits and other stipulations on debate and amendment of Senate bills are arranged by unanimous consent agreements worked out by the leadership and the bill's sponsors. Because bills do not go to the Senate Rules Committee for specific rules, and because the Senate revises its general rules very infrequently, the Rules and Administration Committee devotes more of its attention to such administrative duties as assigning office and parking space and overseeing the Senate's general operations.

SEE ALSO *Cannon, Joseph G.; Committees, congressional; Rayburn, Sam; Rules of the House and Senate; Smith, Howard W.; Unanimous consent agreements*

SOURCES Walter J. Oleszek, *Congressional Procedures and the Policy Process* (Washington, D.C.: Congressional Quarterly, 1989).

RULES OF THE HOUSE AND SENATE

In order to get business done and to operate as fairly as possible, each house of Congress has established rules of procedure. The Constitution (Article 1, Section 4) allows the House and Senate to establish their own separate rules. In the 1st Congress, both houses appointed special committees to propose rules. From the beginning, the rules of the House favored majority rule, while the rules of the Senate protected the rights of the minority. The difference between the two has acted as an additional check and balance on the powers of the federal government.

The first rules of the House dealt with the Speaker's powers, the proper behavior of members, the procedures of debate, the handling of bills, and the operations of the House as a committee of the whole (a device to enable the whole House to act as a committee, in order to limit debate and speed its procedures). Two hundred years later, despite periodic revision, the basic rules of the House still address these issues. House Speaker Thomas B. Reed argued that the rules of the House were designed to promote order and prevent "pandemonium." Although the smaller Senate had the luxury of allowing every member to have a say, the larger House needed tighter rules to get things accomplished. Beginning in the 1840s, the House adopted rules limiting how much time members could speak on any issue—to prevent filibustering (talking a bill to death) or other obstructive tactics by the minority. Regardless of which party has held the majority, its members have promoted rules to give the majority power to act.

From the beginning, Senate rules differed from House rules. For instance, the Senate does not operate as a committee of the whole, and it had no other means of limiting debate until it adopted its first cloture rule in 1917. Although various revisions of the rules have strengthened the majority's ability to act, the Senate has remained a body of equals. Even the most junior member of the minority may speak at length on any Senate bill and therefore has a chance to affect the bill's final shape.

The rules of both the House and Senate remain few in number. A few outmoded rules have been dropped, and a few new rules added. But whenever either body applies or interprets a rule, it establishes a precedent, or model, and the precedents are so numerous that they fill thick volumes. These accumulating precedents have enabled Congress to function and to meet the ever-changing needs of the nation without having to constantly change its rules.

SEE ALSO *Checks and balances; Cloture; Committee of the whole; Filibuster; Precedents, congressional; Rules committees*
SOURCES Robert C. Byrd, "Rules," in *The Senate, 1789–1989: Addresses on the History of the United States Senate*, vol. 2 (Washington, D.C.: Government Printing Office, 1991). Neil McNeil, *Forge of Democracy: The House of Representatives* (New York: David McKay, 1963).

RULES OF THE SUPREME COURT

During its first term, in 1790, the Supreme Court established rules for its activities. Since then, the Court has occasionally revised the rules. The rules and revisions are published in the *United States Reports*.

Changes in the rules may be proposed by one or more of the justices, by members of the bar, or by committees of lawyers and members of the federal judiciary that the Court creates to review the rules. By tradition, the justices agree upon revisions of the rules by consensus, not by a formal majority vote.

The rules cover various aspects of the Court's work. For example, there are rules to be followed by attorneys in Court proceedings. Rule 38 regulates an advocate's behavior during the oral argument, when a case is heard by the Court. The attorney presenting an oral argument may speak no longer than 30 minutes and may not read the oral argument. The rule says, "The Court looks with disfavor on any oral argument that is read from a prepared text." There are rules on the format, content, and length of certain documents involved in Court proceedings. For example, Rule 33 says that a lawyer's brief, submitted to the Court in advance of the oral argument in a case, must not be more than 50 typeset pages in length. Rule 34 specifies the contents and format of a brief and states, "Briefs must be compact, logically arranged with proper headings, concise, and free from burdensome, irrelevant, immaterial, or scandalous matter." One group of rules specifies the duties of the Court's officers, such as the clerk, librarian, and reporter of decisions. Another category of rules pertains to the Court's jurisdiction, or the types of cases it has the authority to review and hear. As of 1993, there were 48 rules of the Court.

RUNNING MATE

SEE *Ticket*

RUSSELL, RICHARD B., JR.

- Born: Nov. 2, 1897, Winder, Ga.
- Political party: Democrat
- Education: Gordon Institute, graduated, 1915; law department of the University of Georgia at Athens, graduated, 1918
- Senator from Georgia: 1933–71
- Died: Jan. 21, 1971, Washington, D.C.

A "senator's senator," Richard Russell, through seniority, chaired such powerful committees as Armed Services and Appropriations, and through personal integrity he earned a deep respect from his colleagues. Senator Norris Cotton (Republican–North Carolina) noted that Russell "engaged in debate only on rare occasions. When he did so, he spoke quietly, but a

silence fell upon the Senate and every member listened attentively, which is about the highest tribute a senator can receive." Russell became an authority on a range of issues from agriculture to military policy. But he also led the Southern caucus in the Senate and devoted his great parliamentary skills to defending racial segregation and opposing civil rights legislation. Some called him the last general of the Confederacy. Russell paid dearly for this stand. Despite the prestige he earned in the Senate, his unbending defense of segregation prevented him from becoming a national leader and achieving the Democratic nomination for President that he sought. After Russell's death, the Senate named its first office building in his honor.

SEE ALSO *Civil rights*
SOURCES Gilbert C. Fite, *Richard B. Russell, Jr., Senator from Georgia* (Chapel Hill: University of North Carolina Press, 1991).

RUTLEDGE, JOHN
Associate Justice, 1790–91
Chief Justice (unconfirmed), 1795

- Born: Sept. 1739, Charleston, S.C.
- Education: privately tutored at home; studied law at the Middle Temple, London
- Other government service: South Carolina Commons House of Assembly, 1761–76; attorney general of South Carolina, 1764–65; Stamp Act Congress, 1765; Continental Congress, 1774–76, 1776–78; governor of South Carolina, 1779–82; judge of the Court of Chancery of South Carolina, 1784–91; chief, South Carolina delegation to the Constitutional Convention, 1787; South Carolina Ratifying Convention, 1788; chief justice, South Carolina Court of Common Pleas, 1791
- Appointed by President George Washington to be an associate justice Sept. 24, 1789, as one of the original members of the U.S. Supreme Court; appointed by Washington as a recess appointment July 1, 1795, to be chief

justice; replaced Chief Justice John Jay, who resigned

• Supreme Court term: confirmed by the Senate as an associate justice Sept. 26, 1789, by a voice vote; resigned Mar. 5, 1791; sworn in as recess appointment to position of chief justice Aug. 12, 1795; the Senate rejected his appointment as chief justice by a vote of 14 to 10 and his service was terminated on Dec. 15, 1795
• Died: June 21, 1800, Charleston, S.C.

John Rutledge was one of the founders of the United States. He was a member of the Continental Congress and the Constitutional Convention of 1787. He was also a member of the committee that wrote the first constitution of South Carolina in 1776.

In 1789 President George Washington appointed Rutledge to be one of the original associate justices of the U.S. Supreme Court. Rutledge resigned in 1791, having written no opinions for the Supreme Court. He left the Supreme Court to become chief justice of South Carolina, which at that time was considered a more important position.

In 1795 President Washington appointed Rutledge to replace John Jay as chief justice of the United States. Jay had resigned to become governor of New York. Rutledge presided over the Court (without Senate confirmation) from August 12 to December 15, 1795, while the Congress was in recess. However, the Senate refused to confirm his nomination because of political disagreements with Rutledge, who had spoken publicly against a treaty negotiated by John Jay with the British government. The Senate had ratified the Jay Treaty in 1794 and many members were angered by Rutledge's promotion of public criticism of the Senate about the matter. So President Washington named Oliver Ellsworth to be the chief justice, and the Senate confirmed this appointment.

Rutledge was so shaken by the Senate's rejection of his nomination that he tried to drown himself. He recovered from this suicide attempt but spent the rest of his life in seclusion. He died at the age of 60 in Charleston, South Carolina.

SEE ALSO *Nominationss, confirmation of*

RUTLEDGE, WILEY B.
Associate Justice, 1943–49

• Born: July 20, 1894, Cloverport, Ky.
• Education: University of Wisconsin, B.A., 1914; University of Colorado, LL.B., 1922
• Previous government service: judge, U.S. Court of Appeals for the District of Columbia, 1939–43
• Appointed by President Franklin D. Roosevelt Jan. 11, 1943; replaced James F. Byrnes, who resigned
• Supreme Court term: confirmed by the Senate Feb. 8, 1943, by a voice vote; served until Sept. 10, 1949
• Died: Sept. 10, 1949, York, Maine

Wiley B. Rutledge was a strong supporter of President Franklin Roosevelt's New Deal. As dean of the University of Iowa Law School, Rutledge spoke against the Supreme Court majority that opposed President Roosevelt's policies in key Court cases. The President rewarded Rutledge with an appointment to the U.S. Court of Appeals for the District of Columbia. As an appellate court judge, Rutledge consistently supported the President's New Deal. When James F. Byrnes retired from the Court in 1942, President Roosevelt picked Rutledge to replace him.

During his six years on the Court, Justice Rutledge was a strong defender of 1st Amendment freedoms. His only lapses from this position were his votes with the majority in the Japanese-American internment cases of World War II (e.g., *Korematsu* v. *United States* and *Hirabayashi* v. *United States*), in which he supported the government's right to detain Japanese Americans on the basis that they might be a threat to national security.

SOURCES Fowler Harper, *Justice Rutledge and the Bright Constellation* (Indianapolis: Bobbs-Merrill, 1965).

S

SALARIES

Congress sets the salaries of the President, Supreme Court justices, and other members of the executive and judicial branches. To prevent salaries from being used as a weapon, the Constitution (Article 2, Section 1, and Article 3, Section 1) prohibits Congress from raising or lowering a President's salary during that President's term or from lowering the salaries of federal judges who serve lifetime terms.

In 1789 Congress fixed the salary of the President at $25,000 per year, the salary of the chief justice at $4,000, and the salary of an associate justice at $3,500.

The President's salary was raised to $50,000 in 1873 and to $75,000 in 1909. From 1949 to 1968 it was $100,000, from 1969 to 2000 it was $200,000, and in 2000 it was increased to $250,000. The salary is subject to federal income tax. Since 1949, Presidents have also received an expense account of $50,000, which in 1951 was made subject to federal income tax. In 1906 Congress authorized $25,000 annually for traveling expenses, a sum that it increased to $40,000 in 1948 and to $100,000 in 1969. That year the President was also given a $12,000 entertainment allowance.

Since 1978, Congress has provided the President with an annual appropriation of $1 million in discretionary funds, which may be used for personnel and services needed for the national interest.

The 1989 Ethics Reform Act provided an annual salary of $124,000 for the chief justice and $118,600 for the associate justices. In 2000 the associate justices received an annual salary of $173,600, and the chief justice was paid $181,400.

From six dollars a day to annual salaries Congress also sets the salaries of its own members, a power that has caused it no end of trouble. Members of the Continental Congress had been paid by their states. To give the U.S. Congress more independence, the Constitution provided that the federal government would pay their salaries. Representative James Madison highly disapproved of legislative bodies increasing their own salaries. While serving in the Virginia legislature, he declined a raise that had been voted on while he was a member. In the 1st Congress, Madison proposed 12 amendments to the Constitution, 10 of which became the Bill of Rights. But to Madison's disappointment, the states failed to ratify his amendment to prohibit Congress from receiving any pay raise until after the next general House election.

During the 1st Congress, senators and representatives set their pay at six dollars per diem (a day) for every day that Congress met. The sum came to less than $1,000 a year, but that was still higher than the average citizen's income. Some members accused their colleagues of dragging out business just so they could collect more days' pay. To correct this tendency, Congress adopted an annual salary of $1,500 in 1816. However, voters angrily disapproved and defeated many members for reelection. The next Congress returned to a per diem salary, at eight dollars a day.

Not until 1856 did Congress manage to set an annual salary of $3,000. Civil War inflation pushed this up to $5,000 in 1866.

At the end of the 42nd Congress, in 1873, Congress increased its members' salaries to $7,500, but made the pay increase retroactive to 1871. In effect, members voted themselves a $5,000 bonus. Newspapers so strongly denounced this "salary grab" that the 43rd Congress repealed the salary increase. Congressional salaries remained at $5,000 for the rest of the 19th century. During the 20th century, salaries steadily increased along with the cost of living, so that by 1989 members were receiving $89,000 a year.

Limits on outside income Critics have complained that elected representatives should not earn higher salaries than their average constituents do. Members of Congress respond by pointing to the expense of maintaining a family and home in both Washington and their home state. Ethics laws have also limited their outside incomes. Whereas Daniel Webster had carried on an active law practice as a senator, arguing many cases before the Supreme Court, modern senators and representatives are restricted in the amount of private business they can conduct while serving in office. An ethics code adopted in 1977 prohibited members from earning more than 15 percent of their congressional salaries in outside income. The code did permit members to supplement their income by giving speeches for fees, called honoraria. But honoraria often came from special interest groups that hoped to shape legislation. In 1989 the House voted to raise members' salaries over the next two years to $125,100 and to ban honoraria. The Senate chose a smaller pay increase, to $101,900, but allowed senators to earn the difference in honoraria. In 1991 after continued public criticism, the Senate abandoned honoraria and raised its salaries to equal those paid to House members. Congress also established automatic cost-of-living increases for its members in the future, which by 2000 raised salaries to $141,300.

Once again the pay raise caused a storm of public protest. The states responded by voting for the still-pending amendment on congressional salaries, which was finally ratified in 1992, 202 years after James Madison had proposed it. The 27th Amendment to the Constitution requires that in the future, members of Congress must stand for reelection before any new pay raise can take effect.

SEE ALSO *Ethics; Ex-Presidency; Vice President; White House Office*

SOURCES Robert C. Byrd, "Congressional Salaries," in *The Senate, 1789–1989: Address on the History of the United States Senate,* vol. 2 (Washington, D.C.: Government Printing Office, 1991).

SALUTE TO THE PRESIDENT

According to military tradition, as a head of state, a President or ex-President is entitled to a 21-gun salute. The same salute is given to Presidents of other republics or to monarchs of foreign nations. Heads of foreign governments, such as prime ministers, are entitled to 18-gun salutes. To commemorate the independence of the United States, the 21-gun salute is often fired in the following sequence: 1-7-7-6.

SAN ANTONIO INDEPENDENT SCHOOL DISTRICT V. RODRIGUEZ

- 411 U.S. 1 (1973)
- Vote: 5–4
- For the Court: Powell
- Concurring: Stewart
- Dissenting: Douglas, Brennan, White, and Marshall

Demetrio Rodriguez was a Mexican American living in San Antonio, Texas. His children, along with many other Mexican-American students, attended the Edgewood Independent Schools. Rodriguez and other Mexican-American parents were upset about the poor educational facilities and programs provided in their school district. They believed that public funds for schools were administered unfairly in Texas. It seemed to them that school districts with mostly higher-income families received more resources than those with mostly Mexican-American students or students of lower economic status.

Demetrio Rodriguez complained to leaders of the Mexican American Legal Defense and Education Fund (MALDEF) about unequal funding of Texas schools that deprived the Mexican-American students and other students from low-income families of fair educational opportunities. MALDEF filed suit against Texas on behalf of Rodriguez and several other San Antonio parents. The suit charged that the Texas system for financing schools was unconstitutional because it violated the "equal protection of the laws" provision of the 14th Amendment.

The Issue MALDEF argued that a high-quality education is a fundamental constitutional right of individuals. This right, acording to MALDEF, was denied to Mexican-American children and others from low-income families who were required to attend public schools with few resources and poor facilities. At fault was the Texas school finance system, which distributed funds unequally—providing much more for some public schools than others. Was this system, as MALDEF claimed, a violation of the 14th Amendment?

Opinion of the Court The right to an education, the Supreme Court decided, is not a fundamental right guaranteed by the Constitution. Justice Lewis Powell wrote, "[A]t least where wealth is concerned the Equal Protection Clause does not require absolute equality or precisely equal advantages. So, the Texas system for financing public schools does not violate the Fourteenth Amendment."

Dissent Justice Thurgood Marshall disagreed with the Supreme Court's opin-

ion. He wrote, "[T]he majority's holding can only be seen as a retreat from our historic commitment to equality of educational opportunity and as unsupportable acquiescence in a system which deprives children in their earliest years of the chance to reach their full potential as citizens."

Significance The *Rodriguez* decision seemed to impede attempts to fundamentally reform distribution of funds to public schools within a state. The Court appeared to validate state funding systems designed to maintain grossly unequal and unfair distributions of resources to public schools. Since the *Rodriguez* decision, however, several states have decided, without the coercion of a U.S. Supreme Court decision, to reform and equalize their school funding systems.

SANFORD, EDWARD TERRY
Associate Justice, 1923–30

- Born: July 23, 1865, Knoxville, Tenn.
- Education: University of Tennessee, B.A., 1883; Harvard, A.B., 1884, M.A., 1889; Harvard Law School, LL.B., 1889
- Previous government service: special assistant to the U.S. attorney general, 1906–7; assistant U.S. attorney general, 1907–8; federal judge, U.S. District Court for the Middle and Eastern Districts of Tennessee, 1908–23
- Appointed by President Warren G. Harding Jan. 24, 1923; replaced Mahlon Pitney, who retired
- Supreme Court term: confirmed by the Senate Jan. 29, 1923, by a voice vote; served until Mar. 8, 1930
- Died: Mar. 8, 1930, Washington, D.C.

Edward Terry Sanford served only seven years on the Supreme Court, after 15 years of service as a federal district judge in Tennessee. His one notable achievement came in the area of constitutional rights. Writing for the Court in *Gitlow* v. *New York* (1925), Justice Sanford denied free speech and press rights to a publisher who advocated violent overthrow of the government. However, he also wrote that the 1st Amendment freedoms of speech and press "are among the fundamental personal rights and liberties protected by the due process clause of the Fourteenth Amendment from impairment by the states."

Two years later, in *Fiske* v. *Kansas* (1927), Justice Sanford wrote the opinion for the Court when it overturned, for the first time, a state law on grounds that it violated the 1st and 14th Amendments to the Constitution in denying an individual his freedom of speech. Thus, Justice Sanford laid the foundation for the later Court decisions to "incorporate" most of the Bill of Rights into the due process clause of the 14th Amendment, thereby prohibiting state governments from violating the Bill of Rights.

SEE ALSO *Gitlow v. New York; Incorporation doctrine*

SANTA CLARA COUNTY V. SOUTHERN PACIFIC RAILROAD CO.

- 118 U.S. 394 (1886)
- Vote: 9–0
- For the Court: Harlan

The state of California tried to collect taxes owed by the Southern Pacific and Central Pacific railroads. Advocates for the railroad companies claimed that the due process clause of the 14th Amendment made the state tax levy against them unconstitutional. The 14th Amendment says that no state shall "deprive any person of life, liberty, or property without due process of law." The railroad company advocates argued that the state tax levy was an unconstitutional denial of their rights to property.

The Issue Was a corporation protected against state interference with its rights in the same way that a person was protected? If not, the California taxes on the railroads should be enforced. If so, the taxes could be declared invalid.

Opinion of the Court The Supreme Court did not directly address the 14th Amendment issue in its opinion. Indeed, Chief Justice Morrison Waite announced, even before the Court heard oral arguments, that the Court would not deal with the question of "whether the provision in the Fourteenth Amendment to the Constitution which forbade a state to deny to any person within its jurisdiction the equal protection of the Constitution, applied to these corporations. We are all of the opinion that it does."

Having established that the Court would apply the 14th Amendment protection of constitutional rights to corporations in the same way as it did to individuals, the Court focused on the narrow issue of whether the state of California could tax fences on the railroad companies' property. The Court decided against the state of California, ruling that the state tax law was a violation of the 14th Amendment due process rights of the corporation, defined by the Court as a person.

Significance Corporations were established in constitutional law as "persons" within the meaning of the 14th Amendment. By using the due process guarantees of the 14th Amendment, corporation lawyers were able to protect businesses from many kinds of state government regulations put forward in behalf of the public good. This view of corporations as persons protected by the 14th Amendment was not fully overturned until the 1930s. In *West Coast Hotel Co.* v. *Parrish* (1937), for example, the Court upheld a state law regulating wages of women workers of a private business. The Court refused to protect the rights of the business as a person under the 14th Amendment.

SEE ALSO *West Coast Hotel Co. v. Parrish*

SCALIA, ANTONIN
Associate Justice, 1986–

- Born: Mar. 11, 1936, Trenton, N.J.
- Education: Georgetown University,

B.A., 1957; Harvard Law School, LL.B., 1960
• Previous government service: general counsel, White House Office of Telecommunications Policy, 1971–72; chairman, Administrative Conference of the United States, 1972–74; assistant U.S. attorney general, Office of Legal Counsel, 1974–77; judge, U.S. Court of Appeals for the District of Columbia Circuit, 1982–86
• Appointed by President Ronald Reagan June 24, 1986; replaced William H. Rehnquist, who became chief justice
• Supreme Court term: confirmed by the Senate Sept. 17, 1986, by a 98–0 vote

Antonin Scalia is the first American of Italian ancestry to become a Supreme Court Justice. He is one of seven children of Eugene and Catherine Scalia, who came to the United States from Italy. Scalia is the first Roman Catholic to be appointed to the Court since William Brennan in 1957.

Justice Scalia has been a strong force on the Court in decisions protecting the constitutional rights of individuals and demanding equal protection of the laws. He has also favored government regulations that protect the safety and security of the community, even if this would mean limitations on the rights of certain individuals. For example, he wrote the opinion for the Court in *Vernonia School District* v. *Acton* (1995), which permitted a drug-testing program for student athletes and restricted, in the context of school, their 4th Amendment rights to freedom from unreasonable searches and seizures.

Scalia often argues for an "original intent" method of interpreting the Constitution. For example, in cases about individual rights, he urges reliance on the intentions of the Constitution's framers as guides to the Court's decisions.

SEE ALSO *Vernonia School District v. Acton*
SOURCES Richard A. Brisbin, Jr., *Justice Antonin Scalia and the Conservative Revival* (Baltimore, Md.: Johns Hopkins University Press, 1997).

SCANDALS, CONGRESSIONAL

As collective bodies, the Senate and House of Representatives have had their share of heroes and scoundrels. Honorable men and women, concerned about the national issues of their day, have occupied the chambers alongside colleagues more interested in personal gain. With critical issues and multimillion-dollar appropriations at stake, lobbyists have at times resorted to unscrupulous methods, including bribery and other special favors, in return for members' votes. Media exposure of these scandals and outraged public opinion have spurred Congress to revise some of its rules and ethical standards to prevent further abuses of power and position.

Railroad scandals Beginning in the 1850s, Congress voted large grants of land and money to stimulate railroad construction. Competing railroad entrepreneurs offered shares of stock to key members of Congress to win support for their projects. In 1857 a freshman representative revealed that he had been offered $1,500 to vote to aid a Minnesota railroad. The House committee investigating these charges recommended that four members be expelled, but they resigned from office. In 1873 Congress was shaken by a larger railroad scandal known as Credit Mobilier (the name of a construction company involved in building the first transcontinental railroad). Representative Oakes Ames (Republican–Massachusetts) acted as a lobbyist for Credit Mobilier and distributed stock to powerful senators and representatives "where it will do the most good for us." The *New York Sun* broke the story with the headline "How the Credit Mobilier Bought Its Way through Congress." Senate and House investigations led to the censure of two representatives and the tarnishing of the reputation of many others.

"The Treason of the Senate" During

the Progressive Era at the start of the 20th century, muckraking magazine writers attacked the Senate as a "millionaires' club" composed of wealthy men or those indebted to wealthy business interests. In 1906 David Graham Phillips published a series of nine articles in *Cosmopolitan* magazine entitled "The Treason of the Senate." By "treason," Phillips meant that some senators were working for big business rather than for the public interest. The "Treason of the Senate" and other muckraking articles led to the defeat or retirement of several powerful senators and gave a boost to the progressive goal of direct election of senators, which the 17th Amendment achieved in 1913.

Campaign financing scandals As the cost of campaigning for Congress escalated, members running for reelection sought campaign funds from a variety of sources, some of which raised questions about conflict of interest. In 1963 when the Senate investigated the business activities of the secretary to the Senate Democratic majority, Bobby Baker, he told of arranging unreported gifts and contributions from business interests to senators. The Senate responded by requiring senators to file more complete statements about their campaign financing and fund-raising. In the 1970s the House investigated a Korean-American businessman, Tongsun Park, accused of making illegal gifts to members of the House. The press labeled this incident "Koreagate," after the recent Watergate scandal. Even more shocking was the Federal Bureau of Investigation's Abscam (short for "Arab scam") operation, in which an FBI agent masqueraded as an Arab sheikh and offered money to various members of Congress in return for favorable legislation. As a result of Abscam, the House expelled one member, two other representatives and a senator resigned, and several others were defeated for reelection.

In 1991 the Senate Ethics Committee investigated the Keating Five—five senators who had intervened with federal bank regulators on behalf of savings and loan banker Charles Keating. Since Keating had made large campaign contributions to these senators, the question arose about whether they had exceeded the efforts they would normally have made for a constituent. The committee criticized their judgment, and the Senate reprimanded one senator for his involvement. The Keating scandal renewed calls for campaign financing reform.

SEE ALSO *Campaign financing, congressional; Censure; Credit Mobilier scandal (1872–73); Ethics; Expulsion from Congress; House bank scandal (1992); Salaries*
SOURCES Bobby Baker, *Wheeling and Dealing: Confessions of a Capitol Hill Operator* (New York: Norton, 1978). George E. Mowry and Judson Grenier, eds., *The Treason of the Senate* (Chicago: University of Chicago Press, 1964). W. Allan Wilbur, "The Credit Mobilier Scandal," in *Congress Investigates: A Documented History, 1792–1974*, edited by Arthur M. Schlesinger, Jr., and Roger Bruns (New York: Bowker, 1975).

SCANDALS, PRESIDENTIAL

SEE *Agnew, Spiro T.; Censure; Clinton, Bill; Harding, Warren G.; Impeachment; Iran-Contra Investigation (1986); Nixon, Richard M.; Reagan, Ronald; Watergate Investigation (1973–74)*

SCANDALS, SUPREME COURT

SEE *Chase, Samuel; Impeachment*

SCHECHTER POULTRY CORP. V. UNITED STATES

- 295 U.S. 495 (1935)
- Vote: 9–0
- For the Court: Hughes

During the early 1930s President Franklin

D. Roosevelt fought the Great Depression by proposing many economic recovery programs. The centerpiece of his efforts was the National Industrial Recovery Act (NIRA) of 1933, managed by the National Recovery Administration (NRA).

Under that law, Congress granted the President authority to approve codes of fair competition for different industries. Drawn up by trade and industry groups themselves, each of these codes included standards of minimum wages and maximum hours of work. Presidential approval of the code for an industry gave that code the force of law.

By 1935 many industries had started to ignore the NIRA. The government decided to bring a test case before the Supreme Court in the hope that a ruling in favor of NIRA codes would encourage industries to accept the codes.

A case involving four brothers who ran a poultry business became a key test of Roosevelt's program. The Schechters bought live poultry outside New York State and sold it in New York City. The government convicted the brothers of violating several provisions of the NIRA live poultry code in order to keep their prices below those of competitors. Prosecutors also charged them with selling thousands of pounds of diseased chickens to a local butcher. The Schechters appealed to the Supreme Court. The press called the suit the "sick chicken case."

The Issue The case involved three questions: Did the economic crisis facing the nation justify resorting to the NIRA? Did the Constitution allow Congress to delegate so much power to the President? And did the law come under Congress's power to regulate interstate commerce?

Opinion of the Court The NIRA lost on all counts. The Supreme Court ruled that the economic problems of the nation did not justify the NIRA. Chief Justice Charles Evans Hughes wrote that "extraordinary conditions do not create or enlarge constitutional power."

Second, the Court said that under the Constitution only Congress has the power to make laws. If Congress wanted to delegate any of this power to the President, it had to set clear standards to guide the executive branch in making detailed applications of the general law. The NIRA was unconstitutional because, in effect, it gave trade and industry groups unregulated power to create any laws they wanted.

Finally, the Court recognized that although the Schechters bought their poultry in many states, they processed and sold it only in New York. Thus, the Schechters' operation was a local concern not directly affecting interstate commerce, and so it was beyond federal control.

Significance The decision at first appeared to devastate President Roosevelt's New Deal economic recovery program. But by 1937 the Supreme Court began upholding new laws passed to fulfill New Deal objectives. The National Labor Relations Act of 1935, for example, was upheld by the Court in *National Labor Relations Board v. Jones & Laughlin Steel Corp.* (1937).

The *Schechter* case established the principle that in domestic affairs Congress may not delegate broad legislative powers to the President without also outlining clear standards to guide the President in employing these powers. This principle stands today.

SOURCES Frank Freidel, "The Sick Chicken Case," in *Quarrels That Have Shaped the Constitution,* edited by John A. Garraty (New York: Harper & Row, 1987).

SCHENCK V. UNITED STATES

- 249 U.S. 47 (1919)
- Vote: 9–0
- For the Court: Holmes

During World War I, Congress passed the Espionage Act of 1917. This law made it illegal to encourage insubordination in the armed forces or to use the mails to distribute materials urging resistance to the government.

Charles Schenck, general secretary of the Socialist party in the United States, was an outspoken critic of America's role in the war. Schenck printed and mailed about 15,000 leaflets to men eligible for the draft. The leaflets denounced the draft as involuntary servitude (slavery) and therefore a violation of the 13th Amendment. The pamphlets also argued that participation in World War I did not serve the best interests of the American people.

Schenck was arrested and convicted of violating the Espionage Act of 1917. At his trial, Schenck claimed his 1st Amendment right to free speech had been violated. The 1st Amendment states: "Congress shall make no law ... abridging the freedom of speech, or of the press."

The Issue Did the Espionage Act of 1917, under which Schenck was arrested, violate the 1st Amendment protection of free speech? The *Schenck* case also posed a larger question about potential limitations on free speech. For the first time in its history, the Supreme Court faced directly the question of whether the government might limit speech under special circumstances.

Opinion of the Court The Court decided against Schenck, ruling that the Espionage Act of 1917 did not violate the 1st Amendment rights of free speech and free press.

Justice Oliver Wendell Holmes wrote the Court's opinion. He set forth a test to determine when government might limit free speech. Holmes said, "The most stringent protection of free speech would not protect a man in falsely shouting fire in a theatre and causing a panic." When spoken or written words "create a clear and present danger" of bringing about evils that Congress has the authority to prevent, the government may limit speech.

Holmes reasoned that during peacetime the 1st Amendment would have protected Schenck's ideas. During a wartime emergency, however, urging men to resist the draft presented a "clear and present danger" to the nation. Holmes declared: "When a nation is at war, many things that might be said in time of peace are such a hindrance to its efforts that their utterance will not be ... protected by any constitutional right."

Significance The *Schenck* decision established important precedents. First, it set up the "clear and present danger" test. This formula was applied to many subsequent free speech cases. In addition, the decision announced that certain speech may be permissible in peacetime but not in wartime. Thus, the *Schenck* case established that the 1st Amendment protection of free speech is not an absolute guarantee. Under conditions such as those Holmes described, the government may constrain speech.

Later, in another free speech case, (*Abrams* v. *United States,* 1919), Holmes wrote a dissenting opinion that modified the "clear and present danger" test set forth in *Schenck*. In his *Abrams* dissent, Holmes emphasized that a "clear and present danger" must be directly connected to specific actions that would bring about evil consequences. If the imminent danger could not be demonstrated, then speech could not be lawfully limited. In the 1950s and 1960s, the modified version of Holmes's "clear and present danger" test prevailed in the Court's opinions. In *Yates* v. *United States* (1957), for example, the Court protected the freedom of expression of Communist party members. And in *Brandenburg* v. *Ohio* (1969), the Court protected free speech by a racist Ku Klux Klan leader.

SEE ALSO *Abrams v. United States; Brandenburg v. Ohio; Freedom of speech and press; Seditious libel; Yates v. United Staes*

SCOTT V. SANDFORD

- 19 How. 393 (1857)
- Vote: 7–2
- For the Court: Taney
- Dissenting: Curtis and McLean

When the Constitution was written in 1787, it permitted slavery. Many of the framers owned slaves; others opposed slavery. During the Constitutional Convention they hotly debated the issue of how to deal with slavery, and the problem continued to plague the new nation. By the 1850s some states had forbidden slavery, while others still protected it.

In 1854 Dred Scott, a slave, was taken by his master to Rock Island, Illinois, a town in a free state. His master later took him to the Wisconsin Territory (an area that is now part of Minnesota), where the Missouri Compromise of 1820, a federal law, had forbidden slavery. His master then brought Scott back to Missouri, a slave state. Scott brought suit against his master, claiming that he was a free man because he had resided in areas that had banned slavery.

The Issue The case involved three issues: (1) Scott had lived in the free state of Illinois. Had he become free while living there? Should Missouri have to recognize that freedom? (2) Scott had traveled to a federal territory that Congress had declared a free territory in the Missouri Compromise of 1820. Had he become free while living there, and should Missouri have to recognize that freedom? (3) Did the Supreme Court have the jurisdiction, or power, to hear this case?

Scott claimed that his master had freed him by taking him to Illinois, where slavery was not allowed. Therefore, any slave taken there became free. Once Scott became free in Illinois, no Missouri law could turn him into a slave again. Scott's lawyers further argued that Missouri must recognize the laws of any other state in the Union.

Scott also claimed that he was free under the Missouri Compromise. Passed by Congress and recognized as the law of the land since 1820, the Missouri Compromise prohibited slavery in all the federal territories north of Missouri. When Scott's master took him to Fort Snelling in the Wisconsin Territory, Scott had also become free there. Even if Missouri chose not to recognize the laws of Illinois, the Constitution required all states to recognize the laws of Congress, as the supremacy clause of the Constitution (Article 6, Clause 2) clearly stated.

Finally, Scott's lawyers argued that the Supreme Court did have the power to hear this case. Article 3, Section 2, of the Constitution established the jurisdiction, the authority to hear cases, of the federal courts. This jurisdiction extended to cases "between citizens of different states." Scott's master was now dead, leaving Scott technically under the control of his dead master's brother-in-law, John F. A. Sanford, who lived in New York. (The case is called *Scott v. Sandford* because a court clerk misspelled the name of the defendant.) Scott claimed that if he was free, then he had to be a citizen of Missouri. As such, he could sue a citizen of New York in federal court.

Opinion of the Court The Supreme Court ruled against Scott on all three issues. In an extraordinary decision, all nine judges wrote opinions that totaled 248 pages. Chief Justice Roger B. Taney's 55-page opinion of the court expressed the collective view of the majority.

Taney first argued that Scott could not sue in a federal court because he was not a citizen of the United States. Taney said that no black person, slave or free, could be a citizen. Taney wrote, "The question is simply this: Can a negro, whose ancestors were imported into this country and sold as slaves, become a member of the political community formed and brought into existence by the Constitution of the United States?" Taney answered his own question: "We think they are not . . . included, and were not intended to be included, under the word 'citizens' in the Constitution." Rather, Taney asserted that at the time the Constitution was written, blacks were "considered as a subordinate and inferior class of beings, who had been subjugated by the dominant race, and whether emancipated or not . . . had no rights or privileges but such as those who held the power and the Government might choose to grant them."

Having concluded that Scott had no

right to sue in a federal court, Taney might have stopped. However, the issue of slavery in the federal territories was an important political question, and Taney wanted to let the nation know where the Court stood on it. So he examined Scott's other claims.

The Court easily disposed of the claim to freedom based on Illinois law. Taney held that Scott lost whatever claim to freedom he had while in Illinois when he left the state, and no law or precedent obligated Missouri to enforce the Illinois law.

Scott's claim based on the Missouri Compromise presented more complications. Considering the Missouri Compromise, passed by Congress in 1820, as the law of the land would obligate the state of Missouri to recognize it. Taney, however, decided that the ban on slavery in the Missouri Compromise was unconstitutional. He reasoned that the territories belonged to all the citizens of the United States. Under the Constitution's 5th Amendment, no one could deprive a person of his property without "due process of law" and "just compensation." But the Missouri Compromise would deprive men like Scott's owner of their property simply for entering federal territories. Thus, the Court held that the Missouri Compromise was unconstitutional. For only the second time, the Supreme Court declared an act of Congress unconstitutional. This power of judicial review of acts of Congress had first been used by the Court in *Marbury* v. *Madison* (1803).

Dissent   In a 69-page dissent, Justice Benjamin R. Curtis took Taney to task at every point. Curtis pointed out that at the time of the ratification of the Constitution blacks voted in a number of states, including Massachusetts, Pennsylvania, and North Carolina. Thus, Curtis argued, free blacks had always been citizens of the nation, and if Scott was free the Court had jurisdiction to hear his case. Curtis also argued in favor of the constitutionality of the Missouri Compromise, which he pointed out had existed as accepted law for more than three decades and served as the basis of the sectional understanding that had kept the North and South together in one Union.

Significance   Taney had hoped to settle the issue of slavery in the territories through the *Scott* verdict. Instead, Taney's decision itself became a political issue. Abraham Lincoln and Stephen A. Douglas argued over its merits in their famous debates of 1858. Instead of lessening sectional tensions, Taney's decision exacerbated them and helped bring on the Civil War.

When the Civil War was finally over, the 13th Amendment (1865) ended slavery. The 14th Amendment (1868) gave blacks citizenship. Thus, by amending the Constitution, the people overturned the *Scott* decision.

SEE ALSO *Jurisdiction*

SOURCES Don E. Fehrenbacher, *The Dred Scott Case: Its Significance in American Law and Politics* (New York: Oxford University Press, 1978). Don E. Fehrenbacher, "The Dred Scott Case," in *Quarrels That Have Shaped the Constitution,* edited by John A. Garraty (New York: Harper & Row, 1987).

SEAL, PRESIDENTIAL

The Presidential seal is the symbol of the Presidential office. To ensure the authenticity of a document, the seal appears on any Presidential order or commission to federal office and on any document published in the President's name. Representations of the Presidential seal appear on *Air Force One* and *Marine One* and are placed on lecterns at which the President speaks.

The seal consists of a coat of arms encircled by 50 stars representing the states of the Union and the words "Seal of the President of the United States." The coat of arms consists of a shield placed upon the breast of an American eagle. In its right talon the eagle holds an olive branch, symbolizing peace; in its left talon it holds a bundle of 13 gray arrows, representing the original colonies. Its beak grasps a gray scroll inscribed with the Latin words *E Pluribus Unum* ("Out of many, one"). Behind and above the eagle is a radiating glory (rays of light that emanate from a single point), on which appears an arc of 13 gray cloud puffs and a constellation of 13 gray five-pointed stars. This coat of arms is almost identical to the Great Seal of the United States.

The eagle on the coat of arms faced left, toward the gray arrows, until President Harry Truman ordered that it face right, looking toward the olive branch of peace. SEE ALSO *Flag, Presidential*

SEARCHES AND SEIZURES

The 4th Amendment to the U.S. Constitution says, "The right of the people to be secure in their persons, houses, papers, and effects, against unreasonable searches and seizures, shall not be violated, and no Warrants shall issue, but upon probable cause, supported by Oath or affirmation, and particularly describing the place to be searched, and the persons or things to be seized."

The principle in the 4th Amendment is clear: the privacy of the individual is protected against arbitrary intrusion by agents of the government. In 1949 Justice Felix Frankfurter wrote (*Wolf* v. *Colorado*): "The security of one's privacy against arbitrary intrusion by the police is basic to a free society. The knock at the door, whether by day or by night, as a prelude to a search, without authority of law but solely on the authority of the police, did not need the commentary of recent history to be condemned as inconsistent with the conception of human rights enshrined in the history and the basic constitutional documents of English-speaking peoples."

The 4th Amendment protection against unreasonable searches and seizures is reinforced by the clause that requires a warrant, or court authorization, for such searches and seizures. A warrant should not be issued, of course, unless there is a finding of "probable cause" by a neutral magistrate or judge.

The 4th Amendment principle of personal security against unlawful intrusion is clear enough. But the exact meaning of the key phrases and their precise application in specific cases requires interpretation and judgment—the duties of the federal courts. What constitutes "unreasonable searches and seizures"? What exactly is the meaning of "probable cause"? Are there any situations that justify a warrantless search by government officials? If so, what are they, and what are the justifications?

In making judgments about 4th Amendment rights, the federal courts attempt to balance liberty and order—the rights of the individual to freedom from tyranny and the needs of the community for stability, security, and safety. Judges must decide when to provide more or less latitude for the rights of individuals suspected of criminal behavior.

The Supreme Court ruled on what is "unreasonable" in *Weeks* v. *United States* (1914). Evidence seized illegally by federal government agents—without probable cause or a search warrant—must be excluded from a defendant's trial, according to the Court. This exclusionary rule applied, however, only to federal government officials. The Court did not establish the exclusionary rule as a limitation on state governments until 1961, in *Mapp* v. *Ohio*.

The Supreme Court established a "good faith" exception to the exclusionary rule in *United States* v. *Leon* (1984). The Court ruled that evidence seized as the result of a mistakenly issued search warrant can be used in a trial as long as the warrant was issued on good faith that there was probable cause for issuing it.

Judges, not law enforcement officers, are supposed to determine whether or not there is probable cause for issuing a search warrant. Evidence seized by police with a valid search warrant can, of course, be used against the defendant in a trial. There are, however, exceptions to the requirement of a warrant to justify a search and seizure of evidence. The Supreme Court ruled, for example, in *Terry* v. *Ohio* (1968) that police may stop and search a suspect's

The Evolution of the 4th

Amendment Rights

- *Weeks* v. *United States* (1914) A person may require that evidence obtained in a search shall be excluded from use against him in a federal court if the evidence was seized illegally—without probable cause or a search warrant.
- *Carroll* v. *United States* (1925) Federal agents can conduct searches of automobiles without a warrant whenever they have a reasonable suspicion of illegal actions.
- *Olmstead* v. *United States* (1928) Wiretaps by federal agents are permissable where no entry of private premises has occurred.
- *Wolf* v. *Colorado* (1949) The 4th Amendment protections apply to searches by state officials as well as federal agents. However, state judges are not required to exclude evidence obtained by searches in violation of 4th Amendment rights.
- *Mapp* v. *Ohio* (1961) Evidence obtained in violation of 4th Amendment rights must be excluded from use in state and federal trials.
- *Katz* v. *United States* (1967) Electronic surveillance and wiretapping are within the scope of the 4th Amendment because it protects whatever an individual wants to preserve as private, including conversations and behavior, even in a place open to the public.
- *Terry* v. *Ohio* (1968) The police may stop and frisk, or search, a suspect's outer clothing for dangerous weapons without first obtaining a warrant if they suspect that a crime is about to be committed.
- *Chimel* v. *California* (1969) Police may search without a warrant only the immediate area around the suspect from which he could obtain a weapon or destroy evidence. But a person's entire dwelling cannot be searched merely because he is arrested there.
- *Marshall* v. *Barlow's, Inc.* (1978) Federal laws cannot provide for warrantless inspections of businesses that are otherwise legally regulated by a federal agency. A federal inspector must obtain a search warrant when the owner of the business to be inspected objects to a warrantless search.
- *United States* v. *Ross* (1982) Police officers may search an entire vehicle they have stopped without obtaining a warrant if they have probable cause to suspect that drugs or other contraband is in the vehicle.
- *United States* v. *Leon* (1984) Evidence seized on the basis of a mistakenly issued search warrant can be introduced in a trial if the warrant was issued in good faith—that is, on presumption that there were valid grounds for issuing the warrant.
- *New Jersey* v. *T.L.O.* (1985) School officials do not need a search warrant or probable cause to conduct a reasonable search of a student. The school officials may search a student if there are reasonable grounds for suspecting that the search will uncover evidence that the student has violated or is violating either the law or the rules of the school.
- *California* v. *Greenwood* (1988) The police may search through garbage bags and other trash containers that people leave outside their houses in order to obtain evidence of criminal activity. This evidence may subsequently be used as the basis for obtaining a warrant to search a person's house.
- *Michigan* v. *Sitz* (1990) The police may stop automobiles at roadside checkpoints and examine the drivers for signs of intoxication. Evidence

obtained in this manner may be used to bring criminal charges against the driver.

• *Minnesota* v. *Dickerson* (1993) Police do not need a warrant to seize narcotics that were found when frisking or quickly searching a suspect for concealed weapons. Evidence seized in this way can be used to bring criminal charges against a suspect.

• *Vernonia School District* v. *Acton* (1995) Public school officials may carry out a policy of drug testing for students involved in interschool athletic programs

• *Wilson* v. *Arkansas* (1995) Police must announce themselves before entering a premises. If the knock and announce rule is violated, then an otherwise warranted search is invalidated.

• *Chandler* v. *Miller* (1997) State laws cannot require candidates for public offices to be tested for drugs. This requirement constitutes an unreasonable search.

• *Maryland* v. *Wilson* (1997) When making a traffic stop, police may order a passenger as well as a driver out of the vehicle without requiring either probable cause or reasonable suspicion.

• *Illinois* v. *Wardlow* (2000) Unprovoked flight by a suspect at the mere sight of a police officer may, in the context of other compelling factors, provide the "reasonable suspicion" necessary to justify a "stop-and-frisk" search of the person.

• *Bond* v. *United States* (2000) Without "reasonable suspicion" of illegal behavior, law enforcement officers cannot move down the aisle of a bus and squeeze baggage stored in overhead racks to find out if any contain illegal contents. Such behavior violates a passenger's 4th Amendment rights.

outer clothing for a gun or other weapons without a warrant if they suspect a crime is about to be committed. Further, police may stop and search automobiles without first obtaining a warrant if they have a reasonable suspicion that illegal goods are inside or that illegal actions are about to take place.

The accompanying table of cases on 4th Amendment rights demonstrates the evolution of constitutional rights in the 20th century. As it shows, the incorporation of the 4th Amendment into the due process clause of the 14th Amendment did not occur until 1949, in the case of *Wolf* v. *Colorado*. Since that time, however, most of the 4th Amendment cases have involved actions at the state level of government. On balance, decisions in these cases have gradually enhanced the rights of individuals against the power of government.

SEE ALSO *Bill of Rights; Exclusionary rule; Incorporation doctrine; Katz v. United States; Mapp v. Ohio; New Jersey v. T.L.O.; Olmstead v. United States; Probable cause; Terry v. Ohio; United States v. Leon; United States v. Ross; Weeks v. United States; Wolf v. Colorado*

SEATING IN CONGRESS

The center aisle in the chambers of both the Senate and House of Representatives divides the political parties. As the presiding officer looks into the chamber, Republicans sit to the left of the center aisle, Democrats to the right. Each senator has a desk, and the more senior senators tend to sit along the center aisle and toward the front, where it is easier to catch the presiding officer's attention to gain recognition to speak. Junior senators occupy seats in the rear and far ends of the chamber, and they move forward and inward with seniority. Some senators prefer to remain in back-row seats or to occupy a specific desk for sentimental purposes, because it belonged to a relative or to a famous predecessor. Senators find it prestigious to sit at the desks of Henry Clay, John C. Calhoun, or Daniel Webster. Modern senators carve their name into the desk drawers, alongside the names of their predecessors. The majority and minority leaders occupy the front desks on either side of the center aisle.

In 1914, after House membership had increased to 435, desks in the chamber were replaced with rows of leather-covered chairs. House members simply take a vacant chair on their party's side of the chamber. When members wish to address the House, they must speak from lecterns in the "well" of the chamber—the lower level at the foot of the Speaker's desk. Managers of legislation may also speak from two long tables on each side of the aisle.

SECRECY IN CONGRESS

Congress has always been the most open branch of the federal government. Yet Congress has also done much of its work in secret and has expended much energy trying to plug "leaks" of secrets to the media.

The Continental Congress and the Congress under the Articles of Confederation debated entirely in closed session, and the Constitution was also written in secret session. The Constitution did not require Congress to conduct its business in public. It specified only that each house keep a journal of its proceedings "and from time to time publish the same, excepting such parts as may in their judgment require secrecy" (Article 1, Section 5). This was the only mention of secrecy in the Constitution. Because House members would stand for direct election by the people in just two years, however, they wanted their constituents to know what they were doing. The House immediately opened its doors and debated and voted in public session. By contrast, the Senate, elected by state legislatures, met entirely in secret session from 1789 until 1794. Even after the Senate constructed a gallery, it opened its doors only for legislative sessions. Executive sessions, which dealt with treaties and nominations, remained secret until 1929. Similarly, many committees of both the House and Senate met in closed-door executive sessions, especially when "marking up" a bill (making final changes before reporting it from the committee).

Legislative bodies are not designed to keep secrets. For every person or group with a reason to keep a secret, there is usually someone else with a reason to publish it. Members of Congress, staff, and the executive branch have all leaked secret information to provoke some legislative action or public response. Leaking is a mutual act between the person releasing the information and the journalist who receives it and publishes it. Each one benefits by getting the story out. Sometimes, however, no single individual leaks a story, but an enterprising journalist pieces it together by gathering observations from a large number of sources.

Angry reaction to leaks   Having done more of its business in secret, the Senate has often reacted angrily to leaks. In 1811 and 1841 the Senate censured senators accused of releasing secret information. In 1848 and 1871 the Senate held newspaper correspondents prisoner in Capitol committee rooms, in unsuccessful attempts to force them to reveal their sources. In 1892 the Senate fired its executive clerk when he was suspected of being the source of frequent leaks from executive sessions. But the next time that the Senate met in secret, reporters went out of their way to print even more details, thereby proving the fired clerk's innocence.

Events climaxed in 1929 when a United Press reporter published a nomination vote from a secret session. Until then the Senate had believed secrecy necessary to protect the privacy of nominees and the sensitivity of foreign nations with whom the United States had signed treaties. But in 1929 the Senate concluded that it could not suppress such important information. Senators voted to open all executive sessions except for the very few dealing with highly classified national security issues.

Although Congress now does much less business in secret, in 1992 it once again investigated a leak. During the Senate Judiciary Committee's hearings on the nomination of Clarence Thomas to the Supreme Court, two reporters learned that the committee had received charges that the nominee had sexually harassed a former member of his staff, Anita Hill. Hill had not wished to appear in public, but she agreed to testify after the story broke. The Senate appointed a special counsel to investigate the source of the leak, but he concluded that so many members of the committee and staff had the information that it was impossible to determine who had leaked it. The special counsel condemned the practice of leaking because it ran contrary to the atmosphere of mutual cooperation and respect needed to conduct legislative business.

SEE ALSO *Censure; Media coverage of Congress*
SOURCES Donald A. Ritchie, *Press Gallery: Congress and the Washington Correspondent* (Cambridge: Harvard University Press, 1991).

SECRETARY OF DEFENSE

The secretary of defense is the administrator of the Department of Defense and the principal civilian adviser to the President on military matters. The secretary serves as a member of the President's "inner cabinet" of advisers and, by law, as a member of the National Security Council. With the chair of the Joint Chiefs of Staff, the secretary participates in the formulation of military strategy, reviews recommendations of the Pentagon's weapons acquisition committees, and recommends new weapons systems to the President. The secretary has the primary responsibility for preparing the military budget and defending it before military subcommittees of the House and Senate Appropriations Committees. He serves as the principal spokesperson for the administration when testifying before the House and Senate Armed Services Committees.

The President issues military orders to the secretary of defense, who transmits them through the Joint Chiefs of Staff to the military commands of the service branches. Each command operates under the supervision of CINCs, the commanders in chief of operational forces. Each CINC reports to the Joint Chiefs, who, in turn, report to the secretary of defense and the President. A Presidential decision to move troops, to engage enemy forces, or to use nuclear weapons is always transmitted through the secretary of defense, who may lawfully countermand the Presidential orders if there is reason to believe that the President is not physically or mentally competent to make the decision.

SEE ALSO *Cabinet; National Security Council*

SECRETARY OF STATE

The secretary of state is the administrator of the Department of State and the principal spokesperson for the President on U.S. foreign policy. The secretary serves as a member of the President's "inner cabinet" of advisers and, by law, as a member of the National Security Council. The secretary has the primary responsibility for preparing the budget for foreign affairs programs, including diplomatic missions, foreign aid to developing nations, and contributions to multinational organizations such as the World Bank, the Inter-American Development Bank, and the International Monetary Fund. The secretary defends foreign affairs programs before subcommittees of the House and Senate Appropriations Committees and is the principal spokesperson for the administration before the House Foreign Affairs Committee and Senate Foreign Relations Committee. The President may also assign the secretary to communicate foreign policy to foreign heads of state or to serve as the principal U.S. diplomat at international conferences.

As head of the first department of government established in 1789, the secretary is the first cabinet officer in line to succeed to the Presidency in the event there is no Vice President, Speaker of the House, or president pro tempore of the Senate to assume the office. A Presidential resignation is submitted to the secretary of state.

Though some secretaries are highly influential advisers and policymakers, others have merely administered the State Department. Thomas Jefferson, the first secretary of state, resigned from George Washington's cabinet because his pro-French policies were not adopted. For the first two decades of the 19th century, each secretary of state was an influential shaper of foreign policy, and each became the next President: James Madison, James Monroe, and John Quincy Adams. Daniel Webster ran U.S. foreign policy when President John Tyler and the Whig Congress remained stalemated in domestic matters. William Seward wrote a memorandum to Abraham Lincoln in which he offered to run foreign policy, but Lincoln wrote back that as President he would retain final responsibility; Seward's main accomplishment was buying Alaska from Russia. Franklin Roosevelt used Presidential assistants to implement his policies, bypassing his secretary of state, Cordell Hull. President Harry Truman, by contrast, relied heavily on George Marshall, who proposed the Marshall Plan for economic recovery in Western Europe after World War II, and Dean Acheson. Acheson was the architect of the U.S. policies of collective security—making alliances to confront aggressor nations—and containment of communist aggression.

Dwight Eisenhower's secretary of state, John Foster Dulles, initiated the policy of "brinkmanship," which involved pushing a situation to the brink by threatening to use the armed forces (including nuclear weapons) to prevent communist regimes from expanding their influence. Dean Rusk served in the administrations of John F. Kennedy and Lyndon Johnson; he was preoccupied with resisting communist aggression in Southeast Asia, and he defended the Johnson administration against charges that it was not willing to negotiate a peace with North Vietnam.

Richard Nixon's secretary of state, William Rogers, was overshadowed by National Security Adviser Henry Kissinger: his one major initiative, the Rogers Plan for Mideast Peace, went nowhere. Eventually, he was succeeded by Kissinger, who as secretary of state engaged in successful "shuttle diplomacy" between Jerusalem and Cairo to bring about a disengagement of opposing forces in the Sinai Peninsula after the Yom Kippur War of 1973. Cyrus Vance, Jimmy Carter's secretary of state, resigned as a matter of honor after Carter ordered a U.S. raid to free diplomats held hostage by Iran; Vance had been kept in the dark about the raid and had not been able to keep his promise to the Senate to brief it in advance of any military action.

Ronald Reagan's first secretary of state, Alexander Haig, suggested to the President that he be the "vicar" of U.S. foreign policy, but Reagan never gave him full responsibility, and Haig was involved in conflicts with Vice President George Bush and National Security Adviser Richard Allen. He offered to resign so many times that eventually Reagan accepted. Secretary George Shultz opposed Reagan's plan to sell arms to Iran and was frozen out of policy-making. But after the Iran-Contra scandal erupted, Shultz became the dominant figure in the Reagan administration because he had the confidence of Congress. George Bush's secretary of state was his close political adviser and campaign manager, James Baker. The two dominated foreign policy in much the way Nixon and Kissinger had done, though Baker failed to convince Iraq to pull out of Kuwait and his Middle East Peace Conference failed to achieve an agreement between Israel and the Arab states.

Madeleine Albright was the first woman to be appointed secretary of state, and Bill Clinton nominated her in part to make history. She was neither a close political adviser nor a national security official he relied upon prior to her appointment. Clinton assigned Albright highly public roles in dealing with Congress, particularly the chairman of the Senate Foreign Relations Committee, Jesse Helms, with whom she developed some rapport that was helpful in providing the State Department with funding. Albright had a tendency to substitute bombastic and inflated rhetoric for quiet diplomacy, and often she had little to show for her efforts. Her most constructive work involved the negotiations between Israel and the Palestinians as the two sides worked to develop a framework peace agreement.

SEE ALSO *Cabinet; Decision making, Presidential; National security adviser; National Security Council*

SOURCES Dean Acheson, *Present at the Creation* (New York: Norton, 1969). James Chace, *Acheson: The Secretary of State Who Created the American World* (New York: Simon & Schuster, 1998). Alexander Haig, *Caveat* (New York: Macmillan, 1984). Henry Kissinger, *White House Years* (Boston: Little, Brown, 1979). George Shultz, *Turning Point* (New York: Macmillan, 1993).

SECRETARY OF THE SENATE

The Senate elects a secretary to serve as its chief administrative officer. Historically the equivalent of the clerk of the House of Representatives as well as the more recently created director of non-legislative services for the House, the secretary of the Senate supervises the various clerks, parliamentarians, and other general staff members of the Senate, is responsible for the disbursement of salaries and payment of other expenses, oversees stationery supplies, registers all lobbyists, and handles numerous other duties to make sure that the Senate functions properly.

As one of its first items of business in 1789, the Senate elected Samuel Allyn Otis as the first secretary. Otis's chief function was to keep the legislative journal that the

Constitution required, making rough notes during the proceedings and having clerks copy them in fine handwritten script into a "smooth journal." Otis purchased supplies for the Senate and began many of the practices that are continued today. In the absence of the Vice President or president pro tempore, the secretary can sign legislation and preside over the Senate, as Secretary of the Senate Leslie Biffle did for two days in 1947. The secretary (or one of the bill clerks working for the secretary) also delivers messages and bills from the Senate to the House.

SEE ALSO *Clerk of the House of Representatives; Director of non-legislative services; Officers of the House and Senate*

SOURCES Robert C. Byrd, "Secretary of the Senate," in *The Senate, 1789–1989: Addresses on the History of the United States Senate*, vol. 2 (Washington, D.C.: Government Printing Office, 1991).

SECRET SERVICE, U.S.

The U.S. Secret Service is a unit of the Department of the Treasury that is responsible for ensuring the safety of the President and Vice President and their families, the President-elect and Vice President–elect and their families, major Presidential and Vice Presidential candidates and their families, and former Presidents and their families. The Secret Service also protects visiting heads of foreign states or governments and other foreign visitors to the United States when designated to do so by the President.

The director of the Secret Service is chosen by the secretary of the Treasury from the ranks of service personnel. The 1,800 special enforcement agents are trained in hand-to-hand combat, firearms, emergency medicine, safe and evasive driving, surveillance, and field investigation at the Federal Law Enforcement Facility in Brunswick, Georgia, and the service's school in Beltsville, Maryland.

The Secret Service Office of Investigations has jurisdiction over federal crimes involving currency, counterfeiting, fraudulent electronic transfers of funds, and other financial crimes.

The Secret Service's Office of Protective Operations provides security at the White House and other Presidential offices, at the official residence of the Vice President in the District of Columbia, and at foreign diplomatic missions in Washington, D.C., and throughout the United States.

The White House Detail is assigned to the President. It protects the President in the Oval Office (a button enables him to summon agents at any time) and on trips within the United States and abroad. It arranges for all security and coordinates efforts of the Federal Bureau of Investigation and local law enforcement agencies in the area a President visits, making sure that all areas are safe and secure. It ensures that no surveillance devices are in use in the White House or any place the President visits.

The Office of Protective Research conducts background checks on individuals who have made threats against the President or other people protected by the Secret Service. It keeps tabs on more than 50,000 individuals who are viewed as potential threats to the President. Some 400 people on the "watch list" are placed under surveillance when the President is in their vicinity.

The White House is guarded by 500 Uniformed Division officers of the Secret Service, who patrol the outer and middle perimeters. The inner perimeter and the mansion itself are secured by more than 100 agents in civilian clothes from the Presidential Protective Detail. The Technical Security Division guards against surveillance and bugging of the White House, and agents screen all visitors to the White House for weapons. All packages entering the White House are examined. Each year about 250 mentally disturbed people and 400 visitors carrying guns are apprehended as they enter the White House on guided tours.

The Secret Service was established during the Civil War, when the Union Army organized a group of agents under the command of Colonel L. C. Baker for counterintelligence (finding Confederate spies) and detection of counterfeit currency. Some of the agents were transferred to the Treasury Department in July 1865. In the 1870s the Secret Service investigated crimes against blacks in the South committed by the Ku Klux Klan, a white supremacist group. In 1898 President William McKinley ordered it to gather military and foreign intelligence during the Spanish-American War, and it also did such work during World War I. After the war its intelligence roles were taken over by the Federal Bureau of Investigation and military intelligence agencies.

In 1901, after the assassination of President McKinley, his successor, Theodore Roosevelt, ordered the Secret Service to protect the President. Beginning with two agents, the protective detail expanded to 40 agents by 1940. Congress authorized the Secret Service to protect the President in 1906, the President-elect in 1908, and the Vice President in 1962. Retired Presidents, widows of Presidents, and their minor children came under protection in 1965. (Widows lose protection if they remarry.) In 1971 foreign heads of state and other individuals designated by the President, such as Presidential candidates, and in 1976 candidates' wives, were included. The Uniformed Division was transferred from the District of Columbia Police by President Warren Harding in 1922 and was made a part of the Secret Service in 1930.

SEE ALSO Assassinations, Presidential
SOURCES Rhodri Jeffreys-Jones, *American Espionage: From Secret Service to CIA* (New York: Free Press, 1977). Gregory Matusky and John P. Hayes, *U.S. Secret Service* (New York: Chelsea House, 1988). Dennis V. N. McCarthy, *Protecting the President: The Inside Story of a Secret Service Agent* (New York: Morrow, 1985). Philip Melanson, *The Politics of Protection: The U.S. Secret Service in the Terrorist Age* (New York: Praeger, 1984).

SECTIONALISM

Sectional, or regional, loyalties were present in Congress from the beginning, but they became stronger during and after the 1820s. As the North grew industrial, it sought protective tariffs (taxes on foreign goods imported into the United States) to protect its products. Because the South remained agricultural, it opposed tariffs that would raise the prices of the manufactured goods it needed. Southerners defended slavery, while an anti-slavery movement grew in the North. The new Western states had their own demands for roads and other internal improvements. Moreover, when Southerners migrated West, they wanted to be able to bring their slaves, but Northerners objected to slavery in the Western territories.

Congress served as the battleground for sectional rivalries and alliances. Although both the Whig and Democratic parties were national organizations, electing members of Congress from all regions, increasingly members crossed party lines to stand together to defend their common sectional interests. John C. Calhoun (Democrat–South Carolina) articulated the Southern position in Congress, while Daniel Webster (Whig–Massachusetts) often spoke for New England. From the 1820s to the 1850s, Henry Clay (Whig–Kentucky) and other congressional leaders worked out one compromise after another to defuse sectional tensions. But as the differences between the sections grew more pronounced, particularly over slavery, compromise became impossible. When the new Republican party won the Presidential election of 1860, the Southern states seceded and the nation plunged into Civil War.

Sectional identities persisted after the Civil War, notably in the Democratic party's long control of the "solid South." But the war had so drained emotions that sectional tensions never again reached their earlier levels. In the modern Congress, various caucuses continue to bring together members from the same region who seek a common agenda to promote the interests of their region.

SEE ALSO Calhoun, John C.; Clay, Henry; Compromise of 1850; "Solid South"; Webster, Daniel

SOURCES David M. Potter, The Impending Crisis, 1848–1861 (New York: Harper & Row, 1976).

SECURITIES AND EXCHANGE COMMISSION

After the stock market crash of 1929, a congressional investigation estimated that perhaps half of the stocks offered for sale during the Roaring Twenties had been fraudulent or otherwise misleading. The major stock exchanges operated essentially as private clubs, under their own rules, with almost no outside supervision. At the start of Franklin Roosevelt's New Deal, in 1933, Congress passed the Securities Act to require accurate information for all stock offerings. The following year saw the passage of the Securities and Exchange Act, which created the Securities and Exchange Commission (SEC).

The SEC is an independent regulatory agency that administers federal laws to protect everyone who buys stocks. The commission also regulates firms that provide investment advice. The SEC includes five members who are nominated by the President and confirmed by the Senate for five-year terms. No more than three of the commissioners may be members of the same political party. The President designates the commission's chairperson.

Within the SEC, the Division of Corporation Finance ensures that companies issuing stock comply with federal disclosure requirements. The Division of Market Regulation supplements the rules enacted by the securities exchanges to further protect investors. The Division of Investment Management enforces three measures enacted during the infancy of the SEC: the

Public Utility Holding Company Act of 1935, the Investment Company Act of 1940, and the Investment Advisors Act of 1940.

The SEC polices Wall Street practices, seeking to stop those who use inside information, who make misleading claims, or who otherwise attempt to manipulate the markets illegally for their own advantage. The investigative arm of the SEC is its Division of Enforcement, which can refer cases to the Department of Justice with recommendations for criminal prosecution.

SEDITIOUS LIBEL

Seditious libel is the crime of making public statements that threaten to undermine respect for the government, laws, or public officials. The Sedition Act of 1798 made it a crime to criticize, ridicule, or erode the authority of the federal government, the President, or other federal officials. This law was used by government officials to prosecute members of the Republican party, headed by Thomas Jefferson, who were rivals to the ruling Federalist party, headed by President John Adams. After Jefferson's victory in the Presidential election of 1800, the Sedition Act of 1798 was allowed to expire.

Controversy about seditious libel emerged during World War I, with passage of the Sedition Act of 1918. In *Abrams* v. *United States* (1919) the Supreme Court upheld the federal government's use of this law to convict Jacob Abrams of distributing leaflets that severely criticized President Woodrow Wilson and the U.S. government. The Court's decision in *Abrams* was based on the "clear and present danger" test stated by Justice Oliver Wendell Holmes in *Schenck* v. *United States* (1919). Justice Holmes, however, wrote a stinging dissent against the Court's use of the "clear and present danger" test in *Abrams* to limit freedom of speech and press. Holmes stressed that a "clear and present danger" exists only when speech

can be connected immediately and directly to specific acts of lawless behavior threatening the security of the United States. If the imminent danger could not be demonstrated, said Holmes, then speech could not be lawfully limited.

Arguments about the constitutionality of seditious libel laws under the 1st Amendment, however, continued until the 1960s, when the U.S. Supreme Court made landmark decisions about this traditional limitation on freedom of speech and press.

In *New York Times Co.* v. *Sullivan* (1964) the Court ruled against a civil libel suit by a public official who tried to collect damages from critics who had denounced him in a newspaper advertisement. In rejecting the suit, the Court compared it to seditious libel prosecutions undertaken to prevent negative speech about the government. The Court concluded that such efforts to limit freedom of speech and press were not permitted by the U.S. Constitution.

In *Garrison* v. *Louisiana* (1964) the Supreme Court overturned a criminal libel conviction. And in *Brandenburg* v. *Ohio* (1969) the court used ideas from Justice Holmes's dissent in *Abrams* to strike down a state law on seditious libel. Thus, the Court acted against seditious libel prosecutions, civil or criminal, and thereby protected the freedom to criticize or otherwise speak out against government actions or officials.

SEE ALSO *Abrams v. United States; Brandenburg v. Ohio; Freedom of speech and press; New York Times Co. v. Sullivan; Schenck v. United States*

SEGREGATION, DE FACTO AND DE JURE

De jure (Latin for "from the law") segregation is the separation of people on the basis of race as required by law. For example, after the Civil War and the ending of slavery by the 13th Amendment to the

Constitution (1865), the governments of the former slave states found new ways to discriminate against black Americans. They enacted laws to require separate public facilities for blacks and whites. Blacks were required, for example, to attend separate schools, to use separate public rest rooms, and to use separate public drinking fountains. The separate facilities for blacks were supposed to be equal to the facilities provided for whites. This "separate but equal" doctrine was endorsed by the Supreme Court decision in *Plessy* v. *Ferguson* (1896). In reality, however, the facilities for black people were rarely, if ever, equal in quality to those provided for whites.

Racial separation that exists as a matter of custom rather than as a legal requirement is known as *de facto* (Latin for "in fact") segregation. For example, one neighborhood may include only white families, and another nearby neighborhood may include only black families. However, this racial segregation may have developed informally in response to social and economic factors, not as a requirement of the law.

De jure segregation has been declared unconstitutional by the U.S. Supreme Court. In *Brown* v. *Board of Education* (1954) the Court ruled against de jure racial segregation in public schools. In subsequent cases the Court outlawed racial discrimination in other areas of public life. In 1964 Congress passed the Civil Rights Act, which outlawed de jure segregation.

The Court has ruled in *Milliken* v. *Bradley* (1974) that courts of law can remedy de facto segregation only if it was caused by specific acts of government. In *Washington* v. *Seattle School District No. 1* (1982) the Court upheld voluntary acts by state agencies to overcome de facto segregation.

SEE ALSO *Brown v. Board of Education; Civil rights; Equality under the Constitution; Plessy v. Ferguson*

SELECTION OF SUPREME COURT JUSTICES

SEE *Appointment power; Nominations, confirmation of*

SELECTIVE SERVICE SYSTEM

"Greetings" began letters to millions of young men, informing them that they had been drafted into military service. The United States had traditionally been opposed to a large standing army and had tended to rely on militia and volunteers to fight its wars. The need for troops during the Civil War caused both the Union and the Confederacy to conscript soldiers (although it was possible to hire someone as a replacement). The draft was revived during World War I and then ended when the war was over.

After war erupted again in Europe in 1939, but before the United States had entered it, the government established the first peacetime draft. The Selective Service System was formally created when President Franklin D. Roosevelt signed the Selective Training and Service Act in 1940. It was replaced by the Selective Service Act of 1948, which regulated the draft from 1948 to 1973, during times of peace as well as times of war. The Selective Service System was assigned to provide manpower as needed for the armed forces and to provide alternative service programs for those men classified as conscientious objectors.

Exemptions from the draft for higher education made the system increasingly unfair in the post–World War II era, as the burden fell more heavily on the poor and on racial minorities. Due to the unpopularity of the Vietnam War, when protestors burned their draft cards, refused to appear for induction, and in some cases even left the country rather than be drafted, the military shifted to an all-volunteer system beginning in 1973. Registration requirements were suspended in 1975. In 1980, following the Soviet Union's invasion of Afghanistan, draft registration was resumed under the Military Selective Service Act. Currently, all men between the ages of 18 and 25 are required to register for a potential military draft.

SELF-INCRIMINATION, PRIVILEGE AGAINST

The 5th Amendment to the U.S. Constitution guarantees that "no person . . . shall be compelled in any criminal case to be a witness against himself." Thus, a criminal defendant has the right to refuse to answer questions that could result in a conviction for a crime.

The 5th Amendment right to avoid self-incrimination was extended to the states when the U.S. Supreme Court incorporated this right into the due process clause of the 14th Amendment in *Malloy* v. *Hogan* (1964). In *Miranda* v. *Arizona* (1966) the Court required law enforcement officers to inform suspects of their 5th Amendment right to remain silent.

Critics have complained that the Court's decision in the *Miranda* case helps criminals resist prosecution. Justice Arthur Goldberg, however, saw the 5th Amendment as a great guarantee of individual rights. In *Murphy* v. *Waterfront Commission of New York* (1964) Goldberg wrote, "[T]he privilege [of avoiding self-incrimination] while sometimes a shelter to the guilty, is often a protection to the innocent."

SEE ALSO *Incorporation doctrine; Miranda v. Arizona; Rights of the accused*

SENATE

All states are represented equally in the U.S. Senate by two senators (in contrast to the House of Representatives, where a state's representation is in proportion to the size of the state's population). Senators serve six-year terms and are divided into three "classes," so that only one class, or one-third of the Senate, is up for election every two years. With two-thirds of its membership carrying over after each election, the Senate is a "continuing body." These longer terms (House members serve only two years) were intended to insulate the Senate—more than the House—from sudden shifts in public opinion.

The equality of the states' representation in the Senate, regardless of the size of the population, was designed to protect the smaller states. The Senate adopted rules that further enhanced minority rights. A small minority of senators, even a minority of one, can use the rules to delay or defeat objectionable legislation. The Senate's toleration of unlimited debate, in the form of the filibuster, has been its most notable difference from the House, whose rules favor the majority.

Although both houses of Congress share essentially the same powers, the Senate has the sole power of "advice and consent," to confirm the President's nominations and to ratify treaties. The Vice President serves as president (or presiding officer) of the Senate, and the senators elect their other officers. Like the House, the Senate determines its own rules and disciplines its own members. The Senate also sits as a court of impeachment once the House has voted to impeach, or formally accuse, a federal officer.

Initially, the Senate met in secret session, and even after it opened its doors in 1794 it operated for years in the shadow of the House. But during the 1830s the Senate emerged as a powerful counterforce to the strong Presidency of Andrew Jackson. Such rivals to Jackson as Henry Clay and Daniel Webster used the Senate as their forum, and a new political party, the Whigs, developed around them. Because senators were evenly divided between free and slave states, the Senate became the center of efforts to preserve the Union. Senators sought legislative compromise to calm popular passions, but decades of compromise could not prevent the Civil War.

Senate leadership The decades after the Civil War saw powerful committee chairmen exert strong party leadership over the Senate. By 1900 journalists were pointing to the Senate Four—Republicans Nelson Aldrich, William Allison, John C. Spooner, and Orville Platt—as being so influential that they could "block and defeat anything that the president or the House may desire." Press criticism of the Senate as a "millionaires' club," more responsive to powerful corporations than to public opinion, resulted in the 17th Amendment in 1913. It gave the privilege of electing senators to the voters rather than to state legislatures.

Throughout its first century, the Senate acted as a body of equals without official floor leaders. The position of majority leader emerged in 1913, when Democratic Caucus chairman John Worth Kern took on the role of directing his party's initiatives on the floor. The parties formalized the posts of majority and minority leader in the 1920s, and the leaders took the front-row seats on either side of the center aisle. Senate rules give the leaders the right of "first recognition," meaning that the presiding officer must recognize them to speak before any other senators.

A clublike atmosphere The atmosphere of the Senate has been compared to that of an exclusive club. Within that club developed an "inner club" made up of powerful committee chairmen and ranking minority party members. The "inner club" drew its membership largely from conservative Southern Democratic committee chairmen and generally excluded junior members and Northern liberals. During the 1950s Majority Leader Lyndon B. Johnson (Democrat–Texas) began to change this structure by appointing freshmen senators to important committees rather than making them spend years in apprenticeships on lesser committees. Johnson's successor as majority leader, Mike Mansfield (Democrat–Missouri),

furthered the trend by spreading power more equally among all senators.

While the upper houses of most parliaments (such as the British House of Lords) have declined in influence in the 20th century, the Senate remains a powerful legislative body. As the Constitution intended, the Senate serves to balance the House, just as the Congress as a whole checks and balances the executive and judiciary branches of the government.

SEE ALSO *Advice and consent; Bicameral; Committees, congressional; Filibuster; House-Senate Relations; "Inner club"; Leadership in Congress; "Millionaires' club"; Nominations, confirmation of; Treaty powers*

SOURCES Richard A. Baker, *The United States Senate: A Bicentennial History* (Malabar, Fla.: Krieger, 1987). George E. Reedy, *The U.S. Senate: Paralysis or a Search for Consensus?* (New York: Crown, 1986). Donald A. Ritchie, *The Senate* (New York: Chelsea House, 1988).

SENATE JUDICIARY COMMITTEE

Established in 1816, the Judiciary Committee is one of the standing, or permanent, committees of the U.S. Senate. In 1868 the Senate directed the Judiciary Committee to examine and screen, for the full Senate, all Presidential nominations to the Supreme Court. Since then, one of the highly visible and very important duties of the committee is its investigations and recommendations about Presidential nominations to the Supreme Court.

The full Senate sends the President's judicial nominations to the Judiciary Committee for review. The committee holds public hearings to consider the merits of each person nominated to fill a vacancy on the Supreme Court. The nominee is invited to appear before the committee to answer questions about his or her background, qualifications, and ideas about law and the U.S. Constitution.

In 1925 Harlan F. Stone became the first nominee to appear before the committee for a hearing. He was subsequently confirmed by the Senate. Since 1955, when John Marshall Harlan II appeared before the Senate Judiciary Committee, all nominees have participated in formal committee hearings.

The committee concludes its hearings on Supreme Court nominations with a vote and a recommendation to the full Senate. The committee's recommendation tends to be decisive. A likely negative committee vote sometimes influences the nominee to withdraw from the process. In 1968 President Lyndon Johnson withdrew his nomination of Abe Fortas for the office of chief justice, when it became clear during the confirmation hearings that the Senate Judiciary Committee would vote against Fortas. A negative recommendation sent by the committee to the full Senate for discussion and vote usually ends in the defeat of the nominee.

SEE ALSO *Appointment power; Nominations, confirmation of*

SENATORIAL COURTESY

When senators vote against a nomination because the home-state senator objects to that nominee, they are showing "senatorial courtesy." They expect that other senators will reciprocate by voting against any objectionable nominee from their own state. The first instance of "senatorial courtesy" took place in 1789, when the Senate rejected the nomination of Benjamin Fishbourn to be a naval officer of the port of Savannah. The two senators from Georgia preferred another candidate and convinced their colleagues to vote against Fishbourn. President George Washington then submitted another nomination that was acceptable to the Georgia senators. "Senatorial courtesy" has given senators great influence over such appointments as federal judges and U.S. attorneys from their state.

SENIORITY IN CONGRESS

Advancement in Congress—increased power and privilege—generally comes through seniority. The longer that members serve, the more senior they become on their committees, leading to the chairmanship of important subcommittees and eventually to the chair of the full committee. Members also receive room assignments through seniority, gaining larger, better-placed offices with more impressive views the more often they are reelected and the more senior they become. Seniority is dated from the time that a member is sworn in. When groups of new members are sworn into the House together as a new "class," members draw lots for office space and other privileges. The Senate, by contrast, uses a formula to determine each member's seniority ranking within that class. The formula includes, in order of importance: previous service in the Senate, service as Vice President, previous service in the House of Representatives, previous service as a state governor, and the size of the population of the senator's state. For a while some outgoing senators resigned just before the end of their term, to allow the governor to appoint their successor and give him a few days' lead in seniority over the rest of the class. But the parties changed their rules in 1980 to prohibit this practice by not recognizing the extra days toward seniority.

The seniority system favors smaller states and districts where one party predominates. When these states repeatedly reelect the same senators and representatives, they gain political power in Congress as those members advance in seniority to become committee chairs and ranking members. Arizona kept Carl Hayden (Democrat) in the House for 15 years and in the Senate for 41, where he became chairman of the Senate Appropriations Committee. Mississippi returned Jamie Whitten (Democrat) regularly to the House for more than 50 years, and he

Ten Longest-
Serving Senators
as of the Second
Session of the 106th
Congress, 2000

1. J. Strom Thurmond *(Democrat until 1964/Republican since 1964– South Carolina)*, 1954–present = 44 years, 5 months
2. Carl Hayden *(Democrat–Arizona)*, 1927–69 = 41 years, 10 months (plus 15 years in the House)
3. John Stennis *(Democrat– Mississippi)*, 1947–89 = 41 years, 2 months
4. Robert C. Byrd *(Democrat–West Virginia)*, 1959–present = 41 years (plus 8 years in the House)
5. Russell Long *(Democrat–Louisiana)*, 1948–87 = 38 years
6. Richard Russell *(Democrat– Georgia)*, 1933–71 = 38 years
7. Edward M. Kennedy *(Democrat– Massachusetts)*, 1962–present = 37 years, 2 months
8. Daniel K. Inouye *(Deomcrat– Hawaii)*, 1963–present = 37 years
9. Francis Warren *(Republican– Wyoming)*, 1890–93, 1895-1929 = 37 years
10. James Eastland *(Democrat– Mississippi)*, 1941, 1943–78 = 36 years, 3 months

chaired the House Appropriations Committee. In 1999, Senator Strom Thurmond (Republican–South Carolina) had served for 43 years.

In 1975 House rules weakened the seniority system by providing that at the beginning of a Congress the members of the majority party could vote to remove a chairman, and could elect a new chair who

was not necessarily the next most senior member. Several senior House members have lost their committee chairmanships under this rule, including Representative Whitten. In 1992, after Whitten's ill health limited his ability to lead his committee, the Democratic Caucus voted to remove him as chairman of the Appropriations Committee. In general, this reform made committee chairmen more accountable to other members. The reduction of seniority also decentralized power and diminished party leadership.

Ten Longest-
Serving
Representatives
as of the Second
Session of the 106th
Congress, 2000

1. Jamie Whitten *(Democrat– Mississippi)*, 1941-95 = 53 years, 2 months
2. Carl Vinson *(Democrat–Georgia)*, 1914–65 = 50 years, 2 months
3. Emmanuel Celler *(Democrat–New York)*, 1923–73 = 49 years, 10 months
4. Sam Rayburn *(Democrat–Texas)*, 1913–61 = 48 years, 10 months
5. Sid Yates *(Democrat–Illinois)*, 1949- 63, 1965–99 = 48 years
6. Wright Patman *(Democrat–Texas)*, 1929–76 = 47 years
7. Joseph G. Cannon *(Republican–Illinois)*, 1873–91, 1893–1913, 1915- 23 = 46 years
8. Adolph Sabath *(Democrat–Illinois)*, 1907–52 = 45 years, 10 months
9. John D. Dingell *(Democrat–Michigan)*, 1955–present = 45 years
10. George Mahon *(Democrat–Texas)* 1935–79 = 44 years

SENIORITY ON THE SUPREME COURT

Certain rules and procedures of the Supreme Court are based on seniority, that is, the length of time each justice has served on the Court. Only the chief justice is exempt from considerations of seniority.

The senior associate justices, those with the longest periods of service, may choose to occupy the larger chambers, or offices, in the Supreme Court Building. The four senior justices also get the better (more spacious) places around the Court's conference table. The most junior justice serves as the doorkeeper during the Court's private conferences. He or she is also the designated receiver and sender of messages during the conferences.

In the Courtroom, the chief justice is seated at the center. The senior associate justice sits to the right of the chief, and the second most senior to his left. The other justices take their places in alternating order of seniority, with the most junior associate justice at the far left of the bench.

During the conferences, the justices speak in order of seniority, from the most senior to the most junior. By speaking first, the senior justices are able to shape the terms of arguments on issues. And, in any case in which the chief justice is not part of the Court's majority, the senior associate justice in the majority has the duty of assigning the writing of the Court's opinion. (If the chief justice is part of the majority, he assigns the writing of the opinion.)

SEPARATE BUT EQUAL DOCTRINE

In 1896 in *Plessy* v. *Ferguson,* the Supreme Court ruled that a state law requiring racial segregation in public transportation was constitutional as long as the separate facilities were equal. This "separate but equal" doctrine was used to justify racial segregation in public schools and a wide variety of other public facilities. In 1954 the Court overturned the "separate but equal" doctrine in *Brown* v. *Board of Education.*

SEE ALSO *Brown* v. *Board of Education; Civil rights; Equality under the Constitution; Plessy* v. *Ferguson; Segregation, de facto and de jure*

SEPARATION OF POWERS

Suspicious of any concentration of power, the framers of the Constitution distributed power among the three branches of the federal government: the legislative, the executive, and the judicial. The legislative branch (Congress) has the power, according to Article 1 of the Constitution, to make certain kinds of laws. In Article 2, the Constitution says that the executive branch (headed by the President) has the power to enforce or carry out laws. The judicial branch (headed by the Supreme Court) is established in Article 3 of the Constitution to interpret and apply the law in federal court cases.

Further, legislative power is divided between the two houses of Congress: the Senate and the House of Representatives. Both houses must pass a bill for it to become law.

The Constitution, however, also *implies* many overlapping powers, which each of the branches have claimed. Presidents have asserted the right to make foreign policy exclusively, without consulting Congress. Congress has attempted to "micromanage" the executive branch by enacting legislation that specifically defines how these laws must be administered. The courts have been accused of "legislating" by actively interpreting legislation in ways that Congress had not intended.

Even so, the separation of powers among the three branches of the federal government is the fundamental constitutional means for achieving limited government and protecting the people against abuses of power. Limited government means that officials cannot act arbitrarily.

Rather, they are bound by the higher law of the Constitution, which guides and limits their use of power in order to protect the liberties of the people and prevent tyranny. James Madison summarized this view of the need for separation of powers in *The Federalist* No. 47: "The accumulation of all powers, legislative, executive, and judiciary, in the same hands, whether of one, a few, or many, and whether hereditary, self-appointed, or elected, may justly be pronounced the very definition of tyranny."

In *The Federalist* No. 48, Madison emphasized that the separation of powers in the U.S. Constitution is complemented by a system of checks and balances, whereby one branch can block or check an action of another branch in order to maintain a balance of power in the government. Madison said that unless the separate branches of government "be so far connected and blended [balanced] as to give each a constitutional control [check] over the others the degree of separation . . . essential to a free government can never in practice be duly maintained."

In military policy, for instance, the President serves as commander in chief of the armed forces, but Congress is authorized to raise and fund an army and navy and votes to declare war. In foreign policy, Presidents appoint U.S. ambassadors and negotiate treaties, but the Senate confirms or rejects those nominations and treaties. Both the House and Senate vote to fund foreign aid and other U.S. diplomatic efforts. In determining fiscal policy, the President submits a budget for the federal government to Congress, but Congress enacts its own version of the budget, appropriates all money, and raises revenue to pay for federal spending. The President may veto, or reject, any revenue and appropriation bill, but by a two-thirds vote of both houses Congress can override that veto.

Judicial review   The Supreme Court uses the power of judicial review to check the executive and legislative branches of government and to maintain the separation of powers. This power enables the Court to declare acts of the executive or legislative branches unconstitutional. Thus, the Court can declare null and void actions of the other branches that exceed or contradict their powers as expressed in the Constitution.

The Court established its power of judicial review in the case of *Marbury* v. *Madison* (1803). Since that time, the Court has exercised this power to declare more than 150 acts of Congress and the President unconstitutional. In *Youngstown Sheet & Tube Co.* v. *Sawyer* (1952), for example, the Court ruled that President Harry Truman's use of an executive order to temporarily take control of privately owned steel mills was unconstitutional. Writing for the Court, Justice Hugo Black explained: "In the framework of our Constitution, the President's power to see that the laws are faithfully executed refutes the idea that he is to be a lawmaker. The Constitution limits his functions in the lawmaking process to the recommending of laws he thinks wise and the vetoing of laws he thinks bad."

In *Clinton* v. *City of New York* (1998) the Court struck down the Line Item Veto Act, which Congress had passed and President Bill Clinton had signed in 1996. This federal statute gave the president the power to "cancel" an item in an appropriations bill passed by Congress and of which he otherwise approved. Clinton's use of the line-item veto was challenged by some members of Congress who protested when he used it to veto their projects. The Court ruled that the law at issue violated Article 1, Section 7, of the Constitution. The principle of the separation of powers was maintained against an act to extend the chief executive's power into an area of government reserved by the Constitution for Congress.

As the preceding examples indicate, each branch of the government has some influence over the actions of the others, but no branch can exercise its powers without cooperation from the others. Each branch has some say in the work of the others as a way to check and limit their powers, but no branch may encroach unconstitutionally upon the domains of the other branches. In this system of separation of powers, with its checks and balances, no branch of the government can accumulate too much power. But each branch, and the government generally, is supposed to have enough power to do what the people expect of it. So the government is supposed to be both limited and strong: strong enough to be effective in maintaining order, stability, and security for the people, but not strong enough to threaten their liberty.

Justice Louis D. Brandeis nicely summed up the founders' purposes and reasons for separation of powers in a dissenting opinion in *Myers* v. *United States* (1926): "The doctrine of the separation of powers was adopted by the Convention of 1787, not to promote efficiency but to preclude the exercise of arbitrary power. The purpose was not to avoid friction but, by means of the inevitable friction incident to the distribution of the governmental powers among three departments, to save the people from autocracy."

SEE ALSO *Checks and balances; Constitution, U.S.; Constitutional democracy; Constitutionalism; Federalist, The; Impeachment; Independent judiciary; Judicial activism and judicial restraint; Judicial power; Judicial review; Marbury v. Madison; Reversals of Supreme Court decisions; Youngstown Sheet & Tube Co. v. Sawyer*

SOURCES George Carey, *The Federalist: Design for a Constitutional Republic* (Urbana: University of Illinois Press, 1991). Martin Diamond, *The Founding of the Democratic Republic* (Itasca, Ill.: F. E. Peacock, 1981). Louis Fisher, *Constitutional Conflicts between Congress and the President* (Princeton, N.J.: Princeton University Press, 1985). Louis Fisher, *Constitutional Dialogues* (Princeton, N.J.: Princeton University Press, 1988). Richard M. Pious, "A Prime Minister for America," *Constitution* 4, no. 3 (Fall 1992): 4–14. M. J. C. Vile, *Constitutionalism and the Separation of* *Powers* (New York: Oxford University Press, 1967).

SEQUOIA

SEE *Yacht, Presidential*

SERGEANT AT ARMS

The House of Representatives and Senate each elect a sergeant at arms to enforce the rules and regulations and to oversee the protection of members, staff, and visitors. On April 7, 1789, the Senate elected James Mathers as its doorkeeper, to guard the doors of the chamber, which were kept closed and barred to the public during early debates. On May 12, 1789, the House elected Joseph Wheaton as sergeant at arms, taking that title from the equivalent post in the British House of Commons. In 1798 the Senate, too, adopted the title of sergeant at arms.

The first sergeant at arms purchased firewood to heat the chambers in winter and guarded the chambers during the months when Congress was in recess. These functions have expanded over time. Today the Senate sergeant at arms supervises much of the maintenance of the Senate wing of the Capitol and office buildings and supervises a wide assortment of staff members, from computer specialists to janitors, carpenters, and barbers. The House assigns these functions differently, placing many of them under the clerk of the House, the doorkeeper, and the director of non-legislative services.

The House sergeant at arms carries the mace (silver rods lashed together and topped by a silver eagle), which is the symbol of the authority of the House. If debate grows heated and disorderly, the sergeant at arms lifts the mace high to remind members to restore order.

The House and Senate have also authorized their sergeants at arms to "arrest" absent members to bring them to the chambers to establish a quorum, the minimum number of members needed to conduct business. The sergeants at arms serve on the Capitol Police Board to oversee policing of the Capitol complex. They supervise parking, and they maintain crowd control during political demonstrations at the Capitol. The sergeants at arms have also become protocol officers who greet official visitors and lead processions of members at Presidential inaugurations, State of the Union messages, and other joint sessions and ceremonial meetings.

SEE ALSO *Capitol Police; Doorkeepers; Mace of the House of Representatives; Officers of the House and Senate; Quorum*

SOURCES Robert C. Byrd, "Sergeant at Arms," in *The Senate, 1789–1989: Addresses on the History of the United States Senate,* vol. 2 (Washington, D.C.: Government Printing Office, 1991).

SERIATIM OPINIONS

Seriatim is the Latin word for "severally," or "in a series." When appellate court judges render seriatim opinions, each one presents a separate judgment on a case; no one writes an opinion for the court as a whole. From its origin until 1803, the U.S. Supreme Court followed the practice of writing seriatim opinions. But under Chief Justice John Marshall this practice stopped and the Court began the practice, which is nearly always employed today, of having one justice write a majority opinion for each case decided by the Court.

SEE ALSO *Concurring opinion; Dissenting opinion; Majority opinion; Opinions of the Supreme Court; Plurality opinion*

SESSIONS OF CONGRESS

Each Congress is divided into at least two sessions. The first session takes place during the year following the election, and the second session follows the year after that. Originally, the Constitution provided that Congress would begin its sessions on the first Monday in December, more than a

year after the election had been held. In 1933 the 20th Amendment moved the beginning of each session up to January 3. The 20th Amendment was designed to end the many lame-duck sessions that had occurred between an election and the start of the next Congress. These sessions were called lame-duck sessions because many of the members had retired or been defeated and were rapidly approaching the end of their term in office. Since the passage of the 20th Amendment, only a few lame-duck sessions have been held to take care of unfinished business. The last one, in 1982, addressed appropriations and budget issues.

Sessions generally run until the fall, although they may go right through December. If the Congress has adjourned, the President can call it back into a special session, which might be designated a third session of that Congress. The last such third session occurred during the 76th Congress (1939–41), when President Franklin D. Roosevelt called Congress back into session following the outbreak of war in Europe.

Legislation introduced but not acted upon during the first session remains alive and keeps the same number during the second session. But any unfinished business dies with the second session, and its sponsors must begin anew in the next Congress.

Representative Clem Miller (Democrat–California) compared the opening day of a new session to the first day of school, when everything seems brand-new and everyone seems hopeful:

Congressmen flood the tunnel that connects the offices with the Capitol. The hubbub is fierce. . . . Everywhere hands are grabbed. They set off smartly in platoons of four or six, waves of men and women proceeding along the gentle incline. Deep smiles of greeting, halloos, and backslapping. This may appear to outsiders as part of the ordinary political spectacle, the general over-friendliness of the trade; but it is much more than that. The emotions are real. The affection is a heartfelt display. It is the camaraderie of the shared experience. These people, these congressmen, have all been through the mill. They have returned from the indifferent cruelties of the political wars.

SEE ALSO *Lame-duck sessions of Congress*
SOURCES Clem Miller, *Member of the House: Letters of a Congressman* (New York: Scribners, 1962).

SHADOW SENATORS

People who live in territories that belong to the United States are represented in Congress by delegates in the House of Representatives and sometimes also by "shadow senators." The House provides all delegates with offices, staff, and committee assignments and permits them to speak in the House chamber. Shadow senators, by contrast, receive little official recognition, serve on no committees, and do not participate in Senate debates. Rather than representing constituents, shadow senators devote most of their attention to lobbying efforts to turn their territory into a state. The first shadow senators were elected by the Tennessee legislature in 1796 to promote statehood. Michigan, California, Minnesota, Oregon, and Alaska also employed shadow senators. Following in this tradition, in 1990 the District of Columbia elected the Reverend Jesse Jackson as a shadow senator to advocate making Washington, D.C., a state.

SEE ALSO *Delegates to the House of Representatives*

SHARED POWERS

SEE *Separation of powers*

SHERMAN ANTITRUST ACT (1890)

During the 1880s Americans worried about the emergence of trusts, or combi-

nations of businesses that tended to reduce competition. Trusts occurred whenever a single board of trustees controlled the management of many different companies. By consolidating these companies, trusts could monopolize, or dominate, production and set prices in a particular industry. Newspapers and magazines accused the Standard Oil Trust, the Sugar Trust, and other large-scale industries of improperly suppressing competition. Defenders of the trusts asserted that such consolidation allowed more efficient production and lower prices. Opponents argued that a lack of competition placed consumers, small businesses, and farmers at the mercy of these monopolies, which could charge whatever prices they wanted.

In 1890 Congress responded to these public concerns by passing—almost unanimously—the Sherman Antitrust Act. Named for its chief sponsor, Senator John Sherman (Republican–Ohio), this act sought to end monopolies and make illegal any restriction on trade. However, the Sherman Act lacked any effective means of enforcement, and it failed to stop the growth of big business. During the 1890s the federal courts further weakened the Sherman Act by interpreting it to permit mergers and other forms of business consolidation. During the Progressive Era (1900–14), reformers continued the fight to "bust" the trusts. In 1914 Congress created the Federal Trade Commission in an effort to regulate business practices rather than try to abolish big business, as the Sherman Act had tried to do.

SHERMAN, JAMES
Vice President

- Born: Oct. 24, 1855, Utica, N.Y.
- Political party: Republican
- Education: Hamilton College, B.A., 1878
- Military service: none
- Previous government service: mayor of Utica, 1885; U.S. House of Representatives, 1887–91, 1893–1909

- Vice President under William Howard Taft, 1909–12
- Died: Oct. 30, 1912, Utica, N.Y.

As a Republican, James ("Sunny Jim") Sherman pulled a major upset in overwhelmingly Democratic Utica, New York, to become its mayor in 1884. A member of the U.S. House of Representatives for 20 years, he chaired the Indian Affairs Committee and served on the Rules Committee. He was a close ally of the powerful Speakers Thomas Reed and Joseph Cannon.

When William Howard Taft of Ohio was nominated for President in 1908, Sherman was chosen to represent eastern Republican interests and balance the ticket. He did next to nothing as Vice President. When President Taft asked him to help pass a Republican bill in Congress, Sherman replied that "acting as a messenger boy is not part of the duties of a Vice President."

He was renominated for Vice President by the Republicans in 1912 but died while campaigning in his native Utica. The Republican National Committee replaced him on the ticket with Columbia University president Nicholas Murray Butler.

SHIRAS, GEORGE, JR.
Associate Justice, 1892–1903

- Born: Jan. 26, 1832, Pittsburgh, Pa.
- Education: Ohio University, 1849–51; Yale College, B.A., 1853; studied law at Yale and privately
- Previous government service: none
- Appointed by President Benjamin Harrison July 19, 1892; replaced Joseph P. Bradley, who died
- Supreme Court term: confirmed by the Senate July 26, 1892, by a voice vote; retired Feb. 23, 1903
- Died: Aug. 2, 1924, Pittsburgh, Pa.

George Shiras, Jr., was a successful lawyer before his appointment to the Supreme Court. However, he had no prior experience in government service, unlike all other Supreme Court justices.

Justice Shiras strongly supported property rights and economic liberty. Thus, he voted to strike down or limit federal and state regulations of businesses in the cases of *United States* v. *E. C. Knight* (1895) and *Allgeyer* v. *Louisiana* (1897). In *Wong Wing* v. *United States* (1896), however, Justice Shiras wrote for the Court in protecting the rights of illegal aliens against unduly harsh punishments that disregarded 5th and 6th Amendment rights of due process and trial by jury.

SOURCES Winfield Shiras, *Justice George Shiras, Jr. of Pittsburgh* (Pittsburgh: University of Pittsburgh Press, 1953).

SLAUGHTERHOUSE CASES

- 16 Wall. 36 (1873)
- Vote: 5–4
- For the Court: Miller
- Dissenting: Field, Bradley, Chase, and Swayne

In 1869 the Louisiana legislature passed a law incorporating the Crescent City Live-Stock Landing and Slaughter House Company. This law required that all butchering of animals in New Orleans had to be done at the facilities of the new Crescent City Company. According to state officials, the reason for passing this law was to protect the health and safety of the community. They claimed that local butchers were causing pollution and spreading diseases by using unsanitary procedures when they slaughtered animals to be processed into food products. By combining all butchering work in one place, the state officials claimed they could regulate this work in order to reduce health risks.

The local butchers were outraged. The new law forced them to take their business to one location and pay high fees for slaughtering their animals there. They argued that the new law was passed primarily to benefit the owners of the Crescent City Company, not the public good.

The local butchers formed their own organization, the Butchers' Benevolent Association, and hired a lawyer, John A. Campbell, who had been a U.S. Supreme Court justice. Campbell sued the Crescent City Company for depriving the local butchers of their right to property. He argued that this is a basic right of individuals, protected by the privileges and immunities clause of the 14th Amendment, which says, "No state shall make or enforce any law which shall abridge the privileges or immunities of citizens of the United States." Further, Campbell argued that the state law at issue deprived the local butchers of their property rights primarily for the private profit of the Crescent City Company and not for the good of the community, as had been claimed.

In 1870 the issue went to the Louisiana Supreme Court, which upheld the state law and rejected the suit of the Butchers' Benevolent Association. The butchers appealed to the U.S. Supreme Court.

The Issue   Did the Louisiana law creating the Crescent City Live-Stock Landing and Slaughter House Company violate the property rights of local butchers under the privileges and immunities clause of the 14th Amendment?

Opinion of the Court   In a close vote (5 to 4), the Court upheld the Louisiana law at issue and decided against the suit brought by the Butchers' Benevolent Association. Writing for the Court, Justice Samuel F. Miller held that the Louisiana state government had not violated the 14th Amendment by creating the Crescent City Company and giving it control of the slaughterhouse business in New Orleans.

Justice Miller argued that the 14th Amendment's privileges and immunities clause did not protect the butchers' property rights or their right to work. Further, he narrowly interpreted the privileges and immunities clause to pertain only to very few rights of national citizenship that states could not abridge or take away. According to Justice Miller, rights of property and labor were

not among these few fundamental rights protected by the 14th Amendment from abridgment by state governments. Rather, these rights were subject to state regulation for the good of the community, said Justice Miller. He also argued that the primary purpose of the 14th Amendment (which was enacted after the Civil War) was to protect the rights of African Americans and not to expand or add to the rights of white people.

Dissent   Justice Stephen J. Field argued that property rights and the right to labor *were* among the privileges and immunities protected from state interference by the 14th Amendment. Justices Joseph Bradley and Noah Swayne also contended that the Louisiana law violated the 14th Amendment by depriving the butchers of property without due process of law. Finally, all of the dissenting justices rejected the Court's argument that the 14th Amendment was designed to protect the rights only of black Americans.

Significance   Justice Miller's opinion for the Court strictly limited future applications of the privileges and immunities clause of the 14th Amendment. This clause might have been used to allow federal government protection for a wide range of fundamental rights, including the federal Bill of Rights, against infringement by state governments. The *Slaughterhouse* decision, by rejecting a broad interpretation of the privileges and immunities clause, made this constitutional provision virtually useless as a guarantee of the most important individual rights. Individuals therefore had to depend upon their state constitutions and governments for protection of their basic rights. This put black people, newly freed from slavery, at a disadvantage in seeking such protection from southern state governments dominated by former slaveholders. One positive outcome of the *Slaughterhouse* decision, however, was the encouragement given to states in the 1870s and 1880s to regulate economic activities for the good of the community; that is, to protect public health, safety, or morals.
SEE ALSO *Property rights*

SMITH, HOWARD W.

- Born: Feb. 2, 1883, Broad Run, Va.
- Political party: Democrat
- Education: Bethel Military Academy, graduated, 1901; law department of the University of Virginia, graduated, 1903
- Representative from Virginia: 1931–67
- Died: Oct. 3, 1976, Alexandria, Va.

As a member of the House Rules Committee for 32 years, including 12 as its chairman, Howard Smith fought for limited government and against nearly all federal programs for education, health, housing, or civil rights. Smith used the full powers of the Rules Committee, as well as his own command of the rules and precedents of the House of Representatives, to frustrate his opponents. During the 1950s the Rules Committee was divided evenly between liberals and conservatives, and a tie vote could prevent legislation from reaching the floor. Sometimes, if Smith thought his side might lose a vote, he would simply go home, knowing that the committee could not meet without its chairman and that bills could not reach the House floor until the committee had acted. In 1961, fearing that the committee would block President John F. Kennedy's legislative programs, liberal Democrats led a revolt against Chairman Smith. They proposed to expand the size of the committee to add more liberal members. Speaker Sam Rayburn (Democrat–Texas) threw his support behind this effort, which won by a slim margin of 217 to 212. Smith continued to fight against social programs, but his power to obstruct had been greatly diminished.

SEE ALSO *Rayburn, Sam; Rules committees*
SOURCES Bruce J. Dierenfield, *Keeper of the Rules: Congressman Howard W. Smith of Virginia* (Charlottesville: University Press of Virginia, 1987).

SMITH, MARGARET CHASE

- Born: Dec. 14, 1897, Skowhegan, Maine
- Political party: Republican
- Representative from Maine: 1940–49
- Senator from Maine: 1949–73
- Died: May 29, 1995, Skowhegan, Maine

When Representative Clyde Smith (Republican–Maine) died in 1940, his wife, Margaret Chase Smith, ran for election to complete his term. She won four more terms in the House before being elected to the Senate. In an era when it was still uncommon for women to enter politics and serve in Congress, Smith avoided the more traditional "women's issues"—such as health and education—and joined the Senate Armed Services Committee, where she established her legislative reputation.

In 1950, when Senator Joseph R. McCarthy began making reckless accusations about alleged communists in government, Senator Margaret Chase Smith asked what proof he had to back up his charges against government officials. McCarthy promised to produce evidence, but he never found anything that convinced her. When other senators seemed unwilling to confront McCarthy, Smith decided that someone had to speak out. On June 1, 1950, she rose in the Senate to deliver her "Declaration of Conscience." She called on the Senate to do some serious soul-searching about the abuse of its powers and privileges. She condemned the loose, unsupported charges that amounted to character assassination, and she defended as basic principles of American life "the right to criticize; the right to hold unpopular beliefs; the right to protest; the right of independent thought."

At the time, very few of Smith's colleagues rallied to her support. It took the Senate another four years before it censured McCarthy for the behavior that Margaret Chase Smith had first taken the floor to denounce.

SEE ALSO *McCarthy, Joseph R.; Women in government*

SOURCES Margaret Chase Smith, *Declaration of Conscience* (Garden City, N.Y.: Doubleday, 1972).

SMITH V. ALLWRIGHT

- 321 U.S. 649 (1944)
- Vote: 8–1
- For the Court: Reed
- Dissenting: Roberts

Lonnie Smith, an African American, lived in Harris County, Texas. On July 27, 1940, Smith was stopped from voting in the Democratic party's primary election for selecting the party's nominees for U.S. senator, representative to Congress, and several state offices. Smith met all the Texas qualifications for eligibility to vote. He was denied the ballot by Democratic party election officials only because of his race.

Smith sought help from the National Association for the Advancement of Colored People (NAACP). One of the NAACP lawyers who helped him was Thurgood Marshall, a future justice of the U.S. Supreme Court. Lonnie Smith sued Allwright, a Democratic party election judge, for illegally denying him the right to vote.

The Issue The 15th Amendment to the Constitution clearly protected Lonnie Smith's right to vote: "The right of citizens of the United States to vote shall not be denied or abridged by the United States or any State on account of race, color, or previous condition of servitude." In addition, Section 1 of the 14th Amendment protected Smith's rights against state government interference.

However, the Democratic party was a private organization, not part of the Texas state government. So party officials claimed they could deny Smith the right to participate in a Democratic party primary election without violating the 14th and 15th Amendments, which limited only the

federal and state governments, not private associations. They argued that as long as Smith was allowed to vote in the final general election, where he could choose between the Democratic and Republican candidates, his constitutional right to vote was protected.

Smith and his lawyers disagreed. They pointed out that the Democratic party dominated politics and government in Texas. The candidates who won the Democratic party primary election almost always won the subsequent general election. So, by denying Smith and other black citizens the right to vote in the primary election, the Democratic party was preventing them from effectively participating in electing their representatives in government.

Did the 14th and 15th Amendment protections of the right to vote apply to the primary elections of a political party?

Opinion of the Court Lonnie Smith and the NAACP won this case. The Supreme Court held that political party primary elections are operated in association with state government machinery set up to choose state and federal officials. Thus, the 14th and 15th Amendments to the U.S. Constitution could be used to protect Smith's right to vote in the Democratic party primary election. Justice Stanley Reed wrote:

> The United States is a constitutional democracy. Its organic law grants to all citizens a right to participate in the choice of elected officials without restriction by any State because of race. This grant to the people of the opportunity for choice is not to be nullified by a state through casting its electoral process in a form which permits a private organization to practice racial discrimination in the election. Constitutional rights would be of little value if they could be thus indirectly denied.

Significance This decision overturned *Grovey v. Townsend* (1935), which had permitted racial discrimination in the conduct of a party primary election. *Smith*

v. *Allwright* was the beginning of legal developments that culminated in the 1960s in full voting rights for African Americans through the passage of the Voting Rights Act of 1965. This federal law was affirmed by the Court in *South Carolina* v. *Katzenbach* (1966) as constitutional under the 15th Amendment.

SEE ALSO *Civil rights; Equality under the Constitution*

SOURCES Donald W. Rogers, ed., *Voting and the Spirit of Democracy: Essays in the History of Voting and Voting Rights in America* (Urbana: University of Illinois Press, 1992).

SNUFF

Before the Civil War, snuff (tobacco finely ground for inhaling) became so popular among senators that the Senate set a large silver urn, a vaselike container, of snuff on the Vice President's desk. But in 1850 Vice President Millard Fillmore complained, "I cannot understand what is going on in the Senate on account of the conversation of Senators who come here to get a pinch of snuff." The urn was replaced with two small black-lacquered boxes, located on the ledges just behind and on either side of the Vice President's desk. If you look carefully from the gallery, you can still see these snuffboxes. For tradition's sake the boxes are kept filled, even though senators long ago stopped taking snuff.

SOURCES Robert Rienow and Leona Train Rienow, *Snuff, Sin & the Senate* (Chicago: Follett, 1965).

SOCIAL SECURITY ADMINISTRATION

During the Great Depression of the 1930s, some of the poorest Americans were the oldest. Many people had failed to save adequately for their retirement; others suffered illnesses that consumed their savings. Reformers called for the government to establish old-age pensions, arguing that when elderly people spent these funds they would help the economy recover. President Franklin D. Roosevelt proposed and Congress enacted the Social Security Act of 1935. Originally, the act created a Social Security Board, but in 1946 it was renamed the Social Security Administration (SAA). For many years it operated as part of the Department of Health, Education, and Welfare, until 1995 when it became an independent executive agency. The SAA is directed by a commissioner appointed by the President and confirmed by the Senate for a six-year term.

The SAA administers a national trust fund to which employees, employers, and the self-employed make contributions. When workers retire, they can qualify for monthly cash benefits. The primary forms of social insurance that the SAA administers are Old Age and Survivors Disability Insurance (OASDI) and Supplemental Security Income (SSI). SSI benefits are earmarked for the aged, blind, and disabled.

As the average person's life expectancy increases, a higher proportion of Americans have been drawing Social Security benefits each year. This has raised fears that the system will not be able to meet the needs of the large number of post–World War II "baby boomers" when they retire. Increasing Social Security taxes would place a heavier burden on younger workers. Alternatives have ranged from designating federal budget surpluses for Social Security to privatizing at least part of the system and allowing individuals to invest some of their Social Security taxes in order to increase the amount that would be available when they retire. Voters, however, have remained wary of any dramatic changes to the Social Security system.

SOLICITOR GENERAL

The President of the United States appoints the solicitor general to represent the federal executive department before the Supreme Court. Congress created the position of solicitor general in 1870 as part of the Department of Justice. The solicitor general assists the attorney general of the United States, who heads the Department of Justice.

The main duty of the solicitor general is to argue the executive branch's position in cases being heard by the Supreme Court. The solicitor general maintains offices at both the Justice Department headquarters and the Supreme Court building. As a result, a close working relationship has developed between the solicitor general and the justices of the Court.

Thurgood Marshall, an associate justice from 1967 to 1991, served as solicitor general from 1965 to 1967. In this role, he won the Supreme Court's affirmation of the Voting Rights Act of 1965 in *South Carolina v. Katzenbach* (1966).

SOURCES Andrea. Sachs, "The Government's Advocate," *Constitution* 3, no. 3 (Fall 1991): 4–14. Rebecca Mae Salokar, *The Solicitor General: The Politics of Law* (Philadelphia: Temple University Press, 1992).

"SOLID SOUTH"

After the Civil War and Reconstruction, the Democratic party regained political control of the eleven former Confederate states. Denying the vote to African Americans and intimidating "carpetbaggers" (Southern Republicans, originally from the North, who got their nickname from their luggage made of carpet fabric), Democrats effectively eliminated the Republican party as a political force in the Southern states. For the next century, winning the Democratic primary in a Southern state meant winning the general election. Southerners also repeatedly reelected their senators and representatives, which enabled them to gain seniority in Congress. As a result, whenever the Democrats held the majority in the Senate or House, Southern Democrats tended to chair the most important committees. The "solid South" held its strongest grip on Congress between the 1930s and 1960s. Then the enactment of the Civil Rights Act of 1964 and the Voting Rights Act of 1965 alienated many white Southerners from the Democratic party. At the same time, Republicans adopted a "Southern strategy"—running candidates and making appointments that would appeal to the region's conservative sentiments. The strategy encouraged many Democrats to register or vote as Republicans. The "solid South" made way for a two-party South as Southern voters began electing Republicans as well as Democrats to Congress.

SEE ALSO *Boll Weevils; Carpetbaggers*
SOURCES Dewey W. Grantham, *The Life and Death of the Solid South: A Political History* (Lexington: University Press of Kentucky, 1988).

SOUTER, DAVID H.
Associate Justice, 1990–

- Born: Sept. 17, 1939, Melrose, Mass.
- Education: Harvard College, A.B., 1961; Harvard Law School, LL.B., 1965
- Previous government service: attorney general of New Hampshire, 1976–78; superior judge, New Hampshire, 1978–83; justice, New Hampshire Supreme Court, 1983–90; judge, Federal Court of Appeals of the First Circuit, 1990
- Appointed by President George Bush July 25, 1990; replaced Justice William Brennan, who retired
- Supreme Court term: confirmed by the Senate Oct. 2, 1990, by a vote of 90–9

David H. Souter was President George Bush's first appointment to the Supreme Court. President Bush was determined to nominate a noncontroversial person who would be readily confirmed by the Senate, without conflict and acrimony. The President also wanted a justice who favored judicial restraint and policy-making only by the legislative and the executive branches of government. Souter clearly was the President's man. He had neither written nor publicly said anything controversial enough that could be used to deny his confirmation. Further, he seemed to agree with the President about judicial self-restraint in interpreting the Constitution.

During his confirmation hearings before the Senate Judiciary Committee, Souter performed cautiously and competently. He was confirmed by the Senate and took his seat as the 105th justice of the U.S. Supreme Court.

During his first few years on the Court, Justice Souter has been a capable justice. He has tended to side with the Court's conservative majority, but he clearly has demonstrated intellectual flexibility and independence. For example, he joined the Court's 1993 decision in *Church of the Lukumi Babalu Aye* v. *City of Hialeah,* which struck down a local law banning animal sacrifice as part of a religious ritual. Souter wrote a concurring opinion that protected the 1st Amendment right of free exercise of religion. Souter's concurring opinion, however, was more strongly and broadly stated than the opinion of the Court, written by Justice Anthony Kennedy. Justice Souter has also been a frequent dissenter from the Court majority. For example, he joined with liberals on the Court in dissenting opinions against decisions that restricted the use of race as a factor in drawing boundaries for congressional districts, as in *Bush* v. *Vera* (1996).

SPEAKER OF THE HOUSE

The House of Representatives elects a Speaker to serve as its presiding officer. At first the Speaker performed the role of moderator—modeled after the Speaker of the British House of Commons—directing the flow of legislative business and maintaining order. When Henry Clay became Speaker in 1811, he assumed the additional role of party leader, preserving his right to debate and vote like other members. (The Speaker must step down from the podium and speak from the floor if he wishes to address a specific issue.) Since Clay's time, most Speakers have combined the roles as leader both of the majority party and of the House as a whole.

As the number of members of the House grew, strong Speakers such as Thomas B. Reed, who served in the 1890s, interpreted and enforced the House rules to favor the majority and to block obstructionist tactics by the minority. In 1910, however, progressive reformers protested against the "dictatorial" leadership of Speaker Joseph G. Cannon and stripped away many of his powers, including the authority to name all committee members and appoint the chairs of all committees. Today the Democratic Caucus and Republican Conference make committee assignments, and House committee members elect their own chairs. House reforms also prohibited the Speaker from serving on the Rules Committee.

A majority of votes is needed to elect a Speaker, and the position has often been hotly contested. The longest election took place between December 1855 and February 1856, when it took 133 ballots to elect Nathaniel Banks as Speaker. Since the 1930s it has become common for the majority leader to move up to become Speaker. Sam Rayburn (Democrat–Texas) holds the record of the longest service as Speaker: a total of 17 years, 2 months, and 2 days over three periods from 1940 to 1961.

When not presiding, the Speaker appoints a Speaker pro tem (a Latin phrase meaning "for the time being") to preside in his place. The Speaker, through the House parliamentarian, refers all bills to committee and also appoints the chairs of the committee of the whole (a device by which the House suspends its rules to meet as a committee, to limit debate and amendments). A combination of administrative, legislative, protocol, and political duties makes the Speaker, in the words of Thomas B. Reed, "the embodiment of the House, its power and dignity."

SEE ALSO *Blaine, James G.; Cannon, Joseph G.; Clark, James Beauchamp ("Champ"); Clay, Henry; Committee of the whole; Foley,*

Speakers of the House

Frederick Augustus Muhlenberg (Federalist–Pennsylvania), 1789–91
Jonathan Trumbull (Federalist–Connecticut), 1791–93
Frederick Augustus Muhlenberg (Federalist–Pennsylvania), 1793–95
Jonathan Dayton (Democratic-Republican–New Jersey), 1795–99
Theodore Sedgwick (Federalist–Massachusetts), 1799–1801
Nathaniel Macon (Democratic-Republican–North Carolina), 1801–7
Joseph B. Varnum (Democratic-Republican–Massachusetts), 1807–11
Henry Clay (Democratic-Republican–Kentucky), 1811–14
Langdon Chives (Democratic-Republican–South Carolina), 1814–15
Henry Clay (Democratic-Republican–Kentucky), 1815–20
John W. Taylor (Democratic-Republican–New York), 1820–21
Philip P. Barbour (Democratic-Republican–Virginia), 1821–23
Henry Clay (Democratic-Republican–Kentucky), 1823–25
John W. Taylor (Democratic-Republican–New York), 1825–27
Andrew Stevenson (Democrat-Virginia), 1827–34
John Bell (Whig–Tennessee), 1834–35
James K. Polk (Democrat–Tennessee), 1835–39
Robert M. T. Hunter (Whig–Virginia), 1839–41
John White (Whig–Kentucky), 1841–43
John W. Jones (Democrat–Virginia), 1843–45
John Wesley Davis (Democrat–Indiana), 1845–47

Robert C. Winthrop (Whig–Massachusetts), 1847–49
Howell G. Cobb (Democrat–Georgia), 1849–51
Linn Boyd (Democrat–Kentucky), 1851–55
Nathaniel P. Banks (Republican–Massachusetts), 1856–57
James L. Orr (Democrat–South Carolina), 1857–59
William Pennington (Republican–New Jersey), 1860–61
Galusha A. Grow (Republican–Pennsylvania), 1861–63
Schuyler Colfax (Republican–Indiana), 1863–69
Theodore M. Pomeroy (Republican–New York), 1869
James G. Blaine (Republican–Maine), 1869–75
Michael C. Kerr (Democrat–Indiana), 1875–76
Samuel J. Randall (Democrat–Pennsylvania), 1876–81
J. Warren Keifer (Republican–Ohio), 1881–83
John G. Carlisle (Democrat–Kentucky), 1883–89
Thomas B. Reed (Republican–Maine), 1889–91
Charles F. Crisp (Democrat–Georgia), 1891–95
Thomas B. Reed (Republican–Maine), 1895–99
David B. Henderson (Republican–Iowa), 1899–1903
Joseph G. Cannon (Republican–Illinois), 1903–11
James Beauchamp ("Champ") Clark (Democrat-Missouri), 1911–19
Frederick H. Gillett (Republican–Massachusetts), 1919–25
Nicholas Longworth (Republican–Ohio), 1925–31
John Nance Garner (Democrat–Texas), 1931–33
Henry T. Rainey (Democrat–Illinois), 1933–34

Joseph W. Byrnes (Democrat–Tennessee), 1935–36
William Bankhead (Democrat–Alabama), 1936–40
Sam Rayburn (Democrat–Texas), 1940–47
Joseph W. Martin (Republican–Massachusetts), 1947–48
Sam Rayburn (Democrat–Texas), 1949–52
Joseph W. Martin (Republican–Massachusetts), 1953–54
Sam Rayburn (Democrat–Texas), 1955–61
John W. McCormack (Democrat–Massachusetts), 1962–71
Carl Albert (Democrat–Oklahoma), 1971–77
Thomas P. ("Tip") O'Neill, Jr. (Democrat–Massachusetts), 1977–87
Jim Wright (Democrat–Texas), 1987–89
Thomas S. Foley (Democrat–Washington), 1989–95
Newt Gingrich (Republican–Georgia), 1995–99
J. Dennis Hastert (Republican–Illinois), 1999–

Thomas S.; Garner, John Nance; Gingrich, Newt; Longworth, Nicholas; Muhlenberg, Frederick Augustus; Officers of the House and Senate; Rayburn, Sam; Reed, Thomas B.; Rules committees; Wright, Jim
SOURCES Ronald M. Peters, Jr., *The American Speakership: The Office in Historical Perspective* (Baltimore, Md.: Johns Hopkins University Press, 1990).

SPECIAL ORDERS

While watching the proceedings of the House of Representatives on television, viewers are sometimes surprised to see the cameras show an entirely empty chamber, except for the person speaking. When this occurs, the House is likely to be operating

under special orders. In regular session, the House places strict limits on the amount of time that members may speak. But when no legislative business is planned, members may reserve the chamber under special orders, to speak at length on any topic that concerns them. Even though the House is not in regular session, remarks made during special orders are carried on C-SPAN's television network and are recorded in the next day's *Congressional Record*. However, to alert viewers that the speaker is addressing an empty chamber, and that opponents are not present to rebut the speaker, the television cameras regularly pan the vacant seats.

The Senate has a different form of "special orders," permitting senators to speak for five minutes each on a variety of topics during the Morning Hour, before debate begins on specific legislation.
SEE ALSO *Morning Hour*

SPECIAL PROSECUTOR

SEE *Independent counsel*

SPECIAL RULES

SEE *Rules of the House and Senate*

SPECIAL SESSIONS OF CONGRESS

If an emergency occurs when Congress is not in session, the Constitution empowers the President to call Congress back into special, or extraordinary, session. Prior to the passage of the 20th Amendment in 1933, Congress met for only a limited number of months each year. Up to that date Presidents called the Senate into special session on 46 occasions, usually to confirm nominations to the cabinet or to deal with important treaties. On 27 other occasions, Presidents called both the House and Senate into special session. These special sessions responded to wars, economic crises, and important legislative proposals. For instance, Abraham Lincoln called Congress into special session on July 4, 1861, to deal with the outbreak of the Civil War. Franklin D. Roosevelt called Congress into special session in March 1933 to pass emergency banking and relief legislation during the Great Depression. This session became known as the "first hundred days of the New Deal."

After the 20th Amendment changed the opening date of Congress to January 3, and after Congress began meeting for most of the year, the need for special sessions diminished. Since 1933 Presidents have called Congress back only four times. Franklin Roosevelt called a special session in October 1937 to enact legislation that would establish minimum wages and maximum hours of work. In September 1939 Roosevelt called Congress into special session when Germany invaded Poland and triggered World War II. During the 80th Congress, when Republicans held the majority in Congress, Democratic President Harry S. Truman called Congress back in October 1947 and July 1948 to deal with unfinished domestic legislation. President Truman planned to campaign for reelection against the "Do-Nothing 80th Congress," so he called these sessions to embarrass the Republican majorities by accusing them of not acting on important social matters.

In recent years when Congress has adjourned, it has also authorized the leaders of the Senate and House to call the Congress back in case of emergency.

SPEECH WRITERS, PRESIDENTIAL

The White House employs a staff of aides who draft Presidential speeches, messages to Congress, proclamations, executive orders, greetings to White House visitors, eulogies, opening statements at news conferences, and other public statements and documents.

Each President has used speech writers differently. They may write first drafts for the President to polish, or provide phrases and slogans, or translate complicated policy proposals into language for a mass audience. Some speech writers are influential assistants to the President who offer policy suggestions and may influence White House decision making. Others are wordsmiths with no policy influence.

The speech-writing office is part of the White House Office. It works with the White House Research Unit, which checks the facts contained in any Presidential statement, especially quotations, dates, statistics, and historical references.

Presidents have relied on speech writers since George Washington received help from Thomas Jefferson, James Madison, and Alexander Hamilton on his state papers and farewell address. Andrew Jackson's veto messages to Congress were drafted by his attorney general. Abraham Lincoln wrote his own speeches and documents, including the Gettysburg Address and Emancipation Proclamation. Woodrow Wilson, who had written books and articles as a professor, also wrote his own speeches. Franklin Roosevelt used several speech writers, including playwright Robert Sherwood. Dwight Eisenhower used journalist Emmet Hughes. Most of John F. Kennedy's speeches were drafted by his counsel, Theodore Sorensen; other Kennedy speech writers included historian Arthur M. Schlesinger, Jr., Ambassador to India John Kenneth Galbraith, and White House aide Richard Goodwin. Ronald Reagan relied heavily on Peggy Noonan, one of the first women speech writers in the White House.

Some speech writers have gone on to distinguished careers. Jack Valenti, an aide to Lyndon Johnson, became president of the Motion Picture Association of America. One of Richard Nixon's speech writers, William Safire, became a columnist for the *New York Times;* another, Pat Buchanan, became a talk-show commentator and contender for the Republican Presidential nomination in 1992 and 1996. Two of Jimmy Carter's speech writers, James Fallows and Hendrik Hertzberg, went on to become influential writers and magazine editors.

Several Presidential speech writers have written important memoirs about the Presidencies in which they served. These include Robert Sherwood (*Roosevelt and Hopkins*), Samuel Rosenman (*The Roosevelt I Knew*), Emmet Hughes (*Ordeal of Power*, which is about his years with Eisenhower), Theodore Sorensen (*Kennedy*), Arthur M. Schlesinger, Jr. (*A Thousand Days*), and William Safire (*Before the Fall*).
SEE ALSO *Fireside chat; Gettysburg Address; Messages, Presidential; News conferences, Presidential; State of the Union address; Washington's Farewell Address; White House Office*
SOURCES Peggy Noonan, *What I Saw at the Revolution* (New York: Random House, 1990). Jeffrey Tulis, *The Rhetorical Presidency* (Princeton, N.J.: Princeton University Press, 1987).

SPOILS

SEE *Patronage*

SPONSORING AND COSPONSORING LEGISLATION

The sponsors of a bill are its principal authors. Bills often take their sponsors' names, such as the Gramm-Rudman-Hollings Act, known for its three Senate sponsors, or the Humphrey-Hawkins Act, known for its chief sponsors in the Senate and House of Representatives. To demonstrate the popularity of a bill and to gather further support, sponsors will send out "Dear Colleague" letters, circulating the bill among other members and urging them to cosponsor it. The names of sponsors and cosponsors are printed at the top of each bill and in the *Congressional Record*.
SEE ALSO *"Dear Colleague" letters*

SQUARE DEAL

The Square Deal was the term used by Theodore Roosevelt in his campaigns against financial trusts, business interests that controlled markets or restrained trade, and the domination of the U.S. economy by the "predatory rich." "We demand that big business give people a square deal," he insisted on a nationwide tour in 1901 to rally public support for proposed legislation to regulate corporations. In his 1904 election campaign Roosevelt used the term to describe his domestic program, promising, "I shall see to it that every man has a square deal, no more and no less."

Roosevelt's Square Deal promised a "balance" between the claims of management and labor, producers and consumers. He was not against large corporations per se, and he had no intention of eliminating large accumulations of private wealth. Rather, he intended to act against their tendency to use the powers of national and state governments against labor and consumers. He called for the creation of a new cabinet department of Commerce and Industries, which would be able to regulate industries engaged in interstate commerce. Instead, in 1903 Congress created a Department of Commerce and Labor but did not give it the regulatory powers proposed by the President.

Roosevelt then turned to the courts to reduce excessive corporate power in the marketplace. His most famous lawsuit was filed in 1902 against the Northern Securities Company, a creation of the financier J. P. Morgan. Along with E. H. Harriman and James J. Hill, Morgan had combined several railroads into the company in an effort to obtain a monopoly on rail transport in the Midwest and Far West. The Supreme Court upheld Roosevelt in 1904 and dissolved the merger. Roosevelt also filed suits against Standard Oil and tobacco and meat trusts for violations of the Sherman Anti-Trust Act.

In 1906 Roosevelt consolidated his Square Deal with several legislative victories. Congress passed the Meat Inspection Act, the Pure Food and Drug Act, and the Hepburn Railroad Act, which regulated industries and prevented trusts from fixing prices or providing consumers with unsafe products.

SEE ALSO *Roosevelt, Theodore*

SOURCES Richard Hofstadter, "The Conservative as Progressive," in *The American Political Tradition* (New York: Knopf, 1948). George W. Mowry, *Theodore Roosevelt and the Progressive Movement* (Madison: University of Wisconsin Press, 1946).

STAFF, CONGRESSIONAL

Congress relies on a large staff to get its work done. By the 1990s the House of Representatives was hiring some 11,000 staff members and the Senate another 6,000. Counting the additional support staff of the Architect of the Capitol, Capitol Police, Library of Congress (including the Congressional Research Service), General Accounting Office, Congressional Budget Office, and Office of Technology Assessment, the total number of legislative branch employees topped 30,000. Still, this is a smaller staff than that of some cabinet departments. Critics have called the congressional staff an anonymous bureaucracy of "unelected representatives." Senator Herman Talmadge (Democrat–Georgia) complained:

> We have got a lot of bright-eyed, idealistic young people right out of law school, seeking new worlds to conquer. They spend virtually all of their time writing speeches for Senators, and developing brand new spending programs for Senators to introduce . . . and if you double the

staff you double the amendments and double the costly new programs.

But was the increased staff the cause of the congressional work load or the result of it? In the 19th century clerks were hired only for the months that Congress was in session. Only a few committees, such as the Ways and Means, Finance, Printing, and Claims Committees, had enough work to hire a year-round staff. The first committee clerks handled the mail and supervised the printing of committee reports, hearing transcripts, and other official documents. By 1900 there were still fewer than 300 congressional employees. These staff members got their jobs mostly through patronage—that is, congressional sponsors hired them to reward them for their political activities and party loyalty.

The construction of Senate and House office buildings gave every member of Congress an office and the ability to employ a small personal staff, consisting of a secretary and one or two assistants. When they drafted complex legislation, members of Congress often had to rely on the executive branch agencies to provide the language for the bills, prepare reports, and even ghostwrite their speeches. Lobbyists from corporate law firms also provided assistance in drafting legislation to help their clients.

Legislative Reorganization Acts After World War II Congress sought to modernize its proceedings and gain independent expertise. The Legislative Reorganization Act of 1946 provided a professional, nonpartisan staff for every committee, authorized the creation and government funding of Republican and Democratic policy committees, and expanded members' personal staffs by creating the post of administrative assistant. The Reorganization Act also expanded the Legislative Reference Service, later renamed the Congressional Research Service, to provide nonpartisan expertise on almost every issue with which Congress deals. At the same time, cold war global responsibilities and the growth of government services at home pressured Congress into remaining in session for more months each year to handle an ever-increasing work load. Between the 1940s and 1970s the staff expanded steadily to match this demand on members' time.

Further reorganization in the 1970s provided every committee member with his or her own staff person on that committee and also established a separate staff to serve the minority party's interests on that committee. The combined effect of these reforms was to lessen Congress's dependence on executive agencies, lobbyists, and other outside sources for gathering information and preparing legislation. The reforms also lessened the dependence of minority party members on staffs that previously had been appointed by committee chairmen from the majority party. Even junior members of the majority party gained more independence by having their own staff members participate in the committees' work.

Women and minorities on the staff In 1970 women staff members examined the range of jobs and salaries on Capitol Hill. They protested that women were not employed in the highest posts and were paid less than men doing comparable work. During the next two decades, salaries became more equal and women held more high-level positions, including the elected posts of secretary of the Senate and sergeant at arms. Congress had also exempted itself from civil rights legislation and other bills that provided for fair employment practices. These bills were enforced by the executive branch through the Justice Department, which could not hold jurisdiction over the legislature. Although members of Congress pledged to comply voluntarily with these laws, the hiring of minorities continued to lag.

Congressional staff turnover Members of the congressional staff are not protected by civil service laws. They serve at the pleasure of the member who employed them or the majority party of their house. When the legislative majority switches from one party to the other, many staff members are replaced by people from the incoming majority party. Even without a change in party, there is regular turnover in the staff. Those who work for individual members tend to be relatively young, often fresh out of college. They work long hours at relatively low pay. Energetic and eager, they seek the opportunity to influence government policy and to advance their own careers after they leave Capitol Hill. Committee staff tend to be older, hold postgraduate degrees, and stay longer in their jobs.

Some staff members are "legislative technicians" who draft amendments and prepare analyses of bills for the members. Others handle political functions, answer mail, keep the files, deal with press relations, coordinate members' schedules, provide computer services, operate home-district offices, conduct research, monitor the work of executive agencies and federal funding, and handle innumerable other tasks to enable Congress to function effectively.

SEE ALSO *Legislative Reorganization Acts (1946 and 1970); Patronage*

SOURCES Harrison W. Fox and Susan Webb Hammond, *Congressional Staffs: The Invisible Force in American Lawmaking* (New York: Free Press, 1979). Michael J. Malbin, *Unelected Representatives: Congressional Staff and the Future of Representative Government* (New York: Basic Books, 1980).

STAFF OF THE SUPREME COURT, NONJUDICIAL

More than 319 permanent staff members assist the justices in carrying out the business of the U.S. Supreme Court. Most of these employees of the Court work for one of the five officers, whose jobs were established by law: administrative assistant to the chief justice, clerk of the Court, reporter of decisions, marshal, and librarian.

Administrative assistant to the chief

justice The administrative assistant, with a staff of three, assists the chief justice in management of nonjudicial business, such as the administration of the Judicial Conference of the United States, the Federal Judicial Center, and the Administrative Office of the United States Courts. The administrative assistant also supervises personnel matters and budgets of the Court.

Clerk of the Court The clerk of the court oversees a staff of 25 people. Among other duties, they manage dockets (agendas) and calendars of the Court, keep track of petitions and briefs that are submitted to the Court, notify lower courts of Supreme Court actions and decisions, and advise lawyers, upon request, about rules and procedures of the Court.

Reporter of decisions The reporter supervises a staff of nine people who are responsible for recording, editing, and printing the opinions of the Court. The reporter of decisions oversees the official publication of the Supreme Court case decisions in *United States Reports,* which is printed by the U.S. Government Printing Office.

Marshal With a staff of more than 200 people, the marshal of the Supreme Court manages the security, physical facilities, and payroll of the Court. The marshal receives all important visitors to the Supreme Court Building. He also takes charge of the safety of justices when they carry out formal duties outside the Supreme Court Building.

The marshal declares the beginning of each public session of the Court. He stands at one side of the bench and announces, "The Honorable, the chief justice and the associate justices of the Supreme Court of the United States." As the justices file into the courtroom, the marshal declares, "Oyez, oyez, oyez [Hear ye]: All persons having business before the Honorable, the Supreme Court of the United States, are admonished to draw near and give their attention, for the Court is now sitting. God save the United States and this honorable Court."

Librarian A staff of 25 helps the librarian of the Supreme Court manage more than 250,000 books and several computerized databases. The librarian supervises the library in the Supreme Court Building and arranges for interlibrary loans.

In addition to the five court officers described above, other employees work for the Office of the Legal Counsel, Office of the Curator, Public Information Office, and the Data Systems Office.

Office of the Curator The curator of the Supreme Court has the duty of recording and preserving the history of the Court. Chief Justice Warren Burger established the Office of the Curator in 1973. The office collects and preserves memorabilia, such as photographs, prints, manuscripts, and videotapes, that are related to the lives and work of the justices.

Items from the collections of the curator are used in the two exhibits the curator's staff prepares each year. These exhibits are presented in the lower Great Hall of the Supreme Court Building.

The curator's staff responds regularly to requests for information about the Supreme Court from scholars, the justices, other federal judges, and the general public. The staff also conducts hourly lectures and tours for the thousands of visitors who annually visit the Supreme Court Building.

Office of the Legal Counsel Two attorneys assist the Court with legal research. The attorneys prepare for the justices summaries and analyses of the cases in which the Court has original jurisdiction (cases not on appeal from lower courts, but heard for the first time by the Supreme Court). This office serves as a general counsel for the Court; that is, it provides legal information for the justices upon request. Unlike the justices' law clerks, who serve short terms, the Office of the Legal Counsel provides the continuous legal research services of experienced attorneys.

Public Information Office A staff of four people works for the Public Information Office. This office distributes 4,000 slip opinions on Supreme Court cases— preliminary, unedited full-text reports on opinions that are circulated within three days of decisions. The slip opinions help newspaper reporters and broadcasters to publicize news of Supreme Court opinions quickly; without the slip opinions, they would have to wait for the fully edited and official publication of the Court opinions. The Public Information Office maintains a press room and broadcast booths for the use of journalists. One hundred seventy-five bench copies of the Court's opinions, preliminary full-text reports, are provided to reporters on the day the opinion is announced by the Court. The Public Information Office also transmits the bench copies of opinions electronically to legal data-base services, such as LEXIS and WESTLAW.

SEE ALSO *Clerk of the Court; Clerks of the justices; Reporter of decisions*

STAFF, WHITE HOUSE

SEE *Executive office of the President; White House Office*

STANDING TO SUE

A person who has the right to bring legal action against another party has standing to sue that party. A party who is injured by another party has standing to sue that party, if the injured one can show that his rights were violated. A party has standing to sue the government only if that party has been injured by the government. For example, if local police conduct an illegal search of a person's home, the person has standing to sue the government under the 4th and 14th Amendments to the Constitution.

By contrast, if a person has no justifiable connection to an alleged wrongful action by the government, then the person has no standing to sue in that regard. For example, a citizen of the United States does not have standing to sue the federal government for recognizing a foreign government that has been charged with violations of international law.

STARE DECISIS

SEE *Precedents, judicial*

STATE COURTS

Some cases that go to the Supreme Court originated in the courts of the 50 states. The direct line of appeal, however, is only from the highest appellate court of a state. For example, a case originating in a trial court in Indiana must be appealed first to the Indiana Supreme Court before it can be heard by the U.S. Supreme Court.

In addition, state-level cases may be appealed to the U.S. Supreme Court only if they involve federal questions—issues pertaining to the U.S. Constitution, federal treaties, or federal laws. State courts are required to act in accordance with the Constitution, as well as federal statutes and treaties made under the Constitution. They must recognize the supremacy of federal law—acts of Congress as well as the Constitution—over state law. And they must interpret federal law in accordance with prevailing decisions of the U.S. Supreme Court.

SEE ALSO *Federalism; Judicial review*

STATE LEGISLATURES

Just as many state capitol buildings are modeled after the U.S. Capitol, most state legislatures resemble the U.S. Congress. The state legislatures are mostly bicameral (they have two chambers), with a House and Senate; do most of their work through committees; control appropriations; and oversee the state governors and executive agencies. However, there are also significant differences. Using a device called the line-item veto, for example, most governors can reject a single item in a large appropriation bill, whereas the President must sign or reject an entire bill.

Initially, state legislatures had a close relationship with Congress. Until the ratification of the 17th Amendment to the Constitution in 1913, state legislatures elected U.S. senators, and many members of the House and Senate had previously served in their state legislature. During the early Congresses, some state legislatures also tried to "instruct" their senators on how to vote. But senators showed no inclination to follow their instructions.

In the federal system, the states have also served as "laboratories" of legislation, notably in social matters. State legislatures pioneered in the development of railroad regulations, restrictions against child labor, health and unemployment insurance, and other issues well in advance of the national Congress. At other times, Congress has prompted state legislatures to act by promising to give or withhold federal funds unless the state legislatures complied with federal rules (such as setting a minimum drinking age and maximum speed limits to receive federal highway money).

STATE OF THE UNION ADDRESS

The State of the Union address is the speech the President makes to a joint session of Congress at the beginning of the legislative session. This address is in accordance with Article 2, Section 3, of the Constitution, which provides that the President shall "from time to time give to Congress information of the State of the Union." Since 1945 the speech has been known as the State of the Union address.

In writing or in person Presidents George Washington and John Adams gave their State of the Union messages in person. But to President Thomas Jefferson the practice too closely resembled the British monarch's annual address to the houses of Parliament and was therefore too regal for his tastes. Jefferson also lisped and disliked

public speaking. So he sent his message in writing to be read aloud to Congress by a clerk. This practice continued for the rest of the 19th century and had the effect of diminishing the President's role in setting the legislative agenda. In 1893 a journalist observed that although the President's annual message was "regularly and respectfully submitted to the proper committees for consideration, it is very rare that any suggestion made by the Executive has any practical result."

Then in 1913 President Woodrow Wilson dramatically went to Congress to deliver his State of the Union message in person. This act symbolized Wilson's belief that Presidents should take a more active role in proposing and promoting legislation. Calling for quick passage of a banking bill, he also found it an "urgent necessity" for Congress to pass bills on agriculture, railroads, and mine safety. Wilson's discussion of Presidential priorities deeply offended many constitutional lawyers, who believed that the President should leave national priorities to Congress. Wilson also addressed Congress in person on a tariff act, reminding the lawmakers that he was "a person, not a mere department of government, hailing Congress from some isolated island of jealous power . . . a human being trying to cooperate with other human beings in a common service."

All Presidents since Wilson have continued his practice of addressing Congress in person to build support for their programs. The first message to be broadcast on the radio was delivered by Calvin Coolidge in 1923. It aided his attempt to secure the Republican nomination for President the following year. Franklin Roosevelt announced much of his New Deal program in his State of the Union addresses, which were also broadcast on radio. Harry Truman presented his entire Fair Deal program of civil rights, housing, and medical care in his addresses.

President Dwight Eisenhower's 1953 State of the Union address was the first to be televised. By the 1960s the address was switched to prime-time viewing hours in the evening to attract the maximum audience. Richard Nixon not only gave a State of the Union address but followed it up in 1971 with a State of the World address outlining his vision of U.S. foreign policy. No President since has given two such speeches to Congress.

Preparation of the State of the Union address takes months and is itself part of the process of government decision making about public policy. The President asks department secretaries and outside experts for ideas about new programs. Cabinet councils and Presidential advisory agencies help the President sift through these ideas and determine priorities. The President then calls on speech writers and political advisers in the White House Office to help prepare drafts of the speech.

Determining what goes into the President's speech is the first step in the struggle to turn ideas into new government programs. As Nixon's speech writer Bryce Harlow put it, each cabinet secretary was "demanding that more space be given to their problems, to which I had to respond that the President says he wants this document kept shorter than a two-hour speech." A few weeks before the speech is to be delivered, the White House may leak parts of it to reporters as a "trial balloon." If public reaction, as gauged by the President's pollsters, is favorable, the proposals will remain in the President's speech, but controversial items might be dropped.

A ceremonial occasion Much ceremony accompanies the State of the Union message. Members of the Senate march in procession the length of the Capitol from the Senate to the larger House chamber. Members of the cabinet and the Supreme Court take seats in the front rows of the chamber, and honored guests fill the galleries. The House doorkeeper loudly announces: "Mr. Speaker, the President of the United States," and members rise for a standing ovation. Unlike the British Parliament, whose members listen in respectful silence to their monarch's annual address, members of Congress punctuate

a President's message with applause. Members from the President's party heartily cheer his proposals, while members of the opposition party remain quietly restrained. Modern Presidents have taken the opportunity to talk beyond Congress, to address the nation as a whole as a means of stimulating public support for their programs in the legislative battles that lie ahead.

SOURCES Barbara Hinckley, *The Symbolic Presidency* (New York: Routledge, Chapman & Hall, 1990). Jeffrey Tulis, *The Rhetorical Presidency* (Princeton, N.J.: Princeton University Press, 1987).

STATUTE

A statute is a written law enacted by a legislature. A federal statute is a law enacted by Congress. State statutes are enacted by state legislatures; those that violate the U.S. Constitution may be struck down by the Supreme Court if the issue is appealed to the Court.

STEEL SEIZURE (1952)

In 1952, President Harry Truman seized steel mills across the United States and put them under federal government control during a labor dispute in order to guarantee steel production during the Korean War. The seizure was overturned by the Supreme Court in the case of *Youngstown Sheet and Tube Co.* v. *Sawyer* (1952), one of the few times in U.S. history that a Presidential executive order has been ruled unconstitutional.

During the Korean War wages and prices were regulated by government agencies according to legislation passed by Congress. In 1952 the labor unions were negotiating with the steel companies for an industrywide settlement. The Wage Stabilization Board recommendations for higher wages were accepted by labor but rejected by management. The Office of Price Stability would have permitted price increases only if they were much lower than those desired by industry. With talks at an impasse, the unions went on strike.

Truman felt that he could not let the strike continue when defense industries depended on steel production. The President considered applying the Defense Production Act of 1950 to end the strike, but neither management nor labor was willing to apply its arbitration provisions. Under the Selective Service Act of 1948 the President could seize factories if orders were not being fulfilled. But the government would have to place direct orders with steel plants, the process would take time, and the Defense Department was pressing for immediate action.

Truman also could have applied the Taft-Hartley Act of 1947, which regulated peacetime labor-management relations. Under Title II, National Emergency Provisions, of the act, the President could appoint a board of inquiry to determine the facts and obtain a federal court injunction for a 60-day "cooling off" period. Fifteen days later, the National Labor Relations Board would conduct a secret vote of workers on the last employer offer. If the strike still could not be settled, the President could ask Congress for a law ending the strike.

Truman did not wish to use this law: wildcat strikes might imperil production, and there was no assurance that the courts would grant the injunction or that Congress would impose a settlement if all else failed. Moreover, the President had vetoed the Taft-Hartley bill in 1947 as antilabor, and it was opposed by the Democratic party and his labor allies. If he invoked that law, he would lose face.

Truman decided to seize the mills based on his constitutional authority as President and commander in chief. (Woodrow Wilson in World War I and Franklin Roosevelt in World War II had both seized defense plants to ensure that war production authorized by Congress was maintained.) Truman issued Executive Order 10340, which directed his secretary of commerce "to take possession of and operate the plants and facilities of certain steel companies." Truman delivered a speech to the American people justifying the seizures, but a rebuttal by the president of one of the seized companies was more effective: 43 percent of the public opposed Truman.

The steel companies sued the secretary of commerce. In June the Supreme Court issued its decision. Only three justices of the Supreme Court were impressed with the President's argument that he had constitutional authority to seize the mills. Six justices, in several opinions, ruled against the President. Each emphasized that Congress had legislated the procedures it wished to be used in strike situations. Congress had specifically rejected the possibility of Presidential seizure when it passed the Taft-Hartley Act. The Supreme Court forced Truman to return the mills to the owners, because, in Justice Robert Jackson's words, he had taken his constitutional powers as commander in chief and had "turned inward, not because of rebellion, but because of a lawful economic struggle between industry and labor." Such a struggle could not be resolved unilaterally by the President, the Court ruled, but must follow the laws passed by Congress. The strike lasted seven weeks after the mills were returned to the owners and then was settled.

SEE ALSO *Commander in chief; Executive orders; Truman, Harry S.; Youngstown Sheet & Tube Co. v. Sawyer*

SOURCES Maeva Marcus, *Truman and the Steel Seizure Case* (New York: Columbia University Press, 1977).

STEVENS, JOHN PAUL
Associate Justice, 1975–

- Born: Apr. 20, 1920, Chicago, Ill.
- Education: University of Chicago, B.A., 1941; Northwestern University School of Law, J.D., 1947
- Previous government service: law clerk to Justice Wiley B. Rutledge, 1947–48; associate counsel, Subcommittee on the Study of Monopoly Power, House

Judiciary Committee, 1951; U.S. Attorney General's National Committee to Study the Antitrust Laws, 1953–55; judge, Seventh Circuit Court of Appeals, 1970–75
- Appointed by President Gerald R. Ford Nov. 28, 1975; replaced William O. Douglas, who retired
- Supreme Court term: confirmed by the Senate Dec. 17, 1975, by a 98–0 vote

John Paul Stevens has been an independent thinker on the Supreme Court. He has often written separate concurring opinions and dissenting opinions.

Justice Stevens has tended to support national government authority in cases on federalism, which has restricted the powers and independent activities of state governments. In particular, he has favored broad interpretations of the Constitution's "commerce clause" (Article 1, Section 8), which grants power to Congress to regulate trade among the states.

Justice Stevens has tended to support protection of individual rights, especially 1st Amendment freedoms of religion, speech, and assembly. He wrote notably for the Court, for example, in *Wallace* v. *Jaffree* (1985) to defend strict separation of church and state. In 1997 he led the Court in striking down a federal law designed to ban "indecent" material from the Internet in the case of *Reno* v. *American Civil Liberties Union*.

SEE ALSO *Reno* v. *American Civil Liberties Union; Wallace* v. *Jaffree*
SOURCES Bradley C. Canon, "Justice John Paul Stevens: The Lone Ranger in a Black Robe," in *The Burger Court: Political and Judicial Profiles*, edited by Charles M. Lamb and Stephen C. Halpern (Urbana: University of Illinois Press, 1991).

STEVENSON, ADLAI
Vice President

- Born: Oct. 25, 1835, Christian County, Ky.
- Political party: Democrat
- Education: Illinois Wesleyan University, 1854; Centre College, 1855–57; read law, 1858
- Military service: none
- Previous government service: master in chancery in Illinois, 1860–64; Illinois state's attorney, 1865–69; U.S. House of Representatives, 1875–77, 1879–81; first assistant postmaster general, 1885–89
- Vice President under Grover Cleveland, 1893–97
- Subsequent government service: monetary commission to Europe, 1897
- Died: June 14, 1914, Chicago, Ill.

Active in Democratic politics, Adlai Stevenson campaigned for Stephen A. Douglas against Abraham Lincoln in the 1858 Senate contest. He was appointed master in chancery (state judge) in Illinois in 1860 and served through 1864. He was first assistant postmaster general in Grover Cleveland's first administration, and "Adlai's Axe" chopped down 40,000 Republican postmasters. Because of his actions, the Republican-controlled Senate blocked his nomination for the Supreme Court in 1889. After obtaining the support of the Illinois delegation for Cleveland at the Democratic convention in 1892, he was rewarded with the Vice Presidential nomination, and for the next four years he presided over the Senate that had blocked him from the Supreme Court.

After leaving office, Stevenson served on a monetary commission to Europe in 1897. He ran for Vice President in 1900 on William Jennings Bryan's losing ticket and was defeated in the race for governor of Illinois in 1908.

Stevenson's grandson, Adlai E. Stevenson II, unsuccessfully ran for President twice on the Democratic ticket, in 1952 and 1956. His great-grandson, Adlai E. Stevenson III, served as a U.S. senator from Illinois from 1970 to 1980.

SOURCES Leonard Schlup, "The American Chameleon: Adlai E. Stevenson and the Quest for the Vice Presidency in Gilded Age Politics," *Presidential Studies Quarterly* 21 (Summer 1991): 511–29.

STEVENS, THADDEUS

- Born: Apr. 4, 1792, Danville, Va.
- Political party: Republican
- Education: Dartmouth College, graduated, 1814
- Representative from Pennsylvania: 1849–53, 1859–68
- Died: Aug. 11, 1868, Washington, D.C.

A lame, old man with a weak heart, so feeble that he had to be carried into the House chamber on a chair, Representative Thaddeus Stevens remained influential and powerful enough to win the impeachment of President Andrew Johnson by the House. As chairman of the Ways and Means Committee, Stevens was the leader of the radical Republicans in the House during the Reconstruction era. He used his powers to block the President from readmitting the former Confederate states into the Union until they had pledged full equality for the freedmen, including the right to vote. Southerners detested Stevens as the symbol of what they saw as a fanatical and vindictive Reconstruction, a man who supported voting rights for African Americans only to maintain the Republican party in office. The freedmen, and many Northerners, revered Stevens as a defender of the ideals of the Declaration of Independence, that all people are created equal and endowed with inalienable rights.
SEE ALSO *Reconstruction, congressional*
SOURCES Fawn Brodie, *Thaddeus Stevens: Scourge of the South* (New York: Norton, 1959).

STEWART, POTTER
Associate Justice, 1958–81

- Born: Jan. 23, 1915, Jackson, Mich.
- Education: Yale College, B.A., 1937; fellow, Cambridge University, 1937–38; Yale Law School, LL.B., 1941
- Previous government service: Cincinnati City Council, Ohio, 1950–53; vice mayor of Cincinnati, 1952–53; judge, Sixth Circuit Court of Appeals, 1954–58

- Appointed by President Dwight D. Eisenhower as a recess appointment Oct. 14, 1958; replaced Harold H. Burton, who retired; nominated by Eisenhower Jan. 17, 1959
- Supreme Court term: confirmed by the Senate May 5, 1959, by a 70–17 vote; retired July 3, 1981
- Died: Dec. 7, 1985, Hanover, N.H.

Potter Stewart was an especially strong defender of individual rights protected by the 1st, 4th, and 14th Amendments. For example, in *Katz* v. *United States* (1967), Stewart strengthened the protection of the 4th Amendment against government's invasion of an individual's privacy. He argued that private conversations must be protected against police interception no matter where the conversation takes place. Stewart wrote: "The Fourth Amendment protects people not places." Thus, a microphone placed against the wall of a telephone booth by federal investigators was held to be a violation of the 4th Amendment's ban on "unwarranted searches and seizures" and a violation of the right of privacy.

Justice Stewart had a way with words, and many of his statements in Supreme Court opinions have become famous quotations. For example, he admitted his difficulty in stating an exact definition of pornography in *Jacobellis* v. *Ohio* (1964); Stewart wrote this often-quoted statement about pornography: "I know it when I see it."
SEE ALSO *Katz v. United States*
SOURCES Tinsley E. Yarbrough, "Justice Potter Stewart: Decisional Patterns in Search of Doctrinal Moorings," in *The Burger Court: Political and Judicial Profiles,* edited by Charles M. Lamb and Stephen C. Halpern (Urbana: University of Illinois Press, 1991).

STONE, HARLAN FISKE
Associate Justice, 1925–41
Chief Justice, 1941–46

- Born: Oct. 11, 1872, Chesterfield, N.H.
- Education: Amherst College, B.A.,

1894, M.A., 1897, LL.D., 1913; Columbia University Law School, LL.B., 1898
- Previous government service: U.S. attorney general, 1924–25
- Appointed by President Calvin Coolidge to be an associate justice Jan. 5, 1925; replaced Joseph McKenna, who retired; appointed chief justice by President Franklin D. Roosevelt June 12, 1941; replaced Chief Justice Charles Evans Hughes, who retired
- Supreme Court term: confirmed as an associate justice by the Senate Feb. 5, 1925, by a 71–6 vote; confirmed by the Senate as chief justice June 27, 1941, by a voice vote; served until Apr. 22, 1946
- Died: Apr. 22, 1946, Washington, D.C.

Harlan Fiske Stone was the only university professor ever to become chief justice of the United States. As a Republican appointed by Democratic President Franklin Roosevelt, Stone is one of only two chief justices nominated by a President from a different political party. (Chief Justice Edward White was the other one.)

Before entering federal government service, Stone was a professor and dean of the Columbia University School of Law (1910–23). He served under President Calvin Coolidge as attorney general of the United States before Coolidge named Stone as associate justice of the Supreme Court. The great respect among the other justices for Stone led President Roosevelt to appoint him to the office of chief justice in 1941.

Throughout his term on the Supreme Court, Harlan Fiske Stone followed the principle of judicial self-restraint, which he stated in a dissenting opinion in *United States* v. *Butler* (1936). In this case, the Court struck down as unconstitutional the Agricultural Adjustment Act, which was part of the New Deal. Justice Stone could find no constitutional basis for this decision and claimed it was based on the anti–New Deal policy preferences of the Court's majority, which were used to override the policy-making majority in Congress. Justice Stone wrote that the President and Congress are restrained by the "ballot box

and the processes of democratic government. . . . The only check on our own exercise of power is our own sense of [judicial] self-restraint."

According to Justice Stone, the Court should leave the making of policies and laws to the executive and legislative branches. The Court should not substitute its policy preferences for those of the democratically elected Congress and President because this would be an unconstitutional overextension of the Court's power.

Justice Stone opposed the judicial activism of the justices who opposed, for conservative political reasons, the New Deal programs of President Roosevelt. Later, as chief justice, Stone opposed the judicial activism of liberal justices who wanted to expand the power and benefits of organized labor.

Chief Justice Stone acted strongly to support 1st Amendment freedoms in the "flag salute cases" of 1940 and 1943; he dissented against the Court's majority in *Minersville School District* v. *Gobitis* (1940), which upheld a state law requiring students in public schools to salute the U.S. flag and pledge allegiance to the United States. Three years later, Chief Justice Stone was instrumental in organizing the Court's majority in *West Virginia State Board of Education* v. *Barnette* (1943), which overturned the *Gobitis* decision. Thus, a state law requiring students in public schools to salute the flag was struck down as a violation of the free exercise of religion by Jehovah's Witnesses.

Chief Justice Stone, however, led the majority in the Japanese-American internment cases, which restricted individual rights of Japanese Americans in favor of national security concerns during World War II. For example, in the cases of *Korematsu* v. *United States* (1944) and *Hirabayashi* v. *United States* (1943), Chief Justice Stone voted to uphold federal laws restricting the freedom of Japanese Americans on the presumption, without evidence, that they might aid Japan, a World War II enemy of the United States. Most

Americans today believe these cases were decided unjustly.

SEE ALSO *Hirabayashi v. United States; Judicial activism and judicial restraint; Korematsu v. United States; Minersville School District v. Gobitis; West Virginia State Board of Education v. Barnette*

SOURCES S. J. Konefsky, *Chief Justice Stone and the Supreme Court* (New York: Macmillan, 1946). Alpheus Thomas Mason, *Harlan Fiske Stone: Pillar of the Law* (New York: Viking Press, 1956). Melvin I. Urofsky, *Division and Discord: The Supreme Court under Stone and Vinson, 1941–1953* (Columbia: University of South Carolina Press, 1997).

STORY, JOSEPH
Associate Justice, 1812–45

- Born: Sept. 18, 1779, Marblehead, Mass.
- Education: Harvard College, A.B., 1798; read law with Samuel Sewall and Samuel Putnam in Boston, 1799–1801
- Previous government service: Massachusetts House of Representatives, 1805–8, Speaker, 1811; U.S. representative from Massachusetts, 1808–9
- Appointed by President James Madison Nov. 15, 1811; replaced William Cushing, who died
- Supreme Court term: confirmed by the Senate Nov. 18, 1811, by a voice vote; served until Sept. 10, 1845
- Died: Sept. 10, 1845, Cambridge, Mass.

Joseph Story was one of the greatest justices of the Supreme Court. He worked in close partnership with Chief Justice John Marshall to establish the supremacy of the U.S. Constitution and the federal government over state constitutions and governments. He also acted with Marshall to uphold private property rights and economic liberty as fundamental principles of the Constitution. Finally, his peers generally agreed that Story was the greatest legal scholar and educator of his times.

Justice Story's greatest opinion for the Court was *Martin* v. *Hunter's Lessee* (1816), in which he upheld the constitutionality of Section 25 of the Judiciary Act of 1789. The constitutional question was whether or not the U.S. Supreme Court should have the power of judicial review over decisions of state courts, as specified in Section 25 of the Judiciary Act of 1789. Justice Story successfully argued for the constitutionality of Section 25, which bolstered the supremacy of the federal government in its relationships with the states. This decision was vindicated, once and for all, by Chief Justice John Marshall (with Story's support) in *Cohens* v. *Virginia* (1821).

Most of Chief Justice Marshall's great decisions were products of close collaboration with Justice Story. He endorsed and helped to develop John Marshall's broad construction of the Constitution. Likewise, Justice Story provided substance and technical precision for Chief Justice Marshall's great opinions about commercial law, contracts, and private property. Like Marshall, Story believed that protection of private property rights was necessary for the preservation of free government.

Throughout his long tenure on the Court, Justice Story found time to be a scholar and educator. He reorganized legal education at the Harvard Law School and served there as a distinguished professor of law. He also wrote several volumes that have become classics of legal scholarship. For example, his *Commentaries on the Constitution* (originally published in 1833) influenced constitutional thought throughout the 19th century. Story's achievements as a teacher and scholar made the Harvard Law School the biggest and best in the United States.

Justice Story's influence on the Court declined after the death of John Marshall in 1835, who was replaced as chief justice by Roger B. Taney. Under Taney's leadership, the Court reflected the ideas of Jacksonian democracy, not Marshall's federalism. The Jacksonians, unlike Marshall, tended to resist strong emphasis on federal government power. States' rights and powers were favored more than before, causing Justice Story to become a dissenter on the Court. Despite Story's declining status on the Taney Court, his influence outside the Court remained strong. His published commentaries on various aspects of the law shaped legal thinking long after his death.

SEE ALSO *Cohens v. Virginia; Martin v. Hunter's Lessee*

SOURCES Gerald T. Dunne, *Justice Joseph Story and the Rise of the Supreme Court* (New York: Simon & Schuster, 1970). James McClellan, *Joseph Story and the American Constitution: A Study in Political and Legal Thought* (Norman: University of Oklahoma Press, 1990). R. Kent Newmyer, "The Lost Legal World of Joseph Story," *Constitution* 4, no. 1 (Winter 1992): 58–65. R. Kent Newmyer, *Supreme Court Justice Joseph Story: Statesman of the Old Republic* (Chapel Hill: University of North Carolina Press, 1985).

STRICT SCRUTINY

SEE *Equality under the Constitution; Suspect classifications; Time, place, and manner rule*

STROMBERG V. CALIFORNIA

- 283 U.S. 359 (1931)
- Vote: 7–2
- For the Court: Hughes
- Dissenting: Butler and McReynolds

Yetta Stromberg was a 19-year-old counselor at a summer camp for children in California. She was also an active member of the Young Communist League. Stromberg taught the children about communist ideas and praised the communist government of the Soviet Union. In teaching one of her lessons, Stromberg had the children make a replica of the red flag of the U.S.S.R. She

and the children raised the banner and recited a pledge of allegiance to it.

The sheriff of San Bernardino County arrested Yetta Stromberg for teaching activities that violated a 1919 state law prohibiting the display of a red flag "as an emblem of opposition to organized government." After her conviction under the California law, Stromberg appealed to the U.S. Supreme Court.

The Issue Stromberg argued that the state of California had denied her right to freedom of speech guaranteed by the 1st and 14th Amendments to the U.S. Constitution. California attorneys claimed that the state law used to convict Stromberg was within the state's power to maintain order and safety.

Opinion of the Court Chief Justice Charles Evans Hughes, writing for the Court, overturned the conviction of Yetta Stromberg. The California "red flag law" was declared unconstitutional because it violated "the conception of liberty under the due process clause of the Fourteenth Amendment [which] embraces the right of free speech [in the First Amendment]."

Significance The *Stromberg* case was one of the Court's early uses of the 14th Amendment to incorporate the 1st Amendment's right to free speech—that is, to protect this right from infringement by a state government. The 14th Amendment states, "No State shall . . . deprive any person of life, liberty, or property, without due process of law."

In addition, in *Stromberg* the Court for the first time protected the substance of symbolic speech (a flag display) against state government restriction.

SEE ALSO *Freedom of speech and press; Gitlow v. New York; Incorporation doctrine; Near v. Minnesota*

SOURCES Paul L. Murphy, *The Meaning of Freedom of Speech* (Westport, Conn.: Greenwood, 1972). Rodney Smolla, *Free Speech in an Open Society* (New York: Knopf, 1992).

STRONG, WILLIAM
Associate Justice, 1870–80

- Born: May 6, 1808, Somers, Conn.
- Education: Yale University, B.A., 1828, M.A., 1831
- Previous government service: U.S. representative from Pennsylvania, 1847–51; justice, Pennsylvania Supreme Court, 1857–68
- Appointed by President Ulysses Grant Feb. 7, 1870; replaced Robert C. Grier, who retired
- Supreme Court term: confirmed by the Senate Feb. 18, 1870, by a voice vote; retired Dec. 14, 1880
- Died: Aug. 19, 1895, Lake Minnewaska, N.Y.

William Strong rarely wrote opinions for the Supreme Court during his 10-year term as an associate justice. He tended to side with the majority in decisions supporting property and contractual rights.

Justice Strong had a mixed record in civil rights cases. He joined the Court's majority in the *Slaughterhouse Cases* (1873) to restrict the rights of individuals under the 14th Amendment. However, he wrote for the Court in *Strauder* v. *West Virginia* (1880) the decision to strike down a state law excluding black people from juries. In a related case, *Ex parte Virginia* (1880), Justice Strong upheld a section of the Civil Rights Act of 1875 that banned racial discrimination in jury selection.

Justice Strong retired from the Court in robust health at the age of 72. He wanted to set an example for three colleagues on the Court who continued to serve despite age-related health problems that interfered with their performance. Within two years, the three resigned.

STUDENT RIGHTS UNDER THE CONSTITUTION

Justice Abe Fortas, writing for the U.S. Supreme Court in *Tinker* v. *Des Moines In-*dependent Community School District (1969), stated, "It can hardly be argued that either students or teachers shed their constitutional rights to freedom of speech or expression at the schoolhouse gate." The Supreme Court has ruled that some constitutional rights of students in public schools are the same as those of other people in the United States. Other constitutional rights, however, are not the same for children and adults. For example, people younger than 18 years old are not eligible to vote in public elections. Further, state governments may constitutionally deny to children certain privileges available to adults, such as licenses to drive automobiles or to marry.

The Supreme Court has also held that certain constitutional rights of adults or students outside of school are not necessarily the same for students in a public school. During the 20th century, the U.S. Supreme Court has decided cases about such constitutional rights of students as freedom of speech and press, religious freedom, freedom of assembly and association, protection against unreasonable searches and seizures, and due process of law.

Free speech and press In 1969, the Supreme Court upheld student rights to free speech in a landmark decision, *Tinker* v. *Des Moines Independent Community School District*. The Court ruled that students who wore black armbands to school to protest U.S. involvement in the Vietnam War had a constitutional right to such freedom of expression. In this case and others, however, the Court has affirmed the authority of school officials to regulate freedom of expression with regard to the time, place, and manner of the spoken or written messages. School officials may therefore limit student speech in order to prevent serious disruption of the teaching and learning processes of the school.

For example, in *Bethel School District No. 403* v. *Fraser* (1986), the Court upheld the restriction of a student's speech by school officials because the speech was obscene and therefore disrupted the educational process. Chief Justice Warren Burger, writing for the Court, declared, "The undoubted freedom to advocate unpopular and controversial views in schools and classrooms must be balanced against the society's countervailing interest in teaching students the boundaries of socially appropriate behavior."

In *Hazelwood School District* v. *Kuhlmeier* (1988) the Court upheld restrictions by school officials on the content of articles printed in a school newspaper. The students' writing for this publication was viewed by the Court as part of the school curriculum and therefore subject to regulation by school authorities. Justice Byron White, writing for the Court, argued, "A school need not tolerate student speech that is inconsistent with its basic educational mission, even though the government could not censor similar speech outside the school." The Court in this case emphasized that the constitutional rights of students in public schools are not necessarily and always the same as the rights of individuals in other places. The Court also stressed that the rights of students in extracurricular activities of the school are broader than their rights in activities of the school's formal program of studies. Thus, Justice White concluded, "It is only when the decision to censor a school sponsored publication . . . has no valid educational purpose [or is not part of the school curriculum] that the First Amendment [can be used] to protect students' constitutional rights."

Protection against unreasonable searches and seizures   The Court has ruled (*New Jersey* v. *T.L.O.*, 1985) that the 4th Amendment rights of public school students are not exactly the same as the rights of adults in nonschool settings. In the *T.L.O.* case, the Court permitted school officials to conduct a search of a student's purse without a warrant, on the grounds that this action was reasonable under the circumstances. There was reason to suspect that the search would turn up evidence of violation of either the law or school rules, so the warrantless search was

upheld even though a similar search outside of school would have been ruled unconstitutional.

In line with the *T.L.O.* decision, federal courts have upheld warrantless searches of student lockers when there is a reasonable suspicion of uncovering evidence of actions violating laws or school rules. School authorities may suspend or expel students from school for possession of illegal drugs, alcohol, or weapons uncovered by warrantless searches of lockers or purses. In the 1995 case of *Vernonia School District* v. *Acton,* the Supreme Court sanctioned school-based drug testing of student athletes.

Due process rights   The 5th and 14th Amendments to the Constitution guarantee due process of law—certain legal procedural rights—to individuals charged with breaking the law and to those facing deprivation of life, liberty, or property by the government. In *Goss* v. *Lopez* (1975) the Supreme Court considered the due process rights of students suspended from school for violating school rules. The Court held that public school officials must follow minimal due process procedures when suspending a student from school for 10 days or less. Students facing such suspension, ruled the Court, must at least receive oral or written notice of charges against them and an opportunity for a hearing to present their side regarding the charges. However, the Court said that due process rights for short-term suspensions do not require that the students charged with wrongdoing have the rights to assistance of legal counsel, to question witnesses against them, and to call their own witnesses to refute the charges against them, which are due process rights specified in the 6th Amendment to the Constitution. Further, the Court said that notice of charges and a hearing should be provided before suspension, unless a student's presence in school threatens the safety, property, or educational opportunities of others.

In its *Goss* ruling, the Court emphasized that it was responding only to an issue about suspensions of 10 days or less. It advised school officials that "longer suspensions or expulsion for the remainder of the school term, or permanently, may require more formal procedures."

In *Honig* v. *Doe* (1988) the Supreme Court ruled on the due process rights of disabled students. Before school officials expel a disabled student from school, they must determine whether the offending behavior was caused by the student's disability. If so, the student cannot be expelled from school. However, the disabled student may be suspended from school, for no more than 10 days, even if the offending behavior stemmed from the disability. If the offending behavior was not caused by the student's disability, the student may be expelled, following careful observance of due process rights, just like a student without a disability. However, a disabled student expelled from school may not be totally deprived of educational services by the public school system.

The Supreme Court in *Ingraham* v. *Wright* (1977) decided that school officials may carry out corporal (physical) punishment as a means of disciplining students without providing due process rights to the student. Lower federal courts have, however, spelled out minimal due process procedures for corporal punishment, which involve prior notice to students about the kinds of misbehavior that could result in corporal punishment and administration of such punishment by one school official in the presence of another school official. Even though the Supreme Court has neither banned nor strictly limited corporal punishment in schools, many school districts and some state legislatures have regulated or eliminated this kind of punishment.

Student rights to religious liberty The Supreme Court has upheld the right of students in public schools to free exercise of religious belief. In *West Virginia State Board of Education* v. *Barnette* (1943), the Court overturned a state flag-salute law. The Court held that the state law forced some students (Jehovah's Witnesses) to sa-

lute the flag even though this action violated their religious beliefs.

The Supreme Court has consistently opposed state and local laws that require public school students to pray or otherwise engage in religious activities during the school day or during school-sponsored extracurricular activities. This restriction has been maintained even when the religious content of the prayers or other activities has been nondenominational, nonpreferential, and voluntary, as long as the government has sanctioned the activity. The Court has held (in *Engel* v. *Vitale*, 1962; *Abington School District* v. *Schempp*, 1963; and *Wallace* v. *Jaffree*, 1985) that these kinds of public school–sanctioned religious activities violate the establishment clause of the 1st Amendment to the Constitution.

Further, in *Stone* v. *Graham* (1980) the Court ruled unconstitutional a state law that required copies of the Ten Commandments to be displayed in public school classrooms because it violated the 1st Amendment's establishment clause. And in 1992 (*Lee* v. *Weisman*) the Court prohibited prayers as part of an official public school graduation ceremony. However, students are free to organize, on their own and without school support, voluntary religious programs associated with graduation. In 1993, the Court let stand a decision of the Court of Appeals for the Fifth Circuit (*Jones* v. *Clear Creek Independent School District*) that ruled that a Texas school district's policy allowing students to voluntarily lead prayers at public school graduation ceremonies does not violate the 1st Amendment's establishment clause.

The Supreme Court rulings on prayer and religious programs in public schools do not prohibit individuals from quietly praying, on their own, during the school day or during school-sponsored extracurricular activities. And students may participate voluntarily in religious events before or after class on school grounds, such as "see you at the flag pole" prayer programs. School officials may neither promote nor prevent such activities. Further, the

Court's rulings do not prohibit teaching and learning about religious beliefs in history or literature courses, as long as teachers refrain from the indoctrination of particular religions.

The Court has supported student rights to free speech and free exercise of religion by upholding the federal Equal Access Act in *Board of Education of the Westside Community Schools* v. *Mergens* (1990). This federal law states that it is unlawful for "any public secondary school which receives Federal financial assistance and which has a limited open forum to deny equal access or a fair opportunity to, or discriminate against, any students who wish to conduct a meeting within the limited open forum on the basis of the religious, political, philosophical, or other content of the speech at such meetings." The Court has ruled that the federal Equal Access Act does not violate the establishment clause and does provide opportunity for students to voluntarily form a religious club and hold meetings of their organization on school premises after school hours.

In *Lamb's Chapel* v. *Center Moriches Union Free School District* (1993) the Supreme Court held that a New York public school district violated the freedom of expression and free exercise of religion rights of a church-supported group by not letting it use school facilities to hold a meeting after completion of the formal school day. The public school officials opened school buildings to other community groups for meetings. Thus, it was unlawful, said the Court, for them to deny access to a church group because the group wanted to exhibit and discuss films about their religious beliefs.

Issues on the religious rights of students in public schools have persisted. In *Santa Fe Independent School District* v. *Doe* (2000), for example, the Supreme Court ruled that organized, student-led prayer at a public high school athletic event, such as a football game, is a violation of the 1st Amendment's prohibition against an establishment of religion.

SEE ALSO *Abington School District* v. *Schempp; Bethel School District No. 403* v. *Fraser; Engel* v. *Vitale; Hazelwood School District* v. *Kuhlmeier; New Jersey* v. *T.L.O.; Tinker* v. *Des Moines Independent Community School District; West Virginia State Board of Education* v. *Barnette; Wallace* v. *Jaffree*

SOURCES J. Devereux Weeks, *Student Rights under the Constitution* (Athens: Carl Vinson Institute of Government, University of Georgia, 1992).

SUBCOMMITTEES, CONGRESSIONAL

House and Senate committees distribute their work among various subcommittees to handle specific areas of the committee's jurisdiction. Subcommittees have smaller memberships, their own chair and ranking members, and their own staff. Subcommittees hold hearings, take testimony, and prepare the initial draft of legislation before submitting the bill for approval, revision, or rejection by the full committee. In recent years, both the House and Senate have adopted rules changes to make sure that senior members do not monopolize the chairmanships of subcommittees, as they did in the past. In the Senate, every member of the majority party chairs a subcommittee, and every member of the minority serves as the ranking member of a subcommittee. In the House, junior members also stand a better chance to chair a subcommittee relatively early in their legislative careers. In an effort to streamline business, at the start of the 103rd Congress the House agreed to limit all major committees to no more than six subcommittees and nonmajor committees to no more than five subcommittees.

SEE ALSO *Committees, congressional*

SUBPOENA POWER OF CONGRESS

Congress can subpoena witnesses, or force them to testify under oath, before its committees. This authority comes from the Constitution's grant to Congress of "all legislative powers" (Article 1, Section 1). Witnesses are subpoenaed to provide information that will assist committees in preparing legislation. In the case of *Mc-Grain v. Daugherty* (1927), the Supreme Court recognized that Congress could subpoena even private citizens to testify. The Court noted that since not everyone would volunteer needed information, "some means of compulsion are essential to obtain what is needed." Witnesses who refuse to respond to a congressional subpoena, or refuse to give information (unless they invoke their 5th Amendment protection against self-incrimination) may be found in contempt of Congress and sent to prison.

The most famous use of the congressional subpoena occurred in 1973, when the Senate Select Committee on Presidential Campaign Activities (popularly known as the Watergate Committee) subpoenaed the tape recordings that President Richard M. Nixon had secretly made of White House conversations. This was the first time that Congress had ever subpoenaed a President. Nixon tried to withhold the tapes, claiming executive privilege (the right of the President not to release internal documents of the administration to the Congress). The courts ruled that the President could not use executive privilege as blanket protection, but the White House then released only a heavily edited version of the tapes. In June 1974, in *United States v. Nixon*, the Supreme Court ruled that executive privilege was a limited power and that the President must turn over all of the requested tapes to a special prosecutor investigating the Watergate incident. The opening of these tapes led Congress to begin impeachment proceedings against the President, causing Nixon to resign.

SEE ALSO *Contempt of Congress; Executive privilege; Investigations, congressional; Watergate investigation (1973–74)*

SOURCES James Hamilton, *The Power to Probe: A Study of Congressional Investigations* (New York: Vintage, 1976).

SUBSTITUTE MOTION

A legislative tactic designed to significantly alter a bill in Congress is to offer a substitute motion or a substitute amendment. Such a motion substitutes a different text for part or all of the bill being debated. A majority vote to accept the substitute kills the original version of the bill.

SUBWAYS, CONGRESSIONAL

Because senators and representatives frequently travel back and forth between their offices and the chambers, and have only 15 minutes from the time the bells first ring in which to cast their vote, the Senate and House operate subways that link the Capitol with the various office buildings. The subway dates back to 1909, when the first Senate office building (later named the Russell Building) opened. At that time, senators rode in two battery-powered buses that shuttled through an underground tunnel. In 1912 the buses were replaced by an electric railway train that ran between the buildings at a speed of 20 miles per hour. When the Dirksen and Hart Senate office buildings were constructed, the subway system was extended to connect them with the Capitol. On the House side, only the Rayburn Building, opened in 1965, has subway transportation to the Capitol. However, the Cannon and Longworth buildings are linked to the Capitol by pedestrian walkways. The public may ride on the Senate and House subways except during votes, when the cars are generally reserved for members only.

SUCCESSION TO THE PRESIDENCY

If the President is removed from office because he has been impeached and convicted of a crime, or if he dies, resigns, or cannot discharge the powers and duties of the office, the Constitution (Article 2, Section 1) provides that "the same shall devolve on the Vice President," who completes the remainder of his predecessor's term. There are no provisions for a special election. It is not clear from the text whether the words "the same" refer to the office of President or simply to the "powers and duties" of the office, which would make the Vice President, upon taking over, the "acting President." William Henry Harrison died in 1841, becoming the first President to die in office. His Vice President, John Tyler, took the oath of office as President and refused to be considered acting President, thus settling the issue. The first clause of the 25th Amendment, adopted in 1967, confirms Tyler's position. It states clearly, "In case of the removal of the President from office or of his death or resignation, the Vice President shall become President."

If there are vacancies for both President and Vice President, the same section of the Constitution provides that Congress shall determine "what officer shall then act as President, and such officer shall act accordingly." The language seems to indicate that the person assumes the powers of the office but is acting President. In 1792 Congress passed the first succession law, providing that the president pro tempore of the Senate would be next in line, then the Speaker of the House, until an interim election was held.

After the death of Vice President Thomas Hendricks in November 1885, Senator George F. Hoar (Republican–Massachusetts) pointed out the absence of both a Speaker of the House and a president pro tempore of the Senate during the long break between the Congress that ended its term on March 3 after an election and the next Congress that began on the first Monday in December, as specified by the Constitution (Article 1, Section 4). In 1886 Congress changed the order of succession, starting with cabinet officers in the order in which their departments had been created (the secretary of state would be first), and dropped any provision for an interim election.

But when Harry S. Truman became President following the death of Franklin D. Roosevelt in 1945, Truman thought it wrong to elevate nonelected officials to the Presidency. At Truman's urging, Congress changed the Act of Presidential Succession to put the Speaker of the House and president pro tempore of the Senate (both offices described in the Constitution) ahead of the cabinet members in the line of succession. The acting President would serve "until the expiration of the then current Presidential term," an explicit rejection of the idea of an interim election.

In 1967, the ratification of the 25th Amendment to the Constitution further affected Presidential succession by allowing the President to appoint—with the advice and consent of Congress—someone to fill a vacancy in the Vice Presidency.

When the President delivers the annual State of the Union message, in the presence of the Vice President, Speaker, president pro tempore, the cabinet, and the Congress, one member of the cabinet always remains absent. This assures that one person in the line of succession will be able to assume the Presidency in case some tragedy befalls all the others.

SEE ALSO *Cabinet; Disability, Presidential; Health, Presidential; 25th Amendment; Vice President*

SOURCES Ruth Silva, *Presidential Succession* (Ann Arbor: University of Michigan Press, 1951). Allen Sindler, *Unchosen Presidents* (Berkeley: University of California Press, 1976).

SUMNER, CHARLES

- Born: Jan. 6, 1811, Boston, Mass.
- Political party: Free Soil, Republican
- Education: Harvard University, graduated, 1830; Harvard Law School, graduated, 1833
- Senator from Massachusetts: 1851–74
- Died: Mar. 11, 1874, Washington, D.C.

Outspoken on many issues, Charles Sumner was passionately opposed to the existence and spread of slavery in the United

States. In 1856 Sumner delivered a heated speech against allowing slavery into the Kansas territory and denounced several Southern senators by name. Representative Preston Brooks of South Carolina took special offense at Sumner's sharp criticism of his uncle, Senator Andrew Butler (Democrat–South Carolina). "I have read your speech and it is a libel on South Carolina," said Brooks as he brought his cane down repeatedly on the startled Sumner, who sat writing at his desk in the Senate chamber. For the next two years, the badly injured Sumner was absent from the Senate, recuperating from his wounds. His empty desk stood as a powerful symbol of the tensions between North and South. (Later, efforts in the House to censure Brooks failed on a straight party-line vote. Brooks then resigned and won reelection by his constituents as a show of support.)

Brooks's blows did not end Sumner's controversial career, however. When the Republicans came into the majority, Sumner became an influential committee chairman and a spokesman for civil rights and against racial segregation. In 1875, shortly after his death, Congress passed the major civil rights bill that Sumner had ardently promoted.

SEE ALSO *Civil rights*
SOURCES David Donald, *Charles Sumner and the Coming of the Civil War* (New York: Knopf, 1960). David Donald, *Charles Sumner and the Rights of Man* (New York: Knopf, 1970).

" S U N S H I N E " R U L E S

"Sunshine" rules passed by the House of Representatives in 1973 and by the Senate in 1975 required congressional committees to do most of their work in open session. Previously, committees had held most hearings in public, but all executive sessions—dealing with internal committee business and markups of a bill (in which the final revisions were made prior to reporting the bill to the full chamber)—were done behind closed doors. Many members felt that they could bargain and reach compromises more easily if they were not under public scrutiny. However, reformers believed that the public's business should be done out in the open, where the press and public could watch.

SEE ALSO *Markup sessions*

S U P R E M E   C O U R T
R E P O R T E R

Since 1883 the West Publishing Company has regularly issued the *Supreme Court Reporter,* an unofficial record of U.S. Supreme Court decisions. The contents of the decisions in the *Supreme Court Reporter* are the same as in the official edition, *United States Reports,* which is issued by the U.S. Government Printing Office. Summaries of all cases are prepared by West. In addition, tables of key words, phrases, and statutes are developed to help readers interpret information in the full-text reports of the Court's opinions.

SEE ALSO *United States Reports*

S U S P E C T
C L A S S I F I C A T I O N S

The equal protection clause of the 14th Amendment and the due process clause of the 5th Amendment restrict state and federal governments from discriminating against individuals. Not all discrimination by the government, however, is unconstitutional. The law may treat classes of individuals differently if it is reasonable to do so and there is a compelling government interest. A state government may, for example, discriminate on the basis of age in determining who is eligible to obtain a driver's license because such discrimination is reasonable and serves the compelling government interest of promoting public safety.

Suspect classifications, by contrast, are assumed to be unreasonable and cannot be justified as necessary to achieve a compelling government interest. Government discrimination against suspect classifications of individuals has been judged by the Supreme Court to be unconstitutional. It considers both race and religion to be suspect classifications; therefore, any government discrimination against racial or religious groups is unlikely to be upheld. When discrimination involving suspect classifications is challenged in court, the government has the very difficult, if not impossible, task of demonstrating that the discrimination is necessary to achieve a compelling state interest. This heavy burden of proof is known as the test of strict scrutiny.

In contrast to the ordinary scrutiny of the Court, strict scrutiny is undertaken on the assumption that the challenged government act is unconstitutional. Only in very few cases has a challenged government act passed the test of strict scrutiny.

SUSPENSION OF THE RULES

To enable the House of Representatives to move speedily on noncontroversial matters, members will ask for a "suspension of the rules." If two-thirds of the House votes to suspend, then debate is limited to 40 minutes, and no additional amendments to the bill are permitted. The Senate achieves the same result with a unanimous consent agreement (that is, limitations on debate and amendment can be achieved if no member objects).

SEE ALSO *Rules of the House and Senate; Unanimous consent agreements*

SUTHERLAND, GEORGE
Associate Justice, 1922–38

- Born: Mar. 25, 1862, Buckinghamshire, England
- Education: University of Michigan Law School, 1883
- Previous government service: Utah Senate, 1896–1900; U.S. representative from Utah, 1901–3; U.S. senator from Utah, 1905–17; chairman, advisory

committee to the Washington Conference for the Limitation of Naval Armaments, 1921; U.S. counsel, Norway–United States arbitrations, The Hague, Netherlands, 1921–22
- Appointed by President Warren G. Harding Sept. 5, 1922; replaced Justice John H. Clarke, who resigned
- Supreme Court term: confirmed by the Senate Sept. 5, 1922, by a voice vote; retired Jan. 17, 1938
- Died: July 18, 1942, Stockbridge, Mass.

George Sutherland was a strong advocate of private rights and limited government. He opposed extensive government regulation of businesses as an invasion of property rights and contractual rights. For example, he wrote for the Supreme Court in *Adkins* v. *Children's Hospital* (1923), the decision that struck down a minimum wage law for female workers. Justice Sutherland argued that this law interfered unconstitutionally with a woman's right to negotiate a contract.

Justice Sutherland was capable of defending the civil rights of accused people as vigorously as property rights. In *Powell* v. *Alabama* (1932), he overturned the conviction of black youths sentenced to death for an assault on a white girl because they had been denied their constitutional right to legal counsel (provided by Amendment 6).

Justice Sutherland's views in support of economic liberty and against heavy-handed government regulation of businesses put him at odds with President Franklin Roosevelt's New Deal programs. He was known as one of the Court's "Four Horsemen"—the hard-line opponents of the New Deal. The Court's movement in 1937 toward acceptance of the New Deal influenced Sutherland to retire from the Court in 1938.

SEE ALSO *Powell v. Alabama*

SWAYNE, NOAH H.
Associate Justice, 1862–81

- Born: Dec. 7, 1804, Frederick County, Va.

- Education: studied law privately
- Previous government service: Coshocton County, Va., prosecuting attorney, 1826–29; Ohio House of Representatives, 1830, 1836; U.S. attorney for Ohio, 1830–41; Columbus City councilman, Ohio, 1834
- Appointed by President Abraham Lincoln Jan. 22, 1862; replaced John McLean, who died
- Supreme Court term: confirmed by the Senate Jan. 24, 1862, by a 38–1 vote; retired Jan. 24, 1881
- Died: June 8, 1884, New York, N.Y.

Noah H. Swayne was a zealous foe of slavery, which led him to join the Republican party and support Abraham Lincoln for the presidency. He became President Lincoln's first Supreme Court appointment.

Justice Swayne readily supported Lincoln's Civil War policies. For example, he backed the President's blockade of southern ports in the *Prize Cases* (1863), and he sustained the use of military trials for civilian defendants in *Ex parte Vallandigham* (1864). After the war, Justice Swayne continued to back Republican party programs.

SWEATT V. PAINTER

- 339 U.S. 629 (1950)
- Vote: 9–0
- For the Court: Vinson

Herman Marion Sweatt was a post office worker in Houston, Texas, who wanted to become a lawyer. He applied for admission to the law school of the University of Texas. Sweatt's application to this racially segregated law school was turned down solely because he was black.

Sweatt turned for help to the National Association for the Advancement of Colored People (NAACP) and its chief legal counsel, Thurgood Marshall, who would later become an associate justice of the U.S. Supreme Court.

The NAACP and Sweatt filed suit to de-

mand his admission to the University of Texas. The trial court judge continued, or postponed, the case for six months to give the state government time to set up a law school for black people that could admit Herman Sweatt. At the end of the six-month period, the judge dismissed Sweatt's suit because the state was setting up a law school to which he could be admitted.

Sweatt, however, was not satisfied. He claimed that the new law school for blacks would be greatly inferior to the University of Texas law school. But the Texas courts decided that the two law schools—one for whites and the other for blacks—were "sub-stantially equivalent." Sweatt and the NAACP appealed to the U.S. Supreme Court.

The Issue This case was a test of the "separate but equal" doctrine established by the Court in *Plessy* v. *Ferguson* (1896). Did the separate Texas law schools—one for white students and the other for blacks—satisfy the 14th Amendment requirement that "No state shall . . . deny to any person within its jurisdiction the equal protection of the laws"?

Opinion of the Court The Supreme Court decided in favor of Sweatt. Chief Justice Fred M. Vinson concluded that the new law school for black students could not be equal to the University of Texas law school, which had a long tradition, a highly regarded faculty, and ample resources. The racially segregated law schools of Texas violated the equal protection clause of the 14th Amendment.

Significance This decision was a clear rejection of the long-standing "separate but equal" doctrine set forth in *Plessy* v. *Ferguson* (1896), and it pointed the way to a more sweeping decision against that doctrine that occurred four years later in *Brown* v. *Board of Education* (1954).

SEE ALSO *Brown v. Board of Education; Civil rights; Equality under the Constitution; National Association for the Advancement of Colored People (NAACP), Plessy v. Ferguson; Segregation, de facto and de jure*

T

TAFT-HARTLEY ACT (1947)

During the 1930s, labor union membership in the United States increased rapidly, aided by the Wagner Act of 1935, which had protected the right of workers to organize and strike. Conservatives cited a coal miners' strike during World War II and a wave of strikes across many industries after the war as evidence that labor unions had become too powerful and unrestrained. In 1946 Republicans won control of both the House and Senate for the first time since 1930. Senator Robert A. Taft, Sr. (Republican–Ohio), chair of the Senate Labor and Public Welfare Committee, and Representative Fred Hartley, Jr. (Republican–New Jersey), chair of the House Education and Labor Committee, sponsored the Labor-Management Relations Act of 1947 to regulate union activities. Their legislation became known as the Taft-Hartley Act.

Passed over President Harry Truman's veto, the Taft-Hartley Act allowed states to enact "right to work" laws to outlaw closed shops, companies where only union members could be employed. Taft-Hartley also prohibited jurisdictional strikes, in which different unions struck a company to determine which one would represent its workers, and barred communists from serving as union officers. Taft-Hartley gave Presidents the right to seek a federal court injunction to call off strikes for an 80-day "cooling off" period. This would allow work to continue while management and labor negotiated a contract. Although highly controversial, and strongly opposed by labor unions, the Republican-sponsored Taft-Hartley Act has remained largely unchanged by later Democratic majorities in Congress.

SEE ALSO *Taft, Robert A., Sr.; Veto power*
SOURCES Robert J. Donovan, *Conflict and Crisis: The Presidency of Harry S. Truman, 1945–1948* (New York: Norton, 1977). Susan M. Hartmann, *Truman and the 80th Congress* (Columbia: University of Missouri Press, 1971).

TAFT, ROBERT A., SR.

- Born: Sept. 8, 1889, Cincinnati, Ohio
- Political party: Republican
- Education: Yale University, graduated, 1910; Harvard University Law School, graduated, 1913
- Senator from Ohio: 1939–53
- Senate majority leader: 1953
- Died: July 31, 1953, New York, N.Y.

When Senator John F. Kennedy published *Profiles in Courage*, he commended Senator Robert Taft as a politician who had stood firm for his principles, no matter how unpopular they were. Although a liberal Democrat, Kennedy admired the conservative Republican Taft. Taft had opposed the New Deal's popular social and economic programs and had argued against U.S. participation in World War II. During the cold war, Taft vigorously opposed the increasing military role of the United States, which was seeking to contain communism around the world. He also embroiled himself in the labor unrest of the 1940s by sponsoring the Taft-Hartley Act, which allowed the government to impose "cooling off" periods in nationwide strikes. These controversial stands ruined Taft's repeated attempts to be elected President. But they won praise for Taft from other senators who recognized his unusual degree of honesty, courage, and unwillingness to bend to public pressure.

SEE ALSO *Taft-Hartley Act (1947)*
SOURCES John F. Kennedy, *Profiles in Courage* (New York: Harper & Row, 1955). James T. Patterson, *Mr. Republican: A Biography of Robert A. Taft* (Boston: Houghton Mifflin, 1972).

TAFT, WILLIAM HOWARD
27th President
Chief Justice, 1921–30

- Born: Sept. 15, 1857, Cincinnati, Ohio
- Political party: Republican
- Education: Yale College, B.A., 1878; University of Cincinnati Law School, LL.B., 1880
- Military service: none
- Previous government service: assistant prosecuting attorney, Hamilton County, Ohio, 1881–82; collector of internal revenue for Cincinnati, 1882–83; assistant county solicitor, Hamilton County, 1885–87; justice, Superior Court of Cincinnati, 1887–90; U.S. solicitor general, 1890–92; presiding judge, 6th Circuit Court of Appeals, 1892–1900; president, Philippine Commission, 1900–1901; civil governor of the Philippines, 1901–4; U.S. secretary of war, 1904–8
- Elected President, 1908; served, 1909–13
- Subsequent government service: joint chairman, National War Labor Board,

1917–18; Appointed to Supreme Court by President Warren G. Harding June 30, 1921; replaced Chief Justice Edward D. White, who died
- Supreme Court term: confirmed by the Senate June 30, 1921, by a voice vote; retired Feb. 3, 1930
- Died: Mar. 8, 1930, Washington, D.C.

William Howard Taft viewed the President as "chief magistrate" of the nation—someone who would hear the arguments of lower officials and then make his decision—not as a national leader who would use public opinion to lead the nation in his own direction. Taft argued that Presidential power was limited by the express language of the Constitution and that the President could not use the "general welfare" clause of its preamble to extend his powers further to meet the needs of the people (as his predecessor Theodore Roosevelt had argued). When Taft broke with the former President over conservation policies, he opened a split in the Republican party that guaranteed his defeat for a second term.

Taft is the only President of the United States to also serve as chief justice of the United States. Of the two positions, chief justice was the one to which he most strongly aspired. From his youth to old age, Taft ardently desired to sit on the Supreme Court. When he was 63 years old, his ambition was fulfilled when President Warren G. Harding appointed him to the Court.

Taft was born into a staunch Republican family. His grandfather had been a judge in New England, and his father, Alphonso Taft, had been secretary of war and attorney general in President Ulysses S. Grant's administration and minister to Russia and Austria during Chester Arthur's Presidency. Taft graduated from Yale second in his class, attended law school in Cincinnati, practiced law briefly, and then spent much of his career as a judge. His highest ambition was to serve on the Supreme Court. In a sense his Presidency was a detour to his lifelong goal, one he accepted because of the urging of his brothers and his wife.

After serving for many years as a state and federal judge, and as solicitor general in the U.S. Justice Department, Taft was tapped by President William McKinley in 1900 to serve as president of the U.S. Philippine Commission, set up to administer the islands the United States had won from Spain in the Spanish-American War. Taft believed that the "little brown brothers" on the islands were not ready for self-rule, so he organized a civil government to replace U.S. military rule and was named the first civil governor of the Philippines the following year. While he was working to pacify the island, he twice declined offers of a Supreme Court appointment from Theodore Roosevelt.

In 1904 Taft became Roosevelt's secretary of war. He met secretly with Count Katsura of Japan on July 29, 1905, to discuss a proposed Japanese protectorate (control over politics and the economy) in Korea once the Russo-Japanese War was concluded. Taft's acquiescence paved the way for the success of the Portsmouth Peace Conference that ended the war. In 1906 Taft helped prevent a potential rebellion in Cuba against a U.S.-supported regime. The United States imposed a provisional government under the terms of the Platt Amendment, which permitted U.S. intervention in Cuban affairs.

Roosevelt designated Taft his successor, and he easily won the Republican nomination of 1908. Taft defeated the Democratic nominee, William Jennings Bryan, though in the heat of the campaign he had to leave his front porch in Cincinnati and campaign vigorously in the Midwest—the first time in U.S. history that both major-party candidates actively campaigned among the people for votes.

When Taft was inaugurated, it was the first time since 1837 that a President had successfully transferred power to his preferred successor. But Taft soon disappointed Roosevelt with his inability to provide effective leadership. He held as few press conferences as he could and was un-

able to rally public opinion behind him. While Roosevelt spent a year in Africa hunting big game, Taft allied himself with Republican conservatives and signed the Payne-Aldrich Tariff, which made only minor cuts in the high taxes on imports that had been set in 1897 by the Dingley Tariff Act. By accepting a high tariff he alienated himself from the progressive wing of the party.

Not all Taft's policies were conservative, however. The tariff act contained the first federal tax on corporate profits. Taft enforced the Sherman Anti-Trust Act to a greater extent than the "trust buster" Roosevelt had, winning lawsuits against the Standard Oil Company of New Jersey, American Tobacco Company, Du Pont de Nemours, and the American Sugar Refining Company. He limited the workday of federal employees to eight hours and created a commission to consider workmen's compensation legislation, which would provide money to injured workers. He proposed an amendment to the Constitution that would permit a personal income tax.

Taft called for a new budget process in which the President would have the primary responsibility for formulating an executive budget, but Congress ignored his requests. He got Congress to approve a new department of labor, enlarge the national park system, and create a bureau of mines. Congress extended the jurisdiction of the Interstate Commerce Commission to cover telephones, telegraph lines, underwater cable lines, and radio. A new campaign finance law proposed by Taft required candidates for Congress to make public their campaign expenditures.

In foreign policy Taft won arbitration treaties with Great Britain and France to provide for peaceful resolution of disputes, but these were blocked by the Senate. He barely got Senate approval for a trade agreement with Canada, and the Canadian parliament defeated it. The President instituted a foreign policy of "dollar diplomacy," which he defined as "substituting dollars for bullets" in an attempt to increase U.S. trade and influence abroad. The government worked with commercial banks to dominate the finances of Caribbean and Central American governments: it ran their customs houses (which collected duties on imported goods), helped establish local banks, floated loans for development, and secured contracts and markets for U.S. businesses.

Taft abandoned dollar diplomacy for more forceful intervention when he landed 2,500 marines in Nicaragua to take control of the country, and he also sent troops into Honduras, Cuba, and China to end threats to U.S. property. "Peaceful Bill" did keep U.S. troops out of Mexico during a revolution that erupted in 1910. Taft upset foreign nations by signing a 1912 law that exempted U.S. shipping companies from paying tolls for use of the Panama Canal. This law seemed to violate the Hay-Pauncefote Treaty, which established that all nations would pay the same tolls; Taft construed it to mean all nations except the United States. The law was repealed in 1913 after Taft left office.

Theodore Roosevelt split with his protégé in 1910 after Taft fired Gifford Pinchot, chief of the Division of Forestry and a defender of Roosevelt's conservation policies. Taft sided with his secretary of the interior, Richard Ballinger, who had opened for sale a tract of public land in Alaska that Roosevelt had previously designated not for sale. (Within a year, after a public outcry, Ballinger was forced to resign and the sale was canceled.)

In the fall of 1910 ex-President Theodore Roosevelt made a nationwide tour to 20 cities, where he articulated a progressive program of government regulation known as the New Nationalism. Meanwhile, Congress passed a series of bills providing for low tariffs on wool, cotton, and other goods, which Taft vetoed, further reducing his popularity in the Middle West. In the 1910 midterm elections Democrats won the House of Representatives and increased their Senate seats from 32 to 42; Republican Senate seats dropped from 59 to 49.

By February 1912, Roosevelt was openly campaigning for the Republican Presidential nomination, reversing his pledge not to seek a third term by claiming he had meant he would not seek three consecutive terms. Taft became the first sitting President to campaign for his own renomination. Roosevelt defeated him in most of the 15 Presidential primaries, even in Ohio. But Taft managed to secure the Republican nomination in 1912, in part through his control of Southern delegations that consisted primarily of black officeholders dependent on his patronage and in part through the support of big-city political machines, or organizations. Roosevelt contested these "Taft delegations" with his own supporters. But the Republican National Committee, controlled by Taft, seated 235 of the Southerners who favored him, awarding only 20 to the Roosevelt delegates and ensuring Taft's victory. Roosevelt then ran as a third-party candidate.

It was a bitter campaign. Taft called Roosevelt an egotist and a demagogue; Roosevelt called Taft a weakling and a fathead with the brains of a guinea pig. With the Republican vote split, Democrat Woodrow Wilson won the election. Taft ran a poor third, winning only the eight electoral college votes of Utah and Vermont. Republicans remained in a minority in the House, lost control of the Senate, and lost a majority of state governments. After four years of Taft his party was divided and in shambles. "I am glad to be going," he said as he left office. "This is the lonesomest place in the world."

After leaving the White House, Taft taught constitutional law at Yale Law School and was elected president of the American Bar Association. He served on the National War Labor Board during World War I. Finally, in 1921, he achieved his goal in life: President Warren Harding appointed him to the Supreme Court. Chief Justice Taft was a great judicial administrator. He influenced Congress to pass the Judiciary Act of 1925, which gave the Court almost total authority to choose what cases it would decide. And Taft influenced Congress to appropriate money for construction of the magnificent Supreme Court Building in which the Court conducts its work today. (Since 1860, the Court had been conducting its business on the first floor of the Capitol, in the old Senate chamber.) Chief Justice Taft was also known as a skillful manager of the Court's work load and an adept mediator among his colleagues.

Taft was not, however, as accomplished at formulating doctrine or writing opinions. Though he wrote 249 opinions for the Court, he left no landmark decisions or enduring interpretations of the Constitution. His most significant opinion was in *Myers* v. *United States* (1926). The Court ruled that the President had the power to remove an executive appointee, a postmaster, without the consent of the Senate. Taft said: "I never wrote an opinion I felt to be so important in its effect."

The Tafts, like the Adamses and the Kennedys, are an American political dynasty. Taft's son, Robert Alphonso Taft, became a U.S. senator from Ohio in 1939. Known as Mr. Republican, he was one of the most influential Republican senators ever to serve. He was a contender for the Republican Presidential nomination in 1940, 1948, and 1952 but was never nominated. His son, Robert Taft, Jr., served as majority leader of the Ohio House of Representatives, as a U.S. representative in the 1960s, and as a senator from 1970 to 1976.

SEE ALSO *Office buildings, Supreme Court; Removal power; Roosevelt, Theodore; Wilson, Woodrow*

SOURCES Paolo E. Coletta, *The Presidency of William Howard Taft* (Lawrence: University Press of Kansas, 1973). William Manners, *TR and Will: A Friendship That Split the Republican Party* (New York: Harcourt, Brace & World, 1969). Alpheus Thomas Mason, *William Howard Taft: Chief Justice* (New York: Simon & Schuster, 1964). William Howard Taft, *Our Chief Magistrate and His Powers* (New York: Columbia University Press, 1916).

TANEY, ROGER BROOKE
Chief Justice, 1836–64

- Born: Mar. 17, 1777, Calvert County, Md.
- Education: Dickinson College, B.A., 1795; read law in the office of Judge Jeremiah Chase in Annapolis, Md.
- Previous government service: Maryland House of Delegates, 1799–1800; Maryland Senate, 1816–21; attorney general of Maryland, 1827–31; U.S. attorney general, 1831–33; acting U.S. secretary of war, 1831; U.S. secretary of the Treasury, 1833–34 (appointment rejected by the Senate)
- Appointed by President Andrew Jackson Dec. 28, 1835; replaced John Marshall, who died
- Supreme Court term: confirmed by the Senate Mar. 15, 1836, by a 29–15 vote; served until Oct. 12, 1864
- Died: Oct. 12, 1864, Washington, D.C.

Chief Justice Roger Brooke Taney is linked inseparably with his infamous opinion in *Scott* v. *Sandford* (1857), which sanctioned slavery and denied the rights of black Americans. Yet Taney freed his own slaves, which he inherited. He also has been ranked by legal scholars as one of the great justices in Supreme Court history.

Roger Taney began his career in the federal government as a staunch Jacksonian Democrat. He served President Andrew Jackson's interests ably as U.S. attorney general, acting secretary of war, and secretary of the Treasury.

In 1835, President Jackson appointed Taney to fill a vacancy on the Supreme Court. The Senate, however, rejected the appointment because of disagreements with Taney's performance as secretary of the Treasury. A few months later, Chief Justice John Marshall died, and President Jackson turned again to Taney. This time the Senate confirmed the President's appointment, after a bitter debate, and Roger Taney succeeded John Marshall as chief justice of the United States.

Chief Justice Taney's greatest opinion was *Charles River Bridge* v. *Warren Bridge* (1837). Writing for the Court, Taney rejected the claim of owners of the Charles River Bridge that their charter, granted by the state of Massachusetts, implicitly gave them a monopoly and thereby prevented the state from granting rights to another company to build a second bridge over the same river. The Charles River Bridge Company, which charged passengers a toll for crossing its bridge, did not want any competition from a second company. In deciding against the monopoly claims of the Charles River Bridge Company, Taney sought to balance private property rights with the public good. He wrote: "The object and end of government is to promote the happiness and prosperity of the community. . . . While the rights of private property are sacredly guarded, we must not forget that the community also has rights, and that the happiness and well-being of every citizen depends on their faithful preservation."

With this decision, Chief Justice Taney defined a major, continuing issue of American constitutional law. From Taney's time until today, jurists have tried, as he did, to balance the sometimes competing claims of private property rights and the community's rights.

Taney's tenure on the Court was marked by growing concerns to protect state government powers and rights within the federal system. This trend was in sharp contrast to the Marshall Court's persistent concern with establishing federal government supremacy over the states. The Taney Court emphasized the sovereignty of the states over matters within their jurisdiction, as provided by the U.S. Constitution, such as maintaining public order, building public facilities, and regulating local businesses.

Taney's conception of states' rights shaped his decisions about slavery. He held that the power to maintain slavery or to free slaves belonged solely to the state governments. His views were expressed memorably and disastrously in *Scott* v. *Sandford*

(1857). In this decision, Taney asserted that black Americans could not be citizens of the United States; that the U.S. Constitution protected private property rights, including the right to own slaves; that each state had exclusive power to make decisions about slavery or emancipation of slaves; and that the federal government had no power to ban slavery in the territories of the United States. The *Dred Scott* decision fanned the flames of conflict between the so-called slave states and free states and was one important cause of the Civil War.

SEE ALSO *Charles River Bridge v. Warren Bridge; Federalism; Scott v. Sandford*
SOURCES Walker Lewis, *Without Fear or Favor: A Biography of Chief Justice Roger Brooke Taney* (Boston: Houghton Mifflin, 1965). R. Kent Newmyer, *The Supreme Court Under Marshall and Taney* (Arlington Heights, Ill.: Harlan Davidson, 1986). Carl B. Swisher, *Roger B. Taney* (New York: Macmillan, 1974).

TARIFF OF ABOMINATIONS (1828)

Duties on imports set by the Tariff of 1828 were so high that its opponents denounced it as the Tariff of Abominations. Northern bankers, merchants, and manufacturers favored high duties, or taxes, on imports to protect American goods from foreign competition. Southern planters feared that high tax rates would increase the cost of nearly everything they bought. When Northerners in Congress worked to increase tariff rates, opponents adopted the tactic of adding many excessively high duties to make the whole tariff unattractive enough to defeat. But their strategy backfired, and the highly protective tariff was enacted. The South was so outraged over the Tariff of Abominations that Vice President John C. Calhoun (Democrat–South Carolina) drafted a proposal that states could "nullify," or effectively cancel, offensive federal laws within their own jurisdiction. President Andrew Jackson and his supporters vigorously denied that states had any right of nullification. A constitutional crisis was avoided in 1832, when Congress adopted a new tariff that significantly lowered the rates set by the Tariff of Abominations.

SOURCES Robert V. Remini, *Martin Van Buren and the Making of the Democratic Party* (New York: Norton, 1970).

TAXATION

SEE *Revenue bills*

TAYLOR, ZACHARY
12th President

- Born: Nov. 24, 1784, Orange County, Va.
- Political party: Whig
- Education: tutored through elementary grades
- Military service: Kentucky Militia, 1806; U.S. Army, 1808–49
- Previous civilian government service: none
- Elected President, 1848; served, 1849–50
- Died: July 9, 1850, Washington, D.C.

Zachary Taylor was the second and last Whig to be elected President of the United States, and like his predecessor William Henry Harrison, he did not complete his term of office. Taylor had spent his whole life as a career military officer, on garrison duty in frontier posts and in the thick of battle against Indians in Florida and during the Mexican-American War. He was the first President without experience in elective or appointive office, though not the last. Taylor had never even cast a vote in a Presidential election before being elected to the office.

Taylor was born in Virginia but grew up on a large farm on the Kentucky frontier. He was tutored but never went to school. He entered the army with a commission as a lieutenant, which his cousin, Secretary of State James Madison, ob-

tained for him. He was promoted to major for his defense of Fort Harrison, Indiana, against attacks by the Indian chief Tecumseh. As a colonel, he defeated the Black Hawk Indians in 1832, and he later defeated the Seminole Indians in 1837, rising to the rank of general after the Battle of Lake Okeechobee. In February 1847, Taylor defeated the Mexican general Santa Anna at the Battle of Buena Vista.

The Whigs nominated Taylor in 1848 for the same reasons they had nominated Harrison: he was a war hero. Taylor was also a Southerner and a slaveholder (in 1841 he had bought a Mississippi plantation with many slaves) who would attract support in the South from a party with little popular following there. He won the Whig nomination on the fourth ballot over Henry Clay, Daniel Webster, and Winfield Scott. Helped by a split in the Democratic party, with Martin Van Buren running on a Free-Soil ticket and Lewis Cass running as a regular Democrat, Taylor was elected with fewer popular votes than Cass and Van Buren combined. However, his solid electoral college majority, in part due to electoral votes from four Southern states, proved the soundness of the Whigs' "Southern strategy."

Taylor took little role in policy-making, leaving it to Whig congressional leaders in accordance with the party's view that Presidents should preside but not attempt to govern. After the California gold rush of 1849, Taylor ordered the state's military governor to hold elections in the territory. Ironically, those elections resulted in a state constitutional convention that wrote a state constitution outlawing slavery. The new state government began to function in 1850 and sought admission to the Union, strongly backed by Taylor.

Taylor wanted California, New Mexico, and Utah all to be admitted to the Union. This proposal caused him to split with Whig congressional leaders, who were more mindful of Southern opposition to the admission of "free" states that would outlaw slavery and end the balance in the Union of 15 slave and 15 free states. Taylor took a strong stand against the Southerners in Congress who threatened secession if California entered the Union as a free state, and he threatened senators from Georgia that he would crush any attempt at secession. Taylor was opposed to the Compromise of 1850, proposed by Henry Clay, that resolved the issue. The compromise, consisting of five separate laws, admitted California as a free state and abolished the slave trade in the nation's capital but balanced these measures with a stringent new law for the return of runaway slaves and the organization of Utah and New Mexico state governments without any determination about slavery. Taylor referred to this compromise as the "Omnibus Bill" and probably would have vetoed the measures had he lived.

Taylor's most significant achievement in foreign affairs was the negotiation of the Clayton-Bulwer Treaty (1850) with Great Britain, which provided that any canal built in Central America would be under joint Anglo-American control. This defused a crisis that might have led to hostilities that neither nation wanted.

Taylor died in office on July 9, 1850, of acute gastroenteritis and was succeeded by Millard Fillmore.

SEE ALSO *Fillmore, Millard*

SOURCES Jack K. Bauer, *Zachary Taylor: Soldier, Planter, Statesman of the Old Southwest* (Baton Rouge: Louisiana State University Press, 1985). Elbert B. Smith, *The Presidencies of Zachary Taylor and Millard Fillmore* (Lawrence: University Press of Kansas, 1988).

TENURE OF OFFICE ACT (1867)

The Constitution gives the President the power to make all nominations of executive branch officials with the advice and consent of the Senate. But the Constitution says nothing about how those officials might be removed, other than by impeachment. After the Civil War, a bitter clash took place between radical Republicans in Congress and President Andrew Johnson over Reconstruction of the South. To prevent Johnson from removing hard-line supporters of Reconstruction from office, Congress passed the Tenure of Office Act in 1867. This act required the President to seek the Senate's consent before removing any cabinet officer or other high-ranking official. Despite its passage over his veto, Johnson insisted that the Tenure of Office Act was unconstitutional. In 1868 he ignored the act and fired Secretary of War Edwin Stanton without consulting the Senate. This was the event that triggered Congress's unsuccessful attempt to remove Johnson from the Presidency. In the 1926 case of *Myers* v. *United States,* the Supreme Court finally declared the Tenure of Office Act unconstitutional. Since then, Presidents have been free to fire or ask for the resignation of any of their appointees in the executive branch. But this removal power does not extend to the independent regulatory commissions (such as the Federal Trade Commission and the Securities and Exchange Commission), whose members serve limited terms and function independently of both the executive and legislative branches. Nor can Presidents remove Supreme Court justices and other federal judges, who serve lifetime appointments, subject only to impeachment.

SEE ALSO *Removal power*

TERM LIMITS, CONGRESSIONAL

How long should a member of Congress serve? The Constitution set two years for a House term and six years for a Senate term but put no restriction on how often members could run for reelection. The House should have "an immediate dependence on, and an intimate sympathy with, the people," James Madison wrote in the *Federalist Papers.* "Frequent elections are unquestionably the only policy by which this dependence and sympathy can be effectually secured." Senators, by contrast, serve six-year terms to give them greater distance from the "sudden and violent passions" of public opinion.

Senators are divided into three classes, with one class (or one-third of the Senate) standing for election every two years. When a new state joins the Union, the two new senators will flip a coin to determine which class they will join—meaning who will get the longer or shorter term.

The lack of restriction on how often members could be reelected contrasted sharply with the Congress under the Articles of Confederation (1781–89), where members could serve only three out of every six years. The turnover of membership this limit caused denied the Congress continuity and members with experience in office.

In the 19th century, most members served only briefly in the national legislature before returning to state politics or private life. Even Henry Clay (Whig–Kentucky), who served between 1806 and 1852, actually left Congress and returned several times during those years.

In the 20th century, as advancement in Congress became determined by seniority, continuous service grew more important. As more members aimed to spend their entire career in Congress, it became commonplace for more than 90 percent to win reelection. Although citizens often expressed dissatisfaction with Congress in general, they regularly reelected their own senators and representatives. Turnover occurred more often through voluntary retirement than through election defeats. In 1990, 81 House members had no opponents, and another 168 faced challengers who could not raise enough money to mount a competitive campaign. Out of 435 members of the House, only 15 lost their election.

Opponents of this trend charged that campaign money from political action committees (PACs) heavily favored incumbents (those already holding office) against their challengers. Incumbents also had the benefit of such perks of office as the frank, or free mailing privileges, to keep their names before the voters. Noting that the 22nd Amendment to the Constitution, ratified in 1951, had limited Presidents to no more than two four-year terms, a number of states called for an amendment that would limit representatives to three two-year terms and senators to two six-year terms. The aim would be to rotate more citizens through Congress, so that members would not lose touch with "the real world." Those who opposed term limits warned that such an amendment would replace experienced members with rookies and would deprive voters of the option of reelecting members who had performed well. Instead of a constitutional amendment, they suggested that voters could limit the terms of their senators and representatives simply by voting against them in the next election.

In the 1990s, voter displeasure over the congressional salary increase, the House bank scandal, and other congressional behavior led to a major turnover of membership. Despite the defeat or retirement of many longtime members, newly elected conservative Republicans pressed for formal term limits. A growing number of states approved ballot initiatives to set congressional term limits. But in 1995, the Supreme Court ruled in *U.S. Term Limits, Inc.* v. *Thornton* that only a constitutional amendment could impose such term limits.

SEE ALSO *Campaign financing, congressional; Elections, congressional; Incumbents; Perks, congressional; Public opinion; Seniority in Congress; Term of office, Presidential*

SOURCES Charles O. Jones, *Every Second Year: Congressional Behavior and the Two-Year Term* (Washington, D.C.: Brookings Institution, 1967).

TERM OF OFFICE, PRESIDENTIAL

According to Article 2, Section 1, of the Constitution, the President serves a fixed four-year term. At the Constitutional Convention in 1787, the Virginia Plan with which the delegates began their work left blank the number of years the executive would serve but provided that the executive would be "ineligible a second time." Then the committee of the whole, by a 5-to-4 vote, provided that the President would serve a seven-year term and be ineligible for reelection, rejecting an alternative idea for a three-year term with two reelections permitted. A later proposal by Alexander Hamilton to elect a "Supreme Governour" for a lifetime term was also rejected. Finally, the Committee on Postponed Matters decided on a provision for a four-year term, coupled with eligibility for reelection to an unlimited number of terms.

Until the election of 1936, Congress set the inaugural date for March 4. A lame-duck session of the previously elected Congress lasted from the November election through the following March and often included many defeated members of Congress. The lame-duck Congress was entitled to choose the President and Vice President in case of a deadlock in the electoral college. The Congress elected with the President did not meet until 14 months after the election—unless the President called it into special session.

In 1933, when the 20th Amendment was ratified, this set the Presidential inaugural date for January 20, which shortened substantially the time between election and inauguration. Franklin D. Roosevelt was the first President to be inaugurated under the new system, beginning his second term on January 20, 1937.

The 20th Amendment also provided that the newly elected Congress would meet on January 3 following the election, even before the President assumed office, thus shortening the lame-duck period of the previous Congress. Usually, the outgoing Congress has adjourned prior to the November election and does not come back into session. The new Congress chooses the President and Vice President in case of a deadlock in the electoral college.

The 22nd Amendment, ratified in 1951, provides that no person may be elected President more than twice.

SEE ALSO *Electoral college; Succession to the Presidency; 22nd Amendment; Two-term tradition*

TERMS OF THE SUPREME COURT

A term of the U.S. Supreme Court is the period of time when the Court is in session. The Judiciary Act of 1789 required that the Court terms begin on the first Monday in February and August. The terms of the Court have been changed, from time to time, by Congress. In 1979 the Court began its current practice of holding sessions throughout the year with periodic recesses. According to law, the Supreme Court begins each annual term on the first Monday in October. This practice was started in 1917.

The Court is in session to hear oral arguments on Monday, Tuesday, and Wednesday for two weeks of each month from October until the end of April. A session may also be held on Monday of the third week of the month. During May and June, the Court is in session to deliver opinions on cases heard during the term. However, some opinions are announced earlier in the term. The justices spend time away from the Court during the summer. But they also continue their work on petitions for hearing cases on appeal from lower courts. The justices meet in late September to take care of unfinished business and to prepare for the new term beginning in October.

SEE ALSO *Decision days; Opening day of the Supreme Court*

TERRY V. OHIO

- 392 U.S. 1 (1968)
- Vote: 8–1
- For the Court: Warren
- Concurring: Harlan, Black, and White
- Dissenting: Douglas

A police officer in plain clothes, Martin McFadden, was patrolling downtown Cleveland when he observed two men acting suspiciously. They were walking back and forth in front of a store, pausing to look into the window. They soon were joined by a third man, who talked with them.

Officer McFadden thought the three men were preparing to rob the store. He confronted the three men, identified himself as a police officer, and frisked them to see if they were armed. He found that one of the men, John Terry, was carrying a pistol. A second man also had a concealed weapon. So McFadden arrested them on concealed weapons charges.

Terry and his companions were convicted. Terry, however, appealed to the U.S. Supreme Court. He claimed that his 4th Amendment and 14th Amendment rights had been violated because Officer McFadden had searched him without a warrant.

The Issue Was the warrantless search of Terry a violation of the 4th Amendment protection against unreasonable searches and seizures and the 14th Amendment guarantee of due process of law in state proceedings?

Opinion of the Court The Supreme Court decided against Terry. The policeman's "stop and frisk" action in this case was constitutional because it was reasonable under the circumstances. The Court made its decision "by balancing the need to search against the invasion which the search entails."

Chief Justice Earl Warren concluded, "[W]here a police officer observes unusual conduct which leads him reasonably to conclude . . . that criminal activity may be afoot . . . and that the person . . . may be armed and presently dangerous . . . he is entitled for the protection of himself and others in the area to conduct a carefully limited search of the outer clothing of such persons in an attempt to discover weapons which might be used to assault him."

Significance *Terry* was the first case to recognize "stop and frisk" as a legal practice by police officers under certain conditions. It has become an established exception to the standard requirement of a search warrant. However, police can stop and frisk a person only when they have reason to believe their lives are in danger. The search must be limited to the area of the body in which the police suspect the presence of weapons.

SEE ALSO *Searches and seizures*

TEST CASES

A test case is one in which an individual or a group intentionally violates a law in order to bring a case to court. The purpose is to test the constitutionality of the law. For example, in 1989 Congress passed a law against flag burning. Soon afterward, protesters broke this law because they wanted to bring a test case to the courts. Thus, the case of *United States* v. *Eichman* (1990) was tried and eventually taken to the U.S. Supreme Court. The Court decided that the federal flag-burning law was unconstitutional and overturned it—exactly the outcome desired by those who initiated the test case.

TEXAS V. JOHNSON

- 491 U.S. 397 (1989)
- Vote: 5–4
- For the Court: Brennan
- Concurring: Kennedy
- Dissenting: Rehnquist, White, O'Connor, and Stevens

The Republican party held its 1984 convention in Dallas, Texas. During one of the convention sessions, a group of demonstrators marched through the streets nearby to protest the policies of President Ronald Reagan, a Republican, who was overwhelmingly supported by delegates at the convention.

When the protest march ended, one of the demonstrators, Gregory Johnson, displayed the American flag, soaked it with kerosene, and set it on fire. As the flag burned, the demonstrators cheered. Some of them chanted, "America, the red, white, and blue, we spit on you."

Police officers arrested Johnson and charged him with violating the flag desecration law of the state of Texas. He was convicted and sentenced to one year in jail and a fine of $2,000. The Texas Court of Criminal Appeals reversed the decision, on the grounds that the decision was a violation of his free speech rights and the Texas and U.S. Constitutions, and the state appealed to the U.S. Supreme Court.

The Issue Advocates for Texas argued that its flag desecration law was a constitutional means to preserve the flag as a symbol of national unity. Further, this state law could be used to stop behavior that threatened to disrupt public order. Johnson argued that his conviction under Texas state law was a violation of 1st Amendment guarantees of freedom of expression as extended to the state through the due process clause of the 14th Amendment. Is flag burning, in the circumstances of this case, protected by the U.S. Constitution? Was the Texas statute on flag desecration constitutional?

Opinion of the Court The Supreme Court ruled in favor of Johnson. Justice William Brennan based his opinion on the prevailing free speech doctrine that justifies limitations only when the speech in question incites others directly and imminently to violence or other unlawful behavior. But there was no evidence that Johnson's "symbolic speech" (expression of an idea through an action, such as burning a flag) was an immediate threat to public order and safety. Brennan concluded, "If there is a bedrock principle underlying the First Amendment, it is that Government may not prohibit the expression of an idea simply because society finds the idea itself offensive or disagreeable."

Dissent Chief Justice William Rehnquist emphasized that freedom of expression may be limited in behalf of a legitimate government interest, such as preventing incitement of a riot or the desecration of a revered national symbol. Rehnquist wrote that the American flag is a "visible symbol embodying our Nation." It is not just "another symbol" and therefore deserves special protection against desecration.

Justice John Paul Stevens wrote that the American flag represents values, such as liberty and equality, that "are worth fighting for." Thus, it cannot be "true that the flag . . . is not itself worthy of protection from unnecessary desecration."

Significance This decision was very controversial. Public opinion polls showed that more than 80 percent of Americans opposed it and wanted a constitutional amendment or a federal law to reverse the *Johnson* decision. President George Bush also condemned the Court's decision.

Congress subsequently passed the Flag Protection Act of 1989, which provided penalties of one year in jail and a $1,000 fine for desecration of the American flag. This federal law had a very short life. The Court declared it unconstitutional in *United States* v. *Eichman* (1990). Thus, the Court's position in the *Johnson* case has prevailed.

SEE ALSO *Freedom of speech and press*

TEXAS V. WHITE

- 7 Wall. 700 (1869)
- Vote: 6–3
- For the Court: Chase
- Dissenting: Grier, Miller, and Wayne

In 1861, early in the Civil War, Texas seceded from the Union to join the Confederate States of America. After the war, Texas was temporarily governed under the Reconstruction policies of the federal government. This Reconstruction government of Texas brought suit to recover state-owned bonds (certificates of debt) that the state's Confederate government had sold.

Buyers of these bonds, such as George White, argued that Texas was at that time not a state and therefore could not sue anyone in a federal court. White based his claim on the fact that Texas had not yet been fully restored to the Union.

The Issue Was Texas able to file a suit

in the U.S. Supreme Court, given the facts of its secession, its status as a Confederate state during the Civil War, and its current status under Reconstruction policies? Did the U.S. Supreme Court have jurisdiction in this case?

Opinion of the Court   The Court ruled against White, and Texas was able to get back its bonds. In his opinion, Chief Justice Salmon Chase set forth enduring ideas about the nature of the federal Union. He stated that the Constitution created "an indestructible Union, composed of indestructible States." Thus, secession was illegal, and in a legal sense Texas had never left the Union. Therefore, as a full-fledged state of the federal Union, Texas could file suit in the federal courts.

Significance   Chief Justice Chase's decision established that secession was not valid under the U.S. Constitution. A constitutional argument that had persisted from the founding of the United States through the Civil War was finally settled.

THIRD PARTIES

Early in the history of the United States, two dominant parties emerged and became entrenched as the Democrats and the Republicans. Third parties have frequently risen to challenge their dominance, focusing on issues that the two major parties either ignored or suppressed. Sometimes a third party can supplant one of the major parties, as the Republican party did in the 1850s when it replaced the Whigs by opposing the spread of slavery into the western territories. More often, the major parties absorb the new ideas put forward by the third parties, which eventually disband.

The Tertium Quids, the nation's first third party, was formed in 1801 after John Randolph, the chairman of the House Ways and Means Committee, broke with President Thomas Jefferson on the issue of states' rights. This political group dissolved once Jefferson maneuvered Randolph out of office, but it did set an example for the possibilities of organized dissent through multiparty politics.

Third parties have traditionally formed to strengthen certain groups' support for or opposition to the general direction of American politics. The American Party (or Know-Nothings as they were commonly called) enjoyed a short-lived success in the 1850s by opposing immigration. The Know-Nothings won offices nationwide in the 1854 elections, due in large part to a growing xenophobia, but they were soon absorbed into the broader-based Republican party.

Third-party candidates have often run in Presidential elections. The Populist party, formed to aid beleaguered farmers, ran a strong third in the 1892 Presidential election. As the Socialist party candidate, Eugene V. Debs made four unsuccessful bids for president from 1900 to 1912. Despite their losses, the Populists and Socialists inspired the Democrats and Republicans to adopt many of the reforms they advocated, including a progressive income tax and federal banking and business regulation.

In 1912 former President Theodore Roosevelt broke from the Republican party and ran for president as the Progressive (or Bull Moose) party candidate. Running on a strong reform platform that included woman suffrage, an end to child labor, and greater federal regulation of the economy, Roosevelt ran second in the race, beating Republican President William Howard Taft but losing to the Democrat, Woodrow Wilson.

Third-party candidates seek to affect the outcome of elections by disrupting voter loyalties to the major parties. In 1948 Southern Democrats walked out of the Democratic convention after it adopted a civil rights plank. The States Rights (or Dixiecrat) party ran South Carolina governor Strom Thurmond for president. Meanwhile, former Vice President Henry Wallace also broke with the Democratic party and ran for president as the Progressive party candidate. Despite these defections, President Harry S. Truman held the core of the Democratic party together and scored an upset victory for reelection. Similarly, in 1968 and 1972, Alabama governor George Wallace campaigned as the American party candidate for president in order to oppose the Democratic party's support for civil rights legislation. Wallace captured a large portion of the southern vote with his anti-Washington platform.

Believing that the two-party system had become less flexible due to the growing importance of outside interest groups and multimillion-dollar campaigns, third-party candidates ran increasingly strong challenges in several elections toward the end of the twentieth century. In 1980 Illinois representative John Anderson left the Republicans and ran as an Independent for president, hoping to carve a constituency out of the disenchanted. Attempting to bring people on the outside of the two-party system together by representing a variety of interests, Anderson won 7 percent of the national vote. His effort was a precursor of the Reform party, founded by wealthy businessman H. Ross Perot.

Perot ran for president on the Reform ticket in both 1992 and 1996. In 1992 he received 13 percent of the vote, making the difference that enabled Democrat Bill Clinton to unseat the Republican President George Bush. Despite winning more than 19 million votes—a record for any third party—Perot received no votes in the Electoral College. This constitutional system, by which voters choose electors equal to the number of senators and representatives in their state and which requires a candidate to win a majority of electors to win the Presidency, has continued to force parties to remain national coalitions rather than splintered regional or issue groups. Third parties serve as a testing ground for new issues, and as banner under which disaffected voters can rally, but their failure to gain ground in the Electoral College usually sends their issues and their voters back into the two major parties.

THOMAS, CLARENCE
Associate Justice, 1991–

- Born: June 23, 1948, Savannah, Ga.
- Education: Holy Cross College, B.A., 1970; Yale Law School, LL.B., 1973
- Previous government service: assistant to the Missouri attorney general, 1973–77; legislative assistant to U.S. Senator John Danforth, 1979–81; assistant secretary of education, Civil Rights Division, 1981–82; chairman, Equal Employment Opportunity Commission, 1982–90; judge, U.S. Court of Appeals for the District of Columbia Circuit, 1990–91
- Appointed by President George Bush July 1, 1991; replaced Thurgood Marshall, who retired
- Supreme Court term: confirmed by the Senate Oct. 15, 1991, by a vote of 52–48

Clarence Thomas became, at the age of 43, the second black associate justice of the Supreme Court of the United States. He replaced Thurgood Marshall, the first African American on the Court. Thomas's road to the pinnacle of judicial power, however, was filled with obstacles.

Clarence Thomas rose to prominence from humble origins. He was raised by his grandfather, Myers Anderson, after his father abandoned him. Although poor, Anderson was a proud man with high hopes for his grandson. He pushed Thomas to excel in school and provided discipline and stability for his grandson. Thomas responded with high achievement in school that led him eventually to graduate from Yale Law School in 1973.

Thomas's first job as a lawyer was in Missouri, where he worked for the attorney general, John Danforth. Later, Danforth was elected to the U.S. Senate as a Republican, and Thomas went to Washington as the Senator's legislative assistant.

During the 1980s, Thomas, with support from Senator Danforth, achieved top-level jobs in the U.S. Department of Education and the Equal Employment Opportunity Commission.

In 1990, President George Bush appointed Thomas to the U.S. Court of Appeals for the District of Columbia Circuit. Eighteen months later, Thurgood Marshall resigned from the Supreme Court at the age of 82. On July 1, 1991, President Bush nominated Thomas to replace Justice Marshall. The President said: "If credit accrues to him for coming up through a tough life as a minority in this country, so much the better. It proves he can do it, get the job done. And so that does nothing but enhance the Court, in my view."

Standing next to the President, Clarence Thomas replied: "In my view, only in America could this have been possible. . . . As a child I could not dare dream that I would ever see the Supreme Court, not to mention be nominated to it."

The move from nomination to Senate confirmation was difficult for Thomas and the President. After several days of hearings, the Senate Judiciary Committee was sharply divided along partisan lines in its evaluation of Thomas. The Democrats, with one exception, clearly opposed his nomination, and the Republican members of the committee favored it. The committee vote was deadlocked, seven members for Thomas and seven against him.

Suddenly, the confirmation process became embroiled in controversy. Anita Hill, a former employee of Thomas at the U.S. Department of Education and the Equal Employment Opportunity Commission, charged him with sexual harassment. The Senate Judiciary Committee conducted special sessions to examine these charges by Hill. After three days of intense and acrimonious discussion of this issue, the Senate Judiciary Committee concluded its work and sent Thomas's nomination to the Senate for a final decision. The Senate committee vote remained at seven for Thomas and seven against him.

The Senate voted to confirm Justice Thomas by a vote of 52 to 48. This was the closest vote of approval for a Supreme Court appointment in more than 100 years. Eleven Democrats joined 41 Republicans to vote for Justice Thomas.

Justice Thomas has performed carefully and competently. At first, he usually joined with Justice Antonin Scalia when presenting concurring or dissenting opinions. Since 1994, however, Thomas has often acted independently to challenge conventional legal positions. For example, he wrote the Court's opinion in *Wilson v. Arkansas* (1995), which revived the old English common law "knock and announce" rule to augment the 4th Amendment's protection against unwarranted or unreasonable searches and seizures. This common law rule requires law-enforcement officers to announce their presence before entering a home or place of business.

SOURCES Jane Flax, *The American Dream in Black & White: The Clarence Thomas Hearings* (Ithaca, N.Y.: Cornell University Press, 1998). Scott Douglas Gerber, *First Principles: The Jurisprudence of Clarence Thomas* (New York: New York University Press, 1999).

THOMPSON, SMITH
Associate Justice, 1823–43

- Born: Jan. 17, 1768, Amenia, N.Y.
- Education: College of New Jersey (Princeton), B.A., 1788; read law with James Kent in Poughkeepsie, N.Y.
- Previous government service: New York Assembly, 1800; New York Constitutional Convention, 1801; associate justice, New York Supreme Court, 1802–14; New York State Board of Regents, 1813; chief justice, New York Supreme Court, 1814–18; U.S. secretary of the navy, 1819–23
- Appointed by President James Monroe as a recess appointment Sept. 1, 1823; replaced Henry Brockholst Livingston, who died; nominated by Monroe Dec. 8, 1823
- Supreme Court term: confirmed by the

Senate Dec. 19, 1823, by a voice vote; served until Dec. 18, 1843
- Died: Dec. 18, 1843, Poughkeepsie, N.Y.

Smith Thompson served on the Supreme Court for 20 years. During this lengthy period of service, however, he had only a slight impact on constitutional law. He developed a position on regulation of commerce at odds with the prevailing view of the Court, which gave broad powers of commercial regulation to the federal government. By contrast, Justice Thompson held that states could regulate commerce in all cases except those that conflicted with a federal law. This position was known as the doctrine of concurrent commerce powers; that is, the federal government and the state government could act jointly in most cases to regulate commerce. Thompson's position influenced the judicial thought of Roger B. Taney, John Marshall's successor as chief justice.

Justice Thompson's most significant opinion was his dissent in *Cherokee Nation v. Georgia* (1831). The state of Georgia asserted control over Cherokee lands within the state that had been granted to the Native Americans by a treaty with the federal government. Thompson argued that the Cherokee were an independent and sovereign nation, despite their status as a conquered people, and must be treated like other sovereign nations in legal dealings with the U.S. government. This dissenting opinion became the majority position, expressed by John Marshall, in *Worcester v. Georgia* (1832).

TICKET

A ticket consists of candidates for different offices who appear on an election ballot under the same party symbol and who run as a team. Prior to the election of 1804, tickets were informal because all candidates ran for Presidential electoral votes; the runner-up became Vice President. The 12th Amendment, which took effect that year, called for separate electoral votes for President and Vice President. That year, for the first time, there were distinct candidates for the two positions, and Thomas Jefferson and George Clinton were the winning ticket.

In 1840 Martin Van Buren ran for President with different Vice Presidential candidates on his ticket in each state. That was because the Democratic national convention had resolved not to endorse any one candidate for the Vice Presidency and to leave it instead to state parties to "nominate" their own Vice Presidential candidates to appear on the ballot with Van Buren.

Occasionally, a party has nominated a Vice Presidential candidate from the opposition party. John Tyler ran for Vice President on the Whig ticket in 1840 but was himself a Democrat. In 1864 Republican Abraham Lincoln ran with Democrat Andrew Johnson on the National Unionist ticket to gain votes from Democrats in the border states, such as Tennessee.

Major-party candidates sometimes run simultaneously on minor-party tickets. In 1868, for example, Ulysses S. Grant and Henry Wilson ran not only as Republicans but also on the National Working Men's party ticket. Their opponents, Horace Greeley and Benjamin Brown, ran not only as Democrats but also as Liberal Republicans and as candidates of the Liberal Republican Party of Colored Men. In 1896 William Jennings Bryan received the Presidential nomination of both the Democratic and the Populist parties, and in 1900 Bryan and Adlai Stevenson received the Democratic and Silver Republican nominations.

Of the 54 Presidential elections held between 1789 and 2000, only 8 resulted in the reelection of a President and the incumbent Vice President. The only Presidents who kept their running mates for a second term were George Washington, James Monroe, Woodrow Wilson, Franklin Roosevelt, Dwight Eisenhower, Richard Nixon, Ronald Reagan, and Bill Clinton.

TIME, PLACE, AND MANNER RULE

The U.S. Supreme Court has developed the time, place, and manner rule to determine whether government regulations or limitations of free speech are legal. According to this guideline, regulations about free speech may be constitutional if they are neutral concerning the content of the speech and deal only with the time, place, and manner of speech.

For example, people may talk freely to each other in public, but they may not talk at a time or place that would block traffic. Individuals may freely criticize government officials, but they may not express themselves in a manner that would interfere with the necessary work of the government. Individuals have the right to speak in favor of candidates for election to government offices. But they may not use a loudspeaker in a residential neighborhood at three o'clock in the morning to broadcast their messages because this would unfairly disturb sleeping residents of the community. In *Kovacs* v. *Cooper* (1949), for example, the Court upheld a local law restricting the use of sound-amplifying equipment on public streets.

When a free-speech regulation is challenged in court, the judges always inquire whether the regulation is neutral with regard to the content of the speech. If not, the Court will apply the test of strict scrutiny; that is, a compelling public interest must be demonstrated as justification for regulating the content of speech. Otherwise, the regulation will be overturned as unconstitutional. An example of a compelling public interest that could pass the strict scrutiny test is protecting the safety of individuals who might be endangered by the unregulated speech.

SEE ALSO *Freedom of speech and press*

TINKER V. DES MOINES INDEPENDENT COMMUNITY SCHOOL DIST

- 393 U.S. 503 (1969)
- Vote: 7–2
- For the Court: Fortas
- Concurring: Stewart and White
- Dissenting: Black and Harlan

In December 1965 some students in Des Moines, Iowa, decided to publicly express their opposition to the war in Vietnam by wearing black armbands. Des Moines school administrators, however, decided upon a policy that forbade the wearing of a black armband in school. Students who violated the policy would be suspended from school until they agreed to comply with the policy.

On December 16, Mary Beth Tinker and Christopher Eckhardt wore armbands to school. John Tinker did the same thing the next day. As a consequence, the three students were suspended from school and told not to return unless they removed their armbands. They stayed away from school until the early part of January 1966.

The three students filed a complaint, through their parents, against the school officials. They sought an injunction to prevent the officials from punishing them for wearing black armbands to school.

The Issue Did the school district's policy of prohibiting the wearing of black armbands in school violate the students' 1st Amendment right to free speech, as extended to the states through the due process clause of the 14th Amendment?

Opinion of the Court The Supreme Court decided by a vote of 7 to 2 that the school district had violated the students' right to free speech under the 1st and 14th

Amendments to the Constitution. In previous cases, such as *Stromberg* v. *California,* the Court had ruled that 1st Amendment free speech rights were incorporated by the due process clause of the 14th Amendment, which provides that no state shall "deprive any person of life, liberty [such as free speech], or property, without due process of law."

Justice Abe Fortas wrote the majority opinion, in which he stated that the wearing of black armbands to protest the Vietnam War was a form of "symbolic speech" protected by the 1st Amendment. Therefore, a public school ban on this form of protest was a violation of the students' right to free speech, as long as the protest did not disrupt the functioning of the school or violate the rights of other individuals. Justice Fortas wrote, "First Amendment rights applied in light of the special characteristics of the school environment, are available to teachers and students. It can hardly be argued that either students or teachers shed their constitutional rights to freedom of speech or expression at the school-house gate."

Dissent Justice Hugo Black was one of the two dissenters in this case. He wrote:
While I have always believed that under the First and Fourteenth Amendments neither the State nor the Federal Government has any authority to regulate or censor the content of speech, I have never believed that any person has a right to give speeches or engage in demonstrations where he pleases and when he pleases. This Court has already rejected such a notion. . . .
One does not need to be a prophet or the son of a prophet to know that after the Court's holding today some students in Iowa schools and indeed in all schools will be ready, able, and willing to defy their teachers on practically all orders. . . .
This case, therefore, wholly without constitutional reasons in my judgment, subjects all the public schools in the country to the whims and ca-

prices of their loudest-mouthed, but maybe not their brightest students.

Significance Tinker is one of the most important cases on the constitutional rights of students in public schools. It supports the protection of free expression that does not disrupt the educational purposes of the school or violate the rights of other students.

In subsequent cases involving students in public schools, such as *Bethel School District No. 403* v. *Fraser* (1986) and *Hazelwood School District* v. *Kuhlmeier* (1988), the Court supported the power of public school officials to limit freedom of expression by students if such expression— in these cases, a vulgar speech and the publication of sensitive material in the student newspaper—disrupted the schools' educational mission.

SEE ALSO *Bethel School District No. 403 v. Fraser; Freedom of speech and press; Hazelwood School District v. Kuhlmeier; Student rights under the Constitution*
SOURCES Peter Irons, *The Courage of Their Convictions* (New York: Free Press, 1988).

TODD, THOMAS
Associate Justice, 1807–26

- Born: Jan. 23, 1765, King and Queen County, Va.
- Education: Liberty Hall (Washington and Lee University), B.A., 1783; read law under Harry Innes, Bedford County, Va.
- Previous government service: clerk, federal district for Kentucky, 1789–92; clerk, Kentucky House of Representatives, 1792–1801; clerk, Kentucky Court of Appeals, 1799–1801; judge, Kentucky Court of Appeals, 1801–6; chief justice of Kentucky, 1806–7
- Appointed by President Thomas Jefferson Feb. 28, 1807, to occupy a new seat on the Court
- Supreme Court term: confirmed by the Senate Mar. 3, 1807, by a voice vote; served until Feb. 7, 1826

• Died: Feb. 7, 1826, Frankfort, Ky.

Thomas Todd was a veteran of the American War of Independence. At the age of 16, he served in the Continental Army. Before the war was over, Todd went to college and prepared to become a lawyer. In 1783, Todd moved to the western frontier in Kentucky, where he practiced law and served as a clerk in the government.

During his nearly 19 years on the Supreme Court, Justice Todd wrote only 14 opinions. He mostly followed the leadership of Chief Justice John Marshall, even though he was appointed by President Thomas Jefferson, a political foe of Marshall.

TOMPKINS, DANIEL
Vice President

• Born: June 21, 1774, Fox Meadows, N.Y.
• Political party: Democratic-Republican
• Education: Columbia College, B.A., 1795
• Military service: New York State Militia, 1812–14
• Previous government service: New York State Constitutional Convention, 1801; New York State Assembly, 1803–4; U.S. House of Representatives, 1805; associate justice, New York Court of Appeals, 1805–7; governor of New York, 1807–17
• Vice President under James Monroe, 1817–25
• Died: June 11, 1825, Tompkinsville, N.Y.

Daniel Tompkins was considered for several appointments, including secretary of state, during James Madison's Presidency, but his career was confined to New York State until 1817. During the War of 1812, as governor of New York and commander in chief of the New York State militia and the Third Military District of the United States, Tompkins found it necessary to borrow money to supply his troops. He borrowed much of the money on his own credit. Creditors later seized his personal fortune to repay bills the military had incurred on his signature. At the end of the war Tompkins applied to the Treasury for repayment but his accounts were challenged, leaving him with severe financial problems.

Tompkins was sponsored by New York politicians as a potential Presidential candidate in 1816, but he attracted little support among the Republicans in Congress (the congressional caucus) who would determine the party's choice. James Monroe, who won the Republican nomination, accepted Tompkins as his running mate.

While Vice President, Tompkins tried to clear up his tangled financial affairs. In poor health and drinking heavily, he spent most of his term in New York City. He was defeated for the New York governorship in 1820 but ran for reelection with Monroe and served a second term as Vice President. In 1824, near the end of his second term, Congress finally authorized the Treasury to reimburse him for $95,000 in expenses.

SEE ALSO *Monroe, James*

TORT

A tort is a civil wrong, other than a contract violation, done by one party to another party. By contrast, a crime is a violation of a government's laws; these are the statutes that pertain to wrongs against society, which the government has authority to punish through its law enforcement powers.

Torts involve violations of civil law, not criminal law. They usually are the responsibility of state courts, but the U.S. Supreme Court sometimes becomes involved when the tort law of a state conflicts with the Constitution or federal laws.

TRANSITIONS, PRESIDENTIAL

Many activities occur prior to and immediately after a new President enters office.

Planned transitions occur at the end of a departing President's term and last from the election to shortly after the inauguration. Unplanned transitions occur almost instantaneously when a President dies or resigns; they take several weeks to complete.

The planned transition involves briefings on the policies of the outgoing administration (especially national security secrets); preparation of the inaugural address and the first message to Congress requesting legislation; preparation of revisions to the budget of the outgoing President; recruitment of personnel to fill the 3,000 political appointments that constitute a Presidential administration; and analysis of each department and agency in order to exert maximum White House influence on its operations.

In an unplanned transition the Vice President takes the Presidential oath of office. He then speaks to the nation about the events that led to his succession, usually by addressing a joint session of Congress.

Only recently have Presidents cooperated with their successors in planning smooth transitions. In 1944 Franklin Roosevelt began the custom of briefing his major-party opponent on national security matters, and in 1952 Truman did the same. Dwight Eisenhower established the custom of providing a personal briefing for his successor (John F. Kennedy), and the two men created the precedent of designating aides to serve as liaisons between the incoming and outgoing administrations.

Outgoing Presidents usually want their successors to endorse their last projects. Herbert Hoover, in the midst of the Great Depression, attempted to get President-elect Franklin Roosevelt to support his proposals for economic recovery. Incoming Presidents generally do not give these endorsements because they wish to preserve their freedom of action. Consequently, there is often some friction between outgoing and incoming Presidents; it is rare but not unknown for the outgoing President to skip the inauguration ceremonies entirely.

Until the 1960s the expenses involved in the transition were borne by the winning candidate and his party. In 1960 Kennedy and the Democratic National Committee spent $300,000. Congress later passed the Presidential Transition Act of 1963, which provided $900,000 for the "orderly transfer of a President and the inauguration of a new President." Funds were increased to keep up with inflation. The Presidential Transition Effectiveness Act of 1988 provided that in 1992 the newly elected President would receive $3.5 million and the departing President would receive $1.5 million. Under the new law, the President-elect's transition organization would be required to limit private contributions to no more than $5,000 from a single source and to report all such contributions. These limits and disclosure provisions were designed to prevent big-money contributors from buying influence and access in the new administration.

SEE ALSO *Succession to the Presidency*
SOURCES Carl M. Brauer, *Presidential Transitions: Eisenhower through Reagan* (New York: Oxford University Press, 1986). James P. Pfiffner, *The Strategic Presidency: Hitting the Ground Running* (Chicago: Dorsey, 1988). James P. Pfiffner and R. Gordon Hoxie, *The Presidency in Transition* (New York: Center for the Study of the Presidency, 1989).

"TREASON OF THE SENATE"

SEE *Scandals, congressional*

TREATY OF VERSAILLES

The Treaty of Versailles was the agreement negotiated by the victorious Allied nations with the defeated Central Powers to end World War I. Twice, in 1919 and 1920, the Senate rejected the treaty. These Senate votes were a major defeat for President

Woodrow Wilson, who had gone to Paris to personally negotiate the treaty with the Allied leaders and the defeated Germany and Austria and who led the fight for its ratification.

The treaty was negotiated at a peace conference held between January and June 1919 at the Palace of Versailles outside of Paris, France. It was attended by 32 nations but dominated by Prime Minister David Lloyd George of Great Britain, Prime Minister Georges Clemenceau of France, Prime Minister Vittorio Orlando of Italy, and President Woodrow Wilson of the United States. Wilson shattered precedent by attending the conference in person rather than naming the secretary of state or a special envoy as chief of the delegation. He was the first U.S. President to go to Europe during his term. Wilson's delegation did not include any leaders of Congress. Instead, Wilson took hundreds of experts to advise him about the peoples and politics of Europe.

Wilson's Fourteen Points program renounced territorial gains for the United States and denounced secret understandings. He called for "open covenants openly arrived at." The other Allies, however, had already come to agreement about the spoils of war, especially German colonies in Africa and the division of the Ottoman Empire in the Middle East.

Signed by the defeated German government in June 1919, the Treaty of Versailles was a vindictive settlement. Germany was forced to accept sole responsibility for the war, pay $56 billion in reparations to the victors, and disarm. The French were allowed to occupy German territory for 15 years and to regain the province of Alsace-Lorraine, which Germany had conquered in 1871. Poland was given a corridor to the sea through the German province of Prussia, which cut Germany in two. Altogether, Germany was stripped of 10 percent of its people, one-eighth of its territory, and all its overseas possessions. From the Ottoman Empire the British received mandates, or territories, in Palestine, Trans-Jordan,

and Iraq, and the French received Syria and Lebanon. Japan acquired Germany's Pacific islands.

The only victory for Wilson during the negotiations was the inclusion of a League of Nations as part of the treaty. The league would be an assembly of all sovereign nations, pledged to preserve the independence and territorial integrity of each member.

Wilson returned home in June to press for U.S. participation in the League of Nations. Opposition came from German Americans and Italian Americans and from isolationists in the South and West. Wilson had not consulted with the Senate during the negotiations and had not tried to win over the influential chairman of the Foreign Relations Committee, Republican Henry Cabot Lodge of Massachusetts. Lodge led the fight against the league. He disliked Wilson and believed the United States should retain complete freedom of action in international affairs. Although Lodge was no isolationist, he managed to unite the isolationist wing of his party, known as the Irreconcilables, with his own followers around a series of "fourteen reservations" to the treaty (an echo of Wilson's Fourteen Points). One provided for U.S. withdrawal from the league by concurrent resolution of Congress, a method not subject to Presidential veto. Another provided that the President could not direct troops in a league peacekeeping operation—an attack on the President's power as commander in chief. Still another would have prevented the President from making interim appointments to an international organization when the Senate was in recess.

The most important reservation amended the treaty by stating that the United States would retain complete freedom of action in foreign affairs and that only Congress had the right to commit U.S. forces to military action—not the league or the President.

To get the two-thirds vote needed for ratification, supporters of the treaty needed to forge an alliance with those favoring reservations. But Wilson refused to make any compromises. Instead, he took his case directly to the people, confident that public opinion would force the Senate to accept the treaty and the League of Nations. In September 1919 Wilson embarked on a nationwide speaking tour to rally support. His tour was exhausting and he collapsed on September 25 in Pueblo, Colorado. He returned to Washington and suffered a stroke on October 2.

On November 19 Democrats in the Senate voted down the treaty with the Lodge reservations; then Lodge's Republican coalition voted down Wilson's version of the treaty. Although more than two-thirds of the Senate favored some sort of league, they were caught between Wilson and Lodge, and no treaty could pass. For the first time, the Senate rejected a peace treaty negotiated by the President. The United States never became a member of the League of Nations. Instead, Congress passed a joint resolution in 1921 officially recognizing an end to hostilities with Germany and other Central Powers.

SEE ALSO *Advice and consent; Treaty powers; Wilson, Woodrow*

SOURCES Lloyd E. Ambrosius, *Woodrow Wilson and the American Diplomatic Tradition: The Treaty Fight in Perspective* (Cambridge: Cambridge University Press, 1987). Thomas A. Bailey, *Woodrow Wilson and the Great Betrayal* (Chicago: University of Chicago Press, 1963). Woodrow Wilson, *The Hope of the World* (New York: Harper, 1920).

TREATY POWERS

The Constitution provides that the President "shall have the Power, by and with the Advice and Consent of the Senate, to make Treaties, provided two-thirds of the Senators present concur." The framers expected the Senate to play a major role in the treaty-making process. In fact, most drafts at the Constitutional Convention gave the Senate the power to make treaties, and it was not until 10 days before the convention adjourned that the President was given the major role in negotiating treaties.

The Constitution's requirement of consent by the Senate reflected concerns that treaties reached by the national government might injure the interests of some of the states. In 1786 the Congress under the Articles of Confederation had approved the Jay-Gardoqui Treaty, which conceded American navigation rights on the Mississippi River to Spain. Westerners had seen this treaty as sacrificing their interests in favor of those of New England merchants.

Does the Senate's advice come only when the President submits a treaty draft to the Senate? Or can the Senate advise the President while he is negotiating the treaty? The language of the Constitution does not divide treaty making into separate stages for negotiation and Senate consent. Rather, the President "makes" the treaty with the advice and consent of the Senate, which seems to imply a role for the Senate in the negotiations.

George Washington set the early precedents. While negotiating an Indian treaty, he suggested that "the business may possibly be referred to their [the Senate's] deliberations in their legislative chamber." Washington met with the Senate on August 22, 1789, to obtain its advice. The senators decided they would not commit themselves to any treaty draft that Washington presented to them that day. Washington had to return two days later in order to obtain their consent, but the experience of consultation soured him. He never again consulted in advance with the Senate in person. When he negotiated the Jay Treaty with Great Britain, he consulted with Senate leaders in writing and submitted the full treaty to the Senate only after it was completed.

Since Washington's time, practices have varied. Until 1815 it was the custom for Presidents to send a special message to Congress before starting negotiations and again when treaty drafts had been concluded. Since then, some Presidents have consulted informally with congressional leaders before negotiations, as President Chester Arthur did in 1884 on a treaty with the independent islands of Hawaii. Many have given extensive briefings to senators while negotiations were in progress, as Secretary of State Dean Acheson did with key senators about the North Atlantic Treaty Organization treaty of 1949. One senator, Walter George, actually wrote part of the treaty for the administration.

The composition of the negotiating team may help the President secure Senate consent. President Harry Truman used a Republican, John Foster Dulles, as his chief negotiator for the treaty with Japan at the end of World War II to give it bipartisan support. For arms control negotiations some Presidents have given senators an informal "veto" over members of their negotiating teams or allowed senators to send staff members to negotiating sessions as observers. Since 1962 members of Congress have been advisers on trade agreement negotiations, and President Jimmy Carter named 26 senators as "official advisers" to his arms negotiating team at Geneva in 1977 and 1978.

Sometimes, Presidents have even put members of Congress in their negotiating delegations, as William McKinley did when he included three senators in his Treaty of Paris delegation in 1900. President Woodrow Wilson did not favor this kind of collaboration: he argued that Presidents should negotiate treaties by themselves and then submit them to the Senate. When he negotiated the Treaty of Versailles in 1919, he did not include a single member of the Senate in his delegation, nor did he provide Congress with any information about negotiations. The Senate defeated the treaty. Jimmy Carter almost committed the same error, failing to include senators on his negotiating team or provide them with briefings when he negotiated the Panama Canal Treaty in 1977. To save the treaty in 1979, Carter agreed to amendments negotiated by several senators with the Panamanian government.

The two-thirds provision by which the Senate gives its formal consent has been interpreted since 1953 to mean two-thirds of a quorum (the minimum number of members necessary to transact business). The Senate may amend the treaty before giving its consent, in which case the new language must be accepted by the other nation. The Senate has also altered treaties by means of reservations, which indicate a substantial change in the interpretation of treaty provisions (the new document is sent to the other nation but does not require its consent) and understandings, which clarify relatively minor aspects of the treaty's implementation.

Sometimes the Senate has amended treaties so severely that it caused the other nation to reject the agreement. In 1824, when the United States signed a treaty with Great Britain to suppress the international slave trade, pro-slavery senators so severely amended the treaty that the British rejected the agreement. At other times, nations have accepted Senate amendments as the price necessary for Senate approval. The Supreme Court upheld the Senate's right to amend a treaty, in the 1869 case of *Haver* v. *Yaker,* when the Court ruled that "a treaty is something more than a contract, for the Federal Constitution declares it to be the law of the land. If so, before it becomes a law, the Senate . . . must agree to it. But the Senate are not required to adopt or reject it as a whole, but may modify or amend it."

After the Senate consents to a treaty, the President may ratify it by signifying to the other nation that it is in effect, or he may withhold ratification if he decides not to implement it. He may withhold ratification because circumstances have changed, because he objects to amendments, or because he foresees problems with the other nation's adherence to it.

Between 1789 and 1989 the Senate approved some 1,500 treaties, or about 90 percent of the total it received. It rejected only 20 treaties by formal vote, including a treaty to annex Texas in 1844 and Wilson's Treaty of Versailles in 1919. The other unratified treaties were either withdrawn by the President or never acted upon by the committees. Although most treaties since World War II have been adopted, the Senate has sometimes blocked or amended important Presidential initiatives. These include the heavily amended Panama Canal Treaties of 1979 and the Strategic Arms Limitation Agreements with the Soviet Union that Jimmy Carter withdrew from the Senate after the Soviet invasion of Afghanistan in 1979.

Proposals have been made to lower the approval requirement to three-fifths or an absolute majority of senators present. Another idea is to prevent any amendments or reservations by senators. Such changes would require a constitutional amendment, and the Senate is unlikely to agree to limitations on its treaty powers.

Treaty obligations can be terminated in a variety of ways. Congress may pass a law inconsistent with the terms of the treaty, and the courts will enforce the law at the expense of the treaty. Congress can pass a joint resolution that directs the President to abrogate, or nullify, a treaty. Or the President can request a Senate resolution consenting to abrogation of a treaty. Finally, the President can abrogate a treaty unilaterally, without obtaining the consent of Congress or the Senate, as Jimmy Carter did in 1978 with the Mutual Defense Treaty of 1954 with the Republic of China (Taiwan).

SEE ALSO *Advice and consent; Executive agreements*

SOURCES Louis Fisher, *Constitutional Conflicts between Congress and the President* (Princeton, N.J.: Princeton University Press, 1985). Robert C. Byrd, "Treaties," in *The Senate, 1789–1989: Addresses on the History of the United States Senate,* vol. 2 (Washington, D.C.: Government Printing Office, 1991).

TRIAL BY JURY

A trial involves public examination of a legal issue in a court of law. A jury is a group of supposedly impartial citizens selected to determine the facts and sit in judgment of a defendant in a trial. The jury, at the end of the trial, reaches a verdict of guilty or innocent, which determines whether the defendant is freed or punished.

The right of an individual to a trial by jury is provided in three parts of the U.S. Constitution. Article 3, Section 2, says, "The Trial of all Crime, except in Cases of Impeachment, shall be by Jury." Amendment 6 says, "In all criminal prosecutions, the accused shall enjoy the right to a speedy and public trial." Amendment 7 says, "In Suits at common law, where the value in controversy shall exceed twenty dollars, the right to trial by jury shall be preserved."

The Supreme Court ruled in *Baldwin* v. *New York* (1970) that the right to a trial by jury is provided to any adult accused of a crime if the potential punishment is incarceration for more than six months. And, according to the 7th Amendment, a trial by jury is available to those involved in a common lawsuit (federal civil, or noncriminal, case) if the controversy involves more than $20.

In a trial by jury of a criminal case, the jury has the power to decide whether the accused person is guilty or innocent. The jury also may make decisions, within legally prescribed limits, about degrees of criminal behavior (for example, whether a person is guilty of murder or merely manslaughter) and the severity of punishment for a guilty person.

The traditional size of a jury, 12 people, is based on English legal traditions that were brought to America during the colonial era. However, some states have experimented with smaller juries, especially in trials of less serious crimes. The U.S. Supreme Court ruled in *Williams* v. *Florida* (1970) that a six-person jury is not necessarily a violation of the constitutional guarantee of due process of law. Further, Section 48 of the Federal Rules of Civil Procedure permits the parties in a dispute to agree to a jury of less than 12 members.

Another tradition has been the requirement of a unanimous decision by a jury in reaching a verdict. Some states, however, have experimented with rules that permit verdicts by juries that are less than unanimous. Usually, these rules have required large majorities, such as 9 or 10 jurors, in reaching a verdict. The Supreme Court decided in *Minneapolis and St. Louis Railway Company* v. *Bombolis* (1916) that jury verdicts in state court proceedings based on less than a unanimous vote were not denials of the fair legal procedures required by the due process clause in the Constitution. Later, however, in *Burch v. Louisiana* (1979), the Court overturned a Louisiana law that permitted verdicts to be reached by a 5-to-1 vote of a six-person jury. In contrast to some state court practices, the unanimous verdict rule remains the standard in federal cases involving a jury trial.

SEE ALSO *Bill of Rights; Rights of the accused*

SOURCES David J. Bodenhamer, *Fair Trial: Rights of the Accused in American History* (New York: Oxford University Press, 1992).

TRIMBLE, ROBERT
Associate Justice, 1826–28

- Born: Nov. 17, 1776, Berkeley County, Va.
- Education: read law under George Nicholas and James Brown, Lexington, Ky.
- Previous government service: Kentucky House of Representatives, 1802; judge, Kentucky Court of Appeals, 1807–9, 1810; U.S. district attorney for Kentucky, 1813–17; U.S. district judge for Kentucky, 1817–26
- Appointed by President John Quincy Adams Apr. 11, 1826; replaced Thomas Todd, who died
- Supreme Court term: confirmed by the Senate May 9, 1826, by a voice vote; served until Aug. 25, 1828
- Died: Aug. 25, 1828, Paris, Ky.

Robert Trimble was the son of pioneers who arrived in the territory of Kentucky in 1780. Trimble took advantage of an opportunity to go to school and attended the Bourbon Academy. Later, he prepared for a career in law by studying with two local attorneys. Trimble became a successful lawyer and judge in Kentucky.

Trimble was the only Supreme Court appointment of President John Quincy Adams. He was the first federal district judge to become a justice of the Supreme Court. Like President Adams, he favored a strong federal government. Justice Trimble served briefly on the Court and wrote only 16 opinions before his sudden death from an undiagnosed illness.

TRUMAN COMMITTEE (1941–45)

In 1941, as the United States busily expanded its defense-industry production just before entering World War II, Senator Harry S. Truman (Democrat–Missouri) proposed a special Senate committee to investigate the national defense program. With millions of dollars being spent to mobilize the army and navy, Truman believed that some contractors were misusing government programs for their own profit. The Senate voted unanimously to create the special committee, which Truman was appointed to chair. During the war, the Truman Committee held many hearings to root out corruption and to promote unity among business, labor, and agriculture in support of the war effort. Favorable publicity from the hearings won Senator Truman the nomination to run for Vice President in 1944. The following April, after the death of Franklin Roosevelt, Truman became President.

SOURCES Theodore Wilson, "The Truman Committee," in *Congress Investigates: A Documented History, 1792–1974,* edited by Arthur M. Schlesinger, Jr., and Roger Bruns (New York: Bowker, 1975).

TRUMAN, HARRY S.
33rd President

- Born: May 8, 1884, Lamar, Mo.
- Political party: Democrat
- Education: high school
- Military service: U.S. Army, 1917–19
- Previous government service: road overseer, Jackson County, Mo., 1914; postmaster, Grandview, Mo., 1915; Jackson County judge, 1922–24; Jackson County presiding judge, 1926–34; U.S. Senate, 1934–45; Vice President, 1945
- Succeeded to Presidency, 1945; served, 1945–53
- Died: Dec. 26, 1972, Kansas City, Mo.

Harry Truman was the first President to assume office in the middle of a war. His decision to drop atomic bombs on Japan shortened World War II and reduced U.S. casualties. In the postwar period he presided over the creation of collective security measures (the creation of alliances for mutual defense against aggression) to contain communist expansion in Europe. Although he won an elected term in one of the greatest upsets in U.S. history, subsequent inflation and labor unrest, coupled with his decision to use U.S. troops to defend South Korea, contributed to his unpopularity and his decision not to seek a second elected term.

Truman grew up on a farm near Independence, Missouri. He finished high school and became a railroad worker, mail room boy, bank clerk, and bookkeeper, returning to his grandfather's farm after several years. In World War I he served as a first lieutenant and then captain of artillery, seeing action near the end of the war in the Argonne Forest and at Verdun. In 1919 he married Elizabeth Virginia ("Bess") Wallace. Truman became a partner in a men's haberdashery with an army friend; when the store failed and left him deeply in debt, he refused to declare bankruptcy and spent years paying off creditors. Truman's political career began after he was introduced to the Democratic boss of

Kansas City, Missouri, Tom Pendergast. As a loyal worker in the Pendergast machine, he helped the organization move into rural Jackson County. He became a county judge (an administrative, not a legal, position), and in 1934 the Pendergast machine backed him in a three-way race for the Democratic nomination for U.S. Senate. Truman won the nomination, then campaigned for and won election as a supporter of Franklin Roosevelt's New Deal. In 1940 he again won a three-way race for the Democratic nomination, then won reelection even though Boss Pendergast had been sentenced to prison for income tax evasion and other members of his machine had been convicted of vote fraud. Voters knew that Truman had not been involved in these activities.

In his second term in the Senate, Truman chaired the Special Committee to Investigate the National Defense Program. He uncovered waste, fraud, and corruption and contributed greatly to the successful U.S. war effort.

In 1944 President Franklin Roosevelt dropped Henry Wallace from his ticket and offered the Democratic convention a choice between Harry Truman and Supreme Court justice William O. Douglas. Although a majority of the delegates supported Wallace on the first ballot, they bowed to Roosevelt's wishes and nominated Truman on the second ballot.

President Roosevelt's death on April 12, 1945, elevated Truman to the Presidency. On May 7 Truman announced that the war in Europe had ended. His first important mission was the Potsdam Conference in July 1945, where he met with British prime minister Winston Churchill and Soviet dictator Joseph Stalin to negotiate the fate of Eastern Europe. Returning home, Truman won Senate consent to the charter of the United Nations; for the first time, the United States would be part of a world organization. In July he decided to use the atomic bomb against Japan to end the war in the Pacific. Hiroshima was destroyed on August 6, Nagasaki on August 9. On August 14 Japan surrendered.

In September 1945 Truman presented his domestic Fair Deal program to Congress: new initiatives in health care, civil rights, public housing, and rural development. Much of the legislation was stalled by a conservative coalition of Republicans and Southern Democrats, although Congress did pass the Employment Act of 1946, which established the Council of Economic Advisers. With the slogan "Had Enough?" the Republicans won control of Congress in 1946 and began passing their own measures. Truman vetoed the Taft-Hartley Act, a law regulating strikes, because he thought it was antiunion, but Congress passed it over his veto in 1947. It also passed an income tax reduction bill. Truman intervened in railroad and coal strikes in 1946 and 1947, alienating labor and liberals, and his attempt to continue the wartime Fair Employment Practices Committee (set up to outlaw racial discrimination in employment) upset Southern conservatives, who abolished it.

In 1948 Truman won the Democratic nomination for President with the support of the urban party bosses. In a brilliant election-year tactic, Truman called the Republican-dominated Congress into special session and challenged it to pass his program. While the Republicans stalled, Truman campaigned for reelection against the "Do-Nothing 80th Congress." He made a whistle-stop railroad tour and crowds chanted "Give 'em Hell, Harry." He proposed major new civil rights legislation, including federal protection against lynchings, voting rights measures, prohibition of discrimination in interstate transportation, and a permanent fair practices commission. In the midst of the campaign Truman issued an executive order ending racial segregation in the armed forces. With overwhelming support from blacks, Truman eked out narrow margins of victory in key Northern states and defeated Republican Thomas E. Dewey, Dixiecrat Strom Thurmond, and Progressive Henry Wallace. Truman won less than half the popular vote, in the closest election since 1916.

Truman returned to Washington to savor his victory, proudly holding aloft a copy of the *Chicago Tribune* that carried the election night headline "DEWEY DEFEATS TRUMAN."

Truman's major domestic success after winning reelection was the Housing Act of 1949, which provided for slum clearance and public housing in urban areas. Congress also raised the minimum wage. It stalled, however, on Truman's farm, education, health, labor, and civil rights proposals.

Truman's foreign policy was based on containing communist expansion in Western Europe. Rather than seeking to cultivate the Soviets as allies, Truman believed that they had to "be faced with an iron fist and strong language." Congress created the Defense Department to supervise the Departments of the Army, Navy, and Air Force and established the Joint Chiefs of Staff for military planning. It also created the National Security Council and the Central Intelligence Agency.

In March 1947 the President announced the Truman Doctrine, stating that the United States would "support free peoples who are resisting attempted subjugation by armed minorities or outside pressure." He called for military and economic aid to Greece and Turkey to prevent communist guerrilla movements from seizing power. Then, in June Secretary of State George Marshall announced the European Recovery Program (later known as the Marshall Plan). Between 1948 and 1951 more than $12 billion was granted or loaned to European nations to restore their postwar economies. In the spring and summer of 1948 Truman ordered U.S. airplanes to supply West Berlin, breaking a Soviet blockade of the western part of the city. The Point Four foreign aid program of technical assistance began in 1949, the same year that the North Atlantic Treaty Organization (NATO) committed the United States to the defense of Western Europe. Similarly, the Rio Pact and the Anzus Pact committed the United States to the defense of the Western Hemisphere,

Australia, and New Zealand. Mutual defense treaties were also signed with the Philippines and Japan. The Soviets tested their first atomic bomb in 1949, so in 1950 Truman permitted development of the powerful hydrogen bomb to proceed. It was successfully tested in 1952.

Truman's policy of containment against communist aggression was put to the test. On June 28, 1950, Truman ordered U.S. air and ground forces to repel a North Korean invasion of South Korea. This "police action" was sanctioned by the United Nations Security Council. Truman's conduct of the war was controversial. On the advice of Secretary of State Dean Acheson, he did not ask Congress for a declaration of war. He allowed General Douglas MacArthur to invade North Korea, but when communist Chinese troops entered the war, Truman refused to allow bombing of North Korean supply bases in China because he feared it might lead to all-out war between the United States and China. On April 11, 1951, Truman fired MacArthur for insubordination after the general called for bombing China. MacArthur received a hero's welcome back in the United States and addressed a joint session of Congress.

The Korean War dragged on. Close to 50,000 U.S. troops were killed and 100,000 wounded. The war rekindled inflation and shortages in the economy and contributed to Truman's declining popularity. After Truman seized steel mills on April 8, 1952, during a strike, claiming he had to ensure production as a war measure, the Supreme Court ordered that he return the mills to their owners. This ruling further diminished Truman's popularity.

On March 29, 1952, Truman announced that he would not seek reelection. In his farewell address, he observed that "the President's job is to make decisions. . . . He can't pass the buck to anybody. No one else can do the deciding for him. That's his job." With his job over, he retired to Independence, Missouri, where he wrote his memoirs and oversaw the creation of his Presidential library. "You, more than any man, have saved Western civilization," Winston Churchill told him.

SEE ALSO *Barkley, Alben; Eisenhower, Dwight David; Roosevelt, Franklin D.; Steel seizure (1952); Wallace, Henry*

SOURCES Robert H. Ferrell, *Harry S. Truman and the Modern American Presidency* (Boston: Little, Brown, 1983). David McCullough, *Truman* (New York: Simon & Schuster, 1992). Merle Miller, *Plain Speaking: An Oral Biography of Harry S Truman* (New York: Berkley, 1974). Harry S. Truman, *Memoirs of Harry S. Truman,* vol. 1, *Year of Decisions, 1945* (New York: Da Capo, 1986). Harry S. Truman, *Memoirs of Harry S. Truman,* vol. 2, *Years of Trial and Hope* (New York: Da Capo, 1987). Margaret Truman, *Harry S. Truman* (New York: Morrow, 1973).

12TH AMENDMENT

The 12th Amendment to the Constitution, ratified in 1804, revised the voting system in the electoral college. The Constitution of 1787 provided that each elector would cast two ballots for President. The person with the most votes would become President and the runner-up would assume the Vice Presidency, provided each received support from a majority of all the electors appointed. If two candidates with such support received an equal number of votes, the House of Representatives was to choose between them.

In the election of 1796, Federalist John Adams received a majority of electoral college votes, but Anti-Federalist Thomas Jefferson was runner-up and became Vice President. In the election of 1800 every Republican elector cast one ballot for Thomas Jefferson and the other for his running mate, Aaron Burr. Because Jefferson and Burr received the same number of votes, the election went into the House of Representatives. Many Federalists preferred Burr to Jefferson, but at the last minute, Alexander Hamilton intervened and on the 36th ballot some Federalists abstained, ensuring Jefferson's election as President.

The Senate then elected Burr Vice President, according to the original intentions of the Jeffersonians.

In 1803 Congress passed the 12th Amendment, which was ratified by the states and adopted on September 25, 1804. It provided that each elector would cast a separate ballot for President and Vice President, thus preventing the situation that had occurred in 1800. The new system ensured that the majority that elected a President would also elect his running mate from the same party, preventing a recurrence of the results in 1796.

Because only one ballot can be cast for each office (rather than two for President under the original system), only one candidate can win a majority vote for President, preventing a recurrence of the results in 1800. If no candidate wins an electoral college majority for President, the House chooses from among the top three, with each state casting a single vote. If no candidate wins a majority for the Vice Presidency, the Senate chooses between the top two, with each senator casting one vote. In the event the House fails to elect a President, the person chosen by the Senate as Vice President acts as President until the House does elect a President.

SEE ALSO *Burr, Aaron; Electoral college; Jefferson, Thomas; Ticket*
SOURCES Richard P. McCormick, *The Presidential Game* (New York: Oxford University Press, 1982).

25TH AMENDMENT

The 25th Amendment to the Constitution, ratified on February 10, 1967, deals with Presidential disability. If a President is disabled, the 25th Amendment provides that the Vice President acts as President (but does not assume the office of President) until the incumbent can resume the office. The President can declare disability and invite the Vice President to act as President. Or the Vice President, together with a majority of the cabinet, can find the President to be disabled, in which case the Vice President can act as President. In either case the President determines when to resume the duties of the office.

If the Vice President and the cabinet disagree with the President's decision, the final determination is made by Congress. A two-thirds vote by each chamber is required to permit the Vice President to continue to act as President in the event the President wishes to resume the powers of his office. These provisions have not yet been applied to any President.

The 25th Amendment also provides for filling vacancies in the Vice Presidency. The President can nominate a Vice President, who takes office upon confirmation by a majority vote of both chambers of Congress. This provision was used in 1973, when Spiro Agnew resigned from the Vice Presidency and Gerald Ford was nominated by President Richard Nixon and confirmed by Congress. It was also used by Ford to fill the vacancy created when he became President after Nixon's resignation.

SEE ALSO *Agnew, Spiro T.; Disability, Presidential; Ford, Gerald R.; Health, Presidential; Nixon, Richard M.; Resignation, Presidential; Succession to the Presidency*
SOURCES John Feerick, *From Failing Hands: The Story of Presidential Succession* (New York: Fordham University Press, 1965). Robert E. Gilbert, *The Mortal Presidency* (New York: Basic Books, 1992).

22ND AMENDMENT

The 22nd Amendment to the Constitution, ratified on February 27, 1951, limits the Presidential term. It provides that no person may be elected President more than twice. No Vice President who succeeded to the office of President, nor any other person in the line of succession who acted as President, and served for more than two years of a term to which someone else had been elected, could be elected to the Presidency more than once.

The wording of the amendment clarifies two situations: When a President dies or leaves office during his term, the Vice President succeeds to the office and becomes President, rather than simply acting as President. On the other hand, anyone else in the line of succession becomes acting President.

Could a former President run for the Vice Presidency, then succeed to the Presidency and serve a third term? The 12th Amendment provides that "no person Constitutionally ineligible to the office of President shall be eligible to that of Vice President of the United States." If a President is deemed to be "ineligible to the office" after two terms, this provision would prevent electors in the electoral college from electing that person Vice President.

Could a former President be appointed under provisions of the 25th Amendment to the Vice Presidency, then consented to by Congress? Could he then become President in the event of a vacancy? Again, if a two-term President is deemed "ineligible to the office," Congress could not elect the ex-President to the Vice Presidency.

However, a former President who then was named to the cabinet or who became Speaker of the House or president pro tempore of the Senate would be in the line of succession to become acting President in the event of a double vacancy. Such positions are not covered by the 12th Amendment, which deals only with the election of Vice Presidents.

SEE ALSO *Succession to the Presidency; Term of office, Presidential; Vice President*

TWINING V. NEW JERSEY

- 211 U.S. 78 (1908)
- Vote: 8–1
- For the Court: Moody
- Dissenting: Harlan

New Jersey charged Albert Twining with the crime of reporting false information to a state government bank examiner. Twining refused to testify at his state court trial, an action that the judge interpreted, in his charge to the jury, as an admission of guilt.

Under New Jersey law, the judge could make such an interpretation.

Twining was convicted and the New Jersey Supreme Court upheld the conviction. Twining, however, argued that he had a constitutional right to protection against giving evidence against himself. He pointed to the 5th Amendment to the U.S. Constitution, which says, "No person shall be . . . compelled in any criminal case to be a witness against himself." Twining appealed to the U.S. Supreme Court.

The Issue Did the New Jersey trial court judge's instructions to the jury violate the 5th Amendment guarantee of protection against self-incrimination? If so, could this part of the federal Bill of Rights be applied to a state government through the due process clause of the 14th Amendment, which says, "No state shall . . . deprive any person of life, liberty, or property, without due process of law"?

Opinion of the Court Justice William H. Moody recognized that the trial judge violated the self-incrimination clause of the 5th Amendment. However, he upheld the conviction of Twining because, in the Supreme Court's view, the self-incrimination clause in the federal Bill of Rights could not be applied to a state government via the due process clause of the 14th Amendment. However, the Court stated that this due process clause could in principle incorporate some fundamental rights in the federal Bill of Rights, if these rights were judged essential to the idea of fairness in due process of law. Justice Moody provided this guideline for future decisions about which rights could be incorporated and applied to state governments: "Is it [the right in question] a fundamental principle of liberty and justice which inheres in the very idea of free government and is the inalienable right of a citizen of such a government?"

The Court decided that the 5th Amendment's self-incrimination clause was not one of the "fundamental principles" of the federal Bill of Rights that could be applied to state governments through the 14th Amendment. But Justice Moody's guidelines did open the way for future applications to the states of selected rights in the federal Bill of Rights.

Dissent Justice John Marshall Harlan concluded that the 5th Amendment's self-incrimination clause did apply to the states through the 14th Amendment. In his opinion, this right to remain silent was a fundamental part of the principle of liberty embedded in the Constitution.

Significance The Supreme Court rejected *total incorporation*—the idea that Amendments 1 to 8 of the federal Bill of Rights could be completely applied to the states through the due process clause of the 14th Amendment. However, the Court did provide an opening for *selective incorporation*—the idea that certain parts of the federal Bill of Rights could be applied to the states on a case-by-case basis. During the 20th century, the Court has selectively incorporated most provisions of the federal Bill of Rights through the due process clause of the 14th Amendment, thereby applying these fundamental rights to the states.

SEE ALSO *Incorporation doctrine; Rights of the accused; Self-incrimination, privilege against*

TWO-TERM TRADITION

The Constitutional Convention of 1787 did not place any limits on the number of terms a President could serve. The two-term tradition was begun by George Washington, although his decision to leave office was made primarily because of criticism in the press. Thomas Jefferson, upon his retirement in 1809, stated that "rotation in office" was his reason for leaving the White House, in order to prevent the danger of a President being reelected for life. The Republican and Democratic Presidents who followed him just assumed that no President should serve more than two terms.

The Whig party carried this one step further and in its 1840 platform stated that a President should not stand for reelection. Democratic President James K. Polk pledged in his election campaign that he would serve only one term. Republican Presidents Abraham Lincoln and Ulysses S. Grant reestablished the two-term tradition after the Civil War.

In 1940, faced with the outbreak of war in Europe, Franklin D. Roosevelt decided that the international crisis was too grave for him to leave office, and he decided to run for a third term. Although his Vice President and some other party leaders opposed his decision, Roosevelt was reelected to a third and then a fourth term, putting an end to the two-term tradition. After the war, the Republican-controlled Congress passed the 22nd Amendment to limit Presidents to two elected terms.

SEE ALSO *Jefferson, Thomas; Roosevelt, Franklin D.; Term of office, Presidential; 22nd Amendment; Washington, George*

TYLER, JOHN
10th President

- Born: Mar. 29, 1790, Charles City County, Va.
- Political party: Democrat, elected on Whig ticket
- Education: College of William and Mary, B.A., 1807
- Military service: Virginia militia, 1813
- Previous government service: Virginia House of Delegates, 1811–16, 1823–25, 1838–40; U.S. House of Representatives, 1817–21; governor of Virginia, 1825–27; U.S. Senate, 1827–36; Vice President, 1841
- Succeeded to Presidency, 1841; served, 1841–45
- Died: Jan. 18, 1862, Richmond, Va.

John Tyler was the first Vice President to succeed to the Presidency. He established the precedent that the successor becomes President and is not the Vice President "acting as President." He also demonstrated that the constitutional prerogatives of the office can check and balance Congress, even when it is dominated by a party such as the Whigs, who insisted on their right to set national policy.

Tyler came from a family of wealthy Virginia plantation owners. He studied law under his father, practiced briefly, and went into politics. He served in the Virginia legislature and became governor in 1825, then U.S. senator in 1827. Tyler voted against the high tariffs of 1828 and 1832. He supported President Andrew Jackson's veto of internal improvements. But he broke with Jackson over South Carolina's nullification of, or decision not to enforce, federal tariffs, casting the only vote in the Senate against the Force Bill of 1833, which gave Jackson the power to use federal force to ensure compliance with the tariff. Tyler was instrumental in forging the compromise tariff of 1833, which ended the crisis. He voted against the rechartering of the Second Bank of the United States and voted to uphold Jackson's veto of the bill, but he joined in the Senate censure of Jackson over the removal of federal deposits from the Bank. In 1836 he resigned his seat rather than adhere to the instructions of his state legislature to vote to expunge the resolution of censure, and he broke his connections with the Democratic party.

In 1836 Tyler ran for Vice President as a regional Whig candidate but lost to the Democratic ticket. In 1840 he was nominated for the Vice Presidency on the Whig ticket, along with General William Henry Harrison for President. Although opposed to the Bank, the Whigs were attracted to Tyler because they believed correctly that he could help carry Southern states.

President Harrison died of pneumonia within a month of taking the oath. John Tyler was in an awkward position. It was not clear from the wording of the Constitution whether the Vice President succeeded to the office of President or only exercised the "powers and duties" of the office, serving merely as acting President. Tyler took the Presidential oath and issued a statement to the American people

couched in the form of an inaugural address. The House promptly passed a resolution referring to him as President, while the Senate defeated a resolution referring to him as Vice President. But much of the nation referred to Tyler as "His Accidency" and did not recognize him as President.

The Whig cabinet moved to take control from the President. At the first cabinet meeting, Secretary of State Daniel Webster told Tyler that his predecessor had settled questions by majority vote of the cabinet. Tyler responded that he alone would be responsible for his administration, and he called for the resignation of anyone who did not accept his view.

Tyler faced a dilemma: Should he allow the Whigs, led by Senator Henry Clay, to pass their economic program? Or should he pursue his own domestic program, which came much closer to the ideas of the Democrats? Tyler did not command a majority in Congress, and the Whigs proceeded to pass their own banking bill, which he vetoed twice. With the help of Democrats, Tyler's vetoes were sustained. The Whig cabinet resigned, and the Whig party issued a statement disassociating itself from the Tyler administration. Whigs demanded that he resign and be succeeded by the president pro tempore of the Senate—a Whig who would hold office until a special election could be held. Tyler refused and made recess appointments of Democrats to his cabinet. Eventually, the Whigs passed a resolution of censure against Tyler, claiming that his use of the veto on policy grounds was unconstitutional.

Tyler was effective even though he was a President without a party. He resolved Dorr's Rebellion, a civil war between two political factions in Rhode Island. He reorganized the navy. A few days before he left office, Tyler won his most important victory: Congress admitted Texas to the Union.

Tyler was a political failure. He did not win the Democratic Presidential nomination in 1844. Historians generally rate him ineffective because of the deadlock in domestic policies. But he showed that a President without a shred of popular or congressional support could still exercise the power to stalemate congressional majorities.

After leaving the Presidency, Tyler returned to the Democratic party. He supported the Compromise of 1850 and the Kansas-Nebraska Act, both of which were designed to defuse slavery tensions and save the Union. In 1860 he spoke out against secession, believing a new compromise could be reached, and early in 1861 he sponsored the Richmond Convention, a last-ditch attempt to avert war between the regions. After the collapse of that effort, he urged Virginia to secede from the Union. He died on January 18, 1862, shortly after being elected to the Confederate House of Representatives.

SEE ALSO *Harrison, William Henry; Succession to the Presidency*

SOURCES Robert J. Morgan, *A Whig Embattled: The Presidency under John Tyler* (Lincoln: University of Nebraska Press, 1954). Norma Lois Peterson, *The Presidencies of William Henry Harrison and John Tyler* (Lawrence: University Press of Kansas, 1989).

U

UNANIMOUS CONSENT AGREEMENTS

Unanimous consent agreements are motions that the Senate or House of Representatives adopts as long as no member objects to them. Many unanimous consent requests deal with routine business, such as "Madam President, I ask unanimous consent to dispense with the reading of the journal" or "Mr. Speaker, I ask unanimous consent to revise and extend my remarks in the *Congressional Record.*" To these requests the presiding officer will respond: "Without objection, so ordered."

The Senate also uses unanimous consent agreements, which are worked out in advance by the majority and minority leaders and managers of a bill, to set the details of how it will consider a bill, how long it will debate each amendment, whether all amendments must be germane (relevant) to the bill's subject matter, and when the final vote will be taken. Sometimes whole bills are adopted by unanimous consent, if members are able to agree in advance to all of the bill's provisions. Unanimous consent agreements help the leadership move noncontroversial matters quickly through the Senate. However, a single senator's objection can stop a unanimous consent agreement, giving the minority another chance to stop or delay the majority from acting. The House generally uses special rules to achieve the same results as unanimous consent agreements.

SEE ALSO *Rules of the House and Senate*

UNITED STATES AGENCY FOR INTERNATIONAL DEVELOPMENT

When Europe lay in ruins following World War II, and communists seemed to be making inroads, the United States launched an ambitious aid program known as the Marshall Plan (for Secretary of State George Marshall, who proposed it). Following the Marshall Plan, the United States—as the world's wealthiest nation and leader of the Western anticommunist countries—continued a policy of foreign aid. Not only would aid assist developing nations economically but it would help them become new markets for U.S. goods.

The United States Agency for International Development (AID) is the federal agency that implements the nation's foreign aid and humanitarian aid programs. Although it long operated as an independent agency, AID is now part of the Department of State.

Congress created the agency in 1961, when it passed the Foreign Assistance Act. This law reorganized the foreign assistance programs and provided for the separation of military and nonmilitary aid. AID became the first U.S. foreign assistance program that had as its primary focus long-range economic and social development assistance.

AID provides assistance largely to Africa, the Near East, Latin America, the Caribbean, Eastern Europe, and Asia. The agency's goals include the protection of human health and the environment, the encouragement of broad-based economic growth and agricultural development, the stabilization of world population growth, support for democratic reforms and good government, and the promotion of education and training programs.

UNITED STATES REPORTS

All decisions of the Supreme Court of the United States are recorded in an authorized publication, the *United States Reports.* This series of volumes was initially compiled by Alexander J. Dallas, the Court's first reporter (1790–1800). Dallas's work was approved by the Court, although he held no official position and sold the publication of his work for profit. The position of reporter of the Supreme Court was not established by Congress until 1816.

Private publishers issued the *United States Reports* until 1922. Since then, the U.S. Government Printing Office has been the publisher.

The Court's decisions are not reported exclusively in the *United States Reports.* They also appear, for example, in *Supreme Court Reporter; United States Law Week,* a weekly publication that covers Supreme Court news and proceedings, including the full text of all Court decisions on cases; and the legal databases LEXIS and WESTLAW. However, the only official report of the Court's decisions is in *United States Reports.* This is the version that must be cited in all briefs and memoranda to the Court, and it should be listed first in any multiple listing of sources of a citation.

SEE ALSO *Reporter of decisions*

UNITED STATES V. CURTISS-WRIGHT EXPORT CORP.

• 299 U.S. 304 (1936)
• Vote: 7–1
• For the Court: Sutherland
• Dissenting: McReynolds
• Not participating: Stone

In 1934, Bolivia and Paraguay were at war with each other. Both countries needed military weapons from abroad, and American weapons makers were eager to sell to them. At the same time, the American public and Great Britain wanted the United States to help end the war by stopping all arms sales to the two nations.

On May 28, 1934, Congress passed a joint resolution giving President Franklin Delano Roosevelt authority to place an embargo, or ban, on selling weapons to Bolivia and Paraguay. Four days later, Roosevelt declared the embargo in effect because he believed it would help restore peace. The federal government later indicted the Curtiss-Wright Corporation for violating the embargo by selling armed aircraft to Bolivia. Curtiss-Wright claimed that the Constitution did not allow Congress to give the President power to declare an embargo.

The Issue   Did Congress's joint resolution unconstitutionally delegate legislative power to the executive branch? Or did Congress have the authority to delegate broad discretionary powers in foreign affairs to the President?

Opinion of the Court   The Supreme Court ruled to uphold the President's embargo. The Court distinguished between the powers exercised by Congress and the President in "external" (foreign) affairs and "internal" (domestic) affairs. The Court said that the national government could take action in conducting foreign affairs that might exceed its authority to direct domestic policy.

Writing for the majority, Justice George Sutherland reasoned that since the United States had existed as a sovereign nation before the adoption of the Constitution, it retained powers to influence international affairs that were neither implied nor listed in the Constitution. These powers stemmed from the simple unspoken reality that the United States existed in a world of nations and must have powers to meet its international responsibilities just as other sovereign nations did. This idea established a new precedent, the doctrine of inherent powers.

Further, the Court ruled that Congress could delegate broad discretionary powers to the President to cope with foreign affairs issues. This verdict contrasted with the Court's ruling on domestic affairs, which limited Congress to delegating legislative powers to the President only if it also set clear guidelines for using those delegated powers.

Dissent Although Justice James McReynolds dissented in this case, he filed no opinion.

Significance The *Curtiss-Wright* decision recognized the broad responsibility of the executive branch of the national government for foreign affairs, giving the President great freedom in directing the nation's foreign policy. Justice Sutherland wrote: "[T]he President alone has the power to speak as a representative of the nation." He described the President's power in foreign affairs as "plenary [full] and exclusive." The President is "the sole organ of the federal government in . . . international relations." This decision thereby provided the foundations for strong and decisive Presidential leadership in world affairs.

SOURCES Robert A. Divine, "The Case of the Smuggled Bombers," in *Quarrels That Have Shaped the Constitution,* edited by

John A. Garraty (New York: Harper & Row, 1987).

UNITED STATES V. DARBY LUMBER CO.

- 312 U.S. 100 (1941)
- Vote: 9–0
- For the Court: Stone

In 1938, the U.S. Congress passed the Fair Labor Standards Act, which set minimum wages, maximum hours, and overtime pay regulations for workers in businesses involved in interstate commerce—that is, in shipping their products across state lines. Enactment of this federal law was based on Congress's power "to regulate Commerce . . . among the several States" (Article 1, Section 8, of the Constitution).

The Darby Lumber Company claimed that the Fair Labor Standards Act was unconstitutional, so it filed suit to prevent enforcement of this federal law.

The Issue The Darby Lumber Company argued that Congress exceeded its powers under the commerce clause of the Constitution when it passed the Fair Labor Standards Act. It claimed that, according to the 10th Amendment to the Constitution, the power to regulate wages, hours of work, working conditions, and so forth belongs to the states. (The amendment states, "The powers not delegated to the United States by the Constitution, nor prohibited by it to the States, are reserved to the States respectively, or to the people.") This claim was based on the Supreme Court's decision in *Hammer* v. *Dagenhart* (1918). Was enactment of the Fair Labor Standards Act a constitutional exercise of the commerce power, or did this federal law violate the 10th Amendment of the Constitution? Further, did the Fair Labor Standards Act violate the due process clause of the 5th Amendment by taking away the right of employers and workers to bargain freely about wages and working conditions?

Opinion of the Court The Supreme Court upheld the Fair Labor Standards Act. Writing for the Court, Justice Harlan F. Stone based his opinion on the dissent of Justice Oliver Wendell Holmes in *Hammer* v. *Dagenhart* (1918). Agreeing with Holmes, Stone argued that the federal government's power to regulate commerce among the states should be interpreted broadly. Thus, the power to regulate wages and working conditions can, said Justice Stone, be tied to the power to regulate interstate commerce. Stone wrote, "The conclusion is inescapable that *Hammer* v. *Dagenhart . . .* should be and now is overruled."

Significance This decision expanded the federal government's power to regulate national economic affairs. Further, this opinion rejected the argument, advanced in *Hammer* v. *Dagenhart,* that the 10th Amendment strictly limits the enumerated, or specifically listed, powers of Congress. Instead, it established a broad interpretation of the Congress's commerce power.

SEE ALSO *Commerce power; Federalism; Hammer v. Dagenhart*

UNITED STATES V. E. C. KNIGHT CO.

- 156 U.S. 1 (1895)
- Vote: 8–1
- For the Court: Fuller
- Dissenting: Harlan

In 1890 Congress passed the Sherman Antitrust Act, which seemed to outlaw business monopolies. A monopoly has control over the means of producing and selling a product or service. The Sherman Antitrust Act provided that "every contract, combination in the form of trust or otherwise, or conspiracy, in restraint of trade or commerce among the several states, or with foreign nations, is hereby declared to be illegal." So, according to this federal law, any business that acted to restrain trade by controlling most or all of a particular business activity would seem to be illegal.

In the late 19th century the American Sugar Refining Company was the dominant maker of sugar in the United States. It was known as the Sugar Trust. In 1892 the Sugar Trust acquired four Philadelphia sugar refineries, including the E. C. Knight Company. As a result, the American Sugar Refining Company controlled 98 percent of sugar manufacturing in the United States. The federal government filed suit under the Sherman Antitrust Act to prevent the "restraint of trade or commerce among the several states" by the American Sugar Refining Company's takeover of nearly all the sugar refining businesses in the United States.

The Issue Was the Sugar Trust in violation of the Sherman Antitrust Act? Did its control of 98 percent of the sugar refining business in the United States constitute an illegal restraint of trade or commerce?

Opinion of the Court In its first interpretation of the Sherman Antitrust Act, the Supreme Court decided against the federal government. It upheld the lower court's dismissal of the government's suit. The Sherman Antitrust Act, according to the Court, did not apply to a trust that refined 98 percent of the sugar sold throughout the United States.

Writing for the Court, Chief Justice Melville Fuller argued that a monopoly of the production of refined sugar did not necessarily lead to an illegal restraint of trade, which was what the Sherman Antitrust Act prohibited. Fuller said that production and commerce were two very different kinds of business activity. He wrote that only the distribution or sale of a product (such as refined sugar) was subject to federal regulation under the commerce clause of the Constitution (Article 1, Section 8). By contrast, Congress did not have the power under the Constitution to regulate the manufacturing of a product that occurred within the boundaries of a state. This power, according to Fuller, belonged to the government of the state in which a manufacturing company was located. So the federal government suit against the Sugar Trust exceeded the scope of the Sherman Antitrust Act, and it could not be applied to E. C. Knight.

Dissent Justice John Marshall Harlan argued that the Sugar Trust's near monopoly of the production of refined sugar gave it power to dominate the distribution and sale of this product. For example, the Sugar Trust could control the market price of refined sugar. Therefore, the Sugar Trust was in violation of the Sherman Antitrust Act.

Justice Harlan argued for a broad interpretation of the federal government's commerce power. He believed that Congress had the authority to regulate business to prevent any interference with free trade among the states. He wrote, "The general [federal] government is not placed by the Constitution in such a condition of helplessness that it must fold its arms and remain inactive while capital combines . . . to destroy competition."

Significance The *E. C. Knight* decision opened the way to large-scale combinations of manufacturing businesses whose production activities had been ruled beyond the scope of the Sherman Antitrust Act. Further, this decision diminished the power of the federal government to regulate economic activity.

The *E. C. Knight* ruling prevailed until the end of the 1930s, when the Court took a different position on the federal government's power, under the commerce clause, to regulate the economy. For example, in *National Labor Relations Board v. Jones & Laughlin Steel Corp.* (1937) and *West Coast Hotel Co. v. Parrish* (1937), the Court upheld federal and state laws regulating wages and working conditions of private businesses. These decisions emphasized a broad interpretation of the federal government's commerce power, which could include the interrelated issues of production and distribution of goods and services. After the erosion of the *Knight* decision in 1937, the federal government exercised broad authority to regulate economic activity for the public good.

SEE ALSO *Commerce power; National Labor Relations Board v. Jones & Laughlin Steel Corp.; West Coast Hotel Co. v. Parrish*

UNITED STATES V. LEON

- 468 U.S. 897 (1984)
- Vote: 6–3
- For the Court: White
- Concurring: Blackmun
- Dissenting: Brennan, Marshall, and Stevens

In 1981 the police in Burbank, California, received information about drug dealing by two residents of their city. So the police began to regularly watch the Burbank home of the two suspects, where they spotted an automobile owned by Alberto Leon, another suspected drug dealer.

The Burbank police obtained a search warrant from a local judge, searched the residence, and found illegal drugs belonging to Alberto Leon. This evidence led to Leon's arrest and conviction.

The Issue Leon's lawyer argued that the search warrant used by the Burbank police was not valid because there was no "probable cause" for the police to request it or for the judge to issue it. As a result, the evidence against Leon gathered by the police should have been thrown out under the exclusionary rule established in *Mapp v. Ohio* (1961), according to which evidence obtained in violation of a person's constitutional rights cannot be used to prosecute the person. Should the evidence against Leon be excluded because it was obtained through procedures that violated the 4th Amendment guarantee to "the right of the people to be secure in their persons, houses, papers, and effects, against unreasonable searches and seizures"? Or should the Supreme Court permit an exception to the exclusionary rule when the police make a "good faith" mistake in obtaining and using a search warrant?

Opinion of the Court The Supreme Court acknowledged that the police used an invalid search warrant to obtain evidence against Leon. Nonetheless, the Court ruled against Leon and permitted a "good faith" exception to the exclusionary rule. The exclusionary rule is not a constitutional right, said Justice Byron White, but merely serves to limit oppressive police actions. However, when police act on "good faith" to obtain valid evidence of criminal behavior, the exclusionary rule does not apply to the case.

Dissent Justice William Brennan, who had established the exclusionary rule in *Mapp* v. *Ohio*, opposed any "good faith" exception to this rule. He feared that this exception would lead to an increase in illegal police behavior in gathering evidence against people suspected of criminal behavior.

Significance The *Leon* decision narrowed the exclusionary rule protections under the 4th Amendment of the Constitution. This outcome was hailed by many law enforcement officials, who often felt frustrated by judicial decisions that permitted a criminal to avoid conviction because of a technical error by the police. However, defenders of the exclusionary rule argued against any exceptions to it because of their strong commitment to 4th Amendment rights.

SEE ALSO *Exclusionary rule; Mapp v. Ohio; Searches and seizures*

UNITED STATES
V. NIXON

- 418 U.S. 683 (1974)
- Vote: 8–0
- For the Court: Burger
- Not participating: Rehnquist

Beginning with George Washington, several Presidents have asserted the right to withhold information from Congress or from a court. The right of the President to do this has come to be called *executive privilege*. Presidents have often made such claims in the area of foreign affairs. In 1974, however, President Richard Nixon claimed executive privilege for another reason.

In the spring of 1972, employees of President Nixon's reelection committee burglarized the Democratic party headquarters in the Watergate office complex in Washington and planted illegal electronic bugging equipment. Eventually, seven of President Nixon's top aides, including former attorney general John Mitchell, were indicted for their role in planning the Watergate break-in, as it came to be known, and for obstructing justice by trying to cover up their actions. During Senate hearings on the break-in and the cover-up, a Nixon aide admitted that there were secretly recorded tapes of Nixon's conversations with his aides. A special prosecutor investigating the Watergate break-in subpoenaed the tapes for use as evidence in the criminal investigations.

President Nixon refused to surrender the tapes. He claimed that the principle of executive privilege protected the record of his private conversations from such a subpoena. He argued that the actions of many past Presidents clearly established the tradition of executive privilege. He also claimed that to allow another branch of government, the courts, to obtain the tapes would destroy the separation of powers established by the Constitution and would weaken the Presidency.

The Issue Did the constitutional principle of separation of powers and the tradition of executive privilege prevent the courts from requiring the President to turn over material needed as evidence in a criminal trial?

Opinion of the Court The Supreme Court ordered President Nixon to turn over the tapes and other documents to the trial court for use as evidence. The Supreme Court rejected the claim that either separation of powers or executive privilege could make the President immune from the judicial process. The Court's ruling established the precedent that unless important military or diplomatic secrets affecting national security were involved, the need to ensure a fair trial outweighed the principle of executive privilege. The decision limited the concept of executive privilege by determining that a President could not use it to prohibit disclosure of criminal conduct.

At the same time, the Court's decision acknowledged the constitutionality of executive privilege in certain other situations. The Constitution does not mention executive privilege, and until the Court reached this decision, legal scholars had frequently debated whether any real constitutional basis supported the doctrine.

In *United States* v. *Nixon,* Chief Justice Warren Burger, a Nixon appointee, said that Presidents and their aides must be free to consider alternatives as they make decisions. In order to do so, they must possess the confidence to express themselves freely without fear that the public will gain access to their ideas. Thus, Burger wrote, "[Executive] privilege is fundamental to the operation of government and inextricably rooted in the separation of powers under the Constitution."

Significance President Nixon obeyed the Court's decision and turned over the tapes to the special prosecutor. Nixon claimed the demand for the tapes was a political maneuver by his enemies. However, this claim could not stand up in the face of a unanimous Court decision written by a Nixon appointee and supported by two other Nixon appointees. The tapes revealed that Nixon had participated in the cover-up. When the contents of these tapes became public knowledge, even Nixon's strongest supporters in Congress believed that he could no longer remain in office. Some Republican congressmen said they would have to vote for his impeachment, and leading Republican senators publicly announced that they saw no way he could avoid conviction. Nixon became the first U.S. President to resign from office.

SEE ALSO *Executive privilege; Separation of powers; Watergate investigation (1973–74)*

UNITED STATES V. O'BRIEN

- 391 U.S. 367 (1968)
- Vote: 7–1

- For the Court: Warren
- Concurring: Harlan
- Dissenting: Douglas
- Not participating: Marshall

In the 1960s, the United States was fighting a war in Vietnam. The war was controversial, and many Americans protested against the selective service system, which drafted young men into the armed forces of the United States. Some of the antiwar protests involved the destruction of draft registration cards, which were issued to all men eligible for induction into the U.S. military. Congress in 1965 amended the Selective Service Act to make it a crime for anyone to "destroy or mutilate" a draft registration card.

On March 31, 1966, David O'Brien burned his draft card during an antiwar demonstration at an entrance to a South Boston courthouse. Agents of the Federal Bureau of Investigation (FBI) saw O'Brien burn his draft card and arrested him for violating the Selective Service Act, as amended in 1965.

The Issue David O'Brien claimed that he had publicly burned his draft card to express his opposition to the Vietnam War. This "symbolic speech" was, in his opinion, permissible because of his 1st Amendment right to free speech. His attorney pointed to the Supreme Court's opinion in *Stromberg* v. *California* (1931), which ruled that symbolic speech was protected from government prohibition by the 1st Amendment.

The federal government's attorney argued that O'Brien's actions seriously interfered with its legitimate business because he wanted "to influence others to adopt his anti-war beliefs" and thwart the government's ability to conduct the war. The government argued that the requirements of national security justified limitations on symbolic speech.

Was the 1965 amendment to the Selective Service Act, which banned destruction of draft cards, a valid limitation on free speech? Or was this federal statute an unconstitutional violation of the 1st Amendment?

Opinion of the Court The Supreme Court upheld the 1965 law and rejected David O'Brien's claims that it violated his right to free speech. Chief Justice Earl Warren wrote:

> We cannot accept the view that an apparently limitless variety of conduct can be labeled "speech" whenever the person engaging in the conduct intends thereby to express an idea. However, even on the assumption that the alleged communicative element in O'Brien's conduct is sufficient to bring into play the First Amendment, it does not necessarily follow that the destruction of a registration certificate is a constitutionally protected activity. This Court has held that when "speech" and "nonspeech" elements are combined in the same course of conduct, a sufficiently important governmental interest in regulating the nonspeech element can justify incidental limitations on First Amendment freedoms.... [W]e think it clear that a government regulation is sufficiently justified if it is within the constitutional power of the Government; if it furthers an important or substantial governmental interest; if the governmental interest is unrelated to the suppression of free expression; and if the incidental restriction on alleged First Amendment freedoms is no greater than is essential to the furtherance of that interest.

Significance The Supreme Court provided guidelines for subsequent decisions about when the government could regulate symbolic speech. These guidelines required the government to have a valid, compelling interest, such as the necessity for a military draft, unrelated to the purpose of suppressing free speech. Moreover, any restrictions on free speech could be no broader than was necessary to carry out that valid interest. The *O'Brien* guidelines, or tests, for deciding permissible limits on free speech are now an established part of constitutional law.

SEE ALSO *Freedom of speech and press; Stromberg v. California*

UNITED STATES V. ROSS

- 456 U.S. 798 (1982)
- Vote: 6–3
- For the Court: Stevens
- Concurring: Blackmun and Powell
- Dissenting: White, Marshall, and Brennan

Detective Marcum of the Washington, D.C., Metropolitan Police received a telephone call about criminal activity in a local neighborhood. The caller reported that a man was selling drugs in the vicinity of 439 Ridge Street. The informer described the drug seller and his automobile in detail.

Marcum and two other police officers, Detective Cassidy and Sergeant Gonzales, quickly went to check out the reported drug dealing on the city streets. They found the car of the alleged drug dealer and used the license plate number to obtain information about the owner, Albert Ross.

The police officers stopped Albert Ross's car, asked him to step outside, and searched him. Sergeant Gonzales, looking through the automobile window, noticed a bullet on the front seat. He entered the car, searched it for weapons, and found a pistol in the glove compartment. The officers arrested Ross for violating the local firearms code.

The officers unlocked the trunk of the car and found a bag and a small pouch. Plastic envelopes in the bag contained white powder, which later proved to be heroin. The pouch contained $3,200 in cash.

Ross was charged with possession of an illegal substance, heroin, with intent to sell it. He, in turn, accused the police of violating his constitutional rights by searching his car and containers in the car without first obtaining a search warrant. His attorney filed a motion asking that the evidence obtained without a warrant be excluded from Ross's trial. Ross's motion was denied, and he was convicted. His attorney appealed and the case eventually went to the U.S. Supreme Court.

The Issue The 4th Amendment to the Constitution guarantees the "right of the people to be secure in their persons, houses, papers, and effects against unreasonable searches and seizures ... and no warrants shall issue, but upon probable cause." However, cars have been treated differently from houses ever since *Carroll v. United States* (1925), when the Supreme Court held that police could search an automobile without a warrant when they had a reasonable suspicion of criminal activity. The justification for this exception to the usual 4th Amendment requirements was that a car can be quickly driven away while police take time to obtain a search warrant. The opportunity to obtain evidence of illegal activity would then be lost.

If cars could be stopped by police and searched without a warrant, legal questions still remained about how far such a search could extend. Was it legal for police to search a car's glove compartment or trunk without a warrant? Can police examine containers spotted in a car, such as boxes or pouches, without obtaining a warrant from a magistrate?

Opinion of the Court Justice John Paul Stevens held that police officers do not need to obtain a warrant before they search compartments of a car or containers found in the vehicle. They can conduct such searches as long as they can demonstrate "probable cause" to believe that they will find evidence of illegal activity. This is the same standard needed to obtain a search warrant prior to conducting a search and seizing evidence.

Justice Stevens wrote, "If probable cause justifies the search of a lawfully stopped vehicle, it justifies the search of every part of the vehicle and its contents that may conceal the object of the search."

Dissent Justices Thurgood Marshall, William Brennan, and Byron White argued that the Court's decision gave a police officer the same authority as a judge to determine probable cause. They said that this was a wrongful blurring of the constitutional separation of judicial powers and executive or law enforcement powers. Justice Marshall feared that the Court's opinion was "a first step toward an unprecedented 'probable cause' exception to the warrant requirement." If this exception were to occur, Marshall said, the constitutional rights of individuals would be unjustly limited.

Significance The Court's decision in *Ross* extended the automobile exception to 4th Amendment requirements established in *Carroll v. United States* (1925). In effect, the *Ross* decision gave the power to determine "probable cause" to police officers rather than to a court.

Since the *Ross* case, the Court has continued to support the automobile exception to usual search and seizure standards. As a result, the 4th Amendment protections against automobile searches are minimal.

SEE ALSO *Carroll v. United States; Probable cause; Searches and seizures; Terry v. Ohio*

UNITED STATES V. UNITED STATES DISTRICT COURT

- 407 U.S. 297 (1972)
- Vote: 8–0
- For the Court: Powell
- Concurring: Burger, Douglas, and White
- Not participating: Rehnquist

In 1968 Congress passed the Omnibus Crime Control and Safe Streets Act, which provided for court-approved electronic surveillance to fight certain kinds of crimes. This law also provided that "nothing contained [in the section about electronic surveillance] shall limit the constitutional power of the President to take such measures as he deems necessary to protect the United States against the overthrow of the Government."

President Richard Nixon used this section of the act to use electronic surveillance (telephone wiretaps, for example) to monitor American citizens suspected of activities dangerous to the security of the United States. The Nixon administration did so without first showing "probable cause" and obtaining a warrant, or permission, from a court, as required by the 4th Amendment.

Electronic surveillance had been used by the Nixon administration against defendants accused of bombing a Central Intelligence Agency office in Ann Arbor, Michigan. Before their trial, the defendants petitioned the U.S. District Court for the Eastern District of Michigan to require the federal government to produce any information about them obtained from electronic surveillance. The U.S. attorney general, John Mitchell, said that such information existed, but he refused to release it. The district court, however, ruled that the Nixon administration's use of electronic surveillance violated the 4th Amendment and ordered the federal government to turn over the requested information. The federal government appealed this ruling to the U.S. Supreme Court.

The Issue The Nixon administration argued that disclosure of the requested information "would prejudice the national interest." Further, the Nixon administration held that Article 2 of the Constitution implied that the President had power to use electronic surveillance or any other means necessary to gather information to protect the federal government from destruction. Did the needs of national security, for which the President is responsible under the U.S. Constitution, outweigh the protection of individual rights guaranteed by the U.S. Constitution, such as the 4th Amendment right to protection against unwarranted governmental searches and seizures of one's private possessions? Was the federal government required to obey the district court's order to disclose certain information obtained through electronic surveillance conducted without a warrant?

Opinion of the Court The Supreme court upheld the federal district court's order. The Court stressed that this case involved protection of 1st and 4th Amendment rights. It viewed the electronic surveillance project of the Nixon administration as a discouragement to free and open exchange of information by individuals critical of the government.

Significance The decision in this case was a strong statement about the primary importance of constitutional rights. Not even pervasive social upheavals and threats to national security could justify denial of fundamental rights of liberty and justice for all individuals.

SOURCES Alvin F. Westin, "Civil Liberties in the Technology Age," *Constitution* 3, no. 1 (Winter 1991): 56–64.

UNITED STATES V. VIRGINIA

- 518 U.S. 515 (1996)
- Vote: 7–1
- For the Court: Ginsburg
- Dissent: Scalia
- Not participating: Thomas

In 1990, a female student (never identified) in a Virginia public high school filed a complaint with the U.S. Department of Justice. She charged the Virginia Military Academy (VMI), a state-supported institution of higher education, with illegal sex discrimination in violation of the 14th Amendment's equal protection clause.

In 1990, VMI and the Citadel in South Carolina were the only government supported all-male military colleges in the United States. Both institutions had long, proud records of distinguished service and achievement. And they were committed to the preservation of their venerable traditions, especially their men-only admissions policies. The time-honored principles and practices of VMI and the Citadel were suddenly and critically threatened by the legal complaint of an anonymous high school senior, who charged that the VMI office of admissions failed to acknowledge or respond to her application to attend the college. The case initiated by the 1990 complaint against VMI reached the U.S. Supreme Court after more than five years in lower federal courts.

After losing the first round in the federal district court, the U.S. Department of Justice took the case to the 4th U.S. Circuit Court of Appeals, which decided that the all-male policy violated the 14th Amendment's guarantee of "equal protection of the laws." Instead of ordering immediate admission of women to VMI, however, the appeals court remanded the case to the district court of original jurisdiction to explore alternative remedies to the nullified admissions policy. In response, VMI created a plan to offer state-supported military education for women in the Virginia Women's Institute for Leadership (VWIL), which it established at nearby Mary Baldwin College. The U.S. government appealed this outcome of the appellate court's decision to the U.S. Supreme Court.

The federal government's lawyers charged that the VWIL plan did not satisfy the 14th Amendment's guarantee of equal protection. Further, they claimed it did not even meet the now discredited standard of *Plessy* v. *Ferguson* (1896)—"separate but equal"—and thereby was a disgraceful attempt to avoid compliance with constitutional law.

Advocates for the state of Virginia defended the VWIL plan as an equitable alternative that provided new opportunities for women. At the same time, it preserved a hallowed and publicly useful tradition of all-male military education that had demonstrated its worth by producing leaders who, generation after generation, served the common good in Virginia and the United States. Further, the counsel for Virginia claimed that women were not capable of performing competently under the physically and psychologically stressful "adversative" method of training used at VMI.

The Issue   Does the 14th Amendment's guarantee of "equal protection of the laws" prohibit a state government from maintaining an all-male military college? Or is such a policy justified by serving important governmental objectives that contribute uniquely and compellingly to the common good?

Opinion of the Court   Justice Ruth Bader Ginsburg's opinion ended the 157-year tradition of all-male education at VMI, and by extension at the Citadel in South Carolina. Justice Ginsburg wrote, "While Virginia serves the state's sons [at VMI] it makes no provision whatever for her daughters. That is not equal protection" as guaranteed by the U.S. Constitution. Ginsburg's opinion rejected Virginia's claim that the VWIL program at Mary Baldwin College provided an equal opportunity for the state's women. Further, the justice pointed out that women successfully attended and graduated from the United States Military Academy. This repudiated the Virginia counsel's claim that women could not meet standards at VMI suitable only for males. Justice Ginsburg concluded, "Women seeking and fit for a VMI-quality education cannot be offered anything else." (Justice Thomas did not participate in the Court's decision because his son, Jamal, was a student at VMI.)

Dissent   Justice Antonin Scalia objected strongly to the Court's decision. He lamented, "Today the Court shuts down an institution that has served the people of the Commonwealth of Virginia with pride and distinction for over a century and a half." He argued that single-sex public schools should and could be constitutionally permitted for those who wanted them.

Significance   The Court's opinion in the VMI case requires government to make an "exceedingly persuasive justification" based on a compelling public interest for the maintenance of a single-sex public school or even private school that receives public funds.

Both VMI and the Citadel complied with the Court's decision. VMI, however, did it reluctantly at first. The school's superintendent called the decision "a savage disappointment" and proposed that VMI should become a private school without obligation to comply with the Court's ruling in this case. But the VMI Board of Visitors rejected this proposal and approved the admission of women beginning in 1997.

UNITED STATES V. WONG KIM ARK

- 169 U.S. 649 (1898)
- Vote: 6–2
- For the Court: Gray
- Dissenting: Fuller and Harlan
- Not participating: McKenna

Wong Kim Ark was born in San Francisco, California, in 1873. His parents had gone to California from China. They were not citizens of the United States but retained their status as subjects of the emperor of China.

Wong Kim Ark traveled to China in 1894. When he returned to California one year later, federal agents refused him admission to the United States because, they said, he was Chinese and not a citizen of the United States. Wong Kim Ark claimed U.S. citizenship because he was born in the United States.

The Issue The 14th Amendment says, "All persons born or naturalized in the United States, and subject to the jurisdiction thereof, are citizens of the United States and of the State wherein they reside." The federal government argued that Wong Kim Ark was not a citizen of the United States because his parents were Chinese. Thus, neither Wong Kim Ark nor his parents were "subject to the jurisdiction" of the United States. Rather, claimed the federal government, they were subject to the jurisdiction of China. Did a person

of Chinese descent, born in the United States, have the right of U.S. citizenship?

Opinion of the Court The Supreme Court's decision favored Wong Kim Ark. Justice Horace Gray held that the common law tradition and the 14th Amendment clearly guaranteed U.S. citizenship to all people born in the country. The ethnic identity or place of birth of the person's parents could not be used to deny citizenship to a person born in the United States.

Significance This case immediately established the citizenship rights of people of Asian descent born in the United States. It also established the general rule of *jus soli* (a Latin term meaning the "right based on soil")—the determination of citizenship by place of birth. The *Wong Kim Ark* case rejected the general rule of *jus sanguinis* (a Latin term meaning the "right based on blood")—the determination of citizenship by the ethnicity of the parents. Given the rule of *jus soli*—embodied in the 14th Amendment—Wong Kim Ark was entitled to all privileges and rights of U.S. citizenship on equal terms with any other citizen, whether naturalized (by legal procedure) or natural-born, as he was.

SEE ALSO *Citizenship*

UNITED STEELWORKERS OF AMERICA V. WEBER

- 443 U.S. 193 (1979)
- Vote: 5–2
- For the Court: Brennan
- Dissenting: Burger and Rehnquist
- Not participating: Powell and Stevens

The United Steelworkers of America, a labor union, made an agreement with the Kaiser Aluminum and Chemical Company to set up a training program to develop the skills of workers at a Kaiser plant in Gramercy, Louisiana. Half of the places in the program were reserved for black workers. In the past, black workers in this region had been denied opportunities to become highly skilled craftworkers, and most of them worked at low-paying, menial jobs. The company's voluntary and temporary plan was designed to overcome past job discrimination and to create new opportunities for black workers.

Brian Weber, a white unskilled worker and a member of the union, applied for a position in the new job training program. He was rejected. However, black workers with less seniority than Weber were selected in order to fill the 50 percent quota reserved for black workers in the new training program.

Seniority refers to the amount of time a worker has been employed in a job. Labor unions often use seniority as a standard for distributing benefits of one kind or another; those with more years of service get preference in promotions to better jobs or positions in job training programs.

Weber charged that his rejection for admission to the job training program was unfair because it was based on race, not the usual standard of seniority. He claimed this was a violation of Title VII of the Civil Rights Act of 1964, which forbids an employer to discriminate against an employee "because of such individual's race, color, religion, sex, or national origin." Weber sued the union and his employer.

The Issue Was the plan for selecting applicants to the job training program, set up by the United Steelworkers of America in agreement with the Kaiser plant, a violation of Title VII of the Civil Rights Act of 1964? Was Brian Weber illegally denied admission to the new job training program at the Kaiser plant in Gramercy, Louisiana?

Opinion of the Court The Supreme Court held that the plan for selecting applicants to the job training program did not violate the Civil Rights Act of 1964. Justice William Brennan wrote that the plan for selecting applicants was in line with the intent of the Civil Rights Act to "break down old patterns of racial segregation and hierarchy."

Brennan emphasized that the race-based quota in the plan was temporary and

resulted from a voluntary agreement between a labor union and an employer. Further, he said, the purpose was not to maintain a racial balance but to overcome a long-standing racial imbalance in employment opportunity.

Dissent Chief Justice Warren Burger and Justice William Rehnquist argued that the plan for admission to the job training program conflicted with the words and the intent of the 1964 Civil Rights Act. According to the dissenters, the federal law clearly prohibits discrimination on the basis of race in selecting participants for a job training program.

Significance This was the first case in which the Court decided an issue about an employer's affirmative action plan—a program that gives favored treatment to members of certain groups supposed to have suffered from past discrimination in employment opportunities. The decision encouraged private employers to experiment with temporary and voluntary affirmative action plans.

SEE ALSO *Affirmative action*

UNLIMITED DEBATE

SEE *Filibuster*

"UPPER HOUSE"

Because neither the Senate nor the House of Representatives is superior to the other, there is technically no "upper" or "lower" house. However, the Senate has been called the "upper house" because its members serve longer terms, represent whole states, and—in the smaller body—have more individual influence over legislation than most House members. Many representatives run for the Senate, but only a few former senators have gone on to serve in the House. The term *upper house* dates back to the 1st Congress, when the smaller Senate met upstairs above the larger House chamber.

V

VAN BUREN, MARTIN
8th President

- Born: Dec. 5, 1782, Kinderhook, N.Y.
- Political party: Democrat
- Education: elementary school; read law, 1796–1803
- Military service: none
- Previous government service: judge, Columbia County, N.Y., 1811–12; New York Senate, 1813–17; attorney general of New York, 1816–17; U.S. Senate, 1821–28; governor of New York, 1829; U.S. secretary of state, 1829–31; Vice President, 1833–37
- Elected President, 1836; served, 1837–41
- Died: July 24, 1862, Kinderhook, N.Y.

Born six years after the signing of the Declaration of Independence, Martin Van Buren was the first President who was born a citizen of the United States. (All prior Presidents had been born British subjects.) With Andrew Jackson, he founded the Democratic party and developed the ideas that led to the two-party system in the United States. His Presidency was a failure, in large measure because of monetary policies begun by his predecessor and continued in his own administration.

Van Buren was the son of a tavern keeper whose forebears had come from Holland 150 years before, and Dutch was still spoken in his home. He received no formal education after his local elementary school but read law for seven years in a lawyer's office and began practicing in 1803. Van Buren's wife died in 1819 after bearing four children; he never remarried. He was a successful lawyer, served as attorney general of New York State, and in 1821 he organized a convention to write a new constitution for New York. By the 1820s he was considered for the U.S. Supreme Court. But Van Buren was by instinct a politician whose canny maneuvers gave him the nickname Little Magician, and he was more interested in a political career than serving as a judge.

Van Buren's chief contribution to U.S. politics was the development of the two-party system. In his book *Inquiry into the Origins and Development of Political Parties in the United States* (1867), he argued that the public interest would be best served with two parties (rather than one or many): one would govern and the other would offer the voters an alternative. Prior to Van Buren's time, the Federalists did not believe there should be a Democratic-Republican party, and the Democratic-Republicans did all they could to bury the Federalists. The result was one-party government in the so-called Era of Good Feeling during James Monroe's Presidency. But Van Buren recognized that this was actually an "era of bad feelings" in which sectional animosities had replaced party competition. His goal was the re-creation of the old struggle between Federalists and Democratic-Republicans, with each party containing followers from all across the Union—and each acknowledging the legitimacy of the other.

Van Buren came to his understanding of two-party politics through his experience in New York. There he led a faction of the Democratic-Republicans who instituted the spoils system—giving government appointments to political allies—by removing a large number of opposition officeholders. After winning election to the U.S. Senate, Van Buren used his patronage powers to create and dominate the Albany Regency—a small group of politicians who organized a political machine and ran the state through the post–Civil War period.

As a U.S. senator, Van Buren renewed the alliance between Southern and New York Democratic-Republicans. He opposed the election of John Quincy Adams and the policies of his administration, especially any federal funding of internal improvements such as the Cumberland Road. He also opposed the extension of slavery into Florida. In 1828, while running for governor of New York, he strongly supported Andrew Jackson's second campaign for the White House. After Jackson won, Van Buren became his secretary of state in 1829, resigning the governorship of New York. He was successful in difficult diplomatic negotiations with France, Great Britain, and Turkey. Later, he was denied Senate confirmation to be minister to Great Britain by a single vote.

Between 1828 and 1832 Van Buren and Jackson created the Democratic party. Instead of trying for a single, all-embracing party, with no principles or program, they put together a party that was not all-inclusive. They opposed the national banking system and favored state banks, and they opposed national funding of internal improvements. Moreover, Van Buren pushed Jackson to institute New York's spoils system in the national government, which froze out many politicians. Jackson's opponents united in the 1830s to form the opposition Whig party. Through Van Buren's efforts, the first stable two-party system had been created.

In 1832 the first Democratic party convention nominated Van Buren to be Jackson's running mate. As Vice President, he served Jackson well as a political adviser and supported him loyally in the "bank wars." In May 1835, with Jackson's endorsement, Van Buren won the Democratic nomination for the Presidency by a unanimous vote of the convention. In his Presidential campaign Van Buren pledged "to tread generally in the footsteps of President Jackson." He reaffirmed Jackson's opposition to the Second Bank of the United States and pledged to uphold the rights of slave owners where slavery already existed. He won the election against four Whig regional candidates.

In one of his last major decisions Andrew Jackson issued the Specie Circular, which ordered that paper money not be accepted for payment in the sale of government lands. There was a run on specie (metal currency), and it flowed from the Eastern banks to the Western banks that needed it. Then the Treasury withdrew its surplus funds from state banks for distribution to state governments, which further reduced deposits of specie in the state banks, particularly large commercial banks in the Northeast. Soon these banks cut back on loans and extensions of credit needed for businesses all along the Eastern seaboard. In May 1837, two months after Van Buren's inauguration, the New York banks suspended payments of specie on demand to their depositors. Within a week banks across the nation followed suit.

Unfortunately for Van Buren, the Panic of 1837, the first serious economic setback the United States had experienced since 1789, destroyed whatever confidence the nation had in his leadership. Of 788 banks, 618 failed when depositors removed their funds. No one could obtain loans or credit, factories closed, and farms were foreclosed, leading to an economic depression. Van Buren refused to endorse a policy of easy money, and he opposed any expansion of credit by the national government. In his inaugural address, he said that "the less Government interferes with private pursuits, the better for general prosperity." The government did intervene minimally to repair the immediate damage: it ended further distribution of surplus revenue from the Treasury and issued $10 million in new Treasury notes to be used to pay government bills and put new funds in circulation. Van Buren refused to spend money on public works to relieve the depression, claiming these expenditures were unconstitutional. His Treasury ran surpluses, which further deflated the currency and weakened the economy.

Van Buren proposed to sever all financial relationships between state banks and the Treasury. He proposed the establishment of an independent treasury system with "subtreasuries" in large cities into which national government funds would be deposited. This would replace Jackson's system in which "pet" banks, owned by state Democratic politicians, controlled federal funds and used them in speculative schemes that had undermined the banking system. The measure, however, would reduce the amount of money available for loans by banks and therefore would further contract the credit system. Whigs argued that the subtreasuries would only make the depression worse. After three years of trying, Van Buren finally won congressional passage of his measure with the argument that the government's funds would be safe only in the government's own bank vaults. Van Buren signed the bill on July 4, 1840, hailing it as the "Second Declaration of Independence." Whigs vowed to make it a campaign issue in the next election.

Van Buren was controversial in handling sectional crises and foreign affairs. He vowed to veto any law changing the status of slavery in the nation's capital (which at that time was legal), leading John Quincy Adams to call him a "northern man with southern feelings." He won over Northern Democrats to oppose the abolitionist cause. He got Southerners to delay their attempts to annex Texas after Texas requested it in 1837. Like the attempts of other Presidents to keep sectional peace, these efforts only delayed the inevitable conflict between North and South and lost him support in both regions.

In foreign affairs Van Buren kept the nation at peace and its borders secure. He prevented two crises with Great Britain from becoming wars. One involved aid by U.S. citizens to Canadians in rebellion against British rule; British forces sank the *Caroline*, a U.S. boat supplying the rebels. Van Buren issued a proclamation warning Americans not to violate neutrality laws.

The second issue involved the disputed boundary between Maine and the Canadian province of New Brunswick. Timber poachers from New Brunswick crossed over into the disputed territory. The governor of Maine ordered troops to the area. Then British forces went on alert. Van Buren managed to work out a truce between the governors of Maine and New Brunswick, won a withdrawal of the militias, and laid the groundwork for a territorial compromise.

Van Buren continued Jackson's policy of removing Southern Indians to Oklahoma, supervising the transfer of 20,000 Cherokee in 1838. In Florida, he fought a long and bloody war against the Seminole Indians, leading to the removal of 3,500 of the 4,000 Indians and the capture of many runaway slaves who had taken refuge with them—all at the cost of 1,500 casualties to U.S. forces.

The hard economic times led to "Martin Van Ruin's" defeat in 1840 at the hands of the popular Whig candidate William Henry Harrison. After leaving the White House, Van Buren devoted his efforts to regaining the Presidency. He was a leading contender for the Democratic nomination in 1844, receiving more than half of the ballots cast but not the necessary two-thirds. He lost the nomination because his stand against the annexation of Texas eroded his support: he correctly foresaw that it would lead to war with Mexico. In 1848 he was nominated by the Free-Soil party, a coalition of New York abolitionists, "conscience" Whigs, and others opposed to the extension of slavery. Van Buren received no electoral college votes but won 10 percent of the popular vote, enough to defeat the Democratic candidate, Lewis Cass, and pave the way for

Whig candidate Zachary Taylor to win. Thereafter Van Buren played no role in national politics.

SEE ALSO *Harrison, William Henry; Jackson, Andrew*

SOURCES Donald B. Cole, *Martin Van Buren and the American Political System* (Princeton, N.J.: Princeton University Press, 1984). John Niven, *Martin Van Buren: The Romantic Age of American Politics* (New York: Oxford University Press, 1983). Major Wilson, *The Presidency of Martin Van Buren* (Lawrence: University Press of Kansas, 1984).

VANDENBERG, ARTHUR H.

- Born: Mar. 22, 1884, Grand Rapids, Mich.
- Political party: Republican
- Education: studied law at the Universtiy of Michigan at Ann Arbor
- Senator from Michigan: 1928–51
- Died: Apr. 18, 1951, Grand Rapids, Mich.

Senator Arthur Vandenberg first won national attention as an isolationist—someone who believed that the United States should defend its own interests and should avoid international organizations and "entangling alliances." But the Japanese attack on Pearl Harbor in December 1941 shattered the illusion that the United States could stand alone, protected on both sides by vast oceans. Vandenberg came to believe that the United States must take a greater role in keeping the peace after World War II ended. On January 10, 1945, he rose in the Senate to deliver what the *Cleveland Plain Dealer* called "a shot heard round the world." In it he abandoned isolationism and embraced international cooperation, urging other senators to follow him. Because Vandenberg was a prominent Republican, his conversion to internationalism made him a leader in building a bipartisan foreign policy under Democratic President Harry S. Truman. As

chairman of the Foreign Relations Committee during the 80th Congress, he strongly supported Truman's program for combatting the Soviet Union during the cold war. Vandenberg also introduced the Senate resolution that cleared the way for U.S. participation in NATO (the North Atlantic Treaty Organization). This pact with Canada and 10 Western European nations was the first mutual defense treaty that the United States entered into since its alliance with France during the American Revolution.

SEE ALSO *Bipartisan foreign policy; Vandenberg Resolution (1948)*

SOURCES Arthur H. Vandenberg, Jr., ed., *The Private Papers of Senator Vandenberg* (Boston: Houghton Mifflin, 1952).

VANDENBERG RESOLUTION (1948)

As U.S. relations with the Soviet Union worsened during the early years of the cold war, President Harry S. Truman determined that the United States must enter a military alliance to defend Western Europe against a Soviet invasion. However, since George Washington's farewell address warned against entering into "entangling alliances," the United States had steadfastly opposed joining any military alliances. Senator Arthur H. Vandenberg (Republican–Michigan) lobbied strongly for congressional support of Truman's foreign policies. To test whether the Senate would give the two-thirds vote necessary to pass a treaty setting up a military alliance, Vandenberg introduced a resolution in the Senate in June 1948 calling for the United States to pursue "regional and other collective agreements" for defense against communism. The Senate passed the Vandenberg Resolution by a vote of 64 to 4, clearing the way for the North Atlantic Treaty Organization (NATO). NATO included Belgium, Canada, Denmark, France, Great Britain, Iceland, Italy, Luxembourg, the Netherlands, Norway, Portugal, and the United States (Greece, Turkey, West Germany, and Spain later joined, while France withdrew).

SEE ALSO *Treaty powers; Vandenberg, Arthur H.*

VAN DEVANTER, WILLIS
Associate Justice, 1911–37

- Born: Apr. 17, 1859, Marion, Ind.
- Education: Indiana Asbury University (DePauw University), B.A., 1878; University of Cincinnati Law School, LL.B., 1881
- Previous government service: city attorney, Cheyenne, Wyo., 1887–88; Wyoming Territorial Legislature, 1888; chief justice, Wyoming Territory Supreme Court, 1889–90; assistant U.S. attorney general, 1897–1903; judge, U.S. Court of Appeals for the Eighth Circuit, 1903–1910
- Appointed by President William Howard Taft Dec. 12, 1910; replaced William Moody, who retired
- Supreme Court term: confirmed by the Senate Dec. 15, 1910, by a voice vote; retired June 2, 1937
- Died: Feb. 8, 1941, Washington, D.C.

Willis Van Devanter moved, as a young man, from his settled community in Indiana to Cheyenne in the Wyoming Territory. On the last western frontier, he built a successful career in law and politics that led him back east to federal government service in Washington, D.C.

Van Devanter served 26 years on the Supreme Court, where he exercised great influence on his colleagues during most of his long term. He rarely wrote opinions; his average number of opinions per year was only 14. (Most justices wrote more than 30 per year.) Justice Van Devanter influenced the other justices through face-to-face discussions about the cases before the Court. He often influenced the direction and substance of opinions written by others.

Justice Van Devanter argued persis-

tently for limited government and against the expansion of the federal government's power to regulate businesses and the relationships between employers and workers. Accordingly, he reacted strongly against the New Deal programs of President Franklin D. Roosevelt. He succeeded in influencing the Court to strike down several New Deal laws during President Roosevelt's first term of office. However, by 1936 the tide had turned against him. Public opinion was strongly on the side of Roosevelt's New Deal. The President's new appointments to the Court reflected this public mood and Roosevelt's views. As a result, Van Devanter decided to retire from the Court in 1937.

VERNONIA SCHOOL DISTRICT V. ACTON

- 515 U.S. 646 (1995)
- Vote: 6-3
- For the Court: Scalia
- Concurring: Ginsburg
- Dissent: O'Connor, Stevens, and Souter

Vernonia, Oregon, a small community of about 3,000 people, faced a serious problem of drug use among students of the local public schools. So the Vernonia School Board approved an anti-drug policy, which required random drug testing of students wanting to participate in interschool athletics.

Vernonia's drug-testing program required all middle-school and high-school student athletes to provide a urine sample at the beginning of their team's season. During the remainder of the season, on a weekly basis, 10 percent of the team members would be chosen at random for a new test. Athletes refusing to take the test would be prevented from participating in interschool sports activities for two years. Students with a positive test result would be suspended from participating in the school's sports program for an unspecified period while undergoing counseling to remedy their problems.

The drug-testing policy seemed to be acceptable among parents in Vernonia. No one objected to the policy when the school board approved it in 1989. However, when James Acton wanted to join his school's seventh-grade football team, his parents challenged the drug-testing policy. They refused to sign a urinalysis consent form to permit their son to take the test. And they filed suit in the federal district court in 1991 to stop the drug-testing policy because, in their opinion, it violated the 4th Amendment's prohibition against "unreasonable" searches.

The federal district court in Oregon dismissed the Actons' suit. They appealed to the Court of Appeals for the 9th District, which favored the Actons' complaint and voided the Vernonia drug-testing program. However, this decision conflicted with a 1988 ruling of the 5th Circuit Court of Appeals that permitted random drug testing in public schools of Indiana, Illinois, and Wisconsin. So the *Acton* case went on appeal to the U.S. Supreme Court, which was called upon to resolve the conflicting appellate court opinions.

The Issue Did the Vernonia School District's mandatory drug-testing policy violate the 4th Amendment rights of students? The Acton family claimed it called for unreasonable searches of a student's body and thereby violated the person's rights under the Constitution's 4th Amendment. The school district's lawyers argued that a compelling public interest—preventing illegal drug use among preadults—justified limitations on the 4th Amendment rights of students in public schools.

Opinion of the Court The Supreme Court upheld the Vernonia drug-testing policy. The Court concluded that the school board's objective on behalf of the community to protect the public against drug abuse, a rampant problem, outweighed the minimal limitations of an individual's 4th Amendment rights associated with the drug-testing regulations. The Court pointed out that only members of sports teams were subjected to drug-testing and that participation in interschool athletics was voluntary.

Writing for the Court, Justice Antonin Scalia said, "The most significant element in this case is . . . that the Policy was undertaken in furtherance of the government's responsibilities, under a public school system, as guardian and tutor for children entrusted to its care." He pointed out that "when the government acts as a guardian and tutor the relevant question is whether the search is one that a reasonable guardian and tutor might undertake." And he concluded that given the mission of public schools, and the circumstances of this case, the searches required by the school board's policy were "reasonable" and thereby permissible under the Constitution's 4th Amendment.

Dissent According to Justice Sandra Day O'Connor, the Vernonia School Board's policy permitted "suspicionless searches" of students, and this violated their 4th Amendment rights. She wrote that innocent students could be "open to an intrusive bodily search" [even though most of them] have given school officials no reason whatsoever to suspect they use drugs at school." Justice O'Connor concluded that it would be "far more reasonable" to restrict drug testing to students who caused disciplinary problems at school.

Significance Federal government officials praised the Court's decision as supportive of their war against illegal drug use. Lee Brown, President Bill Clinton's adviser on drug policy, called the ruling "a victory for kids." But a leader of the American Civil Liberties Union criticized the Court for failing to protect the rights of students in schools. He said, "It makes students second-class citizens." The *Acton* case is a prime example of the ongoing controversy in a free society about how to balance the community's legitimate needs for order and safety against the individual's constitutional rights to liberty.

VETO POWER

From the Latin for "I forbid," the veto is the device Presidents use to reject legislation that Congress has passed. Article 1, Section 7, of the Constitution provides that the President may return any legislation he disapproves of to Congress with an explanation of his objections (although the word *veto* does not appear in the Constitution). The Constitution provides that all measures that require the concurrence of both chambers are to be presented to the President of the United States. The only exceptions are resolutions to adjourn and constitutional amendments.

The President may sign the measure, allow it to become law if he does not sign it within 10 days, or return it to the chamber in which it originated together with his objections. Congress may pass the law over the President's objection by a two-thirds vote in each chamber.

A President who sends a bill back to Congress may not change his mind and recall it; President Ulysses S. Grant attempted to do so twice but Congress refused to return the bills to him.

One form of Presidential veto, known as the pocket veto, cannot be overridden by Congress. Using this technique, the President in a sense places a bill in his pocket and refuses to sign it or return it to Congress. If Congress has adjourned or is in recess for more than ten days, the absence of the President's signature kills the bill. When Congress returns to session, it must start all over again if it wishes to revive the bill.

The Constitution allows for no item-by-item veto. The President may not veto part of a bill and approve the remainder—a power that 43 state governors do have. His veto strikes down the entire measure. In 1877 President Rutherford B. Hayes recommended that the President be given a line-item veto, and between 1877 and 1888 several such constitutional amendments were introduced in Congress, but none were passed. Presidents Dwight Ei-

senhower and Ronald Reagan also proposed the line-item veto for congressional spending bills and were similarly rebuffed. President Bill Clinton also supported the idea, but as part of reforming the budget process, by law, not as a constitutional amendment. In 1995 Congress did pass a law giving the President the line-item veto. President Clinton exercised this power sparingly, but many in Congress—including some who had supported the line-item veto—protested when he used it to veto their projects. In 1998 the Supreme Court declared that the line-item veto was an unconstitutional delegation of Congress's "power of the purse."

Unconstitutional vs. unwise laws
The practice of government executives nullifying laws was well known to the framers of the Constitution. In colonial times the king and royal governors often vetoed laws passed by colonial legislatures. Indeed, that was one of the reasons for rebelling mentioned in the Declaration of Independence. After the Revolution, New York State had a Council of Revision made up of the governor, chancellor, and state judges who could nullify laws that seemed to violate the state constitution.

The Constitution does not specify the grounds on which the President may exercise his veto. Initially, many commentators believed that the President could veto legislation only if he believed the measure to be unconstitutional. President George Washington agreed and tried to avoid vetoing bills, using the power only twice. He believed that Presidents should defer to the will of Congress and use this power only as an emergency measure. Prior to 1832, only 6 of 21 vetoes were made for other than constitutional reasons. The issue came to a head when Andrew Jackson vetoed a bill rechartering the Second Bank of the United States. Jackson claimed that he could veto the bill because of policy disagreement, while the opposition Whig party proclaimed that a President could veto a bill only on constitutional grounds. When John Tyler vetoed bills of the Whig congressional ma-

Presidential Vetoes of Congressional Legislation			
President	Total Vetoes	Regular Vetoes	Pocket Vetoes	Overridden
George Washington	2	2	0	0
John Adams	0	0	0	0
Thomas Jefferson	0	0	0	0
James Madison	7	5	2	0
James Monroe	1	1	0	0
John Quincy Adams	0	0	0	0
Andrew Jackson	12	5	7	0
Martin Van Buren	1	0	1	0
William H. Harrison	0	0	0	0
John Tyler	10	6	4	1
James K. Polk	3	2	1	0
Zachary Taylor	0	0	0	0
Millard Fillmore	0	0	0	0
Franklin Pierce	9	9	0	5
James Buchanan	7	4	3	0
Abraham Lincoln	7	2	5	0
Andrew Johnson	29	21	8	15
Ulysses S. Grant	93	45	48	4
Rutherford B. Hayes	13	12	1	1
James A. Garfield	0	0	0	0
Chester A. Arthur	12	4	8	1
Grover Cleveland	414	304	110	2
Benjamin Harrison	44	19	25	1
Grover Cleveland	170	42	128	5
William McKinley	42	6	36	0
Theodore Roosevelt	82	42	40	1
William H. Taft	39	30	9	1
Woodrow Wilson	44	33	11	6
Warren G. Harding	6	5	1	0
Calvin Coolidge	50	20	30	4
Herbert Hoover	37	21	16	4
Franklin D. Roosevelt	635	372	263	9
Harry S. Truman	250	180	70	12
Dwight D. Eisenhower	181	73	108	2
John F. Kennedy	21	12	9	0
Lyndon B. Johnson	30	16	14	0
Richard M. Nixon	43	26	17	7
Gerald R. Ford	66	48	18	12
Jimmy Carter	31	13	18	2
Ronald Reagan	78	39	39	9
George Bush	44	29	15	1
Bill Clinton	22	22	0	2

jority, a select committee of Congress argued that he had misused his power. In 1842 Senator Henry Clay proposed a constitutional amendment to permit Congress to override a President's veto by a majority vote of each chamber. Neither this proposed amendment nor resolutions to impeach Tyler passed the House. Since the Civil War, most vetoes have been exercised because the President believed laws to be unwise rather than unconstitutional.

In recent years Presidents have sometimes allowed bills to become law but have indicated that they will not enforce a specific provision they believe to be unconstitutional. President Richard Nixon refused to obey a provision of a 1971 military procurement bill requiring him to declare a cease-fire and negotiate with North Vietnam for a prisoner exchange in return for U.S. withdrawal from Indochina. He claimed that "the so-called Mansfield Amendment is unconstitutional, and without force or effect" because it infringed on his powers as commander in chief.

Presidents have also used "signing statements," which are released when they sign measures passed by Congress, to provide their own interpretation of the law. When President Reagan signed the Beirut Resolution of 1982, authorizing him to keep a marine contingent in Lebanon for peacekeeping, he issued a statement arguing that nothing in the resolution could have the effect of limiting or interfering with his powers as commander in chief to station troops anywhere he wished.

The President is assisted in making decisions about whether to sign or veto bills by the Office of Management and Budget, which conducts a review of every bill passed by Congress and sent to the President. Often, cabinet secretaries and White House aides comment as well.

The veto power often becomes a threat that the President can use to influence legislation. Because an override requires a two-thirds vote of both houses, fewer than 7 percent of Presidential vetoes have been overridden. So Presidents can intervene early in the legislative process with threats of a veto unless pending legislation is modified to meet their objections, and sometimes more than one-third of a chamber will sign a pledge in advance to back up the President if he vetoes a bill. This makes the White House an integral part of the legislative process from beginning to end.

SEE ALSO *Creation of the Presidency; Jackson, Andrew; Legislative veto; Line-item veto; Office of Management and Budget; Pocket veto*

SOURCES Carleton Jackson, *Presidential Vetoes: 1792–1945* (Athens: University of Georgia Press, 1967). Robert J. Spitzer, *The Presidential Veto: Touchstone of the American Presidency* (Albany: State University of New York Press, 1988). Charles Zinn, *The Veto Power of the President* (Washington, D.C.: Government Printing Office, 1951).

VICE PRESIDENT

The Vice President is the officer designated by the Constitution to succeed to the office of President in case of a vacancy created by the death, disability, impeachment, or resignation of the President.

The Vice Presidency was an afterthought for the Constitutional Convention, put into the document in order to provide for orderly succession without resorting to election of someone from Congress to fill the vacancy. The Vice President is not a member of either the executive or the legislative branch. Constitutionally, the Vice President is not a subordinate of the President, who has no power to issue orders to the Vice President and who cannot remove him from office. (The Vice President can be removed only by impeachment.) But Vice Presidents have found that the way they gain influence in Washington is by subordinating themselves to the President. By doing so, they have become, since Dwight Eisenhower's administration, part of the inner circle of senior political advisers to the President.

The Vice President has no constitutional responsibilities other than serving as president of the Senate, presiding over that body (except in Presidential impeachment trials, when the chief justice of the United States presides), and voting only to break ties. The Vice President may address the Senate only with the Senate's permission. He may also interpret the Senate rules, but his decisions may be—and have been—overruled by a majority vote of the Senate. John Adams, the first Vice President, felt perplexed about the dual nature of his job. "I am Vice President," he told the Senate. "In this I am nothing, but I may be everything. But I am president also of the Senate. When the President comes into the Senate, what shall I be?"

Vice Presidents presided over the Senate on a regular basis until 1953, when Richard M. Nixon occupied an office near the White House and spent more time on executive than on legislative business. Vice Presidents have increasingly tended to preside only when their vote might be needed to break a tie or during ceremonial occasions. Modern Vice Presidents preside about 1 percent of the time the Senate is in session. The Senate elects a president pro tempore to preside in the Vice President's absence. The president pro tem, in turn, designates junior members of the majority party to take turns, usually for an hour at a time, presiding over the Senate.

Vice Presidents have only a few statutory duties. Since 1949 they have served on the National Security Council, and they are on the Board of Regents of the Smithsonian Institution (which operates various museums in the capital). They name five cadets to the U.S. Military Academy, U.S. Naval Academy, and Air Force Academy. They appoint senators to various independent commissions, including the Migratory Bird Conservation Commission, the Harry S. Truman Scholarship Foundation, and the Advisory Commission on Intergovernmental Relations. Vice Presidents are usually assigned by the President to chair various commissions. They generally chair the Space Council; other commissions deal with nondiscriminatory practices in government contracts and efforts at deregulating the economy. They usually serve as the White House liaison with the National Governors Association and the U.S. Conference of Mayors. The Vice President participates in cabinet meetings, a custom established by Warren Harding. Since Eisenhower's time, Vice Presidents have presided over cabinet meetings in the absence of the President; Richard Nixon chaired 20 such meetings during Eisenhower's illnesses and trips.

Until the 1960s, Vice Presidents had their main offices on Capitol Hill near the Senate chamber. President John F. Kennedy asked Lyndon Johnson to take a suite of offices in the Old Executive Office Building, and today the Office of the Vice President is located on the second floor of that building. He has smaller offices in the Capitol and in the West Wing of the White House.

In 1970 the federal budget allocated funds for the first time to the Office of the Vice President under the line item "Special Assistance to the President." More than $2.5 million was spent on the Vice President's staff in 1992.

Units of the Vice President's Office include the chief of staff, scheduling and advance office, domestic policy staff, legal counsel, national security adviser, press office, and speech writers. The office is assisted by the Office of Administration in the White House with support functions such as payroll and personnel. The Vice President's wife has five aides.

Since 1974 the Vice President has had an official residence on Massachusetts Avenue in the District of Columbia, the former Admiral's House at the Naval Observatory. It has 12 rooms on three floors and is situated on 12 landscaped acres. The Vice President receives a $171,500 salary, a taxable expense allowance of $10,000, and $90,000 for entertaining. Six navy stewards serve as the mansion staff. The first Vice President to occupy the residence was Walter Mondale, beginning in 1977. Vice President George Bush and his wife, Barbara, presided over a complete refurbishing of the mansion, using $200,000 in private contributions.

The Vice President receives no additional pay as president of the Senate but does receive more than $1 million in expenses for his office on Capitol Hill. As president of the Senate, the Vice President has 40 additional staff aides. The Vice Presidential plane is known as *Air Force Two.* The Vice Presidential seal is an eagle with spread wings and a claw full of arrows, with a starburst at its head.

Vice Presidents receive protection from the Uniformed Division of the Secret Service. When they leave office, they may be assigned Secret Service protection for six months at the discretion of the new administration. Unlike former Presidents, they have no right to address the Senate or to stay in the residence on Jackson Place.

In modern times the Vice President has generally become the favorite to win his party's Presidential nomination and succeed to the office. Since 1960, Vice Presidents Richard Nixon, Hubert Humphrey, Walter Mondale, George Bush, and Al Gore all won subsequent Presidential nominations.

SEE ALSO *Cabinet; Disability, Presidential; Electoral college; Executive power; National Security Council; Nominating conventions, Presidential; Secret Service, U.S.; Succession to the Presidency; Ticket; 12th Amendment; 25th Amendment*

SOURCES Joel K. Goldstein, *The Modern American Vice Presidency* (Princeton, N.J.: Princeton University Press, 1982). Paul C. Light, *Vice-Presidential Power: Advice and Influence in the White House* (Baltimore, Md.: Johns Hopkins University Press, 1984). Ronald C. Moe, "The Institutional Vice Presidency," in *The Presidency in Transition,* edited by James Pfiffner and Gordon Hoxie (New York: Center for the Study of the Presidency, 1989). Marie D. Natoli, *American Prince, American Pauper: The Contemporary Vice Presidency in Perspective* (Westport, Conn.: Greenwood,

1985). Timothy Walch, ed., *At the President's Side: The Vice Presidency in the Twentieth Century* (Columbia: University of Missouri Press, 1997). Donald Young, *American Roulette: The History and Dilemma of the Vice Presidency* (New York: Viking, 1974).

VINSON, FRED M.
Chief Justice, 1946–53

- Born: Jan. 22, 1890, Louisa, Ky.
- Education: Centre College, B.A., 1909, LL.B., 1911
- Previous government service: commonwealth's attorney, 32nd District of Kentucky, 1921–24; U.S. Representative from Kentucky, 1924–29, 1931–38; judge, U.S. Court of Appeals for the District of Columbia Circuit, 1938–43; director, U.S. Office of Economic Stabilization, 1943–45; administrator, Federal Loan Agency, 1945; director, U.S. Office of War Mobilization and Reconversion, 1945; U.S. secretary of the Treasury, 1945–46
- Appointed by President Harry S. Truman June 6, 1946; replaced Harlan Fiske Stone, who died
- Supreme Court term: confirmed by the Senate June 20, 1946, by a voice vote; served until Sept. 8, 1953
- Died: Sept. 8, 1953, Washington, D.C.

Fred M. Vinson became the 13th chief justice of the United States in 1946. This was the capstone of a long and meritorious career in all three branches of the federal government. Chief Justice Vinson served only seven years, until his death in 1953, as chief justice. These were years of tumult and controversy involving the Court in issues of patriotism and loyalty to the United States and issues of civil liberties and equal protection against racial discrimination.

Chief Justice Vinson acted strongly against individuals he viewed as a threat to the government of the United States. In *Dennis* v. *United States* (1951), for example, he upheld the Smith Act, which provided for criminal convictions of anyone advocating violent overthrow of the U.S. government. In the *Dennis* case, several leaders of the American Communist party were punished.

Chief Justice Vinson supported equal rights for black Americans in several opinions. For example, he led the Court in overturning state laws that unfairly discriminated against black people in *Sweatt* v. *Painter* (1950) and *McLaurin* v. *Board of Regents* (1950). These rulings helped to set the stage for the Court's landmark decision in *Brown* v. *Board of Education* (1954), which marked the beginning of the end of racial segregation in public schools and other institutions.

SEE ALSO *Dennis v. United States; Sweatt v. Painter*

SOURCES Jan S. Palmer, *The Vinson Court Era* (New York: AMS Press, 1990). C. Herman Pritchett, *Civil Liberties and the Vinson Court* (Chicago: University of Chicago Press, 1954).

VOTING IN CONGRESS

Members of Congress cast hundreds of votes during each session on a multitude of issues. Some votes, usually on routine or less controversial issues, are cast by voice. The presiding officer orders, "All in favor say aye, all opposed nay," noting whether the ayes or nays have it. When voting by voice, the votes of individual members are not identified. By contrast, a roll call vote records the names of all who voted for or against the bill as well as those who were absent or who simply answered "present" without voting.

Different percentages of the vote are needed for different functions in Congress. A majority of 51 percent of the votes cast is necessary to pass an amendment, a bill, or a resolution, to set rules and elect officers, to overturn a ruling of the presiding officer, and to confirm nominations. It takes three-fifths of the senators to invoke cloture and cut off debate. Two-thirds of the vote is needed for the Senate to approve a treaty or to remove an impeached official from office. A two-thirds vote of both the House and Senate is also necessary to override a Presidential veto.

The Senate, with 100 members, votes aloud during a roll call vote, with the legislative clerk recording whether a senator voted aye or nay. Votes in the Senate generally take 15 minutes, although the leadership sometimes will stretch the time to accommodate members hurrying to the chamber from a distance. To keep its voting time down, the House, with 435 voting members, has adopted an electronic voting system. Each representative has a card to insert into one of the small boxes on the back of the benches near the entrances to the House chamber. Using the card, a member can vote yes, no, or present. Members' votes are then lit up on a large scoreboard above the press gallery, with a green light indicating a yes vote and a red light indicating a no. Vote tallies are shown electronically on either side of the chamber. Because being absent during a vote can hurt members politically when they run for reelection, they instruct their party leaders to announce the reason, such as illness or a trip out of town, that prevented them from voting. If absent members wish to show how they would have voted, they can arrange in advance to pair their vote with another absent member who would have voted the opposite way. Paired votes are listed in the *Congressional Record,* indicating the members' position on the bill and that their votes would not have changed the eventual outcome.

Any number of reasons affect the way members of Congress cast their votes. In a dissenting opinion in the case of *Edwards* v. *Aguillard* (1987), Supreme Court Justice Antonin Scalia suggested—somewhat sarcastically—some of the factors that might influence a legislator's vote:

He may have thought the bill would provide jobs for his district, or may have wanted to make amends with a faction of his party he had alienated on another vote, or he may

680 Voting In Congress

have been a close friend of the bill's sponsor, or he may have been repaying a favor he owed the Majority Leader . . . or he may have been pressured to vote for a bill he disliked by a wealthy contributor or by a flood of constituent mail, or he may have been seeking favorable publicity, or he may have been reluctant to hurt the feelings of a loyal staff member who worked on the bill, or he may have been settling an old score with a legislator who opposed the bill, or he may have been mad at his wife who opposed the bill, or he may have been intoxicated and utterly unmotivated when the vote was called, or he may have accidentally voted "yes" instead of "no," or, of course, he may have had (and very likely did have) a combination of some of the above motives.

SEE ALSO *Pair voting*

W

WADE, BENJAMIN F.

- Born: Oct. 27, 1800, Springfield, Mass.
- Political party: Republican
- Education: studied medicine in Albany, N.Y., 1823–25; studied law in Ohio
- Senator from Ohio: 1851–69
- President pro tempore: 1865–69
- Died: Mar. 2, 1878, Jefferson, Ohio

"Bluff" Ben Wade won the South's hatred for his uncompromising opposition to slavery before the Civil War and his demand for the federal government to protect the rights of the freedmen after the war. Wade entered the Senate during the debate over the Kansas-Nebraska Act of 1854, which he loudly opposed. He declared himself a believer in the sentiments of the Declaration of Independence, that "all men are created equal." Southern senators demanded to know if Wade meant that slaves were the equals of white men. "Yes," replied Wade. "Why not equal? Do they not have their life by Almighty God?" During the war, he sponsored the Wade-Davis Bill, calling for military rule over the defeated South and requiring a majority of voters to take a loyalty oath before their state could be readmitted to the Union. President Abraham Lincoln, who wanted a speedier Reconstruction, pocket vetoed the Wade-Davis Bill. Wade broke even more sharply with Lincoln's successor, Andrew Johnson, over Reconstruction. As president pro tempore, Wade would have become President of the United States had

the Senate not failed by a single vote to remove Johnson from office.

SEE ALSO *Reconstruction, congressional; Veto power; Wade-Davis Bill (1864)*
SOURCES Hans L. Trefousse, *Benjamin Franklin Wade: Radical Republican from Ohio* (New York: Twayne, 1963).

WADE-DAVIS BILL (1864)

As the North progressed toward victory in the Civil War, Senator Benjamin F. Wade (Republican–Ohio) and Representative Henry Winter Davis (Unionist–Maryland) introduced a bill to reconstruct the Southern states after the war ended. In harsh language, the Wade-Davis Bill demanded that a majority of voters in the Confederate states must swear an "Ironclad Oath" of allegiance to the Union and that the former slaves must be assured their equality with whites. President Abraham Lincoln had proposed a much more lenient plan of reconstruction that would have required only 10 percent of each state's voters to demonstrate their allegiance to the Union in order for their state to be readmitted. Lincoln pocket vetoed the Wade-Davis Bill, slipping it into his pocket so that Congress would not have the opportunity to override his veto. Wade and Davis angrily accused President Lincoln of acting like a dictator. The Wade-Davis Bill served as an indication of the even greater battles that would follow between the executive branch and the legislature over reconstruction of the South.

SEE ALSO *Reconstruction, congressional;
Veto power*
SOURCES Eric Foner, *Reconstruction:
America's Unfinished Revolution, 1863–
1877* (New York: Harper & Row, 1988).

WAGNER,
ROBERT F.

- Born: June 8, 1877, Nastatten, Germany
- Political party: Democrat
- Education: College of the City of New York, graduated, 1898; New York Law School, graduated, 1900
- Senator from New York: 1927–49
- Died: May 4, 1953, New York, N.Y.

Short, stocky, with a heavy New York accent (saying "woik" for "work"), Robert F. Wagner may have appeared to be a typical machine politician. But he proved to be one of the most effective legislators of the New Deal era. Wagner worked best behind closed committee doors, making his case for legislation, reaching necessary compromises, and rounding up votes before going into debate on the Senate floor. Wagner sponsored a long list of important legislation, but his two greatest achievements occurred in 1935: the Wagner Act, guaranteeing labor's right to organize into unions, and the Social Security Act to provide old-age pensions to most Americans. Milton Handler, a young New Dealer who watched Wagner firsthand, credited Wagner's legislative success to these qualities:

First, his ingrained, humanitarian, progressive philosophy; second, his uncanny capacity to recruit good men to do the detail work for him; third, his masterful ability to maneuver bills through the legislative mill; and fourth, and most important of all, his willingness and determination to stick to his basic conviction through thick and thin—in a word, his "guts."

SOURCES J. Joseph Huthmacher, *Senator Robert F. Wagner and the Rise of Urban Liberalism* (New York: Atheneum, 1968).

WAITE,
MORRISON R.
Chief Justice, 1874–88

- Born: Nov. 29, 1816, Lyme, Conn.
- Education: Yale College, B.A., 1837
- Previous government service: Ohio House of Representatives, 1850–52; president, Ohio Constitutional Convention, 1873–74
- Appointed by President Ulysses S. Grant Jan. 19, 1874; replaced Salmon P. Chase, who died
- Supreme Court term: confirmed by the Senate Jan. 21, 1874, by a 63–0 vote; served until Mar. 23, 1888
- Died: Mar. 23, 1888, Washington, D.C.

Morrison R. Waite had no judicial experience before his appointment as chief justice, and he had never presented a case before the Supreme Court. President Ulysses S. Grant appointed Waite to head the Supreme Court because of his effectiveness in representing the United States in an international arbitration case in Geneva.

At first, Chief Justice Waite was not respected by other members of the Supreme Court because of his lack of experience. He eventually won their acceptance and respect for his hard work and leadership of the Court.

Chief Justice Waite often decided in favor of the power and rights of state governments. For example, in his most notable opinion, *Munn* v. *Illinois* (1877), Chief Justice Waite upheld an Illinois law that set maximum rates that could be charged by grain elevator owners. He supported the power of the state of Illinois to regulate the use of private property "when such regulation becomes necessary for the public good."

In the *Munn* case, and similar cases involving state laws, Waite believed that the political process, not the Courts, was the correct avenue for opponents of the laws. In *Munn* v. *Illinois,* Waite wrote: "For protection against abuse by legislatures, the people must resort to the polls, not to the courts." Waite believed that the legislative branch of government, not the judicial branch, should always take the lead in making public policy. The judiciary, he argued, should restrain itself to questions of legal interpretation.

Under Waite's leadership, the Court tended to narrowly interpret the rights of black Americans under the 14th and 15th Amendments to the U.S. Constitution. Waite argued that most civil rights were associated with state citizenship, which should be guaranteed by the state governments, not the federal government. This viewpoint, which often prevailed on the Court at this time, meant that the civil rights of black Americans varied considerably depending upon the state in which they lived. In many states, their rights were not equal to those of white Americans, and the Supreme Court, under Waite, was reluctant to intervene into the states' affairs to secure these rights.

SEE ALSO *Judicial activism and judicial restraint; Munn v. Illinois*

SOURCES Peter C. Magrath, *Morrison R. Waite: The Triumph of Character* (New York: Macmillan, 1963).

WALLACE, HENRY
Vice President

- Born: Oct. 7, 1888, Adair County, Iowa
- Political party: Republican, then Democrat
- Education: Iowa State College, B.S., 1910
- Military service: none
- Previous government service: secretary of agriculture, 1933–40
- Vice President under Franklin D. Roosevelt, 1941–45
- Subsequent government service: U.S. secretary of commerce, 1945–46
- Died: Nov. 18, 1965, Danbury, Conn.

Henry Wallace was associate editor (1911–24) and then editor (1924–33) of the most influential farmers' magazine of his day, *Wallace's Farmer*. He was also president of the Pioneer Hi-Bred Corn Company, which specialized in new, high-yield strains of corn. Although a Republican, he was appointed by Franklin Roosevelt, a Democrat, to be secretary of agriculture in 1933, to help Roosevelt appeal to Midwestern progressives and win their support for his New Deal program. Wallace implemented the New Deal farm policy, developing new programs for soil conservation, production quotas, and farm price supports through the Agricultural Adjustment Administration. In 1936 he became a Democrat.

Roosevelt chose Wallace to be his Vice Presidential nominee in 1940 to retain the farm vote and solidify support on the political left, though he surprised party leaders by not choosing someone from the South for geographic balance. The Democratic convention balked at his choice. But Roosevelt insisted, making Wallace's nomination a condition of his own candidacy, and the delegates backed down. He did ask Wallace not to deliver an acceptance speech to the angry delegates.

As Vice President, Wallace traveled to Latin America as a goodwill ambassador and served as chair of the Economic Defense Board in 1941, renamed the Board of Economic Warfare in 1942. He lost the position of economic defense coordinator in 1943 after frequent battles with Secretary of Commerce Jesse Jones. Opposition to Wallace by leading conservative Democrats in Congress led Roosevelt to drop him from the ticket in 1944. Instead, Roosevelt appointed him secretary of commerce, and newly elected Vice President Harry Truman persuaded key senators to consent to the nomination.

Wallace kept his post when Truman became President but soon broke with him over the President's strong anticommunist stance. In 1946, after making a speech criticizing Truman's "get tough" policy, Wallace was forced by Truman to resign. Two years later Wallace ran for President on the Progressive party ticket, hoping to play a spoiler role and see to Truman's defeat. But he won no electoral votes and could not prevent Truman's reelection.

SEE ALSO *Truman, Harry S.*

SOURCES John M. Blum, ed., *The Price of Vision: The Diary of Henry A. Wallace, 1942–46* (Boston: Houghton Mifflin, 1973). John. C. Culver and John Hyde, *American Dreamer: The Life and Times of Henry A. Wallace* (New York: Norton, 2000). Norman Markowitz, *The Rise and Fall of the People's Century: Henry A. Wallace and American Liberalism, 1941–1948* (New York: Free Press, 1973).

WALLACE V. JAFFREE

- 472 U.S. 38 (1985)
- Vote: 6–3
- For the Court: Stevens
- Concurring: Powell and O'Connor
- Dissenting: Burger, White, and Rehnquist

From 1978 to 1982 the Alabama legislature passed three laws pertaining to prayer in public schools. The 1978 law authorized schools to provide a daily minute of silence for meditation. A 1981 law provided for a similar period "for meditation or voluntary prayer." A third law, enacted in 1982, allowed teachers to lead "willing students" in a prescribed prayer.

In 1982 Ishmael Jaffree filed suit against the school board of Mobile County to challenge the 1981 and 1982 Alabama laws permitting a period of silence and prayer in public schools. Jaffree decided to file this suit after his three children reported that their teachers had led prayers in school. Jaffree claimed that the 1981 and 1982 Alabama statutes on prayer in public schools violated the establishment clause of the 1st Amendment to the U.S. Constitution, which prohibited the states from making laws regarding the establishment of religion. He cited Supreme Court decisions such as *Engel* v. *Vitale* (1962) and *Abington School District* v. *Schempp* (1963) to support his argument. In both cases, the Court found that state-mandated religious activities in public schools were unconstitutional.

A federal district court ruled against Jaffree, stating that the *Engel* and *Schempp* cases were decided incorrectly. This district court ruling was overturned by the U.S. Court of Appeals for the 11th Circuit. The Court of Appeals followed the precedents of the *Engel* and *Schempp* cases and held that the 1981 and 1982 Alabama laws violated the establishment clause of the 1st Amendment as applied to the states through the 14th Amendment. The state of Alabama appealed the federal appellate court's decision to the U.S. Supreme Court.

The Issue The Supreme Court summarily upheld the appellate court's decision to strike down the 1982 statute, which clearly authorized teachers and students to set aside time for expression of prayer in public schools. According to the Court, this was a clear violation of the 1st Amendment's establishment clause. Therefore, the Court agreed to hear oral arguments only about the 1981 statute, which authorized the moment of silence for "meditation or voluntary prayer." Does a state law authorizing a moment of silence in a public school, for the express purpose of prayer, violate the 1st Amendment provisions on religion: "Congress shall make no law respecting an establishment of religion, or prohibiting the free exercise thereof"?

Opinion of the Court The Court decided for Jaffree and overturned the Alabama law at issue in this case because of the law's religious purpose and intentions. Justice John Paul Stevens relied upon the Court's previous rulings in *Abington School District* v. *Schempp* (1963) and *Lemon* v. *Kurtzman* (1971) to justify the *Jaffree* decision.

Dissent Justice William Rehnquist argued for a totally new interpretation of the 1st Amendment's establishment clause. He rejected the idea of a "wall of separation" between church and state. And he opposed the precedents of *Schempp* and *Lemon* as bases for making decisions about establishment clause issues. Instead, Rehnquist claimed that the 1st Amendment was designed only to prevent the government from favoring one religion over another. As long as all religions were treated neutrally or equally (nonpreferentially), said Rehnquist, the government could provide support for religion in public schools.

Significance This case is notable for what it did not decide. The question of a legislated moment of silence without specific provision for prayer was not addressed. As a result, moments of silence continue to be observed in the public schools of more than 25 states, including Alabama.

SEE ALSO *Abington School District v. Schempp; Engel v. Vitale; Establishment clause; Lemon v. Kurtzman; Religious issues under the Constitution*
SOURCES Peter Irons, *The Courage of Their Convictions* (New York: Free Press, 1988).

WALL STREET INVESTIGATION (1932–34)

In terms of the evidence it uncovered and the legislation it stimulated, one of the most successful congressional investigations was the Senate banking committee's inquiry into the causes of the stock market crash of 1929 and the Great Depression that followed. Ferdinand Pecora, an Italian immigrant who had been an assistant district attorney in New York, served as the committee's counsel and so dominated the hearings that they became known as the Pecora investigation. Pecora subpoenaed the records of major bankers and stockbrokers and called them to testify. J. P. Morgan, Jr., the nation's most prominent banker, was among those whose testimony made national headlines. (During a break in the hearings, a circus promoter slipped a midget into Morgan's lap, and the next day's news photos used the incident as a symbol of the congressional humbling of a powerful banker.) The Pecora investigation led to major banking and stock mar-

ket reforms, most notably the creation of the Securities and Exchange Commission to provide federal regulation of the nation's stock exchanges.

SEE ALSO *Investigations, congressional; Regulation of commerce*
SOURCES Donald A. Ritchie, "The Wall Street Exposé," in *Congress Investigates: A Documented History, 1792–1974*, edited by Arthur M. Schlesinger, Jr., and Roger Bruns, vol. 4 (New York: Bowker, 1975).

WARE V. HYLTON

- 3 Dall. 199 (1796)
- Vote: 4–0
- For the Court: seriatim opinions by Chase, Paterson, Wilson, and Cushing
- Not participating: Ellsworth and Iredell

The Treaty of Paris (1783), which ended the American War of Independence, guaranteed that prewar debts owed by Americans to British subjects would be recoverable. The state of Virginia, however, had passed legislation during the war to protect citizens of Virginia who had debts to British creditors against demands for repayment of the debts. Ware, the financial agent of a British subject, sought payment of a debt owed his client by Daniel Hylton, a Virginia citizen, so Ware took his case to a federal court.

The Issue Article 6 of the Constitution says that "all Treaties made, or which shall be made, under the Authority of the United States, shall be the supreme Law of the Land; and the Judges in every State shall be bound thereby, any Thing in the Constitution or Laws of any State to the Contrary notwithstanding." Given the precise wording of the Constitution about treaties as supreme law, was it possible for Virginia to violate a provision of the 1783 Treaty of Paris about payment of debts to British subjects?

Hylton's attorney was John Marshall, a future chief justice of the United States. Marshall argued that a U.S. treaty could not override a state law enacted before the

Constitution was written in 1787 and before the Treaty of Paris was ratified. Ware argued that the Virginia law at issue violated the U.S. Constitution and, therefore, should be struck down by the Court.

Opinion of the Court   The Supreme Court decided against Hylton and the state of Virginia. It ruled that the Treaty of Paris was part of the supreme law of the United States and its provisions took precedence over any state law that conflicted with it. The Court declared the state law unconstitutional and therefore null and void. Justice Samuel Chase wrote, "A treaty cannot be the supreme law of the land . . . if any act of a state legislature can stand in its way. . . . [L]aws of any states, contrary to a treaty shall be disregarded [as] . . . null and void."

Significance   John Marshall lost the only case he argued before the Supreme Court, which he later dominated for 34 years. Ironically, the Court's sweeping defense of federal supremacy over conflicting state laws was in keeping with Marshall's subsequent opinions for the Court.

This case marks the Court's first use of judicial review to strike down a state action because it violated the U.S. Constitution. This power, implied by Article 6 of the U.S. Constitution, is spelled out in Section 25 of the Judiciary Act of 1789.

SEE ALSO *Federalism; Judicial review*

WAR HAWKS

A group of zealous young Southern and Western members of the House of Representatives known as the "war hawks" seized the initiative from President James Madison in 1812 and prodded the nation into war with Great Britain. The war hawks were expansionists who wanted the United States to add both Canada and Florida to its territory. They also wanted the United States to take tougher military action against American Indians. And they wanted the country to stand firm and defend its national honor against the British policy of seizing former British sailors off

of American ships (called "impressment" of sailors). When the 11th Congress met in December 1811, the war hawks elected the charismatic Henry Clay to be Speaker on his first day in the House. President James Madison reluctantly supported the congressional demands for war with Great Britain. In most respects, the War of 1812 proved a disaster for the United States. While Clay was in Belgium, negotiating a peace treaty to end the war, British troops overran Washington and burned the Capitol building and White House. The peace treaty achieved none of the gains that the war hawks had originally sought. Only General Andrew Jackson's victory over the British at New Orleans (after the peace treaty had been signed) saved the national pride after this misadventure.

SEE ALSO *Clay, Henry*

SOURCES Robert V. Remini, *Henry Clay: Statesman for the Union* (New York: Norton, 1991).

WAR POWERS

Only Congress has the constitutional power to declare war (Article 1, Section 8). Except for foreign aggression or invasion, which the President can repel on his own authority as commander in chief, the framers of the Constitution expected that decisions about peace or war would be made by Congress. But of the more than 220 situations in which the armed forces have been used (half of them involving fighting for more than 30 days), only 5 have involved declarations of war: the War of 1812, the Mexican-American War, the Spanish-American War, World War I, and World War II.

Because of the constitutional separation of war powers, there has been much disagreement and friction between the executive and legislative branches.

Thomas Jefferson believed that giving Congress the power to declare war was "an effectual check to the Dog of war by transferring the power of letting him loose from the Executive to the legislative, from those who are to spend to those who are to pay." Congress must appropriate all money necessary to raise and equip American armed forces and to send them into battle.

Twice in the 19th century, Congress pressed reluctant Presidents into war. In 1812 congressional "war hawks" favored war with Great Britain, despite President James Madison's reservations, and in 1898 Congress pushed a dubious President William McKinley into war with Spain. A more divided Congress endorsed President James K. Polk's call for war with Mexico in 1846. After a long and difficult period of neutrality, Congress supported Woodrow Wilson's call for the United States to enter World War I. It took the Japanese bombing of Pearl Harbor on December 7, 1941, for Congress to declare war on Japan and Germany during World War II. Since 1941 there have been no formal declarations of war.

Cases in which the President has used the armed forces on his own authority, without congressional authorization, have included actions against pirates or bandits threatening U.S. foreign commerce, such as President Thomas Jefferson's use of the navy against the Barbary pirates in the Mediterranean Sea in the early 1800s. They have included rescue missions involving the lives and property of Americans, such as President Jimmy Carter's unsuccessful attempt to rescue diplomats held hostage by Iran in 1979. Presidents have ordered retaliatory actions, such as the bombing raid against Libya in 1986, which followed Libyan terrorist attacks against U.S. service personnel in Germany.

Presidents have ordered the military to protect U.S. freedom of the seas, as John Adams did when he ordered U.S. forces into an undeclared naval war with France. They have used the military to temporarily occupy other nations, including Haiti (1915–34), Nicaragua (1912–25), and Cuba (1906–9). Presidents have used force to overthrow unfriendly regimes, such as Ronald Reagan's invasion of Grenada in 1983. They have supported friendly regimes against civil insurrections, such as

the use of military advisers in El Salvador in the 1980s. They have used hundreds of thousands of troops to aid friendly nations against external aggression (South Korea in 1950, South Vietnam in 1964, and Kuwait in 1990).

Presidents claim that they can make war on their own constitutional authority as commander in chief. They argue that their duty to see that the laws are faithfully executed gives them an "international police power" to see that other nations pay their debts, protect U.S. lives and property, and abide by international law. In addition, the President executes treaty commitments, and certain treaties require the United States to guarantee the security of other nations. Presidents argue that they can use the armed forces in these cases without waiting for congressional approval. They also argue that their oath of office, the executive power, and the commander in chief clause of the Constitution all provide them with the authority to make decisions about peace and war in all other circumstances.

During the cold war, beginning in the late 1940s and lasting through the 1980s, when a "balance of terror" seemed to require that the United States and Soviet Union each have the ability to retaliate against a nuclear attack by the other side, Presidents argued that it was unrealistic to assume that Congress could participate in the decision to use nuclear weapons. Presidents argued that only if they had the power to retaliate without waiting for Congress to agree would the other side respect U.S. retaliatory power. In the 1940s Congress embraced a bipartisan foreign policy, in which the two parties came together to support the national interest, and generally deferred to the President in foreign and military affairs. In 1964, when President Lyndon Johnson asked Congress to enact the Gulf of Tonkin Resolution—permitting him to use U.S. armed forces in retaliation for North Vietnam's alleged assaults on U.S. ships—only two senators dissented. Congress adopted the Gulf of Tonkin Resolution, which Johnson considered a declaration of war. Congressional and public dissatisfaction with the course of the Vietnam War, however, disrupted the bipartisan foreign policy and strained relations between the executive and legislative branches.

Presidential war making becomes controversial if it leads to protracted hostilities, large numbers of dead and wounded, and large expenditures. The President risks splitting his own party, and may be forced to withdraw attempts to win renomination and reelection (as Harry Truman did during the Korean War and Lyndon Johnson did during the Vietnam War). On the other hand, a President who wins a quick and decisive military engagement will find his popularity soaring. This happened to Ronald Reagan after the invasion of Grenada and to George Bush after the invasion of Panama and the defeat of Iraqi forces in Kuwait.

If Congress wishes to oppose the President, it can do so in several ways. It can revoke any resolutions supporting the President (as Congress did in 1970 when it revoked the Gulf of Tonkin Resolution). Congress can cut off appropriations for Presidential war making. During the Vietnam War, it barred troops from engaging in operations in Thailand and Laos (1969) and from using ground forces in Cambodia (1970) and bombing Cambodia (1973). But usually, Congress votes for appropriations requested by the President as well as other authority (such as drafting troops). It does so, in spite of any doubts, because most members do not want to be vulnerable to charges in an election year that they voted to deny weapons and supplies to troops fighting the enemy.

The federal courts almost always find Presidential war making to be constitutional. Cases brought by soldiers drafted to fight in Presidentially ordered combat are usually decided in favor of the President, on the grounds that his power as commander in chief allows him to send troops into combat. The courts have never ruled that Presidential war making was unconstitutional.

Despite the steady shift of war powers from Congress to the Presidency, Congress as a representative body still serves as an extension of public opinion. Recalling the lessons of the unpopular Vietnam War, Presidents seek to achieve national unity by winning congressional support for their foreign and military policies.

SEE ALSO *Commander in chief; Cuban Missile Crisis; Gulf of Tonkin Resolution (1964); Johnson, Lyndon B.; Lincoln, Abraham; Persian Gulf debate (1991); Separation of powers; War Powers Resolution (1973)*

SOURCES Louis Fisher, *Presidential War Power* (Lawrence: University Press of Kansas: 1995). Arthur M. Schlesinger, Jr., *The Imperial Presidency* (Boston: Houghton Mifflin, 1973).

WAR POWERS RESOLUTION (1973)

The War Powers Resolution (WPR) was an act passed by Congress in 1973, over President Richard Nixon's veto, to "insure that the collective judgment of both the Congress and the President will apply to the introduction of United States armed forces into hostilities." The War Powers Resolution restricted Presidential war making to situations in which Congress had declared war or had given the President specific permission to use the armed forces in hostilities or in which the nation, its territories, possessions, or armed forces had been attacked.

The President was required "in every possible instance" to consult with Congress before introducing U.S. armed forces into hostilities. After every such introduction he was to "consult regularly with the Congress" until the forces had been removed. He was required to report to Congress within 48 hours after the introduction of forces into combat or situations in which hostilities were imminent and to report every six months thereafter.

The President was given a maximum of 60 days to use the armed forces without congressional permission; after that time he would have to obtain a declaration of war, other congressional approval, or an extension of the time limit. If he did not gain congressional approval, he had 30 days to withdraw the forces from hostilities.

Presidents Gerald Ford, Jimmy Carter, Ronald Reagan, and George Bush routinely evaded or ignored provisions of the WPR, arguing that it was an unconstitutional infringement on their powers as commander in chief. President Gerald Ford evacuated Americans and Europeans from South Vietnam, Laos, and Cambodia in 1975, when communist forces seized power in those nations, without invoking the consultation clause of the WPR. He also attempted a rescue of the crew of the merchant ship *Mayaguez* after it was seized by Cambodian communists in 1975, without invoking the resolution. In 1980 President Carter ignored the consultation clauses of the WPR when he ordered military forces to try to rescue diplomatic hostages held by Iran for more than a year. In 1982 President Ronald Reagan sent marines into Lebanon, where they remained for months exposed to hostile fire, without invoking the 60-day "clock." When he bombed Libya in 1986, he offered members of Congress a briefing while the planes were in midair, rather than consulting with them about whether the bombing should occur.

In 1989, without consulting Congress, President Bush sent forces into Panama to capture General Manuel Noriega and bring him back to the United States to face drug trafficking charges. (Bush did, however, comply with other provisions of the law.) Bush was authorized by Congress to use military force against Saddam Hussein of Iraq, but Congress did not use the provisions of the WPR.

Presidents do not use the WPR if their use of the armed forces involves peacekeeping or antiterrorist actions or for humanitarian assistance, such as the 1992–93 operation in Somalia and the 1993 airdrops of food in Bosnia and Herzegovina, or if covert operations are involved. Presidents never trigger the 60-day clock that starts when they use the armed forces. If Congress wishes to set a time limit, it must do so itself by passing a joint resolution. But that resolution itself is subject to a Presidential veto, which then must be overridden by a two-thirds vote of each house to go into effect. In practice, a President who fails to obey the terms of the WPR can continue using the armed forces until two-thirds of each chamber of Congress decides to force him to withdraw, a most unlikely situation.

The courts have never ordered a President to comply with the WPR. In *Crockett v. Reagan* (1982), a case involving U.S. military advisers in El Salvador, a federal court declined to start the WPR's 60-day clock, ruling that it was a "political question" between Congress and the President, not subject to judicial consideration. By the 1990s, many constitutional scholars believed that sooner or later the federal courts would declare some or all of the key provisions of the War Powers Resolution to be unconstitutional.

SEE ALSO *Commander in chief; Gulf of Tonkin Resolution (1964); Nixon, Richard M.; War powers*

SOURCES Thomas Eagleton, *War and Presidential Power* (New York: Liveright, 1974). Jacob Javits, *Who Makes War? The President versus Congress* (New York: Morrow, 1973).

WARREN, EARL
Chief Justice, 1953–69

- Born: Mar. 19, 1891, Los Angeles, Calif.
- Education: University of California at Berkeley, B.L., 1912, J.D., 1914
- Previous government service: deputy city attorney, Oakland, Calif., 1919–20; deputy assistant district attorney, Alameda County, Calif., 1920–23; chief deputy district attorney, Alameda County, 1923–25; district attorney, Alameda County, 1925–39; attorney general of California, 1939–43; governor of California, 1943–53

- Appointed by President Dwight D. Eisenhower as a recess appointment Oct. 2, 1953; replaced Chief Justice Fred M. Vinson, who died; nominated by Eisenhower Jan. 11, 1954
- Supreme Court term: confirmed by the Senate Mar. 1, 1954, by a voice vote; retired June 23, 1969
- Died: July 9, 1974, Washington, D.C.

Earl Warren, the son of immigrants from Norway, had a profound influence on constitutional law in the United States. As the 14th chief justice of the United States, he presided over a judicial revolution in the 1950s and 1960s.

Warren's public life before becoming chief justice gave little hint of what he would do on the Court. His career was conducted exclusively in California local and state politics from 1919 until 1953, when he joined the Supreme Court. During World War II, as attorney general and governor of California, Warren vigorously supported the federal order removing people of Japanese ancestry from the Pacific Coast of the United States and confining them in grim camps. He believed, without any evidence, that these people could threaten the national security of the United States during its war with Japan. At the end of his life, Warren expressed remorse: "I have since deeply regretted the removal order and my own testimony advocating it, because it was not in keeping with our American concept of freedom and the rights of citizens."

Governor Warren moved to the Supreme Court through his participation in the Presidential election of 1952, when he helped Dwight D. Eisenhower win the Republican party nomination for President. After winning the Presidency, Eisenhower rewarded Earl Warren with the appointment to the office of chief justice.

Eisenhower later said this appointment was "the biggest damn-fool mistake I ever made." Supreme Court scholars, however, have lauded Warren as one of the Court's all-time great justices. What did Warren do to disappoint Eisenhower and win the acclaim of scholars?

Earl Warren presided over the Supreme Court during a period of great controversy and change. Under his leadership, the Court stated new ideas on equal protection of the laws, the rights of persons accused of crime, freedom of expression, and representation in government.

Chief Justice Warren's greatest opinion was written in 1954, at the beginning of his 16-year term. In *Brown* v. *Board of Education*, Chief Justice Warren skillfully influenced the Court's unanimous decision to strike down state laws that required separate schools to be provided for black and white students. This decision overturned the 1896 ruling in *Plessy* v. *Ferguson* that had sanctioned racial segregation in public facilities.

Several decisions of the Warren Court greatly expanded the constitutional rights of those suspected or accused of crime. For example, state law enforcement officials were required to exclude illegally obtained evidence in criminal proceedings (*Mapp* v. *Ohio*, 1961), to guarantee the right to competent legal assistance for an accused person (*Gideon* v. *Wainwright*, 1963), and to inform people of their right against self-incrimination (*Griffin* v. *California*, 1965, and *Miranda* v. *Arizona*, 1966). These decisions overruled earlier Court rulings that had allowed the states to deviate from strict observance of the federal Bill of Rights. The Warren Court moved decisively to apply the rights of an accused person, as outlined in the federal Bill of Rights, to all of the states under the due process clause of the 14th Amendment to the U.S. Constitution.

The Warren Court's most significant ruling on freedom of expression came in *New York Times Co.* v. *Sullivan* (1964). The Court held that a public official may not sue and recover damages for libel against a person who has written untrue statements about him unless there was a complete and reckless disregard for truth. The Court's intention was to remove barriers to the free flow of information about government officials that is a necessary part of the democratic process.

Chief Justice Warren considered the Court's rulings on a series of "reapportionment cases" to be its most important contribution to constitutional law. These decisions, beginning with *Baker* v. *Carr* (1962) and culminating in *Reynolds* v. *Sims* (1964), established the principle of "one person, one vote" in state and federal elections. State governments were required to apportion, or divide, the state, for purposes of political representation, into districts based solely on population, with the districts as nearly equal in population as was possible. This decision ended the practice of creating districts to unfairly inflate representation in government of some groups at the expense of other groups.

Chief Justice Warren believed it was the Court's responsibility to protect the civil liberties and rights of individuals against overbearing majorities acting privately or through their representatives in government. Warren also believed that the Court should be an active partner with the other branches of government in achieving social justice and protection of the individual against the powers of the state.

SEE ALSO *Brown v. Board of Education; Incorporation doctrine; Judicial activism and judicial restraint; Miranda v. Arizona; Reynolds v. Sims*

SOURCES Ed Cray, *Chief Justice: A Biography of Earl Warren* (New York: Simon & Schuster, 1997). Lucas A. Powe, Jr., *The Warren Court and American Politics* (Cambridge: Harvard University Press, 2000). Bernard Schwartz, *Superchief: Earl Warren and His Supreme Court* (New York: New York University Press, 1983). G. Edward White, *Earl Warren: A Public Life* (New York: Oxford University Press, 1982).

WASHINGTON, BUSHROD
Associate Justice, 1798–1829

- Born: June 5, 1762, Westmoreland County, Va.
- Education: College of William and

Mary, B.A., 1778; read law with James Wilson in Philadelphia, Pa.
- Previous government service: Virginia House of Delegates, 1787; Virginia Ratifying Convention, 1788
- Appointed by President John Adams as a recess appointment Sept. 29, 1798; replaced James Wilson, who died; nominated by Adams Dec. 19, 1798
- Supreme Court term: confirmed by the Senate Dec. 20, 1798, by a voice vote; served until Nov. 26, 1829
- Died: Nov. 26, 1829, Philadelphia, Pa.

Bushrod Washington was George Washington's favorite nephew, who inherited his uncle's property at Mount Vernon. He served in the Continental Army under his Uncle George during the War of Independence. He studied law under James Wilson, whom Bushrod Washington succeeded on the Supreme Court.

Bushrod Washington served on the Supreme Court for 31 years, but he wrote no important decisions. Rather, his contributions came as an ardent supporter of Chief Justice Marshall's opinions. His ties to John Marshall were so close that another associate justice, William Johnson, said that they "are commonly estimated as a single judge."

Justice Washington and Chief Justice Marshall were together on the Supreme Court for 29 years. They disagreed only three times.

WASHINGTON, GEORGE
1st President

- Born: Feb. 22, 1732, Westmoreland County, Va.
- Political party: none
- Education: schooling through age 15
- Military service: adjutant, Southern District of Virginia, 1752; lieutenant colonel and colonel, Virginia Regiment, 1754; commander of Virginia Military, 1755–58; commander in chief of Continental Army, 1775–83
- Previous government service: surveyor, Culpeper County, Va., 1749–51; Vir-

ginia House of Burgesses, 1759–74; justice of the peace, Fairfax County, Va., 1760–74; First Continental Congress, 1774; Second Continental Congress, 1775; presiding officer, Constitutional Convention, 1787
- Elected President, 1789; served, 1789–97
- Died: Dec. 14, 1799, Mount Vernon, Va.

George Washington was the victorious commander in chief of the American military during the revolutionary war, the presiding officer at the Constitutional Convention of 1787, and the first President of the United States. Without Washington's leadership the country might have remained a British colony and evolved into a member of the British Commonwealth of Nations. And without Washington's work at the convention there would be no office of the Presidency as we know it today.

George Washington was born on one of six plantations owned by his father, Augustine Washington. George's father died in 1743, leaving the family 10,000 acres and 50 slaves. Thereafter George was raised by his half-brother Lawrence, who was 14 years his senior, at the Epsewasson plantation at Little Hunting Creek, which Lawrence renamed Mount Vernon. His schooling ended at age 15, when he became a plantation supervisor and land surveyor. After Lawrence married a daughter of Colonel William Fairfax, one of the largest and most powerful landowners in Virginia, George was invited to survey Fairfax lands in the Shenandoah Valley, receiving 550 acres in compensation. Between 1749 and 1751 he was surveyor of Culpeper County. In 1752, after Lawrence died, George inherited the 2,500-acre estate (with its 18 slaves) at Mount Vernon, becoming a large plantation owner at age 20.

Washington was soon influential in public affairs. In February 1753 he was named a major and adjutant of the Virginia Militia. In October he was sent by Governor Robert Dinwiddie to the frontier on Lake Erie to warn the French against occupying lands claimed by Great Britain, but the French rejected the ultimatum. The following year he was commissioned a lieutenant colonel and returned to the West. On May 28 he fought an engagement with the French that led to his promotion to colonel. He then constructed Fort Necessity and awaited a French counterattack. On July 4 the superior French forces captured the fort, accepted Washington's surrender, and let him return to Virginia, but only after he signed capitulation papers (written in French) admitting that he had fired on French officers while they had been under a flag of truce—a statement Washington later disavowed, saying he had not understood the language. These battles marked the start of the French and Indian War in the Americas and of the Seven Years War throughout the world.

Washington accompanied General Edward Braddock on an expedition against Fort Duquesne—near where Pittsburgh stands today—in 1755. The general disregarded Washington's advice on how to fight the Indians allied with the French. On July 9 Braddock was killed during the fighting, and Washington prevented the British defeat from becoming a complete rout. "I had four bullets through my coat, and two horses shot under me," Washington later wrote. On his return he was named commander of the Virginia Militia. By 1758 he had defeated the French at Fort Duquesne and renamed it Fort Pitt.

In 1759 Washington resigned his commission with the rank of brigadier general and married a widow named Martha Dandridge Custis, who had two children by her previous marriage and plantations of 15,000 acres, much of the land near Williamsburg, Virginia. Washington resumed tobacco farming, served in the Virginia House of Burgesses, and was a justice of the peace. He began opposing British colonial policies, particularly the Royal Proclamation of 1763, which discouraged settlement in the West (where Washington owned land in the Ohio Valley), and the Stamp Act of 1765, which taxed imports.

After the governor disbanded the House of Burgesses for protesting the Stamp Act, Washington played a major role in their unauthorized meetings at Raleigh Tavern in 1770 (when it drew up resolutions calling on people not to import British goods, so that they would not pay the hated stamp tax) and in 1774 (when it called for a meeting of a continental congress). He was a delegate to the First Continental Congress of 1774, where he declared, "I will raise one thousand men, subsist them at my own expense, and march myself at their head for the relief of Boston." On June 15, 1775, the Second Continental Congress named Washington commander in chief of the Continental Army. He refused to take any pay for the position.

Washington assumed command of his volunteers in Cambridge, Massachusetts, on July 3, 1775, shortly after the Battle of Bunker Hill. He forced the British to evacuate Boston in March 1776 and concentrate their forces in New York. Washington was defeated at the Battle of Long Island in August and at the Battles of Manhattan and White Plains. He retreated into New Jersey and then into Pennsylvania. On Christmas night, 1776, he crossed the Delaware River and defeated British forces at Trenton, New Jersey. Then he captured Princeton and Morristown. But British reinforcements forced his withdrawal, and he was defeated at Brandywine Creek and Germantown, leading to the loss of Philadelphia. The Conway Conspiracy, a plot to replace Washington with General Horatio Gates, the hero of the Battle of Saratoga, went nowhere, as Congress reaffirmed its support for the beleaguered commander. Washington's forces regrouped at Valley Forge, Pennsylvania, in October 1777. Three thousand of his troops deserted.

Although badly supplied, the troops who stuck it out during the harsh winter emerged from Valley Forge in the spring of 1778 as a disciplined army with superb morale. And the French had decided to help the Americans. With the British withdrawing from Philadelphia and regrouping in New York to await the arrival of a French fleet, Washington won the Battle of Monmouth in June 1778. He then surrounded and kept British forces in New York at bay while other military units fought in the South and won in the Northwest. But in 1780 there were new defeats: Charleston, South Carolina, fell and General Gates lost the Battle of Camden. Some troops mutinied when rations were cut.

In 1781 Washington's forces feigned preparations for an attack on New York. He and the French general Rochambeau secretly went south to face the British in Virginia. They joined up with another French general who was commanding American troops, the Marquis de Lafayette, and lay siege to the British. The arrival of a French fleet in the midst of the Yorktown campaign of 1781 forced British general Lord Charles Cornwallis to surrender his 8,000-man force on October 19, 1781. This defeat ended hostilities. Washington then took his army to Newburgh, New York, to await the articles of peace, which were signed in November 1782, to become effective January 20, 1783. On March 15, 1783, Washington quelled a mutiny by senior officers who wished to disperse Congress and name Washington as an American king. His refusal to join the "Newburgh mutiny" and his insistence on preserving civil government made him the most influential political figure in the country.

Washington retired from the army on December 4, 1783, bidding farewell to his officers at Fraunces' Tavern in New York City. He resumed farming at Mount Vernon and toured the lands Congress had given him in the West. In 1785 Mount Vernon was the setting for a conference between representatives from Maryland and Virginia, who settled issues involving navigation on the Potomac River. That meeting led to the Annapolis Convention of 1786, which, in turn, called for a new constitutional convention for the following year.

In 1787 James Madison and others prevailed upon Washington to attend the Constitutional Convention in Philadelphia, and on May 25 he was named presiding officer. His participation ensured the success of the enterprise, especially because Washington played the key role in ensuring ratification of the new constitution by Virginia.

By unanimous vote of the electoral college on February 4, 1789, Washington was elected the first President of the United States. On April 30, he was inaugurated on the balcony of Federal Hall in New York City. In his inaugural address to Congress he appealed for a Bill of Rights to be added to the Constitution. He refused to accept a salary as President.

Washington had several goals for his Presidency. The first was to establish precedents, or set examples, that would preserve a republican form of government after his term of office. He also aimed to put the finances of the nation on a sound footing, to normalize relations with the British, and to develop the frontier. The methods that he and his Treasury secretary, Alexander Hamilton, devised to achieve these goals created divisions within his administration.

Hamilton wanted a "strong and energetic executive" who would dominate Congress and take control of policymaking. He wanted to levy taxes on whiskey and other goods to raise revenues and pay government debts. He also wanted an alliance (or at least a treaty of friendship) with the British in order to encourage British investment in new U.S. industries.

The President generally supported Hamilton in his plans for industrialization, assumption of the states' revolutionary war debts, creation of a national bank, protective tariffs on imported goods to help U.S. industry, excise taxes on whiskey to raise revenue, and strict neutrality in the wars between Great Britain and France. Hamilton was opposed on many of these policies by Secretary of State Thomas Jefferson, who proposed closer relations with the French and disagreed with Hamilton's revenue measures, his idea of a national bank, and his plans to industrialize the nation.

Near the end of his first term, Washington accepted Jefferson's resignation. Now firmly in the camp of the Federalists organized by Hamilton, Washington was reelected by a unanimous vote of the electoral college in February 1793. He then allowed Hamilton to raise revenues through a whiskey excise tax. When Western farmers rebelled against paying the tax, Washington and Hamilton used military force to put down the Whiskey Rebellion in the summer of 1794. Washington cemented the alliance with Great Britain with Jay's Treaty, ratified in 1795. He accepted the resignation of his new secretary of state, Edmund Randolph, because Randolph had been bribed by the French to oppose the treaty. Washington's strong government secured the West as well: the new frontier state of Kentucky was created in 1792, and Tennessee joined the Union in 1796.

Washington retired after his second term at the age of 64, publishing a farewell address to the nation on September 17, 1796, that warned of the perils of "foreign entanglements" and of "the baneful effects of the spirit of party" in domestic affairs. On July 4, 1798, in the midst of a crisis with France, Congress named him commander in chief of the Army of the United States, but he never took actual command of forces. For the last years of his life he pursued agricultural interests at Mount Vernon and enjoyed his family, especially Martha's grandchildren, two of whom he adopted after the death of their father. He died of pulmonary complications suffered during a snowstorm on December 14, 1799. In Philadelphia, one of his officers, Henry Lee, gave the famous eulogy, "First in war, first in peace, and first in the hearts of his countrymen."

SEE ALSO *Adams, John; Articles of Confederation; Creation of the Presidency; Washington's Farewell Address*

SOURCES Richard Brookhiser, *Founding Father: Rediscovering George Washington* (1996; reprint, New York: Free Press, 1997). Marcus Cunliffe, *George Washington: Man and Monument,* rev. ed. (Boston:

Little, Brown, 1982). James Thomas Flexner, *Washington: The Indispensable Man* (New York: New American Library, 1979). Ralph Ketcham, *Presidents above Party: The First American Presidency, 1789–1829* (Chapel Hill: University of North Carolina Press, 1984).

WASHINGTON'S FAREWELL ADDRESS

Washington's Farewell Address was the message to the American people published by outgoing President George Washington on September 17, 1796. Washington wrote it during the height of a divisive Presidential campaign. In it he outlined three principles that he believed the new nation should follow in public affairs. First, sectional antagonisms should be put to rest. Second, "the baneful effects of the spirit of party" should be muted because they threatened liberty by subordinating people to demagogic leaders and hampering the ability of the President to promote the national interest. Third, U.S. diplomacy should "steer clear of permanent alliances" and "trust to temporary alliances for extraordinary emergencies."

The address was controversial. Washington's political opponents, such as James Madison, saw it as nothing more than a defense of Washington's term in office. Politicians took little heed of Washington's advice: in the 19th century the two-party system was established and sectional animosity increased until the Civil War. The United States did follow one piece of his advice: it did not enter into permanent military alliances with other nations until the end of World War II.

SEE ALSO *Washington, George*

WATERGATE INVESTIGATION (1973–74)

At 2:00 A.M. on June 17, 1972, five Cuban men were arrested while breaking into the Democratic National Committee offices at the Watergate office complex in Washington, D.C. These men named Gordon Liddy, counsel to the Committee to Re-Elect the President (CREEP), as an accomplice, but President Richard M. Nixon insisted that the "White House had no involvement whatsoever" in this "third-rate burglary." Liddy, in turn, could be linked to Operation Gemstone, an administration program to investigate and harass political opponents.

To keep Gemstone from becoming public knowledge, Nixon and his two top aides, H. R. Haldeman and John D. Erlichman, decided to get the Central Intelligence Agency to impede the pending FBI investigation of the break-in by having the CIA claim that it was a matter of national security. White House involvement in the burglary and in Gemstone was covered up successfully through the fall of 1972, and Nixon won a landslide victory over his Democratic opponent, George McGovern.

Persistent stories in the *Washington Post* and other newspapers, however, linked administration officials to the break-in, wiretapping, illegal use of campaign contributions, forged documents to embarrass rival candidates, and other political "dirty tricks."

The Watergate burglars were provisionally sentenced to long prison terms by federal judge John Sirica, who hoped to prod them into talking in order to reduce their sentences. John Dean, the White House counsel, realized that he might be implicated, and he confessed his role in the matter to the Justice Department and implicated Nixon's top aides in the cover-up. On April 30, 1973, Nixon accepted the resignations of Haldeman and Erlichman.

The Senate appointed a Select Committee on Presidential Campaign Activities, chaired by Sam Ervin (Democrat–North Carolina), a folksy "country lawyer" and a specialist in civil liberties. In May 1973 the committee began nationally televised hearings that captured public attention for the next three months. John Dean testified that the President had taken part in an elaborate cover-up of improper activities, although he had no evidence. But then an aide to Haldeman, Alexander Butterfield, admitted that the White House had taped conversations in the Oval Office. Both the Senate committee and the Justice Department's special prosecutor, Archibald Cox, demanded that Nixon turn over any recorded conversations involving Watergate. Nixon turned over some of the tapes but told Cox he could not have the rest, citing his right to the confidentiality of conversations in his office, a claim known as executive privilege.

Cox went to court to obtain the evidence, and Nixon ordered his attorney general, Elliot Richardson, to fire Cox. Richardson refused and was himself fired by the President; finally, Solicitor General Robert Bork, the next-ranking official in the Justice Department, agreed to carry out Nixon's order. This Saturday Night Massacre unleashed a fire storm of protest. Shortly thereafter the House Judiciary Committee opened an impeachment inquiry.

The House committee deliberated until July 24, 1974, when it voted to recommend that the full House pass three articles of impeachment. It accused Nixon of obstruction of justice (his attempt to use the CIA to impede an FBI investigation), abuse of power (misuse of the CIA, FBI, and Internal Revenue Service to harass his political enemies), and refusal to turn over evidence to Congress. It concluded that the President had "acted in a manner contrary to his trust as President and subversive of constitutional government," causing "manifest injury to the people of the United States."

After that vote, the Supreme Court, in *United States* v. *Nixon* (1974), ordered the President to turn over his tapes and other evidence to the federal district court judge who was trying the Watergate crimes, for use by the new special prosecutor, Leon Jaworski. One of the tapes did show that Nixon had engaged in a cover-up and a conspiracy to obstruct justice, which is a federal crime and an impeachable offense.

Shortly afterward, a delegation of senior Republican senators, led by Arizona conservative Barry Goldwater, advised Nixon that the Senate would probably convict him if an impeachment trial were held. Nixon resigned from office on August 9, 1974. He was later pardoned for all Watergate-related crimes by his successor, Gerald Ford.

The Watergate scandal symbolized a dangerous imbalance in the federal system of checks and balances. It was the product of an excessive growth of Presidential power and of Presidential efforts to circumvent the legislative branch. The Senate investigation helped Congress restore its public image and regain some of its lost authority.

SEE ALSO *Ervin, Samuel J., Jr.; Ethics; Executive privilege; Ford, Gerald R.; Impeachment; Independent counsel; Investigations, congressional; Nixon, Richard M.; United States v. Nixon*

SOURCES Philip B. Kurland, "The Watergate Inquiry, 1973," in *Congress Investigates: A Documented History, 1792–1974,* edited by Arthur M. Schlesinger, Jr., and Roger Bruns, vol. 5 (New York: Bowker, 1975). Stanley L. Kutler, *The Wars of Watergate* (New York: Knopf, 1990). Bob Woodward and Carl Bernstein, *All the President's Men* (New York: Warner, 1974).

WAYNE, JAMES M.
Associate Justice, 1835–67

- Born: 1790, Savannah, Ga.
- Education: College of New Jersey (Princeton), B.A., 1808; read law under Charles Chauncey in New Haven, Conn.
- Previous government service: Georgia House of Representatives, 1815–16; mayor of Savannah, 1817–19; judge, Savannah Court of Common Pleas, 1820–22; judge, Georgia Superior Court, 1822–28; U.S. Representative from Georgia, 1829–35
- Appointed by President Andrew Jack-

son Jan. 7, 1835; replaced William Johnson, who died
- Supreme Court term: confirmed by the Senate Jan. 9, 1835, by a voice vote; served until July 5, 1867
- Died: July 5, 1867, Washington, D.C.

James M. Wayne served 32 years as an associate justice of the U.S. Supreme Court. During this time he was torn by his conflicting loyalties to the South and to the federal Union. He was a slaveholder from Georgia who believed in the power and right of each state to decide, without federal interference, about the institution of slavery. He was also committed to the preservation of the United States of America.

When the Civil War erupted, Justice Wayne remained loyal to the Union and remained on the Supreme Court. His son, by contrast, resigned from the U.S. Army and became the adjutant general of the Confederate state of Georgia. In 1861, Georgia declared Justice Wayne an "enemy alien" and confiscated his property.

During the Civil War, Justice Wayne supported President Abraham Lincoln's policies in the *Prize Cases* (1863), upholding Lincoln's blockade of Southern ports, and in *Ex parte Vallandigham* (1864), which permitted the conviction of a civilian Confederate sympathizer in a military court.

SOURCES Alexander A. Lawrence, *James Moore Wayne: Southern Unionist* (Chapel Hill: University of North Carolina Press, 1943).

WAYS AND MEANS COMMITTEE

One of the oldest and most important committees of the House of Representatives, the Ways and Means Committee originates all revenue (tax and tariff) bills. As the name implies, the committee is responsible for finding the ways and means of financing the operations of the federal government. (The equivalent committee in the Senate is the Finance Committee.) Because the Constitution (Article 1, Sec-

tion 7) assigns the origination of revenue bills to the House, the House created the Ways and Means Committee first as a select committee in 1789 and then converted it to a standing committee in 1802. In the 19th century, chairmen of the Ways and Means Committee often functioned as floor leaders of the House, and 21 Speakers served on the committee.

SEE ALSO *Revenue bills*
SOURCES Donald R. Kennon and Rebecca M. Rogers, *The Committee on Ways and Means: A Bicentennial History, 1789–1989* (Washington, D.C.: Government Printing Office, 1989).

WEBSTER, DANIEL

- Born: January 18, 1782, Salisbury, N.H.
- Political party: Federalist, Whig
- Education: Dartmouth College, graduated, 1801; studied law
- Representative from New Hampshire: 1813–17
- Representative from Massachusetts: 1823–27
- Senator from Massachusetts: 1833–41, 1845–50
- Died: October 24, 1852, Marshfield, Mass.

During his long career in Congress, Daniel Webster won fame as an orator and as the chief spokesman for New England's interests. He most notably promoted protective tariffs (taxes on foreign imports that would make it easier for American industry to develop) and national banking policies (the creation of a government-sponsored national bank to control the supply of money). Webster also devoted his debating skills to defending the Union against those who talked of secession, most notably in his famous reply to South Carolina senator Robert Y. Hayne in 1830. When Hayne promoted the idea that states could nullify, or overrule, federal laws, Webster responded that the United States was not a government of states but a "popular Government, erected by the people." Warning of the possibility of civil war, Webster denounced as foolish the notion of "Liberty first and Union afterwards." He declared instead for "Liberty *and* Union, now and forever, one and inseparable."

At the end of his career Webster risked his entire reputation with a memorable speech in favor of the Compromise of 1850. Seeking to organize the Western territories in a way that would appease both pro-slavery opinion in the South and antislavery sentiment in the North, Henry Clay (Whig–Kentucky) put together an omnibus bill with something for all sides. For New England, the bill's most controversial feature was its fugitive slave provision, which would permit slave owners to reclaim their slaves who had fled to freedom in the North. To win New England's support, Clay persuaded Webster to throw his prestige behind the compromise. On March 7, 1850, Webster rose in the Senate and said: "Mr. President—I wish to speak today not as a Massachusetts man, not as a Northern man, but as an American, and a member of the Senate of the United States." Abolitionists and free-soil advocates, who opposed the spread of slavery into the territories, denounced Webster's March 7 speech as a betrayal. People in Massachusetts formed vigilance committees to protect runaway slaves. Webster's public standing plunged, and his Presidential aspirations were destroyed as a result of his efforts to hold the Union together through compromise.

SEE ALSO *Compromise of 1850; Oratory, congressional*

SOURCES Irving H. Bartlett, *Daniel Webster* (New York: Norton, 1978). Richard N. Current, *Daniel Webster and the Rise of National Conservatism* (Boston: Little, Brown, 1955).

WEBSTER V. REPRODUCTIVE HEALTH SERVICES

- 492 U.S. 490 (1989)
- Vote: 5–4

- For the Court: Rehnquist
- Concurring: Scalia and O'Connor
- Dissenting: Blackmun, Brennan, Marshall, and Stevens

In 1986 the state of Missouri passed a law that placed certain restrictions on the performance of abortions. This law was challenged as an unconstitutional violation of women's rights by Reproductive Health Services, a federal organization providing assistance for women seeking abortions. A district court and circuit court of appeals struck down the Missouri law because it placed restrictions on a woman's right to choose an abortion, which was established in *Roe* v. *Wade* (1973). The state of Missouri appealed to the U.S. Supreme Court.

The Issue   At issue was the constitutionality of the Missouri law restricting a woman's right to an abortion, which violated the precedent established by the Court in *Roe* v. *Wade.*

Opinion of the Court   Chief Justice William Rehnquist reported the opinion of a divided Court. A bare majority upheld two of several provisions of the Missouri law: "[W]e uphold the Act's restrictions on the use of public employees and facilities for the performance or assistance of nontherapeutic abortions [those not necessary to save a mother's life]." The other provision of the Missouri law upheld by the Court was a requirement that "before a physician performs an abortion on a woman he has reason to believe is carrying an unborn child of twenty or more weeks . . . the physician shall first determine if the unborn child is viable [capable of life outside the womb]." Thus, the *Webster* decision modified the second-trimester rule in *Roe* v. *Wade,* which held that all regulations on abortion rights during the fourth through sixth months of pregnancy must be related to protecting the health of the mother. The *Webster* decision, however, stopped short of overturning *Roe,* which antiabortion advocates had wanted.

Dissent   Justice Harry Blackmun, author of the Court's opinion in *Roe* v. *Wade,* wrote a passionate dissent. He wrote, "Today, *Roe* v. *Wade* (1973) and the fundamental right of women to decide whether to terminate a pregnancy survive but are not secure." According to Justice Blackmun, the Court's decision in the *Webster* case "implicitly invites every state legislature to enact more and more restrictive abortion regulations in order to provoke more and more test cases, in the hope that sometime down the line the Court will return the law of procreative freedom to the severe limitations that generally prevailed in this country before January 22, 1973."

Significance This case fueled the heated public controversy about the abortion rights issue. Pro-choice groups, who favored abortion rights, saw the Court's decision as an assault on their position. Their opponents cheered it as the beginning of the end for *Roe* v. *Wade.* Both sides increased their attempts to influence state government officials to support their views in this ongoing dispute.

SEE ALSO *Abortion rights; Roe v. Wade*

WEEKS V. UNITED STATES

- 232 U.S. 383 (1914)
- Vote: 9–0
- For the Court: Day

Local police and U.S. marshals suspected Weeks of criminal behavior. His house was searched twice, first by local police and then by a U.S. marshal. Incriminating evidence was found and used to charge Weeks with the crime of sending lottery tickets through the mail.

Neither search of Weeks's home was authorized by a search warrant. So Weeks petitioned a federal court for the return of his property because it had been taken in violation of the 4th and 5th Amendments to the Constitution. The 4th Amendment requires government officials to obtain a warrant before they can search a person's home. The 5th Amendment says that no person can be "deprived of life, liberty, or property, without due process of law." Weeks's petition for return of his property went to the U.S. Supreme Court.

The Issue Did the warrantless search of Weeks's house by a federal officer violate his constitutional rights? Could Weeks's property, taken in a warrantless search, be kept by the government and used against Weeks in court?

Opinion of the Court Justice William R. Day narrowed the case to the consideration of Weeks's 4th Amendment rights, which clearly were violated by the federal marshal's warrantless search of his home. The judgment against Weeks was reversed because the evidence used against him was obtained illegally. His illegally seized property was returned to him and could not be used in any trial.

Significance This case was the origin of the exclusionary rule, which requires that evidence obtained in violation of a person's constitutional rights must be excluded from any legal proceedings against him. Prior to the *Weeks* case, courts admitted illegally seized evidence because the rights of the individual were considered secondary to society's need for the punishment of criminal behavior.

SEE ALSO *Exclusionary rule; Searches and seizures*

WEST COAST HOTEL CO. V. PARRISH

- 300 U.S. 379 (1937)
- Vote: 5–4
- For the Court: Hughes
- Dissenting: Sutherland, Butler, McReynolds, and Van Devanter

Elsie Parrish worked as a chambermaid at the Cascadian Hotel in Wenatchee, Washington. Her pay was $12 for a 48-hour week. This was less than the amount required by the state of Washington's minimum wage law. So Elsie Parrish brought suit against her employer. The state supreme court decided in favor of Parrish, but the hotel owners appealed to the U.S. Supreme Court.

The Issue One year earlier, in *Morehead* v. *New York ex rel. Tipaldo* (1936), the Court ruled a New York State minimum wage law unconstitutional. The Court argued for liberty of contract between employer and employee to decide without government regulation about wages and hours of work. This liberty of contract was held to be protected from state government regulations by the due process clause of the 14th Amendment. Did the state of Washington's minimum wage law violate the 14th Amendment?

Opinion of the Court   The Court upheld the state minimum wage law and reversed the decisions in *Morehead* v. *New York ex rel. Tipaldo* (1936) and *Adkins* v. *Children's Hospital* (1923), upon which the *Morehead* decision was based. In *Adkins*, the Court declared unconstitutional an act of Congress that established a minimum wage for children and women workers in the District of Columbia. The dissenting view in *Morehead*—by Chief Justice Charles Evans Hughes and Justices Louis Brandeis, Benjamin Cardozo, and Harlan Fiske Stone—was the foundation for the Court's opinion in this case, written by Hughes. Justice Owen Roberts joined the four *Morehead* dissenters to form the Court majority in this case.

Chief Justice Hughes rejected the idea of liberty of contract set forth in the *Adkins* and *Morehead* cases. He wrote:

The Constitution does not speak of freedom of contract. It speaks of liberty and prohibits the deprivation of liberty without due process of law. In prohibiting that deprivation the Constitution does not recognize an absolute and uncontrollable liberty. . . . The liberty safeguarded is liberty in a social organization which requires the protection of law against the evils which menace the health, safety, morals, and welfare of the people. Liberty under the Constitution is thus necessarily subject to the restraints of due process, and regulation which is adopted in the interests of the community is due process.

Significance   Justice Roberts's vote in support of the Washington State minimum

wage law was a complete change from his vote in the *Morehead* case, and it made the difference in the *Parrish* case. Reporters called it "the switch in time that saved nine." This reference was to the court-packing plan of President Franklin D. Roosevelt. He had been frustrated by several of the Court's decisions against his New Deal programs involving government regulation of businesses on behalf of the public good. So the President had proposed that Congress enact legislation to enable him to appoint six new justices to the Supreme Court. After the *Parrish* decision, however, the President backed away from his plan to alter the membership of the Court.

The *Parrish* decision provided legal support for Congress to pass the Fair Labor Standards Act in 1938, which included a minimum wage provision for businesses involved in interstate commerce. The *Parrish* decision also provided a precedent for federal court decisions against liberty of contract claims that would endanger important community interests and the public good.

SEE ALSO *Court-packing plan (1937)*

WESTLAW

West Publishing Company has a computerized research service—WESTLAW—that contains a database of all Supreme Court decisions since 1790. Data on current decisions are sent electronically to the WESTLAW database from the Court and can be accessed via computer on the same day the decision is made. The database contains the full text of all decisions of the Court, summaries of recent decisions, and reports about changes in Supreme Court rules. The WESTLAW database also contains information about orders, such as the schedule for oral arguments, stays of execution, and invitations or permissions to file amicus curiae (friend of the court) briefs on cases scheduled to be heard by the Court, and cases accepted on appeal or denied review by the Court.

SEE ALSO *LEXIS*

WEST VIRGINIA STATE BOARD OF EDUCATION V. BARNETTE

- 319 U.S. 624 (1943)
- Vote: 6–3
- For the Court: Jackson
- Concurring: Black, Douglas, and Murphy
- Dissenting: Frankfurter, Roberts, and Reed

The government of West Virginia made a law that required students in public schools to salute the flag and pledge allegiance to it. Refusal to comply with this act would be considered insubordination punishable by expulsion from school. Readmission to school would be granted only on condition that the student comply with the flag-salute law. Furthermore, expelled students would be considered unlawfully absent from school, and their parents or guardians would be liable to prosecution.

Some children and their parents, who were Jehovah's Witnesses, refused to obey the flag-salute law on the grounds that it violated their religious beliefs. They viewed the flag of the United States as a "graven image," and their religion forbade them to "bow down to" or "worship a graven image." They argued that God's law was superior to the laws of the state. In turn, the local school authorities, backed by the West Virginia Board of Education, moved to punish the children and parents who would not obey the law. Thus, several West Virginia Jehovah's Witnesses families, including the family of Walter Barnette, sued for an injunction to stop enforcement of the flag-salute law.

The Issue Did the West Virginia flag-salute law violate the constitutional right to religious freedom of children professing the religion of Jehovah's Witnesses?

Opinion of the Court The Supreme Court ruled that the West Virginia flag-salute requirement was unconstitutional. Justice Robert H. Jackson said that public officials could act to promote national unity through patriotic ceremonies. However, they could not use compulsion of the kind employed in this case to enforce compliance. In particular, the 1st Amendment to the Constitution (applied to the state government through the due process clause of the 14th Amendment) prohibited public officials from forcing students to salute the flag against their religious beliefs. Justice Jackson concluded with one of the most quoted statements in the annals of the Supreme Court:

> The very purpose of a Bill of Rights was to withdraw certain subjects from the vicissitudes of political controversy, to place them beyond the reach of majorities and officials and to establish them as legal principles to be applied by the courts. One's right to life, liberty, and property, to free speech, a free press, freedom of worship and assembly, and other fundamental rights may not be submitted to vote; they depend on the outcome of no elections. . . .
>
> If there is any fixed star in our constitutional constellation, it is that no official, high or petty, can prescribe what shall be orthodox in politics, nationalism, religion, or other matters of opinion or force citizens to confess by word or act their faith therein. If there are any circumstances which permit an exception, they do not now occur to us.

Dissent Justice Felix Frankfurter concluded that the state school board had the constitutional authority to require public school students to salute the flag. He wrote that by not complying with the law, minorities can disrupt government and civil society, and therefore the Court should support the duly enacted legislation at issue in this case, which clearly reflected the will of the majority in West Virginia. If citizens of West Virginia dislike laws enacted by their representatives in the state legislature, then they should try to influence the legislature to change the laws. According to Justice Frankfurter, the Supreme Court had overstepped its authority in placing its judgment above that of the elected legislature and school boards in West Virginia. "The courts ought to stand aloof from this type of controversy," he concluded.

Frankfurter especially objected to Jackson's argument that questions associated with the Bill of Rights should be beyond the reach of local officials and legislatures. Frankfurter believed judges had a duty to respect and give in to the discretion of legislatures and the laws they passed.

Significance The *Barnette* decision overturned the Court's ruling, only three years earlier, in *Minersville School District v. Gobitis,* which had upheld a Pennsylvania law requiring students in public schools to pledge allegiance to the American flag. The two flag-salute cases show how the Supreme Court can change its mind about the meaning of the Constitution. Applications of the doctrine of *stare decisis*—the use of precedent, or previously decided cases, to decide new cases—create stability in the law. However, allowing for exceptions to *stare decisis* and overruling precedents are ways the Court adapts the Constitution to changing conditions.

The *Barnette* case set a new precedent that the legal system has followed to this day. Federal courts applying the *Barnette* precedent have turned back several attempts by officials to establish new flag-salute requirements.

SEE ALSO *Free exercise clause; Minersville School District v. Gobitis; Religious issues under the Constitution; Student rights under the Constitution*

SOURCES Irving Dillard, "The Flag-Salute Cases," in *Quarrels That Have Shaped the Constitution,* edited by John A. Garraty (New York: Harper & Row, 1987).

WHEELER, WILLIAM
Vice President

- Born: June 30, 1819, Malone, N.Y.
- Political party: Republican

- Education: University of Vermont, 1838–39
- Military service: none
- Previous government service: district attorney, Franklin County, N.Y., 1846–49; New York State Assembly, 1850–51; New York Senate, 1858–60; U.S. House of Representatives, 1861–63, 1869–77; president, New York State Constitutional Convention, 1867–68
- Vice President under Rutherford B. Hayes, 1877–81
- Died: June 4, 1887, Malone, N.Y.

When the Republican party nominated William Wheeler for the Vice Presidency in 1876, he was a political unknown outside of upper New York State. He got the nomination because while in Congress he had not taken part in the graft and corruption that permeated the Capitol during Ulysses S. Grant's Presidency. The Republican ticket, headed by Rutherford B. Hayes, won by a one-vote margin in the electoral college after an election commission awarded the Republicans a number of disputed electoral college votes. Like most 19th-century Vice Presidents, Wheeler claimed no accomplishments during his tenure.

WHIP

Each party in the Senate and House of Representatives elects assistant leaders known as whips, who help the floor leaders count heads and round up party members for quorum calls and votes. The title comes from a fox-hunting expression for the person, called the "whipper-in," who kept the dogs from straying during the chase. A part of the British Parliament as early as 1621, whips did not become official positions in Congress until the 20th century. In 1899 House Republicans established the first whips in Congress to help keep their majority in line. In 1971 Carl Albert (Democrat–Oklahoma) became the first party whip to rise to Speaker of the House (Albert also served as House majority leader). In the Senate James Hamilton

Lewis (Democrat–Illinois) became the first party whip in 1913; the Republicans selected their own whip two years later. As Lewis described his post, "The duties of the Senate whip demand his presence on the floor as constantly as possible. Sometimes the long hours test his physical capacity, but generally he is devoted to 'watchful waiting.' " Whips sometimes stand in for the majority or minority leaders in their absence. They have issued "whip notices" to other members of their party, notifying them of scheduled debates and votes. "The whip's job is not to create policy," House Speaker Thomas P. ("Tip") O' Neill, Jr. (Democrat–Massachusetts) has explained, "but to determine whether the votes are there for the policy that has already been determined."

In the Senate the position of whip took on a more bipartisan tone when Republican whip Don Nickles of Oklahoma and Democratic whip Harry Reid of Nevada began issuing joint whip notices in 1999. This practice recognized the parties' mutual need to keep all senators well informed of the schedule of potential votes. By contrast, House whips grew more partisan. After the Republican victory in 1994, Republican whip Tom Delay of Texas spearheaded much of the effort to enact the Republican legislative program, while his counterpart, David Bonior, just as vigorously promoted the Democratic alternatives.

SEE ALSO *Leadership in Congress*
SOURCES Robert C. Byrd, "Party Whips," in *The Senate, 1789–1989: Addresses on the History of the United States Senate*, vol. 2 (Washington, D.C.: Government Printing Office, 1991).

WHITE, BYRON R.
Associate Justice, 1962–93

- Born: June 8, 1917, Fort Collins, Colo.
- Education: University of Colorado, B.A., 1938; Rhodes Scholar, Oxford University, 1939; Yale Law School, LL.B., 1946

- Previous government service: law clerk to Chief Justice Fred M. Vinson, 1946–47; deputy U.S. attorney general, 1961–62
- Appointed by President John F. Kennedy Mar. 30 , 1962; replaced Charles E. Whittaker, who retired
- Supreme Court term: confirmed by the Senate Apr. 11, 1962, by a voice vote; retired June 28, 1993

Byron R. White was an excellent scholar-athlete at the University of Colorado. He ranked first in his class as a scholar, and he was a star on the varsity teams in football, basketball, and baseball. His prowess as a running back in football brought him national fame as an All American and earned him the nickname of Whizzer.

After graduation from college Whizzer White played one season for the Pittsburgh Steelers and led the National Football League in yards gained as a running back. Then he went to England as a Rhodes Scholar to study at Oxford. There he met John F. Kennedy, a future President of the United States.

During World War II, White joined the navy and served in the Pacific theater of the war, where he again met John Kennedy, an officer in the navy. Later, when Kennedy campaigned for President, Byron White supported him, which led to his appointment to the Supreme Court by Kennedy.

Justice White consistently supported equal protection of the law and civil rights of minorities, especially black Americans. However, he was cautious about expanding the rights of people suspected of criminal activity. For example, he dissented from the Warren Court majority in *Miranda* v. *Arizona* (1966) to argue that the Court's decision would unduly hamper efforts by police to obtain a confession from those suspected of criminal behavior. And he wrote for the Burger Court majority in *United States* v. *Leon* (1984) to establish a "good faith" exception to the exclusionary rule established by the Warren Court in *Mapp* v. *Ohio* (1961). The *Leon* case established that when police act on good faith to obtain evidence of criminal behavior without a valid search warrant, the evidence does not have to be excluded from the trial. Justice White also wrote for the Court in *New Jersey* v. *T.L.O.* (1985), which permitted public school officials to disregard the 4th Amendment protection against "unwarranted searches and seizures" when inspecting the personal belongings of students in school who are presumed to be hiding evidence of unlawful behavior.

SEE ALSO *New Jersey v. T.L.O.; United States v. Leon*

SOURCES Dennis J. Hutchinson, *The Man Who Once Was Whizzer White: A Portrait of Justice Byron R. White* (New York: Free Press, 1998). Daniel C. Kramer, "Justice Byron R. White: Good Friend to Polity and Solon," in *The Burger Court: Political and Judicial Profiles,* edited by Charles M. Lamb and Stephen C. Halpern (Urbana: University of Illinois Press, 1991).

WHITE, EDWARD D.
Associate Justice, 1894–1910
Chief Justice, 1910–21

- Born: Nov. 3, 1845, Lafourche Parish, La.
- Education: Mount St. Mary's College, 1856; Georgetown University, B.A., 1861; studied law under Edward Bermudez in New Orleans
- Previous government service: Louisiana Senate, 1874; associate justice, Louisiana Supreme Court, 1878–1880; U.S. senator from Louisiana, 1891–94
- Appointed by President Grover Cleveland to be an associate justice Feb. 19, 1894; replaced Samuel Blatchford, who died; appointed by President William Howard Taft to be chief justice Dec. 12, 1910; replaced Melville Fuller, who died
- Supreme Court term: confirmed by the Senate as associate justice Feb. 19, 1894, by a voice vote; confirmed by the Senate as chief justice Dec. 12, 1910, by a voice vote; served until May 19, 1921

- Died: May 19, 1921, Washington, D.C.

Edward D. White was the first associate justice to be promoted to chief justice of the U.S. Supreme Court. It seems that President William Howard Taft appointed him, instead of a much younger man, in order to keep open the possibility that Taft himself might become chief justice after retirement from the Presidency.

During his 27 years on the Court, White's single major contribution to legal doctrine was his controversial "rule of reason" used to interpret the Sherman Antitrust Act. This federal law was written to outlaw all combinations of businesses for the purpose of restraining trade. White, however, argued that only "unreasonable" restraints were banned by the Sherman Antitrust Act. Of course, what is "reasonable" or "unreasonable" is a matter of interpretation that may vary from one person to another. Chief Justice White's "rule of reason" doctrine gained a majority in *Standard Oil* v. *United States* (1911), which decided that the Standard Oil monopoly had to be broken up.

White was succeeded as chief justice by William Howard Taft in 1921. The former President's long-standing ambition to be chief justice was fulfilled at last.

SOURCES Robert B. Highsan, *Edward Douglass White: Defender of the Conservative Faith* (Baton Rouge: Louisiana State University Press, 1981).

WHITE HOUSE

The White House is the official residence of the President of the United States. Originally called the President's Palace, the President's House, or the Executive Mansion, it was officially proclaimed the White House by President Theodore Roosevelt in 1901.

The site for the White House was determined by George Washington and Pierre L'Enfant, the French architect who developed the master plan for the capital city in 1791. The building was designed by the Irish architect James Hoban, who won a medal worth $500 in a contest judged by three commissioners of the District of Columbia.

The White House cornerstone was laid on October 13, 1792, and the sandstone building was completed in November 1800, just in time for occupancy by John and Abigail Adams. Thomas Jefferson, one of the losers in the design competition, started construction of the East and West Wings during his Presidency, working with architect Benjamin Latrobe. He patterned them after his plantation at Monticello.

On August 24, 1814, during the War of 1812, the British burned the White House to the ground. Only the shell—and the kitchen's ironware and stove—remained. James Hoban supervised the rebuilding of the entire structure by September 1817. Hoban built the South Portico during James Monroe's Presidency and the North Portico during Andrew Jackson's Presidency. At that time the first plumbing and sewer lines were put in. Martin Van Buren installed a furnace, James Polk installed gas lighting, and Franklin Pierce installed bathrooms with running water in the family quarters. The first telephone was put in by Rutherford Hayes, and Chester Arthur installed an elevator.

The interior was rebuilt in 1902 by architect Charles McKim. The family rooms were enlarged and each bedroom was given its own bath. The West Wing was enlarged and a Presidential office included, and the State Dining Room was enlarged by one-third for diplomatic receptions. Plumbing, heating, and electrical wiring were modernized. An East Wing to accommodate guests at official functions was built. The East Room was redecorated in a colonial revival style for the wedding of Teddy Roosevelt's daughter Alice to Nicholas Longworth. After the work was completed, a time capsule containing memorabilia of the period was placed under the marble floor of the Great Hall entrance.

The next major overhaul took place in Calvin Coolidge's administration in 1927.

A third floor with 18 rooms for guests and servants was added, and the roof was replaced. A sun room was built on top of the South Portico. During Franklin Roosevelt's Presidency, the West Wing was rebuilt and underground office space was added. The East Wing was converted to office space for the growing Presidential staff. An indoor swimming pool was added.

From 1949 to 1950, during Harry Truman's Presidency, the entire building was gutted. It was then rebuilt and reinforced with steel beams and a new foundation. Among the improvements were a balcony on the second floor of the South Portico, a grand stairway leading from the family quarters to the first-floor state rooms, and central air-conditioning.

Starting in 1978, the exterior paint was scraped down to wood and stone, and much ornate carving was revealed. The exterior restoration and repainting was completed in 1993.

The White House contains 132 rooms, 29 bathrooms, and 29 fireplaces, all cared for by a chief usher and 96 housekeepers. The National Park Service has 36 workers who take care of its 18.7 acres. The U.S. Secret Service provides protection for White House occupants.

White House furnishings are selected by the curator of the White House (a post established by Lyndon Johnson in 1964) in consultation with the First Family. All furnishings are public property and are inventoried annually. Jacqueline Kennedy created a White House Fine Arts Committee chaired by Henry Francis Du Pont, founder of the Winterthur Museum (a decorative arts museum in Delaware) to advise on the restoration of the state rooms. She also created a Special Committee on Paintings. The White House displays selections from the 444 paintings and sculptures in its permanent collection. Most of the paintings in the collection were done by American artists, but it also includes works by the French painters Paul Cézanne and Claude Monet.

The White House Historical Association and the White House Preservation Committee are private organizations that raise money to preserve furnishings and acquire new pieces. Jimmy and Rosalynn Carter created the White House Endowment Fund, which is supported by private contributions and provides financial support for the maintenance and renovation of first-floor museum rooms.

Ronald and Nancy Reagan spent more than $1 million in private donations to redecorate the second and third floors, using primarily 19th-century American furnishings. Since 1925 Congress has appropriated $50,000 for Presidents to paint and decorate the living quarters at the start of each term.

The first floor contains five state rooms, and Congress requires that it be maintained in "museum character." Patricia Nixon, working with White House curator Clement Conger and the restoration architect Edward Vason Jones, redid the entire first floor in early 18th-century styles.

The state rooms include the East Room ballroom, 80 feet long and 40 feet wide, where press conferences are held. Seven deceased Presidents lay in state there. President Grover Cleveland was married in the East Room. For his daughter Nellie's wedding Ulysses Grant decorated it in a neoclassical style, with Corinthian columns, heavy wooden mantels, and gilt carved framed mirrors. Today it has a polished oak floor, carved wood paneling, and golden drapes.

The State Dining Room, where official state dinners are held, contains a long centerpiece for the table from the Monroe administration. It has wooden paneling and golden silk draperies. Dinners in the State Dining Room may seat as many as 140 guests. Nancy Reagan created a complete dinnerware set executed by Lenox, which includes 220 place settings of 19 pieces each. (Along with the other White House china, it is displayed in the China Room on the ground floor. The White House silver is located in the Vermeil Room, also on the ground floor.) The Family Dining Room has rarely been used for meals since Jacqueline Kennedy installed a President's Dining Room and kitchen on the second floor in 1961. It serves as a pantry during state dinners.

The Blue Room, a small oval room facing onto the South Portico, is used for small formal dinners and entertaining. It has the original French furniture used in Monroe's day.

The Red Room is used by First Ladies to entertain after dinners and for teas, and Dolley Madison held receptions there. Rutherford B. Hayes was sworn in as President in the Red Room before his public inauguration ceremony. Eleanor Roosevelt held press conferences there for women reporters.

The Green Room was used by Thomas Jefferson for meals and by James Monroe for card games. It became a drawing room for small receptions, teas, or dinners. The carpet is green, as are the silk wall coverings.

The second floor contains the family living quarters. It has 13 rooms, including the Yellow Oval Room, where Presidents receive visitors and entertain guests. It opens onto the balcony and looks over the Mall. Next to it is the President's study, and at the end of the hall is the President's bedroom and dressing room. On the other side is the Treaty Room (which served as the cabinet room in the 19th century), then the Lincoln Bedroom and sitting room (once the Presidential office). The "Queen's Bedroom," which has been occupied by Queen Elizabeth (the queen mother) and Elizabeth II, both of Great Britain, and Queen Wilhelmina of the Netherlands, and sitting room are on the opposite side of the hall. There are three other bedrooms for personal guests. There are no bedrooms for foreign heads of state or other official guests; they stay at Blair House, across the street.

Jacqueline Kennedy did the key restoration of the family quarters. She commissioned New York decorator Sister Parish to design a "country home in the city" on the second floor. An important change was to install a kitchen and dining room opposite the President's bedroom, so the First Family would not have to eat on the first floor.

The third floor contains the White House solarium. It is used as a nursery when the First Family has small children. Teenage children have used it for parties and to entertain their friends—without Secret Service intrusion.

On the lower level are offices for some of the staff of the National Security Council. The White House Communications Agency, also located in the basement, operates the Signal Board, which connects the President with senior staff members, top military commanders, and national security officials.

There are two annexes off the main mansion. The West Wing, containing Presidential offices, was destroyed in a fire in 1929. It was completely rebuilt and now contains the Oval Office, the Cabinet Room, and offices for the President's principal aides. Three dining rooms on the lower level of the West Wing, known as the White House Mess, can serve almost 100 staffers at a time. The Rose Garden, outside the President's office, was created during the Kennedy Presidency.

The East Wing contains staff offices, the Visitors' Office (which coordinates public tours), and the Family Theater. The President's doctor and nurses have a medical suite in the White House residence. The White House garage has military chauffeurs to drive the Presidential limousine and cars for senior aides on official business.

The public may visit the state rooms of the White House on most weekdays. There are also annual spring and fall garden tours, an annual Easter egg roll for children, the lighting of the National Christmas Tree, and three nights of candlelight tours to see Christmas decorations. More than 1.2 million people tour the White House each year. On February 14, 1962,

"A Tour of the White House with Mrs. John F. Kennedy," a television program broadcast by CBS, had an estimated audience of 80 million people.

SEE ALSO *Children of Presidents; Executive Office Buildings; First Lady; Kennedy, Jacqueline; Madison, Dolley; Oval Office; Secret Service, U.S.*

SOURCES Lonnelle Aikman, *The Living White House* (Washington, D.C.: White House Historical Association, 1982). William Seale, *The White House: The History of an American Idea* (Washington, D.C.: The American Institute of Architects Press, 1992).

WHITE HOUSE OFFICE

The White House Office is the collective name for the President's assistants. It was created by Reorganization Act No. 1 of 1939, on the recommendation of the Brownlow Commission, a Presidential study group. It concluded that to perform his many functions "the President needs help."

Until 1939 the President had no senior aides on his payroll, though Congress did provide salaries for clerks and for the residence staff. Presidents relied on assistant secretaries, the top-level political appointees of the executive departments, who were informally assigned to handle Presidential business, such as liaison with Congress.

In 1937 the Brownlow Commission recommended that the President be assisted by six senior aides, who ideally would have "a passion for anonymity" in their work. By the end of World War II the number had increased to 45, by the end of Dwight Eisenhower's administration it was up to 400, and there were more than 600 staffers during Richard Nixon's administration.

To run the White House Office, President Eisenhower appointed a chief of staff, assisted by a deputy chief of staff. (John Kennedy and Lyndon Johnson did not follow Eisenhower's innovation, but all Presidents since then have had a chief of staff.) There are also five or six senior political advisers known as "counselors to the President" or "special assistants" who have direct access to him. There are about 50 deputies to these top officials and about 100 assistants to these deputies. These senior aides (including White House speech writers) earn salaries equal to those of under secretaries and assistant secretaries of the departments. The remaining 400 or so staffers serve primarily as managers, secretaries, clerks, or technicians.

The White House Office prepares the President's speeches, does the advance work for the President's public appearances, and handles his schedule and appointments. The Office of Congressional Liaison helps the President persuade Congress to pass his legislative program, and the Office of Intergovernmental Affairs keeps in contact with governors and mayors. The Political Affairs Office keeps the President in close touch with his party's leaders. The Public Liaison Office helps the President gain support from special interest groups and their lobbyists. The Cabinet Secretariat makes sure that department secretaries implement Presidential decisions. The press secretary organizes news conferences and is responsible for preparing the President for questions he may face. The White House counsel ensures that the President is familiar with the legal and constitutional issues involved in decisions he makes.

Other units in the White House include the White House Military Office, which handles the "football," a briefcase that contains communications codes that allow the President to launch a nuclear attack; the White House physician, responsible for monitoring the President's physical condition; and the White House Communications Agency, which keeps the President in touch with military, diplomatic, intelligence, and other national security communications networks.

The senior staff works out of the East and West Wings and the basement of the White House itself, and lower-level aides

work in the Old Executive Office Building next door.

SEE ALSO *Counsel, Office of; Decision making, Presidential; Executive Office Buildings; Executive Office of the President; Office of Administration; Physician to the President; Press secretary; Speech writers, Presidential; White House*

SOURCES Bradley Patterson, *The Ring of Power: The White House Staff and Its Expanding Role in Government* (New York: Basic Books, 1988).

WHITNEY V. CALIFORNIA

- 274 U.S. 357 (1927)
- Vote: 9–0
- For the Court: Sanford
- Concurring: Brandeis and Holmes

Charlotte Anita Whitney was a socialist who helped to found the Communist Labor Party (CLP), an organization dedicated to bringing about fundamental changes in the political and economic systems of the United States, by violent means if necessary. The ultimate goal of the CLP was public ownership of the means of production of goods and services and a redistribution of wealth to benefit the masses of workers. California police arrested Whitney because of her socialist and CLP activities.

The state charged Whitney with violating the California Criminal Syndicalism Act of 1919. According to this law, criminal syndicalism was defined as "advocating, teaching or aiding . . . sabotage . . . or unlawful acts of force and violence . . . as a means of accomplishing a change in industrial ownership or control, or effecting any political change."

Whitney was tried and convicted solely on the basis of her involvement with the CLP, an organization that advocated the use of violent revolution to bring about social changes.

The Issue   At first, the Supreme Court refused to hear the *Whitney* case on the grounds that no federal issue was involved. But Whitney's attorneys proved that in the California Court of Appeals, questions had been raised about possible conflicts of the California Criminal Syndicalism Act with the due process and equal protection clauses of the 14th Amendment. So the Supreme Court accepted the case.

Did the California law used to convict Charlotte Anita Whitney violate her 14th Amendment rights? Moreover, did it also violate her 1st Amendment right of free speech as applied to the states through the due process clause of the 14th Amendment?

Opinion of the Court The Court upheld the California Criminal Syndicalism Act. Justice Edward Sanford concluded that the state's power and duty to maintain public safety and order outweighed the claims of the defendant about protection of her individual rights.

In his concurring opinion, Justice Louis D. Brandeis argued that Whitney's attorneys should have used the "clear and present danger" doctrine, developed in preceding cases by Brandeis and Oliver Wendell Holmes, to distinguish between mere expression of ideas and ideas that would result in actions that would endanger public safety and order. Whitney had claimed that the California law violated the U.S. Constitution, but, said Brandeis, "she did not claim that it was void because there was no clear and present danger of serious evil" that would result from her speech and actions. This version of the "clear and present danger" doctrine had been expressed by Justice Oliver Wendell Holmes in *Abrams* v. *United States* (1919).

Justice Brandeis set forth an often-quoted statement about the latitude and limits of free speech:

[A]lthough the rights of free speech and assembly are fundamental, they are not in their nature absolute. Their exercise is subject to restriction, if the particular restriction proposed is required to protect the State from destruction or from serious injury, political, economic, or moral. . . .

[T]o justify suppression of free speech there must be reasonable ground to fear that serious evil will result if free speech is practiced. . . .

[N]o danger flowing from speech can be deemed clear and present unless the incidence of the evil apprehended is so imminent that it may befall before there is opportunity for full discussion. If there be time to expose through discussion the falsehoods and fallacies, to avert the evil by the process of education, the remedy to be applied is more speech, not enforced silence. Only an emergency can justify repression. Such must be the rule if authority is to be reconciled with freedom. Such, in my opinion, is the command of the Constitution. It is therefore always open to Americans to challenge a law abridging free speech and assembly by showing that there was no emergency justifying it.

Significance Justice Brandeis's concurring opinion has the tone of a dissent. It immediately influenced the life of Charlotte Anita Whitney. The California governor, C. C. Young, pardoned her only a few months after the Supreme Court decision; he gave reasons similar to the ideas in Justice Brandeis's opinion.

In 1969 the Supreme Court overturned the *Whitney* decision in its ruling in *Brandenburg* v. *Ohio*. The ideas of Justice Brandeis influenced the Court's reasoning in this case; it pointed out a defense of free speech rights that could have prevailed for Whitney, if only she and her attorney had used this line of reasoning to support her case.

SEE ALSO *Abrams v. United States; Brandenburg v. Ohio; Freedom of speech and press*

WHITTAKER, CHARLES E.
Associate Justice, 1957–62

- Born: Feb. 22, 1901, Troy, Kans.
- Education: University of Kansas City Law School, LL.B., 1924
- Previous government service: federal judge, U.S. District Court for Western Missouri, 1954–56; judge, U.S. Eighth Circuit Court of Appeals, 1956–57
- Appointed by President Dwight D. Eisenhower Mar. 2, 1957; replaced Stanley Reed, who retired
- Supreme Court term: confirmed by the Senate Mar. 19, 1957, by a voice vote; retired Mar. 31, 1962
- Died: Nov. 26, 1973, Kansas City, Mo.

Charles E. Whittaker was appointed to the Supreme Court in 1957, after serving briefly as a federal district court judge in Missouri and as a judge of the U.S. Eighth Circuit Court of Appeals. He had risen to these distinguished positions through hard work and persistence.

Justice Whittaker's brief term on the Court was undistinguished. He wrote few opinions, none of them memorable, and he was generally viewed as the weakest thinker on the Court. He retired due to poor health.

WILMOT PROVISO

Antislavery advocates in Congress devised the Wilmot Proviso as a legislative tactic to stop the spread of slavery into the vast Southwestern territories that the United States had acquired from its war with Mexico between 1846 and 1848. This proviso (an amendment that sets a provision or requirement) stipulated that no federal funds could be spent to acquire any territory that permitted slavery. Seeking someone to sponsor the bill who had the best chance of winning recognition to speak in the House, the antislavery group chose David Wilmot (Democrat/Republican–Pennsylvania), who had not been unfriendly to Southern interests. The amendment, which became known as the Wilmot Proviso, was attached repeatedly to many bills. Although it passed the House, the Wilmot Proviso was never enacted by the Senate. Even without passage, the Wilmot Proviso became a rallying point for the new Republican party and equally an object of scorn by defenders of slavery.

SOURCES David M. Potter, *The Impending Crisis, 1848–1861* (New York: Harper & Row, 1976).

WILSON, HENRY
Vice President

- Born: Feb. 16, 1812, Farmington, N.H.
- Political parties: Whig, Free-Soil, Know-Nothing, Republican
- Education: no formal education
- Military service: none
- Previous government service: Massachusetts Assembly, 1841–44; Massachusetts Senate, 1844–46, 1850–52; U.S. Senate, 1855–73
- Vice President under Ulysses S. Grant, 1873–75
- Died: Nov. 22, 1875, Washington, D.C.

Henry Wilson was a self-made business entrepreneur who parlayed shoe factories into a large fortune. A member of several political parties, he deserted each, in turn, because it did not take a sufficiently strong stand against slavery. He was elected to the Massachusetts Assembly as a Whig in 1840 and to its senate in 1844. He was a founder of the Free-Soil party in 1848 and a member of the Know-Nothing party from 1853 to 1855. In the 1850s he lost three successive elections for governor of Massachusetts. After his election to the Senate in 1885 he joined the Republican party and was a leading member of its abolitionist wing. As chair of the Senate's committee on military affairs, he led the drive for war preparedness and opposed any compromise with the South just prior to the Civil War. After the war he strongly supported the 14th and 15th Amendments to the Constitution, which provided citizenship and voting rights for freed black men.

Wilson was defeated for the Republican Vice Presidential nomination in 1868 but won it in 1872. During Ulysses Grant's second term a series of scandals engulfed the administration, but Wilson was not involved. He accomplished nothing in office, and his failing health kept him from realizing his own Presidential ambitions.

SEE ALSO *Grant, Ulysses S.*

SOURCES Ernest McKay, *Henry Wilson: Practical Radical* (Port Washington, N.Y.: Kennikat Press, 1971).

WILSON, JAMES
Associate Justice, 1789–98

- Born: Sept. 14, 1742, Fifeshire, Scotland
- Education: University of St. Andrews, Scotland; read law in the office of John Dickinson, Philadelphia, Pa.
- Previous government service: first Provincial Convention at Philadelphia, 1774; Continental Congress, 1775–77, 1783, 1785–87; Constitutional Convention, 1787; Pennsylvania Ratifying Convention, 1787
- Appointed by President George Washington Sept. 24, 1789, as one of the original members of the U.S. Supreme Court
- Supreme Court term: confirmed by the Senate Sept. 26, 1789, by a voice vote; served until Aug. 21, 1798
- Died: Aug. 21, 1798, Edenton, N.C.

James Wilson traveled to the British colony of Pennsylvania from rural Scotland and helped to found a new nation, the United States of America. He served in the Continental Congress during the American War of Independence and participated influentially in the Constitutional Convention of 1787. Historians have rated him as one of the most important framers of the Constitution because many of his ideas were included in the final draft of this document.

In 1789, President George Washington appointed Wilson to the first Supreme Court of the United States. He was generally viewed as the best legal scholar among the original appointments to the Court. However, Justice Wilson's performance did not match his potential, and he contributed little of lasting significance as a Supreme Court justice.

His brief term on the Court was marred by heavy personal problems, including great indebtedness. Wilson's worries led to illness and death, in poverty, at the age of 55.

SOURCES Page Smith, *James Wilson: Founding Father* (Chapel Hill: University of North Carolina Press, 1956).

WILSON, WOODROW
28th President

- Born: Dec. 28, 1856, Staunton, Va.
- Political party: Democrat
- Education: Davidson College, 1876; College of New Jersey (Princeton), B.A., 1879; University of Virginia Law School, 1880; Johns Hopkins University, Ph.D., 1886
- Military service: none
- Previous government service: governor of New Jersey, 1911–12
- Elected President, 1912; served, 1913–21
- Died: Feb. 3, 1924, Washington, D.C.

Woodrow Wilson was the only Democratic President elected between 1896, when William Jennings Bryan was defeated, and 1932, when Franklin Roosevelt was elected. Wilson was a political scientist who once wrote, "The President is at liberty, both in law and in conscience, to be as big a man as he can." Wilson's Presidency demonstrated the validity of his observation: His two terms were characterized by successes in instituting a progressive domestic program. His foreign policies were marked by victory in World War I and military interventions in several nations.

Wilson was born in Virginia and lived in Georgia and the Carolinas during the Civil War. His father's church was used as a temporary hospital for wounded Confederate soldiers. After attending Davidson College for a year to study for the ministry, he withdrew for health reasons and later went to the College of New Jersey (Princeton), where he distinguished himself as a debater. After graduating in 1879 he studied law at the University of Virginia and practiced briefly and without much success in Atlanta before deciding to study history and political science at Johns Hopkins University. His doctoral dissertation, which became a highly regarded book, *Congressional Government,* analyzed the weakness of the Presidency and the strength of the standing committees in Congress. (Wilson is the only President ever to earn a doctorate and the only one who was a political scientist.)

Wilson embarked on a career as a college professor, teaching briefly at Bryn Mawr College (newly established to teach women) and Wesleyan University (where he also served as football coach) before returning to Princeton in 1890 as a professor of jurisprudence and political economy. He published a five-volume *History of the American People.* In 1902 Wilson became president of Princeton.

Wilson soon gained a national reputation for his innovative educational reforms at Princeton, which were designed to emphasize academics and de-emphasize its elitism. In 1908 he published *Constitutional Government in the United States,* in which he described the growth of Presidential power in Theodore Roosevelt's administration.

Two years later Democratic political bosses in New Jersey, seeking a candidate with a reputation for honesty and incorruptibility, visited Wilson at Princeton and offered him the party's nomination for governor. Wilson accepted and won the election. He broke with the party bosses who had supported him so he could establish a reputation as his own man rather than a follower of the bosses. Instead, he backed reform laws to provide for direct primaries for nominations (taking the nominating power away from the bosses), an ethics law for elected government officials, workmen's compensation, a pure food law, and a commission to regulate such public utilities as electricity.

In 1912 Wilson was a contender, although not the favorite, for the Democratic Presidential nomination. He won the nomination on the 46th ballot, defeating the favorite, House Speaker Champ Clark.

With the Republicans split, Wilson was able to win the Presidency with 42 percent of the popular vote, defeating Theodore Roosevelt and William Howard Taft. The Democrats retained Democratic control of the House and won a six-seat margin in the Senate.

Wilson capped his meteoric rise to the White House by demonstrating energetic leadership and domination of Congress. He influenced the roster of committee members so that supporters of his New Freedom program served on key committees. He imposed party discipline on congressional Democrats, who bound themselves to vote for measures put forward by their President. He broke precedent by giving an address to a special session of Congress called in April 1913, instead of sending the legislature a written annual message, as every President since Thomas Jefferson had done. He held regular news conferences and made every effort to rally public opinion around his legislative proposals.

Wilson won passage of a large number of progressive measures. The Underwood Tariff of 1913 lowered the duties on imported manufactured goods, which benefited consumers. The tariff act also contained a provision for the first income tax limited to wealthy individuals. The Federal Reserve Act of 1913 reorganized the banking system in order to prevent the sort of financial instability that caused panics and depressions. The Federal Trade Commission was established in 1914 to end unfair trade practices. The Clayton

Anti-Trust Act of 1914 provided new legal weapons against monopolies (companies that eliminated competition and thus raised prices) while recognizing the rights of workers to organize in labor unions and engage in strikes. In 1916 Wilson got Congress to approve federal land banks to provide low-interest loans to farmers, workmen's compensation for injuries received on the job, an eight-hour day for railroad workers, and laws prohibiting child labor. However, Wilson also promoted racial segregation in government departments in the capital.

In foreign affairs Wilson pursued an interventionist policy against small nations. In 1914 he ordered the military to seize the port of Veracruz, Mexico, to prevent a shipment of German weapons from reaching the revolutionary government of Victoriano Huerta. The crisis ended after European mediators succeeded in getting Huerta to resign. In 1915 the United States occupied the Caribbean islands of Haiti and Santo Domingo and took control of their financial affairs in order to pay back banks that had loaned money to these nations. In 1916 Wilson sent General John J. Pershing into Mexico with orders to pursue the guerrilla leader Pancho Villa, who had crossed into U.S. territory and killed 19 Americans. But Pershing's expedition was unsuccessful, and after several clashes with Mexican troops it was withdrawn early in 1917.

In 1914, at the beginning of World War I, Wilson issued a Neutrality Proclamation that stated that the United States would not take sides in the conflict. But Germany's policy of unrestricted submarine warfare caused Wilson to protest and eventually to tilt U.S. policy toward Great Britain and France. Although the British also interfered with U.S. shipping, only the German action resulted in the loss of American lives. On May 17, 1915, the Germans sank a British ocean liner, the *Lusitania,* resulting in the loss of 1,198 lives, among them 128 Americans. Early in 1916 Germany announced it was ending its submarine warfare, and Wilson then cam-

paigned for reelection on the slogan "He kept us out of war." Wilson won a close election against Republican Charles Evans Hughes, receiving 52 percent of the popular vote.

In December 1916 Germany announced its willingness to negotiate an end to the war. Wilson then called for a peace conference and on January 22, 1917, outlined his ideas for "peace without victory" in Europe. But nine days later, as if in answer, the Germans torpedoed Wilson's initiative by announcing a resumption of unrestricted submarine warfare. On February 3, 1917, Wilson broke diplomatic relations with Germany. Wilson armed U.S. merchant ships on March 5. On March 18 the Germans sank three U.S. merchant vessels, and on April 6 Congress granted Wilson's request for a declaration of war against Germany. The U.S. expeditionary force under General Pershing broke the long stalemate at the Second Battle of the Marne. (Other troops entered Russia on the side of the anticommunist White Russians fighting the Bolsheviks, and they remained until 1920.)

As the Allied victory drew near, Wilson announced his Fourteen Points, a set of principles to guide the victors, in an address to Congress on January 8, 1918. He proposed a system of open diplomacy without state secrets, freedom of the seas, arms reductions, and a "general association of nations" to guarantee all nations their independence and secure borders.

Germany acknowledged its defeat and signed an armistice on November 11, 1918. Meanwhile, Wilson had campaigned for Democratic candidates in the 1918 midterm elections on the basis of his peace proposals, making them a partisan issue. He thus sacrificed the possibility that Republicans would support his plans. Republicans took control of both houses of Congress.

In December 1918 Wilson sailed for the peace negotiations in Paris. He excluded Republican legislators from his delegation, which was a departure from the traditional practice of bipartisan foreign policy. The

European allies had already decided to reward themselves with territories and reparations (financial compensation from their defeated enemies), and Wilson was forced to give up most of his Fourteen Points. Nevertheless, he returned with a draft covenant, or constitution, for a League of Nations, which was included in the Treaty of Versailles that the Allies signed on June 28, 1919.

Wilson submitted the treaty to the Republican-controlled Senate for its advice and consent. Some Republican progressives turned isolationist and were prepared to vote against any treaty at all. Other Republicans, led by Senator Henry Cabot Lodge of Massachusetts, would accept a treaty only if it placed strict limitations on the power of the President to commit the United States to peacekeeping duties under Article X of the League of Nations covenant.

Wilson refused to make any concessions. He crossed the nation on a speaking tour in support of the league. On September 25, 1919, in Pueblo, Colorado, he collapsed. He was brought back to Washington, where he suffered a stroke on October 2. For two months Wilson was totally incapacitated. For the remainder of his term, though he understood fully what was happening around him, he was unable to do more than listen, dictate letters, talk for a few minutes, and scrawl his signature. He did not sign acts of Congress, which became laws without his signature. For four months his cabinet did not meet; for another four it met without him. Cabinet secretaries were unable to discuss government business with him. His wife and the White House physician controlled all access to him. When Secretary of State Robert Lansing inquired if the President was so disabled he should resign, they vigorously denied it. No one in government wanted Vice President Thomas Marshall, whom they considered incompetent, to take over.

Paralyzed and totally dependent on his wife as his link to the outside world, Wilson was in no position to control the outcome of the struggle for the Treaty of Versailles. The Senate approved it with a series of "reservations" sponsored by Senator Lodge. Wilson called on his supporters to vote against that version of the treaty. In November, a coalition of Republicans who opposed any version of the treaty and Democrats defeated Lodge's version. (In 1921, by a simple resolution, Congress declared the war with Germany over.)

Wilson was awarded the Nobel Peace Prize in December 1920, but that prize was small consolation for his political defeat. After his retirement from office, he remained in Washington, D.C., but he was too ill to take part in public affairs. On Armistice Day, 1923, he made his last public speech, in which he foretold eventual U.S. participation in the League of Nations. "I have seen fools resist Providence before," he warned. "That we shall prevail is as sure as God reigns." He died in Washington on February 3, 1924. The United States never joined the League of Nations, though Wilson's goal was ultimately realized when the country took the lead in creating the United Nations at the end of World War II.

SEE ALSO *Checks and balances; Disability, Presidential; Health, Presidential; Marshall, Thomas; New Freedom; Roosevelt, Theodore; State of the Union address; Taft, William Howard; Treaty of Versailles; Treaty powers*

SOURCES N. Gordon. Levin, *Woodrow Wilson and World Politics* (New York: Oxford University Press, 1970). Arthur S. Link, *Woodrow Wilson and the Progressive Era, 1910–1917* (New York: Harper & Row, 1954). Gene Smith, *When the Cheering Stopped: The Last Years of Woodrow Wilson* (New York: Morrow, 1964).

WOLF V. COLORADO

- 338 U.S. 25 (1949)
- Vote: 6–3

- For the Court: Frankfurter
- Dissenting: Douglas, Murphy, and Rutledge

Dr. Wolf, a Colorado physician, was suspected of performing abortions secretly, in violation of state laws. But the police were unable to obtain evidence to prove their suspicions. A deputy sheriff assigned to the case took Dr. Wolf's appointment book from his office, without the doctor's knowledge. The police contacted people listed in this appointment book about Dr. Wolf's medical practice. Through these interviews the police gained enough evidence to convict Wolf of conspiracy to commit abortions.

The Issue   Wolf said his constitutional rights had been violated. He pointed to the 4th Amendment to the U.S. Constitution: "The right of the people to be secure in their persons, houses, papers, and effects, against unreasonable searches and seizures, shall not be violated." He also pointed to the 14th Amendment: "No state . . . shall deprive any person of life, liberty, or property, without due process of law."

Wolf's attorney asked the Supreme Court to overturn his client's conviction because it was based on illegally obtained evidence. He cited the Court's decision in *Weeks* v. *United States* (1914). In that case, evidence obtained in violation of the 4th Amendment was excluded from consideration by prosecutors.

Were Wolf's 4th Amendment rights violated? Are the 4th Amendment guarantees against unreasonable searches and seizures incorporated by the due process clause of the 14th Amendment and thus applicable to the states? Should evidence obtained in violation of the 4th Amendment be excluded by judges from consideration at the trial of a defendant?

Opinion of the Court   Justice Felix Frankfurter agreed that the 4th Amendment was applicable to the states through the 14th Amendment. He wrote eloquently about the fundamental right of the individual to be secure against arbitrary intrusion by agents of the government. Frankfurter said, "The security of one's privacy against arbitrary intrusion by the police is basic to a free society. The knock on the door, whether by day or by night, as a prelude to a search, without authority of law but solely on the authority of the police [is] inconsistent with the conception of human rights enshrined in the history and basic constitutional documents of English-speaking peoples."

The Supreme Court held that 4th Amendment protection applies to searches by state officials as well as by federal agents. However, the exclusionary rule established in the *Weeks* case was not applied to the states. State judges were not required to exclude evidence obtained by searches in violation of 4th Amendment rights, so Wolf's conviction was upheld.

Dissent   Justice William O. Douglas argued that the exclusionary rule must be used to enforce 4th Amendment rights. Without the exclusion of illegally obtained evidence, he noted, the constitutional protections against unreasonable searches and seizures are practically worthless.

Significance   This was the first time that 4th Amendment rights were incorporated by the 14th Amendment and applied to the states, a precedent that has been followed ever since the *Wolf* case. In 1961, in *Mapp* v. *Ohio,* the Court accepted the dissenting position of the *Wolf* case and applied the exclusionary rule to the states, thus overturning the *Wolf* decision.

SEE ALSO *Exclusionary rule; Incorporation doctrine; Mapp v. Ohio; Searches and seizures; Weeks v. United States*

WOMAN SUFFRAGE

The Constitution left the question of who should have the right to vote to the states. Initially, women who owned property could vote in New Jersey, but by 1808 this right had disappeared even there, and throughout the 19th century women could not vote. In 1848 delegates to the Women's Rights Convention in Seneca Falls, New

York, demanded that women have the right to vote. After the Civil War, the woman suffrage campaign spread, led by Susan B. Anthony. Woman suffragists held conventions in Washington, lobbied members of Congress, and testified before congressional committees. In 1913 women paraded down Pennsylvania Avenue and militant protestors began picketing the White House, even chaining themselves to its fence, to draw attention to their campaign. When President Woodrow Wilson delivered his State of the Union message to Congress in December 1916, women in the galleries unfurled a large banner that read, "Mr. President, What Will You Do For Woman Suffrage?" (Ever since that incident, visitors have been prohibited from leaning over the railings of the galleries.) Several states, mostly in the West, individually gave women the right to vote in both state and national elections, and in 1916 Montana elected suffrage leader Jeannette Rankin to the House of Representatives. World War I, fought to "make the world safe for democracy," finally spurred Congress to pass the 19th Amendment to the Constitution, granting women the vote, in 1919, and the states ratified it in 1920.

SEE ALSO *Women in government*

SOURCES Eleanor Flexner, *Century of Struggle: The Woman's Rights Movement in the United States* (Cambridge: Harvard University Press, 1975).

WOMEN IN GOVERNMENT

Women in Congress Regardless of their party or political philosophy, women have always found themselves a minority within the "old boy" Congress. When Catherine May (Republican–Washington) entered the House in 1959, she requested assignment to the Joint Atomic Energy Committee, only to be told that the committee's ranking Republican "just can't see a woman on that committee." It took four

terms before Representative May got on the committee. Other women members faced the same institutional obstacles and banded together in the Congressional Caucus for Women's Issues to defend their interests and to promote their legislative agenda.

The 19th Amendment gave women nationwide the right to vote in 1920, but a woman had already entered Congress four years earlier. Jeannette Rankin (Republican–Montana) won election after successfully leading the woman suffrage movement in her state. She lost a race for the Senate in 1918. The first woman senator, Rebecca Felton (Democrat–Georgia), was appointed to a vacancy in 1922 and served for only a single day. Women were often appointed to fill out unexpired Senate terms, especially widows who succeeded their husbands. Hattie Carraway (Democrat–Arkansas) was appointed to take her late husband's Senate seat in 1931 and was expected to hold it only until the next election. Instead she enlisted the help of Senator Huey P. Long (Democrat–Louisiana), who campaigned with her and helped her win election in 1932. Six years later Carraway was reelected. Margaret Chase Smith (Republican–Maine) won election to her late husband's House seat in 1940 and then was elected senator in 1948. Smith served 24 years in the Senate and became an influential member of the Armed Services Committee. In 1968 Representative Shirley Chisholm (Democrat–New York) became the first African-American woman to serve in Congress. And in 1973 Yvonne Brathwaite Burke (Democrat–California) became the first member of Congress to be granted maternity leave.

More women have served in the House, where they are called "gentlewomen" in debate. Representative Rose DeLauro (Democrat–Connecticut) described the House as "a very competitive place," where it is important to build coalitions. Because all women in Congress do not think alike, they do not always vote together. As DeLauro explained, "You build coalitions among women and you build coalitions among men."

In 1991 the Senate Judiciary Committee conducted hearings on the nomination of Clarence Thomas to be a Supreme Court justice and heard allegations that he had sexually harassed a female employee. Watching the televised hearings, many women became angry when they realized that no women served on the Judiciary Committee. Pointing out that women constituted only 2 percent of the U.S. Senate, more women ran for Congress in the next election. Frequently called the Year of the Woman, 1992 saw 24 new women members elected to the House and 4 new women senators. These included Barbara Boxer and Dianne Feinstein, elected to the Senate as Democrats from California, and the first black woman senator, Carol Moseley-Braun (Democrat–Illinois).

For a century the sign on the swinging doors just outside the Senate chamber read "Senators Only." It was a men's rest room. Although women had served in the Senate since 1922, not until after the 1992 election was a nearby room hastily converted into a women's rest room. It was a small symbol of a major change in American politics.

Women in the Executive Branch
Even before the 19th Amendment was passed in 1920, many women lobbied for reform as members of clubs or as social workers. When President Franklin D. Roosevelt's New Deal made social welfare a priority of the federal government, many of these female reformers began to work at the national level. This new governmental focus coupled with the lobbying efforts of Eleanor Roosevelt and Molly Dewson, the head of the Women's Division of the Democratic National Committee, meant that more women than ever before helped shape U.S. policy in the 1930s.

Mary Anderson, an organizer of the Women's Trade Union League (WTUL, founded in 1903), was made assistant director of the wartime government bureau Women in Industry Service. When this bureau was replaced by the Women's Bureau of the Department of Labor in 1920, Anderson became its first director, improving women's access to employment, fair wages, and the vote.

Roosevelt gave another labor advocate, Frances Perkins, a place in his administration: she served as secretary of labor from 1933 to 1945, becoming the first female cabinet member and exercising great influence over labor legislation during her tenure. In addition, Roosevelt appointed Mary McLeod Bethune, the child of former slaves, to direct the Division of Negro Affairs of the National Youth Administration. Bethune's experience as an educator and founder of a school for black women made her the ideal manager of this New Deal agency, which worked to increase educational opportunities for African Americans. When Ruth Bryan Owen became Roosevelt's minister to Denmark in 1933, she made history as the first female U.S. ambassador.

Women continued to hold a range of positions in the executive branch in the period during and after World War II. The journalist and parliamentary expert Oveta Culp Hobby organized a military unit for women as director of the Women's Interest Section of the War Department in 1941. As the first American female colonel, she became head of the Women's Auxiliary Army Corps (WAAC) in 1942, which became the Women's Army Corps (WAC) in 1943. Her public service continued after the war: from 1952 to 1955, Hobby served as the first secretary of the Department of Health, Education, and Welfare, making her the only woman to serve in President Dwight D. Eisenhower's cabinet. Beginning in the 1980s Elizabeth Dole held two different cabinet posts, exemplifying the range of positions newly available to women. As the first female secretary of transportation, she increased automobile safety regulations and led the campaign to raise the drinking age to 21 under Ronald Reagan's administration. As secretary of labor under President George Bush, she began the "Glass Ceiling Study" to examine barriers to job promotion for women and minorities.

Women continue to perform key executive branch functions as cabinet secretaries. By the time of the 2000 elections, Donna Shalala had become the longest-serving secretary of health and human services in U.S. history, having begun her work under President Bill Clinton in January 1993. She was instrumental in directing and implementing welfare reform during her seven years as secretary. Alexis Herman was sworn in as the 23rd secretary of labor on May 1, 1997, becoming the first African American to hold the position. She had served previously as assistant to the President, as director of the White House Public Liaison Office, and as deputy director of the Presidential Transition Office in 1992.

Under President Clinton, Janet Reno and Madeleine Albright served in positions once considered the sole domain of men. Reno became the first female attorney general on March 12, 1993, just 33 years after she was denied a position in one of Miami's biggest law firms because of her sex. When Clinton made Albright the 64th secretary of state in 1997, she became the highest-ranking woman in the U.S. government. During Clinton's first term, Albright had served as U.S. representative to the United Nations and as a member of the National Security Council.

As of 1998, according to government figures, the representation of women in the permanent executive branch work force exceeds their percentage representation in directly comparable occupations in the regular civilian work force, in 10 of 22 of the executive branch independent agencies.

Women in the Federal Judiciary In 2000, 20 percent of all federal judges were women. Before 1928, there had never been a female federal judge. In that year, however, Genevieve Cline was appointed to the U.S. Customs Court by President Calvin Coolidge. The first female Supreme Court justice was Sandra Day O'Connor,

appointed by President Ronald Reagan in 1981. Ruth Bader Ginsburg, appointed by Bill Clinton in 1993, was the second woman to serve on the Supreme Court.

SEE ALSO *Chisholm, Shirley; Felton, Rebecca Latimer; Rankin, Jeannette; Smith, Margaret Chase*

SOURCES Hope Chamberlin, *A Minority of Members: Women in the United States Congress* (New York: Praeger, 1973). Office of the Historian, U.S. House of Representatives, *Women in Congress, 1917–1990* (Washington, D.C.: Government Printing Office, 1991).

WOODBURY, LEVI
Associate Justice, 1845–51

- Born: Dec. 22, 1789, Francestown, N.H.
- Education: Dartmouth College, B.A., 1809; Tapping Reeve Law School, 1810
- Previous government service: clerk, New Hampshire Senate, 1816; associate justice, New Hampshire Superior Court, 1817–23; governor of New Hampshire, 1823–24; Speaker, New Hampshire House of Representatives, 1825; U.S. senator from New Hampshire, 1825–31, 1841–45; U.S. secretary of the navy, 1831–34; U.S. secretary of the Treasury, 1834–41
- Appointed by President James K. Polk as a recess appointment Sept. 20, 1845; replaced Joseph Story, who died; nominated by Polk Dec. 23, 1845
- Supreme Court term: confirmed by the Senate Jan. 3, 1846, by a voice vote; served until Sept. 4, 1851
- Died: Sept. 4, 1851, Portsmouth, N.H.

Levi Woodbury was a Jacksonian Democrat who served less than six years on the Supreme Court. During his brief term, he tended to side with the majority on the Taney Court. He especially favored the rights and powers of the states in cases regarding conflicts with the federal government. In general, Woodbury's judicial career lacked distinction.

WOODS,
WILLIAM B.
Associate Justice, 1881–87

- Born: Aug. 3, 1824, Newark, Ohio
- Education: Western Reserve College, 1841–44; Yale College, B.A., 1845
- Previous government service: mayor of Newark, Ohio, 1856; Ohio House of Representatives, 1858–62, Speaker, 1858–60, minority leader, 1860–62; chancellor, Middle Chancery District of Alabama, 1868–69; judge, U.S. Circuit Court for the Fifth Judicial Circuit, 1869–80
- Appointed by President Rutherford B. Hayes Dec. 15, 1880; replaced William Strong, who retired
- Supreme Court term: confirmed by the Senate Dec. 21, 1880, by a 39–8 vote; served until May 14, 1887
- Died: May 14, 1887, Washington, D.C.

William B. Woods served briefly on the Supreme Court during the 1880s. His main contributions to constitutional law came through his narrow interpretation of the 14th Amendment. For example, he sided with the Court's majority in the *Civil Rights Cases* (1883) to declare unconstitutional the Civil Rights Act of 1875, which was designed to use federal authority to protect black Americans against abuse of their rights by state government.

Writing for the Court in *Presser* v. *Illinois* (1886), Justice Woods argued that the Bill of Rights restricted only the federal government and could not be applied to the states through the 14th Amendment. This position was not overturned until the second quarter of the 20th century. In general, Justice Woods favored limitations on federal power in favor of state powers and rights.

WORCESTER V.
GEORGIA

- 6 Pet. 515 (1832)
- Vote: 5–1

- For the Court: Marshall
- Dissenting: Baldwin

In the early 19th century, the Cherokee people owned a vast area of land in Georgia. They organized a thriving community with a constitution and republican institutions of government. They clearly meant to live as a free and sovereign, or self-governing, people. Georgia state government officials, however, had a different view of Cherokee destiny. They enacted laws that placed Cherokee lands under the control of Georgia county governments.

The Cherokees objected to Georgia's efforts to rule them. They brought suit directly to the U.S. Supreme Court on grounds that they were an independent nation whose rights had been violated by the state of Georgia. Writing for the Court, Chief Justice John Marshall, in *Cherokee Nation* v. *Georgia* (1831), held that the Court had no jurisdiction, under the U.S. Constitution, to deal with this issue because the Cherokees were "a domestic, dependent nation"—not a truly sovereign nation.

In March 1831 the Georgia militia arrested Samuel A. Worcester and thereby reopened the legal issue of Cherokee rights in the United States. Worcester was a white Christian missionary who lived among the Cherokee people. He was charged by the Georgia government with violation of a law prohibiting "all white persons [from] residing within the limits of the Cherokee nation ... without a license or permit from his excellency the [Georgia] governor." A Georgia state court found Worcester guilty and sentenced him to four years in the state penitentiary. Worcester appealed to the U.S. Supreme Court.

The Issue Worcester's attorneys claimed that the Georgia law he violated was unconstitutional because it conflicted with U.S.–Cherokee treaties, the contract and commerce clauses of the U.S. Constitution, and the sovereign status of the Cherokee nation. Should the national rights of the Cherokees be recognized? Should the Georgia law at issue in this case be declared void?

Opinion of the Court   Chief Justice John Marshall decided against Georgia. He wrote that the Cherokee and other "Indian nations" were "distinct, independent political communities, retaining their original natural rights." This was a dramatic change from the Supreme Court's decision one year earlier in *Cherokee Nation* v. *Georgia.* Marshall overturned Worcester's conviction and ordered his release from prison.

Significance   President Andrew Jackson and the executive branch of the federal government refused to abide by the Court's decision. Worcester remained in jail and served his four-year sentence. The Georgia government moved against the Cherokee people, who were eventually forced to move west of the Mississippi River.

Chief Justice Marshall's *Worcester* opinion departed from his *Cherokee Nation* opinion. Nevertheless, the *Cherokee Nation* opinion prevailed in subsequent cases, to the disadvantage of the people classified in the 1831 case as "domestic, dependent nations."

SOURCES Theda Perdue, *The Cherokee* (New York: Chelsea House, 1988).

WORK LOAD, CONGRESSIONAL

The work load of Congress can be measured in the number of bills and resolutions introduced, referred to committee, discussed in hearings, amended, marked up, debated, and enacted or rejected. After World War II Congress's work load increased dramatically. In the 1940s, 10,000 bills and resolutions, on average, were introduced in each Congress. By the mid-1960s that number had doubled to 20,000. Later the numbers declined because rules changes permitted several members to cosponsor the same bill, eliminating the need for each of them to introduce their own version of the bill. The number of bills passed also declined because of the elimination of the need for many private bills

(to assist specific individuals) and the combining of small pieces of legislation into larger, more complex bills. As a sign of this complexity, the number of pages in the average bill has grown considerably. Both houses have also seen a marked increase in the number of roll call votes, in which members must go to the chambers to have their yeas and nays recorded.

Congress now meets throughout the year because members prefer to spend long weekends and week-long recesses back in their district or state, rather than to adjourn earlier in the year and spend more consecutive months at home. Although members may spend fewer days each week in Washington, they spend longer hours in session each day. The workday has grown from about five hours a day after World War II to about eight hours a day during the 1990s.

Senators and representatives actually spend less of their time on the floor than in committee meetings. The amount of time devoted to committee and subcommittee meetings increased dramatically, reaching a peak in the mid-1970s, when reorganization of the committee structure reduced the number of committees and subcommittees. Individual offices have also recorded an increase in the amount of mail received and sent, telephone calls, and visitors, all of which represent part of the congressional work load.

SEE ALSO *Bills; Committees, congressional; Legislative Reorganization Acts (1946 and 1970); Resolutions, congressional*

SOURCES Norman J. Ornstein, Thomas E. Mann, and Michael J. Malbin, *Vital Statistics on Congress* (Washington, D.C.: American Enterprise Institute, 1994).

WRIGHT, JIM

- Born: December 22, 1922, Fort Worth, Tex.
- Political party: Democrat
- Education: Weatherford College, 1939–40; University of Texas 1940–41
- Representative from Texas: 1955–89

• House majority leader: 1977–87
• Speaker of the House: 1987–89

Jim Wright once noted that Congress could "rise to heights of sparkling statesmanship, and it can sink to levels of crass mediocrity." Although never mediocre, Wright's own career as a representative, majority leader, and Speaker had its spectacular highs and lows. As Speaker, Wright pursued an activist legislative program in opposition to Republican Ronald Reagan in the White House. Together with the restored Democratic majority in the Senate, he pushed for increased social programs and stronger civil rights laws. Wright opposed the Reagan administration's support for the Nicaraguan Contras (the armed opposition to the communist-leaning Sandinista government) and drafted a peace plan that would let Central America solve its own problems. In pursuit of his goals, Wright was never afraid to twist arms, to stretch the rules, and to otherwise use the powers of his office to their fullest. This approach earned him many opponents who resented his aggressive style.

In 1988 Representative Newt Gingrich (Republican–Georgia) raised questions about Wright's ethics, citing the royalties the Speaker had received from his book, *Reflections of a Public Man,* as a cover to evade House restrictions on outside income. The next year, after the House ethics committee investigated the charges and found merit behind them, Wright tearfully resigned as Speaker and as a member of the House.

SEE ALSO *Gingrich, Newt; Speaker of the House*

SOURCES John M. Barry, *The Ambition and the Power* (New York: Viking Penguin, 1989). Jim Wright, *Balance of Power: Presidents and Congress from the Era of McCarthy to the Age of Gingrich* (Atlanta: Turner Publishing, 1996).

Y

YACHT, PRESIDENTIAL

The first yacht placed into official service was the U.S.S. *Mayflower,* assigned to President Theodore Roosevelt in 1902. It was used by Roosevelt, William Howard Taft, Warren Harding, and Calvin Coolidge to entertain personal and government guests. President Herbert Hoover ordered the yacht moth-balled in the interest of economy, and it sank in a Philadelphia naval yard in 1931.

President Franklin D. Roosevelt used the U.S.S. *Sequoia,* which was placed in service in 1933, and the U.S.S. *Potomac,* put in service in 1936. The U.S.S. *Williamsburg,* put in service in 1945, was used by Roosevelt and Harry Truman. A 64-foot cabin cruiser used by Presidents from Truman through Lyndon Johnson was renamed by each succeeding President for someone in his family. It was taken out of service in 1969.

To symbolize a more austere Presidency, President Jimmy Carter sold the *Sequoia* in 1977. A private group, the Presidential Yacht Trust, bought it from a private owner and has refitted it, though no President has accepted the Trust's offer to sail it again.

A Presidential yacht is owned by the U.S. government. Its expenses are part of the navy budget, and its crew consists of naval personnel.

YATES V. UNITED STATES

- 354 U.S. 298 (1957)
- Vote: 6–1
- For the Court: Harlan
- Dissenting: Clark
- Not participating: Brennan and Whittaker

Congress passed the Smith Act in 1940 to limit the political activities of radical opponents of the U.S. government, such as the Communist Party of the United States (CPUSA). The Smith Act made it a crime for anyone knowingly to advocate the forcible overthrow of the U.S. government or to organize or participate in any group committed to the purpose of violent revolution against the U.S. government. Oleta O'Connor Yates was one of 14 members of the CPUSA convicted for violating the Smith Act.

The Issue Could the Smith Act be used to prohibit advocacy of violent overthrow of the government merely as an idea (but not as a direct incitement to forcible political revolution)? Was the Smith Act a violation of the 1st Amendment to the Constitution, which guarantees the individual's rights to freedom of speech, press, petition, and assembly? Should the convictions of Yates and her associates be upheld or reversed?

Opinion of the Court The convic-

tions of Yates and her associates were reversed, but the Smith Act was not ruled
unconstitutional. Rather, the Supreme
Court's interpretation of the Smith Act
was narrowed to the point of making it
virtually unenforceable. Justice John Marshall Harlan emphasized the difference between advocating ideas (abstractions) and
advocating immediate illegal action directed toward violent overthrow of the
government. Harlan ruled that Yates and
her associates were doing merely the former. Yates and the others therefore had
been wrongly convicted under an incorrect
interpretation of the Smith Act, said Justice Harlan.

Significance The *Yates* opinion took
the "teeth" out of the Smith Act. Given the
Court's restrictive interpretation of the
law, it became very difficult to enforce. After the *Yates* case, there were no more
prosecutions carried out to enforce the
Smith Act.

SEE ALSO *Freedom of speech and press*

YIELDING

Any member of Congress who has been
recognized by the presiding officer and is
speaking may yield the floor to another
speaker—or refuse to yield. If other members wish to interrupt the speaker, they will
address the chair and ask, "Will the gentleman [or gentlewoman] from [the
speaker's state] yield?" This device enables
two members to engage in a colloquy, or
back-and-forth debate, over a particular
point. If the speaker wishes to continue his
remarks after such an interruption, the
speaker will stipulate that by yielding for a
question, he is not giving up the right to
regain the floor.

Speakers also yield as a courtesy to
other members who may have an amendment to introduce or a short statement to
make and do not wish to remain for long
in the chamber.

YOUNGSTOWN SHEET & TUBE CO. V. SAWYER

- 343 U.S. 579 (1952)
- Vote: 6–3
- For the Court: Black
- Concurring: Frankfurter, Douglas, Jackson, Burton, and Clark
- Dissenting: Vinson, Reed, and Minton

In the spring of 1952, the United States was
in the midst of the Korean War, and the
nation's steelworkers were about to go on
strike. Harry Truman and his advisers
feared a long strike could bring disaster:
U.S. troops in Korea might run short of
weapons and ammunition.

The President acted forcefully. On
April 8, a few hours before the expected
start of the strike, Truman issued Executive Order No. 10340. This order directed
Secretary of Commerce Charles Sawyer to
take control of the nation's steel mills temporarily and to keep them running. The
steel companies accepted the order but
moved to fight Truman's action in court.

Taking temporary control of the steel
mills was not the only alternative open to
Truman. The President had another way
to deal with the strike. He chose not to use
it.

In 1947 Congress had passed the Taft-
Hartley Act. Under this law, the President
could get a court order delaying the strike
for 80 days. During this "cooling off" period, the steelworkers' union and the mill
owners would have tried to settle their
differences.

Truman disliked the Taft-Hartley Act.
He thought it was anti-labor. He had vetoed it in 1947, but Congress had overridden his veto. He had never used the law
and would not do so in the steel strike.

Furthermore, Truman believed the
blame for the strike did not lie with the
steelworkers. The union had already post-

poned the strike four times in an effort to reach a settlement. Government arbitrators had recommended a compromise, which the union had accepted. The steel companies had rejected those recommendations, even though in 1951 the companies earned their greatest profits in more than 30 years. President Truman believed the steel companies were using the emergency of the Korean War to force the steelworkers to accept low wages. Under such circumstances Truman held the companies, and not the workers, responsible for the crisis in the industry, and he decided to seize the steel mills.

The steel companies quickly challenged Truman's action in the federal district court in Washington, D.C. Within a few days the case went to the Supreme Court.

The Issue   President Truman's order was a remarkable assertion of Presidential power. The President was not carrying out or acting under a law passed by Congress. No law authorized a President to seize and operate the steel mills. By his order, President Truman was, in effect, making law—a power reserved to Congress by Article 1 of the Constitution.

Had the President overstepped the constitutional boundary that separated the functions of the legislative and executive branches? Or did the Constitution give Truman powers to protect the nation in times of national emergency?

The steel companies argued that the President's order clearly violated the Constitution. They said neither the Constitution nor existing laws gave him authority to seize private property. In addition, Congress had already set up procedures to handle the strike in the Taft-Hartley Act. Thus, they claimed the President had exceeded his constitutional authority.

The President argued that his authority, as chief executive under Article 2 of the Constitution, gave him power to keep steel production going in times of national emergency. In addition, he argued that his power as commander in chief allowed him to take actions necessary to protect the lives of U.S. troops. This power included

ensuring a steady flow of steel to produce weapons.

Opinion of the Court   On June 2 the Supreme Court ruled against the President. The Court judged Truman's seizure of the steel mills an unconstitutional exercise of power.

Justice Hugo L. Black, in the majority opinion, said that the President had no power, as either chief executive or commander in chief, to seize private property—even temporarily and during a national emergency. Black said that the power to authorize such an action belonged to Congress, not to the President. Thus, Truman could not seize the steel mills unless Congress passed legislation enabling him to do so. Because Congress had not done so, the seizure was illegal.

Black noted that, in writing the 1947 Taft-Hartley Act, Congress had considered letting Presidents seize factories in the event of strikes but had rejected the idea. Thus, by his executive order Truman had attempted to make his own law. Yet the Constitution, Black said, did not permit him to do so. The Constitution limited the President "to the recommending of laws he thinks wise and the vetoing of laws he thinks bad."

Dissent   Three justices, all Truman appointees, issued a strong dissent. They argued that during a grave national crisis, such as the Korean War, the Constitution allowed the President to exercise unusual powers. Chief Justice Fred Vinson wrote, "Those who suggest that this is a case involving extraordinary powers should be mindful that these are extraordinary times." Vinson added that Truman's actions followed the tradition of taking extraordinary actions in times of crisis established by such Presidents as Abraham Lincoln, Grover Cleveland, Woodrow Wilson, and Franklin Roosevelt.

Significance   The *Youngstown* decision required the government to return the steel mills to their owners immediately. Truman promptly complied with the Court's ruling even though he strongly disagreed with it. The steel strike began, and it lasted for 53 days. When it ended, the steel companies agreed to a contract within one cent of the settlement recommended by the government arbitrators. Truman never used the Taft-Hartley Act to intervene. The President did claim that in the summer and fall of 1952 the strike caused some shortages of ammunition.

In this decision, the Court clearly established that there are limits on the powers a President can derive from the Constitution, even during a national emergency. For nearly 20 years Presidential power had been growing through a series of crises including the Great Depression and World War II. The *Youngstown* decision had the effect of slowing this steady growth.

This case shows how strong Presidents can try to expand the powers of the office. It also demonstrates how the Supreme Court can act to preserve the separation of powers inherent in the U.S. constitutional system.

SEE ALSO *Constitutionalism; Separation of powers; Steel seizure (1952)*

SOURCES Robert J. Donovan, "Truman Seizes Steel," *Constitution* 2, no. 3 (Fall 1990): 48–57. Maeva Marcus, *Truman and the Steel Seizure Case: The Limits of Presidential Power* (New York: Oxford University Press, 1992). Alan F. Westin, *The Anatomy of a Constitutional Law Case: Youngstown Sheet & Tube v. Sawyer* (New York; Columbia University Press, 1990).

Z

ZORACH V. CLAUSON

- 343 U.S. 306 (1952)
- Vote: 6–3
- For the Court: Douglas
- Dissenting: Black, Frankfurter, and Jackson

In 1948 the New York City public schools introduced a "released time" program for religious education, under which students could leave the public schools before the end of the regular school day to attend religious classes of their choosing. During the 1940s and 1950s these programs were widespread. Tessim Zorach, a resident of New York City, complained that the city school system's "released time" program violated the establishment clause of the 1st Amendment.

The Issue The 1st Amendment of the Constitution prohibits government from enacting laws "respecting an establishment of religion." Does this mean that there must be complete separation of church and state? Or does this establishment clause permit certain kinds of governmental association with religion, as long as the government does not discriminate in its treatment of different religions?

Opinion of the Court Justice William O. Douglas upheld the New York City "released time" program because the religious instruction was not carried out in public school buildings. Rather, public school students could choose to participate, during the official school day, in religious instruction outside the public schools. Douglas emphasized that a "re-

leased time" program in Champaign, Illinois, had been declared unconstitutional only because religious instruction was provided in the public school buildings during the school day (*Illinois ex rel. McCollum* v. *Board of Education*, 1948).

Justice Douglas wrote these often-quoted words in support of permissible governmental accommodation of religion:

> We are a religious people whose institutions suppose a Supreme Being. . . . When the state encourages religious instruction or cooperates with religious authorities by adjusting the schedule of public events to sectarian needs, it follows the best of our traditions. For it then respects the religious nature of our people and accommodates the public service to their spiritual needs. To hold that it may not would be to find in the Constitution a requirement that the government show a callous indifference to religious groups. That would be preferring those who believe in no religion over those who do believe.

Dissent Justice Hugo Black emphasized that the location of religious instruction involved in "released time" programs was not relevant. It was the connection between government-supported public schools and the content of the religious instruction that, according to Black and the other dissenters, was not permitted by the 1st Amendment as applied to the states through the 14th Amendment. Black wrote that the resources and authority of the public schools had been unconstitutionally put at the service of private religious groups.

Significance "Released time" programs expanded in the wake of the *Zorach* decision. However, they declined in use and importance in the 1970s and 1980s. The enduring importance of the *Zorach* case is the argument for a constitutional accommodation of government and religion provided by Justice Douglas. In line with this opinion, the Court ruled in *Zobrest* v. *Catalina School District* (1993) that local government funds could be used to pay for a sign-language interpreter to assist a deaf student at a private school operated by the Catholic church.

SEE ALSO *Establishment clause; Religious issues under the Constitution*

SOURCES Robert S. Alley, *The Supreme Court on Church and State* (New York: Oxford, 1988).

ZURCHER V. THE STANFORD DAILY

- 436 U.S. 547 (1978)
- Vote: 5–3
- For the Court: White
- Dissenting: Stewart, Marshall, and Stevens
- Not participating: Brennan

In April 1971 a group of demonstrators seized the administrative offices of Stanford University Hospital. They blocked entrances and would not permit people to move freely through the facility. The Palo Alto city police confronted the demonstrators and a riot resulted. Several police officers were injured. The *Stanford Daily*, a student newspaper, published a report of the riot that included pictures.

The identities of the rioters could not be determined from the pictures published in the newspaper. The police, however, thought the photographer might have other pictures in his office that could be used to identify some of the rioters. They obtained a warrant and searched the offices of the *Stanford Daily*, but they found no additional pictures. However, while

they searched for pictures the police saw confidential papers in the newspaper's files. These papers included information about the management of the newspaper and the personal activities of students.

The *Stanford Daily* brought suit against the police. The student publishers claimed that the police's search of their offices violated their constitutional rights under the 1st, 4th, and 14th Amendments.

The Issue The students argued that a reasonable police search of a newspaper office should be based on a subpoena, not a warrant. A subpoena is an order requiring a person to appear before a court of law. A subpoena issued by a local court would have required representatives of the student newspaper to submit to police, for their examination, any pictures in their possession about the riot. This procedure, the students said, would have eliminated the possibility of police seeing confidential documents in their files not related to the purpose of the search. The city government replied that the warrant was legally obtained and the subsequent search properly conducted.

Was there a violation of the student newspaper's 4th Amendment rights to protection against unreasonable searches? And did the case involve a violation of the 1st Amendment guarantee of a free press?

Opinion of the Court Justice Byron White ruled against the *Stanford Daily*. He referred to the intentions of those who proposed and ratified the federal Bill of Rights: they did not, he wrote, "forbid warrants where the press was involved." Justice White emphasized that the press should not have special privileges with regard to the authorization of search warrants. Further, he contended that requiring a subpoena before the issuance of a search warrant would unduly interfere with effective enforcement of the law.

Dissent Justice Potter Stewart argued that the search without a subpoena was a violation of 1st and 4th Amendment rights because police were able to examine sensitive papers having no relationship to the purpose of the search. This kind of invasion of privacy, wrote Stewart, could intimidate newspaper publishers and thereby interfere with freedom of the press.

Significance The *Zurcher* decision prompted Congress to pass the Privacy Protection Act of 1980. This law prohibits federal government agents from carrying out searches and seizures in newspaper offices on "work-product materials unless the reporter or writer is suspected of committing a crime or there is some life-threatening situation." This federal law does not apply to state or local police, however. Thus the *Zurcher* ruling stands as a legal precedent.

SEE ALSO *Freedom of speech and press; Searches and seizures*

APPENDIX 1

The Constitution of the United States

WE the PEOPLE of the UNITED STATES, in order to form a more perfect union, establish justice, ensure domestic tranquility, provide for the common defense, promote general welfare, and secure the blessings of liberty to ourselves and our posterity, do ordain and establish this Constitution for the United States of America.

ARTICLE 1.

Sect. 1. All legislative powers, herein granted, shall be vested in a Congress of the United States, which shall consist of a Senate and House of Representatives.

Sect. 2. The House of Representatives shall be composed of Members chosen every second year by all the people of the several States, and the Electors in each State shall have the qualifications requisite for Electors of the most numerous branch of the State Legislature.

No person shall be a Representative who shall not have attained to the age of 25 years, and been seven years a citizen of the United States, and who shall not, when elected, be an inhabitant of that State in which he shall be chosen.

Representatives and direct taxes shall be appointed among the several States which may be included within this Union, according to the respective numbers which shall be determined by adding to the whole number of free persons, including those bound to service for a term of years, excluding Indians not taxed, three fifths of all other persons. The actual enumeration shall be made within three years after the first meeting of the Congress of the United States, and within every subsequent term of ten years, in such manner as they shall by law direct. The number of Representatives shall not exceed one for every thirty thousand, but each State shall have at least one representative; and until such enumeration shall be made, the State of New-Hampshire shall be entitled to choose three, Massachusetts eight, Rhode-Island and Providence Plantation one, Connecticut five, New-York six, New-Jersey four, Pennsylvania eight, Delaware one, Maryland six, Virginia ten, North-Carolina five, South-Carolina five, and Georgia three.

When vacancies happen in the Representation from any State, the Executive authority thereof shall issue writs of election to fill such vacancies.

The House of Representatives shall choose their speaker and other officers, and shall have the sole power of impeachment.

Sect. 3. The Senate of the United States shall be composed of two Senators from each State, chosen by the Legislature thereof, for six years; and each Senator shall have one vote.

Immediately after they shall be assembled in consequence of the first election, they shall be divided as equally as may be into three classes. The seats of the Senators of the first class shall be vacated at the expiration of the second year, of the second class at the the expiration of the fourth year, and of the third class at the expiration of the sixth year; so that one third may be chosen every second year, and if vacancies happen, by resignation or otherwise, during the recess of the Legislature of any State, the Executive thereof may make temporary appointments until the next meeting of the Legislature, which shall then fill such vacancies.

No person shall be a Senator who shall not have attained to the age of thirty years, and been nine years a citizen of the United States and who shall not, when elected, be an inhabitant of that State for which he shall be chosen.

The Vice-President of the United States shall be President of the Senate, but shall have no vote, unless they be equally divided. The Senate shall choose their other officers, and also a President pro tempore, in the absence of the Vice-President, or when he shall exercise the office of President of the United States.

The Senate shall have the sole power to try all impeachments. When sitting for that purpose, they shall be on oath of affirmation. When the President of the United States is tried, the Chief Justice shall preside; and no person shall be convicted without the concurrence of two thirds of the members present.

Judgement in cases of impeachment, shall not extend further than to removal from office, and disqualification to hold and enjoy any office of honour, trust or profit, under the United States; but the party convicted shall nevertheless be liable and subject to indictment, trial, judgement and punishment, according to law.

Sect. 4. The times, places and manner, of holding elections for Senators and representatives, shall be prescribed in each State by the Legislature thereof; but the Congress may at any time, by law, make, or alter such regulations, except as to the place of choosing Senators.

The Congress shall assemble at least once every year, and such meeting shall be on the first Monday in December, unless they shall by law appoint a different day.

Sect. 5. Each house shall be judge of the elections, returns and qualification, of its own members, and a majority of each shall constitute a quorum to do business; but a smaller number may adjourn from day to day, and may be authorized to compel the attendance of absent members, in such manner, and under such penalties, as each House may provide.

Each House may determine the rules of its proceedings, punish its members for disorderly behavior, and, with the concurrance of two thirds, expel a member.

Each House shall keep a journal of its proceedings, and from time to time publish the same, excepting such parts as may in their judgement require a secrecy; and the yeas and nays of the members in either House on any question shall, at the desire of one fifth of those present, be entered on the journal.

Neither house, during the session of Congress, shall, without the consent of the other, adjourn for more than three days, nor to any other place than that in which the two Houses shall be sitting.

Sect. 6. The Senators and Representatives shall receive a compensation for their services, to be ascertained by law, and paid out of the treasury of the United States. They shall in all cases, except treason, felony and breach of peace, be privileged from arrest during their attendance at the session of their respective Houses, and in going to and returning from the same; and for any speech or debate in either House, they shall not be questioned in any other place.

No Senator or Represenative shall, during the time for which he was elected, be appointed to any civil office under the authority of the United States, which shall have been created, or the emoluments whereof shall have been increased, during such time; and no person holding any officer under the United States shall be a member of either House, during his continuance in office.

Sect. 7. All Bills for raising revenue shall originate in the House of Representatives;

but the Senate may propose or concur with amendments, as on other bills.

Every bill which shall have passed the House of Representatives and the Senate shall, before it become a law, be presented to the President of the United States; if he approve, he shall sign it; but if not, he shall return it, with his objections, to that House in which it shall have originated, who shall enter the objections at large on their journal, and proceed to reconsider it. If after such reconsideration two thirds of that House shall agree to pass the bill, it shall be sent together with the objections, to the other House, by which it shall likewise be reconsidered, and if approved by two thirds of that house, it shall become a law. But in all cases the votes of both Houses shall be determined by yeas and nays, and the names of the persons voting for and against the bill shall be entered on the journal of each House respectively. If any bill shall not be returned by the President within ten days (Sundays excepted) after it shall have been presented to him, the same shall be a law in like manner as if he had signed it, unless Congress by their adjournment prevent its return, in which case it shall not be a law.

Every order, resolution or vote, to which the concurrence of the Senate and House of Representatives may be necessary (except on a question of adjournment) shall be presented to the President of the United States; and before the same shall take effect, shall be approved by him, or being disapproved by him, shall be repassed by two thirds of the Senate and House of Representatives, according to the rules and limitations prescribed in the case of a bill.

Sect. 8. The Congress shall have power: To lay and collect taxes, duties, imposts and excises. To pay the debts and provide for the common defense and general welfare of the United States; but all duties, imposts and excises, shall be uniform throughout the United States;

To borrow money on the credit of the United States; To regulate commerce with foreign nations and among the several States, and with Indian tribes;

To establish a uniform rule of naturalization, and uniform laws on the subject of bankruptcies, throughout the United States;

To coin money, regulate the value thereof, and of foreign coin, and fix the standard of weights and measures;

To provide for the punishment of counterfeiting the securities and current coin of the United States;

To establish post-offices and post-roads;

To promote the progress of science and useful arts, by securing for limited times to authors and inventors the exclusive right to their respective writings and discoveries;

To constitute tribunals inferior to the Supreme Court;

To define and punish piracies and felonies committed on the high seas and offences against the law of nations;

To declare war, grant letters of marque and reprisal, and make rules concerning captures on land and water;

To raise and support armies, but no appropiation of money to that use shall be for a longer term than two years;

To provide and maintain a navy;

To make rules for the government and regulation of the land and naval forces;

To provide for calling forth the militia to execute the laws of the Union, suppress insurrections, and repel invasions;

To provide for organizing, arming and disciplining the militia, and for governing such part of them as may be employed in the service of the United States, reserving to the States respectively the appointment of the officers, and the authority of training the militia according to the discipline prescribed by Congress;

To exercise exclusive legislation, in all cases whatsoever, over such district (not exceeding ten miles square) as may, by cession of particular States, and the acceptance of Congress, become the seat of the government of the United States, and to exercise like authority over all places purchased by the consent of the Legislature of the State in which the same shall be, for the erection of forts, magazines, arsenals, dock-yards, and other need buildings;—and,

To make all laws which shall be necessary and proper for carrying into execution the foregoing powers, and all other powers vested by this Constitution in the government of the United States, or in any department or officer thereof.

Sect. 9. The migration or importation of such persons as any of the States now existing shall think proper to admit, shall not be prohibited by the Congress prior to the year one thousand eight hundred and eight; but a tax or duty may be imposed on such importation, not exceeding ten dollars for each person.

The privilege of the writ of habeas corpus shall not be suspended, unless when in cases of rebellion or invasion the public safety may require it.

No bill of attainder, or ex post facto law, shall be passed.

No capitation or other direct tax shall be laid, unless in proportion to the census or enumeration herein before directed to be taken.

No tax or duty shall be laid on articles exported from any State. No preference shall be given by any regulation of commerce or revenue to the ports of one State over those of another: Nor shall vessels bound to or from one State, be obliged to enter, clear, or pay duties, in another.

No money shall be drawn from the treasury, but in consequence of appropriations made by law; and a regular statement and account of the receipts and expenditures of all public money shall be published from time to time.

No title of nobility shall be granted by the United States: And no person holding any office of profit or trust under them shall, without the consent of the Congress, accept of any present, emolument, office or title, or any kind whatever from any King, Prince, or foreign State.

Sect. 10. No State shall enter into any treaty, alliance or confederation; grant letters or marque and reprisal; coin money; emit bills of credit; make any thing but gold and silver coin a tender in payment of debts; pass any bill of attainder, ex post facto law, or law impairing the obligation of contracts, or grant any title of nobility.

No State shall, without the consent of Congress, lay any imposts or duties on imports or exports, except what may be absoutely nescessary for executing its inspection laws; and the new produce of all duties and imposts, laid by any State, on imports or exports, shall be for the use of the treasury of the United States; and all such laws shall be subject to the revision and control of the Congress. No State shall, without the consent of Congress, lay any duty on tonnage, keep troops or ships of war in time of peace, enter into any agreement or compact with another State, or with a foreign power, or engage in war, unless actually invaded, or in such imminent danger as will not admit of delay.

ARTICLE II.

Sec 1. The excutive power shall be vested in the President of the United States of America. He shall hold his office during the term of four years, and, together with the Vice-President, chosen for the same term, be elected as follows.

Each State shall appoint, in such manner as the Legislature thereof may direct, a number of Electors, equal to the whole number of Senators and Representatives to which The State may be entitled in the Congress; but no Senator or Representative, or person holding an office of trust or profit under the United States, shall be appointed an Elector.

The Electors shall meet in their respective States, and vote by ballot for two persons, of whom one at least shall not be an inhabitant of the same state with themselves. And they shall make a list of all the persons voted for, and of the number of votes for each; which list they shall sign and certify, and transmit sealed to the seat of the government of the United States, directed to the President of the Senate. The President of the Senate shall, in the presence of the Senate and House of Representatives, open all certificates, and the votes shall be counted. The person having the greatest number of votes shall be the President, if such number be a majority of the whole number of Electors appointed; and if there be more than one who have such majority, and have an equal number of votes, then the House of Representatives shall immediately choose by ballot one of them for President; and if no person have a majority, then from the five highest on the list the said House shall in like manner choose a President. But in choosing the President the votes shall be taken by States, the representation from each State having one vote: a quorum for this purpose shall consist of a member or members from two thirds of the States and a majority of all States shall be necessary to a choice. In every case, after the choice of President, the person having the greatest number of votes of the Electors, shall be the Vice-President. But if there should remain two or more who have equal votes, the Senate shall choose from them by ballot the Vice-President.

The Congress may determine the time of choosing the Electors, and the day on which they shall give their votes; which day shall be the same throughout the United States.

No person, except a natural born citizen, or a citizen of the United States at the time of the adoption of this Constitution, shall be eligible to the office of President; neither shall any person be eligible to that office, who shall not have attained to the age of thirty-five years, and been fourteen years a resident of the United States.

In case of the removal of the President from office, or of his death, resignation, or inability to discharge the powers and duties of the said office, the same shall devolve on the Vice-President; and the Congress may by law provide for the case of removal, death, resignation, or inability, both of the President and Vice-President, declaring what officer shall then act as President, and such officer shall act accordingly, until the disability be removed, or a President shall be elected.

The President shall, at stated times, receive for his services a compensation, which shall neither be increased nor diminished during the period for which he shall have been elected, and he shall not receive within that period any other emolument from the United States, or any of them.

Before he enter on the execution of his office, he shall take the following oath or affirmation:

"I do solemnly swear (or affirm) that I will faithfully execute the office of President of the United States; and will, to the best of my ability, preserve, protect and defend, the Constitution of the United States."

Sect. 2. The President shall be Commander in Chief of the army and navy of the United States, and of the militia of the several states, when called into the actual service of the United States; he may require the opinion, in writing, of the principal officer in each of the executive departments, upon any subject relating to the duties of their respective offices, and he shall have power to grant reprieves and pardons for offenses against the United States, except in cases of impeachment.

He shall have power, by and with the advice and consent of the Senate, to make treaties, provided two thirds of the Senators present concur; and he shall nominate, and by and with the advice and consent of the Senate shall appoint Ambassadors, other public Ministers, and Consuls, Judges of the Supreme Court, and all other offices of the United States, whose appointments are not herein otherwise provided for, and which shall be established by law. But the Congress may by law vest the appointment of such inferior officers as they think proper in the President alone, in the courts of law, or in heads of departments.

The President shall have power to fill all vacancies that may happen during the recess of the Senate, by granting commissons, which shall expire at the end of their next session.

Sect. 3. He shall from time to time give to the Congress information of the State of the Union, and recommend to their consideration such measures as he shall judge necessary and expedient; he may, on extraordinary occasions, convene both Houses, or either of them, and in case of disagreement between them, with respect to the time of adjournment, he may adjourn them to such time as he shall think proper; he shall receive Ambassadors and other public Ministers; he shall take care that the laws be faithfully executed, and shall commission all the officers of the United States.

Sect. 4. The President, Vice-President, and all civil officers of the United States, shall be removed from office, on impeachment for and conviction of treason, bribery, or other high crimes and misdemeanors.

ARTICLE III.
Sect. 1. The judicial power of the United States shall be vested in one Supreme Court, and in such Inferior Courts as the Congress may from time to time ordain and establish. The judges, both of the Supreme and Inferior Courts, shall hold their offices during good behavior; and shall, at stated times, receive for their services a compensation, which shall not be diminished during their continuance in office.

Sect. 2. The judicial power shall extend to all cases in law and equity, arising under this Constitution, the laws of the United States, and treaties made, or which shall be made, under their arthority; to all cases affecting Ambassadors, other public Ministers, and Consuls; to all cases of admiralty and maritime jurisdiction; to controversies to which the United States shall be a party; to controversies between two or more States, between a State and a citizen of another State, between citizens of different States, between citizens of the same state

claiming lands under grants of different States, and between a State, or the citizens thereof, and foreign States, citizens or subjects.

In all cases affecting Ambassadors, other public Ministers and consuls, and those in which a State shall be party, the Supreme Court shall have original jurisdiction. In all the other cases before mentioned, the Supreme Court shall have appellate jurisdiction, both as to law and fact, with such exceptions and under such regulations as the Congress shall make.

The trial of all crimes, except in cases of impeachment, shall be by jury; and such trial shall be held in the State where the said crimes shall have been committed; but when not committed within any State, the trial shall be at such place or places as the Congress may by law have directed.

Sect. 3. Treason, against the United States, shall consist only in levying war against them, or in adhering to their enemies, giving them aid and comfort. No person shall be convicted of treason, unless on the testimony of two witnesses to the same overt act, or on concession in open court.

The Congress shall have power to declare the punishment of treason, but no attainder of treason shall work corruption of blood, or forfeiture, except during the life of the person attained.

ARTICLE IV.
Sect. 1. Full faith and credit shall be given in each State to the public acts, records and judicial proceedings, of every other State. And the Congress may by general laws prescribe the manner in which such acts, records and proceedings, shall be proved, and the effect thereof.

Sect. 2. The citizens of each State shall be entitled to all privileges and immunities of citizens in the several states. A person, charged in any State with treason, felony, or other crime, who shall flee from justice, and be found in another State, shall, on demand of the executive authority of the State from which he fled, be delivered up, to be removed to the State having jurisdiction of the crime.

No person, held to service or labour in one State, under the laws thereof, escaping into another, shall, in consequence of any law or regulation therein, be discharged from such service or labour; but shall be delivered up, on claim of the party to whom such service or labour may be due.

Sect. 3. New States may be admitted by the Congress into this Union; but no new State shall be formed to erected within the jurisdiction of any other State; nor any State be formed by the junction of two or more States, or parts of States, without the consent of the Legislatures of the States concerned, as well as of the Congress.

The Congress shall have power to dispose of and make all needful rules and regulations, respecting the territory or other property belonging to the United States; and nothing in this Constitution shall be so construed, as to prejudice any claims of the United States, or of any particular State.

Sect. 4. The United States shall guarantee, to every State in this Union, a republican form of government, and shall protect each of them against invasion; and, on application of the Legislature, or of the Executive (when the Legislature cannot be convened) against domestic violence.

ARTICLE V.
The Congress, whenever two thirds of both houses shall deem it necessary, shall propose amendments to this Constitution; or, on the application of the Legislatures of two thirds of the several States, shall call a Convention, for proposing amendments; which, in either case, shall be valid, to all intents and purposes, as part of this Constitution, when ratified by the Legislature of three fourths of the several States, or by conventions in three fourths thereof, as the one or the other mode of ratification may be proposed by the Congress: Provided, that no amendment which may be made prior to the year one thousand eight hundred and eight shall in any manner affect the first and fourth clauses, in the ninth section of the first article; and that no State, without its consent, shall be deprived of its equal suffrage in the Senate.

ARTICLE VI.
All debts contracted, and engagements entered into, before the adoption of this Constitution, shall be as valid against the United States under this Constitution, as under the Confederation.

This Constitution, and the laws of the United States which shall be made in pursuance thereof, and all treaties made, or which shall be made, under the authority of the United States, shall be the supreme law of the land; and the Judges in every State, shall be bound thereby; any thing in the constitution or laws of any State to the contrary notwithstanding.

The Senators and Representatives before mentioned; and the members of the several State Legislatures, and all executive and judicial officers, both of the United States and of the several States, shall be bound by oath or affirmation to support this Constitution; but no religious test shall ever be required as a qualification to any office, or public trust, under the United States.

ARTICLE VII.
The ratification of the Conventions of Nine States shall be sufficient for the establishment of this constitution, between the States so ratifying the same.

Done in Convention, by the unanimous consent of the States present, the seventeenth day of September, in the year of our Lord one thousand seven hundred and eighty-seven, and of the Independence of the United States of America the twelfth. In witness whereof, we have hereunto subscribed our names.

GEORGE WASHINGTON, President and Deputy from Virginia.
New-Hampshire, John Langdon, Nicholas Gilman.

Massachusetts, Nathaniel Gorham, Rufus King.
Connecticut, William Samuel Johnson, Roger Sherman.
New-York, Alexander Hamilton.
New Jersey, William Livingston, David Brearley, William Paterson, Jonathan Dayton. Pennsylvania, Benjamin Franklin, Thomas Mifflin, Robert Morris, George Clymer, Thomas Fitzsimons, Jared Ingersoll, James Wilson, Gouverneur Morris.
Delaware, George Read, Gunning Bedford, jun., John Dickinson, Richard Bassett, Jacob Broom.
Maryland, James M'Henry, Daniel of St. Tho. Jenifer, Daniel Carrol.
Virginia, John Blair, James Madison, jun.
North-Carolina, William Blount, Richard Dobbs Spaight, Hugh Williamson.
South-Carolina, John Rutledge, Charles Cotesworth Pinckney, Charles Pinckney, Pierce Butler.
Georgia, William Few, Abraham Baldwin.

Attest, ... WILLIAM JACKSON, Secretary.

The Bill of Rights

Amendment I
Congress shall make no law respecting an establishment of religion, or prohibiting the free exercise thereof; or abridging the freedom of speech, or of the press; or the right of the people peaceably to assemble, and to petition the Government for a redress of grievances.

Amendment II
A well regulated Militia, being necessary to the security of a free State, the right of the people to keep and bear Arms, shall not be infringed.

Amendment III
No Soldier shall, in time of peace be quartered in any house, without the consent of the Owner, nor in time of war, but in a manner to be prescribed by law.

Amendment IV
The right of the people to be secure in their persons, houses, papers, and effects, against unreasonable searches and seizures, shall not be violated, and no Warrants shall issue, but upon probable cause, supported by Oath or Affirmation, and particularly describing the place to be searched, and the persons or things to be seized.

Amendment V
No person shall be held to answer for a capital, or otherwise infamous crime, unless on a presentment or indictment of a Grand Jury, except in cases arising in the land or naval forces, or in the Militia, when in actual service in time of War or public danger; nor shall any person be subject for the same offense to be twice put in jeopardy of life or limb; nor shall be compelled in any criminal case to be a witness against himself, nor be deprived of life, liberty, or property, without due process of law; nor shall private property be taken for public use, without just compensation.

Amendment VI
In all criminal prosecutions, the accused shall enjoy the right to a speedy and public trial, by an impartial jury of the State and district wherein the crime shall have been committed, which district shall have been previously ascertained by law, and to be informed of the nature and cause of the accusation; to be confronted with the witnesses against him; to have compulsory process for obtaining witnesses in his favor, and to have the Assistance of Counsel for his defence.

Amendment VII
In suits at common law, where the value in controversy shall exceed twenty dollars, the right of trial by jury shall be reserved, and no fact tried by a jury, shall be otherwise reexamined in any Court of the United States, than according to the rules of the common law.

Amendment VIII
Excessive bail shall not be required, nor excessive fines imposed, nor cruel and unusual punishments inflicted.

Amendment IX
The enumeration in the Constitution, of certain rights, shall not be construed to deny or disparage others retained by the people.

Amendment X
The powers not delegated to the United States by the Constitution, nor prohibited by it to the States, are reserved to the States respectively, or to the people.

Amendment XI
The judicial power of the United States shall not be construed to extend to any suit in law or equity, commenced or prosecuted against one of the United States by citizens of another State, or by citizens or subjects of any foreign State.

Amendment XII
The electors shall meet in their respective States, and vote by ballot for President and Vice President, one of whom, at least, shall not be an inhabitant of the same State with themselves; they shall name in their ballots the person voted for as President, and in distinct ballots the person voted for as Vice President, and they shall make distinct lists of all persons voted for as President, and of all persons voted for as Vice President, and of the number of votes for each, which lists they shall sign and certify, and transmit sealed to the seat of the government of the United States, directed to the President of the Senate;—The President of the Senate shall, in the presence of the Senate and House of Representatives, open all the certificates and the votes shall then be counted;—The person having the greatest number of votes for President, shall be the President, if such number be a majority of the whole number of electors appointed; and if no person have such majority, then from the persons having the highest numbers not exceeding three on the list of those voted for as President, the House of Representatives shall choose immediately, by ballot, the President. But in choosing the President, the votes shall be taken by States, the representation from each State having one vote; a quorum for this purpose shall consist of a member of members from two-thirds of the States, and a majority of all the States shall be necessary to a choice. And if the House of Representatives shall not choose a President whenever the right of choice shall devolve upon them, before the fourth day of March next following, then the Vice President shall act as President, as in the case of the death or other constitutional disability of the President.

The person having the greatest number of votes as Vice President, shall be the Vice President, if such number be a majority of the whole number of electors appointed, and if no person have a majority, then from the two highest numbers on the list, the Senate shall choose the Vice President; a quorum for the purpose shall consist of two-thirds of the whole number of Senators, and a majority of the whole number shall be necessary to a choice. But no person constitutionally ineligible to the office of the President shall be eligible to that of Vice President of the United States.

Amendment XIII
Section 1. Neither slavery nor involuntary servitude, except as a punishment for crime whereof the party shall have been duly convicted, shall exist within the United States, or any place subject to their jurisdiction.
Section 2. Congress shall have power to enforce this article by appropriate legislation.

Amendment XIV
Section 1. All persons born or naturalized in the United States, and subject to the jurisdiction thereof, are citizens of the United States and of the State wherein they reside. No State shall make or enforce any law which shall abridge the privileges or immunities of citizens of the United States;

nor shall any State deprive any person of life, liberty, or property, without due process of law; nor deny to any person within its jurisdiction the equal protection of the laws.

Section 2. Representatives shall be apportioned among the several States according to their respective numbers, counting the whole number of persons in each State, excluding Indians not taxed. But when the right to vote at any election for the choice of electors for President and Vice President of the United States, Representatives in Congress, the executive and judicial officers of a State, or the members of the legislature thereof, is denied to any of the male inhabitants of such State, being twenty-one years of age, and citizens of the United States, or in any way abridged, except for participation in rebellion, or other crime, the basis of representation therein shall be reduced in the proportion which the number of such male citizens shall bear to the whole number of male citizens twenty-one years of age in such State.

Section 3. No person shall be a Senator or Representative in congress, or elector of President and Vice President, or hold any office, civil or military, under the United States, or under any State, who, having previously taken an oath, as a member of Congress, or as an officer of the United States, or as a member of any State legislature, or as an executive or judicial officer of any State, to support the Constitution of the United States, shall have engaged in insurrection or rebellion against the same, or given aid or comfort to the enemies thereof. But Congress may by a vote of two-thirds of each house, remove such disability.

Section 4. The validity of the public debt of the United States, authorized by law, including debts incurred for payment of pensions and bounties for services in suppressing insurrection or rebellion, shall not be questioned. But neither the United States nor any State shall assume or pay any debt or obligation incurred in aid of insurrection or rebellion against the United States, or any claim for the loss or emancipation of any slave; but all such debts, obligations and claims shall be held illegal and void.

Section 5. The Congress shall have power to enforce, by apropriate legislation, the provisions of this article.

Amendment XV

Section 1. The right of citizens fo the United States to vote shall not be denied or abridged by the United States or by any State on account of race, color, or previous condition of servitude.

Section 2. The Congress shall have power to enforce this article by appropriate legislation.

Amendment XVI

The Congress shall have power to lay and collect taxes on incomes, from whatever source derived, without apportionment among the several States, and without regard to any census or enumeration.

Amendment XVII

Section 1. The Senate of the United States shall be composed of two Senators from each State, elected by the people thereof, for six years; and each Senator shall have one vote. The electors in each State shall have the qualifications requisite for electors of the most numerous branch of the State legislatures.

Section 2. When vacancies happen in the representation of any State in the Senate, the executive authority of such State shall issue writs of election to fill such vacancies: *Provided,* that the legislature of any State may empower the executive thereof to make temporary appointments until the people fill the vacancies by electino as the legislature may direct.

Section 3. This amendment shall not be so construed as to affect the election or term of any Senator chosen before it becomes valid as part of the Constitution.

Amendment XVIII

Section 1. After one year from the ratification of this article the manufacture, sale, or transportation of intoxicating liquors within, the importation thereof into, or the exportation thereof from the United States and all territory subject to the jurisdiction thereof for beverage purposes is hereby prohibited.

Section 2. The Congress and the several States shall have concurrent power to enforce this article by appropriate legislation.

Section 3. This article shall be inoperative unless it shall have been ratified as an amendment to the Constitution by the legislatures of the several States, as provided in the Constitution, within seven years from the date of the submission hereof to the States by the Congress.

Amendment XIX

Section 1. The right of citizens of the United States to vote shall not be denied or abridged by the United States or by any State on account of sex.

Section 2. Congress shall have power to enforce this article by appropriate legislation.

Amendment XX

Section 1. The terms of the President and Vice President shall end at noon on the 20th day of January, and the terms of Senators and Representatives at noon on the 3d day of January, of the years in which such terms would have ended if this article had not been ratified; and the terms of their successors shall then begin.

Section 2. The congress shall assemble at least once in every year, and such meeting shall begin at noon on the 3d day of January, unless they shall by law appoint a different day.

Section 3. If, at the time fixed for the beginning of the term of the President, the President elect shall have died, the Vice President elect shall become President. If a President shall not have been chosen before the time fixed for the beginning of his term, or it the President elect shall have failed to qualify, then the Vice President elect shall act as President until a President shall have qualified; and the Congress may by law provide for the case wherein neither a President elect nor a Vice President elect

shall have qualified, declaring who shall then act as President, or the manner in which one who is to act shall be selected, and such person shall act accordingly until a President or Vice President shall have qualified.

Section 4. The Congress may by law provide for the case of the death of any of the persons from whom the House of Representatives may choose a president whenever the right of choice shall have devolved upon them, and for the case of the death of any of the persons from whom the Senate may choose a Vice President whenever the right of choice shall have devolved upon them.

Section 5. Sections 1 and 2 shall take effect on the 15th day of October following the ratification of this article.

Section 6. This article shall be inoperative unless it shall have been ratified as an amendment to the Constitution by the legislatures of three-fourths of the several States within seven years from the date of its submission.

Amendment XXI

Section 1. The eighteenth article of amendment to the Constitution of the United States is hereby repealed.

Section 2. The transportation or importation into any State, Territory, or possession of the United States for delivery or use therein of intoxicating liquors, in violation of the laws thereof, is hereby prohibited.

Section 3. This article shall be inoperative unless it shall have been ratified as an amendment to the Constitution by conventions in the several States, as provided in the Constitution, within seven years from the date of the submission hereof to the States by the Congress.

Amendment XXII

Section 1. No person shall be elected to the office of the President more than twice, and no person who has held the office of President, or acted as President, for more than two years of a term to which some other person was elected President shall be elected to the office of the President more than once. But this article shall not apply to any person holding the office of President when this article was proposed by the Congress, and shall not prevent any person who may be holding the office of President, or acting as President, during the term within which this article becomes operative from holding the office of President or acting as President during the remainder of such term.

Section 2. This article shall be inoperative unless it shall have been ratified as an amendment to the Constitution by the legislatures of three-fourths of the several States within seven years from the date of its submission to the States by the Congress.

Amendment XXIII

Section 1. The District constituting the seat of Government of the United States shall appoint in such manner as the Congress may direct:

A number of electors of President and Vice President equal to the whole number of Senators and Representatives in Congress to which the District would be entitled if it were a State, but in no event more than the least populous State; they shall be in addition to those appointed by the States, but they shall be considered, for the purposes of the election of President and Vice President, to be electors appointed by a State, and they shall meet in the District and perform such duties as provided by the twelfth article of amendment.

Section 2. The Congress shall have power to enforce this article by appropriate legislation.

Amendment XXIV

Section 1. The right of citizens of the United States to vote in any primary or other election for President or Vice President, for electors for President or Vice President, or for Senator or Representative in Congress, shall not be denied or abridged by the United States or any State by reason of failure to pay any poll tax or other tax.

Section 2. The Congress shall have power to enforce this article by appropriate legislation.

Amendment XXV

Section 1. In case of the removal of the President from office or of his death or resignation, the Vice President shall become President.

Section 2. Whenever there is a vacancy in the office of the Vice President, the President shall nominate a Vice President who shall take office upon confirmation by a majority vote of both Houses of Congress.

Section 3. Whenever the President transmits to the President pro tempore of the Senate and the Speaker of the House of Representatives his written declaration that he is unable to discharge the powers and duties of his office, and until he transmits to them a written declaration to the contrary, such powers and duties shall be discharged by the Vice President as Acting President.

Section 4. Whenever the Vice President and a majority of either the principal officers of the executive departments or of such other body as Congress may by law provide, transmit to the President pro tempore of the Senate and the Speaker of the House of Representatives their written declaration that the President is unable to discharge the powers and duties of his office, the Vice President shall immediately assume the powers and duties of the office as Acting President.

Thereafter, when the President transmits to the President pro tempore of the Senate and the Speaker of the House of Representatives his written declaration that no inability exists, he shall resume the powers and duties of his office unless the Vice President and a majority of either the principal officers of the executive department or of such other body as Congress may by law provide, transmit within four days to the President pro tempore of the Senate and the Speaker of the House of Representatives their written declaration that the President is unable to discharge the powers and duties of his office. Thereupon Congress shall decide the issue, assembling within forty-eight hours for that purpose if not in session. If the congress, within twenty-one days after receipt of the latter written declaration, or, if Congress is not in session, within twenty-one days after Congress is required to assemble, determines by two-thirds vote of both Houses that the President is unable to discharge the powers and duties of his office, the Vice President shall continue to discharge the same as Acting President; otherwise, the President shall resume the powers and duties of his office.

Amendment XXVI
Section 1. The right of citizens of the United States who are eighteen years of age or older, to vote shall not be denied or abridged by the United States or by any State on account of age.
Section 2. The Congress shall have power to enforce this article by appropriate legislation.

Amendment XXVII
No law varying the compensation for the services of the Senators and Representatives shall take effect, until an election of Representatives shall have intervened.

APPENDIX 2

Presidents, Vice Presidents, and Terms of Office

President	Term of Service	Vice President
George Washington	Apr. 30, 1789–Mar. 4, 1793	John Adams
George Washington	Mar. 4, 1793–Mar. 4, 1797	John Adams
John Adams	Mar. 4, 1797–Mar. 4, 1801	Thomas Jefferson
Thomas Jefferson	Mar. 4, 1801–Mar. 4, 1805	Aaron Burr
Thomas Jefferson	Mar. 4, 1805–Mar. 4, 1809	George Clinton
James Madison	Mar. 4, 1809–Mar. 4, 1813	George Clinton
James Madison	Mar. 4, 1813–Mar. 4, 1817	Elbridge Gerry
James Monroe	Mar. 4, 1817–Mar. 4, 1821	Daniel Tompkins
James Monroe	Mar. 4, 1921–Mar. 4, 1825	Daniel Tompkins
John Quincy Adams	Mar. 4, 1825–Mar. 4, 1829	John C. Calhoun
Andrew Jackson	Mar. 4, 1829–Mar. 4, 1833	John C. Calhoun
Andrew Jackson	Mar. 4, 1833–Mar. 4, 1837	Martin Van Buren
Martin Van Buren	Mar. 4, 1837–Mar. 4, 1841	Richard M. Johnson
William Henry Harrison	Mar. 4, 1841–Apr. 4, 1841	John Tyler
John Tyler	Apr. 6, 1841–Mar. 4, 1845	
James K. Polk	Mar. 4, 1845–Mar. 4, 1849	George Dallas
Zachary Taylor	Mar. 4, 1849–July 9, 1850	Millard Fillmore
Millard Fillmore	July 10, 1850–Mar. 4, 1853	
Franklin Pierce	Mar. 4, 1853–Mar. 4, 1857	William King
James Buchanan	Mar. 4, 1857–Mar. 4, 1861	John C. Breckinridge
Abraham Lincoln	Mar. 4, 1861–Mar. 4, 1865	Hannibal Hamlin
Abraham Lincoln	Mar. 4, 1865–Apr. 15, 1865	Andrew Johnson
Andrew Johnson	Apr. 15, 1865–Mar. 4, 1869	
Ulysses S. Grant	Mar. 4, 1869–Mar. 4, 1873	Schuyler Colfax
Ulysses S. Grant	Mar. 4, 1873–Mar. 4, 1877	Henry Wilson
Rutherford B. Hayes	Mar. 4, 1877–Mar. 4, 1881	William Wheeler
James A. Garfield	Mar. 4, 1881–Sept. 19, 1881	Chester Alan Arthur
Chester Alan Arthur	Sept. 20, 1881–Mar. 4, 1885	
Grover Cleveland	Mar. 4, 1885–Mar. 4, 1889	Thomas Hendricks
Benjamin Harrison	Mar. 4, 1889–Mar. 4, 1893	Levi Morton
Grover Cleveland	Mar. 4, 1893–Mar. 4, 1897	Adlai Stevenson
Wiliam McKinley	Mar. 4, 1897–Mar. 4, 1901	Garret Hobart
William McKinley	Mar. 4, 1901–Sept. 14, 1901	Theodore Roosevelt
Theodore Roosevelt	Sept. 14, 1901–Mar. 4, 1905	
Theodore Roosevelt	Mar. 4, 1905–Mar. 4, 1909	Charles Fairbanks
William Howard Taft	Mar. 4, 1909–Mar. 4, 1913	James Sherman
Woodrow Wilson	Mar. 4, 1913–Mar. 4, 1917	Thomas Marshall

President	Term of Service	Vice President
Woodrow Wilson	Mar. 4, 1917–Mar. 4, 1921	Thomas Marshall
Warren G. Harding	Mar. 4, 1921–Aug. 2, 1923	Calvin Coolidge
Calvin Coolidge	Aug. 2, 1923–Mar. 4, 1925	
Calvin Coolidge	Mar. 4, 1925–Mar. 4, 1929	Charles Dawes
Herbert D. Hoover	Mar 4, 1929–Mar. 4, 1933	Charles Curtis
Franklin D. Roosevelt	Mar. 4, 1933–Jan. 20, 1937	John Nance Garner
Franklin D. Roosevelt	Jan. 20, 1937–Jan. 20, 1941	John Nance Garner
Franklin D. Roosevelt	Jan. 20, 1941–Jan. 20, 1945	Henry Wallace
Franklin D. Roosevelt	Jan. 20, 1945–Apr. 12, 1945	Harry S. Truman
Harry S. Truman	Apr. 12, 1945–Jan. 20, 1949	
Harry S. Truman	Jan. 20, 1949–Jan. 20, 1953	Alben Barkley
Dwight D. Eisenhower	Jan. 20, 1953–Jan. 20, 1957	Richard M. Nixon
Dwight D. Eisenhower	Jan. 20, 1957–Jan. 20, 1961	Richard M. Nixon
John F. Kennedy	Jan. 20, 1961–Nov. 22, 1963	Lyndon B. Johnson
Lyndon B. Johnson	Nov. 22, 1963–Jan. 20, 1965	
Lyndon B. Johnson	Jan. 20, 1965–Jan. 20, 1969	Hubert H. Humphrey
Richard M. Nixon	Jan. 20, 1969–Jan. 20, 1973	Spiro T. Agnew
Richard M. Nixon	Jan. 20, 1973–Aug. 9, 1974	Spiro T. Agnew
		Gerald R. Ford
Gerald R. Ford	Aug. 9, 1974–Jan. 20, 1977	Nelson Rockefeller
Jimmy Carter	Jan. 20, 1977–Jan. 20, 1981	Walter F. Mondale
Ronald Reagan	Jan. 20, 1981–Jan. 20, 1985	George Bush
Ronald Reagan	Jan. 20, 1985–Jan. 20, 1989	George Bush
George Bush	Jan. 20, 1989–Jan. 20, 1993	J. Danforth Quayle
Bill Clinton	Jan. 20, 1993–Jan. 20, 1997	Albert Gore, Jr.
Bill Clinton	Jan. 20, 1997–Jan. 20, 2001	Albert Gore, Jr.

APPENDIX 3

Presidential Election Results

Year	Name	Party	Popular Vote	Electoral College Vote
1789	George Washington	Federalist	—	69
1792	George Washington	Federalist	—	132
1796	John Adams	Federalist	—	71
	Thomas Jefferson	Democratic-Republican	—	68
1800	Thomas Jefferson	Democratic-Republican	—	73
	John Adams	Federalist	—	65
1804	Thomas Jefferson	Democratic-Republican	—	162
	Charles C. Pinckney	Federalist	—	14
1808	James Madison	Democratic-Republican	—	122
	Charles C. Pinckney	Federalist	—	47
1812	James Madison	Democratic-Republican	—	128
	George Clinton	Federalist	—	89
1816	James Monroe	Democratic-Republican	—	183
	Rufus King	Federalist	—	34
1820	James Monroe	Democratic-Republican	—	231
	John Quincy Adams	Democratic-Republican	—	1
1824	John Quincy Adams	Democratic-Republican	108,740	84
	Andrew Jackson	Democratic-Republican	153,544	99
	William Crawford	Democratic-Republican	46,618	41
	Henry Clay	Democratic-Republican	47,136	37
1828	Andrew Jackson	Democrat	647,286	178
	John Quincy Adams	National Republican	508,064	83
1832	Andrew Jackson	Democrat	687,502	219
	Henry Clay	National Republican	530,189	49
	Electoral votes not cast		2	
1836	Martin Van Buren	Democrat	765,483	170
	William Henry Harrison	Whig	550,816	73
	Hugh White	Whig	146,107	26
	Daniel Webster	Whig	41,201	14
	Total for the 3 Whigs		739,795	113
1840	William Henry Harrison	Whig	1,274,624	234
	Martin Van Buren	Democrat	1,127,781	60
1844	James K. Polk	Democrat	1,338,464	170
	Henry Clay	Whig	1,300,097	105
1848	Zachary Taylor	Whig	1,360,967	163
	Lewis Cass	Democrat	1,222,342	127

Year	Name	Party	Popular Vote	Electoral College Vote
	Martin Van Buren	Free-Soil	291,263	—
1852	Franklin Pierce	Democrat	1,601,117	254
	Winfield Scott	Whig	1,385,453	42
	John P. Hale	Free-Soil	155,825	—
1856	James Buchanan	Democrat	1,832,955	174
	John Frémont	Republican	1,339,932	114
	Millard Fillmore	Whig-American	871,731	8
1860	Abraham Lincoln	Republican	1,865,593	180
	John C. Breckinridge	Democratic	848,356	72
	Stephen Douglas	Democrat	1,382,713	12
	John Bell	Constitutional Union	592,906	39
1864	Abraham Lincoln	Unionist (Republican)	2,206,938	212
	George McClellan	Democrat	1,803,787	21
	Electoral votes not cast			81
1868	Ulysses S. Grant	Republican	3,013,421	214
	Horatio Seymour	Democrat	2,706,829	80
	Electoral votes not cast			23
1872	Ulysses S. Grant	Republican	3,596,745	286
	Horace Greeley	Democrat	2,843,446	
	Thomas Hendricks	Democrat	—	42
	Benjamin Brown	Democrat	—	18
	Charles Jenkins	Democrat	—	2
	David Davis	Democrat	—	1
1876	Rutherford B. Hayes	Republican	4,036,572	185
	Samuel Tilden	Democrat	4,284,020	184
	Peter Cooper	Greenback	81,737	—
1880	James A. Garfield	Republican	4,453,295	214
	Winfield S. Hancock	Democrat	4,414,082	155
	James B. Weaver	Greenback-Labor	308,578	—
1884	Grover Cleveland	Democrat	4,879,507	219
	James G. Blaine	Republican	4,850,293	182
	Benjamin Butler	Greenback-Labor	175,370	—
	John St. John	Prohibition	150,369	—
1888	Benjamin Harrison	Republican	5,447,129	233
	Grover Cleveland	Democrat	5,537,857	168
	Clinton Fisk	Prohibition	249,506	—
	Anson Streeter	Union Labor	146,935	—
1892	Grover Cleveland	Democrat	5,555,426	277
	Benjamin Harrison	Republican	5,182,690	145
	James B. Weaver	People's	1,029,846	22
	John Bidwell	Prohibition	264,133	—
1896	William McKinley	Republican	7,102,246	271
	William J. Bryan	Democrat	6,492,559	176
	John Palmer	National Democratic	133,148	—
	Joshua Levering	Prohibition	132,007	—
1900	William McKinley	Republican	7,218,491	292
	William J. Bryan	Democrat	6,356,734	155

Year	Name	Party	Popular Vote	Electoral College Vote
	John C. Wooley	Prohibition	208,914	—
	Eugene V. Debs	Socialist	87,814	—
1904	Theodore Roosevelt	Republican	7,628,461	336
	Alton B. Parker	Democrat	5,084,223	140
	Eugene V. Debs	Socialist	402,283	—
	Silas Swallow	Prohibition	258,536	—
	Thomas Watson	People's	117,183	—
1908	William Howard Taft	Republican	7,675,320	321
	William J. Bryan	Democrat	6,412,294	162
	Eugene V. Debs	Socialist	420,793	—
	Eugene Chafin	Prohibition	253,840	—
1912	Woodrow Wilson	Democrat	6,296,547	435
	William Howard Taft	Republican	3,486,720	8
	Theodore Roosevelt	Progressive	4,118,571	86
	Eugene V. Debs	Socialist	900,672	—
	Eugene Chafin	Prohibition	206,275	—
1916	Woodrow Wilson	Democrat	9,127,695	277
	Charles E. Hughes	Republican	8,533,507	254
	A. L. Benson	Socialist	585,113	—
	J. Frank Hanly	Prohibition	220,506	—
1920	Warren Harding	Republican	16,143,407	404
	James M. Cox	Democrat	9,130,328	127
	Eugene V. Debs	Socialist	919,799	—
	P. P. Christensen	Farmer-Labor	265,411	—
	Aaron Watkins	Prohibition	189,408	—
1924	Calvin Coolidge	Republican	15,718,211	382
	John W. Davis	Democrat	8,385,283	136
	Robert La Follette	Progressive	4,831,289	13
1928	Herbert C. Hoover	Republican	21,391,993	444
	Alfred E. Smith	Democrat	15,016,169	87
	Norman Thomas	Socialist	267,835	—
1932	Franklin D. Roosevelt	Democrat	22,809,638	472
	Herbert C. Hoover	Republican	15,758,901	59
	Norman Thomas	Socialist	881,951	—
	William Foster	Communist	102,785	—
1936	Franklin D. Roosevelt	Democrat	27,752,869	523
	Alfred M. Landon	Republican	16,674,665	8
	William Lemke	Union	882,479	—
	Norman Thomas	Socialist	187,720	—
1940	Franklin D. Roosevelt	Democrat	27,307,819	449
	Wendell Willkie	Republican	22,321,018	82
1944	Franklin D. Roosevelt	Democrat	25,606,585	432
	Thomas E. Dewey	Republican	22,014,745	99
1948	Harry S. Truman	Democrat	24,179,345	303
	Thomas E. Dewey	Republican	21,991,291	189
	Strom Thurmond	Dixiecrat	1,176,125	39
	Henry Wallace	Progressive	1,157,326	—
	Norman Thomas	Socialist	139,572	—
	Claude A. Watson	Prohibition	103,900	—

Year	Name	Party	Popular Vote	Electoral College Vote
1952	Dwight D. Eisenhower	Republican	33,936,234	442
	Adlai Stevenson II	Democrat	27,314,992	89
	Vincent Hallinan	Progressive	140,023	—
1956	Dwight D. Eisenhower	Republican	35,590,472	457
	Adlai Stevenson II	Democrat	26,022,752	73
	T. Coleman Andrews	States' Rights	111,178	—
	Walter B. Jones	Democrat	—	1
1960	John F. Kennedy	Democrat	34,226,731	303
	Richard M. Nixon	Republican	34,108,157	219
	Harry Byrd	Democrat	—	15
1964	Lyndon B. Johnson	Democrat	43,129,566	486
	Barry Goldwater	Republican	27,178,188	52
1968	Richard M. Nixon	Republican	31,785,480	301
	Hubert H. Humphrey	Democrat	31,275,166	191
	George Wallace	American Independent	9,906,473	46
1972	Richard M. Nixon	Republican	47,170,179	520
	George McGovern	Democrat	29,171,791	17
	John Hospers	Libertarian	—	1
1976	Jimmy Carter	Democrat	40,830,763	297
	Gerald R. Ford	Republican	39,147,793	240
	Ronald Reagan	Republican	—	1
1980	Ronald Reagan	Republican	43,904,153	489
	Jimmy Carter	Democrat	35,483,883	49
	John Anderson	Independent candidacy	5,719,437	—
1984	Ronald Reagan	Republican	54,455,074	525
	Walter F. Mondale	Democrat	37,577,137	13
1988	George Bush	Republican	48,881,278	426
	Michael Dukakis	Democrat	41,805,374	111
	Lloyd Bentsen	Democrat	—	1
1992	Bill Clinton	Democrat	43,727,625	370
	George Bush	Republican	38,165,180	168
	Ross Perot	Independent candidacy	19,236,411	0
1996	Bill Clinton	Democrat	45,628,667	379
	Bob Dole	Republican	37,869,435	159
	Ross Perot	Independent candidacy	7,874,283	0
2000	George W. Bush	Republican	49,820,518	271
	Albert Gore Jr.	Democrat	50,158,094	267

NOTES

- In 1872, the Democratic Presidential nominee, Horace Greeley, died after the popular votes were cast but before the electors had met. Since the Democrats had lost the election to the Republican candidate, President Ulysses S. Grant, the Democratic electors felt no need to unite behind a single candidate. Instead, they split their votes among four Democratic politicians who had not run for the Presidency or received any popular votes in the election.
- In 1956 a Stevenson elector cast his ballot for Walter B. Jones.
- In 1960 Senator Harry Byrd of Virginia won the electoral votes in his state from an

uncommitted slate of electors that had won the popular vote, and he also picked up an electoral vote in Oklahoma from a Nixon elector.

- In 1968 a Nixon elector voted for George Wallace.
- In 1972 a Nixon elector voted for John Hospers.
- In 1976 a Ford elector voted for Ronald Reagan.
- In 1988 a Dukakis elector voted for Lloyd Bentsen for President, even though Bentsen was running on the Democratic ticket for Vice President.

SOURCES
The statistics given here are the best estimates available based on currently accepted data; election statistics vary widely from source to source. 1789–1968 data from U.S. Bureau of the Census, *Historical Statistics of the United States, Colonial Times to 1970,* Washington, D.C.: Government Printing Office, 1975. 1972–88 data from *Presidential Elections since 1789,* 5th ed., Washington, D.C.: Congressional Quarterly, 1991.

APPENDIX 4

Table of Congresses

(Senate listed above, House listed below in italics)

Congress	Years & President(s)	Majority Party	Minority Party	Others	Total
1st	1789–91	Pro-Administration–18	Anti-Administration–8		26
	Washington	*Pro-Administration–37*	*Anti-Administration–28*		*65*
2nd	1791–93	Federalist–16	Anti-Federalist–13	1 vacant	30
	Washington	*Federalist–39*	*Anti-Federalist–30*		*69*
3rd	1793–95	Federalist–16	Anti-Federalist–14		30
	Washington	*Federalist–54*	*Anti-Federalist–51*		*105*
4th	1795–97	Federalist–21	Democratic-Republican–11		32
	Washington	*Democratic-Republican–59*	*Federalist–47*		*106*
5th	1797–99	Federalist–22	Democratic-Republican–10		32
	J. Adams	*Federalist–57*	*Democratic-Republican–49*		*106*
6th	1799–1801	Federalist–22	Democratic-Republican–10		32
	J. Adams	*Federalist–60*	*Democratic-Republican–46*		*106*
7th	1801–03	Democratic-Republican–17	Federalist–15	2 vacant	34
	Jefferson	*Democratic-Republican–68*	*Federalist–38*	*1 vacant*	*107*
8th	1803–05	Democratic-Republican–25	Federalist–9		34
	Jefferson	*Democratic-Republican–103*	*Federalist–39*		*142*
9th	1805–07	Democratic-Republican–27	Federalist–7		34
	Jefferson	*Democratic-Republican–114*	*Federalist–28*		*142*

Congress	Years & President(s)	Majority Party	Minority Party	Others	Total
10th	1807–09 Jefferson	Democratic-Republican–28	Federalist–6		34
	Jefferson	*Democratic-Republican–116*	*Federalist–26*		*142*
11th	1809–11 Madison	Democratic-Republican–27	Federalist–7		34
	Madison	*Democratic-Republican–92*	*Federalist–50*		*142*
12th	1811–13 Madison	Democratic-Republican–30	Federalist–6		36
	Madison	*Democratic-Republican–107*	*Federalist–36*		*143*
13th	1813–15 Madison	Democratic-Republican–28	Federalist–8		36
	Madison	*Democratic-Republican–114*	*Federalist–68*		*182*
14th	1815–17 Madison	Democratic-Republican–26	Federalist–12		38
	Madison	*Democratic-Republican–119*	*Federalist–64*		*183*
15th	1817–19 Monroe	Democratic-Republican–30	Federalist–12		42
	Monroe	*Democratic-Republican–146*	*Federalist–39*		*185*
16th	1819–21 Monroe	Democratic-Republican–37	Federalist–9		46
	Monroe	*Democratic-Republican–160*	*Federalist–26*		*186*
17th	1821–23 Monroe	Democratic-Republican–44	Federalist–4		48
	Monroe	*Democratic-Republican–155*	*Federalist–32*		*187*
18th	1823–25 Monroe	Democratic-Republican–43	Federalist–5		48
	Monroe	*Democratic-Republican–189*	*Federalist–24*		*213*
19th	1825–27 J. Q. Adams	Jacksonian–26	Adams–22		48
	J. Q. Adams	*Adams–109*	*Jacksonian–104*		*213*
20th	1827–29 J. Q. Adams	Jacksonian–27	Adams–21		48
	J. Q. Adams	*Jacksonian–113*	*Adams–100*		*213*
21st	1829–31 Jackson	Democrat–25	National Republican–23		48
	Jackson	*Democrat–136*	*National Republican–72*	5	*213*
22nd	1831–33 Jackson	Democrat–24	National Republican–22	2	48
	Jackson	*Democrat–126*	*National Republican–66*	21	*213*
23rd	1833–35 Jackson	National Republican–26	Democrat–20	2	48
	Jackson	*Democrat–143*	*National Republican–63*	34	*240*

Congress	Years	President	Majority party	Minority party	Other	Total
24th	1835–37	Jackson	Democrat-26	National Republican-24	2	52
			Democrat-143	*National Republican-75*	*24*	*242*
25th	1837–39	Van Buren	Democrat-35	Whig-17		52
			Democrat-128	*Whig-100*	*14*	*242*
26th	1839–41	Van Buren	Democrat-30	Whig-22		52
			Democrat-125	*Whig-109*	*8*	*242*
27th	1841–43	W. H. Harrison / Tyler	Whig-29	Democrat-22	1 vacant	52
			Whig-142	*Democrat-98*	*2*	*242*
28th	1843–45	Tyler	Whig-29	Democrat-23		52
			Democrat-147	*Whig-72*	*3*	*223*
29th	1845–47	Polk	Democrat-34	Whig-22	2 vacant	58
			Democrat-142	*Whig-79*	*6 (1 vacant)*	*228*
30th	1847–49	Polk	Democrat-38	Whig-21	1	60
			Whig-116	*Democrat-110*	*4*	*230*
31st	1849–51	Taylor / Fillmore	Democrat-35	Whig-25	2	62
			Democrat-113	*Whig-108*	*11 (1 vacant)*	*233*
32nd	1851–53	Fillmore	Democrat-36	Whig-23	3	62
			Democrat-127	*Whig-85*	*21*	*234*
33rd	1853–55	Pierce	Democrat-38	Whig-22	2	62
			Democrat-157	*Whig-71*	*6*	*234*
34th	1855–57	Pierce	Democrat-39	Whig/Republican-22	1	62
			Whig/Republican-100	*Democrat-83*	*51*	*234*
35th	1857–59	Buchanan	Democrat-41	Republican-20	5	66
			Democrat-132	*Republican-90*	*15*	*237*
36th	1859–61	Buchanan	Democrat-38	Republican-26	2 (2 vacant)	68
			Republican-116	*Democrat-83*	*39*	*238*
37th	1861–63	Lincoln	Republican-31	Democrat-15	3 (1 vacant)	50
			Republican-108	*Democrat-44*	*31*	*183*
38th	1863–65	Lincoln	Republican-33	Democrat-10	9	52
			Republican-85	*Democrat-72*	*27*	*184*

Congress	Years & President(s)	Majority Party	Minority Party	Others	Total
39th	1865–67 Lincoln, A. Johnson	Republican–39	Democrat–11	4	54
		Republican–136	*Democrat–38*	*19*	*193*
40th	1867–69 A. Johnson	Republican–57	Democrat–9	2 vacant	68
		Republican–173	*Democrat–47*	*4 (2 vacant)*	*226*
41st	1869–71 Grant	Republican–62	Democrat–12		74
		Republican–171	*Democrat–67*	*5*	*243*
42nd	1871–73 Grant	Republican–56	Democrat–17	1	74
		Republican–136	*Democrat–104*	*3*	*243*
43rd	1873–75 Grant	Republican–47	Democrat–19	7 (1 vacant)	74
		Republican–199	*Democrat–88*	*5*	*292*
44th	1875–77 Grant	Republican–46	Democrat–28	1 (1 vacant)	76
		Democrat–182	*Republican–103*	*8*	*293*
45th	1877–79 Hayes	Republican–40	Democrat–35	1	76
		Democrat–155	*Republican–136*	*2*	*293*
46th	1879–81 Hayes	Democrat–42	Republican–33	1	76
		Democrat–141	*Republican–132*	*20*	*293*
47th	1881–83 Garfield, Arthur	Republican–37	Democrat–37	2	76
		Republican–151	*Democrat–128*	*14*	*293*
48th	1883–85 Arthur	Republican–38	Democrat–36	2	76
		Democrat–196	*Republican–117*	*12*	*325*
49th	1885–87 Cleveland	Republican–42	Democrat–34		76
		Democrat–182	*Republican–141*	*2*	*325*
50th	1887–89 Cleveland	Republican–39	Democrat–37		76
		Democrat–167	*Republican–152*	*6*	*325*
51st	1889–91 B. Harrison	Republican–51	Democrat–37		88
		Republican–179	*Democrat–152*	*1*	*332*
52nd	1891–93 B. Harrison	Republican–47	Democrat–39	2	88
		Democrat–238	*Republican–86*	*8*	*332*

Congress	Years	President				
53rd	1893–95	Cleveland	Democrat–44	*Republican–40*	4	*88*
			Democrat–218	*Republican–124*	14	*356*
54th	1895–97	Cleveland	Republican–44	*Democrat–40*	6	*90*
			Republican–254	*Democrat–93*	10	*356*
55th	1897–99	McKinley	Republican–44	*Democrat–34*	12	*90*
			Republican–206	*Democrat–124*	27	*357*
56th	1899–1901	McKinley	Republican–53	*Democrat–26*	10 (1 vacant)	*90*
			Republican–187	*Democrat–161*	9	*357*
57th	1901–03	McKinley	Republican–56	*Democrat–32*	2	*90*
		T. Roosevelt	Republican–200	*Democrat–151*	6	*357*
58th	1903–05	T. Roosevelt	Republican–57	*Democrat–33*		*90*
			Republican–297	*Democrat–176*	8	*386*
59th	1905–07	T. Roosevelt	Republican–58	*Democrat–32*		*90*
			Republican–215	*Democrat–135*		*386*
60th	1907–09	T. Roosevelt	Republican–61	*Democrat–31*		*92*
			Republican–223	*Democrat–167*	1	*391*
61st	1909–11	Taft	Republican–60	*Democrat–32*		*92*
			Republican–219	*Democrat–172*		*391*
62nd	1911–13	Taft	Republican–52	*Democrat–44*		*96*
			Democrat–230	*Republican–162*	2	*394*
63rd	1913–15	Wilson	Democrat–51	*Republican–44*	1	*96*
			Democrat–291	*Republican–134*	10	*435*
64th	1915–17	Wilson	Democrat–56	*Republican–40*		*96*
			Democrat–230	*Republican–196*	9	*435*
65th	1917–19	Wilson	Democrat–54	*Republican–42*		*96*
			Republican–215	*Democrat–214*	6	*435*
66th	1919–21	Wilson	Republican–49	*Democrat–47*		*96*
			Republican–240	*Democrat–192*	2 (1 vacant)	*435*
67th	1921–23	Harding	Republican–59	*Democrat–37*		*96*
			Republican–302	*Democrat–131*	2	*435*

Congress	Years & President(s)	Majority Party	Minority Party	Others	Total
68th	1923–25 Harding Coolidge	Republican–53	Democrat–42	1	96
		Republican–225	Democrat–207	3	435
69th	1925–27 Coolidge	Republican–54	Democrat–41	1	96
		Republican–247	Democrat–183	5	435
70th	1927–29 Coolidge	Republican–48	Democrat–46	1 (1 vacant)	96
		Republican–238	Democrat–194	3	435
71st	1929–31 Hoover	Republican–56	Democrat–39	1	96
		Republican–270	Democrat–164	1	435
72nd	1931–33 Hoover	Republican–48	Democrat–47	1	96
		Democrat–217	Republican–217	1	435
73rd	1933–35 F. Roosevelt	Democrat–59	Republican–36	1	96
		Democrat–313	Republican–117	5	435
74th	1935–37 F. Roosevelt	Democrat–69	Republican–25	2	96
		Democrat–322	Republican–103	10	435
75th	1937–39 F. Roosevelt	Democrat–76	Republican–16	4	96
		Democrat–334	Republican–88	13	435
76th	1939–41 F. Roosevelt	Democrat–69	Republican–23	4	96
		Democrat–262	Republican–169	4	435
77th	1941–43 F. Roosevelt	Democrat–66	Republican–28	2	96
		Democrat–267	Republican–162	3	435
78th	1943–45 F. Roosevelt	Democrat–57	Republican–38	1	96
		Democrat–222	Republican–209	2	435
79th	1945–47 F. Roosevelt Truman	Democrat–57	Republican–38	1	96
		Democrat–242	Republican–191	2	435
80th	1947–49 Truman	Republican–51	Democrat–45		96
		Republican–246	Democrat–188	1	435

Congress	Years	President	Party	Party	Other	Total
81st	1949–51	Truman	Democrat–54	Republican–42		96
			Democrat–263	Republican–171	1	435
82nd	1951–53	Truman	Democrat–49	Republican–47		96
			Democrat–235	Republican–199	1	435
83rd	1953–55	Eisenhower	Republican–48	Democrat–47	1	96
			Republican–221	Democrat–213	1	435
84th	1955–57	Eisenhower	Democrat–47	Republican–47	2	96
			Democrat–232	Republican–203		435
85th	1957–59	Eisenhower	Democrat–49	Republican–47		96
			Democrat–234	Republican–201	1	435
86th	1959–61	Eisenhower	Democrat–65	Republican–35		100
			Democrat–283	Republican–153	1	437
87th	1961–63	Kennedy	Democrat–64	Republican–36		100
			Democrat–263	Republican–174		437
88th	1963–65	Kennedy / L. Johnson	Democrat–66	Republican–34		100
			Democrat–259	Republican–176		435
89th	1965–67	L. Johnson	Democrat–68	Republican–32		100
			Democrat–295	Republican–140		435
90th	1967–69	L. Johnson	Democrat–64	Republican–36		100
			Democrat–247	Republican–187	*1 vacant*	435
91st	1969–71	Nixon	Democrat–57	Republican–43		100
			Democrat–243	Republican–192		435
92nd	1971–73	Nixon	Democrat–54	Republican–44	2	100
			Democrat–255	Republican–180		435
93rd	1973–75	Nixon / Ford	Democrat–56	Republican–42	2	100
			Democrat–242	Republican–192	1	435
94th	1975–77	Ford	Democrat–60	Republican–38	2	100
			Democrat–291	Republican–144		435
95th	1977–79	Carter	Democrat–61	Republican–38	1	100
			Democrat–292	Republican–143		435

Congress	Years & President(s)	Majority Party	Minority Party	Others	Total
96th	1979–81 Carter	Democrat–58	Republican–41	1	100
		Democrat–277	Republican–158		435
97th	1981–83 Reagan	Republican–53	Democrat–46	1	100
		Democrat–242	Republican–192		435
98th	1983–85 Reagan	Republican–54	Democrat–46		100
		Democrat–269	Republican–166		435
99th	1985–87 Reagan	Republican–53	Democrat–47		100
		Democrat–253	Republican–182		435
100th	1987–89 Reagan	Democrat–55	Republican–45		100
		Democrat–258	Republican–177		435
101st	1989–91 Bush	Democrat–55	Republican–45		100
		Democrat–260	Republican–174	1 vacant	435
102nd	1991–93 Bush	Democrat–56	Republican–44		100
		Democrat–267	Republican–167	1	435
103rd	1993–95 Clinton	Democrat–57	Republican–43		100
		Democrat–258	Republican–176	1	435
104th	1995–97 Clinton	Republican–54	Democrat–46		100
		Republican–233	Democrat–201	1	435
105th	1997–99 Clinton	Republican–55	Democrat–45		100
		Republican–227	Democrat–207	1	435
106th	1999–2000 Clinton	Republican–55	Democrat–45		100
		Republican–222	Democrat–211	1 (and 1 vacant)	435
107th	2000–2002 Bush	Republican–50	Democrat–50		100
		Republican–221	Democrat–212	2	435

Source: Martis, Kenneth C. *The Historical Atlas of Political Parties in the United States Congress, 1789–89.* New York: Macmillan, 1989.

APPENDIX 5

Terms of the Justices of the U.S. Supreme Court

President/Justice	Oath Taken	Term End
George Washington		
John Jay*	19 Oct. 1789	R 29 June 1795
John Rutledge	15 Feb. 1790	R 5 Mar. 1791
William Cushing	2 Feb. 1790	D 13 Sept. 1810
James Wilson	5 Oct. 1789	D 21 Aug. 1798
John Blair, Jr.	2 Feb. 1790	R 25 Oct. 1795
James Iredell	12 May 1790	D 20 Oct. 1799
Thomas Johnson	R 19 Sep. 1791	
	6 Aug. 1792	R 16 Jan. 1793
William Paterson	11 Mar. 1793	D 9 Sept. 1806
John Rutledge*†	R 12 Aug. 1795	15 Dec. 1795
Samuel Chase	4 Feb. 1796	D 19 June 1811
Oliver Ellsworth*	8 Mar. 1796	R 15 Dec. 1800
John Adams		
Bushrod Washington	R 9 Nov. 1798	
	4 Feb. 1799	D 26 Nov. 1829
Alfred Moore	21 Apr. 1800	R 26 Jan. 1804
John Marshall*	4 Feb. 1801	D 6 July 1835
Thomas Jefferson		
William Johnson	8 May 1804	D 4 Aug. 1834
Henry Brockholst Livingston	R 20 Jan. 1807	
	2 Feb. 1807	D 18 Mar. 1823
Thomas Todd	4 May 1807	D 7 Feb. 1826
James Madison		
Joseph Story	3 Feb. 1812	D 10 Sept. 1845
Gabriel Duvall	23 Nov. 1811	R 14 Jan. 1835
James Monroe		
Smith Thompson	10 Feb. 1824	D 18 Dec. 1843
John Quincy Adams		
Robert Trimble	16 June 1826	D 25 Aug. 1828

President/Justice	Oath Taken	Term End
Andrew Jackson		
John McLean	11 Jan. 1830	D 4 Apr. 1861
Henry Baldwin	18 Jan. 1830	D 21 Apr. 1844
James M. Wayne	14 Jan. 1835	D 5 July 1867
Roger B. Taney*	28 Mar. 1836	D 12 Oct. 1864
Philip P. Barbour	12 May 1836	D 25 Feb. 1841
John Catron	1 May 1837	D 30 May 1865
Martin Van Buren		
John McKinley	9 Jan. 1838	D 19 July 1852
Peter V. Daniel	10 Jan. 1842	D 31 May 1860
John Tyler		
Samuel Nelson	27 Feb. 1845	R 28 Nov. 1872
James K. Polk		
Levi Woodbury	R 23 Sept. 1845	
	3 Jan. 1846	D 4 Sept. 1851
Robert C. Grier	10 Aug. 1846	R 31 Jan. 1870
Millard Fillmore		
Benjamin R. Curtis	R 10 Oct. 1851	R 30 Sept. 1857
Franklin Pierce		
John A. Campbell	11 Apr. 1853	R 30 Apr. 1861
James Buchanan		
Nathan Clifford	21 Jan. 1858	D 25 July 1881
Abraham Lincoln		
Noah H. Swayne	27 Jan. 1862	R 24 Jan. 1881
Samuel F. Miller	21 July 1862	D 13 Oct. 1890
David Davis	10 Dec. 1862	R 4 Mar. 1877
Stephen J. Field	20 May 1863	R 1 Dec. 1897
Salmon P. Chase*	15 Dec. 1864	D 7 May 1873
Ulysses S. Grant		
William Strong	14 Mar. 1870	R 14 Dec. 1880
Joseph P. Bradley	23 Mar. 1870	D 22 Jan. 1892
Ward Hunt	9 Jan. 1873	R 27 Jan. 1882
Morrison R. Waite*	4 Mar. 1874	D 23 Mar. 1888
Rutherford B. Hayes		
John Marshall Harlan	10 Dec. 1877	D 14 Oct. 1911
William B. Woods	5 Jan. 1881	D 14 May 1887
James A. Garfield		
Stanley Matthews	17 May 1881	D 22 Mar. 1889

President/Justice	Oath Taken	Term End
Chester A. Arthur		
Horace Gray	9 Jan. 1882	D 15 Sept. 1902
Samuel Blatchford	3 Apr. 1882	D 7 July 1893
Grover Cleveland		
Lucius Q. C. Lamar	18 Jan. 1888	D 23 Jan. 1893
Melville W. Fuller*	8 Oct. 1888	D 4 July 1910
Benjamin Harrison		
David Brewer	6 Jan. 1890	D 28 Mar. 1910
Henry B. Brown	5 Jan. 1891	R 28 May 1906
George Shiras, Jr.	10 Oct. 1892	R 23 Feb. 1903
Howell E. Jackson	4 Mar. 1893	D 8 Aug. 1895
Grover Cleveland		
Edward D. White	12 Mar. 1894	P 18 Dec. 1910
Rufus W. Peckham	6 Jan. 1896	D 24 Oct. 1909
William McKinley		
Joseph McKenna	26 Jan. 1898	R 5 Jan. 1925
Theodore Roosevelt		
Oliver Wendell Holmes, Jr.	8 Dec. 1902	R 12 Jan. 1932
William R. Day	2 Mar. 1903	R 13 Nov. 1922
William H. Moody	17 Dec. 1906	R 20 Nov. 1910
William H. Taft		
Horace H. Lurton	3 Jan. 1910	D 12 July 1914
Charles E. Hughes	10 Oct. 1910	R 10 June 1916
Edward D. White*†	19 Dec. 1910	D 19 May 1921
Willis Van Devanter	3 Jan. 1911	R 2 June 1937
Joseph R. Lamar	3 Jan. 1911	D 2 Jan. 1916
Mahlon Pitney	18 Mar. 1912	R 31 Dec. 1922
Woodrow Wilson		
James C. McReynolds	5 Sept. 1914	R 31 Jan. 1941
Louis D. Brandeis	5 June 1916	R 13 Feb. 1939
John H. Clarke	1 Aug. 1916	R 18 Sept. 1922
Warren G. Harding		
William H. Taft*	11 July 1921	R 3 Feb. 1930
George Sutherland	2 Oct. 1922	R 17 Jan. 1938
Pierce Butler	2 Jan. 1923	D 16 Nov. 1939
Edward T. Sanford	5 Feb. 1923	D 8 Mar. 1930
Calvin Coolidge		
Harlan F. Stone	2 Mar. 1925	P 2 July 1941

President/Justice	Oath Taken	Term End
Herbert C. Hoover		
Charles E. Hughes*†	24 Feb. 1930	R 1 July 1941
Owen J. Roberts	2 June 1930	R 31 July 1945
Benjamin N. Cardozo	14 Mar. 1932	D 9 July 1938
Franklin D. Roosevelt		
Hugo L. Black	19 Aug. 1937	R 17 Sept. 1971
Stanley F. Reed	31 Jan. 1938	R 25 Feb. 1957
Felix Frankfurter	30 Jan. 1939	R 28 Aug. 1962
William O. Douglas	17 Apr. 1939	R 12 Nov. 1975
Frank Murphy	18 Jan. 1940	D 19 July 1949
Harlan F. Stone*†	3 July 1941	D 22 Apr. 1946
James F. Byrnes	8 July 1941	R 3 Oct. 1942
Robert H. Jackson	11 July 1941	D 9 Oct. 1954
Wiley B. Rutledge	15 Feb. 1943	D 10 Sept. 1949
Harry S. Truman		
Harold H. Burton	1 Oct. 1945	R 13 Oct. 1958
Fred M. Vinson*	24 June 1946	D 8 Sept. 1953
Tom Clark	24 Aug. 1949	R 12 June 1967
Sherman Minton	12 Oct. 1949	R 15 Oct. 1956
Dwight D. Eisenhower		
Earl Warren*	R 5 Oct. 1953	
	2 Mar. 1954	R 23 June 1969
John M. Harlan II	28 Mar. 1955	R 23 Sept. 1971
William J. Brennan, Jr.	R 16 Oct. 1956	
	22 Mar. 1957	R 20 July 1990
Charles E. Whittaker	25 Mar. 1957	R 31 Mar. 1962
Potter Stewart	R 14 Oct. 1958	
	15 May 1959	R 3 July 1981
John F. Kennedy		
Byron R. White	16 Apr. 1962	R 28 June 1993
Arthur J. Goldberg	1 Oct. 1962	R 25 July 1965
Lyndon B. Johnson		
Abe Fortas	4 Oct. 1965	R 14 May 1969
Thurgood Marshall	2 Oct. 1967	R 1 Oct. 1991
Richard M. Nixon		
Warren E. Burger*	23 June 1969	R 26 Sept. 1986
Harry A. Blackmun	9 June 1970	R 3 Aug. 1994
Lewis F. Powell, Jr.	7 Jan. 1972	R 26 June 1987
William H. Rehnquist	7 Jan. 1972	P 26 Sept. 1986
Gerald R. Ford		
John Paul Stevens	19 Dec. 1975	

President/Justice	Oath Taken	Term End
Ronald Reagan		
Sandra Day O'Connor	25 Sept. 1981	
William H. Rehnquist*†	26 Sept. 1986	
Antonin Scalia	26 Sept. 1986	
Anthony M. Kennedy	18 Feb. 1988	
George Bush		
David H. Souter	9 Oct. 1990	
Clarence Thomas	1 Nov. 1991	
Bill Clinton		
Ruth Bader Ginsberg	10 Aug. 1993	
Stephen G. Breyer	3 Aug. 1994	

NOTES
President/Justice column:
Presidents are listed in boldface lines; the justices whom they appointed are beneath.
* = chief justice
† = nomination for promotion to chief justice only; see prior listing for service as associate justice
Oath Taken column:
R = recess appointment; the justice took the office before being confirmed by the Senate; he may have taken a second oath after confirmation
Term End column:
D = died
P = promoted to chief justice; see separate listing for service as chief justice
R = retirement/resignation

VISITING THE WHITE HOUSE

The public may visit the White House on Tuesday through Saturday, 10 A.M. until 12 noon. On the ground floor, visitors may look through the doors of the Vermeil Room and Library; upstairs, on the first floor, they may visit the East Room ballroom, where press conferences are held; the State Dining Room, where official state dinners are held; the Blue Room, used for small formal dinners and entertaining; the Red Room, used by First Ladies to entertain after dinners and for teas; and the Green Room, now used for small receptions, teas, or dinners. Secret Service Tour Officers are available to answer questions.

The second floor contains the family living quarters.

Congressional guided tours are available by contacting the local or Washington office of your congressional representative or senator at least eight to ten weeks in advance.

The White House also sponsors annual spring and fall garden tours, an annual Easter egg roll for children, the lighting of the National Christmas Tree, and three nights of candlelight tours to see Christmas decorations. More than 1.2 million people tour the White House each year.

The White House Visitor Center, located at the southeast corner of 15th and E Streets is open seven days a week, from 7:30 A.M. until 4 P.M.

VISITING CONGRESS

Although you can follow the debates of the House and Senate on television, there is much more of Congress to see during a visit to Capitol Hill. Free public tours of the Capitol are available without appointment during the day, and the galleries are open as long as the House and Senate are in session. (From outside the Capitol you can tell which house is meeting because a flag will fly over the House or Senate wing whenever that chamber is in session.) To obtain gallery passes, go to the offices of your senator or representative in the Senate and House office buildings. Subways and tunnels link these office buildings to the Capitol.

Because Congress does the largest share of its work in committee, you should visit one of the many committee hearings in addition to the floor debates. Each morning the Washington newspapers publish lists of open committee meetings, the subjects of the testimony, and the rooms where these committees will meet (in one of the House or Senate office buildings). Seats are usually available, but those hearings that draw the most media attention will also draw the largest audience, and visitors sometimes must wait in line for available space.

Spend some time on the Capitol grounds as well, to view the Mall from the terraces on the West Front, explore the grotto designed by Frederick Law Olmsted, survey the variety of trees (which are labeled by species), and visit the Botanical Gardens at the base of Capitol Hill. Surrounding the Capitol's East Front plaza, every building that you see represents some function that once took place within the Capitol, including the Supreme Court (which left the Capitol for its own building in 1935) and the Library of Congress (which moved into the first of its three main buildings in 1897). Like the Capitol and congressional office buildings, the Supreme Court and Library of Congress are open and have public exhibition areas.

The Capitol grounds are regularly the scene of much activity: the motorcade of a visiting dignitary, the television cameras set up on the lawn for news broadcasts, school bands performing on the Capitol steps, demonstrators promoting a cause, or the National Symphony Orchestra entertaining in honor of a national holiday. As a citizen, you are a constituent of Congress and a welcomed guest. Make the most of your visit.

VISITING THE SUPREME COURT BUILDING

The public may visit the Supreme Court Building at 1 First Street, S.E., Washington, D.C., every week of the year, Monday through Friday, from 9:00 A.M. until 4:30 P.M. except on legal holidays. More than 700,000 people annually visit the Supreme Court Building. Visitors have access only to certain parts of the ground floor and first floor of the Supreme Court Building.

Visitors can see a film about the Court in a room on the ground floor. Staff members of the curator's office also give lectures about the Court and its history. Courtroom lectures are presented daily, every hour on the half hour, from 9:30 A.M. to 3:30 P.M., when the Court is not in session.

The courtroom includes seats for about 300 visitors, which are available on a first come, first seated basis. Demand is usually high. The Court is in session to hear oral arguments in the Court chamber (courtroom) from 10:00 A.M. to noon and from 1:00 to 3:00 P.M. on Monday, Tuesday, and Wednesday, for two-week periods each month, beginning on the first Monday in October until the end of April of each year. A session may also be held on Monday of the third week of the month. From mid-May through June, the courtroom sessions convene at 10:00 A.M. The Court uses these sessions to deliver its opinions on cases heard previously.

The exhibit hall on the ground floor contains portraits and statues of the justices and other displays of documents and memorabilia relating to the work of the Court. The curator prepares two exhibits a year using the Court's collections of photographs, prints, films, manuscripts, and other memorabilia. The curator's office also collects decorative and fine arts.

The kiosk of the Supreme Court Historical Society, on the ground floor next to the exhibit hall, sells books and other materials that provide visitors with additional information about the Supreme Court Building and the operations of the Court.

All Presidents
The White House
1600 Pennsylvania Avenue
Washington, D.C. 20500
Tel. 202-456-2203
www.whitehouse.gov

John Adams and John Quincy Adams
John Adams and John Quincy Adams
Birthplace
Quincy Historical Society
133-141 Franklin Street
Quincy, Mass. 02269
Tel. 617-773-1177

Adams National Historic Site
135 Adams Street
Quincy, Mass. 02269
Tel. 617-770-1175
www.nps.gov/adam

Chester Alan Arthur
Chester A. Arthur Historic Site
(birthplace replica)
Fairfield, Vt. 05455
Tel. 802-828-3051

James Buchanan
Wheatland, home of James Buchanan
1120 Marietta Avenue
Lancaster, Pa. 17603
Tel. 717-392-8721
www.wheatland.org

George Bush
George Bush Presidential Library and
Museum
Texas A&M University
1000 George Bush Drive West

College Station, Tex. 77845
Tel. 409-260-9552
http://bushlibrary.tamu.edu

Jimmy Carter
Jimmy Carter Library
One Copenhill Avenue
Atlanta, Ga. 30307
Tel. 404-331-3942
http://carterlibrary.galileo.peachnet.edu

Grover Cleveland
Grover Cleveland Birthplace
207 Bloomfield Avenue
Caldwell, N. J. 07006
Tel. 201-226-1810

Calvin Coolidge
Calvin Coolidge Homestead
Route 100A
Plymouth Notch, Vt. 05056
Tel. 802-672-3773

Dwight David Eisenhower
Dwight D. Eisenhower Library
SE Fourth Street
Abilene, Kans. 67410
Tel. 785-263-4751/1-877-RINGIKE
www.eisenhower.utexas.edu

Eisenhower Birthplace State Historic Site
208 East Day Street
Denison, Tex. 75020
Tel. 903-465-8908
www.eisenhowerbirthplace.org

Eisenhower National Historic Site
Gettysburg National Military Park
97 Taneytown Road

Gettysburg, Pa. 17325
Tel. 717-338-9114
www.nps.gov/eise/home

Millard Fillmore
Replica of birthplace
Fillmore Glen State Park
Moravia, N. Y. 13118
Tel. 315-497-0130

Millard Fillmore House
24 Shearer Avenue
East Aurora, N.Y. 14052
Tel. 716-652-8875

Gerald R. Ford
Gerald R. Ford Library
1000 Beal Avenue
Ann Arbor, Mich. 48109-2114
Tel. 734-741-2218
www.ford.utexas.edu

Gerald R. Ford Museum
303 Pearl Street
Grand Rapids, Mich. 49504
Tel. 616-451-9263
www.ford.utexas.edu

James A. Garfield
James A. Garfield National Historic Site
Lawnfield
8095 Mentor Avenue
Mentor, Ohio 44060
Tel. 440-255-8722
www.nps.gov/jaga

Ulysses S. Grant
Grant's Birthplace State Memorial
U.S. 52 and State Route 232
Point Pleasant, Ohio 45163
Tel. 513-553-4911

U. S. Grant's Home State Historic Site
500 Bouthillier St.
Galena, Ill. 61036
Tel. 815-777-3310

Appomattox Court House National
Historic Park
McLean House
Appomattox, Va. 24522

Tel. 804-352-8987
www.nps.gov/apco

General Grant National Memorial
Grant's Tomb
Riverside Drive and 122nd Street
New York, N.Y. 10003
Tel. 212-666-1640
www.nps.gov/gegr

Warren G. Harding
Harding Home and Museum
380 Mount Vernon Avenue
Marion, Ohio 43302
Tel. 740-387-9630
www.ohiohistory.org/places/harding

Benjamin Harrison
President Benjamin Harrison Memorial
Home
1230 North Delaware Street
Indianapolis, Ind. 46202
Tel. 317-631-1888

William Henry Harrison
William Henry Harrison Museum
Grouseland
3 West Scott Street
Vincennes, Ind. 47591
Tel. 812-882-2096

Rutherford B. Hayes
Rutherford B. Hayes Center
Spiegel Grove
Fremont, Ohio 43420
Tel. 419-332-2081/1-800-998-7737
www.rbhayes.org

Herbert C. Hoover
Herbert Hoover Library-Museum
Parkside Drive
West Branch, Iowa 52358
Tel. 319-643-5301
http://hoover.nara.gov

Herbert Hoover National Historic Site
Parkside Drive and Main Street
West Branch, Iowa 52358
Tel. 319-643-2541
www.hooverassoc.org

Andrew Jackson
The Hermitage, home of Andrew Jackson
4580 Rachel's Lane
Hermitage, Tenn. 37076
Tel. 615-889-2941
www.thehermitage.com

Thomas Jefferson
Monticello, home of Thomas Jefferson
Thomas Jefferson Memorial Foundation
Charlottesville, Va. 22902
Tel. 804-984-9822
www.monticello.org

Jefferson Memorial
Washington, D.C.

Andrew Johnson
Andrew Johnson National Historic Site
College and Depot Streets
Greeneville, Tenn. 37743
Tel. 423-638-3551
www.nps.gov/anjo

Lyndon B. Johnson
Lyndon Baines Johnson Library and
Museum
University of Texas
2313 Red River Street
Austin, Tex. 78705-5702
Tel. 512-916-5137
www.lbjlib.utexas.edu

John F. Kennedy
John Fitzgerald Kennedy Library and
Museum
Columbia Point
Boston, Mass. 02125
Tel. 617-929-4500
www.cs.umb.edu/jfklibrary/

John Fitzgerald Kennedy National
Historic Site
83 Beals Street
Brookline, Mass. 02146
Tel. 617-566-7937

Abraham Lincoln
Lincoln Birthplace National Historic Site
2995 Lincoln Farm Road
Hodgenville, Ky. 42748

Tel. 270-358-3137
www.nps.gov/abli

Abraham Lincoln Library and Museum
Highway 25 East
Harrogate, Tenn. 37752
Tel. 423-869-6235
www.Imunet.edu/Museum

Lincoln Boyhood National Memorial
Lincoln City, Ind. 47552
Tel. 812-937-4541
www.nps.gov/libo

Lincoln Home National Historic Site
426 South Seventh Street
Springfield, Ill. 62701
Tel. 217-492-4241, ext. 221
www.nps.gov/liho

Lincoln's Tomb State Historic Site
Oak Ridge Cemetery
Springfield, Ill. 62702
Tel. 217-782-2717

Ford's Theatre National Historic Site
511 10th Street., N.W.
Washington, D.C. 20004
Tel. 202-426-6924
www.nps.gov/foth/index2

Lincoln Memorial
23rd Street, N.W.
Washington, D.C.
www.nps.gov/line/home

James Madison
Montpelier, home of James Madison
Route 20
Orange County, Va. 22957
Tel. 540-672-2728
www.montpelier.org

Octagon House
1799 New York Avenue, S.W.
Washington, D.C. 20006
Tel. 202-638-3105

William McKinley
National McKinley Birthplace Memorial
40 North Main Street

Niles, Ohio 44446
Tel. 330-652-1704
www.mckinley.lib.oh.us/memorial

James Monroe
James Monroe Museum and Memorial
Library
908 Charles Street
Fredericksburg, Va. 22401
Tel. 540-654-1043

Ash Lawn–Highland, home of James
Monroe
Albemarle County, Route 795
Charlottesville, Va. 22901
Tel. 804-293-9539
http://monticello.avenue.org/ashlawn

Richard M. Nixon
Richard Nixon Presidential Library and
Birthplace
Yorba Linda, Calif. 92686
Tel. 714-993-3393
www.nixonfoundation.org

Franklin Pierce
Franklin Pierce Homestead
Routes 31 and 9
Hillsboro, N.H. 03244
Tel. 603-478-3165
www.conknet.com/hillsboro/historic/
homestead

The Pierce Manse
14 Penacook St.
Concord, N.H. 03301
Tel. 603-225-2068/603-224-7668
www.newww.com/free/pierce

James K. Polk
Ancestral Home of James Knox Polk
301 West 7th Street
Columbia, Tenn. 38401
Tel. 931-388-2354
www.jameskpolk.com

Ronald Reagan
Ronald Reagan Birthplace
Main Street
Tampico, Ill.

Ronald Reagan Presidential Library
40 Presidential Drive
Simi Valley, Calif. 93065
Tel. 805-522-8444
www.reagan.utexas.edu

Franklin D. Roosevelt
Franklin D. Roosevelt Library
259 Albany Post Road
Hyde Park, N. Y. 12538
Tel. 914-229-8114
www.academic.marist.edu/fdr/

Home of Franklin D. Roosevelt National
Historic Site
Route 9
Hyde Park, N.Y. 12538
Tel. 914-229-9115
www.nps.gov/hofr

Little White House Historic Site
Highway 85 West
Warm Springs, Ga. 31830
Tel. 706-655-5870

Franklin D. Roosevelt Memorial
900 Ohio Drive, S.W.
Washington, D.C. 20242
www.nps.gov/fdrm/home

Theodore Roosevelt
Theodore Roosevelt Birthplace National
Historic Site
28 East 20th Street
New York , N.Y. 10003
Tel. 212-260-1616
www.nps.gov/thrb/

Sagamore Hill National Historic Site
20 Sagamore Hill
Oyster Bay, N.Y. 11771
Tel. 516-922-4788
www.nps.gov/sahi/

Theodore Roosevelt Island National
Memorial
Washington, D.C.
www.nps.gov/this/

William Howard Taft
William Howard Taft National Historic
Site
2038 Auburn Avenue
Cincinnati, Ohio 45202
Tel. 513-684-3262
www.nps.gov/wiho/

Zachary Taylor
Zachary Taylor National Cemetery
4701 Brownsboro Road
Louisville, Ky. 40202

Harry S. Truman
Harry S. Truman Library and Museum
U.S. Highway 24 and Delaware Street
Independence, Mo. 64050
Tel. 816-833-1400
www.trumanlibrary.org

Harry S. Truman Birthplace State
Historic Site
1009 Truman Avenue and 11th Street
Lamar, Mo. 64759
Tel. 417-682-2279
www.mostateparks.com/trumansite

Harry S. Truman National Historic Site
223 Main Street
Independence, Mo. 64050
Tel. 816-254-9929
www.nps.gov/hstr

John Tyler
Sherwood Forest Plantation
Route 5
Charles City, Va. 23020
Tel. 804-829-5377
www.sherwoodforest.org

Martin Van Buren
Martin Van Buren National Historic Site
(Lindenwald)
1013 Old Post Road
Kinderhook, N.Y. 12106
Tel. 518-758-9689
www.nps.gov/mava/

George Washington
Mount Vernon, home of George
Washington
George Washington Parkway South
Mt. Vernon, Va. 22121
Tel. 703-780-2000
www.mountvernon.org

Washington Monument
Washington, D.C.

Valley Forge Historical Society Museum
Route 23
Valley Forge, Pa. 19481
Tel. 610-783-0535
www.ushistory.org/valleyforge

Woodrow Wilson
Wilson Birthplace
20 North Coalter Street
Staunton, Va. 24401
Tel. 540-885-0897
www.woodrowwilson.org

Woodrow Wilson House
2340 S Street, N.W.
Washington, D.C. 20008
Tel. 202-387-4062
www.woodrowwilsonhouse.org

**Other Sources of Information about
Presidents**

The White House Office
1600 Pennsylvania Avenue, N.W.
Washington, D.C. 20500
Tel. 202-456-1414
*This is the address and the telephone
number that you can use to let the
president know your opinions.*

White House Historical Association
740 Jackson Place, N.W.
Washington, D.C. 20503
Tel. 202-737-8292
www.whitehousehistory.org/whha/

FURTHER READING

Many of the entries in this volume contain references to books dealing with that specific subject. The following volumes will be useful for further study.

U.S. CONGRESS
General References

Bernstein, Richard B., and Jerome Agel. *Into the Third Century: The Congress*. New York: Walker, 1989.

Biographical Directory of the United States Congress, 1774–1989. Washington D.C.: Government Printing Office, 1989.

Cohen, Richard W. *Washington at Work: Back Rooms and Clean Air*. New York: Macmillan, 1992.

Congressional Quarterly. *Guide to Congress*. Washington, D.C.: Congressional Quarterly, 1991.

Davidson, Roger H., and Richard C. Sachs, eds. *Understanding Congress: Research Perspectives*. Washington, D.C.: Government Printing Office, 1991.

Dodd, Lawrence C., and Bruce I. Oppenheimer. *Congress Reconsidered*. Washington, D.C.: Congressional Quarterly, 1993.

Goehlert, Robert U., and Fenton S. Martin. *The United States Congress: An Annotated Bibliography, 1980–1993*. Washington, D.C.: Congressional Quarterly, 1995.

Josephy, Alvin. *On the Hill: A History of the United States Congress*. New York: Simon & Schuster, 1979.

Mann, Thomas E., and Norman J. Ornstein, eds. *Congress, the Press, and the Public*. Washington, D.C.: American Enterprise Institute, 1994.

Oleszek, Walter J. *Congressional Procedures and the Policy Process*. Washington, D.C.: Congressional Quarterly, 1989.

Smock, Raymond W., ed. *Landmark Documents on the U.S. Congress*. Washington, D.C.: Congressional Quarterly, 1999.

The House of Representatives

Cheney, Richard B., and Lynne V. Cheney. *Kings of the Hill: Power and Personality in the House of Representatives*. New York: Continuum, 1983.

Currie, James. *The United States House of Representatives*. Malabar, Fla.: Krieger, 1987.

Davidson, Roger H., Susan Webb Hammond, and Raymond W. Smock, eds. *Masters of the House: Congressional Leadership over Two Centuries*. New York: Westview, 1998.

Galloway, George B., and Sidney Wise. *History of the House of Representatives*. New York: Crowell, 1976.

McNeil, Neil. *Forge of Democracy: The House of Representatives.* New York: McKay, 1963.
Ragsdale, Bruce A. *The House of Representatives.* New York: Chelsea House, 1989.

The Senate

·Baker, Richard A. *The Senate: A Bicentennial History.* Malabar, Fla.: Krieger, 1987.
Baker, Richard A., and Roger H. Davidson, eds. *First among Equals: Outstanding Senate Leaders of the Twentieth Century.* Washington, D.C.: Congressional Quarterly, 1991.
Byrd, Robert C. *The Senate, 1789–1989: Addresses on the History of the United States Senate.* 2 vols. Washington, D.C.: Government Printing Office, 1989–1991.
Hess, Stephen. *The Ultimate Insiders: U.S. Senators in the National Media.* Washington, D.C.: Brookings Institution, 1986.
Reedy, George E. *The U.S. Senate: Paralysis or a Search for Consensus?* New York: Crown, 1986.
Ritchie, Donald A. *The Senate.* New York: Chelsea House, 1988.
White, William S. *Citadel: The Story of the U.S. Senate.* New York: Harper, 1956.

Using Congressional Documents

Congress publishes extensive documentation on its activities. These published documents date back to the 1st Congress in 1789 but have multiplied over time as the work load of Congress has increased. The starting place for most research on Congress is the *Congressional Record,* which is a record of most everything spoken and done on the floor of the House and Senate. The index to the *Record* identifies each member's speeches, together with bills and resolutions introduced and the subjects that Congress debated. The *Congressional Record* covers all debates since 1873. For earlier debates, the *Annals of Congress* covers 1789 to 1824; the *Register of Debates* covers 1825 to 1837; and the *Congressional Globe* covers 1833 to 1873. In addition, both the House and Senate publish journals that provide summaries of all floor activities, including bills introduced, referred to committee, amended, voted upon, and signed into law. These journals do not include members' speeches. The Senate also publishes an executive journal containing all nominations and treaties.

Congress does a great deal of its work in committee and publishes the transcripts of most of the hearings it holds in public. The Congressional Information Service (CIS) publishes *CIS U.S. Congressional Hearing Index,* which lists each of these hearings by committee, by subject, and by witness. CIS has also produced similar guides to the previously unpublished hearings of the House and Senate (*CIS Index to Unpublished U.S. Senate Committee Hearings* and *CIS Index to Unpublished U.S. House of Representatives Committee Hearings*). In addition to hearing transcripts, Congress publishes many reports to furnish background material in support of bills, to record members' experiences during foreign travel, and to cover a wide range of other legislative interests. These reports can be located through the *CIS Serial Set Index.* The *Congressional Record,* hearings, reports, and CIS indexes and microfiche editions of congressional documents can be found in the government documents section of most large public libraries and university libraries.

Congressional Quarterly Inc. (CQ) also produces a variety of helpful tools for research on Congress, including a weekly magazine and an annual almanac for each session of Congress since 1945. CQ's *Guide to Congress* and *Congress A to Z* are handy one-volume encyclopedias on congressional history, practices, and procedures. CQ's multivolume *Congress and the Nation* series summarizes the wide range of legislation Congress has dealt with since 1945. In addition, CQ publishes a variety of books about specific congressional and political issues that are available at most larger libraries.

THE PRESIDENCY
General References

Burns, James McGregor. *Presidential Government: The Crucible of Leadership.* Boston: Houghton Mifflin, 1966.

Congressional Quarterly. *The Presidency A to Z.* Washington, D.C.: Congressional Quarterly, 1992.

Kane, Joseph N. *Facts about the Presidents.* 5th ed. New York: H. W. Wilson, 1989.

Levy, Leonard W., and Louis Fisher, eds. *Encyclopedia of the American Presidency.* 4 vols. New York: Simon & Schuster, 1993.

Nelson, Michael. *Congressional Quarterly Guide to the Presidency.* Washington, D.C.: Congressional Quarterly, 1989.

Pious, Richard M. *The Presidency.* Boston: Allyn & Bacon, 1995.

Schick, Frank L. *The Records of the Presidency: Presidential Papers & Libraries from Washington to Reagan.* Phoenix, Ariz.: Oryx, 1989.

Anecdotal Treatments of the Presidency

Boller, Paul F., Jr. *Presidential Anecdotes.* New York: Penguin, 1989.

Boller, Paul F., Jr. *Presidential Campaigns.* New York: Oxford, 1985.

Frank, Sid, and Arden Melick. *The Presidents: Tidbits and Trivia.* Rev. ed. New York: Hammond, 1990.

Hay, Peter. *All the Presidents' Wives: Anecdotes of the Women behind the Men in the White House.* New York: Penguin, 1989.

Brief Biographical Treatments

Armbruster, Maxim E. *The Presidents of the United States.* New York: Horizon Press, 1982.

Bailey, Thomas A. *Presidential Saints and Sinners.* New York: Free Press, 1981.

Bailey, Thomas A. *The Pugnacious Presidents: White House Warriors on Parade.* New York: Free Press, 1980.

Freidel, Frank. *The Presidents of the United States of America.* 12th ed. Washington, D.C.: White House Historical Association, 1989.

Magill, Frank N., ed. *The American Presidents: The Office and the Men.* 3 vols. Danbury, Conn.: Grolier, 1989.

The Development of the Presidency

Barrileaux, Ryan J. *The Post-Modern Presidency: The Office after Ronald Reagan.* New York: Praeger, 1988. A study of recent Presidential prerogatives.

Berman, Larry. *The New American Presidency.* Boston: Little, Brown, 1987. A history of the modern Presidency, with prescriptions for reforming the office.

King, Gary, and Lyn Ragsdale. *The Elusive Executive: Discovering Statistical Patterns in the Presidency.* Washington, D.C.: Congressional Quarterly, 1988.

Koh, Harold. *The National Security Constitution.* New Haven: Yale University Press, 1991. An examination of the Iran-Contra case and its aftermath.

Leuchtenberg, William E. *In the Shadow of FDR: From Harry Truman to Ronald Reagan.* Rev. ed. Ithaca, N.Y.: Cornell University Press, 1985.

Lowi, Theodore. *The Personal President: Power Invested, Promise Unfulfilled.* Ithaca, N.Y.:

Cornell University Press, 1985. An examination of the excesses of the post-Watergate Presidency.

Milkis, Sidney, and Michael Nelson. *The American Presidency.* Washington, D.C.: Congressional Quarterly, 1990.

Pious, Richard M. *The American Presidency.* New York: Basic Books, 1979. Presents a theory of Presidential power as constitutional prerogative.

Riccards, Michael P. *A Republic If You Can Keep It: The Foundations of the American Presidency, 1700–1800.* Westport, Conn.: Greenwood, 1987. Traces the history of self-government in the colonies and states.

Rose, Richard. *The Postmodern President.* Chatham, N.J.: Chatham House, 1989. Discusses how changes in American economic power have changed the role of the President in world politics.

Rossiter, Clinton. *The American Presidency.* New York: Harcourt Brace & World, 1956. Classic account of the duties of the President.

Rossiter, Clinton. *Constitutional Dictatorship.* New York: Harcourt Brace & World, 1963. A study of Lincoln's use of power during the Civil War.

Rubin, Richard. *Press, Party, and Presidency.* New York: Norton, 1981. Discusses changes in Presidential leadership with regard to public opinion and relations with media.

Schlesinger, Arthur M., Jr. *The Imperial Presidency.* Boston: Houghton Mifflin, 1973. Examines how Truman, Eisenhower, Kennedy, and Johnson paved the way for Nixon's abuses of power.

Tulis, Jeffrey. *The Rhetorical Presidency.* Princeton, N.J.: Princeton University Press, 1987. A study of Presidential speech making.

First Ladies on Life in the White House

Carter, Rosalynn. *First Lady from Plains.* Boston: Houghton Mifflin, 1984.

Ford, Betty. *The Times of My Life.* New York: Harper & Row, 1978.

Reagan, Nancy, and William Novak. *My Turn: The Memoirs of Nancy Reagan.* New York: Random House, 1988.

Roosevelt, Eleanor. *This I Remember.* 1949. Reprint, Westport, Conn.: Greenwood Press, 1975.

Leadership

Burns, James MacGregor. *Leadership.* New York: Harper & Row, 1978.

Patterson, Bradley. *The Ring of Power.* New York: Basic Books, 1990. A discussion of the operations of the White House, by a former aide.

Reedy, George. *The Twilight of the Presidency.* New York: New American Library, 1970. Discusses the dangers of a large Presidential staff, by a former press secretary.

Pictorial Histories

The American Heritage Pictorial History of the Presidents. New York: Simon & Schuster, 1968.

Durant, John, and Alice Durant. *Pictorial History of the American Presidents.* New York: A. S. Barnes, 1969.

Presidential Decision Making

Barber, James David. *The Presidential Character.* 4th ed. Englewood Cliffs, N.J.: Prentice-Hall, 1992. Psychological studies of modern Presidents.

Graff, Henry F. *The Tuesday Cabinet.* Englewood Cliffs, N.J.: Prentice-Hall, 1970. An account of Lyndon Johnson's advisers during the Vietnam War.

Greenstein, Fred. *The Hidden-Hand Presidency.* New York: Basic Books, 1982. Discusses the techniques used by Eisenhower to win political victories.

May, Ernest R., ed. *The Ultimate Decision.* New York: George Braziller, 1960. Examines the decisions Presidents make to go to war.

Neustadt, Richard. *Presidential Power and the Modern Presidents.* New York: Free Press, 1990. Discusses the way Presidents use power and influence to get others to do what they want.

Pyle, Christopher, and Richard M. Pious, eds. *The President, Congress, and the Constitution.* New York: Free Press, 1984. An examination of constitutional law cases involving Presidential power.

Sorensen, Theodore. *Decision-Making in the White House.* New York: Columbia University Press, 1963. Discusses crisis decision making in the Kennedy White House.

Presidential Elections

Fischer, Roger A. *Tippecanoe and Trinkets Too: The Material Culture of American Presidential Campaigns, 1828–1984.* Urbana: University of Illinois Press, 1988.

Jamieson, Kathleen Hall. *Packaging the Presidency: A History and Criticism of Presidential Campaign Advertising.* 2nd ed. New York: Oxford University Press, 1992.

McCormick, Richard P. *The Presidential Game.* New York: Oxford University Press, 1982.

McGinnis, Joe. *The Selling of the President.* New York: Penguin, 1988.

Melder, Keith. *Hail to the Candidate: Presidential Campaigns from Banners to Broadcasts.* Washington, D.C.: Smithsonian Institution Press, 1992.

Polsby, Nelson W., and Aaron Wildavsky. *Presidential Elections: Contemporary Strategies of American Electoral Politics.* 7th ed. New York: Free Press, 1988.

Reinsche, J. Leonard. *Getting Elected: From Radio and Roosevelt to Television and Reagan.* New York: Hippocrene, 1988.

Schlesinger, Arthur M., Jr., and Fred L. Israel, eds. *The Coming to Power: Critical Presidential Elections in American History.* New York: Chelsea House, 1981.

Schlesinger, Arthur M., Jr., ed. *History of American Presidential Elections, 1789–1984.* 5 vols. New York: Chelsea House, 1986.

Tugwell, Rexford G. *How They Became President.* New York: Simon & Schuster, 1964.

Wayne, Stephen J. *The Road to the White House: The Politics of Presidential Elections.* New York: St. Martin's, 1992.

Presidents on the Presidency

Carter, Jimmy. *Keeping Faith: Memoirs of a President.* New York: Bantam, 1982.

Eisenhower, Dwight D. *The White House Years.* Garden City, N.Y.: Doubleday, 1965.

Ford, Gerald R. *A Time to Heal.* New York: Harper & Row, 1979.

Hoover, Herbert. *Memoirs.* 3 vols. 1951–52. Reprint, New York: Garland, 1979.

Johnson, Lyndon B. *The Vantage Point.* New York: Holt, Rinehart & Winston, 1971.

Nixon, Richard M. *RN: The Memoirs of Richard Nixon.* New York: Grosset & Dunlap, 1978.

Reagan, Ronald. *An American Life.* New York: Simon & Schuster, 1990.

Roosevelt, Theodore. *An Autobiography.* New York: Macmillan, 1919.

Taft, William Howard. *Our Chief Magistrate and His Powers.* New York: Columbia University Press, 1916.

Truman, Harry. *Memoirs.* 2 vols. Garden City, N.Y.: Doubleday, 1955.

Wilson, Woodrow. *Constitutional Government in the United States.* New York: Columbia University Press, 1908.

U.S. SUPREME COURT
General References

Abraham, Henry J. *The Judicial Process.* New York: Oxford University Press, 1993.

Baum, Laurence. *The Supreme Court.* Washington, D.C.: Congressional Quarterly, 1992.

Biskupic, Joan, and Elder Witt. *The Supreme Court at Work.* 2nd ed. Washington, D.C.: Congressional Quarterly, 1997.

Cooper, Phillip J. *Battles on the Bench: Conflict Inside the Supreme Court.* Lawrence: University Press of Kansas 1999.

Hall, Kermit L., ed. *The Oxford Companion to the Supreme Court of the United States.* New York: Oxford University Press, 1992.

Harrell, Mary Ann, and Burnett Anderson. *Equal Justice Under Law: The Supreme Court in American Life.* Washington, D.C.: Supreme Court Historical Society, 1982.

Jost, Kenneth. *The Supreme Court A to Z.* 2nd ed. Washington, D.C.: Congressional Quarterly, 1998.

Katzmann, Robert A. *Courts and Congress.* Washington, D.C.: Brookings Institution, 1997.

Lazarus, Edward. *Closed Chambers: The Rise, Fall, and Future of the Modern Supreme Court.* New York: Penguin, 1999.

Marcus, Maeva. *Origins of the Federal Judiciary.* New York: Oxford University Press, 1992.

McCloskey, Robert G., and Sanford Levinson, eds. *The American Supreme Court.* 2nd ed. Chicago: University of Chicago Press, 1994.

O'Brien, David M. *Storm Center: The Supreme Court in American Politics.* 5th ed. New York: Norton, 1999.

Perry, Barbara A. *The Priestly Tribe: The Supreme Court's Image in the American Mind.* Westport, Conn.: Praeger, 1999.

Perry, H. W., Jr. *Deciding to Decide: Agenda Setting in the United States Supreme Court.* Cambridge: Harvard University Press, 1991.

Schwartz, Bernard. *A History of the Supreme Court.* New York: Oxford University Press, 1993.

Semonche, John E. *Keeping the Faith: A Cultural History of the U.S. Supreme Court.* Lanham, Md.: Rowman & Littlefield, 1998.

Shapiro, Fred R., ed. *American Legal Quotations.* New York: Oxford University Press, 1993.

Shnayerson, Robert. *The Illustrated History of the Supreme Court of the United States.* New York: Abrams, 1986.

Wagman, Robert J. *The Supreme Court: A Citizen's Guide.* New York: Pharos Books, 1993.

Wiecek, William M. *Liberty under Law: The Supreme Court in American Life.* Baltimore, Md.: Johns Hopkins University Press, 1988.

Witt, Elder. *Guide to the U.S. Supreme Court.* Washington, D.C.: Congressional Quarterly, 1989.

Witt, Elder. *The Supreme Court and Individual Rights.* Washington, D.C.: Congressional Quarterly, 1988.

The Bill of Rights

Meltzer, Milton. *The Bill of Rights: How We Got It and What It Means.* New York: Crowell, 1990.

Schwartz, Bernard. *The Great Rights of Mankind: A History of the American Bill of Rights.* Madison, Wis.: Madison House, 1992.

Constitutional History and Issues

Anastaplo, George. *The Constitution of 1787: A Commentary.* Baltimore, Md.: Johns Hopkins University Press, 1989.

Bailyn, Bernard, ed. *The Debate on the Constitution: Federalist and Antifederalist Speeches, Articles, and Letters During the Struggle Over Ratification.* 2 vols. New York: Library of America, 1993.

Bernstein, Richard B., and Jerome Agel. *Amending America: If We Love the Constitution So Much, Why Do We Keep Trying to Change It?* New York: Random House, 1993.

Bowen, Catherine Drinker. *Miracle at Philadelphia: The Story of the Constitutional Convention.* 1966. Reprint, Boston: Little, Brown, 1987.

Burt, Robert A. *The Constitution in Conflict.* Cambridge: Harvard University Press, 1992.

Collier, Christopher, and James Lincoln Collier. *Decision in Philadelphia: The Constitutional Convention of 1787.* New York: Random House, 1986.

Cox, Archibald. *The Court and the Constitution.* Boston: Houghton Mifflin, 1987.

Currie, David P. *The Constitution in the Supreme Court: The First Hundred Years.* Chicago: University of Chicago Press, 1985.

Currie, David P. *The Constitution in the Supreme Court : The Second Century, 1888–1986.* Chicago: University of Chicago Press, 1994.

Currie, David P. *The Constitution of the United States: A Primer for the People.* Chicago: University of Chicago Press, 1988.

Epstein, Lee, and Thomas G. Walker. *Constitutional Law for a Changing America.* Washington, D.C.: Congressional Quarterly, 1992.

Friendly, Fred W., and Martha J. H. Elliott. *The Constitution: That Delicate Balance.* New York: Random House, 1984.

Garraty, John A., ed. *Quarrels That Have Shaped the Constitution.* New York: Harper & Row, 1987.

Hall, Kermit L., ed. *By and for the People: Constitutional Rights in American History.* Arlington, Ill.: Harlan Davidson, 1991.

Kelly, Alfred H., Winfred A. Harbison, and Herman Belz. *The American Constitution: Its Origins and Development.* New York: Norton, 1990.

Ketchum, Ralph. *Framed for Posterity: The Enduring Philosophy of the Constitution.* Lawrence: University Press of Kansas, 1993.

Leuchtenberg, William E. *The Supreme Court Reborn: The Constitutional Revolution in the Age of Roosevelt.* New York: Oxford University Press, 1996.

Levy, Leonard W., Kenneth L. Karst, and Dennis J. Mahoney, editors. *Encyclopedia of the American Constitution.* 4 vols. New York: Macmillan, 1986.

Lutz, Donald S. *The Origins of American Constitutionalism.* Baton Rouge: Louisiana State University Press, 1988.

Peck, Robert S. *We the People: The Constitution in American Life.* New York: Abrams, 1987.

Ritchie, Donald A. *The U.S. Constitution.* New York: Chelsea House, 1989.

Urofsky, Melvin I. *A March of Liberty: A Constitutional History of the United States.* New York: Knopf, 1988.

Justices

Friedman, Leon, and Fred L. Israel, eds. *The Justices of the United States Supreme Court, 1789–1991.* 5 vols. Rev. ed. New York: Chelsea House, 1992.

Woodward, Bob, and Scott Armstrong. *The Brethren: Inside the Supreme Court.* New York: Simon & Schuster, 1979.

Yalof, David A. *Pursuit of Justices: Presidential Politics and the Selection of Supreme Court Nominees.* Chicago: University of Chicago Press, 1999.

Legal History

Friedman, Lawrence M. *A History of American Law.* 2nd rev. ed. New York: Simon & Schuster. 1986.

Hall, Kermit L. *The Magic Mirror: Law in American History.* New York: Oxford University Press, 1989.

Hall, Kermit L., William M. Wiecek, and Paul Finkelman. *American Legal History: Cases and Materials.* New York: Oxford University Press, 1991.

Horowitz, Morton J. *The Transformation of American Law, 1780–1860.* New York: Oxford University Press, 1992.

Horowitz, Morton J. *The Transformation of American Law, 1870–1960: The Crisis of Legal Orthodoxy.* New York: Oxford University Press, 1992.

Schwartz, Bernard. *Main Currents in American Legal Thought.* Durham, N.C.: Carolina Academic Press, 1993.

Trials and Decisions

Arbetman, Lee, and Richard L. Roe. *Great Trials in American History.* St. Paul, Minn.: West, 1985.

Guitton, Stephanie, and Peter H. Irons, eds. *May It Please the Court: The Most Significant Oral Arguments Made Before the Supreme Court Since 1955.* New York: New Press, 1994.

Hall, Kermit L., ed. *The Oxford Guide to United States Supreme Court Decisions.* New York: Oxford University Press, 1999.

Irons, Peter. *The Courage of Their Convictions. Sixteen Americans Who Fought Their Way to the Supreme Court.* New York: Penguin, 1990.

Irons, Peter, ed. *May It Please the Court: The First Amendment: Live Recordings and Transcripts of the Oral Arguments Made Before the Supreme Court in Sixteen Key First Amendment Cases.* New York: New Press, 1998.

Johnson, John W. *Historic U.S. Court Cases, 1690–1990, An Encyclopedia.* New York: Garland, 1992.

Lively, Donald E. *Landmark Supreme Court Cases: A Reference Guide.* Westport, Conn.: Greenwood, 1999.

Schwartz, Bernard. *Decision: How the Supreme Court Decides Cases.* New York: Oxford University Press, 1996.

The Authors

JOHN J. PATRICK is director of the Social Studies Development Center, professor of education, and director of the ERIC Clearinghouse for Social Studies/Social Science Education at Indiana University. He is the author of two textbooks, *American Political Behavior* and *History of the American Nation*, as well as many resources for history and legal edcuation. He was the chief consultant to the video series *The U.S. Constitution* and senior consultant to the civic education program in Poland.

RICHARD M. PIOUS is professor of political science at Barnard College and the Graduate Faculties of Columbia University, where he teaches courses on presidential politics. He is the author of *The American Presidency; The President, Congress and the Constitution;* and the textbook *American Politics and Government;* and a biography of Richard Nixon. He was the editor of the Academy of Political Science's centennial volume, *The Power to Govern,* and the editor of reprint series in American constitutional law and the history of the presidency.

DONALD A. RITCHIE is the Associate Historian of the U.S. Senate Historical Office and the author of *Press Gallery: Congress and the Washington Correspondents* (which won the Richard Leopold Prize of the Organization of American Historians); *A Necessary Fence: The Senate's First Century; The Senate; The U.S. Constitution;* and *James M. Landis: Dean of the Regulators.* He is coauthor of a high school textbook, *History of a Free Nation.* In 1990 he won the James Madison prize for the best article on the history of the federal government.

INDEX